**Springer Proceedings in Business and Economics**

Springer Proceedings in Business and Economics brings the most current research presented at conferences and workshops to a global readership. The series features volumes (in electronic and print formats) of selected contributions from conferences in all areas of economics, business, management, and finance. In addition to an overall evaluation by the publisher of the topical interest, scientific quality, and timeliness of each volume, each contribution is refereed to standards comparable to those of leading journals, resulting in authoritative contributions to the respective fields. Springer's production and distribution infrastructure ensures rapid publication and wide circulation of the latest developments in the most compelling and promising areas of research today.

The editorial development of volumes may be managed using Springer Nature's innovative EquinOCS, a proven online conference proceedings submission, management and review system. This system is designed to ensure an efficient timeline for your publication, making Springer Proceedings in Business and Economics the premier series to publish your workshop or conference volume.

This book series is indexed in SCOPUS.

Sebastian Kot · Bilal Khalid · Adnan ul Haque
Editors

# Corporate Practices: Policies, Methodologies, and Insights in Organizational Management

International Conference on Entrepreneurship and the Economy in an Era of Uncertainty 2023

Springer

*Editors*
Sebastian Kot
Faculty of Management
Częstochowa University of Technology
Czestochowa, Poland

Bilal Khalid
KMITL Business School
King Mongkut's Institute of Technology
Ladkrabang
Bangkok, Thailand

Adnan ul Haque
Faculty of Business and Management
Yorkville University
Fredericton, NB, Canada

ISSN 2198-7246 ISSN 2198-7254 (electronic)
Springer Proceedings in Business and Economics
ISBN 978-981-97-0995-3 ISBN 978-981-97-0996-0 (eBook)
https://doi.org/10.1007/978-981-97-0996-0



This Springer imprint is published by the registered company Springer Nature Singapore Pte Ltd.
The registered company address is: 152 Beach Road, #21-01/04 Gateway East, Singapore 189721, Singapore

Paper in this product is recyclable.

# Preface

The 3rd International Conference on Entrepreneurship and Economy in an Era of Uncertainty took place on November 15–17, 2023, in Pattaya, Thailand. The conference was organized in collaboration with agreement, King Mongkut's Institute of Technology Ladkrabang in Thailand, Stamford International University in Thailand, and Częstochowa University of Technology in Poland.

Few academic initiatives are as vibrant and revolutionary as the study of economics and entrepreneurship. Understanding these disciplines is becoming increasingly important as the world changes and offers new opportunities and challenges. This is especially true in these unpredictable times when our economic environments and entrepreneurial pursuits are shaped by swift changes on the global stage and unanticipated disruptions. The 3rd Global Conference on Economy and Entrepreneurship in the Era of Uncertainty is evidence of our dedication to bringing these important topics to light. In an atmosphere of cooperation and research, the conference was convened to explore the various dimensions of economics and business, examining how they adapt and thrive unpredictably.

The rapid advancement of technology is causing a significant shift in the global economy that is leading to the emergence of the digital economy and Industry 4.0. Despite being influenced by a number of variables, this evolution emphasizes how important entrepreneurship is to promoting sustainability and economic success. We are holding this conference in this exciting and changing environment, focusing on the revolutionary potential of technology and how it affects accounting, sustainability, management, and the entrepreneurial spirit in businesses. It is critical to acknowledge the benefits of technology adoption in addition to the difficulties that businesses and society confront. Digital technologies, which provide creative solutions to consumers and businesses, have been essential in reducing the disruptions brought about by various economic issues. Thus, Industry 4.0 and the digital economy have advanced more quickly. Notably, a large number of these technologies are now generally available and are incorporated into the operations of a broader spectrum of businesses.

The principal aim of this conference is to promote an extensive discourse on the latest advancements in the digital economy, innovations, and their significant implications for modern economies. We want to investigate the various ways that technology affects business ventures, management approaches, green projects, and accounting procedures in businesses and institutions in this forum. The conference community is indispensable for spreading the newest developments and encouraging international cooperation. We are ready to explore the dynamic relationship between technology and entrepreneurship as a group here, knowing that combining these two factors will propel economies forward and build resilience. We hope to be a part of the continuous change in the economic landscape by exchanging knowledge and insights with one another, which will promote innovation and sustainable growth worldwide. Professionals from Bahrain, Bulgaria, Canada, China, Czech Republic, Hungary, India, Indonesia, Iraq, Israel, Latvia, Malaysia, Pakistan, Philippines, Poland, Portugal, Romania, Saudi Arabia, Singapore, Slovakia, Slovenia, South Africa, South Korea, Thailand, Ukraine, Vietnam took part in the 2023 conference. These partnerships brought a wealth of varied viewpoints and mutually beneficial skills to the conference, highlighting the international scope of the scholarly discourse.

During the meeting, we mutually acknowledged the profound significance of convening the 3rd Global Conference on Entrepreneurship and Economy in an Era of Uncertainty. The collective recognition of this significance shows our dedication to cultivating a deeper awareness of the obstacles and possibilities that lie ahead in our constantly evolving global landscape. The conference fostered meaningful dialogues, generated novel concepts, and eventually enhanced the ongoing global discourse on entrepreneurship and economics. It aims to transform the current era of uncertainty into a phase of exploration, adjustment, and advancement.

Collectively, we commenced this scholarly expedition, positioned to unearth the discernments that will mold the trajectory of entrepreneurship and economics, even amidst the most unpredictable circumstances the world has faced in recent history, first with the COVID-19 pandemic in 2020 and other global conflicts.

Following the opening ceremony, a plenary session occurred during which various speakers presented on various topics. One presentation focused on the impact of globalization on the management of culture in enterprises and discussed logistics and humanitarian aid. Another presentation centered around rethinking sustainable transportation and the role of shared mobility in urban environments. Additionally, a strategy for personal development and unlocking inner potential was shared, and the importance of sustainable development goals and their contribution to transforming higher education was emphasized.

The Young Researchers Workshop held during the conference offered a unique opportunity for attendees to gain valuable insights and expertise in academic publishing, particularly in high-indexed Scopus journals. This masterclass was expertly conducted by distinguished panelists and editors who collectively brought a wealth of experience and knowledge. Along with prioritizing publication in high-impact Scopus journals, this masterclass offered many advantages that extended beyond the confines of the conference setting. Some advantages include enhanced research quality; participants were encouraged to refine their research methodologies, ensuring their contributions were rigorous, innovative, and impactful. The masterclass was a networking hub, connecting young researchers with established academics in their respective fields. This networking opportunity can open doors to collaborative research projects, career development, and long-lasting professional relationships. Participants were equipped with strategies and practical tips for navigating the often intricate process of manuscript submission and peer review. This knowledge can significantly increase the likelihood of successful publication in high-indexed Scopus journals, further enhancing their academic portfolios. Attendees were mentored on the importance of research visibility. High-indexed Scopus journals offer a wide readership and a strong reputation in the academic community. Having research published in such journals can significantly enhance the visibility and impact of a researcher's work, thus contributing to their academic career advancement. Beyond publishing, the masterclass also focused on developing academic skills, such as academic writing, presentation techniques, and effective communication. These skills are transferable and valuable for researchers in various academic careers. Participants could seek personalized advice and guidance from the expert facilitators. This mentorship can extend beyond the workshop, supporting young researchers' academic pursuits. Interacting with accomplished scholars can be a motivating and inspirational experience, encouraging young researchers to pursue excellence in their academic pursuits.

Throughout the 3-day conference, attendees engaged in a series of activities, including six distinct sessions, master classes, knowledge exchange with peers, and deliberations on various topics about entrepreneurship, creative and innovative enterprises, sustainable communities, business and organizational management, and innovations in the digital economy. These discussions encompassed subjects such as digitalization in education, the Internet of Things (IoT), sustainable environments, and the challenges of managing projects across diverse borders, etc.

The conference received a lot of submissions which were all subjected to an extensive and rigorous review process; a double blind peer review approach was used for all submitted papers. The editors of the conference conducted the initial assessment and scrutiny of the papers, and they were checked for plagiarism to proceed to the next stage. The papers that made it to the next stage were subsequently forwarded to at least two reviewers for a blind peer review process. After the peer review procedure was concluded, a technical evaluation and assessment of the papers for plagiarism, proficiency in English, and overall organization was performed. Consequently, a collection of superior scholarly articles was generated, showcasing exemplary methodologies and empirical findings about the subject matter of the conference. All the manuscripts that made to this stage further assessment and substantial extension before being accepted for publishing in the Springer Proceedings in Business and Economics series.

For the first section, "Entrepreneurial Mindset," six papers were selected. The first paper in this theme track discusses a casual model of entrepreneurial intention in undergraduate students. The authors examined how creative activities and projects by universities and colleges influence entrepreneurial intention in undergraduate students of a mid-size governmental university in Thailand. The second paper in this theme track explored the factors involved in predicting the entrepreneurial mindset and the relationship between the entrepreneurial mindset and success. The study aims to understand how the entrepreneurial mindset is created and to analyze how this attitude affects entrepreneurial success. The third paper in track evaluated personal growth and self-discovery with an emphasis on unlocking inner greatness. This was considered vital in a world of chances and challenges where individuals seek to fulfill their full potential. The study placed a major focus on the establishment of explicit objectives and the development of a forward-thinking mentality as fundamental initial measures. The fourth submission addresses the influence of heuristics and cognitive biases on the decision-making processes within committees focused on special education. This study examines the various elements that impact the decision-making process, including perceptual, implementation-related, and general factors. Additionally, it investigates the consequences of these factors on the internal conversations among committee members. The fifth paper explores the concept of society as a quasi-organic organism, examining how culture manifests itself physically through verbal, material, and geographical forms and evaluating culture as a concept distinct from biology and deeply ingrained in the human experience, both molding and being formed by our neuroplastic brains. The final article in this looked at the relevance of psychological, cognitive, and neurological flexibility in fulfilling twenty-first-century demands. It explores how education and perception shape people and society, evaluating how they affect the social and educational environment and how well they meet twenty first-century needs.

The second theme track borders on "Entrepreneurship and Innovation." Ten papers were selected. The first paper on the theme examined the use of brand mascots in marketing campaigns for tourist destinations and their impact on building brand awareness. The second submission focuses on examining entrepreneurship among the Roma community, a significant minority group in Europe, looking into the awareness and intentions for entrepreneurship among young individuals of Roma ethnicity pursuing education and seeking personal and professional development opportunities. The third paper in this track compares women's entrepreneurship in India across time to gain significant insights and reveal India's global women's entrepreneurship status through extensive studies. The fourth paper assesses the contribution of skills to entrepreneurial intentions among transgender people who help them integrate into society. The fifth paper investigated the effects of Education 4.0 on HEIs and assessed its impact through survey-based quantitative research. The sixth paper explored the impact of instant messengers that would result in behavioral changes in the consumer and the effects of digital channels on messages. The seventh article proposed a model that will shape the adoption patterns of battery electric vehicles (BEVs) within the consumer demographic of Thailand. The eighth paper investigated the dynamic nature of online platform interaction within the specific context of fresh fruit e-commerce in China utilizing multiple factors: perceived value, product quality, social media influence, familiarity with e-commerce platforms, and online shopping convenience. The ninth paper explored the relationship between specific entrepreneurial characteristics and entrepreneurial spirit among Indonesians. The final paper in theme expands upon the current body of literature about student satisfaction at public universities in Malaysia by examining the influence of readiness for e-learning, training for e-learning, and motivation for e-learning.

The third theme track covers "Creative and Innovative Enterprises." Nine papers were selected for this theme track. The first paper in this theme track assessed the use of social networks by younger users in individual EU countries, focusing on gender characteristics and age, and the importance of social networks for e-commerce. The second paper offers a framework of value co-creation for enterprises and discusses the relevance of six groups of participants or actors involved in value co-creation processes for enterprises. The third paper reviewed SMEs' adoption of Industry 4.0 (I4.0) tools in supply chain financing (SCF) and discusses the benefits of I4.0 and SCF for SMEs, the barriers to adoption and implementation, and a systems theory-based methodology for adopting SCF I4.0 tools to accelerate I4.0 SCF adoption. The fourth paper analyzed the support of the Regional Operational Program of the Silesian Voivodeship 2014–2020 to increase innovativeness, innovative activity, and the implementation of innovation in the EU projects in the SMEs in the Silesian Voivodeship. The fifth article aimed to identify and develop a set of strategic measures that address the challenges identified in integrating digital technologies. The sixth paper attempted to identify post-pandemic proficiencies in demand and examined how educational institutions promote them to boost employability. The seventh submission aimed to inscribe the issues leaders confront in nurturing creativity at individual and team levels. The eighth paper used a systematic review to examine the influence of social media on destination marketing in China and reviewed the use of short videos as a destination marketing social media tool. The final paper in the theme track aims to identify ongoing research directions common to resilience and dynamic capabilities, utilizing the Scopus database from 2020 to 2023.

The fourth theme track covers "Entrepreneurship, Accounting, and Venture Capital." Ten papers were selected for this theme track. The first paper in this theme track presented an experimental method based on the dynamics of road and bridge works prices, reducing the risk of exceeding construction investment costs. The second submission in this track investigated the impact of the COVID-19 pandemic, especially the lockdowns and restrictions, on various economies, with a focus on how these measures affected enterprises, mainly service-based businesses. The third submission explored whether the gender of the CEO influences the motives leading to creative accounting and the influence of the gender of the CEO on the implementation of creative accounting by employees under the direction of the CEO. The fourth paper examined the effect of profitability and leverage on dividend policy decisions for Jordanian firms that are listed on the Amman Stock Exchange (ASX) using a panel econometric model. The fifth paper in this track examined how perceived pleasure and trust related to utilizing mobile payments were perceived, as well as how these factors affected users' intentions to keep using the service. The sixth article investigates the impact of revenue streams on nonprofit organizations' total annual revenue, financial performance, and financial stability. The seventh paper for this theme track investigated the effect of integrating sustainability reporting and

Eco-innovation activities on the firm value. The eighth article attempts to build a model framework to help Chinese mobile payment operators identify factors that affect consumers' use of mobile payment to expand consumer groups and enhance the competitiveness of mobile payment companies. The ninth article investigated the volatility spillover from three leading capital markets, New York, Shanghai, and Japan Stock Exchange on the Stock Exchange of Thailand, using Dynamic Conditional Correlation Multivariate GARCH (DCC-MGARCH). The final paper for this theme track evaluated the factors influencing purchasing decisions of nutritional supplements for the elderly in Thailand, focusing on health consciousness, quality assurance, social influence, accessibility, and perceived benefits.

The fifth theme track covers "Business and Organizational Management." The theme had 18 papers. The first paper in this theme track addresses the urgent need for a unified EU-level regulation of telework. This topic has gained critical importance due to the COVID-19 pandemic. The second submission presented the policy research for the management efficiency of the research facility. The third submission aims to determine how European pandemic-related restrictions and the armed conflict in Ukraine influenced seaport cargo volumes. The fourth paper examined the impact of CSR toward employees on organizational trust, organizational commitment, and customer orientation behavior and the mediating role of organizational trust and organizational commitment in the relationship between perceived CSR toward employees and customer orientation behavior. The fifth paper ascertained whether company internationalization and globalization can produce new circumstances that alter Poland's firm management paradigm. The sixth article scrutinized the role of Poland in ensuring the logistics of humanitarian aid provided to Ukraine by the international community in wartime. The seventh study for the theme track explored the interplay between authentic leadership, employee resilience, and employee work performance. The eighth submission investigated the factors influencing the organizational survival of retail food businesses during the COVID-19 outbreak in Thailand to develop a conceptual framework. The ninth paper attempted to create a tool to collect qualitative research data on Thai prosumers' performance on social media. The tenth article examined the impact of the feminine leadership style and feminine organizational culture on the organization's overall performance in contrasting economies. The eleventh paper intended to calculate the efficiency score for selected countries, describe their innovation profiles, and compare the most effective and the least effective. The twelfth submission explored the influence of the COVID-19 pandemic on work values and the reality of career choices among university students. The thirteenth paper explores the intricate dynamics of factors influencing customer retention within the parcel delivery sector. The fourteenth submission for the theme track analyzed the mediating role of psychological capital in the relationship between psychological empowerment and innovative work behavior in marketing employees at a private Bank in Bali. The fifteenth article investigated the complex roles that employers, workplace climate, and acceptance play in shaping the experiences of employees with disabilities from the employees' perspective. The sixteenth research submitted for the theme was a quantitative case study report seeking to explore the teachers' emotions, emotional regulation strategies, and withdrawal behaviors the unique population of the Arab sector Israel. The final paper in the track explored the correlation between the leadership of the Arab Scout movement counsels and the community engagement of its members.

The sixth theme track covers "Organizational Performance and Sustainability." The theme had 9 papers. The first paper in this theme track presented the available ways and methods of measuring the phenomenon of reputation as the modern challenge for responsible and sustainable development of the perceived image of entities as their very fragile intangible assets. The second submission examined innovative approaches to online reputation management during a global pandemic. The third paper focuses on developing sustainable mobility in cities in Poland, Europe, and worldwide, explicitly emphasizing the sharing economy's role. The fourth submission in this theme track examines the relationship between green marketing strategies and how they impact consumer perceptions of brands. The fifth paper focuses on highlighting the significance of Psychological Capital as a mediator variable between Psychological Empowerment and Service Behavior and Service Climate and Service Behavior of the employees in the banking sector in south India. The sixth submission investigates the potential of Fourth Industrial Revolution technologies in advancing Agenda 2030 of the SDGs. The seventh paper examines how the food sector has changed from traditional competitiveness to supply chain competition, emphasizing sustainability, environmental awareness, and ethics. The eighth submission for this theme track discourses the pressing issue of climate change and the drivers behind it by exploring the relationship between $CO_2$ emissions and various economic indicators of 22 European countries from 1992 to 2019. The final submission for this theme track discusses the increasing importance of green technology in response to global environmental challenges and the urgent need for environmental sustainability. It highlights the relatively new concept of green innovation and the limited amount of research conducted on this topic.

We want to express our sincere gratitude to our esteemed keynote speakers, distinguished panelists, and dedicated authors who have played a pivotal role in shaping the success of this conference. Their invaluable contributions in the form of submissions and the subsequent meticulous review process, guided by the insightful feedback from our diligent reviewers, have been instrumental in making this event a resounding success. We extend our heartfelt appreciation to the diligent members of the Program Committee for their unwavering commitment to providing astute reviews ensuring the quality and relevance of the conference content.

As we reflect on the achievements of this conference, we are filled with hope and anticipation for the future. We aspire that this conference will continue to thrive as an annual tradition, serving as a distinguished platform for the convergence of scientists and practitioners. In the years to come, we look forward to witnessing the exchange of ideas, the sharing of the latest breakthroughs, and the collaborative exploration of the ever-evolving landscape of the global business economy.

We would like to express our sincere appreciation to all the authors who submitted their work for consideration in this publication. Your dedication to advancing knowledge and contributing to academic discourse is genuinely commendable. We are grateful for the effort and expertise you have shared with us. We would also like to extend our heartfelt thanks to the reviewers who carefully evaluated the submitted works. Your insightful feedback and constructive criticism have been invaluable in maintaining the quality and rigor of the content included in this publication. Your commitment to scholarly excellence is deeply appreciated. It is through the collaborative efforts of authors and reviewers that this publication has achieved its scholarly significance. We extend our deepest gratitude to each and every individual who has contributed to the realization of this endeavor.

Czestochowa, Poland
Bangkok, Thailand
Fredericton, Canada
November 2023

Sebastian Kot
Bilal Khalid
Adnan ul Haque

# Program Committee

A. Hariharasudan, Kalasalingam University, India
Agata Mesjasz, Częstochowa University of Technology, Poland
Beata Gavurova, Academy of Economic Studies, Romania
Beata Ślusarczyk, Częstochowa University of Technology, Poland
Belaid Aouni, Qatar University, Qatar
Budsabawan Maharakkhaka, Stamford International University, Thailand
Daniel Meyer, University of Johannesburg, South Africa
Fauzia Jabeen, Abu Dhabi University, United Arab Emirates
Hafezali Iqbal Hussain, Taylors University, Malaysia
Hana Stverkova, VŠB-Technical University of Ostrava, Czechia
Ismi Rajiani, Lambung Mangkurat University, Indonesia
Iwona Otola, Częstochowa University of Technology, Poland
Janusz Michałek, WSB University, Poland
Jean Marc Dautrey, Stamford International University, Thailand
Jhalukpreya Surujlal, North West University, South Africa
József Popp, John von Neumann University, Hungary
Judit Olah, John von Neumann University, Hungary
Jumadil Saputra, Universiti Malaysia Terengganu, Malaysia
Katarzyna Szczepańska-Woszczyna, WSB University, Poland
Lucian-Ionel Cioca, Lucian Blaga University of Sibiu, Romania
Manuela Tvaronaviciene, Vilnius Gediminas Technical University, Lithuania
Maria Fekete-Farkas, Hungarian University of Agriculture and Life Sciences, Hungary
Mariusz Urbański, Road and Bridge Research Institute, Poland
Marlena Grabowska, Częstochowa University of Technology, Poland
Martina Rašticová, Mendel University in Brno, Czechia
Natalia Konovalova, RISEBA University of Applied Sciences, Latvia
Natanya Meyer, University of Johannesburg, South Africa
Nusanee Meekaewkunchorn, Bansomdejchaopraya Rajabhat University, Thailand
Pensri Jaroenwanit, Khon Kaen University, Thailand

Piyada Paowadueng, Khon Kaen University, Thailand
Radovan Bacik, University of Presov, Slovakia
Robert Jeyakumar, Multimedia University, Malaysia
Robert Stefko, University of Presov, Slovakia
Robert Ulewicz, Częstochowa University of Technology, Poland
Singha Chaveesuk, King Mongkut's Institute of Technology Ladkrabang, Thailand
Slimane Ed-Dafali, Chouaib Doukkali University, Morocco
Veronika Fenyves, University of Debrecen, Hungary
Wiliam Philip Wall, Stamford International University, Thailand
Wittika Thangchan, Khon Kaen University, Thailand
Wornchanok Chaiyasoonthorn, King Mongkut's Institute of Technology Ladkrabang, Thailand
Yasri, Universitas Negeri Padang, Indonesia
Yuriy Bilan, Rzeszow University of Technology, Poland
Yusliza Mohd Yusoff, Universiti Malaysia Terengganu, Malaysia
Zoltan Bujdoso, Hungarian University of Agriculture and Life Sciences, Hungary

# Reviewers

A. Hariharasudan, Kalasalingam University, India
Adnan ul Haque, Yorkville University, Canada
Armenia Androniceanu, Academy of Economic Studies, Romania
Beata Gavurova, Technical University of Kosice, Slovakia
Beata Ślusarczyk, Częstochowa University of Technology, Poland
Daniel Meyer, University of Johannesburg, South Africa
Fauzia Jabeen, Abu Dhabi University, United Arab Emirates
Hafezali Iqbal Hussain, Taylors University, Malaysia
Hana Stverkova, VŠB-Technical University of Ostrava, Czechia
Ismi Rajiani, Lambung Mangkurat University, Indonesia
Iwona Otola, Czestochowa University of Technology, Poland
Janusz Grabara, Jan Dlugosz University, Czestochowa, Poland
Janusz Michałek, WSB University, Poland
Judit Olah, John Von Neumann University, Hungary
Jumadil Saputra, Universiti Malaysia Terengganu, Malaysia
Katarzyna Grondys, Czestochowa University of Technology, Poland
Katarzyna Szczepańska-Woszczyna, WSB University, Poland
Klaudia Smoląg, Czestochowa University of Technology, Poland
Magdalena Biel, Czestochowa University of Technology, Poland
Manuela Tvaronaviciene, Vilnius Gediminas Technical University, Lithuania
Maria Fekete-Farkas, Hungarian University of Agriculture and Life Sciences, Hungary
Mariusz Urbański, Road and Bridge Research Institute, Poland
Muhammad Imran, Universiti Utara Malaysia, Malaysia
Natanya Meyer, University of Johannesburg, South Africa
Nusanee Meekaekunchorn, Bansomdejechaopraya Rajabhat University, Thailand
Paula Pypłacz, Czestochowa University of Technology, Poland
Pensri Jaroenwanit, Khon Kaen University, Thailand
Radovan Bacik, University of Presov, Slovakia
Robert Jeyakumar, Multimedia University, Malaysia
Robert Stefko, University of Presov, Slovakia

Robert Ulewicz, Czestochowa University of Technology, Poland
Singha Chaveesuk, King Mongkut's Institute of Technology Ladkrabang, Thailand
Veronika Fenyves, University of Debrecen, Hungary
Wiliam Philip Wall, Stamford International University, Thailand
Wornchanok Chaiyasoonthorn, King Mongkut's Institute of Technology Ladkrabang, Thailand
Yusliza Mohd Yusoff, Universiti Malaysia Terengganu, Malaysia

# Contents

**Entrepreneurial Mindset**

**A Casual Model of Entrepreneurial Intention in Undergraduate Students** ... 3
Porngarm Virutamasen, Piyapong Klaikleng, Kageeporn Wongpreedee, and Navidreza Ahadi

**Decoding Entrepreneurial Mindset: From Metacognitive Awareness, Growth Orientation and Opportunities Capitalization to Entrepreneurial Success** ... 21
Nina Szczygiel, Dina Ramos, and Nicole Jesus

**Rising to Your Potential: Unlocking Your Inner Greatness** ... 39
William Philip Wall

**Cognitive Biases and Heuristics in Decision-Making Processes Affecting Budget and Perceptions in Special Education Committees and the Potential Contribution of Expanding Psychological Flexibility Among Decision-Makers** ... 47
Hila Fuchs and Slawomir Banaszak

**The Quasi-Organic Society Living Culture Body and Its Business Applications** ... 77
Ariel Fuchs, Hila Fuchs, Eva Benkova, Daniel Galily, and Tatyana Petkova

**The Importance of Psychological and Cognitive Flexibility in Educational Processes to Prepare and Acquire the Skills Required in the Twenty-First Century** ... 91
Hila Fuchs, Eva Benkova, Arie Fishbein, and Ariel Fuchs

## Entrepreneurship and Innovation

**Influence of Brand Mascots on Enhancing Awareness of Vietnam's Tourism** ..... 117
Trinh Le Tan, Thi Tra My Le, Hoang Quynh My Phan, Truong Son Phuong Phan, Linh Giang Nguyen, and Thuy Phuoc Tan Le

**Entrepreneurship Among Young People of Roma Origin—Attitudes and Perceptions** ..... 133
Silviya Georgieva

**Factors Affecting Performance of Women Entrepreneurs': A Study of Rural Women Entrepreneurs in Emerging Indian Market** ..... 153
Dhanashree Katekhaye and Róbert Magda

**Transgender Entrepreneurs: An Alternative Path to Social Integration** ..... 171
Gnana Sanga Mithra S, Aravind B. R, Bhuvaneswari G, Suriya S, Sathish R, and Edhaya Chandran E

**Investigating the Role of Education 4.0 in the Performance of HEIs** ..... 183
D. Sri Dhivya, A. Hariharasudan, E. Balamurali, Zdzislawa Dacko-Pikiewicz, and Janusz Michałek

**Internet of Things: Effectiveness of Instant Messengers on Consumer Behaviour as a Digital Marketing Channel** ..... 205
Easwaramoorthy Rangaswamy, Stephanie Lim Mei Ling, Nishad Nawaz, and Gemini Velleringatt Joy

**An Acceptance Model for the Adoption of Battery Electric Vehicles in Thailand** ..... 231
Thana Sithanant, Burin Sukphisal, and Nayika Kamales

**Factors Influencing Online Platform Engagement in Fresh Fruit E-commerce in China** ..... 247
Lin Tang and Nuttawut Rojniruttikul

**Bridging the Gap Between Entrepreneurial Personality and Entrepreneurship Education Program** ..... 263
Jumadi, Ismi Rajiani, and Ersis Warmansyah Abbas

**Student Acceptance Level for E-Learning in Public Universities of Malaysia** ..... 273
Muhammad Imran, Ali Raza, A. K. Mahbubul Hye, and Maadi Bakor Omar

**Creative and Innovative Enterprises**

**The Importance of Social Networks for E-commerce: An Analysis of Young Users' Perspectives in the European Union** ..... 291
Richard Fedorko, Radovan Bačík, Martin Rigelský, Jakub Horváth, and Štefan Kráľ

**Towards an Integrated Model of Value Co-creation for Enterprises** ..... 305
Thi Bich Hanh Tran

**Industry 4.0 Adoption in Supply Chain Financing for Small and Medium Enterprises: A Systems Theory Approach** ..... 321
Navidreza Ahadi, Gladness Monametsi, Shahryar Sorooshian, and Porngarm Virutamasen

**An Assessment of Innovativeness, Innovative Activity and Innovation Implementation in EU-Funded Projects in the Śląskie Voivodship in Poland** ..... 335
Monika Raczyńska and Joanna Kurowska-Pysz

**Digital Transformation in Organizations from Sibiu Country, Romania** ..... 351
Adriana Milea and Lucian-Ionel Cioca

**Navigating Pandemic and AI Influences on Employability Competencies** ..... 369
Negar Sohaee, Farnaz Azadjoutabari, Amey Jadhav, and Kaustubh Kulkarni

**Knowledge Sharing by Leadership Perks up Creativity: An Empirical Evidence Based on Multilevel Survey** ..... 393
GholamReza Zandi, Imran Ahmed Shahzad, Ayesha Kanwal, Khawar Naheed, Muhammad Sadiq Shahid, and Sandy Low Bee Choo

**Social Media and Destination Marketing in China: A Systematic Review of Short Videos** ..... 413
Congying Liu, Ahmad Edwin Bin Mohamed, and Muhammad Zulqarnain Arshad

**A Bibliometric Analysis of Dynamic Capabilities and Resilience Using VOSviewer** ..... 437
Iwona Otola and Marta Szczepańczyk

**Entrepreneurship, Accounting, and Venture Capital**

**Innovative Price Indexing for Managing Road and Bridge Projects: Mitigating Cost Overruns** ..... 451
Mariusz Urbański, Katarzyna Grondys, Marcin Świtała, and Wiesław Liszewski

**State Aid as a Form of Alleviating the Negative Effects of the COVID-19 Pandemic on the Economy** ........................ 467
Beata Ślusarczyk and Magdalena Biel

**CEO Gender's Impact on Creative Accounting Motives and Manipulation: Evidence from Slovakia** ........................ 479
Jakub Michulek and Anna Krizanova

**Do Profitability and Leverage Influence Dividend Policy? Evidence from Emerging Countries** ............................... 495
Amanj Mohamed Ahmed, Mária Fekete-Farkas, and István Hágen

**Southeast Asian Youth's Long-Term Desire to Use Mobile Payments** .................................................... 511
Yasri Yasri, Astra Prima Budiarti, Rizki Sri Lasmini, Gerald Goh Guan Gan, Theeraphab Phetmalaikul, Lita Bacalla, and Naila Beltran

**Revenue Structure, Financial Stability and Financial Performance of NPOs in Developing Countries: Does Revenue Diversity Lead to Better Performance?** ........................... 523
Akeel Almagtome, Enaam Almusawi, Hussein Furaijl, Ahmed Al-Yasiri, and Zahira Alfartoosi

**Eco-Innovation Accounting, Sustainability and Firm Value: An Integrated Perspective** ..................................... 543
Akeel Almagtome and Anmar Aljaafari

**Determinants of Willingness to Use Mobile Payment Application in China** ................................................... 557
Shulan Chen, Wornchanok Chaiyasoonthorn, and Singha Chaveesuk

**Volatility Linkage Between the Stock Exchange of Thailand and Major Stock Markets** ..................................... 569
Budsabawan Maharakkhaka, Boonyachote Suteerawattananon, and Sutatt Ramasoot

**Exploring Influential Factors in the Purchasing of Nutritional Supplements for the Elderly** ................................... 587
Yuhang Wang and Nuttawut Rojniruttikul

**Business and Organizational Management**

**Balancing Flexibility and Fairness: Legal Implications for Defining Decent Telework in the EU in an Era of Digitalization** .... 605
Marta Urbane

**Policy Research for Management Efficiency of Research Facility** ...... 615
Donghun Yoon

**European Seaport Cargo Management: Adaptations Amidst the Global Economic Crisis** ........ 627
Katarzyna Grondys

**How Does Perceived CSR Toward Employees Influence Customer Orientation Behavior: The Moderating Role of Internal Communication** ........ 643
Thinh-Van Vu

**The Impact of the Globalization on the Management Culture in Polish Enterprises** ........ 663
Bartosz Jeżyna and Sebastian Kot

**Logistics of Polish Humanitarian Aid for Ukraine** ........ 677
Olha Husieva and Sebastian Kot

**Effects of Authentic Leadership on Employee Work Performance, Moderated by Employee Resilience** ........ 695
Pitchaya Srimongkolkul and Jumpoth Boriraj

**Factors Influencing Organizational Survival of Retail Food Businesses in Thailand: A Conceptual Perspective** ........ 711
Auyporn Naklamthong, Wornchanok Chaiyasoonthorn, and Singha Chaveesuk

**The Creation of Tools to Collect Qualitative Research Data for Prosumer Performance** ........ 725
Arissa Sa-ardnak, Wornchanok Chaiyasoonthorn, and Singha Chaveesuk

**Impact of Feminine Leadership Style and Feminine Organizational Culture on the Overall Performance of the Organization: Comparative Analysis** ........ 735
Riffat Faizan

**The Efficiency Estimation in Universities Intellectual Capital: Evidence from EU Countries** ........ 749
Natália Slyvkanyč and Jozef Glova

**Factors Effecting on Work Values Towards Career Choices Among University Students** ........ 765
Nagatheesan V. Marimuthu, Saralah Devi Mariamdaran Chethiyar, Muhammad Zulqarnain Arshad, Kharrtheek Devarajah, Yadu K. Damodaran, and Muhammad Ali Arshad

**Factors Influencing Customer Retention in the Parcel Delivery Industry** ........ 789
Zonghong Wu and Nuttawut Rojniruttikul

**Psychological Empowerment, Psychological Capital, and Innovative Work Behavior: A Path to Organizational Success** .... 807
Ida Bagus Ketut Surya, I. Gede Riana, Tjokorda Gde Raka Sukawati, and I. Putu Astawa

**Managing Employees with Disabilities: The Impact of Employer Behavior and Workplace Climate from an Employee Perspective in Israel** .... 817
Eslam Hujerat

**Experience of Emotions, Emotion Regulation, and Withdrawal Behavior of Arab Teachers in Israel Primary Schools** .... 841
Nagham Farah

**The Scouts Movement Leadership in the Arab Society in Israel and Its Effect on Community Engagement of Its Members** .... 867
Adham Farah

**Organizational Performance and Sustainability**

**Reputation Analysis of Selected European and US Brands in the Context of the COVID-19 Pandemic** .... 895
František Pollák, Peter Markovič, Michal Konečný, and Mária Kmety Barteková

**Reputation of Family-Owned Businesses: Parent Companies vs. Their Brands in the Context of Global Pandemic** .... 917
Peter Markovič and František Pollák

**Rethinking Sustainable Transportation: The Role of Shared Mobility in Urban Environments** .... 939
Marcin Kubera and Beata Ślusarczyk

**Green Marketing and Brand Perception: Unveiling the Consumer Perspective** .... 951
Lucia Sujanska and Margareta Nadanyiova

**Psychological Empowerment and Service Culture: Fostering Sustainable Service Behavior in the Banking Sector** .... 963
Vairamani Sathyamoorthi, Sikkander Basheer Inayath Ahamed, Nishad Nawaz, Anandhan Hariharasudan, and Ravindran Kandasamy

**The Role of Fourth Industrial Revolution (4IR) Technologies in Achieving Sustainable Development Goals** .... 985
Everjoy Chipo Makazhe and Tafadzwa Clemetine Maramura

**A Test of an Instrument for Measuring the Model of White Supply Chain Management for Sustainable Performance in the Food Industry** ........ 999
Waraporn Suksanchananun, Wornchanok Chaiyasoonthorn, and Singha Chaveesuk

**Thresholds of Sustainability: Analyzing the Interplay Between Carbon Dioxide Emissions, Economic Growth, and Urbanization in the European Union** ........ 1023
Jana Chovancová, Igor Petruška, and Peter Adamišin

**Managerial Approach in Green Innovation: Theoretical Framework** ........ 1039
Anuphat Thirakulwanich and Katarzyna Szczepańska-Woszczyna

# Entrepreneurial Mindset

# A Casual Model of Entrepreneurial Intention in Undergraduate Students

**Porngarm Virutamasen, Piyapong Klaikleng, Kageeporn Wongpreedee, and Navidreza Ahadi**

**Abstract** This research describes how entrepreneurial intention is developed, giving the importance of creative activities and projects provided by universities. Thus, the antecedents of entrepreneurial intention were investigated among undergraduate students of a mid-size governmental university in Thailand. It was argued in this framework that creative activities organized by the university or the college contributed to instilling entrepreneurial intention in undergraduate students. Self-administered survey data from 400 undergraduate students were collected and analyzed using the structural equation model technique to verify the hypothesis relationships. The findings indicated that creative activities supported by the university significantly affected entrepreneurial intention among undergraduate students via entrepreneurial self-efficacy. Additional results also revealed the significant influence of individual growth mindset and individual creativity among students, which correlate well with entrepreneurial self-efficacy. The paper concludes with suggestions for extended research and implications for educators and policymakers in education regarding entrepreneurial intention strategies development among students.

**Keywords** Entrepreneurship · Entrepreneurial Intention · Entrepreneurial Self-Efficacy · Creative Activity

## 1 Introduction

The subject matter of entrepreneurship has garnered significant scholarly and academic interest in recent decades [1]. It has been regarded as a key activity contributing to the economy by creating new jobs. It is strongly associated with the socio-economic evolution of developed and developing countries [2]. Two

P. Virutamasen (✉) · K. Wongpreedee · N. Ahadi
College of Creative Industry, Srinakharinwirot University, Bangkok, Thailand
e-mail: porngarm@g.swu.ac.th

P. Klaikleng
Educational and Psychological Test Bureau, Srinakharinwirot University, Bangkok, Thailand



S. Kot et al. (eds.), *Corporate Practices: Policies, Methodologies, and Insights in Organizational Management*, Springer Proceedings in Business and Economics,
https://doi.org/10.1007/978-981-97-0996-0_1

major streams of research have been carried out on this issue: (1) Entrepreneurial intention and (2)—entrepreneurial education. Entrepreneurial intention reflects the person's willingness and readiness to pursue entrepreneurship as a career choice and to get involved in entrepreneurial activities [3]. Most previous studies on entrepreneurial intention have focused on exploring personal traits and personalities that affect an individual's entrepreneurial intention [4]. Within this stream of research, entrepreneurial self-efficacy has been proposed to have a direct impact on entrepreneurial intention, where individuals with high levels of entrepreneurial self-efficacy tend to deal successfully with the entrepreneurship process and the challenging conditions attached to the process [2, 5]. Moreover, many other factors have also been examined.

The other stream has been focused on entrepreneurship education, which is associated with nurturing creative skills that can be applied in real life [6]. With its recognition as a powerful tool for creating jobs and improving economic power, the number of courses and training programs on entrepreneurship and the related ones provided by universities and higher education institutions is increasing, with the purpose of students' motivation and confidence development leading to entrepreneurship as a career choice at the end. Past research has shown that entrepreneurship education has had a positive impact on students' entrepreneurial intentions. In particular, arguments have been that several supportive dimensions, such as entrepreneurship education, entrepreneurial passion, entrepreneurial orientation, entrepreneurial self-efficacy, and entrepreneurial mindset, are associated with developing an entrepreneurial intention for new business creation and start-ups [7].

This study continues the stream of research on entrepreneurial intention, highlighting the importance of creative activities provided by the university as a part of the entrepreneurship education ecosystem and other individual traits, namely growth mindset and individual creativity. In particular, this research argues that creative activities provided by universities, which are counted as an entrepreneurship education ecosystem, together with an individual growth mindset and creativity, can lead to entrepreneurial intention through the mediating role of entrepreneurial self-efficacy. This study provides contributions to the literature on entrepreneurship as follows:

First, most of the previous studies have investigated entrepreneurship education in the context of Europe [8], India [9], and China [1]. At the same time, more research needs to be published internationally in the context of Thai students. Second, existing research studies have been focused on personal traits such as family business [10], entrepreneurial alertness [11], and entrepreneurial self-efficacy [12], but much less have included growth mind-set and individual creativity in the research framework to determine entrepreneurial intention among students. Finally, this study provides an extension model by taking entrepreneurial self-efficacy as a mediator to explain the relationship among creative activities provided by the university, individual growth mind-set, and creativity further to predict the entrepreneurial intention among Thai undergraduate students.

The paper begins with the literature, and the theoretical background underlying the research framework is reviewed, followed by the research model and related hypotheses. The research methodology and data analysis are described subsequently.

The paper concludes with a discussion and conclusion, highlighting managerial implications and suggestions for future research.

## 2 Literature Review

### 2.1 *Entrepreneurial Intention*

Entrepreneurial intention is a starting point of the challenging process of being an entrepreneur. Hence, it has received considerable attention from scholars to explore various factors that may lead to entrepreneurial intention. According to [13], entrepreneurial intention is a self-acknowledged belief to start a new career. Some scholars have studied entrepreneurial intention from a social cognitive theory perspective [2, 14–16]. One of the most important personal factors that have demonstrated a significant influence on entrepreneurial intention is entrepreneurial self-efficacy [2, 17]. Previous studies also investigated how entrepreneurs' different traits and personalities can affect their entrepreneurial intentions [5].

Another antecedent factor that has been claimed to have a significant influence on entrepreneurial intention is the entrepreneurial ecosystem, which was defined by [18] as a group of interrelated factors of economic, social, and institutional that stimulate the creation and development of entrepreneurial opportunities.

Additionally, some scholars examined entrepreneurial intention among students in colleges and universities [19, 20], while some have focused their research on the relationship between appropriate teaching and learning methods in colleges and entrepreneurial intention [21].

### 2.2 *Entrepreneurial Self-Efficacy*

Self-efficacy was expressed for the first time from the social cognitive theory proposed by [22] as individual self-belief to attain goal-oriented tasks. In the light of entrepreneurship research, entrepreneurial self-efficacy has been given several definitions [23, 24]. This research paper refers to entrepreneurial self-efficacy as the degree to which a person believes in his skills and abilities to accomplish the required duties to start a new business venture [14]. Entrepreneurship is a long and challenging journey that requires commitment and persistence. Therefore, it is predicted that an individual with a high degree of entrepreneurial self-efficacy is likely to be ready and able to face challenging conditions while establishing a new business [14, 20, 25, 26]. Many studies show that entrepreneurial self-efficacy is a leading indicator of entrepreneurial intention and attitude [2, 5, 14, 25, 27]. In particular, several research studies found that self-efficacy played a significant mediating role, either direct or indirect, in entrepreneurial intention [28, 29]. Some scholars also have entrepreneurial self-efficacy related to an entrepreneurial mindset, suggesting that these two factors will help formulate entrepreneurial intention [30, 31].

## 2.3 Individual Creativity

Individual creativity has been claimed to be associated with entrepreneurship because creativity is particularly crucial for entrepreneurial activities, and entrepreneurship itself is a creative activity. In entrepreneurship, individual creativity refers to the process by which entrepreneurs combine existing resources and generate new ideas to start innovative businesses [32]. Recently, many researchers have explored individual creativity's influence on entrepreneurial intention [32–34]. Results of these studies demonstrated that individuals with high levels of creativity were more likely to become entrepreneurs or start new businesses than those with lower levels of creativity [32–34]. Moreover, a study by [35] revealed that entrepreneurs with creativity had inspiration and strong leadership, which would enable them to lead organizations successfully with differentiated products and services that outperformed competitors.

## 2.4 Growth Mindset

The concept of a growth mindset is essential, emphasizing self-awareness of one's weaknesses and the intention to improve these weaknesses to achieve personal goals. Research in the field has shown that a Growth Mindset has a positive impact on seeking entrepreneurial opportunities and entrepreneurial intention. This mindset encourages individuals to view their weaknesses as opportunities for learning and gaining new experiences, ultimately leading to positive outcomes [36–39].

## 2.5 Creative Activities Supported by University/college

This research uses the definition of entrepreneurship promotion from educational institutions as provided by [7], which states that "learning activities related to the development of knowledge, skills, abilities, and attitudes, and the role of educational institutions in promoting entrepreneurship skills are crucial". Educational management must promote the intention to become entrepreneurs to ensure that learners' future tendencies include engaging in entrepreneurship during or after their education. Therefore, the strategy for promoting entrepreneurship skills should include fostering the intention to become entrepreneurs in both classroom teaching and extracurricular activities, as well as creating a university or faculty environment conducive to learning and developing entrepreneurial skills. Universities should not only provide physical support but also create a learning environment that encourages future entrepreneurship exchanges [40].

## 2.6 Related Research Work

Yousaf et al. [41] examined education management to promote entrepreneurship and entrepreneurial intentions by considering self-perceived abilities and attitudes toward entrepreneurship as mediating variables. The research analyzed the conceptual framework for developing entrepreneurship by measuring the intention to become an entrepreneur. This research was correlational.

The research findings suggest that education management in entrepreneurship, self-perceived abilities, and attitudes toward starting new businesses impact entrepreneurial intention, with self-perceived abilities and attitudes acting as mediating variables. For future research, it is recommended to explore causal relationship models of promoting entrepreneurial intentions within various social and cultural settings.

Pitisutti and Kaewjaroen [42] studied the factors influencing students' intention in entrepreneurship-focused programs at Phayao University. The objective was to investigate the impact of planned behavior theory and entrepreneurial characteristics on students' intentions to become entrepreneurs. The research used a survey method involving 202 students. Data analysis employed multiple regression analysis. The research findings concluded that planned behavior theory and entrepreneurial characteristics impact students' intentions to become entrepreneurs in the entrepreneurship program. For future research recommendations, it is suggested to study economic and social factors influencing the intention to become entrepreneurs.

Wathanakom [43] conducted a study on the factors influencing the intention of undergraduate students to become entrepreneurs. The objective was to examine the influence of factors related to perceived entrepreneurial capability and attitudes toward entrepreneurship on the intention to become an entrepreneur. The study discovered a need for a deeper comprehension of the critical factors contributing to success. Traditionally, an entrepreneur's path commences to be entrepreneurial, recognizing opportunities, initiating business endeavors, and assembling the necessary resources for a successful venture. This intention to be entrepreneurial is a fundamental precursor to engaging in entrepreneurial activities, aligning with the theory of planned behavior. As a result, researchers are keen on identifying the pivotal factors influencing entrepreneurial intention.

Daniel [44] studied the promotion of an entrepreneurial mindset using the design thinking concept for entrepreneurship education management. The objective was to foster an entrepreneurial mindset among first-year students at Harvard University, totaling 66 students over two academic years, where entrepreneurship courses were taught using design thinking. Data analysis was conducted using surveys assessing satisfaction and entrepreneurial mindset at the end of the semester. The research findings were as follows:

1. Collaborative learning, creativity, and autonomy should be integrated into classroom teaching practices.
2. Teaching methods using design thinking should align with course content and objectives.
3. Instructors should possess facilitation skills to aid the learning process.
4. Understanding levels of students' learning mindsets vary, emphasizing a multidisciplinary team of instructors.

Kumar and Shuk [45] conducted a study on creativity, proactive personality, and entrepreneurial intention with a focus on self-perceived entrepreneurial capability as a mediating variable. The research aimed to investigate the roles of creativity and proactive personality in influencing entrepreneurial intentions and to examine how self-perceived entrepreneurial capability mediates these relationships. Data were collected from 484 management students through structured questionnaires. Structural equation modeling was used for data analysis. The research findings indicate that self-perceived entrepreneurial competence is a good predictor of entrepreneurial intention. Intrapreneurial personality influences entrepreneurial intentions and is influenced by creative thinking.

Furthermore, the research shows that self-perceived entrepreneurial competence is a variable transmitted from creative thinking and intrapreneurial personality to entrepreneurial intention. For future research, it is advisable to explore additional factors such as passion, family business ownership, social and family support, and perceived barriers. Additionally, examining economic structure in different contexts may be worthwhile. For future research recommendations, it is suggested to establish a design thinking process for entrepreneurship education management.

Jiatong et al. [46] studied the impact of entrepreneurship promotion from educational institutions, entrepreneurial identity, and creativity on entrepreneurial intentions mediated by self-perceived entrepreneurial capability. The research findings indicated that self-perceived entrepreneurial capability influenced the relationship between entrepreneurship promotion from educational institutions, entrepreneurial identity, and creativity.

In addition, Badri and Hachich [47] also investigated the effects of entrepreneurship promotion from educational institutions on the entrepreneurial intentions of students from two universities in Tunisia. The research suggested that personal characteristics such as age, gender, and educational level were significant variables affecting the intention to become an entrepreneur or start a startup business. The research framework is presented as follows:

**Hypothesis 1:**
Entrepreneurial self-efficacy is positively related to entrepreneurial intention.

**Hypothesis 2:**
Growth mindset is positively related to entrepreneurial intention.

**Hypothesis 3:**
Individual creativity is positively related to entrepreneurial intention.

**Hypothesis 4:**
Growth mindset is positively related to entrepreneurial intention, and having entrepreneurial self-efficacy mediates the relationship.

**Hypothesis 5:**
Growth mindset is positively related to entrepreneurial intention, having individual creativity mediate the relationship.

**Hypothesis 6:**
Creative activities provided by university is positively related to entrepreneurial intention, having growth mindset, individual creativity, and entrepreneurial self-efficacy mediate the relationship.

### 2.7 *Research Framework*

See Fig. 1.

## 3 Research Methodology

This research aims to study the causes of undergraduate students' intention to become entrepreneurs using a Casual research methodology and a Quantitative method. The research has two main objectives, which are:

1. To examine the role of creative activities supported by university in developing entrepreneurial intentions among undergraduate students.
2. To propose strategies for enhancing the entrepreneurial intentions of undergraduate students.

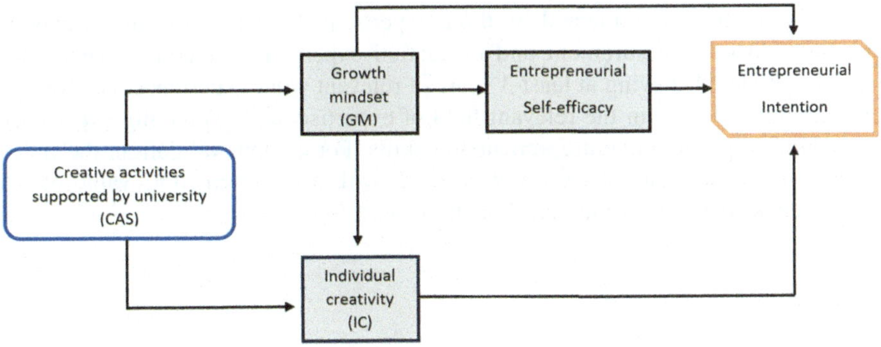


**Fig. 1** Research Framework

The following sections will provide a detailed explanation of the research methodology and procedures. This study is a quantitative research approach. Several scholars who have studied entrepreneurship have guided this research, including [1, 19, 48]. Each variable consists of no fewer than three questions. This research comprises the following processes (Table 1):

1. Literature Review: In this phase, the study involves a comprehensive examination of relevant theories, concepts, and prior research related to Entrepreneurial Intention (EI), Creative Activities Supported by University/College (CAS), Growth Mindset (GM), Entrepreneurial Self-efficacy (ES), and Individual Creativity (IC).
2. Research Execution:

   2.1. Operational Definitions of Variables: This section defines the variables used in the research, providing practical definitions for terms like Entrepreneurial Intention, Entrepreneurial Self-efficacy, Growth Mindset, Individual Creativity, and Creative Activities Supported by University/College.

   2.2. Selection of Study Population: The research specifies the population or group under investigation.

   2.3. Development of Research Instruments: For this study, research instruments take the form of questionnaires that gather data related to the variables. There are five key variables, each with at least three corresponding questions:
      1. Creative activities supported by university/college (CAS).
      2. Growth mindset (GM).
      3. Entrepreneurial self-efficacy (ES).
      4. Individual creativity (IC).
      5. Entrepreneurial intention (EI).

## *3.1 Content Validation*

Content validation is conducted by three experts, including two business experts and one research measurement and evaluation expert. The selection criteria for experts include: (1) having at least 3 years of relevant work experience, (2) holding a postgraduate degree in the relevant field of expertise, and (3) having experience in teaching or promoting entrepreneurship skills. For content validation, the Index of Objective-Congruence (IOC) will be used, with a minimum IOC value of 0.5 considered acceptable for the questions to be used.

**Table 1** Research tool questions

| Variables | Queries |
|---|---|
| Creative activities supported by university/college | 1. You have participated in training related to entrepreneurship in the department/faculty/university<br>2. The department/faculty/university offers sufficient courses related to entrepreneurship for you to study<br>3. The department/faculty/university provides guest speakers or special instructors to impart knowledge about entrepreneurship sufficiently<br>4. You have had the opportunity to engage in activities that help develop entrepreneurial skills through the department/faculty/university, such as organizing product sales events or product design activities<br>5. The department/faculty/university has faculty members who provide advice on entrepreneurship |
| Growth mindset | 6. You are confident that your knowledge and abilities are accurate and do not need any changes<br>7. You believe that it is normal for you to change your thoughts constantly<br>8. When you learn something new and find it conflicting with your existing knowledge, you are willing to change your thoughts<br>9. You know how to change your thoughts in certain situations or for specific reasons<br>10. You believe that the thoughts of others contribute to you having new ideas |
| Individual creativity | 11. When faced with problems, you can find new solutions to solve them<br>12. You have different ways of managing and addressing problems with new approaches<br>13. You can design new things that can be used as practical innovations<br>14. You can present your new ideas to others in a way that they are willing to accept<br>15. You are a creative thinker |

(continued)

**Table 1** (continued)

| Variables | Queries |
|---|---|
| Entrepreneurial self-efficacy | 16. You are confident that you will be able to achieve success in being an entrepreneur<br>17. You are confident that you can find new opportunities or avenues for business ventures<br>18. You are confident in your ability to create innovative and creative products<br>19. You recognize that your unique ideas will help you plan your business<br>20. You are confident that you will succeed with business and development ideas |
| Entrepreneurial intention | 21. Your career goal is to become a business owner<br>22. You are determined to have your own business<br>23. You have started planning your own business venture<br>24. You are interested in becoming an entrepreneur in the future<br>25. You intend to have a business of your own |

## *3.2 Reliability Testing*

Reliability testing is performed using Cronbach's Alpha on a sample of 100 individuals who are not part of the research study. Based on the results, adjustments were made to the questionnaire before its actual use.

## *3.3 Data Collection*

Data were collected based on a questionnaire developed by the researchers. The participants were undergraduate students studying in fields related to the creative industry. A purposive random selection method were employed.

## *3.4 Statistical Analysis*

Statistical analysis includes descriptive statistics, t-tests, ANOVA, correlation coefficient calculations, and the Structural Equation Model (SEM) for more complex analyses.

## 4 Results

Examining the relationships between variables in the causal model of entrepreneurial intention revealed that all variables in the model have a positive relationship. The highest relationship was found between entrepreneurial self-efficacy and individual creativity, with a statistically significant correlation of 0.758 at the 0.05 significance level. On the other hand, entrepreneurial intention had the lowest relationship with the growth mindset, with a correlation of 0.373, which was also statistically significant at the 0.05 level. Details are presented in Table 2.

The analysis of the influence between variables in the causal model of entrepreneurial intention revealed that the model, according to theory, fits the empirical data well ($\chi 2(1, 211) = 2.634$, $p = 0.105$, RMSEA = 0.088, SRMR = 0.015). Each independent variable can explain entrepreneurial intention by 46.1%.

When considering the influence between variables in the model, it was found that self-perceived entrepreneurial ability has a direct positive influence on entrepreneurial intention with a size of 0.832, which is statistically significant at the 0.05 level. On the other hand, individual creativity has a direct negative influence on entrepreneurial intention with a size of -0.256, which is also statistically significant at the 0.05 level. In addition, the growth mindset has a direct positive influence on entrepreneurial intention with a size of 0.038, which is not statistically significant. However, it has an indirect influence on entrepreneurial intention through individual creativity and self-perceived entrepreneurial ability with a size of 0.222, which is statistically significant at the 0.05 level.

The analysis also found that university support and promotion through creative activities have an indirect influence on entrepreneurial intention through other variables in the model, with a size of 0.097, which is statistically significant at the 0.05 level. Additionally, university support and promotion through creative activities have an indirect influence on individual creativity through the growth mindset with a size of 0.274, which is statistically significant at the 0.05 level. Similarly, the growth

**Table 2** The correlation coefficients between variables in the causal model of students' entrepreneurial intentions

| | CAS | GM | IC | SE | EI |
|---|---|---|---|---|---|
| CAS | 1 | | | | |
| GM | 0.481* | 1 | | | |
| IC | 0.384* | 0.623* | 1 | | |
| SE | 0.531* | 0.595* | 0.758* | 1 | |
| EI | 0.428* | 0.373* | 0.397* | 0.660* | 1 |
| *M* | 2.871 | 3.660 | 3.547 | 3.401 | 3.450 |
| *SD* | 1.142 | 0.626 | 0.714 | 0.795 | 1.010 |

*$p < 0.05$; CAS = Creative activities supported by university/college; GM = Growth mindset; IC = Individual creativity; SE = Entrepreneurial self-efficacy; EI = Entrepreneurial intention

mindset has a direct positive influence on individual creativity with a size of 0.570, which is statistically significant at the 0.05 level. Details are presented in Table 3 and Fig. 1.

## 5 Conclusion, Discussion and Managerial Implication

The volatile economic conditions and disruptive technological changes that impact market competitiveness have significantly drawn attention to the concepts of entrepreneurship and entrepreneurial development. It is widely recognized that entrepreneurs are income generators and job creators who continuously seek opportunities to start new businesses. Entrepreneurs are, therefore, crucial for revitalizing, fortifying, and advancing a country's economy.

In Thailand, the government has consistently promoted and fostered entrepreneurship through various projects and activities facilitated by collaboration between the public and private sectors. This research aims to study the causal factors influencing the intention to become a new entrepreneur among university students at the tertiary level. The objective is to analyze the role of creative activities supported by the university in developing entrepreneurial intention among undergraduate students and to provide guidance/strategies to universities and faculties in curriculum management and administration that align with the country's policies and directions for developing new entrepreneurs.

The study incorporates variables from two main concepts: the growth mindset and individual creativity, as well as entrepreneurial self-efficacy (SE). The research findings support our proposed research framework, indicating that university-supported activities help promote entrepreneurial potential among students and can lead to the development of entrepreneurial intentions. This is achieved through the growth mindset, individual creativity, and entrepreneurial self-efficacy.

The results of this research support the work of [21], which found that fostering an entrepreneurial intention can be learned through education, especially when coupled with activities that enhance students' entrepreneurial intentions. The study demonstrates that such activities stimulate creativity in students and cultivate a strong growth mindset. Consequently, students believe that their skills and knowledge can be enhanced through learning and effort. This creative mindset and framework instill confidence in students to create or manage their businesses in the future, a quality widely recognized as essential for entrepreneurs [19, 41].

Another critical and clear result from this research is the direct relationship between entrepreneurial self-efficacy and entrepreneurial intentions, which is consistent with the findings of several scholars [49, 50]. Students with a high level of self-efficacy regarding their entrepreneurial capabilities are confident that they can establish their businesses and overcome various challenges during the startup phase. They are also more likely to identify business opportunities, take risks, and maintain a positive attitude toward entrepreneurship as a career. This self-efficacy in

**Table 3** The influence between variables in the causal model of undergraduate students

| Dependent variable | GM | | | IC | | | SE | | | EI | | |
|---|---|---|---|---|---|---|---|---|---|---|---|---|
| | DI | IN | TE | DI | IN | TE | DI | IN | TE | DI | IN | TE |
| Initial variable | | | | | | | | | | | | |
| CAS | 0.481* | – | 0.481* | 0.110* | 0.274* | 0.384* | – | 0.213* | 0.213* | – | 0.097* | 0.097* |
| GM | – | – | – | 0.570* | – | 0.570* | 0.422* | – | 0.422* | 0.038 | 0.222* | 0.260* |
| IC | – | – | – | – | – | – | – | – | – | 0.256* | | 0.256* |
| SE | – | – | – | – | – | – | – | – | – | 0.832* | – | 0.832* |
| $r^2$ | 0.231 | | | 0.397 | | | 0.331 | | | 0.461 | | |
| $\chi^2(1, 211) = 2.634$, $p = 0.105$, RMSEA = 0.088, SRMR = 0.015 | | | | | | | | | | | | |

*$p < 0.05$; CAS = Creative activities supported by university/college; GM = Growth mindset; IC = Individual creativity; SE = Entrepreneurial self-efficacy; EI = Entrepreneurial intention; DI = Direct effect; IN = Indirect effect; TE = Total effect

their entrepreneurial abilities results from their participation in university-supported entrepreneurial creative activities.

The research findings also highlight the significant roles of individual growth mindset and individual creativity, which can be enforced by creative activities supported/provided by universities. This aligns with the research by [51], which suggests that entrepreneurship can be nurtured through socialization processes, particularly within educational institutions. Furthermore, it highlights the benefits of entrepreneurial, creative activities in promoting both the growth mindset and individual creativity. Additionally, recommendations from [51] propose that educational institutions should incorporate practical entrepreneurship courses into their curriculum to stimulate students' desire and intentions to become entrepreneurs further.

Additionally, these research findings imply the importance of designing curriculum activities to develop entrepreneurship among university students, especially for policymakers in the public education sector, top-level education institution administrators, curriculum managers, and corporate leaders collaborating to develop students into entrepreneurs, which is essential for national development.

For policymakers in the public sector, it is crucial to promote and systematically support entrepreneurship by establishing agencies that assist entrepreneurs in accessing skills training and funding. This can also include providing tax privileges for new entrepreneurs. Furthermore, educational institutions should actively formulate education policies to foster genuine entrepreneurship from primary to university levels.

For educational institution administrators, advocating for entrepreneurship-related courses, modules, and other creative activities that cultivate entrepreneurial intentions is essential. This can involve integrating entrepreneurship content and skills into the curriculum, fostering networks with successful entrepreneurs to inspire and serve as role models, and enabling students to engage in business planning and entrepreneurial activities during their studies. Creating a conducive environment for these activities, both inside and outside the classroom, is also essential.

For private sector organizations, strong collaboration with educational institutions is crucial in developing students into entrepreneurs. This can be achieved through various creative activities, such as mentoring students in business start-up projects for university-level entrepreneurship competitions, offering internship opportunities within organizations, and partnering with courses or universities to create entrepreneurial development programs for students jointly.

For researchers interested in this study area, it is essential to consider various environmental factors that may impact entrepreneurial intentions. One factor to explore is whether students come from a business background or if there is a family business involved. Research can investigate whether these factors influence the likelihood of students developing entrepreneurial intentions. Another essential aspect is conducting longitudinal research to track the continuous effects of students with high entrepreneurial intentions. This would involve following up on whether these students start businesses and, if not, the reasons why they do not. This longitudinal approach would provide valuable insights into the development of entrepreneurs. It could help identify barriers or challenges that need to be addressed at the policy level to support aspiring entrepreneurs. It is worth noting that the research in question focused solely on undergraduate students at one state university. Therefore, caution should be exercised when applying the research findings to different contexts, universities, or countries. Comparisons should be made carefully, considering the unique contextual factors influencing entrepreneurial intentions and activities in various settings. Further research that involves different student groups, faculties, or international perspectives would contribute to a more comprehensive understanding of the topic and its implications.

## 6 Limitations and Future Research

The study focused on a specific mid-size governmental university in Thailand. The findings may not be universally applicable as entrepreneurial intention can be influenced by various contextual factors such as culture, economic conditions, and institutional support. Future research should include a more diverse sample of universities or consider a multi-institutional study for better generalizability. While the study examines direct relationships between variables like growth mindset, entrepreneurial self-efficacy, creative activities, and entrepreneurial intention, it could benefit from exploring potential mediating variables. These could include perceived barriers to entrepreneurship, risk perception, and tolerance, self-determination and autonomy, and the influence of social support and networks. Understanding how these factors mediate the relationships can provide a more comprehensive understanding of entrepreneurial intention formation in undergraduate programs. Comparative research across different universities or educational systems within Thailand and other countries could provide valuable insights into the role of education and cultural contexts in shaping entrepreneurial intentions and behaviors. Qualitative research exploring the pedagogical approaches and teaching methods that are most effective in enhancing entrepreneurial intention and creativity among students could provide practical insights for educators and curriculum designers. Furthermore, investigating the role of gender and cultural differences in entrepreneurial intention and the impact of creative activities on these intentions could further enrich our understanding of how diverse populations respond to entrepreneurship education.

## References

1. Jiatong, W., Murad, M., Bajun, F., Tufail, S.M., Mirza, F., Rafiq, M.: Impact of entrepreneurial education, mindset, and creativity on entrepreneurial intention: Mediation role of entrepreneurial self-efficacy. Front. Psychol. **12**, 1–13 (2021)

2. Hassan, A., Saleen, I., Anwar, I., Hussain, S.A.: Entrepreneurial intention of Indian University students: The role of opportunity recognition and entrepreneurship education. Educ. Train. **62**(7–8), 843–861 (2020)
3. Akinwale, Y.O., Ababtain, A.K., Alaraifi, A.A.: Structural equation model analysis of factors influencing entrepreneurial interest among university students in Saudi Arabia. Journal of Entrepreneurship Education **22**(4), 1–14 (2019)
4. Elnadi, M., Gheith, M.H.: Entrepreneurial ecosystem, entrepreneurial self-efficacy, and entrepreneurial intention in higher education: Evidence from Saudi Arabia. The International Journal of Management Education **2**, 1–13 (2021)
5. Alammari, K., Newvery, R., Haddoud, M.Y., Beaumont, E.: Post-materialistic values and entrepreneurial intention—The case of Saudi Arabia. J. Small Bus. Enterp. Dev. **36**(1), 158–179 (2019)
6. Kalyoncuoglu, S., Aydintan, B., Goksel, A.: The Effect of entrepreneurship Education on entrepreneurial intention: An experimental study on undergraduate business students. J. Manag. Res. **9**, 72–91 (2017)
7. Cui, J., Bell, R.: Behavioral entrepreneurial mindset: How entrepreneurial education activity impacts entrepreneurial intention and behavior. Int. J. Manag. Educ. **20**(2), (2021)
8. Boldureanu, G., Ionescu, A.M., Mercu, A., Bedrula-Grigoruta, M.V., Boldureanu, D.: Entrepreneurship education through successful entrepreneurial models in higher education institutions. Sustainability **12**(3), 1267–1278 (2020)
9. Jena, R.K.: Measuring the impact of Business Management Students' attitude towards entrepreneurship education on entrepreneurial intention: a case study. Comput. Hum. Behav. **107**, (2020)
10. Douglas, E.J., Shepherd, D.A., Venugopal, V.: A multi-motivational general model of entrepreneurial intention. J. Bus. Ventur. **36**, (2021)
11. Urban, B.: Entrepreneurial alertness, self-efficacy, and social entrepreneurship intentions. J. Small Bus. Enterp. Dev. **27**(3), 489–507 (2020)
12. Ceresia, F., Mendola, C.: Am I an entrepreneur? entrepreneurial self-identity as an antecedent of entrepreneurial intention. Adm. Sci. **10**(3), 46 (2020)
13. Hsu, D.K., Burmeister-Lamp, K., Simmons, S.A., Foo, M.d., Hong, M.C., Pipes, J.D.: I know I can, but I don't fit: perceived fit, self-efficacy, and entrepreneurial intention. J. Bus. Ventur. **34**, 311–326 (2019)
14. Zhao, H., Seibert, S.E., Hills, G.E.: The mediating role of self-efficacy in the development of entrepreneurial intentions. J. Appl. Psychol. **90**, 1265 (2005)
15. Gutierrez, P.I.R., Pastor Perez, M., del P., Galicia, P.E.A.: University entrepreneurship: how to trigger entrepreneurial intention of undergraduate students. J. Sci. Technol. Policy Manag. **10**(4), 927–950 (2019)
16. Sahin, F., Karadag, H., Tuncer, B.: Big five personality traits, entrepreneurial self-efficacy and entrepreneurial intention: a configurational approach. Int. J. Entrep. Behav. Res. **25**, 1188–1211 (2019)
17. Baello, C.M., Ahuja, D., Finkley, N., Rao, R.: Enhanced Oral Health Care Services for PLWHA-Midlands Region, South Carolina. In Open Forum Infectious Diseases, vol. 7, No. Supplement_1, pp. S535–S536. US: Oxford University Press (2020, October)
18. Audretsch, D.B., Belitski, M.: Entrepreneurial ecosystems in cities: establishing the framework condition. J. Technol. Transf. **42**(5), 1030–1051 (2017)
19. Altinay, L., Madanoglu, M., Daniele, R., Lashley, C.: The influence of family tradition and psychological traits on entrepreneurial intention. Int. J. Hosp. Manag. **31**(2), 489–499 (2012)
20. Karabulut, A.T.: Personality traits on entrepreneurial intention. Procedia Soc. Behav. Sci. **229**, 12–21 (2016)
21. Kuratko, D.G., Fisher, G., Audretsch, D.B.: Unraveling the entrepreneurial mindset. Small Bus. Econ. J. **1**, 1–11 (2020). https://doi.org/10.1177/0972150919844395
22. Bandura, A.: Self-Efficacy: The Exercise of Control. Macmillan (1997)
23. Boyd, N.G., Vozikis, G.S.: The influence of self-efficacy on the development of entrepreneurial intentions and actions. Entrep.: Theory Pract. **18**(4), 63–77 (1994)

24. Tsai, K.H., Chang, H.C., Peng, C.Y.: Extending the link between entrepreneurial self-efficacy and intention: a moderated mediation model. Int. Entrep. Manag. J. **12**, 445–453 (2016)
25. Memon, M., Soomro, B.A., Shah, N.: Enablers of entrepreneurial self-efficacy in a developing country. Educ. + Train. **61**(6), 684–699 (2019). https://doi.org/10.1108/ET-10-2018-0226
26. Sidek, S., Zainol, F.A.: Psychological traits and business performance of entrepreneurs in small construction industry in Malaysia. Int. Bus. Manag. **2**(1), 170–185 (2011)
27. Schmutzler, J., Andonova, V., Diaz-Serrano, L.: How context shapes entrepreneurial self-efficacy as a driver of entrepreneurial intentions: a multilevel approach. Entrep. Theory Pract. **43**(5), 880–920 (2019)
28. McGee, J.E., Peterson, M.: The long-term impact of entrepreneurial self-efficacy and entrepreneurial orientation on venture performance. J. Small Bus. Manage. **57**, 720–737 (2019). https://doi.org/10.1111/jsbm.12324
29. Burnette, J.L., Pollack, J.M., Forsyth, R.B., Hoyt, C.L., Babij, A.D., Thomas, F.N., Coy, A.E.: A growth mindset intervention: enhancing students' entrepreneurial self-efficacy and career development. Entrep. Theory Pract. **44**(5), 878–908 (2020)
30. Laalo, H., Heinonen, J.: Governing the entrepreneurial mindset: business students' constructions of entrepreneurial subjectivity. Eur. Educ. Res. J. **15**(6), 696–713 (2016)
31. Handayati, P., Wulandari, D., Soetjipto, B.E., Wibowo, A., Narmaditya, B.S.: Does entrepreneurship education promote vocational students' entrepreneurial mindset? Heliyou **6**, (2020)
32. Shi, Y., Yuan, T., Bell, R., Wang, J.: Investigating the relationship between creativity and entrepreneurial intention: the moderating role of creativity in the theory of planned behavior. Front. Psychol. **11**, 1209 (2020). https://doi.org/10.3389/fpsyg.2020.01209
33. Chia, C.-C., Liang, C.: Influence of creativity and social capital on the entrepreneurial intention of tourism students. J. Entrep. Manag. Innov. **12**, 151–168 (2016). https://doi.org/10.7341/20161227
34. Murad, M., Li, C., Ashraf, S.F., Arora, S.: The influence of entrepreneurial passion in the relationship between creativity and entrepreneurial intention. Int. J. Glob. Bus. Compet. **16**, 51–60 (2021)
35. Chen, M.H.: Entrepreneurial leadership and new ventures: creativity in entrepreneurial teams. Creat. Innov. Manag. **16**(3), 239–249 (2007)
36. Burnette, J.L., Pollack, J.M., Forsyth, R.B., Hoyt, C.L., Babij, A.D., Thomas, F.N., Coy, A.E.: A growth mindset intervention: enhancing students' entrepreneurial self-efficacy and career development. Entrep. Theory Pract. **44**, 878–908 (2019)
37. Thomas, A., Passaro, R., Quinto, I.: Developing entrepreneurship in the digital economy: the ecosystem strategy for startups growth. Strat. Behav. Digit. Econ. 1–20, (2019)
38. Dweck, C.S.: Self-Theories: Their Role in Motivation, Personality, and Development. Psychology Press (2000)
39. Jaafar, M., Abdul-Aziz, A.R., Maideen, S.A., Mohd, S.Z.: Entrepreneurship in the tourism industry: issues in developing countries. Int. J. Hosp. Manag. **30**(4), 827–835 (2011)
40. Iscaro, V., Castaldi, L.: Experimen/taLab: a virtual platform to enhance entrepreneurial education through training. Ind. High. Educ. **31**(1), 97–110 (2017)
41. Yousaf, U., Ali, S.A., Ahmed, M., Usman, B., Sameer, I.: From entrepreneurial education to entrepreneurial intention: a sequential mediation of self-efficacy and entrepreneurial attitude. Int. J. Innov. Sci. **13**(3), 364–380 (2021)
42. Pitisutti, P., Kaewjaroen, T.: Development of home economics entrepreneur indicators for undergraduate students. J. Multidiscip. Soc. Sci. **18**(1), 37–44 (2022)
43. Wathanakom, N., Khlaisang, J., Songkram, N.: The study of the causal relationship between innovativeness and entrepreneurial intention among undergraduate students. J. Innov. Entrep. **9**, 1–13 (2020)
44. Daniel, A.D.: Fostering an entrepreneurial mindset by using a design thinking approach in entrepreneurship education. Ind. High. Educ. (2016). https://doi.org/10.1177/0950422216653195

45. Kumar, R., Shukla, S.: Creativity, proactive personality, and entrepreneurial intention: examining the mediating role of entrepreneurial self-efficacy. Glob. Bus. Rev. 1–18, (2019)
46. Jiatong, W., Murad, M., Bajun, F., Tufail, M.S., Mirza, F., Rafiq, M.: Impact of entrepreneurial education, mindset, and creativity on entrepreneurial intention: mediating role of entrepreneurial self-efficacy. Front. Psychol. **12**, 724440 (2021)
47. Badri, R., Hachicha, N.: Entrepreneurship Education and Its Impact on Students' Intention to Start Up: A Sample Case Study of Students from Two Tunisian Universities, 182–190, (2019)
48. Quan, X.: Prior experience, social network, and levels of entrepreneurial intentions. J. Educ. Bus. **87**, 94–101 (2012)
49. Bagheri, A., Lope Pihie, Z.A.: The moderating role of gender in shaping entrepreneurial intentions: implications for vocational guidance. Int. J. Educ. Vocat. Guid. **14**, 255–273 (2014)
50. Carr, J.C., Sequeira, J.M.: Prior family business exposure as intergenerational influence and entrepreneurial intent: a theory of planned behavior approach. J. Bus. Res. **60**(10), 1090–1098 (2007)
51. Henderson, R., Robertson, M.: Who wants to be an entrepreneur? young adult attitudes to entrepreneurship as a career. Career Dev. Int. **5**(6), 279–287 (2000)

# Decoding Entrepreneurial Mindset: From Metacognitive Awareness, Growth Orientation and Opportunities Capitalization to Entrepreneurial Success

**Nina Szczygiel, Dina Ramos, and Nicole Jesus**

**Abstract** The paper conceptualizes the entrepreneur as an entity navigating dynamic and uncertain environments. It aims to examine the factors predicting the entrepreneurial mindset and the relationship between the entrepreneurial mindset and success. The study aimed to understand how the entrepreneurial mindset is shaped and to examine how this mindset influences entrepreneurial success. The results suggest that an entrepreneurial mindset is mainly characterized by the ability to identify and act on opportunities, an orientation toward growth based on adaptability, an ongoing pursuit of personal development, and heightened metacognitive awareness. Notably, the trait of perseverance in the face of rejections and adverse events emerges as highly relevant. External elements, including the environmental context and external forces, play a role in shaping the success of an entrepreneur. Nevertheless, it is the internal attributes of the individual that form the essential foundation of this achievement. The research contributes by critically examining existing approaches and adds depth to comprehending the entrepreneurial mindset and its practical applications in predicting and nurturing entrepreneurial success.

**Keywords** Entrepreneurial mindset · Entrepreneurial success · Growth orientation · Metacognition · Metacognitive awareness

N. Szczygiel (✉) · D. Ramos
GOVCOPP, University of Aveiro, Campus de Santiago, 3810-193 Aveiro, Portugal
e-mail: nina.szczygiel@ua.pt

N. Szczygiel · D. Ramos · N. Jesus
DEGEIT, University of Aveiro, Campus de Santiago, 3810-193 Aveiro, Portugal

 
S. Kot et al. (eds.), *Corporate Practices: Policies, Methodologies, and Insights in Organizational Management*, Springer Proceedings in Business and Economics,
https://doi.org/10.1007/978-981-97-0996-0_2

# 1 Introduction

Efforts to understand what makes an entrepreneur successful have persisted for several decades, with the recent focus on the entrepreneurial mindset concept, a vague yet compelling explanation [1]. While these and related issues, such as strategies for success and reasons for failure, feature significantly in the literature, the depth and breadth of studies indicate a clear need for ongoing updates and support in the field [2]. Beyond a theory assuming that the entrepreneurial mindset is crucial for entrepreneurial behaviour [1], the practical implications of this theme are of paramount importance. Indeed, success—or lack thereof—holds significant ramifications for entrepreneurs themselves and their communities, justifying the interest in ensuring ways to achieve it [3].

Entrepreneurial success has proven elusive in literature. While environmental evidence and exogenous factors undeniably influence entrepreneurial outcomes, interest in the individual subject and their differences has persisted. Generally, contemporary entrepreneurship research focuses on understanding the psychological nature and development of the entrepreneur [4]. For some authors, the personality profile and specific characteristics of these individuals clarify the nature of success in entrepreneurship [5]. Since McClelland's [6] investigations, the number of studies on the personality traits of entrepreneurs has increased. Despite the abundance of research of this nature, the results remain essentially mixed and inconclusive, yet research persists [7, 8].

Acknowledging the relationship between individual differences and entrepreneurial success and recognizing the prevailing academic emphasis on cognitive models, this research embarks on an exploration of the entrepreneurial mindset. More precisely, the study aims to grasp how the entrepreneurial mindset is formed and the extent to which it predicts entrepreneurial success. To achieve this objective, an empirical study was undertaken, employing a mixed-methods approach.

Central to this research is exploring the theoretical delineation of the entrepreneurial mindset to offer enhanced clarity regarding its components and their intricate relationships with entrepreneurial behaviors. This theoretical depth is imperative for the pragmatic application of the entrepreneurial mindset concept. A recent systematic review by Naumann [9] has brought attention to the fact that, despite extensive research efforts, some approaches to studying the entrepreneurial mindset need to be revised. The present study examines and extends existing approaches, expands the geographic focus in alignment with the recommendation of Naumann [9], and contributes to a nuanced understanding of the entrepreneurial mindset and its practical implications for predicting and fostering entrepreneurial success.

## 2 Literature Review

Numerous studies emphasize the entrepreneurial mindset as a critical factor in entrepreneurial success. According to McGrath and MacMillan [10], the entrepreneurial mindset involves thinking about business with a focus on embracing the benefits of uncertainty. Uncertainty arises from the inability to assign probabilities to subsequent events, primarily due to a need for more information about cause-and-effect relationships [11]. It comprises concepts such as risk and ambiguity [12]. An organization's capability to navigate uncertainty can contribute to its competitive advantage [13].

McGrath and MacMillan [10] assert that individuals exhibiting an entrepreneurial solid sense also demonstrate a robust mindset. They have identified five crucial characteristics of the entrepreneurial mindset. In this sense, entrepreneurs: (1) Vigilantly seek and passionately explore new opportunities that enable them to profit from changes and disruptions in business practices, including the creation of entirely new business models; (2) Diligently seek opportunities and act on them rather than merely staying alert; (3) Select only the best opportunities and avoid exhausting themselves and their organizations by pursuing every option exhaustively; (4) Focus on adaptable execution, that is, act instead of constantly analyzing new ideas and are capable of changing course as the real opportunity and the way to exploit it evolve, and (5) Take charge of everyone within their domain.

Ireland et al. [14] argue that an essential aspect of the entrepreneurial mindset encompasses active engagement within an entrepreneurial framework. The wealth creation potential of this mindset is amplified when employed within an entrepreneurial structure. This structure includes goal definition, creating an opportunity record, and determining the articulated time for launching the exploratory strategy of an entrepreneurial opportunity. The authors emphasize the consistent use of this entrepreneurial structure in all projects, and this perspective aligns with the entrepreneurial mindset as approached by McGrath and MacMillan [10].

A study by Haynie and colleagues [15] that sought to investigate the foundations of the entrepreneurial mindset by associating previously studied cognitive processes with higher-order cognitive processes allowed for the development of a metacognitive model of the entrepreneurial mindset in an attempt to elucidate the development of metacognitive strategies in a challenging environment. However, before understanding the metacognitive model, it is essential to grasp the central elements involved in cognitive processes and how they relate to entrepreneurship.

Cognitive processes are central to entrepreneurial and business activities as they shape the entrepreneur's approach to processing information and decision-making, impacting their strategies for perceiving and creating opportunities. Research has studied cognitive processes to uncover the link between cognition and behavior, exploring how entrepreneurs acquire, store, and retrieve information to make decisions and achieve goals, and has sought to understand how entrepreneurs align their cognitive processes with their entrepreneurial objectives. Consistent with this idea, Gartner [16] argues that cognition is critical in entrepreneurship.

To understand the entrepreneurial mindset fully, it is vital to delve into metacognition, which involves thinking about one's thinking processes. *Metacognition* is the higher-order cognitive function that enables individuals to plan, monitor, and regulate their cognitive activities [17]. Metacognitive processes involve (a) planning; that is, entrepreneurs plan their actions and strategies by setting goals, outlining steps, and anticipating challenges. Effective planning contributes to goal-directed behavior; (b) monitoring, that is, entrepreneurs continuously monitor their cognitive processes, evaluating the effectiveness of their strategies and adjusting as needed. This self-awareness enhances decision-making, and (c) regulation, namely, entrepreneurs regulate their cognitive processes by implementing changes based on monitoring outcomes. This adaptive quality enables them to navigate uncertainties and changing circumstances.

Therefore, entrepreneurial mindset is characterized by cognitive and metacognitive processes that enable individuals to identify opportunities, make decisions, and navigate the uncertainties inherent in entrepreneurship. Understanding how cognitive and metacognitive processes interact provides valuable insights into the foundations of entrepreneurial thinking.

## *2.1 Hypotheses Development*

McGrath and MacMillan [10] and Ireland et al. [14] assert that entrepreneurs actively seek new opportunities that can bring them wealth. Benedict and Venter [18] affirm that those with an entrepreneurial mindset can identify opportunities and envision creative ways to capitalize on them. Indeed, market information asymmetries, such as demographic, social changes, or regulatory shifts, fuel entrepreneurial opportunities [14, 19]. Consequently, these opportunities may only be equally recognizable to some individuals; only a fraction can detect them [20]. Mullins [21] adds that successful entrepreneurs think expansively, discovering and seizing small opportunities that others may overlook because they can perceive their future potential. Therefore, it is reasonable to assume that the identification and capitalization of entrepreneurial opportunities are key activities for entrepreneurs capable of achieving success. Therefore, the following hypothesis is proposed:

**Hypothesis 1 (H1):**
The ability to identify and capitalize on opportunities is an integral part of the entrepreneurial mindset.
Murphy and Dweck [22] posit that individuals who perceive their mindset as growth-oriented believe that learning and experience will lead to significant development in their behavior. This mindset, characteristic of an entrepreneur, encompasses traits such as flexibility, creativity, continuous innovation, and renewal, proving relevant for entrepreneurs [14]. According to McGrath and MacMillan [10], successful entrepreneurs must combine their best learning with the ability to sense, act, and mobilize quickly. This implies that these individuals must be open to learning to

exhibit flexible behavior. Given that they operate in uncertain and dynamic environments and considering that an entrepreneurial mindset involves the ability to adapt to these circumstances [15], the following hypothesis is proposed:

**Hypothesis 2 (H2):**
Having a growth orientation is an integral part of the entrepreneurial mindset.

According to Haynie et al. [15], the metacognitive model that focuses on increasing awareness of one's interactions with the environment, self-awareness, thought processes, and past experiences directly impacts the functioning and development of an entrepreneur's mindset. Entrepreneurs commonly exhibit high levels of metacognitive awareness, given the high uncertainty, novelty, and dynamism they operate. Increased metacognitive awareness leads to greater use of metacognitive resources for formulating and evaluating strategies, consequently assisting in choosing the strategy that best suits the successful completion of entrepreneurial tasks. Therefore, the following hypothesis is proposed:

**Hypothesis 3 (H3):**
High metacognitive awareness is an integral part of the entrepreneurial mindset.
Some authors have argued that individuals and opportunities are at the core of the entrepreneurial phenomenon [3, 20] and that individuals displaying a strong entrepreneurial sense also demonstrate a strong mindset [10]. Thus, we can assert that an entrepreneurial mindset and its psychological resources are essential for driving success in entrepreneurship [14, 23, 24]. Therefore, the following hypothesis is proposed:

**Hypothesis 4 (H4):**
The individual's entrepreneurial mindset explains entrepreneurial success.

## 3 Methodology

Research on the entrepreneurial mindset has often utilized personality assessment instruments specifically designed for something other than this purpose. In other words, most studies have employed instruments measuring personality (e.g., [25]), motivations, or entrepreneurial intentions (e.g., [26]) as proxies for the entrepreneurial mindset. Except for the measure developed by Davis and colleagues [27], which requires paid training for certification, only some instruments have been devised specifically to analyze the entrepreneurial mindset comprehensively. With this in mind, and to understand better the phenomenon of entrepreneurial mindset and its relevance in achieving success, a mixed-methods study, incorporating data gathered from different sources, was carried out.

## 3.1 Research Instruments

The research was based on an interview and it further employed a questionnaire comprising two scales aimed to assess two of the constructs under study: growth orientation and metacognitive awareness.

### 3.1.1 Interview

For the interview, a guide consisting of four parts was developed. The interview guide included the following elements: (I) personal information, (II) recognition and action on entrepreneurial opportunities, (III) characteristics of an entrepreneurial mindset, and (IV) attainment of entrepreneurial success. After obtaining some basic information from the respondents for a general characterization of the sample, the goal in the second part was to understand how the respondents regard and act on entrepreneurial opportunities. The focus was on comprehending what these entrepreneurs think about opportunities as a critical activity for wealth creation, how they identify and adapt to them, and whether setting goals contributes to the identification and capitalization of these opportunities and, consequently, to entrepreneurial success. Eleven questions were formulated based on authors such as McGrath and MacMillan [10], Ireland and colleagues [14], Shane and Venkataraman [20], and Morris [19]. The third part of the interview was dedicated to analyzing the lines of thinking proposed by Mullins [21]. Finally (IV), an effort was made to understand the respondents' perception of the concept of entrepreneurial success, provided that its definition is not consensual in the literature [2, 28].

### 3.1.2 Growth Orientation Questionnaire

The questionnaire assessing growth orientation was based on Vandewalle's [29] Work Domain Goal Orientation Instrument. While the original instrument consists of 13 questions, the research incorporated 5, focusing on evaluating individual growth mindset. All items were measured on a 7-point Likert scale, where one corresponds to "strongly disagree" and 7 to "strongly agree" with the proposed statement. The instrument analyzing growth orientation included the following items: (1) I am willing to choose challenging tasks in my work where I can learn a lot from them (LGO1); (2) I frequently seek opportunities to develop new skills and knowledge (LGO2); (3) I enjoy complex and challenging tasks where I can learn new skills (LGO3); (4) For me, developing skills at work is critical enough that I take risks to develop them (LGO4); and (5) I prefer situations at work that require a high level of competence and talent (LGO5).

#### 3.1.3 Metacognitive Awareness Questionnaire

The second questionnaire analyzed the respondents' metacognitive awareness, drawing on the Generalized Measure of Adaptive Cognition developed by Haynie and Shepherd [30]. This questionnaire consists of five parts: Goal Orientation (GO), Metacognitive Knowledge (MK), Metacognitive Experience (ME), Metacognitive Choice (MC), and Monitoring (M). The Likert scale ranges from 1 ("not very much like me") to 7 ("very much like me").

#### 3.1.4 Secondary Data

To enrich the results of this research, a selection of lectures, articles and other contents available in the internet was included to the analysis and analyzed with the content analysis (of which results will be referred as 'content' with the respective material number).

### *3.2 Sample*

Given the challenging nature of measuring entrepreneurial success, the initial sample selection was based on evaluating the success of potential respondents' ventures based on economic factors. More specifically, the screening focused on the companies with the highest revenue per district in Portugal (there are 18 districts in Portugal). The included companies were contacted via email and phone. However, due to the context of the pandemic at the time of data collection, most companies experienced adverse conditions, which resulted in several rejections. Therefore, smaller-sized companies were included in the study. The final sample composition was based on data related to the ventures, such as the number of employees (ranging from a minimum of 11 to a maximum of 250) and the business volume (ranging from 2 million euros to 50 million euros), characteristic factors of small and medium-sized enterprises.

### *3.3 Data Collection Procedures*

After contacting the selected companies, ten entrepreneurs agreed to participate in this research. Interviews and questionnaires have the same sample size since these are two instruments that complement each other. Each respondent completed the questionnaires before starting the respective interview. Some of these contacts were made in person; however, the majority were conducted using online communication platforms.

# 4 Results and Discussion

## *4.1 Identification and Capitalization of Opportunities*

Concerning the entrepreneurial inclination of recognizing prospects, individuals continually engage in proactive endeavors to explore novel business opportunities. They emphasized the constant nature of this search and its role in expanding their worldview and benefiting their entrepreneurial efforts (Interview 3). They highlighted the importance of being attentive to new opportunities and actively seeking to add value to their surroundings (Interview 2, 7). McGrath and MacMillan [10] propose that a robust mindset characterizes individuals with a strong entrepreneurial sense. Authors such as Benedict and Venter [18] and Ireland et al. [14] argue that this mindset is, in part, explained by the ability to detect and recognize opportunities, a key component in defining entrepreneurship.

The results of the present study align with this perspective of transforming small opportunities into big ones since entrepreneurs expressed their belief that small projects can give rise to significant ventures (Interview 10). Participants emphasized the importance of seeing what others don't see and discovering challenges others overlook (Interview 2). They recognized that small opportunities have growth potential and contribute to gradual, sustained success (Interviews 4 and 7). The ability to perceive and act on small opportunities and take incremental steps toward goals was crucial for long-term success (Content 13). In line with these findings, Mullins [21] notes that entrepreneurs think big and perceive and seize small opportunities, often undervalued by many, knowing the potential these opportunities can achieve over time.

Regarding capitalizing on opportunities above creativity and innovation, the results showed that participants mentioned the expression "we don't have to reinvent the wheel" multiple times. This underscores the idea that not all opportunities must come from groundbreaking ideas or innovations. Kuratko and Hodgetts' [31] myth that entrepreneurs are always inventors was dispelled, emphasizing that entrepreneurs can succeed by following their unique path (Content 7). Participants recognized that doing things differently only sometimes requires extreme creativity or innovation. Recent studies suggest that identifying opportunities plays a more significant role than creativity in achieving entrepreneurial success [32]. Entrepreneurs from the present study stressed the importance of understanding that opportunities can be found by approaching challenges differently, emphasizing that following the majority may not lead to future success (Content 11).

Shane and Venkataraman [20] propose that the population recognizes opportunities differently, with only individuals able to identify entrepreneurial opportunities. Regarding recognizing opportunities differently from others, entrepreneurs from the study have echoed this idea, emphasizing that only some see opportunities in the same way or identify those with true potential. They believed that being attentive to the world, recognizing problems, and identifying solutions set entrepreneurs apart

(Interviews 3, 1, 9, 5 and 7). This unique ability to perceive opportunities differently may contribute to the success of entrepreneurial ventures.

About acting upon opportunities and taking risks; while some participants emphasized the importance of identifying opportunities, others highlighted the necessity of taking action and being willing to take risks [33–35]. They argued that capitalizing on opportunities required putting values, sacrifices, and devotions into action (Content 9). This orientation toward action and risk-taking was a strong justification for entrepreneurial success. These results highlight a complex interplay of mindset, opportunity recognition, and action-taking in the entrepreneurial process. Entrepreneurs not only actively seek opportunities but also recognize the importance of seizing small chances, capitalizing on opportunities without the need for groundbreaking innovations, and differentiating themselves by perceiving opportunities differently from others. Moreover, the emphasis on taking action and embracing risks further underlines the dynamic nature of entrepreneurship.

## 4.2 *Growth Orientation*

In terms of entrepreneurial learning objectives orientation, the study has found that entrepreneurs exhibit a strong orientation toward learning objectives. This signifies their eagerness to self-develop, acquire new skills, master unfamiliar situations, and enhance competence [29]. The literature emphasizes entrepreneurial adaptability across opportunities, thoughts, and social aspects, and our sample of entrepreneurs echoes this view. Adaptability, particularly resilience and adjusting to new scenarios, is crucial in the entrepreneurial context (Interviews 1, 6, 8, and 10). This adaptability extends to addressing resource scarcity; entrepreneurs creatively gather and transform necessary resources through collaboration or alternative means (Interviews 4, 7, and 9). The findings align with the idea that entrepreneurial characteristics can be learned and taught, emphasizing the significance of personal development [6, 36]. Personal development involves gaining new experiences, experimenting with new ideas, and promoting similar opportunities for others (Interview 4). Entrepreneurial responsibility and personal development are intertwined with how entrepreneurs perceive negative events. Successful entrepreneurs view rejections as temporary setbacks and obstacles in the creative process, understanding that failure is a regular part of the journey [35].

Regarding the value of perseverance in entrepreneurship, participants recognize the immense value of perseverance, deeming it crucial in the face of challenges, often ranking it higher than the business idea itself (Interview 7). Entrepreneurs critically assess the source of rejections, deriving pleasure from attempting what others deem impossible. They understand that the greatest reward comes from achieving what others thought was unattainable (Content 17). Finally, the results indicate a positive attitude toward learning from negative events. Entrepreneurs perceive rejection as an opportunity for improvement, underscoring the importance of trial and error in refining strategies (Interview 3).

The results support the idea that entrepreneurs are oriented toward learning objectives, indicative of a growth mindset. This aligns with the notion that a growth mindset, as proposed by Dweck [37] and Hultén and Tumunbayarova [38], is directly related to an individual's personal development, validating the hypothesis regarding the characteristic nature of an entrepreneurial mindset oriented toward growth.

## *4.3 Metacognitive Awareness*

### 4.3.1 Goal Orientation

The analysis reveals that the entrepreneurs in the present study exhibit a strong goal orientation, aligning with the literature that emphasizes the connection between goal setting and entrepreneurial success [10, 39, 30]. The results show that goal orientation motivates entrepreneurs, driving effort and providing direction (Interviews 7 and 8). Entrepreneurs stress the significance of setting ambitious goals, even if they seem impossible, using skeptics' doubts as motivation (Content 9).

### 4.3.2 Metacognitive Knowledge

Participants have demonstrated a solid grasp of metacognitive knowledge, both internally (understanding personal strengths and weaknesses) and externally (awareness of how others perceive their businesses). This knowledge aids in controlling fears, doubts, and insecurities, crucial for maintaining focus and strength during challenging times (Content 4). The entrepreneurs' scores on the Likert scale suggest a high level of metacognitive knowledge, aligning with the literature [30].

### 4.3.3 Metacognitive Experience

Entrepreneurs leverage past experiences, memories, intuitions, and emotions in decision-making, recognizing the value of intuition in strategic decisions [40]. While there's a discrepancy in the quantitative results regarding dependence on intuition, overall, entrepreneurs exhibit a reliance on metacognitive experiences.

### 4.3.4 Metacognitive Choice

The analysis indicates that entrepreneurs display cognitive adaptability, using metacognitive knowledge and experiences to generate alternative decision frames. However, there's a notable variation in scores for the component MC3, suggesting that entrepreneurs, driven by a strong orientation for action, might not dwell extensively on considering all options after making a decision.

#### 4.3.5 Monitoring

Entrepreneurs value feedback and actively engage in monitoring to reassess goals and strategies, reinforcing the importance of feedback from various sources (Interview 4, Content 15). The results confirm entrepreneurs' utilization of monitoring practices. The analysis affirms that entrepreneurs in this study possess robust metacognitive awareness, a key characteristic of an entrepreneurial mindset. Their goal orientation, coupled with a keen understanding of metacognitive knowledge and experiences, enables them to adapt cognitively, make strategic choices, and actively monitor their progress, contributing to their success in navigating uncertain entrepreneurial environments.

### *4.4 Entrepreneurial Success*

#### 4.4.1 Success Aligned with Individual Goals

As highlighted in the literature, the definition of success in entrepreneurship is not unanimous, and this was confirmed by this study: "The success of the entrepreneur can be many things. For some, it is starting a company; for others, it is having 1000 employees" (Interview 2). According to the findings, the definition is linked to individual goals: "(…) it is essential to identify our goal and work towards it – that is why I always emphasize that defining the goal is crucial for success" (Interview 10); and "The definition of success varies according to the objectives you have defined and the life stage you are in" (Interview 5). This aligns with Zhokhova et al.'s [41] definition that sees entrepreneurial success as the ability to achieve objectives provided that this definition can be divided into two main perspectives: economic (e.g., [42, 43]) and non-economic [2, 28, 43].

#### 4.4.2 Non-Economic Benefits Preferred Over Economic Benefits

Although some entrepreneurs express both perspectives, the results suggest a strong inclination toward non-economic benefits as measures of entrepreneurial success: "The goals of what I am creating always differ a lot – they are constantly changing. I know people who create businesses with a business model focused on rapid capitalization, and then they leave. These people probably have wealth as their main goal, which goes against what I think" (Interview 8). Indeed, this form of advantage is perceived as particularly attractive to entrepreneurs. Coupled with personal and social skills, as highlighted by [44], it enables the development of the determination and resilience needed to confront the challenges and losses they might encounter, as emphasized by Powell and Eddleston [45].

### 4.4.3 Money as a Minor Reason for Entrepreneurs

Despite the significant reference to money, especially in preliminary studies, it does not seem to be the main motive for entrepreneurs [2, 46]: "The economy doesn't work without generating value. Money is just a tool to make things real. It's not about money; it's just a means for things to happen. The important thing is to generate value; if you don't generate it, it means little" (Interview 6). When creating a company, the focus should be on "what are some of the other problems that probably affect the future of humanity the most?" rather than "what is the best way to make money" (Content 18). The participant of Content 3's analysis claims to have resources like money and influence to do more and better, and he carries them with joy, always aiming for the best for society, especially for young people (Content 3).

### 4.4.4 Non-Economic Benefits

Non-economic benefits can be measured by entrepreneurs' status and satisfaction with their needs [47]. Some of the benefits found in the literature [6, 28, 48] and corroborated in the present study are: (1) making money ("Entrepreneurial success is being able to have financial sustainability for yourself and your loved ones and being able to create value for other people. That is, creating value in the sense that your product or service delivers value to the lives of your customers and being able to achieve financial sustainability, generate wealth for the people in your network and project" (Interview 2)); (2) satisfaction and personal fulfillment ("Entrepreneurial success turns out to be personal gratification and satisfaction when you achieve your goal and the challenge you set for yourself. Entrepreneurial success occurs when what you desire materializes, what you dreamed of becomes viable and real" (Interview 8), "Entrepreneurial success is linked to personal fulfillment as an entrepreneur. That is when you feel fulfilled" (Interview 1). Work fills a significant part of a person's life, and for them to be truly satisfied, they need to believe that they are doing excellent Work in what they love most (Content 6)); (3) freedom and independence ("Time is the most valuable asset we have, and no matter how much money you make, nothing pays for our time (…) I have a lot of schedule flexibility, and I believe that comes after much work when you reach a minimum level of success in your company, where you already have a large team and can delegate much work – not everything goes through you, and everything does not depend on you anymore" (Interview 7)); and (4) growth opportunities ("I believe that anyone who likes to develop looks at the chance to grow from new challenges as a great advantage in this profession" (Interview 9); "The goal is always to grow more, wisdom is a reward that money does not bring you" (Interview 3)). As Alstete [2] states, the benefits are not the same for all entrepreneurs, and they may seek only one reward or set of them. The same seems to happen with the motivations that lead an individual to undertake. It is noted that our interpretation of the literature is that motivations (such as independence, personal development, perception of wealth instrumentalization, and approval) are strongly related to the definition of personal goals or benefits. This means that other works may reinforce the results discussed here [6, 7, 20, 36, 49].

#### 4.4.5 Entrepreneurial Success Regarded as a Continuous Process Rather Than a Milestone

The results indicate that entrepreneurial success is not viewed as a single, static achievement. Instead, it is seen as an ongoing process, with individuals continuously striving for improvement and growth: "Success is always something that is ahead. It is a thing of the present and future" (Interview 3).

To conclude, entrepreneurial success, as unraveled through interviews and content analysis, intricately links with individual goals, with non-economic benefits taking precedence. The narrative emphasizes a dynamic trajectory, propelled by intrinsic factors and an entrepreneurial mindset. It seems clear that the entrepreneurs in this study exhibit a multifaceted view of success, with an emphasis on individual goals and a preference for non-economic benefits. Their definitions of success align with ongoing processes of improvement and personal fulfillment, reflecting a dynamic and evolving perspective on entrepreneurial success. This nuanced understanding provides a foundation for further exploration into the complex interplay between individual goals, non-economic benefits, and the continuous pursuit of success in entrepreneurial endeavors. Findings align seamlessly with existing literature, portraying entrepreneurial success as a multifaceted phenomenon.

## 5 Conclusions

The literature has directed its attention to the entrepreneurial mindset as a predictor of success, well explained by characteristics such as the identification and capitalization of opportunities, an orientation toward growth with a focus on adaptation and personal development), and elevated metacognitive awareness. The study has corroborated the findings from previous research, this time from a Portuguese and European perspective, allowing for the validation of the established hypotheses and concluding that how an entrepreneur thinks can indeed influence the achievement of personal success. Also, it suggests that perseverance holds significant value in the entrepreneurial journey, emphasizing the development of a positive capacity to cope with negative events and rejections as crucial for success. These elements, along with the orientation to define and pursue objectives, are intrinsic to the entrepreneurial mindset. Finally, it is concluded that the definition of success is individual and related to each person's goals, which, in turn, are linked to their motivations.

From the discussed results, there is no singular formula for entrepreneurial success. This is because each individual has a highly personal definition of success, implying a unique and individualized process to achieve it. Nevertheless, if we were to assume a common precept for achieving success, it would likely align with the conclusions of Tang [50], who states that the success of an entrepreneurial journey lies in the ability to identify opportunities and take necessary actions to overcome challenges throughout the process, requiring both cognitive and motivational reinforcement from an entrepreneur. This statement encapsulates some of the key takeaways from the results of this study: (1) the identification of opportunities is an entrepreneurial habit, with the emphasis not just on recognizing them but also on taking action and assuming risks; (2) the entrepreneur must develop capabilities such as adaptation (given the changing environments) and perseverance to overcome negative events and rejections (as these are regular elements of the journey); (3) the entrepreneur possesses a strong orientation toward their objectives, highly correlated with their motivations for entrepreneurship. Regarding objectives, in addition to their strong presence in the literature, they proved to be pervasive across the results of all the study hypotheses. This realization leads to the understanding that the entrepreneur exists in an atmosphere composed of their objectives—a concept inseparable from an entrepreneurial mindset and success.

The principal limitation of this study lies in the relatively small sample size. A larger sample would have allowed us to generalize results to a broader population. Moreover, while recognizing the vague and complex nature of the concept of success, the study opted to use an economic perspective as a measure of success. This decision, though pragmatic for enhancing results in the current literature, brings forth limitations. The societal recognition of successful entrepreneurs is primarily linked to the monetary outcomes of their ventures, often overshadowing non-economic benefits such as personal fulfillment. This limitation prompts the need for future research to explore alternative success metrics.

Future investigations could focus on entrepreneurs with well-established businesses, particularly those demonstrating high profits. Most prior studies concentrated on the analysis of students or startup entrepreneurs. To achieve more robust and significant results, a more extensive and more diverse sample, including established market players, could be considered. Also, research endeavors should diversify their geographical focus beyond the North American perspective, as observed in this study. Exploring entrepreneurial mindsets and success criteria in different cultural and regional contexts can contribute to a more comprehensive understanding of the subject.

**Acknowledgements** This work was financially supported by the Research Unit on Governance, Competitiveness and Public Policies (UIDB/04058/2020) + (UIDP/04058/2020), funded by national funds through FCT - Fundação para a Ciência e a Tecnologia.

## References


1. Pidduck, R.J., Clark, D.R., Lumpkin, G.T.: Entrepreneurial mindset: dispositional beliefs, opportunity beliefs, and entrepreneurial behavior. J. Small Bus. Manage. **61**(1), 45–79 (2021). https://doi.org/10.1080/00472778.2021.1907582
2. Alstete, J.W.: On becoming an entrepreneur: an evolving typology. Int. J. Entrep. Behav. Res. **8**(4), 222–234 (2002). https://doi.org/10.1108/13552550210436521
3. Markman, G.D., Baron, R.A.: Person–entrepreneurship fit: Why some people are more successful as entrepreneurs than others. Hum. Resour. Manag. Rev. **13**(2), 281–301 (2003). https://doi.org/10.1016/S1053-4822(03)00018-4
4. Obschonka, M., Stuetzer, M.: Integrating psychological approaches to entrepreneurship: the Entrepreneurial Personality System (EPS). Small Bus. Econ. **49**(1), 203–231 (2017). https://doi.org/10.1007/s11187-016-9821-y
5. Lackéus, M. Entrepreneurship in education. What, why, when, how. OECD-LEED (2015).
6. McClelland, D. C. The achieving society. 2nd ed.. Van Nostrand (1961).
7. Herron, L., Sapienza, H.J.: The entrepreneur and the initiation of new venture launch activities. Entrep. Theory Pract. **17**(1), 49–55 (1992). https://doi.org/10.1177/104225879201700106
8. Stewart, W.H., Watson, W.E., Carland, J.C., Carland, J.W.: A proclivity for entrepreneurship: A comparison of entrepreneurs, small business owners, and corporate managers. J. Bus. Ventur. **14**(2), 189–214 (1999). https://doi.org/10.1016/S0883-9026(97)00070-0
9. Naumann, C.: Entrepreneurial mindset: a synthetic Literature review. Entrep. Bus. Econ. Rev. **5**(3), 149–172 (2017). https://doi.org/10.15678/EBER.2017.050308
10. McGrath, R.G., MacMillan, I.C.: The entrepreneurial mindset: strategies for continuously creating opportunity in an age of uncertainty. Harvard Business Press (2000).
11. Hoskisson, R.E., Busenitz, L.W.: Market uncertainty and learning distance in corporate entrepreneurship entry mode choice. In M. A. Hitt, R. D. Ireland, S. M. Camp, D. L. Sexton (eds). Strategic Entrepreneurship: creating a new mindset (pp. 151–172). Blackwell (2002).
12. Priem, R.L., Love, L.G., Shaffer, M.A.: Executives' perceptions of uncertainty sources: a numerical taxonomy and underlying dimensions. J. Manag. **28**(6), 725–746 (2002). https://doi.org/10.1177/014920630202800602
13. Brorström, B.: The world's richest municipality: the importance of institutions for municipal development. J. Econ. Issues **36**(1), 55–78 (2002). https://doi.org/10.1080/00213624.2002.11506443
14. Ireland, R.D., Hitt, M.A., Sirmon, D.G.: A model of strategic entrepreneurship: the construct and its dimensions. J. Manag. **29**(6), 963–989 (2003). https://doi.org/10.1016/S0149-2063(03)00086-2
15. Haynie, M., Shepherd, D., Mosakowski, E., Earley, P.C.: A situated metacognitive model of the entrepreneurial mindset. J. Bus. Ventur. **25**(2), 217–229 (2010). https://doi.org/10.1016/j.jbusvent.2008.10.001
16. Gartner, W.B.: "Who Is an entrepreneur?" is the wrong question. American Journal of Small Business **12**(4), 11–32 (1989). https://doi.org/10.1177/104225878801200401
17. Flavell, J.H.: Metacognition and cognitive monitoring: a new area of cognitive developmental inquiry. Am. Psychol. **34**(10), 906–911 (1979). https://doi.org/10.1037/0003-066X.34.10.906
18. Benedict, E.A., Venter, P.F.: Education, entrepreneurial mindset and innovation: necessary ingredients for increasing entrepreneurial activity in South Africa. Int. J. Entrep. Innov. Manag. **11**(2), 239–253 (2010). https://doi.org/10.1504/IJEIM.2010.030071
19. Morris, M.H.: Entrepreneurial Intensity: sustainable Advantages for Individuals, Organizations, and Societies. Greenwood Publishing (1998).
20. Shane, S., Venkataraman, S.: The promise of entrepreneurship as a field of research. Acad. Manag. Rev. **25**(1), 217–226 (2000). https://doi.org/10.2307/259271
21. Mullins, J.: The counter-conventional mindsets of entrepreneurs. Bus. Horiz. **60**(5), 597–601 (2017). https://doi.org/10.1016/j.bushor.2017.05.003
22. Murphy, M.C., Dweck, C.S.: Mindsets shape consumer behavior. J. Consum. Psychol. **26**(1), 127–136 (2016). https://doi.org/10.1016/j.jcps.2015.06.005

23. Baluku, M.M, Kikooma, J.F., Otto, K.: Positive mindset and entrepreneurial outcomes: the magical contributions of psychological resources and autonomy. J. Small Bus. Entrep. **30**(6), 1–26 (2018). https://doi.org/10.1080/08276331.2018.1459017
24. Chang, A.A.R., Qureshi, J.A., Najib, S., Salman, F.: Learning the Chinioti way: exploring the legacy of a family business community leaders' success based on the entrepreneurial mindset and values of Chinioti Sheikhs. Investig. Pensam. Crítico **10**(3), 109–135 (2021). https://doi.org/10.17993/3cemp.2021.100347.109-135
25. Costa, P.T., McCrae, R.R.: Revised NEO personality inventory. Professional manual. Psychological Assessment Resources, Inc., NEO-PI-R) and NEO five-factor inventory (NEO-FFI) (1992)
26. Stewart, W.H., Roth, P.L.: Risk propensity differences between entrepreneurs and managers: a meta-analytic review. J. Appl. Psychol. **86**(1), 145–153 (2001). https://doi.org/10.1037/0021-9010.86.1.145
27. Davis, M.H., Hall, J.A., Mayer, P.S.: Developing a new measure of entrepreneurial mindset: Reliability, validity, and implications for practitioners. Consult. Psychol. J.: Pract. Res. **68**(1), 21–48 (2016). https://doi.org/10.1037/cpb0000045
28. Carter, N.M., Gartner, W.B., Shaver, K.G., Gatewood, E.J.: The career reasons of nascent entrepreneurs. J. Bus. Ventur. **18**(1), 13–39 (2003). https://doi.org/10.1016/S0883-9026(02)00078-2
29. Vandewalle, D.: Development and validation of a Work Domain Goal Orientation Instrument. Educ. Psychol. Measur. **57**(6), 995–1015 (1997). https://doi.org/10.1177/0013164497057006009
30. Haynie, M., Shepherd, D.: A measure of adaptive cognition for entrepreneurship research. Entrep. Theory Pract. **33**(3), 695–714 (2009). https://doi.org/10.1111/j.1540-6520.2009.00322.x
31. Kuratko, D.F., Hodgetts, R.M.: Entrepreneurship: A Contemporary Approach, 4th edn. The Dryden Press (1994).
32. Chen, M.H., Chang, Y.Y., Lin, Y.C.: Exploring creative entrepreneurs' happiness: cognitive style, guanxi and creativity. International Entrepreneurship and Management Journal **14**, 1089–1110 (2018). https://doi.org/10.1007/s11365-017-0490-3
33. Antoncic, J.A., Antoncic, B., Gantar, M., Hisrich, R.D., Marks, L.J., Bachkirov, A.A., Li, Z., Polzin, P., Borges, J.L., Coelho, A., Kakkonen, M.L.: Risk-taking propensity and entrepreneurship: the role of power distance. J. Enterprising Cult. **26**(1), 1–26 (2018). https://doi.org/10.1142/S0218495818500012
34. Caliendo, M., Fossen, F., Kritikos, A.: The impact of risk attitudes on entrepreneurial survival. J. Econ. Behav. Organ. **76**(1), 45–63 (2010). https://doi.org/10.1016/j.jebo.2010.02.012
35. Scarborough, N. M. Effective small business management: An entrepreneurial approach. 10th ed. Pearson Prentice Hall (2012).
36. Carvalho, P.M.R., González, L.: Modelo explicativo sobre a intenção empreendedora. Comportamento Organizacional e Gestão **12**(1), 43–65 (2006)
37. Dweck, C.S.: Mindsets and human nature: promoting change in the Middle East, the schoolyard, the racial divide, and willpower. Am. Psychol. **67**(8), 614–622 (2012). https://doi.org/10.1037/a0029783
38. Hultén, P., Tumunbayarova, Z.: Building students' entrepreneurial mindsets: Results from an intervention at a Russian university. The International Journal of Management Education, 18(2) (2000). https://doi.org/10.1016/j.ijme.2020.100380
39. Filardi, F., Barros, F.D., Fischmann, A.A.: Homo empresario al emprendedor contemporáneo: las características de evolución de emprendedores de 1848 a 2014. Revista Ibero Americana de Estratégia **13**(3), 123–140 (2014). https://doi.org/10.5585/ijsm.v13i3.2130
40. Miller, C., Ireland, R.D.: Intuition in strategic decision making: friend or foe in the fast-paced 21st century. Acad. Manag. Exec. **19**(1), 19–30 (2005)
41. Zhokhova, V., Sokolova, D., Lehtyanskaya, L.: Success factors of social entrepreneurship: a case study of the Russian Far East. In: 6th International Conference on Social, Economic, and Academic Leadership, Prague, Czech Republic (2020). https://doi.org/10.2991/assehr.k.200526.017

42. McMullen, J.S., Shepherd, D.A.: Entrepreneurial action and the role of uncertainty in the theory of the entrepreneur. Acad. Manag. Rev. **31**(1), 132–152 (2006). https://doi.org/10.5465/amr.2006.19379628
43. Wach, D., Stephan, U., Gorgievski, M.: More than money: developing an integrative multi-factorial measure of entrepreneurial success. Int. Small Bus. J. **34**(8), 1–24 (2015). https://doi.org/10.1177/0266242615608469
44. Petříková, D., Soroková, T.: Managerial and entrepreneurial skills as determinants of business. Pol. J. Manag. Stud. **14**(1), 184–194 (2016)
45. Powell, G.N., Eddleston, K.A.: Linking family-to-business enrichment and support to entrepreneurial success: Do female and male entrepreneurs experience different outcomes? J. Bus. Ventur. **28**(2), 261–280 (2013). https://doi.org/10.1016/j.jbusvent.2012.02.007
46. Hormozi, A.M.: Becoming an entrepreneur: how to start a small business. Int. J. Manag. **21**(3), 278–328 (2004)
47. Singh, S.H., Bhowmick, B., Eesley, D., Sindhav, B.: Grassroots innovation and entrepreneurial success: Is entrepreneurial orientation a missing link? Technol. Forecast. Soc. Chang. **164**, 119582 (2019). https://doi.org/10.1016/j.techfore.2019.02
48. Timmons, J.A., Spinelli, S.: New Venture Creation: Entrepreneurship for the 21 Century, 7th edn. McGraw-Hill (2007).
49. Parreira, P., Salgueiro-Oliveira, A., Castilho, A., Melo, R., Graveto, J., Gomes, J.H., Vaquinhas, M., Carvalho, C., Mónico, L., Brito, N.: Entrepreneurial motivations questionnaire: AFC and CFA in academy. BMC Health Serv. Res. **16**(3), 69 (2016). https://doi.org/10.1186/s12913-016-1423-5
50. Tang, J.-J.: Psychological capital and entrepreneurship sustainability. Front. Psychol. **11**, 866 (2020). https://doi.org/10.3389/fpsyg.2020.00866

# Rising to Your Potential: Unlocking Your Inner Greatness

**William Philip Wall**

**Abstract** This research analyzed personal growth and self-discovery, focusing on unlocking inner greatness. This was necessary and important in a world of opportunities and challenges where individuals strive to realize their full potential. The study emphasized setting clear goals and cultivating a visionary mindset as foundational steps. Continuous self-reflection, learning, and a persistent attitude were highlighted as crucial for navigating the journey effectively, alongside building a supportive network that fosters positivity and minimizes negativity. Embracing failure as a stepping stone to success and celebrating achievements sustained motivation and resilience. The significance of prioritizing both physical and mental well-being, as well as the ability to adapt to changing circumstances, emerged as critical factors in maintaining growth. Lastly, the research underscored the value of giving back and drawing insights from diverse sources, showcasing the interconnectedness of personal development and broader societal impact.

**Keywords** Inner Greatness · Giving Back · Unlocking · Self-Discovery · Vision

## 1 Introduction

Every individual is born with an inherent potential to attain extraordinary heights, although only a few succeed in realizing such greatness. As a leader, to cultivate and inspire your inherent greatness, it is imperative that you consciously assess your habits and proactively replace them when they no longer align with your objectives. The realization of greatness cannot be merely achieved through self-perception or contemplation of greatness [1]. It is a virtue that necessitates nurturing, investment, and a deliberate approach. Striving for inner greatness mandates upholding an unwavering belief in your capacity to excel. According to [2], the vast tapestry of human existence, everyone possesses a unique reservoir of untapped potential, a wellspring

W. P. Wall (✉)
Stamford International University, Bangkok, Thailand
e-mail: William.wall@stamford.edu



S. Kot et al. (eds.), *Corporate Practices: Policies, Methodologies, and Insights in Organizational Management*, Springer Proceedings in Business and Economics,
https://doi.org/10.1007/978-981-97-0996-0_3

of greatness that lies dormant, waiting to be discovered and unleashed. However, all too often, this potential remains dormant, obscured by the cacophony of daily life and the constraints of self-doubt. It is a universal journey, one of self-discovery and empowerment, to unlock the inner greatness that lies within every one of us.

The path of self-discovery and personal growth that comes with realizing your potential and unleashing your inner greatness can change your life and the world around you. It involves identifying and utilizing the innate talent, passion, and tenacity reserves inside each of us. When we decide to live up to our full potential, we not only achieve our own goals and desires but also serve as an example for others [3]. Our accomplishments are proof of the human spirit's limitless ability for development and invention. To reach our full potential, we must work together. This has a positive ripple effect that inspires and uplifts people around us and ourselves. It serves as a potent reminder that every one of us can overcome obstacles, shatter down walls, and gradually change the course of history.

In this article, we will explore the intricate facets of personal development, resilience, and self-belief, offering insights and strategies to help you navigate the often-challenging path toward realizing your full potential. From uncovering hidden talents to overcoming self-doubt, this exploration aims to inspire and equip you with the tools necessary to embark on a transformative journey toward realizing your inner greatness.

## *1.1 The Vision—What Can You See?*

Unlocking your inner greatness to rise to your potential starts with a simple yet profoundly transformative question: 'What can you see?' This question is a powerful catalyst for self-discovery and personal development, as it encourages individuals to embark on a journey of introspection, reflection, and purposeful action [4].

In essence, this question prompts individuals to engage in a deeper examination of their aspirations, capabilities, and the boundless possibilities that lie before them. It serves as a clarion call to assess one's current state, unearthing dormant talents, and nurturing aspirations, envisioning their desired future, and charting a deliberate course toward achieving it. Through introspection and guided exploration, individuals can unlock their inner greatness and set themselves on a path to ascend to their highest capabilities [1]. Answering this question is guided by the following aspects:

**Self-Reflection:** this is the first critical aspect, that entails first looking inward to gain a deeper understanding of oneself. "What can you see?" compels individuals to reflect on their strengths, weaknesses, values, and passions (Gebauer, Lowman & Gordon, 2008). This self-examination unveils the unique attributes and talents that can be harnessed to reach our full potential.

**Goal Setting:** The question propels people to set clear and meaningful goals. By envisioning what we can see in our future, a person gains clarity on their objectives. These goals become the stepping stones towards unlocking our potential.

**Overcoming Obstacles:** In addition to identifying strengths, self-discovery entails weaknesses and areas that may require improvement. It also involves recognizing the obstacles and challenges that may impede the intended progress. This awareness enables us to devise strategies to overcome these hurdles.

**Continuous Growth:** Unlocking inner greatness and realizing personal growth is an ongoing process. As the individual evolves and learns more about him/herself, the goals and vision also evolve. Therefore, regularly revisiting the question "What can you see?" ensures that we stay attuned to our evolving aspirations and adjust our actions accordingly.

**Aspiration and Motivation:** The question is a source of inspiration and motivation. The concept of fueling our intrinsic motivation is rooted in the notion of recognizing the immense untapped potential that is inside us.

**Embracing Change:** The question promotes the development of adaptation by embracing change. We become more adaptable to change, innovative thinking, and grab new chances as we grow and our perspective broadens.

The process of unlocking one's inner greatness and reaching one's full potential is a continuous and transforming endeavor. The question of "What can you see?" is not merely a question; it is a call to action, a commitment to self-improvement, and a guiding light on the path to personal excellence. By consistently pondering this question, individuals can harness their inner greatness and embark on a journey of self-discovery that leads to realizing their fullest potential.

## 2 Cultivating Inner Greatness

### *2.1 Taking Advantage of Your Natural Capabilities*

**Acknowledging your Uniqueness:** Every person has a unique set of abilities, traits, and skills that come together to form their potential. Identifying and embracing your individuality is the first step towards unleashing the potential hidden inside you. It is critical to understand that your potential is not a comparison to another person but a reflection of who you are.

**The Power of Self-Belief:** It is only possible to reach your full potential if you have faith in yourself and your abilities. The power of self-belief is attained by developing a sense of confidence and a constructive mental attitude (Taylor, 2011). It is essential to realize that limiting thoughts and self-doubt may both operate as obstacles that will prevent you from reaching your full potential. In their place, cultivate beliefs and thoughts that are self-affirming.

## 2.2 Navigating the Path of Self-Discovery

**Self-Exploration:** Going on the road of self-discovery is like opening the doors to your inner greatness. To explore the deepest parts of yourself, you need time, patience, and a strong desire to do so. In this complicated process, you are the mapper, planning your thoughts, feelings, and wants. It is about removing the layers of social standards, outside influences, and past events to get to the heart of who you are [5].

**Reflecting on Values, Interests, Passions, and Goals:** Reflection is at the heart of getting to know yourself. This self-reflection includes thinking about your values and the driving principles that determine how you make choices and act. It is about figuring out what you care about, what makes you feel alive, and what you value. Also, spend time doing things that you are interested in and that make your heart beat fast with energy. Find your hobbies, the things that not only keep you interested but also give you a deep sense of satisfaction [6]. Lastly, take a close look at your goals. Your goals are the plans of your hopes and dreams. Self-discovery helps you get all these parts to work together in a way that makes sense to your true self.

**Self-Assessment:** A thorough self-evaluation is a crucial step toward self-discovery. It means looking at yourself in the mirror of truth and being honest about your strengths and flaws without judging yourself or being biased. Knowing your strengths is like having a powerful tool in your hands. It gives you the power to build on your natural skills, do well, and contribute to the world around you [7]. At the same time, knowing your flaws is not a sign that you are not good enough; it is an improvement plan. It is a chance to improve yourself and turn your weaknesses into strengths through hard work and persistence.

## 2.3 Setting a Purpose and Ambitious Vision

**The Vision:** Your path to greatness will be easier if you have a clear vision. Your vision is the most vital component of the journey. It is a clear picture of what you want to achieve. A strong vision gives you energy and the drive to solve problems and keep going when things get tough. It is like the guide star that keeps reminding you of where you want to go [8]. Your vision gives you direction and drive, which helps you stay on track when distractions or problems arise.

**Setting Goals:** To achieve your vision, you must set short-term and long-term goals. To set practical goals, you need to break down your ideas into steps that you can take. Make a plan with SMART goals (specific, measured, achievable, relevant, and time-bound). Review your goals often and make changes as you go [9]. Effective goal setting turns your vision into steps you can take, which makes your dreams come true. It is how to get from where you are now to where you want to be.

## 2.4 *Taking Action and Continuous Growth*

**Take First Steps:** To discover your true greatness, you have to take action. Use your knowledge, skills, and your insights to help you accomplish your goals. Take consistent steps towards your goals that are steady and planned. Change happens when people take action. Take action to close the gap between where you are now and where you want to be. Action is the dynamic force that will get you there [10]. It is the concrete manifestation of your dedication to personal development and growth.

**Embracing a Learning Spirit:** Getting to be great is a never-ending process. Learn as long as you can. Look for ways to grow personally and professionally. Learn more, get new skills, and be able to change to changing situations. Every interaction and experience can help you grow, whether with a book, a class, a mentor, or a person in your life. The road to uncovering your inner greatness is a dynamic process driven by action and a dedication to continuous education throughout one's life [11]. You realize that the journey itself is just as significant as the destination as you continue to move forward, bringing you closer to realizing your full potential. First is to ask, "What can you see?" then, once you have answered that question, let your actions and insatiable need for knowledge illuminate the path to your best possible self.

## 2.5 *Overcoming the Obstacles*

**Overcoming Fears and Failure:** The fear of failure in your goals might prevent you from reaching your full potential. Learn from your mistakes and use them to propel you towards success [12]. Appreciate that every obstacle presents you with an opportunity to learn something new and improve as a person. Learn from your mistakes and use them to fuel your motivation and resiliency.

**Determination and Resilience:** The road to achieving your full potential can be challenging. The path will inevitably include several obstacles and setbacks [13]. Develop your capacity for perseverance and resilience. It is, therefore, necessary to acquire the capacity to respond positively to setbacks by recommitting yourself to achieving your goals with even more enthusiasm.

# 3 Keeping the Momentum

Unlocking your inner greatness is a lifetime journey of self-discovery, focused action, and continuous growth. However, the journey does not end with an initial burst of excitement or the simple realization that you have potential. Instead, it goes far beyond that and includes persistence, consistency, and a firm commitment [14]. You have to keep going if you want to go on the journey of a lifetime and see the results of your hard work.

## 3.1 Keeping the Vision Alive

As you move forward on your road to greatness, it is important to stick to the goal you have made. Your goal is the North Star that keeps you going in the right direction, even when the seas of life get rough [15]. Here are three aspects that are critical to keeping the vision alive.

i. **Revisit your vision often:** The pressures and distractions of life can make it hard to see clearly. Set aside time to think about your goals, dreams, and a clear picture of what you want to accomplish. This keeps your goal clear and your loyalty to it strong.
ii. **Adapt and Refine:** You may find that your idea changes over time. It's a normal part of growing up. Don't be afraid to make changes to your goals and dreams as you learn and grow [16]. Your ability to change your mind about things can be a sign of how mature and adaptable you are.
iii. **See yourself succeeding:** Take time every day to see yourself succeeding. This practice helps you stay focused on your goal and gives you more confidence and drive [17]. Think about yourself reaching your goals and let that picture push you forward.

## 3.2 Commitment to Action

Keeping the progress going also requires you to act with unwavering dedication. At the start, it's easy to be excited, but as the journey goes on, problems may test your commitment. Here's how to keep your promise:

i. **Consistent Effort:** No one becomes great in one day. It's the result of daily, consistent effort. Make a plan that helps you reach your goals and stick to it, even when you don't feel like it [18].
ii. **Accountability:** Tell someone you trust about your goals, or even better, find someone to hold you accountable. Having someone to check in with can give you the support and drive you need to stick to your goals.
iii. **Resilience:** Expect failures and problems along the way. Instead of seeing them as problems, look at them as chances to grow and learn. Your ability to keep going even when things are hard shows how committed you are [19].
iv. **Celebrate Small Wins:** No matter how small your wins may seem, acknowledge and celebrate them. These wins keep you going and tell you that you are making progress.

The trip of a lifetime, the search for your inner greatness, is a unique and never-ending goal. To be successful, it is essential to keep the momentum going by sticking to your goal and taking constant, focused action [20]. With each step you take, you get closer to your best potential, knowing that the journey shows how strong and determined you are. So, keep the idea alive, stay dedicated, and welcome this journey with open arms. It is the journey of a lifetime.

## 4 Conclusions

The aspect of "Rising to Your Potential: Unlocking Your Inner Greatness" gives a deep understanding of how self-discovery and personal growth can be an ongoing journey. During this enlightening journey, we have talked about how important it is to develop our inner greatness and how we have a vast amount of untapped potential. We started by asking ourselves, "What can you see?" This creative point of view points us toward a purpose-driven life full of desire and success. We have learned that developing inner greatness means using our natural skills, following the complicated path of self-discovery, setting big goals, taking consistent action, and working hard to overcome problems. It is a long way, and you must be committed and strong, but the benefits are endless. However, the road continues when you realize and achieve what you want. "Keeping the Momentum" is the last key to keeping your greatness inside you. It means not only keeping the idea alive but also making a promise to take action all the time. It is about ensuring that your actions always match your goals so that your inner greatness is not just a spark that goes out but a fire that never goes out.

## References


1. Taylor, P.: The soul of leadership: unlocking your potential for greatness. JAMA **306**(8), 884–885 (2011)
2. Moss, L.: The Intent to Live: Achieving Your True Potential as an Actor. Bantam (2005)
3. Koestenbaum, P.: Leadership, New and Revised: The Inner Side of Greatness, a Philosophy for Leaders, vol. 174. John Wiley & Sons (2002)
4. Purves, D., Lotto, R.B.: Why We See What We Do: An Empirical Theory of Vision. Sinauer Associates (2003)
5. Gebauer, J., Lowman, D., Gordon, J.: Closing the Engagement Gap: How Great Companies Unlock Employee Potential for Superior Results. Penguin (2008)
6. Schippers, M.C., Ziegler, N.: Life crafting as a way to find purpose and meaning in life. Front. Psychol. **10**, 2778 (2019)
7. Daniel, R.: Self-assessment in performance. Br. J. Music Educ. **18**(3), 215–226 (2001)
8. Grossman, J., Cawn, B.: Ambitious Leadership: A Case Study of Setting a Vision for Ambitious Instruction. New Leaders (2016)
9. Ogbeiwi, O.: Why written objectives need to be really SMART. Br. J. Healthc. Manag. **23**(7), 324–336 (2017)
10. Anderson, J., Costa, A., Kallick, B.: Habits of mind: A journey of continuous growth. Learn. Lead. Habits Mind **16**, 60 (2008)
11. Epstein, M.: Self-driven continuous dislocations and growth. In: Mechanics of Material Forces, pp. 129–139. Springer, US, Boston, MA (2005)
12. Allen, S.L., Davis, K.S., Rousseau, P.C., Iverson, P.J., Mauldin, P.D., Moran, W.P.: Advanced care directives: overcoming the obstacles. J. Grad. Med. Educ. **7**(1), 91–94 (2015)
13. Tumbleson, B.E., Burke, J.J.: When life hands you lemons: overcoming obstacles to expand services in an embedded librarian program. J. Libr. Adm. **50**(7–8), 972–988 (2010)
14. Garrison, W.H.: Democracy, experience, and education: promoting a continued capacity for growth. Phi Delta Kappan **84**(7), 525–529 (2003)
15. McDonald, A.: Keeping the vision alive: maintaining motivation and promoting effective learning. Procedia Soc. Behav. Sci. **3**, 190–193 (2010)

16. Both, G.: Keeping Autonomous Driving Alive: An Ethnography of Visions, Masculinity and Fragility, p. 148. Verlag Barbara Budrich (2020)
17. Kerouac, J., Ginsberg, A.: Keeping vision alive. Emerg. Buddh. Am. Lit. 123, (2009)
18. Slack, F.J., Orife, J.N., Anderson, F.P.: Effects of commitment to corporate vision on employee satisfaction with their organization: an empirical study in the United States. Int. J. Manag. **27**(3), 421 (2010)
19. Dvir, T., Kass, N., Shamir, B.: The emotional bond: vision and organizational commitment among high-tech employees. J. Organ. Chang. Manag. **17**(2), 126–143 (2004)
20. Loewe, M., Rippin, N.: Translating an ambitious vision into global transformation: the 2030 agenda for sustainable development (No. 7/2015). Discussion Paper (2015)

# Cognitive Biases and Heuristics in Decision-Making Processes Affecting Budget and Perceptions in Special Education Committees and the Potential Contribution of Expanding Psychological Flexibility Among Decision-Makers

**Hila Fuchs and Slawomir Banaszak**

**Abstract** Amendment 11 to the Israeli Special Education Law came into force in January 2019. The amendment entailed a fundamental change in the concept of special education. Accordingly, guidelines were drawn up for the work of the special education committees. The decisions made in the special education committees have an impact on many areas of individual lives. Therefore, it is important to discuss, analyze and understand the decision-making processes in the committees and examine the challenges and necessary improvements. This study examines the influence of heuristics and cognitive biases on decision-making processes in special education committees. It also seeks to understand the relationship between cognitive biases that influence decisions and psychological inflexibility to determine the potential contribution of psychological flexibility to committee decisions. The study combines a qualitative analysis of 60 open-ended questionnaire with committee chairpersons and a content analysis of 50 committee protocols and decisions that describing the positions of different committee members during decision discussions with a theoretical-literary analysis of cognitive biases from the field of behavioral economics and its connection to components of psychological flexibility and inflexibility. The study found that many factors influence decision-making processes in special education committees. It also concluded that implementing components of psychological flexibility can improve decision-making processes and decision-making accuracy.

H. Fuchs (✉)
Gaia College Research Institute, Jerusalem, Israel
e-mail: hila@gaia.college

S. Banaszak
Adam Mickiewicz University, Poznan, Poland
e-mail: s.ban@amu.edu.pl

H. Fuchs
Management, Gaia College Research Institute, Jerusalem, Israel

 
S. Kot et al. (eds.), *Corporate Practices: Policies, Methodologies, and Insights in Organizational Management*, Springer Proceedings in Business and Economics,
https://doi.org/10.1007/978-981-97-0996-0_4

**Keywords** Decision making · Special education law · Heuristics · Psychological flexibility · Professional committees

# 1 Introduction

## *1.1 Eligibility and Characterization Committees in Special Education—Background*

In recent decades, changes in perception have led to more positive attitudes toward people with diverse needs in general and students with special needs in particular [46]. Today, students with special needs are provided by law with comprehensive special education services as part of the general education system. This reality was almost non-existent a few decades ago. The State of Israel, as part of the international community, has signed and is committed to international treaties on the rights of children and persons with disabilities. In the early years of the state, the attitude towards disabilities was characterized by adapting to the world in terms of the nursing approach [47]. People with disabilities and students with special needs belonged to the Ministry of Social Affairs and received social benefits. It was not until about forty years after the establishment of the state, in 1988, that a special education law was enacted. With this law, special educational services for students with special needs in special institutions were legally established in the state education system. Over the years, other processes took place in Israel in terms of parallel processes and the establishment of humanistic and ecological social approaches [1]. These processes, which included the transition from a caring approach toward disabilities to a social approach, emphasized society's responsibility toward individuals and the right of each individual to equal opportunity, and led to a number of movements in special education and students' rights [2].

In recent years, with the advances in social concepts emphasizing acceptance and equality, and with the events that have taken place in the world and in Israel in parallel with the educational, social and governmental processes, there has been a significant increase in the number of special education students. In recent years, the number of students with special educational needs has steadily increased. Since 2015, the budget for special education support has increased by 68%. During these years, the number of students with special educational needs increased by 35%. Over the last five years, the budget has increased by 47%, compared to an increase of only 21% in the general budget of the Ministry of Education. In the current school year, the budget for special education is NIS 16 billion, accounting for 23.5% of the Ministry of Education's budget [48]. The numerical increase significantly impacted the special education budgets and the relative part of the budget in the general education budget. At the same time as the trend of increase in quantity and budget, challenges appeared characterized by inefficient management of the budget, lack of tools and resources, lack of transparency in resource allocation, non-standard placement, lack of professional tools and effective estimates in the decision-making processes of the placement committees and difficulty of the headquarters in controlling and monitoring decision-making, processes and resource allocation. Also, problems were found in the conduct of the placement committees and claims of a need for more professional tools and non-uniform standards (MOE 2023). The need for change brought with it several processes and committees over the years, ultimately leading to Amendment 11 to the Special Education Law. The amendment entered into force in January 2019. It brought semantic and essential changes that concern both the general social perception and the perception of social responsibility, as well as the perception of special education services, special education students, and their rights. The amendment is based on concepts emphasizing social responsibility for the inclusion and integration of the individual with a disability and the need to act to realize his right to equal participation in society. The right to equal participation was expressed simultaneously as the law was amended in the "CEO's Circular" to promote inclusion in the education system (2021). The CEO's circular dealt with integrating students with diverse needs in the education system, emphasizing a social and ecological concept. He defined the goal of inclusion and the need to respond by expanding circles: the student, the kindergarten/class framework, the educational staff, the educational institution, the parents, and the community. He emphasized A systemic concept and the joint responsibility and commitment for adapted targets while referring to all the factors and the various areas of function. The circular emphasizes the system's commitment to detection processes, forward-thinking, adaptation, assimilation, follow-up implementation, and improvement. They also defined the preliminary processes, criteria, and conditions for examining a student's referral to committees according to law [3].

As part of the amendment to the law and the concept underlying it, the procedure for determining eligibility and characteristics in special education has changed. As part of the change, two committees were established whose role is to replace the placement committees: an eligibility and characterization committee that holds exclusive authority and responsibility for the question of the student's eligibility for special education services, determining the level of functioning and characterization of his disability as a basis for determining the basket of services he will receive and the multi-professional staff committees that are held at the school and are responsible for the segmentation of supports in the future for the committee's decision and the parents' choice. For each committee, the necessary preliminary documents and processes are defined: the list of attendees, the discussion processes, the adoption of the decision, its validity, and the various options the decision allows. The change in the guidance in the practice and essence of the special education committees is intended to make precise and optimize the professional tools and standards in order to lead a course of precision and optimal integration; however, in practice, the decision-making processes remain vague, and the discussion in the committee still lacks professional tools and standards that will allow for an accurate and unbiased decision regarding the student's needs and under the possibilities, the boundaries, and vision of the system.

### 1.2 The Importance of the Research

The decisions made by the special education committees affect many areas. The committees are statutory institutions that represent a functional image, and their decisions are legally valid. They discuss the rights of individuals and aim to realize these rights; therefore, they contain elements of a legal nature. The decisions are based on state and public policies and have the power to influence and determine public and political policies in the future. The decisions are discussed in educational policy and educational semantics and are made by experts with knowledge and experience in special education. The committees have educational and developmental consequences on an individual and societal level and are of societal importance. The decisions of the committees are of budgetary significance as they affect the allocation of budgets for special educational services. Furthermore, the decisions are linked to the responsibility to uncover, adapt and establish an educational, social and systemic approach. They have a moral and value-related significance as they affect the future of society. Therefore, it is important to discuss, analyze and understand the decision-making processes in the committees, how they can be optimized and how they can be brought closer to the vision that underlies the change in the law, which provides for a change in the special education committees' understanding of internal and communicative processes. An understanding of the internal processes of each of the processes that take place within the partnership in discussion and the processes that are influenced by various environmental factors within the committee, alongside an understanding of their role and influence in the decision-making processes, can help to broaden and deepen awareness of the challenges that can affect the decision-making process and influence its outcomes. Understanding the implications and challenges will enable the impact of different tools on decision-making processes to be explored. Familiarity with mechanisms and tools has had a positive impact on decision-making processes, such as psychological flexibility. Understanding the relationship between these tools and factors that intervene in the decision-making process and the decision-making process in general can be a starting point for the development of tools and models for handling, improving and accuracy of decision-making processes and their outcomes.

## 2 Theoretical Background

### 2.1 Decision-Making Processes

A decision is defined as a conscious and practical reference to an existing situation and combines a choice among multiple courses of action. The decision-making process is a cognitive process [4]. This process combines external and internal factors such as the individual's personality, value system, and beliefs [5] in combination with the information and resources available to him or her [6]. Intuition, common sense, and life experience are used in decision making [7]. Decisions can be complex and complicated, and despite attempts to be precise, misjudgments can often occur decisions affecting social and economic policy are characterized by great complexity and uncertainty, which makes it difficult to predict the consequences of future decisions [8]. Decision-making processes can be classified according to the conditions under which the decision is made: a situation of complete certainty, in which the decision requires control over as many variables and their influence as possible; decisions under conditions of uncertainty, in which there is usually a choice between two alternatives. It is not possible to estimate the outcomes of the decision and determine whether it will lead to success or failure; decisions under conditions of risk, where even if all choices between different options lead to the best decision, it is not certain that the goal of the decision will be achieved [49].

Behavioral economics is based on psychological and economic aspects. It analyzes processes and impacts that occur based on multiple demands and limited resources. It deals with decision-making processes, choices and actions under complex conditions and situations of uncertainty and their consequences. The main principles of behavioral economics come from different fields of knowledge, and it is possible through them to analyze, understand and formulate courses of action in different fields of action and different disciplines such as law and justice, public policy, social sciences, health and education (Weissbalai 2022) This study is concerned with decision-making under conditions of uncertainty. Studies have shown that decision processes under uncertainty are based on a combination of intuition, common sense, and life experience [9] identifies two systems as the basis of decision processes. System one is fast and intuitive. Decisions made in this system rely largely on feelings and rules of thumb associated with memories and identification of similarities and associations. System two is characterized by slow decision-making processes that are rational and calculated [10].

It has also been found that in situations with high mental load, schedules, and under uncertain conditions, people tend to rely on rules of thumb and intuition, which can lead to cognitive biases, perceptual and judgment errors. Therefore, these biases are repetitive and predictable [11].

In addition, studies have indicated that experts with experience and knowledge are more affected by systematic biases and misjudgments [12]. This is because when intuitive thinking is activated, the control mechanisms do not work efficiently and therefore errors are caused based on the assumption of knowledge and expertise. The causes of errors can be manifold. Errors can result from administrative and organizational constraints, such as bureaucracy, lack of resources or time to understand and address challenges in depth. Errors can also be due to the personality of the decision makers, their flexibility, their willingness to accept criticism, their ability to work under pressure, and more. As mentioned earlier, other sources of error include the tendency to apply rules of thumb and systematic bias [13]. Decision-making processes are studied through the study of truth and rationality, along with an understanding of the limits of human perception and the realization that a state of absolute certainty about the correctness of a particular decision is nearly impossible. Various constraints that intervene in decision-making require that a rational thought process be preferred to a particular thought process (ibid.). Various studies have found different effects of cognitive biases, motivational biases, logical fallacies, emotional biases, and more [14]. The desire to cope with the complexity and challenges posed by cognitive limitations leads to a tendency to simplify uncertain reality through rules of thumb. These rules are called heuristics [15]. These responses are inflexible in human consciousness over many years and become established as patterns. Consciousness creates filters through which people perceive reality. The products of consciousness are perceived as reality itself. They replace unmediated experience and guide human behavior. In addition, various strategies are developed to intervene in or avoid psychological events based on the link created by consciousness between an internal event and potential harm (ibid.). Human cognition can psychologize almost any stimulus, greatly enhancing discrimination between stimuli or combinations of stimuli that are perceived as negative or aversive by their verbal representation. In any situation, people are subject to a sense of regret for what is no longer here, anxiety even in the absence of actual stimuli, and worry about potential dangers even if they never occurred [16]. The mind's infinite capacity to make arbitrary connections can lead a person to ignore the objective and subjective value of stimuli and illogically associate them with positive or negative emotions [17]. Therefore, to understand human behavior, one must also analyze cognition [16]. Therefore, to effect change in a person's experience of a particular event, the contextual role of the event must be manipulated [18]. Heuristics are guidelines. They act on experience and in ways that are consistent with logic, but they are correct only for some situations and events. They involve shortcuts and biases in the reliability of factual and systematic knowledge, which can lead to errors. According to Kahneman and Tversky [19], there are limited useful heuristics in decision-making processes. It is important to understand how systematic errors arise in order to gain insights for optimizing decision processes that are consistent with the values and goals underlying the issue under discussion. In addition, decision-making processes in changing or complex situations require precision in recognizing, evaluating, and understanding the situation [20]. In situations where decisions must be made involving humanity, morality, and values, information processing processes require correct identification and analysis of moral values to avoid erroneous conclusions [21]. Decisions have emotional consequences; they are a source of concern, pride, regret, guilt, change, and transcendence. Every decision is rooted in emotion. It depends on emotional resilience, social environment, a tendency toward optimism, and an overestimation of ability that can lead to arrogance, opacity, excessive indifference, and aversion to risk or loss [22].

Eligibility and characterization committees are based on a humanistic concept that incorporates natural rights and issues of morality, values, and responsibility. Studies claim that the use of cognitive biases in decisions related to morals and values sometimes helps individuals protect their egos [23]. It can lead to ignoring the moral elements when dealing with complex situations and diverting attention from the elements that have the potential for moral harm when making decisions [24]. Cognitive processes and skills play a central role in analysis and decision-making processes. Lack of attention and distractions resulting from the use of heuristics in decision-making processes can lead to unethical decisions [25]. When stress levels are high, the processing system does not function efficiently [26], and there is a tendency for automatic responses based on fixed patterns and existing attitudes. For example, Kaniel [27] states that anxiety or avoidance in emotionally arousing situations leads to one-dimensional, concrete, and categorical thinking characterized by the adoption of biases and labeling processes. In this situation, decisions may be made based on parameters that are sometimes completely at odds with the facts [27].

Kahneman and Tversky [19] have identified three key heuristics underlying cognitive biases in decision processes. The representativeness heuristic is a rapid cognitive process based on the tendency to automatically associate a particular person with a particular group based on a central characteristic, while ignoring other factors of weight and importance. The association is based on labeling and ignores elements such as the size of the group and the possibility that the item belongs to it because of its size [19]. Several cognitive biases are characteristic of this heuristic: ignoring sample size manifests itself in ignoring prevalence as an element in decision making and conveying impressions of samples of different sizes in the same way; similarity between cause and effect leads to a search for causes and effects that are similar. There is also an assumed correspondence between causes and outcomes: Biased perception of randomness and the tendency to attribute causal regularity to a random sequence, due to the natural tendency to think in patterns and the illusion of validity that gives too much weight to first impressions.

In decision-making processes, it can be economical to invest time and mental resources in representativeness, but it can lead to bias and error [12]. It can lead to superficial or biased judgment based on biased testimony or biased thinking, making it difficult to focus on the uniqueness of the case. At the same time as cataloging, there is a tendency to search for the information that matches the expectations and attitudes that correspond to the intuitive decision according to confirmation bias. There is also a tendency to ignore information and data that contradict the original assumption in the context of selection bias and to make decisions based on arbitrary comparison rather than relying on the analysis of the unique case.

The availability heuristic is characterized by intuitive cognitive processes based on relying on the information available in memory rather than on the analysis of facts and objective probability depending on the case or situation. Decision making is based on evaluating examples that come to mind. Availability is usually influenced by salient memories, without regard to their frequency or objective probability. Relying on this heuristic can lead to errors and overestimation of risk. The frequency estimate in this heuristic is influenced by the ease with which cases can be recalled in memory, sometimes regardless of how they happened or how frequent they objectively were. In the same way, the degree of efficiency and accuracy of memory retrieval is also influenced. Difficulty in retrieving something from memory has been associated with low frequency ratings, rather than criticizing the processes of memory retrieval. The availability heuristic is also influenced by how easy it is to retrieve things from the imagination. In most cases, it is easier to imagine dramatic descriptions and salient examples related to the decision topic. These examples can influence the decision-making process. Another bias that belongs to the availability heuristic is the framing bias. According to the framing bias, decision processes are influenced by how alternatives are presented for selection. In addition, phenomena associated with fears, anxieties, and strong emotions are perceived to be more frequent and available than reality and influence decision processes. The domino effect, which is also one of the biases of the availability heuristic, tends to predict a particular influence of one domain on another domain as the basis for a decision. Not relying on these biases in decision-making processes often leads to an incorrect and exaggerated assessment of risks and thus to a decision that does not reflect the facts.

The anchoring heuristic is a cognitive process in which people fixate on the initial intuitive assessment and use it as an anchor point and comparison for decision making. This assessment is an anchor point and sets standards in the decision-making process. This happens even when its accuracy is not certain and even when it is wrong. According to the anchor heuristic, the anchor point remains fixed, and if it is shown to be wrong, there is a tendency to improve it. This bias also results from insufficient activation of critical faculties and the difficulty of abandoning a belief or position once it has been established, even when there is evidence to the contrary. Their use often leads to incorrect risk assessments, incorrect judgments, and incorrect decisions. In addition to heuristics, other cognitive biases can influence attitudes as a basis for decision-making processes, such as distorted or damaged deliberation and processing; the limitations of human memory as a basis for analyzing reality and making decisions; emotional components as part of a position, basis for identification, perception of morality, environmental influences, and psychodynamic components [28]. Emotional biases arise, among other things, on the basis of arbitrary relationships that arise naturally in the mind within the framework of human cognitive abilities. They eliminate the objective and subjective value of events in experience and irrationally link them to various emotions [29].

Eligibility and characterization committees raise complex issues related to students with disabilities and involve addressing issues of morality and values. Individuals experience an encounter with a disability or issues related to disability and inclusion as a challenging situation that requires coping and adjustment. Encountering a new or challenging situation creates a need for control. The need for control leads to a tendency to help when encountering another person's challenge or difference. The tendency to help and treat helps the individual cope with existential anxiety about dysfunction. In addition, helping creates a sense of separation between the person and the situation and helps to feel safe.

## 2.2 *Psychological Flexibility*

Psychological flexibility is the ability to experience the present consciously and without bias and to act according to individual values [17]. It forms the basis for appropriate decision-making and behavioral processes, even when decisions and actions are accompanied by complex psychological events [50]. These processes help an individual change the role of his or her internal experience, behavior, and communication by flexibly facing challenges [51]. According to Hayes & Wilson (2003), six parallel and interrelated processes form the basis of psychological flexibility: acceptance is the state of being ready, willing, and able to experience private events without attempting to change their frequency, content, or form (Burke and Moore 2015). Acceptance implements flexible and efficient patterns of behavior that are consistent with the individual's goals and values [30]. Cognitive defusion is the ability to distinguish between thoughts, feelings, physiological sensations, and impulses when evaluating real events while being fully aware of the present and choosing effective and relevant behaviors (Burke and Moore 2015). Present moment mindfulness is an active, attentive, full, non-judgmental awareness of the present moment (Burke and Moore 2015). "I as observer" is A multidimensional awareness of oneself as more than the sum of one's personal experiences (Burke and Moore 2015). This capacity is expressed in the individual's ability to see themselves and others as more complex than the set of labels associated with them and to avoid being identified by their thoughts about themselves [30]. Values are Selected principles (Burke and Moore 2015) chosen by the individual [31] define processes and are associated with patterns of action that guide and organize the individual's behavior (ibid.) and give it meaning (Burke and Moore 2015). Values are like a compass that guides an ongoing process toward specific and achievable goals [32], committed actions is reinforce effective behaviors that help individuals achieve values, based goals [30]. These behaviors should be tailored to each individual's values and not motivated by external factors. They should also be evaluated regularly and adjusted as needed. Ultimately, values-based behaviors should be the end goal. Psychological flexibility depends on a person's ability to efficiently balance the mental energy they invest in current events in their immediate environment and the energy they can invest in important future situations [33]. Automatic processes such as heuristics, stereotypes, and habits help us interpret and respond to the environment in a balanced way. However, this process leads individuals to make inferences about themselves, others, and the world around them based on limited knowledge and misconceptions [34]. Psychological flexibility helps design efficient processes based on heuristics.

Heuristics are simple mental procedures that help find quick but incomplete answers and solutions to difficult questions and decision making [9]. Heuristics help us navigate social environments and deal with myriad verbal and nonverbal information in social interactions [33]. Heuristics and stereotypes enable us to make inferences and determine responses to inferences on a daily basis [35]. Heuristics and stereotypes resist rethinking and changing [36], that make it difficult to recognize other relevant information or to gain new insights and prevent us from experiencing and participating in different personal situations [37] Presence, Mindfulness, and Values. This requires that we recognize the tendency to decide and choose according to automatic patterns that lead to social judgments and preferences based on habits. The limitations of cognitively biased social judgments, habits, and preferences and the fact that automatic, habit-based responses ultimately limit flexible, original, and predictive decisions and outcomes [33].

Psychological flexibility involves full awareness of an individual's feelings and thoughts, as well as behavior that is consistent with his or her values [38]. Studies have shown that psychological flexibility affects behavior, performance levels, biases, and the ability to cope with, accept, and learn new things [16]. The ability of an individual with psychological flexibility to experience negative thoughts and emotions without subsequently intervening or judging allows them to experience these types of thoughts and emotions without perceiving them as real and therefore without being affected by them [39]. In this situation, the individual's ability to respond and behave in accordance with his or her true values is preserved [39]. Category formation and labeling are natural and normal processes when they occur immediately and automatically [33]. However, when a person is unable to disengage from a particular thought, or when emotions and thoughts are perceived as objective representations of reality rather than temporal products of the mind [40], labeling may indicate a lack of acceptance and openness and lead to negative consequences [33]. The inability to accept frustration or deal with unwanted experiences directly reduces the effective use of attentional skills and decision-making abilities. This leads to energy being invested in trying to avoid or change irrevocable experiences [41], causing a lack of psychological availability for adaptation and acceptance [33]. Psychological flexibility occupies a key position in coping with situations of psychological distress. Moreover, it has been found to be significantly positively related to prudence and presence in decision-making processes. It enables to deal effectively with new and challenging situations and to develop alternative views and ideas. Juanchich et al. [42] found a link between psychological flexibility and effective decision-making processes. They found that greater cognitive reflection predicted positive decision-making outcomes in real life [43].

# 3 Methods

## *3.1 The Purpose of the Study*

The purpose of this study is to examine how various cognitive biases from the fields of behavioral, cognitive psychology, and behavioral economics are expressed and influence the decision-making processes of committees discussing the provision of responses to students with diverse needs, and how psychological flexibility can reduce cognitive biases and help adjust, streamline, and correct committee discussion decisions and their short- and long-term outcomes. Eligibility and characterization committee discussion management and decision making contain elements and aspects that touch on legislation, education, society, perceptions and values, attitudes and policies toward disabilities, public policy, and budget. The implications for committee decision making and the potential consequences of committee decisions are examined in the context of budgetary, conceptual, social, educational, developmental, value-based, and legal significance. The study is based on the assumption that knowledge of various cognitive biases from cognitive psychology and behavioral economics, and the simultaneous application of an implementation model to expand psychological flexibility among decision makers, can help improve the accuracy of committee decisions and their future impact. The research aims to provide insights that will form the basis for designing a unique practice for decision-making processes in committees of this type. This is because of the multidimensional consequences of committee decisions at the individual and corporate levels.

## 3.2 Research Paradigm

The research is an integrative, interdisciplinary qualitative research that combines concepts and theories from the fields of education, special education, and disabilities studies with concepts and theories from the fields of cognitive psychology, behavioral economics, contextual and functional theories, and theories of human cognition that underlie psychological flexibility.

## 3.3 Research Design

The study will combine a qualitative analysis of open-ended questionnaire of chairpersons of eligibility and characterization committees, an analysis of content in committee protocols and decisions that occurred from 2019–2023, and a theoretical-literary analysis of cognitive biases from the fields of behavioral economics and third wave cognitive-behavioral psychology on the components of psychological flexibility and inflexibility. The study will also address the ability of psychological inflexibility components to contribute to flexibility and the reduction of common biases in suitability committee discussions and decision-making processes based on the definition of the components, an explanation of their application in committee discussions, and examples from studies related to the various aspects that emerge in committee discussions that can contribute to a deeper understanding and form the basis for building a model that can help in the decision-making processes in eligibility and characterization committee discussions.

## 3.4 Research Population and Sample

The study population from which the first sample was sampled included the chairperson of the Eligibility and Characterization Committees, aged 45–60, with knowledge, experience, and training in special education and 3–5 committee days per week for years or more. Who agreed to participate in the study.

Data was collected from (Table 1) 60 participants. Most of the participants were women (85.00%) with an average age of 49.63 years. All participants had an academic education (100.00%) and 15–20 years of experience in education (53.33%).

Table 1 The first sample

| | N | % | Mean |
|---|---|---|---|
| Gender | | | |
| • Female | 51 | 85.00 | |
| • Male | 9 | 15.00 | |
| Age | | | 49.63 |
| Education | | | |
| • 2nd Degree | 57 | 95.00 | |
| • 3rd degree | 3 | 5.00 | |
| Years of experience in education | | | |
| • 10–15 years | 12 | 20.00 | |
| • 15–20 years | 32 | 53.33 | |
| • More than 20 years | 16 | 26.66 | |
| Years of seniority in the current position | | | |
| • Since the first year | 44 | 73.33 | |
| • Since the third year and more | 16 | 26.66 | |

The study population from which the second sample was drawn included various eligibility and characterization committee members between the ages of 35–65 who agreed to participate in the study.

Data from the second sample were collected from (Table 2) 87 participants who participated in various combinations on 50 committees according to the characterizations in Amendment 11 of the Special Education Act. Most of the participants were women (77.00%) and had a mean age of 43.72 years. All participants had an academic education (100.00%). 28 of the participants were school psychologists (32%), 34 of the participants were special education teachers (39%), 6 of the participants were community education officers (6.80%), and 13 of the participants were representatives of parent organizations (14.90%).

## 3.5 Research Question

How are the effects of cognitive biases reflected in the Eligibility and Characterization Committee's discussions and decisions, and how can increasing committee members' psychological flexibility help optimize and improve the accuracy of the committee's decision-making processes.

**Table 2** The second sample

| | N | % | Mean |
|---|---|---|---|
| Committee member | | | |
| • Chairperson | 6 | 6.8 | |
| • Educational psychologist | 28 | 32.1 | |
| • Special Education supervisor | 34 | 39.08 | |
| • Municipality education supervisor | 6 | 6.8 | |
| • Parents organization representor | 13 | 14.9 | |
| Gender | | | |
| • Female | 67 | 77.01 | |
| • Male | 20 | 22.9 | |
| Age | | | 43.72 |
| Education | | | |
| • 2nd Degree | 79 | 90.8 | |
| • 3rd degree | 8 | 9.19 | |
| Years of seniority in the current position | | | |
| • Since the first year | 56 | 64.36 | |
| • Since the third year and more | 31 | 35.63 | |

## 3.6 Research Tools

The research was designed using an interdisciplinary approach combining theoretical and qualitative research.

1. Short personal details questionnaire addressing to gender, age, education, experience, role and seniority.
2. Open ended questionnaire that examines hidden, clear, and prominent perceptions of characteristics and challenges addressing to the committees' discussions and decisions. The questionnaire contains ten general questions concerning to the process before, during and after committee discussions; the partnership and relationship with the educational staff, committee members, and the supervisors; correlations and gaps in perceptions; decision parameters; decision making process; advantage, challenges; role perception and personal motivation and individual experience.
3. Committees' discussion protocol and decision protocol content analyzing.
4. Analyzing psychological flexibility literature according to earlier stages results

## 3.7 Research Process

The theoretical part refers to behavioral economic principles and elements of psychological flexibility. It explores possible relationships between them in relation to decision-making processes in general and in eligibility and characterization committees in particular. The study examined the protocols, guiding thoughts, and decisions of eligibility and characterization committees between the years 2019 and 2023. All texts were thoroughly scanned and selected, representative quotes of the content were chosen, key themes were noted, and classification into major and minor categories was performed. In addition, principles of behavioral economics and elements of flexibility and psychological inflexibility were traced in the content that came up in discussion among committee members and examined for reasons and decisions.

**The research was conducted in three phases:**

*In the first phase*, include open ended questionnaire filled by the chairs of the eligibility and characterization committees about the characterizations and main challenges in the decision-making processes in the committees were qualitatively analyzed.

*In the second phase,* protocols paper, documents of the committees, justifications and decisions of the committees from 2019–2023 were qualitatively analyzed. The content was analyzed in terms of the characteristics of various biases typical of decision-making processes in behavioral economics and psychology.

*In the third phase*, articles and studies on psychological flexibility were analyzed with regard to findings on biases in decision-making processes in special education committees. In the final phase, the various elements examined in the research were linked to provide practical insights and a basis for building a model.

## 4 Results

In the first stage, the analysis of the qualitative data focused on examining the challenges in the decision-making processes from the perspective of the committee chairperson. The second stage focused on the heuristics and biases that influence decision-making during the discussion of the committee members. The qualitative part is based on a content analysis using the multiple case study paradigm [44]. According to the constructivist approach [52], the text was analyzed in a thematic analysis based on the continuous stages. It referred to text segments as analytical units [54]. The analysis process was based on coding to link the different content segments and examine the meanings [53] and the themes that characterized the data. The coding process involved categorization based on the information analysis and alignment with the concepts relevant to the data. The categorization formed the basis for interpretation and meaning. The categories were examined in relation to other categories [52]. The analysis included an evaluation of the open-ended questionnaire, which included general and specific questions about the management of the committee, as well as general and specific questions about decision-making processes and impacts during the process. The content also involved relating to the literature review the relationship between psychological flexibility and inflexibility components to relevant factors such as self-regulation, perceptions of disability, impulsivity, values and more.

## 4.1 Challenges and Characteristics

The content collected using the open-ended questionnaire brought to light some challenges and characteristics in the decision-making processes of special education committees (Fig. 1).

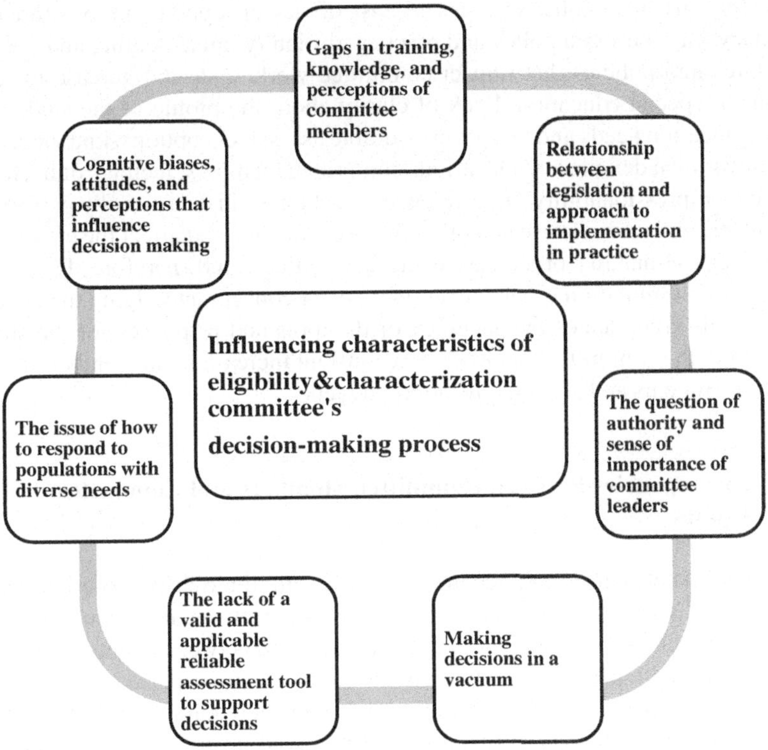


**Fig. 1** Challenges and characteristics in the decision-making processes of special education committees

## 4.2 *Characterization Committees in Various Counties*

From the data collected from 60 chairs of and characterization committees in various counties, it appears that:

### 4.2.1 The Framework of the Discussion

The framework of the discussion is clear in terms of the order and organization of the discussion, the participants in the discussion and the order of speakers, the documents and functional levels and areas tested during the discussion, and the parameters that serve as the basis for the committee's decision. At the same time, committee chairs report frequent policy changes, a sense of lack of support and sometimes even legitimacy, gaps between policy and practice, difficulty implementing and enforcing procedures and policies that impact committee work, a steady increase in student referrals to special education, Lack of clarity about the profile of the student with special education needs and lack of measurable assessment options, knowledge gaps and motivational deficits among various committee members, feelings of irrelevance and even "impressionability," interference and changes in decisions by performance committees, and more. These and other factors influence and affect the effectiveness of the decision-making processes in the committees, and therefore do not allow processes of assimilation of an educational-social concept underlying the change in the law. This complicates the accuracy of the tools and responses for the students discussed in the committee and leads to a constant increase in the number of special education students and special education budgets.

### 4.2.2 Discrepancies Between Committee Members and Committee Chairs

Discrepancies between committee members and committee chairs experience significant discrepancies in knowledge, perceptions, perspectives, and attitudes between the committee chair and other committee members and between committee members and education staff, parents, and students. committee chairs reported their consistent, comprehensive, and in-depth training to enhance their knowledge, skills, understanding, and professionalism regarding all practical, legal, and perceptual issues related to special education, Amendment 11 to the Special Education Act, eligibility and characterization committees, processes of exhausting opportunities, concepts and processes related to inclusion and integration, processes of functional assessment, transformations and processes in the concept of disability, and educational approaches. Also, the requirements for the position of Chair of the Eligibility and Characterization Committees, as published in the notice pursuant to the legislative amendment, were in line with the basic idea of appointing a person who has knowledge, experience and training in the field of special education, as well as familiarity with and conviction in humanistic social concepts, to lead the processes in the field and in the committees, while participating in the promotion, reception and implementation of processes of inclusion and integration of students with special needs in regular education. The various members of the committee work in special education. However, they do not participate in as thorough and intensive training as the committee chairs and sometimes are not even familiar with routine procedures. The chair is a fixture on the committees and guides the various parties in the processes that precede and follow committee discussions. Committee members usually rotate. Roles are fixed, but characters differ from discussion to discussion, and so perceptions, attitudes, tendencies, and decisions are not uniformly shaped. In addition, committee chairs reported a sense of mission around a concept that emphasizes inclusion and integration, an equal right to participate and be included in society, and the need for changes in perceptions and practices in this area to expand the capacity to deal with and respond to students with diverse needs in regular classes. Because of the wide variation among representatives on different committees and even within the same committee, it is impossible to indicate a consistent level of knowledge, skill, and perception among the various partners. According to an evaluation report by the National Board for Evaluation and Measurement of Decision Making, committee discussions can be deliberations by committee members that interfere with the decision-making process and put resource interests ahead of the best interests of students and the promotion of inclusion (June 2023).

### 4.2.3 Authority, Importance, and Support

Another point from the committee chairs' open ended questionnaire relates to the need for more certainty and consistency in policies and procedures and the lack of support from decision makers. Despite the evaluation report's findings (June 2023) that education teams refrain from referring students for fear of quotas, in practice committee chairs report lack of quotas, lack of goals, lack of feedback, and loopholes in procedures that allow for increasing numbers of requests and approvals. There is also a proliferation of Committee with exceptional approval even though they do not meet the criteria for referral to this type of committee. There is also a complete neglect of budgetary discourse alongside the approval of special education budgets in huge amounts. Additionally, to approval of special education services despite a lack of staff and resources that does not allow the right to support to be implemented. special education can be helpful for students that really need it but it has its prices. There is a potential for personal and systemic harm due to the ease of approving services in committees. The reports also note that appeals committees should be part of the same office and under the same perceptual umbrella, but these committees typically do not support the processes that take place in the eligibility and characterization committees. They often very easily uphold appeals and overturn the professional committee's decision. This assertion also emerges from the reports of committee chairs who see the essential value of their work, their professionalism, their sense of purpose, and their perception of their role compromised. This is tantamount to a desire for more support from the department and special education leaders. Special education committees deal with decisions that affect budget, law, education, society, policy, and personality. Despite the great importance and multi-faceted implications, the discussion in practice must follow an orderly decision-making process. In the experience of committee chairs, characterization of decisions is often biased and sometimes arbitrary.

### 4.2.4 Measurement, Assessment and Criteria

Another problem is the lack of clarity about the profile of the student with special needs, which is characterized by the need to be able to truly reliably measure and evaluate the student's performance within the educational framework and the factors that influence his or her performance. In addition, the impact of a change in certain factors on the student's performance must be measured. Committee chairs feel that the preparation processes for committee discussion often occur within the pedagogical framework to coordinate positions for presentation to the committee. As a result, there can be significant discrepancies between the student's performance in the educational framework and the presentation of the functional picture to the committee. Without measurement tools, it is only sometimes possible to accurately present the functional picture. The National Board of Evaluation and Measurement's evaluation report (NBEM 2023) supports these findings, saying that the results show that, in most cases, schools know the rules of the game and come to committees while they and parents present a consistent and agreed-upon position (MOE 2023). In the first two years of committee work, education teams completed a functional-level questionnaire (RAMA 2022) created and validated by the Department of Testing and Evaluation. This was the first step in creating a functional profile assessment tool to be measured with standardized instruments. Just as committee preparation often focuses on staff and parent goals to achieve the highest level of support, the Functioning Level Questionnaire became from being a valid, reliable, and representative instrument to one whose goal is to achieve the highest level of support. Committee chairs reported that as the first year of implementation of the change in the law progressed and the educational teams gained experience in completing the questionnaire, the discrepancy between the results of the questionnaire and the student's performance increased. In addition, the instructions for weighing the questionnaire in determining the level of functioning changed during the first year. From a questionnaire that had a significant weight in determining the level of performance at the beginning of the implementation of the change in the law, it became another document in the stack of documents submitted to the committee. By the third year of committee work, the requirement to complete the questionnaire was removed, even for new students submitted to the committee for discussion.

### 4.2.5 Perceptions, Attitudes, and Biases

The Eligibility and Characterization Committees discuss students who are facing challenges. Even when the student's situation does not require special education, it always touches the heart and recruits. It is often difficult to separate situations of identification from the student's perception of real need alongside the moral sense of obligation to do the right thing, which often makes it difficult to make an accurate and effective decision. The content that emerged from chairs of eligibility and characterization committees' open ended questionnaire indicates that the granting of a parent's and staff's request for special education services is viewed as a moral and caring act of making the request. This approach leaves no room for consideration of the exact needs of the student. Similarly, there is often a misconception among committee members that not granting eligibility for special education services to a student who needs them will result in greater harm than granting eligibility to a student who does not. This approach often ignore from the prices that exist in special education. It emphasizes the complexity and lack of supports in mainstream schools and tends to approve supports. The perception of the benefits of special education, along with the perception of the harm caused by its absence, tips the scales in favor of eligibility, even though it may not accurately reflect the student's situation and may even affect his or her future and the future of society.

### 4.2.6 The Question of Sources

The lack of a defined and clear profile of students with special education needs and the desire to provide an answer to students referred to the committee sometimes results in the confirmation of eligibility for special education services to students for whom this is not the right solution, or even to students for whom this will not help at all and whose needs can be met elsewhere. Students who are at risk of dropping out of school because they are not in school, students who are part of the regular education system but need adjustments in graduation, students who need help or support in the medical field, students who need an environment that allows them to express their abilities and does not focus specifically on academic skills, students who need to intervene in parental routines, and more. The challenges presented to the committee touch on emotions and motivate a desire to help, but they do not look at the big picture. Committee members feel the need to provide an answer. Because the committee believes it can provide a special education answer, it tends to affirm eligibility in these cases without considering whether it has value. The need to provide an answer often makes one forget that there are committees and departments whose job it is to provide specific answers to these areas. In most cases, it is not beneficial to the function to provide a response from special education rather than customized responses.

In summary, the experience of the chairs of eligibility and characterization committees suggests that the decision-making processes in the committees could be improved, constructive, and precise. Committee decisions are based on a lack of clarity in procedures and policies, gaps in knowledge of procedural and in-depth processes, gaps in perceptions and motivation of various committee members, a lack of an accurate profile defining the special education student, a lack of knowledge and understanding of the situation in the field, a lack of budgetary implications, discrepancies between the committee's decision and its ability to implement it optimally, the lack of systematic evidence, the influence of attitudes, emotions, charisma, interpersonal relationships, and personal experiences, the conflation of moral issues, the misjudgment of the cost–benefit ratio, the lack of involvement or consequences for committee members in their decisions, and more. An analysis of committee discussions and.

## *4.3 Decisions in Terms of Heuristics and Their Components Revealed the Following Results*

Committee members tend to look at performance in a particular area rather than overall performance in determining eligibility for special education services. This is even though the educational system is charged with promoting overall development. In many cases, the focus is on the student's academic performance. In these cases, despite the student's good social and emotional skills and success in non-academic occupations, the committee classifies him as a special education student. This is even though his general functioning is not at all like that of a special education student and he is engaged in a targeted challenge in a particular area. The tendency in the committee's discussion to emphasize academics, especially for students with good skills and abilities in various areas whose academic area is not their strong skills, preserves traditional notions of the educational system emphasizing academics over other and additional areas. This concept is contrary to the essence of the Committee, which emerged from a humanistic and ecological concept. A concept that emphasizes the right of every student to participate equally in society and strives for an inclusive society that accepts and promotes all its members. A one-dimensional reference in the committee fails to express the multitude of qualities and abilities of individuals, labels them and their overall abilities, and can be detrimental to their sense of worth, resilience, and capability. These feelings have a critical impact on his functional prognosis. In addition, there is a tendency to approve preschool claims based on the notion that preschoolers can only benefit from special services and support without considering the many benefits of learning from and emulating children with normal development. This is consistent with the representativeness heuristic. According to this heuristic, there is a tendency to automatically associate a particular individual with a particular group in terms of a central but unique characteristic. Another feature of the representativeness heuristic, which assumes a similarity between cause and effect, is reflected in committee members' discussions and decisions in that committee members tend to predict performance based on a diagnosis without considering abilities, strengths, skills, compensatory mechanisms, and support resources. Committee members often assume that a delay in oral skills over a long period of time will inevitably lead to integration difficulties, even when social and communication skills are completely normal, as does the tendency to think that learning disabilities will inevitably lead to significant educational gaps without considering mechanisms of resilience, motivation, memorization, and investment. Another assumption that is repeatedly voiced is that the student's functional prognosis depends on the socioeconomic level of the parents. Special education eligibility is often based on the assumption that parents with low socioeconomic levels do not have the resources to support and help their children. Therefore, their level of functioning will be low. This ignores the relationship between family members, parental investment and warmth, the student's strengths and abilities, and more. This position is contrary to the concept underlying the amendment and the natural right to equality and opportunity. Confirmation bias, as part of the representativeness heuristic, is expressed in discussions among committee members and in committee decisions by the fact that some committee members often tend to confirm eligibility for special education services even before they have received the full picture. This is due to a positive perception of special education. In these cases, information presented during the discussion that does not support the decision is ignored, such as showing progress after supports are provided, showing areas of strength that can support the challenging area of functioning, not providing supports to explore the potential for progress, attributing functioning to a specific situation in a specific time period and not as inherent to the student's functioning. Selectivity bias, which is characterized by the tendency to look for, interpret, prefer, and remember information that confirms our beliefs or hypotheses while paying less attention to information that supports alternative options, and which is also part of the representativeness heuristic, is expressed in the committee by the tendency to look for features of the diagnosis that are stated in the accepted document, especially in cases of psychiatric documents. When there are no clear features, there is a tendency to assign features of the diagnosis to functional features that are not necessarily related, such as characterizing academic difficulties as anxiety in students with an anxiety disorder document, even though there is an untreated attention deficit disorder, and that a psycho-didactic diagnosis has not been performed in the past, even though educational personnel have made recommendations over the years. There is also a tendency to emphasize the needs of the individual while ignoring systemic consequences, such as a lack of staff and resources. Assimilation of a perception of exclusion and marginalization alongside a self-perception of incompetence. Another feature of the representativeness heuristic is the tendency to weight irrelevant components as part of the decision parameters. The committee's discussion is aimed at examining the student's functioning and support needs in the school environment. Committee members do not recognize the importance of other factors such as well-being, community support, marital status, parental behavior, adolescent development, and more. The committee's decision is often based on parameters that are not defined in special education, such as a complex family situation, fear of dropping out of school, other siblings in special education, and lack of support at home. In addition, sometimes challenging behavior is already present at home but needs to be addressed at school. Even in these cases, sometimes the Board tends to affirm eligibility for special education services, even if they are not the exact solution to the student's needs, and sometimes they are not appropriate for any of the student's needs. Biased testimony or biased thinking are also characteristics of representativeness. Since the beginning of the implementation of Amendment 11 to the Special Education Act and given the significant increase in requests for special education services in recent years, the profile of the student with special education needs has become blurred. At the same time, over the years, education teams and parents have become more aware of the parameters that can drive the issue of rights during committee discussions. There are cases when the representation of the student in the committee by the educational staff, by the parents and sometimes by the student himself is the result of a careful preparation aimed at obtaining resources from the committee. It is only sometimes possible to recognize these situations. Therefore, biased statements sometimes lead to an inaccurate decision. Also, the thought or perception that the special school can provide a solution for every student, the perception that the mainstream school does not have the resources or ability to provide a solution for the student, the perception that there are not enough resources in the system rather than the perception that there is a need to be accurate with resources-all of these can influence the committee's thinking and decision.

A positive contrast effect occurs when something is perceived to be better than it normally would be because it is compared to something worse. When the weighting is equal but opposite, a negative contrast effect occurs. Sometimes closely spaced appointments on the same day can influence the committee's decision. Very complex and multidisciplinary cases are presented alongside cases where the challenge is undiscipline and has a specific functional impact. The preference for relying on information from memory rather than analyzing facts and probabilities in the availability heuristic is reflected in the committee's sometimes basing its decision on recollection of details said in the past about the student or in the student's environment, on another student with a functional picture that is remembered as similar to the functional picture presented to the committee, on recollection of resources and care in the regular school versus resources and care in the special school, on recollection of student processes that are perceived as similar in function, or even on personal memories that evoke identification. The effect of extreme events and dramatic memories as anchors for a decision, regardless of their frequency, is also a feature of the availability heuristic. Regarding this feature, observation of decisions made by eligibility and characterization committees shows that cases with a complex personal history are almost always immediately approved as eligible for special education services, and sometimes even without examining the entire functional picture or adjusting the special education service response to the case. In addition, a dramatic element in a student's history often drives the decision, even if he or she does not have a functional profile that requires special education services. Perceptions of special education as positive and supportive for students with various types of challenges and perceptions of mainstream education as inadequate in the face of challenges lead to a preference for special education, even though special education excels in various areas and even though students who were in special education wanted to transfer to mainstream education because of negative experiences and feelings of not belonging and being inadequate. It follows the framing bias based on decision making about the possible alternatives as a feature of the availability heuristic. Another feature of the availability heuristic, according to which phenomena related to fears and anxieties tend to be perceived more frequently, is reflected in the decisions of the committee by the fact that students with behavioral difficulties or students who come with a mental health document tend to evoke feelings of helplessness and difficulties in dealing with both the educational staff and the members of the committee, which affects the decisions about them, even if there are no preparatory processes in the educational environment that can support their functioning. The tendency is that students of this type are more likely to need special education services, although the responses found within the services for students entitled to special education support often do not meet their needs and often do not support them. Even when it is determined that the student is struggling academically, some committee members tend to assert that without support, there will be emotional, social, and risk effects that significantly impact developmental prognosis and future functioning.

The reliance on an anchor point as part of the anchor heuristic, the adherence to it, and the decision based on it manifests itself in the discussion sometimes appearing as if the decision had already been made before the discussion began based on some preliminary information provided in the preparatory materials for the discussion. In these cases, committee members who hold to their position sometimes hold to their position even when there is really no reason to do so because they believe it is the better option. The anchoring heuristic is characterized by the difficulty of abandoning an initial position even when it has been proven wrong. For example, some committee members tend to claim that the gaps today are not large and do not meet the criteria for intensive support, but if support is not provided, larger gaps will result based on this claim, they decide that special education services are needed to prevent this from happening. Another example is relying on the diagnosis even though there are conflicting reports from the team or vice versa to have a solid basis for a decision.

A misperception of risk also characterizes the anchoring heuristic, reflected in the committee's discussion of the underestimation of the mainstream education and the overestimation of special education without questioning the accuracy, appropriateness, identity, and characteristics of the staff. The decision is based on the common perception that special education is a magic solution. However, reality only sometimes proves this. These perceptions are expressed in the argument that without the right to special education, the student will continue to accumulate deficits and have no chance of success. Another common claim is that without special education eligibility, the student will end up in risky situations. Yet there is often no connection between these two claims, because risky situations do not occur specifically with special education treatment, but with dramatic behaviors or psychological characteristics that require services in an inclusive setting. In cases of school dropout, youth development, and vocational training. Special education does not provide solutions. Sometimes, being part of a special education school can actually exacerbate risky situations, such as learning and imitating the peer group within the special education. In addition, the entitlement to special education services is a recurring topic in the entitlement to special education services.

## 5 Discussion and Summary

The structure of human cognition as the basis for cognitive and psychological processes is the source of bias toward events and situations in general and in decision-making processes in particular. The filters that consciousness produces as a survival process shape the individual's point of view and perception of reality. Human cognition tends to psychologize almost any stimulus. Consciousness relates to psychological events as reality itself. And because psychological events are potentially harmful, reactive strategies are developed to deal with them. The mind establishes arbitrary relationships that cause individuals to ignore the objective and subjective value of stimuli and illogically associate them with an emotional experience. This mechanism influences general behavior and decision-making processes [17]. Therefore, to make decision processes more accurate, it is important to develop an awareness of cognition and the contextual role of responses [18]. Biased, one-dimensional responses based on rules of thumb, patterns, and context are expressions of psychological inflexibility. This study examined the biases that arise in committee decision-making processes according to the components of psychological inflexibility in order to optimize decision-making processes in suitability and characterization committees. The components of psychological inflexibility are interrelated with the components of psychological flexibility. Analysis of the relationships and equilibria will explain the challenges in the decision-making processes and how the processes can be optimized and refined to provide an appropriate response to the student and protect the student's rights. Understanding bias and its influence will allow consideration of the potential contribution of expanding psychological flexibility as a tool for accuracy and optimization of decision-making processes in eligibility and characterization committees.

Psychological inflexibility, the opposite of psychological flexibility and associated with cognitive patterns such as repetition compulsion and stress [45], rigid patterns of behavior and functioning limit the ability to act according to values and goals and according to the demands of the situation [33].

The psychological flexibility model consists of six components that form the basis for flexible behavior and coping. Acceptance means accepting private events without trying to change them (Burke and Moore 2015). It promotes flexible, purposeful behavior [30] by leading to nonjudgmental observation of psychological Cognitive Defusion is the ability to distinguish thoughts, feelings, and sensations when evaluating real events, which enables mindful awareness and effective behavior (Burke and Moore 2015). It creates a separation between thoughts and reality and facilitates their examination as products of consciousness: committed action, reinforcing effective behaviors that help individuals achieve value-based goals [30]. Committed action involves an individual's awareness of values that are important to him or her, concrete goals based on those values, directing and organizing behavior in ways that lead to the achievement of goals, recognizing internal obstacles that may arise and interfere with action, and overcoming those obstacles with a commitment to act in accordance with the difficulty and not fight it [30]. Mindfulness in the present means being aware of the present moment without judgment (Burke and Moore 2015). It allows one to experience the whole moment, not just its components, and shifts focus away from psychological events, changing one's perspective and behavior [30]. "I as observer" is a multidimensional self-awareness that transcends personal experience (Burke and Moore 2015). It helps individuals see themselves and others as more complex than labels and prevents them from identifying with thoughts about themselves [30]. Values, as described in the selected principles (Burke and Moore 2015), are individual choices [31] that shape personality and guide behavior by providing a sense of purpose (Burke and Moore 2015). Unlike specific and attainable goals [32], values act as a constant compass that is unique to each person and not measurable by general standards [30]. They serve as personal axioms that are influenced by society, culture, and language [31], and cannot be compared to other values or used as criteria for evaluating other values.

The model also proposes six different components that constitute psychological inflexibility. Experience avoidance is the opposite of acceptance and is defined as an attempt to distance oneself in some way from unwanted experiences. Lack of contact with the present moment is the opposite of the present moment and is defined as not paying attention to one's experiences in a particular moment. Self as content is the opposite of self as observer and involves judging experiences, resulting in a narrowed view of self. Fusion is the opposite of defusion and means being trapped in unwanted inner experiences. Inaction is the opposite of engaged action and is defined as an inability to behave in a way that is consistent with what is important in life. Lack of contact with values is the opposite of values and is defined as disconnection from the areas of life that are most meaningful to oneself. The elements that characterize psychological inflexibility can be summarized as a tendency to act according to familiar patterns based on past experiences that are consistent with how the individual perceives and defines him or herself. Leaning on the past rather than the present and on a familiar general experience rather than a unique presence and experience helps the individual to stay away from or avoid unpleasant experiences, struggles, and challenges. In this situation, the individual acts automatically and is limited, does not encounter reality in the present, is not attentive to the real and unique needs that arise, and is not attentive to his inner values. His way of working and specifically in this case, the decision-making processes he carries out are based on automation, security or avoidance. All these features are found in the decision-making processes of eligibility and characterization committees, which are analyzed according to the features of Kahneman and Tversky's heuristics. The decision processes in eligibility and characterization committees present difficult challenges and dissonances as they deal with issues of value and morality. They are confronted with the need to provide an answer to the individual while serving a systemic concept, creating policy, establishing a concept, and thinking about education as a foundation for society and the decision that has the potential for influence and change. They touched experiences, memories, feelings, attitudes and perceptions. They evoked compassion and identification, required training, knowledge, skill and professionalism, assertiveness and values, presence, precise attention, attentive care, a broad but unique perspective, courage, openness, reflective processes and awareness.

Psychological flexibility is the cornerstone of individuals being aware of their thoughts and emotions and recognizing them as different from reality. This awareness enables individuals to act in accordance with their values, even in the face of conflicting thoughts and feelings [55]. Research shows a positive correlation between psychological flexibility, empathy, and compassion and a negative correlation with bias and prejudice (ibid.). Social problems often arise from a lack of compassion, judgment, knowledge, and environmental pressures (Stroud et al. 2008). Consequently, increasing psychological flexibility can address many of these social problems [55]. Conversely, labeling, prejudice, and false beliefs can lead to problematic and avoidant decision-making and behaviors [55]. A values-based approach to attention and action can help resolve conflicts based on biased beliefs and promote greater tolerance for understanding others and their needs (ibid.).

Social processes and social policy in a society characterized by individuals with psychological flexibility will prioritize compassion as a shared value and ensure that social institutions such as government, law enforcement, business, education, the economy, and civic life function for the benefit of their members. In addition, psychological flexibility empowers individuals to distinguish between thoughts, feelings, and reality, leading to effective, value-based decision-making. It reduces behaviors driven by social pressures, social perceptions, and comparisons, thus having profound effects on individuals, society, and culture [55].

Analysis of the components of psychological flexibility and rigidity in relation to the various biases that influence eligibility and characterization committee decisions leads to the conclusion that psychological flexibility can influence decision-making processes related to the allocation of resources, supports, and services for people with diverse needs. Research findings also suggest that psychological inflexibility and principles of behavioral economics can provide insight into potential biases and heuristics that may influence these types of decisions. An analysis of open ended questionnaire of the committee chairpersons, as well as an analysis of committee members' discussions about committee decisions, shows that several factors can influence decision-making processes and their outcomes. Many studies have examined the effects of psychological flexibility on awareness processes, self-regulation, emotion regulation, connection to values, values-driven behavior, acceptance, judgment avoidance, and connection to needs in the here and now, as well as evaluation and control skills [43].

## *5.1 Conclusions*

Psychological flexibility includes self-awareness of thinking and feeling patterns as well as presence and acceptance that allow judgment avoidance. Awareness of decision-making processes and recognizing the presence and influence of different heuristics and biases have a positive effect on the accuracy of decisions.

Psychological flexibility is based on a functional approach with a behavioral orientation. It helps to act according to values and to regulate impulsiveness and emotional influences. The connection to values guides decisions based on perception and purpose rather than momentary effects. Understanding the principles of behavioral economics and how biases that can impact decisions can be regulated using the extension of psychological flexibility increases the potential for a deep understanding of the challenges in decision-making processes and for creating an infrastructure for behavioral interventions that will accurately help with decision-making processes.

### 5.2 *Contribution*

Awareness of biases and heuristics, accuracy of needs, presence and reference to the situation in the here and now combined with a functional and behavioral approach will help to better control and assess skills in decision-making processes. These processes include effective management of complex decision-making processes under conditions of uncertainty, risk management from a broad perspective, and a focused and informed reference to the unique situation. The study suggests that a combination of insights from behavioral economics along with the application of psychological flexibility components can enable committee members to make more professional, objective, present, egalitarian, attentive, compassionate, and accurate decisions. Decisions that prioritize the well-being of students and their rights. This, along with fidelity to intrinsic values, courage, authenticity and a willingness to effect good and genuine social change.

### 5.3 *Limitations*

The conclusions of this study must be examined in light of several limitations, the most important of which have to do with the study population and study design.

First, this is a qualitative study, which is not about statistical generalization, but about a unique understanding of the topic under study. Like all qualitative research, it can be based on the researcher's interpretation and proximity to the research subject.

The sample in this type of research is relatively small if you include all committee chairs, school psychologists, special education supervisor representatives, agency representatives, and parent representatives who attend committees on an ongoing basis in the relevant research population.

Open ended questionnaire were assigned to a group of eligibility and characterization committee chairs. The individuals in this position applied in advance for a position aimed at changing the education system. The requirements for this position included a belief in a comprehensive and integrated approach. In addition, the chairs of the eligibility and characterization committees have undergone many training processes guided by this concept.

The study presents many challenges from the perspective of the chairs of suitability and characterization committees and can therefore highlight a particular concept and examine the challenges in decision-making processes in the light of this concept. From the perspective of the other committee members, other challenges would have arisen in the decision-making processes also, In any qualitative analysis, there is a risk that personal interpretations and judgments will interfere with the data analysis.

## *5.4 Follow-Up Studies*

In follow-up studies, it makes sense to underpin the research results with quantitative questionnaires that can be used to statistically check for the presence of various biases. This is done alongside questionnaires to investigate psychological flexibility. This type of investigation can support the conclusions of the research.

In addition, it is important to follow the committee's decisions and the students' educational processes to verify the accuracy of the decision made by the committee with regard to the various biases that were brought up in the discussion.

In the future, after collecting statistical data based on research, it is useful to develop an applied model for committee decision making and examine both the effectiveness of its application and its results.

## References

1. Goldstein, D.G., Gigerenzer, G.: Models of ecological rationality: the recognition heuristic. Psychol. Rev. **109**(1), 75–90 (2002)
2. Fuchs, H., Amar, I.: The ability to self-advocate, the right to be heard and the independent status of the student in eligibility and characterization committees. In: Mind, Body and Soul academic conference. Mahut Center, Levinsky-Wingate Academic Center. Tel Aviv. Israel. (2023)
3. PAS-Psychological Advisory Service: Relationships, connection and educational partnership between the education staff and the students' parents. State of Israel, Ministry of Education, Pedagogical Administration, Senior Division. (2019)
4. Korobkin, R.: The problems with heuristics for law. UCLA School of Law, Research Paper No, 04–1. Los Amgeles, CA (2004)
5. Shapira, H.: Conversations on Game Theory. Kinneret, Zmora-Bitan (2008)
6. Janis, I.L., Mann, L.: Decision Making: A Psychological Analysis of Conflict, Choice, and Commitment. Free press (1977)
7. Zakai, D.: Making Good, Correct Decisions and Without Regrets. Prolog Pub (1998)
8. Abramson, E.L., Paul, C.R., Petershack, J., Serwint, J., Fischel, J.E., Rocha, M., ... Li, S.T.T.: Conducting quantitative medical education research: From design to dissemination. Acad. Pediatr. **18**(2), 129–139 (2018)
9. Kahneman, D.: The human side of decision making. J. Invest. Consult. **13**, 9–14 (2012)
10. Albrechtsen, J.S., Meissner, C.A., Susa, K.J.: Can intuition improve deception detection performance? J. Exp. Soc. Psychol. **45**(4), 1052–1055 (2009)
11. Heukelom, F.: Kahneman and Tversky and the origin of behavioral economics. Tinbergen Institute Discussion Paper and Universiteit van Amsterdam (2006)
12. Brehm, S.S., Kassin, S., Steven, F.: Social Psychology, 6th edn. N.Y: Houghton Mifflin Company (2005)

13. Ben Noon, C.: Cognitive biases and judicial decisions - intuition and orderly thinking in the work of the judge. Shaari Mishpat, 5. (2016). [Hebrew] Available at SSRN: https://ssrn.com/abstract=2732292
14. Korteling, J.E., Toet, A.: Cognitive Biases. Encyclopedia of Behavioral Neuroscience (2020)
15. Mart, R., Pardalos, P.M., Resende, M.G.: Handbook of heuristics. Springer Publishing Company, Incorporated. Springer (2018)
16. Hayes, S.C., Strosahl, K.D., Wilson, K.G.: Acceptance and Commitment Therapy: The Process and Practice of Mindful Change, 2nd edn. Guilford Press (2012)
17. Marom, S., Gilboa-Schechtman, E., Moore, N., Myers, J.: Cognitive Behavioral Therapy for Adults Therapeutic Principles. Tel Aviv: Dyunon Publication. [Hebrew] (2011)
18. Chiles, J., Strosahl, K.: Clinical Manual for Assessment and Treatment of Suicidal Behavior. American Psychiatric Publishing (2004)
19. Kahneman, D., Tversky, A.: Choices, Values, and Frames. New York: Cambridge, UK: Russell Sage Foundation. (2000)
20. McKenzie, J., Woolf, N., van Winkelen, C., Morgan, C.: Cognition in strategic decision making: A model of non-conventional thinking capacities for complex situations. Manag. Decis. **47**(2), 209–232 (2009)
21. Hammond, J., Keeney, R., Raiffa, H.: The hidden traps in decision making. Harv. Bus. Rev. **84**(1), 118–126 (2006)
22. Lerner, J.S., Li, Y., Valdesolo, P., Kassam, K.S.: Emotion and decision making. Annu. Rev. Psychol. **66**, 799–823 (2015)
23. Greenwald, A.G.: The Totalitarian Ego: The fabrication and revision of personal history. Am. Psychol. **35**, 603–618 (1980)
24. Taylor, S.E., Brown, J.D.: Illusion and well-being: a social psychological perspective on mental health. Psychol. Bull. **103**, 193–210 (1988)
25. Reshef, A.: Identifying Moral Issues in a Complex Environment. Doctorate Dissertation. Hebrew University (2008)
26. Baddeley, A., Logie, R.: Auditory imagery and working memory. In: Reisberg, D. (ed.) Auditory Imagery, pp. 179–198. Lawrence Erlbaum, Hillsdale, NJ (1992)
27. Kaniel, S.A.: Thinking Education: Cognitive Education for Controlling Consciousness. Tel Aviv University: Ramot Publishing. [Hebrew] (2006)
28. Liu, J., Ando, H.: Emotion eliciting and decision making by psychodynamic appraisal mechanism. In 2008 Conference on Human System Interactions (pp. 645–650). IEEE. (2008)
29. Fuchs, H.: Psychological flexibility and attitudes towards individuals with disabilities. Cult.-Soc.-Educ. **21**(1), 145–159. Poznan: Adam Mickiewicz University Press. ISSN: 2300–0422, ISSN (Online): 2719–2717. (2022). https://doi.org/10.14746/kse.2022.21.9
30. Yuval, I.: Acceptance and Commitment: Theory and Practice. In: Maron, S., Gilboa-Schechtman, E., Moore, N., & Myers, J. (eds.) Cognitive Behavioral Therapy for Adults. Tel Aviv: Dyunon Publication. [Hebrew] (2011)
31. Dahl, J.: ACT and Health Conditions. In: Blackledge, J.T. Ciarrochi, J., Deane, F.P. (eds.) Acceptance and Commitment Therapy: Contemporary Theory Research and Practice, pp. 119–149). Australian Academic Press (2009)
32. Luoma, J.B., Hayes, S.C., Walser, R.D.: Learning ACT: An Acceptance & Commitment Therapy Skills-Training Manual for Therapists. New Harbinger; Oakland, CA (2007)
33. Kashdan, T.B., Rottenberg, J.: Psychological flexibility as a fundamental aspect of health. Clin. Psychol. Rev. **30**, 865–878 (2010)
34. Dunning, D., Heath, C., Suls, J.M.: Flawed self-assessment: Implications for health, education, and the workplace. Psychol. Sci. Public Interes. **5**(3), 69–106 (2004)
35. Shah, A.K., Oppenheimer, D.M.: Heuristics made easy: an effort-reduction framework. Psychol. Bull. **134**(2), 207–222 (2008)
36. Kammrath, L.K., Peetz, J., Hara, K., Demarco, A., Wood, K., Kirkconnell, J., ... Allen, T.: It'sa matter of time: the effect of depletion on communal action in romantic relationships is moderated by relationship length. J. Pers. Soc. Psychol. **109**(2), 276 (2015)

37. Funder, D. C.: On the accuracy of personality judgment: a realistic approach. Psychol. Rev. **102**(4), 652 (1995)
38. Palladino, C.L., Ange, B., Richardson, D.S., Casillas, R., Decker, M., Gillies, R.A., ... Stepleman, L.: Measuring psychological flexibility in medical students and residents: a psychometric analysis. Med. Educ. Online **18**(1), 20932 (2013)
39. Masuda, A., Price, M., Anderson, P.L., Schmertz, S.K., Calamaras, M.R.: The role of psychological flexibility in mental health stigma and psychological distress for the stigmatizer. J. Soc. Clin. Psychol. **28**(10), 1244–1262 (2009)
40. Safran, J.D., Segal, Z.V.: Cognitive Therapy: An Interpersonal Process Perspective. Basic Publication, New York (1990)
41. Wegner, D.M.: Ironic processes of mental control. Psychol. Rev. **101**(1), 34 (1994)
42. Juanchich, M., Gourdon-Kanhukamwe, A., Sirota, M.: "I am uncertain" vs "It is uncertain". How linguistic markers of the uncertainty source affect uncertainty communication. Judgm. Decis. Mak. **12**(5), 445–465 (2017)
43. Gautam, A., Mathur, R.: Influence of mindfulness on decision making and psychological flexibility among aircrew. J. Psychosoc. Res. **13**(1), 199–207 (2018)
44. Stake, R.E.: Multiple Case Study Analysis. Guilford press (2013)
45. Bruno, F., Vozzo, F., Arcuri, D., Maressa, R., La Cava, E., Malvaso, A., ... Chiesi, F.: The longitudinal association between Perceived Stress, PTSD Symptoms, and Post-Traumatic Growth during the COVID-19 Pandemic: the role of coping strategies and psychological inflexibility. Curr. Psychol. 1–16 (2022)
46. Fuchs, H. (2021). Attitudes of parents and children towards people with disabilities and their integration into society. Culture-Society-Education, **20**(2), 91–109. Poznań: Adam Mickiewicz University Press.
47. Fuchs, H. (2021). Psychological flexibility and attitudes towards disability—Psycho-socio educational study of the relations between parents and children. Ph.D Dissertation. Faculty of Educational Studies of AMU. Adam Mickiewicz University, Poznan. https://hdl.handle.net/10593/26450
48. Weissbalai, E. (2022). The special education system in Israel. Jerusalem: Knesset Israel Publication. [In Herew].
49. Ruggeri, K., Alí, S., Berge, M. L., Bertoldo, G., Bjørndal, L. D., Cortijos-Bernabeu, A., ... & Folke, T. (2020). Replicating patterns of prospect theory for decision under risk. Nature human behaviour, **4**(6), 622–633.
50. Burke, K., & Moore, S. (2015). Development of the parental psychological flexibility questionnaire. Child Psychiatry & Human Development, 46, 548–557.
51. Rolffs, J.L., Rogge, R.D., & Wilson, K.G. (2018). Disentangling components of flexibility via the hexaflex model: Development and validation of the Multidimensional Psychological Flexibility Inventory (MPFI). Assessment, **25**(4), 458–482.
52. Lincoln, Y., & Guba, E.G. (1985). Naturalistic inquiry. Newbury Park, CA: Sage.
53. Ryan, G.W., & Bernard, H.R. (2000). Techniques to identify themes in qualitative data.F ield Methods, **15**(1), 85–109. https://doi.org/10.1177/1525822X02239569
54. Shkedi, A. (2003). Words of meaning—qualitative research—Theory and practice. Raanana: Ramot Publicaiton. [in Hebrew].
55. Biglan, A. (2009). The role of advocacy organizations in reducing negative externalities. Journal of Organizational Behavior Management, **29**(3–4), 215–230. https://doi.org/10.1080/01608060903092086
56. Stroud, C. B., Davila, J., & Moyer, A. (2008). The relationship between stress and depression in first onsets versus recurrences: a meta-analytic review. Journal of Abnormal Psychology, **117**(1), 206. Chicago

# The Quasi-Organic Society Living Culture Body and Its Business Applications

**Ariel Fuchs, Hila Fuchs, Eva Benkova, Daniel Galily, and Tatyana Petkova**

**Abstract** This paper delves into the idea of society as a quasi-organic entity, exploring how culture, through its verbal, material, and spatial expressions, forms a physical-phenotypic manifestation. While culture has historically been an abstract concept and material surrounding, it is a concept separate from biology, and it is deeply interwoven into human experience, both shaping and being shaped by our neuroplastic brains. Dawkins' "extended phenotype" concept hints at this connection, suggesting that culture can be perceived as the phenotype of collective human behavior, an extension of our biological nature—our quasi-organic society. From the beginning of civilization, humans have been influenced and molded by evolving cultural norms. Nevertheless, the nexus between culture and biology still needs to be discussed. Drawing parallels between organisms that modify their environment and humans who shape their surroundings driven by cultural "memes," we emphasize that culture does not merely influence biology—it resides within it. Grounded in Émile Durkheim's idea that societies operate like organisms and Dawkins' understanding of the extended phenotype, this work asserts that our material culture is the tangible expression of the cultural memes within our brains. This perspective challenges traditional notions, urging a more integrated understanding of culture and biology.

**Keywords** Quasi-organic Society · Meme · Extended Phenotype · Culture

---

A. Fuchs (✉)
Gaia College, Jerusalem, Israel
e-mail: Ariel@gaia.college

H. Fuchs
University of Ljubljana, Ljubljana, Slovenia

E. Benkova
University of Presov, Presov, Slovakia

D. Galily · T. Petkova
South-West University, "Neofit Rilski", Blagoevgrad, Bulgaria

 
S. Kot et al. (eds.), *Corporate Practices: Policies, Methodologies, and Insights in Organizational Management*, Springer Proceedings in Business and Economics,
https://doi.org/10.1007/978-981-97-0996-0_5

# 1 Introduction

## *1.1 A Nest-Living Body*

Biologically, the phenotype is the physical expression of the genotype, which contains all the genetic information of the body. The term phenotype is used to represent the physical embodiment of any gene from the set of genetic knowledge found in each genotype. Some phenotypes have higher flexibility options than others for adapting to changing environments. Dawkins proposes in his book [1, 2]. The ant nest or bee nest is the extended phenotype of the social insect.

On the one hand, the extended phenotype unites all the units of life and, with its help, creates a large, quasi-organic living body. Furthermore, on the other hand, the extended phenotype is an external trigger that gives each part of the "body" its role. The genes of one body, with the help of the extended phenotype, claims Dawkins [2], unite into one big body. All the genes of that body are equal. However, from the moment they are born, they come into contact with their physical environment, with the expanded phenotype of the nest (one whole living body), and become a cell (within the nest-body)—the phenotype required by the system. Each living unit, each ant, becomes a cell within the new body, the living spatial body of the ant nest. The environment is the trigger. The individual extended phenotype, then, is combined with other extended phenotypes of the social group to create the social extended phenotype, and it forms the basis for small living systems to connect with large living systems and thus create a larger survival machine, which is a good basis for their survival. Furthermore, above all—they are the basis for creating the quasi-organic social body.

To strengthen the metaphor between the behavior of a nest and an organic body, Dawkins (ibid.) gives several examples of symbiotic-evolutionary systems between animals that end up functioning as one real living body. For example, there is one snail that suffers from a certain parasite on the back of its shell that causes the snail to invest more energy in its shell, and thus it becomes thicker. The parasite exerts some hidden chemical effect on the snail, and this forces the snail to exceed its preferred shell thickness. It is also possible that the parasite values the life of the slug in this way, and therefore, both the genes of the slug and the genes of the parasite can benefit from it. Dawkins calls this kind of behavior an "extended phenotype" because it is as if the parasite's gene has reached out of its body and is changing things in the world outside of it. In evolution, it will cease to be a parasite, cooperate with its host regularly, and perhaps merge with its tissues until it is no longer possible to recognize it as a parasite. Another parasite infects the ambrosia tree fever beetle and reproduces through the beetle's eggs. Over the years, the bacterium and the beetle may discover the survival advantage of this cooperation and join in one body.

Similarly, inside each of our body cells, there are tiny bodies called mitochondria. The mitochondrion is a chemical factory responsible for supplying most of the energy that the cell of the human body consumes. Mitochondria are a symbiotic genetic tract attached to our cell type at an earlier stage of evolution. Furthermore, each of our genes is a symbiotic unit, and we, each of us, is a huge colony of symbiotic genes. We are nothing but remnants of ancient parasitic fusions.

We see that there are several steps here. First, there is a gene that joins another gene, and a cell is created that is the phenotype of the genes. Each cell in the body is a phenotype representing part of the genetic DNA. The extended phenotypic of each cell are all the products it produces, the result of which is outside the boundaries of its phenotypic body. These external products and these extended vacancies create an environment. The environment connects the appropriate and is the external trigger for the creation of the entire body and sometimes even for the phenotypic activation of the parts of the genome.

When a living body connects to another living body, based on the analogy of social insects, a new living body is created—a nest-living body. Each living organism that is a part of a social-nest, in this analogy, is one cell within the social-quasi-organic-nest. The environment, in this analogy, is the phenotype of the of the social-quasi-organic-nest living body.

## *1.2 Unit of Survive*

### 1.2.1 Memes Jump from Head-to-Head, According to Dawkins, Dent, and Blackmore

Richard Dawkins' conceptualization of memes in "The Selfish Gene" [1] offered a groundbreaking analogy between biological and cultural evolution. By proposing that ideas, behaviors, styles, or cultural practices propagate within a culture in a manner analogous to genes, Dawkins added a novel layer of understanding to how cultures evolve, change, and persist. A meme, by Dawkins, is a cultural unit in its cognitive form—a cultural memory unit. His main claim there is that the cultural world external to a person and the social dynamics in space, survive in the mind and are passed on by "jumping" head-to-head, in this sense material culture lives as genes. There (ibid., Chapter 10), he claims that just as man is the survival machine of his genes, he is also the survival machine of his memes.

Dawkins [2] writes, "Most of the things that distinguish man from other animals can be summed up in one single word—culture. ... Cultural transmission is similar to genetic transmission. ... The gene, the DNA molecule, is an entity that reproduces itself. ... the new (cultural) replicating unit can be called a new name—meme. As an example of memes, you can bring pleasantries, ideas, pottery methods, clothing fashion, and building arches. Just as genes spread themselves by jumping from body to body, so memes spread themselves by jumping from brain to brain—a process that can be called imitation. ... Memes must be seen as living structures, not only through the metaphor but also in the technical sense. When you plant a fertile meme in me, you introduce a parasite into my brain. ... Memes seem to be in constant mutation ... and yet there is enough fidelity in copying to make it a viable unit of natural selection. … the evolution of combinations of water that adapt to each other is like the evolution of combinations of genes that adapt to each other".

Dawkins (ibid.) suggests that Memes are the Culture Genes. Just as genes are responsible for physical traits and are passed on from one generation to the next through reproduction, memes are cultural ideas or practices that are transmitted from one mind to another through communication. Both genes and memes are information units, but while genes exist in the DNA, memes exist in the brain and are expressed behaviorally.

The well-known philosopher Dennett [3] took the theory of memes one step further and claimed that memes are the tools used for thought—these are the variables that enter the cognitive algorithms of each of us. The Psychologist Blackmore and Blackmore [4, 5] suggest that the Cultures experience an evolutionary process. They claim that just as populations evolve over time due to changes in gene frequencies, cultures evolve as memes spread, mutate, and compete. Some memes may die out, while others may combine to form more complex ideas or cultural practices.

Dawkins [2] also discussed how certain memes can be seen as parasitic, meaning they spread even if they do not confer any benefit to the individual or society. Examples include conspiracy theories or certain urban legends. Dawkins' idea was revolutionary not just because it offered a new way to think about culture but also because it suggested that our ideas, behaviors, and cultural practices are only sometimes consciously chosen or deliberately passed on. Instead, they can propagate independently, using human minds as their hosts.

Over the years, meme theory has been both celebrated and criticized. Some believe it offers valuable insights into cultural evolution, while others think the analogy between genes and memes is oversimplified. Regardless of one's stance, the meme concept has undoubtedly left a significant mark on various academic disciplines, and the term itself has become a cultural meme, especially in the internet age, where "internet memes" are a pervasive phenomenon.

### 1.2.2 The "Social Nest" as the Survival Unit According to De Waal

De Waal [6] wrote one of the first books dealing with the "intermediate unit" as the social frame as the unit of survival based on an examination of chimpanzees and roach monkeys. At the opening of his book, he presents his theory as an attempt to examine the social survival unit as the survival unit of the organism. De Waal specifies that this survival unit is found between the two survival units accepted to this day—between the micro-gene unit is the "selfish gene" theory, which began with the writings of Dawkins [1] and claims that the gene is the survival unit allowed by nature to survive. The macro unit "Gaia" began with the writings of Lovelock [7]. In this context, we can also mention Margolis [8], who claims that the entire ecology is a huge survival unit that works together to survive [9].

De Waal [6] presents in his book many examples from observations he made on chimpanzees and cockroach monkeys through which he examines the "social nest," which functions as a survival unit and by the way he deals with the origins of good and evil "in humans and other animals". In his book, he states numerous times that his observations represent an early evolutionary stage in the development of the human social unit in all its components. During his observations, he identifies the roots of morality and justice. De Waal claims that cruelty and evil, within the social framework, constitute only five percent of all chimpanzee behaviors, and all those manifestations of "gestures of threat and intimidation" originate from—interest in food, interest in partners, or protecting the weak and young.

To emphasize the protection of the weak among the chimpanzees, he cites many examples from his observations in which an alpha male (the dominant male) is seen protecting the weak. Beyond that, de Waal tells of a case in which an alpha male lost his high place in the hierarchy because, during conflicts, he repeatedly intervened for the benefit of the powerful and his allies and not the benefit of the weak and needy. This book presents an innovative worldview that claims that the chimpanzees and the other apes that De Waal describes throughout the book indeed contain within them the roots of interpersonal interaction of the human species and the roots of love.

The interpersonal interaction in the examples he gives certainly gives a feeling that the social system, especially among the chimpanzees, is the unit of survival. However, beyond that, it is a unit that varies in the intensity of its interactions based on the size of the territory or the intensity of the external danger. In the book, he gives several examples of external pressures that led to the creation of a large group of chimpanzees that increased the individual's survival ability. However, the more severe the external pressures, the more difficult and restrictive the social struggle and structure become. The alpha male is stronger in the social hierarchy, is more complex, and social obligations are more difficult to fulfill. De Waal also compares these data to the groups of chimpanzees he studied in captivity.

This is strikingly like the description of human groups in Africa characterized by a much more coercive social framework than the social frameworks we know in the Western world. The rules are much more understandable, and much less room for discretion is given. The social codes should be understandable and clear [10]. From the studies, it appears that in the primates that are in the group, the interpersonal connection increases the ability to survive. We can go from the primates to the human groups isolated in space–time to assume that social connection increases their ability to survive for them as well.

### 1.2.3 The Decline of the West According to Spengler

Spengler wrote "The Decline of the West" against the background of the end of World War I after studying the Mexican, Chinese, and Western cultures. In his book, Spengler suggests seeing culture as a living organism. Oswald Spengler's interpretation of Culture and Civilization is a central theme in his seminal work "The Decline of the West," where he presents a cyclical model of history. For Spengler, cultures are akin to living organisms—they are born, grow, mature, and ultimately decline and die. He claimed that, like a living organisms, culture has a uniform structure and a lifespan. Every culture is born, matures, withers, and dies. According to Amler, every culture has life, and every culture is destined to die, no culture in the world can be immune from its expected death. So even though the contents of each culture are different, and each culture is different, unique, and one-off, unlike other cultures in terms of symbolism, religion, values, art, poetry, relationships, and dynamics between people, the life structure of the culture is the same.

Spengler divided the cultural lifespan into four periods. Every culture has spring, summer, winter, and autumn. Each period has a cultural-verbal, cultural-material, or cultural-spatial expression that characterizes it. These are of course accompanied by a social form that is its basis. Spring—characterized by books and poetry, art, religion, and spirituality. Summer—characterized by the aristocracy, active philosophy instead of religion, and the blossoming of the arts. Fall—signs are evident.

Fatigue, institutionalization, does not have the vitality of previous periods; there is no creation, but there is an institutionalized existence for all ways of life. It has legitimacy for everything, but this is legitimacy without being realized. Winter—is the period of the sunset of the culture, in which the culture sinks spiritually, dealing with organizations and arrangements instead of strength and creativity. It becomes a mass culture, exploitative, city, proletarian, and dictatorial in its foundation—even if it does not have dictators, it relies on technology more than creativity and constantly has ambitions to spread. This is the stage where culture becomes civilization and that is the end of culture. This stage can last even 1000 years (the case of the Roman Empire lasted several centuries).

Regarding space, Spengler claimed that the perception of space affects language, the interaction between people, and psychology. The space contains the "primary symbol" of the cultural reality, and every culture has its primary symbol, on which the worldview of humans is based. In the Greek world for example, which is characterized by limited space and time, everything has a beginning and an end and the spatial structure is finite, therefore the Greek sculpture is self-contained, wholeness, and perfection. The socialist sculpture, compared to the Greek, in which the figure looks to the horizon, to the new world, represents the primary cultural symbol of the aspiration for progress. Greek architecture, for example, is very closed within itself compared to Gothic churches that radiate infinity.

In Spengler's view Culture is characterized by growth, vitality, and the flourishing of arts, philosophy, and religion. It represents the early and middle phases of a society's historical arc. Culture, in this sense, is a dynamic process; it is organic, creative, and the expression of the soul of a people. It is the time when a society is defining itself, forming its identity, and expressing its innermost values through its collective activities and creations. And Civilization is what becomes of Culture after it has passed its peak of life and begins to ossify. It is the final stage of societal development, marked by the hardening of its cultural forms into rigid structures. This stage is characterized by the predominance of critical over creative faculties, a turn toward materialism, the city's rise at the expense of the countryside, the domination of politics over religion and philosophy, and the spread of uniformity over unique cultural expressions.

Spengler uses the metaphor of seasons to describe the life cycle of cultures and civilizations: cultures blossom in their spring and summer (akin to the 'becoming' in your quote), while civilizations enter their autumn and winter (the 'thing become'). As a civilization reaches this stage, according to Spengler, it exhibits a decline in its creative capacities and an increase in skepticism, cynicism, and preoccupation with the material aspects of life.

Civilizations in this context are often seen as more technologically advanced, more heavily urban, and more complex regarding bureaucracy and infrastructure. However, they lack the spiritual and creative vigor that defines the cultural phase. Spengler was particularly concerned with Western civilization, which he believed was declining, having lost the creative impetus of its cultural youth.

While Spengler's work was highly influential in the early twentieth century, it is important to note that a particular cultural and historical context shaped his views. His theories reflect a form of historical determinism that needs to be supported in contemporary historiography. However, his perspective on the cyclical nature of societies and his distinction between Culture and Civilization still provide a provocative lens through which to view human history.

## *1.3 The Cultural Gene*

### 1.3.1 The Material Expression of the Social Order by Hillier and Hanson

A sociobiological thought like the views of Dawkins, Dennett, and Blackmore formed the basis for the idea of the "inverted genotype" as it appears in Hillier and Hanson [11, 12], Hillier and Hanson align with Dawkins' concept of memes as units of cultural information that replicate and spread through human carriers. In this framework, memes influence the formation of our built environment, influencing our social practices and cultural evolution.

It is an intriguing perspective that posits our physical surroundings as a kind of cultural genome—a repository and replicator of the social norms and values of a society. This view allows urban planners, architects, and sociologists to analyze and interpret the built environment as a direct outcome of the invisible social 'code' within a community. Such an approach may not provide a physical location for these 'social genes' or 'memes' as traditional genetics does for biological genes. However, it acknowledges that the 'instructions' or 'rules' guiding the formation of social spaces are embedded within the culture and collective behaviors of people. In a sense, the environment becomes a record of these memes, preserving and propagating the social structure through time and space.

### 1.3.2 The Cultural Gene by Sauer

Sauer [13] is considered the first thinker of historical geography. In his well-known article "Introduction to Historical Geography," he claimed that culture is a spatial "energy field" that functions as a living body with "genetic" (or "memetic" according to Dawkins) foundations. Sauer's concept crosses the biological-individual lifetime since the living existence is the culture and not the individual (man). The genetically based (memetic) spatial "cultural landscape" constitutes the physical body of the living culture. This landscape exists before man's birth, enters his consciousness, animates the landscape with his existence, and the landscape remains after his death. Thus, just as the biological genes survive by jumping from body to body, in transitions between generations, so also the "cultural genes" (as Sauer calls them) or "memes" (as Dawkins calls them) jump from head-to-head. Head in the transition from generation to generation based on cultural time–space units of the "cultural landscape".

Sauer in historical geography saw that cultures are born and die just like living beings. Throughout their lives, they are always in a process of change based on the human cultural communication units. The changes are constant but preserve cultural stability. That is until a collection of changes becomes so extreme that they lose their original cultural self. At this stage, according to Sauer, cultures die, and new cultures are born that also contain some of the previous cultures but mostly new ideas.

### 1.3.3 The Meme Machine—A Living Culture

Understanding cultural transmission and replication through the lens of biological processes is a complex endeavor that spans multiple disciplines, including biology, psychology, anthropology, and sociology. The approaches mentioned by Lewens [14] seek to bridge the gap between the biological underpinnings of humans as a species and the vast, intangible realm of culture.

The Historical Approach for cultural evolution looks at the evolution of human cognitive capacities and how these capacities have shaped our ability to create and transmit culture. By examining the historical progression of human cognition, researchers can infer how certain cultural traits may have arisen and persisted. This includes the study of hominin evolution, the development of language, and the emergence of complex social structures.

The Kinetic Theories for cultural evolution, also known as interactionist theories, focus on the dynamic interactions between individuals that result in cultural phenomena. Such theories often examine the processes of learning, imitation, and social influence that led to the diffusion of cultural traits. Kinetic theories might use models from population genetics, like diffusion equations, to describe how cultural elements spread through a group.

The Selectionist Approach for cultural evolution borrows directly from Darwinian ideas, positing that cultural traits are subject to a form of selection similar to biological traits. Ideas, beliefs, and practices that offer some advantage—survival, reproduction, or social prestige—become more widespread. Just as genes compete for survival through the success of the organisms they inhabit, cultural traits compete for psychological and social success. This selection can be at the level of individual humans, groups, or even entire societies and may involve both conscious and unconscious processes.

Each of these perspectives provides a different mechanism by which culture might be transmitted and replicated:

- The historical approach might look at long-term changes and the incremental accumulation of cultural knowledge.
- The Kinetic theories focus on the immediate processes and interactions that spread culture from person to person.
- The Selectionist approach considers the broader dynamics of competition, adaptation, and survival within the cultural landscape.

Combining these approaches can give a more complete picture of cultural evolution. For instance, selectionist ideas can help explain why certain cultural traits persist over time, while kinetic theories can illuminate the mechanisms by which these traits spread through populations.

The nature of our brain sets it apart from static repositories of knowledge like pages, papyrus, or cave paintings. Rather than a mere storage unit, the brain is a dynamic, living organ where experiences do not just reside—they interact, evolve, and are continually reshaped. These experiences, from memories to beliefs, are not just inscribed but are embedded within a network of living neurons.

Culture encompasses two primary dimensions. The verbal-conceptual pertains to intangible ideas, beliefs, and norms, and the material represents the tangible manifestations of these conceptual beliefs. Often, these two facets are intricately intertwined, making it difficult to separate one from the other. However, archaeology, with its focus on tangible remnants from the past, predominantly delves into material culture. As noted by Gould and Schiffer [15], this discipline offers a unique lens to study the material aspects of bygone cultures exclusively. A significant subset of research, as highlighted by Buchli [16, 17], is so hard to obtain and manage, being root and living in our neural memes.

### *1.4 Profound Symbiosis Between Our Biological Phenotype and Cultural Evolution*

Dawkins' notion of "the extended phenotype" refers to the tangible, external expressions derived from an organism's genotype [18]. In essence, while a phenotype depicts the direct physical manifestations of genetic information, the extended phenotype pushes this concept beyond the organism's body. It represents the external structures or behaviors resulting from an organism's genetic makeup. For instance, a beaver's dam or a spider's web exemplifies their respective extended phenotypes. In social insects, individual behaviors lead to unique extended phenotypes—the nest that becomes a quasi-organic entity. These behaviors contribute to the overarching social nest phenotype that characterizes the entire group.

From the dawn of humanity, there is evidence of our ceaseless drive to extend our physical presence, utilizing the world around us for our benefit. This notion can be traced back to Thompson's 1929 "Demographic Transition Theory" as referenced by Kirk [19] and Caldwell [20]. As we honed our survival instincts, not only did our biological fortifications strengthen—through means like fortified walls, advances in medicine, and enhanced hygiene practices—but so did our material extensions in the form of refined technology, improved materials, and more efficient fuel sources.

Harari [21] notes that in our quest for survival and comfort, humans have often reshaped and, at times, depleted the environment around them. This relentless drive to adapt and dominate can be likened to the concept of the "expanded phenotype" proposed by Dawkins [2]. As humans create innovations ranging from simple pockets to complex structures like bridges and houses or intangibles like mathematical formulas, we expand our physical and conceptual boundaries. In this continuum, where the genetic-phenotypic biological body meets the phenotypic-extended technological body, culture is the bridging force, acting as the "when" in Dawkins' paradigm.

The profound symbiosis between our biological phenotype and cultural evolution is evident in the trajectory of human longevity. With the agricultural revolution roughly 11,500 years ago, humans shifted from nomadic hunting to a sedentary lifestyle centered on cultivation and food production [22]. This monumental change, accompanied by ensuing cultural advancements, has substantially augmented our life expectancy. From a mere 26 years during the Bronze and Iron Ages to an average of 67.2 years globally in 2010, and even reaching 83 years in Japan recently [23]. Nevertheless, when considering longevity, it is not just the individual's biological form that persists. The material-cultural constructs outlive the individual, enduring for centuries. These constructs are "open and self-organizing complex systems" [24]. Modern humans are now born into pre-existing material-cultural systems, live within them, and leave them behind as legacies that continue long after their biological existence ceases.

This material struggle takes place over the minds and bodies of the human race. While many of our phenotypic body systems exhibit an intrinsic ability to adapt and respond to environmental changes, the brain stands out in its unparalleled adaptability. Often referred to as the 'wisdom of the body,' this inherent flexibility is most pronounced within the brain, which is why our primary focus gravitates towards this complex organ. This profound brain adaptability, distinct from other body systems, is the place where most of ours memes live. But the other parts of our body also contain some meme knowledge and it adapts, as much as possible, to environmental information. Alternatively, as Merleau-Ponty writes in The Phenomenology of the Body [25, 26].

## *1.5 Results*

These results provide a rich understanding of the interplay between our biology and the cultural environment, revealing the intricate ways in which culture is not only a product of human evolution but a contributing force to it. In our opinion the results call for a view of human beings as both creators and bearers of culture, continuously engaged in a dynamic process where culture and biology co-evolve. This perspective has far-reaching implications for various fields, from anthropology and psychology to urban planning and education, influencing how we conceive of human nature, social structures, and the potential trajectory of our species' future development.

The main results stemming from this comprehensive literature review, which spans concepts from evolutionary biology to phenomenology, are:

1. Neurobiological Embodiment of Culture:
    - The brain's neuroplasticity allows for the physical embodiment of cultural experiences, with every experience actively molding our neural pathways.
    - Culture, through the mechanism of memes, is encoded in the brain, influencing and reshaping our neural networks and, by extension, our behaviors and perceptions.
2. Extended Phenotype in Human Evolution:
    - Human-made environmental modifications and cultural artifacts can be viewed as extended phenotypes directly arising from our genotypic predispositions and innovations.
    - Technological and cultural advancements are not just survival tools but are integral to the evolutionary process, influencing the selection pressures acting upon us.
3. Symbiosis Between Biological and Cultural Evolution:
    - There is a profound interdependence between biological evolution and cultural changes, each driving and informing the other.
    - Cultural shifts, such as the transition to agriculture, have significantly impacted human biology, affecting our health, longevity, and social organization.
4. Material-Cultural Systems as Legacy:
    - The constructs of human culture, including technology, architecture, and social systems, outlive individual human beings, contributing to a cultural legacy that impacts successive generations.
    - These material-cultural systems are seen as "open and self-organizing complex systems," where the individual is both a contributor and recipient of cultural heritage.
5. Existential and Phenomenological Perspectives:
    - Human consciousness and self-awareness are deeply entwined with cultural contexts, challenging the notion of an isolated, individual existence separate from the environment.
    - The concept of being "thrown into nature" underscores the inherent link between individual subjectivity and the world, with cultural experiences shaping and being shaped by this interplay.

## 1.6 Discussion, or How These Results Can Be Used in the Business World

The insights derived from understanding the interplay between biology and culture have several applications in the field of business and management. Here's a discussion on how the results can inform and enhance practices within these areas:

1. Human-Centric Design and Innovation:
   - Recognizing that technological and environmental modifications are extensions of human capabilities can drive more human-centric product design and innovation.
   - Businesses can utilize this approach to create products and services that align better with innate human behaviors and cultural nuances, enhancing user experience and adoption rates.
2. Cultural Competency in Global Business:
   - The embodiment of culture within individuals underscores the importance of cultural competency and sensitivity in global business practices.
   - Managers can be trained to understand cultural memes and their impact on behavior, which can lead to more effective marketing strategies, communication, and product development tailored to diverse cultural backgrounds.
3. Leadership and Organizational Culture:
   - The understanding that culture lives within us and is passed on like memes suggests that leadership and management styles can significantly influence an organization's culture.
   - Leaders can foster a positive workplace culture that promotes adaptability, learning, and innovation by intentionally embodying and transmitting productive cultural memes.
4. Employee Training and Development:
   - The concept of neuroplasticity can be applied to employee training programs. Understanding that experiences rewire the brain can lead to more effective and adaptive learning strategies, encouraging lifelong learning and skill development.
   - By creating training programs that consider the 'living' nature of knowledge and skills within employees, organizations can better prepare their workforce for change and innovation.
5. Change Management:
   - The results highlight the adaptability and resilience of human beings in response to environmental and cultural changes.

- This knowledge can be leveraged in change management initiatives, by aligning new business strategies with innate human and cultural propensities, thereby reducing resistance and enhancing the assimilation of new practices.

6. Sustainability and Corporate Responsibility:
   - The legacy of material-cultural systems suggests businesses have a role in contributing to sustainable and enduring cultural constructs.
   - Companies can integrate sustainability into their core values and operations, ensuring that their business practices contribute positively to the cultural and environmental legacy they leave behind.
7. Longevity and Strategy Planning:
   - Understanding that cultural shifts can affect biological evolution provides businesses with a long-term perspective on the impact of their strategies.
   - Businesses can plan by considering how their actions will influence not just immediate profits but also the long-term well-being and development of their consumers and society at large.
8. Recruitment and Diversity:
   - Acknowledging the role of cultural diversity in the workplace can enhance creativity and innovation.
   - By recruiting individuals from diverse cultural backgrounds, businesses can benefit from a wide range of perspectives and ideas, leading to more robust problem-solving and innovation.

In conclusion, the dynamic relationship between our biological makeup and cultural evolution presents rich opportunities for businesses and management to develop more effective, sustainable, and adaptive practices. It underscores the need for a nuanced approach that considers the complex human dimensions of business activities, from product design to organizational leadership, and highlights the potential for businesses to play a constructive role in shaping cultural legacies.

## References


1. Dawkins, R.: The Selfish Gene. Oxford university press (2016)
2. Dawkins, R.: The Extended Phenotype: The Long Reach of the Gene. Oxford University Press (2016)
3. Dennett, D.C.: Kinds of Minds: Toward an Understanding of Consciousness. Basic Books (2008)
4. Blackmore, S., Blackmore, S.J.: The Meme Machine, vol. 25. Oxford Paperbacks (2000)
5. Ermakov, D., Ermakov, A.: Memetic approach to cultural evolution. Biosystems **204**, 104378 (2021)
6. De Waal, F.B., Waal, F.D.: Good Natured. Harvard University Press (1996)
7. Lovelock, J.: Gaia. Oxford University Press (1979).

8. Margulis, L.: The Symbiotic Planet: A New Look at Evolution. Weidenfeld and Hutchinson (1998).
9. Lovelock, J., Margulis, L.: The Gaia Hypothesis. New York (2007)
10. Goody, E.N.: Parenthood and social reproduction. In: Thelen, T., Alber, E. Politics and Kinship, pp. 236–251. Routledge (2021)
11. Hillier, B., Hanson, J.: The Social Logic of Space. Cambridge university press (1989)
12. Fuchs, A.: Home Internal Structure and the Personality Structure of Parents and Children in the City of Tel Aviv. Tel Aviv Uni, MA Thesis. (2001). [Hebrew]. NLI Library: 990022832710205171
13. Sauer, C.O.: Foreword to historical geography. Annals of the Association of American Geographers **31**(1), 1–24 (1941).
14. Lewens, T.: Cultural Evolution: Conceptual Challenges. OUP Oxford (2015)
15. Gould, R.A., Schiffer, M.B. (eds.).: Modern Material Culture: The Archeology of Us. Elsevier (2014)
16. Buchli, V. (ed.).: The Material Culture Reader. Routledge (2020)
17. Fuchs, A.: Psychological Flexibility and Attitudes towards Disability. PhD Dissertation, Faculty of Educational Studies, Adam Mickiewicz Uni, Poznan (2021)
18. De Vienne, D.: What is a phenotype? History and new developments of the concept. Genetica **150**(3–4), 153–158 (2022)
19. Kirk, D.: Demographic transition theory. Popul. Stud.. Stud. **50**(3), 361–387 (1996)
20. Caldwell, J.C.: Demographic Transition Theory. Springer Science & Business Media (2007)
21. Harari, Y.N.: Sapiens: A Brief History of Humankind. Random House (2013).
22. Bowles, S., Choi, J.K.: The neolithic agricultural revolution and the origins of private property. J. Polit. Econ. **127**(5), 2186–2228 (2019)
23. Imai, T., Miyamoto, K., Sezaki, A., Kawase, F., Shirai, Y., Abe, C., ... Shimokata, H.: Traditional Japanese diet score—association with obesity, incidence of ischemic heart disease, and healthy life expectancy in a global comparative study. J. Nutr., Health Aging **23**, 717–724 (2019)
24. Portugali, J.: Schrödinger's what is life?—complexity, cognition and the city. Entropy **25**(6), 872 (2023)
25. Ataria, Y.: Phenomenology of the body. In: Ataria, Y. (ed.) Consciousness in Flesh: An Unapologetic Phenomenological Study, pp. 1–37. Springer International Publishing, Cham (2022)
26. Merleau-Ponty, M.: Selections from Phenomenology of Perception. Sel. Read. Philos. Percept. **15** (2002)
27. Dawkins, R.: Viruses of the mind. Dennett His Crit.S: Demystifying Mind **13**, e27 (1993)

# The Importance of Psychological and Cognitive Flexibility in Educational Processes to Prepare and Acquire the Skills Required in the Twenty-First Century

**Hila Fuchs, Eva Benkova, Arie Fishbein, and Ariel Fuchs**

**Abstract** This research examines the crucial roles of cognitive and psychological flexibility in cultivating essential 21st-century skills. Cognitive flexibility is delineated as the capacity to adapt one's thinking and problem-solving approaches in the face of novel, evolving circumstances. Psychological flexibility is characterized by the ability to modify emotional and behavioral responses in alignment with overarching values and objectives despite challenges or stressors. The synthesis of current literature reveals a profound intersection between these forms of flexibility and competencies, such as critical thinking, problem-solving, creativity, and emotional intelligence, which are pivotal for thriving in a rapidly changing global landscape. The research underscores the necessity of integrating flexibility-oriented strategies into educational curricula and assessments through a comprehensive review of educational methodologies and cognitive-behavioral theories, including Acceptance and Commitment Therapy (ACT) and its impact on educational outcomes. By drawing on meta-analytical findings and theoretical discourse, the study elucidates how cognitive and psychological flexibility underpin individual adaptability and well-being but also the holistic development of students. The findings advocate for a shift towards more personalized and resilience-focused educational practices that foster these forms of flexibility, thereby equipping learners with the tools necessary to navigate and succeed in the twenty-first century's dynamic and multifaceted environments. The novelty of this study lies in its integrative approach to understanding the confluence of cognitive and psychological flexibility as foundational to mastering 21st-century skills. Unlike prior research, which often investigates cognitive and psychological flexibility in isolation, this work examines their synergistic impact on a suite of

H. Fuchs (✉) · A. Fuchs
Gaia College Research Institute, Jerusalem, Israel
e-mail: hila@gaia.college

E. Benkova
University of Presov, Presov, Slovakia

A. Fishbein
Ono Academic College, Kiriat Ono, Israel

 
S. Kot et al. (eds.), *Corporate Practices: Policies, Methodologies, and Insights in Organizational Management*, Springer Proceedings in Business and Economics,
https://doi.org/10.1007/978-981-97-0996-0_6

competencies that are essential in a rapidly evolving world. This article discusses psychological flexibility, cognitive flexibility, and neurological flexibility. It examines the role and suitability of the functions subsumed under these terms for twenty-first century needs. The article refers to educational and perceptual processes that shape the individual and society. To this end, it examines educational processes and concepts, their impact on educational and social reality, and their adaptation to the demands of twenty-first century reality. In addition, the study presents and enumerates the skills required in the twenty-first century and analyzes their different components, as well as the relationship between the required skills and qualifications and the components of psychological flexibility and cognitive flexibility. The integration between the different parts that takes place throughout the review and analysis process establishes a link between the flexibility mechanisms and their components, the demands brought by the challenges of the time, and the skills required for the individual to adapt appropriately and function effectively. Both at the level of the individual and at the systemic level, according to which the individual is an essential factor in shaping society.

**Keywords** Psychological flexibility · Cognitive flexibility · Educational processes

## 1 Introduction

This study refers to flexibility as a core component of the skills required for students and graduates of the education system in the twenty-first century. The flexibility mechanisms studied include psychological flexibility and cognitive flexibility and refer to neurological flexibility and the relationships and connections between the different types of flexibility.

The research concept was created addressing the skills needed for the twenty-first century. This is a period characterized by accelerated technological developments that lead to the need to deal with rapid changes and growing uncertainty. In addition to technological development, this period is characterized by frequent changes in values, goals, social and personal perceptions, needs, qualifications, and skills. This reality requires rapid and multidimensional adjustments. Therefore, changes in perspective, the participation of individuals in assessment processes, and tools for measurement and evaluation are required.

By its very nature, the education system is committed to and responsible for the development and growth processes of individuals through the provision of knowledge, skills, tools, values, and participation in shaping the ability of individuals to participate in and influence the quality of society.

As mentioned above, the purpose of education is to fill an essential part of the process in which the individual becomes a functioning, active and contributing person in society. The system aims to include and address all areas of the individual's development and prepare them to become an influential part of society.

In practice, there is a widening gap between the skills and tools needed to accelerate development and the skills and tools provided by the education system.

Beyond the attempts and proposals for innovative and developmental reforms and programs, the core structures that govern the system's functioning are based on the notions of survival and measurable achievement that have characterized the system since its inception. Gaps between needs and resources create challenges. These challenges impact and are absorbed by the system's work, shape the work plan, and are reflected in services and outcomes.

Challenges impact the system and are expressed in various forms and ways. At the level of human resources, there is a significant decline in applications to academic programs in education and teaching, significant attrition and resignation rates, and a weakening of the status and authority of education teams. At the level of resource management, one can cite inefficient allocation of time, irrelevant curricula, excessive preoccupation with measuring and evaluating educational performance, lack of processes and responses, and inaccuracy of criteria.

It is also possible to observe over the years an increase in behavioral, emotional, social, communication, and mental difficulties among students, a lack of specific knowledge and resources, and an increase in the violation of the students' right to active and equal participation in society as a result of a lack of tools and resources and their referral to special education.

Emphasizing and measuring achievement using fixed and uniform indicators and criteria creates a reality of comparison and violates the right to equal opportunity. In addition, working with students with diverse needs and a variety of needs, along with a lack of knowledge and skills, harms the sense of competence and motivation of educational teams. The challenging reality requires to deal with the needs of the hour, putting aside the orderly and consistent creation of differentiated and adapted teaching programs. Therefore, the system has led to a policy of cataloging, paving and exclusion. This is despite the proliferation of studies and findings that point to benefits in the acceptance of differential supports within the general population and the well-known prices that individuals and society pay for processes of segregation and perceptions that enable it. In addition, research shows that in many cases it is impossible to demonstrate a direct correlation between academic success and quality of life [1]. Therefore, it is important to study and isolate the influencing parameters to allow for different models of success.

Diagnostics is another tool in addition to achievement testing and academic skills assessment. Most diagnoses are based on the medical model. This model is based on a dichotomous distinction between health and disease states. Accordingly, it treats students with emotional, mental, or academic difficulties as sick students that require individualized treatment [2]. The education system strives to see itself as a significant and influential factor in the general perception of society, promoting humanistic and ecological approaches. In practice, however, the liberal discourse that emphasizes multiculturalism, inclusion, and diversity struggles to conceal policies based on competition and fear of mixing the other and the different [3].

The concept applied in the education system is based on age-old fears derived from the medical and neoliberal models, expressed in the fear of how students with poor academic prognosis will affect school representation [4]. This is accompanied by increasing diagnostic categories related to childhood disorders and disabilities and a push for professional intervention [5]. The study aims to discuss the potential impact of flexibility mechanisms on educational processes in light of the needs and challenges of the twenty-first century, with a focus on relevant and valuable preparation of students for the skills required in that period.

## 2 The Approaches Underlying the Research

The study was largely based on a *transformative, integrated approach.* This approach uses parallel and complementary strategies throughout the study to structure and create long-term goals and plans related to individual and social issues. It aims to influence awareness and implement actions for change and improvement [6].

### *2.1 The Ecological Holistic Approach*

Considers reality as a product of sensory reception and human experience. According to this approach, humans perceive the world through their senses. Understanding of the world is crystallized through the construction of interpretations of phenomena and events. These interpretations are adapted to the accumulated knowledge of science through language and discourse. In the ecological approach, knowledge is a subjective structure constructed through social interaction that allows for adaptation but does not overlap between concepts in reality [7]. Science does not reveal the theories and disclose the laws of nature, but the structure of the theories is based on experience. Therefore, reality is constructed from the perceptions of its participants and has no fixed representation (ibid.). The approach advocates the interdependence of the various components of the world. It emphasizes the importance of each factor [8]. An ecological approach is a democratic approach that sees the importance of each element and promotes cooperation, mutual respect, and the right to be different (ibid.). According to this approach, man is an inseparable part of the system he operates. Since he is the only living being with consciousness and reflective capacity, he is simultaneously responsible for how he views the world, how he interprets it, what his personal perceptions are, and what knowledge structures he adopts [9].

## 2.2 *Approaches and Processes as a Basis for Cognitive Flexibility and Psychological Flexibility*

**The behavioral science approach** views behavior as the primary subject of psychology and emphasizes the need to apply behavioral science to improve society and culture. It involves the application of learning principles to develop a proven method for changing overt behavior [10]. This method focuses on learning theories based on stimulus–response and classical and operant conditioning [11]. *The behavioral approach* assumes a triangular relationship between the context in which the behavior occurs, the behavior, and the outcome of the behavior. Thus, some outcomes will reinforce a particular behavior, while others will result in a reduction. Behavior therapy intervention focuses on external and internal behaviors that are perceived as challenging and aims to achieve adaptive, socially meaningful behavior [12].

**The cognitive-behavioral approach** addresses the connections between cognition and behavior, as well as the emotional state and overall functioning of the organism. This theory assumes a connection between the way the individual perceives the events in his life and his feelings, physiological reactions, and behavior. According to this approach, an individual's feelings and behavior are influenced by the interpretation he gives to the events in his life rather than by the events themselves [13, 14]. Cognitive behavioral intervention methods use strategies to change thinking, feelings, and behavior [15]. The intervention works on the individual's belief system, behavioral strategies, understanding of beliefs, and patterns of behavior that guide and shape them [16]. The goal of the intervention is to achieve and establish cognitive change in the thinking and belief system to bring about stable emotional and behavioral change [17].

**Functional contextualism** is holistic, focuses on context, and is value-based. It states that we can only understand the world through our interactions with it. The interactions we experience are always historically and contextually bounded; therefore, there is no way or purpose to test what is right and true. It is based on openness and acceptance of all events and emphasizes selected values as important components of a meaningful life [12]. Functional contextualism examines the causes and effects of ongoing interactions among organisms in various historical and contemporary contexts. Core components of approaches based on functional contextualism include a focus on the whole event, sensitivity to the role of context in understanding the nature and function of the event, emphasis on a pragmatic criterion of truth, and specific scientific goals for which the standards must be applied [12]. Functional contextualism is a philosophical product of the pragmatic approach [18, 19, 20]. All forms of contextualism define the criterion of truth as "what works successfully" [21], i.e., the truth content of an assertion is measured in terms of its practical results and utility [12].

**Human consciousness** has evolved over the course of evolution into a highly developed entity that operates almost continuously with the faculties of reasoning, imagination, memory, classification, association, explanation, analysis, comparison, judgment, and prediction. These cognitive abilities have provided humans with significant evolutionary advantages, including the ability to react and act in a variety of situations and events. Many cognitive abilities and advantages have helped humans dominate the planet. At the same time, they are the source of human suffering that because consciousness can make arbitrary connections between an unlimited number of objects and between one object and another. Any situation, event, or object can be arbitrarily linked to anything, positive or negative, regardless of its value [22]. In our rich, complex, and multidimensional world of experience, consciousness naturally produces judgments, evaluations, and one-dimensional and biased associations. These reactions remain in consciousness in their heavy form for many years, and it is not easy to change them (ibid.). Consciousness creates filters through which people perceive reality. The products of consciousness are perceived as reality, replacing unmediated experience and controlling human behavior. (ibid.). According to relational framing theory, consciousness is the basis of language, and language is central to shaping human experience in general and amplifying human suffering [22].

**Human language and cognition** depend on the relational framework, as associations and relationships are shaped by a specific reinforcement history [23]. Thinking, understanding, speaking, or listening occurs by inferring the relationship between words and events, words and words, and events and events [12].

Relational framework theory is a functional theory from the field of behavior analysis that addresses the relationship between behavior and environment [24] and uses behavioral science tools to arrive at an understanding of human cognition and language [22]. Human language and cognition depend on the framework of relationships, as associations and relationships are shaped by a specific reinforcement history [23]. The theory assumes that the behavior of cognitive structure is related to the behavior of language units [12] and that higher-order cognition and associative learning are not contradictory functions [25]. It also assumes that linguistic units, such as cognitive structures, are connected through experience.

**Relational frame theory** emerges because of cognitive language activity related to the event, rather than as a result of the formal properties of the participants [12]. Human cognition can make infinite arbitrary connections between different types of stimuli and use them in endless contexts [26]. Human cognition can convert almost any stimulus into a psychological stimulus. Therefore, the perception of stimuli or combinations that are perceived as negative or aversive through their verbal representations is significantly increased [22]. Relational operants alter natural learning processes and therefore modify or activate stimulus control. On this basis, according to relational framework theory, it is necessary to analyze cognition to understand human behavior [12]. To effect a change in a person's experience of a particular event, the contextual role of the event must be manipulated [27].

## 2.3 Flexibility Component as Part of a Functional Assessment

There are several definitions for the concept of flexibility. Flexibility is defined as the ability to respond efficiently and quickly to changing situations, external and internal influences, a transition between tasks, and situations of uncertainty in the context of routine actions [28]. It is also the ability to cope with and adapt to a wide range of possible environments, changing circumstances, changing environmental factors, or instability in the environment [29] and as the ability to cope with increasing expectations and demands without requiring additional resources or compromising performance [30]. Interpersonal flexibility is the ability of individuals to adapt to changing interpersonal situations. Many personality theories assert that flexibility is a key component of a healthy personality [31]. Several theories refer to interpersonal flexibility. They all define two basic elements. The first is a diverse range of available behaviors, and the second is the ability to adapt these behaviors to the demands of different situations [32].

According to Herr [33], interpersonal flexibility is an important component of global society in its various aspects. Herr [33] emphasizes that although it is an important skill, it does not develop spontaneously, but requires guidance and investment to cultivate.

## 2.4 The Twenty-First Century

The twenty-first century is characterized by significant and frequent change, uncertainty, and a need for skills that enable optimal adaptation and adjustment during movement.

Studies have shown that fixed skills, tools, and standards that served during the Industrial Revolution are becoming less relevant in a technological world that changes frequently [34].

Today's world requires individual critical thinking, creativity, information management, technological literacy, communication, self-direction, continuous learning, ethical awareness, cultural awareness, and flexibility [35].

Various researchers see the educational framework as a key social actor and claim that the educational system does not prepare its students for the demands of the twenty-first century. According to them, curricula need to be changed, designed, and adapted to needs, and there should be investment in skills development and teaching, rather than focusing on teaching irrelevant content and information (ibid.).

Various studies looking at the impact of flexibility mechanisms on the individual have demonstrated a positive relationship between flexibility and adaptive skills in the emotional domain, coping with challenging life situations, mental health, self-compassion, quality of life, and pro-social behavior [36].

In the twenty-first century, flexibility becomes even more important as a required skill because one often has to deal with people from different backgrounds, societies, and cultures. These require flexibility and adaptability. A frequently changing world brings with it a high degree of uncertainty. Flexibility drives one to navigate between changing situations, identify needs, act quickly, efficiently and responsibly, and bring skills to the forefront. A person with a high level of flexibility will adapt better to change and act more efficiently and accurately in different environments and situations [37, 38].

This research asserts that real change in the education system that helps to adapt to the changing demands of the world and to students with different needs requires a clear and precise executive-functional definition of the skills required for students and graduates in the education system. The creation and implementation of a clear instrument that sees flexibility as a core component develops students' reflective capacity and relies on different assessment methods. This instrument will assess skills, qualifications, and goals as the basis for differentiated, functional, and holistic work plans.

Functional definitions of learning refer to learning as a change in behavior based on experience. From these definitions, it can be inferred that learning is a function of the impact of experience on behavior.

## *2.5 Definition of Learning*

Lachmann [39] defined learning as a process based on behavior. Therefore, a change in behavior is a result of the learning process. The assumption that the core of learning is a change that occurs in the organism was abstractly described by Hall [40] as an internal change. Ormord [41] argued that this change sometimes involves specific mental processes.

According to the mechanistic approach, learning is only one process among many processes that determine behavior. Therefore, learning can occur even when there is no behavior change. From a mechanistic perspective, a change in behavior is the result of a specific factor that acted near the time when a change in behavior was observed [42]. Thus, from a mechanistic perspective, learning is defined as a change in the organism due to experience.

Another approach that can bridge the gap between the functional and mechanistic approaches assumes that experience triggers changes in the organism that lead to behavioral change over time. On this basis, the proposed approach views learning as a developmental process that manifests itself in a change in the organism's behavior as a result of frequent environmental experiences [43]. Regardless of whether one takes a functional, mechanistic approach or a bridging and unifying approach, learning processes are based on change. According to Kashdan [44], healthy coping and comprehensive learning involve various skills that respond to a dynamic and unpredictable world whose fundamental nature is change and renewal [44].

According to relational framework theory (source), relational operants that shape individual consciousness alter the way direct learning processes occur and modify or activate stimulus control. The products of consciousness are perceived as reality itself, substituting for unmediated experience and controlling human behavior, including one's will and motivation to engage in new learning and accept change [12].

A study that examined the relationship between learning processes, environmental influences, attitudes and perceptions, flexibility, and coping with challenges and change showed a relationship between rigidity and inhibitions and lack of availability to learning and between flexibility and openness to learning. The results showed a relationship between the degree of flexibility and diversity of perspectives, openness, and readiness for learning and learning. It was also found that processes that pose challenges and dilemmas that require flexibility influence learning and openness to new opinions, attitudes, ideas, and perspectives [36]. Thus, we can conclude the importance of flexibility in promoting learning.

Studies that address the connection between brain science and educational and learning processes see flexibility as a fundamental and common principle in both brain science and human development processes [45]. According to this concept, the individual is an active factor with responsibility and commitment to the learning process. Experimentation, renewal, and change are based on learning processes and therefore require flexibility.

## 2.6 *Flexibility Mechanisms*

Three expressions of flexibility are involved in developmental and learning processes. Genetic flexibility allows biological variation during different developmental periods [46].

Neurological flexibility is expressed in the design of connections between structures in the nervous system and different brain regions [47]. Another flexibility is the flexibility required for the existence and development of human experience. Flexibility is required for interactions with the environment and interactions between internal and external experiences [48]. Flexibility is based on the autonomy of individuals to act in their environment and is a distinguishing characteristic between humans and technical systems [48]. Neurological flexibility is the result of learning. It manifests in processes in the brain and is enabled by interactions between the emotional system and the external environment [49]. Neurological flexibility is a process in which functional flexibility develops cognitive abilities that help to act and interact in the world. [50]. Several researchers agree with the assertion that learning occurs as a result of changes in neural connections in the brain [36, 51, p. 102, 52, 53]. Accordingly, any learning process, whether emotional, cognitive, or motor, relies on the creation and strengthening of connections between neurons. This process takes place between pairs of cells and mainly in neuronal networks. Thousands of neurons are organized into interconnected systems capable of remembering and processing complex knowledge [54]. These processes are an expression of the neuroplasticity of the brain and nervous system. Neuroplasticity is the ability of the system to change its organism [55, 56]. Learning is manifested in the change and improvement of connections and the action of cells in the brain [; Holtmaat and Svoboda 2009]. Studies have shown that neuronal connections can change in different parts of the brain, so that synaptic plasticity leads to learning behavior and memory formation [57]. Although almost all neuronal connections have a capacity for plasticity, different factors can promote and support the learning process, while others inhibit or even prevent it [58]. These factors are related to cognitive, emotional, and environmental conditions [57]. Contributing factors: Researchers have identified a group of neurotransmitters involved in the processes of motivation and attention. Dopamine, for example, is a neurotransmitter that is released in situations of reinforcement or anticipation of reinforcement. Acetylcholine is a neurotransmitter that is released in new or unexpected situations [59]. When neurotransmitters are active, their presence promotes neuroplasticity and learning processes. Blocking neurotransmitters inhibits these processes [58]. When the neurotransmitter dopamine is active, it travels through pathways that connect the limbic system, which is responsible for processing emotions, to the frontal lobe of the brain, which is responsible for planning and control. The pathway passes through systems that receive sensory and motor information from many areas of the brain. These systems are involved in the selection and organization of goal-directed actions. Thus, there is a link between dopamine and motivation [60]. Delaying factors: the limbic system, which is responsible for processing emotions, is also related to synaptic connections and learning processes (Immordino-Yang 2015). This system includes the hippocampus and the amygdala. These structures play a role in emotional processing, survival mechanisms, and the transfer of information to memory. The amygdala emotionally characterizes stimuli after experience. The characteristics are transferred to the hippocampus and stored in memory. When a person encounters a similar or identical stimulus, the amygdala activates a response that corresponds to the emotional characterization of that stimulus. Negative characterizations trigger a sense of survival threat and cause the activation of survival mechanisms and the release of cortisol in response to stress [61]. Cortisol receptors are located in the brain in highly concentrated areas responsible for memory. High cortisol levels damage the strength of connections between synapses and therefore inhibit memory-related processes, such as encoding and retrieval [62]. Therefore, high cortisol levels negatively affect learning processes [57].

Cognitive flexibility involves acquiring and applying cognitive processes and strategies to deal with unfamiliar and unexpected situations [63]. As such, it is a characteristic of normal executive functions. It is mainly characterized by the ability to adjust attentional control and task representation, which ultimately translates into changing strategy and adapting to change. It is responsible for a person's ability to process different components of complex information simultaneously, to process multiple ideas, to think diversely, to shift perspective, to switch between tasks, to change goals according to circumstances or context, and to regulate thoughts and behaviors [64, 65]; to distinguish between what is essential and what is not [66]; to face and benefit from challenges and opportunities in a complex and changing world [67]. For cognitive flexibility to be successfully implemented, several characteristics of management functions must work together. In a changing environment, there is a need to direct attention and identify the change and required action strategies, delay earlier reactions, and redefine and manipulate the target in real-time to successfully move from one situation to another. Thus, cognitive flexibility is not only the result of different management functions, but also manifests itself in a changed response to the new target [68]. The prefrontal cortex is the central neurological structure associated with cognitive flexibility processes linked to planning and control abilities [69]. According to Wen's (Shana) diagram, cognitive flexibility consists of awareness, adaptation, and security [70]. Awareness is the individual's ability to consider different possibilities, manage them, and make decisions based on their placement in an upper category [71]. Adaptation is the individual's ability to adapt to changing environmental conditions. Self-confidence is expressed in the individual's ability to express and act in different situations, including situations of uncertainty [72]. Kaniel [73] defines self-reflection as "metacognition" or "inner eye" that enables a person to see him/herself and take responsibility. According to Kaniel [73], reflection and metacognition arise in complex situations that require a combination of cognition, emotion, and behavior. The application of reflection is relevant to the various functional areas required in education. For example, several studies point to the effects of negative automatic thoughts on emotional behavior [74]. Other studies emphasize the importance of reflection processes for improving skills and abilities in academic settings [75]. Flexibility enables the maintenance of high levels of cognitive performance. They point to the ability to integrate developmental achievements as a foundation and horizon for future achievement [17].

The individual's ability to monitor the focus of his attention and to control cognitive processes from spontaneous to controlled and back again enables the establishment of associations. The cognitive and regulatory cognitive processes enable learning and creativity [18]. Cognitive flexibility as a metacognition related to the ability to transform cognition according to new situations or challenges [19]. Beckmann [17] distinguishes cognitive flexibility from intelligence on the basis of flexibility involving the use of metacognition and acceptance of dynamic nature. Flexibility enables the maintenance of a high level of cognitive performance, which is expressed in the ability to integrate developmental achievements in the present and provide a foundation and horizon for future achievements [19].

Studies have shown that the development of cognitive flexibility skills has a positive effect on the learner's autonomy, their ability to think reflectively and their learning processes [76], Problem solving and cognitive skills [77]. A positive relationship was also found between cognitive flexibility and academic performance [78], initiative, creativity and quality of life [79].

**Psychological flexibility** is the ability to experience the present consciously and without bias and to act according to the values one has chosen to live by [22]. Psychological flexibility provides the foundation for appropriate decision-making and attentive and conscious behavior, even when decisions and actions are accompanied by severe and painful psychological events [80]. These processes lead to a wide range of physical and cognitive strategies [81] and help individuals change the role of their internal experience through flexible behavior in the face of thoughts and events [82]. According to Hayes and Wilson (2003) and Hayes et al. [83], six parallel and interrelated processes form the basis of psychological flexibility: Acceptance—the state of being ready, willing, and able to experience private events without attempting to change their frequency, content, or form [80]. Cognitive difusion—the ability to distinguish between thoughts, feelings, physiological sensations, and impulses when evaluating real events, while being fully aware of the present and choosing effective and relevant behaviors [80]. Present moment mindfulness—an active, attentive, complete, non-judgmental awareness of the present moment [80]. "I as observer"—A multidimensional awareness of oneself as more than the sum of one's personal experiences [80]. Values—Selected principles that shape personality [80], are freely chosen by the individual [81], define processes, and are associated with patterns of action that guide, organize, and give meaning to the individual's behavior (ibid.) [80]. Engaged action—reinforcing effective patterns of behavior that help individuals achieve values-based goals [84]. The scales of processes that form the foundations of psychological flexibility are dynamic and responsible for shaping the individual's patterns of interaction with his or her environment (ibid.). In general, psychological flexibility includes awareness of the present, adaptation to situations and events, having a flexible perspective and balancing conflicting needs, and behaving in a manner consistent with values [44]. The six core processes can be divided into "Acceptance" and "Cognitive Defusion," which refers to an open response style. It supports openness to direct and unmediated experiences. The pair "Awareness of the Present Moment" and "I as Context" is a focused response style. It supports a conscious and flexible connection with the present. The pair "values" and "engaged action" indicates an active response style. It supports connections with meaningful values through daily activities [85]. There is a parallel between the processes that constitute psychological flexibility and similar processes defined as self-control [86], emotional regulation [53], and self-regulation [87].

Hailikari et al. [52] found a relationship between psychological flexibility, cognitive-attributive strategies and academic emotions. They also indicate that psychological flexibility is positively associated with expectations of success, willingness to engage in new academic tasks, and positive emotions.

Psychological flexibility and cognitive flexibility are two important concepts in adjustment, mental health and function but the relationship between them has not been explored. In this review, cognitive flexibility was examined using cognitive behavioral theories and psychological flexibility was examined using acceptance and commitment therapy.

Although cognitive flexibility and psychological flexibility have developed in different waves, they represent different developments and perspectives in cognitive behavioral approaches. Therefore, there are inevitably many similarities between the two structures, in addition to significant differences in perception. Studies have shown that both structures are significantly and positively related to improved mental health, well-being, adaptability, coping, meaning, and quality of life [88].

A comprehensive meta-analysis of Van Laar and colleagues [89] based on a review of 75 academic sources published between 2000–2016. They found a broad consensus regarding 12 key competencies. The 12 competencies are critical thinking, information management, collaboration, communication, problem solving, creativity and innovation, lifelong learning, self-direction, flexibility, cultural awareness, ethical awareness, and technical and digital skills (ibid.).

To highlight the importance of the flexibility component as a core component of functional assessment processes and the skills required in the twenty-first century, it is important to point out the relationship between the required skills and the components of flexibility mechanisms discussed in this study. The basic components of neurological, psychological, and cognitive flexibility include qualities such as acceptance, listening, presence, seeing out of context, cognitive separation, values, engaging in obligatory action, diverse thinking, focused attention, broad perspective and ability to take a variety of viewpoints, awareness and reflectivity, analyzing situations, identifying and defining needs and goals, regulating and planning thoughts and behavior, thinking outside the box, and the ability to act effectively and adaptively. A close examination of the skills presented reveals that the components of flexibility, in varying composition and dosage, are fundamental to the definition of the skills defined in the work of Van Laar and colleagues [89].

## 3 Methodology—The Approaches Underlying the Research

The systematic literature review was conducted in five phases according to the PRISMA 2020 guidelines [90]. The first phase consisted of an initial search of the literature for search terms such as: "cognitive flexibility," "psychological flexibility," "twenty-first century skills," "education" and "academic achievement" in the electronic databases PubMed (n = 75), PsycINFO (n = 117) and ERIC (n = 91).

Inclusion and exclusion criteria were defined to identify full, peer-reviewed base knowledge studies in English. The studies are base knowledge and full text available and full-text accessibility that examined the relationship between cognitive flexibility, psychological flexibility, various components of twenty-first century skills, and education. We excluded non-empirical articles and duplicate papers. Based on the inclusion and exclusion criteria, 157 papers were excluded as ineligible regarding years range and language. In addition, 21 papers were excluded based on the type of paper, which included peer-reviewed only. Based on the inclusion and exclusion criteria, 16 duplicate papers were excluded using Microsoft Excel software. In the second phase, the inclusion and exclusion criteria for the main topics were not applied to 44 papers. In the fourth phase, 9 papers were carefully screened for eligibility by applying the inclusion and exclusion criteria to exclude papers that contained only opinions and were not based on knowledge. In the fifth phase, the full text of the remaining 36 papers was thoroughly reviewed for relevance to our criteria and research questions. The process described is summarized in a PRISMA flowchart (Fig. 1).

The four reviewers performed data extraction. Disagreements were resolved through discussion.

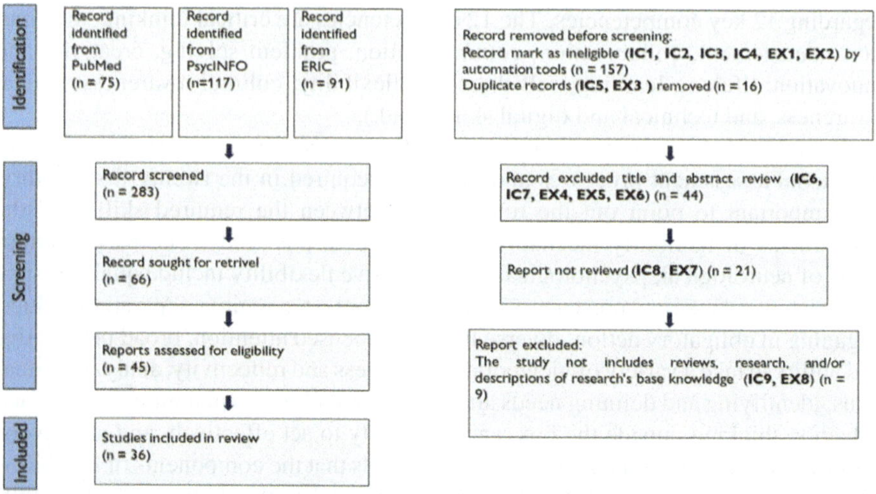


**Fig. 1** The systematic literature review according to the PRISMA 2020 guidelines

For integration and synthesis, a narrative synthesis approach was used. The studies were collected and grouped according to main categories. Then, the connection between different parameters was analyzed.

# 4 The Connection Between 21st Skills and Flexibility Mechanism

Critical thinking is the cognitive and analytical ability to examine claims, approaches, and basic assumptions underlying various processes. While deepening analysis, research, and precision provide a variety of perspectives and openness [91]. Flexibility mechanisms include acceptance, attention, cognitive separation, broad perspective, understanding of context, and analytical skills.

## *4.1 Creativity and Innovation*

Creativity and innovation are characterized by creativity, originality, and relevance to develop responses that meet the need and situation [92]. Flexibility mechanisms include acceptance, attention, cognitive separation, broad perspective, understanding the context, moving between different situations, implementing ideas and executing them, and efficiency.

## 4.2 *Entrepreneurship*

Entrepreneurship is defined as expressing creativity through development, adapting a response to a need, experimenting under uncertain conditions, learning from failure, and having the courage to try [93]. Flexibility mechanisms also include acceptance, attentiveness, cognitive separation, broad perspective, understanding context, mindfulness, recognizing needs, focusing attention, diverse thinking, and the ability to cope.

## 4.3 *Cooperation and Communication*

Cooperation and communication are defined as social and communication skills based on verbal skills, self-confidence, self-expression, broad perspective, cooperation, leadership, high understanding of social situations, recognizing others, and the big picture of the group, which translate into effective actions in the areas of knowledge, initiative, task management, and use of group resources [94] and is based on flexibility mechanisms such as a broad perspective, the ability to move between situations, acceptance, presence, openness, identification of needs, and effective and needs-based action.

## 4.4 *Self-direction, Lifelong Learning, and Flexibility*

Self-direction, lifelong learning, and flexibility represent the ability to cope and adapt under uncertain conditions, adapt to a changing environment, acquire different skills and knowledge, self-direct, be mentally flexible, and take initiative while being aware of changes in the environment and needs [95]. In addition, elements of flexibility such as adaptability, presence, listening, cognitive detachment, broad perspective, adapting to the situation, and adapting action to the need are emphasized.

## 4.5 *Ethical, Social, and Legal Awareness*

Ethical, social, and legal awareness encompasses the power and dangers of accessing technology and databases [96, 97]. Addressing the many challenges posed by reality requires an awareness and ability to independently identify ethical issues and to distinguish and regulate ethically, socially, and legally problematic behaviors. Recognize social and legal ethics. It refers to flexibility mechanisms such as awareness, values, value-based action and contextual understanding.

## 4.6 Reciprocal Connection Between Psychological and Cognitive Flexibility

Individuals with a higher degree of cognitive flexibility showed a correspondingly high degree of increased psychological flexibility. This indicates dynamic interactions between the two abilities. The positive relationship between cognitive and psychological flexibility enables deeper processes and better adaptation to changing circumstances.

## 4.7 Implications for Twenty-First Century Skills

Analysis of the various texts suggests a positive correlation between psychological flexibility and cognitive flexibility, as well as between flexibility skills and mastery of twenty-first century skills such as problem solving, communicative thinking, creativity and good communication skills.

## 4.8 Implications for Education

Psychological flexibility and cognitive flexibility are associated in the literature with innovation, initiative, cooperation and leadership. These qualities are key in the changing world and in finding and adapting to the professional demands of the twenty-first century.

## 4.9 Well-Being and Compliance

Psychological flexibility and cognitive flexibility are associated with better self-regulation skills, emotion regulation and resilience, which influence overall well-being and quality of life.

## 4.10 Prediction of Educational Effects

Psychological flexibility has been found to be a significant predictor of student engagement and persistence. Cognitive flexibility is a strong predictor of academic success.

### 4.11 Holistic Development

The study emphasizes the importance of a holistic approach to development in educational systems. It also highlights the development of flexibility mechanisms, a key component for success in the present and future in a changing world and the skills required for the twenty-first century.

### 4.12 Assessment and Training Methods

Due to the importance and centrality of flexibility mechanisms in the development of the adult and their adaptation to the twenty-first century, it is important to integrate teaching and assessment methods that emphasize and develop cognitive flexibility and psychological flexibility.

Cultural awareness refers to the discernment and understanding of the different characteristics and needs of different and diverse cultures, as well as optimal communication based on cultural, historical, geographic, and general knowledge. Combined with the ability to adapt to global trends while balancing maintaining uniqueness and adopting global characteristics [98], this requires flexibility mechanisms that are part of the possibility of diversity and adaptation.

## 5 Discussion and Summary

Cognitive and psychological flexibility are essential components of many fundamental skills necessary for success in the twenty-first century in a rapidly changing world.

Cognitive flexibility is considered a key component of critical thinking and problem-solving skills. It is expressed in the ability to adapt to changing situations and to think about problems in new and creative ways. Effectively solving complex problems and adapting to changing circumstances requires a broad, diverse perspective and flexible thinking to arrive at possible solutions. Psychological flexibility is the ability to adapt to changing emotional, cognitive, and behavioral situations. It is considered a key component of social and emotional intelligence. Effectively managing complex environmental and internal situations requires skills in self-regulation, acceptance, empathy, and openness to different perspectives and ideas. Research has shown that individuals with higher levels of cognitive and psychological flexibility are more likely to possess important twenty-first century skills, such as critical thinking, problem solving, creativity, and social and emotional intelligence [35]. Cognitive and psychological flexibility are important attributes of twenty-first century education. The research emphasize these concepts relate to education.

***Cognitive flexibility*** refers to the adaptation of thinking and problem-solving approaches to changing circumstances, information, or perspectives. In the context of education, cognitive flexibility is critical because of required skills like Adaptability, critical thinking and creativity. According to adaptability the twenty-first century is characterized by rapid change and evolving technology. Students must be able to adapt quickly to new information and skills. According to critical thinking: cognitive flexibility enables students to think critically and consider multiple points of view, which is essential for informed decision making and problem solving according to creativity: It promotes creative thinking by allowing students to explore different ideas and approaches.

***Psychological flexibility*** involves adjusting behavior and responses to be consistent with values and goals, even in difficult feelings and challenging situations. It is relevant to education for the reasons concerning to resilience, motivation and interpersonal skills. Addressing resilience: psychological flexibility helps students cope with stress, setbacks, and academic pressure. Addressing motivation: It encourages students to pursue long-term educational goals by aligning their actions with their values. Addressing Interpersonal Skills: It promotes effective communication, empathy, and collaboration, which are essential in the twenty-first century workplace.

Assessing and expanding cognitive and psychological flexibility is important for several reasons. The 21st-century skills are critical for success in the modern world. Therefore, educational assessment should not be limited to traditional measures such as exams but should also focus on these essential skills. It is necessary to emphasize Holistic development; assessing flexibility and reflectivity provides a more holistic approach to education. This recognizes that success goes beyond memorization, including adaptability, creativity, and emotional intelligence. The focus should be on individualized learning and assessment that incorporate flexibility and reflection. It can help educators identify students' strengths and weaknesses. This information can serve as the basis for personalized learning and growth. The education system should prepare the students for the future in which they may need to adapt to a rapidly changing career landscape; promoting and assessing these skills can help them better cope with uncertainty. It is important to improve instructional practices and use assessment tools that focus on flexibility and reflection. Tools that can provide educators with valuable feedback on the effectiveness of their teaching practices and curriculum design. This can lead to more adaptive and innovative teaching practices.

Cognitive flexibility, the ability to adapt to changing situations and to look at problems in new and creative ways, is considered a key component of critical thinking and problem-solving skills. To effectively solve complex problems and adapt to changing circumstances, individuals must be able to view problems from multiple perspectives and think flexibly about possible solutions.

Psychological flexibility, the ability to adapt one's thoughts, feelings, and behaviors to changing situations, is a key component of social and emotional intelligence. To navigate complex social situations and build positive relationships with others, people need to be able to regulate their emotions, show empathy, and be open to other perspectives and ideas.

This research has shown that individuals with higher levels of cognitive and psychological flexibility are more likely to possess important twenty-first century skills, such as critical thinking, problem solving, creativity, and social and emotional intelligence. For example, a study published in the Journal of Educational Psychology found that college students with higher levels of cognitive flexibility were more likely to perform well on complex problem-solving tasks. These findings suggest that cognitive and psychological flexibility are important components of many key skills needed for success in the twenty-first century. Developing these skills may be important for people who want to succeed in a rapidly changing world.

# 6 Practical Recommendation

The findings of the literature review, which examines the relationship between cognitive and psychological flexibility and twenty-first century skills, form the basis for practical recommendations for educators, curriculum designers and policy makers. The review shows that improving pedagogical practices and focusing them on developing and cultivating cognitive and psychological flexibility skills will help students adapt to the changing demands of the twenty-first century.

## *6.1 Recommendations for Educator*

Cognitive and psychological flexibility training as part of the curriculum: Learning based on problem solving, posing challenges and encouraging students to think about different ways to solve problems.

Growth from mistakes: encouraging adaptive and coping thinking that sees challenges as opportunities for learning and development. By combining challenges with quality processes of learning from mistakes.

Diversity of teaching methods: Using different teaching strategies according to different learning styles and promoting cognitive flexibility. Learning is based on discussions, simulations, role plays, joint projects and initiatives.

Development of reflection abilities and habits: Development of reflective exercises and skills that improve the level of self-awareness and the ability to accept, adapt and act in changing situations and in the face of challenges.

Promoting mindfulness: a practice that expands psychological flexibility. It helps to broaden perspective, manage stress, recognize feelings and thoughts, and be present in reality, distinguishing authentic reactions from patterned responses.

## 6.2 Recommendations for Curriculum Designers

Integrate interdisciplinary learning: Design curricula that cross traditional boundaries of subjects of study. It encourages the application of knowledge in different contexts and the development of a broad perspective.

Incorporate social-emotional learning (SEL): Integrating SEL skills into the curriculum helps to expand the skills of emotion regulation, acceptance of others, acting on values, and presence, which are components of psychological flexibility.

Incorporate real-world problem solving: Use real-world events and scenarios to teach complex problem solving. Real world events are seen as relevant in the eyes of students and they are encouraged to develop and apply different cognitive strategies and adapt their approaches to the demands of reality.

Constructive use of technology: Technology can be used to facilitate adaptive learning experiences that are tailored to educational objectives. Technology can be used to expose students to different perspectives and strategies and motivate them to develop different skills.

## 6.3 Recommendations for Policy Makers

Support for professional development: It is important to create and provide opportunities for regular, ongoing and relevant professional development for teachers. To increase their knowledge and skills in modern teaching strategies that promote cognitive and psychological flexibility.

To cultivate collaborative learning environments: To develop learning and working environments in educational institutions that foster collaboration, creativity and open communication.

Allocating resources for well-being: Beit Samar should ensure that it has the necessary resources to support students' psychological well-being as a basis for developing psychological flexibility.

Change assessment and measurement methods: Incorporate indices of cognitive and psychological flexibility into assessment practices to provide a relevant assessment of student readiness for the twenty-first century.

Invest in research: It is important to fund, promote, and develop research initiatives that help to better understand the impact of cognitive and psychological flexibility on learning processes, learning outcomes, functioning, and well-being. And to understand the effectiveness and accuracy of interventions to improve these skills.

# References

1. Razer, M., Friedman, V.J., Warshofsky, B.: Schools as agents of social exclusion and inclusion. Int. J. Incl. Educ. **17**(11), 1152–1170 (2013)

2. Jones, K.L.: Ecological model in school psychology: What are the historical trends in school psychology research? Doctor of Philosophy Thesis, University of Memphis, Electronic Theses and Dissertations, 2366. Identifier 6784 (2021)
3. Bauman, Z.: Work, Consumerism and the New Poor. McGraw-Hill Education (UK) (2004)
4. Ball, S.J.: 14 New states, new governance and new education policy. In: Apple, M.W., Ball, S.J., Gandin, L.A. (eds.) The Routledge International Handbook of the Sociology of Education. Routledge (2009)
5. Graham, L.J., Sweller, N., Van Bergen, P.: Detaining the usual suspects: charting the use of segregated settings in New South Wales government schools, Australia. Contemp. Issues Early Child. **11**(3), 234–248 (2010)
6. Mertens, D.M.: Transformative mixed methods research. Qual. Inq. **16**(6), 469–474 (2010)
7. Von Glasersfeld, E.: Knowing without metaphysics: aspects of the radical constructivist position. In: Steier, F. (ed.) Research and Reflexivity, pp. 12–29. Kitchener, Ontario: Kitchener-Waterloo. London: Sage (1989)
8. Keiny, S.: Ecological Thinking: A New Approach to Educational Reform. University Press of America, New York (2002)
9. Maturana, H.R., Varela, F.J.: The Tree of Knowledge: The Biological Roots of Human Understanding. Shambhala, Boston (1987)
10. Hayes, S., Hoffman, S.: The third wave of cognitive behavioral therapy and the rise of process-based care. World Psychiatry **16**(3), 245–246 (2017)
11. David, D., Hofmann, S.G.: Another error of descartes? implications for the "third wave" cognitive-behavioral therapy. J. Cogn. Behav. Psychother. **13**(1), 115–124 (2013)
12. Hayes, S.C.: Acceptance and commitment therapy, relational frame theory, and the third wave of behavioral and cognitive therapies. Behav. Ther. **35**(4), 639–665 (2004)
13. Beck, A.T.: Thinking and Depression: II. Theory and Therapy. Arch. Gen. Psychiatry **10**(6), 561–571 (1964)
14. Ellis, A.: Reason and Emotion in Psychotherapy. Oxford, England: Lyle Stuart (1962)
15. Kendall, P.C. (ed.): Child and Adolescent Therapy: Cognitive-Behavioral Procedures, 4th edn. New York: Guilford Press (2012)
16. Alford, B.A., Beck, A.T.: The relation of psychotherapy integration to the established systems of psychotherapy. J. Psychother. Integr. **7**, 275–289 (1997)
17. Beckmann, J.F.: The umbrella that is too wide and yet too small: Why dynamic testing has still not delivered on the promise that was never made. J. Cogn. Educ. Psychol. **13**(3), 308–323 (2014)
18. Fox, K.C., Christoff, K.: Metacognitive facilitation of spontaneous thought processes: when metacognition helps the wandering mind find its way. In: Fleming, S.M., Frith, C.D. (eds.) The Cognitive Neuroscience of Metacognition, pp. 293–319. Springer, Berlin, Heidelberg (2014)
19. Preiss, D.D.: Metacognition, mind wandering, and cognitive flexibility: understanding creativity. J. Intelligence **10**(3), 69 (2022)
20. Biglan, A., Hayes, S.C.: Should the behavioral sciences become more pragmatic? The case for functional contextualism in research on human behavior. Appl. Prev. Psychol.: Curr. Sci. Perspect. **5**, 47–57 (1996)
21. Hayes, S.C., Hayes, L.J., Reese, H.W.: Finding the Philosophical core: a review of Stephen C. Peppers World Hypotheses: a study in evidence. J. Exp. Anal. Behav. **50**(1), 97– 111 (1988)
22. Marom, S., Gilboa-Schechtman, E., Moore, N., Myers, J.: Cognitive Behavioral Therapy for Adults Therapeutic Principles. Tel Aviv: Dyunon Publication. [Hebrew] (2011)
23. Berens, N.M., Hayes, S.C.: Arbitrarily applicable comparative relations: experimental evidence for a relational operant. J. Appl. Behav. Anal. **40**(1), 45–71 (2007)
24. Hayes, S.C., Brownstein, A.J.: Mentalism, behavior-behavior relations, and a behavior-analytic view of the purposes of science. Behav. Analyst **9**, 175–190 (1986)
25. De Houwer, J., Hughes, S., Barnes-Holmes, D.: Associative learning as higher order cognition: learning in human and nonhuman animals from the perspective of propositional theories and relational frame theory. J. Comp. Psychol. **130**(3), 215 (2016)

26. Liberman, N., Trope, Y.: The psychology of transcending the here and now. Science **322**(5905), 1201–1205 (2008)
27. Chiles, J., Strosahl, K.: Clinical Manual for Assessment and Treatment of Suicidal Behavior. American Psychiatric Publishing (2004)
28. Holweg, M.: The three dimensions of responsiveness. Int. J. Oper. Prod. Manag. **25**(7), 603–622 (2005)
29. Gupta, Y.P., Somers, T.M.: The measurement of manufacturing flexibility. Eur. J. Oper. Res. **60**(2), 166–182 (1992)
30. Zhang, S.J., Chen, Y.Q., Sun, H.: Emotional intelligence, conflict management styles, and innovation performance: An empirical study of Chinese employees. Int. J. Confl. Manag. **26**(4), 450–478 (2015)
31. Scott, W.A.: Structure of natural cognitions. J. Pers. Soc. Psychol. **12**(4), 261–278 (1968)
32. Chesnokova, O., Subbotsky, E.: Social creativity in primary-school children: how to measure, develop and accept it. Procedia Soc. Behav. Sci. **146**, 141–146 (2014)
33. Herr, E.L.: Contexts and influences on the need for personal flexibility for the 21st century, part II. Can. J. Couns. Psychother. **27**(4) (1993)
34. Brugger, F., Gehrke, C.: Skilling and deskilling: technological change in classical economic theory and its empirical evidence. Theory Soc. **47**, 663–689 (2018)
35. OECD.: The Future of Education and Skills - Learning Framework 2030. OECD publications (2018)
36. Fuchs, H.: Psychological flexibility and attitudes towards individuals with disabilities. Cult.-Soc.-Educ. **21**(1), 145–159 (2022). Poznań: Adam Mickiewicz University Press https://doi.org/10.14746/kse.2022.21.9
37. Karakas, F.: New paradigms in organizational development in the 21st century: Positivity, spirituality, and complexity. Organ. Dev. J. **27**(1) (2009)
38. Koh, E., Hong, H., Seah, J.: Learner adaptivity: an initial conceptualization. Adaptivity as a Transformative Disposition: for Learning in the 21st Century, 15–30 (2014)
39. Beebe, B., Lachmann, F.M., Jaffe, J.: Mother—infant interaction structures and presymbolic self-and object representations. Psychoanal. Dialog. **7**(2), 133–182 (1997). https://doi.org/10.1080/10481889709539172
40. Hall, W.P.: Biological nature of knowledge in the learning organisation. Learn. Organ. **12**(2), 169–188 (2005)
41. Ormrod, J.E.: Educational Psychology: Developing Learners, 6th edn. Upper Saddle (2008)
42. Chiesa, M.: Radical behaviorism and scientific frameworks: from mechanistic to relational accounts. Am. Psychol. **47**(11), 1287 (1992)
43. De Houwer, J., Barnes-Holmes, D., Moors, A.: What is learning? On the nature and merits of a functional definition of learning. Psychon. Bull. Rev. **20**, 631–642 (2013)
44. Kashdan, T.B., Rottenberg, J.: Psychological flexibility as a fundamental aspect of health. Clin. Psychol. Rev. **30**(7), 865–878 (2010)
45. Goldberg, H.: Growing brains, nurturing minds—neuroscience as an educational tool to support students' development as life-long learners. Brain Sci. **12**(12), 1622 (2022)
46. Kandel, E.R.: The molecular biology of memory storage: a dialogue between genes and synapses. Science **294**(5544), 1030–1038 (2001)
47. Magistretti, P.J.: Neuron–glia metabolic coupling and plasticity. J. Exp. Biol. **209**(12), 2304–2311 (2006)
48. García-Carrasco, J., Hernández-Serrano, M.J., Martín-García, A.V.: Plasticity as a framing concept enabling transdisciplinary understanding and research in neuroscience and education. Learn. Media Technol. **40**(2), 152–167 (2015)
49. Vincent, J.D., Lledo, P.M.: The Custom-Made Brain: Cerebral Plasticity, Regeneration, and Enhancement. Columbia University Press (2014)
50. García Carrasco, J.: Leer en la cara y en el mundo. Herder (2007)
51. Herculano-Houzel, S.: Do you know your brain? A survey on public neuroscience literacy at the closing of the decade of the brain. Neuroscientist **8**(2), 98–110 (2002)

52. Hailikari, T., Nieminen, J., Asikainen, H.: The ability of psychological flexibility to predict study success and its relations to cognitive attributional strategies and academic emotions. Educ. Psychol. **42**(5), 626–643 (2022)
53. Thompson, R.A.: Emotion regulation: a theme in search of definition. Monogr. Soc. Res. Child Dev. **59**(2/3), 25–52 (1994)
54. Immordino-Yang, M.H.: Emotions, Learning, and the Brain: Exploring the Educational Implications of Affective Neuroscience (the Norton Series on the Social Neuroscience of Education). WW Norton & Company (2015)
55. Butts, D.A., Weng, C., Jin, J., Alonso, J.M., Paninski, L.: Temporal precision in the visual pathway through the interplay of excitation and stimulus-driven suppression. J. Neurosci. **31**(31), 11313–11327 (2011)
56. Holtmaat, A., Svoboda, K.: Experience-dependent structural synaptic plasticity in the mammalian brain. Nat. Rev. Neurosci. **10**(9), 647–658 (2009)
57. Owens, M.T., Tanner, K.D.: Teaching as brain changing: exploring connections between neuroscience and innovative teaching. CBE Life Sci. Educ. **16**(2), fe2 (2017)
58. Takeuchi, T., Duszkiewicz, A.J., Morris, R.G.: The synaptic plasticity and memory hypothesis: encoding, storage and persistence. Philos. Trans. R. Soc. B: Biol. Sci. **369**, 1–14 (2014)
59. Schultz, W., Dickinson, A.: Neuronal coding of prediction errors. Annu. Rev. Neurosci. **23**(1), 473–500 (2000)
60. Sapolsky, R.M.: Behave: The Bestselling Exploration of Why Humans Behave as They Do. Random House (2017)
61. LeDoux, J.E.: The Emotional Brain: The Mysterious Underpinnings of Emotional Life. Simon and Schuster (1998)
62. De Kloet, E.R., Oitzl, M.S., Joëls, M.: Stress and cognition: are corticosteroids good or bad guys? Trends Neurosci. **22**(10), 422–426 (1999)
63. Canas, J., Quesada, J., Antoli, A., Fajardo, I.: Cognitive flexibility and adaptability to environmental changes in dynamic complex problem-solving tasks. Ergonomics **46**(5), 482–501 (2003)
64. Miyake, A., Friedman, N.P., Emerson, M.J., Witzki, A.H., Howerter, A., Wager, T.D.: The unity and diversity of executive functions and their contributions to complex "frontal lobe" tasks: a latent variable analysis. Cogn. Psychol. **41**(1), 49–100 (2000)
65. Jurado, M.B., Rosselli, M.: The elusive nature of executive functions: a review of our current understanding. Neuropsychol. Rev. **17**, 213–233 (2007)
66. Monsell, S.: Task switching. Trends Cogn. Sci. **7**(3), 134–140 (2003)
67. Dağ, İ., Gülüm, İ.V.: The mediator role of cognitive features in the relationship between adult attachment patterns and psychopathology symptoms: cognitive flexibility. Turk. J. Psychiat. **24**(4) (2013)
68. Dajani, D.R., Uddin, L.Q.: Demystifying cognitive flexibility: implications for clinical and developmental neuroscience. Trends Neurosci. **38**(9), 571–578 (2015)
69. Canas, J.J., Fajardo, I., Salmeron, L.: Cognitive flexibility. Int. Encycl. Ergon. Hum. Factors **1**(3), 297–301 (2006)
70. Crocker, A.: Cognitive Flexibility (2018)
71. Anderson, A.K.: Affective influences on the attentional dynamics supporting awareness. J. Exp. Psychol. Gen. **134**(2), 258 (2005)
72. Bilgin, M.: Developing a cognitive flexibility scale: validity and reliability studies. Soc. Behav. Personal. Int. J. **37**(3), 343–353 (2009)
73. Kaniel, S.: Developing teachers' and learners' autonomy through reflection and meta-consciousness. In: Eriksson, G., Wallace, B. (eds.) Diversity in Gifted Education: International Perspectives on Global Issues, pp. 20–27. Routledge (2006)
74. Yavuzer, Y., Karataş, Z.: Associations between popularity and aggression in Turkish early adolescents. Curr. Psychol. **40**, 5420–5429 (2021)
75. Chang, B.: Reflection in learning. Online Learn. **23**(1), 95–110 (2019)
76. Orakçı, Ş: Exploring the relationships between cognitive flexibility, learner autonomy, and reflective thinking. Think. Ski. Creat. **41**, 100838 (2021)

77. İdawati, I., Setyosari, P., Kuswandi, D., Ulfa, S.: Investigating the effects of problem-solving method and cognitive flexibility on improving university students' metacognitive skills. J. Educ. Gift. Young Sci. **8**(2), 651–665 (2020)
78. Toraman, Ç., Özdemir, H.F., Aytuğ Koşan, A.M., Orakçı, Ş.: Relationships Between Cognitive Flexibility, Perceived Quality of Faculty Life, Learning Approaches, and Academic Achievement (2020)
79. Arán Filippetti, V., Krumm, G.: A hierarchical model of cognitive flexibility in children: extending the relationship between flexibility, creativity and academic achievement. Child Neuropsychol. **26**(6), 770–800 (2020)
80. Burke, K., Moore, S.: Development of the parental psychological flexibility questionnaire. Child Psychiatry Hum. Dev. **46**(4), 548–557 (2015)
81. Dahl, J.: ACT and Health Conditions. In: Blackledge, J.T., Ciarrochi, J., Deane, F.P. (eds.) Acceptance and Commitment Therapy: Contemporary Theory Research and Practice. Australian Academic Press, pp. 119–149 (2009)
82. Rolffs, J.L., Rogge, R.D., Wilson, K.G.: Disentangling components of flexibility via the hexaflex model: development and validation of the Multidimensional Psychological Flexibility Inventory (MPFI). Assessment **25**(4), 458–482 (2018)
83. Hayes, S.C., Strosahl, K., Wilson, K.G.: Acceptance and Commitment Therapy: An Experiential Approach to Behavior Change. The Guilford Press, New York (1999)
84. Vigoda-Gadot, E., Yuval, F.: The state of bureaucracy: public opinion about the performance of government agencies in Israel. Int. J. Public Opin. Res. **16**(1), 63–80 (2004)
85. Hayes, S.C., Strosahl, K.D., Wilson, K.G.: Acceptance and Commitment Therapy: The Process and Practice of Mindful Change, 2nd edn. Guilford Press (2012)
86. Finkenauer, C., Engels, R., Baumeister, R.: Parenting behaviour and adolescent behavioural and emotional problems: the role of self-control. Int. J. Behav. Dev. **29**(1), 58–69 (2005)
87. Moilanen, K.L.: The adolescent self-regulatory inventory: the development and validation of a questionnaire of short-term and long-term self-regulation. J. Youth Adolesc. **36**, 835–848 (2007)
88. Aslan, Ş, Türk, F.: Comparison of concepts of cognitive flexibility and psychological flexibility. Psikiyatride Guncel Yaklasimlar **14**(1), 119–130 (2022)
89. Van Laar, E., Van Deursen, A.J., Van Dijk, J.A., De Haan, J.: The relation between 21st-century skills and digital skills: a systematic literature review. Comput. Human Behav. **72**, 577–588 (2017)
90. Page, M.J., McKenzie, J.E., Bossuyt, P.M., Boutron, I., Hoffmann, T.C., Mulrow, C.D., ... Moher, D.: The PRISMA 2020 statement: an updated guideline for reporting systematic reviews. BMJ **372** (2021)
91. Cottrell, P.L.: Industrial Finance, 1830–1914: The Finance and Organization of English Manufacturing Industry. Routledge (2013)
92. Brynjolfsson, E., McAfee, A.: The Second Machine Age: Work, Progress, and Prosperity in a Time of Brilliant Technologies. WW Norton & Company (2014)
93. Fayolle, A., Gailly, B.: From craft to science: teaching models and learning processes in entrepreneurship education. J. Eur. Ind. Train. **32**(7), 569–593 (2008)
94. Kennedy, K., Farley, J.: Counseling gifted students: school-based considerations and strategies. Int. Electron. J. Elem.Tary Educ. **10**(3), 361–367 (2018)
95. Petkova, T., Chukov, V.: The Social Space and the Mobile Human. In: Collection of the 3rd International Conference on Studies in Humanities and Social Science (2019). https://doi.org/10.32591/coas.e-conf.03.06057c
96. Schwab, K.: The Fourth Industrial Revolution. Currency (2017)
97. Straker, L., Pollock, C., Maslen, B.: Principles for the wise use of computers by children. Ergonomics **52**(11), 1386–1401 (2009)
98. Brooks, J.S., Normore, A.H.: Educational leadership and globalization: literacy for a glocal perspective. Educ. Policy **24**(1), 52–82 (2010)

# Entrepreneurship and Innovation

# Influence of Brand Mascots on Enhancing Awareness of Vietnam's Tourism

**Trinh Le Tan, Thi Tra My Le, Hoang Quynh My Phan, Truong Son Phuong Phan, Linh Giang Nguyen, and Thuy Phuoc Tan Le**

**Abstract** Building brand awareness is an important step in enhancing the familiarity and recall of visitors to a tourist destination. Using brand mascots in marketing campaigns is one of the critical methods to build brand awareness. Using mascots helps travelers recall meaningful qualities and improves the image of popular attractions, allowing the country's tourism sector to grow considerably and deliver significant economic advantages, especially while Vietnam's tourism economy is recovering from the COVID-19 pandemic. However, the mascot image has yet to be effectively utilized in the tourism industry. The purpose of this research is to investigate the influence of brand mascots on increasing awareness of the tourism industry in Vietnam among the Gen Z generation. We used a Pilot Study to adjust the scale to suit the Vietnamese context. Also, we employed the quantitative method using the analytical tools of EFA, CFA, and SEM to measure the outcomes in this 165-student population study. According to the results of the survey, young people are very interested in and appreciate brand mascots. Mascot traits have a significant influence on tourism destinations' trustworthiness, attractiveness, attitude, and recognition. Furthermore, the data indicate that a mascot is an excellent communication strategy for increasing brand awareness. This research has partly contributed to encouraging marketers to take advantage of the power of the mascot brand to enhance the awareness of visitors to Vietnam's tourism industry in the future.

**Keywords** Brand mascot · Brand awareness · Gen Z · Tourism · Vietnam

T. Le Tan (✉) · T. T. M. Le · H. Q. M. Phan · T. S. P. Phan · L. G. Nguyen · T. P. T. Le
Business Department, FPT University, Danang, Vietnam
e-mail: Tantl2@fe.edu.vn

 
S. Kot et al. (eds.), *Corporate Practices: Policies, Methodologies, and Insights in Organizational Management*, Springer Proceedings in Business and Economics,
https://doi.org/10.1007/978-981-97-0996-0_7

## 1 Introduction

Brand mascots are characters that help to reinforce and "humanize" the brand, which marketers are interested in and use in brand marketing methods. Mascots allow businesses to quickly convey stories with distinctive messages or ethnic heritage to customers, thus helping brands boost their popularity, transform, and strengthen consumer recognition.

Utilizing data provided by World Data spanning the period from 1995 to 2020, it is evident that the COVID-19 pandemic has had a significant and adverse effect on the financial performance of Vietnam's tourism sector. Before the pandemic, revenue was at 11.83 billion U.S. dollars, representing 3.6% of GDP. However, tourism revenue is only predicted to be 3.23 billion USD by 2020, a 73% decrease from 2019. This is a significant setback for Vietnam, a country with many potential and natural advantages in this industry. As a result, restoring the tourism industry immediately is a critical and urgent task. Vietnam has already reopened, and the tourism industry is exhibiting indications of revival, with a growth rate of 50%-75% [1]. Unfortunately, the number of tourists fell 17 times compared to the same period in 2019, and it will take some time for Vietnam's tourism to recover. As a result, a plan for promoting the tourist industry's rapid development and promoting Vietnam's image to more worldwide friends is demanded.

Many studies have demonstrated the efficiency of brand mascots in promoting brand awareness, but most have primarily focused on the F&B industry. Only studies on the impact of mascots on children through the characters on product packages to improve brand recognition and increase sales have been published. Mascot characters not only enhance product consumption but also help build product usage habits, laying the groundwork for creating and extending new product lines. This is a crucial marketing component that aids in brand identification. Despite the success of F&B, there are few studies on the effect of mascots on tourists' opinions of a nation in the tourism industry. Japan pioneered the idea of mascots representing provinces to promote tourism, and it has already had some success. Most research on those mascots focuses on why those particular mascots are effective rather than on the benefits of using mascots to promote tourism or how to create a mascot with a positive impact on tourism [2]. Besides that, in this study, we also rely on the results of two research models, The Awareness Pyramid [3] and Dimensions of Brand Knowledge [4], to develop hypotheses. As a result, the analysis in this study will be on the rationale for using mascot characters to promote tourism and the creation and implementation of mascots in the Vietnamese tourism industry. Since, in Vietnam, the mascot brand is still a "mystery" that is rarely used for development, and conquering the tourism business after the COVID pandemic is still a key challenge today. This study aims to construct a proposed model related to the Brand Mascots component affecting tourists' awareness of Vietnam's tourism image.

## 2 Literature Review

The Dimensions of Brand Knowledge model [4] avers that brand awareness includes recognizing and recalling brands from customers. The brand recognition factor is explained as a brand's ability to be recognized among competitors in the same industry. Related aspects of trustworthiness, attractiveness, and attitude influence brand recognition. Most previous studies also use the Brand Knowledge model [4] to construct brand awareness in different industries. Through this model, brand awareness related to Vietnam Tourism Vietnam will develop strategies aligned with future development orientations and the brand mascot.

### *2.1 Brand Mascot Identification and Relationship of the Four Characters in Brand Mascot*

Brand mascots are cartoon characters created especially for advertising or other commercial objectives [5]. According to mascot studies, mascots provide significant advantages for recognizing and remembering the products and businesses they represent [6]. Brand character brings the brand to life by integrating human characteristics like emotion, perception, and personality. They also enable companies to establish a positive brand identity and relationship [7]. Mascots are considered to embrace the power of recognition, which is utilized to interpret and process events in our daily lives [8]. Mascots' effect on brand recognition may be explained in three ways. For starters, customers can immediately recall unique, endearing, and engaging mascots. The second is the mascots' function in making a personal connection with customers. Finally, using social media and other mass communication to increase customer happiness and sharing for advertising campaigns [9]. A mascot may give limitless options to promote brand awareness and recognition [10].

### *2.2 Hypotheses and Research Model*

#### 2.2.1 Familiar Character

Licensed characters are live or animated figures that were produced for entertainment purposes. In contrast, trade characters were created as part of an advertising effort and constantly featured in ad campaigns linked with a particular food product or brand [11]. Popular characters appear in films, comic books, television shows, and other forms of media [12]. This particular bond with characters encourages ongoing media exposure, resulting in the character becoming a well-known personality for the youngster [13]. Children see familiar characters in things such as apparel, packaged meals, school supplies, and the media. Products with representations of well-known characters sell for billions of dollars [14].

### 2.2.2 Familiarity and Trustworthiness

The endorsement of the brand mascot might have a convincing impact [15]. Consumers perceive mascots as actual persons who place their faith in the mascot's appearance and knowledge [16]. One of the positive effects of the mascots can be mentioned: to encourage children to avoid eating unhealthy fast snacks, several nutritious food businesses have included images of the familiar character on the package to persuade them to utilize this food more [17]. We have formulated the following hypothesis from the above references: Familiarity and Trustworthiness.

Hypothesis 1 Familiarity positively affects Trustworthiness

### 2.2.3 Familiarity and Attractiveness

Children, in particular, are inclined to form parasocial relationships with media characters, which reflect emotional attachments based on the characters' attractiveness and the message they express [18]. To catch children's attention, these announcements have frequently incorporated popular cartoon characters in recent years [19]. Children create "parasocial relationships" with beloved characters, which represent emotionally charged friendships based on the beauty of the characters and the messages they portray, and these relationships can influence their diet-related results [20]. According to de Droog et al., familiar characters create a favorable, rich, emotive reaction, which may lead to youngsters preferring things that include such characters [18]. Subsequently, the second hypothesis regarding the influence of familiarity and beauty was formulated.

Hypothesis 2 Familiarity Positively Affects Attractiveness

### 2.2.4 Trustworthiness

Customers' attitudes and brand-related actions, including purchases, attitudinal and behavioral loyalty, perceptions of brand value, brand commitment, and brand referrals, are all influenced by trustworthiness [21]. According to the findings of Garretson and Neirich's study, brand trustworthiness positively affected brand attitudes while also moderating other mascot attributes on brand attitude [13]. Brand characters are seen as a trait that successfully establishes an emotional connection between customers and a brand, and they have a favorable influence on consumers' sentiments about the brand [22]. The following hypothesis is to test the impact of Trustworthiness on Attitude.

Hypothesis 3 Trustworthiness Positively Affects Attitude

### 2.2.5 Attractiveness

The combination of many components of the mascot, such as design, color, and other qualities, enhances its attractiveness to young customers, improving the brand's attitude [23]. Harun and colleagues say changing product appearances leads to diverse buyer perceptions [24]. Their findings suggest youngsters are more readily convinced and drawn to items with charming or pleasant graphics and, conversely, to products with weird and unattractive packaging [24]. Attractive mascots have a more significant effect on client attitudes [25]. These characteristics give customers a familiar attitude and a desire for the mascot to become a friend in real life [25]. The following hypothesis is to test the impact of Attractiveness on Attitude.

Hypothesis 4 Attractiveness Positively Affects Attitude

### 2.2.6 Attitude

Brand attitude is essential for high brand equity outcomes such as expected performance and recognition [26]. A consumer attitude that leads to a focused brand, according to [27], is reliant not only on brand awareness but also on market preferences [27]. When the customer is given a comprehensive notion of the commercial, they may determine if it has been seen previously. People like what they are comfortable with [28]. As a result, attitudes toward celebrities can impact product perception [29]. The following hypothesis was proposed to test the impact of Attitude on Brand Recognition.

Hypothesis 5 Attitude Positively Affects Brand Recognition

### 2.2.7 Brand Recognition

Brand recognition is the rapidity with which a customer recognizes and distinguishes a brand when one of its aspects, such as a logo or a slogan, is exhibited [30]. In other words, customers must accurately differentiate the brand based on what they have already seen or heard [31]. When a consumer makes a purchasing choice, one of the goals of brand awareness is recognition because the choice may be dependent on the brands the customer was exposed to when making the decision rather than the brand name or product category [32]. Building brand recognition is an important brand strategy for promoting and increasing the brand's impact in the market, contributing to increased brand awareness [31]. Because one of the primary goals of an advertising campaign is to raise brand awareness, it is also beneficial to identify whether the target market makes purchasing decisions based on brand recall or recognition [33]. The rationale behind formulating this hypothesis is to examine the influence of Brand Recognition on Brand Awareness.

Hypothesis 6 Brand Recognition Positively Affects Brand Awareness

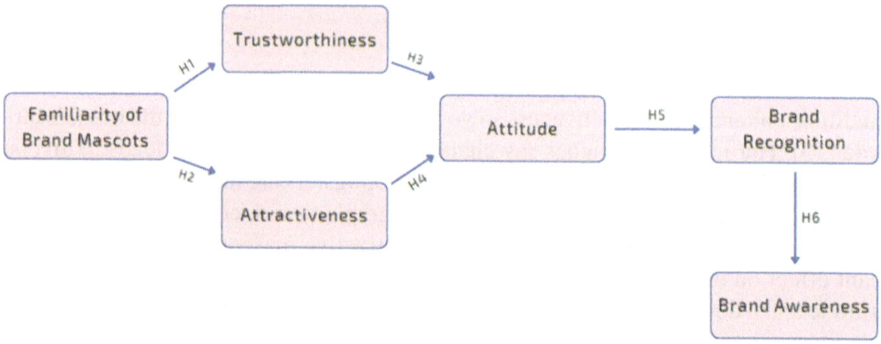


**Fig. 1** Research model

### 2.2.8 Brand Awareness

"Brand awareness" refers to the strength of a brand's presence in the consumer's consciousness [34]. Customers' capacity to recall the brand in numerous configurations is connected with the power of a brand node or brand footprint in memory [4]. As a result, marketers always begin their brand strategy by raising brand awareness using various communication channels such as advertising, personal selling, advertising, direct marketing, and so on[31]. Brand awareness is critical for tourist attractions since a location must be known to receive tourists at any given moment.

According to Chigora's 2015 research, brand knowledge can help improve tourists' appreciation for tourist destinations [35]. A well-known location receives more visitors than its competitors [35]. Brand awareness is crucial for tourist destinations because a location must be known to accept guests at any given time [36]. This means that improving the visual quality of icons and images to raise awareness enhances the survival of any destination in the global market [37]. This may be observed at a tourist site when a tourist is aware of its existence and remembers it for a long time so that when the desire for a vacation comes, the mind will transport the tourist to the exact location kept in memory [35] (Fig. 1).

## 3 Research Method

### *3.1 Sample*

The study adopted Green's formula $N \geq 50 + 8$ m, where m is the number of factors in the research model [38]. The study model has six factors; hence, the minimal sample size is 98 answers. The official research included 165 students ages from 1995 to 2010 and of varied genders. We have invited students, mostly from Da Nang, Vietnam, to participate in an online survey. After selecting them, we recorded 150 people who matched our survey criteria. Authors have used nonprobability sampling with convenience to save cost and time. To construct a proposed model in this study, authors have reviewed previous studies with theoretical models and external factors related to brand mascots. Most previous studies were cited from Scopus or ISI databases to ensure validation and quality. The measurement scale in this proposed research model was adjusted from a pilot study with ten students. The questionnaire was constructed from items and made an official survey with 165 students. Analytic Result was shown through SPSS software and AMOS 20.0.

### 3.2 *Quantitative Research*

Quantitative methods objectively measure the data collected through survey questionnaires. This results in an accurate analysis. Cronbach's Alpha reflects the degree of tight correlation between observed variables in the same component, determining which observed variables are eligible for inclusion in the scale and which are not. Before examining EFA factors in quantitative research, we will utilize Cronbach's Alpha test technique to exclude wrongly observed variables in a factor. Factor EFA (Exploratory Factor Analysis) aids in evaluating two sorts of values on the scale: concurrent and discriminant. Confirmatory Factor Analysis (CFA) is an equally significant component for examining the quality of observed variables and validating the factor structures as exploratory factor analysis (EFA). The next step of the study will use the SEM tool in the AMOS software to fill in the factors collected from the survey. The nature of SEM analysis to produce results is the same as multivariate regression in SPSS. It means determining, based on the p-value coefficients, whether the study's hypotheses are met or not.

### 3.3 *Pilot Study*

A pilot study was conducted with a sample size of 10 students from FPT Danang University. During this examination, we made necessary modifications to the scale and words to align them with the specific context of Vietnam. Subsequently, an official measurement scale table was established, denoted as Table 1.

### 3.4 *Questionnaire*

The survey was divided into three sections: (1) respondents' demographics; (2) questions on the impact of brand mascots on promoting tourist awareness in Vietnam; and (3) respondents' perspectives on the employment of brand mascots in Vietnam's tourism industry. This questionnaire, like the earlier studies, used a 5-point Likert

**Table 1** Scales for factors that influence Brand Mascots

| Variables | Items | Sources |
|---|---|---|
| Familiar of brand mascot | Friendliness<br>Uniqueness<br>Humor<br>Attractiveness | [33] |
| Trustworthiness | Product quality<br>Products used by mascots or endorsements in their life<br>Consumer can take and asses the information from the product | [39] |
| Attractiveness | Designing the plot<br>Cute goods and color<br>Put in social media<br>Emphasis of face expression | [40] |
| Attitude | Nostalgia (child-parent)<br>Attractiveness of Brand Mascot<br>Would like to live the same experience as the character does<br>Project their own feelings on the character | [41] |
| Recognition | Familiar<br>Trust<br>Recall<br>Brand's logo | [32] |
| Brand awareness | Be aware of the brand<br>Some characteristics of a brand come to the customer's mind quickly<br>Recall the symbol or logo of a brand quickly<br>Can recognize brand among other competing brands | [39] |

scale, with the level of strongly disagreeing climbing to entirely agreeing on a range of 1 to 5. The survey was written in Vietnamese to make it more relevant and easier to comprehend and respond to questions. Following that, it was translated into English, and the statistical results were presented in the next section.

# 4 Result

## *4.1 Testing Scales for Concepts with Cronbach's Alpha*

See Table 2

**Table 2** Cronbach's alpha of scales

| No. | Scale | Code | Corrected Item-Total Correlation | Cronbach's α if Item Deleted | Cronbach's α |
|---|---|---|---|---|---|
| 1 | Familiar of brand mascot | BM1 | 0.798 | 0.854 | 0.895 |
| | | BM2 | 0.747 | 0.873 | |
| | | BM3 | 0.764 | 0.867 | |
| | | BM4 | 0.767 | 0.866 | |
| 2 | Trustworthiness | TR1 | 0.811 | 0.893 | 0.915 |
| | | TR2 | 0.829 | 0.879 | |
| | | TR3 | 0.849 | 0.862 | |
| 3 | Attractiveness | AT1 | 0.668 | 0.926 | 0.909 |
| | | AT2 | 0.824 | 0.872 | |
| | | AT3 | 0.856 | 0.860 | |
| | | AT4 | 0.843 | 0.868 | |
| 4 | Attitude | AD1 | 0.881 | 0.934 | 0.950 |
| | | AD2 | 0.898 | 0.929 | |
| | | AD3 | 0.897 | 0.929 | |
| | | AD4 | 0.841 | 0.946 | |
| 5 | Recognition | RE1 | 0.852 | 0.926 | 0.941 |
| | | RE2 | 0.884 | 0.916 | |
| | | RE3 | 0.836 | 0.931 | |
| | | RE4 | 0.870 | 0.920 | |
| 6 | Brand awareness | BA1 | 0.740 | 0.857 | 0.886 |
| | | BA2 | 0.762 | 0.850 | |
| | | BA3 | 0.764 | 0.849 | |
| | | BA4 | 0.740 | 0.857 | |

Extraction: 82.964
KMO: 0.906
Sig: 0.000

N = 165 participants were chosen for the formal research's sample size utilizing the sample evaluation procedure. Following this stage, no variables were turned down.

## 4.2 Concept Testing Scales Using EFA

Using the Principal Axis Factoring with the Promax rotation extraction method, the following testing standards were used: paying attention to the bar that the maximum factor loading for each item was 0.5; paying attention to the bar that the variance between the maximum factor loading and any factor loading| must be 0.3; the total average variance extracted was 50% [20]; KMO was 0.5; and Bartlett's test was used (Table 3).

**Table 3** Results of official research using EFA

| | Factor | | | | | |
|---|---|---|---|---|---|---|
| | 1 | 2 | 3 | 4 | 5 | 6 |
| BM1 | | | 0.873 | | | |
| BM2 | | | 0.830 | | | |
| BM3 | | | 0.770 | | | |
| BM4 | | | 0.813 | | | |
| TR1 | | | | | | 0.705 |
| TR2 | | | | | | 0.838 |
| TR3 | | | | | | 0.832 |
| AT2 | | | | | 0.708 | |
| AT3 | | | | | 0.750 | |
| AT4 | | | | | 0.978 | |
| AD1 | 0.869 | | | | | |
| AD2 | 0.995 | | | | | |
| AD3 | 0.949 | | | | | |
| AD4 | 0.658 | | | | | |
| RE1 | | 0.847 | | | | |
| RE2 | | 0.915 | | | | |
| RE3 | | 0.887 | | | | |
| RE4 | | 0.917 | | | | |
| BA1 | | | | 0.750 | | |
| BA2 | | | | 0.815 | | |
| BA3 | | | | 0.871 | | |
| BA4 | | | | 0.796 | | |

## 4.3 *Scales for Idea Testing in CFA*

The scale of the research model is in line with market data, as shown by the results of the CFA analysis (Chi-square = 245,200, df = 194, CMIN/df = 1.264, CFI = 0.983, TLI = 0.828, RMSEA = 0.041). Indicators thought to be evaluated while evaluating Model Fit include the following, as stated by [43] in Multivariate Data Analysis, 7th edition:

The optimal CMIN/df is 2, while CMIN/df 5 is fine.

CFI 0.9 is excellent, 0.95 is excellent, and 0.8 is satisfactory.

A GFI of 0.9 is considered adequate, whereas a GFI of 0.95 is excellent.

In general, an RMSEA of 0.08 is considered satisfactory, whereas an RMSEA of 0.03 is exemplary.

Using the aforementioned standards, we give the following assessment of the survey's indicators: The CMIN/df and CFI indices are both excellent, coming in at

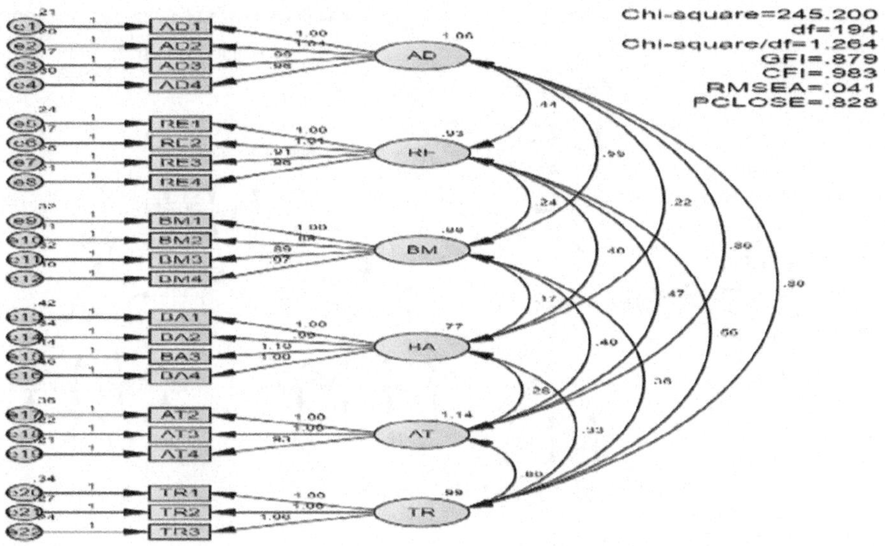


**Fig. 2** The critical measurement outcome from the CFA (standardization)

CMIN/df = 1.264 2 and CFI = 0.983 > 0.95, respectively. There is a high quality standard for the RMSEA index (RMSEA = 0.041 0.08). However, when compared to Hair et al. requirements, the GFI index fell short [43]. Our GFI in this survey was 0.879, which is below Hair's recommended threshold of 0.9. According to the findings of previous studies [42;43], our GFI index is within safe ranges (Fig. 2).

## 4.4 *Using SEM Analysis to Validate the Research Model*

Based on the findings from the structural analysis, it is observed that the model under investigation possesses a total of 203 degrees of freedom. Additionally, the Chi-square value obtained for this model is 371.891, with a statistically significant p-value of 0.000. This figure, however, suggests that the model reaches a satisfactory level with market data (CMIN/df = 1,832) after being adjusted with CMIN/df. Many other assessment metrics also look good (CFI = 0.945, TLI = 0.937, RMSEA = 0.73), so this model fits the data well (Fig. 3).

## 4.5 *Regression Weights Testing the Model Estimate*

The bootstrapping method verifies that the calculated regression coefficients in the SEM analysis model are accurate (Table 4).

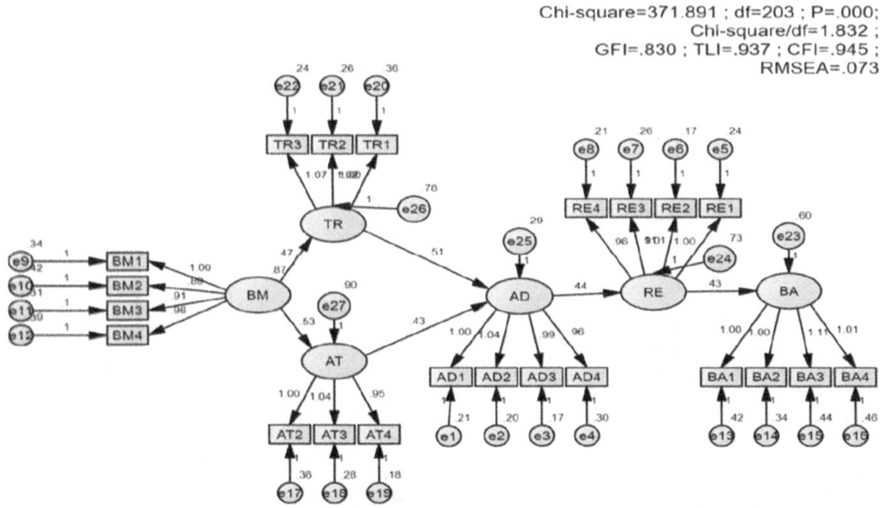


**Fig. 3** The SEM model analytical results (standardization)

**Table 4** Computed values based on Regression Variables

| Relationship | Estimate | S.E. | C.R. |
|---|---|---|---|
| TR ← BM | 0.475 | 0.093 | 5.130 |
| AT ← BM | 0.528 | 0.099 | 5.343 |
| AD ← TR | 0.506 | 0.079 | 6.370 |
| AD ← AT | 0.434 | 0.071 | 6.127 |
| RE ← AD | 0.440 | 0.074 | 5.942 |
| BA ← RE | 0.426 | 0.078 | 5.493 |

- The following are the findings from an experiment on the effect of well-known brand mascots on brand recognition in the Vietnamese tourism industry, and the significance of regulatory variables:
- H1 discusses how the company mascot's familiarity influences consumers' perception of their reliability. If we assume H1, we get an estimated value of 0.475%, a standard error of 0.935%, and a probability of less than 0.05%. The first hypothesis (H1) is correct.
- In H2, we see how the brand's mascot's familiarity influences its desirability. Assuming H2, we get an estimated value of 0.528, a standard error of estimation of 0.99, and a significance level of P = *** (infinitesimal) 0.05. The second hypothesis, H2, is true.
- Brand trustworthiness has an effect on consumer perception, as stated in Headline 3. Estimated value for H3 is 0.506, standard error (SE) is 0.079, and the significance level is P = *** (infinite) 0.05. The third null hypothesis (H3) fails.

- The influence of a brand's beauty on consumer perception is discussed in H4. Estimated value for H4 is 0.434, Standard Error of the Estimate is 0.71, and the Probability of Error is *** (infinitesimal) 0.05. The validity of H4 is confirmed.
- An individual's mentality toward a brand has a direct bearing on how well they remember that brand, as stated in H5. An assumed value of 0.44 for H5 is calculated, with a standard error of 0.74 and a significance level of P = *** (infinitesimal) 0.05. As a result, H5 is a correct hypothesis.
- The importance of familiarity with a brand is discussed in the sixth heading. Estimated value for H6 is 0.426, Standard Error of the Estimate is 0.78, and the Probability of Error is *** (infinitesimal) 0.05. The validity of H6 is confirmed.

## 5 Discussion

Vietnam's tourism sector has recently been grappling with the challenges posed by the COVID-19 pandemic, making its recovery a crucial area of focus. This study emerged in this context, attempting to fill a significant gap in the academic literature: mascots' role in enhancing the appeal and recognition of Vietnam's tourism. While mascots have long been recognized as potent tools in brand marketing across various industries, their influence on tourism, especially within the Vietnamese context, still needs to be explored. To investigate this thoroughly, our study utilized a quantitative methodology, analyzing data from a survey with a sample size of N = 165 students. Among the many available analytical methods Cronbach's alpha analysis, exploratory factor analysis, canonical correlation analysis, structural equation modeling, model estimation with bootstrapping, and multigroup analysis. These analyses were conducted with the aid of SPSS 22 and AMOS 20.

Our research framework comprised six thematic areas, all of which revolved around the fundamental principles of brand identity. Among these were mascot recognition, brand credibility, brand attractiveness, brand attitude, and brand recognition. As the results were analyzed, it became clear that brand mascots are crucial in influencing consumer brand recognition within Vietnam's tourism sector. Significant variables associated with these mascots, particularly their familiarity, correlate positively with increased brand recognition. The literature portrayed mascots as offering attractive advantages in facilitating the identification and recall of the products and enterprises they symbolize. By incorporating human attributes such as emotion, perception, and personality, mascots effectively animate the brand, presenting a wide array of possibilities for enhancing brand awareness and recognition [6, 7, 10].

One notable finding from our research was the inherent efficacy of mascots when they are seen as accessible and distinctive by the viewers, which was also supported by scholars [13, 14, 18]. De Droog et al. [18] earlier found that the presence of known characters elicits a positive and emotionally engaging response among young individuals. Consequently, this emotional connection may influence their preference for products or experiences incorporating these characters because of the trust that the brand has created [13, 21]. The unique characteristics of a brand not only generate curiosity but also contribute to the establishment of a memorable brand identity [16, 17]. Furthermore, mascots have been recognized as crucial in effectively conveying the brand's narrative in marketing initiatives, amplifying the message's impact on the intended demographic. Using brand mascots can serve as a strategic maneuver for Vietnam's tourism industry as it endeavors to revitalize itself in the aftermath of the epidemic. The study provides evidence that their impact can effectively stimulate brand recognition and trust, which is crucial in recruiting tourists from local and international markets..

### *5.1 Implication*

In theoretical contribution: This study has combined brand mascot factors with the Dimensions of Brand Knowledge model in the tourism industry. In practical contribution: Vietnam's tourism advertising efforts have yet to make extensive use of mascots in recent years. Marketers have chosen celebrity influence over brand mascots even though mascots positively affect customer brand awareness. To determine the precise effect and impact of mascots on Vietnam's tourism business, further research papers or trials will be required in the future. We conclude with two suggestions for future investigation based on the results of this one. In Vietnam, there is a need for additional research on the impact of symbols on the tourism industry at each level of the "marketing funnel" model. Since then, evidence has accrued indicating that the mascot brand plays a vital role in determining whether or not to use the services provided by Vietnam's tourist attractions. Second, given the abundance of world-famous attractions in Vietnam, we require papers that dissect every facet of those spots in great detail. A mascot representing all of Vietnam's tourist destinations is possible.

## References


1. McGale, L.S., Halford, J.C.G., Harrold, J.A., Boyland, E.J.: The influence of brand equity characters on children's food preferences and choices. J. Pediatr. **177**, 33–38 (2016)
2. Rafiq, M.R., Rai, I.H., Hussain, S.: The impact of logo shapes redesign on brand loyalty and repurchase intentions through brand attitude. Int. Rev. Manag. Mark. **10**(5), 117 (2020)
3. Aaker, D.A., Equity, M.B.: Capitalizing on the Value of a Brand Name. N. Y. **28**(1), 35–37 (1991)
4. Hoolwerff, D.: *Does your mascot match your brand's personality? An empirical study on how visual characteristics of a brand mascot can function as a tool for transmitting an archetypical brand personality* (Master's thesis, University of Twente). (2014)
5. Mohanty, S.S.: Growing importance of mascot & their impact on brand awareness–a study of young adults in Bhubaneswar City.Int. J. Comput. Eng. & Manag. **17**(6), 42–44 (2014)
6. Callcott, M.F., Lee, W.N.: A content analysis of animation and animated spokes-characters in television commercials. J. Advert. **23**(4), 1–12 (1994)

7. Soltani, A., Pieters, J., Young, J., Sun, Z.: Exploring city branding strategies and their impacts on local tourism success, the case study of Kumamoto Prefecture, Japan. Asia Pac. J. Tour. Res. **23**(2), 158–169 (2018)
8. Brown, S.: It's alive inside! A note on the prevalence of personification. Ir. Mark. Rev. **21**(1), 3 (2011)
9. Shah, S.S.H., Aziz, J., Jaffari, A.R., Waris, S., Ejaz, W., Fatima, M., Sherazi, S.K.: The impact of brands on consumer purchase intentions. Asian J. Bus. Manag. **4**(2), 105–110 (2012)
10. Caufield, K.: Analyzing the effects of brand mascots on social media: Johnson City Power Board case study. (2012)
11. Castonguay, J., Kunkel, D., Wright, P., Duff, C.: Healthy characters? An investigation of marketing practices in children's food advertising. J. Nutr. Educ. Behav. **45**(6), 571–577 (2013)
12. Callcott, M. F., Lee, W. N.: Establishing the spokes-character in academic inquiry: Historical overview and framework for definition. ACR North American Advances. (1995).
13. Hémar-Nicolas, V., Gollety, M.: Using brand character when targeting children: what for? An exploration of managers' and children's viewpoints. Young Consum. **13**(1), 20–29 (2012)
14. Danovitch, J.H., Mills, C.M.: The influence of familiar characters and other appealing images on young children's preference for low-quality objects. Br. J. Dev. Psychol. **35**(3), 476–481 (2017)
15. Bennett, D.E., Thompson, P.: Use of anthropomorphic brand mascots for student motivation and engagement: A promotional case study with Pablo the penguin at the University of Portsmouth Library. New Rev. Acad. Librariansh. **22**(2–3), 225–237 (2016)
16. Garretson, J.A., Niedrich, R.W.: Spokes-characters: Creating character trust and positive brand attitudes. J. Advert. **33**(2), 25–36 (2004)
17. Batada, A., Seitz, M.D., Wootan, M.G., Story, M.: Nine out of 10 food advertisements shown during Saturday morning children's television programming are for foods high in fat, sodium, or added sugars, or low in nutrients. J. Am. Diet. Assoc. **108**(4), 673–678 (2008)
18. Kraak, V.I., Story, M.: Influence of food companies' brand mascots and entertainment companies' cartoon media characters on children's diet and health: a systematic review and research needs. Obes. Rev. **16**(2), 107–126. (2015)
19. Salehzadeh, R., Pool, J.K.: Brand attitude and perceived value and purchase intention toward global luxury brands. J. Int. Consum. Mark. **29**(2), 74–82 (2017)
20. Bond, B.J., Calvert, S.L.: A model and measure of US parents' perceptions of young children's parasocial relationships. J. Child. Media **8**(3), 286–304 (2014)
21. Becerra, E.P., Badrinarayanan, V.: The influence of brand trust and brand identification on brand evangelism. J. Prod. & Brand. Manag. **22**(5/6), 371–383. (2013)
22. Weszka, P.: FIFA World Cup brand elements and local inspirations. Sport Mark. Q. **20**(3), 174 (2011)
23. Green, S.B.: How many subjects does it take to do a regression analysis. Multivar. Behav. Res. **26**(3), 499–510 (1991)
24. Harun, A., Samsuriv, N., Mohd Fadil, M. Z., Naseri, R. N. N., & Cheng, S. B.: Source credibility in Nestlé's breakfast cereal anthropomorphic mascots. International J. INTI. **24**(SI), 22–26. (2020)
25. Prapawong, S., Kongdee, N., Jintapitak, M.: Creation of Storytelling and Background of Institute's Educational Mascots: Case Study of College of Arts, Media and Technology, Chiang Mai University. In 2020 Joint International Conference on Digital Arts, Media and Technology with ECTI Northern Section Conference on Electrical, Electronics, Computer and Telecommunications Engineering (ECTI DAMT & NCON), pp. 282–286. IEEE. (2020)
26. Rossiter, J. R., Percy, L.: Advertising communication models. ACR North American Advances. (1985)
27. Hoffner, C.: Children's wishful identification and parasocial interaction with favorite television characters. J. Broadcast. Electron. Media **40**(3), 389–402 (1996)
28. Im, H.H., Kim, S.S., Elliot, S., Han, H.: Conceptualizing destination brand equity dimensions from a consumer-based brand equity perspective. J. Travel Tour. Mark. **29**(4), 385–403 (2012)

29. MacInnis, D.J., Shapiro, S., Mani, G.: Enhancing brand awareness through brand symbols. ACR North American Advances. (1999)
30. Khurram, M., Qadeer, F., Sheeraz, M.: The role of brand recall, brand recognition and price consciousness in understanding actual purchase. Journal of Research in Social Sciences **6**(2), 219–241 (2018)
31. Aaker, D.A.: Building strong brands. Simon and Schuster. (2012)
32. Chigora, F., Zvavahera, P.: Awareness completes brand loyalty: Reality of Zimbabwe tourism destination. Business and Management Horizons **3**(2), 60–69 (2015)
33. What can we learn from the marketing of Mickey Mouse? (n.d.). Retrieved October 7, 2023, from https://metia.com/blog/what-can-we-learn-from-the-marketing-of-mickey-mouse/ (2016)
34. Gartner, W.C., Ruzzier, M.K.: Tourism destination brand equity dimensions: Renewal versus repeat market. J. Travel Res. **50**(5), 471–481 (2011)
35. Gerbing, D.W., Anderson, J.C.: An updated paradigm for scale development incorporating unidimensionality and its assessment. J. Mark. Res. **25**(2), 186–192 (1988)
36. Kotler, J.A., Schiffman, J.M., Hanson, K.G.: The influence of media characters on children's food choices. J. Health Commun. **17**(8), 886–898 (2012)
37. Allison, A.: Portable monsters and commodity cuteness: Poke´ mon as Japan's new global power. Postcolonial Studies **6**(3), 381–395 (2003)
38. Hair, J.F., Black, W.C., Babin, B.J., Anderson, R.E.: Advanced diagnostics for multiple regression: A supplement to multivariate data analysis. Advanced Diagnostics for Multiple Regression: A Supplement to Multivariate Data Analysis. (2010)
39. Baumgartner, H., Homburg, C.: Applications of structural equation modeling in marketing and consumer research: A review. Int. J. Res. Mark. **13**(2), 139–161 (1996)
40. Doll, W. J., Xia, W., & Torkzadeh, G.: A confirmatory factor analysis of the end-user computing satisfaction instrument. MIS Q. 453–461 (1994)
41. Brownell, T. R. The influence of brand-equity mascots used by US food, beverage, and restaurant companies on the diet of American children and parents (Doctoral dissertation, Virginia Tech) (2017)

# Entrepreneurship Among Young People of Roma Origin—Attitudes and Perceptions

**Silviya Georgieva**

**Abstract** There has been a growing research interest in young people with entrepreneurial intentions and in minorities who contribute to the development of the economy and society through their business initiatives. At the same time, there needs to be more research on entrepreneurship among the Roma community. The Roma ethnic group is the most significant minority in Europe, according to data from various institutions. A lot of research looks at their culture, demographics, and socio-economic challenges, but their entrepreneurial activity should be more often studied. This is especially valid for studying the awareness and intentions for entrepreneurship among young people of Roma ethnicity who are getting an education and are looking for their realization. The novelty of the research is the in-depth study of the attitudes to entrepreneurship and the desire to develop entrepreneurial activities in the future by pupils of secondary schools and university students of Roma origin. The aim is to explore the awareness of students from secondary schools and universities of Roma origin regarding the benefits and opportunities that entrepreneurship provides for their development and the advancement of the community. The methodology includes a survey through a structured questionnaire, which covers 442 respondents. Two-dimensional distributions and statistically significant differences analyze the data found between specific characteristics. The results show that young people of Roma origin need more knowledge and encouragement to choose and develop an entrepreneurial career. Institutions and organizations should be more active in their work with the youth of this ethnic group, especially in terms of entrepreneurship.

**Keywords** Ethnic entrepreneurship · Roma · Entrepreneurship · Social inclusion · Youth entrepreneurship

S. Georgieva (✉)
UNWE, Sofia, Bulgaria
e-mail: s.georgieva@unwe.bg



S. Kot et al. (eds.), *Corporate Practices: Policies, Methodologies, and Insights in Organizational Management*, Springer Proceedings in Business and Economics,
https://doi.org/10.1007/978-981-97-0996-0_8

# 1 Introduction

Entrepreneurship among young individuals, particularly those belonging to minority groups, is of considerable importance and magnitude. Therefore, it is crucial to gain an exhaustive understanding of the perspectives of young individuals belonging to the Roma ethnic group, who constitute the biggest minority population in Europe, regarding the establishment and growth of their enterprises. Developing entrepreneurial activities by young people is the subject of several national and European policies and numerous studies. In Bulgaria, of all types of entrepreneurship, youth entrepreneurship is the focus of strategic documents and attracting the attention of researchers. Youth entrepreneurship is reflected in a number of national documents, such as The Updated National Strategy for Poverty Reduction and Promotion of Social Inclusion 2030, The National Youth Strategy 2021–2030, The National Strategy for Small and Medium-sized Enterprises 2021–2027, etc. Despite these targeted efforts to promote it among young people, their encouragement and support to start their own business, the data show that more effective actions are needed in this area. Tracking the trend for companies started by young people shows that it is not an upward trend [1]. Similar findings have also been made in other European countries [2].

In Europe, the Roma are the largest minority group [3], while of the three largest ethnic groups in Bulgaria, the Roma is the youngest [4]. At the same time, the people of this ethnic group face several economic and social problems. In many documents and policies of institutions at the highest level [3–5], main challenges such as education, healthcare, accommodation, social exclusion and segregation, employment, etc., faced by the Roma are considered. However, the entrepreneurial intentions of young people from the Roma ethnic group are rarely explored and highlighted in policies, documents, and studies. There needs to be more research to shed light on their expectations, barriers, the support required, and motivations for starting their own business. Even more noticeable is the need to understand the attitudes and aims of people of Roma origin towards entrepreneurship; due to the findings, they are not so active in creating self-employment [6]. Although entrepreneurship can contribute to solving some of the problems faced by the Roma ethnic group, it is not among the main priorities of many strategic documents and policies at different levels.

The challenge is the effective promotion and adequate support purposefully addressed to the start-up by young people from minority groups, specifically young people of Roma ethnicity. Formulating policies to stimulate their business initiatives requires specific knowledge of their understanding of entrepreneurship, needs, and fears. Insufficiently thorough research on Roma entrepreneurship creates a gap between the formulated policies and achieving the desired results regarding the socio-economic challenges of the Roma community. This gap calls for studying entrepreneurial intentions as a possible pathway contributing to more employment and reducing poverty, discrimination, and segregation.

For all these reasons, this paper aims to clarify the understanding and expectations of young people of Roma ethnicity of entrepreneurial activity. The answers of 442 pupils and students from the Roma community have been analyzed. The obtained results emphasize the role of entrepreneurship training, as well as the importance of the existing family business; the influence of place of residence and gender is clarified. The results can be a starting point for formulating effective policies to promote entrepreneurship among young people of Roma ethnicity and create a favorable ecosystem for starting their businesses.

The understanding and expectations of the opportunities that entrepreneurship provides for labor self-realization, satisfaction with expression and usefulness for oneself and other people, and the risk-taking accompanying this activity through the prism of young people of Roma origin should be considered as an intersection of youth entrepreneurship, the current situation of the Roma ethnic group and the state of Roma entrepreneurship.

## 2 Literature Review

### *2.1 Youth Entrepreneurship*

The study of youth entrepreneurship requires consideration of many aspects of the subject, such as intentions, motivation, challenges, and practical approaches to support young people who want to start their businesses. Among the first questions to be clarified, however, is which people we define as young. In Bulgarian legislation, this is resolved by the text in the additional regulations of the Youth Act, where the term "youth" refers to people from 15 to 29 years of age [7]. In a study on this type of entrepreneurship, young people are classified into the following three subgroups: from 15 to 19 years old, from 20 to 24 years old, and from 25 to 29 years old. The typology considers their differences in terms of the stage at which they are trained in the education system, as well as their opportunities to perform some form of economic activity [8]. Age as a determinant, among other factors, is found in the segmentation of women entrepreneurs. It shows that young ladies with higher education are motivated by a desire for independence and rely on sustainable competitive advantages of their business. Older women with less education are more often entrepreneurs out of necessity. These differences should be considered in the formation and implementation of support programs according to the characteristics of individual groups of entrepreneurs [9].

Tracking the development trend of youth entrepreneurship in Bulgaria shows a few particular reasons for optimism. Data, for example, for 2020 indicate that the number of unemployed self-employed youth is just over 16.7 thousand. At the same time, 38% of young people have the opinion that they need to acquire more knowledge about entrepreneurship, as well as to accumulate financial skills related to setting up their own business [1]. Similar findings have been made in several other countries in Europe. A study of entrepreneurial attitudes shows that there are fewer young people with the desire to start a business. In just five years, students aspiring to entrepreneurship as their career and professional development decreased from 70 to 36% [2].

The reasons for the hesitations of young people to choose entrepreneurship as their path of development is the result of many factors, among which is accepting that this activity is associated with risk and the probability of failure. Clarifying the impact of fear of failure and its influence on the desire to start one's own business shows that some subgroups can be distinguished among young people, as they are not a homogeneous community. More non-entrepreneurship oriented are in the age range between 15 and 24 in both countries subject to the study—Germany and Greece. At the same time, those aged between 25 and 34 in Greece already show a level of entrepreneurship comparable to other older age groups. Gender differences were also reported in the study, with the tendency of the younger people these differences to decrease [10]. The driving forces for starting their own business differ for each age group. Some of them are dominated by the desire to create employment for themselves and those close to them, while others—want to show their qualities and skills, as well as to receive recognition for their results.

Among the assumptions that explain why a small part of young people start their businesses are the lack of capacity to create innovations and the courage to start such a venture. The higher degree of social relations and the accelerated intensity of social conditions enhance the motivation of youth regarding their entrepreneurial endeavors [11]. Innovations, on the other hand, are vital to the existence and sustainable development of companies. Research results show that product innovation directly and positively affects the performance of business organizations. At the same time, other process innovations and external factors have a positive and significant but indirect influence on their performance [12].

The development of youth entrepreneurship and its support goes through the study of motives, problems, states, policies, and other aspects. Fifteen years ago, regarding this type of entrepreneurship in Bulgaria, the finding needed more research. It was specified that it was considered in the context of the employment of young people and their participation in the labor market. Knowledge could have helped form policies for its promotion and development [8]. Since then, youth entrepreneurship has been the subject not only of research but also of attention from various institutions and organizations. It should be noted that the youth activities that are supported by the municipal and state authorities are diverse, and along with the promotion of professional and personal success and opportunities for full involvement in free time, emphasis is also placed on entrepreneurship as part of the measures for the development of non-formal education along with art, culture, science, sports, volunteering, etc. [7].

In strategic documents, a typology of entrepreneurship is also made, and emphases are laid in the process of their promotion and development. Among the critical types of entrepreneurship that must be supported to contribute to the region's growth and increase the competitiveness of the Bulgarian economy is youth entrepreneurship, along with women's, high-tech, family, etc. It is considered that young people, women, the unemployed, the elderly, and migrants need training, mentoring, and counseling [13]. The purpose of support for these types of entrepreneurship is to ensure equal access to employment, overcoming poverty through generating income from one's activity, developing new ideas, and competitiveness.

Considering the needs of specific groups, especially youth, to support their active involvement in entrepreneurial activities is also related to considering stereotypes and myths that affect and shape the attitude toward starting one's own business. Among them are the following: a desire to avoid risk, as well as regarding failure; not providing a second chance to perform; lack of confidence to start entrepreneurial initiatives; lack of training in economics and instability of legislation [14]. It can be summarized that setting up a business, especially for young people, is associated with several challenges, among which are the cultural and institutional ecosystem, as well as the availability of funds to start an entrepreneurial initiative [15]. In this sense, there are different approaches to encouraging young entrepreneurs, good practices, and accumulated experience. For example, even decades ago, some countries offered one-stop-shop services. Consultancy and training services are provided, as well as 'starter unit space' and 'backup services' for future entrepreneurs [16].

Education institutions and their knowledge are a prerequisite for developing a positive attitude towards entrepreneurship and a desire to achieve financial independence through one's own business, to realize achievements, and to build up authority in society. Of great interest are studies that examine the role of the education system in building more and more successful entrepreneurs, including even ones among social groups that are relatively less likely to engage in entrepreneurial activity. The place of universities for developing entrepreneurship among groups that could be represented better in starting their own business considers their importance. It identifies six key considerations that target the university ecosystem [17].

The importance of education, along with economic, institutional, sociocultural, and other factors, is vital in shaping young people striving for success in entrepreneurship. It is, therefore, essential to explore young people's understanding and expectations for the benefits and opportunities provided by starting their own business. It is necessary to be clear about why young people start their businesses. Whether they are primarily related to financial motives and lack of employment or rather a desire to develop, prove, and express themselves, get recognition from the public, and strive to be helpful to the people around them. Particular attention should be paid to the youth of the Roma community, as they have additional challenges to deal with, apart from the ones already listed and typical for all young people regardless of their origin.

## *2.2 Roma Entrepreneurship*

The last census in Bulgaria in 2021 shows the following "picture" of the population in the country: almost 85% of the inhabitants identify themselves as belonging to the Bulgarian ethnic group, and the second largest ethnic group is the Turkish one—about 8%. Those who self-identified as belonging to the Roma ethnic group are just over 4% or 266,720. It is an essential fact that the youngest ethnic group of the three main ones in the country is the Roma. Children up to 14 from this ethnic group are almost 27% [4].

These data confirm the delineated trends from previous population censuses. The last one done ten years ago, in 2011, shows in some aspects a similar demographic situation. Then, there were 280,979 self-identified people whose mother tongue was Romany. All people voluntarily answered this question and indicated their ethnicity and mother tongue. The data confirm the tendency for the Roma ethnic group in the country to be the third largest after Bulgarian and Turkish ones [18]. From a geographical point of view, the Roma live on the territory of the entire country, with a greater concentration of this ethnic group found in the following six areas: Sliven, Montana, Shumen, Dobrich, and Yambol [4].

The Roma are the largest ethnic minority in Europe. Data show that 10–12 million Roma inhabit our continent. About half of them live in EU member states. Despite the adopted policies, strategies, and measures, a large part of the Roma ethnic group faces misunderstanding, prejudice, and exclusion from the community [19]. Part of these challenges can be successfully overcome by popularizing, supporting, and developing entrepreneurial activities among people of the Roma ethnicity.

The problems listed above that the people of the Roma ethnic group face are visible in Bulgaria as well. Among them, poverty, social exclusion, and lack of education are often mentioned and the focus of policies. The data show that in Bulgaria, out of the three main ethnic groups, the Roma have the worst indicators in terms of higher and secondary education graduates, respectively 0.8% and about 14%. In general, the problems with their early dropping out of the education system, segregation, and non-participation in employment, education, and training stand out. In the context of these data, the finding regarding poverty and social exclusion is wholly expected. Among those who self-identified as Roma, the share of people with low incomes is the highest—just over 66%. For comparison, in 2020, poverty among people of Bulgarian ethnicity was almost 18%, the lowest level of all ethnic groups [5]. This analysis is also confirmed by the data in another strategic document, according to which the Roma, along with the unemployed and economically inactive people, young people, children, the elderly, single parents, the disabled, and people of foreign origin, are among the vulnerable groups, who are most at risk of poverty and social exclusion [20]. These challenges require the implementation of various policies by the state authorities, including providing opportunities for people from this ethnic group to start their businesses, as well as previously forming positive attitudes towards entrepreneurship and prerequisites leading to such a choice.

Entrepreneurial intentions among young people of Roma origin are of particular interest due to the opportunities that entrepreneurship provides to ensure employment, financial independence, expression, and benefits for the community that can be achieved by this ethnic group, which is also characterized by specific additional problems. According to the analyses, however, it was found that the people of the Roma ethnicity could be more active in creating self-employment within the formal economy [6].

Strategic, programmatic, and other documents, studies, and publications comment on the problems of the Roma community in various contexts—education, health care, accommodation, social exclusion and segregation, employment, etc. [3–5]. Other challenges to this ethnic group are being studied and are of interest—for example, a study of the Roma community in the context of education and stereotypes. A survey on this topic is focused on Roma students, referred to as ethnic "others" in Bulgarian schools [21]. At the same time, entrepreneurship is not highlighted as a strong focus for solving these problems.

Employment, education, health care, and housing are among the main problems faced by people of the Roma ethnicity and are the focus of implemented policies. Roma aged between 20 and 64 are employed in paid work at around 43%, below the EU average of 70% in 2015. The situation for young people is even more alarming since 63% of them aged 16–24 lack training, education, or employment. This percentage is much above the average—12% for the EU [22].

The representatives of this ethnic group also realize the problems. In a survey conducted among Roma, they admit that the main reason why they cannot find a job in the first place is insufficient qualifications—22.3%, and in second place with a significant difference, according to them, it is because of their ethnicity—14.6%, 11.5% do not have a job because they have health problems—illness or physical disability [23].

At the same time, as already stated, entrepreneurial activity among the Roma ethnic group is not high, which leads to several consequences. The reported obstacles to starting a business in general terms are the following: slow and complicated registration, requiring a lot of funds; the need for licenses, which requires time and effort; high administrative costs; high fiscal and other obligations; complex procedures related to bankruptcy, etc. discourage potential entrepreneurs from starting a business. These highly limiting barriers to starting one's business activity are especially valid for those who need more free resources. This group is most likely to include the Roma, who are disproportionately hindered by the obstacles to starting an entrepreneurial activity [24]. In another study aimed at Roma entrepreneurship, among the indicated barriers to starting one's business activity are the following: discrimination in the market, low level of skills, low level of capital and lack of access to financing, and the welfare trap [6].

Although it is a powerful means of overcoming poverty and social exclusion, entrepreneurship development is not explicitly planned and emphasized as an opportunity in the EU Roma Strategic Framework for Equality, Inclusion, and Participation for 2020–2030, for example. However, projects and activities promoting entrepreneurship among the Roma can be indicated. In an initiative that covers entrepreneurship among the Roma, 3,600 entrepreneurs from seven countries have been charted, 130 entrepreneurs from the Roma ethnic group are trained, prepared, and included in the activity of financial institutions—40 people, supported through digitalization and mentoring—90 businesses, facilitated applying for a loan—2,500 [25].

In Bulgaria, the Trust for a Social Alternative develops long-term "Employment and Entrepreneurship". This program is aimed at creating potential entrepreneurial activity skills, as well as studying models for providing funding for start-up and developing businesses by representatives of underprivileged communities, among which are mainly the Roma [26]. Although entrepreneurship is an alternative often not particularly emphasized in policies, projects, and programs, it should be noted that, according to experts, entrepreneurs in the Roma community have increased in the period from 2011 to 2019 [27].

These data, as well as the findings of previous research, make it necessary to reveal the attitudes among young people of the Roma ethnicity regarding entrepreneurial activity as offering different opportunities and what motivates and can support the setting up of their businesses.

Based on the literature review, the following research questions have been formulated, to which an answer is sought in the study:

Is there a statistically significant difference in the attitudes of young people of Roma ethnicity towards entrepreneurship depending on whether they study Entrepreneurship?

Is there a statistically significant difference in the attitudes of young people of Roma ethnicity towards entrepreneurship depending on whether or not their families have their businesses?

Is there a statistically significant difference in the attitudes of young people of Roma ethnicity towards entrepreneurship depending on where they live?

Is there a statistically significant difference in the attitudes of young people of Roma ethnicity towards entrepreneurship depending on whether their gender?

## 3 Methodology

### *3.1 Purpose, Research Questions and Methods*

The object of this research is an investigation of the young people of Roma origin who are part of the education system in the country. The aim is to study and analyze the understandings and expectations of secondary school students and university students for entrepreneurial activity, more specifically, what benefits and opportunities they think establishing and managing their own business provides. Several main questions are included in a module that explores the awareness of young Roma people of the potential of entrepreneurship to make a positive change for the individual, their family, and close ones, as well as for society as a whole. These questions cover respondents' understanding of the following:

- whether they consider that entrepreneurship ensures a good financial situation, by generating good income from entrepreneurial activity;
- whether it provides a chance for the expression of personal abilities, qualities, trainings, as well as achievements in the field of business;
- whether entrepreneurship enables the business owner to be useful to a diverse range of people through the activity he develops;
- whether through entrepreneurship a person can become an authority for others and the community as a whole;

- whether respondents admit that entrepreneurial activity is associated with high risk.

The survey results were processed using SPSS. Some basic features are identified with crucial questions. In this way, two-dimensional distributions in the form of crosstabs were obtained. Approximate Significance was analyzed, i.e., whether and between which characteristics statistically significant differences are found.

### 3.2 *Characteristics of the Questionnaire and Scope of the Study*

The questionnaire as a whole is divided into separate modules. The first questions are aimed at providing information that gives basic data to the respondents. The following modules contain several questions aimed at clarifying awareness of benefits, capacity to exploit opportunities, assessment of the environment that may encourage or hinder entrepreneurial activities, evaluation of options, and one's intentions.

An additional text has been prepared for the survey cards with an explanation of the purpose of the research, the approximate time required to answer the questions and the way of marking the answers. It is especially emphasized that participation in the survey is entirely voluntary and guaranteed anonymous. Information is provided about the researcher and contact details—names, phone numbers, and email. Providing the contacts allows for feedback.

As part of the study, 442 students and pupils of Roma origin were surveyed. Respondents differ in various characteristics—gender, age, entrepreneurship training (some are studying or have studied such a discipline), and specifics of the education institution where they look. In addition, respondents live and study in settlements of different sizes.

### 3.3 *Organization of the Study*

The research was conducted within two months. It was implemented with the help of the "Arete" Youth Foundation and several schools that train students of Roma origin. YF "Arete" is an organization that works exceptionally actively with young people with significant potential but experiencing social and economic difficulties. Students who are scholars of the organization and expressed a desire to participate in the study filled in the prepared survey card. Several pre-selected schools, in which pupils of entirely or predominantly Roma origin are educated, were also included in the study. The schools are located in settlements of different sizes. Education institutions situated in Sofia, as well as in a town that is a municipal center, as well as a school that is in a village, were surveyed. Representatives of the school management were previously informed about the objectives and structure of the questionnaire, as well as the most suitable period for conducting the research.

## 4 Results

An analysis has been made of the answers received from the surveyed 442 young people of Roma ethnicity about their intentions regarding entrepreneurial activity based on the following characteristics:

- Presence of Entrepreneurship in training
- Having a business in the respondents' family
- Place of residence and gender of the respondents

Attitudes towards entrepreneurship have been checked and analyzed regarding the perception of the statements that "owning a business provides a good income," "owning a business provides benefits for the entrepreneur, his relatives, and the whole society,"; "owning a business allows for personal achievements and expression," "owning a business provides entrepreneurs with authority in the community," "owning a business is associated with high risk-taking."

A statistically significant difference is found depending on whether Entrepreneurship is included in the training program when assessing the statements that "owning a business provides benefits for the entrepreneur, his family, and the community" and that "entrepreneurship establishes the authority of business owners in society."

Young people studying some forms of Entrepreneurship are much more emphatic about the benefits of establishing and managing their own business. 31% accept this as "absolutely true," 49% as "true," and a neutral position taken 15% of respondents from this group.

Of the group of young people who do not study Entrepreneurship, 22% (9% less) are those who answer that it is "absolutely true" that entrepreneurship is beneficial to individuals and the community as a whole, 41% believe that this statement is "true," and 32% are those who hesitate (Table 1). The data show that the study of Entrepreneurship is a prerequisite for its more complex understanding and perception as an activity that provides many benefits for both the individual and the whole community.

In general, when analyzing the answers to this question, it can be concluded that entrepreneurship is perceived as beneficial to the individual, the entrepreneur's relatives, and society, and it is supported as "true" by the most significant number of respondents - 47%. 29% are even more adamant that this is "absolutely true." Almost 5% do not associate establishing their own business with benefits to the specified groups, and about 20% do not accept it as true or false.

A statistically significant difference is found when evaluating the statement that "owning a business provides entrepreneurs with high authority in society."

Here again, young people studying Entrepreneurship are more emphatic. 23% are confident about this, 51% define this statement as "true," and 17% are hesitant.

**Table 1** Have you studied entrepreneurship? / Do you agree that owning a business provides benefits for the entrepreneur, the family and the community?

| Q_8_3. Do you agree that owning a business provides benefits for the entrepreneur, the family and the community? | Q_6. Have you studied entrepreneurship? (%) | |
|---|---|---|
| | No | Yes |
| Absolutely true | 22 | 31 |
| True | 41 | 49 |
| Neither true nor false | 32 | 15 |
| False | 3 | 2 |
| Absolutely false | 2 | 3 |

Cramer's V = 0,190; Approximate Significance = 0,003

Of the group of young people who do not study Entrepreneurship, 11% accept this statement as "absolutely true," 41% as "true," and 32% cannot decide whether it is true or not (Table 2).

These results show that knowledge of the nature of entrepreneurship and understanding of its benefits gives a large proportion of respondents the belief that entrepreneurs are individuals who have authority among other people in the community. Perceiving entrepreneurship in this way would encourage some young people to consider it an attractive path for their professional development in the future.

Among the total sample size of 442 participants, it was found that 48% hold the belief that engaging in business activities grants entrepreneurs a certain level of authority within society. Furthermore, 20% of the respondents expressed a high degree of certainty in this belief, while nearly 12% had an opposing viewpoint. About a fifth of the young people have yet to know this issue.

**Table 2** Have you studied entrepreneurship?/Do you agree that owning a business provides entrepreneurs with high authority in society?

| Q_8_5. Do you agree that owning a business provides entrepreneurs with high authority in society? | Q_6. Have you studied entrepreneurship? (%) | |
|---|---|---|
| | No | Yes |
| Absolutely true | 11 | 23 |
| True | 41 | 51 |
| Neither true nor false | 32 | 17 |
| False | 13 | 6 |
| Absolutely false | 3 | 3 |

Cramer's V = 0, 215; Approximate Significance = 0,000

A statistically significant difference is found at Approx. Sig between 0.05 and 0.1 at a 90% confidence level regarding statements that owning a business enables achievements and expression and provides a good income.

There is a statistically significant difference at a 90% level of confidence (Approx. Sig = 0.060) regarding the statement that owning a business provides opportunities for achievements and performances depending on whether the youth study Entrepreneurship or not. Young people studying Entrepreneurship are more emphatic. Of them, 56% consider this statement "true," 30% - "absolutely true," and 10% hesitate. Of those who are not studying Entrepreneurship, respectively, 48% answered that it is "true," 25% - "absolutely true," and 19% hesitated. Under the conditions mentioned above, a statistically significant difference at a 90% level of confidence is also found for the understanding that owning a business provides good income depending on whether the youth study Entrepreneurship or not (Approx. Sig = 0.057). Greater support is again demonstrated by young people studying Entrepreneurship. Of these, 54% consider this statement "true," 31% accept it as "absolutely true," and 11% are hesitant. In respondents who do not study Entrepreneurship, 50% answered that this statement is "true," 26% define it as "absolutely true," and 21% hesitate, i.e., ten percent more than the other group.

Generally speaking, the statement that owning a business provides a good income is supported as "true" by almost 53% and rated as "absolutely true" by 30% of all 442 respondents. Only 4% believe this does not correspond to reality and that entrepreneurial activity cannot be relied upon to obtain good income.

No statistically significant difference is found regarding the understanding that owning a business is related to taking many risks according to whether or not the respondents study Entrepreneurship at school/university.

There is a statistically significant difference in the perception of the risk accompanying entrepreneurship and the existence or lack of owning a business by family member/s of those included in the study.

The results show that the vast majority of respondents, almost 82%, do not have direct observation over entrepreneurial activity, as their families or a member of the extended family do not have their own business. For this reason, it is of great interest how the risk directly related to entrepreneurship is assessed by the youth whose families have business experience and those who do not and whether there is a difference in the judgments of these two groups of respondents.

A significant proportion, precisely 46%, of the younger generation hailing from families engaged in entrepreneurial endeavors hold the belief that business ownership entails a substantial degree of risk-taking. About 17% are those who answer that this is "absolutely true," but this is also the share of those who hesitate, as well as those for whom it is not true that entrepreneurship is high-risk. Among young people whose families do not have their businesses, there is higher support for the finding that entrepreneurship is associated with many risks. 38% admit it is "true," but another 27%, 10% more than the previous group, say it is "absolutely true." In addition, the proportion of those who hesitate about whether this statement is true or not is about 6% more or 23% (Table 3).

**Table 3** Does someone in your family have his/her own business? / Do you agree that owning a business involves a lot of risk?

| Do you agree that owning a business involves a lot of risk? | Q_5. Does someone in your family have his/her own business? (%) | |
|---|---|---|
| | No | Yes |
| Absolutely true | 27 | 17 |
| True | 38 | 46 |
| Neither true nor false | 23 | 17 |
| False | 8 | 17 |
| Absolutely false | 4 | 3 |

Cramer's V = 0, 163; Approximate Significance = 0,019

These data suggest that youth with family experience with entrepreneurship would be more inclined to accept the risk of starting their own business and, therefore, decide to be entrepreneurs. Most young people whose families have no business experience would be more conservative regarding risk. It would have a more challenging time daring to start their own business. As a result, it follows that the education system and society must create mechanisms to encourage and actively support young people who have ideas and desire to realize them.

Somewhat surprisingly, the 442 respondents show little certainty regarding the statement that starting one's own business is associated with taking a high risk. Almost 40% consider it "true" that much uncertainty accompanies entrepreneurial activity, and another 25% are sure of this. Nearly 22% are hesitant about the truth of this statement, and just over 13% do not associate entrepreneurship with high risk-taking.

The extent to which owning a business enables personal achievements and expression according to whether some of the family (Approx. Sig = 0.096) of the respondents have a business also shows the presence of a statistically significant difference at a 90% level of confidence. 65% of young people whose families have a company accept this as "true," almost 26% say it is "absolutely true," and only 7% think it is neither true nor false. 51% of those who do not have a family business answer that the statement is "true" for them, 29% is "completely true" and 13% are hesitant.

A frequently made distribution of whether establishing one's own business provides an opportunity for personal achievements and expression shows that almost 54% of all respondents accept that it is "true"; another 29% are even more emphatic. Only slightly more than 5% are of the opposite opinion and do not perceive entrepreneurship as providing opportunities to demonstrate personal qualities, abilities, and skills and achieve high results.

There is no statistically significant difference regarding claims that owning a business provides a good income, benefits the entrepreneur, his family, and the community, and includes authority in society according to owning or not a business by family member/s of those included in the study.

Statistically significant differences are found regarding the understanding that owning a business enables the entrepreneur to benefit himself, his relatives, and society, depending on the place of residence of the respondents.

Among the cohort of young individuals hailing from rural areas, a substantial majority unequivocally assert that the act of establishing and operating a business yields advantageous outcomes for the entrepreneur, their immediate circle, and the wider community. 58% of this group expresses this opinion. Of the respondents who live in a village, 59% believe that entrepreneurship is beneficial and indicated that it is "true." At the same time, 48% of young people from the capital have the same opinion, as well as 39% of those who live in a big town (Table 4).

The specified results show that young people accept entrepreneurship as something that benefits different social groups. Awareness of this fact would encourage more young people to choose to start their own business as their career path. There are some differences in the definiteness of the answers depending on where the respondents live and study. A strong impact is likely the environment, which provides them with varying degrees of opportunities to directly observe the activities of entrepreneurs who support their relatives and other people from the community, to know personally, and to follow good examples and role models.

Statistically significant differences are not found regarding the understanding that owning a business is a source of good income, enables performance and achievements, is associated with many risks, and builds the authority of entrepreneurs in the community, depending on where the respondents live.

The analyses of the data obtained from the research show that there are no statistically significant differences regarding the assessment of "owning a business as providing a good income," "allowing personal achievements and expression," "enabling the entrepreneur to be beneficial to himself, his relatives and the whole

**Table 4** Residence/ Do you agree that owning a business provides benefits for the entrepreneur, his close people and the community?

| Q_8_3. Do you agree that owning business provides benefits for the entrepreneur, his close people and the community? | Q_3. Residence (%) | | | |
|---|---|---|---|---|
| | Village | Small town | Big town | Sofia |
| Absolutely true | 19 | 58 | 35 | 28 |
| True | 59 | 16 | 39 | 48 |
| Neither true nor false | 19 | 11 | 17 | 21 |
| False | 3 | 10 | 5 | 1 |
| Absolutely false | 0 | 5 | 4 | 2 |

Cramer's V = 0, 150; Approximate Significance = 0,003

community," "associated with a lot of risks," "provides authority in the community" by men and women. Gender is not a factor that leads to significant changes in the conceptions regarding the specified statements.

## 5 Discussion

Entrepreneurial attitudes are discussed through the prism of respondents' expectations and understandings by evaluating the statements that:

- "Own business provides good income."
- "Own business provides utility for the entrepreneur, the family, and the whole society."
- "Own business allows for personal achievement and expression."
- "Own business provides authority to entrepreneurs in the community," "own business is associated with high risk."

This analysis was done according to the formulated research questions based on the literature reviewed and the studies on the topic.

The share of young people who start their own business is relatively small. This is indicated by the data and findings in a number of countries in Europe [1, 2] etc.). For this reason, it is of interest to what extent and how entrepreneurship education affects young people's understanding of starting their businesses. Among the reported main obstacles that young people face and that can be overcome to some extent through training are, for example, the provision of financial means, problems arising from the ecosystem [15]; overcoming some stereotypes, including the attitude to risk and failure; insufficient self-confidence to work as an entrepreneur [14]. Moreover, over a third of young people consider that they need more knowledge for entrepreneurship [1].

A statistically significant difference is found depending on the *presence or absence of entrepreneurship training* regarding the assessment that *owning a business benefits the entrepreneur, his family, and the community,* as well as that *it builds the authority of entrepreneurs in society*. A statistically significant difference is found at a 90% confidence level for the statements that *owning a business provides an opportunity for achievements and expression* and is a source of *good income.* No statistically significant difference in owning a business *is associated with taking many risks according to whether or not respondents study Entrepreneurship.*

Family business has a particular influence on the perception of entrepreneurship by the youth. It is found that the limiting factor for starting one's own business is also the need for more courage [11]. Family business experience and "learning by doing" in the family firm can favorably influence entrepreneurial intentions. The usefulness, prestige, and authority associated with the creation and development of a successful business are also related to overcoming poverty, which is among the severe problems for the Roma ethnic group [22], as well as rejection and segregation [21].

There is a statistically significant difference in the perception of the *risk accompanying entrepreneurship and the presence or absence of owning a business by family member/s* of those included in the study. A statistically significant difference exists regarding the conception that *owning a business enables achievements and expression depending on the presence or absence of family business* (Approx. Sig = 0.096) at a 90% confidence level. There is no statistically significant difference regarding the statements that owning a company *provides a good income, owning a business benefits the entrepreneur, his family, and the community, and it gives authority in society* according to *owning or not a business by family member/s* of the young people surveyed.

The place of residence and the specifics of the local environment shape understandings and expectations towards entrepreneurship. In the municipal and state policies, among other alternatives for developing the informal education of the youth, attention is also paid to entrepreneurship [7]. Dynamics in social relations and conditions influence the motivation and entrepreneurial aspirations of young people [11]. Encouraging young people to start and develop a business, even in remote areas, can be done through various elements of technical (infrastructure) support. There are several forms of such support [16]. Higher education institutions are also part of the ecosystem that supports youth entrepreneurial careers [17].

Statistically significant differences are found regarding the understanding that owning a business enables the entrepreneur to be *beneficial to their relatives, and society*, depending on *the place of residence of the respondents.* Statistically significant differences are not found regarding the statements that owning a business provides *an opportunity to receive good income, as well as an opportunity for expression and achievements, it is associated with many risks, it builds the authority of entrepreneurs in the community depending on the place of residence of the respondents.*

Women's entrepreneurship is a subject of great interest from academics and policymakers. Several studies look for differences in entrepreneurial intentions depending on gender. In others, the specifics of individual subgroups of female entrepreneurs are explored [9]. The distinctive culture and traditions of the Roma ethnic group determine the role and position of women in the family and society. Therefore, it is necessary to analyze whether there are gender differences in entrepreneurial intentions.

*There are no statistically significant differences* regarding the perception of "owning a business as providing a good income," "allowing for personal achievements and expression," or "allowing the entrepreneur to be beneficial to him/herself, their relatives, and the whole community," "associated with a lot of risks," "providing authority in the community" according to *the gender* of the respondents.

The results show the strong impact of entrepreneurship training among young people in forming attitudes towards establishing and developing their own business, as well as the family's experience in entrepreneurship and, to some extent, their place of residence. These circumstances should be considered by policy-making institutions and organizations supporting Roma youth in their choice of professional development, including their encouragement to start their own business.

## 6 Conclusion

The socio-economic challenges (education, healthcare, housing, rejection, discrimination, employment, etc.) faced by the Roma require the adoption and implementation of targeted policies. Although entrepreneurship can contribute to solving some of these problems, including unemployment, social exclusion, rejection, poverty, etc., this opportunity still needs to be emphasized more strongly in the target and implemented activities in this area. There are some gaps in the available research regarding the entrepreneurial intentions, motivations, expectations, and challenges of the youth from this ethnic group. For these reasons, the focus of the publication is to research and analyze the expectations and intentions of Roma youth regarding the establishment of their own business by considering the influence of entrepreneurship training, business ownership by the youth's families, place of residence, and gender of the respondents. The survey conducted among 442 young people of Roma origin shows the following results:

A statistically significant difference, depending on the presence or absence of entrepreneurship training, is found for the statements that owning a business provides benefits for the entrepreneur, his family, and the community, as well as that it builds the authority of entrepreneurs in society. A statistically significant difference is found at a 90% confidence level for the statements that owning a business provides an opportunity for achievements and expression and is a source of good income. There is a statistically significant difference in the perception of the risk accompanying entrepreneurship and the presence or absence of owning a business by family member/s. At a 90% confidence level, a statistically significant difference exists regarding owning a business as enabling achievements and expression. Statistically significant differences are found regarding the understanding that owning a business allows for the entrepreneur to be beneficial to himself, his relatives, and society, depending on the place of residence of the respondents. There are no statistically significant differences depending on gender in terms of these statements. The obtained results show the influence of entrepreneurship training, the existence of a family business, place of residence, and gender.

These conclusions can be taken into account when planning and forming policies for the development of entrepreneurship among young people of Roma ethnicity. In this regard, the following recommendations can be made to policymakers:

1. The identified role of entrepreneurship education regarding young people's understanding of their own business suggests the even stronger presence of such disciplines in the educational process. This will result in a better perception of entrepreneurial activities, as well as their inclination to consider entrepreneurship as a future career.
2. Family business influences the formation of attitudes towards entrepreneurship. Therefore, it would be helpful to include internships or practice in companies within the educational process. This will give the young people an opportunity to get acquainted with the entrepreneur's work. Short visits or meetings with successful entrepreneurs, including those of Roma origin, would be useful.

3. Digitization of education will reduce the differences in the perception of entrepreneurship regardless of where young people live.

The study limitations are related to the fact that young people of Roma origin who are surveyed are part of the education system. Consequently, the specified results are irrelevant for young people of Roma origin who are not part of training, education, and employment. The research is limited only to young people of Roma origin from Bulgaria who live and study in the country. No international analyses and comparisons are made. In addition, the study is cross-sectional (e.g., the data are collected at a specific time) and not longitudinal, which shows a snapshot of the problem but cannot indicate the trends of its development.

Future research can be focused on the factors, restrictions, and motivations that determine the decision of Roma youth to start their own business, as well as the policies that effectively support such a choice. Research on a particular group of young people who have dropped out of education, training, and employment can contribute to forming more target measures for their integration, including through entrepreneurship. The importance of the topic in a European and global context also implies conducting international research, comparing the results, searching for good practices, and making recommendations for policy formation.

**Acknowledgements** This work was financially supported by the University of National and World Economy—UNWE Research Programme.

## References

1. National Assembly: The National Youth Strategy (2021–2030). https://www.strategy.bg/StrategicDocuments/View.aspx?lang=bg-BG&Id=1603 (2023), Last accessed 01 July 2023
2. Bikse, V., Lusena-Ezera, I., Rivza, B.: Performance trends in youth entrepreneur's capacity prerequisite for the entrepreneurship development of Latvia. Pol. J. Manag. Stud. **14**(1), 40–50 (2016)
3. European Commission: Communication from the Commission to the European Parliament and the Council a Union of Equality: EU Roma Strategic Framework for Equality, Inclusion and Participation for 2020 – 2030, (2020)
4. National Statistical Institute: Ethnocultural characteristics of the population as of September 7. https://www.nsi.bg/sites/default/files/files/pressreleases/Census2021-ethnos.pdf (2021). Last accessed 09 April 2023.
5. Council of Ministers: National Strategy of the Republic of Bulgaria for equality, inclusion and participation of the Roma (2021 - 2030). https://www.strategy.bg/StrategicDocuments/View.aspx?lang=bg-BG&Id=1541 (2022). Last accessed 10 April 2023.
6. Organization for Economic Cooperation and Development: Inclusive Entrepreneurship – Focus on the Roma Community. In SME and Entrepreneurship Policy in the Slovak Republic, Chapter 8 edited by Kris Bschmans and Jonathan Potter, OECD Publishing, Paris (2021).
7. National Assembly: Youth Act SN. Vol. 31, 20 April 2012. last modified and add. SN. No. 61, August 2022, (2012).
8. Rangelova, R.: The Development of Youth Entrepreneurship in Bulgaria. In Youth Entrepreneurship and Local Development in Central and Eastern Europe, edited by Paul Blokker and Bruno Dallago. Routledge Taylor & Francis Group, London and New York (2008).

9. Georgieva, S.: Women's Entrepreneurship—Segmentation and Management Dimensions. Pol. J. Manag. Stud. **26**(2), 144–161 (2022)
10. Tubadji, A., Dietrich, H., Angelis, V., Haas, A., Schels, B.: Fear-of-failure and cultural persistence in youth entrepreneurship. J. Small Bus. Entrep. **33**(5), 513–538 (2021)
11. Rahmatiah, Wiroto, D. W., Taan, H.: Business continuity, motivation, and social conditions of young entrepreneurs. Econ. Sociol. **12**(4), 166–182 (2019)
12. Vladimirov, Z.: SME innovations and performance: the mediating role of product innovation. Int. Rev. Entrep. **14**(2), 209–234 (2016)
13. Council of Ministers: National Strategy for Small and Medium Enterprises 2021–2027. https://www.mi.government.bg/strategy-policy/godishna-programa-za-prilagane-na-naczionalnata-strategiya-za-malkite-i-srednite-predpriyatiya/. (2021). Last accessed 12 April 2023
14. Noga, M., Brzeziński, A.: Economics, Education and Youth Entrepreneurship: International Perspectives. Routledge Taylor & Francis Group, London and New York (2022)
15. Blokker P., Dallago, B.: Economic Transformation and the Challenge of Youth Entrepreneurship in Central and Eastern Europe (Introduction). In Youth Entrepreneurship and Local Development in Central and Eastern Europe, edited by Paul Blokker and Bruno Dallago. Routledge Taylor & Francis Group, London and New York (2008).
16. Coles, B., MacDonald, R.F.: From New Vocationalism to the Culture of Enterprise. In Youth in Transition: The Sociology of Youth and Youth Policy, edited by Claire Wallace and Malcolm Cross, Routledge Library Editions: British Sociological Association, (Volume 6). Routledge Taylor & Francis Group, London and New York (1990)
17. O'Brien, E., M. Cooney, T., Blenker, P.: Expanding university entrepreneurial ecosystems to under-represented communities. J. Entrep. Public Policy **8**(3), 384–407 (2019)
18. National Statistical Institute: Population and housing census in the Republic of Bulgaria, Population by ethnic group and mother language. https://censusresults.nsi.bg/census/reports/2/2/r9.aspx (2011). Last accessed 09 April 2023
19. European Commission: Roma in EU. (2020), https://commission.europa.eu/strategy-and-policy/policies/justice-and-fundamental-rights/combatting-discrimination/roma-eu/roma-equality-inclusion-and-participation-eu_bg. Last accessed 09 April 2023
20. Council of Ministers: Updated National Strategy for Poverty Reduction and Promotion of Social Inclusion 2030. https://www.strategy.bg/StrategicDocuments/View.aspxlang=bg-BG&Id=1345? (2020). Last accessed 10 April 2023
21. Lambrev, V., Traykov, B., Kirova, A.: Constructing Roma students as ethnic 'others' through orientalist discourses in Bulgarian schools. Int. Stud. Sociol. Educ. **27**(1), 23–41 (2018)
22. European Parliament: Implementation of National Roma Integration Strategies: combating negative attitudes towards people with Romani background in Europe. European Parliament resolution of 17 September 2020 on the implementation of National Roma Integration Strategies: combating negative attitudes towards people with Romani background in Europe (2020/2011(INI)https://www.europarl.europa.eu/doceo/document/TA-9-2020-0229_EN.html (2019). Last accessed 15 April 2023
23. Bogdanov, G., Vankova, Zv., Zahariev, B., Yordanov, I., Kabakchieva, P., Mihailova, Sp.: Report on the public policies for the Roma integration in Bulgaria and the main problems of the socio-economic inclusion of the Roma community (project). „„EU INCLUSIVE project – Data transfer and good practices exchange between Romania, Bulgaria, Spain and Italy regarding the inclusion of the Roma population", „Open society", Sofia (2012).
24. Bogdanov, L., Angelov, G.: Roma integration in Bulgaria: necessary reforms and economic effects. (2007), https://osis.bg/wp-content/uploads/2018/04/OSI_Publication_Roma_1.pdf. Last accessed 15 April 2023

25. Roma Economic Development Initiative: https://redi-ngo.eu/about-redi-2/. Last accessed 3 April 2023
26. Trust for Social Alternatives: http://socialachievement.org/bg/kakvo-pravim/programni-oblasti/ikonomichesko-razvitie-i-dostyp-do-zaetost/zaetost-i-predpriemachestvo/. Last accessed 15 April 2023
27. EuroNewsBulgaria:https://euronewsbulgaria.com/news/6788/romskite-predpriemachi-sa-se-utroili-za-desetiletie--e-konomika-23112022. Last accessed 4 July 2023

# Factors Affecting Performance of Women Entrepreneurs': A Study of Rural Women Entrepreneurs in Emerging Indian Market

**Dhanashree Katekhaye and Róbert Magda**

**Abstract** This research paper seeks valuable insights into the current landscape of women's entrepreneurship in India while offering a comparative analysis spanning previous periods. Through detailed analyses, the study will illuminate India's contemporary global standing in women's entrepreneurship. Recognizing the pivotal role that women play in propelling economic advancement, it becomes imperative to delve into the factors that influence the achievements of female entrepreneurs within the Indian context. The principal objective of this study is to analyze problems faced by rural women entrepreneurs and their impact on their performance. Employing a quantitative descriptive methodology, the research employs a convenience sampling technique to collect data through a self-administered questionnaire targeting women entrepreneurs in India. The study encompasses a dataset of 335 samples. The analytical framework encompasses descriptive, reliability, validity analyses, as well as and ANOVA procedures. The study's findings underscore the factors that significantly shape women entrepreneurs' performance, encompassing their educational attainment, previous entrepreneurial experience, business training, capital access, comprehension of business intricacies, governmental support, and asset ownership. Conversely, variables such as age, marital status, market entry, and physical infrastructure availability are found to exert minimal influence on the level of success achieved by women entrepreneurs.

**Keywords** Woman entrepreneurs · Entrepreneurship · Development · Performance · India

D. Katekhaye (✉)
Dr. Ambedkar Institute of Management Studies and Research, Nagpur, India
e-mail: dhanashree_katekhaye@daimsr.edu.in

R. Magda
John Von Neumann University, Kecskemét, Hungary

Northwest University, Vanderbijlpark, South Africa



S. Kot et al. (eds.), *Corporate Practices: Policies, Methodologies, and Insights in Organizational Management*, Springer Proceedings in Business and Economics,
https://doi.org/10.1007/978-981-97-0996-0_9

# 1 Introduction

Entrepreneurship holds a vital role in a country's growth and progress, particularly in fostering industrial development. It originates from an individual's creative drive, evolving into business ownership, economic stability, and capital formation. Entrepreneurial skills are crucial for industrialization, curbing poverty and unemployment, marking a shift toward a market economy where the presence of women entrepreneurs is growing. Despite this, women's involvement in income generation must still be increased. In micro, small, and medium enterprises, women's entrepreneurship proves essential, driving innovation and job creation. Women entrepreneurs carry out multifaceted roles in establishing businesses, requiring knowledge, skills, and familial backing. However, gender-related challenges like cultural barriers, legal and financial limitations, mobility constraints, and restricted network access hinder their startup and growth. Women entrepreneurs contribute to poverty reduction and female empowerment. Government and developmental bodies are incentivizing and supporting women entrepreneurs through various programs.

Women serve as the cornerstones of economic growth in numerous developing nations. According to the Global Entrepreneurship Monitor (GEM) findings, women entrepreneurs are responsible for creating employment opportunities, fostering wealth, and driving innovation across 37 surveyed countries. Remarkably, in many of these countries, the expansion rate of women establishing new businesses outpaces that of male entrepreneurs. [1]

Entrepreneurs have a pivotal function in every economy, employing their abilities and proactive approach to foresee demands and introduce fresh concepts to the market. An entrepreneur is a person who establishes a novel business, assuming a significant portion of the risks while reaping a substantial share of the benefits. Those entrepreneurs who effectively navigate the hazards of starting a venture receive not only financial gains but also recognition and ongoing prospects for expansion.

A female entrepreneur is an individual who willingly takes on demanding roles to fulfill her requirements and attain financial autonomy. Numerous women possess this characteristic, yet they have yet to be allowed to display their capabilities, resulting in their unawareness of their true potential. In India, women assume greater responsibilities in nurturing children and cultivating a harmonious home environment infused with care and fondness. Within the realm of the family, women efficiently coordinate a range of tasks, adeptly managing multiple activities without being perturbed by challenges.

The presence of women-led enterprises is experiencing a significant uptrend across the economies of nearly every nation. The latent entrepreneurial capabilities of women have been undergoing a gradual transformation, aligning with an increasing recognition of their role and economic standing within society. Proficiency, expertise, and the capacity to adjust within the business realm constitute the primary factors driving women's engagement in entrepreneurial pursuits.

Female entrepreneurs play a crucial role in advancing the economic progress of any nation, with their contribution becoming particularly essential in enhancing the economic status of developing nations like India.

In order to foster the well-being and affluence of developing economies, it is of utmost importance to recognize women entrepreneurs as novel catalysts for enduring economic expansion [2].

The present comprehension of the interrelationships among the determinants of business achievement indicates that establishing distinct associations between specific factors contributing to individual success and the enduring performance of small and medium enterprises (SMEs) owned by women, particularly in developing nations, is still constrained. Numerous research works emphasize the importance of women entrepreneurs as a crucial yet undervalued asset for promoting sustainable economic expansion [3–5].

### *1.1 Objectives of Study*

1. To analyses the problems faced by rural woman entrepreneurs and its impact on their performance in India.
2. To determine the various factors influencing entrepreneurial success.
3. To provide overview of the dynamics of female entrepreneurs in India

### *1.2 Research Hypotheses*

With reference to above research questions, the following hypotheses were formulated:

**H0:** There is no significant relationship between the problems faced by rural women entrepreneurs and their performance.

**H1:** There is significant relationship between the problems faced by rural women entrepreneurs and their performance.

## 2 Literature Review

Women entrepreneurs exert significant influence across a diverse array of economic domains. A "Female Entrepreneur" is an individual who places economic self-sufficiency above personal requirements, displaying resolute determination to bring about positive transformations with an emphasis on exceptional quality. According to the Government of India, women entrepreneurship entails women possessing and directing an enterprise, holding a minimum of 51% of the capital investment, and ensuring that at least 51% of the workforce opportunities are accessible to women.

At present, Small and Medium Enterprises (SMEs) overall, and entrepreneurship specifically, constitute an essential foundation for sustainable economic advancement. The contribution of women to this sphere has gained increased prominence [6].

Women often encounter challenges such as inadequate leadership, planning, and insufficient allocation of financial resources while running their businesses. Despite possessing these qualities, many women have not been provided the platform to exhibit their talents, resulting in a lack of awareness about their true capabilities. A comparison between the fundamental attributes required for entrepreneurs and the inherent characteristics of Indian women unveils substantial potential in the entrepreneurial capabilities of Indian women. Recognizing, extracting, and showcasing this potential is essential for its utilization in productive and service sectors, contributing to the nation's development. A significant portion of the global impoverished population comprises women, with two-thirds of illiterate individuals being female. The majority of out-of-school children are also girls. The ongoing world food price crisis disproportionately affects women, as many go without regular meals, often sacrificing their sustenance to ensure their children are fed.

As stated by Brush and Hisrich [7], several challenges have hindered the growth of numerous women-led entrepreneurial ventures, preventing them from progressing from small to medium scale. These challenges include disparities in accessing land and property, which in turn restricts women's ability to secure loans for their businesses. This financial constraint confines their business growth to the micro-enterprise level. This study aims to evaluate the various factors impacting the performance of women-led entrepreneurial ventures within Iringa Municipality. Despite the generally acknowledged contribution of small enterprises to development, women entrepreneurs within this sector need to overcome significant barriers that impede their sustained growth and progression.

Furthermore, the field of women in entrepreneurship has been widely disregarded both within society and within the realm of social sciences [7]. According to Franco and Winqvist [8] and Reynolds and White [9], not only do women exhibit a lower participation rate in entrepreneurship compared to men, but they also frequently opt to initiate and oversee enterprises in different sectors than those typically chosen by men; To determine the primary factors influencing performance, an intensive and meticulous systematic analysis of contemporary empirical research was undertaken.

As per the opinion of Kyalo [10], Jha, Makkad, and Mittal [11]. Nasri and Muhammad [12]; Salah and Kaplan [13]; The thorough examination of the connection between each factor and the performance of female entrepreneurs is thus elaborated upon below, aiming to establish a coherent conceptual framework (Fig. 1).

The entrepreneurial landscape has witnessed a significant rise in women entrepreneurs, contributing to economic growth and societal development. However, the performance of women entrepreneurs is influenced by many factors. This article explores the various dimensions that impact the success of women entrepreneurs, categorizing them into social and demographic factors, environmental factors, and training and development factors.

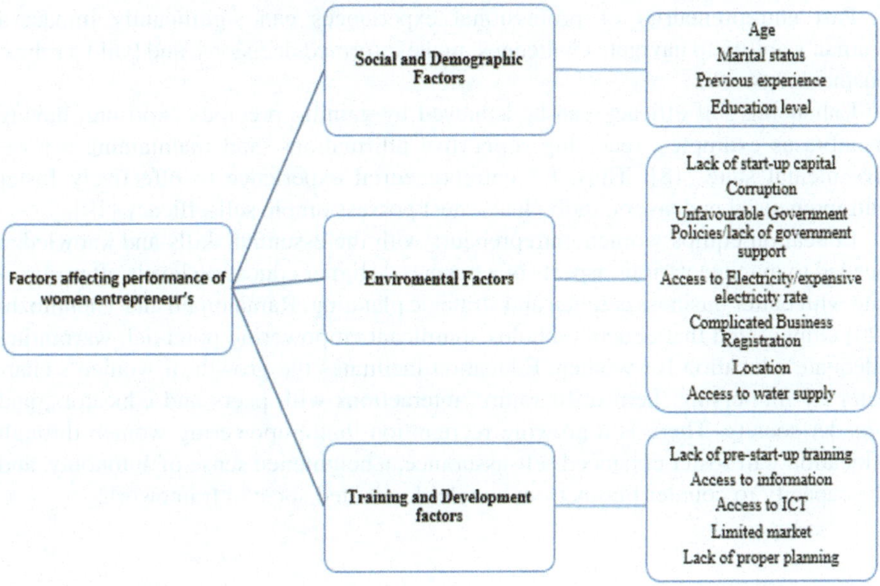


**Fig. 1** Conceptual framework based on literature

## *2.1 Social and Demographic Factors*

Age is pivotal in shaping an entrepreneur's experience and decision-making abilities. Younger entrepreneurs may need more experience, while older entrepreneurs might need help adapting to new technologies and trends. The tendency for women to establish their own businesses after being employed in paid positions could contribute to the prevalence of middle-aged women entrepreneurs. Furthermore, women aged 36 and above who have already raised their children, along with those aspiring to initiate businesses following retirement from their paid employment, might account for the inclination towards entrepreneurship during middle age. This notion is supported by research on women entrepreneurs, as various studies have underscored the concentration of women entrepreneurs within the middle age bracket [13]. The exploration of women entrepreneurs has consistently emphasized the middle age group, as evidenced by studies conducted by Celebi [14], Ufuk and Ozgen [15], and Yetim and Tatlıdil [16].

Marital status can influence the level of support and responsibilities a woman entrepreneur experiences. Single entrepreneurs may have more flexibility, while those with families might face challenges balancing work and family commitments. Most research investigations have indicated that their spouse can influence the decision regarding one's chosen occupation. Unmarried individuals possess the liberty to select employment in alignment with their preferences, whereas married individuals often experience the influence of their partner on their decision-making. This phenomenon is reflected in studies conducted by Verbake and de Graaf [17].

Past entrepreneurial or professional experiences can significantly impact a woman's ability to navigate challenges, make informed decisions, and build a robust business network.

Enhancing self-efficacy can be achieved by gaining previous exposure, having mentors as examples, receiving supportive affirmations, and maintaining a positive mental state [18]. Thus, for entrepreneurial experience to effectively foster entrepreneurial endeavors, individuals must possess ample self-efficacy [19].

Education equips women entrepreneurs with the essential skills and knowledge needed to manage various aspects of a business. Higher education levels often correlate with better business acumen and strategic planning. Ramanujam and Thenmozhi [20] emphasized that education holds significant empowering potential, warranting adequate education for women. Education facilitates the growth of women's character by immersing them in literature, interactions with peers and educators, and broader society. There is a growing recognition that empowering women through education will foster enhanced self-assurance, a heightened sense of autonomy, and the capacity to counter biases from a male-dominated societal framework.

## 2.2 *Environmental Factors*

Insufficient access to funding is a common obstacle faced by women entrepreneurs. Limited financial resources can hinder business expansion, product development, and marketing efforts. The issue of securing funding to maintain their businesses is encountered by both male and female entrepreneurs, with women facing even greater difficulties in Rwanda [21]. Financial institutions often harbor skepticism regarding women's competence in effectively managing a business and are inclined to avoid having women as clients Blaire[22].

High levels of corruption within the business environment can deter women entrepreneurs from entering the market or growing their businesses. Corrupt practices can lead to unfair competition and operational challenges. Apparition and colleagues [23] also support this notion by demonstrating that an individual's perception of government initiatives against corruption and their confidence in their entrepreneurial abilities and knowledge can exert a more significant influence on entrepreneurial intentions compared to societal norms and governmental regulations.

Policies that do not provide adequate support for women entrepreneurs can hinder growth. Lack of access to business incentives, grants, and resources can limit business expansion. The interplay between the broader economic landscape and governmental regulations significantly influences these contrasting dynamics [24]. In periods of high taxation and economic downturns, opportunity-driven entrepreneurs might reduce spending and delay investments. However, they are also inclined to initiate businesses when tax policies and government size are more favorable. Conversely, necessity-driven entrepreneurs transition from the labor force into entrepreneurship due to unfavorable economic circumstances [25].

Reliable and affordable access to electricity is crucial for business operations. High electricity costs can increase operational expenses and impact profitability. The research conducted by Grimm and Hartwiga [26] demonstrates that the availability of electricity has a favorable influence on micro and small enterprises (MSEs) in the topmost profit category. This discovery implies that these MSEs may need to surpass a significant threshold to experience the advantageous outcomes stemming from full access to electricity.

Most formalization strategies have concentrated on enhancing the business regulatory framework by streamlining the procedures for business registration and reducing associated costs Bruhn and McKenzie [27]. Cumbersome and time-consuming business registration processes can discourage women from formalizing their ventures. Simplified registration procedures can encourage more women to enter the market.

Location and Access to Basic Infrastructure: Business location impacts accessibility to markets, suppliers, and customers. Access to water supply, transportation, and other infrastructure can help business activities. Some aspects of infrastructure, such as transportation networks, energy supply, and healthcare systems, are fundamental for various economic endeavors, while specific components hold particular significance for entrepreneurial activities [28].

## *2.3 Training and Development Factors*

Comprehensive training programs for aspiring women entrepreneurs must equip them with business skills, financial literacy, and industry insights before launching their ventures. Entrepreneurship increasingly garners attention in the present era, particularly as traditional employment prospects in government and private sectors become less promising. Consequently, governments emphasize fostering entrepreneurial competencies across various educational and training tiers, aiming to cultivate a culture of entrepreneurship. Additionally, entrepreneurship is viewed as a prompt remedy to address unemployment, particularly among recent graduates.

Adequate access to information, technology, and the internet enables women entrepreneurs to stay informed about market trends, reach broader audiences, and manage their businesses more effectively. Digitization has significantly transformed how information is sourced, accessed, and utilized in guiding the resource orchestration process. For instance, Welter et al. [29] contend that digitalization's impact on various entrepreneurial tasks has reduced the hierarchical nature of information and resource distribution that has historically shaped the social frameworks in which entrepreneurs function.

Limited market exposure can restrict the growth potential of women-led businesses. Diversification strategies and innovative marketing approaches can help expand the customer base. O'Neill [30] suggests that small and medium-sized enterprises (SMEs) must enhance and adapt their current resources and capabilities to capitalize on emerging prospects, such as evolving markets and shifting consumer characteristics. This adaptation is not only crucial for their survival in a challenging environment but also offers the potential to access novel product markets.

Inadequate business planning can lead to operational inefficiencies, financial instability, and missed growth opportunities. Strategic planning is crucial for sustainable business development.

A complex interplay of social, environmental, and training factors influences the performance of women entrepreneurs. Addressing these challenges requires a holistic approach involving policymakers, government agencies, NGOs, and the private sector to create an enabling environment that fosters gender equality, equitable access to resources, and support mechanisms for women entrepreneurs. By recognizing and addressing these factors, societies can empower women entrepreneurs to achieve their full potential and contribute to economic progress.

## 3 Research Methodology

In this research, a quantitative descriptive methodology was utilized, employing the convenience sampling technique. The data-gathering process involved the distribution of self-administered questionnaires to female entrepreneurs in India. The researcher selected the Vidarbha region for their study. A total of 335 women entrepreneurs from small and medium-sized enterprises registered with the District Industries Centre were selected using convenience sampling and included in the study. The analysis encompassed performing descriptive statistical analysis, evaluating the reliability and validity of the data, and employing ANOVA for data analysis.

Table 1 shows sample entrepreneurs in various districts or DICs (District Industries Centers) and their corresponding block or taluka areas. For instance, in Nagpur, there were 81 sample entrepreneurs from the Umred&Pardi block, and this pattern continues for other districts such as Gondia, Amravati, Wardha, and Bhandara, with respective sample sizes of 64, 55, 63, and 72. The total number of sample entrepreneurs across all districts and block/taluka areas amounted to 335. This data allows researchers to examine and compare the experiences and challenges faced by women entrepreneurs in different geographical regions within the surveyed districts.

**Table 1** Distribution of Sample rural woman entrepreneurs

| Sr.no | Districts/DICs | Block/ Taluka | Sample entrepreneurs |
|---|---|---|---|
| 1 | Nagpur | Umred&Pardi | 81 |
| 2 | Gondia | Tiroda | 64 |
| 3 | Amravati | Dhamngaon | 55 |
| 4 | Wardha | Pulgaon | 63 |
| 5 | Bhandara | Lakhani | 72 |
| | Total | | 335 |

## 4 Result and Discussion

In essence, this research enriches the understanding of women's entrepreneurship in India by providing a comprehensive overview of current conditions and a meticulous analysis of success-driving factors. As women continue to be key drivers of economic growth, the insights derived from this study can inform policies and strategies to nurture a conducive environment for women entrepreneurs. The analysis of the results, based on a sample size of 335 participants from the Vidarbha region in India, provides valuable insights into their perceptions and experiences regarding various factors affecting women entrepreneurs' performance. The mean scores and standard deviations offer a comprehensive understanding of the participants' responses.

Table 2 illustrates the problems and challenges faced by women entrepreneurs. The participants' Marital status garnered a mean rating of 3.82, reflecting a moderate distribution of marital statuses among the participants and a standard deviation of 0.047, indicating some diversity in responses. Lack of start-up capital was rated at 4.07 on average, with a relatively higher mean and a standard deviation of 0.059, suggesting notable variation in the perceived impact of this factor. Education level received a mean rating of 3.52, revealing a somewhat diverse distribution of educational backgrounds, with a more significant standard deviation of 0.087, indicating varying levels of education among participants. Education holds significant empowering potential, warranting adequate education for women. Education facilitates the growth of women's character by immersing them in literature, interactions with peers and educators, and broader society. The dependence on the rural entrepreneurs on the access to information and intermediaries is relatively high. They need these middlemen to broadcast their products and services. Several authors, like Saxena [31] and Smallbone [32], have explained similar challenges. They also state communication and transport as a main hindrance to entrepreneurship.

Sen and Grace [34] consider the part that increased technology plays in the role of public libraries to contribute to community resilience, though not precisely in rural contexts. The constancy of a country's environment is very encouraging, enhancing the entrepreneurial career. Politics is a superior part of the environment. Various types of political efforts can hamper the way of entrepreneurship. Khanka [35] pointed out that security is an essential factor for entrepreneurship development. The analysis also highlights other factors such as corruption, access to electricity, market limitations, and proper planning, each associated with mean ratings and standard deviations that provide insights into the participants' experiences and perceptions. As per Lowergren M.[33], suggested that at the high school level, entrepreneurship study basics should be introduced in all Fields of study because all students may require such entrepreneurial competencies. The consistently present standard deviations indicate varying degrees of dispersion in the participants' responses, suggesting differing perspectives on these factors. This information is pivotal for understanding the nuanced nature of these variables and their potential influence on women entrepreneurs' performance.

**Table 2** Problems and challenges faced by of women entrepreneur's

| | Sample (n) | Mean | Std. Deviation |
|---|---|---|---|
| Marital status | 335 | 3.82 | 0.047 |
| Lack of start-up capital | 335 | 4.07 | 0.059 |
| Education level | 335 | 3.52 | 0.087 |
| Lack of pre-start-up training | 335 | 3.82 | 0.066 |
| Access to information | 335 | 3.84 | 0.067 |
| Corruption | 335 | 3.74 | 0.071 |
| Previous experience in entrepreneurship | 335 | 3.76 | 0.074 |
| Unfavourable Government Policies/lack of government support | 335 | 4.02 | 0.023 |
| Access to Electricity/expensive electricity rate | 335 | 3.83 | 0.049 |
| Complicated Business Registration | 335 | 3.88 | 0.052 |
| Access to ICT | 335 | 3.77 | 0.031 |
| Limited market | 335 | 3.92 | 0.041 |
| Access to water supply | 335 | 3.81 | 0.022 |
| Lack of proper planning | 335 | 3.96 | 0.032 |
| Location | 335 | 3.95 | 0.03 |

*Source* Analysis based on primary data

Analysis highlights crucial factors affecting the performance/ success of a woman entrepreneur (Table 3). Based on the provided mean scores and standard deviations, several key points emerge. Funding, with a mean of 3.89, stands out as a notably important factor, indicating its significance for entrepreneurial success. Other significant factors include idea generation, with a mean of 3.78, and training, with a mean value of 3.46, reinforcing the importance of innovation and continuous learning. Marketing, with a mean value of 3.45 and satisfaction mean of 3.32, also holds relevance, suggesting the role of effective promotion and personal fulfillment. Adaptation to the environment had a mean of 3.23, and scalability had a mean of 3.23, indicating the need for flexibility and growth potential. While the standard deviations are moderately high across all factors, indicating varying opinions, this compilation underscores the multifaceted nature of success for women entrepreneurs, encompassing factors ranging from strategic decisions to cultural alignment and technological integration.

**Table 3** Factors affecting the performance/success of a women entrepreneurs

| Statement | Mean | Std. Deviation |
|---|---|---|
| Idea | 3.78 | 2.96 |
| Chief Executive Officer decisions | 3.24 | 2.72 |
| Marketing | 3.45 | 2.91 |
| Funding | 3.89 | 3.08 |
| Evaluation culture | 3.12 | 2.61 |
| Adaptation to the Environment | 3.23 | 2.7 |
| Team work | 3.41 | 2.76 |
| Timing | 3.22 | 2.68 |
| Culture and values | 3.15 | 2.63 |
| Satisfaction | 3.32 | 2.82 |
| Training | 3.46 | 2.95 |
| Diversity | 3.17 | 2.65 |
| Scalability | 3.23 | 2.71 |
| Advisors | 3.25 | 2.69 |
| Digitalization | 3.31 | 2.81 |

*Source* Analysis based on primary data

## *4.1 Hypothesis Testing*

The summary of the model in the context of multiple regressions indicates a robust and positive correlation between the variables that act as independent factors influencing the efficacy of women entrepreneurs and the level of customer satisfaction. (Table 4).

This connection is supported by a statistically significant correlation coefficient (R) of 0.874, at a significance level 0.05. The study highlights a range of factors that impact women entrepreneurs, encompassing challenges like insufficient initial capital, bureaucratic hurdles from the government, inadequate preparatory

**Table 4** Summary of the Model (Factors affecting the performance/ success of woman entrepreneurs)

| Model Summary[b] | | | | | | | | | |
|---|---|---|---|---|---|---|---|---|---|
| **Model** | **R** | **R Square** | **Adjusted R Square** | **Std.Error of the estimate** | **Change Statistics R Square Charge** | **F Change** | **df1** | **df2** | **Sig.F Change** |
| 1 | 0.874* | 0.853 | 0.852 | 0.18325 | 0.874 | 642.325 | 7 | 349 | 0.000 |

*Source* Analysis based on primary data
* signifies a statistically significant result ($p < 0.05$)

training, difficulties in securing bank loans, instances of corruption, complications in procuring production equipment, unfavorable governmental policies, restricted access to affordable electricity, intricate business registration procedures, limited reach of information and communication technology (ICT), constrained market scope, insufficient access to water supply, inadequate planning, and disadvantageous business location.

The reliant variable, which signifies the issues confronted by women entrepreneurs, is reasonably explained by these autonomous factors, indicating an R square value of 0.853. This signifies that a substantial 85.3% of the variations in the predicaments faced by women entrepreneurs can be attributed to the performance of their enterprises. Consequently, 85.3% of potential alterations in the extent to which these factors influence women entrepreneurs' performance are interrelated with the challenges they come across.

The model summary demonstrates a robust and positive correlation between the problems faced by rural women entrepreneurs and their performance. This correlation is supported by a statistically significant correlation coefficient (R) of 0.874 at a significance level 0.05.

The R-square value of 0.853 indicates that approximately 85.3% of the variations in the challenges faced by women entrepreneurs can be attributed to the independent variables, underscoring a solid relationship.

An ANOVA (Independent variables as predictors to factors affecting the performance of women entrepreneurs. Table 5. shows The ANOVA analysis indicates (Table. 6) the problems faced by rural women entrepreneurs and their performance. This is supported by a significant F-value of 784.310 and a P-value less than 0.05 ($P = 0$), signifying that there is a notable impact on the factors affecting the performance of women entrepreneurs.

The coefficients of the independent variables display a positive direction and possess statistical significance at a level of $P < 0.05$. These findings suggest that specific variables related to service quality, including factors like location ($B = 0.437$, $P = 0.000$), successful acquisition of a bank loan ($B = 0.827$, $P = 0.000$), limited market access ($B = 0.389$, $P = 0.012$), and unfavorable governmental policies ($B = 0.275$, $P = 0.02$), exert a positive and noteworthy influence on the performance of women entrepreneurs. The ANOVA analysis reveals that the influence of independent variables on problems faced by rural women entrepreneurs' satisfaction is statistically significant. This is substantiated by a significant F-value of 784.310 and a p-value

**Table 5** ANOVA Test

| ANOVA* | | | | | | |
|---|---|---|---|---|---|---|
| **Model** | | **Sum of Squares** | **df** | **Mean Square** | **F** | **Sig** |
| 1 | Regression | 158.134 | 8 | 37.253 | 784.310 | 0.000 |
| | Residual | 7.652 | 287 | 0.41 | | |
| | Total | 172.122 | 334 | | | |

*Source* Analysis based on primary data

**Table 6** Factors influencing entrepreneurial success

| Model | Unstandardized Coefficients | | Unstandardized Coefficients | | |
|---|---|---|---|---|---|
| | B | Std. Error | Beta | T | Sig |
| (Constant) | 0.784 | 0.049 | | 16.208 | 0 |
| Lack of start-up capital | 0.662 | 0.131 | 0.391 | 1.246 | 0.218 |
| Too much Government Bureaucracy | 0.019 | 0.129 | 0.318 | 1.344 | 0.149 |
| Lack of pre-start-up training | 0.196 | 0.125 | 0.112 | 4.128 | 0.54 |
| Getting a Bank loan | 0.827 | 0.118 | 1.048 | 4.715 | 0.00 |
| Corruption | 0.34 | 0.164 | 0.741 | -3.588 | 0.028 |
| Finding equipment for production | -0.297 | 0.133 | 0.337 | 2.711 | 0.106 |
| Unfavourable Government Policies | 0.275 | 0.128 | 0.381 | 1.599 | 0.002 |
| Access to Electricity/ expensive electricity rate | 0.312 | 0.147 | 0.214 | 2.384 | 0.311 |
| Complicated Business Registration | 0.416 | 0.173 | 0.29 | 3.898 | 0.358 |
| Access to ICT | 0.296 | 0.122 | 0.551 | 1.487 | 0 .168 |
| Limited market | 0.389 | 0.047 | 0.177 | 2.415 | 0.12 |
| Access to water supply | 0.25 | 0.158 | 0.322 | 2.804 | 0.254 |
| Lack of proper planning | 0.38 | 0.114 | 0.274 | 3.149 | 0.287 |
| Location | 0.437 | 0.184 | 0.612 | 6.276 | 0.00 |

*Source* Analysis based on primary data

of 0, signifying that at least one of the predictor variables significantly impacts the factors affecting women entrepreneurs' performance.

Among these variables, the most substantial standardized coefficient (Beta) corresponds to "responsiveness," with a value of 1.048. Furthermore, this variable demonstrates the highest t-statistic (4.128) and a significant p-value of 0.00. These outcomes suggest that an increase of one standard deviation in responsiveness is connected with an unstandardized effect of 0.807 on performance.

The regression analysis reveals important insights into the factors influencing entrepreneurial success. The model indicates that several variables exhibit statistically significant relationships with entrepreneurial outcomes. Table 6 illustrates that the need for start-up capital shows a positive coefficient (B = 0.662, p = 0.218), albeit not statistically significant, suggesting that insufficient funding might hinder success. Meanwhile, government bureaucracy (B = 0.019, p = 0.149) and corruption (B = 0.34, p = 0.028) demonstrate positive relationships with entrepreneurial success, with the latter showing a negative impact. Corrupt practices can lead to unfair competition and operational challenges, availability of pre-start-up training (B = 0.196, p = 0.54) and acquiring a bank loan (B = 0.827, p < 0.001) have positive effects on entrepreneurial success, implying that proper training and financial support play crucial roles. Surprisingly, unfavorable government policies (B = 0.275, p = 0.002) and complicated business registration processes (B = 0.416, p = 0.358) exhibit positive relationships, indicating unexpected effects. Limited market access (B = 0.389, p = 0.12) and lack of proper planning (B = 0.38, p = 0.287) also show positive associations with success. Additionally, the location stands out with a significant positive influence on entrepreneurial outcomes (B = 0.437, p < 0.001). The other variables, such as access to electricity, access to ICT, access to water supply, and finding equipment for production, display varying degrees of influence, although not all are statistically significant. The findings underscore the multifaceted nature of entrepreneurial success and suggest avenues for further research and policy interventions to foster a conducive environment for entrepreneurs. The analysis supports the alternative hypothesis H1, indicating a significant relationship between the independent variables and the factors affecting the performance of women entrepreneurs in India. This research provides valuable insights into the complex dynamics of women's entrepreneurship in the Indian context and highlights key factors that influence their success.

## 4.2 *Limitation of Study*

This study on women's entrepreneurship in India has important insights, but it has several limitations. It used convenience sampling, potentially introducing bias. The sample size may not represent the diversity of women entrepreneurs in India. Self-administered questionnaires may result in response bias. Cross-sectional data offers only a snapshot, possibly missing long-term effects. It may not account for all variables influencing success or regional variations in India. Changes over time and transferability to other contexts are concerns. Qualitative analysis could provide deeper insights. Finally, recall and social desirability bias should be considered. Despite these limitations, the study contributes to understanding women's entrepreneurship in India and informs future research and policy development.

## 5 Conclusion

This research paper presents an exploration of women's entrepreneurship in India, contributing novel insights to the current understanding of this dynamic field. The study's unique aspects include examining the present status of women's entrepreneurship in India and a comparative analysis that contextualizes this status within the global landscape. The overarching aim of this research is to shed light on the burgeoning success of women entrepreneurs, which is attributed to their inherent traits, aspirations, and contributions to economic growth. Recognizing the substantial role played by women in driving economic development, this study seeks to dissect the intricate web of variables that underlie their success in the Indian context. Employing a methodology grounded in convenience sampling, this study utilizes a quantitative descriptive approach. Data is collected through self-administered questionnaires distributed to 335 women entrepreneurs in Vidarbha, India. The analysis employs a combination of descriptive, reliability, validity, and ANOVA techniques to derive meaningful insights.

The analysis supports the alternative hypothesis H1, indicating a significant relationship between the independent variables and the factors affecting the performance of women entrepreneurs in India. This research provides valuable insights into the complex dynamics of women's entrepreneurship in the Indian context and highlights key factors that influence their success. Overall, your hypothesis testing analysis is well-written and informative, making it a valuable resource for understanding the research findings related to women's entrepreneurship in India. The results of the investigation results underscore the vital contribution of a range of factors in molding the effectiveness of women entrepreneurs. Aspects including educational attainment, previous entrepreneurial background, business training, capital accessibility, comprehension of business operations, government backing, and ownership of assets stand out as crucial determinants of performance. In contrast, variables like age, marital status, market entry, and physical infrastructure exert only a modest impact on the degree of success achieved by women entrepreneurs.

Detailed analyses, summarized in tables, provide a nuanced understanding of participants' perceptions and experiences across various influencing factors. These insights range from age distribution to the significance of factors like lack of start-up capital, education level, and market accessibility, showcasing diverse perspectives among respondents. Moreover, the study delves into key success factors for women entrepreneurs, highlighting factors such as funding, idea generation, training, marketing, and satisfaction, among others. The presented analysis underscores the multifaceted nature of entrepreneurial success, where a balance of factors ranging from strategic decision-making to cultural alignment and technological integration is crucial. The analysis also provides insights into the specific variables that have a significant impact on the performance of women entrepreneurs in India. This information can be valuable for policymakers, organizations, and researchers interested in supporting and promoting women's entrepreneurship.

Furthermore, the research employs regression analysis to uncover the intricate relationships between independent variables and entrepreneurial success. The analysis underscores the significance of government bureaucracy, pre-start-up training, bank loan accessibility, and more, highlighting their complex interplay in determining entrepreneurial outcomes.

This research enriches the understanding of women's entrepreneurship in India by providing a comprehensive overview of current conditions and a meticulous analysis of success-driving factors. As women continue to be key drivers of economic growth, the insights derived from this study can inform policies and strategies to nurture a conducive environment for women entrepreneurs.

## References

1. Reynolds, P.D., Hay, M., Bygrave, W.D., Camp, S.M., and Autio, E.: Global Entrepreneurship Monitor 2000 Executive Report, Babson Park, MA and London, UK, Babson College and London Business School (2000).
2. Ogundana, M., Simba, A., Dana,L., Liguori,E.:Women entrepreneurship in developing economies: A gender-based growth model. J. Small BusinessManagement **122**, 59 -70 (2021)
3. Minniti, M.,Naudé, W.:What do we know about the patterns and determinants of female entrepreneurship across countries? European. J. Dev. **22**, 277–293 (2010)
4. Sarker, S., Palit, M.: Determinants of success factors of women entrepreneurs in Bangladesh-A study based on Khulna region. Business Economic. Research **4**, 237 (2014)
5. Nsengimana, S., Tengeh, R. K., Iwu, C. G.:The sustainability of businesses in Kigali, Rwanda: an analysis of the barriers faced by women entrepreneurs. Sustainability 91372 (2017).
6. Box, M., Segerlind, T.: Entrepreneurial teams, gender, and new venture survival:contextsand institutions. SAGE Open **8**, 215824401877702 (2018)
7. Brush, C., Hisrich, R.D.: Women-owned businesses: Why do they matter? In: Acs, Z.J. (ed.) Are Small Firms Important? Their Role and Impact: Boston, pp. 111–127. Kluwer Academic Publisher, MA (1999)
8. Franco, A., Winqvist, K.:The entrepreneurial gap between women and men. Brussells: Eurostat: Statistics in Focus (2002)
9. Reynolds, P.D., White, S.B.: The Entrepreneurial Process: Economic Growth, Men, Women, and Minorities. Quorum Books, Westport, Connecticut (1997)
10. Kyalo, M. E.: Factors influencing performance of women entrepreneurs in Kenya: A case of bungoma south. A Research Report Submitted in Partial Fulfillment of the Requirement for the Award of Master of Arts Degree in Project Planning and Management of University Of Nairobi, Kenya. (2016).
11. Jha, P., Makkad, M., Mittal, S.: Performance-oriented factors for women entrepreneurs—A scale development perspective. J. Entrep. Emerg. Econ. **10**(2), 329–360 (2018)
12. Nasri, N., Muhammad, S.: Factors affecting female entrepreneurial intentions in Kabul, Afghanistan. J. Entrep. Emerg. Econ. **1**(1), 22–34 (2018)
13. Ecevit, Y: Research on Small Business Owners Women Entrepreneurs .The report prepared for the General Directorate of the Status of Women and Their Problems, 8–17(1996)
14. Celebi N.:Women Entrepreneurs in Small Business in Tourism Marketing: and Their Encouragement. Turkish Republic The Prime Minister for Women's Status and Problems Head Office.Ankara Turkey, 9–20(1997)
15. Ufuk, H., Ozgen, O.: The Profile of Women Entrepreneurs: A Sample FromTurkey". Int. J. Consum. Stud. **25**(4), 299–308 (2001)

16. Yetim N, Tatlıdil E.: Social and Cultural Dynamics of Women Entrepreneurs: The Case of Small and Medium-Size Clothing in Adana and Mersin enterprises Turkey, 491–507 (2004).
17. Verbakel, E., De Graaf, P.M.: Partner effects on labour market participation and job level: Opposing mechanisms. Work Employ Soc. **23**(4), 635–654 (2009)
18. Sweida G.:The Woman Entrepreneur's Paradox: Entrepreneurial Intention, Entrepreneurial Self-efficacy, and Behavior. PhD dissertation, The Claremont Graduate University, Claremont, CA(.2018)
19. Schlaegel, C., Koenig, M.: Determinants of entrepreneurial intent: a meta-analytic test and integration of competing models. Entrep. Theory. Pract. **38**, 291–332 (2014)
20. Ramanujam, K., Thenmozhi, R.:Empowerment of women.Kison world, 62–75(2006).
21. Rwanda.: Access to Finance. Statistics-publication, National Institute of statistics,Vol. 2 (2012).
22. Blaire.:Rwanda gender gap,Banks must stop failing female entrepreneurs,189–208(2015).
23. Aparicio M, Sebastian, David U, David A.:Institutional factors, opportunity entrepreneurship and economic growth Panel data evidence. Technol. Forecast. Soc. Chang., 45–61(2016).
24. Fairlie, R.W., Kapur, K., Gates, S.: Is employer-based health insurance a barrier to entrepreneurship? J. Health Econ. **30**(1), 146–162 (2011)
25. Shiller, R.J.: Narrative economics. American Economic Review **107**(4), 967–1004 (2017)
26. Straka, M., Oláh, J., Kassakorn, N.: Impact of Green Supply Chain Integration on SMEs Technological and Economic Performance. Global Journal of Entrepreneurship and Management **2**(1), 12–30 (2021)
27. Bruhn, M., Mckenzie, D.: Entry regulation and formalization of microenterprises in developing countries. The World Bank Research Observer **29**(2), 186–201 (2014)
28. Venkataraman, S.: The distinctive domain of entrepreneurship research. In: Katz, J., Brockhaus, R. (eds.), Advance in entrepreneurship, firm emergence, and growth Vol. 3, (1997)
29. Welter, F., Baker, T., Wirsching, K.: Three waves and counting: The rising tide of contextualization in entrepreneurship research. Small Bus. Econ. **52**(2), 319–330 (2019)
30. O'Neill, H.: Turnaround and recovery: What strategy do you need. Long Range Plan. **19**(1), 80–88 (1986)
31. Saxena, S.: Problems Faced by Rural Entrepreneurs and Remedies to Solve. J.Of Bus. Manag. **3**(1), 23–29 (2012)
32. Smallbone,D.: Fostering entrepreneurship in rural areas. In: Potter, J., Hofer, A.R. (eds.), Strengthening entrepreneurship and economic development in East Germany: lessons from local approaches, pp. 161–187 (2009)
33. Lowergren,M.: Entrepreneurship Education:Developing Project-based learning. National Council for Graduate Entrepreneurship, (2006).
34. Sen, A., Grace, D.: Community Resilience and the Role of the Public Library. Libr. Trends **61**(3), 513–541 (2013)
35. Khanka,S.:Entrepreneurial Development.10th Indian Reprint, New Delhi: S. Chand and Company Ltd.(2009).

# Transgender Entrepreneurs: An Alternative Path to Social Integration

**Gnana Sanga Mithra S, Aravind B. R, Bhuvaneswari G, Suriya S, Sathish R, and Edhaya Chandran E**

**Abstract** This study aims to assess the contribution of skills to entrepreneurial intentions among transgender people who help them integrate into society. A quantitative method was used to collect data from 132 transgender people using a semi-structured interview schedule. The present study tries to understand the development of transgender individuals through entrepreneurship, which will help them to integrate into mainstream society. Regression and correlation analyses were used to determine the determinants of entrepreneurial opportunities among transgender entrepreneurs in Tamil Nadu. Based on the skill set and nature of business, it is concluded that there are significant differences in influencing factors for trans-entrepreneurship, such as experience, personal, family, economic, employment, and market factors, because their regression coefficient is significant. The study only included male-to-female transgender people and was limited to Tamil Nadu. More research is required before these conclusions can be drawn from other settings and circumstances.

**Keywords** Transgender entrepreneurs · Skills · Economic development

G. S. M. S (✉)
Vinayaka Mission's Law School, Vinayaka Mission's Research Foundation (DU), Chennai, India
e-mail: sangamithra0212@gmail.com

A. B. R
School of Liberal Arts and Special Education (SLASE), Kalasalingam Academy of Research and Education, Krishnankoil, India

B. G
School of Social Sciences and Languages (SSL), Vellore Institute of Technology, Chennai, India

S. S
PG Department of Development Studies, Madras School of Social Work, Chennai, India

S. R
Department of Commerce, Academy of Maritime Education and Training (DU), Chennai, India

E. C. E
Vinayaka Mission's Law School, Vinayaka Mission's Research Foundation (DU), Chennai, India



S. Kot et al. (eds.), *Corporate Practices: Policies, Methodologies, and Insights in Organizational Management*, Springer Proceedings in Business and Economics,
https://doi.org/10.1007/978-981-97-0996-0_10

## 1 Introduction

In his reference work Sexual Hygiene and Pathology, Psychiatrist John F. Oliven of Columbia University coined Transgender in 1965. Transgender people are shrouded in the mystery community. This disastrous community is forced to live on the outskirts of society, feared and despised, never loved and welcomed. Outsiders are not permitted to inquire about their personal lives. They live more like bonded laborers than free democratic citizens of the country. When they enter this lifestyle, they are entangled in a web of deception and abuse at every turn. For many years, the Indian Census has not recognized the third gender. Only in 2011 did the Census Department collect data on transgender people for employment, literacy, and caste, but they were lumped in with men. There is some evidence that the transgender population is growing. Both the Central and State Ministries of Law and Social Justice must recognize the plight of transgender people. It is strange to realize that the public calls these sexual minorities derogatory names, does not recognize them for being trapped in the wrong gender and has always kept them at a distance. Despite some recognition and social acceptance, they are still looked down upon not only in Indian societies but also globally. Formal legislation must be passed to transform a social changeover with acceptance, respect, and dignity.

"The nation (India) closed two-thirds of its overall gender gap (66.8% in the ranking," according to the report. However, the situation of women on the outskirts of Indian society is precarious. Despite a slight performance improvement, it has dropped four positions since the previous edition, as countries rated lower than India have gained ground. "The significant gender gap in India is attributed to religious and historical cultures. Compared to other countries, the mechanism is much slower due to prevailing perceptions within Indian societal culture".

Nowadays, more middle-class women are stepping forward to launch businesses and contribute to the Indian economy. However, economic empowerment for women is not a single entity, and its lifeblood is drawn from various sources within our social structure, such as caste, class, faith, and regional compulsions. Thus, economic empowerment for women results from these forces interacting with one another. "The Global Gender Gap Report (2019) of the World Economic Forum placed India in 112th position in the Global Gender Gap Index 2020 among 153 economies. India had come down four stages in the ranking from the 108th position in 2018, appointing the widening gender gap".

Transgender studies have recently received increased attention from researchers. Transgender studies are now concentrating on interdisciplinary fields, incorporating discourses from the social sciences, life sciences, arts, and psychology. Such intertwined studies have aided in the interpretation of gender, identity, and desire in a variety of contexts [1]. The current study investigates the entrepreneurial challenges transgender entrepreneurs face for intrinsic value on knowledge of the transgender community and sound economic reasons. Because of the phenomenon's complexity, the best method of examining the challenges faced by the transgender entrepreneur appears to be the grounded theory method, which facilitates the collection of realities and the extraction of the entrepreneurial challenges faced by transgender entrepreneurs.

## 2 Literature Review

Entrepreneurs face numerous challenges when starting a business, including an unstable bureaucratic environment, poor economic conditions, and complicated rules and regulations [1]. Transgender entrepreneurs are an under-researched and marginalized group within entrepreneurship research [2]. Entrepreneurs face similar challenges in all developing countries, such as business laws, and small businesses are difficult to assess because contract and property assets are poorly designed, poor infrastructure, limited access to financial capital, corruption, poor economic policies, limited financial opportunities, and a lack of managerial skills [3]. It has been over thirty years since literature about women entrepreneurship has been in print [3], and women entrepreneurs are regarded as valuable assets to the country, employing 40% of the workforce [4].

Women entrepreneurs have been breaking the "glass ceiling" for many years and paved their way in a male-dominated society, proving successful [4]. Gender was a primary hurdle that women entrepreneurs encountered, and there is a significant gender disparity in the choosing of entrepreneurship as a vocation between men and women [5]. Other hurdles include bias, working capital, insufficient confidence, marketing, mistrust of lenders, mistrust of family support, collateral security, ignorance, and procedures related to the law [5]. India has long been known as a diverse country that welcomes all the world's cultures and traditions. However, due to a lack of information on gender nonconforming people, the Families of transgender people have flatly refused to disown their children for defying gender norms that are laid down by society [6]. When there is a difference between the person's sex and when an individual's gender role is defined, the individual is referred to as a Eunuch, and they are now referred to as transgender people. Transgender people face a slew of obstacles in their lives, the majority of which are physical and legal [6]. They also face disrespect, discrimination, being downtrodden, being forced to leave their parents, child catching, human trafficking, unwanted attention, rape abuse, verbal abuse, physical abuse, no identity proof, low economic status, poor housing, no property ownership, and a lack of education.

When compared to cisgender people, transgender people have a significant increase in health disparities. A transgender individual's main occupation is begging and commercial sex work, and even if the transgender individual finds other means of employment, they continue to engage in commercial sex work [6]. Transgender women do not like to engage in employment opportunities due to discrimination and exploitation. Most transgender people are unhappy with their current living situation and suffer from a variety of psychological issues, such as depression and low self-esteem [7]. Post-Traumatic Stress Disorder (PTSD), Major Depressive Episode (MDE), Obsessive–Compulsive Disorder (OCD), panic disorders, and suicidal tendencies. Despite the trauma and abuse that transgender people have experienced, some sporadic transgender people have taken up self-employment and become entrepreneurs [8]. As a result, it is critical to understand the difficulties that a transgender person faces when pursuing entrepreneurship as a career.

## 3 Data and Method

The current study took a descriptive research approach to examine the factors that contribute to transgender empowerment through entrepreneurship. Descriptive research is acceptable because participants are observed in their natural environment, resulting in accurate and trustworthy data. It also attempts to describe how behavior occurs. "[9] defines target population as any group of people who share one or more characteristics in which the researcher is interested." "This group includes respondents of various ages, marital status, place of residence, educational levels, occupations, and income levels. The population chosen is sufficiently representative to answer the research questions." According to [10], sampling size refers to the number of elements included in the study. "The current study employs non-probability sampling techniques." The study of transgender entrepreneurs in Tamil Nadu employs convenient sampling. For an infinite population, the sample size is fixed at 132. A web-based and paper-based survey was used to collect data. A web-based survey was chosen because it was the most acceptable medium for contacting the survey's target demographic. It is the most cost-effective data collection method for the study, and it also allows respondents to complete the survey at their convenience. Previous web-based surveys have had a significant impact on the survey process. Unlike other types of surveys, web-page design skills and computer programming experience are critical in creating Web-based surveys [10]. Web-based surveys can be used to check for errors or omissions in responses so that they can be corrected quickly and accurately. In addition, a paper-based survey was conducted to collect data for the study.

- Hypothesis 1: A positive relationship exists between education and increased transgender participation in communication and decision-making.
- Hypothesis 2: Empowerment helps in accelerating entrepreneurial skills leading transgender self-development.
- Hypothesis 3: New Media has created a positive impact on Transgender's career development.

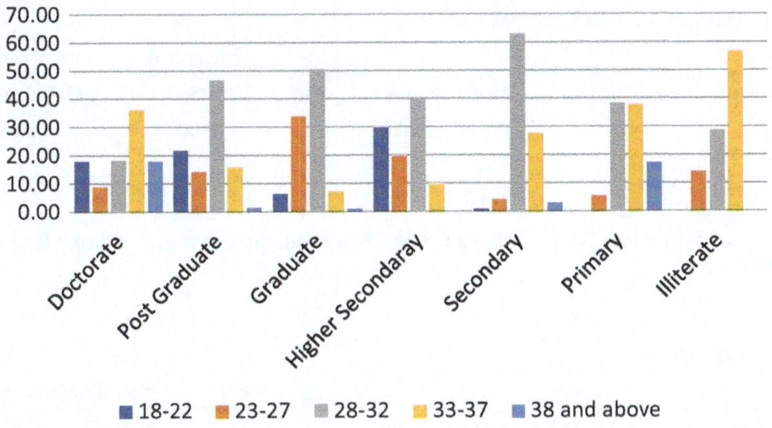


**Fig. 1** Educational status of the respondents

# 4 Results

## *4.1 Empirical Analysis*

The findings revealed that the respondents are classified into five age groups: 18–22 years; 23–27 years; 28–32 years; 33–37 years, and above 38 years. Based on their age group, their educational status is categorized as a doctorate, postgraduate, graduate, higher secondary, secondary, primary, and illiterate. The analysis shows that women in the age group of 28–32 constitute 49.32% of the respondents. Women above the age group of 38 form the least 3.10%. In the age group of 18–22, 18% of them are doctorates, 22% of them are postgraduates, 6.64% of them are graduates, 30% of them have completed higher secondary education and 1.12% of them have completed primary education. There was no illiterate in the age category. More respondents are graduates in the category of 23–27 (34.07%) and 28–32 (50.44%) (Fig. 1).

## *4.2 Wilcoxon Signed Ranks Test*

In the Wilcoxon Signed Ranks Test shown above, since the P value is less than 0.01, the null hypothesis is rejected at a 1% level of significance [11]. The results prove a positive relationship between empowerment and increased participation of women in communication and decision-making. Such participation has ultimately led to a gendered impact on policymaking (Table 1).

The correlation coefficient to the assistance by empowerment in accelerating entrepreneurial skills leading to women's self-development is 0.719. It indicates

**Table 1** Transgender's decision-making

| | | N | Mean rank | Sum of ranks |
|---|---|---|---|---|
| Decision making—Education | Negative ranks | 132[a] | 258.50 | 133,386.00 |
| | Positive ranks | 0[b] | 0.00 | 0.00 |
| | Ties | 0[c] | | |
| | Total | 132 | | |

a. Pain Score Post < Pain Score Pre b. Pain Score Post > Pain Score Pre c. Pain Score Post = Pain Score Pre

**Table 2** Correlation

| | | New media | Self development |
|---|---|---|---|
| New media | Karl-Pearson Correlation | 1 | 0.719** |
| | Sig. (2-tailed) | | 0.000 |
| | N | 132 | 132 |
| Self-development | Karl-Pearson Correlation | 0.719** | 1 |
| | Sig. (2-tailed) | 0.000 | |
| | N | 132 | 132 |

**. Correlation is significant at the 0.01 level (2-tailed)

a 71% positive relationship between the assistance by education in accelerating the entrepreneurial skills leading to self-development of women and the help by education in accelerating the entrepreneurial effort on coordination and is significant at a 1% level. It is concluded that education helps in accelerating entrepreneurial skills leading to the self-development of Transgender [12] (Table 2).

The following conceptual framework explains the entire process of transgender empowerment through education, awareness, and enhancing entrepreneurial skills: The age and educational qualifications of the respondents are expected to have a significant impact on the empowerment process. Demographic factors influence tool use as well. The purpose of accessing information, the type of information, and the time utility all influence the process's outcome. Education-acquired knowledge and skills can provide material benefit, cognitive change, perception change, relational change, and technical competency [13]. These factors are most likely to facilitate empowerment. As a result, this study analyses data along these conceptual framework lines.

### *4.3 Occupation and Income*

An occupational discrepancy has a substantial effect on an individual's socioeconomic stand-up, which is connected to their capability to admittance resources such as seeking a job, purchasing a home, and so on. It may be more difficult for an individual to find work, advance in their career, obtain a loan, or purchase a home if they are experiencing occupational disparity. "Occupational status can predict outcomes such as social position and money, both of which have long-term consequences for the individual and their dependants". The labour force is highly segregated by gender, which explains why there are still so many gaps and inequities between men and women with comparable degrees. Gender-based inequality is characterized by a division of work. It has an impact on the structure both in terms of economics and identity creation [14]. Studies demonstrate, however, that the total picture of gender and labour has not been analysed. The significance of these challenges is critical to the future structure of our workforce.

It is inferred from Table 4.4 that the respondents from different occupational categories have been classified under different income groups. Out of 516 respondents, only one person is from the automobile industry and another is a doctor. They fall under the income group of Rs.11000 -25,000 and Rs.50001–75,000 respectively. Nearly 1.36% of the respondents run shops and online sales as well. They fall under four income groups: Rs.25001–50,000, Rs.50001–75,000, Rs.75001–1,00,000 and above Rs.1,00,000 constituting 0.73%, 2.02%, 1.10% and 3.19% respectively. About 13.20% of the employees are company workers out of which 11.83% earn about Rs.11000–25,000 annually. The respondents whose monthly income falls under the category of Rs. 25,001 to 50,000 are 2.19%. The respondents who earn above Rs 1 lakh are 28.72%. The categories of respondents who are in the income brackets of Rs 50,001–75,000 and of Rs 75,001–1 Lakh are 12.12% and 16.3% respectively. As discussed above, there is only one doctor-respondent and her income falls under the category of Rs 50,001–75,000. The number of respondents who are doing full time business is 12 and among them 2.15% earn about Rs 11,000–25,000; 6.06% come under Rs 50,001–75,000; 3.26% earn Rs 75,001–1 lakh; and only 1.6% falls under above 1 lakh category. The respondents who work as Government employees are 3.3% out of which nearly 8.51% earn more than Rs 1 lakh. The income categories of Rs 11,000 - 25,000 and of Rs 75,001–1 lakh are 3.23%. Only 1.4% of them come under the category of Rs. 25,001 to 50,000 (Table 3).

Private employees constitute about 3.88% of the total respondents, out of which 0.73% earn Rs 25,001–50,000, 3.03% earn Rs 50,001–75,000, 10.87% earn Rs 75,001–1 lakh and 6.38% earn more than 1 lakh. Students constitute about 13.79% of the total respondents. By using New Media, they also earn income under the category of Rs 11,000–25,000, there are about 25.43% of the students and in the next 4 categories, their shares are about 35.04%, 2.02%, 1.09% and 1.06% respectively. Finally, teachers also took part as respondents of this research and 1.01% of them fall under the category of Rs 50,001–75,000.

The findings of the survey revealed that transgender entrepreneurship in Chennai has had a positive impact on the lives of transgender individuals. The majority of respondents (67.4%) reported that entrepreneurship had provided them with an alternative source of income, which was not based on sex work or begging. This has helped them to gain financial independence and improve their standard of living. Transgender entrepreneurship has also helped to challenge the negative stereotypes

**Table 3** Income level

| | 11,000–25,000 | | 25,001–50,000 | | 50,001–75,000 | | 75,001–100,000 | | Above 100,000 | | |
|---|---|---|---|---|---|---|---|---|---|---|---|
| Occupation | N | % | N | % | N | % | N | % | N | N | % |
| Automobile Industry | 1 | 1.08 | 0 | 0 | 0 | 0 | 0 | 0 | 0 | 0 | 0.19 |
| Both Online & Physical store | 0 | 0 | 1 | 0.73 | 2 | 2.02 | 1 | 1.10 | 3 | 3.19 | 1.36 |
| Company Worker | 11 | 11.83 | 3 | 2.19 | 2 | 12.1 | 15 | 16.3 | 27 | 28.7 | 13.2 |
| Doctor | 0 | 0 | 0 | 0 | 1 | 1.01 | 0 | 0 | 0 | 0 | 0.19 |
| Full time Business | 2 | 2.15 | 0 | 0 | 6 | 6.06 | 3 | 3.26 | 1 | 1.06 | 2.33 |
| Government Employee | 3 | 3.23 | 2 | 1.46 | 1 | 1.01 | 3 | 3.26 | 8 | 8.51 | 3.30 |
| Home-maker | 21 | 22.58 | 47 | 34.31 | 6 | 26.2 | 27 | 29.3 | 22 | 23.4 | 27.7 |
| Online Business | 2 | 215 | 3 | 2.19 | 0 | 10.1 | 5 | 5.43 | 9 | 9.57 | 5.63 |
| Own Business | 15 | 16.13 | 6 | 4.38 | 0 | 10.1 | 0 | 0 | 5 | 5.32 | 6.99 |
| Part-time Business | 19 | 20.43 | 26 | 18.98 | 5 | 25.2 | 26 | 28.2 | 12 | 12.7 | 20.9 |
| PrivateEmployee | 0 | 0 | 1 | 0.73 | 3 | 3.03 | 10 | 10.8 | 6 | 6.38 | 3.88 |
| Student | 19 | 20.43 | 48 | 35.04 | 2 | 2.02 | 1 | 1.09 | 1 | 1.06 | 13.7 |
| Teacher | 0 | 0 | 0 | 0 | 2 | 1.01 | 1 | 1.09 | 0 | 0 | 0.39 |
| Total | 93 | 100 | 33 | 100 | 0 | 100 | 92 | 100 | 94 | 100 | 100 |

associated with transgender individuals [15]. The respondents reported that their businesses had received positive responses from the community, which had helped to break down barriers and promote acceptance. However, the survey also revealed that transgender entrepreneurs in Chennai face several challenges. The most common challenge reported by the respondents was discrimination and stigma. Many respondents reported that they had faced discrimination in the job market, which had forced them to turn to entrepreneurship as a means of income. Others reported that they had faced discrimination from customers or landlords, which had made it difficult to start or run their businesses. Another challenge reported by the respondents was a lack of access to resources and support [16]. Many respondents reported that they had not received any support or training to start their businesses, which had made it difficult to manage their finances or market their products or services.

## 5 Impact of Entrepreneurship on Transgender Entrepreneurs

The survey revealed that entrepreneurship had a positive impact on the lives of transgender entrepreneurs in Chennai. The majority of respondents (82.6%) reported that entrepreneurship had helped them to gain financial independence and improve their standard of living. They reported that they were able to support themselves and their families without engaging in sex work or begging. Entrepreneurship had also helped to improve their self-esteem and self-confidence [16]. The respondents reported that they felt more respected and valued in society as entrepreneurs, which had helped to boost their self-esteem and confidence.

*Emergence of Transgender Entrepreneurship in South India*
In recent years, there has been a rise in transgender entrepreneurship in South India. This is due to various factors, including the increased awareness of transgender issues, the availability of funding and resources, and the support of NGOs and the government. One example of transgender entrepreneurship in South India is the Chennai-based transgender beauty salon, Shanthi Salon. The salon was started in 2014 by Shanthi, a transgender woman, with the help of a local NGO. Shanthi was able to secure funding and resources to start the salon, which has since become a popular destination for beauty services in Chennai. The salon employs transgender individuals who have been trained in beauty services. Another example of transgender entrepreneurship is the Bangalore-based café, Café Positive. The café was started in 2016 by a group of transgender individuals who were part of the Hijra community. The café offers a variety of food and beverages and provides employment opportunities for transgender individuals.

*Impact of Transgender Entrepreneurship on the Lives of Transgender Individuals*
Transgender entrepreneurship has had a positive impact on the lives of transgender individuals in South India. It has provided them with an alternative source of income, which is not based on sex work or begging. It has also allowed them to gain access

to education and training, which is necessary for starting and running a business. Transgender entrepreneurship has also helped to challenge the negative stereotypes associated with transgender individuals. It has shown that transgender individuals can run successful businesses and contribute to the economy.

*Policies and Initiatives to Promote Transgender Entrepreneurship in South India* The government and NGOs in South India have taken various initiatives to promote transgender entrepreneurship. One such initiative is the Tamil Nadu Transgender Welfare Board, established in 2008. The board provides financial assistance to transgender individuals who want to start their businesses. The board also provides training and education programs to help transgender individuals develop the necessary skills for starting and running a business. Another initiative is the Trans Empowerment Network, a Bangalore-based NGO that provides entrepreneurship training to transgender individuals [17]. The NGO offers a six-month training program that covers various aspects of starting and running a business, including marketing, finance, and operations.

## 5.1 Recommendations

i. Implement Inclusive Policies: Develop and implement policies that explicitly support transgender entrepreneurs, offering equal access to resources, funding, and business opportunities.
ii. Access to Financial Resources: Establish financial programs specifically tailored to the needs of transgender entrepreneurs, providing them with access to grants, loans, and venture capital.
iii. Educational and Skill Development Initiatives: Create skill development and business training programs targeted at transgender individuals, equipping them with the knowledge and skills needed to succeed as entrepreneurs.
iv. Mentorship and Networking Opportunities: Set up mentorship programs that connect transgender entrepreneurs with experienced business leaders and mentors who can provide guidance, advice, and industry insights.
v. Awareness Campaigns: Launch awareness campaigns to educate the general public about transgender issues, dispel myths, and reduce stigma.
vi. Collaboration with NGOs and Advocacy Groups: Partner with non-governmental organizations (NGOs) and transgender advocacy groups to ensure that policies and initiatives are aligned with the actual needs of the transgender community.
vii. Creating Safe Spaces: Establish safe and supportive physical spaces where transgender entrepreneurs can work, network, and collaborate without fear of discrimination or harassment.
viii. Government and Corporate Initiatives: Encourage government agencies and corporations to procure goods and services from transgender-owned businesses.

## 6 Conclusion

Transgender entrepreneurship has the potential to contribute to the economic growth and development of Chennai and should be encouraged and supported. By promoting and supporting transgender entrepreneurship, we can break down barriers and promote acceptance of transgender individuals in society [18]. This research article highlights the importance of creating a supportive environment for transgender entrepreneurs to thrive and succeed. In conclusion, the emergence of transgender entrepreneurs as a catalyst for social integration presents a promising alternative path toward a more inclusive and harmonious society in Chennai. As we navigate the complexities of modern life, it is increasingly evident that economic growth and societal progress are intertwined, and the promotion of transgender entrepreneurship stands as a testament to this synergy. The findings discussed in this research underscore the significance of fostering an environment that nurtures and supports transgender entrepreneurs [19]. Beyond their economic contributions, these individuals possess the power to dismantle the walls of prejudice and discrimination that have marginalized them for far too long. By recognizing their potential, extending a helping hand, and creating avenues for their entrepreneurial aspirations, we not only tap into a wellspring of innovative ideas but also pave the way for greater societal acceptance.

## References


1. Blei, D.M.: Probabilistic topic models. Commun. ACM **55**(4), 77–84 (2012). https://doi.org/10.1145/2133806.2133826
2. Brickell, C.: The sociological construction of gender and sexuality. Sociol. Rev. **54**(1), 87–113 (2006). https://doi.org/10.1111/j.1467-954X.2006.00603.x
3. Gnana Sanga Mithra, S., & Vijayalakshmi, V. (2019). Changing trends in socio-economic conditions of transgender in Chennai city. Int. J. Eng. Adv. Technol. **9**(1), 194–196. https://doi.org/10.35940/ijeat.A1116.109119.
4. Hjorth, D., & Steyaert, C.: Narrative and discursive approaches in entrepreneurship: A second movements in entrepreneurship book. Edward Elgar Publishing (2005) https://books.google.com/books?id=9-g4AgAAQBAJ
5. Alsos, A.G., Ljunggren, E., Hytti, U.: Gender and innovation: State of the art and a research agenda. Int. J. Gend. Entrep. **5**(3), 236–256 (2013). https://doi.org/10.1108/IJGE-06-2013-0049
6. Brush, C.G., De Bruin, A., Welter, F.: A gender-aware framework for women's entrepreneurship. Int. J. Gend. Entrep. **1**(1), 8–24 (2009). https://doi.org/10.1108/17566260910942318
7. Kelley, D. J., Singer, S., & Herrington, M. (2012). Global entrepreneurship monitor 2011 global report. Global Entrepreneurship Research Association, London Business School.
8. Moroz, P.W., Hindle, K.: Entrepreneurship as a process: Toward harmonizing multiple perspectives. Entrep. Theory Pract. **36**(4), 781–818 (2012). https://doi.org/10.1111/j.1540-6520.2011.00452.x
9. Calas, M. B., & Smircich, L.: 1.8 from the 'woman's point of view' ten years later: Towards a feminist organization studies. In S. R. Clegg, C. Hardy, T. Lawrence, & W. R. Nord (eds.) The Sage handbook of organization studies (pp. 284). SAGE Publications Inc. (2006) https://books.google.com/books?id=TuE0NRH2U7UC

10. E, E. C., & S, G. S. M.: Digital humanities and game ethics: Investigating the impact of representation in gaming. Stud. Media Commun. **11**(7), 159 (2023) https://doi.org/10.11114/smc.v11i7.6266
11. Jiartana, I. W., Riana, I. G., Wibawa, I. M. A., Surya, I. B. K.: Organisational citizenship behaviour in public service: integrating public service motivation and sense of community. Pol. J. Manag. Stud. **27** (1), (2023)
12. OECD/The European Commission. The missing entrepreneurs: Policies for inclusive entrepreneurship in Europe. OECD Publishing (2019) https://doi.org/10.1787/3ed84801-en
13. Pandey, T.: Women entrepreneurship in business trends; challenging issue for growth. IJRDO-J. Appl. Manag. Sci. **1**(10), 18–20 (2016). https://ijrdo.org/index.php/ams/article/view/2389/2037
14. Kisel'akova, D., Hairul, H., Gallo, P., Gallo, P., Cabinova, V., & Onuferova, E.: Total quality management as managerial competitiveness in enterprises worldwide. Pol. J. Manag. Stud. **21**(2), 195–209 (2020). https://doi.org/10.17512/pjms.2020.21.2.14
15. Setyaningsih, S., Czako, K.F., Vasic, T., Vasic, T., Kelle, P.: Crosss-analysis of supply chain management drivers for small and Medium-sized enterprisses. Polish Journal of Management Studies **23**(1), 352–369 (2021)
16. Papanikolaou, Y., Foulds, J. R., Rubin, T. N., Tsoumakas, G. Dense distributions from sparse samples: Improved gibbs sampling parameter estimators for LDA. J. Mach. Learn. Res. **18** 1–58 (2017). https://www.jmlr.org/papers/volume18/16-526/16-526.pdf
17. Mirchandani, K.: Feminist insight on gendered work: New directions in research on women and entrepreneurship. Gend. Work. Organ. **6**(4), 224–235 (1999). https://doi.org/10.1111/1468-0432.00085
18. Gnana Sanga Mithra, S., Vijayalaskmi, V.: A mathematical model for breaching the blockades-mainstreaming transwomen and transmen in Chennai by using block fuzzy cognitive. J. Interdiscip. Math. **25**(3), 827–838 (2022). DOI: https://doi.org/10.1080/09720502.2021.2015100
19. McMullen, J.S., Dimov, D.: Time and the entrepreneurial journey: The problems and promise of studying entrepreneurship as a process. J. Manage. Stud. **50**(8), 1481–1512 (2013). https://doi.org/10.1111/joms.12049

# Investigating the Role of Education 4.0 in the Performance of HEIs

D. Sri Dhivya, A. Hariharasudan, E. Balamurali, Zdzislawa Dacko-Pikiewicz, and Janusz Michałek

**Abstract** Integrating emerging technologies, such as artificial intelligence, big data, and the Internet of Things (IoT) into education is known as Education 4.0, revolutionizing Higher Education Institutions (HEIs). This transformation goes beyond the classroom and impacts the entire system, including student enrolment and retention. By adopting Education 4.0, institutions can improve their curriculum, teaching methods, and overall learning outcomes while increasing operational efficiency. However, this shift presents challenges, such as the need for institutions to reskill their workforce to keep up with the rapidly evolving technological landscape. This study aims to examine the effects of Education 4.0 on HEIs and assess its impact. The study's methodology examines the impact of Education 4.0 on HEIs through survey-based quantitative research. The study assesses the effectiveness of Education 4.0 in various areas, such as psychological readiness, innovative pedagogical approaches and engagement and motivation, digital literacy, and learning outcomes in teaching and learning. The study is unique in its focus on implementing Education 4.0 in HEIs. The methodology used in this study involved survey research design, and institutions were selected based on a random sampling technique. The data was collected among students, faculty, and administrators of HEIs in the southern region of Tamil Nadu, India, through a questionnaire and analyzed using descriptive statistics. The results indicate that Education 4.0 significantly improves many aspects of HEIs. However, the study's limitations highlight the need for further research to address gaps and expand on these findings.

D. S. Dhivya
Department of English, Kalasalingam Academy of Research and Education, Krishnankoil, India

A. Hariharasudan (✉)
Kalasalingam Academy of Research and Education, Krishnankoil, India
e-mail: dr.a.hariharasudhan@gmail.com

E. Balamurali
Department of Science and Humanities, Sri Krishna College of Engineering and Technology, Coimbatore, India

Z. Dacko-Pikiewicz · J. Michałek
WSB University, Dabrowa Górnicza, Poland



S. Kot et al. (eds.), *Corporate Practices: Policies, Methodologies, and Insights in Organizational Management*, Springer Proceedings in Business and Economics,
https://doi.org/10.1007/978-981-97-0996-0_11

**Keywords** Education 4.0 · Higher education institutions · Innovative methods · Psychological readiness

## 1 Introduction

The evolution of education has always been linked to technology and societal changes. With Education 4.0, we are at a turning point where digital tech, abundant information, and global demands reshape education. Education 4.0 aligns with the Fourth Industrial Revolution, blurring physical, digital, and biological boundaries, impacting industries, economies, and daily lives [1]. Education 4.0 is akin to Industry 4.0, leverages technology for adaptable, interconnected learning environments that transcend traditional boundaries [2]. It departs from standardized education, offering personalized, data-driven experiences [3]. This approach enhances critical skills, like critical thinking and digital literacy [4], fostering active learning and innovation [5]. In the age of Education 4.0, Higher Education Institutions (HEIs) hold a pivotal role in reshaping education and technology [6]. HEIs leverage global connectivity to attract diverse learners and educators through online courses and virtual classrooms, promoting cross-cultural understanding [7]. Education 4.0 offers HEIs numerous advantages, including streamlined administration, data-driven decision-making, AI-driven personalized learning, enhanced student engagement, and improved collaboration [8]. HEIs align their curricula with industry demands, enhancing graduates' employability and positioning them as dynamic leaders in the digital education landscape.

India's National Education Policy (NEP) 2020 aligns with Education 4.0 principles, emphasizing technology integration, personalized learning, and interdisciplinary approaches [9]. NEP 2020 focuses on building a robust digital infrastructure for online and blended learning, fostering collaboration between academia, industry, and research [10]. These initiatives enhance employability, drive innovation, and nurture entrepreneurship, reflecting Education 4.0's core principles [11]. NEP 2020 complements the industry integration emphasis of Education 4.0. In light of the increasing number of institutions embracing the principles of Education 4.0 within their academic frameworks, this study aims to delve into the tangible impact and effectiveness of Education 4.0 implementation in the light of psychological readiness, innovative pedagogical approach, engagement and motivation, digital literacy and learning outcomes, specifically within Higher Education institutions. Focusing on the southern region of Tamil Nadu, India, this research aims to comprehensively assess the extent to which Education 4.0 strategies have been integrated. By employing a survey method and random sampling techniques, this study provides a detailed understanding of how these institutions have embraced Education 4.0, shedding light on the challenges, successes, and overall outcomes among students, faculty, and administrators. The insights derived from this research contribute to the broader discourse on the transformation of higher education in the digital era.

## 2 Review of Literature

### 2.1 *Psychological Readiness*

A recent study underscores the significance of psychological readiness for Education 4.0 [12]. Students need adaptability, digital literacy, and self-directed learning skills to excel in a tech-driven educational landscape. Collaboration and communication competencies are vital for virtual teamwork [13]. Faculty must embrace technology, offer a student-centric approach, and cater to diverse learning styles [14]. Administrators should adapt to labor market changes, prioritize critical thinking, and foster industry-aligned curricula [15]. Encouraging a culture of lifelong learning is vital, given Education 4.0's impact on job skills [16]. Psychological readiness, encompassing adaptability, digital literacy, and lifelong learning, empowers stakeholders to thrive in Education 4.0 [17].

H1 The psychological readiness of the participants significantly enhances the performance of HEIs by implementing Education 4.0

### 2.2 *Innovative Pedagogical Approach*

Innovative pedagogical approaches are central to Education 4.0, with HEIs leading the way [18]. These approaches prepare students for a technology-driven world by fostering adaptive learning, critical thinking, and digital fluency [19]. Studies highlight the effectiveness of project-based learning and the flipped classroom model [20]. HEIs align with the emphasis on lifelong learning, offering ongoing education and personalized learning [21]. Blended learning, gamification, virtual reality, and augmented reality enhance teaching methods [22]. Work-integrated learning and industry partnerships promote practical skill development [23]. Microcredentials and just-in-time learning address specific skill needs [24]. Innovative pedagogies empower graduates for success in the dynamic Education 4.0 landscape [25]. HEIs enrich education for students, faculty, and administrators alike, enhancing engagement, critical skills, and real-world relevance [26].

H2 Innovative pedagogical approach of the participants significantly enhances the performance of HEIs by implementing Education 4.0

### 2.3 *Engagement and Motivation*

Studies underscore the significance of interactive learning environments, with gamified elements and digital platforms enhancing student engagement [27]. Integrating real-world relevance into the curriculum connects theory to practical applications, invigorating learning [28]. Collaborative projects mirror modern work environments, promoting teamwork and problem-solving [29]. Innovative teaching methods like flipped classrooms, case-based learning, and interactive discussions rejuvenate faculty's enthusiasm for teaching [30]. Ongoing professional development helps faculty adapt to evolving educational technologies and methodologies. Meaningful assessment approaches showcase the practical application of instructional efforts, renewing faculty motivation [31]. Collaborative efforts between institutions and administrators through guest lectures, workshops, and industry partnerships enrich the curriculum and motivate administrators by shaping future professionals [32]. Emphasis on applied learning aligns with administrators' preferences, motivating them to contribute to workforce-aligned educational initiatives [33]. These insights emphasize the motivation-driven benefits of collaboration in the context of Education 4.0.

H3 Engagement and motivation of the participants significantly enhance the performance of HEIs by implementing Education 4.0

## 2.4 *Digital Literacy*

The importance of digital literacy for students is underscored, encompassing technological proficiency, information evaluation, and cybersecurity awareness [34][35]. Faculty's ability to leverage digital tools and enhance the learning experience is pivotal through technological integration [36]. Digital communication skills facilitate meaningful virtual interactions, emphasizing faculty's adaptability [37]. The demand for employees with strong digital skills is rising, making digital literacy crucial for workplace success [38]. Administrators seek individuals skilled in data literacy for informed decision-making, along with remote work competence [39]. This multifaceted digital literacy is pivotal for Education 4.0's success, benefiting students, faculty, and administrators in higher education institutions [40]. These skills prepare stakeholders to thrive in a technology-driven educational and professional landscape.

H4 Digital literacy of the participants significantly enhances the performance of HEIs by implementing Education 4.0

## 2.5 *Learning Outcomes*

The study underscores the importance of defining learning outcomes in Education 4.0, emphasizing critical thinking, problem-solving, and digital literacy for students [41][42]. Collaboration, communication, adaptability, and lifelong learning are essential for thriving in evolving workplaces [43][44]. Faculty should possess innovative teaching skills and technological integration proficiency [45]. A student-centred approach, understanding individual needs, is vital [46]. Graduates need

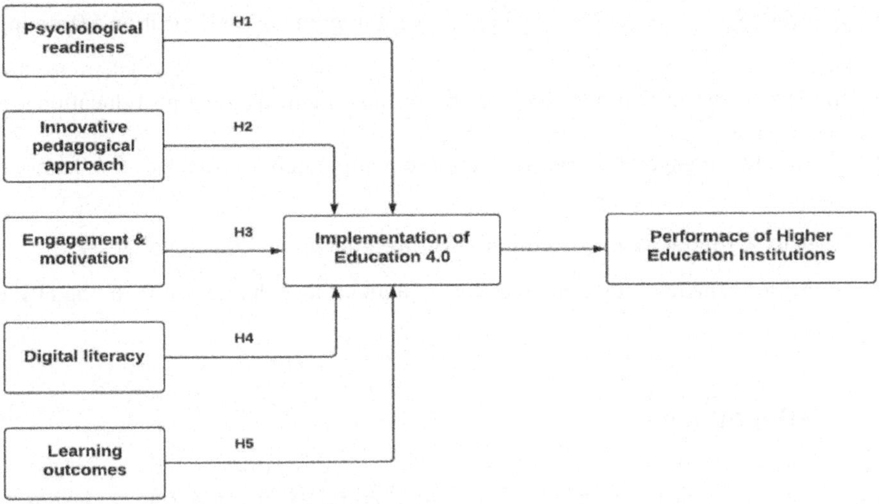


**Fig. 1** Hypothesis framework of the study

applied skills like critical data analysis and effective communication [47]. Learning outcomes must adapt to meet dynamic needs in Education 4.0, tailored for students, faculty, and administrators. Critical thinking, digital literacy, collaboration, adaptability, and practical skills are pivotal for success in this technology-driven landscape (Fig. 1).

H5 Learning outcomes of the participants significantly enhance the performance of HEIs by implementing Education 4.0

## 2.6 *Statement of the Problem*

Education 4.0 has garnered significant interest across various schools and Higher Education Institutions (HEIs). However, limited research exists, particularly in the southern region of Tamil Nadu, regarding its implementation and potential to enhance HEIs performance among students, faculty and administrators. The study aimed to assess the impact of HEIs by implementing Education 4.0.

### 2.6.1 Objectives

The study aims to assess the influence of Education 4.0 in Higher Education Institutions (HEIs) through a survey approach by investigating the perspectives of students, faculty, and administrators.

- To investigate the psychological readiness for implementing Education 4.0 among HEIs.
- To explore innovative pedagogical approaches for implementing Education 4.0 among HEIs.
- To examine engagement and motivation for implementing Education 4.0 among HEIs.
- To analyse digital literacy for implementing Education 4.0 among HEIs.
- To examine the learning outcomes for implementing Education 4.0 among HEIs.

## 3 Methodology

The research employed a robust quantitative approach using a survey design to explore phenomena within a specific population. Random sampling was used to select participants based on study objectives. The focus was on Higher Education Institutions in southern Tamil Nadu, India, involving students, faculty, and administrators. The research framework (Fig. 2) guided the study, initially involving 20 HEIs in a pilot phase. Data collection was conducted via surveys and analyzed with descriptive statistics in SPSS version 21.

### *3.1 Participants*

Before distributing the questionnaire, colleges provided consent, ensuring participants' anonymity and data confidentiality. The study included students, faculty, and Higher Education Institution (HEI) administrators. Out of 150 institutions, 145 were randomly sampled. In the pilot phase, 20 HEIs were selected, and a Likert Scale questionnaire with ratings from 1 (Strongly Disagree) to 5 (Strongly Agree) was administered. The same questionnaire was used for data collection from the 145 institutions, covering students, faculty, and administrators. Demographic information was collected via a questionnaire, and data were stored and analyzed using SPSS version 21.

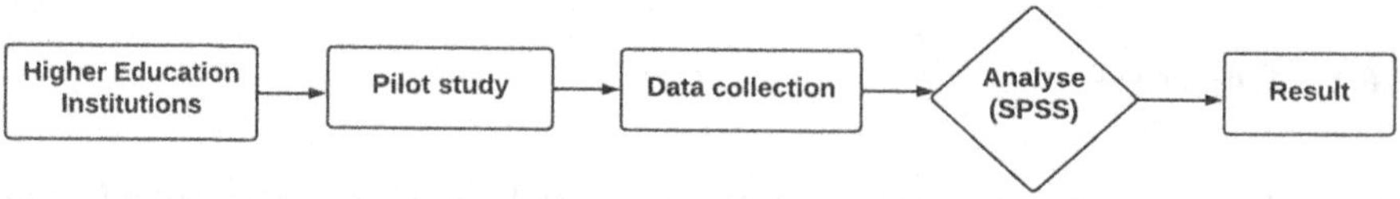


**Fig. 2** Research framework

**Table 1** Reliability statistics

| Cronbach's alpha | N of items |
|---|---|
| 0.985 | 30 |

## *3.2 Instruments*

Data collection involved a self-developed questionnaire using a 5-point Likert scale (1 - Strongly Disagree to 5 - Strongly Agree). The questionnaire, created using Google Forms, was shared within a WhatsApp group, ensuring comprehensive responses to all questions. It was strategically structured, covering variables like psychological readiness, innovative pedagogical approaches, engagement, digital literacy, and learning outcomes relevant to Education 4.0 in HEIs, totaling 30 questions. The questionnaire underwent content validation by field experts, including administrators and faculty, and achieved a high Cronbach's Alpha value of 0.985 in SPSS, indicating strong internal consistency among the measured variables (Table 1).

## *3.3 Procedure*

A pilot study involving 20 HEIs utilized the same questionnaire, which was later used for data collection across all HEIs. Participants received the questionnaire via WhatsApp through their respective institutions. Administrative officers of the institutions played a key role in data collection, assisted by the researchers, and collected multiple responses from individual institutions, typically 2 to 3. The questionnaire effectively encapsulated the study's core essence, aiding participant understanding. Following data collection, all information was analyzed using descriptive statistics in SPSS version 21.

# 4 Results

Utilized for analyzing, summarizing, and presenting outcomes tied to a dataset extracted from either a sample or an entire population, descriptive statistics are showcased. Table 2 outlines the occurrence and proportion of participants' genders. In this ongoing study, a total of 427 participants took part, with 284 (66.5%) being male and 143 (33.5%) females. With all fields designated as obligatory, no errors were triggered. Thus, the valid overall percentage equals 100%.

Presenting the incidence and distribution of participants' ages, Table 3 exhibits its dataset. The age spectrum of the total participants spans from 17 to 66. Specifically, there are 134 participants within the 17–20 age bracket, 188 participants aged

**Table 2** Gender of the participants

| | | Frequency | Percent | Valid percent | Cumulative percent |
|---|---|---|---|---|---|
| Valid | Male | 284 | 66.5 | 66.5 | 66.5 |
| | Female | 143 | 33.5 | 33.5 | 100.0 |
| | Total | 427 | 100.0 | 100.0 | |

between 21 and 30, 90 participants falling within the 31–40 age range, 24 participants aged between 40 and 50, and 4 participants in the 50–66 age range.

Presented in Table 4 are the frequency and proportion of participant regions. Among the 427 participants, 190 (44.5%) are affiliated with rural regions, while 237 (55.5%) hail from urban areas. No discrepancies have arisen, resulting in a comprehensive, valid percentage of 100%.

Table 5 displays the occurrence and ratio of participant designations. Within the cohort of 427 participants, 147 (34.4%) are students from various HEIs, while 145 (34.0%) are faculty of HEIs and 135 (31.6%) are administrators of HEIs. No discrepancies have surfaced, yielding a comprehensive, valid percentage of 100%.

Table 6 presents the descriptive statistics concerning the entire participant pool, showcasing the mean value for each question. Questions Q1 to Q30 are designed to validate the research, with the 'N' column indicating the number of participating individuals in the current study. The 'Range' column illustrates the span between the highest and lowest values on the Likert scale across all questions, consistently standing at 4. In the 'Minimum' column, the least Likert scale value of 1 is recorded for all questions, reflecting participants' lowest responses. The 'Maximum' column reveals the peak Likert scale value of 5 for each question, indicating participants' highest responses. Meanwhile, the 'mean' column displays the average value for each question, showcasing a minimum mean value of 3.75 and a maximum of 4.13. Standard Deviation ('Std. Deviation') outlines the extent of deviation from the mean for each question, with all values surpassing 1. Lastly, the 'variance' column highlights participants' variability, ranging from 1.085 to 1.495.

Presented in Table 7 are the overall percentage values for each question, determined by the Likert scale ratings. Within the 5-point Likert scale, the highest rating of 5 corresponds to "strongly agree," followed by 4 for "agree," 3 for "neutral," 2 for "disagree," and 1 for "strongly disagree." As per the findings from Table 7, a notable observation emerges: a considerable number of participants strongly agreed with the premises of the ongoing study.

Figure 3 illustrates the perspectives of the participants who responded to the research. Among the 427 participants, their feedback is distributed as follows: 569 (4%) strongly disagree, 827 (6%) disagree, 1683 (13%) express neutrality, 4352 (34%) agree, and 5379 (42%) strongly agree with the study.

The information presented in Table 8 offers a comprehensive breakdown of the responses to the questions, encompassing the percentage and actual participant counts expressing strong agreement among students, faculty, and administrators within the

**Table 3** Age of the participants

| | | Frequency | Percent | Valid percent | Cumulative percent |
|---|---|---|---|---|---|
| Valid | 17 | 3 | 0.7 | 0.7 | 0.7 |
| | 18 | 35 | 8.2 | 8.2 | 8.9 |
| | 19 | 38 | 13.6 | 13.6 | 22.5 |
| | 20 | 58 | 13.6 | 13.6 | 36.1 |
| | 21 | 13 | 3.0 | 3.0 | 39.1 |
| | 22 | 8 | 1.9 | 1.9 | 41.0 |
| | 23 | 12 | 2.8 | 2.8 | 43.8 |
| | 24 | 11 | 2.6 | 2.6 | 46.4 |
| | 25 | 30 | 7.0 | 7.0 | 53.4 |
| | 26 | 21 | 4.9 | 4.9 | 58.3 |
| | 27 | 17 | 4.0 | 4.0 | 62.3 |
| | 28 | 15 | 3.5 | 3.5 | 65.8 |
| | 29 | 28 | 1.9 | 1.9 | 67.7 |
| | 30 | 33 | 7.7 | 7.7 | 75.4 |
| | 31 | 20 | 4.7 | 4.7 | 80.1 |
| | 32 | 22 | 5.2 | 5.2 | 85.2 |
| | 33 | 15 | 3.5 | 3.5 | 88.8 |
| | 34 | 6 | 1.4 | 1.4 | 90.2 |
| | 35 | 15 | 3.5 | 3.5 | 93.7 |
| | 36 | 5 | 1.2 | 1.2 | 94.8 |
| | 37 | 3 | 0.7 | 0.7 | 95.6 |
| | 38 | 2 | 0.5 | 0.5 | 96.0 |
| | 39 | 1 | 0.2 | 0.2 | 96.3 |
| | 40 | 1 | 0.2 | 0.2 | 96.5 |
| | 42 | 4 | 0.9 | 0.9 | 97.4 |
| | 43 | 1 | 0.2 | 0.2 | 97.7 |
| | 44 | 2 | 0.5 | 0.5 | 98.1 |
| | 45 | 2 | 0.5 | 0.5 | 98.6 |
| | 46 | 1 | 0.2 | 0.2 | 98.8 |
| | 48 | 1 | 0.2 | 0.2 | 99.1 |
| | 53 | 1 | 0.2 | 0.2 | 99.3 |
| | 54 | 2 | 0.5 | 0.5 | 99.8 |
| | 66 | 1 | 0.2 | 0.2 | 100.0 |
| | Total | 427 | 100.0 | 100.0 | |

**Table 4** Region of the participants

| | | Frequency | Percent | Valid percent | Cumulative percent |
|---|---|---|---|---|---|
| Valid | Rural | 190 | 44.5 | 44.5 | 44.5 |
| | Urban | 237 | 55.5 | 55.5 | 100.0 |
| | Total | 427 | 100.0 | 100.0 | |

**Table 5** Designation of the participants

| | | Frequency | Percent | Valid percent | Cumulative percent |
|---|---|---|---|---|---|
| Valid | Student | 147 | 34.4 | 34.4 | 34.4 |
| | Faculty | 145 | 34.0 | 34.0 | 68.4 |
| | Administrator | 135 | 31.6 | 31.6 | 100.0 |
| | Total | 427 | 100.0 | 100.0 | |

Higher Education Institutions (HEIs). Table 8 reveals that the most substantial proportion of students (49.0%) expressed a strong agreement with the statement that 'Education 4.0 can enhance understanding by addressing doubts anytime.' Moreover, among faculty, the highest response (42.8%) indicated strong agreement with the notion that 'Blended learning (a fusion of technology and traditional methods) in Education 4.0 aids in comprehending concepts more effectively.' For administrators, the dominant sentiment (54.8%) affirmed that Education 4.0 has heightened my utilization of digital tools and technologies. Conversely, the lowest proportion of participants (24.8%) strongly concurred with the statement that 'I believe online learning can be more effective than traditional classroom learning'.

Figure 4 illustrates the perceptions of various participants, including students, faculty, and administrators, concerning variables like Psychological Readiness, Innovative Pedagogical Approach, Engagement and Motivation, Digital Literacy, and Learning Outcomes for the integration of Education 4.0 to enhance HEIs performance. Notably, students and faculty aligned in their support for learning outcomes, whereas administrators favored engagement and motivation as key factors for the implementation of Education 4.0 aimed at improving HEIs performance.

Figure 5 portrays the collective study responses through a line graph. The graph illustrates a predominant trend of strong agreement among the majority of participants in the study.

Figure 6 presents the tally of responses received for the ongoing study regarding the factors that contribute to the advancement of Higher Education Institution (HEIs) performance through the implementation of Education 4.0. Among these, 'Psychological Readiness' garnered 1065 responses, 'Innovative Pedagogies' obtained 1066 responses, 'Engagement and Motivation' received 1083 responses, 'Digital Literacy' garnered 1068 responses, and 'Learning Outcomes' reached a total of 1098 responses.

**Table 6** Descriptive statistics

| | N | Range | Minimum | Maximum | Mean | Std. Deviation | Variance |
|---|---|---|---|---|---|---|---|
| Q1 | 427 | 4 | 1 | 5 | 4.01 | 1.223 | 1.495 |
| Q2 | 427 | 4 | 1 | 5 | 3.75 | 1.224 | 1.498 |
| Q3 | 427 | 4 | 1 | 5 | 3.99 | 1.110 | 1.232 |
| Q4 | 427 | 4 | 1 | 5 | 4.13 | 1.065 | 1.135 |
| Q5 | 427 | 4 | 1 | 5 | 4.03 | 1.080 | 1.166 |
| Q6 | 427 | 4 | 1 | 5 | 4.06 | 1.042 | 1.085 |
| Q7 | 427 | 4 | 1 | 5 | 4.04 | 1.062 | 1.128 |
| Q8 | 427 | 4 | 1 | 5 | 4.04 | 1.086 | 1.180 |
| Q9 | 427 | 4 | 1 | 5 | 4.01 | 1.092 | 1.192 |
| Q10 | 427 | 4 | 1 | 5 | 4.04 | 1.077 | 1.160 |
| Q11 | 427 | 4 | 1 | 5 | 4.02 | 1.136 | 1.291 |
| Q12 | 427 | 4 | 1 | 5 | 3.98 | 1.108 | 1.227 |
| Q13 | 427 | 4 | 1 | 5 | 4.02 | 1.126 | 1.267 |
| Q14 | 427 | 4 | 1 | 5 | 4.03 | 1.082 | 1.170 |
| Q15 | 427 | 4 | 1 | 5 | 3.99 | 1.130 | 1.277 |
| Q16 | 427 | 4 | 1 | 5 | 4.08 | 1.058 | 1.118 |
| Q17 | 427 | 4 | 1 | 5 | 4.08 | 1.109 | 1.230 |
| Q18 | 427 | 4 | 1 | 5 | 3.99 | 1.076 | 1.157 |
| Q19 | 427 | 4 | 1 | 5 | 4.07 | 1.081 | 1.169 |
| Q20 | 427 | 4 | 1 | 5 | 4.08 | 1.055 | 1.113 |
| Q21 | 427 | 4 | 1 | 5 | 4.00 | 1.113 | 1.239 |
| Q22 | 427 | 4 | 1 | 5 | 4.03 | 1.093 | 1.194 |
| Q23 | 427 | 4 | 1 | 5 | 4.00 | 1.068 | 1.141 |
| Q24 | 427 | 4 | 1 | 5 | 4.00 | 1.142 | 1.305 |
| Q25 | 427 | 4 | 1 | 5 | 4.03 | 1.098 | 1.205 |
| Q26 | 427 | 4 | 1 | 5 | 4.07 | 1.094 | 1.198 |
| Q27 | 427 | 4 | 1 | 5 | 4.07 | 1.078 | 1.161 |
| Q28 | 427 | 4 | 1 | 5 | 4.02 | 1.093 | 1.195 |
| Q29 | 427 | 4 | 1 | 5 | 4.07 | 1.055 | 1.113 |
| Q30 | 427 | 4 | 1 | 5 | 4.06 | 1.088 | 1.184 |
| Valid N (listwise) | 427 | | | | | | |

## 4.1 *Hypothesis Testing*

Hypothesis testing involves assessing the validity of a proposed claim by analyzing data and helping to draw reliable conclusions in research and decision-making. The following Hypotheses are validated with the help of the result findings.

**Table 7** Aggregated percentage value of the questionnaire

| Questions | Strongly Disagree (%) | Disagree (%) | Neutral (%) | Agree (%) | Strongly Agree (%) |
|---|---|---|---|---|---|
| Q1 | 7.5 | 6.3 | 10.1 | 29.7 | 46.4 |
| Q2 | 7.0 | 10.3 | 17.3 | 31.4 | 34.0 |
| Q3 | 4.9 | 5.9 | 14.8 | 34.0 | 40.5 |
| Q4 | 4.0 | 5.4 | 10.8 | 33.0 | 46.8 |
| Q5 | 4.0 | 7.7 | 9.8 | 38.6 | 39.8 |
| Q6 | 3.5 | 4.9 | 15.5 | 34.2 | 41.9 |
| Q7 | 3.5 | 6.6 | 13.8 | 35.1 | 41.0 |
| Q8 | 4.4 | 5.9 | 12.9 | 35.4 | 41.5 |
| Q9 | 4.0 | 6.8 | 14.5 | 33.3 | 41.5 |
| Q10 | 4.0 | 5.9 | 14.3 | 33.5 | 42.4 |
| Q11 | 5.2 | 6.1 | 14.3 | 30.7 | 43.8 |
| Q12 | 4.7 | 6.8 | 13.6 | 35.4 | 39.6 |
| Q13 | 4.9 | 6.8 | 12.2 | 33.3 | 42.9 |
| Q14 | 3.5 | 8.0 | 11.9 | 35.1 | 41.5 |
| Q15 | 5.2 | 6.3 | 14.3 | 32.8 | 41.7 |
| Q16 | 4.0 | 5.9 | 10.8 | 37.2 | 42.2 |
| Q17 | 4.0 | 8.2 | 9.1 | 33.0 | 45.7 |
| Q18 | 3.7 | 6.1 | 17.6 | 32.8 | 39.8 |
| Q19 | 4.0 | 5.9 | 13.8 | 32.3 | 44.0 |
| Q20 | 3.7 | 5.6 | 12.4 | 35.1 | 43.1 |
| Q21 | 5.4 | 5.9 | 11.7 | 37.0 | 40.0 |
| Q22 | 4.0 | 7.0 | 13.3 | 33.7 | 41.9 |
| Q23 | 3.7 | 6.1 | 16.6 | 34.4 | 39.3 |
| Q24 | 5.9 | 5.9 | 12.4 | 34.2 | 41.7 |
| Q25 | 4.0 | 7.5 | 12.2 | 34.0 | 42.4 |
| Q26 | 4.2 | 6.1 | 13.1 | 32.1 | 44.5 |
| Q27 | 4.4 | 5.2 | 12.4 | 34.7 | 43.3 |
| Q28 | 4.7 | 5.9 | 13.1 | 35.8 | 40.5 |
| Q29 | 3.3 | 6.6 | 13.1 | 34.4 | 42.6 |
| Q30 | 4.0 | 6.6 | 12.9 | 33.0 | 43.8 |

H1 The Psychological Readiness of the Participants Significantly Enhances the Performance of HEIs by Implementing Education 4.0

Table 6 presents descriptive statistics outcomes. Q1 to Q6, addressing the research hypothesis, show means ranging from 3.75 to 4.13 and standard deviations from 1.042 to 1.136. Table 7 reveals that 46.8% strongly agreed, while 7.5% disagreed

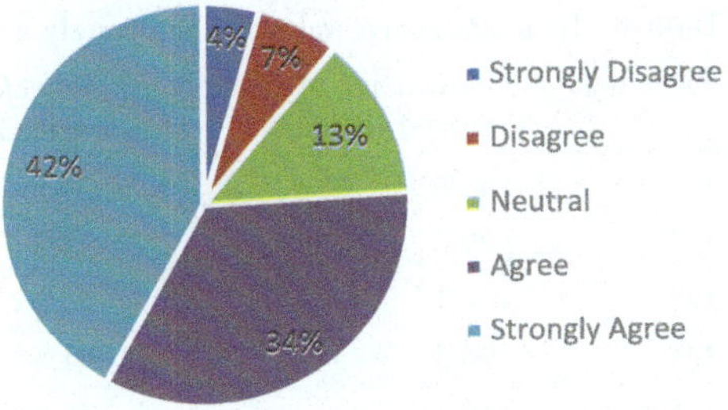


**Fig. 3** Perception of the participants

with the research. In Table 8, strong agreement percentages are displayed. Administrators showed the highest acceptance at 52.6%, especially regarding technology in HEI learning support. Faculty had the lowest strong agreement at 24.8%, particularly about online learning. Figure 4 reflects participant impressions; students (356), faculty (310), and administrators (389) strongly agreed on psychological readiness. Figure 6 shows cumulative factors enhancing HEIs performance, with 19.8% strongly agreeing that psychological readiness significantly uplifts HEIs through Education 4.0, confirming H1.

H2 Innovative pedagogical approach of the participants significantly enhances the performance of HEIs by implementing Education 4.0

Table 6 presents descriptive statistics outcomes. Q7 to Q12, addressing the research hypothesis, show means ranging from 3.98 to 4.04, and standard deviations between 1.077 and 1.130. Table 7 reveals that 35.4% strongly agreed, while 5.2% disagreed with the research. In Table 8, strong agreement percentages are displayed. Administrators exhibit the highest acceptance at 53.3%, particularly for active learning strategies using Education 4.0. However, students show the lowest strong agreement at 34.7% for the same strategies improving their knowledge. Figure 4 reflects participant impressions, with students (332), faculty (327), and administrators (398) strongly agreeing with the innovative pedagogical approach. Figure 6 indicates cumulative factors enhancing HEIs performance, with 1066 responses, representing 19.8% strongly agreeing that innovative pedagogical approaches significantly uplift HEIs through Education 4.0, confirming H2.

H3 Engagement and motivation of the participants significantly enhance the performance of HEIs by implementing Education 4.0

Table 6 displays the outcomes of the study's descriptive statistics. Questions Q13 to Q18, addressing the research hypothesis, show means ranging from 3.99 to 4.08, and standard deviations between 1.058 and 1.130. Table 7 reveals that 45.7% strongly agreed, while 5.2% disagreed with the research. In Table 8, strong agreement percentages are displayed. Administrators exhibit the highest acceptance at 54.1% for the implementation of Education 4.0, which enables a more customized approach to learning. Faculty records the lowest strong agreement at 34.5% for Education 4.0 enhancing the capacity to actively involve and inspire individuals. Figure 4 reflects participant impressions, with students (352), faculty (322), and

**Table 8** Total percentage value of the strongly agreed for the questionnaire

| Questions | Percentage of strongly agreed students | Percentage of strongly agreed faculty | Percentage of strongly agreed administrators |
|---|---|---|---|
| Q1 | 47.6 | 39.3 | 52.6 |
| Q2 | 29.3 | 24.8 | 48.9 |
| Q3 | 36.1 | 35.2 | 51.1 |
| Q4 | 48.3 | 41.4 | 51.1 |
| Q5 | 36.1 | 38.6 | 45.2 |
| Q6 | 44.9 | 34.5 | 39.3 |
| Q7 | 34.7 | 35.9 | 53.3 |
| Q8 | 43.5 | 33.8 | 47.4 |
| Q9 | 37.4 | 35.9 | 51.9 |
| Q10 | 40.8 | 36.6 | 50.4 |
| Q11 | 40.8 | 42.8 | 48.1 |
| Q12 | 35.4 | 40.7 | 43.0 |
| Q13 | 38.8 | 40.0 | 50.4 |
| Q14 | 41.5 | 36.6 | 46.7 |
| Q15 | 34.7 | 37.9 | 54.1 |
| Q16 | 39.5 | 36.6 | 51.1 |
| Q17 | 49.0 | 36.6 | 51.9 |
| Q18 | 36.1 | 34.5 | 49.6 |
| Q19 | 38.8 | 39.3 | 54.8 |
| Q20 | 38.8 | 37.9 | 53.3 |
| Q21 | 38.1 | 35.9 | 46.7 |
| Q22 | 38.8 | 37.2 | 50.4 |
| Q23 | 36.1 | 36.6 | 45.9 |
| Q24 | 37.4 | 39.3 | 48.9 |
| Q25 | 37.4 | 40.7 | 51.1 |
| Q26 | 44.2 | 38.6 | 51.1 |
| Q27 | 44.2 | 37.2 | 48.9 |
| Q28 | 36.7 | 37.9 | 47.4 |
| Q29 | 44.9 | 35.2 | 48.1 |
| Q30 | 42.2 | 35.9 | 54.1 |

administrators (410) strongly agreeing with engagement and motivation. Figure 6 shows cumulative factors enhancing HEIs performance, with 1083 responses, representing 20% strongly agreeing that engagement and motivation significantly uplift HEIs performance through Education 4.0, confirming H3.

H4 Digital literacy of the participants significantly enhances the performance of HEIs by implementing Education 4.0

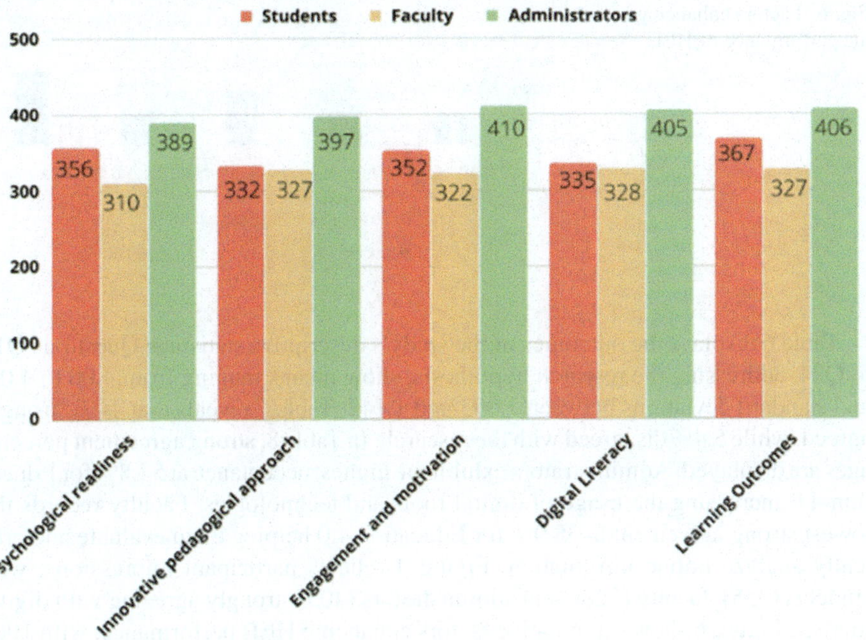


Fig. 4 Impression of the participants

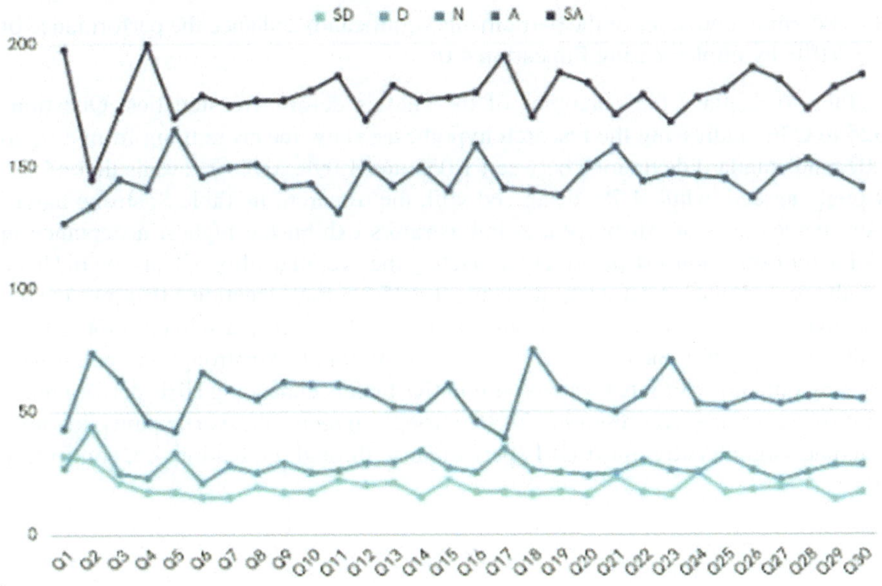


Fig. 5 Overall responses of the study

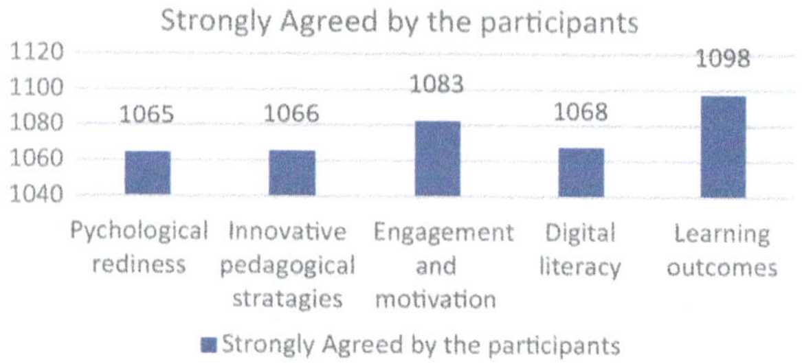


**Fig. 6** Factors enhancing the performance of HEIs

Table 6 displays the outcomes of the study's descriptive statistics. Questions Q19 to Q24, addressing the research hypothesis, show means ranging from 4.00 to 4.08, and standard deviations between 1.093 and 1.142. Table 7 reveals that 44% strongly agreed, while 5.4% disagreed with the research. In Table 8, strong agreement percentages are displayed. Administrators exhibit the highest acceptance at 54.8% for Education 4.0 increasing the usage of digital tools and technologies. Faculty records the lowest strong agreement at 35.9% for Education 4.0 helping them evaluate and critically analyze online information. Figure 4 reflects participant impressions, with students (335), faculty (328), and administrators (405) strongly agreeing with digital literacy. Figure 6 shows cumulative factors enhancing HEIs performance, with 1068 responses, representing 19.8% strongly agreeing that participants' digital literacy significantly uplifts HEIs performance through Education 4.0, confirming H4.

H5 Learning outcomes of the participants significantly enhance the performance of HEIs by implementing Education 4.0

Table 6 displays the outcomes of the study's descriptive statistics. Questions Q25 to Q30, addressing the research hypothesis, show means ranging from 4.02 to 4.07, and standard deviations between 1.055 and 1.098. Table 7 reveals that 44.5% strongly agreed, while 4.7% disagreed with the research. In Table 8, strong agreement percentages are displayed. Administrators exhibit the highest acceptance at 54.1% for Education 4.0, positively impacting the overall quality of learning in HEIs. Faculty records the lowest strong agreement at 35.2% for Education 4.0 improving the effectiveness of assessment and feedback. Figure 4 reflects participant impressions, with students (367), faculty (327), and administrators (406) strongly agreeing with learning outcomes. Figure 6 shows cumulative factors enhancing HEIs performance, with 1098 responses, representing 20.4% strongly agreeing that participants' learning outcomes significantly uplift HEIs performance through Education 4.0, confirming H5.

## 5 Discussion

In today's world, the prominence of Education 4.0 is undeniable. It serves as a key catalyst in bolstering the performance of (HEIs). This study investigates the impacts of Education 4.0 implementation on the participants within HEIs. By scrutinizing the effects on individuals engaged in HEIs, this research contributes to understanding the influence of Education 4.0.

This study highlights the importance of psychological readiness in implementing Education 4.0 in Higher Education Institutions (HEIs). It focuses on psychological awareness and acceptance among educators, administrators, and students, emphasizing the need to embrace new teaching methods and technology. Unlike previous research that centered on faculty development, this study advocates for comprehensive tech-enhanced training to boost faculty and students' confidence, and competence, addressing psychological barriers [15, 31, 48]. Additionally, it underscores the significance of effective change management strategies in HEIs, including transparent communication and inclusivity, to facilitate successful Education 4.0 integration.

In Education 4.0, innovative pedagogical approaches are key in reshaping HEIs. Our study emphasizes these approaches, including project-based learning, flipped classrooms, gamification, and experiential learning, using technology for engaging experiences. This aligns with prior research highlighting their transformative potential [49] and their alignment with learner-centric education and critical thinking [50]. Faculty development is crucial for effective implementation, fostering a conducive learning environment in line with Education 4.0 principles. Our study parallels previous findings on innovative teaching methods [31, 45, 49], such as blended learning for language learners.

The current study emphasizes the importance of engagement and motivation strategies in Education 4.0. Through interactive simulations, gamified assessments, and personalized learning, students take ownership of their education, leading to increased engagement and motivation. This aligns with previous findings that active student engagement through innovative methods significantly improves motivation, understanding, and academic performance [27]. Educators benefit from these strategies, experiencing increased teaching effectiveness and satisfaction [51]. Furthermore, the study underscores the alignment of graduates' skills with administrators' expectations, making students more attractive to potential employers. This supports Education 4.0's focus on practical, industry-relevant skills [11], ultimately better preparing students for the dynamic workforce [52, 53].

The study emphasizes technology's vital role in Education 4.0, highlighting the need for digital skills among students, faculty, and administrators. This digital literacy aligns with prior research emphasizing its significance in modern education [25, 42]. It also supports the growing importance of digital skills in technology-enhanced learning environments characteristic of Education 4.0 [53]. Educators using technology for innovative teaching should possess digital competencies for effective design and assessment [48, 51], fostering dynamic learning environments [50].

Strong digital skills prepare individuals for the evolving job market, aligning with the study's focus on leveraging digital tools and adapting to technological advancements [40].The study shows Education 4.0 transforms Higher Education Institutions (HEIs), enhancing learning outcomes. Students gain practical skills beyond traditional education, aligning with previous research highlighting Education 4.0's impact [24]. Technology and learner-centric approaches improve education quality, echoing holistic outcomes [51]. Dynamic learning environments, with interactive elements, equip students with industry-relevant skills, bridging theory and practice. Graduates possess domain knowledge and valued multidisciplinary skills, making them attractive to modern workplaces, as seen in HEIs emphasizing skills development and experiential learning [10, 15].

Numerous studies have explored Education 4.0 broadly and in Higher Education Institutions (HEIs). Yet, few focus on its implementation within these institutions. This study stands out by centering on participants' perceptions of how Education 4.0 enhances HEIs. It gauges students, faculty, and administrators' viewpoints, shedding light on their insights and experiences. This multifaceted approach distinguishes our research, delving into both theoretical implications and practical execution. The study's unique contribution lies in assessing Education 4.0's impact on HEIs comprehensively, from learning experiences to teaching methods and job market skills. This holistic understanding can guide HEIs in refining their strategies and offerings.

## 6 Conclusion

In summary, Education 4.0 significantly enhances HEI performance through technology integration, with administrators benefiting the most, followed by students and faculty. This global shift toward tech-driven education is crucial for preparing individuals for the modern professional landscape. Key factors include learning outcomes, engagement, digital literacy, innovative pedagogies, and psychological readiness. Institutions must seamlessly integrate technology, and policymakers should incorporate Education 4.0 into curricula for skill enhancement. Challenges, like learner distractions and faculty tech preparation, exist. Future research should expand the study's scope. Education 4.0 transforms HEIs globally, guiding them toward a tech-driven educational landscape aligned with future demands.

## References

1. Hariharasudan, A., Kot, S.: A scoping review on Digital English and Education 4.0 for Industry 4.0. Soc. Sci. **7**(11), 227 (2018)
2. Srivani, V., Hariharasudan, A., Pandeeswari, D.: English language learning using education 4.0 in Karimnagar, India. World J. Engl. Lang. **12**(2), 325 (2022)
3. Srivani, V., Hariharasudan, A., Nawaz, N., Ratajczak, S.: Impact of Education 4.0 among engineering students for learning English language. PLoS One **17**(2), 1–12 (2022)

4. Dhivya, D. S., Hariharasudan, A., Ragmoun, W., Alfalih, A.A.: ELSA as an Education 4.0 tool for learning business english communication. Sustain. **15**(4), 3809 (2023)
5. Thavabalan, P., Mohan, S., Hariharasudan, A., Nawaz, N.: English for business communication: An interventional study with employees of Indian printing industry at Sivakasi. Asian ESP J. **17**, 90–107 (2021)
6. Thavabalan, P., Mohan, S., Hariharasudan, A., Krzywda, J.: English as business lingua franca (Belf) to the managers of Indian printing industries. Pol. J. Manag. Stud **22**(2), 549–560 (2020)
7. Szczepańska-Woszczyna, K., Gatnar, S.: Key competences of research and development project managers in high technology sector. Forum Sci. Oecon. **10**(3), 107–130 (2022)
8. Hariharasudan, A., Rahiman, H.U., Nawaz, N., Panakaje, N.: Strategic influence of business English in management education. Pol. J. Manag. Stud. **23**(2), 180–195 (2021)
9. Palese, E., LaMance, R., Tardy, C.M.: Internationally mobile students' language views in an Inner Circle English writing course. Syst. **112**, 102950 (2023)
10. Miranda, J.: The core components of education 4.0 in higher education: Three case studies in engineering education. Comput. Electr. Eng. **93**, 245 (2021)
11. Manivasakan, S., Parija, S.: Education 4.0 in higher education institutions: The need. J. Sci. Dent. **12**(1), 1–2 (2022)
12. Nawaz, N., Durst, S., Hariharasudan, A., Shamugia, Z.: Knowledge management practices in higher education institutions comparative study. Pol. J. Manag. Stud. **22**(2), 291–308 (2020)
13. Sun, T., Wang, C.: College students' writing self-efficacy and writing self-regulated learning strategies in learning English as a foreign language. Syst. **90**(3), 102221 (2020)
14. Bin Saeed, B., Afsar, B., Hafeez, S., Khan, I., Tahir, M., Afridi, M.A.: Promoting employee's pro-environmental behavior through green human resource management practices. Corp. Soc. Responsib. Environ. Manag. **26**(2), 424–438 (2019)
15. Stuss, M.M., Szczepańska-Woszczyna, K., Makieła, Z.J.: Competences of graduates of higher education business studies in labor market I (results of pilot cross-border research project in Poland and Slovakia). Sustain. **11**(18), 4988 (2019)
16. Srivani, V., & Hariharasudan, A.: Influence of education 4.0 on english language instruction in Telangana's engineering institutions. J. Intercult. Commun., **23**(2), 50–57 (2023)
17. Saha, M.: English teachers' attitudes towards learners: Effects on the rural pedagogies in Bangladesh. Ampersand **10**, 100107 (2023)
18. Ziegler, N.: Interdisciplinary research at the intersection of CALL, NLP, and SLA: Methodological implications from an input enhancement project. Lang. Learn. **67**(S1), 209–231 (2017)
19. Walsh, J.N., Rísquez, A.: Using cluster analysis to explore the engagement with a flipped classroom of native and non-native English-speaking management students. Int. J. Manag. Educ. **18**(2), 100381 (2020)
20. Goh, P.S.C., Abdul-Wahab, N.: Paradigms to drive higher education 4.0. Int. J. Learn., Teach. Educ. Res. **19**(1), 159–171 (2020)
21. Putri, A.S., Prasetyo, Z.K., Purwastuti, L.A., Prodjosantoso, A.K., Putranta, H.: Effectiveness of STEAM-based blended learning on students' critical and creative thinking skills. Int. J. Eval. Res. Educ. **12**(1), 44–52 (2023)
22. Huizenga, J., Admiraal, W., Dam, G. tem., Voogt, J.: Mobile game-based learning in secondary education: Students' immersion, game activities, team performance and learning outcomes. Comput. Hum. Behav. **99**, 137–143, Oct. (2019)
23. Eady, L., Michelle J., Lockyer.: Tools for learning: technology and teaching. In Learning to Teach in the Primary School, p. 71, pp. 71–89 (2013)
24. Zoghbor, W.S.: Teaching English pronunciation to multi-dialect first language learners: The revival of the Lingua Franca Core (LFC). Syst. **78**, 1–14 (2018)
25. Villalobos-Zúñiga, G., Cherubini, M.: Apps That Motivate: a Taxonomy of App Features Based on Self-Determination Theory. Int. J. Hum Comput Stud. **140**, 102449 (2020)
26. Escobar Fandiño, F.G., Muñoz, L.D., Silva Velandia A.J.: Motivation and E-Learning English as a foreign language: A qualitative study. Heliyon **5**(9), (2019)

27. Rus, D.: Creative methodologies in teaching English for engineering students. Procedia Manuf. **46**, 337–343 (2020)
28. Escobar Fandiño, F.G., Muñoz, L.D., Silva Velandia, A.J.: Motivation and E-Learning English as a foreign language: A qualitative study. Heliyon **5**(9), (2019)
29. Plutsky, S.: Faculty perceptions of students' business communication needs. Bus. Commun. Q. **59**(4), 69–76 (1996)
30. Dhivya, D. S., Hariharasudan, A., Nawaz, N.: Unleashing potential: Multimedia learning and Education 4.0 in learning Professional English Communication. Cogent Soc. Sci. **9**(2), 2248751 (2023)
31. Gajek, A., Fabiano, B., Laurent, A., Jensen, N.: Process safety education of future employees 4.0 in Industry 4.0. J. Loss Prev. Process. Ind. **75**, 104691 (2022)
32. Li, M., Yu, Z.: Teachers' satisfaction, role, and digital literacy during the COVID-19 Pandemic. Sustain. **14**(3), (2022)
33. Matsumoto-Royo, K., Ramírez-Montoya, M.S.: Core practices in practice-based teacher education: A systematic literature review of its teaching and assessment process. Stud. Educ. Eval. **70**, 101047 (2021)
34. Abdulrahaman, M.D.: Multimedia tools in the teaching and learning processes: A systematic review. Heliyon **6**(11), e05312 (2020)
35. Abdulrahaman, M.D., Faruk, N., Oloyede, A.A., Surajudeen-bakinde, N.T., Olawoyin, L.A.: Heliyon multimedia tools in the teaching and learning processes : A systematic review. Heliyo **6**, e05312 (2020)
36. Wang, K., Li, B., Tian, T., Zakuan, N., Rani, P.: Evaluate the drivers for digital transformation in higher education institutions in the era of industry 4.0 based on decision-making method. J. Innov. Knowl. **8**(3), 100364 (2023)
37. Fleaca, E., Stanciu, R.D.: Digital-age learning and business engineering education-a pilot study on students' E-skills. Procedia Manuf. **32**, 1051–1057 (2019)
38. Şimon, S., Kilyeni, A., Suciu, L.: Strategies for improving the english pronunciation of the 1st Year 'Translation-interpreting' students. Procedia Soc. Behav. Sci. **191**, 2157–2160 (2015)
39. Eshet-Alkalai, Y.: Digital literacy: A conceptual framework for survival skills in the digital era. J. Educ. Multimed. Hypermedia **13**, 93–106 (2004)
40. Ibrahim, N.: The importance of implementing collaborative learning in the english as a second language (ESL) classroom in Malaysia. Procedia Econ. Financ. **31**(15), 346–353 (2015)
41. Liu, P.L.: Mobile English vocabulary learning based on concept-mapping strategy. Lang. Learn. Technol. **20**(3), 128–141 (2016)
42. Richards, J.C.: Curriculum approaches in language teaching: Forward, central, and backward design. RELC J. **44**(1), 5–33 (2013)
43. Nachoua, H.: Computer-assisted language learning for improving students' listening skill. Procedia Soc. Behav. Sci. **69**, 1150–1159 (2012)
44. Wang, X., Cheng, Z.: Cross-Sectional Studies: Strengths, weaknesses, and recommendations. Chest **158**(1), S65–S71 (2020)
45. Ye, J., Zhang, X., Zhou, L., Wang, D., Tian, F.: Psychological mechanism linking green human resource management to green behavior. Int. J. Manpow. **43**(3), 844–861 (2022)
46. Habók, A., Magyar, A., Molnár, G.: Investigating the relationship among english language learning strategies, language achievement, and attitude. Front. Psychol. **13**, 867714 (2022)
47. Mayer, R.E.: Applying the science of learning: Evidence-based principles for the design of multimedia instruction. Am. Psychol. **63**(8), 760–769 (2008)
48. Haderer, B., Ciolacu, M.: Education 4.0: artificial intelligence assisted task-and time planning system. Procedia Comput. Sci. **200**, 1328–1337 (2022)
49. Farias-Gaytan, S., Aguaded, I., Ramirez-Montoya, M.S.: Transformation and digital literacy: Systematic literature mapping. Educ. Inf. Technol. **27**(2), 1417–1437 (2022)
50. Mohamad Alakrash, H., Abdul Razak, N.: Towards the education 4.0, readiness level of EFL students in utilising technology-enhanced classroom. Int. J. Innov., Creat. Chang. **13**(10), 161–182 (2020)

51. Van, L.K., Dang, T.A., Pham, D.B.T., Vo, T.T.N., Pham, V.P.H.: The effectiveness of using technology in learning english. AsiaCALL Online J. **12**(2), 24–40 (2021)
52. Khan, A.A., Laghari, A.A., Shaikh, Z.A., Dacko-Pikiewicz, Z., Kot, S.: Internet of Things (IoT) security with blockchain technology: A state-of-the-art review. IEEE Access. **10**, 122679–122695 (2022)
53. Anaelka, A.H.: Education 4.0 made simple: Ideas For teaching. Int. J. Educ. Lit. Stud. **6**(3), 92 (2018)

# Internet of Things: Effectiveness of Instant Messengers on Consumer Behaviour as a Digital Marketing Channel

**Easwaramoorthy Rangaswamy, Stephanie Lim Mei Ling, Nishad Nawaz, and Gemini Velleringatt Joy**

**Abstract** Digital marketing has been evolving as technology has been changing. With the advent of the Internet of Things (IoT), digital marketing tools and approaches must be studied as organizations face intense competition. The research aims to study the impact of instant messengers that would result in behavioral changes in the consumer. Further, digital marketing channels' effects are also analyzed. Reviews were done, and the research gap highlighted the need for the study. In the methodology context, realism was used as the research philosophy. Quantitative research with an online survey method was used to collect primary data. The sample size of the study is 54 respondents from Singapore. Results showed that digital marketing channels in the form of instant messengers need to be better used by entities to differentiate themselves in the market. The study also found that millennials are more responsive compared to non-Millennials. Therefore, it is imperative to customize the strategy for digital marketing channels. Similarly, those belonging to the millennial generation exhibit a greater propensity to prioritize attributes such as product quality or differentiation over price. The study indicated that the brand reputation of an organization is crucial irrespective of the channel options. This applies to both millennials and non-millennials, which is the novelty of the current study.

---

E. Rangaswamy
Amity Global Institute, Singapore, Singapore
e-mail: erangaswamy@singapore.amity.edu

S. L. M. Ling
PropertyGuru Group, Singapore, Singapore

N. Nawaz (✉)
Department of Business Management, College of Business Administration, Kingdom University, Riffa, Kingdom of Bahrain
e-mail: n.navaz@ku.edu.bh

G. V. Joy
VIT Business School, VIT University, Vellore, India
e-mail: geminivjoy@vit.ac.in



S. Kot et al. (eds.), *Corporate Practices: Policies, Methodologies, and Insights in Organizational Management*, Springer Proceedings in Business and Economics,
https://doi.org/10.1007/978-981-97-0996-0_12

**Keywords** Digital marketing · Consumer behaviour · Instant messaging · Social media

## 1 Introduction

This study approaches IoT (Internet of Things) from the perspective of Digital marketing, which is becoming an essential and increasing competition for businesses when it comes to marketing. The number of active Internet users has reached almost 5.19 billion people, which encompasses 64% of the global population. Of this total, 4.88 billion, or 59.9% of the world's population, were social media users [1]. In the twenty-first century, it is becoming essential for businesses to have a web presence. Furthermore, the survey found that the post-COVID-19 pandemic not only forces these traditional businesses with no online presence to adopt but also pushes companies to accelerate the digitalization of their customers and supply-chain interactions and internal operations by 3 to 4 years. [2, 3].The digital marketing industry has been increasingly popular as a channel, with businesses spending over USD 204 billion in 2017. [4]. With the COVID-19 pandemic accelerating the shift towards an even more digitalized world, a survey on "COVID-19 and E-commerce" conducted by the United Nations Conference on Trade and Development (UCTAD) shows that more than half of the 3700 respondents shop more frequently now and have suggested that this will have a lasting effect even as the world begins to recover.

As forecasted by eMarketer, media advertisement spending globally will increase from 325.02 billion to 526.17 billion by 2024. [5]. This means that businesses would need to look into being smarter in their advertisement spending rather than relying on existing channels to get a share of voice in order to attract the attention of potential customers [6]. [7] The authors highlighted that social media has become an essential communication element. Their study has assessed social media usage and investigated the popularity of tools and forms in social networks. Similarly, [8] highlighted that with the spread of the COVID-19 pandemic and the increasing importance of e-commerce, the study of online consumer behavior is particularly relevant. Petrosyan [1] also attempted to analyze the impact of the IoT concept on the operations of modern organizations and the implementation of changes related to its use.

Currently, 74.4% of small and medium businesses (SMB) intend to spend on social media for marketing purposes [9]; they are mainly spent on an advertisement that lacks personalization and is recognized by marketers to have a 74% strong or extreme impact on marketing [10]. A survey done in 2018 shared that 77% of respondents found that email marketing is the top digital marketing channel used for personalization. However, relying on this approach could be counterproductive, as research done in 2017 suggests that only 10% of respondents felt that email marketing was beneficial [9]. Ironically, there was no result in utilizing social platforms for personalization [11]. This is unfortunate as messenger platforms like Facebook had over 126 million monthly users in 2018, which suggests a missed opportunity [12]. [1] Asper the Ani indicated that as of 2022, in the context of global internet usage, it can be seen that the usage is higher among individuals between 15 and 24 years across all regions. The study even shows that among the young people in Europe, which represents the most significant usage penetration, 98%. Also, it can be seen that the worldwide average for the age group 15–24 years was 75% in the context of internet usage. As such, it is crucial for the current study to also look at the effectiveness of instant messengers on consumer behavior as a digital marketing channel among millennials and non-Millennials.

## 1.1 Problem Statement

With the prevailing change in the business environment at the advent of technological innovations, organizations must reinvent their business strategies. Consumer behavior has been changing due to medial social penetration, and organizations could use instant messengers effectively as a tool for digital marketing channels. Awareness among the consumers of such messengers needs to be studied along with the factors consumers tend to consider before making decisions. Further, there is also a need to evaluate channel preferences among consumers in the context of Millennials and non-Millennials. Digital marketing has taken the lead, and there has been an urgent need for marketers to reshape their strategies, especially in the communication channel. The different types of channels used for digital marketing that consumers are familiar with need to be studied. Also, the marketing channel preference impacts the consumer's decision-making process. Further, the various factors that a consumer would consider in the decision-making process before acting on a marketing communication is an area that marketers would like to understand and plan their different strategies that would impact the effectiveness of the communication that can be applied to Instant Messaging. The above research problems are to be studied, and the present study addresses the research gap in IoT (Internet of Things).

## 1.2 Research Questions

This research aims to study the effectiveness of Instant Messenger as a communication channel for digital marketing. Research questions set the elementary understanding through collecting relevant information in the form of qualitative and quantitative forms of information. The research questions attempt to collect information so that research objectives are duly met. The following are the research questions of this study,

- What are the different types of channels used for digital marketing that consumers are familiar with?
- What are the various factors that a consumer would consider in the decision-making process before acting on a marketing communication?

- Does the marketing channel preference impact the consumer's decision-making process?
- What are the different strategies that impact the effectiveness of the communication that can be applied to Instant Messaging?

Some digital channels have seen a reduced impact, and understanding the effectiveness of internet messaging as a digital marketing channel in the marketing space would help marketers be more effective communicators. The primary objective of the research is to study the effectiveness of Messenger on consumer behavior as a digital marketing channel in the context of among Millennials and non Millennials and is as follows:

- To analyze the different types of channels used for digital marketing.
- To study the factors a customer will consider when deciding to act on a marketing communication.
- To evaluate the preference and effectiveness of consumer behavior based on the communication channel used for digital marketing.
- To suggest various strategies to improve the effectiveness of Instant Messaging as a communication channel

### *1.3 Significance of the Study*

Digital marketing is becoming essential and increasingly competitive for businesses when it comes to marketing [13]. Many companies have invested heavily in different digital marketing channels to gain market share, such as search marketing, social media marketing, email marketing, etc. With consumers being exposed to many digital advertisements daily, businesses must be more thoughtful when targeting customers. The strategy used to approach customers significantly impacts consumers' buying behavior [4]. In social media marketing, as highlighted by [14], companies need to be more effectively using instant messaging services as a marketing channel. Companies may use social media to a greater extent to reach customers as consumers are increasingly adopting it. This research will evaluate whether it could be a better alternative to the existing marketing channels in terms of the effectiveness of consumer behavior [3].

## 2 Literature Review

This section summarises the published literature related to this study. The in-depth review of the previously conducted literature research helped to identify research gaps that the present study will focus on. This review will first understand the background of the current digital marketing industry, how big it is, and the current practices in the market. After which, an examination of the impact on the customer's purchasing behavior based on the current digital marketing practices. In particular, Facebook can be utilized for social media and instant messaging marketing. Therefore, it would be interesting to find out the impact of consumer behavior using Facebook as a channel for digital marketing. [15]. Understanding the difference in impact helped identify any gaps in the market. Lastly, the engagement rate and the utilization of instant messaging to understand whether it is even worth exploring further [16].

## *2.1 Background of Digital Marketing Industry*

Digital marketing as an industry is getting increasingly popular as a channel, with over USD 204 billion spent in 2017. Even though 74.4% of small and medium businesses (SMB) intend to spend on social media for marketing purposes [14], they are mainly spent on advertisement that lacks personalization and are recognized by marketers to have a 74% strong or extreme impact on marketing [17]. A survey done in 2018 shared that 77% of respondents found that email marketing is the top digital marketing channel used for personalization [18]. Even research in 2017 found that only 10% of respondents felt that email marketing was beneficial [10], whereas there was no result in utilizing social platforms for personalization [10]. This is unfortunate as Facebook Messenger had over 126 million monthly active in 2018, which suggests a missed opportunity (eMarketer, 2018).

## *2.2 Understanding Digital Marketing's Impact on Customer's Purchase Decisions*

A study on the impact of digital marketing on customer purchase decisions was conducted by [18]. The objective is to examine the implication of digital marketing in the consumer purchase decision and to find out that consumers are aware of digital marketing and channels that influence their purchase decision. This study is carried out with over 50 respondents through a survey, and the results are analyzed using the chi-square test. The findings indicated that consumers are aware of digital channels and prefer to buy things digitally and suggested that educational qualification has no role in purchasing online. Overall, it concluded that an effective reach of advertisement for convenience goods would increase the sales of goods purchased through digital channels. [16] supported the findings towards digital purchases, particularly on Facebook. However, it did conclude that while Facebook advertisement has a positive effect on the buying behavior of young consumers, the Facebook environment does not. Further support by [19] also found that SMEs need to fully utilize the potential of digital tools to maximize the opportunities they provide [20]. As such, digital marketing tools must be carefully used to ensure that organizations can impact the customer's purchase decisions. Irrespective of the social media tool that the consumers use, marketers need to ensure that they reach out, especially to different segments, at least in the context of age groups that tend to align with the various social media platforms.

## 2.3 Effects of Social Media Advertisement on Consumer Behaviour

The effects of social media advertisements like Facebook and the environment on the buying behaviors of young consumers were studied [16]. The study's objective is to determine the impacts of emotional and environmental responses on the buying behavior of young consumers. Over 309 Facebook users of both genders participated in the survey in Pakistan. The findings indicated that Facebook advertisements and their environment significantly affect consumers' buying behavior. They concluded that females have moderating effects on Facebook advertisements and no moderating impact on the Facebook environment. In support, [4] found that social media platforms enable easy buying decisions as they provide a highly engaged and comprehensive level of information to consumers to influence their behavior. Interestingly, [21] suggests that customers now demand real-time replies to their queries and expect personalized company recommendations. The studies show that the level of engagement is vital in the social media platform irrespective of the tools used. The responses from the organizations are expected to be fast, reliable, and customized to the customers' queries. Engagement level needs to be at the highest, and any lapse would be adversely seen, and a faster spread of negative word of mouth is possible. Such effects of social media advertising on consumer behavior must be addressed.

## 2.4 Consumer's Engagement Rate Using Instant Messaging

Emerging Digital Marketing Strategies Using Mobile Instant Messaging was studied by Bell and Waters [22] to explore strategies to improve customer engagement with instant mobile messaging (MIMs). The study included interviews with four marketing managers from three United States organizations who utilize MIMs as a marketing tool to improve customer engagement strategies. The findings indicated that MIMs have a 35% engagement rate higher than other channels and suggest that the name-based plan needs to work to engage customers. Overall, the study concluded that marketing managers should review the underlying principles in each strategy and adapt accordingly to their situation. In support of the study made by [6] [18], they have also considered Mims's benefits and traits that positively influence consumer satisfaction. However, Koufaris and Hampton-Sosa [23] argued that the cognitive engagement dimension and the emotional engagement dimension affect the level of satisfaction. However, only the emotional engagement dimension affects behavior-based [24] customer relationship management(CRM) performance, while social engagement does not affect satisfaction and CRM performance. Moreover, this study confirms the relationship between customer satisfaction and customer behavior-based relationship performance [25]. The reviews indicated clearly that engagement rates among consumers and marketers are vital. Marketers need to react fast and need engagement strategies revamped to address the needs of the consumers online. Such requirements would be beyond the cognitive and emotional aspects that the consumers would look for. Apart from influencing the consumers' decisions, effective engagement with the consumers would also help improve the satisfaction level of the consumers.

### 2.5 Current Utilization of Common Instant Messaging as a Digital Marketing Channel

Even though Facebook is the most popular social network in the world, with over 2,603 million active users, which is 603 million ahead of its runner-up, Youtube [26], which suggests that it is an underutilized channel to build a meaningful relationship with consumers, a recent study [19] about the usage of digital marketing channels in SMEs examines factors that influence the adoption and use of digital marketing channels in SMEs and provide insights into the utilization and goals of digital marketing and examines factors that influence the adoption and use of digital marketing channels in SMEs. A survey was done with 421 survey respondents working in SMEs, of which 16 were managers.

The findings suggest that SMEs need to use the full potential of digital tools. They concluded that this is why they are not benefiting from the opportunities and questions if they have understood the fundamental changes like communication due to digitalization. In support, another study also concluded that customers' decision processes in marketing evolve and will do so from a decision process in which they are highly responsive to marketing to one in which they are less responsive [13]. In addition, another study also concluded that Facebook Messenger (Chatbot) has higher support than Email Marketing [21]. It can be seen that beyond the passive comments, consumers expect marketers to be more engaged with instant responses to their queries. The digital tools related to instant messaging and engaging consumers are crucial and would shape or reshape the market opportunities for the organizations. Adopting such digital marketing channels would need to be embraced as consumer communication is evolving rapidly due to technological advancements. The difference between the Millennials and non-Millennials would also be crucial in this context.

## 2.6 Gap Analysis

A *research gap* is a study activity between standards and actual delivery differences [27]. The overall literature analysis reflected that most of the researchers focused on the industry as a whole; however, there are very few who focused explicitly on instant messenger and its influence as a digital marketing channel. There is a potential research gap as there is a need to study the different types of channels used for digital marketing. Factors that affect the consumer's choice of communication channel must be studied elaborately. Furthermore, evaluating preference and effectiveness on consumer behavior based on the communication channel used for digital marketing is crucial. Engagement strategies need to be reviewed, as consumer behavior is evolving due to technological evolution. The literature does not elaborate on the factors contributing to consumer behavior's impact on MIMs. There is likely a crucial difference between Millennials and non-Millennials in digital marketing. In this research, the focus will review the effectiveness and provide insights of instant messenger on consumer behavior as a digital marketing channel and will fill the gap by examining the process in context with consumer buying behavior.

## 2.7 Conceptual Model

The research uses an explorative research framework by which hypotheses are explored using the survey method and realism as the research philosophy. The data collection is done through research questions to collect a comprehensive data set to examine the various research objectives and enable the proper findings. The study needs to cover the strategy's development split into consumer behavior and digital marketing. For consumer behavior, there are a few factors explored, including age group, gender, job position, type of product/service, and item price, to determine which factors have the most significant influence over consumer behavior [28]. For digital marketing, further exploration of sub-categories of the type of communication channel needs to be studied. Finally, the findings are presented to determine the best combination of the two categories and provide recommendations accordingly.

As such, the above literature review section shows that digital marketing is an important communication channel and that it is essential for any company to use it as a tool to drive more sales. However, to ensure that it is an effective channel, companies need to be on social media [29]. Instant messaging has become essential in the industry. However, it currently needs to be more utilized now[30]. This research will further explore this medium and conclude its effectiveness in meeting the high demands of consumer's expectations and providing positive customer behavior in the ever-changing digital era [31]. In this context, hypotheses were constructed to support the overall design and framework of the research. This study will further test the following hypothesis:

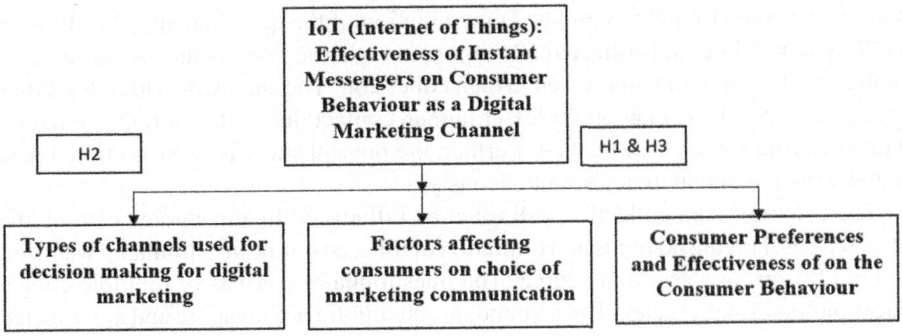


**Fig. 1** Research framework

**Hypothesis 1:**
There will be no significant difference between millennials and the effectiveness as a target audience for Instant Messengers.

**Hypothesis 2:**
Compared to the other digital marketing channels, Instant Messaging is the most effective communication channel.

**Hypothesis 3:**
There is no significant difference between the Millennials of the respondents with regards to the factors affecting consumer's behaviour towards digital marketing. As such the Conceptual Framework is provided in Fig. 1.

## 3 Research Methods

In this section, a summary of the research methodology and the methods of research will be explained and justified. In the research approach,[2] the inductive mono-method approach is used for this research as data is explored to develop theories from which will then be subsequently related to the literature in subsequent discussion. Due to the limitation of time and resources, it would be appropriate to choose mono-method quantitative research as a data collection technique, as [11] suggests that it is much easier to plan and execute. As quantitative focuses on frequencies and numbers, it does not target the experience and meaning but the data collected, which are subjected to rigorous analysis. This justifies the approach because the research does not start with any predetermined theories or conceptual frameworks, even though there is a clearly defined purpose and research question. This research has undertaken the mono-method quantitative survey as a primary data resource so that reliable data is gathered in numerical form. This strategy can efficiently obtain perspective and understand consumer behavior at one point through a questionnaire and can pick more than one variable. As this survey is conducted anonymously, the responses are honest compared to other methods. Dissemination of the questionnaire was through a QR code/weblink and collected 52 responses from the participants. A survey also enables scale in quantity and speed in data collection. The survey provides flexibility online as respondents may prefer lesser human contact due to the current pandemic, thus justifying this chosen method. Further, the present study is cross-sectional data as the survey was conducted simultaneously.

The extent of data collection will often be influenced by the amount of time the research has. Having no funds and limitation of time, an online questionnaire was used as the [22] primary research source. The questionnaire consists of multiple-choice questions and Likert scales. The respondents are public in Singapore and are selected based on convenience sampling. The design of quantitative research is often treated with three activities: sampling, measuring, and procedures for inference. [32]. The questionnaire was structured into four sections, namely, demographics, and the last three sections address each of the research objectives. There are six multiple-choice questions in the demographics section to find the gender, age group, qualification level, employment status, marital status, and annual income level. The demographics are instrumental in helping us understand whether there is a specific relationship between the demographics and the research objectives. Due to the limitation of time and cost factors during the COVID-19 pandemic, the sample size for this research was set to 52 with convenience sampling. The data collection window was two weeks after the ethics approval and conducted with respondents aged 18 and above. A small sample size of 10 was used for a pilot test to ensure that research questions were structured understandably so that data collection and analysis could be accurate. For future studies, a larger sample size could be considered if resources were more flexible and available during that period. Even though the study had a sample size of 52, which may not be representative, the sample size is still a statistically significant sample. As such, the results can be generalized. For instance, Roscoe (1975) in [33] proposes the rules of thumb for determining sample size as "sample sizes larger than 30 and less than 500 are appropriate for most research".

Content validity and construct validity were conducted for the study. Content validity was shown by discussing the research instrument with three industry experts who are digital marketing experts. Also, construct validity was demonstrated by seeking views from the statistician on the variables and tests used in the study. To measure reliability, the researcher used Cronbach's Alpha to determine the reliability of the test. Reliability is the extent to which a test produces similar results until constant condition regardless of occasion [22]. According to the Cronbach's Alpha reliability test, the reliability score of the test is 0.88. Using Cronbach's Alpha test, the value should be as close to 1 as possible; however, any figure above 0.7 is considered reliable and within the acceptable range [17]. Therefore, the data is deemed to be reliable for further quantitative analysis.

## 4 Results

The demographic profile of the respondents was analyzed in this section. Based on whether the respondents will respond to common digital marketing channels, 52 completed online surveys were conducted. The profile of the respondents was exhibited independently for each demographic variable, such as age, gender, education, employment status, income level, and marital status. This study's broad digital marketing experience was familiarity, level of exposure, and engagement with different digital marketing channels. Most participants were female (63.5%), while the rest were males (36.5%). Most participants (71.2%) were millennials (24–30 years old in 2020), while the rest, 28.8%, were non-millennials. Concerning the participant's education level, most of the participants' highest education levels (51.9%) are bachelor's degrees. In contrast, the rest are broken down into tertiary education (26.9%), master's degrees (17.3%), and secondary and below (3.8%). Furthermore, the current employment status of the participants shows that 76.9% are working, whereas 11.5% are self-employed, and the remaining 11.5% are unemployed. Most of the participants' marital status (63.5%) are married, whereas only 36.5% are single. The majority of the participants' current monthly income level (SGD) (32.7%) are between \$2500 - \$5000 working, whereas the rest are broken down into < \$2500 (9.6%), \$5001-\$7500(25%), \$7501 - \$10,000 (19.2%), \$10 000 - \$15 000 (7.7%) and \$15,001 - \$20,000.

### *4.1 Factors that a Customer Will Consider When Deciding to Act on a Marketing Communication*

To study the various factors that a customer will consider when deciding to act on a marketing communication, the following tests were performed.

The data collected in Table 1 was to analyze if the consumer's behavior towards digital marketing channels has any significance and gender. The results for the chi-square tests indicate that the P value is all above 0.05. Hence, it concludes that there is no significance between the consumer's behavior towards digital marketing channels and the marital status.

The data collected in Table 2 was to analyze if the consumer's behavior towards digital marketing channels has any significance and marital status. The results for the chi-square tests indicate that the P value is above 0.05, except for instant messaging. Hence, it concludes that there is no significance between the consumer's behavior toward digital marketing channels and marital status except for influencer marketing.

The data collected in Table 3 was to analyse the significance between consumer's behaviour towards digital marketing channels and educational level. The results indicates that the P value is all above 0.05. Hence, it concludes that there is no significance between the consumer's behaviour towards digital marketing channels and the educational level.

**Table 1** Gender and factors affect consumer behaviour towards digital marketing

| Digital marketing channel | Gender | N | Mean | SD | P-Value | $H_O$ |
|---|---|---|---|---|---|---|
| Influencer | Male | 19 | 3.84 | 1.642 | 0.813 | **A** |
| | Female | 33 | 3.73 | 1.701 | | |
| Email | Male | 19 | 3.79 | 1.357 | 0.812 | **A** |
| | Female | 33 | 3.33 | 1.514 | | |
| Social Media | Male | 19 | 1.79 | 1.134 | 0.283 | **A** |
| | Female | 33 | 2.00 | 1.118 | | |
| Instant messaging | Male | 19 | 4.63 | 1.461 | 0.270 | **A** |
| | Female | 33 | 4.94 | 1.478 | | |
| Google search | Male | 19 | 2.84 | 1.214 | 0.518 | **A** |
| | Female | 33 | 3.03 | 1.510 | | |
| Forum | Male | 19 | 4.11 | 1.883 | 0.521 | **A** |
| | Female | 33 | 3.97 | 1.468 | | |

*Note* SD: Standard Deviation; Nore: A: Accepted

**Table 2** Marital status and factors affect consumer behaviour towards digital marketing

| Factors | Marital status | N | Mean | SD | P Value | Ho accepted |
|---|---|---|---|---|---|---|
| Influence | Married | 33 | 3.58 | 1.714 | 0.273 | A |
| | Single | 19 | 4.11 | 1.560 | | |
| Email | Married | 33 | 3.93 | 1.368 | 0.496 | A |
| | Single | 19 | 3.68 | 1.635 | | |
| Social media | Married | 33 | 1.97 | 1.159 | 0.696 | A |
| | Single | 19 | 1.84 | 1.068 | | |
| Instant messaging | Married | 33 | 5.15 | 1.176 | 0.034 | A |
| | Single | 19 | 4.26 | 1.759 | | |
| Google search | Married | 33 | 3.00 | 1.414 | 0.797 | A |
| | Single | 19 | 2.89 | 1.140 | | |
| Forum | Married | 33 | 3.91 | 1.684 | 0.522 | A |
| | Single | 19 | 4.21 | 1.512 | | |

The data collected in Table 4 was to analyze the significance between consumer behavior towards digital marketing channels and educational level. The results indicate that the P value is all above 0.05. Hence, it concludes that there is no significance between the consumer's behavior toward digital marketing channels and the income level. Further, the data collected in Table 5 was to analyze the importance of consumer behavior toward digital marketing channels and Age groups. The results indicate that the P value is all above 0.05. Hence, it concludes that there is no significance between the consumer's behavior towards digital marketing channels and the Age Group.

**Table 3** Education level and factors affect consumer behaviour towards digital marketing

| Digital marketing channel | Educational level | N | Mean | SD | P-Value | A |
|---|---|---|---|---|---|---|
| Influencer | Secondary & below | 2 | 3.00 | 1.414 | 4.99 | **A** |
| | Tertiary (GCE "A"Level, Diploma, higher NITEC, NITEC) | 14 | 4.07 | 1.492 | | |
| | Bachelor's degree | 27 | 3.89 | 1.695 | | |
| | Master's degree | 9 | 3.11 | 1.900 | | |
| | Total | 52 | 3.77 | 1.664 | | |
| Email | Secondary & below | 2 | 3.00 | 0.000 | 0.656 | **A** |
| | Tertiary (GCE "A"Level, Diploma, higher NITEC, NITEC) | 14 | 3.57 | 1.555 | | |
| | Bachelor's degree | 27 | 3.33 | 1.468 | | |
| | Master's degree | 9 | 4.00 | 1.500 | | |
| | Total | 52 | 3.50 | 1.462 | | |
| Social media | Secondary & below | 2 | 1.50 | 0.707 | 0.065 | **A** |
| | Tertiary (GCE "A"Level, Diploma, higher NITEC, NITEC) | 14 | 1.43 | 0.646 | | |
| | Bachelor's degree | 27 | 1.96 | 1.126 | | |
| | Master's degree | 9 | 2.67 | 1.414 | | |
| | Total | 52 | 1.92 | 1.118 | | |
| Instant messaging | Secondary & below | 2 | 5.50 | 0.707 | 0.484 | **A** |
| | Tertiary (GCE "A"Level, Diploma, higher NITEC, NITEC) | 14 | 5.21 | 1.188 | | |
| | Bachelor's degree | 27 | 4.74 | 1.483 | | |
| | Master's degree | 9 | 4.33 | 1.871 | | |
| | Total | 52 | 4.83 | 1.465 | | |
| Google search | Secondary & below | 2 | 2.50 | 2.121 | 0.967 | **A** |
| | Tertiary (GCE "A"Level, Diploma, higher NITEC, NITEC) | 14 | 3.00 | 1.519 | | |
| | Bachelor's degree | 27 | 3.00 | 1.414 | | |
| | Master's degree | 9 | 2.89 | 1.269 | | |

(continued)

**Table 3** (continued)

| Digital marketing channel | Educational level | N | Mean | SD | P-Value | A |
|---|---|---|---|---|---|---|
| | Total | 52 | 2.96 | 1.400 | | |
| Forum | Secondary & below | 2 | 5.50 | 0.707 | 0.541 | A |
| | Tertiary (GCE "A"Level, Diploma, higher NITEC, NITEC) | 14 | 3.71 | 1.267 | | |
| | Bachelor's degree | 27 | 4.07 | 1.685 | | |
| | Master's degree | 9 | 4.00 | 2.000 | | |
| | Total | 52 | 4.02 | 1.615 | | |

The data collected in Table 6 was to analyze the significance between consumer behavior toward digital marketing channels and Employment status. The results indicate that the P value is all above 0.05. Hence, it concludes that there is no significance between the consumer's behavior towards digital marketing channels and the Employment status.

The data collected in Table 7 was to analyse which demographic had significance on social media as a digital marketing channel most likely to be responded to. The results indicates that the P value is all above 0.05 except education. Hence, it concludes that there is no significance between the consumer's likelihood to respond on social media except for education level.

### *4.2 Preference and Effectiveness on the Consumer Behaviour Based on the Communication Channel Used for Digital Marketing*

To evaluate the preference and effectiveness on the consumer behaviour based on the communication channel used for digital marketing, the following tests were performed in Table 8

The data collected in Table 8 was to analyze which age group (Millennial or non-millennial) had significance on preferred communication method. The results indicate that the P value is all above 0.05. Hence, it concludes that there is no significance between the age group and preferred communication method.

**Table 4** Income level and factors affect consumer behaviour towards digital marketing

| Digital marketing channel | Educational level | N | Mean | SD | P | A |
|---|---|---|---|---|---|---|
| Influencer | Secondary & below | 2 | 3.00 | 1.414 | 4.99 | **A** |
| | Tertiary (GCE "A"Level, Diploma, higher NITEC, NITEC) | 14 | 4.07 | 1.492 | | |
| | Bachelor's degree | 27 | 3.89 | 1.695 | | |
| | Master's degree | 9 | 3.11 | 1.900 | | |
| | Total | 52 | 3.77 | 1.664 | | |
| Email | Secondary & below | 2 | 3.00 | 0.000 | 0.656 | **A** |
| | Tertiary (GCE "A"Level, Diploma, higher NITEC, NITEC) | 14 | 3.57 | 1.555 | | |
| | Bachelor's degree | 27 | 3.33 | 1.468 | | |
| | Master's degree | 9 | 4.00 | 1.500 | | |
| | Total | 52 | 3.50 | 1.462 | | |
| Social media | Secondary & below | 2 | 1.50 | 0.707 | 0.065 | **A** |
| | Tertiary (GCE "A"Level, Diploma, higher NITEC, NITEC) | 14 | 1.43 | 0.646 | | |
| | Bachelor's degree | 27 | 1.96 | 1.126 | | |
| | Master's degree | 9 | 2.67 | 1.414 | | |
| | Total | 52 | 1.92 | 1.118 | | |
| Instant messaging | Secondary & below | 2 | 5.50 | 0.707 | 0.484 | **A** |
| | Tertiary (GCE "A"Level, Diploma, higher NITEC, NITEC) | 14 | 5.21 | 1.188 | | |
| | Bachelor's degree | 27 | 4.74 | 1.483 | | |
| | Master's degree | 9 | 4.33 | 1.871 | | |
| | Total | 52 | 4.83 | 1.465 | | |
| Google search | Secondary & below | 2 | 2.50 | 2.121 | 0.967 | **A** |
| | Tertiary (GCE "A"Level, Diploma, higher NITEC, NITEC) | 14 | 3.00 | 1.519 | | |
| | Bachelor's degree | 27 | 3.00 | 1.414 | | |
| | Master's degree | 9 | 2.89 | 1.269 | | |

(continued)

**Table 4** (continued)

| Digital marketing channel | Educational level | N | Mean | SD | P | A |
|---|---|---|---|---|---|---|
| | Total | 52 | 2.96 | 1.400 | | |
| Forum | Secondary & below | 2 | 5.50 | 0.707 | 0.541 | **A** |
| | Tertiary (GCE "A"Level, Diploma, higher NITEC, NITEC) | 14 | 3.71 | 1.267 | | |
| | Bachelor's degree | 27 | 4.07 | 1.685 | | |
| | Master's degree | 9 | 4.00 | 2.000 | | |
| | Total | 52 | 4.02 | 1.615 | | |

**Table 5** Age group and factors affect consumer behaviour towards digital marketing

| Digital marketing channel | Employment Status | N | M | SD | P Value |
|---|---|---|---|---|---|
| Influence | Unemployed | 6 | 3.83 | 1.835 | 0.650 |
| | Working | 40 | 3.85 | 1.642 | |
| | Self Employed | 6 | 3.17 | 1.835 | |
| | Total | 52 | 3.77 | 1.664 | |
| Email | Unemployed | 6 | 3.33 | 0.816 | 0.498 |
| | Working | 40 | 3.43 | 1.551 | |
| | Self employed | 6 | 4.17 | 1.329 | |
| | Total | 52 | 3.50 | 1.462 | |
| Social media | Unemployed | 6 | 2.00 | 0.632 | 0.388 |
| | Working | 40 | 1.83 | 1.107 | |
| | Self employed | 6 | 2.50 | 1.517 | |
| | Total | 52 | 1.92 | 1.118 | |
| Instant messaging | Unemployed | 6 | 5.00 | 2.000 | 0.500 |
| | Working | 40 | 4.78 | 1.330 | |
| | Self employed | 6 | 5.00 | 2.000 | |
| | Total | 52 | 4.83 | 1.465 | |
| Google search | Unemployed | 6 | 2.83 | 1.722 | 0.311 |
| | Working | 40 | 3.00 | 1.392 | |
| | Self employed | 6 | 2.17 | 0.983 | |
| | Total | 52 | 2.96 | 1.400 | |
| Forum | Unemployed | 6 | 4.00 | 1.789 | 0.999 |
| | Working | 40 | 4.03 | 1.672 | |
| | Self employed | 6 | 4.00 | 1.265 | |
| | Total | 52 | 4.02 | 1.615 | |

*Note* N No of respondents, M: Mean, SD: Standard Deviation

**Table 6** Employment status and factors affect consumer behaviour towards digital marketing

| Digital marketing channel | Educational level | N | Mean | SD | P Value |
|---|---|---|---|---|---|
| Influencer | 18–23 years old | 1 | 2.00 | | 0.729 |
| | 24–39 years old | 37 | 3.86 | 1.636 | |
| | 40–55 years old | 12 | 3.67 | 1.923 | |
| | Over 56 years old | 2 | 3.50 | 0.707 | |
| | Total | 52 | 3.77 | 1.664 | |
| Email | 18–23 years old | 1 | 3.00 | | 0.761 |
| | 24–39 years old | 37 | 3.51 | 1.609 | |
| | 40–55 years old | 12 | 3.67 | 1.073 | |
| | Over 56 years old | 2 | 2.50 | 0.707 | |
| | Total | 52 | 3.50 | 1.462 | |
| Social Media | 18–23 years old | 1 | 1.00 | | 0.549 |
| | 24–39 years old | 37 | 1.97 | 1.093 | |
| | 40–55 years old | 12 | 2.00 | 1.279 | |
| | Over 56 years old | 2 | 1.00 | 0.000 | |
| | Total | 52 | 1.92 | 1.118 | |
| Instant messaging | 18–23 years old | 1 | 6.00 | | 0.274 |
| | 24–39 years old | 37 | 4.92 | 1.278 | |
| | 40–55 years old | 12 | 4.25 | 1.960 | |
| | Over 56 years old | 2 | 6.00 | 0.000 | |
| | Total | 52 | 4.83 | 1.465 | |
| Google search | 18–23 years old | 1 | 4.00 | | 0.872 |
| | 24–39 years old | 37 | 2.89 | 1.487 | |
| | 40–55 years old | 12 | 3.08 | 1.240 | |
| | Over 56 years old | 2 | 3.00 | 1.414 | |
| | Total | 52 | 2.96 | 1.400 | |
| Forum | 18–23 years old | 1 | 5.00 | | 0579 |
| | 24–39 years old | 37 | 3.84 | 1.608 | |
| | 40–55 years old | 12 | 4.33 | 1.775 | |
| | Over 56 years old | 2 | 5.00 | 0.000 | |
| | Total | 52 | 4.02 | 1.615 | |

## *4.3 Hypotheses Testing*

Hypothesis 1: There will be no significant difference between Millennials and the effectiveness as a target audience for Instant Messengers. The data collected in Table 9 was to analyze if Millennials were an influential target audience for instant messaging as a digital marketing channel. The results from Table 5.1 indicate that the P value is 0.049. Since the P value is less than 0.05, hypothesis 1 is accepted.

**Table 7** Demographics that most likely to respond to digital marketing channel (social media)

| Digital marketing channel | Educational level | N | Mean | SD | P Value |
|---|---|---|---|---|---|
| What is your Gender? | Most likely | 25 | 1.56 | 0.507 | 0.465 |
| | 2 | 13 | 1.77 | 0.439 | |
| | 3 | 9 | 1.56 | 0.527 | |
| | 4 | 3 | 2.00 | 0.000 | |
| | 5 | 2 | 1.50 | 0.707 | |
| | Total | 52 | 1.63 | 0.486 | |
| What is your Age? | Most likely | 25 | 2.36 | 0.700 | 0.714 |
| | 2 | 13 | 2.15 | 0.376 | |
| | 3 | 9 | 2.33 | 0.500 | |
| | 4 | 3 | 2.00 | 0.000 | |
| | 5 | 2 | 2.50 | 0.707 | |
| | Total | 52 | 2.29 | 0.572 | |
| What is the highest education level you have completed? | Most likely | 25 | 2.68 | 0.748 | 0.038 |
| | 2 | 13 | 2.54 | 0.660 | |
| | 3 | 9 | 3.33 | 0.707 | |
| | 4 | 3 | 3.33 | 0.577 | |
| | 5 | 2 | 3.50 | 0.707 | |
| | Total | 52 | 2.83 | 0.760 | |
| Marital status | Most likely | 25 | 1.40 | 0.500 | 0.637 |
| | 2 | 13 | 1.31 | 0.480 | |
| | 3 | 9 | 1.33 | 0.500 | |
| | 4 | 3 | 1.67 | 0.577 | |
| | 5 | 2 | 1.00 | 0.000 | |
| | Total | 52 | 1.37 | 0.486 | |
| What is your monthly Income level in SGD? | Most likely | 25 | 3.24 | 1.200 | 0.372 |
| | 2 | 13 | 2.38 | 1.193 | |
| | 3 | 9 | 3.22 | 1.856 | |
| | 4 | 3 | 2.67 | 1.155 | |
| | 5 | 2 | 3.50 | 0.707 | |
| | Total | 52 | 3.00 | 1.328 | |

Hence, we concluded that there is a significant difference between the different age groups(Millennials/non-Millennials) and consumer's behavior in engaging with instant messaging as a marketing channel.

Hypothesis 2: Compared to the other digital marketing channels, Instant Messaging is the most effective communication channel.

The data collected in Table 10 analyzed which digital marketing channel consumers would respond to regarding ranking (1 = most likely to respond to, 6

**Table 8** Preferred method of communication

| Preferred Methods of Communication | N | M | SD | P-Value |
|---|---|---|---|---|
| Online | 23 | 1.78 | 0.42 | 0.613 |
| Offline | 4 | 1.50 | 0.57 | |
| Not to be contacted | 2 | 1.50 | 0.70 | |
| Both online and offline | 23 | 1.69 | 0.47 | |
| Total | 52 | 1.71 | 0.45 | |

*Note* N: No of respondents, M: Mean, SD: Standard Deviation, S. Er: Standard Error, LB: Lower Bound, UB: Upper Bound, MiM: Minimum, MxM: Maximum

**Table 9** Millennials engagement with instant messaging

| Independent Sample Test | | *t*-test for equality of Means | | | | |
|---|---|---|---|---|---|---|
| | | F | P | t | df | Sig (2-tailed) |
| If you were being served an advertisement which of the following digital marketing channels will you most likely to respond to? Rank the following in order of most to least likely (1= mot like Whatsapp | Equal variances assumed | 4.09 | .048 | -0.70 | 50 | 0.48 |
| | Equal not variances assumed | | | 0.50 | 18.45 | 0.55 |

*Note* F: Frequency, MD: Mean Difference, SD: Standard Deviation, S. Er: Standard Error Difference, LB: Lower Bound, UB: Upper Bound, MiM: Minimum, MxM: Maximum

= least likely). The results from Table 4.24 indicate that instant messaging is ranked the lowest among all the channels. Therefore, hypothesis 2 is rejected. From the result, in terms of ranking, consumers would respond to this marketing channel in the following order: Social media, Google Search, Email, Influencer, Forum, and Instant Messaging. Hence, it is concluded that there is a significant difference between the different age groups(Millennials/non-Millennials) and the consumer's behavior in engaging with instant messaging as a marketing channel.

**Table 10** Marketing channel most likely to respond

| Digital marketing channel | N | Mean | SD |
|---|---|---|---|
| Influencer | 52 | 3.77 | 1.664 |
| Email | 52 | 3.50 | 1.462 |
| Social media | 52 | 1.92 | 1.118 |
| Instant messaging | 52 | 4.83 | 1.465 |
| Google search | 52 | 2.96 | 1.400 |
| Forum | 52 | 4.02 | 1.615 |

Hypothesis 3: There is no significant difference between the millennials of the respondents with regards to the factors affecting consumer's behaviour towards digital marketing.

The data collected in Table 11 was to analyze whether the factors affecting consumer behavior toward digital marketing correlate with whether the consumer is a millennial or not a millennial. The results from Table 4.10 indicate that the P value of all the factors except product and price has a P less than 0.05. Secondly, the data concludes that for Millennials, the factors influencing the consumer's behavior in rank are brand reputation, product, price, type of promotion, personalization, where the advertisement is, and competition. Whereas for non-Millennials, the factors influencing the consumer's behavior in order of rank are brand reputation, price, type of promotion, product, where the advertisement was found, personalization, and competition.

Instant Messaging as a marketing channel, from the respondent's perspective, does not seem as effective as other common mediums, even though instant messaging has the highest usage among all the tracks. However, different results also show

**Table 11** Millennials and factors affect consumer behaviour towards digital marketing

| Factors | Age group | N | Mean | SD | P Value |
|---|---|---|---|---|---|
| Competition | Non-Millennial | 15 | 6.20 | 0.862 | 0.457 |
| | Millennial | 37 | 5.92 | 1.341 | |
| | Total | 52 | 6.00 | 1.221 | |
| Personalization | Non-Millennial | 15 | 5.07 | 1.534 | 0.215 |
| | Millennial | 37 | 4.41 | 1.787 | |
| | Total | 52 | 4.60 | 1.729 | |
| Price | Non-Millennial | 15 | 2.93 | 1.163 | 0.048 |
| | Millennial | 37 | 3.76 | 1.383 | |
| | Total | 52 | 3.52 | 1.365 | |
| Product | Non-Millennial | 15 | 3.47 | 1.807 | 0.04 |
| | Millennial | 37 | 2.51 | 1.325 | |
| | Total | 52 | 2.79 | 1.525 | |
| Type of promotion | Non-Millennial | 15 | 3.27 | 1.387 | 0.247 |
| | Millennial | 37 | 3.86 | 1.766 | |
| | Total | 52 | 3.69 | 1.675 | |
| Where the advertisement was shown | Non-Millennial | 15 | 4.27 | 2.282 | 0.31 |
| | Millennial | 37 | 4.89 | 1.868 | |
| | Total | 52 | 4.71 | 1.993 | |
| Brand reputation | Non-Millennial | 15 | 2.47 | 1.506 | 0.85 |
| | Millennial | 37 | 2.38 | 1.516 | |
| | Total | 52 | 2.40 | 1.498 | |

a significance between those exposed to the medium and their perception of their likelihood to respond to it.

## 5 Research Contributions

The study found that there are a few common digital marketing channels that advertisers commonly use. The findings indicate that consumers are most likely to respond to advertisements in rank from Social media, Google Search, Email, Influencers, Forums, and Instant Messaging [30]. Instant messaging as a digital marketing channel concerning the age groups and their relationship with instant messaging was studied. The results show a significant difference between the consumer's age groups (Millennials/non-Millennials) and the consumer's likelihood to respond to the advertisement on the medium. Therefore, advertisers should focus their efforts on the millennial group as their primary target audience to get the most effective response rate to optimize the conversion rates of their campaigns. The results also agree with Hypothesis 1 that Millennials would be more effective as a target audience of instant messaging as a digital marketing channel [2]. In the context of exposure, results show a significant difference between the consumer's age groups (Millennials/non-Millennials) and the consumer's likelihood to respond to the advertisement on the medium. [2]. Therefore, advertisers should focus their efforts on the millennial group as their primary target audience to get the most effective response rate to optimize the conversion rates of their campaigns. The results also agree with Hypothesis 1 that Millennials would be more effective as a target audience of instant messaging as a digital marketing channel.

Regarding marital status and the relationship with instant messaging, the results found a significant relationship between the respondent's marital status and their likeliness to respond to instant messaging [34]. Therefore, advertisers should focus their efforts on single individuals compared to married individuals, who are more likely to respond to digital marketing efforts through that medium. In the context of the Factors that affect effectiveness on consumer behavior, results found no significant relationship between the respondent's gender and their likeliness to respond to the standard digital marketing channel. Therefore, advertisers need not focus on gender differentiation when marketing digitally. It also found no significant relationship between the respondent's marital status and their likeliness to respond to common digital marketing channels apart from instant messaging. Therefore, advertisers can focus on something other than marital status for the most common digital marketing channels apart from instant messaging, where singles are more likely to respond than married individuals.

Regarding the educational level, results found no significant relationship between the respondent's academic level and their likeliness to respond to the standard digital marketing channel. Therefore, advertisers must focus on something other than educational level differentiation when marketing digitally. Also, results found no significant relationship between the respondent's income level and their likeliness to respond to common digital marketing channels. Therefore, advertisers need to focus on something other than income-level differentiation when marketing digitally. Lastly, the results found no significant relationship between the respondent's employment status and their likeliness to respond to common digital marketing channels. Therefore, advertisers need to focus on something other than employment status differentiation when marketing digitally.

Strategies to improve the effectiveness of Instant Messaging as a communication channel are also crucial in online vs. offline. Results found no significant relationship between the respondent's preferred mode of communication and their age group to respond to standard digital marketing channel advertisements. However, based on frequencies, there is an equal inclination towards online only or both online and offline communication. Therefore, advertisers need not focus their efforts on communication mode and stick to the method that they are most comfortable with. Lastly, in the product context, results found a significant relationship between the respondent's perception of the product as a factor and their age group. It also indicates that millennial views product more highly as compared to non-Millennials. Therefore, advertisers should focus their efforts on ensuring that the product's quality is good, especially if their name's target audience is Millennials.

## *5.1 Limitations and Future Research Avenue*

Although there has been an effort in this paper to discuss and analyze certain factors contributing to consumer behavior in instant messaging as a digital channel, several limitations can be identified. Firstly, the sample size could be more significant. This is due to the limited time and resources for this project. To attain a more accurate analysis, future research could consider getting a larger size. Secondly, another limitation of this study is the demographics of the respondents. In terms of demographics, the respondents were mainly residing in Singapore only. It could be interesting to compare how different countries react to instant messaging as a channel. In addition, a better spread of age group is recommended as most respondents are Millennials. This is due to the limitation of the survey distribution, and more Millennials are active in social media. It is easier for them to navigate their way through an online questionnaire.

Furthermore, based on the data collected, only a few respondents have been exposed to the instant messenger as a digital marketing channel, even though they use it frequently. Based on this, their answers could be skewed based on their perception rather than an actual representation of their response. For future tests, a larger sample size could be used, or if resource permits and regulation of social meet-ups relaxes, to allow respondents to be exposed to an instant messaging ad before attempting the question.

## 6 Conclusion

The present study has addressed the research gap in the context of consumer buying behavior using an explorative research framework by which hypotheses are explored using the survey method and realism as the research philosophy. The data collection is done through research questions so that a comprehensive data set is collected to examine the various research objectives and enable the correct findings. The study has indicated that the perception of the effectiveness of instant messaging as a marketing channel could be better as compared to the other digital marketing channels and finally concluded that Millennials were more responsive towards instant messenger as a digital channel compared to non-Millennials. Instant messengers as a marketing channel should be more utilized and could still allow marketers to differentiate themselves from competitors. Based on the results, it is highly likely that Millennials were more responsive than non-Millennials. The product and price factors are the critical differentiator between targeting Millennials and non-Millennials. Millennials rank product quality higher than price, whereas non-Millennials are more price-conscious. The study also highlighted that regardless of the channel, marketers should ensure their brand's reputation is vital as it is the most crucial factor for consumers in the buyer behavior for both age groups (Millennials/non-Millennials).

## References


1. Petrosyan, A.: Worldwide digital population 2023. Statista (2023)
2. Granheim, S.I., Løvhaug, A.L., Terragni, L., Torheim, L.E., Thurston, M.: Mapping the digital food environment: A systematic scoping review. Obes. Rev. **23**(1), (2022) https://doi.org/10.1111/obr.13356.
3. Appel, G., Grewal, L., Hadi, R., Stephen, A.T.: The future of social media in marketing. J. Acad. Mark. Sci. **48**(1), 79–95 (2020)
4. Chivandi, A., Samuel, M.O., Muchie, M.: Social media, consumer behavior, and service marketing. Consum. Behav. Mark., 25 (2020)
5. Guttmann, A..: 2018 Small Business Marketing Trends. 2018 Small Business Marketing Trends https://www.statista.com/statistics/467219/local-merchant-media-marketing-choice-usa (2018). Accessed 05 Oct. 2018
6. Pancholi, V.R., Patel, B.P.: Enhancement of cloud computing security with secure data storage using AES. Int. J. Innov. Res. Sci. Technol. **2**(9), 18–21 (2016)
7. Kisiołek, A., Karyy, O., Halkiv, L.: Social media in marketing management of higher education institutions in the context of poland and ukraine. Polish J. Manag. Stud. **24**(1), (2021)
8. Gu, S., Ślusarczyk, B., Hajizada, S., Kovalyova, I., Sakhbieva, A.: Impact of the covid-19 pandemic on online consumer purchasing behavior. J. Theor. Appl. Electron. Commer. Res. **16**(6), 2263–2281 (2021)
9. Statista Research Department: Personalized Marketing Channels Use 2018. Evergage Inc. https://www.statista.com/statistics/451788/digital-marketing-channels-with-personalized-communication(2021). Accessed 07 Aug. 2020
10. Evergage: 2018 Trends In Personalization. Evergage Inc. http://www.evergage.com/wp-content/uploads/2018/04/Evergage-2018-Trends-in-Personalization-Survey.pdf (2018). Accessed 07 Aug. 2020

11. Sahay: Peeling Saunders'S Research Onion. Peeling Saunders'S Research Onion. https://www.researchgate.net/profile/Arunaditya_Sahay2/publication/309488459_Peeling_Saunder's_Research_Onion/links/5813283508aedc7d89609ea8/Peeling-Saunders-Research-Onion.pdf (2016). Accessed 17 Nov. 2020
12. Ceci, L.: Number of facebook messenger users in the United States from 2018 to 2022. eMarketer. https://statista.com/statistics/558283/number-of-fb-messenger-users-usa (2018). Accessed 07 Aug. 2020
13. Valentini, S., Montaguti, E., Neslin, S.A.: Decision process evolution in customer channel choice. J. Mark. **75**(6), 72–86 (2011)
14. Duffett, R.G.: Effect of instant messaging advertising on the hierarchy-of-effects model amid teenagers in South Africa. Electron. J. Inf. Syst. Dev. Ctries. **72**(1), 1–21 (2016)
15. Yudhana, A., Riadi, I., Anshori, I.: Identification of digital evidence facebook messenger on mobile phone with National Institute of Standards Technology (Nist) Method. J. Ilm. Kursor. **9**(3), (2018)
16. Rehman, F.U., Ilyas, M., Nawaz, T., Hyder, S.: How Facebook advertising affects buying behavior of young consumers: The moderating role of gender. Acad. Res. Int. **5**(4), 395–404 (2014)
17. Taber, K.S.: The use of Cronbach's alpha when developing and reporting research instruments in science education. Res. Sci. Educ. **48**(6), 1273–1296 (2018)
18. Padmavathy, C., Lee, S.A., Pattusamy, M., Dey, M.K., Swapana, M.: The role of perceived benefits and personality traits on mobile instant messaging users' responses. Asia Pacific J. Mark. Logist. (2018)
19. Taiminen, H.M., Karjaluoto, H.: The usage of digital marketing channels in SMEs. J. Small Bus. Enterp. Dev. (2015)
20. Rathod, A.Y., Pandya, S., Doshi, N.: IoT and Modern Marketing: Its Social Implications. International Conference on Advanced Communication Technology, ICACT 2020, 407–413 (2020). https://doi.org/10.23919/ICACT48636.2020.9061210
21. Balasudarsun, N.L., Sathish, M., Gowtham, K.: Optimal ways for companies to use Facebook Messenger Chatbot as a Marketing Communication Channel. Asian J. Bus. Res. **8**(2), 1–17 (2018)
22. J. Bell and S. Waters, Ebook: doing your research project: a guide for first-time researchers. Mcgraw-hill education, UK (2018)
23. M. Koufaris and W. Hampton-Sosa, "Customer trust online: examining the role of the experience with the Web-site," Dep. Stat. Comput. Inf. Syst. Work. Pap. Ser. Zicklin Sch. Business, Baruch Coll. New York, 2002.
24. Princes, E., Manurung, A.H., So, I.G., Abdinagoro, S.B.: A closer look at the consumer conformity in industry 4.0: Purchase intention redefined. Polish J. Manag. Stud. **22**(1), 401–417 (2020). https://doi.org/10.17512/pjms.2020.22.1.26
25. Parwekar, P., Gupta, G.: Cloud data for marketing in tourism sector. Smart Innovation, Systems and Technologies **165**, 143–153 (2020). https://doi.org/10.1007/978-981-15-0077-0_16
26. S. N. C. Microsoft, Microsoft. SME digital transformation study, SME Digital Transformation Study. https://news.microsoft.com/en-sg/2020/10/22/over-80-of-singapore-smes-embrace-digital-transformation-more-than-half-report-slowdowns-due-to-covid-19-asme-microsoft-study-2020 (2020). Accessed 26 Nov 2020
27. Upadhyaya, M.: Customer Satisfaction Measurement: an empirical Study of the Need-Gap Analysis in the Service Industry. J. Econ. Bus. Res. **19**(2), 54–61 (2013)
28. Akre, V., Rajan, A., Ahamed, J., Al Amri, A., Al Daisi, S.: Smart digital marketing of financial services to millennial generation using emerging technological tools and buyer persona. In: ITT 2019—Information Technology Trends: Emerging Technologies Blockchain and IoT, pp. 120–125. (2019) https://doi.org/10.1109/ITT48889.2019.9075106.
29. Rocsana, B.-M.-T., Ovidiu, B. Factors influencing online consumer behavior in the era of iot. Mater. Sci. Forum. **957** MSF, 81–89 (2019). https://doi.org/10.4028/www.scientific.net/MSF.957.81.

30. Quach, S., Thaichon, P., Martin, K.D., Weaven, S., Palmatier, R.W.: Digital technologies: tensions in privacy and data. J. Acad. Mark. Sci. (2022). https://doi.org/10.1007/s11747-022-00845-y
31. Kaczorowska-Spychalska, D.: Shaping consumer behaviour in the fashion industry by interactive communication forms. Fibres Text. East. Eur. **26**(4), 13–19 (2018). https://doi.org/10.5604/01.3001.0012.1307
32. Zyphur, M.J., Pierides, D.C.: Is quantitative research ethical? Tools for ethically practicing, evaluating, and using quantitative research. J. Bus. Ethics **143**(1), 1–16 (2017)
33. U. Sekaran., Bougie, R.: Research Methods for Business: A Skill Building Approach. John Wiley & Sons (2016)
34. Imanova, G.E., Imanova, G.: Digital marketing technologies selection under Z-environment. Adv. Intell. Syst. Comput. **1306**, 378–387 (2021). https://doi.org/10.1007/978-3-030-64058-3_47

# An Acceptance Model for the Adoption of Battery Electric Vehicles in Thailand

**Thana Sithanant, Burin Sukphisal, and Nayika Kamales**

**Abstract** The primary objective of this study is to propose a model that will shape the adoption patterns of battery electric vehicles (BEVs) within the consumer demographic of Thailand. BEVs have emerged as a promising avenue for addressing critical environmental concerns, including air pollution, fossil fuel dependency, and climate change. Despite the successful integration of BEVs in various global markets, the penetration in Thailand remains notably limited in contrast to nations such as the United States, China, and Europe, especially Norway. The investigation begins by delineating the fundamental characteristics of BEVs, followed by a meticulous integration of theoretical underpinnings derived from the Unified Theory of Acceptance and Use of Technology (UTAUT) and the Car Technology Acceptance Model (CTAM). These theoretical frameworks serve as a robust foundation for the analysis. In tandem with this theoretical framework, a host of pivotal determinants from multiple BEV adoption reviews is scrutinized, encompassing aspects like pricing structures, regulatory policies implemented by governmental bodies, the accessibility and robustness of charging infrastructures, the dimensions of environmental consciousness, experiential considerations related to driving, household composition, and residential placement. Consequently, these multifarious determinants are synthesized and result in a novel conceptual framework, thereby engendering a nuanced and insightful comprehension of the pivotal drivers that collectively shape the landscape of BEV adoption within Thailand. Further empirical investigations will be undertaken to a more profound awareness of the intricate dynamics that propel the broader integration of BEVs nationwide.

**Keywords** Battery electric vehicle · Adoption · UTAUT · CTAM

T. Sithanant (✉) · B. Sukphisal · N. Kamales
KMITL Business School, King Mongkut's Institute of Technology Ladkrabang, 10520 Bangkok, Thailand
e-mail: 63611005@kmitl.ac.th

B. Sukphisal
e-mail: burin.su@kmitl.ac.th

 
S. Kot et al. (eds.), *Corporate Practices: Policies, Methodologies, and Insights in Organizational Management*, Springer Proceedings in Business and Economics,
https://doi.org/10.1007/978-981-97-0996-0_13

## 1 Introduction

The global carbon footprint associated with fossil fuel usage is undergoing an alarming expansion, attributable to the prevailing fossil fuel crisis and the escalating environmental concerns that have attained heightened prominence due to their substantial repercussions on the Earth's ecological equilibrium. This trajectory is anticipated to persist in its upward trajectory over temporal horizons. This situation contributes to the emission of greenhouse gases, prominently including carbon dioxide, which stands as the principal instigator of worldwide temperature elevation and subsequent climate alterations [1]. Nevertheless, a cluster of nations across the globe has acknowledged the gravity of this predicament and embarked upon diverse initiatives aimed at mitigation [2]. A prospective avenue to address the quandary posed by fossil fuel consumption lies in the transition from internal combustion engine vehicles to electric vehicles [3, 4]. However, realizing this paradigm shift remains an accomplishment limited to a few nations [5], among which Norway is a noteworthy exemplar [6]. Notably, a significant milestone was reached in the year 2020, wherein Norway emerged as the first nation in history to witness a dominant proportion (54.3%) of new vehicle registrations comprising battery electric vehicles (BEVs), surpassing the conventional combustion engine vehicles (CFVs) [7, 8]. The triumph of Norway has aroused considerable interest among other nations, fostering a desire to comprehend the pivotal success factors that underlie its achievement [9]. In Thailand, the ramifications of this technological transition are poised to resonate not only in the environmental sphere but also across the spectrum of domestic automobile manufacturing and its ancillary downstream industries, encompassing vehicle servicing, electronics, power generation, and battery production [10, 11]. Thailand, too, has endeavored to promote the adoption of electric vehicles for a substantial period; nevertheless, a discernible disparity persists when juxtaposed with the Norwegian paradigm [12, 13]. In light of these considerations, the present analysis is steered towards a comprehensive exploration and comparative examination of the interrelationships and factors influencing the consumer adoption of battery electric vehicles within the Thai context. The outcomes emanating from this endeavor hold the potential to inform the formulation of an encompassing roadmap, benefitting all stakeholders vested in orchestrating a national transformation. Furthermore, this study could serve as a strategic compass for policymakers, offering insights for articulating proactive initiatives, goal delineation, strategic blueprints, and the synchronization of infrastructural imperatives to be realized in the times ahead. Given these imperatives, an incisive investigation into the determinants propelling Thai consumers' inclination towards embracing BEVs assumes profound significance.

# 2 Literature Review

## 2.1 Definitions

In Thailand's current vehicle market, there are four types of electric vehicles (EVs). The Thailand Automotive Institute gives full definitions for these types as follows:

### 2.1.1 Hybrid Electric Vehicles (HEVs)

HEVs combine internal combustion engines (ICEs) and electric motors. ICEs perform the main function of driving, while the electric motors will only provide power when the vehicles start, and during acceleration. The batteries in HEVs are in a closed loop, meaning they will be recharged by the engine's deceleration or acceleration, but not by any external source such as electricity mains [14].

### 2.1.2 Plug-In Hybrid Electric Vehicles (PHEVs)

PHEVs are similar to HEVs, but the difference is that they have larger batteries and can be charged from electricity mains. However, PHEVs have a limited electric range, usually less than 100 km, before swapping to the internal combustion engine once all the batteries are drained [14].

### 2.1.3 Fuel Cell Electric Vehicles (FCEVs)

FCEVs can be considered another type of EV as the structures consist of a fuel cell stack and a high-pressure tank used to store hydrogen in liquid form. The working principle is that hydrogen and oxygen are sent to the fuel cells to react and generate the electricity that charges the battery. Electricity is then sent to the electric motor to drive the vehicle [14].

### 2.1.4 Battery Electric Vehicles (BEVs)

BEVs are purely electrically operated, and no other source of power is involved except for the electricity that is stored in the batteries. The batteries can be charged using electricity converters from power outlets [14].

Compared to other vehicles, BEVs have the longest pure electric driving range and the highest battery capacity, which also means they take the longest time to charge [14]. As a result, customers who wish to use BEVs must dramatically change their driving habits compared to other EVs or standard FCVs. This suggests that the variables that influence consumers are also very different [15]. This analysis is limited to considerations affecting BEVs only, and not those aligned with HEVs, PHEVs and FCEVs.

## 2.2 The Review of Theory

In this section, the aim is to explore and describe all relevant theories, elements, and additional factors that will be constructed for the development of the final acceptance framework for adopting battery electric vehicles in Thailand.

### 2.2.1 Unified Theory of Acceptance and Use of Technology (UTAUT)

In 2003, Venkatesh, Morris, G. B. Davis, and F. B. Davis proposed the Unified Theory of Acceptance and Use of Technology (UTAUT). The aim was to anticipate user intentions to embrace technology and the succeeding usage behavior [16]. Four key elements comprise the primary constructs of UTAUT: (1) performance expectancy, (2) effort expectancy, (3) social influence, and (4) facilitating conditions [16]. UTAUT was derived from eight previous dominant models that vary from human behavior, computer science, and information technology. Eight models are (1) The theory of reasoned action (TRA), (2) motivational model (MM), (3) model of PC utilization (MPCU), (4) the theory of planned behavior (TPB), (5) technology acceptance model (TAM), (6) combined theory of planned behavior and technology acceptance model (TAM and TPB), (7) diffusion of innovation theory (DOI) and (8) social cognitive theory (SCT) [16]. Figure 1 illustrates the concept of UTAUT, and the four key elements can be described as follows:

*Performance expectancy:* The extent to which a person believes that using the system can assist that person to improve job performance [16].

*Effort expectancy:* The level of ease affiliated with using the system [16].

*Social influence:* The extent to which a person assumes that others think that such person should have used the new system [16].

*Facilitating conditions:* The extent to which an individual assumes that the system's organizational and technological infrastructure is in place to facilitate its use [16].

While the first three elements directly affect usage intentions and usage behavior, the fourth factor only impacts use behavior. Age, gender, experience, and voluntariness of use are considered the moderators to influence the four key elements of usage intention and use behavior [16].

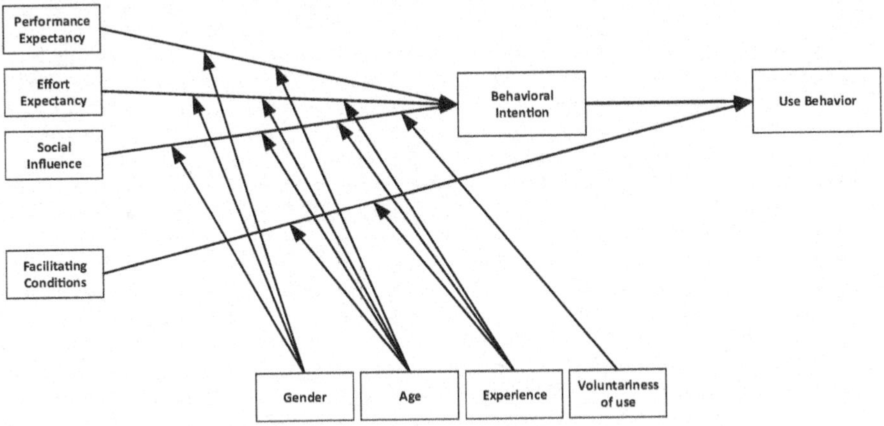


**Fig. 1** Original model for the unified theory of acceptance and use of technology (UTAUT) [16]

### *2.3 Car Technology Acceptance Model (CTAM)*

In 2012, Osswald, Wurhofer, Trösterer, Beck, and Tscheligi proposed the Car Technology Acceptance Model (CTAM). This model was designed specifically to predict information technology usage in cars [17]. Its constitution introduces four additional elements over the original UTAUT, which are (1) attitudes towards using technology, (2) perceived safety, (3) self-efficacy, and (4) anxiety [17]. CTAM aims to explore the popularity of modern information technology in cars, such as GPS and access to mobile phones via the car's dashboard. Although CTAM is derived from UTAUT, its questionnaires are adapted slightly to match the car context (e.g., the questionnaire is altered, and employment is replaced with driving). With high prediction accuracy, CTAM was later widely accepted for the prediction of the adoption of the emerging technology that was being used in cars.

In 2019, the University of Cambridge researchers Hewitt, Politis, Amanatidis, and Sarkar introduced the Autonomous Vehicle Acceptance Model (AVAM). This model focuses on user acceptance of autonomous vehicles. AVAM was adapted from existing user acceptance models for generic technologies, UTAUT and CTAM. While CTAM questions are worded to focus mainly on in-car technology, AVAM intends to cover whole-car technologies such as autonomous vehicles [18] (Fig. 2).

All four additional elements can be defined as follows:

**Anxiety:** The extent to which a person feels apprehension, unease, or arousal when confronted with a situation. [18].

**Perceived safety:** The extent to which a person assumes that using a system will affect that person's well-being [18].

**Attitude towards using technology:** The magnitude of a user's overall affective response to a system. This component aims to represent the user's beliefs on system use and its consequences. [18].

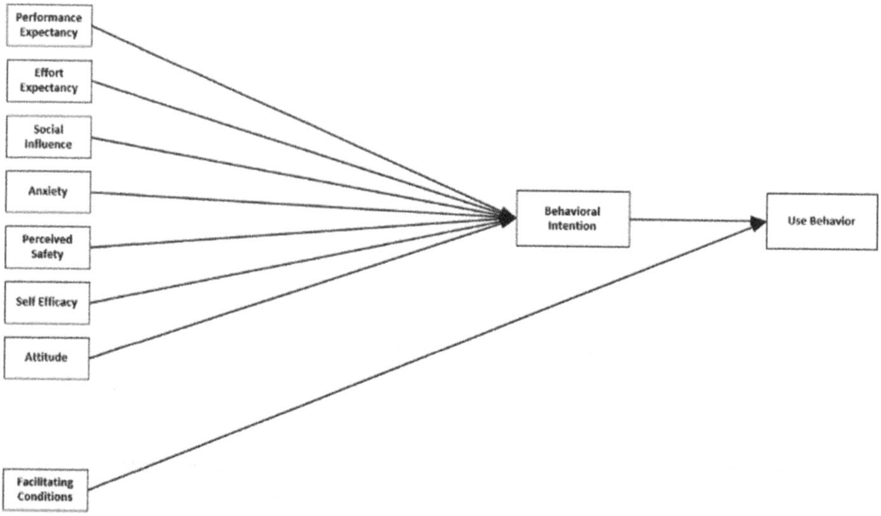


**Fig. 2** Autonomous vehicle acceptance research model (AVAM) inherited from CTAM, as proposed by Hewitt [18]

**Self-efficacy:** The determinant of a person's confidence in his or her ability to use technology (such as GPS) to accomplish a task [18].

## *2.4 Review of Other Factors Related to BEV*

As a modern automotive product, a BEV is very distinct from a CFV in terms of technology [14]. These distinctions may be potential influences on the adoption rate. One of the distinctions is that BEVs consume electricity stored in the battery and need to be recharged by electrical outlets. In contrast, CFVs consume gasoline or petrol stored in a tank and must be refilled at gas stations. These distinct characteristics of BEVs will require those who adopt them to adapt their mindsets and daily behaviors [19]. So, it is evident that a comprehensive understanding can only be achieved through something other than UTAUT or CTAM. To furnish a more comprehensive analysis, it is imperative to incorporate additional constructs and factors into the examination. Beyond the traditional CTAM constructs, the following elements shall be deliberated upon as supplementary determinants: environmental concern, price value, charging infrastructure, and government policy. Furthermore, it is essential to undertake a meticulous reassessment and customization of each constituent of the CTAM framework to render it applicable and relevant to the specific context of BEVs.

### 2.4.1 Performance Expectancy

The reason for owning and driving a car is to move from one place to another within the known limitations of specific vehicles. BEVs and CFVs are not much different in terms of performance expectancy. However, the driving distance of BEVs has been identified as one of the major obstacles to customer acceptance [20, 21]. As a result, promoting BEVs to consumers remains a challenge unless the driving distance is increased significantly compared to CFVs.

### 2.4.2 Effort Expectancy

In general, a person who normally drives CFVs can switch to drive BEVs without much effort or long periods of trial and error. The ease of use of BEVs should be intrinsic. Nevertheless, the impact of technical factors that influence effort expectancy, such as engine power, top speed, acceleration, and responsiveness, have also been verified as positively related to the adoption rate [22, 23].

### 2.4.3 Social Influence

Many scholars who study BEV adoption focus on social influence, which refers to an individual's sense of exception or pressure from external sources or individuals. These references may be both intangible and prescriptive in nature. Thus, subjective social norms have a positive effect on intention [24, 25]. Likewise, the study of Barth, Jugert, and Fritsche found that the impact of social influence was even higher than that of economic factors [26].

### 2.4.4 Anxiety

Range anxiety is described as the fear of a BEV's battery being depleted in the middle of a trip [27]. In the past, range anxiety about BEVs was considered a roadblock to adoption [27]. Now, however, the situation seems to be improved as battery technology has advanced tremendously, though there is still concern among consumers [28]. Graham-Rowe et al. [28] explained that the restricted range of BEVs has a negative impact on consumer behavior unless travel schedules are well planned, which reduces range anxiety. Range anxiety can also be alleviated if drivers have had extensive experience with BEVs [28].

### 2.4.5 Perceived Safety

When it comes to automobile adoption, safety has always been the top priority. Thai people are very concerned about driving BEVs during heavy rain because there is a high risk of flooding, which may result in an electrical short circuit. Thus, carmakers that can show BEVs can handle this issue will persuade the public to consider the adoption of BEVs [29].

### 2.4.6 Self-Efficacy

People with high self-efficacy are more likely to adopt BEVs and see them as a challenge to master rather than a threat to escape. In a study conducted in the United States, self-efficacy was found to be a major factor in predicting behavioral intentions [30].

### 2.4.7 Attitude

This component is intended to represent users' attitudes toward BEV use and its consequences. Attitudes are often considered to be important psychological variables that affect adoption decisions [31]. Several researchers have investigated attitudes towards several subjects, including technology affiliation, the environment, comfort, and image, and concluded that attitudes were the most accurate predictors of consumer intention [31, 32].

### 2.4.8 Environmental Concern

BEVs are being marketed all over the world because of their zero-carbon emissions and environmental friendliness. These environmental advantages are driving factors for consumer adoption intentions [32–34]. This means that, to accelerate the rate of adoption, the promotion of BEVs in Thailand should emphasize the characteristics of environmental sustainability.

### 2.4.9 Charging Infrastructure

One of the most discussed topics among the previous studies is the charging of BEVs as this is the main distinction from CFVs. The charging issue is the major factor for those whose intention is to use BEVs to change their daily lives. The charging infrastructure problems are not limited to long charging times and inadequate charging facilities, but also the standardization of charging hardware. The negative effect of charging time cannot be overlooked unless the charging period can be adequately reduced and the availability of charging infrastructure is sufficient [35]. Also, the number and location of public domain charging stations will have a positive effect on market penetration [22]. Some consumers intend to charge their BEVs at home with domestic charging infrastructure [36, 37]. In order to accommodate charging facilities at home, however, consumers will most likely be required to upgrade their home electric supplies with another lump sum investment. Potential promotional policies could include some incentives to cover this added cost [37].

### 2.4.10 Price Value

Price value is defined as an individual's perceived trade-off between the costs and benefits of using technology [38]. The price value is considered a positive impact towards intentions when the benefits are greater than the costs. Compared to traditional fuel engine vehicles (CFVs), the high upfront cost of BEVs is the first barrier to entry for BEVs, whereas the lower operational cost is asserted in favor of adoption. This price factor is discussed in the majority of studies [36, 38–41]. However, consumers take into consideration the initial cost of BEVs more than any long-term savings [39, 40]. Although the cost advantages of BEVs may appeal to certain customers, these advantages are not immediately apparent. However, short-term countermeasures, such as substantial cash promotions, should also encourage the majority of targeted customers. This suggests that the Thai government could issue rebates or use a tax policy to induce a higher adoption rate.

### 2.4.11 Government Policy

The widespread acceptance of BEVs appears heavily dependent on government assistance during the market promotion period. As evidence from Norway in 2020 shows, Norway is proud to be the world capital of BEVs with more than half of its newly registered vehicles being pure electric types [7]. The process of transforming the country began in 2008, which was when Oslo formulated its CO2 emission reduction plan, and electric vehicles were a major part from the start. The government has played a key role in this accomplishment as it laid out clear action goals for many establishments throughout the country [8]. From many previous studies, one of the most powerful policies is financial subsidies [20, 26, 42–44]. As the major barrier to adoption is the much higher cost of BEVs, government policies, including monetary incentives, preferential tax rates, free parking, and driving privileges have been demonstrated to positively influence consumer adoption intentions. Not only will this policy of subsidization directly impact consumer intentions, but also act as a moderator to the consumer price value factor. Moreover, these effects were found to increase when more aggressive policies were issued [41, 45]. Another major policy that positively affects the adoption rate is the setup of charging stations and standardization, as discussed earlier from various studies [20, 37, 46]. This is in line with the establishment plan from Norway. Since 2008, the Norwegian government has embarked on a program to construct at least two fast-charging stations every 50 km on all main roads. This infrastructure will eventually cover the whole country and targets 2025 as its deadline [8]. It seems obvious that commitments from the government can significantly influence customer intentions.

#### 2.4.12 Facilitating Conditions

Facilitating conditions refer to an individual's perception of the technical support that is available for using a technology or system [16]. For BEVs, it can be understood that an ample source of batteries, available learning tools and information, and resources for maintenance, as well as after sales services exist [47]. This relationship between facilitating conditions and use behavior for BEVs was found to be positive [47].

#### 2.4.13 Driving Experience

Driving experience is practically defined as the direct experience of previous driving with BEVs [48]. In fact, experience can significantly moderate the relationship between social influence and behavioral intention [16]. Also, experience can have a moderating effect on the relationship between facilitating conditions and behavioral intention. Furthermore, there was a moderating effect of driving experience towards range anxiety as inexperienced drivers had relatively more anxiety about driving BEVs than experienced drivers [28, 48].

#### 2.4.14 Voluntariness of Use

Voluntariness of use is the degree to which the use of technology is perceived as voluntary or the result of self-determination [16]. While CTAM and AVAM do not incorporate this element, research has shown that the connection between BEV usage behavior and facilitating conditions could be influenced by the voluntariness of use, as confirmed by [49].

#### 2.4.15 Household Composition

Family and household factors influence the adoption of BEVs, in addition to individual considerations. The larger the family, the more likely customers are to embrace a BEV [50]. Similarly, the number of vehicles in a family is a significant factor; customers in families with more vehicles are more likely to own at least one BEV [20]. This is quite positive for the Thai market as Thai people tend to live in larger family groups compared to others.

#### 2.4.16 Living Location

Living location is accounted for as a variable to impact BEV adoption [15]. Consumers who live outside of urban areas tend to be early adopters. Because of their long commutes, they can be more economical by using BEVs [38]. However, aspects of location in Thailand can generate different results as there are people who live in the vicinity of a town, but the long traveling time can have a similar effect to a long traveling distance because of traffic congestion.

## 3 Proposed Conceptual Framework and Hypotheses

The amalgamation of insights garnered from the synthesis of UTAUT, CTAM, and various other critical determinants influencing Battery Electric Vehicle (BEV) adoption has culminated in the formulation of the acceptance model presented in Fig. 3.

In summary, all hypotheses can be derived as the following:

H1: Adoption of BEVs could be affected by performance expectancy.

H2: Adoption of BEVs could be affected by effort expectancy.

H3: Adoption of BEVs could be affected by social influence.

H4: Adoption of BEVs could be affected by anxiety.

H5: Adoption of BEVs could be affected by perceived safety.

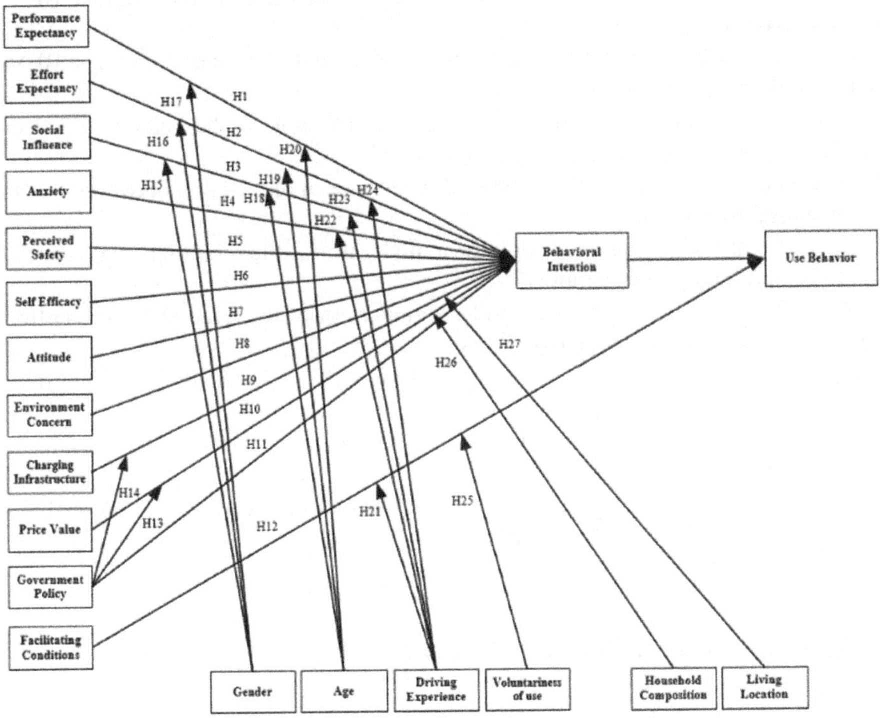


**Fig. 3** Proposed framework for the adoption of battery electric vehicles in Thailand based on CTAM

H6: Adoption of BEVs could be affected by self-efficacy.
H7: Adoption of BEVs could be affected by attitude.
H8: Adoption of BEVs could be affected by environmental concerns.
H9: Adoption of BEVs could be affected by charging infrastructure.
H10: Adoption of BEVs could be affected by price value.
H11: Adoption of BEVs could be affected by government policy.
H12: Usage behavior of BEVs could be affected by facilitating conditions.

H13: The relationship between price value and the decision to embrace BEVs may be moderated by government policy.

H14: The relationship between the charging infrastructure and intention to embrace BEVs may be moderated by government policy.

H15: The relationship between social influence and decision to embrace BEVs may be moderated by gender.

H16: The relationship between effort expectancy and decision to adopt BEVs may be moderated by gender.

H17: The relationship between effort expectancy and decision to adopt BEVs may be moderated by gender.

H18: The relationship between social influence and decision to embrace BEVs may be moderated by age.

H19: The relationship between effort expectancy and decision to embrace BEVs may be moderated by age.

H20: The relationship between effort expectancy and decision to embrace BEVs may be moderated by age.

H21: The driving experience could be a moderator to the relation between facilitating conditions and usage behavior of BEVs.

H22: The driving experience could be a moderator of the relation between anxiety and intention to adopt BEVs.

H23: The driving experience could be a moderator of the relation between social influence and intention to adopt BEVs.

H24: The driving experience could be a moderator of the relation between effort expectancy and intention to adopt BEVs.

H25: The relationship between usage behavior of BEVs and facilitating conditions may be moderated by voluntariness of use.

H26: The relationship between price value and adoption of BEVs could be moderated by household composition.

H27: The relationship between the charging infrastructure and adoption of BEVs could be moderated by living location.

## 4 Conclusion and Further Research

BEVs are expected to be one of the products that can help alleviate global environmental problems in the future. Many countries have already adopted BEVs, and they are widely used. Nevertheless, there is still a massive gap in Thailand compared to other nations. One of the reasons is that BEVs are very distinct from CFVs, and the adopters must adjust their daily behaviors compared to those using CFVs. These distinctions of BEVs may influence the adoption rate as a result. This study aims to provide guidelines for constructing solutions to the problem.

The study has reviewed the relevant literature on the parameters influencing consumers' adoption of BEVs. This study explores and describes the factors that affect battery electric vehicle adoption, as well as introduces a new conceptual framework. The framework uses technology acceptance models, including UTAUT and CTAM, to clarify and predict battery-electric vehicle adoption. Apart from that, this study reviews and introduces other factors, including price value, government policy, charging infrastructure, and environmental concerns, as relevant additional factors that directly impact the adoption rate, with driving experience, household composition, and living location as the moderating factors. This study synthesized those factors with UTAUT and CTAM into a new conceptual framework. The proposed framework will be further conducted empirically using statistical analysis. The results from the empirical test will provide valuable insights for policymakers, enabling them to gain a comprehensive understanding of the determinants crucial for the widespread adoption of Battery Electric Vehicles (BEVs). Such insights enable stakeholders to formulate informed action plans, establish targets and strategies, and effectively coordinate future tasks and infrastructure development.

## 5 Limitations

It is critical to contextualize our proposal within the framework of certain limitations. Notably, there are several unexplored factors, including those about battery lifespan, environmental conditions such as flooding, and the influence of insurance policies on Battery Electric Vehicles (BEVs). This omission may restrict the extent to which our findings can be generalized. Future investigations should elucidate the mediating factors that underlie the relationships among these variables, thereby enhancing our comprehension of this multifaceted phenomenon. Nonetheless, this study boasts several strengths that warrant acknowledgment. The utilization of UTAUT and CTAM as the foundational construct has proven to be a robust and reliable framework. These inherent strengths bolster the accuracy of our findings and mitigate the impact of potential confounding variables, consequently reinforcing the robustness and reliability of our conclusions.

## References


1. Scientific Consensus: Earth's Climate is Warming, NASA. https://climate.nasa.gov/scientific-consensus/
2. World climate change report card: These countries are meeting goals, Environment. https://www.nationalgeographic.com/environment/article/climate-change-report-card-co2-emissions.
3. Electric cars help limit climate change despite blackspots in India, Poland, Climate Home News. https://www.climatechangenews.com/2020/03/23/electric-cars-help-limit-climate-change-despite-blackspots-india-poland/
4. Batteries, Charging, and Electric Vehicles, Energy.gov., https://www.energy.gov/eere/vehicles/batteries-charging-and-electric-vehicles
5. Ortar, N., Ryghaug, M.: Should all cars be electric by 2025? The electric car debate in Europe. Sustain. **11**(7), 1868 (2019)
6. Hannisdahl, O. H., Malvik, H. V., Wensaas, G. B.: The future is electric! The EV revolution in Norway—Explanations and lessons learned. In: 2013 world electric vehicle symposium and exhibition (EVS27), pp. 1–13. IEEE. (2013, November)
7. Bilsalget i desember og hele 2020, Opplysningsrådet for veitrafikken, https://ofv.no/bilsalget/bilsalget-i-desember-2020
8. Norway Sets Global Electric Car Record in 2020, Life in Norway, https://www.lifeinnorway.net/norway-sets-global-electric-car-record-in-2020. Accessed 06 January2021
9. What can the world learn from Norway as an EV superpower? Silicon Republic. https://www.siliconrepublic.com/machines/norway-ev-ireland-lessons
10. Impact of the Transition to Electrical Vehicles on Workers in Automotive Parts Manufacturing in Thailand, http://library.fes.de/pdf-files/bueros/thailand/17393.pdf
11. Chantharaphaha, K.: Future Directions of Electric Vehicles and the Thai Automobile Industry. Asian Adm. & Manag. Rev. **3**(1), (2020)
12. EV History, Electric Vehicles Association of Thailand 2015. http://www.evat.or.th/15708247/ev-history
13. EVs on a roll. https://www.bangkokpost.com/business/2045139/evs-on-a-roll
14. Electric vehicle learning center. Thailand Automotive Institute, https://thaiauto.or.th/2012/th/services/ev/
15. Brückmann, G., Willibald, F., Blanco, V.: Battery Electric Vehicle adoption in regions without strong policies. Transportation Research Part D: Transp. Environ. **90**, 102615 (2021)
16. Venkatesh, V., Morris, M.G., Davis, G.B., Davis, F.D.: User acceptance of information technology: Toward a unified view. MIS Q. **27**(3), 425–478 (2003)
17. Osswald, S., Wurhofer, D., Trösterer, S., Beck, E., Tscheligi, M.: Predicting information technology usage in the car: towards a car technology acceptance model. In: Proceedings of the 4th international conference on automotive user interfaces and interactive vehicular applications, pp. 51–58. (2012, October)
18. Hewitt, C., Politis, I., Amanatidis, T., Sarkar, A.: Assessing public perception of self-driving cars: The autonomous vehicle acceptance model. In: Proceedings of the 24th international conference on intelligent user interfaces, pp. 518–527. (2019, March)
19. Haustein, S., Jensen, A.F., Cherchi, E.: Battery electric vehicle adoption in Denmark and Sweden: Recent changes, related factors and policy implications. Energy Policy **149**, 112096 (2021)
20. Hackbarth, A., Madlener, R.: Willingness-to-pay for alternative fuel vehicle characteristics: A stated choice study for Germany. Transportation Research Part A: Policy Pract. **85**, 89–111 (2016)
21. Egbue, O., Long, S.: Barriers to widespread adoption of electric vehicles: An analysis of consumer attitudes and perceptions. Energy Policy **48**, 717–729 (2012)
22. Jensen, A.F., Cherchi, E., Mabit, S.L.: On the stability of preferences and attitudes before and after experiencing an electric vehicle. Transportation Research Part D: Transp. Environ. **25**, 24–32 (2013)

23. Mau, P., Eyzaguirre, J., Jaccard, M., Collins-Dodd, C., Tiedemann, K.: The 'neighbor effect': Simulating dynamics in consumer preferences for new vehicle technologies. Ecol. Econ. **68**(1–2), 504–516 (2008)
24. Moons, I., De Pelsmacker, P.: Emotions as determinants of electric car usage intention. J. Mark. Manag. **28**(3–4), 195–237 (2012)
25. Afroz, R., Masud, M.M., Akhtar, R., Islam, M.A., Duasa, J.B.: Consumer purchase intention towards environmentally friendly vehicles: an empirical investigation in Kuala Lumpur. Malaysia. Environ. Sci. Pollut. Res. **22**(20), 16153–16163 (2015)
26. Barth, M., Jugert, P., Fritsche, I.: Still underdetected–Social norms and collective efficacy predict the acceptance of electric vehicles in Germany. Transp. Res. Part F: Traffic Psychol. Behav. **37**, 64–77 (2016)
27. Yuan, Q., Hao, W., Su, H., Bing, G., Gui, X., Safikhani, A.: Investigation on range anxiety and safety buffer of battery electric vehicle drivers. J. Adv. Transp. 1–11 (2018)
28. Graham-Rowe, E., Gardner, B., Abraham, C., Skippon, S., Dittmar, H., Hutchins, R., Stannard, J.: Mainstream consumers driving plug-in battery-electric and plug-in hybrid electric cars: A qualitative analysis of responses and evaluations. Transp. Res. Part A: Policy Pract. **46**(1), 140–153 (2012)
29. Thananusak, T., Rakthin, S., Tavewatanaphan, T., Punnakitikashem, P.: Factors affecting the intention to buy electric vehicles: Empirical evidence from Thailand. Int. J. Electr. Hybrid Veh. **9**(4), 361–381 (2017)
30. Oliver, J.D., Rosen, D.E.: Applying the environmental propensity framework: A segmented approach to hybrid electric vehicle marketing strategies. J. Mark. Theory Pract. **18**(4), 377–393 (2010)
31. Hoen, A., Koetse, M.J.: A choice experiment on alternative fuel vehicle preferences of private car owners in the Netherlands. Transportation Research Part A: Policy Pract. **61**, 199–215 (2014)
32. Beck, M.J., Rose, J.M., Greaves, S.P.: I can't believe your attitude: a joint estimation of best worst attitudes and electric vehicle choice. Transp. **44**(4), 753–772 (2017)
33. Noppers, E.H., Keizer, K., Bolderdijk, J.W., Steg, L.: The adoption of sustainable innovations: Driven by symbolic and environmental motives. Glob. Environ. Chang. **25**, 52–62 (2014)
34. Liu, T., Wang, Q., Su, B.: A review of carbon labeling: Standards, implementation, and impact. Renew. Sustain. Energy Rev. **53**, 68–79 (2016)
35. Peters, A., Dütschke, E.: How do consumers perceive electric vehicles? A comparison of German consumer groups. J. Environ. Policy & Plan. **16**(3), 359–377 (2014)
36. Plötz, P., Schneider, U., Globisch, J., Dütschke, E.: Who will buy electric vehicles? Identifying early adopters in Germany. Transp. Res. Part A: Policy Pract. **67**, 96–109 (2014)
37. Skippon, S., Garwood, M.: Responses to battery electric vehicles: UK consumer attitudes and attributions of symbolic meaning following direct experience to reduce psychological distance. Transp. Res. Part D: Transp. Environ. **16**(7), 525–531 (2011)
38. Venkatesh, V., Thong, J.Y., Xu, X.: Consumer acceptance and use of information technology: extending the unified theory of acceptance and use of technology. MIS Q. **36**(1), 157 (2012)
39. Dumortier, J., Siddiki, S., Carley, S., Cisney, J., Krause, R.M., Lane, B.W., Rupp, J.A., Graham, J.D.: Effects of providing total cost of ownership information on consumers' intent to purchase a hybrid or plug-in electric vehicle. Transp. Res. Part A: Policy Pract. **72**, 71–86 (2015)
40. Bjerkan, K.Y., Nørbech, T.E., Nordtømme, M.E.: Incentives for promoting battery electric vehicle (BEV) adoption in Norway. Transp. Res. Part D: Transp. Environ. **43**, 169–180 (2016)
41. Aasness, M. A., Odeck, J.: The increase of electric vehicle usage in Norway—incentives and adverse effects. Eur. Transp. Res. Rev. **7**(4), (2015)
42. Helveston, J.P., Liu, Y., Feit, E.M.D., Fuchs, E., Klampfl, E., Michalek, J.J.: Will subsidies drive electric vehicle adoption? Measuring consumer preferences in the US and China. Transp. Res. Part A: Policy Pract. **73**, 96–112 (2015)
43. Li, W., Long, R., Chen, H.: Consumers' evaluation of national new energy vehicle policy in China: An analysis based on a four paradigm model. Energy Policy **99**, 33–41 (2016)

44. Sang, Y.N., Bekhet, H.A.: Modelling electric vehicle usage intentions: an empirical study in Malaysia. J. Clean. Prod. **92**, 75–83 (2015)
45. Ko, W., Hahn, T.-K.: Analysis of Consumer Preferences for Electric Vehicles. IEEE Trans. Smart Grid **4**(1), 437–442 (2013)
46. Lai, I., Liu, Y., Sun, X., Zhang, H., Xu, W.: Factors influencing the behavioural intention towards full electric vehicles: An empirical study in Macau. Sustain. **7**(9), 12564–12585 (2015)
47. Wahl, L. S., Hsiang, W. H., Hauer, G.: The intention to adopt battery electric vehicles in Germany: driven by consumer expectancy, social influence, facilitating conditions and ecological norm orientation. Innovations for Metropolitan Areas: Intelligent Solutions for Mobility, Logistics and Infrastructure designed for Citizens, pp. 79–92 (2020)
48. Rauh, N., Franke, T., Krems, J. F.: Understanding the impact of electric vehicle driving experience on range anxiety. Human Factors: J. Hum. Factors Ergon. Soc. **57**(1), 177–187 (2015)
49. Khazaei, H., Khazaei, A.: Electric vehicles and factors that influencing their adoption moderating effects of driving experience and voluntariness of use (conceptual framework). J. Bus. Manag. **18**(12), 60–65 (2016)
50. Zhang, Y., Yu, Y., Zou, B.: Analyzing public awareness and acceptance of alternative fuel vehicles in China: The case of EV. Energy Policy **39**(11), 7015–7024 (2011)

# Factors Influencing Online Platform Engagement in Fresh Fruit E-commerce in China

**Lin Tang and Nuttawut Rojniruttikul**

**Abstract** The rapid expansion of e-commerce and technology integration into everyday life has brought about significant transformations in consumer behavior, particularly in China. This study explores the dynamic realm of online platform engagement in the context of fresh fruit e-commerce in China. It investigates various dimensions, including perceived value, product quality, social media influence, e-commerce platform familiarity, and online shopping convenience. The study surveyed 385 consumers who actively engage in online purchases of fresh fruits. Reliability and validity tests were performed to ensure the robustness of the data. Multiple linear regression analysis was conducted for hypothesis testing. The results indicate that perceived quality, e-commerce platform familiarity, and online shopping convenience have a significant and positive influence on online platform engagement, while perceived value and social media influence do not exhibit statistically significant effects on the same engagement. Moreover, the demographic characteristics of consumers in this sector highlight a diverse population. These findings offer valuable insights for both academia and industry. They contribute to a deeper understanding of consumer preferences and behaviors within the digital realm, providing businesses with data-driven insights to enhance customer experiences and develop informed strategies. The study also has implications for policymakers, informing them about the dynamics and challenges in the fresh fruit e-commerce sector.

**Keywords** Perceived value · Perceived quality · Social media influence · E-commerce platform familiarity · Online shopping convenience

---

L. Tang · N. Rojniruttikul (✉)
King Mongkut's Institute of Technology Ladkrabang, Bangkok, Thailand
e-mail: nuttawut.ro@kmitl.ac.th



S. Kot et al. (eds.), *Corporate Practices: Policies, Methodologies, and Insights in Organizational Management*, Springer Proceedings in Business and Economics,
https://doi.org/10.1007/978-981-97-0996-0_14

## 1 Introduction

The surge of e-commerce and the rapid fusion of technology into everyday life has brought about substantial transformations in consumer behavior and shopping patterns globally [1]. This transformation is particularly conspicuous in China, where the e-commerce landscape has burgeoned and evolved astoundingly [2]. Amidst this evolutionary tide, the engagement of consumers with online platforms has emerged as a critical and compelling realm of exploration, especially within the context of fresh fruit e-commerce [3].

The tapestry of online platform engagement is intricate and multifaceted, interweaving various dimensions such as perceived value, product quality, convenience, technological familiarity, and the influence of social media [4]. These dimensions intersect and exert mutual influence, collectively shaping the decisions and experiences of consumers in the sphere of fresh fruit e-commerce.

In the contemporary landscape of fresh fruit e-commerce in China, online platform engagement has ascended to paramount significance. This ascent is driven by technological advances, socio-economic shifts, and consumer-centric factors [5]. The rapid digital metamorphosis experienced by China in recent years finds its reflection in the e-commerce domain, particularly in the context of fresh fruit procurement. This transformation has given rise to a complex web of interactions, preferences, and behaviors that delineate the present state of online platform engagement [6].

The ubiquity of smartphones and enhanced internet connectivity has democratized online shopping, rendering it accessible to a substantial portion of Chinese consumers [7]. E-commerce platforms have responded with user-friendly interfaces and seamless mobile applications facilitating effortless engagement [8]. The infusion of innovative technologies such as artificial intelligence, virtual, and augmented reality has further enriched the user experience, empowering consumers to inspect and select fresh fruits virtually [9].

By dissecting these dimensions and understanding their impact, this study endeavors to unearth the driving forces that impel consumers to engage with specific online platforms for fresh fruit purchases [10]. These insights illuminate the path towards optimizing the online shopping experience, customizing strategies to align with consumer preferences, and prognosticating future trends in the dynamic realm of e-commerce [11].

The culmination of this research aspires to offer a comprehensive portrayal of the intricate factors at play in online platform engagement within the realm of fresh fruit e-commerce in China [12]. The insights derived from empirical data can steer businesses and stakeholders towards more informed decision-making, elevating the quality of online shopping experiences and contributing to the continuous evolution of e-commerce practices [13]. The proliferation of e-commerce in China has not only revolutionized consumer behaviors but has also significantly impacted the way food is procured. Among various food categories, fresh fruit e-commerce has mainly stood out. In recent years, the popularity of purchasing fresh fruits online has surpassed that of many other food groups. This surge in online fresh fruit sales can be attributed to several factors.

Importantly, this research is poised to delve into the intricate factors that mold consumers' engagement with online platforms to acquire fresh fruits in China [14]. As the ecosystem of online shopping continues to expand, comprehending the underlying dynamics that orchestrate consumers' interactions with these platforms becomes paramount, not only for businesses but also for policymakers in shaping the evolving landscape of e-commerce [4].

## 2 Literature Review

### *2.1 Perceived Value*

The concept of perceived value in the context of e-commerce plays a pivotal role in shaping consumers' attitudes and behaviors. In this literature review, we delve into existing research to explore the relationship between perceived value, fresh fruit purchases, and online platform engagement.

Perceived value, a multidimensional construct, represents the consumer's overall assessment of the benefits received relative to the costs incurred in an e-commerce transaction [15]. In the context of online shopping for fresh fruits, consumers assess the perceived value not only in terms of the monetary cost but also other factors like product quality, convenience, and the overall online shopping experience.

Studies have highlighted the significance of perceived value in driving consumers' preferences in fresh fruit e-commerce. For instance, a previous study found that consumers who perceived a higher value in freshness, quality, and convenience of fresh fruit purchases online were more likely to engage with e-commerce platforms [16]. This is consistent with the notion that consumers seek value not only in terms of price but also the overall quality of the product and the convenience of the shopping process.

The influence of perceived value on online platform engagement has been well-documented. Research demonstrated that consumers who perceive a high value in their online shopping experiences, which encompasses factors like perceived value for money, product quality, and convenience, tend to be more engaged with e-commerce platforms [17]. The overall value perception enhances user satisfaction and trust, leading to higher levels of engagement.

The literature suggests that perceived value is a critical factor in driving online platform engagement in fresh fruit e-commerce. Consumers who perceive value in terms of product quality, freshness, and the overall shopping experience are more likely to engage with online platforms for their fresh fruit purchases. As such, H1 positing a significant positive relationship between perceived value and online platform engagement aligns with the existing body of research and is grounded in the understanding that consumers place significant importance on the value they derive from their e-commerce interactions [15–17].

This review underscores the importance of considering perceived value as a critical determinant of online platform engagement in fresh fruit e-commerce. It provides a strong rationale for the proposed hypothesis and sets the stage for further empirical investigation. Therefore, the following hypothesis is proposed:

H1: Perceived value of fresh fruits significantly influences online platform engagement.

## 2.2 *Perceived Quality*

Perceived quality represents a consumer's judgment of the overall excellence or superiority of a product or service [15]. In e-commerce, perceived quality extends beyond the physical attributes of the product. It includes the quality of the shopping experience, such as website design, customer service, and delivery reliability [18].

Research has indicated that the perceived quality of fresh fruits is a significant factor for consumers engaging with e-commerce platforms. In a previous study, it was found that consumers who perceived the online purchase of fresh fruits as offering high quality in terms of freshness, packaging, and adherence to promised standards were more likely to engage with e-commerce platforms [19]. This suggests that the perceived quality of fresh fruits is crucial in attracting consumers to these platforms.

The impact of perceived quality on online platform engagement is well-documented. Research highlights that when consumers perceive high product quality and a quality shopping experience in their e-commerce interactions, they are more inclined to engage with online platforms [20]. The perception of quality fosters trust, customer satisfaction, and brand loyalty, ultimately leading to higher levels of engagement.

The literature suggests that the perceived quality of fresh fruits is a driving force behind online platform engagement in fresh fruit e-commerce. Consumers who perceive high quality in the products they purchase and in the overall shopping experience are more likely to engage with online platforms for fresh fruit procurement. Therefore, the following hypothesis is proposed:

H2: Perceived quality of fresh fruits significantly influences online platform engagement.

## 2.3 *Social Media*

Social media has transformed consumer behavior and engagement within the realm of e-commerce. It has become a powerful platform for influencing consumer perceptions, decisions, and brand loyalty [21]. Social media influence encompasses various dimensions, including user reviews, recommendations from friends and influencers, and interactive content that guides consumer choices.

In the context of fresh fruit e-commerce, the influence of social media is palpable. Consumer reviews, photographs, and recommendations on social media platforms play a pivotal role in shaping consumer perceptions of fresh fruits [22]. Users frequently share their experiences with specific fresh fruit brands, and such peer endorsements and user-generated content can significantly influence the decisions of potential buyers.

Research indicates that social media influence has a substantial impact on online platform engagement. Consumers who encounter positive reviews, endorsements, and user-generated content on social media are more likely to engage with e-commerce platforms [21]. This influence extends to the fresh fruit e-commerce sector, where users are drawn to online platforms with a strong social media presence and positive reviews.

The literature underscores that social media influence is a driving force behind online platform engagement in fresh fruit e-commerce. Users are swayed by the recommendations and endorsements they encounter on social media platforms. As a result, the following hypothesis is proposed:

H3: Social media influence of fresh fruits significantly influences online platform engagement.

## 2.4 E-commerce Platform Familiarity

Consumer familiarity with e-commerce platforms has gained prominence in understanding online shopping behavior. It refers to the user's experience and comfort level with a specific e-commerce platform, which can significantly impact their shopping habits [23]. A familiar platform often leads to smoother transactions, greater trust, and a more positive overall experience.

In fresh fruit e-commerce, consumers familiar with a particular platform may have specific advantages. They are more likely to navigate the platform with ease, find their preferred fresh fruit vendors, and be comfortable with the ordering process [24]. Familiarity can be a critical factor in enhancing the user experience.

Research has shown that consumers' familiarity with e-commerce platforms significantly influences their online platform engagement. Familiarity often reduces the perceived risks associated with online shopping and can positively affect users' intentions to engage with a platform [23]. In the context of fresh fruit e-commerce, consumers familiar with the platform are more likely to engage with it due to the reduced cognitive effort required.

The literature suggests that e-commerce platform familiarity is a crucial factor affecting online platform engagement. It implies that consumers comfortable with a platform are likelier to engage with it when purchasing fresh fruits. Thus, the following hypothesis is proposed:

H4: E-commerce platform familiarity of fresh fruits significantly influences online platform engagement.

## 2.5 Online Shopping Convenience

Online shopping convenience is a central determinant of consumer behavior in digital commerce. It encompasses ease of use, accessibility, transaction efficiency, and user-friendliness [25]. Convenience is a crucial driver for consumers' choice to shop online, as it streamlines the purchase process and enhances the shopping experience.

In the context of fresh fruit e-commerce, the convenience of online shopping becomes particularly relevant. Consumers often perceive shopping for fresh fruits in traditional markets or physical stores as time-consuming and effort-intensive. Online platforms offer the convenience of browsing, comparing, and ordering fresh fruits from the comfort of one's home [26]. The ability to access a wide variety of fresh fruits with ease and have them delivered to one's doorstep contributes to the overall convenience of the shopping process.

Research has demonstrated that the convenience of online shopping significantly influences online platform engagement. A convenient shopping process is often associated with higher levels of engagement [25]. In fresh fruit e-commerce, consumers who find the process convenient are more likely to engage with the platform, increasing their interaction and repeat visits.

The literature suggests that online shopping convenience influences online platform engagement. In fresh fruit e-commerce, a convenient shopping process will likely encourage consumers to engage with the platform more actively. Therefore, the following hypothesis is proposed:

H5: Online shopping convenience of fresh fruits significantly influences online platform engagement.

Drawing upon insights derived from prior research and the hypotheses posited in this study, the multifaceted phenomenon of online platform engagement takes center stage. It has garnered substantial attention in e-commerce, with its significance further magnified by the global pandemic. The outbreak of COVID-19 undeniably expedited the worldwide transition towards online shopping, rendering the investigation of online platform engagement more pertinent than ever. In light of these considerations, the following conceptual framework is proposed:

Within the ever-evolving realm of e-commerce, this framework delves into the intricate interplay of factors that impact consumers engaged in the online purchase of fresh fruits in China. The conceptual model comprises five crucial dimensions, with each dimension contributing to the overall level of engagement on online platforms (Fig. 1).

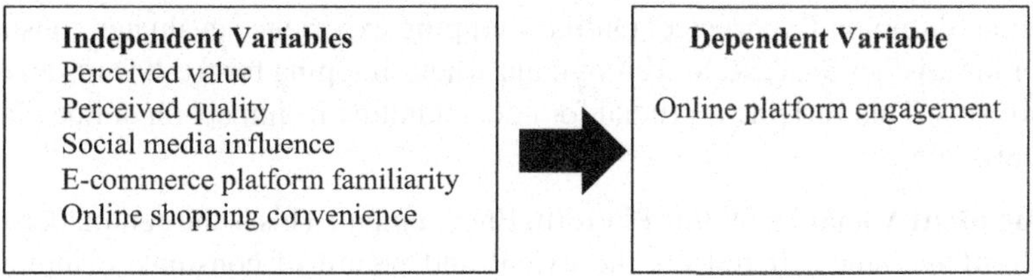


**Fig. 1** Conceptual framework

# 3 Methodology

## *3.1 Population and Sample*

This study primarily focuses on customers actively participating in the rapidly expanding online fresh fruit market in China, encompassing the digital landscape of fresh fruit e-commerce. The research data were collected from a sample of 385 customers who had actively engaged with various online platforms for fresh fruit e-commerce in China, including prominent platforms such as Taobao, JD.com, Tmall, Pinduoduo, Meituan Dianping, Dingdong Maicai, and Freshhema (Hema Xiansheng). Given the unavailability of precise information regarding the exact size of the overall population, a pragmatic approach was employed, utilizing convenience sampling to collect data from this targeted population efficiently.

## *3.2 Variables*

**Independent Variables:**

1 Perceived Value: This variable evaluates the perceived worth and benefit that consumers associate with the fresh fruits available on online platforms. It aims to explore how consumers' perceptions of value affect their engagement with these platforms.
2 Perceived Quality: Perceived quality assesses consumers' judgments regarding the quality and attributes of fresh fruits available on digital platforms. The study aims to understand how perceived quality influences consumer engagement.
3 Social Media Influence: This variable examines the extent to which social media platforms and their influence impact consumers' decisions and behaviors when engaging with fresh fruit e-commerce platforms.
4 E-commerce Platform Familiarity: E-commerce platform familiarity considers the consumers' level of acquaintance and experience with the online platforms used for fresh fruit purchases. It seeks to understand how familiarity affects consumer engagement.

5 Online Shopping Experience: Online shopping experience evaluates consumers' overall satisfaction, ease, and enjoyment when shopping for fresh fruits on digital platforms. This variable is crucial for understanding its impact on online platform engagement.

**Dependent Variable**: Online Platform Engagement: This is the central dependent variable of the study. It reflects the extent and nature of consumers' interaction, involvement, and participation with online platforms for fresh fruit e-commerce. It measures the depth of engagement and evaluates what factors drive or inhibit it.

## *3.3 Research Instrument*

The primary data collection tool employed in this study is a meticulously structured questionnaire. A comprehensive review informed the construction of the questionnaire of pertinent literature and expert consultation within the field. This questionnaire encompasses two sections: the initial section gathers fundamental demographic information, while the subsequent section delves into the essential independent and dependent variables. Respondents' agreement with statements is assessed using a 5-point Likert scale, ranging from "strongly agree" to "strongly disagree." ot survey was conducted involving a sample of 30 participants. The primary objective of this pilot survey was to evaluate the reliability of the questionnaire. The collected data were subjected to analysis to ascertain the internal consistency of the questionnaire items. This analysis included the calculation of Cronbach's alpha coefficient, with a threshold set at 0.70, indicating that the questionnaire's reliability is met.

The questionnaire underwent a rigorous content validity assessment, overseen by three experts in the field. These experts executed an Item Objective Congruence (IOC) analysis, evaluating each questionnaire item in alignment with the research objectives. Items with an IOC value equal to or greater than 0.50 were deemed relevant, demonstrating adherence to the content validity criteria.

## *3.4 Data Collection*

Data for this study was acquired through the distribution of an online questionnaire via the "Questionnaire Star" platform. This digital approach was selected to enhance sample validity. The survey was systematically conducted throughout regular weekdays and holidays, spanning one month or more. This meticulous time frame was chosen to ensure that data collection encompassed varying consumer behaviors and preferences, contributing to the robustness of the study. The collected data is presently undergoing rigorous analysis, employing appropriate statistical techniques. The purpose of this analysis is to scrutinize the research hypotheses. The analytical methods applied include:

**Descriptive Statistics:** The dataset is initially subjected to descriptive statistical analysis, which encompasses the calculation of mean values and standard deviations. This process furnishes a comprehensive overview of the dataset.

**Multiple Regression Analysis:** To evaluate the relationships between the independent variables and the dependent variable, multiple regression analysis is being employed. This sophisticated analytical technique allows for a detailed examination of the associations within the data.

## 4 Results

### *4.1 Demographic Information*

Table 1 provides a comprehensive overview of the demographic information for the 385 customers in the study.

The results presented in Table 1 indicate that approximately 60.8% of the customers were male, while 39.2% were female. The study encompassed a diverse age range, with the highest representation observed in the 31–40 years old category (38.4%). Young adults, aged 21–30 years, comprised about 20.8% of the sample, while the category of "60 years old or older" had the lowest representation, accounting for only about 2.1% of the customers.

In terms of marital status, the majority of customers were classified as "Single," making up approximately 76.1% of the sample. Around 22.6% of the customers were "Married," with a small percentage falling into the "Others" category (1.3%). Regarding educational attainment, a significant portion of the customers held a "Bachelor degree" (52.5%). "Master degree" holders constituted approximately 22.6% of the sample. The categories of "High School or lower" and "Doctoral degree" had lower representation, at around 10.9% and 3.6%, respectively.

Customers' monthly income displayed a diverse distribution, with the largest group having a monthly income in the "4,001–6,000 yuan" range (21.8%). The "15,000 yuan and above" income category had the lowest representation, accounting for approximately 11.9% of the customers.

### *4.2 Level of Each Variable*

Table 2 displays the mean and standard deviation for the variables under study.

Table 2 presents the mean and standard deviation for each of the variables under investigation, along with the corresponding level of measurement.

Perceived Value: The mean score for perceived value is 3.466 with a standard deviation of 0.696. This indicates a relatively high level of perceived value among the customers.

**Table 1** Demographic information (n = 385)

| Demographic Characteristic | Category | Frequency | Percentage |
|---|---|---|---|
| Gender | Male | 234 | 60.8 |
| | Female | 151 | 39.2 |
| Age | Under 20 years old | 5 | 1.3 |
| | 21–30 years old | 80 | 20.8 |
| | 31–40 years old | 148 | 38.4 |
| | 41–50 years old | 85 | 22.1 |
| | 51–60 years old | 59 | 15.3 |
| | 60 years old or older | 8 | 2.1 |
| Marital status | Single | 293 | 76.1 |
| | Married | 87 | 22.6 |
| | Others | 5 | 1.3 |
| Education | High School or lower | 42 | 10.9 |
| | Vocational School | 40 | 10.4 |
| | Bachelor degree | 202 | 52.5 |
| | Master degree | 87 | 22.6 |
| | Doctoral degree | 14 | 3.6 |
| Monthly income | Less than 2,000 yuan | 23 | 6.0 |
| | 2,000–4,000 yuan | 41 | 10.6 |
| | 4,001–6,000 yuan | 84 | 21.8 |
| | 6,001–8,000 yuan | 73 | 19.0 |
| | 8,001–10,000 yuan | 50 | 13.0 |
| | 10,001–15,000 yuan | 68 | 17.7 |
| | 15,000 yuan and above | 46 | 11.9 |

**Table 2** Mean and standard deviation for each variable

| Variables | Mean | S.D | Level |
|---|---|---|---|
| Perceived value | 3.466 | 0.696 | High |
| Perceived quality | 3.256 | 0.761 | Moderate |
| Social media influence | 3.425 | 0.735 | High |
| E-commerce platform familiarity | 3.407 | 0.727 | High |
| Online shopping experience | 3.725 | 0.737 | High |
| Online platform engagement | 3.322 | 0.771 | Moderate |

Perceived Quality: Customers have rated perceived quality with a mean of 3.256 and a standard deviation of 0.761. The standard deviation suggests a moderate level of agreement in the responses regarding perceived quality.

Social Media Influence: Social media influence has a mean score of 3.425 and a standard deviation of 0.735, signifying a high level of social media influence in customers' decisions.

E-commerce Platform Familiarity: With a mean of 3.407 and a standard deviation of 0.727, customers demonstrate a high degree of familiarity with e-commerce platforms.

Online Shopping Experience: The mean for online shopping experience is 3.725, with a standard deviation of 0.737, indicating a high level of satisfaction with online shopping convenience.

Online Platform Engagement: Customers have rated their online platform engagement with a mean of 3.322 and a standard deviation of 0.771. This suggests a moderate level of online platform engagement among the respondents.

## *4.3 Regression Analysis*

In this section, the results of the multiple linear regression analysis conducted to investigate the impact of various independent variables on online platform engagement within the domain of fresh fruit e-commerce are presented. Table 3 below provides a comprehensive overview of the regression analysis results.

The results in Table 3 provide insights into the impact of each independent variable on online platform engagement within the specific domain of fresh fruit e-commerce. The $R^2$ value, which stands at 0.569, signifies the proportion of the variance in online platform engagement explained by the independent variables included in the model. An $R^2$ of 0.569 suggests that these variables collectively account for 56.9% of the variance in online platform engagement. A detailed analysis of each variable follows:

**Perceived Value**: The B (unstandardized coefficient) for Perceived Value is 0.025, with a Beta (standardized coefficient) of 0.023. These values indicate that the perceived value of fresh fruits has a slight positive influence on online platform engagement. However, the t-value of 0.399 suggests that this effect lacks statistical

**Table 3** Multiple linear regression analysis results

| Variables | B | Beta | t | p-value |
|---|---|---|---|---|
| Constant | 0.089 | | 0.569 | 0.570 |
| Perceived value | 0.025 | 0.023 | 0.399 | 0.690 |
| Perceived quality | 0.164 | 0.162 | 2.788 | 0.006*** |
| Social media influence | 0.088 | 0.084 | 1.847 | 0.066 |
| E-commerce platform familiarity | 0.369 | 0.348 | 6.613 | 0.000*** |
| Online shopping experience | 0.283 | 0.270 | 5.467 | 0.000*** |
| $R^2 = 0.569$; SEE = 0.5096; sig = 0.000*** | | | | |

*** $p < 0.001$

significance at the conventional significance level (p-value of 0.690). Consequently, perceived value does not significantly predict online platform engagement within this context.

**Perceived Quality**: For Perceived Quality, the B value is 0.164, accompanied by a Beta of 0.162. These values are notably higher compared to those associated with Perceived Value. This suggests that the perceived quality of fresh fruits has a more substantial and positive impact on online platform engagement. The t-value of 2.788 is statistically significant, as indicated by the p-value of 0.006. Therefore, perceived quality significantly predicts online platform engagement.

**Social Media Influence**: With a B value of 0.088 and a Beta of 0.084, Social Media Influence exhibits a positive effect on online platform engagement. However, it does not achieve statistical significance at the standard threshold (t-value of 1.847 and p-value of 0.066). This indicates that social media influence does not significantly impact online platform engagement.

**E-commerce Platform Familiarity**: The B value for E-commerce Platform Familiarity is 0.369, with a Beta of 0.348. The substantial t-value of 6.613 and a highly significant p-value of 0.000 underscore the strong and statistically significant positive impact of e-commerce platform familiarity on online platform engagement.

**Online Shopping Experience**: The Online Shopping Experience is characterized by a B value of 0.283 and a Beta of 0.270. The t-value of 5.467, along with a p-value of 0.000, indicates a robust and statistically significant favorable influence on online platform engagement.

## 5 Conclusion and Discussion

In the realm of fresh fruit e-commerce within China, this study has offered comprehensive insights into the multifaceted phenomenon of online platform engagement. It has systematically investigated how specific variables, such as perceived value, perceived quality, social media influence, e-commerce platform familiarity, and the online shopping experience, influence consumers' engagement with digital platforms. The conclusions drawn from this research carry substantial implications for understanding consumer behavior in the dynamic context of e-commerce, particularly within the fresh fruit sector in China.

The findings have shed light on the following key insights:

**Perceived value:** This study indicates that within the domain of fresh fruit e-commerce in China, the perceived value of products may not significantly predict online platform engagement. It is plausible that, given the high competitiveness of the fresh fruit e-commerce market, other factors play a more substantial role in shaping consumer engagement [27].

**Perceived quality:** In contrast, the perceived quality of fresh fruits emerged as a pivotal determinant of online platform engagement. Consumers who place higher importance on the quality of fresh fruits available on these platforms tend to exhibit more significant engagement [28].

**Social media influence:** The results indicate that social media influence is not a statistically significant predictor of online platform engagement within the context of this study. This suggests that social media, as a factor, may not wield significant influence over consumer behavior in the fresh fruit e-commerce sector in China. [29]

**E-commerce Platform Familiarity:** The research underscores the significant role of familiarity with e-commerce platforms. Consumers who are well-acquainted with these platforms exhibit a greater propensity for engagement. This highlights the importance of user-friendly and intuitive interfaces in fostering familiarity and enhancing the user experience [30].

**Online Shopping Experience:** The study accentuates the profound influence of the online shopping experience on online platform engagement. Consumers who enjoy positive, efficient, and enjoyable shopping experiences within these platforms are more likely to engage actively [31].

While this study primarily contributes to the understanding of consumer behavior in fresh fruit e-commerce within China, it also encompasses demographic information, such as gender and age. This inclusion is consistent with previous research studies on the subject. Previous empirical research in this region has indicated the average frequency of sustainability-related activities and awareness in consumer attitudes. Factors that affect this rate, namely age and gender, have also been determined [32]. Therefore, the implications of this study extend to a broader context of consumer engagement in the digital age. It underscores the multifaceted nature of online platform engagement and emphasizes the need for a holistic approach to align with consumer preferences.

## 6 Recommendation

Based on the findings of this study on the factors influencing online platform engagement in fresh fruit e-commerce in China, several recommendations can be made to enhance both academic research and industry practices.

**Enhancing Perceived Quality:** E-commerce platforms should focus on improving the perceived quality of fresh fruits they offer. This can be achieved by implementing rigorous quality control measures and ensuring that delivered products match the advertised descriptions. Regular quality assessments and adherence to safety standards can help build consumer trust and engagement.

**E-commerce Platform Familiarity:** E-commerce platforms should work on user-friendly interfaces and seamless mobile applications, ensuring that consumers of varying technological familiarity can navigate and use their platforms with ease. Continuous improvements in platform design, guided tutorials, and accessible customer support can aid consumers in becoming more familiar with online platforms.

**Optimizing Online Shopping Experience:** A positive online shopping experience can significantly impact consumer engagement. E-commerce businesses should continue to invest in technologies like virtual reality and augmented reality to enhance the online shopping experience. Additionally, improving website speed, responsiveness, and personalized product recommendations can provide a more satisfactory experience.

## 7 Limitations and Recommendation for Future Research

1. This research employs a cross-sectional design, capturing a snapshot of online platform engagement. Longitudinal or experimental designs could offer a deeper understanding of how these factors evolve and their causal relationships.
2. The study relies on self-reported data, which may be subject to biases such as social desirability. Future research could explore alternative methods like observational data or mixed-method approaches to mitigate these biases.
3. This study focuses on online fresh fruit consumers in China. The factors influencing online platform engagement may vary in different cultural or regional contexts. Expanding the research to a broader international audience or specific regions within China can provide more nuanced insights.

## References


1. Smith, A.: The impact of e-commerce on global consumer behavior. Journal of Consumer Trends **5**(2), 123–136 (2019)
2. Li, Y., Zhang, Q., Wang, H.: The rapid evolution of e-commerce in China. International Journal of E-Commerce **16**(3), 45–58 (2020)
3. Wang, L., Sun, S.: Online platform engagement in fresh fruit e-commerce. E-commerce Research Quarterly **12**(4), 311–326 (2018)
4. Chen, X., Liu, W., & Wu, Y: Exploring dimensions of online platform engagement. Journal of Consumer Research **8**(1), 57–72 (2021)
5. Liu, Q., Wu, Z., Wang, F.: Socio-economic shifts and consumer-centric e-commerce in China. Journal of E-commerce Development **14**(3), 201–215 (2019)
6. Huang, J., Guo, L., Zhang, M.: The influence of social media on consumer preferences in e-commerce. Social Media Studies **3**(2), 89–104 (2017)
7. Wu, Y., Zhang, L., Yang, S.: Democratization of online shopping in China. E-commerce Trends **7**(4), 285–298 (2020)
8. Zhang, J., Chen, H., Lee, T.: User-friendly interfaces and seamless mobile applications in e-commerce. Mobile Commerce Quarterly **11**(1), 75–88 (2018)
9. Guo, W., Wang, L., Zhang, S.: Innovative technologies in e-commerce. International Journal of E-Commerce Technology **15**(2), 129–142 (2019)
10. Wu, X., Li, C.: Unveiling the driving forces behind consumer engagement. E-commerce Behavior Research **22**(3), 215–228 (2021)
11. Xu, Q., Chen, Y., Li, J.: Prognosticating future trends in e-commerce. Journal of Future Commerce **9**(4), 351–366 (2020)
12. Zhang, Y., Chen, H.: Online platform engagement in fresh fruit e-commerce. E-commerce Insights **14**(2), 163–176 (2019)
13. Huang, M., Zhang, R., Chen, X.: Empirical insights into online platform engagement. International Journal of E-commerce Studies **18**(1), 59–74 (2021)

14. Dai, W., Wu, L., Li, H.: Shaping the evolving landscape of e-commerce in China. E-commerce Policy Review **24**(4), 311–326 (2018)
15. Zeithaml, V.A.: Consumer perceptions of price, quality, and value: A means-end model and synthesis of evidence. J. Mark. **52**(3), 2–22 (1988)
16. Kim, J., Kim, S.: The role of perceived value in online shopping: The case of the Republic of Korea. International Journal of Retail & Distribution Management **45**(11), 1111–1123 (2017)
17. Huang, P.L., Lurie, N.H.: The role of online shopping platform in enhancing customer engagement. J. Retail. **95**(4), 436–446 (2019)
18. Parasuraman, A., Zeithaml, V.A., Malhotra, A.: E-S-QUAL: A multiple-item scale for assessing electronic service quality. J. Serv. Res. **7**(3), 213–233 (2005)
19. Chen, Y., Ganesan, S.: An empirical investigation of online consumer purchasing behavior. Commun. ACM **55**(9), 98–106 (2012)
20. Bhatti, M.A., Mushtaq, R., Latif, H.: Service quality, perceived value, and customer loyalty in e-commerce. J. Electron. Commer. Res. **20**(3), 200–214 (2019)
21. Smith, A.N., Zook, Z.: Antecedents and consequences of social media utilization in small and medium-sized hotels. Tour. Manage. **63**, 204–213 (2017)
22. Zhang, L., Fang, L.: Impact of electronic word-of-mouth on online purchase intention: A modification of the theory of planned behavior. IEEE Access **7**, 95781–95791 (2019)
23. Smith, L.K., Johnson, M.J.: User familiarity and usage intentions in social commerce: An exploratory study. Inf. Syst. Front. **20**(6), 1327–1340 (2018)
24. Kim, S.Y., Lee, J.E.: The impact of online shopping experience on risk perceptions and online purchase intentions: Does product category matter? Sustainability **11**(17), 4654 (2019)
25. Li, X., Zhang, Y.: Online shopping convenience, self-efficacy, and purchase intention: An empirical study. J. Consum. Mark. **36**(7), 1009–1019 (2019)
26. Chen, S., Sun, L., Liu, X.: Understanding consumers' online shopping intention: A perspective of convenience theory. Comput. Hum. Behav. **108**, 106294 (2020)
27. Marbach, J., Lages, C., Nunan, D.: Who are you and what do you value? Investigating the role of personality traits and customer-perceived value in online customer engagement. J. Mark. Manag. **32**, 5–6 (2016)
28. Rungtrakulchai, R.: The Impacts of Customer Engagement on Brand Equity in E-commerce. Journal of Business Administration and Languages **10**(1), 94–104 (2022)
29. Weng Marc Lim, W.M. & Rasul, T.: Customer engagement and social media: Revisiting the past to inform the future. Journal of Business Research. 148: 325–342 (2022)
30. Algharabat, R.S., Rana, N.P.: Social Commerce in Emerging Markets and its Impact on Online Community Engagement. Inf. Syst. Front. **23**, 1499–1520 (2021)
31. Bilal, A.: A A-khateeb & Fakher Jaoua: The Impact of Attitude Towards Online Shopping in Strengthening the Relationship Between Online Shopping Experience and E-Customer Engagement. International Journal of Customer Relationship Marketing and Management **14**(1), 25 (2023)
32. Kita, P., Cvirik, M., Jewski, G.M., Mazalanova, V.K.: Design of a tool to measure the behavioral aspect of conscious and sustainable consumer attitudes. Forum Scientiae Oeconomia. **11**(2), 133–146 (2023)

# Bridging the Gap Between Entrepreneurial Personality and Entrepreneurship Education Program

**Jumadi, Ismi Rajiani, and Ersis Warmansyah Abbas**

**Abstract** Indonesia's transition towards a market-based economy necessitates reevaluating the role of entrepreneurship education within the country. Employing a cultural approach, this study investigates the relationship between specific entrepreneurial characteristics and entrepreneurial spirit among Indonesians. While numerous personality traits have been linked to successful entrepreneurs, this study focuses on five attributes: risk-taking propensity, tolerance for ambiguity, internal locus of control, innovativeness, and independence. These traits may not be widely ingrained within the traditional culture of Indonesia, potentially hindering the effectiveness of entrepreneurship promotion efforts. Accordingly, the study contends that entrepreneurship education programs in Indonesia must be adapted to address the unique cultural landscape of the nation. These programs should be designed to cultivate and instill the necessary entrepreneurial characteristics, acknowledging the cultural nuances that shape the entrepreneurial spirit among the Indonesian population. By doing so, entrepreneurship education programs can effectively align with the goals and vision of the reformation, ultimately fostering a vibrant ecosystem of innovative and competitive entrepreneurs throughout Indonesia.

**Keywords** Entrepreneurs · Risk-taking propensity · Tolerance for ambiguity · Internal locus of control · Innovativeness · Independence

## 1 Introduction

Entrepreneurship is inextricably linked to education in developing countries like Indonesia. Education is critical in nurturing and developing entrepreneurial potential by providing students with the knowledge, skills, and attitudes necessary to start and run a successful business. In Indonesia, entrepreneurship is a compulsory subject in most universities. This is because entrepreneurship can help reduce unemployment,

---

Jumadi · I. Rajiani (✉) · E. W. Abbas
Lambung Mangkurat University, Banjarmasin, Indonesia
e-mail: rajiani@ulm.ac.id



S. Kot et al. (eds.), *Corporate Practices: Policies, Methodologies, and Insights in Organizational Management*, Springer Proceedings in Business and Economics,
https://doi.org/10.1007/978-981-97-0996-0_15

promote economic development, and foster a sense of self-reliance and independence [1]. In addition, entrepreneurs can help solve social problems and serve as role models for others. The connection between entrepreneurship and education is particularly strong in developing countries because entrepreneurship can be a powerful tool for economic growth and social change [2]. By investing in entrepreneurship education, the Indonesian government is investing in the country's future.

While entrepreneurship education is undoubtedly important in nurturing entrepreneurial intention, cultural and personality characteristics play an equally significant role [3]. Culture shapes individuals' values, beliefs, and attitudes toward entrepreneurship. In some cultures, entrepreneurship is highly valued and seen as a desirable career path. In others, entrepreneurship may be viewed with suspicion or even disdain [4]. In cultures that emphasize collectivism, individuals may be more likely to prioritize the group's needs over their own goals [5]. This can make it difficult for individuals to pursue entrepreneurial ventures, which often require a high degree of individualism and self-reliance.

Personality characteristics also play a role in influencing entrepreneurial intention. Individuals with a risk-taking propensity, tolerance for ambiguity, and self-efficacy are more likely to be attracted to entrepreneurship. Conversely, individuals who are low in these traits may be more likely to avoid entrepreneurial ventures [6].To be effective, entrepreneurship education must consider the cultural and personality characteristics of the students it serves. For example, in cultures where entrepreneurship is not highly valued, entrepreneurship education programs may need to focus on changing students' attitudes toward entrepreneurship [1]. Similarly, programs may need to provide students with the skills and knowledge to overcome cultural barriers to entrepreneurship.

In addition to addressing cultural and personality factors, entrepreneurship education programs can also help to create a more supportive environment for entrepreneurs. This can be done by providing students access to mentors, networking opportunities, and financial resources [7]. By creating a supportive environment, entrepreneurship education programs can increase the likelihood that students will turn their entrepreneurial intentions into reality.

Two main hypotheses have been proposed to explain the economic predicament: the structural hypothesis and the cultural hypothesis [8]. The structural hypothesis attributes Indonesian economic underperformance to structural impediments erected by non-Indonesians, notably the Dutch colonial government and Chinese immigrants. In contrast, the cultural hypothesis posits that Indonesian values hinder economic advancement. Despite implementing numerous programs to boost entrepreneurship in Indonesia, progress could be more active [9]. This suggests that the structural hypothesis has limited explanatory power.

Indonesia scores high on the collectivism dimension, emphasizing group harmony and social obligations [10]. This cultural value may discourage individuals from taking risks and pursuing entrepreneurial ventures. Additionally, a study found that Indonesia scores low on the need for achievement dimension, associated with a desire for success and personal accomplishment [11]. This cultural value can also discourage entrepreneurial activity. Therefore, it is evident that cultural factors play a significant role in shaping entrepreneurial behavior in Indonesia. While structural impediments may have contributed to Indonesia's economic difficulties in the past, cultural values are likely to have a more enduring impact on entrepreneurial activity in the country. In light of the limited explanatory power of the structural hypothesis, it is time to provide further attention to the cultural hypothesis, which proposes that Indonesian values are instrumental in obstructing economic advancement. Specifically, this research identifies cultural characteristics of Indonesians that may account for the extent to which selected personality characteristics are significant predictors of entrepreneurial spirit.

Culture has a significant impact on personality. Indonesians score high on the collectivism dimension, emphasizing group harmony and social obligations [12]. This cultural value can discourage individuals from taking risks and pursuing entrepreneurial ventures. Additionally, Indonesians score low on the individualism dimension, which is associated with a focus on personal achievement and self-reliance [10]. This cultural value can also discourage entrepreneurial activity.

Given the established link between culture and personality, the objective of this article is to develop a model of the predictor personality characteristics that identify individuals with more versus less entrepreneurial spirit. By examining the relationship between cultural characteristics, personality characteristics, and entrepreneurial spirit, this research aims to contribute to a deeper understanding of the factors influencing entrepreneurial behavior in Indonesia.

## 2 Entrepreneurial Personality Theory

Economic factors, such as market incentives and capital availability, are necessary for the establishment and growth of entrepreneurial ventures [5]. However, while economic factors are necessary for entrepreneurship to thrive, more is needed. For individuals to be motivated to start their businesses, there must also be non-economic factors that foster entrepreneurial inclination. Such non-economic factors include culture, psychological, and personality characteristics [13]. As this study is on the spirit of entrepreneurship rather than the extent to which such entrepreneurial activities exist, economic factors should be discussed in detail. Instead, the focus is on non-economic factors, such as personality characteristics influencing the entrepreneurial spirit.

Entrepreneurial spirit pertains to the entrepreneurial outlook and stance [14]. As an entrepreneur is often defined as an individual who undertakes new, innovative, and risky ventures, entrepreneurial spirit is often referred to as possessing such personality characteristics as risk-taking propensity [15]. These characteristics enable a person to be entrepreneurial. In line with this definition, numerous personality characteristics have been associated with entrepreneurs. Some more commonly observed and cited ones include risk-taking propensity, tolerance for ambiguity, persistence, achievement orientation, internal locus of control, innovativeness, and independence [6].

Entrepreneurs are generally believed to take more risks than managers because entrepreneurs bear the ultimate responsibility for the consequences of their decisions. A possible reason for this higher risk-taking behavior is that entrepreneurs view business situations more positively and perceive them as opportunities. At the same time, non-entrepreneurs may see little potential in them [16]. As a result, entrepreneurs are more likely to undertake these perceived opportunities than less entrepreneurial individuals.

Among Southeast Asians, the risk-taking propensity is uncommon [17]. Southeast Asians, including Indonesians, avoid uncertainty and seek assurance [18]. Indonesian culture is classically uncertainty-avoiding, tending to generate predictable behavior and discourage rule-breaking [19]. Asal *bapak senang* (keeping the father happy), a characteristic of many Indonesian relationships, is partly practiced to minimize risk among individuals [20]. Therefore, based on the above discussion, risk-taking propensity is a differentiating cue for entrepreneurial spirit because it is not a common characteristic among Indonesians. An individual who is willing to take risks and face uncertainty is more likely to have an entrepreneurial spirit compared to one who avoids uncertainty.

Thus, the following proposition is proposed:

HI: Low risk-taking propensity hampers Indonesians to be an entrepreneur.

Entrepreneurs face a high degree of uncertainty introduced by the dynamic business world. In addition to setbacks and surprises, an entrepreneurial environment often needs more organization, structure, and order. However, entrepreneurs thrive in such ambiguous environments [21]. Therefore, entrepreneurs are said to have a higher tolerance for ambiguity and enjoy situations without structure and procedure [22]. As with risk-taking propensity, tolerance for ambiguity is a significant predictor of entrepreneurial spirit. Indonesians are generally averse to uncertainty and seek assurance. This cultural characteristic can discourage individuals from pursuing entrepreneurial ventures, which are inherently uncertain. Therefore, individuals who are willing to tolerate ambiguity and are comfortable with unstructured and unpredictable situations are more likely to have an entrepreneurial spirit [23].

Thus, the following proposition is proposed:

H2: Low tolerance for ambiguity hampers Indonesians to be an entrepreneur.

Entrepreneurs are generally characterized by a high internal locus of control [24]. Individuals with a high internal locus of control believe they control their life events [25]. As a result, when they encounter failures, they attribute them to their actions rather than external factors [26].

In contrast, Indonesian culture is generally characterized by a high external locus of control. This is due in part to the strong influence of Islam in Indonesian society [27]. Islam teaches that divine law is immutable and absolute (*takdir*) [28]. As a result, many Indonesians believe their lives are predetermined by fate or supernatural forces.

The concept of *takdir* can discourage entrepreneurial behavior because it can lead individuals to believe they have little control over their success or failure [6]. This can make it difficult for individuals to take the risks necessary for entrepreneurial success. However, it is essential to note that the relationship between Islam and entrepreneurial behavior is complex. While *takdir* can discourage entrepreneurial activity, it can motivate individuals to work hard and achieve their goals. Additionally, Islam emphasizes the importance of striving for success in this life, which can encourage individuals to pursue entrepreneurial ventures [29]. Therefore, the impact of Islam on entrepreneurial behavior varies depending on the individual's interpretation of religious teachings. Individuals who interpret *takdir* as a call to action may be more likely to be entrepreneurial than those who interpret it as a sign that their lives are predetermined [30]. Thus, the following proposition is proposed:

H3: External locus of control hampers Indonesians to be an entrepreneur.

Entrepreneurs are often discontented with routine and regularity, which leads them to generate new ideas [31] and become more innovative [32]. Their willingness to make mistakes is also an advantage in overcoming the barriers to creativity [33]. However, Indonesia is not generally known for its innovativeness [34]. One reason for this is the country's paternalistic environment. The well-defined hierarchy, with its explicit roles for each member, can inhibit creativity and innovation. In such an environment, individuals may be discouraged from challenging the status quo or proposing new ideas.

Additionally, the concept of face is an important one in Indonesian culture. Face is a measure of social value, and the potential loss of face from failure can discourage individuals from taking risks [35]. This can be a barrier to innovation, as it can prevent individuals from trying new things that may not be successful. Therefore, in a culture where innovativeness is not encouraged, it becomes a differentiating cue that distinguishes individuals with an entrepreneurial spirit from those without [36]. Individuals willing to challenge the status quo, take risks, and embrace failure are more likely to be successful entrepreneurs [37].

Thus, the following proposition is proposed:

H4: Innovativeness hampers Indonesians to be entrepreneurs.

Entrepreneurs are also tending to be self-reliant and independent [38]. They can work on their own and need less social support than non-entrepreneurs. An individualistic culture promotes entrepreneurship by allowing individuals to act autonomously and make changes without being constrained by social norms or expectations [39]. Additionally, individuals may become entrepreneurs because they are dedicated to values that conflict with those of their previous employers [40]. This can lead them to seek independence by starting their businesses.

In contrast, Indonesian culture is generally characterized by collectivism [10]. In collectivist cultures, social bonding is essential in many aspects of life. Businesses in Indonesia are often patrimonialistic, meaning that they are characterized by paternalism, hierarchy, responsibility, mutual obligation, a family atmosphere, personalism, and protection [41]. Given the relationship between independence and entrepreneurship, it is expected that more independent individuals are more likely to have an entrepreneurial spirit. However, the collectivist nature of Indonesian culture can discourage independence. Individuals in collectivist cultures are expected to conform to social norms and to prioritize the needs of the group over their own needs. This can make it difficult for individuals to assert their independence and pursue their entrepreneurial goals. Therefore, individuals who can overcome the cultural barriers to independence in Indonesia are more likely to be successful entrepreneurs.

Thus, the following proposition is proposed:

H5: The presence of dependence hinders the entrepreneurial endeavors of individuals in Indonesia.

The compatibility of individual attributes with cultural norms is a subject of paramount importance in the context of cross-cultural management and human resource practices. In the case of Indonesia, a country renowned for its rich and diverse cultural tapestry, there are distinct attributes that may pose challenges when attempting to align them with the prevailing cultural norms. In this narrative, we shall examine five specific attributes—risk-taking propensity, tolerance for ambiguity, internal locus of control, innovativeness, and independence—and elucidate how these traits may be problematic to match Indonesian culture.

Indonesian culture is predominantly rooted in collectivism and a strong sense of community. Risk-taking propensity, an attribute often associated with entrepreneurial endeavors and individualistic societies, may not align with the traditional values of Indonesian society. In Indonesia, the emphasis is placed on preserving harmony, and decisions are frequently made considering the collective rather than individual interests. Risk-taking behavior is seen as disruptive and potentially detrimental to social cohesion, making it challenging to integrate this attribute into the cultural fabric.

Tolerance for ambiguity is a trait that relates to an individual's capacity to handle uncertain and unclear situations. Indonesian culture, while dynamic and adaptable, still values structured and hierarchical systems. Tolerance for ambiguity might be perceived as a lack of respect for established norms and authority, potentially undermining one's ability to navigate the traditional hierarchies and structures in Indonesian organizations.

An internal locus of control represents a belief in personal control over one's life and decisions. Indonesian society, however, often emphasizes a more fatalistic outlook, which attributes life events to fate, destiny, or a higher power. An individual displaying a strong internal locus of control may be perceived as challenging the prevailing cultural narrative and diminishing the significance of these external factors, making it difficult to align with the Indonesian worldview.

Innovation is often celebrated in many parts of the world as a driver of progress and competitiveness. However, in the Indonesian context, where conformity and tradition are highly valued, excessive innovativeness might be suspected. Straying too far from established practices could disrupt the harmony and balance Indonesian culture strives to maintain.

Independence, in the sense of self-reliance and individual decision-making, may be at odds with the Indonesian culture's emphasis on interdependence and strong social ties. Group consensus and cooperation are integral to social cohesion in Indonesia, and extreme independence could be perceived as self-centered or disruptive to these collective values.

The congruence of individual attributes with the cultural context is complex and multifaceted. The attributes listed—risk-taking propensity, tolerance for ambiguity, internal locus of control, innovativeness, and independence—may need to harmonize more effortlessly with the prevailing Indonesian cultural norms, often rooted in collectivism, tradition, and a sense of communal responsibility. Understanding and addressing these cultural disparities is pivotal for organizations and individuals seeking to thrive in the Indonesian milieu, and it underscores the need for cultural sensitivity and adaptability in cross-cultural interactions and management practices. The misalignment of specific attributes with Indonesian culture poses significant challenges for entrepreneurship education programs in universities. Adapting these programs to the local cultural context is crucial to effectively nurture the next generation of entrepreneurs in Indonesia while respecting and acknowledging the nation's rich and diverse cultural heritage.

## 3 Implication for Entrepreneurship Education Program

Cultural barriers to entrepreneurship in Indonesia are closely tied to specific personality traits and cultural norms. Indonesian culture often places a strong emphasis on stability and security. As a result, many individuals may be risk-averse and hesitant to venture into entrepreneurship, where uncertainties and risks are inherent. Ambiguity aversion is another cultural trait in Indonesia. People tend to prefer clear, well-defined paths and may be uncomfortable with the uncertainty of entrepreneurial ventures. Indonesian culture, in some instances, tends to attribute success or failure to external factors or fate rather than individual control. This can discourage individuals from taking the initiative and responsibility required for entrepreneurship. Traditional values and norms in Indonesia often prioritize conformity and established norms over innovation and creative thinking. This can hinder entrepreneurial ideas that require innovative solutions.

Entrepreneurship education programs can play a pivotal role in addressing these cultural barriers in the following ways: (1) Emphasizing Personality Development: Entrepreneurship education programs can actively work to nurture and develop personality traits associated with entrepreneurship, such as risk-taking, tolerance for ambiguity, and a stronger internal locus of control. By integrating training and exercises that gradually build these characteristics, students can become more confident in their entrepreneurial endeavors. (2) Providing Knowledge and Skills: Entrepreneurship programs offer students practical knowledge and skills related to starting and managing a business. This equips them with the tools and strategies necessary to navigate the complexities of entrepreneurship, potentially mitigating the perceived risks. (3) Tailoring to the Indonesian Context: To be effective, these programs should align with Indonesian cultural norms and values. This can involve incorporating local case study stories of successful Indonesian entrepreneurs and highlighting how entrepreneurial practices can coexist with cultural values. (4) Linking with Support Initiatives: Collaboration with other initiatives supporting entrepreneurship, such as government policies and mentorship programs, can provide students with a broader support ecosystem. This not only reinforces the importance of entrepreneurship but also connects them with resources and mentors who can guide them through their entrepreneurial journey. (5) Encouraging a Balanced Approach: Entrepreneurship education should promote a balanced approach, encouraging individuals to combine cultural values and norms with innovative thinking. It is not about abandoning one's cultural identity but finding creative ways to channel it into entrepreneurial success.

In sum, entrepreneurship education programs have the potential to address cultural barriers in Indonesia by nurturing the required personality traits, providing practical knowledge, and aligning with local cultural contexts. By doing so, they can empower individuals to overcome cultural barriers and pursue entrepreneurial opportunities more effectively.

## 4 Conclusion

This study highlights the importance of cultural factors when developing entrepreneurship education programs. The five entrepreneurial characteristics examined in this study (risk-taking propensity, tolerance for ambiguity, internal locus of control, innovativeness, and independence) may not be widely ingrained within the traditional culture of Indonesia. As such, entrepreneurship education programs in Indonesia should be adapted to address the unique cultural landscape of the nation. These programs should be designed to cultivate and instill the necessary entrepreneurial characteristics, acknowledging the cultural nuances that shape the entrepreneurial spirit among the Indonesian population. Therefore, entrepreneurship education programs in Indonesia should incorporate cultural considerations into their curriculum. This could involve using culturally relevant examples and case studies, as well as inviting guest speakers who can share their experiences as entrepreneurs in Indonesia. This study is a conceptual paper and does not test any hypotheses. As such, the findings of this study need to be more generalizable to the broader population. Additionally, the study only focuses on a limited number of entrepreneurial characteristics. Future research could explore the relationship between other cultural factors and entrepreneurial spirit.

## References


1. Hadi, S., Abbas, E.W., & Rajiani, I. Should spirituality be included in entrepreneurship education program curriculum to boost students' entrepreneurial intention? Front. Educ. **7** (2022)
2. Tien, N.H., Ngoc, N.M., Trang, T.T.T., Duc, L.D.M., Mai, N.P.: Sustainable development of higher education institutions in developing countries: comparative analysis of Poland and Vietnam. Contemp. Econ. **16**(2), 195–210 (2022)
3. Badghish, S., Ali, I., Ali, M., Yaqub, M.Z., Dhir, A.: How socio-cultural transition helps to improve entrepreneurial intentions among women? J. Intellect. Cap. **24**(4), 900–928 (2022)
4. Romero-Colmenares, L.M., Reyes-Rodríguez, J.F.: Sustainable entrepreneurial intentions: Exploration of a model based on the theory of planned behaviour among university students in north-east Colombia. Int. J. Manag. Educ. **20**(2), 100627 (2022)
5. Rajiani, I., Kot, S., Michałek, J., & Gede Riana, I. Barriers to technology innovation among nascent entrepreneurs in deprived areas. Probl. Perspect. Manag. **21**(3), 614–628 (2023)
6. Basuki, Widyanti, R., & Rajiani, I. Nascent entrepreneurs of millennial generations in the emerging market of Indonesia. Entrep. Bus. Econ. Rev. **9**(2), 151–165 (2021)
7. Bauman, A., Lucy, C.: Enhancing entrepreneurial education: Developing competencies for success. Int. J. Manag. Educ. **19**(1), 100293 (2021)
8. Lim, L.: Work-related values of Malays and Chinese Malaysians. Int. J. Cross Cult. Manag. **1**(2), 209–226 (2001)
9. Broto Legowo, M., Sorongan, F.A.: Accelerating digital transformation during the COVID-19 Pandemic: A model design for Indonesian MSMEs. Binus Bus. Rev. **13**(2), 203–211 (2022)
10. Rajiani, I., Kot, S.: Javanese Indonesia: Human resource management issues in a uniquely collectivist culture. Cult. Manag.: Sci. Educ. **4**(2), 9–21 (2020)
11. Muttaqin, T., Wittek, R., Heyse, L., van Duijn, M.: The achievement gap in Indonesia? Organizational and ideological differences between private Islamic schools. Sch. Eff. Sch. Improv. **31**(2), 212–242 (2019)
12. Smaldino, P.E., Lukaszewski, A., von Rueden, C., Gurven, M.: Niche diversity can explain cross-cultural differences in personality structure. Nat. Hum. Behav. **3**(12), 1276–1283 (2019)
13. Nikulin, D.: Driving forces of informal employment: An empirical study based on Polish enterprise data. Entrep. Bus. Econ. Rev. **11**(3), 93–106 (2023)
14. Khurana, I., Ghura, A.S., Dutta, D.K.: The influence of religion on the humane orientation of entrepreneurs. J. Small Bus. Manage. **59**(3), 417–442 (2021)
15. Salameh, A.A., Akhtar, H., Gul, R., Omar, A.B., & Hanif, S. Personality traits and entrepreneurial intentions: Financial risk-taking as mediator. Front. Psychol. **13** (2022)
16. Dankiewicz, R., Ostrowska-Dankiewicz, A., & Bulut, C. The attitudes of entrepreneurs of the small and medium-sized enterprises sector in Poland to key business risks. Equilibrium. Q. J. Econ. Econ. Policy **15**(3), 511–536 (2020)
17. White, G.O., Rajwani, T., Krammer, S.M.: Legal distance and entrepreneurial orientation of foreign subsidiaries: Evidence from Southeast Asia. J. World Bus. **57**(6), 101382 (2022)
18. Toh, M.Y., Zhang, Y.: Bank capital and risk adjustment responses to economic uncertainty: Evidence from emerging Southeast Asian economies. Res. Int. Bus. Financ. **60**, 101576 (2022)
19. Rajiani, I., Pypłacz, P.: National culture as modality in managing the carbon economy in Southeast Asia. Pol. J. Manag. Stud. **18**(1), 296–310 (2018)
20. Fitriastuti, T., Vanderstraeten, A.: Being Out of the Loop: Workplace deviance as a mediator of the impact of impression management on workplace exclusion. Sustain. **14**(2), 1004 (2022)
21. Zellweger, T., Zenger, T.: Entrepreneurs as scientists: A Pragmatist approach to producing value out of uncertainty. Acad. Manag. Rev. **48**(3), 379–408 (2023)
22. Gandhi, M., Joshi, M.: Entrepreneurial firms and their sustainability in a VUCA world. World review of entrepreneurship, Manag. Sustain. Dev. **19**(6), 542–561 (2023)
23. Kara, A., Dheer, R.J.S.: The relationship between culture and entrepreneurship: the role of Trust. Int. Entrep. Manag. J. (2023). https://doi.org/10.1007/s11365-023-00901-1

24. Uysal, E.K., Karadağ, H., Tuncer, B., Şahin, F.: Locus of control, need for achievement, and entrepreneurial intention: A moderated mediation model. Int. J. Manag. Educ. **20**(2), 100560 (2022)
25. Tyler, N., Heffernan, R., & Fortune, C. A. Reorienting locus of control in individuals who have offended through strengths-based interventions: Personal agency and the good lives model. Front. Psychol. **11** (2020)
26. Zhan, L., Lin, L., Wang, X., Zhang, J., & Zhang, L. Internal but not external locus of control predicts acute stress response. Psychophysiol. **60**(4) (2022)
27. Barton, G., Yilmaz, I., Morieson, N.: Authoritarianism, democracy, Islamic movements and contestations of Islamic religious ideas in Indonesia. Relig. **12**(8), 641 (2021)
28. Lasawali, A., Abidin, A., Idhan, M., Al-Amri, J. S., & Haerunnisa, W. Islamic moderate values in teaching classic Islamic books at modern Islamic boarding schools in Indonesia. Int. J. Curr. Sci. Res. Rev. **6**(8) (2023)
29. Anggadwita, G., Dana, L.P., Ramadani, V., Ramadan, R.Y.: Empowering Islamic boarding schools by applying the humane entrepreneurship approach: the case of Indonesia. Int. J. Entrep. Behav. Res. **27**(6), 1580–1604 (2021)
30. Bourchier, D., Jusuf, W.: Liberalism in Indonesia: Between authoritarian statism and Islamism. Asian Stud. Rev. **47**(1), 69–87 (2022)
31. Mens, J., van Bueren, E., Vrijhoef, R., Heurkens, E.: A typology of social entrepreneurs in bottom-up urban development. Cities **110**, 103066 (2021)
32. Apostu, S.A., Mukli, L., Panait, M., Gigauri, I., Hysa, E.: Economic growth through the lenses of education, entrepreneurship, and Innovation. Adm. Sci. **12**(3), 74 (2022). https://doi.org/10.3390/admsci12030074
33. Etemad, H.: The evolving international entrepreneurship orientations and international entrepreneurship capital in the rapidly changing and digitizing international environments. J. Int. Entrep. (2022). https://doi.org/10.1007/s10843-022-00322-1
34. Octasylva, A.R.P., Yuliati, L.N., Hartoyo, H., Soehadi, A.W.: Innovativeness as the key to MSMEs' Performances. Sustain. **14**(11), 6429 (2022)
35. Mokoginta, K., Arafah, B.: Negotiation in Indonesian culture: A cultural linguistic analysis of bahasa Indonesia textbooks. Theory Pract. Lang. Stud. **12**(4), 691–701 (2022)
36. Chaurasia, S. Concept of entrepreneur and entrepreneurship. Agric. Microbiol. Based Entrep. 3–24 (2022)
37. Pidduck, R.J., Tucker, R.: Meaningful heterodoxies: Advancing entrepreneurship through engagement with unorthodox phenomena. J. Bus. Ventur. Insights **18**, e00319 (2022)
38. Michaelis, T.L., Scheaf, D.J., Carr, J.C., Pollack, J.M.: An agentic perspective of resourcefulness: Self-reliant and joint resourcefulness behaviors within the entrepreneurship process. J. Bus. Ventur. **37**(1), 106083 (2022)
39. Wood, B.P., Ng, P.Y., Bastian, B.L.: Hegemonic conceptualizations of empowerment in entrepreneurship and their suitability for collective contexts. Adm. Sci. **11**(1), 28 (2021)
40. Jachimowicz, J.M., Weisman, H.: Divergence between employer and employee understandings of passion: Theory and implications for future research. Res. Organ. Behav. **42**, 100167 (2022)
41. Ristiawan, R., Huijbens, E., Peters, K.: Projecting development through tourism: Patrimonial governance in Indonesian geoparks. Land **12**(1), 223 (2023)

# Student Acceptance Level for E-Learning in Public Universities of Malaysia

**Muhammad Imran, Ali Raza, A. K. Mahbubul Hye, and Maadi Bakor Omar**

**Abstract** The present study extends the existing literature on student satisfaction in public universities in Malaysia by investigating the role of readiness for e-learning, training for e-learning, and motivation for e-learning. The quantitative approach is adopted for the current research. The study's data was collected from 370 students from public universities in Malaysia through a structured questionnaire. The findings of the study have found a positive and significant relationship between readiness for e-learning, training for e-learning, and student acceptance level toward e-learning in public universities of Malaysia. Besides, the current study also has found the mediating role of motivation for e-learning between readiness for e-learning and student acceptance. This study delves into the intricate web of factors influencing student acceptance of e-learning in the context of Malaysian public universities, focusing on readiness for e-learning, training for e-learning, and motivation for e-learning. These elements are inextricably linked, and understanding their interplay is essential for crafting effective strategies to enhance the adoption of e-learning for higher student satisfaction levels. Additionally, this research explores the mediating role of motivation, shedding light on how it can bridge the gap between readiness for e-learning, training for e-learning, and student acceptance. By unraveling these complexities, this study aims to provide valuable insights and recommendations to bolster the acceptance and effectiveness of e-learning within this specific educational setting.

M. Imran (✉)
Universiti Utara Malaysia, Sintok, Malaysia
e-mail: muhammad.imran@uum.edu.my

A. Raza
School of Economics, Shandong University, Jinan, China

A. K. M. Hye
Shinawatra University, Pathum Thani, Thailand

M. B. Omar
Universiti Utara Malaysia, Sintok, Malaysia



S. Kot et al. (eds.), *Corporate Practices: Policies, Methodologies, and Insights in Organizational Management*, Springer Proceedings in Business and Economics,
https://doi.org/10.1007/978-981-97-0996-0_16

**Keywords** E-learning · Student acceptance · Readiness · Training · Motivation · Malaysian public universities

## 1 Introduction

The rapid growth of technology has led to an increase in the use of e-learning in education [1–2]. Online education offers many advantages, such as flexibility, accessibility, and cost-effectiveness, but it also presents challenges. To be successful in online learning, students must be prepared, motivated, and have the necessary skills and support. E-learning has become a crucial aspect of modern education and a valuable tool for effectively delivering knowledge and skills [3]. With the increasing popularity of e-learning, it is essential to understand the factors contributing to its successful implementation. However, student acceptance of e-learning refers to the degree to which students are willing to participate in e-learning and perceive it as a valuable tool for learning [4]. Student acceptance of e-learning is influenced by several factors, including perceived usefulness, perceived ease of use, perceived enjoyment, perceived credibility, readiness, training, and motivation of students [5]. A student who accepts e-learning recognizes its benefits and is willing to use it for learning. A positive perception and attitude towards e-learning can lead to increased participation and success in online education [6]. Thus, readiness for E-learning refers to the degree to which an individual is prepared to participate in e-learning [7]. It encompasses various components, including technical competence, familiarity with e-learning, motivation, and perceived benefits. A person ready for e-learning has the technical skills to use e-learning technologies and understands how e-learning works. They are also motivated to participate in e-learning and recognize its benefits.

Technical readiness involves having the necessary equipment, software, and Internet access to participate in online courses [8]. Learning readiness consists of the required academic skills, such as critical thinking and problem-solving, to succeed online. Dispositional readiness involves having the right attitude [9] and motivation to participate in e-learning. Along with readiness, e-learning training refers to the preparation and instruction provided to individuals on how to effectively use e-learning technologies and participate in e-learning [10]. This training can take various forms, including online tutorials, webinars, and face-to-face workshops. The purpose of training is to increase an individual's competence and confidence in using e-learning technologies and to maximize the benefits of e-learning.

Furthermore, this includes orientation to the online learning platform, technical support, and training in online learning skills such as time management and communication [11]. Effective training can help students become more comfortable and confident in participating in online learning. In respect of motivation for e-learning refers to the reasons or drives that prompt a student to participate in online education. It encompasses intrinsic motivation, such as a desire for knowledge and self-improvement, and extrinsic motivation, such as career advancement or financial incentives.

Motivation for e-learning can play a significant role in shaping a student's experiences and attitudes towards online education. A motivated student is more likely to engage in the online learning experience, overcome challenges actively, and have a positive experience, leading to increased acceptance of e-learning [12] as the mediating role of motivation for E-learning to the drive or desire to participate in e-learning [13]. It is a crucial factor in the successful implementation of e-learning and can mediate between readiness for e-learning, training for e-learning, and student acceptance. A person motivated to participate in e-learning is more likely to be ready for e-learning, receive e-learning training, and accept e-learning as a valuable tool for learning. Furthermore, motivation for e-learning can enhance the effectiveness of training for e-learning and increase student acceptance of e-learning. The relationship between readiness for e-learning, e-learning training, student acceptance, and motivation for e-learning is complex and interrelated. Readiness for e-learning, training for e-learning, and student acceptance are all important factors that contribute to the successful implementation of e-learning. The mediating role of motivation for e-learning highlights the importance of understanding and addressing the motivations of individuals who participate in e-learning. This understanding can increase the effectiveness of e-learning by growing readiness for e-learning, training for e-learning, and student acceptance.

The remaining study is structured below. The research framework is elaborated in section two, which integrates the literature review. The study's hypotheses are also explained in this section. The third and fourth sections present the research methods with results and discussion. Section fifth offers the study's conclusion with potential policy recommendations.

# 2 Research Framework and Hypotheses Development

## 2.1 *Readiness for E-learning and Student Acceptance for E-learning*

A student who is highly prepared for e-learning is more likely to have a positive experience with online education and be more accepting of e-learning as a viable mode of learning. Conversely, a student who is not well-prepared for e-learning may struggle with online courses and have a negative perception of e-learning, potentially reducing their willingness to participate in the future. The readiness for e-learning and student acceptance of e-learning are closely related and can influence one another. A positive experience with e-learning can increase a student's acceptance of it [14], while a negative experience can decrease it. Educators and institutions must provide support and resources to help students become ready for e-learning to improve their acceptance and overall experience with online education.

According to Akaslan and Law [15], the ability of an organization to benefit from e-learning is called e-learning readiness. Assessing the success and effectiveness of online learning can be done by studying how prepared students are for it from their point of view Drysdale et al. [16]. Only 12% of students chose to study online in the MacKeogh and Fox [17] study, while 20% preferred traditional teaching methods. These results suggest that while many students are in favor of technology, they are not willing to give up face-to-face education. In another study, Jong and Howard [18] found that online students need a more direct connection with their instructors and students. According to Starenko et al. [19], student preparation is another decisive factor in successful e-learning implementation Rasouli et al. [20], Mosadegh et al. [21]. According to George et al. [22], knowledge, technical skills, access to technology, independent learning, computer and internet proficiency, and attitudes toward online learning can all be used to assess student readiness assessment. Thus, when the right learning environment and strategic training are combined, students' preparation and likelihood of success in online learning are enhanced [23].

H1: There is a positive relationship between readiness and student acceptance.

## 2.2 Training for E-learning and Students' Acceptance for E-learning

The term "training" describes initiatives to impart the necessary knowledge of TOK (theory of knowledge) principles, including technical capabilities and organizational skills—developing the capabilities needed to perform a task. Internal computer training promotes a more favorable opinion and a better understanding of the system in adopting information systems [24]. Comprehensive researchers have found that training improves perceived appropriateness and ease of use, improving perceived technology adoption. Similarly, university-provided training programs for an e-learning system can help students accept it because of its apparent benefits and ease of use. With the rise of online, e-learning has emerged as a new, flexible, and adaptable method for students to gain necessary knowledge.

The widespread development of Internet systems and technologies creates enormous opportunities for training and education. Mathieson et al. [25] state that researchers examining perceived resources often focus on people's emotional states rather than offering practical advice for better innovation management. The student's awareness of the resources (support, training, and access to technology) available to him both inside and outside the university he attends is a critical factor in determining whether an e-learning system is acceptable. Effective training can help students become more comfortable and confident in their abilities to participate in online learning, leading to a positive experience and increased acceptance of e-learning. On the other hand, adequate or effective training can lead to satisfaction and clarity, potentially decreasing a student's willingness to participate in future online courses. The e-learning training is a crucial factor in shaping a student's experience with and acceptance of e-learning. Providing comprehensive and user-friendly training can help students overcome challenges and develop positive attitudes toward online education, while lack of training can contribute to negative experiences and decreased acceptance.

H2: There is a positive relationship between training for e-learning and student acceptance for e-learning.

## *2.3 Motivation for E-learning as a Mediator*

Isolation has been well-documented among online learning students [26]. According to Hasan and Khan [27], the technique can be caused by solitude lac, lack of connection in the online space, and a feeling of isolation, which leads to a lack of motivation to study. Learners must be motivated to stay in a learning system. Unmotivated students may find it challenging to concentrate on the learning experience [28]. A variety of factors can impact their degree of satisfaction and encouragement. Suzuki et al. [29] emphasized the significance of innovation, responses, reliability, and intrinsic motivation. According to Sun et al. [30], students' learning' sense of ease of use does have a significant influence on their satisfaction with the system. Based on prior virtual experience with the phenomenon, technology skills, and interests, learners' conceptions of enjoyment may differ. Experienced internet learners may be more comfortable with different forms of educational technology than less experienced students. Learners who have little experience with online learning may feel insecure, which can lead to anxiety. Anxiety can have a negative impact on online learner satisfaction [30].

Consequently, when integrating e-learning into the school environment, remember that someone with easy access to technology and/or the online world may need help to adjust to a digital landscape. They may suffer from "technophobia" or "internet fear," which makes online learning difficult and results in low motivation to learn. As a result, they may experience increased stress and decreased motivation. This fear has indeed been recognized as a symptom of the fast-paced technological changes that will drive social transformation.

The relationship between motivation for e-learning and student acceptance of e-learning is a close one, as motivation can play a significant role in shaping a student's experiences and attitudes towards online education. When students are motivated to participate in e-learning, they are more likely to engage in the online learning experience actively and put in the effort to overcome any challenges they may face. This can lead to a positive experience and increased acceptance of e-learning. On the other hand, if students need more motivation for e-learning, they may be less likely to participate actively in online courses or try to overcome challenges. This can result in a negative experience and decreased acceptance of e-learning.

Motivation for e-learning can have a direct impact on student acceptance of e-learning. A motivated student is more likely to have a positive experience and be more accepting of online education. At the same time, lacking motivation can lead to a negative understanding and decreased acceptance. When students are motivated to participate in e-learning, they are more likely to try to become ready for online learning. For example, they may invest time and effort into developing technical skills, familiarizing themselves with online platforms, and learning how to manage their time and attention while engaged in online activities. Having a high level of readiness for e-learning can lead to a positive experience with online education, which, in turn, can increase a student's acceptance of e-learning [31].

On the other hand, if students need more motivation, they may be less likely to put in the effort to become ready for e-learning, potentially leading to a negative experience and decreased acceptance of online education. However, motivation for e-learning can mediate between readiness for e-learning and student acceptance of e-learning. A motivated student is more likely to become ready for e-learning and have a positive experience. At the same time, a lack of motivation can decrease readiness and contribute to negative attitudes toward e-learning.

H3: There is a mediating role of motivation for e-learning between readiness for e-learning and student acceptance for e-learning.

H4: There is a mediating role of motivation for e-learning between training for e-learning and student acceptance for e-learning.

## 2.4 Research Framework

The research framework employed in the study is portrayed in Fig. 1.

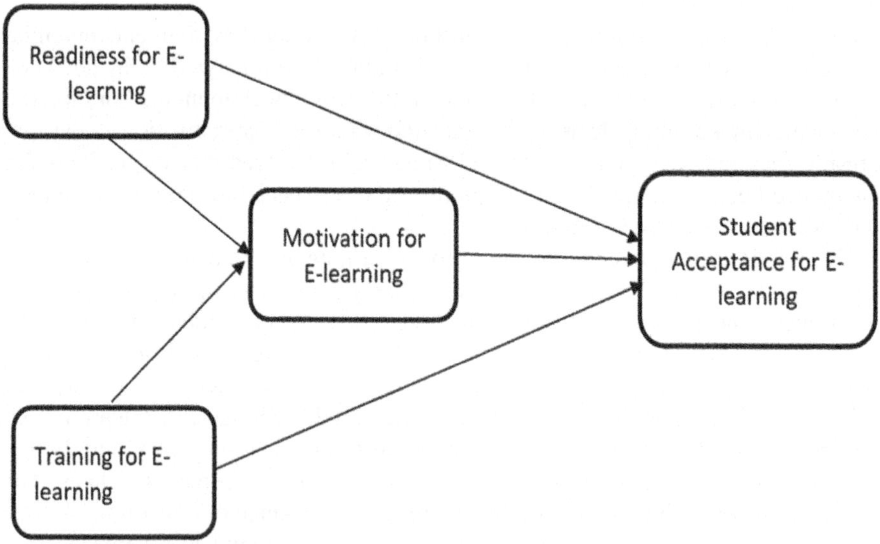


**Fig. 1** Conceptual framework

# 3 Methodology

## 3.1 Data Sources and Study Participants

The quantitative approach will be adopted for the current research. The quantitative method lets researchers know participants' views on points and thoughts about concerns, issues, and situations [32]. The quantitative approach is used for the present study that focuses on defining the student acceptance level regarding online learning and its influential factors. The population of the study is undergraduate students at public universities in Malaysia. The data is collected from 370 students at public universities in Malaysia through a structured questionnaire. The survey technique is more beneficial to understand the respondents' views, thoughts, feelings, and perspectives. The data is collected face-to-face and online. Moreover, the data was analyzed using Smart PLS.

## 3.2 Research Instruments

This paper examines the main constructs such as readiness for e-learning, motivation of e- learning, training for e-learning, and student acceptance for e-learning. All variables are measured on a 5-point Likert scale, ranging from "strongly disagree" to "strongly agree". Measurement items of each variable are presented in Table 1. Some indicators are modified keeping in view the study's objectives.

| Measures of Motivation for E-learning | | | | | | |
|---|---|---|---|---|---|---|
| 1 | I have a strong desire to succeed in the learning process | 1 | 2 | 3 | 4 | 5 |
| 2 | I have planning and anticipation in doing | 1 | 2 | 3 | 4 | 5 |
| 3 | My actions in the student learning process on campus | 1 | 2 | 3 | 4 | 5 |
| 4 | I have high creativity in achieving success in the learning process | 1 | 2 | 3 | 4 | 5 |
| 5 | I can monitor progress and weaknesses in acting in the learning process | 1 | 2 | 3 | 4 | 5 |
| 6 | I have courage in acting and are not afraid to take risks in the learning process | 1 | 2 | 3 | 4 | 5 |
| 7 | I have a high sense of responsibility in the learning process | 1 | 2 | 3 | 4 | 5 |

Where 1= Strongly Disagree (SD), 2= Disagree (D), 3=Neutral (N), 4=Agree (A), 5=Strongly Agree (SA)

| Measures of training for E-learning | | | | | | |
|---|---|---|---|---|---|---|
| 1 | I do not need training on e-learning | 1 | 2 | 3 | 4 | 5 |
| 2 | My teachers do not need training on e-learning | 1 | 2 | 3 | 4 | 5 |

(continued)

(continued)

| | | | | | | |
|---|---|---|---|---|---|---|
| 3 | Technical and administrative personals do not need training | 1 | 2 | 3 | 4 | 5 |
| 4 | The facilities of university are sufficient for e-learning | 1 | 2 | 3 | 4 | 5 |

Where 1= Strongly Disagree (SD), 2= Disagree (D), 3=Neutral (N), 4=Agree (A), 5=Strongly Agree (SA)

| Measures of student acceptance for E-learning | | | | | | |
|---|---|---|---|---|---|---|
| 1 | E-learning can improve the quality of my studies | 1 | 2 | 3 | 4 | 5 |
| 2 | I believe that using e-learning can increase my performance | 1 | 2 | 3 | 4 | 5 |
| 3 | I believe that e-learning is useful for my research | 1 | 2 | 3 | 4 | 5 |
| 4 | E-learning enables me to accomplish my studies more effectively than the traditional method | 1 | 2 | 3 | 4 | 5 |
| 5 | It is easy for me to use e-learning tools (e.g. (WebEx, e-learning Portal etc.) | 1 | 2 | 3 | 4 | 5 |
| 6 | I believe that my teachers find it easy to use (WebEx, e-learning Portal etc.) | 1 | 2 | 3 | 4 | 5 |

Where 1 = Strongly Disagree (SD), 2 = Disagree (D), 3 = Neutral (N), 4 = Agree (A), 5 = Strongly Agree (SA)

# 4 Results

## *4.1 Measurement Model Assessment Results*

### 4.1.1 Convergent Validity

To examine the measurement model, convergent and discriminant validity are primarily used before testing the hypotheses. Convergent validity assesses the correlation among multiple indicators of the same construct and is measured using loadings, average variance extracted (AVE), and composite reliability (CR). Referring to the criteria for convergent validity, factor loadings, CR, and AVE values should be greater than 0.60, 0.70, and 0.50, respectively [33–36]. According to Fornell and Larcker [37], CR should not be less than 0.7, and AVE should not be less than 0.5. Based on the results, all values fall within the mentioned cutoffs, endorsing the model's convergent validity (Table 2).

### 4.1.2 Discriminant Validity

The Heterotrait-Monotrait (HTMT) correlation ratios are used to check the discriminant validity that is also part of the measurement model. Discriminant validity empirically differentiates the constructs from one another and measures the differences

**Table 1** Research instruments

| *Measures of readiness for E-learning* | | | | | | |
|---|---|---|---|---|---|---|
| 1 | You have access to the Internet at home | 1 | 2 | 3 | 4 | 5 |
| 2 | You have access to the Internet at your university | 1 | 2 | 3 | 4 | 5 |
| 3 | I am satisfied with my university network | 1 | 2 | 3 | 4 | 5 |
| 4 | I use the Internet as information source | 1 | 2 | 3 | 4 | 5 |
| 5 | I use e-mail as the main communication tool | 1 | 2 | 3 | 4 | 5 |
| 6 | I use office software for content delivery and demonstration | 1 | 2 | 3 | 4 | 5 |
| 7 | I use web browsers (e.g. Internet Explorer, Google Chrome) confidently | 1 | 2 | 3 | 4 | 5 |
| 8 | I use search engines (e.g. Google, MSN Search) confidently | 1 | 2 | 3 | 4 | 5 |
| 9 | I use digital file management tools confidently | 1 | 2 | 3 | 4 | 5 |
| 10 | I use tools to create learning materials confidently | 1 | 2 | 3 | 4 | 5 |
| 12 | I have information about e-learning | 1 | 2 | 3 | 4 | 5 |
| 13 | I have enough ICT competencies to prepare e-learning materials | 1 | 2 | 3 | 4 | 5 |
| 14 | I feel that I am ready to integrate e-learning in my studies | 1 | 2 | 3 | 4 | 5 |
| 15 | I have enough time to prepare e-learning materials | 1 | 2 | 3 | 4 | 5 |
| 16 | I believe my teachers will like e-learning | 1 | 2 | 3 | 4 | 5 |
| 17 | My university top-level administration understands the e-learning | 1 | 2 | 3 | 4 | 5 |
| 18 | The top-level administration supports the use of e-learning | 1 | 2 | 3 | 4 | 5 |
| 19 | E-learning is applied in all departments of my university | 1 | 2 | 3 | 4 | 5 |
| 20 | E-learning can enhance the theoretical part of my studies | 1 | 2 | 3 | 4 | 5 |
| 21 | E-learning can enhance the practical part of my studies | 1 | 2 | 3 | 4 | 5 |
| 22 | E-learning can be applied to the theoretical part of my studies | 1 | 2 | 3 | 4 | 5 |
| 23 | E-learning can be applied to the practical part of my studies | 1 | 2 | 3 | 4 | 5 |

*Note* Where 1 = Strongly Disagree (SD), 2 = Disagree (D), 3 = Neutral (N), 4 = Agree (A), 5 = Strongly Agree (SA)

**Table 2** Scales and convergent validity results

| | Cronbach's alpha | Composite reliability (rho_a) | Composite reliability (rho_c) | Average variance extracted (AVE) |
|---|---|---|---|---|
| Motivation for e-learning | 0.900 | 0.900 | 0.921 | 0.624 |
| Readiness for e-learning | 0.951 | 0.956 | 0.956 | 0.500 |
| Student acceptance for e-learning | 0.885 | 0.888 | 0.913 | 0.635 |
| Training for e-learning | 0.890 | 0.905 | 0.923 | 0.750 |

*Source* Authors' estimations

**Table 3** Heterotrait-monotrait ratio results

| | Motivation | Readiness | Satisfaction | Training |
|---|---|---|---|---|
| Motivation for e-leaning | | | | |
| Readiness for e-learning | 0.764 | | | |
| Student acceptance for learning | 0.678 | 0.830 | | |
| Training for e-learning | 0.347 | 0.489 | 0.490 | |

*Source* Authors' estimations

between the overlapping constructs. The correlation coefficient under HTMT should not be exceeded to 0.90 [38]. Referring Henseler, et al. [39], though the Fornell-Larcker criterion can measure the discriminant validity, HTMT can efficiently assess the sensitivity rates higher than Fornell-Larcker. Furthermore, all variables' HTMT values should be less than 0.90. It is shown that all HTMT values for all variables are not higher than 0.90, implying that all variables in the current study have discriminant validity (Table 3).

#### 4.1.3 Model-Fit

In Table 4, the results further infer that estimated model fits the observed data reasonably well, as indicated by the similarity in various fit indices between the estimated and saturated models. The SRMR, d_ULS, and d_G values are all consistent between the two models, indicating that estimated model replicates the data patterns nearly as well as the fully saturated model, which is a model with all possible relationships estimated. Furthermore, the chi-square statistic, while not ideal for large datasets, is consistent between the models, and the NFI value of 0.77 suggests an appropriate level of fit.

**Table 4** Model fit results

| | Saturated model | Estimated model |
|---|---|---|
| SRMR | 0.066 | 0.066 |
| d_ULS | 3.391 | 3.391 |
| d_G | 1.189 | 1.189 |
| Chi-square | 2422.43 | 2422.43 |
| NFI | 0.77 | 0.77 |

**Table 5** Path analysis results

| Hypothesis | Beta | Standard deviation | *T* statistics | *P* values |
|---|---|---|---|---|
| H1: Readiness - > student acceptance | 0.717 | 0.040 | 17.754 | 0.000 |
| H2: Training - > student acceptance | 0.125 | 0.060 | 2.072 | 0.038 |
| H3: Readiness - > Motivation - > student acceptance | 0.090 | 0.044 | 2.026 | 0.043 |
| H4: Training - > Motivation - > student acceptance | -0.001 | 0.006 | 0.255 | 0.799 |

#### 4.1.4 Structural Model Assessment

According to structural model, the values of t-statistics should not be less than 1.96 at 0.05 significant level. Thus, the results of table 5 offer valuable insights into the relationships among the variables in this study. Firstly, the direct relationships between readiness for e-learning and student acceptance for e-learning is found significant, hence the H1 is supported. Secondly the direct relationship between training for e-learning and student acceptance for e-learning is also positive significant, thus, H2 is supported. On the other side, the indirect relationship of motivation between readiness for e-learning and student acceptance for e-learning shows positive and significant result, hence H3 is accepted. Besides, the indirect relationship of motivation between training for e-learning and student acceptance for e-learning is found insignificant, hence H4 is not supported.

## 5 Conclusion of the Study

This study has explained crucial insights into the complicated setting of student acceptance of e-learning in Malaysian public universities. As the requirement of the modern era, the educational sector evolves with technological advancements; it becomes necessary to investigate the complex relationship of contributing factors that could shape the students' behavior toward acceptance of technological advancement in the education sector. However, this study has explored the relationship between readiness for e-learning, motivation for e-learning, training for e-learning, and student acceptance for e-learning in universities. However, the findings of the study indicated a strong positive direct relationship between readiness for e-learning, training for e-learning, and student acceptance in public universities of Malaysia. Moreover, this study found an indirect relationship between motivation for e-learning, readiness for e-learning, and student acceptance of e-learning. Hence, the study's findings show the critical role of preparedness and training for e-learning in student acceptance level for e-learning.

Furthermore, this study has emphasized the significance of training programs in enhancing students' acceptance level toward e-learning. The e-learning training can enhance competence and skills, increasing student acceptance levels toward e-learning when individuals perform well.

Moreover, the mediating role of motivation for e-learning expressed that motivated individuals are more likely to experience acceptance due to their pursuit of goals or fulfillment of needs. ReadinessReadiness for e-learning can play a crucial role as a precursor to motivation, ultimately leading to higher levels of student acceptance.

On the other hand, this study found no mediating function of motivation for e-learning between training and student acceptance of e-learning. This outcome suggests that exercise alone may not substantially influence an individual's motivation. Motivation is a multifaceted construct influenced by various factors, including personal goals and intrinsic motivation, which training may not directly address.

Furthermore, concerning the study's implications, this study offers a set of implications, such as the effective implementation of e-learning practices within Malaysian public universities, which can spearhead comprehensive readiness initiatives encompassing technical skills, access to technology, and academic preparedness. Moreover, acknowledging the multifaceted nature of motivation, universities must provide robust motivational support mechanisms. This includes mentorship programs, counseling services, and interventions designed to kindle intrinsic motivation, goal setting, and a sense of belonging in the online learning community. The universities should implement a dynamic feedback loop to gauge student satisfaction and gather insights for continual improvement. This iterative process should inform the ongoing refinement of e-learning platforms and courses, aligning them more closely with student expectations.

It also encourages active faculty engagement with e-learning platforms and equips educators with the necessary support and incentives to harness the full potential of digital teaching methods. Develop robust, long-term strategic plans for e-learning adoption, considering scalability, resource allocation, and alignment with educational objectives. Such foresight ensures the sustained growth and effectiveness of e-learning endeavors.

Thus, this study not only illuminates the transformative potential of e-learning within Malaysian public universities but also furnishes actionable policy recommendations to support student acceptance. By giving due emphasis to readiness, training, and motivation while remaining attuned to the unique needs and expectations of their student cohorts, institutions can navigate the digital frontier of education adeptly. This journey toward a digitally empowered education system promises to equip students with the skills and knowledge required to thrive in an ever-evolving global landscape.

## 6 Limitations and Future Recommendations of the Study

There are a few limitations presented in this study, such as the data only collected from public universities due to time constraints. Future studies should collect the data from public and private universities to generalize the research. The cross-sectional approach has been adopted for this study; the prospective analysis can use the longitudinal approach for data collection. Moreover, only limited factors have been investigated regarding student acceptance of e-learning; future studies can consider more factors as well, such as technostress and digital infrastructure.

## References

1. Korucu, A.T., Alkan, A.: Differences between m-learning (mobile learning) and e-learning, basic terminology and usage of m-learning in education. Procedia Soc. Behav. Sci. **15**, 1925–1930 (2011)
2. Abbas, E.W, Rajiani, I.: Managing e-learning in public universities by investigating the role of culture. Pol. J. Manag. Stud. **20**, (2019)
3. Sandybayev, A.: The impact of e-learning technologies on student's motivation: Student centered interaction in business education. Int. J. Res. Tour. Hosp. (IJRTH) **6**(1), 16–24 (2020)
4. Lee, B.-C., Yoon, J.-O., Lee, I.: Learners' acceptance of f in South Korea: Theories and results. Comput. Educ. **53**(4), 1320–1329 (2009)
5. Ejdys, J., Kozłowska, J.: Acceptance of e-learning at university level during the covid-19 pandemic situation-teachers'and students'perspective. Pol. J. Manag. Stud. **23**(2), 106–129 (2021)
6. Nora, A., Snyder, B.P.: Technology and higher education: The impact of e-learning approaches on student academic achievement, perceptions and persistence. Journal of College Student Retention: Res., Theory & Pract. **10**(1), 3–19 (2008)
7. Smoląg, K., Ślusarczyk, B., Kot, S.: The role of social media in management of relational capital in universities. Prabandhan: Indian J. Manag. **9**(10), 34–41, (2016)
8. Rasmitadila, R., Aliyyah, R.R., Rachmadtullah, R., Samsudin, A., Syaodih, E., Nurtanto, M., Tambunan, A.R.S.: The perceptions of primary school teachers of online learning during the COVID-19 pandemic period. J. Ethn. Cult. Stud. **7**(2), 90–109 (2020)
9. Muangmee, C., Kot, S., Meekaewkunchorn, N., Kassakorn, N., Tiranawatananun, S., Khalid, B.: Students' Use Behavior towards E-Learning Tools during COVID-19 Pandemics: Case Study of Higher Educational Institutions of Thailand. Int. J. Eval. Res. Educ.**10**(4), 1166–1175 (2021)
10. Turnbull, D., Chugh, R., Luck, J.: Transitioning to E-Learning during the COVID-19 pandemic: How have Higher Education Institutions responded to the challenge? Educ. Inf. Technol. **26**(5), 6401–6419 (2021)
11. Jackson, K., Szombathelyi, M.K.: The influence of COVID-19 on sentiments of higher education students-prospects for the spread of distance learning. Econ. & Sociol. **15**(3), 216–247 (2022)
12. Harandi, S.R.: Effects of e-learning on Students' Motivation. Procedia Soc. Behav. Sci. **181**, 423–430 (2015)
13. Davidovitch, N., Eckhaus, E.: Economics of time: advantages of e-learning in proportion to the time utilized and the tradeoff between work and studies. Econ. & Sociol. **15**, 222–235 (2022)
14. Stelmokienė, A., Jarašiūnaitė-Fedosejeva, G., Kravčenko, K.: Relationship between gender equality, employees'perception of distributive justice and wellbeing in eu: the effect of gender and management position. Econ. & Sociol. **16**(1), 123–137 (2023)

15. Akaslan, D., Law, E.L.-C.: E-learning in the Science of Electricity in Higher Education in Turkey in terms of Environment and. Electr. Eng. **577**(56), 32312 (2010)
16. Drysdale, J.S., Graham, C.R., Spring, K.J., Halverson, L.R.: An analysis of research trends in dissertations and theses studying blended learning. Internet High. Educ. **17**, 90–100 (2013)
17. MacKeogh, K., Fox, S.: Strategies for Embedding e-Learning in Traditional Universities: Drivers and Barriers. Electron. J. E-Learn. **7**, 147–154 (2009)
18. Jong, E.d., Howard, E.: Integration in two-way immersion education: Equalising linguistic benefits for all students. Int. J. Biling. Educ. Biling. **12**, 81–99 (2009)
19. Starenko, M., Vignare, K., Humbert, J.: Enhancing student interaction and sustaining faculty instructional innovations through blended learning. Blending Learning: Research Perspectives, pp. 161–178. (2007)
20. Rasouli, A., Rahbania, Z., Attaran, M.: Students' Readiness for E-Learning Application in Higher Education. Malays. Online J. Educ. Technol. **4**, 51–64 (2016)
21. Mosadegh, H., Kharazi, K., Bazargan, A.: Conducting feasibility of e-learning in gas companies in Yazd province. J. Sci. Technol. Inf. **3**, 547–569 (2011)
22. George, P.P., Papachristou, N., Belisario, J.M., Wang, W., Wark, P.A., Cotic, Z., Rasmussen, K., Sluiter, R., Riboli–Sasco, E., Car, L.T.: Online eLearning for undergraduates in health professions: a systematic review of the impact on knowledge, skills, attitudes and satisfaction. J. Glob. Health **4**, (2014)
23. Straka, G.A., Stöckl, M.: New learning formats and venues in the context of information and communication technologies. Vocational education and training: The European research field. Backgr. Rep. **2**, 183–214, (1998)
24. Igbaria, M., Iivari, J., Maragahh, H.: Why do individuals use computer technology? A Finnish case study. Inf. and Manag.**29**, 227–238 (1995)
25. Mathieson, K., Peacock, E., Chin, W.W.: Extending the technology acceptance model: the influence of perceived user resources. ACM SIGMIS Database: DATABASE Adv. Inf. Syst. **32**, 86–112 (2001)
26. Shaw, S., Polovina, S.: Practical experiences of, and lessons learnt from, Internet technologies in higher education. J. Educ. Technol. Soc. **2**, 16–24 (1999)
27. Hasan, N., Khan, N.H.: Online teaching-learning during covid-19 pandemic: students' perspective. Online J. Distance Educ. E-Learn. **8**, 202–213 (2020)
28. Nambiar, D.: The impact of online learning during COVID-19: students' and teachers' perspective. Int. J. Indian Psychol. **8**, 783–793 (2020)
29. Suzuki, T., Geissel, H., Bochkarev, O., Chulkov, L., Golovkov, M., Fukunishi, N., Hirata, D., Irnich, H., Janas, Z., Keller, H.: Nuclear radii of Na and Mg isotopes. Nucl. Phys. A **630**, 661–677 (1998)
30. Sun, P.-C., Tsai, R.J., Finger, G., Chen, Y.-Y., Yeh, D.: What drives a successful e-Learning? An empirical investigation of the critical factors influencing learner satisfaction. Comput. Educ. **50**, 1183–1202 (2008)
31. Latip, M.S.A., Noh, I., Tamrin, M., Latip, S.: Students' acceptance for e-learning and the effects of self-efficacy in Malaysia. Int. J. Acad. Res. Bus. Soc. Sci. **10**, 658–674 (2020)
32. Bougie, R., Sekaran, U.: Research methods for business: A skill building approach. John Wiley, Sons. (2019)
33. Sigdel, B., Photchanachan, S., Uppapong, K., Bhattarai, A.: Revamp of Tourism Industry in Nepal: Women Entrepreneurial Orientation, Competitive Advantage, and Firm Performance. J. Women's Entrep. & Educ. (2023)
34. Arshad, M., Ahmad, M., Ali, M., Khan, W., Arshad, M.: The role of government business support services and absorptive capacity on SMES performance. Int. J. Adv. Sci. Technol. **29**, 1492–1499 (2020)
35. Arshad, M.Z., Arshad, D.: Intellectual capital and SMEs performance in Pakistan: The role of environmental turbulence. Int. J. Entrep. **22**, (2018)
36. Naseem, S., Guang Ji, T., Kashif, U., Arshad, M.Z.: Causal analysis of the dynamic link between energy growth and environmental quality for agriculture sector: a piece of evidence from India. Environ. Dev. Sustain. **23**, 7913–7930 (2021)

37. Fornell, C., Larcker, D.F.: Evaluating structural equation models with unobservable variables and measurement error. J. Mark. Res. **18**, 39–50 (1981)
38. Gaskin, J., James, M.: HTMT plugin for AMOS. IBM SPSS AMOS Version, (2019).
39. Henseler, J., Ringle, C.M., Sarstedt, M.: A new criterion for assessing discriminant validity in variance-based structural equation modeling. J. Acad. Mark. Sci. **43**, 115–135 (2015)

# Creative and Innovative Enterprises

# The Importance of Social Networks for E-commerce: An Analysis of Young Users' Perspectives in the European Union

**Richard Fedorko, Radovan Bačík, Martin Rigelský, Jakub Horváth, and Štefan Kráľ**

**Abstract** Social networks are currently one of the most important means of disseminating information, as almost every Internet user has a social media account. Some users use social media not only for communication but also for purchasing goods and services. The primary goal of the study is to assess the use of social networks by younger users in individual countries of the European Union, focusing on gender characteristics and age. Secondly, the study points out the importance of social networks for e-commerce. The analyses hereunder used secondary data from the Eurostat database for all countries of the European Union for the period between 2013 and 2021. The study focused on internet use and the use of social networks (creating user profiles, sending messages, and posting posts on Facebook, Twitter, etc.). These variables indicate the proportion (in percentage) of the population participating in social networks in the last three months. The analysis of differences was carried out using non-parametric tests—Wilcoxon W test and Kruskal–Wallis H test. K-medoid clustering using the Manhattan distance was also employed. The results indicated differences between individual countries in the intensity of participation on social networks, with France showing the most significant deviation (lowest participation). It was also found that participation is higher among women than among men, and younger generations of users offer higher participation rates than older ones. The obtained results can be useful for better understanding the behavior of different genders and age groups on social networks. Businesses can use these findings to create targeted social media campaigns for specific age or gender groups.

**Keywords** E-commerce · Social networks · Young users · European union

R. Fedorko (✉) · R. Bačík · M. Rigelský · J. Horváth · Š. Kráľ
Faculty of Management and Business, University of Prešov, Prešov, Slovakia
e-mail: richard.fedorko@unipo.sk

 
S. Kot et al. (eds.), *Corporate Practices: Policies, Methodologies, and Insights in Organizational Management*, Springer Proceedings in Business and Economics,
https://doi.org/10.1007/978-981-97-0996-0_17

## 1 Introduction

Social networks are an indispensable tool for e-commerce companies, enabling them to leverage the power of online communities and reach an expansive audience. Text mining, for instance, can generate insights about customers and potential ones. Social media, such as Twitter, also provides e-commerce companies with real-time information about their customers [1]. For example, keywords such as "Baidu," "Tencent," "headlines," "Sina.com," mode," "e-commerce," "retail," and "platform" were closely related to the Chinese tweets. Similarly, keywords such as "China," "Alibaba," "Baidu," "DianPing," "Meituan," "Asia," "e-commerce," and "service" were the most strongly associated English terms with O2O [2]. Social media is also used to coordinate customer service and delivery activities. Additionally, social networks can be used to share information about prices, product quality, customer service, and e-sellers reputation [3]. Research has also shown that social media has a positive influence on consumer behavior and brand equity in e-commerce [4].

Furthermore, social media influencers are increasingly conveying their opinion regarding products and brands through social media postings. Social networks have become a necessity for all online users [5]. Most young internet users use social media to communicate and to shop. Many consumers use Facebook, Twitter, Instagram, and other social apps to research products and find the best deals. Online shopping has become easier with the help of social media since users can easily share their opinions on products with their friends. Social networks have changed how we consume goods and services [6]. Most young users use social media to find the best deals. Many retailers have Facebook pages where they post sales and coupons—these can be found easily by searching for them online. It's much easier to find information this way than through traditional searching methods [7]. Users can also follow specific brands on Twitter or Instagram to see when new sales are starting or ending. Social networking makes it easier to find great bargains without spending hours looking for them. Plus, it's great for businesses looking to advertise their products and gain more customers [8]. Social networks are also helpful in keeping up with new product releases. Many online shops post updates on their websites about new products coming out. However, not many people visit product pages unless they want something new. Instead, they rely on social media to tell them about new releases as they happen. This is especially useful for smaller businesses that cannot post product announcements on their websites. Social networks make it easy to stay informed about new products without directly asking anyone for information [9].

## 2 Literature Review

In In the modern world, social networks offer a multitude of advantages to both buyers and sellers. For buyers, these networks are invaluable for gathering information about products and services. They can use these networks to ask questions about products and services, as well as research them and make requests for quotes [10]. Social networks also allow buyers to communicate with sellers and make offers and requests for information. Once a purchase is made, buyers can use the networks to provide feedback and post reviews without contacting the company directly [11]. For sellers, social networks offer a platform for communicating with buyers and influencing the various stages of the buying process. Through careful planning and technology applications, sellers can increase customer satisfaction and profitability [12]. E-commerce is becoming more significant in the lives of young internet users compared to five years ago; there is a growing trend of young consumers who shop via social media platforms such as Instagram, Pinterest, Facebook, and Snapchat, as well as via messaging apps like WhatsApp and WeChat. Marketers need to understand how social media affects e-commerce, as this will help them create strategies for their business based on how consumers are using these platforms nowadays. E-commerce allows companies and consumers to sell and buy products online. Unlike marketing to residents near a physical store, the potential customer base is much larger and could be located anywhere there is internet. Electronic commerce, also known as electronic commerce, enables businesses and consumers to make online purchases. Many companies and consumers find e-commerce more efficient than brick-and-mortar stores. Businesses save costs, and customers can choose and shop from a wide range of products anywhere in the world at any time of the day [13]. On average, online stores with social media generated 32% more sales than those without an online presence. Being available and active on social media platforms can do wonders for your business.

Additionally, social media engagement has increased by 61% during the COVID-19 pandemic. Therefore, brands that are active on social platforms during this period will see a significant boost in customer acquisition and engagement [14]. Social networks have become increasingly important for online shopping and e-commerce due to their ability to facilitate direct purchases through mobile apps. This is especially true for platforms such as Facebook, Pinterest, and Instagram, which offer natural purchase abilities to their users and the involved enterprises. Additionally, almost seven of the ten individuals who use social media search for a product through them and use a mobile device, according to the Statista portal [15]. This is unsurprising given that most internet users prefer to surf via their smartphone rather than a desktop PC and that the number of online purchases through mobile devices has significantly increased [16]. Social networks are essential for online shopping since they provide secure mechanisms for protecting direct assets through them. Launching means is vital for social media networks as it should guarantee the security of individuals' information and transactions. In addition, the greater the users' security perceptions are, the higher their intention to adopt this type of Mobile Social Commerce (MSC).

Furthermore, social networks are essential for online shopping because they allow users to purchase items directly through social media apps without having to go to a brick-and-mortar store first, and they offer users the opportunity to shop now from them via their mobile apps. Social networks facilitate shopping via direct mobile payments via convenience, reward, and security. Finally, online shopping relies on social networks to provide customer support and to deliver timely updates about inventory and shipping [17]. Social networks make it much easier to shop online. Users can keep up with product releases easily, thanks to social media posts. Plus, Facebook and Twitter make it simple to find great deals on anything you need. Businesses should take note of these trends when creating strategies for their online stores [18]. Social networks, together with other digital technologies, affect the quality of life of individuals and entire organizations in the modern world. Therefore, their constant monitoring and evaluation are important in the development of our society [19].

The study is important as young social media users, or social networks, are currently the group with the greatest purchasing potential in the e-commerce market. For this reason, it is important to investigate and find out the specifics of their purchasing decisions and consumer behavior. Understanding the commonalities of their purchasing behavior will allow retailers to spend more effectively on their marketing strategy while increasing their potential profits. There needs to be more studies in the area of research tackled hereunder. Those that have been written on the topic attack individual countries separately. The study included data for the EU countries in the ISO 3 code, which still needs investigation. The goal of the survey hereunder is to assess the use of social networks by younger users in individual countries of the European Union, focusing on gender characteristics and age.

## 3 Methodology

The purpose of the presented study is to assess the use of social networks by younger users in individual countries of the European Union, focusing on gender characteristics and age. Based on the established objective, the following research questions and research hypotheses were formulated:

RQ1: Are there statistically significant differences in the use of social networks by young Internet users in terms of age?

RQ2: Are there statistically significant differences in the use of social networks by young Internet users in terms of gender?

RH1: We assume that there are statistically significant differences in the use of social networks by young Internet users in terms of age.

RH2: We assume that there are statistically significant differences in the use of social networks by young Internet users in terms of gender.

All EU countries with ISO 3 code were included in the study ($n = 27$: Austria (AUS), Belgium (BEL), Bulgaria (BGR), Croatia (HVR), Cyprus (CYP), Czechia (CZE), Denmark (DNK), Estonia (EST), Finland (FIN), France (FRA), Germany (DEU), Greece (GRC), Hungary (HUN), Ireland (IRL), Italy (ITA), Latvia (LVA), Lithuania (LTU), Luxembourg (LUX), Malta (MLT), Netherlands (NDL), Poland (POL), Portugal (POR), Romania (ROU), Slovakia (SVK), Slovenia (SVN), Spain (ESP), Sweden (SWE)). Data used hereunder (from 2013 to 2021) was obtained from the database of the Statistical Office of the European Union, commonly known as EUROSTAT [20].

The analysis focused on the variable Internet users participating in social networks (creating user profiles, texting, and posting posts on Facebook, Twitter, etc.). This variable represents the percentage of individuals who used the Internet in the last three months. The analytical processes used hereunder consisted predominantly of descriptive analysis and visualization techniques. The analysis of differences was carried out using non-parametric tests—Wilcoxon W test and Kruskal–Wallis H test. K-medoid clustering (PAM) using the Manhattan distance was also employed. The number of clusters was estimated using the silhouette method. The analytical processes were carried out in the R software environment—version 4.2.1 [21] and SPSS (version 26).

## 4 Results

The following section presents and briefly describes the findings arrived at hereunder. The analysis focuses on the description of the findings using the characteristics of descriptive statistics, visualization techniques. The output of the cluster analysis is shown in the conclusion.

Table 1 shows the outputs of the descriptive analysis, where the commonly used statistical characteristics of central tendency, variability and location were used. The first rows show a frequency analysis that points to certain missing data. Focusing on the characteristics of the central tendency, data show that men in all three age categories show slightly lower values of participation in social networks than women. From the given results, the conclusion can be made that the younger generations show a slightly higher social media participation rate than the older generations. Based on the variability results, it can be concluded that women show more homogeneous outputs compared to men. Skewness and kurtosis show slight deviations from a normal statistical distribution. The results show that the rate of use of social networks is relatively high among young Internet users. This may reflect, on the one hand, their higher level of digital skills compared to older generations, but on the other hand, the fact that young users spend time using digital technologies and the Internet.

When analyzing the data set, it is wise to look at the countries themselves. Table 2 shows the average values of participation in social networks by country. The more intense the coloring, the higher the percentage of the population of the given category participating in social networks. At first glance, it is evident that France needs to catch up to the European trend in participation. One of the reasons may be, for example, the Cambridge Analytica affair from 2018, which revealed that the well-known social network Facebook failed to protect the personal data of its users. It was the French who expressed their most significant concern, with 30% of social media users saying they would delete their account and a further 6% doing so immediately [8].

Figure 1 shows the average overall development of indicators for individual years. Data do not show a clear-cut upward trend, as a decline can be perceived in the vast

**Table 1** Descriptive analysis—Internet users participating in social networks

| Variable | Males 16–19 years | Females 16–19 years | Males 20–24 years | Females 20–24 years | Males 25–29 years | Females 25–29 years |
|---|---|---|---|---|---|---|
| Valid | 238 | 238 | 240 | 240 | 240 | 240 |
| Missing | 5 | 5 | 3 | 3 | 3 | 3 |
| Mean | 91.37 | 93.51 | 89.73 | 92.64 | 85.46 | 89.31 |
| Median | 92.37 | 94.58 | 90.73 | 93.56 | 87.03 | 90.45 |
| Std. Deviation | 6.21 | 4.79 | 5.95 | 4.99 | 7.54 | 6.69 |
| Skewness | − 1.15 | − 0.95 | − 1.08 | − 1.11 | − 0.92 | − 0.90 |
| Kurtosis | 1.48 | 0.86 | 1.87 | 1.37 | 1.06 | 0.75 |
| Minimum | 67.79 | 74.51 | 64.42 | 74.29 | 58.96 | 63.36 |
| Maximum | 100 | 100 | 100 | 100 | 99.12 | 100 |
| Percentiles 25 | 88.23 | 90.72 | 86.67 | 89.93 | 81.16 | 85.92 |
| Percentiles 75 | 95.61 | 97.19 | 94.09 | 96.33 | 90.32 | 94.47 |

majority of indicators in 2021. This phenomenon can be explained, on the one hand, by the gradual easing of the COVID-19 pandemic restrictions, when some users began to prioritize more real-life activities and experiences and tried to cut down on the time spent on social networks. Another reason may be information about personal data leaks and concerns about harassment, especially in the case of young users.

Table 3 shows a non-parametric test of differences between individual years. Differences were not confirmed only in the first two cases.

The analysis of differences using non-parametric tests was also carried out taking into account data for men and women and also for individual age groups. The Wilcoxon *W* test confirmed there is a significant difference between men and women ($W$ statistic = 407,001; $p$ value < 0.001) and the Kruskal–Wallis H test confirmed the differences among age groups ($H$ statistic = 149.82; $p$ value < 0.001).

The visualizations in Fig. 2 show that more women than men showed higher participation in social networks. With regard to age, higher values were measured in younger age groups. This can also be explained by the fact that women are generally more sociable than men. They primarily use social networks to maintain contacts, share information or opinions with others, and also shop in various groups or on the marketplace of the given social network. Men tend to use social networks more for obtaining information or contacts [22]. Higher values for younger age groups may indicate a significant impact of digitization and technology on younger users, who consider social networks a part of their identity and an integral part of their daily life, as they were born in this digital era. The following visualizations (Fig. 3–5) show the number for men and women across individual EU countries.

The cluster analysis was carried out as the last. The purpose of this analysis was to assess the individual outputs per countries and to group these countries based

**Table 2** Average values per individual countries—Internet users participating in social networks

| ID | Males 16–19 years | Females 16–19 years | Males 20–24 years | Females 20–24 years | Males 25–29 years | Females 25–29 years |
|---|---|---|---|---|---|---|
| AUS | 92.52 | 94.57 | 86.51 | 91.21 | 79.03 | 86.80 |
| BEL | 94.38 | 93.42 | 92.08 | 95.00 | 88.48 | 92.01 |
| BGR | 90.00 | 91.81 | 91.10 | 92.03 | 87.99 | 89.37 |
| CYP | 95.40 | 95.41 | 94.42 | 95.06 | 92.27 | 90.88 |
| CZE | 94.28 | 95.33 | 94.04 | 93.77 | 86.40 | 89.90 |
| DEU | 87.25 | 90.65 | 86.57 | 90.05 | 80.47 | 84.79 |
| DNK | 96.42 | 98.37 | 92.75 | 96.46 | 91.86 | 94.56 |
| ESP | 91.38 | 92.94 | 89.86 | 93.05 | 85.90 | 88.00 |
| EST | 94.05 | 96.85 | 90.95 | 95.31 | 87.00 | 93.27 |
| FIN | 88.75 | 96.50 | 86.78 | 94.41 | 85.61 | 93.62 |
| FRA | 74.04 | 82.45 | 74.13 | 79.99 | 65.43 | 72.08 |
| GRC | 93.34 | 91.63 | 91.24 | 91.76 | 86.69 | 88.17 |
| HUN | 97.08 | 96.22 | 96.29 | 96.95 | 94.09 | 95.47 |
| HVR | 94.13 | 95.25 | 93.93 | 93.31 | 87.60 | 92.44 |
| IRL | 91.13 | 92.87 | 90.76 | 92.37 | 85.21 | 88.30 |
| ITA | 82.24 | 86.52 | 82.21 | 85.92 | 77.77 | 79.96 |
| LTU | 91.75 | 95.74 | 91.17 | 95.15 | 87.77 | 91.71 |
| LUX | 87.81 | 89.86 | 87.72 | 91.08 | 82.80 | 87.86 |
| LVA | 93.74 | 95.90 | 91.85 | 95.11 | 88.57 | 94.74 |
| MLT | 96.89 | 96.61 | 91.28 | 95.93 | 92.10 | 93.06 |
| NDL | 90.49 | 95.15 | 89.88 | 95.26 | 83.05 | 90.90 |
| POL | 90.85 | 92.38 | 87.83 | 90.23 | 79.68 | 85.68 |
| POR | 94.58 | 96.27 | 91.98 | 95.08 | 89.90 | 90.96 |
| ROU | 88.51 | 90.00 | 89.50 | 88.34 | 86.14 | 87.14 |
| SVK | 92.98 | 92.72 | 92.18 | 93.47 | 87.87 | 90.22 |
| SVN | 91.89 | 94.63 | 84.67 | 91.82 | 78.88 | 84.27 |
| SWE | 90.01 | 94.11 | 89.63 | 91.67 | 86.69 | 93.02 |

on the similarity of the outputs. Average values (average for individual years) of selected indicators were included in this analysis. The indicated clusters represent countries that recorded average values of selected indicators at a similar level. It is clear that France differs the most from among the countries in question. This could be explained by the lower frequency of use of social networks (as mentioned above) due to the concern regarding the protection of personal data (Fig. 6).

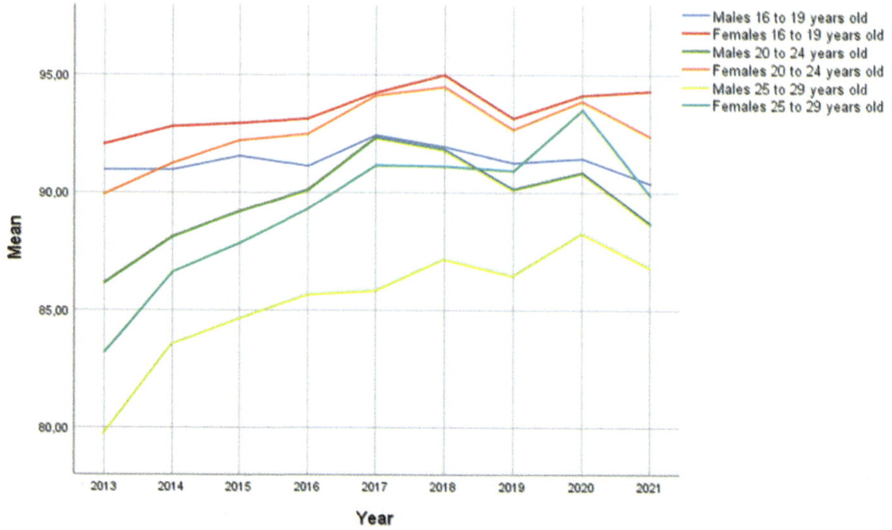


**Fig. 1** Average development—Internet users participating in social networks

**Table 3** Differences between individual years - Internet users participating in social networks

| Statistic | Males 16–19 years | Females 16–9 years | Males 20–24 years | Females 20–24 years | Males 25–29 years | Females 25–29 years |
|---|---|---|---|---|---|---|
| Kruskal–Wallis H | 3.1139 | 9.1660 | 27.9785 | 23.1660 | 29.3622 | 54.5454 |
| df | 8 | 8 | 8 | 8 | 8 | 8 |
| Asymp. Sig | 0.9270 | 0.3284 | < 0.001 | < 0.001 | < 0.001 | < 0.001 |

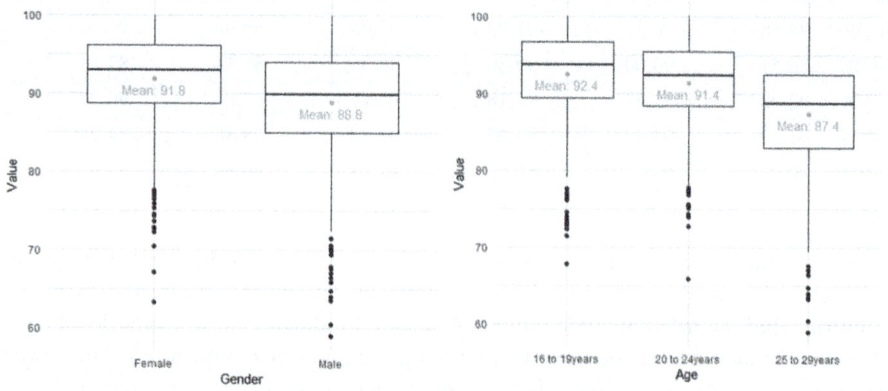


**Fig. 2** Internet user participating in social networks by gender and age

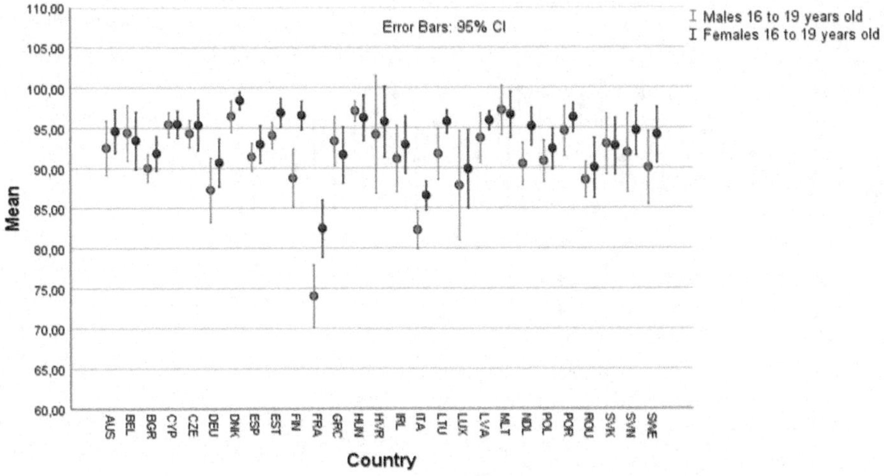


**Fig. 3** Average—Internet user participating in social networks (Males 16 to 19 years old and Females 16 to 19 years old)

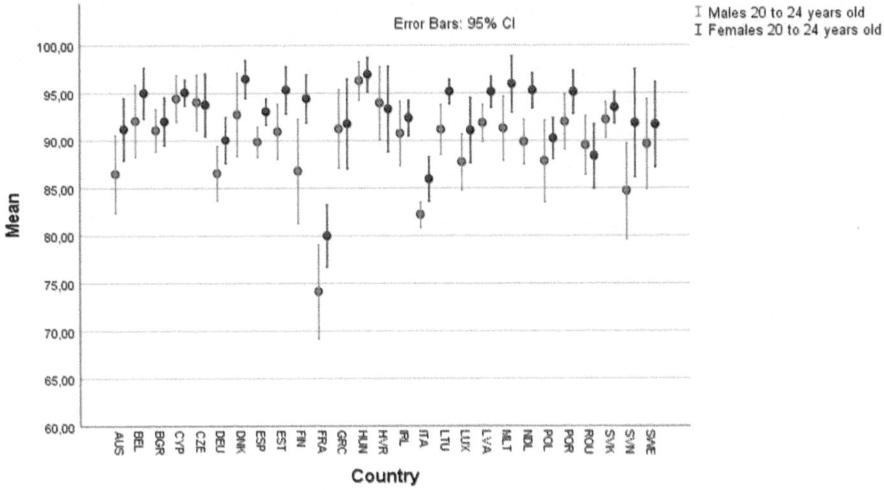


**Fig. 4** Average—Internet user participating in social networks (Males 20 to 24 years old and Females 20 to 24 years old)

## 5 Discussion

The results of the study showed that the rate of use of social networks is relatively high among young Internet users. This is not surprising, as the younger generations of Internet users usually have better digital skills and spend more time using the Internet and social networks than other age groups. This was also confirmed in the research

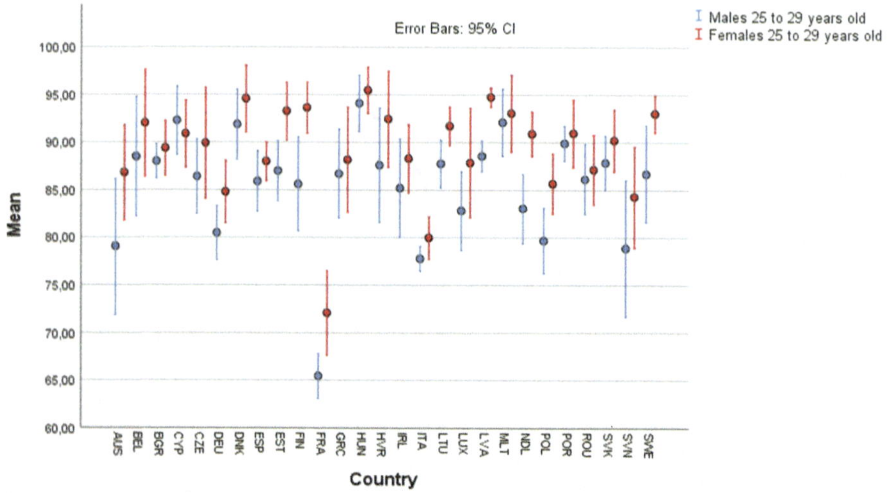


**Fig. 5** Average—Internet users participating in social networks (Males 25 to 29 years old and Females 25 to 29 years old)

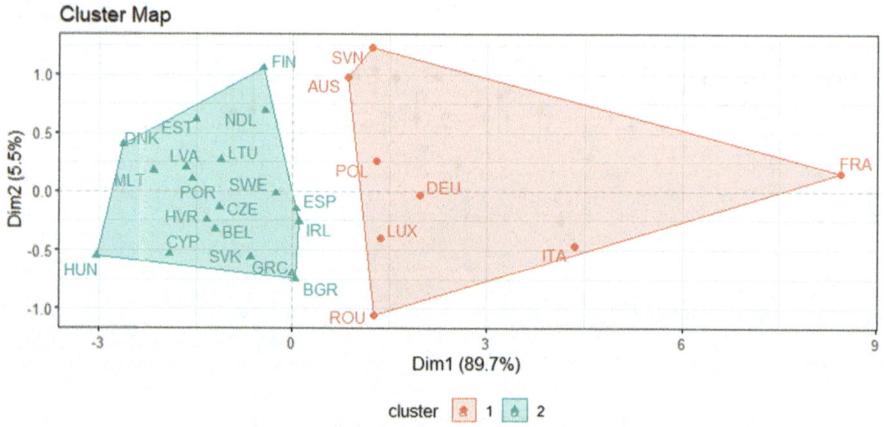


**Fig. 6** Cluster analysis—Internet users participating in social networks

of Alalwan et al. [23], Zhang et al. [24], Sokolova and Kefi [25], and Yoon et al. [26], who states that Generation Z and Millennials use social networks most often, especially for maintaining relationships, sharing and searching for information, and shopping.

The results of our study also showed that from the gender point of view, participation in social networks is slightly higher for women than for men. This may, to some extent, be related to gender differences from a psychological point of view, where women are believed to be more sociable than men, whether it is sharing opinions or maintaining contacts. Similar findings are reported by Roberts et al. [27] and

Dumford et al. [28], who found that women spend, on average, more time than men on social networks and participate more often in various activities such as sharing information and posts. Nadelson et al. [29] even state that women not only use social networks more than men but that they also influence them to a greater extent, for example, when it comes to purchasing decisions [30].

The obtained results further demonstrated that, in terms of age, younger users participate in social networks more than older age groups. Younger Internet users go through various psychological and behavioral changes and usually feel the need to belong. Socializing is a natural process for them, and in today's digital era, which most of them were born into, they find satisfaction in joining online communities on social networks. These young people participate more in social networks, engage in various discussions, present their opinions, maintain relationships, search for information, or purchase online. Thus, the development of digital technologies and the Internet can have a considerable impact on younger Internet users who consider social networks as part of their identity [31–33].

The results also indicated some differences between countries in the participation rate on social networks, with France showing the largest variation, as it recorded the lowest participation among the countries surveyed. This could be explained by the problems social networks reported about personal data protection and security. At the same time, Statista [15] pointed to the fact that many French people have left social networks and limited their use for this very reason. A study by Alkis and Kose [34] also points to similar results, as they found that several French Internet users have reduced their use of social networks precisely because of the perceived security risk and concerns about the misuse of personal data.

As surprising as it may be, data showed that in 2021, there was a year-on-year decrease in the use of social networks by young Internet users, both among men and women, in almost all groups. In 2020, the world faced the COVID-19 pandemic, which meant social contact was limited, thus resulting in a sharp increase in social networks, whether for communicating with loved ones, entertainment, or shopping. This was also confirmed in the studies conducted by Cato et al. [35], Tuck and Thompson [36] and Mohammed and Ferraris [37]. The decline in 2021 could have been caused by the relaxation of measures and behavioral changes of consumers who seem tired of social networks and opt for more physical activities and experiences, thus resulting in limiting the use of social networks [38]. This was confirmed by Lin et al. [39] in their research, as they pointed to the reduced use of social networks due to information overload. Another reason may be the fear of personal data leaks, as confirmed by Sarfraz et al. [40]. Their study showed that it is the security risk and the fear of losing privacy that has a significant impact on young Internet users deactivating and deleting their accounts on social networks.

## 6 Theoretical and Managerial Implications

The research results contribute to the enrichment of theoretical knowledge about the importance of using social networks in electronic commerce. Thus, one of the benefits is the expansion of the theoretical construct of consumer behavior in the conditions of the online environment of the Internet, with a focus on the use of social networks. The theoretical basis of the issue is enriched by adding relevant empirical evidence related to the understanding of consumer purchasing behavior in the Internet environment through the examination of the use of social networks by young consumers and the analysis of differences based on socio-demographic characteristics, namely gender and age.

Social networks are no longer primarily used for communication but are expanding to include social commerce. Social networks are currently shaping users' shopping preferences and creating a need to participate in activities shared by their online community. This is an excellent opportunity for online sellers from the point of view of managerial implications. Many companies use social networks for professional and business purposes, whether to promote the brand, increase visibility, present the company's product portfolio, or build and maintain customer relationships. This study provides useful information on the demographic indicators of young social network users. The obtained results can help us understand the behavior of different genders and age groups on social networks. Marketers can use these findings to create social media campaigns targeting specific age and gender groups.

## 7 Conclusion

Nowadays, social networks play an important role not only in expanding and maintaining social ties but also in mainly influencing the purchasing decisions of users. The study aimed to assess the use of social networks among young users in individual countries of the European Union, focusing on gender and age, based on secondary data from the Eurostat database from 2013 and 2021. From our point of view, the given goal was met. This study expands the existing knowledge in several ways. On the one hand, the paper helps build the theoretical basis of the issue of the use of social networks and points out the importance of the use of social networks in connection with e-commerce; on the other hand, the paper presents original findings that can be applied on a practical level.

Several marketers use social media for professional and business purposes. The obtained results can, therefore, help them better understand the behavior of different genders and age groups on social networks, which sellers can then use to create targeted campaigns aimed at specific groups of users in terms of age or gender. The major limitation of the study is missing data for some years or countries. Future research could obtain data on the use of social networks by older users, which could then be compared with the younger generation of Internet users, either from a gender or age point of view. It might be interesting to study the associations between social media use and other variables, such as the level of digital literacy. As part of further research, the differences in the given indicators between the countries of the European Union and other countries of the world could be examined.

**Acknowledgement** This paper is a partial output of the VEGA grant 1/0694/20 "Relational marketing research—perception of e-commerce aspects and its impact on purchasing behaviour and consumer preferences" and VEGA grant 1/0506/24 "Research on aspects of the e-commerce process in the dimension of buying behavior and consumer preferences with an emphasis on the principles of circular economy".

## References

1. Shen, Ch., Chen, M., Wang, Ch.: Analyzing the trend of O2O commerce by bilingual text mining on social media. Comput. Hum. Behav. **101**, 474–483. (2019)
2. Tseng, et al.: Managing enterprise social media to develop consumer trust. Br. Food J. **124**(12), 4626–4643 (2022)
3. Curzi, V., Lecoq, W., Quéré, N.: The impact of social media on E-commerce decision making process. Int. J. Technol. Bus. **1**(1), 1–9 (2019)
4. Yadav, M., Rahman, Z.: Measuring consumer perception of social media marketing activities in e-commerce industry: Scale development & validation. Telemat. Inf. **34**(7), 1294–1307 (2017)
5. Svatosova, V.: The importance of online shopping behavior in the strategic management of e-commerce competitiveness. J. Compet. **12**(4), 143–160 (2020)
6. Arora, A., et al.: Measuring social media influencer index- insights from Facebook, Twitter and Instagram. J. Retail. Consum. Serv. **49**, 86–101 (2019)
7. Chornous, G., Nikolskyi, I., Wyszyński, M., Kharlamova, G., Stolarczyk, P.: A hybrid user-item-based collaborative filtering model for e-commerce recommendations. J. Int. Stud. **14**(4), 157–173 (2021)
8. Dixon, S.: Cambridge Analytica: share of French people wishing to unsubscribe from Facebook (2018). https://www.statista.com/statistics/1094463/cambrigde-analytica-willingness-to-unsubscribe-from-facebook-france/. Accessed 21 Jun 2023
9. Ch., Hang-sub.: The young generation and their social media. Sociétés **129**(3), 105–113 (2015)
10. Štefko, R., Nastišin, Ľ, Nebeský, Ľ, Fedorko, R.: Consumers' online brand-related activities on facebook as a competitive E-Commerce channel. J. Compet. **15**(1), 91–112 (2023)
11. Diba, H., Vella, J.M., Abratt, R.: Social media influence on the B2B buying process. J. Bus. & Ind. Mark. **34**(7), 1482–1496 (2019)
12. Ramanathan, U., Subramanian, N., Parrott, G.: Role of social media in retail network operations and marketing to enhance customer satisfaction. Int. J. Oper.& Prod. Manag. **37**(1), (2017)
13. Itani, O.S., et al.: Social media and customer relationship management technologies: Influencing buyer-seller information exchanges. Ind. Mark. Manage. **90**, 264–275 (2020)
14. Ali Taha, V. et al.: The use of social media and its impact on shopping behavior of Slovak and Italian consumers during COVID-19 pandemic. Sustain. **13**(4), 1710. (2021)
15. Statista.: Social Media Usage - France. Statistics & Facts. https://www.statista.com/topics/6278/social-media-usage-in-france/#topicOverview. Accessed 21 Jun 2023
16. Saprikis, V., Avlogiaris, G.: Factors that determine the adoption intention of direct mobile purchases through social media apps. Sustain.**12**(11), 449 (2021)
17. WebFX.: Social Media for Ecommerce: A Quick Guide. https://www.webfx.com/industries/retail-ecommerce/ecommerce/social-media/. Accessed 21 Jun 2023
18. Zanzalari, D.: Advantages of E-Commerce. https://www.thebalancemoney.com/advantages-of-ecommerce-1141610. Accessed 21 Jun 2023

19. Hajduová, Z., Smoląg, K., Szajt, M., Bednárová, L.: Digital competences of polish and slovak students—comparative analysis in the light of empirical research. Sustain. **12**(18), 7739 (2020)
20. Eurostat.: (2023) Individuals - internet activities https://ec.europa.eu/eurostat/databrowser/view/ISOC_CI_AC_I__custom_4737108/default/table?lang=en. Accessed 21 Jun 2023
21. R Core Team. R.: A language and environment for statistical computing. R Foundation for Statistical Computing, Vienna, Austria. URL https://www.R-project.org/. Accessed 21 Jun 2023
22. Razoredge.: Men vs. Women. Social Media Usage. https://www.razoredge-media.co.uk/men-vs-women-social-media-usage/. Accessed 21 Jun 2023
23. Alalwan, A.A., Rana, N.P., Dwivedi, Y.K., Algharabat, R.: Social media in marketing: A review and analysis of the existing literature. Telemat. Inf. **34**(7), 1177–1190 (2017)
24. Zhang, Y., Trusov, M., Stephen, A.T., Jamal, Z.: Online shopping and social media: Friends or foes? J. Mark. **81**(6), 24–41 (2017)
25. Sokolova, K., Kefi, H.: Instagram and YouTube bloggers promote it, why should I buy? How credibility and parasocial interaction influence purchase intentions. J. Retail. Consum. Serv. **53**, (2020)
26. Yoon, J.Y., Lee, C., Choi, J., Chang, S.R., Kim, J.: The effect of social media apps on shopping apps. J. Bus. Res. **148**, 23–32 (2022)
27. Roberts, J.A., Yaya, L.H., Manolis, C.: The invisible addiction: Cell-phone activities and addiction among male and female college students. J. Behav. Addict. **3**(4), 254–265 (2014)
28. Dumford, A.D., Miller, A.L., Lee, C.K., Caskie, A.: Social media usage in relation to their peers: Comparing male and female college students' perceptions. Comput. Educ. Open **4**, 100121 (2023)
29. Nadelson, L.S., Berg, W., Fox, B., Grandbouche, P., Harris, M., Kroschel, T.L., Sandoval, S.: Snap, tweet and post: college student social media perceptions and heutagogic practices and uses. Int. J. Higher Educ. **6**(4), 11–27 (2017)
30. Roudposhti, V.M., Nilashi, M., Mardani, A., Streimikiene, D., Samad, S., Ibrahim, O.: A new model for customer purchase intention in e-commerce recommendation agents. J. Int. Stud. **11**(4), 237–253 (2018)
31. Wiederhold, B.K.: Social media use during social distancing. Cyberpsychol., Behav. Soc. Netw. **23**(5), 275–276. (2020)
32. Szymkowiak, A., Melović, B., Dabić, M., Jeganathan, K., Kundi, G.S.: Information technology and Gen Z: The role of teachers, the internet, and technology in the education of young people. Technol. Soc. **65**, 101565 (2021)
33. Jeljeli, R., Farhi, F., Hamdi, M.E.: The mediating role of gender in social media shopping acceptance: From the WOM perspective. Heliyon **8**(10), e11065 (2022)
34. Alkis, A., Kose, T.: Privacy concerns in consumer E-commerce activities and response to social media advertising: Empirical evidence from Europe. Comput. Hum. Behav. **137**, 107412 (2022)
35. Cato, S., Iida, T., Ishida, K., Ito, A., Katsumata, H., McElwain, K.M., Shoji, M.: The bright and dark sides of social media usage during the COVID-19 pandemic: Survey evidence from Japan. Int. J. Disaster Risk Reduct. **54**, 102034 (2021)
36. Tuck, A.B., Thompson, R.J.: Social networking site use during the COVID-19 pandemic and its associations with social and emotional well-being in college students: Survey study. JMIR Format. Res. **5**(9), e26513 (2021)
37. Mohammed, A., Ferraris, A.: Factors influencing user participation in social media: Evidence from twitter usage during COVID-19 pandemic in Saudi Arabia. Technol. Soc. **66**, 101651 (2021)
38. Draskovic, M., Milica, D., Mladen, I., Chigisheva, O.: Preference of institutional changes in social and economic development. J. Int. Stud. **10**(2), 318–328 (2017)
39. Lin, S., Lin, J., Luo, X.R., Liu, S.: Juxtaposed effect of social media overload on discontinuous usage intention: The perspective of stress coping strategies. Inf. Process. Manage. **58**(1), 102419 (2021)
40. Sarfraz, M., Khawaja, K. F., Ivascu, L., Khalil, M. An empirical study on cyber ostracism and students' discontinuous usage intention of social networking sites during the COVID-19 pandemic: A mediated and moderated model. Stud. Educ. Eval. **76**, 101235. (2023)

# Towards an Integrated Model of Value Co-creation for Enterprises

**Thi Bich Hanh Tran**

**Abstract** This study aims to offer a framework of value co-creation for enterprises. Concerning methodology, the study starts with a rigorous review of the types of co-created values from prior research, which proposes a set of differential core values for customers, firms, and society. Then, the study discusses the relevance of six groups of participants or actors involved in value co-creation processes for enterprises. The study also elaborates on two novel mechanisms, including innovation capability and marketing capability, for the actors to co-create resultant values for enterprises. The study proposes a comprehensive model with the actors, the mechanisms, and the accrued values. It concludes with discussions on implications for the Asia Pacific region as it is a strongly developing business context with various activities of value co-creation by enterprises. With the novel framework proposed and new mechanisms discussed, the study provides a meaningful extension to the value co-creation literature. It also allows enterprises to have a holistic view of the value co-creation phenomenon to manage value co-creation processes effectively.

**Keywords** Value co-creation · Value co-creation actors · Mechanisms · Integrated Model Asia Pacific region

## 1 Introduction

With the development of the economy and the intense competition, enterprises are forced to strive hard for continuous changes [6]. To successfully compete in the fiercely competitive markets, firms relentlessly look for effective practices and strategies. Conventionally, focus on internal factors has been well-accentuated as crucial elements for developing enterprises. Recently, value co-creation—an integration of contributions of various stakeholders, including external ones like customers, has

T. B. H. Tran (✉)
Department of Business, Swinburne Vietnam, FPT University, Hanoi, Vietnam
e-mail: hanhttb2@fe.edu.vn



S. Kot et al. (eds.), *Corporate Practices: Policies, Methodologies, and Insights in Organizational Management*, Springer Proceedings in Business and Economics,
https://doi.org/10.1007/978-981-97-0996-0_18

been identified as essential for developing enterprises' businesses [26]. By this recognition, researchers have garnered an increasing interest in learning about dynamics of value co-creation [3, 33, 71]. Herein, value co-creation is defined as creating perceived use value for the enterprise through relationships and interactions among the ecosystem of all actors [26, 34].

Though a growing number of studies of value co-creation have been added, studies of value co-creation have been chiefly dispersed. Research of value co-creation has been commonly from three separate perspectives, including service science, innovation and product development, and marketing and consumer research [17]. While recognizing the contributions of various participants in value co-creation, most studies have merely attended to customers' and suppliers' involvement [2, 39, 54]. Accordingly, most of the proposed frameworks specify value co-creation processes with the company and customers (including business customers and final customers) or suppliers and focal companies. These frameworks help offer valuable insights into specific aspects of business operation, for example, the interaction between customers and enterprises.

Nevertheless, value co-creation of enterprises involves more actors apart from the company (i.e., employees), suppliers, and customers that have been generally studied by existing research [16]. Shashi et al. [47] reckoned that both internal integration and external integration are conducive to the addition of values to the enterprise, which is relevant to business performance. This observation reflects the involvement of all relevant participants in the value co-creation of enterprises. However, the study did not specify the groups of external and internal stakeholders for involvement. According to Kotler and Armstrong [29], for business operations, enterprises involve six groups of stakeholders, including the company per se, customers, suppliers, competitors, intermediaries, and the public. Each group makes specific significant contributions to creating value for enterprises.

Regrettably, no framework, to date, has been identified with the integration of all these relevant participants. This lacuna in research needs to be addressed as a comprehensive model with all participants will enable enterprises to grasp a holistic view of value co-creation management, from which proper practices and strategies can be devised and executed for maximizing values for enterprises and fostering sustainable competitive advantages. This serves as a valuable response to the call for an integration of stakeholders to be strategically managed as an integrated system as opposed to individually optimized fragmented subsystems [56]. The focus on integrating all relevant actors also aligns with the tenet of The Resource-Based Theory of the Firm [64], which is that an enterprise is a unique collection of all resources. Enterprises must acquire valuable, scarce, heterogeneous, inimitable, and irreplaceable resources from various stakeholders to foster and sustain a competitive advantage.

In addition, a review of the existing research suggests that the mechanisms for co-created values have been sparingly studied but remain obscure. According to Drucker [14], two main functions in doing business include innovation and marketing. As such, to catalyze the resultant values, enterprises should channel efforts into leveraging innovation capability and marketing capabilities. If participants' involvement in value co-creation is expected to be conducive to values for enterprises while innovation capability and marketing capability are two critical factors for reaching desirable outcomes, a question raised is, "Can innovation capability and marketing capability serve as two main mechanisms for co-created values of enterprises?" These two mechanisms should be examined to gain insight into the phenomenon of value co-creation in enterprises and to optimize the contributions of relevant partners.

Asia Pacific is a dynamic context with vast differences from the Western context while receiving much attention from business investors. Furthermore, competition in the economies in the region is remarkably increasing, leading to more demands for progressive strategies and practices for calibrating effectiveness in doing business [12]. Strong and unique cultures of economies in the region also distinctly shape many business operations. With such unique characteristics, value co-creation processes in the Asia Pacific region pose dynamics that deserve research attention. In other words, attending to the phenomena of value co-creation in the Asia Pacific region can be a timely response to the economic situation and societal development.

With the reasoning above, this study has three primary purposes. First, it aims at integrating all of the relevant participants or stakeholders of enterprises into the co-creation of values for enterprises. This will be an early research to offer a comprehensive value co-creation framework with contributions of all relevant partners to enterprises, so the study extends the extant literature. Second, the study attempts to address the mediating role of innovation capability and marketing capability in the relationship between the value co-creation of participants and resultant values, which need to be addressed by prior research. Third, with the propositions and discussions, the study addresses implications for the Asia Pacific region to gain insights and effectively manage value co-creation processes in enterprises. This is a valuable addition to literature and practices as value co-creation is happening robustly in the Asia Pacific region.

## 2 Literature Review

### *2.1 Co-created Values for Enterprises*

As various perspectives exist for studying value co-creation, the conceptualizations of co-created values are diverse. From an enterprise's perspective, fundamental values to be concerned about may include values for customers, values for firms, and values for society at large. This pursuit can be resorted to popularly employed marketing philosophies of enterprises in the contemporary economy with an orientation to customers and societal marketing. According to [22, 54], customer values consist of economic value and relational value. Chan et al. [8] provided an extended conceptualization with three components: economic, relational, and enjoyment value. With consideration of two dimensions of motivation (i.e., extrinsic versus intrinsic) and personal orientation (self-oriented versus other-oriented), Holbrook [24] proposed a more specific conceptualization of customer value with four sub-factors comprising economic, social, hedonic, and altruistic. Slightly different, Baumann and Meunier-Fitzhugh [5] present superior value through better fit of the offering, economic value, and skill enhancement to accrue value from an offering as three elements of customer values. With the discussions mentioned earlier, customer value is more widely conceptualized with two main dimensions: economic value and relational value.

Regarding values for firms, Baumann and Meunier-Fitzhugh [5] listed transactional value and relationship value as two key dimensions. Nambisan and Baron [38] proposed four values for firms, including economic value, relationship, value related to innovation and development, and unfavorable value outcomes. Later, a proposal by Xie et al. [68] suggests that values for firms are transactional/economic, marketing, operating, and knowledge value. Though no measure exists for this conceptualized aspect, this conceptualization of values is more aligned with the firm's operational activities and pursuits. The conceptualization of values for society has been relatively consistent, and three values have been identified, including economic, social, and environmental value for society, organizations, and individuals [4].

## 2.2 *Actors for Value Co-creation*

### 2.2.1 Internal Integration

Internal integration entails that the functional departments of enterprises collaborate with each other, have coordination of intra-organizational activities as well as decisions, and form cross-functional teams for achieving goals [30]. Internal integration allows for lateral relations among functional departments which contribute to enhance capability of enterprises for processing information [73]. Internal integration also enables employees in different departments have cooperation in assimilating knowledge obtained from external partners and then combining such knowledge with existing knowledge base in enterprises [18]. Therefore, the study proposes:

*H1*: Internal integration positively affects co-created values of enterprises.

### 2.2.2 Customer Integration

Customer integration for value co-creation refers to that customers directly participate in the design, development and delivery of customized solutions by applying their specialized knowledge and skills and through information sharing and joint production [53, 72]. In accordance with Michel et al. [35], Zhang and Chen [72] and Roy et al. [43], customers involve in value co-creation with enterprises in several different ways such as providing information about their needs, requirements, operations and environmental contexts or engaging in dialog and interactions. When customers participate in co-creation of values to enterprises, they contribute essential resources such as facilities, materials, labor and knowledge and these contributions can help enterprises to create more values such as fulfilment of customers' changing demands [44]. In a similar vein, [65] discloses that close collaboration and information sharing activities of firms with customers offers firm strategic insights into market expectations and opportunities which subsequently leading to a more efficient and effective response towards customer needs [49]. The study hypothesises:

*H2*: Customer integration positively affects co-created values of enterprises.

### 2.2.3 Supplier Integration

Supplier integration refers to that an enterprise works with suppliers to coordinate activities and decisions through information sharing and by involving suppliers in internal operations in order to fulfil customer requirements [16, 70]. By interacting and cooperating with suppliers, enterprise gain valuable resources like knowledge [46, 66] that can be useful for enterprises to create values in use. An effective integration of suppliers also serves as an enabler for enterprise to have cost efficiency and product/service quality which are forms of values to firms. There has been rich theoretical and practical evidence on the relevance of effectiveness of supplier management to benefits accrued for firms. [42] showed that a sound supplier integration enables effective planning and forecasting, product and process design, and transaction management. So, the study proposes:

*H3*: Supplier integration positively affects co-created values of enterprises.

### 2.2.4 Competitor Integration

Cheong et al. [9] presented a model of value network to which competitors participate in co-creating values with focal company. Herein, the study argues that there are ample possibilities for focal company to ally with competitors as temporary complementors, like complementors in making markets. The study addressed the concept of coopetition as a business strategy to which both focal company and competitors simultaneously cooperate and compete. It argues that both participating firms become better off with market shares, profits, and technical improvements. The study also analysed the case of Tesla Motor for integration of competitor's participation into value co-creation process. Additionally, [21] and [32] postulated that in alliance with competitors, learning opportunities for focal company are paramount as competitors bring to the table broad capabilities and skills that are beneficial to the focal enterprise. These pieces of evidence suggests that competitor integration of enterprise is positive for triggering desirable values. Hence, the study proposes:

*H4*: Competitor integration positively affects co-created values of enterprises.

### 2.2.5 Marketing Intermediary Integration

According to Kotler and Armstrong [29], marketing intermediaries are companies involved in helping the focal company to promote, sell, and distributes its products to final customers. Marketing intermediaries of enterprises consist of resellers, physical distribution firms, marketing services agencies, and financial intermediaries. Resellers are known as companies to find customers or make sales of products to customers. They can be called wholesalers and retailers who resell merchandise to final customers. Physical distribution firms are intermediaries to help focal company to stock and move goods from points of origin to destinations. Marketing services agencies are known as advertising agencies, media firms, marketing research firms, and marketing consulting firms that help focal company to promote products to the markets. Financial intermediaries function as organizations to finance transactions associated with buying and selling products. They can be banks, credit companies, and insurance companies. By helping enterprises to sell, promote, and distribute products to customers in a cost efficient way, marketing intermediaries create benefits for enterprises while reducing costs, which is one form of value creation. Therefore, the study proposes:

*H5*: Marketing intermediary integration positively affects co-created values of enterprises.

### 2.2.6 Public Integration

Kotler and Armstrong [29] postulated that public is any group that has an actual or potential interest in or impact on an organization's ability to achieve its objectives. Seven groups of publics are identified in enterprises including financial publics, media publics, government publics, citizen-action publics, local publics, general public, and internal publics [29]. Financial public includes banks, investment analysts and stockholders that affect company's capability to obtain funds. Media public includes newspapers, magazines, TV stations, and blogs and Internet media serving as carriers of news, features, and opinions that pertain to company. Government public include governmental offices or departments that may offer advice or consultancy on legal issues of company's businesses. Citizen-action publics consist of consumer organizations, environmental groups, and minority groups. Local publics includes neighbourhood residents and community organizations. These groups create values to enterprises by providing support to business operations. General public with attitude towards company's products/services may also affect its buying of the products/services of company. Internal publics includes workers, managers, volunteers, and the board of directors. The positive attitude of internal publics can be spilled over to the external publics) [29], therefore creating values for the company. Obviously, each of the publics may influence enterprise in different ways. When enterprises can positively integrate all of these publics into business operations, they can achieve favourable results as these publics contribute certain benefits for enterprises. With this reasoning, the study proposes that:

*H6*: Public integration positively affects co-created values of enterprises.

## 2.3 *Mechanisms for Co-created Values of Enterprises*

### 2.3.1 Innovation Capability as a Mediator

Innovation capability refers to company's ability to continuously transform knowledge and ideas into new products, processes and systems for the benefit of the firm [25, 31]. According to [51], innovation capability of enterprise consists of technological and administrative or managerial innovation. New technologies applied, new products, new services are forms of technological innovation while administrative innovations comprise new procedures, new policies and organizational forms [69].

Integration of value co-creation actors' contribution may be conducive to innovation capability of enterprises for two main reasons. First, participations of various actors enable enterprises to have exposure to ample idea sources which are beneficial for improving capability for performing innovations. Evidence has shown that a sound integration of groups of stakeholders amplifies innovative ideas as ideas for possible innovations can come from any sources such as customers, competitors, suppliers, staff, intermediaries, and publics. To exemplify, according to [10, 30], and [20], external stakeholders contribute to complement internal research and development (R&D) investments. Finger et al. [15] discloses that external integration allows for access to external sources of technology and knowledge while [45] reveals that internal integration promotes knowledge exchange which is necessary for innovation capability. [52] and [66] inserted that internal integration improves innovation of enterprises by facilitating knowledge exchange and enabling a firm to transform acquired resources from partners. Second, a smooth integration of all groups of value co-creation actors allows for a better transformation of ideas into valuable real innovations. Each group of actors hold some resources that can be useful for developing innovative tasks. The quality integration of these actors facilitates effective execution of innovative tasks, so leveraging innovation capability of firms. Meanwhile, with an enhanced capability for innovation performance, enterprises may create more realized values for customers such as higher product quality, achieve more values for firms, and bringing about favourable values for society. The reasoning is that an improvement in innovation capability makes enterprises effective and efficient in creating desirable results or realized values. Jessen and Randoy [27] and [19] revealed that both firm's capability of innovation in both products and processes is a catalyst for its positive outcomes achieved such as financial performance, market position, and bargaining power. Therefore, the study proposes:

*H7*: Innovation capability serves as a mediator in the relationship between value creation actor integration and co-created values of enterprises.

### 2.3.2 Marketing Capability as a Mediator

Marketing capability refers to integrative capability of enterprise to apply collective knowledge, skills and resources that it possesses to "market-related needs of the business, allowing for adding value to its goods and services, adapt to market conditions, take advantage of market opportunities and meet competitive threats" ([58], p. 4). A considerable classifications of marketing capabilities have been proposed. For example, Day [13] conceptualize marketing capability with market sensing (i.e. ability to identify customers' needs) and customer-linking capability (ability to build relationship with customers). Vorhies et al. [59] proposed another conceptualization with marketing exploration capability and marketing exploitation capability. Meanwhile, according to Mohammed et al. [36], marketing capabilities include marketing planning and marketing implementation capability. Interestingly, [37] and [60] specified that marketing capabilities cover company's ability in market/marketing research, pricing, products, relationship, marketing communication, and marketing management. This conceptualization is deemed aligned with specific activities in business operations of company.

With a sound integration of relevant actors, enterprises may calibrate marketing capability in two ways. Foremost, integration of contributions of value co-creation actors allows firms to effectively exploit resources for providing product or service offerings to customers, so serving customers more satisfactorily and smoothly. Besides, integrating contributions from all value co-creation actors entails more solid resources for networks. The reason is that each actor possesses certain relationships that can be beneficial for focal enterprises [34]. With a good integration of actors' involvement, enterprises can learn about market as well as taking advantages of the actors' networks for marketing activities. In this way, marketing capability of enterprises is strengthened. With the enhanced marketing capability, enterprises have more likelihood to create desirable values for customers, for firm per se, and for the society. This is because marketing capability is directly relevant to performances and achievement of results [55, 59]. For example, an improved marketing capability enables enterprises to sustain relationships with customers more effectively, which helps to catalyze more customer relational values for customers. Prior studies have confirmed that marketing capabilities are helpful for appropriating values and creating competitive advantages for enterprises as they are difficult to be duplicated [23, 63] (Fig. 1). Hence, the study proposes:

*H8*: Marketing capability serves as a mediator in the relationship between value creation actor integration and co-created values of enterprises [23, 63].

## 3 Discussions and Implications

In practice, the proposed model can be subject to many contextual variations. The variations can be in the industry context, national context, and regional context. Empirical testing of the framework with the various contextual evidence, especially cross-context evidence, is valuable to offer an insight into the phenomenon of value co-creation by enterprises as the influential linkages or the most robust factors will be identified for managerial implications. Nevertheless, due to a lack of measures for

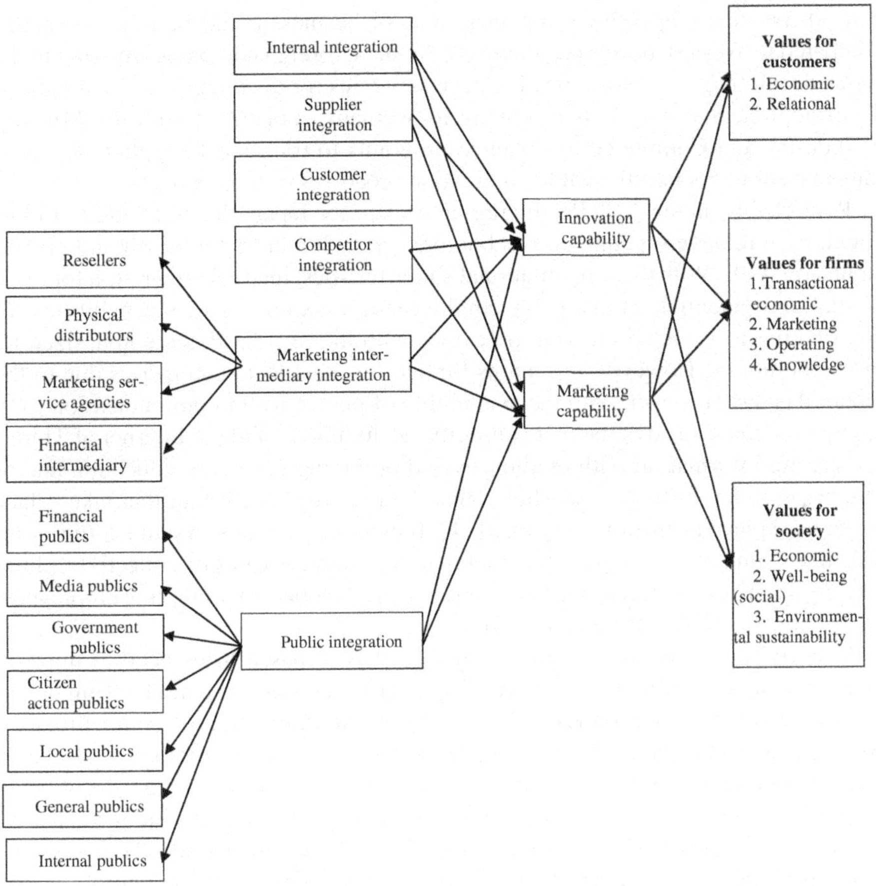


**Fig. 1** The proposed research model

the factors that may take some time for development and validation, the present study conceptually proposed the framework and discussed the relevance of the model for the Asia Pacific economic context. The extent and the degree of integration of actors for firms in the Asia Pacific region may differ from those of Western contexts. In Asia Pacific countries, except for some developed contexts like Australia, New Zealand, Hong Kong, Japan, Korea, and Singapore, where customers are pretty knowledgeable and innovative [47], firms in other countries with less knowledgeable customers may need for investment in educating customers on involvement and participation in the value co-creation process.

In emerging economies like India, China, and Indonesia, in which an increase in the number of middle-class families is captured [28, 40], integration of customers should be cautiously carried out as a large number of customers aspire to be recognized as practical and intelligent consumers while their levels of demands for services/products are also growing [28]. Suppliers are paramount in the Asia Pacific context, but their capabilities for operations of business could be more advanced compared to Western developed contexts. As such, foreign companies moving to the Asian developing economies need to have strategies for the integration of suppliers. To exemplify, Samsung, when moving to Vietnam, cooperated with the Ministry of Industry and Commerce to organize programs to train local suppliers to better integrate suppliers into the value co-creation processes of the company.

Remarkably, in the Asia Pacific region, except for Japan, the population of most countries is relatively young and technology-savvy but lacks more soft and professional job skills. With these populational characteristics, internal integration for firms is vital and potential. Training for employees to maximize staff's capabilities for contributing to value co-creation processes with the firm has been emphasized by big corporations. However, it remains limited for most local enterprises due to the incurred costs. However, with the availability of platforms for communication [67], enterprises can take advantage of supportive technologies and the Internet of Things for sharing information with employees and providing necessary education and/or training to them. Research has shown that the majority of learning that takes place in the workplace is informal learning [11]. Importantly, in most Asian Pacific countries like China, Korea, Japan, and Vietnam, the characteristics of collective culture amplify teamwork and sharing. This feature is an advantage to promoting employees' contributions to co-creating values with firms.

Concerning competitors, a great majority of Asia-based firms need to improve their financial capabilities compared to new market entrants or entrants from developed to developing economies [12]. Therefore, the integration of competitors for Asian firms should be cautiously executed. Such a sound integration will enable firms to acquire necessary resources while avoiding or minimizing the risks of being negatively acquired. Nonetheless, small enterprises in the Asia Pacific context with limited capabilities [28] also need to recognize the positive side of competitors. Enterprises need to be aware that effectively integrating with competitors is one way to co-create values, particularly for improving capabilities that benefit their development.

Regarding the public, with a collectivist culture, public ideas from communities are influential in enterprises in the Asia Pacific region [48]. Internal public and citizen action public may be less prominent compared to those in developed Western economies. However, their influences have become more robust thanks to the emergence of communities and the support of technology for communications [67]. Media publics in these contexts need to be more well-developed and transparent compared to several Western contexts. However, their influences are increasing, particularly in emerging economies where customers' knowledge is substantially leveraged as customers easily access information sources through social media platforms such as Facebook [67].

In addition, while marketing intermediaries in Western economies are advanced with progressive practices due to their long-standing development history, marketing intermediaries in developing Asian economies are less professional in service provision [1]. Because of the need for more expertise and resources, marketing intermediaries may become less involved in value co-creation with enterprises. Many companies in Asian developing contexts face problems of distribution and promotion of products/services [7]. For distribution, the backward and fragmented transportation systems in the region raised many challenges in the delivery of products to final customers [1], limiting the capabilities of distributors to co-create values with focal companies. Therefore, Asia-based firms must be attentive to the selection of compatible distribution partners so that by integrating into value co-creation processes such as joint development of innovative products and marketing events, they can make more favorable contributions to companies. Similarly, with minimal financial and human resources and a need for more expertise, Asia–Pacific-based firms in developing economies preferably hire marketing agencies to perform several marketing functions for the company, like market research, advertising, and so on. The company can facilitate the contributions of these marketing intermediaries into the value co-creation process by eliciting their ideas and feedback for innovative work and providing them with information for their elicited solutions for creative marketing tasks (e.g., creative ideas for an advertisement of a product).

Innovation and marketing have been the foci of businesses for survival and prosperity. These two business functions have been recognized by Drucker [14], and they are still preeminent in the contemporary business world. Enterprises in the Asia Pacific region are in the same line. This means the proposed associations of actors' integration to innovation and marketing capabilities are potentially relevant. Evidentially, enterprises relentlessly strive for innovation and market performance.

Nevertheless, ample empirical evidence is needed to validate both the linkage and the whole model and to confirm whether these two mechanisms are the most influential mechanisms, which is per the theoretical premise or not. Finally, with more attention to societal marketing [29], enterprises become more oriented to benefit society due to business performance. Asia Pacific region with a large population, especially China and India, needs to be more attentive to this. The proposed model, including societal values, reflects the eminent concerns of the business world.

## 4 Conclusion

Though many studies have been recently added to the literature, a comprehensive model integrating all relevant actors for value co-creation needs to be improved, and the mechanisms involved must be made more explicit. This study was carried out to address these theoretical gaps such that the study discusses the involvement of six groups of stakeholders for value co-creation for enterprises and proposes two paths (i.e., innovation capability and marketing capability) for actors' value co-creation to enterprises. The study's attempt is in line with the Resources-based Theory, such that stakeholders' contributions serve as resources for enterprises, and with a sound integration of such resources, enterprises likely achieve better performances, such as creating values for customers, firms, and the society at large. The discussions on the relevance of the model to the Asia Pacific context offer additional insight into the practice of value co-creation for enterprises.

The study has three main contributions. First, it proposed a novel comprehensive framework with a complete list of actors for value co-creation that has yet to be considered in research. While recognition of the involvement of various actors in value co-creation for enterprises has been well-recognized, the existing research either conceptually addressed the actors in general [26] or merely attended to customers and suppliers [41], [61] or analyzed a different categorization of actor embeddedness like structural, relational and cultural [62]. This study offers an advancement with a comprehensive addition of actors and discusses explicitly how each group of actors joins in co-creating values for enterprises. Second, the study proposes two crucial mechanisms that are accentuated in operating businesses [14] while being neglected for study by extant research. These two mechanisms will benefit enterprises to gain a deeper insight into the value co-creation process in enterprises, from which to properly channel efforts and allocate resources for bettering achievement of co-created values. Third, this is an early study to discuss the value co-creation model for the Asia Pacific context. With the different Asia Pacific-specific characteristics, the study provides a better understanding of the application of value co-creation.

The main limitation of the study lies in the need for more empirical validation for the proposed model. Future research is suggested to conduct empirical testing in various contexts for a cross-cultural validation of the model. Future research should also consider evaluating other factors that can exert influences on the relationship between value co-creation actor integration and co-created values to generate more insightful findings about the phenomenon. Last but not least, while the study robustly reviewed the existing literature on the topic, it did not use a more systematic review method like PRISMA. Future research should employ this review method for a more systematic topic review.

**Funding Information** This research is funded by Vietnam National Foundation for Science and Technology Development (NAFOSTED) under grant number 502.02-2018.27

## References

1. ADB.: ADB annual report. Manila, Philippines (2011). Available at https://www.adb.org/documents/adb-annual-report-2011
2. Agrawal, A.K., Rahman, Z.: Roles and resource contributions of customers in value co-creation. Int. Strat. Manag. Rev. **3**(1–2), 144–160 (2015)
3. Alves, H.: Co-creation and innovation in public services. Serv. Ind. J. **33**(7–8), 671–682 (2012)
4. Austin, J.E., Seitanidi, M.M.: Collaborative value creation: A review of partnering between nonprofits and businesses: Part I. Value creation spectrum and collaboration stages. Nonprof. Volun. Sect. Quar. **41**(5), 726–758 (2012). https://doi.org/10.1177/0899764012450777
5. Baumann, J., Le Meunier-FitzHugh, K.: Making value co-creation a reality—Exploring the co-creative value processes in customer-salesperson interaction. J. Mark. Manag. **31**(3–4), 289–316 (2015). https://doi.org/10.1080/0267257X.2014.956137
6. Binkhorst, E., Den Dekker, T.: Agenda for co-creation tourism experience research. J. Hos. Mark. & Manag. **18**(2–3), 311–327 (2009)

7. Chakraborty, A., Mandal, B.: Return migration: A review of the recent experiences. J. Eco. Pol. & Res. **12**(1), 90–99 (2016)
8. Chan, K.M.A., Balvanera, P., Benessaiah, K., Chapman, M., Díaz, S., Gómez-Baggethun, E., Gould, R., Hannahs, N., Jax, K., Klain, S., Luck, G.W., Martín-López, B., Muraca, B., Norton, B., Ott, K., Pascual, U., Satterfield, T., Tadaki, M., Taggart, J., & Turner, N.: Opinion: why protect nature? Rethinking values and the environment. Proc. Nat. Acad. Sci. **113**(6), 1462–1465 (2016)
9. Cheong, T., Song, S.H., Hu, C.: Strategic alliance with competitors in the electric vehicle market: Tesla motor's case. Math. Probl. Eng. (2016). https://doi.org/10.1155/2016/7210767
10. Craighead, C.W., Hult, G.T.M., Ketchen, J.D.: The effects of innovation–cost strategy, knowledge, and action in the supply chain on firm performance. J. Oper. Manag. **27**(5), 405–421 (2009)
11. Cunningham, J., Hillier, E.: Informal learning in the workplace: key activities and processes. Edu. & Train. **55**(1), 37–51 (2013). https://doi.org/10.1108/00400911311294960
12. Dahl, J., others.: Asia-Pacific review 2019: bracing for consolidation—the quest for scale. McKinsey & Company (2019). Available at https://www.mckinsey.com/~/media/mckinsey/industries/financial%20services/our%20insights/bracing%20for%20consolidation%20in%20asia%20pacific%20banking%20the%20quest%20for%20scale/asia-pacific-banking-review-2019-vf.ashx
13. Day, G.S.: The capabilities of market-driven organizations. J. Mark. **58**(4), 37–52 (1994)
14. Drucker, P.F.: The practice of management (1st ed.). New York, Harper (1954)
15. Finger, A.B., Flynn, B.B., Paiva, E.L.: Anticipation of new technologies: supply chain antecedents and competitive performance. Int. J. Oper. Prod. Manag. **34**(6), 807–828 (2014)
16. Flynn, B.B., Huo, B., Zhao, X.: The impact of supply chain integration on performance contingency and configuration approach. J. Prod. Econ. **28**(1), 58–71 (2010)
17. Galvagno, M., Dalli, D.: Theory of value co-creation: A systematic literature review. Manag. Serv. Qual. **24**, 643–683 (2014). https://doi.org/10.1108/MSQ-09-2013-0187
18. Grant, R.M.: Toward a Knowledge-Based theory of the firm. Stra. Manag. J. **17**, 109–122 (1996). http://www.jstor.org/stable/2486994
19. Gupta, A.K.: Innovation dimensions and firm performance synergy in the emerging market: a perspective from Dynamic Capability Theory & Signaling Theory. Technol. Soc. **64** (2021)
20. Haefner, N., Palmié, M., Leppänen, P.T.: With(out) a little help from my friends? Reconciling incongruous findings on stakeholder management, innovation, and firm performance. Entrep. Theory Pract. **47**(1), 142–171 (2023)
21. Hamel, G., Doz, Y., Prahalad, C.K.: Collaborate with your competitors and win. Havard Bus. Rev. **67**(1), 133–139 (1989)
22. Hartline, M.D., Ferrell, O.C.: The management of customer-contact service employees: An empirical investigation. J. Mark. **60**(4), 52–70 (1996)
23. Hooley, G., Greenley, G., Cadogan, J., Fahy, J.: The performance impact of marketing resources. J. Bus. Res. **58**, 18–27 (2005)
24. Holbrook, M.B.: Consumption experience: Customer value, and subjective personal introspection: an illustrative photographic essay. J. Bus. Res. **59**(6), 714–725 (2006)
25. Hurley, R.F., Hult, G.T.M.: Innovation, market orientation, and organizational learning: an integration and empirical examination. J. Mark. **62**(3), 42–54 (1998)
26. Iglesias, O., Ind, N., Alfaro, M.: The organic view of the brand: A brand value co-creation model. J. Bra. Manag. **20**(8), 670–688 (2013)
27. Jessen, J.I., Randoy, T.: The performance effect of innovation in shipping companies. Mari. Pol. & Manag.: Int. J. Ship. & Por. Res. **33**(4), 327–343 (2006)
28. Kharas, H., Gertz, G.: The new global middle class: a cross-over from West to East. In China's emerging middle class: Beyond economic transformation. Brookings Institution Press (2010)
29. Kotler, P., Armstrong, G.: Principles of Marketing (17th ed.). The University of Minnesota Libraries Publishing (2018)
30. Lai, F., Zhang, M., Lee, D.M.S., Zhao, X.: The impact of supply chain integration on mass customization capability: an extended resource-based view. IEEE Trans. Eng. Manage. **59**(3), 443–456 (2012)

31. Lawson, B., Samson, D.: Developing innovation capability in organizations: a dynamic capabilities approach. Int. J. Innov. Manag. **5**(3), 377–400 (2001)
32. Lechler, S., Canzaniello, A., Hartmann, E.: Assessment sharing intra-industry strategic alliances: effects on sustainable supplier management within multi-tier supply chains. Int. J. Prod. Econ. **217**, 64–77 (2019)
33. Lee, J., Gereffi, G., Beauvais, J.: Global value chains and agrifood standards: challenges and possibilities for smallholders in developing countries. Proc. Nat. Acad. Sci. US. Am. **109**(31), 12326–12331 (2012). https://doi.org/10.1073/pnas.0913714108
34. Merz, M.A., Zarantonello, L., Grappi, S.: How valuable are your customers in the brand value co-creation process? The development of a customer co-creation value (CCCV) scale. J. Bus. Res. **82**, 79–89 (2018)
35. Michel, S., Vargo, S.L., Lusch, R.F.: Reconfiguration of the conceptual landscape: a tribute to the service logic of Richard Normann. J. Aca. Mark. Scien. **36**(1), 152–155 (2008)
36. Mohammed, A.A., Rashid, B., Tahir, S.: Customer relationship management (CRM) technology and organization performance: Is marketing capability a missing link? An empirical study in the Malaysian hotel industry. Asi. Soc. Scien. **10**(9), 197–212 (2014)
37. Morgan, N.A., Zou, S., Vorhies, D.W., Katsikeas, C.S.: Experiential and informational knowledge, architectural marketing capabilities, and the adaptive performance of export ventures. Decis. Sci. **34**(2), 287–321 (2003)
38. Nambisan, S., Baron, R.A.: Virtual Customer Environments: Testing a Model of Voluntary Participation in Value Co-creation Activities. J. Prod. Inno. Manag. **26**, 388–406 (2009). https://doi.org/10.1111/j.1540-5885.2009.00667.x
39. Oh, L.B., Teo, H.H.: Consumer value co-creation in a hybrid commerce service delivery system. Int. J. Elec. Com, **14**(2010–3), 35–62 (2014)
40. Pratomo, D., Syafitri, W., Anindya, C.: Expanding middle class in Indonesia. J. Indones. Sustain. Dev. Planning **1**, 307–312 (2020)
41. Priem, R.L.: A consumer perspective on value creation. Aca. Manag. Rev. **32**(1), 219–235 (2007)
42. Ragatz, G.L., Handfield, R.B., Peterson, K.J.: Benefits associated with supplier integration into new product development under conditions of technology uncertainty. J. Bus. Res. **55**(5), 389–400 (2002)
43. Roy, S.K., Singh, G., Hatton, C., et al.: Customers' motives to co-create in smart services interactions. Electron. Commer. Res. **23**, 1367–1400 (2023)
44. Sampson, S.E., Spring, M.: Customer roles in service supply chains and opportunities for innovation. J. Supply Chain Manag. **48**(4), 30–50 (2012)
45. Sawhney, R.: Interplay between uncertainty and flexibility across the value chain: towards a transformation model of manufacturing flexibility. J. Oper. Prod. Manag. **24**(5), 476–493 (2006)
46. Sharma, A., Kumar, V., Borah, S.B.: Complexity in a multinational enterprise's global supply chain and its international business performance: a bane or a boon? J. Int. Bus. Stud. **53**, 850–878 (2022)
47. Shashi, M., Shabani, A., Singh, R.: The impact of interwoven integration practices on supply chain value addition and firm performance. J. Ind. Eng. Int. **15**, 39–51 (2019). https://doi.org/10.1007/s40092-019-0316-8
48. Shavitt, S., Barnes, A.J.: Culture and the consumer journey. J. Retail. **96**(1), 40–54 (2020)
49. Swink, M., Narasimhan, R., Wang, C.: Managing beyond the factory walls: effects of four types of strategic integration on manufacturing plant performance. J. Oper. Manag. **25**(1), 148–164 (2007)
50. Tonby, O., Woetzel, J., Choi, W., Eloot, K., Dhawan, R., Seong, J., Wang. P.: The future of Asia: Asian flows and networks are defining the next phase of globalization. Discussion Paper. McKinsey Global Institute (2019)
51. Tuominen, M., Hyvönen, S.: Organizational innovation capability: a driver for competitive superiority in marketing channel. Int. Rev. Retail. Distrib. Consum. Res. **14**(3), 277–293 (2004)

52. Valle, S., Vazquez-Bustelo, D.: Concurrent engineering performance: incremental versus radical innovation. Int. J. Prod. Econ. **119**(1), 136–148 (2009)
53. Vargo, S., Lusch, R.: Evolving to a new dominant logic for marketing. J. Mark. **68**(1), 1–17 (2004)
54. Vargo, S.L.: Customer integration and value creation. Paradigmatic traps and perspectives. J. Serv. Res. **11**(2), 211–215 (2008)
55. Vicente, M., Antunes, M.J., Malva, M.: The impact of marketing capabilities, technological capabilities and organizational innovation on export performance. Universidade Europeia. ICEMC, 328–337 (2016)
56. Vickery, S.K., Jayaram, J., Droge, C., Calantone, R.: The effects of an integrative supply chain strategy on customer service and financial performance: an analysis of direct versus indirect relationships. J. Oper. Manag. **21**(5), 523–539 (2003)
57. Vorhies, D., Yarbrough, L.: Marketing's role in the development of competitive advantage: Evidence from the motor carrier industry. J. Mark.-Foc. Manag. **2**, 361–386 (1998) 10.1023/A:1009763920828.
58. Vorhies, D.W.: An investigation of the factors leading to the development of marketing capabilities and organizational effectiveness. J. Stra. Mark. **6**, 3–23 (1998)
59. Vorhies, D.W., Orr, L.M., Bush, V.D.: Improving customer-focused marketing capabilities and firm financial performance via marketing exploration and exploitation. J. Aca. Mark. Scien. **39**(5), 736–756 (2011)
60. Vorhies, D.W., Morgan, N.A.: Benchmarking marketing capabilities for sustainable competitive advantage. J. Mark. **69**(1), 80–94 (2005)
61. Walter, A., Ritter, T., Gemuenden, H.G.: Value creation in buyer-seller relationships: theoretical considerations and empirical results from a suppliers perspective. Ind. Mark. Manag. **30**(4), 365–377 (2001)
62. Wajid, M., Khan, M.A., Shirazi, M.U., Summiya, F.: Seed priming modulates germination potential, osmoprotectants accumulation and ionic uptake in wheat seedlings under salt stress. Int. J. Agric. Biol. **22**, 594–600 (2019)
63. Weerawardena, J.: The role of marketing capability in innovation-based competitive strategy. J. Stra. Mark. **11**(1), 15–35 (2003)
64. Wernerfelt, B.: The Resource-Based view of the firm: Ten years after. Stra. Manag. J. **16**(3), 171–174 (1995)
65. Wong, C.Y., Boon-itt, S., Wong, C.W.Y.: The contingency effects of environmental uncertainty on the relationship between supply chain integration and operational performance. J. Oper. Manag. **29**(6), 604–615 (2011)
66. Wong, C., Wong, C.Y., Boon-itt, S.: The combined effects of internal and external supply chain integration on product innovation. Int. J. Prod. Econ. **146**(2), 566–574 (2013)
67. World Bank.: World development report. Washington DC (2019). Available https://documents1.worldbank.org/curated/en/816281518818814423/pdf/Main-Report.pdf
68. Xie, K., Wu, Y., Xiao, J., Hu, Q.: Value co-creation between firms and customers: The role of big data-based cooperative assets. Infor. & Manag. **53**(8), 1034–1048 (2016)
69. Yang, C.C., Marlow, P.B., Lu, C.S.: Assessing resources, logistics service capabilities, innovation capabilities and the performance of container shipping services in Taiwan. Int. J. Prod. Econ. **122**(1), 4–20 (2009)
70. Yeung, J.H.Y., Selen, W., Zhang, M., Huo, B.: The effects of trust and coercive power on supplier integration. Int. J. Prod. Econ. **120**(1), 66–78 (2009)
71. Yi, Y., Gong, T.: Customer value co-creation behavior: scale development and validation. J. Bus. Res. **66**(9), 1279–1284 (2013)
72. Zhang, X., Chen, R.: Examining the mechanism of the value co-creation with customers. Int. J. Prod. Eco. **116**, 242–250 (2008). https://doi.org/10.1016/j.ijpe.2008.09.004
73. Zhang, M., Zhao, X., Qi, Y.: The effects of organizational flatness, coordination, and product modularity on mass customization capability. Int. J. Prod. Econ. **158**, 145–155 (2014)

# Industry 4.0 Adoption in Supply Chain Financing for Small and Medium Enterprises: A Systems Theory Approach

**Navidreza Ahadi, Gladness Monametsi, Shahryar Sorooshian, and Porngarm Virutamasen**

**Abstract** This article examines the adoption of Industry 4.0 (I4.0) tools in supply chain financing (SCF) for small and medium-sized enterprises (SMEs). The paper proposes a strategy for accelerating I4.0 SCF adoption by outlining the benefits of I4.0 and SCF for SMEs, the challenges of adoption and implementation, and developing a model for adopting SCF I4.0 tools using systems theory. The study highlights the significance of understanding the factors driving I4.0 SCF adoption by SMEs to make better strategic decisions. Additionally, it emphasizes the challenges SMEs face in obtaining funding for their businesses and the benefits of using SCF to address SCM and financing limitations for SMEs. This study employs content analysis of existing literature to present a conceptual framework for implementing Industry 4.0 Supply Chain Finance (I4.0 SCF) in Small and Medium-sized Enterprises (SMEs). The study also provides a comprehensive framework for the adoption of I4.0 SCF, which can help SMEs make informed decisions about the use of I4.0 tools in obtaining Supply Chain Financing. Finally, the study maps the adoption strategies onto the Systems framework, showing how I4.0 adoption can be achieved.

**Keywords** Adoption strategy · Industry 4.0 · Small and medium-sized enterprises · Supply chain finance · Systems theory

N. Ahadi (✉) · P. Virutamasen
College of Creative Industry, Srinakharinwirot University, Bangkok, Thailand
e-mail: navidreza@g.swu.ac.th

G. Monametsi
School of Business and Management Studies, Botswana Open University, Gaborone, Botswana

S. Sorooshian
Department of Business Administration, University of Gothenburg, Gothenburg, Sweden



S. Kot et al. (eds.), *Corporate Practices: Policies, Methodologies, and Insights in Organizational Management*, Springer Proceedings in Business and Economics,
https://doi.org/10.1007/978-981-97-0996-0_19

## 1 Introduction

Small and medium-sized enterprises (SMEs) are crucial in many economies worldwide, particularly developing countries [1]. SME development is linked to the quality of life and socio-economic development of a country [2]. Policymakers continue to show interest in SME research, and the COVID-19 pandemic has highlighted the vulnerability of SMEs to economic shocks. To mitigate the pandemic's economic impact, SME financing has taken center stage, given their lower resilience and bigger impact on economies than larger enterprises. Financial constraints SMEs face, such as the inability to cover fixed operating costs, access raw materials, and severe liquidity problems due to restrictions on business operations, can be addressed through supply chain financing (SCF) [3].

This article examines significant patterns, influences, and insights from the literature, providing a solid foundation for our framework. This research also focuses on how Small and Medium-sized Enterprises (SMEs) are implementing Industry 4.0 Supply Chain Finance (I4.0 SCF). Our goals include emphasizing the value of I4.0 SCF for SMEs, identifying the barriers to adoption, and proposing a system theory model to direct SMEs and stakeholders toward successful I4.0 SCF integration. In essence, this article endeavors to understand the critical intersection of I4.0 and SCF within the SME landscape. At the same time, it provides practitioners, decision-makers, and academics with a road map for navigating the constantly changing landscape of present supply chain financing.

[4] state that supply chain financing is a technology-enabled financial process that provides credit to SMEs cost-effectively. Unlike traditional loans, this method of financing allows flexibility in terms of early payments or extended credit at a lower fee, helping to free up crucial working capital and, thus, better supply chain management. Accelerating the adoption of Industry 4.0 supply chain financing will make it easier for SMEs to obtain the operating capital they require to expand their operations and provide them an equal opportunity to compete with more giant corporations.

The methods employed in supply chain finance illustrate the Fourth Industrial Revolution (Industry 4.0), which is based on information and communication technology (ICT) and enables the reorganization of supply chain financing activities by applying new technologies such as cloud-based platforms [5]. These ICT-driven supply chain activities that use Industry 4.0's ICT capabilities for the design and planning, production, distribution, consumption, and reverse logistics are referred to as supply chain 4.0. The SME sector is well-suited for applying this supply chain 4.0 due to the financial gap created by traditional forms of financing, such as banks, which need to be improved to service SME financing needs effectively.

Research has shown that SME innovation capability positively impacts SCF adoption and SCF performance [6] and that SCF positively impacts SME performance [7]. Improved transparency and visibility that Industry 4.0 supply chain finance offers throughout the supply chain are its main advantages. SMEs can better manage inventories, streamline logistics, and identify any possible supply chain bottlenecks or inefficiencies using technologies such as the Internet of Things (IoT), artificial intelligence (AI), blockchain, and nonfungible tokens [8]. They can make better decisions and lower their risk of supply chain interruptions by having greater visibility into the supply chain.

Despite the significant impact of Industry 4.0 tools on SCF [9], their uptake by SMEs is low [10, 11], and the adoption gap continues to widen as technology becomes more sophisticated. [12] recommends encouraging the digital uptake of SMEs and leveraging financial technologies (fintech) and alternative sources of financing. Because supply chain digitization occurs across political, economic, and socio-cultural norms in a globalized world, many drivers behind and challenges to using the potential benefits of Industry 4.0 in SCF must be better understood [13]. Therefore, understanding the factors that drive I4.0 SCF for SMEs is essential in making better strategic decisions.

This paper proposes a strategy for accelerating the adoption of Industry 4.0 supply chain financing for SMEs to address the adoption gap. To achieve this goal, we first outline the benefits and relationship between Industry 4.0 and SCF for SMEs, as well as the challenges of adoption and implementation. We then develop a model for adopting Industry 4.0 SCF tools using systems theory and the innovation diffusion model. The article emphasizes the importance of understanding the factors that drive I4.0 SCF to make better strategic decisions.

We highlight the challenges faced by SMEs in obtaining funding for their businesses and the benefits of using SCF as a solution to address SCM and financing limitations for SMEs. Finally, we map the adoption strategies onto the systems framework, showing how the adoption of Industry 4.0 tools can be achieved. The remainder of this paper is structured as follows: literature review, methodology, results, and conclusion.

## 2 Literature Review

This literature review section provides an overview of the current research on Industry 4.0 and SCF adoption for SMEs. The benefits and challenges of using Industry 4.0 tools in SCF for SMEs are discussed, followed by developing a model for adopting Industry 4.0 SCF tools using systems theory and the innovation diffusion model. Understanding the factors driving ICT-driven supply chains for better strategic decision-making is highlighted.

### *2.1 Supply Chain Management and Supply Chain Finance*

In recent years, integrating supply chain management (SCM) with supply chain finance (SCF) has become increasingly crucial for businesses. SCM is no longer just a logistical-focused business function but rather an all-encompassing value-driven function of a firm that affects its capital structure, risk level, and cost structure. As such, using finance in SCM allows managers to make decisions that increase shareholder value beyond reducing stock levels and speeding up stock turnaround. It plays a significant role in integrating SCF with SCM by optimizing cash flow within the supply chain, which leads to efficient and lower costs of capital. According to Gomm [14], IT serves three primary purposes: it speeds up cash flow by optimizing finance across various aspects of the supply chain, it facilitates SCM collaborations between and amongst the supply chain (e.g., procurement, research, and development) that makes it possible for cash-flow optimization, and it helps with external party coordination, including service providers and financial institutions.

## 2.2 SME Context

While SCM and financing are important for all businesses, small to medium enterprises (SMEs) face unique challenges in obtaining funding for their businesses due to their incongruent nature with financial institutions. This has been a subject of numerous academic articles over the years, and the challenges can be summarized as an inability to meet the exacting loan standards of financial institutions, a lack of technical know-how in dealing with financial matters (on the part of the owner-manager), and financing needs being insufficiently met. Due to these challenges, traditional financing avenues typically available to larger companies are elusive to SMEs. Regarding SCM for SMEs, Abassi et al. [15] identified five challenges: lack of coordination and cooperation between parties, operational risks caused by scalability and unstable demand, limited technological access, lack of rigorous business modeling methodology, and locked working capital. While many countries have introduced policies to address these problems, the problems persist. SCF has been identified as a viable solution to address the SCM and financing limitations of SMEs, offering a multipronged solution to the long-term difficulties of SME financing [16]. Utilizing digital platforms and markets is a key component of Industry 4.0 supply chain financing, which gives SMEs access to a more excellent selection of suppliers and consumers, as well as several financing options. Small and medium-sized businesses (SMEs) can receive financing more swiftly and conveniently by leveraging digital platforms, as opposed to paper-intensive methods or protracted approval procedures. This can assist SMEs in getting the funding they need despite obstacles like poor credit records and a lack of collateral.

## 2.3 Process of Supply Chain Finance

Dervojeda and colleagues [17] explain that the process of SCF involves two parties, the buyer and the seller, who are juxtaposed in their financial interests in the process. SMEs, usually the suppliers, after offering a service or selling their goods, would like to receive payment on the invoice as soon as possible. On the other hand, the buyer would like to delay payment as much as possible. In such cases, SMEs are at liquidity risk, unable to finance their working capital needs. SCF works by introducing a finance institution as an intermediary to alleviate the opposing positions of the buyer and the seller. Once the seller has raised an invoice and the buyer has approved it, the supplier can request early payment from the financial intermediary, allowing the supplier to finance their working capital needs. However, the request for early settlement will come at a discounted rate, although at a much lower rate than a traditional bank loan or an invoice factoring service. On the invoice due date, the buyer pays the due amounts to the financial intermediary.

## *2.4 I4.0 in Supply Chain Finance*

The use of various Industry 4.0 (I4.0) technologies helps to facilitate this process. For example, IoT can track the behaviors of parties and transactions in real-time. Smart contracts can help with the execution of commands of a legal contract between parties involving payments and other legal obligations. Technical integration improves supplier integration and collaborative initiatives [18]. Digital infrastructure enables mobility, connectivity, and cloud computing systems and resources, all of which contribute to ICT growth and advancement, allowing for greater integration and emphasis on ICT in various industries [19–21] investigated cloud computing technology as one of the primary digital infrastructures that improve internet mobility, connectivity, and autonomy. Industry 4.0 SCF might assist SMEs in reducing some of the risks related to global trade. SMEs can more effectively manage currency risks, lower the chance of fraud, and adhere to intricate international trade standards by utilizing digital technologies. This can help SMEs grow their clientele and break into new areas without taking too much risk.

Despite the benefits of I4.0 for SCF, there are numerous challenges of adaptation faced by SMEs. Conflicting attempts to adopt I4.0 as a paradigm have caused organizations uncertainty. Adopting a new paradigm requires a substantial initial cost outlay, which could be increased if mishandled [13]. Issues in choosing I4.0 enablers correctly could increase difficulties in digitization on supply chains and could be costly for businesses, which results in implementation issues and failures [22]. Collaboration challenges include issues with trust and transparency, governance, supplier opportunism, and differences in legal, tax, and patent systems. Planning, control, or coordination of multiple controlling technological entities so that they can work together in a properly established mechanism in the supply chain [13].

In contrast, Supply chain innovation is enhanced by standardizing data collection, processing, and storage [23–25]. Lack of proper data processing can threaten businesses as data is a strategic asset, and businesses are increasingly looking for ways to capitalize on it to create added value, development, and competitive advantage [26, 27]. The threat of ineffective cybersecurity risk mitigation frameworks raises security concerns in ICT infrastructure [25, 28, 29]. Protectionist trade policies, in particular, discourage competition in international trade [22]. Technological advancement will result in job losses and high unemployment rates if the proper training to upgrade employee skills is not provided [30]. According to Lin et al. [31], consumer protections are provided by national policies and laws, as well as legal agreements and frameworks. Some erroneous licensing agreements may result in a bottleneck for SCF I4.0 adopters [22, 32]. Several countries' initiatives similar to Industry 4.0 require standardization frameworks for interoperability [33].

To overcome these challenges, there is a need for a systematic approach to SCF I4.0 adoption. Adopting SCF I4.0 requires collaboration between all parties involved in the supply chain process, including suppliers, buyers, financial intermediaries, and technology providers. This collaboration is critical to ensure that the benefits of SCF I4.0 are realized and that any challenges are addressed. A systematic approach to SCF I4.0 adoption involves using a framework that provides a structured and step-by-step process for organizations. The framework should consider the following vital factors:

1. Business Strategy: The adoption of SCF I4.0 should align with the organization's overall business strategy. The framework should include a process for assessing the organization's current business strategy and identifying areas where SCF I4.0 can support and enhance the strategy.
2. Technology Infrastructure: The adoption of SCF I4.0 requires a robust technology infrastructure. The framework should include a process for assessing the organization's current technology infrastructure and identifying any gaps that need to be addressed.
3. Process Integration: The adoption of SCF I4.0 requires the integration of financial and supply chain processes. The framework should include a process for assessing the organization's current processes and identifying areas where SCF I4.0 can be integrated.
4. Risk Management: The adoption of SCF I4.0 introduces new risks that need to be managed. The framework should include a process for identifying and managing the risks associated with SCF I4.0 adoption.
5. Change Management: The adoption of SCF I4.0 requires a significant change in the organization's processes and culture. The framework should include a process for managing this change and ensuring that all stakeholders are engaged and involved in the adoption process.
6. Performance Measurement: The adoption of SCF I4.0 should be measured to assess the success of the adoption and identify areas for improvement. The framework should include a process for measuring the performance of SCF I4.0 adoption and using this information to continuously improve the adoption process.
7. Collaboration: As previously mentioned, collaboration between all parties involved in the supply chain process is critical for the success of SCF I4.0 adoption. The framework should include a process for fostering collaboration between suppliers, buyers, financial intermediaries, and technology providers.

By using a systematic approach to SCF I4.0 adoption, organizations can ensure that they are able to overcome the challenges associated with adoption and realize the benefits of SCF I4.0. The following section outlines a model for the adoption of SCF I4.0 tools using the systems theory and the innovation diffusion model.

## 3 Methodology

This study utilizes a content analysis of relevant literature to conceptualize and develop a framework for adopting Industry 4.0 Supply Chain Finance (I4.0 SCF) for Small and Medium-sized Enterprises (SMEs). The authors conducted a search using various databases with search terms such as "I4.0, SCF, SMEs" to gather literature that could help identify and categorize critical trends related to the subject matter.

Through this approach, the authors built a framework for adopting I4.0 SCF for SMEs using the systems theory and the innovation diffusion model. The systems theory was used to identify the elements involved in adopting I4.0 SCF for SMEs and their interrelationships. In contrast, the innovation diffusion model was used to identify the different stages of the adoption process and the factors that influence each stage.

The resulting framework provides a systematic approach to adopting I4.0 SCF for SMEs. It can be used by SMEs, financial institutions, and other stakeholders involved in the supply chain process. The framework includes recommendations for addressing the challenges identified in the literature review, such as lack of coordination and collaboration, operational risks, limited access to technology, lack of rigorous business modeling methodology, and locked working capital.

In summary, the methodology used in this study involved a content analysis of relevant literature to conceptualize and develop a framework for adopting I4.0 SCF for SMEs. The framework was built using the systems theory and provides a systematic approach to addressing the challenges SMEs face in adopting I4.0 SCF.

## 4 Results

The adoption of Industry 4.0 (I4.0) in supply chain finance (SCF) for small and medium-sized enterprises (SMEs) requires a systematic approach that considers the integration of different factors. The Systems Theory offers a framework for viewing organizations as systems with integrated parts that must function efficiently. This theory emphasizes the importance of relationships between parts of an organization, which is especially relevant for modern organizations as systems become more complex and interdependent. The theory suggests that organizations should be open and interact with the external environment, thus changing the view of management as mechanical to one of dynamic and coordinated. This approach is crucial for building and sustaining an agile business that can survive in a changing environment. The Systems Theory also provides a multi-pronged approach to achieving the best success for tech adoption, specifically I4.0 for SCF. It is, therefore, relevant for the adoption of new technology in SCF for SMEs [34–36].

The proposed strategy adoption model is anchored on three pillars of industrial innovation, namely policy, science and technology strategy, and business management. Capital and funding are critical factors for effective organizational digital transformation, and the need for IT infrastructure for SMEs requires a heavy initial investment for I4.0 implementation [18, 25]. The short-termism and cost focus exacerbate the funding challenges SMEs face regarding I4.0 adoption compared to multinational corporations (MNCs) [37]. SME funding organizations should, therefore, have targeted funding schemes for I4.0 development, and governments should fund I4.0 initiatives to advance their uptake within their economy. Conversely, SMEs should seek out and be aware of funding opportunities that can help fund specific areas within their business. Supply chain coordination and incentive programs, such as buyback, quantity discounts, and revenue-sharing structures, are effective funding schemes [29, 38].

Corporate vision, norms, values, mission goals, and company objectives shape organizational behaviors. Effective employee engagement and empowerment in government and leadership style are essential, and supportive management styles are necessary for effective I4.0 adoption [18, 25, 39, 40, 44]. Visionary management should be able to effectively communicate and advocate the benefits of I4.0 to stakeholders for and within their businesses. I4.0 should be part of a strategic approach to the business model used for organizational objectives. The disruptive nature of I4.0 to businesses requires change management initiatives that may need more management support, communication, and clearly defined objectives [41]. Developing knowledge-driven digital capabilities for I4.0 depends on the growth of digital skills in various industries. Knowledge-driven personal competencies, social competencies, and technical competencies are all enabled by digital skills. Training and development help to increase awareness of and aptitude of employees so that I4.0 tools are implemented effectively within the business [23, 30, 42–45].

According to [31], different political systems influence strategic initiatives in different countries. The European governments have been at the forefront of policy development around the I4.0 transformation of SMEs. These are targeted policies aimed at specific outcomes for SMEs. For example, Portugal 2020, developed in 2017, has two phases, the first of which involves financing, human resources, and investment support [46]. This phase involves a bottom-up approach to investment in human and infrastructure development. Higher educational programs should focus on digital skills literacy, and a more significant portion of budgets should be dedicated to research and development. Access to the internet should be a priority as it keeps people connected, and it is the basis for access to I4.0 tools. Public and private partnerships should be developed in I4.0 policies.

According to [12, 31, 38], data-driven Industry 4.0 Business Models (BMs) comprise the super patterns Incorporation (Process Innovation), Automation (Product

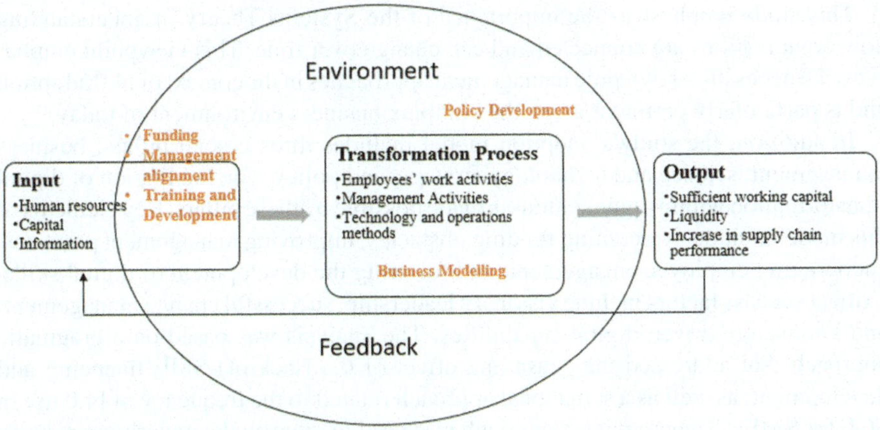


**Fig. 1** I4.0 Supply Chain Financing for SMEs

and Service Innovation), and Expertization (Hybrid of product and process innovation). Numerous business models have been suggested for the I4.0 business transformation process. [41] suggests different models that can be used, including the Digital lean transformation framework [47], the Agile change management model [48], and the Digital transformation conceptual model [49]. SMEs need to utilize the best business models for themselves that may be dependent on the industry or specific objective. For example, a manufacturing firm has different financing needs than a service-oriented firm, and thus, the type of I4.0 tech applied may differ substantially. On a more granular level, SMEs can adopt new business models, such as pay-per-use or subscription-based ones, thanks to Industry 4.0 supply chain financing. These methods can lessen SMEs' reliance on one-time sales and help them create ongoing revenue streams. By providing these models, SMEs may stand out from their rivals and give their clients more for their money.

Based on a systems approach, we have mapped the adoption strategy onto the Systems framework. Figure 1 depicts the adoption strategies mapped onto the framework, showing how I4.0 adoption will be achieved.

## 5 Conclusion, Discussion and Implications

This study provides a comprehensive framework for adopting Industry 4.0 supply chain financing in small and medium-sized enterprises (SMEs). The study highlights the challenges companies face in adopting and implementing I4.0 SCF, which has become increasingly important in the modern context of supply chain management. By considering organizational, cultural, and regulatory factors, this study provides a more comprehensive understanding of adopting I4.0 SCF for SMEs.

This study emphasizes the importance of the Systems Theory in understanding how organizations are connected and can change over time. This viewpoint emphasizes the necessity of dynamic management approaches in the context of I4.0 adoption and is particularly pertinent given the complex business environment of today.

In addition, the study's adoption model includes three crucial pillars: business management, science and technology strategy, and policy. The facilitation of digital transformation within organizations is made possible by these pillars. Key elements of this model include overcoming funding obstacles, improving management practices, encouraging employee engagement, and fostering the development of digital skills. Critical success factors include visionary leadership, successful change management, and knowledge-driven digital capabilities. The analysis was based on a pragmatic approach that addressed the cause and effect of the (lack of) SME financing and development, as well as a semantical approach related to the frequency of I4.0 use in SCF for SMEs. The pragmatic approach was used to identify the underlying reasons for the challenges SMEs face in obtaining financing.

In contrast, the semantical approach was used to identify how much I4.0 is used in SCF for SMEs. The key findings highlight how I4.0 SCF can accelerate the growth and development of SMEs by enabling flexible business models, enabling faster financial transactions, improving supply chain visibility, and lowering trade risks through digital technologies and platforms. Also, it emphasizes the significance of taking various factors, such as organizational dynamics and regulatory environments, into account during the adoption process. It highlights the importance of this integration, identifies challenges and opportunities, and offers a methodical strategy based on systems theory and innovation diffusion model.

Alsmairat et al. [50] emphasize the vital role of innovation in supply chain risk mitigation and improved operational efficiency. This study's insights offer practical guidance for enhancing performance in the manufacturing sector, highlighting the significance of managing supply chain risks and fostering resilience. According to [51], Industry 4.0 presents opportunities and challenges for various enterprises. Rapid adaptation becomes essential when businesses align their strategies, products, and services with evolving customer demands. Several researchers emphasize the importance of supply chain technologies and fintech for generating stakeholder value within the financial supply chain through the lens of working capital management [52–58].

The contribution of this study lies in its approach to adopting I4.0 SCF. Unlike previous studies that have focused on the technical aspects, this study provides a framework that considers the integration of different factors. The framework developed in this study emphasizes the importance of relationships between parts of an organization, which is especially relevant for modern organizations as systems become more complex and interdependent. This approach is crucial for building and sustaining an agile business that can survive in a changing environment. By providing these models, SMEs may stand out from their rivals and provide more value to their clients. The findings of this study have implications for industry practitioners, decision-makers, and policymakers and provide insights into the factors that influence the adoption of ICT-SC. It implies that a holistic approach is necessary for effective I4.0 SCF for SMEs that involves multiple stakeholders, including governments responsible for creating a conducive environment for the uptake of I4.0 tools through a supportive regulatory environment and public and private partnerships to support government efforts and SMEs.

## *5.1 Limitations and Future Research*

There are several limitations to this study. This study is based on content analysis and previous studies to uncover the root causes of the financing challenges encountered by SMEs. It is essential to recognize that supply chain finance and the related field of Industry 4.0 are dynamic and constantly evolving. As this was a conceptual paper offering a model for adopting I4.0 SCF for SMEs, future research can expand this research into an empirical study. The study focus is limited to analysis through the body of literature available at the time of analysis. Therefore, new developments and insights need further investigation.

There are several potential directions for future research in Industry 4.0 Supply Chain Finance (I4.0 SCF) for SMEs. Priority should be given to empirical validation of the suggested framework through studies conducted in real-world scenarios, as this will provide valuable insights and applicability. In-depth case studies of I4.0 SCF implementations that were successful in SMEs can offer nuanced understanding and valuable tactics. Cross-industry analyses can show the adoption patterns and advantages unique to each industry. The long-term effects of I4.0 SCF can be better understood through longitudinal studies that follow the performance of SMEs over time. It is essential to conduct in-depth analyses of the policy and regulatory ramifications associated with adopting I4.0 SCF on both a regional and global scale to foster favorable conditions. Finally, research that focuses on a particular technology can explore the distinct functions and effects of that technology on SME supply chain financing.

## References

1. Woźniak, M., Duda, J., Gąsior, A., Bernat, T.: Relations of GDP growth and development of SMEs in Poland. Procedia Comput Sci **159**, 2470–2480 (2019)
2. Erdin, C., Ozkaya, G.: Contribution of small and medium enterprises to economic development and quality of life in Turkey. Heliyon **6**(2), e03215 (2020)
3. Zutshi, A., Mendy, J., Sharma, G.D., Thomas, A., Sarker, T.: From challenges to creativity: enhancing SMEs' resilience in the context of COVID-19. Sustainability **13**(12), 6542 (2021)
4. Maheshwari, P., Kamble, S.: A comparative approach for sustainable supply chain finance to implement Industry 4.0 in Micro-, Small-, and Medium-sized enterprises. In: Digital transformation and Industry 4.0 for Sustainable Supply Chain Performance, pp. 207–230. Springer International Publishing, Cham (2023)
5. Yee, K.C., Teck, T.S., Sorooshian, S.: Powers of information-technology for supply chains: case of Malaysia. Qual.-Access Success **21**(177), 157–162 (2020)

6. Lu, Q., Liu, B., Song, H.: How can SMEs acquire supply chain financing: the capabilities and information perspective. Ind. Manag. Data Syst. **120**(4), 784–809 (2020)
7. Vu, T., Nguyen, D., Luong, T., Nguyen, T., Doan, T.: The impact of supply chain financing on SMEs performance in Global supply chain. Uncertain Supply Chain Manag **10**(1), 255–270 (2022)
8. Zanjanab, A.G., Ahadi, N., Monametsi, G., Sorooshian, S., Taghipour, A.: The outlook of Non Fungible Tokens (NFTs): an alternative for academic manuscript ownership and scholarly publications. In: 2023 International Conference on Cyber Management And Engineering (CyMaEn), pp. 245–250. IEEE, January 2023
9. Soni, G., Kumar, S., Mahto, R.V., Mangla, S.K., Mittal, M.L., Lim, W.M.: A decision-making framework for Industry 4.0 technology implementation: the case of FinTech and sustainable supply chain finance for SMEs. Technol. Forecast. Soc. Change **180**, Art. 121686 (2022)
10. Ghobakhloo, M., Iranmanesh, M., Vilkas, M., Grybauskas, A., Amran, A.: Drivers and barriers of Industry 4.0 technology adoption among manufacturing SMEs: a systematic review and transformation roadmap. J. Manuf. Technol. Manag. (ahead-of-print) (2022)
11. Mittal, S., Khan, M.A., Romero, D., Wuest, T.: A critical review of smart manufacturing & Industry 4.0 maturity models: implications for small and medium-sized enterprises (SMEs). J. Manuf. Syst. **49**, 194–214 (2018)
12. Kergroach, S.: SMEs Going Digital: policy challenges and recommendations. OECD Going Digital Toolkit Notes, No. 15. OECD Publishing, Paris (2021) https://doi.org/10.1787/c91088a4-en
13. Nicolescu, R., Huth, M., Radanliev, P., De Roure, D.: Mapping the values of IoT. J. Inf. Technol. **33**(4), 345–360 (2018)
14. Gomm, M.L.: Supply chain finance: applying finance theory to supply chain management to enhance finance in supply chains. Int J Log Res Appl **13**(2), 133–142 (2010)
15. Abbasi, W.A., Wang, Z., Alsakarneh, A.: Overcoming SMEs financing and supply chain obstacles by introducing supply chain finance. HOLISTICA–Journal Bus. Public Adm. **9**(1), 7–22 (2018)
16. Liang, X., Zhao, X., Wang, M., Li, Z.: Small and medium-sized enterprises sustainable supply chain financing decision based on triple bottom line theory. Sustainability **10**(11), 4242 (2018)
17. Dervojeda, K., Verzijl, D., Nagtegaal, F., Lengton, M., Rouwmaat, E.: Innovative Business Models: Supply Chain Finance. Business Innovation Observatory, The Netherlands (2014)
18. Yadav, G., Luthra, S., Jakhar, S.K., Mangla, S.K., Rai, D.P.: A framework to overcome sustainable supply chain challenges through solution measures of Industry 4.0 and circular economy: an automotive case. J. Clean. Prod. **254**, 120112 (2020)
19. Pfohl, H.C., Yahsi, B., Kurnaz, T.: The impact of Industry 4.0 on the supply chain. In: Innovations and Strategies for Logistics and Supply Chains: Technologies, Business Models and Risk Management. Proceedings of the Hamburg International Conference of Logistics (HICL), Vol. 20, pp. 31–58. epubli GmbH, Berlin (2015)
20. CGI, Inc.: 4.0 making your business more competitive. CGI Group Inc (2017)
21. Probst, L., Pedersen, B., Lonkeu, O.K., Martinez-Diaz, C., Araujo, L.N., Klitou, D., Rasmussen, M.: Digital Transformation Scoreboard 2017: Evidence of Positive Outcomes and Current Opportunities for EU Businesses. The European Commission, Brussels (2017)
22. Schröder, C.: The Challenges of Industry 4.0 for Small and Medium-Sized Enterprises. Friedrich-Ebert-Stiftung, Bonn (2016)
23. Ahadi, N., Tangthong, S.: Structural equation model of variables affecting firm's market value in precious mineral mining industry: case of Eastern African community. J. Int. Bus. Entrep. Dev. **13**(2), 197–215 (2021)
24. Hamdi, A.E., Maryati, M., Hamdin, M.S.: The potential of nature tourism at Muar and Tangkak Districts, Johor, Malaysia. IOP Conf. Ser.: Earth Environ. Sci. **269**(1), 012008 (2019, July)
25. Omar, Y.M., Minoufekr, M., Plapper, P.: Business analytics in manufacturing: current trends, challenges and pathway to market leadership. Oper. Res. Perspect. **6**, 100127 (2019)
26. Ralston, P., Blackhurst, J.: Industry 4.0 and resilience in the supply chain: a driver of capability enhancement or capability loss? Int. J. Prod. Res. **58**(16), 5006–5019 (2020)

27. Preindl, R., Nikolopoulos, K., Litsiou, K.: Transformation strategies for the supply chain: the impact of Industry 4.0 and digital transformation. Supply Chain. Forum: Int. J. **21**(1), 26–34 (2020)
28. Ahadi, N., Tangthong, S.: Impact of organisation environment on control system and technological innovation for improving the firm performance of gold mining projects: case of Eastern African community. J. Glob. Bus. Adv. **15**(5), 621–642 (2022)
29. Ma, X., Wang, J., Bai, Q.,Wang, S.: Optimization of a three-echelon cold chain considering freshness-keeping efforts under cap-and-trade regulation in Industry 4.0. Int. J. Prod. Econ. **220**, 107457 (2020)
30. Flynn, J., Dance, S., Schaefer, D.: Industry 4.0 and its potential impact on employment demographics in the UK. Adv. Transdiscipl. Eng. **6**, 239–244 (2017)
31. Lin, K.C., Shyu, J.Z., Ding, K.: A cross-strait comparison of innovation policy under Industry 4.0 and sustainability development transition. Sustainability **9**(5), 786 (2017)
32. Ardito, L., Petruzzelli, A.M., Panniello, U.,Garavelli, A.C.: Towards Industry 4.0: mapping digital technologies for supply chain management-marketing integration. Bus. Process. Manag. J. **25**(2), 323–346 (2018)
33. Rajput, S., Singh, S.P.: Connecting circular economy and Industry 4.0. Int. J. Inf. Manage. **49**, 98–113 (2019)
34. Von Bertalanffy, L.: The meaning of general system theory. Gen. Syst. Theory: Found. Dev. Appl. **30**, 53 (1973)
35. Chikere, C.C., Nwoka, J.: The systems theory of management in modern day organizations—a study of Aldgate congress resort limited Port Harcourt. Int. J. Sci. Res. Publ. **5**(9), 1–7 (2015)
36. Sony, M., Naik, S.: Industry 4.0 integration with socio-technical systems theory: a systematic review and proposed theoretical model. Technol. Soc. **61**, 101248 (2020)
37. Masood, T., Sonntag, P.: Industry 4.0: adoption challenges and benefits for SMEs. Comput. Ind. **121**, 103261 (2020)
38. Weking, J., Stöcker, M., Kowalkiewicz, M., Böhm, M., Krcmar, H.:. Leveraging Industry 4.0—a business model pattern framework. Int. J. Prod. Econ. **225**, 107588 (2020)
39. Mohelska, H., Sokolova, M.: Management approaches for Industry 4.0—the organizational culture perspective. Technol. Econ. Dev. Econ. **24**(6), 2225–2240 (2018)
40. Duarte, S., Cruz-Machado, V.: Exploring linkages between lean and green supply chain and the Industry 4.0. In: Proceedings of the Eleventh International Conference on Management Science and Engineering Management, Vol. 11, pp. 1242–1252. Springer (2018)
41. Di Maria, E., Bettiol, M., Capestro, M., Furlan, A.: Do Industry 4.0 technologies lead to more (and better) knowledge? In: European Conference on Knowledge Management, Academic Conferences International Limited. pp. 174–181, September 2018
42. Bellantuono, N., Nuzzi, A., Pontrandolfo, P., Scozzi, B.: Digital transformation models for the I4. 0 transition: lessons from the change management literature. Sustainability **13**(23), 12941 (2021)
43. Liboni, L.B., Cezarino, L.O., Jabbour, C.J.C., Oliveira, B.G., Stefanelli, N.O.: Smart industry and the pathways to HRM 4.0: implications for SCM. Supply Chain. Manag.: Int. J. **24**, 124–146 (2019)
44. Hofmann, E., Sternberg, H., Chen, H., Pflaum, A., Prockl, G.: Supply chain management and Industry 4.0: conducting research in the digital age. Int. J. Phys. Distrib. Logist. Manag. **49**(10), 945–955 (2019)
45. Brinch, M., Stentoft, J., Jensen, J.K.: Big data and its applications in supply chain management: findings from a Delphi study. In: Hawaii International Conference on System Sciences, 2017
46. Interreg Europe: Definition of I4.0 Public Policy Initiative (2020, June 20). https://projects2014-2020.interregeurope.eu/fileadmin/user_upload/tx_tevprojects/library/file_1606752330.pdf
47. Romero, D., Flores, M., Herrera, M., Resendez, H.: Five management pillars for digital transformation integrating the lean thinking philosophy. In: 2019 IEEE International conference on Engineering, technology and Innovation (ICE/ITMC), 1–8. IEEE, June 2019
48. Le Grand, T., Deneckere, R.: COOC: an agile change management method. In: 2019 IEEE 21st Conference on Business Informatics (CBI), Vol. 2, pp. 28–37. IEEE, July 2019

49. Verina, N., Titko, J. Digital transformation: conceptual framework. In: Proceedings of the International Scientific Conference Contemporary Issues in Business, Management and Economics Engineering, pp. 9–10, May 2019
50. Alsmairat, M.A.K., Mushtaha, A.S., Hammad, M.S.A.: Understanding the relationship between supply chain risk and lean operations performance. Pol. J. Manag. Stud. **27**(1), 7–25 (2023)
51. Kemendi, Á., Michelberger, P., Mesjasz-Lech, A.: Industry 4.0 and 5.0—organizational and competency challenges of enterprises. Pol. J. Manag. Stud. **26**(2), 209–232 (2022)
52. Kinelski, G.: Smart city 4.0 as a set of social synergies. Pol. J. Manag. Stud. **26**(1), 92–106 (2022)
53. Toušek, Z., Hinke, J., Gregor, B., Prokop, M., Streimikiene, D.: Shareholder value creation within the supply chain—working capital perspective. Pol. J. Manag. Stud. **26**(1), 310–324 (2022)
54. Sytnik, I., Stopochkin, A., Wielki, J., Edaich, S., Sytnik, B. Prerequisites and scenarios for the EU economy transformation inlight of Industry 4.0 development. J. Int. Stud. **16**(2), 85–101 (2023)
55. Sytnik et al.: Explored new economic model centered on the proactive adoption of Industry 4.0 technologies that holds the potential to facilitate the European Union's economic recovery from the crisis and transition to a higher level of socio-economic development (2023)
56. Dankiewicz, R., Balawejder, B., Chudy-Laskowska, K., Britchenko, I.: Impact factors and structural analysis of the state's financial security. J. Int. Stud. (2071-8330) **15**(4), 80–92 (2022)
57. Diep, N.T.N., Canh, T.Q.: Impact analysis of peer-to-peer Fintech in Vietnam's banking industry. J. Int. Stud. **15**(3), 173–185 (2022)
58. Kireyeva, A.A., Kredina, A., Vasa, L., Satpayeva, Z.T.: Impact of financial technologies on economic development: theories, methods and analysis. J. Int. Stud. **14**(4), 286–303 (2021)

# An Assessment of Innovativeness, Innovative Activity and Innovation Implementation in EU-Funded Projects in the Śląskie Voivodship in Poland

**Monika Raczyńska and Joanna Kurowska-Pysz**

**Abstract** In each subsequent financial perspective, the priorities and conditions for using EU funds and the business environment in which projects co-financed from European funds are implemented change. In the years 2014–2022, the Śląskie Voivodeship used funds from the Regional Operational Program of the Śląskie Voivodeship 2014–2020 to strengthen competitiveness and employment growth in SMEs implementing technological innovations. The Program's entry into the final settlement stage has allowed us to make a comprehensive assessment of the use of EU funds and enterprises' attitudes regarding innovativeness, innovative activity, and the implementation of innovations in SMEs in the voivodship. The work aims to analyze the support of the Regional Operational Program of the Silesian Voivodeship 2014–2020 to increase innovativeness, innovative activity, and the implementation of innovation in the EU projects in the SMEs in the Silesian Voivodeship. The research area was the Śląskie Voivodeship, and the research subject was SMEs that applied for funds in the frame of the Program. The following methods were used: desk research analysis (literature, documents, publicly available secondary data for 2014–2022) and statistical methods. The authors' analysis confirmed the dependence existing, in theory, has been confirmed, e.g., innovation (here: the number of settled, completed projects) is less compared to the innovative activity of enterprises (here: applications selected for co-financing). There is less creative activity than innovativeness, understood as creative attitudes (innovative ideas submitted as approved applications for co-financing).

**Keywords** Innovation · Innovativeness · Innovative Activity · Enterprise · EU Project

M. Raczyńska (✉) · J. Kurowska-Pysz
WSB University, Cieplaka 1C Street, 41-300 Dąbrowa Górnicza, Poland
e-mail: raczynska.monika@gmail.com

J. Kurowska-Pysz
e-mail: jkurowska@wsb.edu.pl

 
S. Kot et al. (eds.), *Corporate Practices: Policies, Methodologies, and Insights in Organizational Management*, Springer Proceedings in Business and Economics,
https://doi.org/10.1007/978-981-97-0996-0_20

## 1 Introduction

Innovation is one of the most desirable features of an enterprise [1], and the ability to identify and implement innovations is one of the critical sources of market competitiveness. Therefore, enterprises are constantly seeking knowledge about innovations and sources of their financing. Technological innovations, measured in terms of new products, services, and processes, are particularly desirable [2]. Implementing technological innovation is often preceded by a time-consuming and expensive process, sometimes including research and development work [3] and periodically conducted in cooperation with science [4]. There is a common view in the research that bringing the innovation process to the stage of implementation and commercialization is a task that can only be achieved by enterprises characterized by an elevated level of innovation and innovative activity [5]. There are some factors favorable to this process within the company, e.g., trust between managers and their staff [6], effective communication [7], and innovation-driven leadership [8]. Some external factors can also support this process, e.g., the availability of intellectual capital required to develop innovation [9] and the availability of information concerning the potential support for innovative companies [10]. However, one of the barriers to developing enterprise innovation is the need for more equity capital or an unacceptable level of risk accompanying the implementation of innovative projects [11] financed with returnable money, e.g., with a loan [12]. There are many more factors related to barriers and stimulants described in literature and practice. One of the tools used to stimulate entrepreneurs' interest in implementing innovations is a subsidy [13], e.g., non-repayable financing of part or all of the costs incurred in connection with the implementation of projects, coming from, e.g., EU funds.

A European project can be a tool to implement the business strategy [14]. It is a specific combination of private and public projects [15], distinguished by, among others, the need to achieve the declared indicators within the required time, relating to, for example, the number of innovations implemented or the increase in employment in the enterprise. It is also characterized by the requirement to maintain the durability of the results for a specified period, which is directly related to the adaptation of the project results to the activities of the organization implementing it. The involvement of EU funds in pro-innovative investments of enterprises serves to improve their competitiveness in the organizational and territorial dimension; it also equalizes the development opportunities of enterprises within the European Community, raises the standard of living of citizens, and strengthens regional economies [16] and the entire European Union [17]. W. Baumol [18] emphasizes that all the economic development since the eighteenth century is due to innovation. Breakthrough innovations create entirely new products and services, business models, and, in some cases, even new markets [19]. The multidimensional impact of innovation on the functioning of enterprises, societies, and economies is beyond doubt; therefore, supporting innovative processes is one of the priorities of the European Union's socio-economic convergence policy. This is expressed in creating an incentive effect by providing subsidies to enterprises that meet the established criteria, which, thanks to these funds, strengthen innovation, develop innovative activity, and, eventually, implement innovations.

Both scientifically and in practice, several activities are undertaken to assess progress in developing innovative economies as ecosystems, including international rankings, like the European Innovation Scoreboard [20], and national and regional statistical systems. Less frequent attempts are made to assess the impact on innovation development in regions regarding instruments based on European funds, such as regional operational programs. This is due to the cyclical nature of these programs based on the 7-year financial perspectives of the European Union (e.g., 2014–2020). However, the results of their implementation can only be observed over a more extended period. This work is an attempt to assess the impact of the Regional Operational Program of the Silesian Voivodeship 2014–2020 (the ROP SLV) to increase innovativeness, innovative activity, and the implementation of innovation in the EU projects in the SMEs in the Silesian Voivodship.

## 2 Innovativeness, Innovative Activity, and Innovation Implementation: Theoretical Background

Schumpeter introduced the concept of innovation to management sciences, pointing out that it involves the formation of a new production function [21], which was identified primarily with technical or organizational innovations. According to E.M. Rogers, an innovation is an idea, practice, or object perceived as new by the one who adopts it [22]. The research and practice of creating and implementing innovations have significantly expanded the contemporary state of knowledge on this subject, firmly accepting the impact of innovations on the economic condition of enterprises. According to M. Porter, innovations should be combined with the booming financial exploitation of new ideas. The process of its implementation covers a comprehensive continuum of technical and organizational changes, from simple modifications of existing products, procedures, and practices that may be new for the company but not necessarily for the industry in which it operates to the creation of fundamentally new products and processes that were not previously known to either the company or the industry in which it operates [23]. Designing and implementing innovations is a complicated and multi-stage process. It can be conducted in enterprises with the necessary competencies [24] and resources, including financial ones, and a favorable organizational climate. The practical implementation of innovations is influenced not only by creativity and promising ideas [25], which determine innovation but also by innovative activity and the ability to implement innovations.

Innovation is a feature of economic entities and economies, meaning the ability and motivation to create, implement, and absorb innovations. Innovation can be considered at the organizational or macroeconomic level. From a macroeconomic perspective, innovation reflects the innovativeness of entities that are part of a given national or regional economic system. Achieving the required level of innovation by an enterprise is necessary to enable the development of various forms of innovative activity. These are all activities inside and outside the enterprise that lead to the introduction of new or improved products, processes, and organizations and the acquisition of new markets. Innovative activity is a dynamic concept that is realized, among others, by undertaking research and development work, staff education, exchanging know-how, joint learning, and other activities necessary to create innovations. The implementation of innovation reflects the results of the innovative activity of an enterprise or enterprise at a given time and in a specific area. The performance of innovation includes, among others, its commercial use within or outside the enterprise by the adopted business assumptions.

The presented definitions indicate that innovation is a crucial attribute of enterprises that encourages and motivates them to undertake various forms of innovative activity within and outside but does not guarantee the development of a solution that may become an innovation. Implementation of innovation, resulting from the effective and efficient innovative activity of the enterprise, including, among others, research and development work, is determined not only by technological considerations, e.g., the feasibility of the solution, but also, among others, economic considerations, e.g., the profitability of this implementation, and social relations, e.g., meeting ethical standards and norms espoused by a given organization and adaptation of innovations in the organization. These relationships are presented in Fig. 1.

For an enterprise to effectively implement an innovation, it must be innovative enough to undertake various forms of creative activity and eventually create an invention that meets the conditions for implementation. The implementation of an invention is, therefore, the final stage of the innovation process and includes all activities related to preparing the organization to accept and apply the invention [31]. The

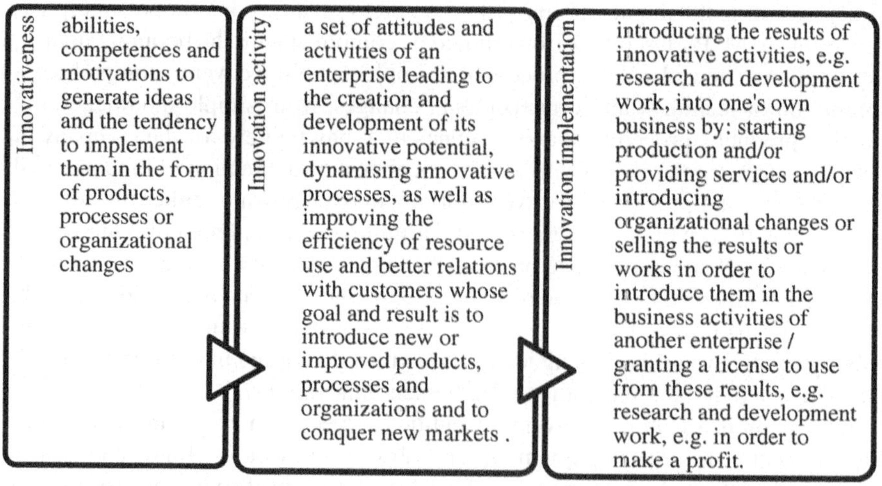


**Fig. 1** Relation among: innovativeness, innovative activity and innovation implementation. *Source* own study based on: [26–30]

efficiency and effectiveness of enterprises in implementing innovations results from, among others, their innovative potential, which includes, among others, financial resources, e.g., their own or external funds that enable financing the costs incurred in connection with the innovation process [32]. Environmental conditions that may facilitate or hinder the development and implementation of innovations are also critical. Such a factor is, among others, the availability of capital, which often determines any innovative activity and risks related to a creative project [33]. The incentive effect, associated with the provision of regional aid (subsidies or preferential loans) to enterprises interested in implementing innovations, may be introduced by stimulating the innovativeness of enterprises, e.g., increased interest in applying for grants, development of innovative activity (including training of staff in management EU projects), and ultimately in the implementation of innovations (including research and development work completed with commercialization). This work analyses these dependencies on the example of using funds from the ROP SLV in projects developing innovations in small and medium-sized enterprises in the Silesian Voivodeship.

## 3 The Development and Implementation of the EU-Funded Projects Focused on Innovation in the Silesian Voivodeship

The primary tool that supports the development and implementation of the EU-funded projects focused on innovation in the Silesia Voivodeship is the ROP SLV. It is one of the EU programs financing commercial projects to implement technological innovation in enterprises. The European Regional Development Fund has invested in the ROP SLV, aiming to reduce differences in the level of development of regions in the EU and to strengthen the EU's economic, social, and territorial cohesion. It was also crucial to boost relations between business and science, aiming for the more vital involvement of universities in the innovation processes [34]. In the programming period 2014–2020, the ROP SLV had the largest budget of funds among all regional operational programs, nearly EUR 3.47 billion, approximately 11% of the entire allocation granted at the beginning of the programming period for regional operational programs in Poland. As a result, fourteen areas (priority axes) were identified. Around EUR 305 million were allocated to Priority Axis III, Strengthening the competitiveness of SMEs, aiming to increase the competitiveness and innovation of SMEs, tailored to regional development needs and the regional smart specializations.

The EU projects implementing technological innovations in enterprises were co-financed by the Programme in the frame of the Priority Axis III Competitiveness of SMEs, Measure 3.2 Innovations in SMEs as one of the following types of projects:

1. Implementation and commercialization of product and process innovations;
2. Investments in SMEs.

Bearing in mind the definition of technological innovation according to the *Oslo Manual* (1992, 1997) [35], it can be recognized when a new or significantly improved product is introduced to the market or when a new or enhanced process is applied in production (technological development and process innovations), whereby the product or process is unique, at least from the point of view of the company introducing it. According to the Oslo Manual, an innovation may mean one notable change or minor incremental changes that constitute a meaningful change [36].

As mentioned above, J.A. Schumpeter focused on technical innovations and the capitalist economy of the early twentieth century, based on large, concentrated mass industry and the most critical factors of production, land, labor, and capital. Nowadays, the importance of knowledge and information has increased. Innovation involves many scientific, technological, organizational, financial, and commercial activities. Empirical research also adopts a broad approach (in the *general sense*) of creation as a "subjective novelty," e.g., referring to any idea, service, or sound that someone perceives as new (it may have existed for a long time but it may be an innovation for a person who sees it as new).

Technological innovation can be perceived as a process innovation or a product innovation. Process innovation is the introduction of new or significantly improved production or delivery methods into practice in the enterprise. In contrast, product innovation is the introduction of a new good or service by a given enterprise or the significant improvement of previously offered goods or services concerning their characteristics or intended use [37]. According to the ROP SLV, two types of technological innovation can be co-financed. Process innovation is focused on implementing into practice in an enterprise a new or significantly improved production or delivery method. This includes significant changes in technology, devices, and/or software. Product innovation is related to a given enterprise's introduction to the market to a new product or service or significantly improved in terms of its functional characteristics or the utility purposes it is intended to serve. This includes improvements in the technical characteristics, components, and materials used and the software that is an integral part of the product, as well as improvements that facilitate the use of the product by the user [29]. According to the rules of the ROP SLV, the technological innovation implemented as a result of the project had to be used in the Silesian Voivodeship for no longer than three years (36 months to the date of submission of the application for the subsidy funded by the ROP SLV). Projects involving introducing an innovative product/service or process to the market, at least on the scale of the Silesian Voivodeship, were supported.

The process of creating, preparing, implementing, and using technological innovation by an enterprise as part of a project co-financed by the ROP SLV can be referred to as the three elements described above: innovation, innovative activity, and innovation implementation. They are necessary to adapt innovations in the enterprise [38] and, simultaneously, require ensuring an appropriate approach to managing the innovation process, including through an EU project [39]. The implementation phases of a project aimed at implementing a technological innovation, based on funding from the ROP SLV, can be assigned to the steps of the innovation process. The innovativeness of the enterprise corresponds to the synthetically presented stages of the EU project:

- initiating the project (defining the problem to be solved, using the company's abilities, motivation, and inclination to create an idea for innovation);
- developing the project and applying for a subsidy (planning the innovation process and its preparation in accordance with the guidelines of the ROP SLV);
- obtaining co-financing from the ROP SLV (meeting the formal and substantive requirements for projects co-financed by the ROP SLV and qualifying the project for implementation. The start of the project, innovative activity, sometimes occurs after submitting the application for co-financing before the results, which is, however, associated with a more significant threat).

If the required level of innovation characterizes the organization, the potential to create an idea for innovation is released. Often, only obtaining funds from the ROP SLV makes it possible to undertake innovative activity and start implementing a project leading to the implementation of innovation. At this stage, the tasks planned in the project are performed, which should lead to the expected results and goals of the project by the guidelines of the ROP SLV. Enterprises that receive support from the ROP SLV implement and settle projects and submit required reports on work progress. Many projects that have yet to receive funding from the ROP SLV are not continued due to the lack of capital necessary to finance them and financial difficulties at further stages of implementation. In this way, many valuable ideas for innovation may fail because, among others, they need more financial resources to develop them.

The implementation of an innovation, as a positive result of innovative activity, can be assigned in an EU project to the stage of adaptation of the innovation, e.g., implementation in one's own business, its commercialization based on the adopted business model within at least three years from the end of the project. Not all projects end with implementing innovations, resulting from circumstances that make project implementation difficult or impossible. Therefore, despite the innovative activity, it is only sometimes possible to execute the invention per the adopted business model and move to the phase of its adaptation by the organization.

## 4 Methodology

The conclusions from the theoretical part of the work prove that the determinant of an enterprise's innovative activity is the appropriate level of innovativeness, and the determinant of the implementation of innovations is a creative activity, e.g., including the implementation of R&D results related to the performance of innovations. Based on these research assumptions, the research problem of the work was formulated, which includes the question about the impact of the use of the ROP SLV funds on innovation, innovative activity, and implementation of innovations in enterprises implementing EU projects.

This formulation of the research problem made it possible to assess the preparation of enterprises in the Silesian Voivodeship for the effective implementation of innovations. The projects concerning the performance of technological innovation are characterized by unique solutions and approaches to planning, organizing, motivating, and controlling systems. They are also subject to detailed EU guidelines and require a specific methodology for managing a project co-financed from EU funds, which is a critical factor determining the success of the innovation implementation.

The work aims to analyze the support of the ROP SLV to increase innovativeness, innovative activity, and the implementation of innovation in the EU projects in the SMEs in the Silesian Voivodship.

The research area was the Śląskie Voivodeship, and the subject of the research was SMEs that applied for funds in the frame of the ROP SLV, under the calls on the Priority Axis III Competitiveness of SMEs, Measure 3.2 Innovations in SMEs. The research concerned the period of 2014–2022.

To achieve the aim of the work, the following methods were used:

- desk research (literature, documents), using the techniques: examination of documents, analysis of secondary data, e.g., source documentation, legal acts, etc.;
- statistical methods; technique: statistical analyses.

The authors analyzed, among others, previous research, as well as publicly available secondary data for the period 2014–2022 on the use of funds from the ROP SLV and the results of the mid-term evaluation [40] of this Program, which provided data for conducting further statistical analyses and formulated conclusions. Quantitative data for statistical analysis were used from the list of projects under Priority Axis III Competitiveness of SMEs, Measure 3.2 Innovations in SMEs, and the ROP SLV 2014–2020.

Considering the study's novelty, it should be emphasized that the EU funds are tools to support the socio-economic development of regions and enterprises, especially in less-developed and backward EU territories [41]. In each subsequent financial perspective, the priorities and conditions for using EU funds and the business environment in which projects co-financed from European funds are implemented change, and this issue requires constant analysis. In 2014–2022, the Silesia Voivodeship used funds from the ROP SLV to strengthen competitiveness and employment growth in SMEs implementing technological innovations. The entry of the ROP SLV into the final stage of settlement has allowed the authors to assess the use of EU funds and the enterprises' attitudes regarding innovativeness, innovative activity, and implementation of innovations in SMEs in the Śląskie Voivodship.

## 5 Results

Table 1 presents data on the number of projects under individual calls for proposals under Priority Axis III named Competitiveness of SMEs, Measure 3.2 Innovations in SMEs, the ROP SLV (2014–2022), which were assessed and settled.

A comprehensive review of the relationship among the number of applications submitted to the calls reflecting the innovativeness of enterprises, the number of projects selected to be implemented under Priority Axis III Competitiveness of SMEs, Measure 3.2 Innovations in SMEs, the ROP SLV reflecting the innovative activities of these companies and the number of settled projects reflecting the innovation implementation is presented in Fig. 1.

Legend: (a) data for nine calls (1 to 9); (b) the date on the first six calls (from 1 to 6), excluding calls for COVID-19; Innovativeness—Number of submitted applications for co-financing [pcs.]; Innovative activity—Applications selected for co-financing [pcs.]; Innovation implementation—Number of settled projects [pcs.]

Source: own study based on: [42]

Figure 2 confirms the dependence existing in theory, innovation implementation (here: the number of settled, completed projects) is less compared to the examples of innovative activity of enterprises (here: applications selected for co-financing). There is less innovative activity than innovativeness understood as innovative ideas submitted as approved applications for co-financing. Figure 2 was developed based on data from Table 1, which are more detailed results than those presented in Fig. 2. Table 1 and Fig. 2 show that up to the sixth competition, under which applications for co-financing were accepted from 30/01/2020 to 30/04/2020, innovation decreased, the activity of enterprises that submitted their ideas to a lesser extent on innovative activity and innovation (Fig. 1). During the sixth call for Action 3.2 Innovations in SMEs of the ROP SLV 2014–2020, only 110 applications were submitted. It was the lowest value for the ROP SLV. In 2017 and 2018, two calls for proposals were finalized, which brought cumulatively more applications (855) than for the competition starting in 2015 (the first call), 630 applications. However, under three subsequent calls for proposals (since 2019: call no. 4, 5, 6), 401 applications have been submitted. Therefore, the number of applications from one call for proposals completed in 2017 (the second call), 555 applications, was not reached. The increase in the number of submitted applications (here: innovativeness) in the competition no. 7 (Table 1) was associated with many changes favouring enterprises in the submission process. A comparison of the number of submitted applications for co-financing for the last three calls for proposals requires more detailed analyses. Until July 23, 2022 (Table 2), 302 projects (17.58% of projects selected for co-financing) for nine calls, and after excluding the last three calls – 193 projects (23.80% of projects selected for co-financing under six competitions) have been suspended. This means that the enterprises applied for termination of the contract for co-financing, or the decision to terminate the contract was made by the subsidising institution, or the enterprise did not sign the contract at all due to various circumstances.

**Table 1** Results of submissions to calls under Priority Axis III Competitiveness of SMEs; Measure 3.2 Innovations in SMEs the ROP SLV (2014–2022) (data on 23/07/2022)

| Call no | Deadline of the call | Number of applications | | | | Project settled [pcs] |
|---|---|---|---|---|---|---|
| | | Submitted [pcs.] | Positively assessed at the formal assessment [pcs.] | Positively assessed in the substantive assessment [pcs.] | Selected for co-financing [pcs.] | |
| 1 | January 18, 2016 | 630 | 404 | 276 | 276 | 206 |
| 2 | February 28, 2017 | 555 | 403 | 210 | 210 | 157 |
| 3 | February 28, 2018 | 300 | 230 | 122 | 122 | 80 |
| 4 | April 18, 2019 | 157 | 130 | 75 | 75 | 41 |
| 5 | December 19, 2019 | 134 | 116 | 60 | 60 | 26 |
| 6 | April 30, 2020 | 110 | 90 | 68 | 68 | 8 |
| 7 | June 24, 2020 | 2146 | 1678 | 1413 | 664 | 182 |
| 8 | May 20, 2021 | 175 | 105 | 99 | 99 | 0 |
| 9 | June 26, 2020 | 144 | 144 | 144 | 144 | 0 |
| Total [pcs.] | | 4351 | 3300 | 2467 | 1718 | 700 |
| Total without the last three calls [pcs.] | | 1886 | 1373 | 811 | 811 | 518 |
| Percentage (in relation to total submitted [pcs.]) [%] | | 100.00% | 75.84% | 56.70% | 39.49% | 16.09% |
| Percentage without the last three calls (in relation to total submitted without the last three competitions [pcs.]) [%] | | 100.00% | 72.80% | 43.00% | 43.00% | 27.47% |

*Legend* Calls analysed separately or after their exclusion are marked
*Source* own elaboration based on: [42]

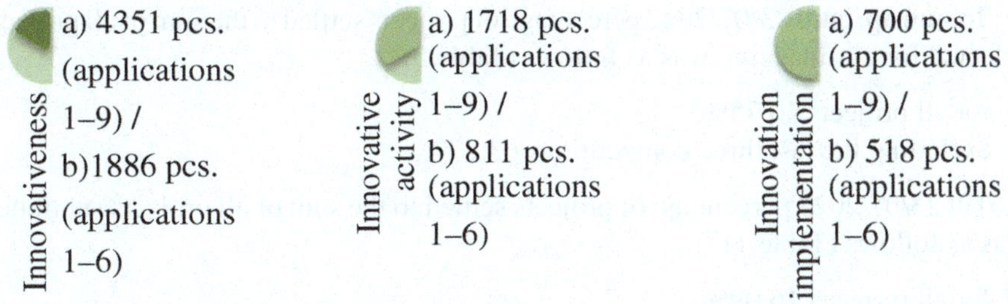


**Fig. 2** Operationalization of innovativeness, innovative activity, innovation implementation on the example of Priority Axis III Competitiveness of SMEs Measure 3.2 Innovations in SMEs, the ROP SLV 2014–2020 in 2014–2022 (data on 23/07/2022)

**Table 2** Aggregate data on projects selected for co-financing, settled, in progress, suspended under Priority Axis III Competitiveness of SMEs, Measure 3.2 Innovation in SMEs, the ROP SLV 2014–2020 in 2014–2022 (data on 23/07/2022)

| Call no {1} | The sum of all projects selected for co-financing {2 = 3 + 4 + 5 + 6} | Project settled {3} | Implementation of the project {4} | Project suspended {5} | Selected for funding {6} |
|---|---|---|---|---|---|
| 1 | 276 | 206 | 1 | 69 | 0 |
| 2 | 210 | 157 | 6 | 47 | 0 |
| 3 | 122 | 80 | 9 | 33 | 0 |
| 4 | 75 | 41 | 14 | 20 | 0 |
| 5 | 60 | 26 | 23 | 11 | 0 |
| 6 | 68 | 8 | 46 | 13 | 1 |
| 7 | 664 | 182 | 411 | 67 | 4 |
| 8 | 99 | 0 | 72 | 19 | 8 |
| 9 | 144 | 0 | 106 | 23 | 15 |
| Together | 1718 | 700 | 688 | 302 | 28 |
| Percentage of selected | 100% | 40.75% | 40.05% | 17.58% | 1.62% |
| Projects without changed calls related to COVID-19: no. 7, no. 8 and no. 9 | 811 | 518 | 99 | 193 | 1 |
| Percentage of selected (without changed calls related to COVID-19: no. 7, no. 8 and no. 9) | 100.00% | 63.87% | 12.21% | 23.80% | 0.12% |

*Legend* Calls analysed separately or after their exclusion are marked
*Source* own study based on: [42]

To sum up, until 23/07/2022 percentage of projects settled to the sum of all projects selected for co-financing was as follows (Table 2):

- for all projects 40.75%,
- excluding the last three competitions 63.87%.

Till 23/07/2022 percentage of projects settled to the sum of all projects submitted was as follows (Table 1):

- for all projects 16.09%,
- excluding the last three competitions 27.47%.

## 6 Discussion and Conclusions

In research, innovativeness, innovative activity, and innovation implementation are defined in various ways. The interdependencies and relationship existing, in theory, were confirmed, i.e., fewer innovations (here: the number of settled, completed projects) compared to examples of innovative activity of enterprises (here: applications selected for co-financing). There are fewer innovative activities than innovativeness (here: innovative ideas (projects) submitted in the call). Only by April 30, 2020, innovativeness decreased, e.g., the attitude of enterprises that presented their ideas regarding innovative activities and innovations to a lesser extent. Until 23/07/2022, the percentage of projects settled about the sum of all projects selected for co-financing was 40.75% for all projects; without the last three competitions, 63.87%. For comparison, the 2016 Special CHAOS Report prepared by The Standish Group International *Special CHAOS Report 2016* shows that less than 36% of projects are completed within the assumed time, budget, and result. Till 23/07/2022, the percentage of projects settled about the sum of all projects submitted was for all projects 16.09%, excluding the last three competitions, 27.47%.

According to research, innovatively active enterprises undertake innovative activity in a narrow scope and incidentally. The studies on medium and large Polish enterprises have identified many innovatively active enterprises and only 5% of innovatively mature enterprises [43]. Those results influence national and international indicators like the European Innovation Scoreboard, described in other articles.

Analyzing the research results, one can also refer to the implementation status of the level of innovation, innovative activity, and innovation implementation planned in the ROP SLV, presented in Table 3.

Table 3 shows the level of implementation of indicator No. 1 in calls: no. 2; no. 3; no. 4, no. 9 will be achieved, as evidenced by the number of completed (settled) projects. However, in recruitment no. 5, this indicator will not be achieved considering the number of settled projects (26 completed) and projects under implementation (23 pcs.). Moreover, it will not be achieved in the call no. 5 indicator no. 3 (planned value 52 pcs.). However, the shortage of indicator values from call no. 5 should be compensated by the surplus of the above-value achieved. Indicators in recruitment, e.g., no. 2; no. 3; no. 4, no. 9. The cumulated published indicators (including several

**Table 3** Comparison of the status of projects and selected assumed indicators for Priority Axis III Competitiveness of SMEs, Measure 3.2 Innovations in SMEs, the ROP SLV (data on 23/07/2022)

| Call no | Sum | 1 | 2 | 3 | 4 | 5 | 6 | 7 | 8 | 9 |
|---|---|---|---|---|---|---|---|---|---|---|
| **Status of the project in the call** | | | | | | | | | | |
| Selected for funding [pcs.] | 28 | 0 | 0 | 0 | 0 | 0 | 1 | 4 | 8 | 15 |
| Project implementation [pcs.] | 688 | 1 | 6 | 9 | 14 | 23 | 46 | 411 | 72 | 106 |
| Project settled [pcs.] | 700 | 206 | 157 | 80 | 41 | 26 | 8 | 182 | 0 | 0 |
| Sum | 1416 | 207 | 163 | 89 | 55 | 49 | 55 | 597 | 80 | 121 |
| **Indicator** | | | | | | | | | | |
| 1. Number of enterprises receiving subsidies [pcs.] | 318 | * | 80 | 28 | 34 | 61 | * | * | * | 115 |
| 2. Number of enterprises supported to introduce products new to the market [pcs.] | 151 | * | 8 | 3 | 29 | 46 | * | * | * | 65 |
| 3. Number of enterprises supported to introduce products new to the enterprises [pcs.] | 300 | * | 80 | 28 | 33 | 52 | * | * | * | 107 |

*Legend* *No value was specified in the guidelines, e.g., the estimated value of the indicator planned to be achieved during the recruitment process was not estimated or not made available
*Source* own study based on: [42]

enterprises) will be possible to achieve. Another case is budget, time, scope, and quality. Those aspects could be analyzed after or during the durability period. As part of the mid-term evaluation [40], the ROP SLV budget for Measure 3.2 Innovations in SMEs was expected to be used (contracted). The ROP SLV was Poland's most significant regional operational program in the 2014–2020 financial perspective, which will be spent until December 31, 2023, by EU guidelines.

Poland also had the largest budget allocated for 2014–2020 under the EU cohesion policy, which proves the country's development needs, including innovations. By June 30, 2023, the budget for Poland has not yet been fully used, like many other EU countries. By June 30, 2023, the planned indicator regarding supported enterprises had not been achieved at the EU level. This may be due to the prolonged period of project implementation, which was influenced by, among others, factors such as the COVID-19 pandemic, the war in Ukraine, or the international energy crisis caused by this conflict.

But despite the above indicators (including several enterprises), it is likely to achieve. Another case is budget, time, scope, and quality. A comparison of the number of submitted applications for co-financing for the last three calls for proposals requires more detailed analyses. However, innovation profile data should not be interpreted as "more is better." The data should be used to understand better the differences in the structure of business types in a country, helping policymakers to design policies that better target different businesses [20].

The following were indicated as recommendations:

- enterprises and Managing Authorities of Operational Programs whose task is to take care of the use of EU funds, and familiarize themselves with the indicators and terminology related to the management of the EU project of implementing technological innovation, especially connected with the new programming period;
- many projects which do not get support may have problems in future or last longer, so it could be good to take care of the project implementation in its whole process related to innovativeness, innovative activity and innovation implementation;
- enterprises that are novice innovators should become acquainted with the principles of using European funds; good practices, for example of more experienced companies, Managing Authorities of Operational Programmes; consulting companies or clusters and networks.

The level of innovativeness and intensity of innovative activities, as well as the number of implemented innovations, determine the international competitiveness of SMEs [44]. However, the EU funds can support only a minority of innovative-driven businesses; therefore, leveraging the innovativeness and competitiveness of the company requires additional support on the national and regional levels.

## 7 Limitations of the Research and Further Directions of Study

The research problem is a complex topic, explored in this work only to a certain extent. The authors focused on the ROP SLV, and similar programs in other Polish regions require separate analysis since they are diverse. The work analyses the results of the ROP SLV 2014–2020 implementation in years 2014–2022. However, some projects are being implemented by the end of 2023. The research results do not consider enterprises' different levels of innovativeness (separate studies), a disadvantage of innovation indicators in the literature.

The need for further research was recognized in the frame of analysis of the 2014–2020 financial perspective, e.g., after the durability period and the end of the ROP SLV 2014–2020 (ex-post) as well as in terms of comparison of research results with results outside the Silesian Voivodeship, Poland (example: [45]), and other programs. An exciting direction for further research can be the recognition of determinants of decline and low innovativeness, innovative activity, and innovation implementation.

## References

1. Szczepańska-Woszczyna, K.: The importance of organizational culture for innovation in the company. Forum Scientiae Oeconomia **2**(3), 27–39 (2014)
2. Barney, J.B., Foss, N.J., Lyngsie, J.: The role of senior management in opportunity formation: direct involvement or reactive selection? Strat. Manag. J. **39**(5), 1325–1349 (2018)
3. Dziallas, M., Blind, K.: Innovation indicators throughout the innovation process: an extensive literature analysis. Technovation **80**, 3–29 (2019)

4. Ismail, N., Kot, S., Abd Aziz, A. S., Rajiani, I.: From innovation to market: integrating university and industry perspectives towards commercialising research output. Forum Sci. Oecon. **8**(4), 99–115 (2020)
5. Bedi, H.S.: Innovativeness, business performance and environmental uncertainty: a multivariate configuration. Int. J. Bus. Innov. Res. **18**(3), 328–345 (2019)
6. Oláh, J., Hidayat Y.A., Popp, J., Lakner, Z., Kovács, S.: Integrative trust and innovation on financial performance in disruptive era, Econ & Sociol **14**(2), (2021)
7. Lakner, Z., Kiss, A., Popp, J., Zéman, Z., Máté, D., Oláh, J.: From basic research to competitiveness: an econometric analysis of the global pharmaceutical sector. Sustainability **11**(11), 3125 (2019)
8. Szczepańska-Woszczyna, K., Kurowska-Pysz, J:. Sustainable business development through leadership in SMEs. Ekonomia i Zarządzanie **8**(3), 57–69 (2016)
9. Kurowska-Pysz, J.: Development of student's professional competences within the framework of science-business cooperation, Pol. J. Manag. Stud. **9** (2014)
10. Monteiro, A.P., Vale, J., Leite, E., Lis, M., Kurowska-Pysz, J.: The impact of information systems and non-financial information on company success. Int. J. Account. Inf. Syst. **45**, 100557 (2022)
11. Wach, K., Maciejewski, M., Głodowska, A.: Inside entrepreneurial orientation: do risk-taking and innovativeness influence proactiveness? Econ & Sociol **16**(1), (2023)
12. Wellalage, N.H., Fernandez, V.: Innovation and SME finance: evidence from developing countries. Int. Rev. Financ. Anal. **66**, 101370 (2019)
13. Dvouletý, O., Srhoj, S., Pantea, S.: Public SME grants and firm performance in European Union: a systematic review of empirical evidence. Small Bus. Econ. **57**, 243–263 (2021)
14. Ahmad, M., Ahmed, Z., Bai, Y., Qiao, G., Popp, J., Oláh, J.: Financial inclusion, technological innovations, and environmental quality: analyzing the role of green openness. Front. Environ. Sci. **10**, 851263, (2022)
15. Trocki, M. (ed.): Zarządzanie projektem europejskim, Wydawnictwo PWE, Warszawa (2006)
16. Borowiecki, R., Makieła, Z.J.: Determinants of development of entrepreneurship and innovation in local areas of economic activity: a case study analysis. Forum Sci. Oecon. **7**(2), 7–24 (2019)
17. Becker, S.O., Egger, P.H., Von Ehrlich, M.: Going NUTS: The effect of EU Structural Funds on regional performance. J. Public Econ. **94**(9–10), pp. 578–590 (2010)
18. Baumol, W.: The free-market innovation machine: analyzing the growth miracle of capitalism, Princeton University Press, Princeton, p 25 (2002)
19. European Commission: A renewed European agenda for research and innovation Europe's chance to shape its future, communication from The Commission to The European Parliament, The European Council, The Council, The European Economic and Social Committee and The Committee of The Regions. COM (2018) 306 final, Bruksela 15.05.2018, p 11 (2018)
20. European Commission, Hollanders, H, Es-Sadki, N.: European Innovation Scoreboard 2022—Methodology Report, The report was written by H. Hollanders and N. Es-Sadki, Maastricht University (UNU-MERIT) as part of the Development of the European Innovation Scoreboard project for the European Commission, Directorate-General for Research and Innovation, This report was prepared and coordinated by Deloitte Belgium, Maastricht University/UNU-MERIT, Valdani Vicari & Associati (VVA), Brussels, pp 29, 34–36 (2022)
21. Schumpeter, J.A.: Business cycles, McGraw-Hill, New York and London, p 87 (1939)
22. Rogers, E.M.: Diffusion of Innovations, Free Press, New York, p 12 (2003)
23. Porter, M.E.: The competitive advantage of nations. The Macmillan Press Ltd., London (1990)
24. Szczepańska-Woszczyna, K., Gatnar, S.: Key competences of research and development project managers in high technology sector. Forum Sci. Oecon. **10**(3), 107–130 (2022)
25. Sońta-Drączkowska, E.: Zarządzanie projektami we wdrażaniu innowacji. Polskie Wydawnictwo Ekonomiczne, Warszawa **60–69**(78), 48–49 (2018)
26. Białoń, L.: Aktywność innowacyjna organizacji, Oficyna Wydawnicza WSM, Warszawa (2008)
27. Hurley, G.T.M., Knight, R.F.G.A.: Innovativeness: it's antecedents and impact on business performance. Ind. Mark. Manag. **33**, 429–438 (2004)

28. Mizgajska, H.: Aktywność innowacyjna polskich małych i średnich przedsiębiorstw w procesie integracji z Unią Europejską, Prace habilitacyjne 4, Wydawnictwo Akademii Ekonomicznej w Poznaniu, Poznań, p 48 (2002)
29. Śląskie Centrum Przedsiębiorczości (Silesian Center for Entrepreneurship): Competition Regulations No. RPSL.03.02.00-IP.01–24–026/20 under the Regional Operational Program of the Silesian Voivodeship for 2014–2020, Priority Axis III Competitiveness of SMEs, Measure 3.2 Innovations in SMEs, Project Type Investments in SMEs , Chorzów 7/2020
30. Wściubiak, Ł.: Aktywność innowacyjna zaawansowanych technologicznie firm produkcyjnych sektora MŚP w Polsce, rozprawa doktorska, promotor: dr hab. inż. H. Mizgajska, prof. nadzw. UEP, Uniwersytet Ekonomiczny w Poznaniu, Wydział Zarządzania, Poznań, pp 19–21, 30 (2010)
31. Hameed, M.A., Counsell, S., Swift, S.: A conceptual model for the process of IT innovation adoption in organizations. J. Eng. Technol. Manag. **29**(3), 358–390 (2012)
32. Valitov, S.M., Khakimov, A.K.: Innovative potential as a framework of innovative strategy for enterprise development. Procedia Economics and Finance **24**, 716–721, (2015)
33. Bradley, S.W., McMullen, J.S., Artz, K., Simiyu, E.M.: Capital is not enough: innovation in developing economies. J. Manag. Stud. **49**(4), 684–717 (2012)
34. Otola, I., Grabowska, M. (Eds.). Business models: innovation, digital transformation, and analytics. CRC Press. (2020)
35. OECD/Eurostat: Oslo Manual. The measurement of scientific and technological activities, Paris (1997)
36. OECD/Eurostat.: Oslo Manual, Guidelines for Collecting, Reporting and Using Data on Innovation, 4th Edition, The Measurement of Scientific, Technological and Innovation Activities, OECD Publishing, Paris/Luxembourg, pp 8, 20–21, 28–29, 34–36, 46, 60–69, 78, 80–81 (2018)
37. OECD/Eurostat.: Oslo Manual: Guidelines for Collecting and Interpreting Innovation Data, 3rd Edition Manuel d'Oslo: principes directeurs pour le recueil et l'interprétation des données sur l'innovation, 3e édition, Paris, 2005, s. 46 (Ministry of Science and Higher Education, Department of Science Strategy and Development—Polish edition; Warsaw 2008, Published in agreement with the OECD (2005/2008)
38. Ober, J.: Adaptacja innowacji w świetle zachowań organizacyjnych-wybrane aspekty. Wydawnictwo Politechniki Śląskiej (2022)
39. Ng, Y.K., Lee, V.H., Foo, A.T.L., Gan, P.L.: The relationship between knowledge management practices and technological innovation: a conceptual framework. Int. J. Manag., Knowl. Learn. **1**(1), 71–89 (2012)
40. Pracownia Badań i Doradztwa "Re-Source" Korczyński Sarapata sp.j. w ramach prowadzonego na zlecenie Urzędu Marszałkowskiego Województwa Śląskiego badania: Ewaluacja mid-term dotycząca postępu rzeczowego RPO WSL 2014–2020 oraz wkładu Programu w realizację unijnej strategii EU 2020 dla potrzeb przeglądu śródokresowego (Research and Consulting Studio "Re-Source" Korczyński Sarapata sp.j.: as part of the study commissioned by the Marshal's Office of the Silesian Voivodeship: Mid-term evaluation regarding the material progress of the ROP SLV 2014–2020 and the Programme's contribution to the implementation of the EU 2020 strategy for the needs of mid-term review), Katowice, p 135, maj (2019)
41. Meyer, D.F., Meyer, N.: Management of small and medium enterprise (SME) development: an analysis of stumbling blocks in a developing region. Pol. J. Manag. Stud. **16**(1), 127–141 (2017)
42. Śląskie Centrum Przedsiębiorczości (Silesian Center for Entrepreneurship): Lists of accepted projects, formally and substantively assessed, selected for co-financing, last accessed 2022/07/23
43. KPMG w Polsce: Dojrzałość innowacyjna przedsiębiorstw w Polsce, p 41 (2013).
44. Tadevosyan, R.: Innovations and international competitiveness: country-level evidence, Econo & Sociol **16**(3), (2023)
45. Raczyńska, M.: Analysis of enterprise innovation management in Poland. In: Lis, M., Szyszka, M. (eds.), Theory and Practice, "Logos Verlag", Berlin, pp 89–99 (2019)

# Digital Transformation in Organizations from Sibiu Country, Romania

**Adriana Milea and Lucian-Ionel Cioca**

**Abstract** The digital transformation of an organization involves the adoption and integration of digital technologies in all operational and strategic aspects of the activity. This process involves much more than just implementing digital solutions; it involves a profound change in the way of thinking and approach regarding the business model, a change that affects both the organizational culture and internal processes, the way of interaction with customers, and business partners. The digital transformation of an organization must be an ongoing process, given that digital technologies and the business environment are constantly evolving. Thus, organizations must be flexible enough to adapt to all the changes that occur quickly. This study aimed to identify and develop a set of strategic measures that address the challenges identified in the context of the integration of digital technologies. The analysis and implementation of these measures can contribute to increasing the degree of digitalization of enterprises/organizations, which will generate a series of positive effects both at the organizational level and on the entire economy; the necessary data were obtained following the analysis of studies and publications available in the scientific literature. Also, this study aimed to provide an image of the state of digitalization of enterprises/organizations in Sibiu County, Romania. By analyzing the data obtained following a survey conducted on a sample of 40 enterprises/organizations, the study sought to identify the degree of integration of digital systems within the organizations, as well as the type of digital solutions implemented and used by them.

**Keywords** Digitalization · Digital transformation · Safety · Health · Romania

A. Milea (✉) · L.-I. Cioca
Faculty of Engineering, Lucian Blaga University of Sibiu, 4 Emil Cioran Street, 550025 Sibiu, Romania
e-mail: adriana.milea@ulbsibiu.ro



S. Kot et al. (eds.), *Corporate Practices: Policies, Methodologies, and Insights in Organizational Management*, Springer Proceedings in Business and Economics,
https://doi.org/10.1007/978-981-97-0996-0_21

# 1 Introduction

Starting in 2014, the European Commission has annually monitored the progress made by the EU member states in the digital field, analyzing aspects such as human capital, connectivity, the integration of digital technology, and digital public services. The results of this analysis were summarized in the Digital Economy and Society Index (DESI) report. According to the DESI 2022 report, Romania ranks 27th out of the 27 EU member states. Also, Romania ranks at the bottom of the rankings that analyze the degree of digitization of small and medium-sized enterprises (SMEs) [31].

Digital transformation is defined as "a continuous process of using new digital technologies in everyday organizational life, which recognizes agility as a basic mechanism for the strategic renewal of an organization's business model, the collaborative approach and, the lastly, culture" [1]. Digital transformation refers to "the deep and accelerated transformation of activities, processes, skills and the business model by fully capitalizing on the changes and opportunities offered by digital technologies to maximize their impact in society, strategically and prioritized, in accordance with the changes present and future[2].

The technological advances that have taken place in recent decades in all sectors of activity, namely the integration of digital technologies within the activities of organizations, have produced significant changes both in terms of productivity and performance of organizations, but it has also had a major impact on safety and workers' well-being [3–5]. The purpose of this study was an informative one to identify the digital systems implemented and used within organizations from Sibiu County, Romania.

For this study 2 objectives were established:

1. Elaboration of a set of strategic measures, which will contribute to increasing the degree of digitization of enterprises/organizations;
2. Identification of the degree of integration of digital systems within enterprises/organizations from Sibiu County, Romania, as well as the type of digital solutions implemented and used by them

By establishing such objectives, our intention was to initiate a reflection on the degree of digitization of organizations from Sibiu County, Romania. It is then essential in this context to also assess the impact of these systems on the safety and health of workers, including how workers perceive their integration into their work.

The paper began with a description of our research methodology, followed by the presentation of the results obtained from the analysis of the collected data. In the last section of the paper, our conclusions following this study were presented, as well as the current limitations of research in this direction, including ours.

## 2 Methodology

The first part of this study involved a theoretical approach, namely an analysis of studies and publications available in the scientific literature, to identify strategic measures that can contribute to increasing the degree of digitalization of organizations.

For this study, the necessary data were obtained by using the Scopus interdisciplinary database, taking into account the fact that researchers most frequently use this database to carry out systematic analyses of the literature and previous scientometric and bibliometric analyses.

To identify the relevant studies, the following document selection criteria were applied:

1. Searching for selected keywords, in article title, abstract and keywords according to the following criteria:
2. "occupational safety and health" OR "occupational health" OR "occupational safety"
3. AND "digitalization" OR "digitalization" OR "digital"
4. Type of documents: articles, conference paper, book chapter, review, conference review, open access
5. The search period: 2010–2023
6. Language: English.

Following the application of this selection, a number of 255 publications were identified. Later, based on the analysis of the title of the documents and the abstract, a number of 25 publications were selected and included in the present study—Fig. 1.

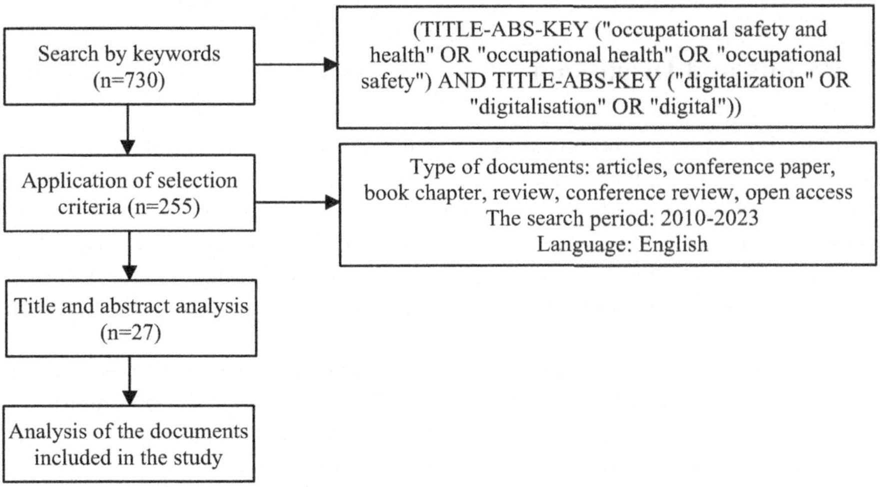


**Fig. 1** The method of selecting the publications included in the study

Studies included in the Web of Science-Core Collection and Google Scholar databases were also analyzed.

The second part of this study included the results obtained from a survey conducted on a sample of 40 enterprises/organizations from Sibiu County, Romania. The analyzed organizations are of different sizes (between 2–2400 employees) and operate in different fields of activity (production, trade, services, etc.) as can be seen in Table 1.

The enterprises/organizations were classified according to the number of employees, as follows: large company (over 250 employees), medium company (between 51–250 employees), small company (between 11–50 employees) and micro-enterprises (between 1–10 employees) (Tables 1 and 2).

For data collection and analysis, the questionnaire was used as a research tool—a Google Forms questionnaire consisting of 26 general, closed, and open questions through which data is requested. The questionnaire was distributed in the second quarter of 2023 through online means of communication (e-mail, Whatsapp application), requesting its completion by the administrators of the selected enterprises/organizations, the worker assigned to organize prevention and protection activities, or another person—appointed by the management of the organization.

The data collected based on these questionnaires were centralized and subjected to fundamental statistical analysis using the Excel application, mainly using histograms to visualize the data distribution. Through this method, the essential components of the digital transformation could be identified.

The second part of this study involves a theoretical approach, namely an analysis of the studies and publications available in the scientific literature, to identify strategic measures that can contribute to increasing the digitalization of enterprises/organizations.

## 3 Results and Discussion

Increasing the degree of digitalization of organizations is essential for their efficiency, competitiveness, and adaptability in a constantly changing world [6]. Digitalization enables the automation and optimization of repetitive processes and tasks, increasing operational efficiency. Digital systems also enable organizations to collect, store, and access information accurately and quickly, which facilitates better-informed decision-making and enables organizations to respond more effectively to market changes.

The technological, social, and organizational changes entailed by integrating digital technologies within organizations have created several opportunities to improve working conditions. However, it has been found that they also present several challenges and emerging risks regarding worker safety and health.

Based on the analysis of publications available in the scientific literature, as well as based on the data collected and analyzed within this study, a set of strategic measures was developed, which addresses the challenges identified in the context

**Table 1** The enterprises/organizations included in the study

| Field of activity | No. organizations | No. total employees | Size of the organization (no. of employees) | Classification of organizations according to no. employee | | | |
|---|---|---|---|---|---|---|---|
| | | | | Large company | Medium company | Small company | Microenterprise |
| Production | 24 | 6704 | 2–2400 | 7 | 11 | 3 | 3 |
| Trade | 12 | 2459 | 4–600 | 4 | 3 | 4 | 1 |
| Services | 4 | 694 | 3–630 | 1 | – | 2 | 1 |
| TOTAL | 40 organizations | | | | | | |

**Table 2** The field of activity of the entreprises/organizations included in the study

| The name of the organization (abbreviated) | Field of activity | |
|---|---|---|
| A | Production | The manufacture of milling products |
| TP | Production | Manufacture of paper and corrugated cardboard and paper and cardboard packaging |
| SF | Production | Manufacture of fruit and vegetable juices |
| GR | Production | Manufacture of paper and corrugated cardboard and paper and cardboard packaging |
| THP | Production | Manufacture of paper and corrugated cardboard and paper and cardboard packaging |
| RT | Production | Carpentry and carpentry works |
| RFR | Production | Wholesale trade of parts and accessories for motor vehicles |
| CGR | Production | Manufacture of abrasive products and other products from non-metallic minerals |
| CT | Production | Manufacture of abrasive products and other products from non-metallic minerals |
| MS | Production | Manufacture of other electrical equipment |
| KA | Production | Manufacture of electronic subassemblies |
| Kuk | Production | Manufacturing of tools |
| HU | Production | Manufacture of other machines and equipment for general use |
| RF | Production | Manufacture of articles from metal threads |
| SFF | Production | Manufacture of other food products |
| TGP | Production | Manufacture of plastic packaging articles |
| MC | Production | The manufacture of milling products |
| P | Production | Manufacture of fruit and vegetable juices |
| DEE | Production | Manufacture of textile articles |
| ABR | Production | Manufacture of textile articles |
| G | Production | Manufacture of underwear |
| RO | Production | Manufacture of paper and corrugated cardboard and paper and cardboard packaging |
| IM | Production | Manufacture of other machines and equipment for general use |
| SPT | Production | Printing activities |
| SSol | Services | Other professional, scientific and technical activities |
| ElC | Services | Construction works of utility projects for electricity and telecommunications |
| CWS | Services | Other business support services activities |
| VS | Services | Activities to create custom software |
| VSo | Services | Activities to create custom software |

(continued)

**Table 2** (continued)

| The name of the organization (abbreviated) | Field of activity | |
|---|---|---|
| Vis | Services | Activities to create custom software |
| VSR | Services | Activities to create custom software |
| SS | Services | Other professional, scientific and technical activities |
| EC | Services | Construction works of utility projects for electricity and telecommunications |
| DPS | Services | Consulting activities for business and management |
| GIT | Services | Activities to create custom software |
| AS | Services | Maintaining and repairing vehicles |
| BSS | Trade | Non-specialized wholesale trade |
| BRI | Trade | Wholesale trade of machines for the textile industry and of sewing and knitting machines |
| SC | Trade | Wholesale of computers, peripheral equipment and software |
| DC | Trade | Clothing retail, in specialized stores |

of the integration of digital technologies within organizations. We recommend that these measures be analyzed, evaluated, and taken into account by each organization because the implementation of these measures can contribute to increasing the degree of digitization of organizations:

- Development of a strategic digitization plan appropriate to the organization's specific needs: identifying areas that require digital improvements; establishing specific digitization objectives; identifying appropriate digital and technical solutions to achieve the objectives; allocation of the necessary resources, etc.;
- Developing an appropriate strategic plan to ensure the professional development and skills of workers, so that they have the ability to adapt to this new stage of economic development: the development of digital skills; professional training regarding the new technologies and equipment used; adequate training on relevant occupational health and safety issues; developing skills (resilience, adaptability to new changes, creativity, etc.); analyzing the current performance of workers and identifying new development and improvement needs to meet current and future job requirements [7–16];
- Designation of a person responsible for the implementation of the digitalization strategy to ensure the effective development of the digitalization process, the achievement of the established objectives, the efficient use of the allocated resources, the identification of the most appropriate digital solutions, etc.;
- Assessing the existing infrastructure in organizations and adapting it (where applicable) to facilitate the integration of new technologies [7];

- Ergonomic assessment of workplaces and establishment of appropriate preventive measures (adaptation of work equipment, worker posture, workload) to prevent musculoskeletal disorders [9, 12];
- The rigorous identification and assessment of risks and the choice of solutions and appropriate safety measures to prevent the risks of occupational injury and illness [5, 17–19];
- Adopting a sociotechnical approach in the organization of workers' activity [4, 20] to facilitate the integration of digital technologies by: consulting and involving workers in the process of integrating digital technologies; adequate training of workers in the use of new technologies; ergonomic workplace organization; ensuring adequate technical support for workers regarding the use of new technologies, etc. [9];
- Evaluation of existing policies and procedures in the field of occupational health and safety and their adaptation to new requirements [21];
- Promoting a culture of worker safety at work and developing a plan of measures to ensure the maintenance of workers' health and well-being: their active involvement in the process of integrating new digital technologies; their involvement in the decision-making process regarding the established safety measures, regarding the process of identification, evaluation and management of workplace-specific risks; the active involvement of workers in the process of developing a program for monitoring workers' health; providing training and professional development programs for workers to facilitate their adaptation to new working conditions; promoting a positive work environment, etc. [16, 22, 23];
- Identification and implementation of appropriate technical and organizational measures to ensure the security and confidentiality of workers' personal data, according to the provisions of Regulation (EU) 2016/679 on data protection [17, 22, 24, 25].

The questionnaire used to obtain the necessary data was structured in 3 parts (Fig. 2).

The first part of the questionnaire included a set of 16 items aimed at identifying the digital solutions implemented/integrated within the surveyed entreprises/organizations, the synthesis of the answers obtained being presented in the following:

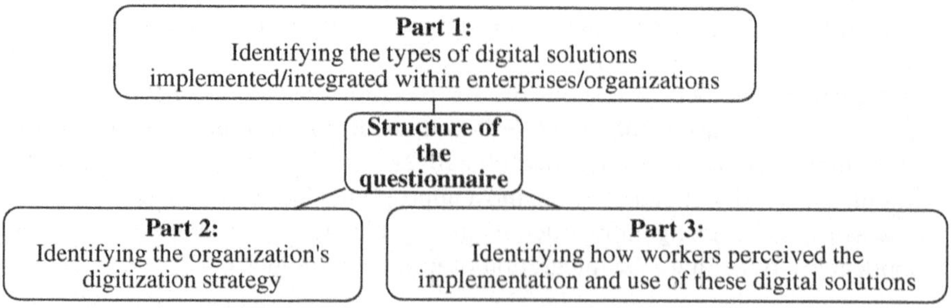


**Fig. 2** The way the questionnaire is structured

- 55% of the analyzed organizations use time and task management software—for organizing and prioritizing activities, for setting deadlines, collaborating with colleagues, tracking progress in completing tasks (Trello; Asana; Todoist; Microsoft To Do; ClickUp; Wrike; etc.)—Fig. 3, point 1;
- 97,5% of organizations use online communication and collaboration platforms for information sharing, real-time collaboration, virtual meetings and collaborative project management (Microsoft Teams; Slack; Google Workspace; Zoom, etc.)—Fig. 3, point 2;
- 35% of organizations have implemented computer monitoring and worker activity analysis software—to monitor work performance and behavior, computer activity, determining active/inactive time spent using applications or websites, activity monitoring on documents (Cyclope; CleverControl; Statlook; etc.)—Fig. 4, point 1;
- 92,5% of organizations use document and information management tools—to store, share and access relevant documents and information, to organize information more efficiently and facilitate remote collaboration (Dropbox; Google Drive; Microsoft SharePoint, etc.)—Fig. 4, point 2;
- 62,5% of organizations have implemented task automation software or workflow automation tools—for easy and quick approval of documents, to help eliminate

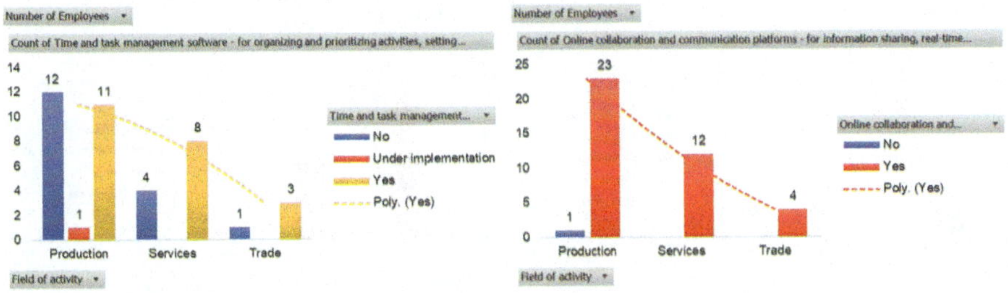


**Fig. 3** Use of digital systems: 1. Time and task management software; 2. Online collaboration and communication platforms

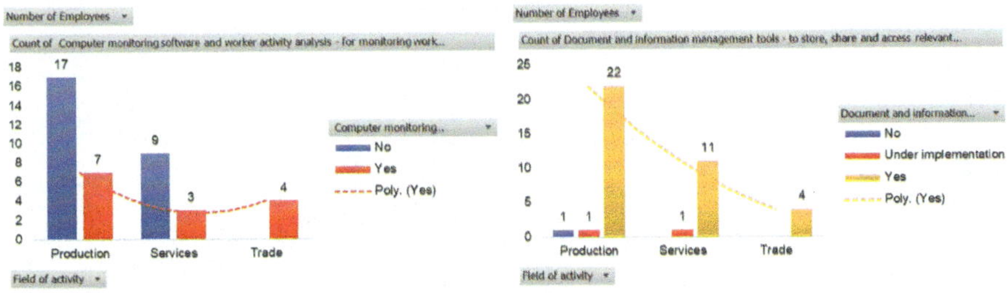


**Fig. 4** Use of digital systems: 1. Computer monitoring software and worker activity analysis; 2. Document and information management tools

repetitive and monotonous tasks, allowing workers to focus on more valuable and creative activities—Fig. 5, point 1;

- 97,5% of organizations use cyber security tools—to protect sensitive information and prevent computer attacks (anti-virus; firewall; two-step authentication; data protection software; etc.)—Fig. 5, point 2;
- 15% of organizations use virtual assistants - digital platforms through which workers can request information in real time and receive answers that help save time that can be invested in other activities—Fig. 6, point 1;
- 30% of organizations use tools for monitoring the location of workers - to collect data about the movement and location of em-ployees: location sensors, accelerometers, etc.—Fig. 6, point 2;
- 60% of organizations have hybrid workspaces, which combine the physical workspace with the virtual environment and are equipped with audiovisual technology, cameras, microphones, etc.—to improve real-time communication with employees, customers, both remotely and in person—Fig. 7, point 1;
- 30% of organizations have integrated workspace management systems—which monitor workspace occupancy, planning and booking workspaces, meeting rooms and contribute to optimizing the use of physical space and its efficient use—Fig. 7, point 2;

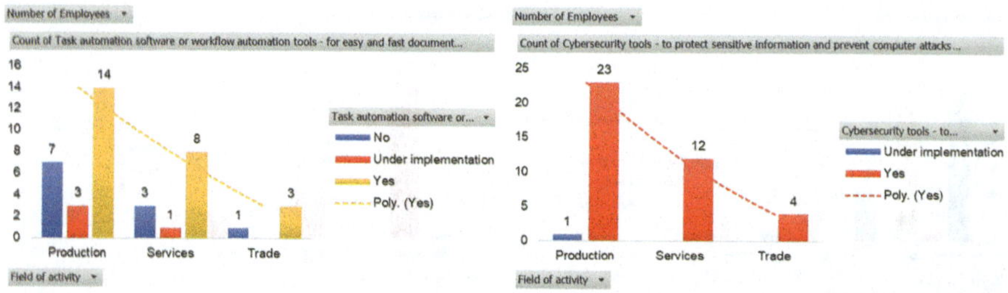


**Fig. 5** Use of digital systems: 1. Task automation software or workflow tools; 2. Cybersecurity tools

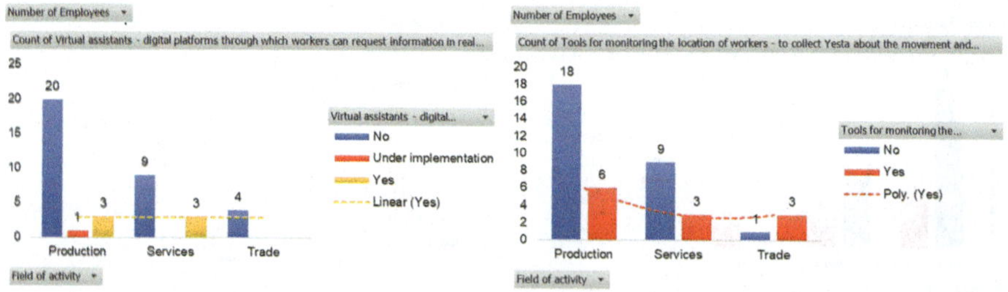


**Fig. 6** Use of digital systems: 1. Virtual assistants; 2. Tools for monitoring the location of workers

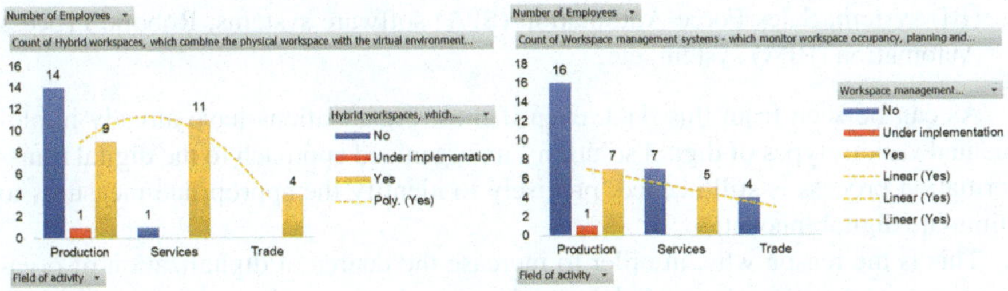


**Fig. 7** Use of digital systems: 1. Hybrid workspaces; 2. Workspace management systems

- 67,5% of organizations have ergonomic, intelligent desks and chairs—to adjust them according to the conformation of the user's body, to detect the posture and movement of employees—Fig. 8, point 1;
- 60% of the organizations have integrated systems to optimize indoor facilities (based on motion sensors, sensors for detecting the presence of workers in the premises, sensors for monitoring air quality, temperature sensors, sensors for detecting the level of illumination)—which have the ability to optimize different systems (lighting, air conditioning, ventilation, security, etc.)—Fig. 8, point 2;

- Most organizations use various health and wellness apps and devices - that monitor and promote worker health and wellness (physical activity trackers, posture monitoring apps, relaxation and stress management programs, wellness coaching apps, other apps/devices);
- 75% of organizations offer workers the opportunity to carry out their activity in a place other than the one organized by the employer—Fig. 9, point 1;
- 35% of organizations have implemented and use various e-learning platforms for training and evaluating employees—Fig. 9, point 2;
- Other types of digital systems implemented by organizations are: time attendance applications, document access control applications (SafetyCloud), interaction Kiosk systems that allow users to interact with different services or information, Enterprise Resource Planning (ERP) software systems, Business Intelligence

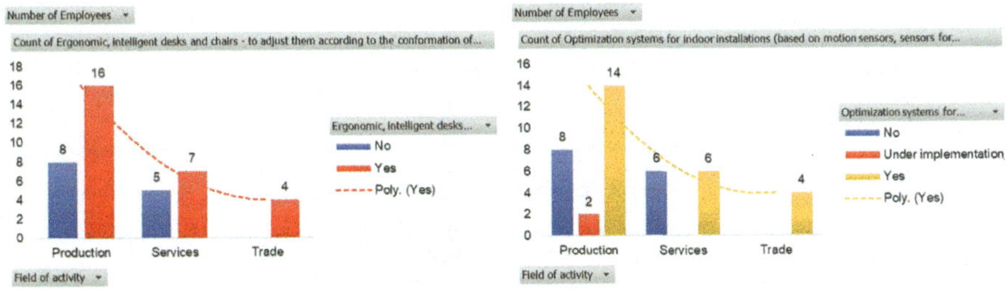


**Fig. 8** Use of digital systems: 1. Ergonomic, smart desks and chairs; 2. Systems for optimizing indoor facilities

(BI) system, Sales Force Automation (SFA) software systems, Robotic Process Automation (RPA) system, etc.

As can be seen from this data, even if most organizations have already implemented various types of digital solutions, an organized approach to the digital transformation process is still needed, precisely to identify the appropriate measures to stimulate digital innovation.

This is the reason why, in order to increase the degree of digitalization of organizations, we have recommended the analysis, evaluation and consideration by each organization of the set of measures developed, presented in the first part of this chapter.

The second part of the questionnaire aimed to identify the digitization strategy of the enterprises/organizations.

From the analysis of the data collected following the survey of the 40 organizations, the following aspects were concluded:

- The main reasons that led organizations to implement digital solutions were: "optimization of activity and its monitoring", "need to keep up with the competition", "ease and speed in obtaining documents", "efficiency, speed, results", "lower costs in the medium and long term", "immediate need", "optimization of processes and increase in employee productivity", "efficiency of internal processes", "optimization", "increase in productivity", etc.
- The results indicated that the analyzed organizations are in the midst of a digital transformation process, but still, most of them (57,5%) have not yet developed a strategy for digitizing their activities and processes, they do not have qualified staff to implement the digitalization strategy (62,5%) and have not designated a person responsible for planning the activities necessary to implement the digitization strategy (50%);
- From the point of view of the resources allocated to support the digitization process, only 15% of the analyzed organizations allocated a dedicated budget, between 1–10% of the profit;
- 75% of organizations stated that workers have the knowledge, skills and abilities to use these digital systems. The assessment of workers is carried out by different methods: by periodic assessments (theoretical or practical) (52,5%), by direct

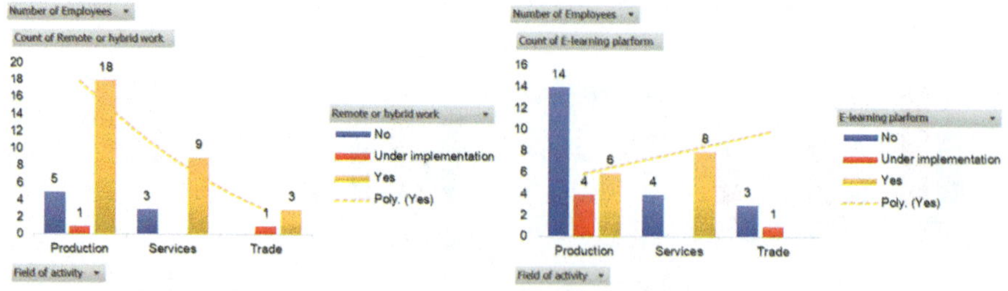


**Fig. 9** Use of digital systems: 1. Remote or hybrid work; 2. E-learning platforms

observation during operational controls (12,5%), by simulations (12,5%) or other methods;

- All organizations noticed the benefits/opportunities obtained following the implementation of these digital solutions: improving the way information is transmitted; improving worker productivity, reducing the time needed to perform some activities; reducing errors, response time to requests; easy access to information; increasing the degree of motivation of workers; improving the efficiency in the organization of the activity; cost reduction as a result of the elimination of some jobs, etc.;
- At the time of implementing these solutions, the organizations also encountered a series of challenges: technical challenges (the ability and/or availability of developers to implement these systems); high costs and long implementation times; high initial workload; employee reluctance to change; the difficulty of integrating new systems with existing systems; the need to adapt work procedures, etc.;
- The evaluation of the successful implementation of digital solutions is carried out through different methods: through external audits; through customer and employee feedback; monitoring the financial results of organizations; by analyzing the periodic reports generated by the IT system; by analyzing the degree of use of the implemented solutions; cost reduction, etc.;
- 85% of organizations have implemented an adequate policy in the field of occupational safety and health, adapted to the new existing conditions—Fig. 10, point 1; 97,5% promotes a culture of worker safety in the workplace;
- 67,5% of the organizations stated that the existing infrastructure allowed the implementation of new digital solutions—Fig. 10, point 2;
- 70% of the organizations stated that the workplaces where the workers carry out their activity were ergonomically designed in order to prevent the occurrence of musculoskeletal disorders;
- Only 30% of the organizations stated that they have implemented a program to monitor workers' health, to identify and adequately address the risks associated with the new working conditions;

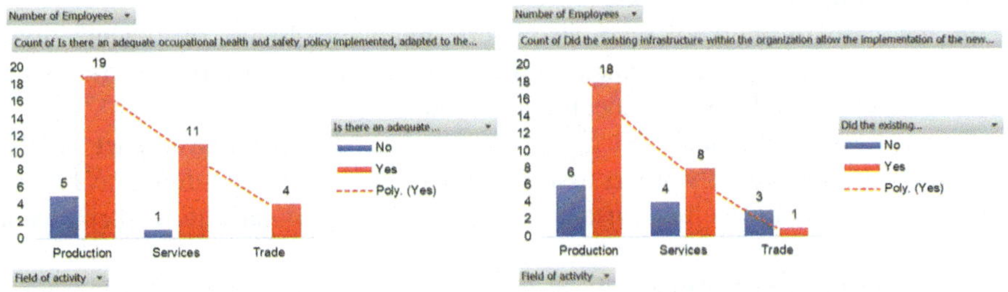


**Fig. 10** 1. There is an adequate occupational health and safety policy in place, adapted to the new existing conditions? 2. The existing infrastructure within the organization allowed the implementation of the new digital solutions (or required an adaptation)?

- In order to facilitate and optimize the integration of digital technologies, the management of the organizations adopted a series of measures: the allocation of the necessary resources; conducting internal and external trainings, courses, audio/ teleconferences; adaptation of the internal regulation; performing external audits; calling on external consultants; increasing the budget allocated for digitization; tracking the implementation strategy adopted at the level of the group to which the organizations belong, etc. [26];
- In order to ensure the security and confidentiality of workers' personal data, a series of measures have been implemented at the level of organizations: the implementation of the provisions of the GDPR regulation; calling on external consultants for the correct implementation of the GDPR rules; developing and implementing strict data security and privacy policies and procedures; conclusion of personal data processing agreements; concluding documents with confidentiality clauses; limiting access to personal data to authorized personnel only; encryption of personal data to protect sensitive information during transmission or storage, etc.;
- The proportion of organizations that have adopted advanced digital technologies is higher in the case of large organizations operating in the field of manufacturing or services and is lower in the case of organizations engaged in trade activities and also decreases with the reduction in the size of the organization;
- It is important to mention that none of the analyzed organizations accessed funds or financing schemes intended for the digitization of SMEs. The funds accessed by them were intended for the development and modernization of activities, the development of products and services, etc.

The third part of the questionnaire was aimed at identifying how the implementation and use of these digital solutions was perceived by employees:

- Even if at the beginning some employees perceived the implementation of these digital solutions neutrally (15%), others with skepticism, reluctance (20%), the majority realized that digital solutions significantly improve processes and work load, can improve efficiency and productivity, and the time gained can be allocated to performing new work tasks;
- In the case of workers who also work remotely, 42,5% of organizations have noticed changes associated with the lack/reduction of direct contact with colleagues, the reduction of social interaction, etc.;
- Only 27,5% of the analyzed organizations noticed a negative impact on the psychosocial health of workers associated with the use of these digital technologies (for example, feelings of anxiety, frustration, demoralization, skepticism, etc.);
- 52,5% of the organizations believe that carrying out the activity also in a telework regime has influenced the balance of workers between professional life and personal life;
- Also, 55% of the organizations assessed in the actual activity carried out by the workers a tendency to intensify work, an increase in the pace of work.

The degree of digitization of organizations can be an impediment to their development [27], digitization being essential for ensuring their competitiveness at the local, national and even global level, in the case of multinational organizations [28]. This aspect can be achieved by developing a clear and well-defined business model, through a set of systematically implemented operations and by using a variety of resources that must be managed and used effectively to ensure the sustainable development of the organization: human, financial, technological (infrastructure), physical (workspaces and appropriate work equipment), knowledge (knowledge, expertise) and relational (with customers, partners) resources [29, 30].

## 4 Conclusions

The proper integration of digital technologies within organizations is the tool that can stimulate their competitiveness in the long term [13, 27, 29] and can ensure the increase of their productivity and performance, which generates positive effects on the entire economy [29]. In addition to these benefits, various barriers and obstacles can prevent or slow down this process, such as limited financial resources, the lack of qualified personnel to implement and manage these technologies, the risk of cyber-attacks and data security breaches, the demonstrated resilience of employees to the changes involved in digitization, etc. Decision-makers within organizations must develop well-thought-out digitization plans, identify appropriate measures to stimulate digital innovation, and, at the same time, ensure all the necessary resources to carry out this complex process.

The European Commission, within its economic and technological development agenda, has placed a significant emphasis on the importance of the digital transformation of businesses, minimal and medium-sized enterprises (SMEs), and to support them, has initiated a series of programs and initiatives such as Digital Single Market Strategy for Europe, Horizon Europe, Digital Europe Programme, European Innovation Council (EIC), European Structural and Investment Funds (ESI funds).

### *4.1 Limitations of the Research*

For this study, were analyzed data obtained over a relatively short period of two weeks. The results obtained may vary in the event of an increase in the size of the analyzed sample. Thus, we recommend conducting additional studies that analyze data collected from a larger number of organizations, with an increase in the time interval allocated for data collection.

There is a possibility that some of the data provided by respondents may be inaccurate, incomplete or randomly selected at the time of completing the questionnaire.

Thus, the data collected and analyzed cannot be fully guaranteed. Thus, we recommend conducting additional studies in this direction. We also recommend further studies to identify the impact of these digital systems on worker safety and health, including how workers perceive their integration into their work.

## References


1. Warner, K., Wäger, M.: Building dynamic capabilities for digital transformation: an ongoing process of strategic renewal. Long Range Plann. **52**(3), 326–349 (2019)
2. Demirkan, H., Spohrer, J., Welser, J.: Digital innovation and strategic transformation. IT Proffesional **18**(6), 14–18 (2016)
3. Sharma, A., Singh, B.: Evolution of industrial revolutions: a review. Int. J. Innov. Technol. Explor. Eng. **9**(11), 66–73 (2020)
4. Xu, X., Lu, Y., Vogel-Heuser, B., Wang, L.: Industry 4.0 and Industry 5.0-Inception, conception and perception. J. Manuf. Syst. **61**(October), 530–535 (2021)
5. Leso, V., Fontana, L., Iavicoli, I.: The occupational health and safety dimension of Industry 4.0. La Medicina del lavoro **110**(5), 327–338 (2018)
6. Afonasova, M., Panfilova, E., Galichkina, M., Ślusarczyk, B.: Digitalization in economy and innovation: the effect on social and economic processes. Pol. J. Manag. Stud. **19**(2), 22–23 (2019)
7. Mourtzis, D., Angelopoulos, J., Panopoulos, N.: Operator 5.0: a survey on enabling technologies and a framework for digital manufacturing based on extended reality. J. Mach. Eng. **22**(1), 43–69 (2022)
8. Gajek, A., Fabiano, B., Laurent, A., Jensen, N.: Process safety education of future employee 4.0 in Industry 4.0. J. Loss Prev. Process. Ind. **75**, (2022)
9. Lindholm, M., Reiman, A., Väyrynen, S.: On future occupational safety and health challenges. Int. J. Occup. Environ. Saf. **4**(1), 108–127 (2020)
10. Noja, G., Pânzaru, C.: Five Possible impacts of Digitalisation in Romania. Eur. Rev. Appl. Sociol. **14**(22), 1–10 (2021)
11. Vasilescu, M., Serban, A., Dimian, G., Aceleanu, M., Picatoste, X.: Digital divide, skills and perceptions on digitalisation in the European Union—towards a smart labour market. PLoS ONE **15**(4), 1–39 (2020)
12. Lenaerts, K., Waeyaert. W., Gillis, D., Smits, I., Hauben, H.: Digital platform work and occupational safety and health: overview of regulation, policies, practices and research (2022)
13. Chenic, A., Burlacu, A., Dobrea, R., Tescan, L., Creţu, A., Stanef-Puica M., et al.: The impact of digitalization on macroeconomic indicators in the new industrial age. Electronics (Switzerland) **12**(7), (2023)
14. Pärli, K.: Impacts of digitalisation on employment relationships and the need for more democracy at work. Ind. Law J. **51**(1), 84–1–8 (2022)
15. Trenerry, B., Chng, S., Wang, Y., Suhaila, Z., Lim, S., Lu, H., et al.: Preparing workplaces for digital transformation: an integrative review and framework of multi-level factors. Front. Psychol. **12**(March), 1–24 (2021)
16. Zhao, H., Zhao, Q., Ślusarczyk, B.: Sustainability and digitalization of corporate management based on augmented/virtual reality tools usage: China and other world IT companies' experience. Sustainability (Switzerland), **11**(17), (2019)
17. Leng, J., Sha, W., Wang, B., Zheng, P., Zhuang, C., Liu, Q., et al.: Industry 5.0: Prospect and retrospect. J. Manuf. Syst. **65**(October), 279–295 (2022)
18. Robla-Gomez, S., Becerra, V., Llata. J., Gonzalez-Sarabia, E., Torre-Ferrero, C., Perez-Oria, J.: Working together: a review on safe human-robot collaboration in industrial environments. IEEE Access 5, 26754–26773 (2017)

19. Hanna, A., Larsson, S., Götvall, P., Bengtsson, K.: Deliberative safety for industrial intelligent human–robot collaboration: regulatory challenges and solutions for taking the next step towards industry 4.0. Robot. Comput.-Integr. Manuf. **78**(June), 102386 (2022)
20. Adriaensen, A., Decré, W., Pintelon, L.: Can complexity-thinking methods contribute to improving occupational safety in industry 4.0? A review of safety analysis methods and their concepts. Safety **5**(4), (2019)
21. Lemos, J., Gaspar, P., Lima, T.: Environmental risk assessment and management in industry 4.0: a review of technologies and trends. Machines **10**(8), 1–14 (2022)
22. Leesakul, N., Oostveen, A., Eimontaite, I., Wilson, M., Hyde, R.: Workplace 4.0: Exploring the implications of technology adoption in digital manufacturing on a sustainable workforce. Sustainability (Switzerland) **14**(6), (2022)
23. Caggiano, A., Grant, R., Peng, C., Li, Z., Simeone, A.: Manufacturing process impacts on occupational health: a machine learning framework. Procedia CIRP **112**(March), 561–566 (2022)
24. Soori, M., Arezoo, B., Dastres, R.: Internet of things for smart factories in industry 4.0, a review. Internet Things Cyber-Phys. Syst. **3**(April), 192–204 (2023)
25. European Agency for Safety and Health at Work.: Smart digital monitoring systems for occupational safety and health: uses and challenges (2023)
26. Burinskienė, A., Seržantė, M.: Digitalisation as the indicator of the evidence of sustainability in the European Union. Sustainability (Switzerland) **14**(14), (2022)
27. Straková, J., Talíř, M., Váchal, J.: Opportunities and threats of digital transformation of business models in smes. Econ. and Sociol. **15**(3), 159–171 (2022)
28. Pekarcikova, M., Izarikova, G., Trebuna, P., Kliment, M.: Digitalisation importance and influence on the competitiveness of industrial enterprises in the time of the covid-19 pandemic. Pol. J. Manag. Stud. **24**(2), 370–385 (2021)
29. Roman, A., Rusu, V.: Digital technologies and the performance of small and medium enterprises. Stud. Bus. Econ. **17**(3), 190–203 (2022)
30. Obermayer, N., Csizmadia, T., Banász, Z.: Companies on thin ice due to digital transformation: the role of digital skills and human characteristics. Int. Multidiscip. J. Soc. Sci. **11**(3), 88–118 (2022)
31. Shaping Europe's digital future Homepage.: https://digital-strategy.ec.europa.eu/ro/policies/desi-romania, last accessed 2023/06/22

# Navigating Pandemic and AI Influences on Employability Competencies

Negar Sohaee, Farnaz Azadjoutabari, Amey Jadhav, and Kaustubh Kulkarni

**Abstract** The COVID-19 epidemic/pandemic has transformed the global business landscape, requiring a comprehensive review of the necessary competencies to navigate it. In this context, it carefully examines the changing dimensions of employability skills in the "new normal," as well as the seismic impact of artificial intelligence (AI) on the job market. Our study's primary objective is to identify post-pandemic proficiencies in demand and examine how educational institutions promote them to boost employability. To achieve this, we undertake a comprehensive survey of higher education institutes, human resource managers, students, and academic overseers to examine the gap between competency development and graduate employability. We aim to understand the discrepancies between graduates' skills and knowledge and employers' demanding requirements in the new normal. A complete examination of the complex values, capacities, and assumptions driving the growing need for new skills and knowledge among aspiring professionals is the key focus of this study. This study's unique contribution lies in its thorough analysis of AI's revolutionary impact and the new normal's demands on employability through a comprehensive exploration of these intricate dynamics. It seeks to understand how higher education institutions foster and improve employable skills in the new normal. Furthermore, it considerably contributes to the ongoing discourse on pedagogy and workforce preparation by revealing the complex interplay between educational provision, AI, and job market changes. Laced with AI's revolutionary dynamics, this research proposes a paradigm shift in educational methods to bridge the gap between graduates' competency and the complex set of labor market's proficiencies.

**Keywords** Artificial Intelligence (AI) · Pandemic · New Normal · Employability · Demanded Skills · Competency

N. Sohaee (✉) · F. Azadjoutabari · A. Jadhav · K. Kulkarni
Yorkville University, Toronto, ON L4K 4N1, Canada
e-mail: nsohaee@yorkvilleu.ca



S. Kot et al. (eds.), *Corporate Practices: Policies, Methodologies, and Insights in Organizational Management*, Springer Proceedings in Business and Economics,
https://doi.org/10.1007/978-981-97-0996-0_22

## 1 Introduction

Knowledge and adaptability are needed to navigate global change. The unexpected COVID-19 outbreak and the rapid growth of artificial intelligence (AI) have transformed work procedures in recent years. These two factors, individually powerful but collectively revolutionary, have forced us to reevaluate employability competencies. The pandemic has created a new 'new normal' with its issues and paradigms. However, AI's entry into mainstream professional fields has added another layer of complexity, compelling a reevaluation of 'fit for the job.' Our study examines the merging of these trends to help educational institutions, students, and businesses navigate this complex terrain.

As a result of the COVID-19 epidemic, the landscape of employability competencies is undergoing significant change, and this study will conduct an in-depth investigation of this phenomenon. The tremendous impact that artificial intelligence (AI) has had and will continue to have on the dynamics of the employment market is another evidence of the complexity of this era. The pandemic prompted widespread demands in different sectors and workforces worldwide to undergo significant changes beginning in the early part of the year 2020. The rapid rise of remote work and service delivery highlighted the need for modified skills set to succeed in the future [1].

The inefficiency of personnel was one of the significant challenges businesses faced during the pandemic, highlighting the importance for educational institutions and industries to work together to close the demand–supply gap. Regarding AI's significant impact on the job market, collaboration becomes more urgent. The current research uses surveys to examine the new ordinary and necessary competencies to determine necessary modifications if problem-based learning is still applicable.

In this ever-changing setting, the capacity to quickly adjust to new circumstances and problem-solve creatively has become an essential component of success. According to [2] Buheji and Sisk (2020) and [3] OECD (2019), the "New Normal" requires not just critical operational strategies but also a mindset that is quick to navigate over unanticipated challenges. The growing popularity of AI in the workplace has highlighted the need for flexible skills. This research responds to them and provides a hidden empirical pathway to help educational institutions design long-term employability and competency developments [4].

In the context of the dynamic relationship between the requirements of the new normal and the potential of revolutionary AI, a comprehensive strategy is required. A strategy that fulfills the demand for critical skills and assists people in developing the essential flexibility needed to succeed in a changing work environment. The research links employability, the new normal, and AI's disruptive influence to create a strategic workforce-ready framework [5].

Research Problem: Research Problem: The pandemic and AI advancement have caused significant work market shifts, creating employability competency gaps. How can educational institutions adapt to these new challenges?

Objective of the Study: The objective of this study is to examine the changing dynamics of employability competencies in considering the COVID-19 epidemic and the significant influence of artificial intelligence. Through analyzing the requirements posed by the "new normal," our objective is to identify the essential skills and evaluate the applicability of problem-based learning. The goal of this research is to offer recommendations to educational institutions on how to create employability and competency development programs that are effective over the long run and can help people succeed in a workplace that is constantly changing.

Research Goal: To advise educational institutions on creating sustainable employability and competency development programs that help individuals succeed in a changing workplace.

## 2 Literature Review

After After the pandemic, remote work became popular, and new business models were needed. The new average of volatility, competition, and technological dependency requires a flexible and adaptable workforce. It means employability skills are now necessary in an AI-driven job market [6], and Problem-solving as well as critical thinking is valued in AI-driven labor markets [7].

The new normal and artificial intelligence are transforming the employment market, requiring quick adaptation to new concepts and solutions. Flexibility, inventiveness, and creativity are valued in this dynamic environment. The COVID-19 pandemic showed the necessity for effective problem-solving and ongoing improvement more than ever and indicates the need to mix human innovation with AI-driven solutions perfectly.

Additionally, COVID-19 and AI changed remote employee training, introducing higher employability skills. This changing climate requires organizations to retrain their staff and recruit talented candidates. Artificial intelligence amplifies these developments, requiring rethinking job duties and their descriptions. In this new normal and with the help of AI, synergistic cooperation between businesses and education systems helps to create a flexible and technologically competent workforce that can thrive during potential changes [8].

The job market is dynamic, so staying ahead is crucial. AI's disruptive generation impacts work with tremendous enthusiasm. This compelling technology transforms IT in businesses, delivering unlimited possibilities for efficiency and value. AI solutions like ChatGPT, Bard, Claude, Midjourney, and others are now more accessible and user-friendly, enabling widespread adoption and making potential AI become a game-changer that surpasses all prior technologies.

Generation AI's growth as a job-shaper is unsurprising in the fast-changing digital industry. The accessibility of AI tools is changing companies' functionality, especially in IT departments. AI's commercialization is inevitable as its accessibility grows, creating a climate for rapid adoption [9, 10].

AI's impact on the job market is most noticeable during labor market polarization. Technology increases the demand for high-skill occupations and the supply of low-skill ones, making middle-skill jobs vulnerable to automation [11]. This increases salary gaps and devalues occupations, emphasizing the necessity for flexible skills that match the changing technology landscape [12, 13].

The relationship between AI and employability skill development emphasizes educational paradigm shifts. Educational institutions must update curricula to provide students with domain-specific knowledge and meta-skills to learn, adapt, and interact in interdisciplinary environments [14]. AI and education disrupt traditional instructional methods, motivating tailored learning paths and immersive technologies that develop cognitive capabilities needed for the new normal [15]. The post-pandemic era and revolutionary AIs potentiate a dynamic world. To be relevant, the future worker must master this landscape's mobility and continue learning. AI's disruptive impact on job market dynamics makes collaboration between individuals, corporations, and educational systems, forming crucible employability skills, which is the key to success. Strategic workforce readiness must address the potential new normal and AI's revolutionary synergy.

## *2.1 Research Questions*

Building on the literature review, this study addresses the following research questions:

- How have the""new normal" and AI changed job market employability skills?
- How important are problem-solving and critical thinking in AI-driven job markets?
- Does AI and remote employee training affect the demand for higher employable skills?
- How can organizations and schools prepare students for the post-pandemic and AI-driven world?

We will study the changing employment landscape and employability skills in an AI-driven world using these research questions.

## *2.2 Influences of AI on Employability Competency*

Employability competency comprises a variety of traits, abilities, knowledge, and attitudes that help an individual succeed in their chosen career. According to [16] Cole and Tibby (2013), employability is a person's perceived ability to find and keep a job. According to the theoretical framework, employability competency is anchored in academic discourse. Practical implications of employability are visible in numerous industries, but theoretical literature provides a thorough grasp of its dynamics. The theoretical approaches emphasize matching human traits to the ever-changing job market. Yorke [17] defines employability, especially in graduates, as a combination of abilities, knowledge, and personal traits that increase the likelihood of success in their sector [17]. Apart from benefiting the person, these achievements benefit the labor, community, and economy [18].

AI has a major influence on job market dynamics today. AI integration has transformed a broad spectrum of expertise. Without any hesitation, traditional skills are important, but cognitive abilities that match AIs are becoming more fundamental. Higher-order cognitive skills, critical thinking, and sophisticated problem-solving become more valuable as regular jobs are utilized with high tech [19]. This requires people to adapt to the new technologies, emphasizing learnability—the ability and willingness to learn new skills [20].

According to theoretical literature, AI and the 'new normal' encourage a growth mentality that values constant learning and skill improvement [21].

In the employability competency framework, attitudes matter most. Attitudes shape an individual's outlook and influence all aspects of their employability [22]. Workplace relationships and approaches depend on attitudes. In the fast-changing work market caused by the COVID-19 pandemic, productivity, adaptation, and preparedness are essential. These mindsets help people handle uncertainty and build resilience. Educational institutions foster these views, equipping students for the changing world [23].

Employability competency includes knowledge, skills, and personal traits together with attitudes. Knowledge—formal schooling and experiential learning—forms the foundation for skill development. Skills apply information, while personal attributes include honesty and action styles like autonomy and meticulousness [23].

Based on theoretical perspectives, modern awareness of employability competency significantly emphasizes sustaining employment in constantly changing and uncertain environments. Adaptability is valued more in today's employment market as AI penetrates more industries. A new era of professional competency has arrived because of AI's capabilities, which call for a combination of specialized and generalist skills [24].

Finally, employability competency is a blend of traits, abilities, attitudes, and knowledge [25]. The new normal emphasizes cognitive skills and a growth mentality due to AI. Adaptability is crucial in uncertain times [26]. Domain and AI-aligned skills must be balanced to support the workforce as AI changes job market dynamics [27]. Educational institutions must prepare students to accept these changing competencies and future challenges and possibilities in any revolutionary period.

## 3 Methodology

This this study examines the changing demands of employable competency in the pandemic and new normal, focusing on AI's impact on work market dynamics. The study uses various research methods to examine the changing skill needs for success throughout this disruptive period.

Our three-tiered data collection approach will include surveys for students, academic institution planners, and recruiters in five major worldwide metropolitan hubs: North America, Europe, Asia, Africa, and Australia. This organized approach will reveal the complex relationship between skill demands, education adaptation, and workforce preparation.

Sample Selection Method in this research is stratified random selection selected participants from diverse sectors, age groups, and employment statuses (full-time, part-time, freelancing). This stratification guarantees that our sample matches our population regarding sector distribution, age, and job status.

## *3.1 Data Collection Process*

- HR Professional Questionnaires: A carefully developed questionnaire is used to get insights from HR professionals and recruiters. This survey seeks. to understand businesses' needs in post-pandemic, and AI-infused knowledge, and skills. Critical comprehension of changing skill requirements will guide the educational system and modify strategic in human resource practice.
- Academic Institution Planner Questionnaires: Curriculum designers will provide insights in this phase. Our goal with these curriculum planners is to match academic curricula to corporate needs. Feedback from these questionnaires will influence timely course outline revisions to match the changing employment landscape.
- Undergraduate and Graduate Student Questionnaires: The third phase gathers student perspectives, concentrating on skills they feel unprepared for. This data will help academic planners to improve course material. Student perspectives provide their skill gaps with the job market demands.

## *3.2 Data Collection Tools and Process*

Our primary tool for getting insights was SurveyMonkey, which collected all the data for this study. We methodically customized our survey questionnaire and improved data quality to meet the needs and interests of our student respondents. In addition to the poll, we created tailored questions for gathering input from human resources managers from various companies and industries.

This comprehensive strategy let us learn how the subject affected professionals in various fields. We tailored our survey questions to each industry's unique viewpoints and developing needs to ensure that our data is well-rounded and accurately represents each sector's issues and potential. This method emphasizes our research's depth and breadth, making it more robust and insightful.

### *3.3 Participant Demographics*

The research includes the participation of 115 individuals from various backgrounds. These individuals were purposefully chosen to represent a variety of stakeholder groups. There are a total of 75 undergraduate and graduate students included in the sample. Most of these students are from Canada, but there is also representation from a few other nations. In addition, the sample consists of twenty human resources professionals or recruiters from various businesses who contributed their insightful perspectives. To further broaden the scope of the investigation, the sample was expanded with twenty more participants hailing from the academic era.

### *3.4 Data Monitoring and Analysis*

Both quantitative and qualitative methods were used to analyze the large dataset. Collecting patterns, trends, and deviations from the norm will provide analytical insights. This study's method is well-suited to provide comprehensive insights into the changing employability skill expectations caused by the pandemic and AI enhancement in each and individual aspect of job settings. This study uses a multidimensional technique with varied participant groups to bridge the gap between skill requirements and educational provision to create a workforce that can navigate the constantly evolving professional landscape.

## 4 Data Analysis

### *4.1 Analysis Analyzing Post-Pandemic Era: Students' Exploration of AI's Impact on Job Markets*

The global pandemic has had a significant effect on the educational system. Thus, instructional practices and socialization have been disturbed, posing significant challenges to students' education [28]. A comprehensive student survey was conducted to understand these challenges. Students will impact future economies globally; therefore, this survey's dataset is crucial.

An analysis of the participants' demographic information revealed that most of the students (84%) were between the ages of 18 and 29, 12% were between the ages of 30 and 39, and 4% ranged in age from 40 to 49. The gender breakdown of the participants revealed that 54.67 percent identified as female, while 45.33 percent identified as male. Most participants held either a high school diploma or a bachelor's degree, followed by those with a master's degree. A smaller proportion of the population had earned either an associate degree or a PhD.

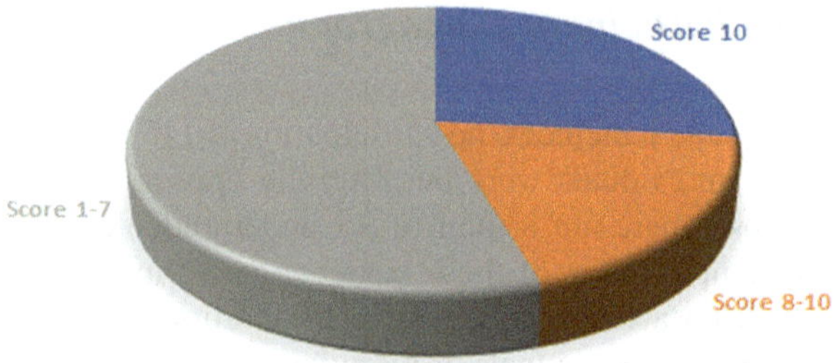


**Fig. 1** Participants' Level of Uncertainty About Job Prospects after the Pandemic & AI's Disruption (10 is worst scenario)

The survey showed that even young generations with the right qualifications are worried about their prospects after the pandemic and AI's workplace disruption. Participants determined their level of uncertainty from 1 to 10, when 10 is the worst scenario, with 26.67% scoring 10, 18.67% scoring 8–10, and the rest 54.66 answered 1–7 (Fig. 1). Due to job issues and AI-driven displacements. According to the survey, almost two-thirds of participants are thinking about changing their careers in the future because they are worried that AI could take their jobs or change their careers. In this uncertain environment, most of the participants (Students) rated their school's preparedness for the future as ranging from 5 to 7 on a scale of 10, with ten being the least prepared. Respondents highlighted interpersonal skills such as self-assurance, a positive outlook, leadership, and strong work ethic as essential for future job success. This raises the question of handling uncertainty and emphasizes the need for long-term skills. These talents are essential for finding and keeping work in the post-pandemic and AI-powered era:

- Problem-solving: In a fast-changing, AI-integrated world, complexity and effectiveness are crucial.
- Creativity and Innovation: AI handles regular chores, freeing humans to create new ideas, products, and services.
- Technology Proficiency: Technology proficiency helps people adapt and contribute to AI-redefined workflows.
- Critical Thinking: To comprehend AI-generated insights and identify credible facts, decision-making are essential.
- Continuous Learning and Adaptability: Rapid technology breakthroughs, including AI, require constant enhancement to stay relevant in changing job environments, therefore prompt adaptation and continuing learning are essential.

These collective capacities enable individuals to succeed in a world transformed by post-pandemic problems and AI's disruptive effects, changing work and success skills.

The study highlights two main issues that online students must face, compounded by AI's growing impact on learning: fewer opportunities for meaningful social interaction and less direct instructor participation. Much screen time, poor physical activity, decreasing concentration, and degrees of social isolation can all reduce their productivity. Among these dynamics, AI's disruptive impact is evident in the

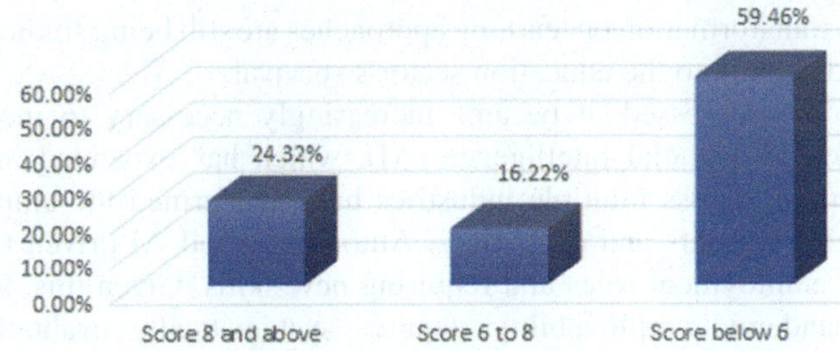


**Fig. 2** Impact of Remote Work & Study on Social Connectivity

learning system. Remote work and study have a significant impact on social connectivity, as 24.32% of respondents scored eight or above. More than 16.22% gave scores between 6 and 8, showing the subtleties of influence (Fig. 2). To provide a holistic and productive learning experience that prepares students for a world of changing technological modalities and social norms, AI must modify learning paradigms.

This study shows that AI's disruptive impact on education and the workforce presents a complete picture of online learning's issues. This includes AI's growing impact on learning. In the emerging AI-driven educational system that encourages collaborative participation, 52% of participants emphasize the importance of increased student contact in online learning. An additional 38% recognize the potential benefits of an enhanced interactive learning environment in an AI-driven educational landscape. Despite challenges, many adjustments provide benefits. Participants stress scheduling flexibility and unique exposure to varied geographic learning situations aided by AI-enabled online education.

Educational institutions must meet and balance interactive learning, AI-augmented pedagogies, and global connectivity, both traditional and AI-driven paradigms, at the same time. This strategic convergence could create a general educational experience that prepares students to thrive in an era of technological change and changing social norms, as well as AI literacy that empowers students to make informed decisions and use AI tools consciously. As AI enters the workplace, students must also exhibit adaptability and a lifelong learning mindset to stay competitive in a fast-paced AI environment. The benefits of AI, such as reduced human error, unbiased decision-making, and pattern discovery, demonstrate the mutual relationship between education and the AI-powered world. AI, education, and employment are intertwined in this dynamic future, creating a universal ecosystem that equips people to handle AI-driven changes with competency and resilience.

Several participants' opinions highlight the changing link between education, AI, and work. Some participants said online classes improved their self-discipline and technical skills. The survey also highlighted people's innate sociability, highlighting the challenges of learning settings without meaningful social connections. In-person learning improves focus, comprehension, and interpersonal skills more than virtual learning. Online education is essential to the education sector's survival. Although the effects of this transformation on learning approaches are still being studied, online education is fundamental to the education sector's survival.

As the research progressed, it became increasingly necessary to include the growing influence of artificial intelligence (AI), which has expanded into work settings. AI adoption across multiple industries has transformed the employment landscape, bringing benefits and challenges. Automation and AI-driven technologies are altering employment roles and requiring new skills. Given this, assessing students' post-pandemic employability requires systematically evaluating AI's growing role.

## *4.2 Academic Field Data Analysis*

This analysis connects the changing educational landscape, learning and adaptation, and AI's impact on employment. It presents a complete paradigm that recognizes the dynamic interaction of various factors in influencing education, employability, and society. The impact of artificial intelligence (AI) on employment skills requires a rethinking of educational goals. Academics say the employment market values technology, data science, problem-solving, creativity, and innovation. Technology and big data analysis have created many jobs in the market. In response, the educational paradigm must shift to focus on cutting-edge technologies that define the present professional scene with AI at the forefront. Notably, 70% of respondents support emphasizing data-centric subjects in school. Despite the rise of technology and machine learning in the workplace, creative thinking is still essential.

Over the past decade or two, remote work paradigms and collaboration tools like Google Docs, Dropbox, Facetime, and Skype have transformed the modern workplace. This change allows workers to collaborate across borders. The COVID-19 pandemic has boosted virtual employment, urging online courses and programs. Online learning prepares students for the workforce in the digital age. In the early pandemic, 90% of academics thought internet tests were unfair. Improvements have made online tests and assignments more effective than during the pandemic. AI's evolution, the modern workplace's transformation, and online learning's dynamic potential present a kaleidoscope of opportunities and challenges that picture the educational journey toward an AI-infused, digitally empowered, and globally connected future.

1. 80% of academic management and professors believe online education promotes student teamwork. The digital learning environment simulates AI-driven workforce collaboration. Remote work requires good communication and coordination, especially in virtual environments. A totally new but essential aspect is learning digital teamwork skills in today's workplace through online education.
2. 90% of academic managers and faculty think online education prepares students for post-COVID-19 remote jobs. Telecommuting has underlined the necessity for independent and successful work from anywhere. These skills grow with

online education, making students valuable to organizations seeking adaptable personnel who can succeed remotely.
3. Online education increases students' virtual communication abilities, which are essential in modern business era, say 90% of academic managers and faculty. Virtual communication is crucial for remote work. Online learning helps students write clear emails, use instant messaging and video conferencing, and detect virtual nonverbal cues.
4. 75% of academic managers and instructors say online education promotes self-discipline. In remote employment, self-direction and efficiency are essential for online learning. Online education teaches students good habits and structured work routines. Virtual learning encourages proactive self-motivation, self-discipline, and work ethic.
5. All academic managers and faculties believe that online education improves students' technology skills and employability. Online courses teach collaboration, information sharing, access, and task fulfillment. This technical proficiency provides individuals confidence in using technology at work, especially in a technologically evolved society.
6. 90 percent of academic managers and faculty agree online learning environments improve soft skills like time management, virtual teamwork, and patience, which are valued in the job market now. These soft skills enable teamwork, workload management, and creative problem-solving in unexpected and challenging situations, ensuring workplace success. Online education gives students a professional edge by developing soft skills.
7. Online education prepares students for technological accountability, said 75% of academic management and professors. Lack of in-person interaction necessitates proactive learning and self-motivation, which raises accountability. As students enter the workforce, task ownership and timely, professional execution are vital.

## *4.3 Human Resource Manager's Perspective*

The COVID-19 epidemic has changed global business. Some businesses closed, but others grew. The pandemic is forcing many firms to adopt remote labor and changing norms. This transition has revealed new talents and expectations that organizations seek in their employees [29].

Artificial intelligence (AI) has further changed job needs and employee skill sets in this dynamic environment [5]. AI's infiltration into numerous industries has changed the abilities needed for modern jobs. Changing the AI landscape redefines the traditional skills set. Technical expertise, self-motivation, and focus are needed in the remote work era. Employers now value self-confidence, active listening, and a positive attitude over teamwork and conflict management.

The pandemic's disruption of firm operations forced a broad evaluation of success abilities. In this context, AI technology has increased the need to evolve skills. Contemporary technical skill requires agility, flexibility, and a deep understanding of technology. Furthermore, AI has made interpersonal skills important competencies due to their importance in navigating the dynamic and technologically advanced workplace.

The epidemic and AI-induced transformation have not been uniformed across age groups. Midlife and seniors struggle with digital jobs. This gap shows that flexible HR techniques are needed to fulfill workforce needs.

Therefore, these disruptive trends are forcing firms to rethink remote work. This strategic shift optimizes processes and prepares personnel for change. Remote work raises issues about employee well-being and effectiveness. Interpersonal skills that improve adaptation and attentiveness are crucial to overcoming loneliness and inactivity. These skills are essential for success in a post-pandemic and AI-shaped professional environment.

The epidemic and AI have altered corporate operations, prompting a complete assessment of abilities to succeed. Technical expertise, agility, and a deep technological grasp are essential, combined with core interpersonal abilities. The transformation affects different age groups unevenly, especially those over 45, but also emphasizes the need for flexible HR strategies. Companies must rethink remote work techniques for operational optimization, well-being, and performance. In this changing paradigm driven by the pandemic and AI integration, learning interpersonal skills like inventiveness and attentiveness is crucial.

Working from home has become the business norm. The incorporation of AI technology has highlighted the need for technical proficiency, self-motivation, and focus. Flexible human resources techniques and remote work models are vital as the workforce adapts to new technology, especially for middle-aged workers who struggle. Educational priorities are reassessed as corporate dynamics change. Fostering human-centered skills like critical thinking, data analysis, and problem-solving is crucial. This proactive strategy meets the changing business landscape, where flexibility to post-pandemic remote work and AI reshapes work settings totally. Thus, flexibility in working hours, places, and arrangements will define the professional landscape in the future.

## 5 Discussion

### *5.1 Upcoming Skills for the New World*

After the epidemic and AI's transformation, enterprises must learn new skills to survive in a changing market. Self-awareness is an essential skill for personal and professional growth. Self-awareness requires understanding and interpreting one's own actions and feelings.

Personal and professional success depends on emotional intelligence "EI", defining as the ability to understand and manage one's own and others' emotions.

Employees with strong EI are more resourceful and effective and emotional intelligence is crucial in the post-pandemic, AI-influenced workplace for the following reasons:

- Empathy: Improves relationships by understanding and bonding.
- Motivation: Essential for internal drive in a changing world [30].
- Self-Regulation: elemental factor for emotional equilibrium
- Relationships: dispute resolution, and teamwork.
- Rising Relevance: Businesses must master these skills as they adapt to complex developments.

### *5.2 Communication Skills in Transition*

After the pandemic and AI's growth, communication skills are being redefined across the professional landscape. The new normal in organizations is online meetings and communication, supported by Zoom and Microsoft Teams. Their use has increased, with millions of users daily [31], acclaimed changing interpersonal relations. In this digital age, building relationships with coworkers and clients is more important than ever, thus technical, analytical, and soft skills are essential [32]. In this fast-changing environment, employability—the ability to find and keep a job—is crucial. Against this backdrop, educational and training institutions play a crucial role in preparing graduates with skills beyond job attainment. The learned skills should help people handle job demands during chaotic times, not just get them jobs [4].

Once a cornerstone, effective communication now supports productivity. The ubiquitous "thumbs up" and video chats have replaced handshakes and face-to-face interactions. The border between work and personal time and place is blurry, and this highlights the fundamental changes in our everyday routines, forcing us to rethink our methods. This transition and the current crises have elevated workplace digital communication ethics. The virtual world promotes connectivity but also allows ethical failings. As real and online encounters blur, a new arena for honesty and respect in digital communication arises. The rise of AI and post-pandemic dynamics emphasize the need for communication skills in this changing world. Technical expertise, sophisticated communication, and ethical integrity are needed to navigate these new streams and build a resilient and flexible career.

### *5.3 Leadership and Critical Thinking: Shaping the Future*

Leadership and critical thinking are fundamental in the time of changes, becoming more important since the COVID-19 epidemic and AI-driven developments. Due to the pandemic's widespread impact, executives must have strong critical thinking and decision-making skills in a variety of businesses. In the fast-changing workplace, Mukherjee (2023) says leaders must have adaptable skills beyond traditional leadership skills. Adaptability, creativity, digital proficiency, emotional intelligence, and the ability to handle complex situations are among these characteristics. Modern company success depends on personal relationships and organizational adaptability. Leaders must understand their employees' goals and create a conductive environment for professional growth [33][33]. Critical thinking is a leader's foundation. Leaders can analyze data, evaluate difficult circumstances, and make informed decisions with this competence. In times of uncertainty and turmoil, it leads leaders through complex difficulties and inspires innovative solutions. Critical thinking improves decision-making, empowering leaders to manage teams and motivate them. Leadership and critical thinking are the key to post-pandemic company success. Effective leaders must make sound decisions and understand their employees' needs to create a harmonious work environment. Thus, leadership motivated by critical thinking helps firms to navigate in the time of uncertainty, seize opportunities, and sustain resilient growth in a world altered by the epidemic and AI.

## *5.4 Quick Response and Adaptability*

The ability to adapt and act quickly in today's dynamic and constantly changing world is currently not only advantageous; but also, it has grown into a basic requirement. Businesses now need to be more agile and flexible than ever before because of the COVID-19 pandemic and the ongoing development of AI technology:

- The COVID-19 Pandemic's Effect on The Workplace: Our workplace has undergone significant change because of the COVID-19 pandemic, which also highlighted the importance of flexibility. Businesses were forced to evaluate their conventional operating models and quickly switch to remote work arrangements. Unexpectedly, productivity wasn't always increased by remote work. Franken et al. (2021) found that working remotely during the COVID-19 pandemic did not necessarily lead to increased productivity. According to Franken's research, remote work dynamics significantly impact employee productivity due to factors such as task complexity, individual preferences, and the quality of the infrastructure [34].
- Skills Development for Facing Change: Despite the need for fast response, post-pandemic dynamics emphasize the need for continual skill development such as adaptability, resilience, and awareness of quick-changing paradigms. This requires individuals to develop a natural ability to adapt and overcome hurdles. This helps people survive in the uncertain climate and exploit post-pandemic possibilities.
- Future Resilience: In this fast-changing world, resilience is essential. Employers value skills that correspond to global remote work acceptance. To succeed in this changing workplace, individuals must be adaptable, pressure-tolerant, accept the unexpected, and prioritize tasks. Traditional job roles and competencies have changed by 2023 [35].

This adjustment emphasizes the revolutionary impact of the COVID-19 pandemic, the rise of the remote workforce, and the dominant role of AI and data science. The demand for employees with adaptability, digital proficiency, and a wider skill set to navigate this new era with resilience and agility is expanding. This major transition coincides with AI, data science, machine learning, and freelancing, especially in uncertain economic times. As workers transition from the modern workforce to the AI age, resilience means adapting to the changing work landscape and technology. Success in the post-pandemic and AI-driven world depends on the ability to quickly adapt and overcome problems since faster work dynamics require skill development to prosper in this ever-changing employment ecosystem.

## *5.5 Creativity and Innovation: Fueling Transformation*

Within the context of rapid technological changes, innovation and creativity are crucial in all fields. Creative thinking and out-of-the-box brainstorming are essential due to the rapid pace of technology. In a world where automation and AI take over, human creativity remains unmatched. Creative vitality spans all businesses and professions, even though it is often linked to art, music, and literature. The corporate landscape is constantly changing in this era. The ability to discover new viewpoints and create up to date solutions is vital in such an atmosphere. The essence of human creativity stands out in an age when machines and AI do everyday tasks. Creative fields are fertile, yet all industries are vibrant with creativity.

Business growth amplifies the requirement for creative thinking. Both individuals and businesses need the ability to foster innovative ideas and disruptive solutions. Companies want professionals who can see problems from several angles and create new ideas that boost growth. In the fast-changing corporate environment of AI, creativity is essential to accomplish. Human brilliance and AI's transformational tide are intertwined, but creativity and invention are essential to thrive and adapt changes in a world shaped by constant evolution.

## *5.6 Change Management: Flexibility Benefits*

Employers today value a skill set more than ever, echoing the global rise in remote work acceptance. Therefore, thrive in this evolving way of work by being adaptable, pressure-tolerant, and accepting the unexpected are important key as well as the task prioritizing and the desire to take on more are intrinsic in this New Normal. This evolving landscape has changed remote worker preparation. As workforce development guardians, corporations must encourage modern workplace talent by retraining and recruiting large corporations' employees for the new normal. A World Economic Forum projection shows a professional recalibration coming. An amazing 42% of essential competencies necessary for present job roles have changed from 2022, creating nearly 133 million new jobs. This revolutionary labor demand resonates with AI, data science, machine learning, and driving freelancing. In the face of uncertain and difficult budgetary conditions, the post-pandemic economy struggles with employability. As the modern professional narrative meets with the age of AI, resilience is embracing adaptability and choosing a path that matches the changing workforce landscape and technology.

### *5.7 Tech Savvy: Exploring New Territory*

COVID-19 has shaken the labor and job market, ushering in a new era of tech-savvy individuals in high demand. The worldwide skills gap was already visible before the pandemic since 82% of open occupations required digital capabilities. The epidemic has increased the need for specific digital skills as companies adapt to modern technology and platforms. Businesses positioned to compete in this fast-changing digital ecosystem must invest in cutting-edge technologies and tech-savvy people. Data literacy, computer programming, big data analytics, the Cloud's ethereal realm, artificial intelligence's virtuosity, blockchain's cryptic nuances, and their symbiotic intricacies will give those who understand the Fourth Industrial Revolution. A solid understanding of the latest technical trends and their professional applications is vital but being a polymath across every system or platform is difficult. As the post-pandemic and AI-driven eras collide, individuals who can interpret technology's encrypted language will enter an odyssey that combines digital fluency with AI's revolutionary powers.

## 6 Result

The COVID-19 pandemic and AI's exponential expansion have changed the career environment [5] (Singh & Tarkar, 2022). In an age where technology and human contact are intertwined, strong intrapersonal and interpersonal skills are essential for career success.

### *6.1 The New Employment Landscape*

This changing situation requires technical and intra and interpersonal skills to succeed. However, defining, measuring, and cultivating these skills are difficult. Policymakers, educators, and employers must collaborate to capitalize on this transformative moment. The Employability Skills Framework takes center stage, necessitating tweaks to tools, media, and resources. This system, based on employability criteria and evaluation inventories, creates a skill set that spans workforce development and education [38].

## 6.2 *Improving Employability Framework Evolution*

Figure 3 shows the Employability Framework as a post-COVID-19 guide. This novel framework is based on Ken Wilber's four-quadrant model of human understanding (1997) [36]. These quadrants reveal the complex relationship between internal and external influences and individual and group dynamics.

- The upper left (UL) quadrant highlights an individual's skills and self-image. Resilience, adaptation, and remote communication rules are here. Post-pandemic employment depends on digital adaptation, multitasking skills, optimism, and self-confidence in the digital age.
- The upper right (UR) quadrant matches skills with the changing work market. This synthesis requires a keen understanding of technical changes, industry demands, and growing prospects to build a sustainable career.
- The lower left (LL) quadrant orchestrates workplace and organizational group dynamics. Collaboration, teamwork, and diversity are essential for innovation and good working relationships.
- The lower right (LR) quadrant links external conditions to collaborative efforts. This convergence requires legislative changes, educational improvements, and strategic corporate alliances to create a new employment ecosystem.

Developing abilities that handle both pandemic concerns and AI prospects is crucial to success in transformative change. This intricate tapestry includes refined communication skills, mastering leadership, unshakeable adaptive agility, unbounded creativity, flawless technology fluency, and a mindfully renovated Employability Skills Framework. These interwoven aspects guide individuals and organizations

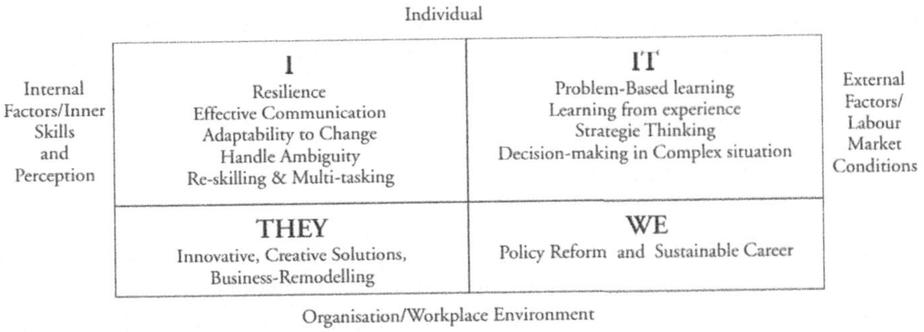


**Fig. 3** Common Employability Skills Framework, National Network

to navigate the ever-changing landscape, promote resilience, and map a course for success in a world of extraordinary transition.

Based on the data we gathered, we came up with the following adjustments to the employability skill frameworks for the post-pandemic and AI era as shown in Fig. 4:

- Personal characteristics: Qualities like self-awareness, emotional intelligence, and resilience are examples of personal characteristics that are essential for managing the difficulties of the post-pandemic and AI-driven world. These abilities allow people to comprehend and control their emotions, adjust to shifting conditions, make wise judgments, and stimulate creativity and innovation in a setting that is fast-changing.
- People Skills: In a virtual and remote work setting, it is essential to have strong interpersonal ties, the ability to lead others, and excellent communication skills. In an increasingly virtual environment, these abilities promote constructive relationships, teamwork, and the capacity to connect with coworkers and clients.
- Applied Knowledge: Having applied knowledge can help people stay competitive in a time when technology is a key component of many different businesses. This knowledge can range from technical proficiency to data literacy and awareness of artificial intelligence (AI). To adjust to the changing needs of the work market, one must have a solid understanding of emerging technologies, data analytics, and digital tools.
- Working Skills: Working skills include the capacity for problem-solving, flexibility, and multitasking that enable people to flourish in situations where change is constant. Professionals with these abilities may successfully navigate uncertainty, accept flexibility, and manage tasks while retaining a good attitude that is crucial for success in the face of shifting work paradigms.

### *6.3 Implications*

The rapid expansion of artificial intelligence (AI) and the transformative effects of the COVID-19 pandemic have disrupted conventional labor structures, presenting new challenges and prospects for individuals and organizations. The results and recommendations given in this study have various implications that can provide guidance for future studies and inform managerial practices.

### *6.4 Theoretical Implications:*

- Reconceptualization of Skill Sets: The existing literature on employability skills has to be updated. It was largely written before the epidemic and during the early stages of AI. Future workforce studies will focus on the critical abilities that were highlighted, including emotional intelligence, resilience, and adaptability.

**Fig. 4** Revitalized Employability Skills Framework in the Post-Pandemic and AI Era

The present study presents an enhanced model that can serve as a foundational framework for future scholarly investigations.

- Workplace Dynamics: Traditional organizational theories need to be reevaluated considering the trend toward remote work and the reliance on AI-driven tools. How do traditional theories of team dynamics, motivation, and leadership change in a modern workplace that prioritizes technology?
- Human-AI Interaction: The integration of AI into business operations offers a wide range of potential research topics. How does AI affect creativity, decision-making, and human relationships in the workplace? This research emphasizes the need for advanced knowledge and a new theoretical framework for human-AI interactions.

## *6.5 Managerial Implications:*

- Talent Development and Retention: Organizations must make significant investments in ongoing learning and development considering the shifting skill requirements. The efficacy of conventional training modules may be insufficient. However, it is crucial to prioritize activities that foster adaptability, emotional intelligence, and technological proficiency.

- Ethical Considerations in a Digital Workplace: As previously said, the blending of personal and professional spheres in remote work environments and the widespread implementation of AI tools call for a reevaluation of workplace ethics. Managers must take the initiative to develop policies and standards that reflect these developments.
- Reimagined Leadership: In a post-pandemic, AI-driven world, there are many differences in the leadership model. The focus is more emphasized on empathy, adaptability, and digital competence. Organizational leaders must acknowledge this change and modify their leadership philosophies accordingly.
- Organizational Structure and Strategy: As remote work increases and AI tools are more widely used, organizations may need to reevaluate their structural and strategic models. Adjusting to the shifting corporate environment might require reevaluating team structures, communication channels, and even fundamental business strategy.

As a result, the research illuminates how the world of labor is fast changing under the influence of outside forces like the pandemic and technological advancement, particularly AI. While the research offers an updated framework for comprehending employable abilities in this modern period, it also emphasizes the need for ongoing adaptation, both in academic studies and corporate activities. The interaction between people and technology, as well as the difficulties and opportunities it brings, will continue to be a focus of study and research as time goes on.

## 7 Conclusion

In the AI era and post-pandemic world, success is a balanced mix of technical brilliance, personal finesse, and adaptability. The changing environment requires professional paths that combine AI knowledge with interpersonal abilities. Successful communication, leadership, resilience, and innovation become essential whenever virtual and physical blur exists.

The revamped Employability Competencies Framework, "A shared language among policymakers, educators, and employers," unites fundamental keys of competencies that introduce a beautiful symphony of skills nurturing across academics, industry, and workforce development. Its quadrants illuminate personal competence, labor market alignment, collaborative synergy, and strategic progression, creating a complete AI-era tapestry.

People are the artists and masterpieces in this tapestry. Continuous upskilling, retraining, and technological adoption are part of the journey. Digital literacy, a deep understanding of AI, and adaptability to its ever-changing era are crucial; however, humans lead and innovate alongside technology as AI conducts the orchestra.

At the intersection of human inventiveness and technology, the story of achievement is multi-dimensional—the harmony of abilities, adaptation, and creativity crescendo careers to new heights. Individuals and organizations find rhythm in the

AI era, navigating the unknown with perseverance, ingenuity, and determination. Finally, it is a well-known opinion now that humans and AI will play an epic show of unlimited potential.

### *7.1 Limitations and Future Proposals*

We acknowledge the limitations of our study and propose future research. Our target demographic may not represent the total workforce. Artificial intelligence evolves quickly; thus, perspectives and difficulties may change faster than expected. Future research could examine AI's effects on niche businesses and their potential. AI's effects on different age groups should also be examined, as employability competencies may vary by generation. This may result in customized frameworks and solutions. Research could also reveal changing dynamics by measuring skill evolution and AI's influence. To conclude, the harmonious coexistence of humans and AI provides unparalleled possibilities, but continual research and adaptability are needed to maximize its potential.

## References

1. Donnelly, R., Johns, J.: Recontextualising remote working and its HRM in the digital economy: an integrated framework for theory and practice,". Int. J. Hum. Resour. Manag. **32**(1), 84–105 (2021)
2. Buheji, M., Sisk, S.: You and the new normal, Author House, UK (2020)
3. OECD.: The Future of Work, OECD Employment Outlook. [Online] Available at: https://www.oecd.org/employment/Employment-Outlook-2019-Highlight-EN.pdf (2019) Accessed 15 April 2020
4. Levenson, A.: A Long Time until the economic new normal, leaders must learn from the pandemic now to position their companies to thrive in the next crisis, Sloan Re-view, MIT, April 10. [Online] Available at: https://sloanreview.mit.edu/article/along-time-until-the-economic-new-normal/ (2020) Accessed 15 April 2020
5. Singh, R., Tarkar, P.: Future of work: how artificial intelligence will change the dynamics of work culture and influence employees' work satisfaction post-covid-19. In: Proceedings of International Conference on Communication and Artificial Intelli-gence: ICCAI 2021 pp. 239–260. Singapore: Springer Nature Singapore, May 2022
6. Bird, D.: Planning your post-COVID-19 return: 8 kinds of attitudes about risk, Enterprisers Project. [Online] Available at: https://enterprisersproject.com/article/2020/6/covid-19-return (2020) Accessed 15 April 2020
7. Shobha, C.V., Johnson, B.: Employability framework in the post-covid scenario—a literature review. Abhigyan **39**(2), 28–36 (2021). [Online] Available at: https://www.proquest.com/scholarly-journals/employability-framework-post-covid-scenario/docview/2632833624/se-2?accountid=142373 Accessed 15 April 2020
8. Meister, J.: The impact of the coronavirus on HR and the new normal of work, Forbes **31** March (2020). [Online] Available at: https://www.forbes.com/sites/jeannemeister/2020/03/31/the-impact-of-the-coronavirus-on-hrand-the-new-normal-of-work/#178b9d232b60 Accessed 15 April 2020

9. Zhang, Y., Xiong, F., Xie, Y., Fan, X., Gu, H.: The impact of artificial intelligence and blockchain on the accounting profession, IEEE. Access **8**, 110461–110477 (2020)
10. Kumar, V., Rajan, B., Venkatesan, R., Lecinski, J.: Understanding the role of artificial intelligence in personalized engagement marketing. Calif. Manage. Rev. **61**(4), 135–155 (2019)
11. Gibbs, M.B.: How is new technology changing job design? IZA World of Labor (2022)
12. Pokrivcakova, S.: Preparing teachers for the application of AI-powered technologies in for-eign language education. J. Lang. Cultural Edu. **7**(3), 135–153, Dec (2019)
13. Chen, L., Chen, P., Lin, Z.: Artificial intelligence in education: a review. IEEE Access **8**, 75264–75278 (2020). https://doi.org/10.1109/ACCESS.2020.2988510
14. UNESCO.: COVID-19 Educational disruption and response. [Online] Available at: https://en.unesco.org/covid19/educationresponse (2020) Accessed 15 April 2020
15. Enang, C.E.: Emerging technologies in teaching and learning of business education programmes in the new normal in tertiary institution in Nigeria. Niger. J. Bus. Educ. (Nigjbed) **9**(2), 64–71 (2022)
16. Cole, D., Tibby, M.: Defining and developing your approach to employability: a framework for higher education institutions, Heslington: The Higher Education Academy (2013)
17. Yorke, M.: Employability in higher education: what it is-what it is not (Vol. 1). York: Higher Education Academy (2006)
18. Buheji, M., Buheji, A.: Planning competency in the new normal–employability competency in post-COVID-19 pandemic. Int. J. Hum. Resour. Stud. **10**(2), 237–251 (2020)
19. Brynjolfsson, E., McAfee, A.: The second machine age: work, progress, and prosperity in a time of brilliant technologies, WW Norton & Company (2014)
20. World Economic Forum, J. (2020), The future of jobs report 2020. Retrieved from Geneva
21. Mangels, J.A., Butterfield, B., Lamb, J., Good, C., Dweck, C.S.: Why do beliefs about intelligence influence learning success? a social cognitive neuroscience model. Soc. Cogn. Affect. Neurosci. **1**(2), 75–86 (2006)
22. Armoogum, N.Y., Ramasawmy, B., Driver, B.M.F.: The need to enhance the employability competences (knowledge, skills, autonomy, and attitudes) of undergraduates in agriculture. evidence from students' perceptions and employers' expectations. Tuning J. High. Educ. **4**(1), 169–219 (2016)
23. Schofer, J.L., Mahmassani, H.S., Ng, M.T.: Resilience of US Rail intermodal freight during the COVID-19 pandemic. Res. Transp. Bus. Manag. **43**, 100791 (2022)
24. Koutroukis, T., Chatzinikolaou, D., Vlados, C., Pistikou, V.: The post-COVID-19 era, fourth industrial revolution, and new globalization: restructured labor relations and or-ganizational adaptation. Societies **12**(6), 187 (2022)
25. Kaur, H., Bains, A.: Understanding the concept of entrepreneur competen-cy. J. Bus. Manag. & Soc. Sci. Res. **2**(11), 31–33 (2013)
26. Inge, R., Rémi, S., Simon, B.: Unraveling the concept of employ-ability, bringing together research on employability in higher education and the work-place. Stud. High. Educ. **45**(12), 2588–2603 (2020). https://doi.org/10.1080/03075079.2019.1623770
27. Shiohira, K.: Understanding the impact of artificial intelligence on skills develop-ment, education 2030, UNESCO-UNEVOC International Centre for Technical and Voca-tional Education and Training (2021)
28. Paudel, P.: Online education: benefits, challenges and strategies during and after COVID-19 in higher education. Int. J. Stud. Educ. (IJonSE) **3**(2), (2021)
29. Meyer, B.H., Prescott, B., Sheng, X.S.: The impact of the COVID-19 pandemic on business expectations. Int. J. Forecast. **38**(2), 529–544 (2022)
30. Wijayati, D.T., Rahman, Z., Rahman, M.F.W., Arifah, I.D.C., Kautsar, A.: A study of artificial intelligence on employee performance and work engagement: the moderat-ing role of change leadership. Int. J. Manpow. **43**(2), 486–512 (2022)
31. Morris B.: Why does Zoom exhaust you? Science has an answer. The Wall Street Journal (2020). [Online] Available at: https://www.wsj.com/articles/why-does-zoom-exhaustyou-science-has-an-answer-11590600269

32. Jones, D.: Reflection: making little things visible. Des. Technol. Educ.: Int. J. **26**(1), 8–11 (2021) Retrieved from https://ojs.lboro.ac.uk/DATE/article/view/2925
33. Mukherjee, C.: Multi-dimensional leader capabilities for organizational agility in the future of work, PQDT-Global (2023)
34. Franken, E., Bentley, T., Shafaei, A., Farr-Wharton, B., Onnis, L.A., Omari, M.: Forced flexibility and remote working: opportunities and challenges in the new nor-mal. J. Manag. Organ. **27**(6), 1131–1149 (2021)
35. Ng, E., Stanton, P.: The great resignation: managing people in a post COVID-19 pandemic world. Pers. Rev. **52**(2), 401–407 (2023)
36. Wilber, K.: An integral theory of consciousness. J. Conscious. Stud. **4**(1), 71–92 (1997)
37. Sohaee, N., Ghasempour, A.: Students' emotional considerations and mental health during crises, In Teaching in the Post COVID-19 Era pp. 717–727. (2021). Doi:https://doi.org/10.1007/978-3-030-74088-7_70.
38. Lulewicz-Sas, A., Kinowska, H., Fryczyńska, M.: How sustainable human re-source management affects work engagement and perceived employability. Econ. & Sociol. **15**(4), (2022). ISSN 2071–789X.

# Knowledge Sharing by Leadership Perks up Creativity: An Empirical Evidence Based on Multilevel Survey

**GholamReza Zandi, Imran Ahmed Shahzad, Ayesha Kanwal, Khawar Naheed, Muhammad Sadiq Shahid, and Sandy Low Bee Choo**

**Abstract** Creativity has been under discussion for decades, and every time researchers address it, new challenges and solutions occur. This study aimed at inscribing the issues confronted by leaders in nurturing creativity at two levels, individual and team. For the same, hypotheses have been developed and tested by a multilayered model concerning dual-focused transformational leadership (TFL) and incorporated intervening mechanisms. For this multi-source survey, data has been collected from employees, team leaders, and managers working in pharmaceutical firms and analyzed through Structure Equation Modeling with the help of SmartPLS. The findings instituted that individual-focused TFL had an affirmative indirect influence on an individual's creativity through individual skill development. In contrast, team-focused TFL influences team creativity over team tacit knowledge sharing and support for creativity. This study also evidenced that tacit knowledge has a moderating impact on skill development and individual creativity. The findings of the current research further proved the direct effect of personality traits on boosting individual creativity. The result found the insignificant moderating effect of openness to experience on the relationship between individual skill development and creativity. Additionally, this study discussed the proof of the given theoretical framework while the study is helpful for leaders and top management from a practical implications point of view. This study has limitations and also recommends future directions.

**Keywords** Transformational Leadership · Team Tacit Knowledge · Support for Creativity · Openness to Experience · Employee Creativity

---

G. Zandi · S. L. B. Choo
Universiti Kuala Lumpur Business School, 54000 Kuala Lumpur, Malaysia

I. A. Shahzad
The University of Faisalabad, Faisalabad, Pakistan

Skema Business School, Lille, France

A. Kanwal · K. Naheed · M. S. Shahid (✉)
Department of Commerce, Bahauddin Zakariya University, Multan, Pakistan
e-mail: sshahidmalik@bzu.edu.pk



S. Kot et al. (eds.), *Corporate Practices: Policies, Methodologies, and Insights in Organizational Management*, Springer Proceedings in Business and Economics,
https://doi.org/10.1007/978-981-97-0996-0_23

# 1 Introduction

Studies of creativity and innovation have been a motivation itself as they remained in the great interest of both practitioners as well as researchers. The concept has been gaining popularity among business managers, particularly in knowledge management literature, as it is crucial for organizations to promote creative ideas [1–3], and it seems obligatory for organizations to be involved in research and development to generate new ideas and efficiently implement the ideas in all departments [4–6]. In order to exploit the potential regarding creativity, firms find a need to collaborate, as firms can meet challenges collectively with diverse knowledge, abilities, and experiences [1]. Moreover, individual creativity is crucial for the foundation of innovative processes and the achievement of competitiveness on a sustainable basis [7, 8]. Therefore, researchers [9] highlighted that innovative firms should develop creative and innovative teams. Therefore, corporate leaders stay close to employees for the continuous production of innovative ideas, products, and processes [10, 11]. This instigated the author to explore the mechanism where creativity and innovation can be channeled in the cut-throat corporate world.

In order to nourish individual creativity and team creativity, firms' interest seems to skyrocket in business literature, and team creativity is grabbing attention as one of the social, contextual, and motivational factors of any organization [2]. Studies suggest that firm intentions to achieve a competitive edge are subject to its focus on teamwork [12, 13]. Organizations that count on research and development depend upon teamwork to gain a competitive advantage [12, 13], where creativity involves R&D activities that heavily depend upon teamwork to gain competitive advantage; some researcher has demonstrated that team-level creativity is crucial to facilitate an efficient usage of teamwork related dexterities likewise social and project management skills. Similarly, individual creativity is also considered to lead organizations in a more competitive environment [6].

Organizations face rapidly growing technology, changing environments, and internalization. So, to lead in such a dynamic environment, an organization must consider individual-level creativity [6], where business literature advocates that managers can encourage and inhibit employees and team creativity by adopting various leadership styles [14, 15]. Previous studies describe that managers, by choosing diverse leadership styles, could inspire their followers and brighten individual and team creativity.

Consequently, this study adopts transformational leadership (TFL) behavior to target individual and team levels. Previous literature predicted discrete impact at both levels and showed individual teams' interchangeable mechanisms in TFL and creativity. Conceptualization of dual-focused predicts unique variance multilevel creativity while limiting the effect of TFL at both levels. Team leaders can inspire and support team members to proactively endorse their abilities and pro-innovative ideas [16] through their transformational in sharing their unique knowledge and achieving the team's goal. Having good communication between transformational leaders and team members encourages the sharing of their tacit knowledge that can be easily shared through their ideas, experiences, and expertise that, in turn, creativity through the generation of new ideas [17].

The research questions the current study has addressed: First, does team-focused TFL have a direct relationship with team tacit knowledge sharing and team creativity and with mediation support for creativity? Second, does individual-focused TFL have a significant relationship with their creativity and skill development directly and with the moderation of openness to experience? Third, is team tacit knowledge sharing moderated on individual creativity? This article has covered the perception of the leaders and followers working in the pharmaceutical industry with multiple years of experience in innovative activities and the need for creativity.

## 2 Literature Review

The Theory of Transformational Leadership was developed to understand the differences in leadership effectiveness [18]. Still, there is a need for further assessment of actionable models that measure profound constructs and concern the validity of transformational leadership style [16, 19, 20]. The theory of creativity involves four substantial panoramas from which three important models are utilized in creativity, i.e., innovative-based studies; the componential theory of organizational creativity involves an interactionist perspective of organizational creativity and an interactionist perspective of organizational creativity. Further to this, it is used in psychological and organizational creativity research. The interactionist perspective of organizational creativity is explained by Woodman et al. [20]. This view expresses that creativity is the outcome of cognitive capability (e.g., divergent wondering), personality, expertise, and motivation, social and contextual effects.

Based on dual-focused transformational leadership, the current study emphasizes the conceptualization of individual-focused TFL and team-focused TFL because previous studies highlighted that team-focused TFL and individual-focused TFL both identified and claimed that individual-focused TFL and Team focused TFL enhance team creativity, individual creativity through individual skill development and team knowledge sharing. The conceptualization of the dual-focused TFL model shows the behavior of transformational leaders who can motivate individuals and teams at the same time [16, 21].

Further, individual-focused TFL pays close attention to individual needs, personal development and excellence, intellectual abilities, and unique characteristics of each member. Team-focused TFL emphasizes common grounds, shared values, and ideology of team members by "articulating a compelling vision, constituting a role model for the team, and fostering acceptance of collective goals" [16]. Individual-focused transformational leadership pays attention to individual employees and cares about their self-development. In contrast, Team-focused transformational leadership focuses on the team and pays more attention to the team's interests. Therefore, individual-focused TFL enhances individual creativity, and team-focused TFL has a positive impact on team creativity because the author suggested that team-focused transformational leadership can build an atmosphere of team trust and cooperation. Consequently, leaders should improve employee creative performance [22, 23].

## *2.1 Team Focused TFL, Team Tacit Knowledge Sharing and Team Creativity*

Organizational leaders encourage employees to discuss and share knowledge and promote open communication to raise questions and find solutions. A leader guides their followers, discusses innovative ideas with team members [24], and ensures that team members are involved in the specific team agenda and organizational activities and are assured about a decision made democratically [25]. Hence, transformational leaders are required to know the state of mind of team members to think creatively and engage in the achievement of collective goals [18].

Moreover, socially influential individuals encourage their followers to share tacit knowledge for the organization's benefit [11]. It is beneficial for an employee to conform to socially significant others' desirable norms and engage TKS because it is an effective way for the employee to engage in social relations with essential persons in his or her firm [26, 27]. To magnify creativity in the team, leaders are required to build open communication among team members and build an environment to exchange information [28]. Another study by Tagger [29] sheds t light on this fact broadly by examining that the probability of reaching a higher level of creativity within the team is because of creative people among the team and production processes because members utilize knowledge that is accessible among the team and collectively member approach these things effectively.

As leaders focus on mutual goals and shared views, the team-based TFL is considered the best leading way to bring each team member on one platform for sharing knowledge-related activities and helping the team to portray its creative abilities. Hence, previous studies define *team knowledge sharing* as "the extent to which team members share task-relevant ideas, information, and suggestions with each other" [30].

Team focused TFL enhances individual knowledge constantly providing and collecting knowledge behavior boost. In addition, Dong et al., [16] describe a positive impact of team focused TFL on team knowledge sharing. Transformational leaders are crucial to know the state of mind of their team members to encourage their involvement for achieving team's goals. Having good communication between transformational leaders and team members encourage sharing of tacit knowledge through their ideas, experiences and expertise that in turn encourage, creativity by the generation of new ideas [18]. Therefore, this study hypothesized the following relationships;

H1: Team Focused TFL has a significant impact on Team Tacit Knowledge Sharing.
H2: Team Tacit Knowledge Sharing has a significant impact on Team Creativity.

#### 2.1.1 Individual Focused TFL, Individual Creativity and Individual Skill Development

Theories of creativity leadership could assist individuals in acquiring work-based skills and knowledge, which are essential ingredients for generating thoughts, ideas, and products in a new way [31]. Further, Parker & Wu [30] prescribed that "leaders can influence the pro-activity of their team members through fostering the development of knowledge, skills, and abilities." Moreover, the basic notion of individual-based TFL is development, which emphasizes the abilities and needs of individuals. As individual-based TFLs may improve creativity at the individual level, their development is considered a principal influencer process. Evidence relevant to this concept indicates that transformational leadership, on an individual basis, influences the development of their employees. Additionally, the employees who follow their leader try to communicate expectations and stimulate them to perform to achieve quality through an inherent need for growth [21, 32]. *Transformational leadership* is a leadership style in which leaders motivate their members to put extra effort into meeting their basic self-actualization needs. So, followers will participate in development ventures envisaged by Dvir et al. [33].

Besides, the transformational leader, through intellectual stimulation, could encourage an individual to become challenged to face problems with a new perspective and defy traditions, but to meet all viewpoints and problems, followers must learn new skills through consecutive development [34] as an individualized consideration leader of transformational behavior, give support and display honor to build understanding related to development needs. By relating these lines, more studies found that supportive leader and supervisor leads followers toward development activities along with their involvement in courses, journal reading, and starting novel projects actively [35, 36]. Therefore, previous research has also highlighted that to motivate followers individually toward the development of skills and abilities, individual-based TFL is needed [16]. Based on this, the following hypothesis has been developed;

H3: Individual Focused TFL has a significant impact on Individual Skill Development.

Accordingly, an insight "Invention is little more than a new combination of those images, which have been previously gathered and deposited in the memory" [37]. Further, it is to be noted that nothing can be made of nothing. He who has laid up no material can produce no combination (Yang et al., 2016). To support the above discussion, it is pointed out that individuals with diverse skills need creative ideas to be involved in diversifiable thinking [34]. It is also argued that employee's involvement in critical and creative thinking and recognizing novel opportunities are based on their knowledge and skills [35].

Conclusively, a high capacity for creativity denoted high skills and competencies available for creative performance, as the capability to view difficulties in new panoramas is significantly associated with individual creativity [36]. Ultimately, Dong et al. [16] conceptualized and recommended that individual-based magnify the creativity of their supporters due to their association with learning and skills attainment, which is the primary use of individual creative action taking and its performance. Further to this, Wang and Howell [37] highlighted that individual-based TFL empowers followers to develop their potential, enhance their skills, and improve their self-efficacy. In this condition, leaders recognize the admirer's needs, admirers' skills, and admirers' capabilities, which formerly coached and tutored followers appropriately, which impacts the admirer's act to complete assignments independently by dazzling an enthusiasm for them [38]. Therefore, the following hypotheses were developed as;

H4: Individual Skill Development has significant impact on Individual Creativity.
H5: Individual Skill Development mediates the relationship between Individual Focused TFL and Individual Creativity.

### 2.1.2 Team Tacit Knowledge Sharing and Openness to Experience

The personality trait "Openness to Experience" is a primogenital trait in the science and arts [38]. This trait is defined as followers who are open-minded, inclined towards the implementation of new ideas, and thirst for knowledge and creativity [39–41]. Openness to experience influences employee's attention and efforts to apply their skills on the job [42] actively. The study of Barrick et al. [43] conducted 11 meta-analyses and evidenced that openness was found to have the most vital relationship with work outcomes in all big five traits. Some studies have outlined high scores about openness by using a "deep" approach, such as Biggs, Kember, & Leung [44], that treat learning situations with intrinsic interest and determination. Training is a part of learning; it shows that individuals with the highest openness score can have high job performance through learning in the form of training. The training of employees for human resources development could enhance the competitive advantage of companies over their counterparts.

Openness to creativity is considered a source to boost creativity in any organization, which create divergent thinking in peoples and motivate them to enhance their abilities to seek novel ideas [45]. These data enable us to evaluate the extent to which different skills contribute to innovative output by enhancing the ability of firms in each country/industry to take advantage of the opportunities [46]. So, this study hypothesized that openness to creativity is positively linked with creativity because creativity-related personality trait, i.e., openness to experience, is closely associated with individual creativity.

A pool of knowledge is generated, which builds individual members' divergent thinking, even though this knowledge enlarges, activates thoughts, and enhances abilities [47]. This means that sharing within the team build opportunity for team members to gain profitable information, and discussion of shared information stimulate them to generate new understandings and tactics for resolving issues. Corresponding with this philosophy, the previous study highlighted that ideas, skills, and experiences are exchanged with other members, which stimulates more different ideas, through which individual member within a team enhances their thoughts that favor creativity. The literature described knowledge sharing in research and development in teams because team members rely on new ideas to handle complex problems and services on a usual basis [48]. Therefore, the study hypothesized the following;

H6: Openness to Experience moderates the relationship between Individual Skill Development and Individual Creativity.
H7: Team TKS moderates the relationship between Individual Skill Development and Individual Creativity.

### 2.1.3 Team Focused TFL, Support for Creativity and Team Creativity

Extant studies have shown that supervisor and coworker support for creativity may stimulate creative performance [49]. However, little more is needed to know about how support impinges on specific phases of the creative process. Business literature has shown that organizational support through its supervisor support facilitates the generation of new ideas among the team members [50, 51]. Further, research has demonstrated that intrinsic motivation enhances problem-solving capabilities and creative behavior [51, 52, 53). Previous studies highlighted that team creativity arises based on an organizational internal climate that involves shared vision, task orientation, support for creativity, and participation safety [54]. Organizational culture utilizes a dynamic team-based approach to facilitate the process of organizational learning, whereas organizational learning is the collaborative process of problem-solving [55].

Because creativity arises from exposure to different perspectives and from combining old with new ways, seeing things through the support of development-oriented team-based leadership [56] that discusses a variety of ideas and opinions to generate more creative solutions through team-oriented leaders, supervisors, and coworkers support that develop the culture of creativity among team members. A team's creativity within team members is only possible with organizational support that may create team members' perceptions that discuss various ideas and opinions and are likely to generate more creative solutions. A team process stimulates team members' creativity, so leader, supervisor, and coworker support is required. Another knowledge-sharing aspect among team members is a need for more organizational support for diversity, which may create individual perceptions precluding communications needed to support creativity and innovation processes [57]. A team-based TFL gives supportive feedback about performance that reinforces the desired behavior and defines when the new behavior is needed [25]. This enabled this study to postulate the following;

H8: Team Focused TFL has significant impact on Support for Creativity
H9: Support for creativity has significant impact on Team Creativity.
H10: Support for creativity mediates the relationship between Team Focused TFL and Team Creativity.

#### 2.1.4 Mediation of Team Tacit Knowledge Sharing, Support for Creativity and Individual Skill Development

Team-based TFL is an influential person helping to foster mutual task attainment by establishing intimate ideas in members to fully involve them in goal fulfillment and appreciate them [58, 59]. Due to this, team members are ready to take a chance because members feel admired, which boosts their inner cognizance and drives them to place their attempts and share knowledge, ideas, and expertise to provide input [60, 61]. So, deliberation of information shared leads to sharing tacit knowledge increasingly to gain collectiveness in creativity.

Team members appeared as the appealing agents for the generation of novel ideas and execution of those ideas envisaged by Gilson, Lim, Luciano, & Choi [61]. The process of creativity starts when the team members share knowledge through coordination, and it is also argued that much of the knowledge is shared when team members meet to share knowledge in a given area, much of which is tacit [62].

Poor firm performance due to lack of business knowledge amongst top management resulted in not being in the best interests of the company's shareholders. Sharing such tacit knowledge creates a flow of novel ideas contributing to successful outcomes, such as new products, processes, and patents. Because tacit knowledge sharing and transformational leadership style improve team performance, creativity as a process starts in the team by sharing tacit knowledge [63]. The study of related literature indicates that tacit knowledge sharing necessitates a positive and direct link with team member creativity [64]. So, based on the above hypothesis, it has been postulated as herein;

H11: Team Tacit Knowledge Sharing mediates the relationship between Team Focused TFL and Team Creativity.

This study has developed the conceptual model presented in Fig. 1.

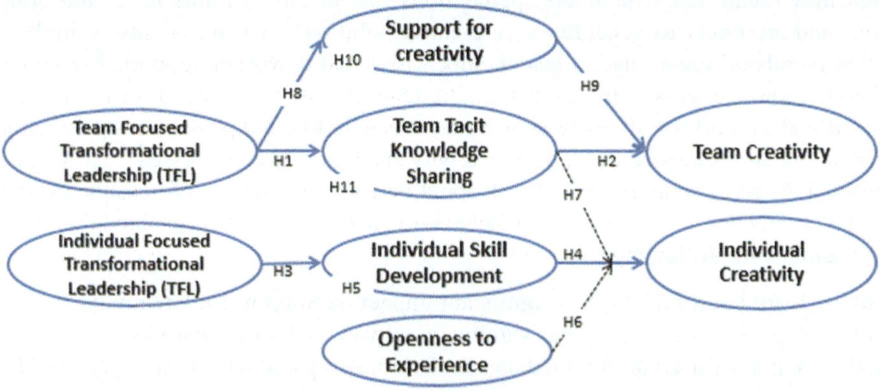


**Fig. 1** Conceptual Framework Showing Proposed Moderation of Environmental Factors on Business Performance and Innovation

**Table 1** Summary of the instrument items

| | | |
|---|---|---|
| Team Focused TFL | 9 | Wang & Howell (2010) |
| Individual Focused TFL | 16 | Wang & Howell (2010) |
| | 5 | Amabile, Conti, Coon, Lazenby, & Herron, (1996) |
| | 6 | Bartol, Liu, Zeng, and Wu (2009) |
| | 6 | Dong et al. (2017) |
| | 4 | Farmer, Tierney, and Kung-McIntyre (2003) |
| | 4 | Farmer, Tierney, and Kung-McIntyre (2003) |
| | 8 | Baer & Oldham (2006) |
| | **58** | |

# 3 Methodology

In this quantitative research, primary data has been collected by employing a fully structured self-administered questionnaire through a snowball probability sampling technique from the managers working in pharmaceutical firms in South Punjab, Pakistan. Respondents have been accessed by referrals from the social network of initial contacts as they were willing to participate and recommend other potential members who meet these research criteria. The sample size was selected using a formula devised by Israel [62], as N = Z2pq/e, because the desired population was large and the variability was also unknown; therefore, assumed p = 0.5 is the maximum variability has been opted. Additionally, this study has been conducted at a 95% confidence level and ± 5% precision, which resulted in a sample size of 385 respondents. Data has been collected at two levels: first from leaders and second from members. This study adopted previously well-established measurement scales; details are summarized in Table 1. A total of 390 responses were collected, of which 382 were used for analysis for this study. The collected data was analyzed in SmartPLS 3.2 by applying the SEM technique.

# 4 Results

## *4.1 Measurement Model*

Table 2 shows the results regarding the internal consistency, reliability, and validity of the model. As Sekaran and Bougie [63] pointed out, a value closer to zero indicates no internal consistency among the construct rather than values closer to one showed strong internal consistency [65]. Cronbach's alpha values have verified internal consistency, and it indicated consistency and equality among the constructs used in the model as values were found greater than 0.80.

**Table 2** Measurement Model Results

| | | | | |
|---|---|---|---|---|
| IC1 | 0.801 | 0.875 | 0.915 | 0.728 |
| IC2 | 0.889 | | | |
| IC3 | 0.86 | | | |
| IC4 | 0.861 | | | |
| **IF1** | **0.738** | **0.93** | **0.938** | **0.505** |
| IF2 | 0.644 | | | |
| IF3 | 0.721 | | | |
| IF5 | 0.622 | | | |
| IF6 | 0.763 | | | |
| IF7 | 0.668 | | | |
| IF8 | 0.808 | | | |
| IF9 | 0.752 | | | |
| **IF1** | **0.738** | **0.93** | **0.938** | **0.505** |
| IF10 | 0.770 | | | |
| IF11 | 0.692 | | | |
| IF12 | 0.677 | | | |
| IF13 | 0.747 | | | |
| IF14 | 0.750 | | | |
| IF15 | 0.662 | | | |
| IF16 | 0.613 | | | |
| **ISD1** | **0.675** | **0.816** | **0.866** | **0.521** |
| ISD2 | 0.632 | | | |
| ISD3 | 0.699 | | | |
| ISD4 | 0.739 | | | |
| ISD5 | 0.789 | | | |
| ISD6 | 0.783 | | | |
| **OE1** | **0.787** | **0.862** | **0.893** | **0.519** |
| OE3 | 0.679 | | | |
| OE4 | 0.728 | | | |
| OE5 | 0.609 | | | |
| OE6 | 0.808 | | | |
| OE7 | 0.818 | | | |
| OE8 | 0.811 | | | |
| **SC1** | **0.783** | **0.827** | **0.878** | **0.59** |
| SC2 | 0.783 | | | |
| SC3 | 0.825 | | | |

(continued)

**Table 2** (continued)

| | | | | |
|---|---|---|---|---|
| SC4 | 0.725 | | | |
| SC5 | 0.719 | | | |
| **TC1** | **0.827** | **0.882** | **0.918** | **0.738** |
| TC2 | 0.841 | | | |
| TC3 | 0.898 | | | |
| TC4 | 0.869 | | | |
| **TF1** | **0.679** | **0.895** | **0.915** | **0.544** |
| TF2 | 0.731 | | | |
| TF3 | 0.757 | | | |
| TF4 | 0.733 | | | |
| TF5 | 0.734 | | | |
| TF6 | 0.745 | | | |
| TF7 | 0.768 | | | |
| TF8 | 0.752 | | | |
| TF9 | 0.734 | | | |
| **TKS1** | **0.738** | **0.832** | **0.877** | **0.545** |
| TKS2 | 0.784 | | | |
| TKS3 | 0.771 | | | |
| TKS4 | 0.725 | | | |
| TKS5 | 0.781 | | | |

The value accepted for measuring composite reliability should be greater than 0.6 for factor loadings [68]. Values for factor loading for all items of the variable of interest are more significant than 0.70 and have fulfilled the acceptable criteria suggested by [68]. Convergent validity was reported through Average Variance Extracted (AVE), which is used to quantify the convergent validity, and AVE specified all the mean values of the quadratic loadings of a set of variables [68] where the cut-off value recommended for AVE was higher than 0.50.

Discriminant validity results reported in Table 4 were accessed by cross-loading criteria and criteria used by Fornell and Larcker [69] using an algorithm technique in SmartPLS software. Discriminant validity measures the degree to which one variable relates to another construct [68]. Fornell & Larcker [69] pointed out that the construct should share more variance with its indicators than with any other construct. Table 3 results showed that diagonal values were more significant than off-diagonal values.

The results reported in Table 3 and 4 showed that the current study fulfilled criteria of measurement model.

**Table 3** Fornell & Larcker Criterion

| | | | | | | | |
|---|---|---|---|---|---|---|---|
| 0.853 | | | | | | | |
| 0.396 | 0.711 | | | | | | |
| 0.664 | 0.296 | 0.722 | | | | | |
| 0.373 | 0.727 | 0.228 | 0.72 | | | | |
| 0.385 | 0.813 | 0.263 | 0.692 | 0.768 | | | |
| 0.762 | 0.402 | 0.591 | 0.38 | 0.431 | 0.859 | | |
| 0.363 | 0.832 | 0.278 | 0.695 | 0.796 | 0.388 | 0.737 | |
| 0.278 | 0.594 | 0.161 | 0.564 | 0.613 | 0.312 | 0.641 | 0.738 |

**Table 4** Structural Model Results

| | | | | |
|---|---|---|---|---|
| TF-TFL - > TKS | 0.641 | 0.647 | 10.495 | 0.0 |
| TKS - > TC | 0.076 | 0.083 | 0.73 | 0.465 |
| IF-TFL - > ISD | 0.296 | 0.318 | 3.89 | 0.00 |
| ISD - > IC | 0.624 | 0.625 | 12.589 | 0.00 |
| OE - > IC (moderating effect) | −0.029 | −0.025 | 0.498 | 0.619 |
| TKS - > IC (moderating effect) | 0.133 | 0.131 | 2.519 | 0.012 |
| TF-TFL- > SC | 0.796 | 0.798 | 23.474 | 0.00 |
| SC- > TC | 0.385 | 0.381 | 3.521 | 0.00 |

## 4.2 *Structural Model Results*

The structural model assessed the theoretical model of the current study, which was evaluated based on obtained values of path coefficients (β) and the coefficient of determination (R2) [68]. Table 4 grouped the structural model results, as "β determined the relationship between the variables investigated in a model" [74], and these values varied from + 1 to -1. The results in Table 5 showed that the hypothesized direct relationships H1, H3, H4, H7, and H8 showed positive relationships, while H2 was found to have insignificant positive relationships. H5 and H6 measured the moderating effect. H5 found that openness to experience has a negative but insignificant effect on individual creativity. H6 is found to have a positive at a significance level of $P < 0.05$ with a t-value of less than 2.58 but more significant than 1.96. Team Tacit Knowledge Sharing strengthens individual creativity. Further to this, the results of the study for H1, H3, H4, H5, H6, H7 and H8 were found significant as the cut-off point for t-values was found more excellent than the cut-off values, i.e. 1.65 at $p < 0.10$, 1.96 at $p < 0.05$, and 2.58 at $p < 0.01$, defined by Hair et al. [68].

Moreover, "$R^2$ measures the combined effect of variances of exogenous variables over endogenous variables" [68]. Results were grouped in Table 5 and found the $R^2$ values that vary from weak to strong.

**Table 5** Regression Analysis (Goodness of fit)

| | |
|---|---|
| 0.512 | Moderate |
| 0.088 | Weak |
| 0.634 | Strong |
| 0.190 | Weak |
| 0.411 | Moderate |

**Table 6** Mediation Analysis Statistics

| | | | | | | |
|---|---|---|---|---|---|---|
| 0.398 | 0.41 | 0.068 | 5.879 | 0.000 | Supported | |
| 0.306 | 0.305 | 0.091 | 3.361 | 0.001 | Supported | Partial Mediation |
| 0.4 | 0.414 | 0.064 | 6.238 | 0.000 | Supported | |
| 0.185 | 0.198 | 0.049 | 3.776 | 0.000 | Supported | Partial Mediation |
| 0.049 | 0.055 | 0.069 | 0.707 | 0.48 | unsupported | No-Mediation |

The mediating effect (Table 6) of individual skill development between individual focused-TFL and individual creativity showed a partial mediation. Support for creativity has partial mediation between Team focused-TFL and team creativity. However, the mediation of team tacit knowledge sharing between Team focused-TFL and Team creativity was found unsupported.

## 5 Discussion

The study hypothesized the positive and significant link between team focused TFL and team tacit knowledge sharing as in H1. This study highlighted that leader resolves friction among the members in to support the teamwork, as reported by the study of Lai [21]. This behavior of the leader encourages team members to share their unique ideas and expertise and more experienced members efficiently provide other members with inimitable knowledge or specialized skills. The result for H2 is insignificant and is rejected. This result indicated that team member's tacit or specialized knowledge does not help the team to create new ideas. The result is inconsistent with Bartol et al. [70]. Baer and Oldham [71] and Farmer et al. (2003) argued that team member tells other members about their knowledge, which helps them to seek new ideas and ways to solve problem.

The relationship between IF-TFL and individual skill development H3 is significantly supported. The result of H3 indicated that transformational leaders have a positive effect, and they focused on the skills development on an individual basis in an organization, indicating as, if the leader focuses on each employee than it will increase its skills. When leaders encourage each employee's development, the employee can increase their skills. The result also indicated that leader helps their employees to develop their skills and get them to look at problems from several aspects as the study of Dong et al. [16] infers that IF- TFL develop employee's skills.

The result for H4 showed a significant positive effect on individual creativity through its skill development. This inferred that when individuals enjoy learning new ideas or methods, they can generate groundbreaking ideas, as discussed in the study of Baer & Oldham [71]. The supported results for H4 designated that employees are proactive and prepare themselves for learning new skills and overcome any skill deficiency related to their work.

The result indicated that employees are ready to learn new skills that help them to adapt to work challenges, as discussed in a few studies [16, 71].

However, moderation of openness to experience individual creativity is not supported by H5. The openness culture neither strengthens nor decreases the effect on individual creativity. The result for H6 moderating effect of team tacit knowledge sharing has a weak positive but significant effect. This showed that when team members share their unique skills, knowledge, abilities, and understandings with their team members, it increases the individual creativity in an organization. The creativeness or skills to contribute to creative ideas in each employee increase. The result for the hypothesized relationship of TF-TFL and support for creativity (H7) and team creativity (H8) is found to have a positive and significant effect. H7 and H8 supported the hypothesis and highlighted that team-focused leadership and a supportive culture help its members develop and generating creative ideas. Support for creativity by the team members enhanced by the supportive behavior of leaders, managers and supervisors. Supportive behaviors help the team to boosts creative abilities of members and unsupportive behavior have a negative impact on personal abilities. Hence, if leaders demonstrate supportive behavior to their members and subordinates, it can increase their capability to perceive efficient and effective usage of shared vision. This study contended that influential leaders, with their powers and dominant locus that inclined to be largely convoluted in the in handling difficult issues and creativity.

H9 hypothesized the mediation of support for creativity between TF-TFL and team creativity.

The result found that support for creativity has partial mediation, this inferred that support for creativity is important factor that help in strengthen the relationship of TF-TFL and team creativity. Supportive culture from the organization is crucial in the process of team creativity. *H10 supported with partial mediation* of individual skill development between IF-TFL and individual creativity. Leader focus on individual employee development is important to increase the creative based initiatives among the employees. However, the result of H11 is not supported and found to insignificant team tacit knowledge sharing is not crucial in the process of team creativity. This is also confirmed with the result of moderating effect found in H6 that it strengthens the individual creativity rather than important in the mechanism team creativity process.

## *5.1 Theoretical Contributions*

Firstly, this study measured dual-focused transformational leadership at individual and team levels and enriched the knowledge-sharing literature, particularly on tacit knowledge-sharing. It has provided a framework for the researchers to move on to further research in knowledge management. Secondly, the current study measured the effect of factors from personal and cultural aspects, i.e., skill development, creativity, and support for creativity," that not only opens a new debate area but also provides a new construct for future researchers. Thirdly, this study measured the impact of team tacit knowledge rather than general knowledge sharing investigated by Dong et al. [16]. The importance of tacit knowledge rather general is highlighted by the study of Mihardjo & Alamsjah [72]; shared within the team is tacit knowledge. This study utilizes this sort of knowledge at the team level. Therefore, this study remains able to advance the understanding of leaders at team development phases that transform the behavior of members.

Fourthly, results demonstrate the likely advantages of team-based TFL, as (1) this leadership behavior helps team members to identify the essence of tacit knowledge sharing within the team, (2) It provides support for creativity by novel mannered thoughts and action upon creatively (3) Sharing tacit knowledge and provide opportunities to share and act creatively freely. Therefore, the current study contributed to the literature that an organization can benefit from TF-TFL, which may increase team tacit knowledge sharing and team creativity and also from a supportive culture. (5) There is a great need to focus on IF-TFL if the organization intends to increase creativity on individual and team levels. By integrating this study, it identifies that individual-level processes and team-level processes could be incurred at a time that impacts creativity and examines the influence of TFL in a dynamic way. So, that multi-level mechanism is incurred in one platform by transformational leadership to boost creativity at both levels. (6) The study moreover found that team tacit knowledge sharing and individual skills development interaction predict individual creativity. There needs to be more studies that have contributed to creativity literature by using dual-focused transformational leadership. Seventh, this study contributed to the creativity literature by focusing on knowledge management, human resource development, leadership behavior, and organizational environmental support on individual and team levels. The current study integrated the factor at a dual level.

Finally, the current study underscores the importance of facilitating knowledge sharing for individual creativity as it may pay off member's improvement. Correspondingly, the ancillary (indirect) result of individual-based leadership on creativity by individual's skill development established a strong effect when the sharing of knowledge among team members was weak. The result of the current study indicated that leaders should emphasize individual members' creativity and development. Knowledge-sharing among teams may be valued, especially when an individual's competencies need to expand to a high level.

### 5.2 Practical Contributions

The hypothetical model of the study has significant recommendations for managers. The first implication is that this study will benefit management to embrace dual TFL for transforming employee behavior, particularly in the field where creativity is needed. The result of this study indicated that while involved in both levels of TFL, team leaders exhibit their role in promoting creativity. This dual-based focus helps team leaders solve issues and problems and enrich the generation of new ideas among the cohorts. To promote creativity among the members, leaders can express their expectations and intellectual-based challenges and offer perceptive, social, and emotional support. Leader at the team level helps their members to involve team-focused behaviors such as enunciating their vision and expediting their recognition of team-based objectives. The outcomes of the current study also propose that leaders of organizations need to encourage their members to create thoughts and offer prospects for creativity through several apparatuses, i.e., (workshops, discussion sessions, and training). At the team focused, leaders may supplement their categorical attention on the sharing of ideas and skills, particularly to enhance creativity among team members and at the individual level. The result of the current study evidenced that sharing of knowledge at both levels has an affirmative effect; it may be worthwhile to reward knowledge-sharing behavior among team members.

### 5.3 Limitations and Future Suggestion

There are some limitations of the current study. This study used the snowball sampling method, a non-probability sampling method. The current study collected data from pharmaceutical firms. The currently used team tacit knowledge sharing as a moderating variable to link with individual creativity. This study used creativity as the dependent variable. There are suggestions for future studies that they can use probability sampling techniques like random sampling to increase the reliability of results. The data can be collected from other service-oriented companies, increasing the generalizability of results. Further studies can use other moderating variables like psychological variables and cultural-based variables. Future studies can also link the variables other team individual skill development and support for creativity that can help the policymakers to increase creativity and innovativeness in an organization.

## References

1. Bovaird, T., Loeffler, E.: Developing Evidence-based co-production: a research agenda. In: The Palgrave handbook of co-production of public services and outcomes pp. 693–713. Palgrave Macmillan, Cham (2021)

2. Luu, T.T., Rowley, C., Dinh, C.K., Qian, D., Le, H.Q.: Team creativity in public healthcare organizations: The roles of charismatic leadership, team job crafting, and collective public service motivation. Public Perform. Manag. Rev. **42**(6), 1448–1480 (2019)
3. Harms, M., Kennel, V., Reiter-Palmon, R.: Team creativity: cognitive processes underlying problem solving. In: Team creativity and innovation pp. 61–86. Oxford University Press (2017)
4. Tidd, J., Bessant, J.R.: Managing innovation: integrating technological, market and organizational change. John Wiley & Sons (2020)
5. West, J., Salter, A., Vanhaverbeke, W., Chesbrough, H.: Open innovation: the next decade (2014)
6. Kremer, H., Villamor, I., Aguinis, H.: Innovation leadership: best-practice recommendations for promoting employee creativity, voice, and knowledge sharing. Bus. Horiz. **62**(1), 65–74 (2019)
7. George, J.M.: 9 Creativity in organizations. Acad. Manag. Ann. **1**(1), 439–477 (2007)
8. Zhang, X., Bartol, K.M.: The influence of creative process engagement on employee creative performance and overall job performance: a curvilinear assessment. J. Appl. Psychol. **95**(5), 862 (2010)
9. Pirola-Merlo, A., Mann, L.: The relationship between individual creativity and team creativity: aggregating across people and time. J. Organ. Behav. **25**(2), 235–257 (2004)
10. Katz, J.H., Herman, G.L., Johnson, M.A., Loewenstein, J.: Cultivating not gatekeeping: a key leadership role in the creative process. BMJ Leader **5**(1), (2021)
11. Shalley, C.E., Gilson, L.L., Blum, T.C.: Interactive effects of growth need strength, work context, and job complexity on self-reported creative performance. Acad. Manag. J. **52**(3), 489–505 (2009)
12. Ilgen, D.R., Hollenbeck, J.R., Johnson, M., Jundt, D.: Teams in organizations: from input-process-output models to IMOI models. Annu. Rev. Psychol. **56**, 517–543 (2005)
13. Shahzad, I.A., Farrukh, M., Ahmed, N.O., Lin, L., Kanwal, N.: The role of transformational leadership style, organizational structure and job characteristics in developing psychological empowerment among banking professionals. J. Chin. Hum. Resour. Manag. (2018)
14. Mainemelis, C., Kark, R., Epitropaki, O.: Creative leadership: a multi-context conceptualization. Acad. Manag. Ann. **9**(1), 393–482 (2015)
15. Mumford, M.D., Scott, G.M., Gaddis, B., Strange, J.M.: Leading creative people: orchestrating expertise and relationships. Leadersh. Q. **13**(6), 705–750 (2002)
16. Dong, Y., Bartol, K.M., Zhang, Z.X., Li, C.: Enhancing employee creativity via individual skill development and team knowledge sharing: influences of dual-focused transformational leadership. J. Organ. Behav. **38**(3), 439–458 (2017)
17. Castellani, P., Rossato, C., Giaretta, E., Davide, R.: Tacit knowledge sharing in knowledge-intensive firms: the perceptions of team members and team leaders. Rev. Manag. Sci., 1–31 (2019)
18. Jackson, C.J.: Transformational leadership and gravitas: 2000 years of no development? Personality Individ. Differ. **156**, 109760 (2020)
19. Jia, J., Liu, H., Chin, T., Hu, D.: The continuous mediating effects of GHRM on employees' green passion via transformational leadership and green creativity. Sustainability **10**(9), 3237 (2018)
20. Woodman, R.W., Sawyer, J.E., Griffin, R.W.: Toward a theory of organizational creativity. Acad. Manag. Rev. **18**(2), 293–321 (1993)
21. Lai, L.: A review of team-focused transformational leadership: past and new trends. J. Serv. Sci. Manag. **12**(2), 172–185 (2019)
22. Golden, J.H., III., Shriner, M.: Examining relationships between transformational leadership and employee creative performance: the moderator effects of organizational culture. The Journal of Creative Behavior **53**(3), 363–376 (2019)
23. Sousa, B., Rocha, A.T.: The role of attachment in public management and place marketing contexts: a case study applied to Vila de Montalegre (Portugal). International Journal of Public Sector Performance Management **5**(2), 189–205 (2019)

24. Hau, Y.S., Kim, B., Lee, H.: What drives employees to share their tacit knowledge in practice? Knowl. Manag. Res. Pract. **14**(3), 295–308 (2016)
25. Zheng, J., Wu, G., Xie, H.: Impacts of leadership on project-based organizational innovation performance: the mediator of knowledge sharing and moderator of social capital. Sustainability **9**(10), 1893 (2017)
26. Hargadon, A.B., Bechky, B.A.: When collections of creatives become creative collectives: a field study of problem solving at work. Organ. Sci. **17**(4), 484–500 (2006)
27. Taggar, S.: Individual creativity and group ability to utilize individual creative resources: a multilevel model. Acad. Manag. J. **45**(2), 315–330 (2002)
28. Farrukh, M., Ting, H., Shahzad, I.A., Hua, Z.: Can incivility impede knowledge sharing behaviour? Int. J. Inf. Syst. Change Manage. **10**(4), 295–310 (2018)
29. Tagger, S.: Individual creativity and group ability to utilize individual creative resources: a multilevel model. Acad. Manag. J. **45**, 315–330 (2002). https://doi.org/10.2307/3069349
30. Parker, S.K., Wu, C.H.: Leading for proactivity: how leaders cultivate staff who make things happen (2014)
31. Schriesheim, C.A., Wu, J.B., Scandura, T.A.: A meso measure? Examination of the levels of analysis of the Multifactor Leadership Questionnaire (MLQ). Leadersh. Q. **20**(4), 604–616 (2009)
32. Chen, C.J., Shih, H.A., Yeh, Y.C.: Individual initiative, skill variety, and creativity: the moderating role of knowledge specificity and creative resources. Int. J. Hum. Resour. Manag. **22**(17), 3447–3461 (2011)
33. Dvir, T., Eden, D., Avolio, B.J., Shamir, B.: Impact of transformational leadership on follower development and performance: a field experiment. Acad. Manag. J. **45**(4), 735–744 (2002)
34. Choi, J.N.: Person–environment fit and creative behavior: differential impacts of supplies–values and demands–abilities versions of fit. Human Relations **57**(5), 531–552 (2004)
35. Antonakis, J., House, R.J.: On instrumental leadership: beyond transactions and transformations. UNL Gallup Leadership Institute Summit, Omaha (2004)
36. Batey, M., Furnham, A., Safiullina, X.: Intelligence, general knowledge and personality as predictors of creativity. Learn. Individ. Differ. **20**(5), 532–535 (2010)
37. Wang, X.H.F., Howell, J.M.: Exploring the dual-level effects of transformational leadership on followers. J. Appl. Psychol. **95**(6), 1134 (2010)
38. McCrae, R.R., Costa Jr, P.T.: Conceptions and correlates of openness to experience. In: Handbook of personality psychology pp. 825–847. Academic Press (1997)
39. Grabowska, M., Otola, I., Szymczyk, K.: Innovation in business models. innovation, digital transformation, and analytics. Boca Raton, CRC Press, In Business Models (2020)
40. Ślusarczyk, B., Tvaronavičienė, M., Haque, A.U., Oláh, J.: Predictors of industry 4.0 technologies affecting logistic enterprises' performance: international perspective from economic lens. Technol. Econ. Dev. Econ. **26**(6), 1263–1283 (2020)
41. Bidjerano, T., Dai, D.Y.: The relationship between the big-five model of personality and self-regulated learning strategies. Learn. Individ. Differ. **17**(1), 69–81 (2007)
42. Chamorro-Premuzic, T., Furnham, A.: Mainly openness: the relationship between the Big Five personality traits and learning approaches. Learn. Individ. Differ. **19**(4), 524–529 (2009)
43. Barrick, M.R., Mount, M.K., Judge, T.A.: Personality and performance at the beginning of the new millennium: what do we know and where do we go next? Int. J. Sel. Assess. **9**(1–2), 9–30 (2001)
44. Biggs, J., Kember, D., Leung, D.Y.: The revised two-factor study process questionnaire: R-SPQ-2F. Br. J. Educ. Psychol. **71**(1), 133–149 (2001)
45. Gong, Y., Kim, T.Y., Lee, D.R., Zhu, J.: A multilevel model of team goal orientation, information exchange, and creativity. Acad. Manag. J. **56**(3), 827–851 (2013)
46. Madjar, N.: Emotional and informational support from different sources and employee creativity. J. Occup. Organ. Psychol. **81**(1), 83–100 (2008)
47. Madjar, N., Oldham, G.R., Pratt, M.G.: There's no place like home? The contributions of work and nonwork creativity support to employees' creative performance. Acad. Manag. J. **45**(4), 757–767 (2002)

48. Frese, M., Teng, E., Wijnen, C.J.: Helping to improve suggestion systems: predictors of making suggestions in companies. J. Organ. Behav. **20**(7), 1139–1155 (1999)
49. Amabile, T.M., Schatzel, E.A., Moneta, G.B., Kramer, S.J.: Leader behaviors and the work environment for creativity: perceived leader support. The Leadership Quarterly **15**(1), 5–32 (2004)
50. Carmeli, A., Reiter-Palmon, R., Ziv, E.: Inclusive leadership and employee involvement in creative tasks in the workplace: the mediating role of psychological safety. Creat. Res. J. **22**(3), 250–260 (2010)
51. Burningham, C., West, M.A.: Individual, climate, and group interaction processes as predictors of work team innovation. Small Group Research **26**(1), 106–117 (1995)
52. Demircioglu, M.A., Berman, E.: Effects of the innovation climate on turnover intention in the Australian public service. Am. Rev. Public Adm. **49**(5), 614–628 (2019)
53. Mumford, M.D., Gustafson, S.B.: Creativity syndrome: integration, application, and innovation. Psychol. Bull. **103**(1), 27 (1988)
54. Lambert, D.M., Graves, N., Slater, F.: Geography as powerful knowledge. Int. Res. Geogr. Environ. Educ. **25**(3), 189–194 (2016)
55. Shin, S.J., Kim, T.Y., Lee, J.Y., Bian, L.: Cognitive team diversity and individual team member creativity: a cross-level interaction. Acad. Manag. J. **55**(1), 197–212 (2012)
56. Detert, J.R., Burris, E.R.: Leadership behavior and employee voice: is the door really open? Acad. Manag. J. **50**(4), 869–884 (2007)
57. Hülsheger, U.R., Anderson, N., Salgado, J.F.: Team-level predictors of innovation at work: a comprehensive meta-analysis spanning three decades of research. J. Appl. Psychol. **94**(5), 1128 (2009)
58. Pietruszka-Ortyl, A.: Determinants of the knowledge diffusion process among professionals in the IT sector. Forum Sci. Oecon. **8**(3), 73–97 (2020). Wydawnictwo Naukowe Akademii WSB
59. Liang, B., van Knippenberg, D., Gu, Q.: A cross-level model of shared leadership, meaning, and individual creativity. J. Organ. Behav. **42**(1), 68–83 (2021)
60. Zandi, G., Aslam, A., Selamat, M.H., Nasir, M.U.: Effect of participative leadership and employees training on organizational productivity: a study of E&E Sector in Malaysia. Acad. Entrep. J. **25**, 1–10 (2019)
61. Gilson, L.L., Lim, H.S., Luciano, M.M., Choi, J.N.: Unpacking the cross-level effects of tenure diversity, explicit knowledge, and knowledge sharing on individual creativity. J. Occup. Organ. Psychol. **86**(2), 203–222 (2013)
62. Israel, G.D.: Determining sample size. 1992. Fact Sheet PEOD **6**, (2020)
63. Sekaran, U., Bougie, R.: Research methods for business: a skill building approach. John Wiley & Sons (2020)
64. Farmer, S.M., Tierney, P., Kung-Mcintyre, K.: Employee creativity in Taiwan: an application of role identity theory. Acad. Manag. J. **46**(5), 6(Davide, 2019)-630.Baer, (2003)
65. Chin, W.W.: The partial least squares approach to structural equation modeling. Mod. Methods Bus. Res. **295**(2), 295–336 (1998)
66. Hair Jr, J.F., Sarstedt, M., Hopkins, L., Kuppelwieser, V.G.: Partial least squares structural equation modeling (PLS-SEM): an emerging tool in business research. European Business Review, (2014)
67. Fornell, C., Larcker, D. F.: Structural equation models with unobservable variables and measurement error: algebra and statistics (1981)
68. Könning, M., Westner, M., Strahringer, S.: Multisourcing on the Rise–Results from an Analysis of more than 1,000 IT Outsourcing Deals in the ASG Region. In Proceedings of the Multikonferenz Wirtschaftsinformatik pp. 06–09, (2019)
69. Bartol, K.M., Liu, W., Zeng, X., Wu, K.: Social exchange and knowledge sharing among knowledge workers: the moderating role of perceived job security. Manag. Organ. Rev. **5**(2), 223–240 (2009)
70. Baer, M., Oldham, G.R.: The curvilinear relation between experienced creative time pressure and creativity: moderating effects of openness to experience and support for creativity. J. Appl. Psychol. **91**(4), 963 (2006)

71. Mihardjo, L., Sasmoko, S., Alamsjah, F., Elidjen, E.: Digital leadership role in developing business model innovation and customer experience orientation in industry 4.0. Manag. Sci. Lett. **9**, (2019)

# Social Media and Destination Marketing in China: A Systematic Review of Short Videos

**Congying Liu, Ahmad Edwin Bin Mohamed, and Muhammad Zulqarnain Arshad**

**Abstract** Traditionally, tourists gain information about a particular destination from tourist boards and journals. However, in the modern era of rapid technological advancements, social media plays a significant role in influencing tourists' decisions regarding their choice of destination. It has changed how information is shared, and one of the famous sources of information sharing is short videos. China mainly operates domestic tourism and must attract international tourists. Therefore, this systematic review examined social media's influence on destination marketing in China and reviewed the use of short videos as a destination marketing social media tool. The study followed the qualitative research approach and started with a keyword search relevant to the purpose of the study. Later on, the papers included in the study ranged from 2010 to 2022. Google Scholar, Web of Science, and Scopus database were used for conducting the study. Since it is a systematic review, the study reported the methodology by following the PRISMA checklist. The study's findings revealed that social media marketing is extensively used to share information related to destinations and thus emerged to influence tourists' decision-making significantly. Additionally, findings revealed that social media is growing, and social media also influences Chinese destination marketing. Importantly, the information shared in the form of short videos, live videos, and user-generated videos positively contributed to the positive image creation of the tourist experience in China, which led to an enhanced intention to travel.

---

C. Liu (✉) · A. E. B. Mohamed
School of Tourism, Hospitality and Event Management, Universiti Utara Malaysia, Sintok, Malaysia
e-mail: liucongying11@gmail.com

A. E. B. Mohamed
e-mail: edwin@uum.edu.my

M. Z. Arshad
School of Business Management, College of Business, Universiti Utara Malaysia, Sintok, Malaysia
e-mail: m.zulqarnain.arshad@uum.edu.my

 
S. Kot et al. (eds.), *Corporate Practices: Policies, Methodologies, and Insights in Organizational Management*, Springer Proceedings in Business and Economics,
https://doi.org/10.1007/978-981-97-0996-0_24

**Keywords** Social Media · Destination Marketing · Systematic Review · PRISMA · China

## 1 Introduction

Rapid advancements in technology, internet usage, and social networks have led to social media exerting an increased influence by affecting consumers' decision-making in virtually every field, specifically in the Chinese tourism industry. The introduction of the Internet and communication technologies aided the contemporary nature of prevailing social media network use. Researchers have come to emphasize the digital communication modes that form consumer behaviors and influence their preferences. Organizational sectors accomplish goals using the Internet and digital communication [1]. Travel business and tourism industry attention has focused on the advanced digital world, with investments made in social media platforms to attain efficient, extensive, and effective marketing and advertising. A single click on social media enables the assessment of a broader range of audiences, thus exerting a substantial effect on the destination. Social media content can target potential audiences and foster their familiarity with a destination [2]. Currently, positive relationships are also established through social media as global companies have adopted social media to assess consumers' needs, wants, and preferences by responding to consumers' information-sharing responses [3]. Social media focuses on audience or consumer connection to enhance brand understanding. In addition to benefiting economic growth, social media currently ensures the most differentiated and cost-effective means of destination marketing. Generally, social is one of the widely used media tools as well [4, 5]. It has emerged to be the need of tourists due to dynamic changes in customer needs [6, 7] that can be addressed by an innovative platform such as social media.

The increased acceptance and adoption of social media have altered business functions, including tourism sector activities. Located in eastern Asia, China is the third largest country globally and continues to draw attention to its tourist destinations. Social media applications influence consumers' decision-making and facilitate their connection with Chinese tourism service product providers. People in China comprise an important tourism segment that ensures greater potential for Chinese tourism industry development [8]. Social media application development, which would benefit the Chinese tourism industry, has aided many consumers searching for tourist destinations. As people share experiences regarding their visit to a specific location, the sharing subsequently increases the probability of others visiting the exact location. Social media thus acts as an intermediary between individuals and tourist destinations. Online destination information influences decision-making on tourism destinations. Since 2011, researchers focused on how social media and other communication technologies are influencing the tourism and travel sectors [8, 9]. Nevertheless, exhaustive reviews of social media use as a destination marketing tool still need to be included, specifically in China, which focuses on short videos and reels as social media tools.

Currently, there are numerous social media addicts, and many influencers are involved in paid promotion and free reviews of specific products or services [10]. Short videos and reels are an advanced social media feature, specifically on Instagram. Visits to a specific tourist destination can increase business when other tourists become aware of the efficient services [11]. Videos and reels uploaded on social media improve the image of a destination. Such videos mainly encompass the person's personal experiences in the form of feedback. Videos are used for the promotion of the destinations [12]. Another study contended that visuals with fewer human distractions are an influencing tool for destination promotion [13] because they tend to build the cognitive image of the tourists [14]. They also stated that the mobile applications have changed the way information is obtained by the tourists [14]. Another study about the video content put forward that the reels on instagram tend to drive user engagement positively. Such content is generated by the tourists who already visited the destinations [15]. So, social media users consider such reviews inspirational and are prompted to replicate the behavior by visiting a specific location [16] and improving the destination image via videos and reels. Despite the enhanced role of social media in promoting tourism activities at various global destinations, research on social media usage and tourism destination decision-making still needs to be explored [17]. The study has the objective of providing a synthesis of the literature on how social media influences destination marketing. Thus, this study conducted a systematic review of social media and destination marketing that focused on using short videos as a social media tool in China. The literature in the context above was reviewed, with the results described in this article on social media and destination marketing.

## 2 Social Media as a Destination Marketing Tool

Recent research demonstrated that social media use substantially influenced the tourism industry, as the number of social media users has increased substantially. Literature from the past decade mapped a positive relationship between social media marketing and intention to travel, and intention to travel to or revisit a specific place [17–19]. In addition to visitor word-of-mouth (WOM), social media users have access to other types of online information, which aids travel intention and destination image development [20, 21]. The variety of social media platforms, information tools, and information production and publishing techniques has significantly altered how destination marketing organizations or tourist destinations use social media. Consumer needs-centric content on the social media platforms of destination marketing organizations and tourist destinations has increased. Such content enables the highlighting of the advantages and disadvantages of each destination choice and aids the research stage of planning to travel [17] and the information- or experience-sharing phase [21].

Besides facilitating consumers to obtain information, social media enables users to generate shareable content.

Zeng and Gerritsen [18] and [19] focused on the potential of user-generated content for strategically managing tourism intentions and choices. Kim and Lee [19] emphasized the key role of social media in transforming how tourists seek, consume, and perceive information on their intended travel destinations. Furthermore, Kim Lee [19] highlighted that tourists could share their travel experiences to influence the destination image through social media platforms, such as Instagram, Facebook, YouTube, and Twitter. Social media has also become the leading tourism organization tool to market specific destinations to target travel consumers. Various tourism information quality factors of social media use substantially influenced the formation of a destination image [19].

Chinese users tend to consume social media to plan their travels and share travel experiences [19, 22]. Several studies examined the influence of social media on travel destination choice [19]. Earlier studies reported that social media information was considered low reliability and low credibility. Therefore, social media did not substantially influence destination choice despite travel information-sharing and consumption [18, 23]. Furthermore, some studies reported the indirect effect of social media on tourists' decisions by reducing dissonance instead of directly influencing travel destination choices [24–26].

In an empirical study, Pan Rasouli [20] highlighted the role of a person's social network and its influence on their decisions to travel and destination image. The estimation results of the random choice model in the study determined that the destination image of a person's social network members influenced their knowledge and perception of a destination. Social media usage constraints, such as those in China, can also influence destination image, affecting consumers' emotional experience [28]. Given that it is one of the most widely-used communication platforms, Ketter [21] emphasized that Facebook was an important communication channel during crises to protect and cultivate a destination image. Ketter evaluated the ability of Facebook to restore the image of Nepal as a tourism destination following the magnitude 7.8 earthquake in 2015 (the Gurkha earthquake) and concluded that social media platforms have unique metrics and act as multifunctional tools. Thus, social media platforms can address diverse audiences and provide formal and informal interaction mechanisms that allow these platforms to become positive destination marketing tools.

## *2.1 Destination Social Media Marketing in the Chinese Context*

The Chinese tourism industry has developed substantially in the past 20 years. Therefore, there has been increased research on how the destination image of China can be improved to increase tourist inflow. Ran, Zhenpeng [22] noted that domestic tourism generates most of the revenue in the Chinese tourism sector and that larger tourism markets, such as the US, do not contribute to tourism sector growth and income. Thus, Ran et al. [30] examined the effect of electronic WOM (eWOM) on Beijing social media concerning US traveler's attitudes and intentions to visit Beijing. The results indicated a strong relationship between eWOM utilitarian function and credibility on destination image.

Nonetheless, destination image did not affect future intentions to travel. Leung et al. [17] reviewed the role of social media in travelers' tourism operations decision-making. The review analyzed literature from 2007 to 2011 to examine how social media-related research evolved in the hospitality and tourism sectors. The content analysis revealed that social media affected travelers' planning processes and enabled travel companies to manage and promote destination images. Shani et al. [31] empirically examined the effect of promotional videos on changing the destination image, where the destination was China. How promotional videos affected short-term US employees' perceptions of their travel intentions for China was tested with an experimental approach. The cultural and nature-related tourism dimensions in the promotional video influenced the participants' behavioral intentions to travel. Shani et al. [31] summarised that China should be promoted as a desirable travel destination that focuses on its cultural and nature-related tourism attractions.

Li et al. [32] commented that web content published by social media peers had become a clear information source for travel planning. Li et al. conducted a content analysis of blog articles to examine how the activities and travel attractions, such as shopping, food, beverages, accommodation, and transportation mechanisms, promoted in the blog posts of peers' social media platforms affected the travel destination image and travel intentions to China. Traveler-generated web content could help create destination images to manage and market destinations, such as China. Yang and Wang [33] discussed the opportunities and challenges encountered by destination marketing organizations following the popularity of social media for travel decision-making. Yang and Wang emphasized that such organizations should develop social media marketing strategies that can influence the effectiveness of their overall marketing strategies and allow them to meet their stakeholders' expectations. Yang and Wang also described the Chinese social media landscape. They discussed the challenges and opportunities overseas destination marketing organizations could adopt to improve travel planning and travel intentions to mainland China.

Kim et al. [22] investigated the role of tourism information content and non-content cues in social media users' destination image formation. The study provided insights into the social media information components on tourism destinations and the influence of social media tourism IQ on travel decision-making, which aided the development of travel intentions. Sotiriadis [20] conducted academic research on consumer behavioral changes in the tourism sector due to social media use and suggested strategies that tourism businesses could adopt to maximize destination image improvement and travel intention and behavior. Zhao, Zhu [23] examined the influence of tourist experiences of Zhangjiajie, China, that were posted on WeChat Moments through images and text on the destination image using aggregated maps and social semantic networks. The results indicated that images promoted the natural aspects, scenery, and landscapes of the destination, and the text acted as an echo of the images. Overall, the images and text contributed to creating an improved image of Zhangjiajie on WeChat Moments.

Fu and Timothy [24] examined the effect of social media constraints on destination image. Negative emotions can disrupt the affective destination image, as internet restrictions in China can negatively affect tourist destinations. Sun et al. [35] examined the projected image of Australia and Chinese consumers' perception of the destination image. Numerous gaps were identified in the perceived and projected destination images. The major tourist attractions were natural resources, natural environment, history and culture, and general infrastructure. Yang and Wang [26] reported that the image of China as a tourist destination (destination image and potential visitors' travel intentions) was negatively affected by misleading information on social media.

## 3 Methodology

Managerial studies use systematic literature reviews to obtain valuable insights and quality results. This study used the systematic literature review as a research methodology, which maintains the principles of authentic results via data collection from published and credible sources. The research methodology involves the three steps of planning, evaluation, and reporting suggested previously [27, 53, 54]. The systematic literature review was conducted over an accurate and sufficient duration to maintain adequacy standards. The analysis was followed by sequential steps that enabled the construction of a database comprising the detailed characteristics of the included studies. The database facilitated the probability of describing different social media and destination marketing perspectives, which ensured the complete explanation of the social media and destination marketing features and characteristics in the literature. To conduct the systematic review, the present study has followed the Preferred Reporting Items for Systematic Reviews and Meta-Analyses (PRISMA) statement. Figure 1 depicts the entire review procedure in PRISMA format (Fig. 1).

The research was initiated by identifying three scientific databases [World of Science (WoS), Scopus, and Google Scholar], where the articles uploaded and maintained by these databases are correctly referenced and cited. Furthermore, the databases above contain articles from reliable journals with better impact factors and increased credibility. The WoS and Scopus databases are appropriate and host complete articles from the scientific publications and communication studies domains. The wide variety of global publishers greatly reflects their contributions to outdoor language growth and development. Google Scholar is also a justified literature source in this study because it is a free tool aggregating academic research on one platform over the past few years [16].

Given the topic's connection to the selected review documents, this review included different journals and conference papers. This study focused on technological perspective variables and digital content, such as the Internet and social media

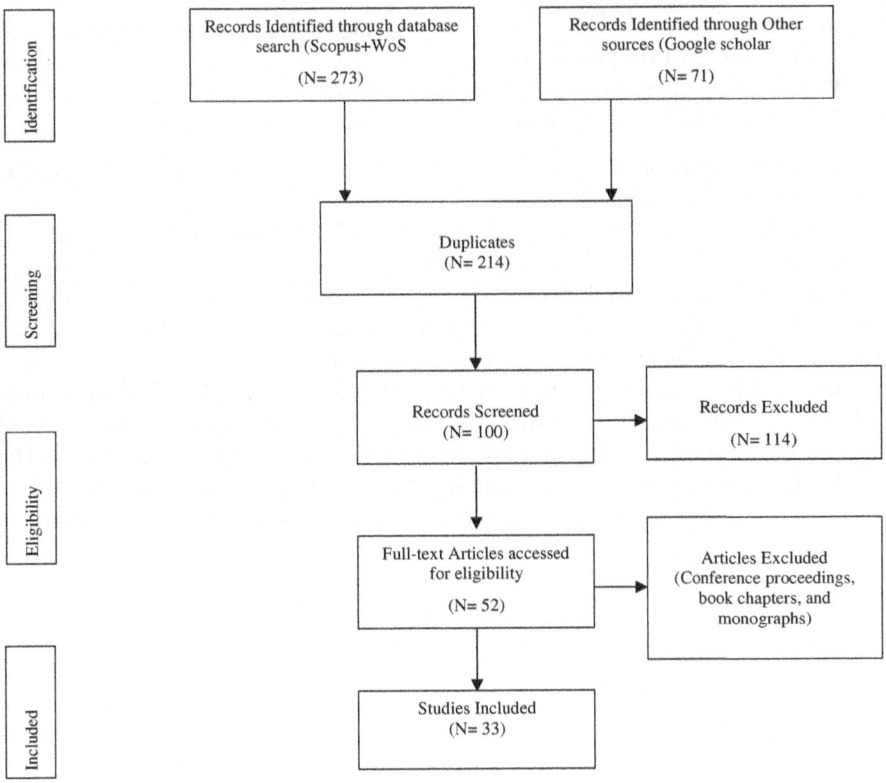


**Fig. 1** Review process. *Note* Self-elaborated

destination marketing. Therefore, the selection of conference papers and journals was considered accurate. To retain quality, no non-cited journal was included, and the inclusion of all appropriately cited articles in quality-oriented journals and conference papers was assured. Different keywords were chosen for the article selection in the three databases to ensure broad research results. In each database, the research was limited to the relevant research topic by using a filter. Google Scholar is the exception in this review, given that it is not a database. Instead, Google Scholar is a search engine and, therefore, does not allow the precise selection and identification of research characteristics. Table 1 lists the two keyword sets used in the search, where a keyword from both sets in the title or abstract was essential; otherwise, the article was excluded.

The Eligibility criterion of the papers for the present study is as follows:

- Type of paper (e.g., literature reviews, case studies, research articles, conference
- papers, etc.);
- Type of journal (i.e., peer-reviewed vs. non peer-reviewed);
- Paper access (i.e., open access vs. paid);

- Topic domain (i.e., management, marketing, psychology vs. sciences)
- The time range of the publication;
- Stage of publication (i.e., published vs. in review)
- The language of the publication.

The eligibility criterion is fixed to ensure that the maximum quality articles may be entertained in the review.

Step 1 of the review research process was conducted using the keywords in Table 1. Table 2 lists the results obtained from the three databases.

In step 2 of the review, duplicate articles were removed. Ninety-one, 81, and 42 duplicate articles were removed from WoS, Scopus, and Google Scholar, respectively, which resulted in the omission of 214 articles (see Table 3).

Step 3 involved selecting only the themes related to the social media and destination marketing research that contributed to the discourse. To modify the outcomes, all such topics were narrowed down into a smaller subsection of possible articles. The article titles and themes were analyzed to extract the most relevant research. Hence, filters were used in Scopus and WoS to narrow the research domains to business

**Table 1** Keyword sets

| | |
|---|---|
| Keyword Set 1 | • Short videos<br>• Videos<br>• Short films<br>• Reels<br>• Social media<br>• Social media marketing<br>• Social media platform names (Twitter, Facebook, Instagram, and Tik Tok Videos) |
| Keyword Set 2 | • Tourism destination<br>• Destination image<br>• Tourist destination selection<br>• Tourist destination image<br>• Destination marketing |

*Note* Self-Elaborated

**Table 2** Step 1

| | WoS | Scopus | Google Scholar | Total |
|---|---|---|---|---|
| Keyword Pair | 152 | 121 | 71 | 344 |

*Note* Self-elaborated

**Table 3** Step 2

| | WoS | Scopus | Google Scholar | Total |
|---|---|---|---|---|
| Duplicates | 91 | 81 | 42 | 214 |

*Note* Self-elaborated

management, social science, and business and management studies. Table 4 lists the results obtained from the databases.

Based on the pre-selected articles, the review focused on contributions with the following features: peer-reviewed publication, international journal article or conference paper, cited by other authors, and written in English. Based on the aforementioned features, conference proceedings, book chapters, and monographs were excluded (see Table 5).

The 52 articles (Table 5) were analysed by reading the abstracts based on the study criteria and the included variables. Relevant articles were included in the review, which involved the final selection, upon which the review results were presented. Accordingly, the aforementioned phase led to the finalisation of 33 articles (see Table 6). The overall research theme is presented in Table 7.

The 33 selected articles were downloaded from the databases, archived locally, and arranged according to the three themes (social media use as a destination marketing tool, destination social media marketing in the Chinese context, and short video

**Table 4** Step 3

| | WoS | Scopus | Google Scholar | Total |
|---|---|---|---|---|
| Titles and Themes | 43 | 34 | 23 | 100 |

*Note* Self-elaborated

**Table 5** Step 4

| | WoS | Scopus | Google Scholar | Total |
|---|---|---|---|---|
| Type | 22 | 19 | 11 | 52 |

*Note* Self-elaborated

**Table 6** Step 5

| | WoS | Scopus | Google Scholar | Total |
|---|---|---|---|---|
| Abstract | 15 | 13 | 5 | 33 |

*Note* Self-elaborated

**Table 7** Overview of research steps

| | | WoS | Scopus | Google Scholar | Total |
|---|---|---|---|---|---|
| Step 1 | Keyword Pair | 152 | 121 | 71 | 344 |
| Step 2 | Duplicates | 90 | 80 | 42 | 214 |
| Step 3 | Titles and Themes | 42 | 33 | 23 | 100 |
| Step 4 | Type | 21 | 18 | 11 | 52 |
| Step 5 | Abstract | 15 | 13 | 5 | 33 |

*Note* Self-elaborated

marketing and short tourism videos on destination tourism in China). The scientific contributions and characteristics of the reviewed research were recorded in an Excel sheet. The title, abstract, methodology type, findings, and any other required information were extracted following careful analysis of the articles and useful information retrieval strategies.

# 4 Results

The following section presents the study results. From 3.1 to 3.5, information is provided regarding the distribution of the articles concerning the year of publication, methodology, publication type, sources, authors, and keyword mapping. Later on, the other sections of the results show the themes identified and the studies conducted on those themes. Finally, the results section presents a detailed analysis of the findings of studies included in the study.

## *4.1 Year-Wise Analysis*

The review was conducted by searching for content published before January 2023. Although no restriction was placed on the start of the timeframe, the closing limitation was December 2022. The earliest article included in this study was published in 2010 (see Fig. 2); thus, the timeframe was 2010–2022. The maximum number of published articles was from the past three years: four, nine, and five were published in 2020, 2021, and 2022, respectively. Regarding the earlier years, one article was published in 2010, 2014, 2016, and 2018; three articles each were published in 2013, 2015, and 2017, and two articles were published in 2019. Overall, 33 articles were included in this review.

## *4.2 Methodological Analysis*

No methodological restriction was imposed on the selected review set, and quantitative and qualitative articles were included. Sixteen out of the 33 included articles were quantitative, where ten articles mapped relations between proposed variables with structural equation modeling (SEM), three articles used simple regression conducted on SPSS, one article used an agglomerative hierarchical clustering technique, and two articles used machine learning-powered artificial intelligence (AI) algorithms.

Seventeen of the 33 articles in this review were qualitative studies. Of these 17 studies, 11 were conducted using content analysis. Most of the aforementioned qualitative studies obtained content from web pages, news articles, or research papers.

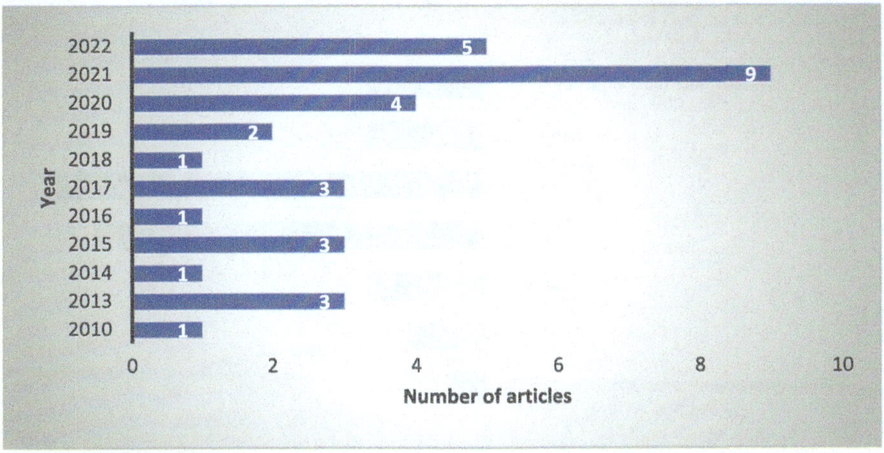


**Fig. 2** Yearly distribution of selected literature. *Note* Self-elaborated

**Table 8** Distribution of methodologies

| Data type | Methodology | Articles (No.) |
|---|---|---|
| Quantitative | Agglomerative hierarchical clustering | 1 |
| | AI algorithm | 2 |
| | Regression | 3 |
| | SEM | 10 |
| Qualitative | Content analysis | 11 |
| | Literature review | 3 |
| | Semi-structured interviews | 3 |

*Note* Self-elaborated

Of the remaining six articles, three were systematic literature reviews and three conducted semi-structured interviews (see Table 8 and Fig. 3).

## *4.3 Source Analysis*

The articles included in this review featured two sources: conferences and journals. Up to 91% of the included articles (30 of 33) were published in well-reputed and peer-reviewed journals, whereas the remaining three were conference proceedings that were recently cited by journal articles. Figure 4 depicts the source type distribution percentages, while Table 9 lists the source names (journals or conferences) and the number of articles from each source.

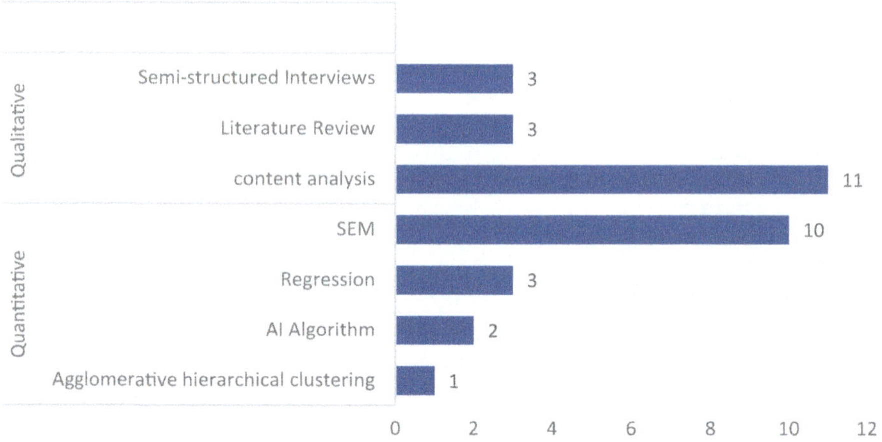


**Fig. 3** Methodological distribution of selected literature. *Note* Self-elaborated

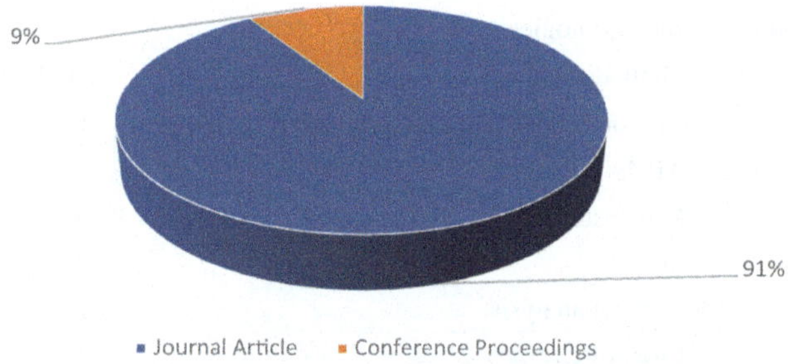


**Fig. 4** Source type-based distribution of selected literature. *Note* Self-elaborated

## 4.4 Author and Co-Occurrence Analysis

The 33 included articles were produced by a total of 91 authors, where 1–5 authors worked on each article. Five articles were written by a single author, six were written by two authors, 11 were written by three authors, 10 were written by four authors, and one was written by five authors (see Table 10 and Fig. 5). The findings paralleled marketing, social, and business research trends, as the majority of such studies involved 3–5 authors.

The co-citation and co-authorship analysis revealed that the 33 articles mainly reflected disjointed authors with a low level of co-authorship and cross-citation. Figure 6 illustrates the co-citation clusters of the 33 articles, which included 91 authors and 31 clusters. Figure 7 depicts the largest co-citation cluster, which contained five authors connected by nine cross-connections.

**Table 9** List of aources

| Source Name | Articles (No.) |
|---|---|
| *Asian Social Science* | 1 |
| *Current Issues in Tourism* | 1 |
| *Frontiers in Business, Economics and Management* | 1 |
| *Future of Tourism Marketing* | 1 |
| *Information & Management* | 1 |
| *International Journal of Contemporary Hospitality Management* | 1 |
| *International Journal of Tourism Research* | 1 |
| *Journal of China Tourism Research* | 1 |
| *Journal of Hospitality and Tourism Insights* | 1 |
| *Journal of Retailing and Consumer Services* | 1 |
| *Journal of Social Sciences and Humanities* | 1 |
| *Journal of Vacation Marketing* | 1 |
| *Audiens* | 1 |
| *South Asian Journal of Tourism and Heritage* | 1 |
| *Tourism Recreation Research* | 1 |
| *Vision* | 1 |
| 2019 16th International Conference on Service Systems and Service Management (ICSSSM) | 1 |
| E3S Web of Conferences | 1 |
| 2020 International Workshop on Electronic Communication and Artificial Intelligence (IWECAI) | 1 |
| *Journal of Hospitality and Tourism Management* | 2 |
| *Tourism Management* | 2 |
| *Tourism Management Perspectives* | 2 |
| *Sustainability* | 3 |
| *Journal of Travel & Tourism Marketing* | 5 |

*Note* Self-elaborated

**Table 10** Number of authors per paper

| Authors per Article (No.) | Articles (No.) | Percentage (%) |
|---|---|---|
| 1 | 5 | 15.2 |
| 2 | 6 | 18.2 |
| 3 | 11 | 33.3 |
| 4 | 10 | 30.3 |
| 5 | 1 | 3 |

*Note* Self-elaborated

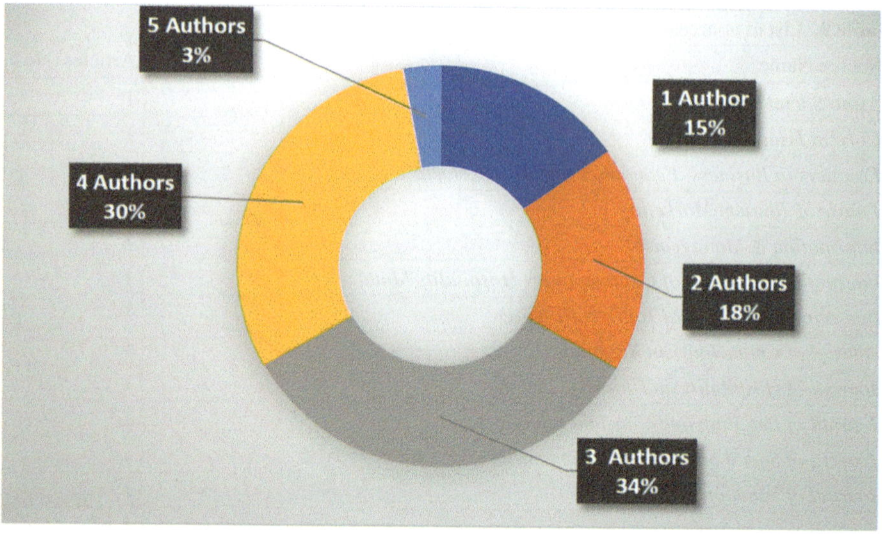


Fig. 5 Number of authors per article. *Note* Self-elaborated

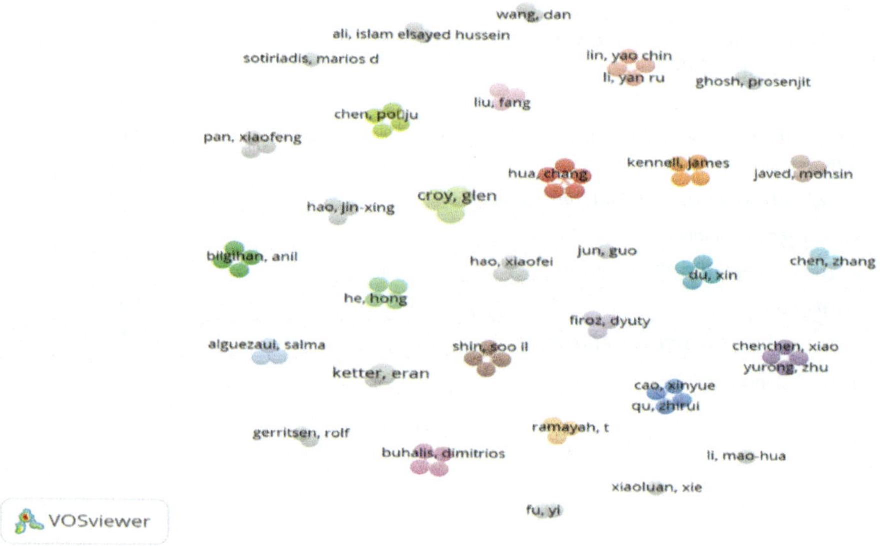


Fig. 6 Author co-citation clusters (All Articles). *Note* Self-elaborated

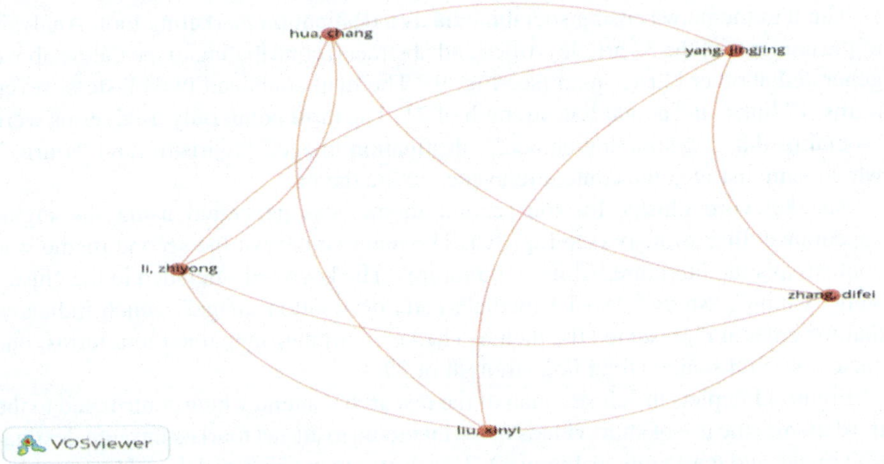


**Fig. 7** Largest author co-citation cluster. *Note* Self-elaborated

## 5 Keyword Analysis

The contents of the included articles were validated via keyword analysis of the titles and abstracts, which yielded a cluster map (see Fig. 8). The cluster map contained two clusters, 16 terms, 97 links, and a total link strength of 475. The map was generated by filtering for terms used at least eight times in the article. The most commonly linked terms were "social medium," “destination image," and "destination choice," which indicated the content relevance to the review topic.

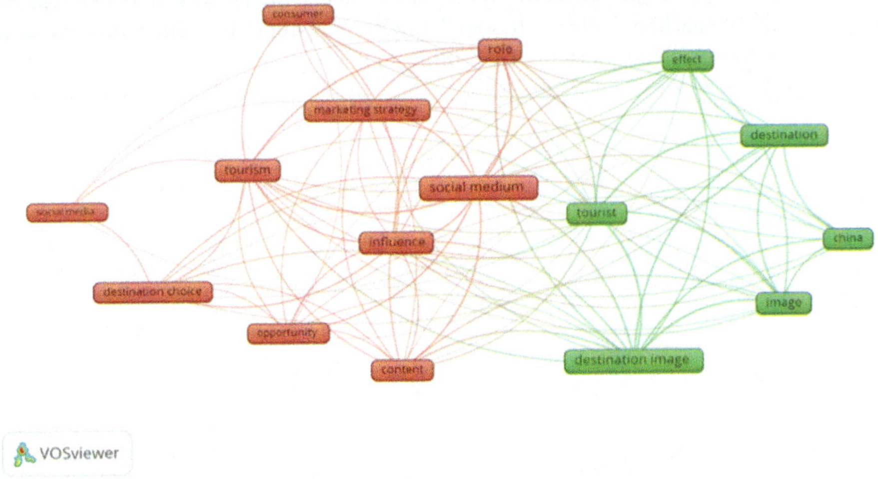


**Fig. 8** Mapping of keywords in title and abstract (All Articles). *Note* Self-elaborated

The first theme was using social media as a destination marketing tool. Analysis of the contents of the 33 articles (titles and abstracts) contributing to the theme above generated another cluster map (see Fig. 9). The map contained two clusters, seven terms, 17 links, and a total link strength of 71. The most commonly used terms were "social media," "destination choice," "destination image," "tourism," and "tourist," which demonstrated the content relevance to the theme.

The keyword cluster for the second theme was generated using the eight-appearance filter strategy (see Fig. 10). The main context of the second theme was context-specific literature (Chinese literature). The keywords included in the cluster were "China", "study", "social media", and "destination image", which indicated that the content represented the theme. The keyword map contained four terms, one cluster, six links, and a total link strength of 27.

Figure 11 depicts the cluster map of the research content, which contributed to the third theme (the use of short videos in social media to attract tourists through destination image and marketing techniques). The cluster map contained three clusters, nine terms, 30 links, and a total link strength of 72. The prominent terms were "China," "Covid," "video," "short video," "destination image," "destination," and "destination marketing," which indicated normality with the generated theme.

## 6 Thematic Findings and Discussion

A thorough analysis of the included articles and their contents enabled the mapping of three themes aligned with the study's aim and objectives. The first theme was social media usage as a destination image-creating and development tool. The relevant articles were not contextually limited to China. The second theme was destination marketing through social media in China, while the last theme was short video usage for destination marketing through social media in China. The three themes were mapped to the reviewed literature (see Table 11).

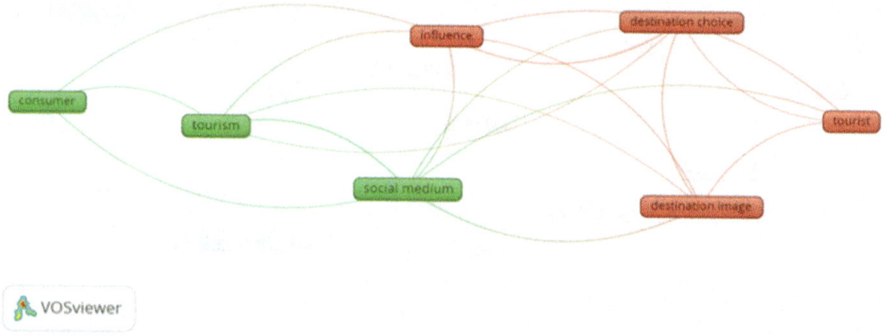


**Fig. 9** Mapping of keywords in title and abstract (Theme 1). *Note* Self-elaborated

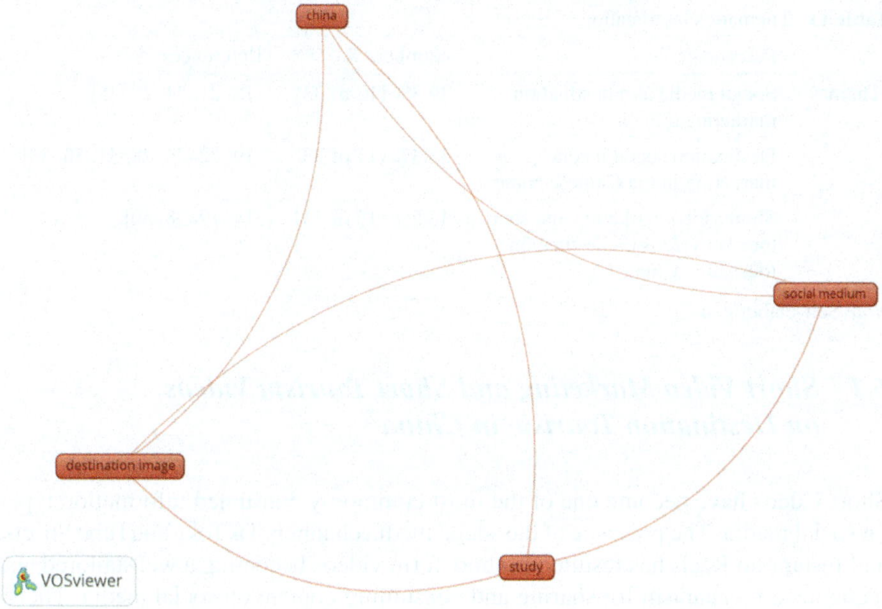


**Fig. 10** Mapping of keywords in title and abstract (Theme 2). *Note* Self-elaborated

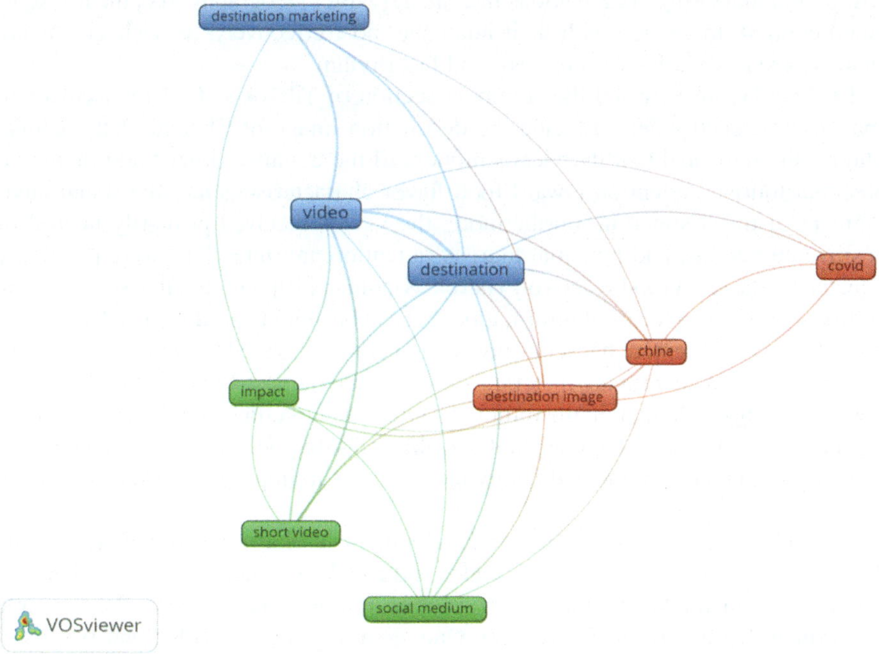


**Fig. 11** Mapping of keywords in title and abstract (Theme 3). *Note* Self-elaborated

**Table 11** Thematic classification

| | Percentage | Number (%) | References |
|---|---|---|---|
| Themes | Social media as a destination marketing tool | 39.3% (13 of 33) | [18–21, 24, 28–35] |
| | Destination social media marketing in the Chinese context | 33.3% (11 of 33 | [19, 22–26, 28, 31, 36–38] |
| | Short video marketing and short tourism videos on destination tourism in China | 45.5% (15 of 33) | [14, 19, 38–50] |

*Note* Self-elaborated

## *6.1 Short Video Marketing and Short Tourism Videos on Destination Tourism in China*

Short videos have become one of the most commonly consumed information types on social media. The presence of the social media channels TikTok, YouTube Shorts, and Instagram Reels has resulted in short-form videos becoming a well-tailored and recognized mechanism for sharing and consuming content on social media. Therefore, an increasing number of potential travelers use short-form content to discover new travel destinations and obtain inspiration to travel to new places. Therefore, destination marketing organizations increasingly use videography, specifically short video content, to engage with their audience most effectively, as such videos are characterized by clarity, conciseness, and fast rhythm.

Li, Xu [51] investigated the comment section of TikTok's short food videos to analyze how such videos affected the destination image of Chengdu City, China. The results indicated that the videos influenced the cognitive image and increased potential tourists' attention toward food flavor characteristics and the social environment of the destination. Furthermore, the videos received primarily neutral or positive comments, and potential tourists' attention and intentions were positively affected by the short food videos on TikTok. Xiaoluan [40] reported that social media platforms are rich in forms of information that can be quickly produced and accessed. Nevertheless, the content has a low production cost, which led to increased development of low-cost advertising materials on social media post-COVID-19. Moreover, it was also suggested that, in the future, destination marketing companies or tourism companies should strengthen the public health and safety focus on their social media by using virtual and augmented reality technologies to improve the user experience [42].

Jun [42] highlighted that tourism development is vital for national sustainable development and growth. The study also indicated that short videos had become a vital tourism marketing tool in the mobile internet era by using the example of Xixinan, China, as the destination. One agency-generated video and one user-generated video were used to examine the effect these short videos can have on the tourism image representation of Xixinan. The agency-generated video focused on nature, culture, folk culture, and other local attractions, whereas the user-generated video focused on the tourist experience. Nonetheless, both videos promoted the image of Xixinan. Kim Lee (19) also highlighted the importance of social and cognitive elements in the content to influence potential tourists' travel decisions. Jun [42] emphasized the role of "short video + live broadcast" in China to enhance outcomes for tourism enterprises. The study used the TikTok and Kwai platforms as examples to examine the challenges encountered during live and short video promotion in the cultural tourism industry.

Shani and Chen [38] were among the first to examine the potential effects of video content on changing the image of China as a travel destination for potential tourists from the US. The study revealed that there were mixed and contrasting representations of China that created a need to modernize the representation of the image of China as a tourist destination. Fong and Firoz [49] emphasized that tourism advertisement videos are currently one of the most appropriate information sources for tourists seeking holiday destinations. Young tourists are more likely to travel to destinations that vary culturally, and the audio and visual information presented in videos have a more substantial influence on these potential tourists to travel to a holiday destination. Li [52] highlighted that potential tourists would more likely be attracted to visit if promotional videos demonstrated the unique features of the destination, such as natural landscapes, architectural and heritage-related cultural infrastructure, seasonal activities, and the uniqueness of the local culture. Shao, Wang [48] examined the visual destination images revealed in user-generated short videos by implementing an AI technology-based algorithm. The study revealed that visual destination images and short videos were excellent information sources to create a positive image of a particular destination in potential tourists' perceptions. Chenchen, Yurong [14] highlighted how TikTok changed tourists' access to information. The study examined tourists' perception of the influence of TikTok videos on destination image perception and intention to travel. The findings demonstrated that the TikTok short videos positively influenced the tourists' perception of the destination image of China and their intention to travel.

Cao, Qu [43] highlighted the importance of short videos for destination management organizations in the current tourism market. The results revealed that short videos aided the promotion of brand attitude. Therefore, short videos can act as an effective marketing tool to improve the destination image. Ketter and Avraham [44] examined the role of YouTube videos in affecting the destination image during and after the pandemic. Stankov, Kennell [46] reported that aerial drone videos and user-generated content in short videos allow potential tourists to be attracted to destinations, as such videos and content tend to highlight the unique and other characteristics of the destination. Du, Liechty [47] discovered that consuming and creating tourism-related short videos on TikTok enhanced how tourists engage with travel content. Furthermore, short video visual and storytelling orientations increased the influence of such content on the travel decision-making process. Celebrity endorsements of destinations in short-form travel videos were also deemed valid in improving the destination image Yang, Zhang [45].

## 7 Conclusion

This study explored the influence of social media content on the destination image of China by conducting a systematic review of 33 articles obtained from WoS, Scopus, and Google Scholar. The publication timeframe was from 2010 to 2022. The included studies involved qualitative and quantitative methodologies and were from journals or conferences. Three themes were extracted from the content: social media use as a destination marketing tool, destination social marketing in China, and short videos as a destination marketing tool. The findings demonstrated that short videos are currently the most effective tool for enhancing destination images, as they are short, precise, clear, and highlight destination attractions in minimal duration. The study has addressed the significant issue that will facilitate destination marketers in China to understand better the importance of social media marketing in attracting tourists. This study makes a valuable contribution to the literature by providing evidence that video content in the form of short videos may attract tourists. Although China has a well-established domestic tourism industry, the study findings established that by focusing on attractive short media content, international tourism can be increased in China. Conclusively, the study has highlighted the importance of social media in promoting tourism compared to the traditional means of destination marketing.

This study encountered several limitations and drawbacks that can be addressed in future research. For example, this study type depended on technical approach decisions, such as selecting the investigation fields, publication languages, and databases, which might lead to excluding relevant articles from the analysis. The inclusion of keywords ("destination promotions", "social media", "reels", and "destination marketing") would lead to a better description of destination marketing. Furthermore, only articles of the highest and most satisfactory quality published in credible journals were considered in the investigation. In that case, valuable clues to future investigation trends in other publications (book chapters, conference papers, and PhD dissertations) might be overlooked. The other limitation is that this review was conducted following the consideration of several databases, with only the most recognised databases used in the review. A multi-sourcing method that compares several databases might yield a broader or wider overview of the research in the relevant field and a practical comprehension of the core developments. This review incorporated recent articles to align with contemporary results. Future researchers can investigate research articles older than those included in this review to obtain results on the gradual change in social media and destination marketing. The research contexts were central to China. Future researchers may alter the context and vary or alter the methodological choices during their research.

## References


Alamäki, A., Rhee, C., Suomala, J., Kaski, T., Kauttonen, J.: Creating effective visuals for destination marketing videos: acenery vs people. J. Vacat. Mark. **29**(1), 141–157 (2023)

Ali Qalati, S., Li, W., Ahmed, N., Ali Mirani, M., Khan, A.: Examining the factors affecting SME performance: the mediating role of social media adoption. Sustainability **13**(1), 75 (2020)

Bakr, G., Ali, I.E.H.: The role of social networking sites in promoting Egypt as an international tourist destination. South Asian J. Tour. Herit. **6**(1), 169–183 (2013)

Boediman, S.F., Hendriarto, P., Satmoko, N.D., Sulistiyani, S., Amar Sani, A.S.: Relevance of social media applications as a marketing strategy for Indonesian tourism destinations (literature analysis study). Bp. Int. Res. Crit.S Inst.-J. (BIRCI-Journal). **4**(3), 5705–5712 (2021)

Boediman, S.F., Hendriarto, P., Satmoko, N.D., Sulistiyani, S., Sani, A.: The relevance of using social media applications strategies to increase marketing potential of Indonesian maritime tourism (Analytical Study of Tourism Journals and Online Marketing). Bp. Int. Res. Crit.S Inst.-J. (BIRCI-Journal). **4**(4), 8791–8799 (2021)

Cao, X., Qu, Z., Liu, Y., Hu, J.: How the destination short video affects the customers' attitude: the role of narrative transportation. J. Retail. Consum. Serv. **62**, 102672 (2021)

Chenchen, X., Yurong, Z., Die, H., Zhenqiang, X.: editors. The impact of Tik Tok video marketing on tourist destination image cognition and tourism intention. 2020 International Workshop on Electronic Communication and Artificial Intelligence (IWECAI) IEEE (2020)

Cheung, M.L., Ting, H., Cheah, J.H., Sharipudin, M.N.S.: Examining the role of social media-based destination brand community in evoking tourists' emotions and intention to co-create and visit. J. Prod. & Brand. Manag. **30**(1), 28–43 (2021)

Du, X., Liechty, T., Santos, C.A., Park, J.: 'I want to record and share my wonderful journey': Chinese Millennials' production and sharing of short-form travel videos on TikTok or Douyin. Current Issues in Tourism **25**(21), 3412–3424 (2022)

Fernández-Cavia, J., Marchiori, E., Haven-Tang, C., Cantoni, L.: Online communication in Spanish destination marketing organizations: the view of practitioners. J. Vacat. Mark. **23**(3), 264–273 (2017)

Fong, Y.L., Firoz, D., Sulaiman, W.I.W.: The impact of tourism advertisement promotional videos on young adults. J. Soc. Sci. Hum.Ities **12**(3), 1–16 (2017)

Fu, Y., Timothy, D.J.: Social media constraints and destination images: the potential of barrier-free internet access for foreign tourists in an internet-restricted destination. Tour. Manag. Perspect. **37**, 100771 (2021)

Filieri, R., Alguezaui, S., McLeay, F.: Why do travelers trust TripAdvisor? Antecedents of trust towards consumer-generated media and its influence on recommendation adoption and word of mouth. Tour. Manag. **51**, 174–185 (2015)

Geer, R., Barnes, A.: Cognitive concomitants of interactive board use and their relevance to developing effective research methodologies. Int. Educ. J. **8**(2), 92–102 (2007)

Ghosh, P., Mukherjee, S.: Understanding tourist behaviour towards destination selection based on social media information: an evaluation using unsupervised clustering algorithms. J. Hosp. Tour. Insights (ahead-of-print) (2022)

Huerta-Álvarez, R., Cambra-Fierro, J.J., Fuentes-Blasco, M.: The interplay between social media communication, brand equity and brand engagement in tourist destinations: an analysis in an emerging economy. J. Destin. Mark. & Manag. **16**, 100413 (2020)

Imran, M., Haque, A.U., Rębilas, R.: Performance appraisal politics and employees' performance in distinctive economies. Pol. J. Manag. Stud. **18**(2), 135–150 (2018)

Javed, A., Iqbal, J., Iqbal., S.M.J., Imran, M.: Sustainable leadership and employee innovative behavior: discussing the mediating role of creative self-efficacy. J. Public Aff. **21**(3), e2547 (2021)

Javed, M., Tučková, Z., Jibril, A.B.: The role of social media on tourists' behavior: an empirical analysis of millennials from the Czech Republic. Sustainability **12**(18), 7735 (2020)

Jun, G.: editor Research on the marketing innovation of "live+ short video" in the culture and tourism industry in we media era. E3S Web of Conferences; EDP Sciences (2021)
Ketter, E., Avraham, E.: # StayHome today so we can# TravelTomorrow: tourism destinations' digital marketing strategies during the Covid-19 pandemic. J. Travel. Tour. Mark. **38**(8), 819–832 (2021)
Ketter, E.: Destination image restoration on facebook: the case study of Nepal's Gurkha Earthquake. J. Hosp. Tour. Manag. **28**, 66–72 (2016)
Kim, S.E., Lee, K.Y., Shin, S.I., Yang, S.B.: Effects of tourism information quality in social media on destination image formation: the case of Sina Weibo. Inf. & Manag. **54**(6), 687–702 (2017)
Kvasnová, D., Maráková, V.: editors. Destination management organisations as the outcome of institutional innovations in the tourism sector. Forum Sci. Oecon. (2018)
Leung, D., Law, R., Hoof Van, H., Buhalis, D.: Social media in tourism and hospitality: a literature review. J. Travel. & Tour. Mark. **30**(1–2), 3–22 (2013)
Lever, M.W., Elliot, S.: Show me a story: social media-based user-generated videos and destination brand engagement. global perspectives on strategic storytelling in destination marketing: IGI Global p. 230–45 (2022)
Li, Y.R., Lin, Y.C., Tsai, P.H., Wang, Y.Y.: Traveller-generated contents for destination image formation: Mainland China travellers to Taiwan as a case study. J. Travel. & Tour. Mark. **32**(5), 518–533 (2015)
Li, W., Chen, Z., Guo, W.: Visual representation of tourism image in short video: comparison between agency-generated video and user-generated Video. Front. Bus., Econ. Manag. **3**(1), 31–39 (2022)
Li, Y., Xu, X., Song, B., He, H.: Impact of short food videos on the tourist destination image—Take Chengdu as an example. Sustainability **12**(17), 6739 (2020)
Li, M.H.: Exploring short video application users' visit intention: applying the stimulus-organism-response model Asian. Social Science **15**(12), 8–19 (2019)
Loyalka, P., Popova, A., Li, G., Shi, Z.: Does teacher training actually work? Evidence from a large-scale randomized evaluation of a national teacher training program. Am. Econ. J.: Appl. Econ. **11**(3), 128–154 (2019)
Lund, N.F., Cohen,S.A., Scarles, C.: The power of social media storytelling in destination branding. J. Destin. Mark. & Manag. **8**, 271–280 (2018)
Maráková, V., Kvasnová, D.: editors. Cooperation as a driving force of innovations in destination marketing management. Forum Sci. Oecon. (2016)
Mirzaalian, F., Halpenny, E.: Exploring destination loyalty: application of social media analytics in a nature-based tourism setting J. Destin. Mark. & Manag. **20**, 100598 (2021)
Pan, X., Rasouli, S., Timmermans, H.: Investigating tourist destination choice: effect of destination image from social network members. Tour. Manag. **83**, 104217 (2021)
Ran, L., Zhenpeng, L., Bilgihan, A., Okumus, F.: Marketing China to US travelers through electronic word-of-mouth and destination image: taking Beijing as an example. J. Vacat. Mark. **27**(3), 267–286 (2021)
Sotiriadis, M.D.: Sharing tourism experiences in social media: a literature review and a set of suggested business strategies. Int. J. Contemp. Hosp. Manag. (2017)
REIcHER, R.Z.: editor Hungarian millennials' attitudes on being online. Forum Scientiae Oeconomia Wydawnictwo Naukowe Akademii WSB (2018)
Shani, A., Chen, P.J., Wang, Y., Hua, N.: Testing the impact of a promotional video on destination image change: application of China as a tourism destination. Int. J. Tour. Res. **12**(2), 116–133 (2010)
Shao, T., Wang, R., Hao, J.X.: Editors. visual destination images in user-generated short videos: an exploratory study on Douyin. 2019 16th International Conference on Service Systems and Service Management (ICSSSM); IEEE (2019)
Song, S., Park, S.B., Park, K.: Thematic analysis of destination images for social media engagement marketing. Ind. Manag. & Data Syst. **121**(6), 1375–1397 (2021)

Stankov, U., Kennell, J., Morrison, A.M., Vujičić, M.D.: The view from above: the relevance of shared aerial drone videos for destination marketing. J. Travel. & Tour. Mark. **36**(7), 808–822 (2019)

Stefko, R., Bacik, R., Fedorko, R.: Spendings on social media as part of marketing budgets. Pol. J. Manag. Stud. **8**, 243–250 (2013)

Stojanovic, I., Andreu, L., Curras-Perez, R.: Effects of the intensity of use of social media on brand equity: an empirical study in a tourist destination. Eur. J. Manag. Bus. Econ. **27**(1), 83–100 (2018)

Stankov, U., Kennell, J., Morrison, A.M., Vujičić, M.D.: The view from above: the relevance of shared aerial drone videos for destination marketing. Future of Tourism Marketing pp. 40–54 Routledge (2021)

Sun, W., Tang, S., Liu, F.: Examining perceived and projected destination image: a social media content analysis. Sustainability **13**(6), 3354 (2021)

Tham, A., Croy, G., Mair, J.: Social media in destination choice: distinctive electronic word-of-mouth dimensions. J. Travel. & Tour. Mark. **30**(1–2), 144–155 (2013)

Tham, A., Mair, J., Croy, G.: Social media influence on tourists' destination choice:importance of context. Tour. Recreat. Res. **45**(2), 161–175 (2020)

Xiaoluan, X.: Research on social media tourism marketing in the post-epidemic period. Jurnal Audiens **2**(2), 279–288 (2021)

Yang, J., Zhang, D., Liu, X., Hua, C., Li, Z.: Destination endorsers raising on short-form travel videos: self-image construction and endorsement effect measurement. J. Hosp. Tour. Manag. **52**, 101–112 (2022)

Yang, X., Wang, D.: The exploration of social media marketing strategies of destination marketing organizations in China. J. China Tour. Res. **11**(2), 166–185 (2015)

Yang, S., Isa, S.M., Ramayah, T.: How are destination image and travel intention influenced by misleading media coverage? Consequences of COVID-19 outbreak in China. Vision **26**(1), 80–89 (2022)

Zeng, B., Gerritsen, R.: What do we know about social media in tourism? A review. Tour. Manag. Perspect. **10**, 27–36 (2014)

Zhao, Z., Zhu, M., Hao, X.: Share the Gaze: representation of destination image on the Chinese social platform WeChat Moments. J. Travel. & Tour. Mark. **35**(6), 726–739 (2018)

# A Bibliometric Analysis of Dynamic Capabilities and Resilience Using VOSviewer

**Iwona Otola and Marta Szczepańczyk**

**Abstract** Unexpected events and the instability and turbulence of the environment are causing attention to be paid to concepts that allow companies to adapt to new conditions. As a result, there has been a growing interest in resilience and dynamic capabilities. These concepts have many things in common at the ontological level. This article aims to identify ongoing research directions common to resilience and dynamic capabilities. The study uses data from the Scopus database from 2020 to 2023. Research trends and keyword co-occurrence analysis were included in the bibliometric analysis, and VOSviewer software was used to visualize the data.

**Keywords** Resilience · Dynamic capabilities · Co-occurrence · Bibliometric analysis · Vosviewer

## 1 Introduction

Both the topics of resilience and dynamic capabilities are widely described in the literature. The concept of resilience has been known in the literature since the 1970s, and a precursor to this theme was Holling (1973), who defined resilience in ecological systems [1]. In contrast, the concept of dynamic capabilities was presented by Teece et al. (1997) at the end of the twentieth century [2]. Although both of these concepts have well-established theoretical backgrounds, there has been a renewed interest in them, given the events of recent years. A turbulent, volatile, and difficult-to-predict environment is causing an increasing number of events that can be categorized as black swans, devastatingly affecting people, businesses, and the natural environment. It, therefore, becomes natural to revisit these concepts in the context of preparedness and coping with disruptive events [3].

In its initial development, the concept of resilience was considered from the perspective of sciences such as engineering, psychology, sociology, ecology, and

I. Otola (✉) · M. Szczepańczyk
Czestochowa University of Technology, 42-201 Czestochowa, Poland
e-mail: iwona.otola@pcz.pl



S. Kot et al. (eds.), *Corporate Practices: Policies, Methodologies, and Insights in Organizational Management*, Springer Proceedings in Business and Economics,
https://doi.org/10.1007/978-981-97-0996-0_25

complex adaptive systems [4, 5]. Still, it has yet to be a research domain in management science. Research on resilience in the management sciences only flourished after 2000 due to the increasing complexity and interdependence of socioeconomic systems and the increasing dynamics of a turbulent environment. How companies can survive despite unfavorable environments is related to their adaptability, agility, and responsiveness. Resilience is a complex concept resulting from the many interactions and linkages between variables occurring in the enterprise itself as well as in its environment. It is these interactions that foster a multi-faceted approach to the concept of resilience to deal with discontinuities and disruptive events [6]. Resilience is recognized as a type of capability that enables companies to respond with agility to unexpected events and to exploit events that could potentially threaten their survival [7]. Duchek [8], while reviewing the literature, distinguishes three views of organizational resilience, which she presents as:

i. the ability to resist disruptive situations and/or the ability to recover from disturbances and return to normal,
ii. the ability to adapt to change through the development, adaptation, integration and reconfiguration of resources, competences and processes,
iii. the ability to anticipate and identify disruptive events and take preventive action.

The first viewpoint is a very conservative approach to resilience, where the primary assumption is that the company will survive and return to the situation before the disruptive event [9]. The second viewpoint combines resilience with dynamic capabilities and learning to emerge stronger from an undesirable crisis and strengthen one's competitive position [10, 11]. A third viewpoint is the critical role of scanning the environment for threat prediction [12], building situational awareness of company stakeholders [13], and the preparation of preventive actions [14].

The concept of dynamic capabilities has its roots in resource theory. Still, unlike that theory, it does not focus on having resources that meet VRIN criteria but on integrating and configuring them in such a way as to maintain a competitive advantage in a changing environment. A rapidly changing, uncertain environment requires companies to find new ways to compete and collaborate to survive and succeed [15]. According to the definition proposed by Teece (1997), dynamic capabilities should lead to competitive advantage in a changing business environment. The authors emphasize that the idea of dynamic capabilities focuses on two aspects. The first refers to the dynamics of the environment, and the second relates to the opportunities provided by the competencies and resources possessed by the company [2]. Wang & Ahmed (2007) have identified three components of dynamic capabilities that 'underpin a firm's ability to integrate, reconfigure, renew and recreate its resources and capabilities in line with external changes' [16]. Among these components, the cited authors included: (i) adaptive capacity, defined by the flexibility of internal resources allowing them to adapt to changing environmental conditions; (ii) absorptive capacity, responsible for the ability to acquire knowledge and the learning process (iii) innovative capacity understood as the innovative orientation of the company about products/methods of production/markets. Another dynamic capability model, well described in the literature, was presented by Teece (2007), who distinguished three categories of capability [17]: (i) sensing - meaning the ability to explore the environment in search of an opportunity, (ii) seizing - is the ability of an organization to mobilize resources and competencies (iii) reconfiguring - the ability to reconfigure its resources and competencies to exploit an identified opportunity.

It is worth emphasizing that the concepts of resilience and dynamic capabilities share common ontological elements in their definitions and characteristics, and they intend to implement change to respond to events in a turbulent environment [18]. According to the theoretical assumptions of both concepts, they draw from and complement each other. Jiang (2019) indicates that dynamic capabilities can assist in building organizational resilience by [19]: '(i) making the best use of organizations' slack resources, (ii) embedding and integrating into organizational functions and processes, and (iii) changing organizations' operational routines.' According to Buzzao & Rizzi (2023), ongoing research indicates 'the possibility of modeling DCs for resilience as specific sets of a firm's abilities to anticipate, survive and thrive in unexpected, sometimes disastrous events and, in a broader sense, turbulent environments' [20]. For this reason, it seems appropriate to explore common thematic areas for both concepts. The fundamental aim of this article is to identify directions of ongoing research related to resilience and dynamic capabilities.

## 2 Research Methodology

Given the large number of scientific resources relating to the topic of dynamic capabilities and resilience, in this paper, we use bibliometric analysis. Indeed, bibliometric analysis helps map cumulative scientific knowledge [21] and allows for an in-depth analysis of research trends [22]. It is a quantitative tool for exploring, measuring, mapping, and analyzing large amounts of existing research [22] and indicates the current direction of queries in the research area under discussion. For the bibliometric analysis, data from the Scopus database from 2020 to 2023 was used. 2020 was chosen as the starting year because the theme of resilience in business management because of a pandemic has become crucial again. It is also worth noting that although both concepts have been known in science for many years, the consideration of these issues together has only become apparent since the pandemic. A search of publications meeting the criteria related to resilience and dynamic capabilities reveals that the first publication appeared in 2006 and was written by Pina e Cunha and Vieira da Cunha [23]. In the following years, there were also single publications. An annual number of publications exceeding ten items have been seen from 2020 (Table 1).

As the topic of resilience is widespread across many academic disciplines, it was decided to narrow the search to Business, Management, and Accounting. The next step was to select relevant phrases, which could be either in the title of the publication, its keywords, or the abstract. The words chosen for the study were resilience and dynamic capabilities. The following query was constructed for the search:

**Table 1** The number of publications in Scopus

| Year | No of publications |
|---|---|
| 2020 | 14 |
| 2021 | 12 |
| 2022 | 59 |
| 2023 | 83 |
| 2020 | 14 |

*Source* Scopus database

TITLE-ABS-KEY ((“resilience” OR “resiliency” OR “resilient”) AND (“dynamic capability” OR “dynamic capabilities”)) AND PUBYEAR > 2019 AND PUBYEAR < 2024 AND (LIMIT-TO (SRCTYPE, “j”) OR LIMIT-TO (SRCTYPE, “p”)) AND (LIMIT-TO (SUBJAREA, “BUSI”)) AND (LIMIT-TO (DOCTYPE, “cp”) OR LIMIT-TO (DOCTYPE, “ar”)) AND (LIMIT-TO (LANGUAGE, “English”)).

As a result, 168 publications meeting the above criteria were identified, including 165 scientific articles and three conference papers. The publications studied include 128 already published and 40 in press. A detailed analysis of the abstracts made it possible to retain all articles. The VOSviewer software was used for further analyses, including data visualization. To eliminate errors in the analyses resulting from different notations of the exact keywords, e.g., dynamic capability and dynamic capabilities, a thesaurus was used (Table 2).

**Table 2** Thesaurus for VOSviewer

| Keywords | Replace by |
|---|---|
| Dynamic capability | Dynamic capabilities |
| Dynamic capability view | Dynamic capabilities view |
| Dynamics capability | Dynamic capabilities |
| Pandemic | Covid-19 |
| Pandemics | Covid-19 |
| Supply chain resiliences | Supply chain resilience |
| Supply chains | Supply chain |
| Supply-chain disruptions | Supply chain disruption |

*Source* Authors’ elaboration

## 3 Analysis of Results

The bibliometric analysis was based on the presentation of journals and article citations, as well as keyword co-occurrence analysis (co-word analysis).

### *3.1 Publication Trend Analysis*

The study identified 88 journals in which the topic of resilience and dynamic capabilities appeared. The 10 journals in which the topic appeared most frequently are shown in Table 3. The International Journal of Production Economics published the most, with 10 research articles. However, when looking at the number of citations, the Journal of Business Research and the International Journal of Logistics Management lead the way.

Due to the short research period, the citation analysis carried out is not perfect, as almost half of the scientific articles (48.5%) were published in 2023. Nevertheless, Table 4 presents the most frequently cited five scientific papers [24–28].

Although the Journal of Business Research and the International Journal of Logistics Management have the highest number of citations, the two most cited scientific articles are in journals outside the list of journals indicated in Table 3.

**Table 3** Number of publications and citations by journals

| Source | 2020 | 2021 | 2022 | 2023 | Citations |
|---|---|---|---|---|---|
| International journal of production economics | 2 | – | 4 | 4 | 194 |
| Ieee transactions on engineering management | – | – | 4 | 4 | 17 |
| International journal of logistics management | – | – | 5 | 4 | 245 |
| Business strategy and the environment | – | – | 3 | 3 | 81 |
| Journal of business research | – | – | 5 | 1 | 263 |
| International journal of operations and production management | 1 | – | 1 | 3 | 59 |
| International journal of production research | – | – | 1 | 4 | 95 |
| Supply chain management | | 1 | – | 4 | 91 |
| International journal of physical distribution and logistics management | – | – | 1 | 3 | 15 |
| Technological forecasting and social change | – | – | – | 4 | 3 |

*Source* Authors' elaboration based on Scopus database

**Table 4** Most cited scientific papers

| Title of publication | Authors | Journal | Year | Citations |
|---|---|---|---|---|
| Firm innovation and supply chain resilience: a dynamic capability perspective | Sabahi, S., Parast, M.M. | International Journal of Logistics Research and Applications | 2020 | 134 |
| Reframing service innovation: COVID-19 as a catalyst for imposed service innovation | Heinonen, K., Strandvik, T. | Journal of Service Management | 2021 | 129 |
| Supply chain management during and post-COVID-19 pandemic: Mitigation strategies and practical lessons learned | Raj, A., Mukherjee, A.A., de Sousa Jabbour, A.B.L., Srivastava, S.K. | Journal of Business Research | 2022 | 98 |
| Achieving supply chain resilience: the role of supply chain ambidexterity and supply chain agility | Aslam, H., Khan, A.Q., Rashid, K., Rehman, S.-U. | Journal of Manufacturing Technology Management | 2020 | 86 |
| Artificial intelligence for supply chain resilience: learning from Covid-19 | Modgil, S., Singh, R.K., Hannibal, C. | International Journal of Logistics Management, | 2020 | 86 |

*Source* Authors' elaboration based on Scopus database

## 3.2 *Keyword Co-occurrence Analysis*

For the co-occurrence keyword mapping analysis, the assumption was made that a keyword must occur at least five times. The analysis of 168 publications identified 826 keywords, but only 36 met the assumed criterion. Table 5 presents the most frequently occurring keywords, along with the link and the total link strength (TLS). For keyword mapping analysis, a link indicates the co-occurrence of a keyword with another keyword, while TLS shows the number of publications in which two keywords appear together [29, 30]. The most frequent keyword was 'dynamic capabilities' (occurred in 79 publications, representing 47% of all publications), which was combined with other keywords 34 times. The TLS indicates 216 publications in which 'dynamic capabilities' were linked to different keywords. It is noteworthy that among the most frequent keywords shown in Table 5, as many as five of them are related to supply chain topics.

The keyword co-occurrence analysis carried out makes it possible to understand the various thematic research directions from the point of view of their grouping into clusters, i.e. network visualization. According to the description of the VOSviewer software in the network visualization, the significance of a keyword is greater the larger its circle and label. In turn, the distance and lines between the keywords indicate the strength of the links between them, with the strength being greater for smaller distances [31] (Fig. 1 and Table 6).

Cluster 1 contains the most keywords with 11 and is concentrated around the topic of the pandemic. The word 'COVID-19' appeared in 47 publications (28% of total

**Table 5** Most highly co-occurring keywords

| Keywords | Link | Occurrences | TLS |
|---|---|---|---|
| Dynamic capabilities | 34 | 79 | 216 |
| Supply chain resilience | 33 | 52 | 175 |
| COVID-19 | 30 | 47 | 141 |
| Resilience | 30 | 47 | 127 |
| Supply chain | 31 | 37 | 156 |
| Enterprise resource management | 25 | 16 | 82 |
| Organisational resilience | 14 | 14 | 25 |
| Innovation | 19 | 12 | 31 |
| Supply chain management | 21 | 9 | 46 |
| Sustainable development | 23 | 9 | 46 |
| Decision making | 19 | 9 | 38 |
| Supply chain disruption | 14 | 9 | 37 |
| Agility | 11 | 9 | 24 |

*Source* Authors' elaboration

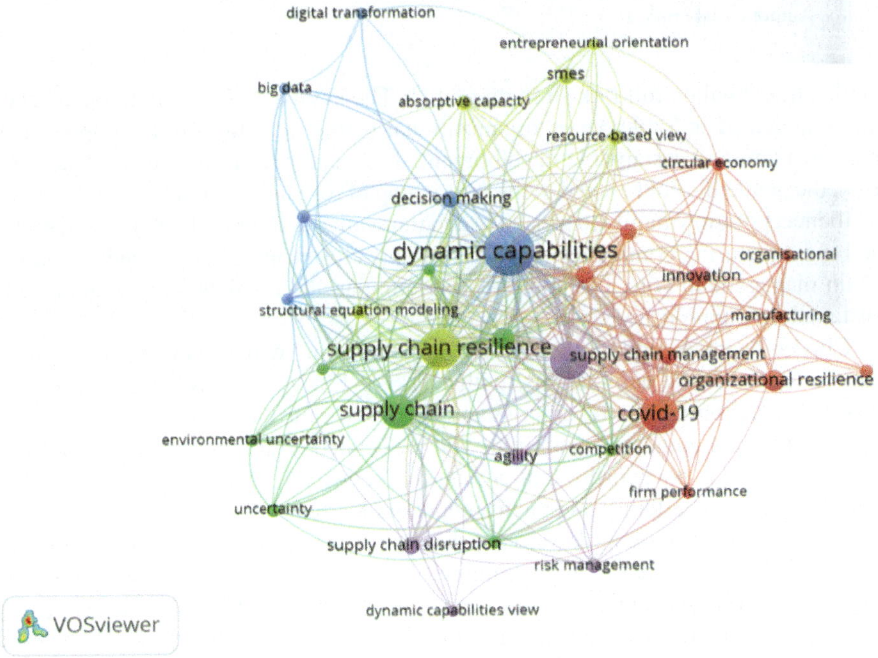


**Fig. 1** Visualization of keyword co-occurrence analysis. *Source* Authors' elaboration using VOSviewer software

**Table 6** Clusters of keyword co-occurrences

| Cluster (No of items and colour) | Keywords |
|---|---|
| 1 (11, red cluster) | Circular economy, covid-19, crisis management, firm performance, innovation, manufacturing, organisational, organisational resilience, supply chain management, sustainability, sustainable development |
| 2 (8, green cluster) | Competition, digital technologies, enterprise resource management, environmental uncertainty, industrial management, supply chain, supply chain performance, uncertainty |
| 3 (6, blue cluster) | Big data, decision making, digital transformation, dynamic capabilities, least squares approximations, supply chain agility |
| 4 (6, yellow cluster) | Absorptive capacity, entrepreneurial orientation, resource-based view, smes, structural equation modelling, supply chain resilience |
| 5 (5, purple cluster) | Agility, dynamic capabilities view, resilience, risk management, supply chain disruption |

*Source* Authors' elaboration

publications) with a full link strength of 141. The keywords with a high occurrence index indicated in Table 5 i.e., organizational resilience, innovation, supply chain management, and sustainable development, also occurred in this cluster. Undoubtedly, the pandemic contributed to the flourishing of research related to organizational resilience, pointing mainly to proactive and innovative actions both in the SME sector and manufacturing companies. Research in this cluster has also focused on supply chain management with a look at creating circular and resilient supply chains and sustainability approaches.

Cluster 2 centers around the keyword 'supply chain,' which occurred in 37 publications (22% of total publications) with a TLS of 156. Another relevant keyword in this cluster is 'enterprise resource management' (occurrence 16, TLS 82). A look at resilience and dynamic capabilities was associated with digital technologies and competition. It is noteworthy that among the keywords, there were two related to insecurity, i.e., uncertainty and environmental uncertainty.

Cluster 3 consists of six keywords, the most common being 'dynamic capabilities,' which, as indicated at the beginning of the analysis, is of the most significant importance. The academic considerations are in digital transformation using 'big data' and targeted 'decision making.' Also relevant in this cluster is the keyword 'least squares approximations,' indicating the research methodology conducted. As in previous clusters, one of the keywords is related to supply chains, in this case, agility.

Cluster 4 mainly revolves around the keyword 'supply chain resilience,' which appeared in 52 publications (31% of total publications) with a TLS value of 175. It was considered in the context of other keywords such as 'resource-based view,' 'entrepreneurial and 'absorptive capacity.' The issues above were mainly linked to research in small and medium-sized enterprises. An important keyword in this cluster was 'structural equation modeling,' indicating the use of this method in the research process.

Cluster 5 consists of five keywords, three of which are significant in this topic, as also indicated by the information in Table 5 i.e., resilience, agility, and supply chain disruption. The most prominent keyword in this cluster is 'resilience,' which appears in 47 publications (28% of total publications) with a TLS of 127. The cluster includes articles addressing the topic of enterprise agility and an orientation toward risk management about dynamic capabilities, often called sensing, seizing, and reconfiguring. Dynamic capabilities and agility have also been discussed in the context of building resilient supply chains and in shaping corporate responses to market uncertainty.

## 4 Conclusions

The bibliometric analysis carried out, although only covering a three-year research period, indicates an increased research interest in resilience in combination with dynamic capabilities. This has undoubtedly been influenced by the pandemic, which has contributed to new insights into how companies operate in an unstable environment. As indicated in the theoretical considerations, both the concepts of resilience and dynamic capabilities are related to adaptation and adjustment activities to changing market conditions. The bibliometric analysis shows topics pertaining to business agility, innovation, and digital developments. These activities are expected to contribute to strengthening the competitive position of enterprises despite lurking threats. However, the central theme in the bibliometric analysis concerns supply chains, which, due to the closure of the economies of various countries, have been broken overnight. The research about supply chains was conducted to answer how to build resilient supply chains and what role dynamic capabilities play in this resilience. The findings serve to analyze further and explore the research gap about resilience as well as dynamic capabilities.

## References


1. Holling, C.S.: Resilience and stability of ecological systems. Annu. Rev. Ecol. Syst. **4**, 1–23 (1973)
2. Teece, D.J., Pisano, G., Shuen, A.: Dynamic capabilities and strategic management. Strateg. Manag. J. **18**(7), 509–533 (1997)
3. Altshuler, A., Schmidt, J.: Why does resilience matter? Global implications for the tourism industry in the context of COVID-19. Worldwide Hosp. Tour. Themes **13**(3), 431–436 (2021)
4. Iftikhar, A., Purvis, L., Giannoccaro, I.: A meta-analytical review of antecedents and outcomes of firm resilience. J. Bus. Res. **135**, 408–425 (2021)

5. Martin-Breen, P., Anderies, J.M.: Resilience: A literature review. Bellagio Initiative, IDS. Brighton (2011)
6. Burnard, K.J., Bhamra, R.: Challenges for organisational resilience. Contin. & Resil. Rev. **1**(1), 17–25 (2019)
7. Lengnick-Hall, C.A., Beck, T.E., Lengnick-Hall, M.L.: Developing a capacity for organizational resilience through strategic human resource management. Hum. Resour. Manag. Rev. **21**(3), 243–255 (2011)
8. Duchek, S.: Organizational resilience: A capability-based conceptualization. Bus. Res. **13**(1), 215–246 (2020)
9. Sheffi, Y.: Resilience reduces risk. Logistics Quarterly **12**(1), 12–14 (2006)
10. Liu, R., Long, J., Liu, L.: Seeking the resilience of service firms: A strategic learning process based on digital platform capability. J. Serv. Mark. **37**(3), 371–391 (2023)
11. Nava, L.: Rise from ashes: A dynamic framework of organizational learning and resilience in disaster response. Bus. Soc. Rev. **127**(S1), 299–318 (2022)
12. YahiaMarzouk, Y., Jin, J.: Linking environmental scanning and organizational learning with organizational resilience of Egyptian SMEs: The moderating role of environmental uncertainty. International Journal of Organizational Analysis ahead-of-print (2022)
13. McManus, S., Seville, E., Vargo, J., Brunsdon, D.: Facilitated Process for Improving Organizational Resilience. Nat. Hazard. Rev. **9**(2), 81–90 (2008)
14. Madani, F., Parast, M.M.: An integrated approach to organizational resilience: A quality perspective. Int. J. Qual. & Reliab. Manag. **40**(1), 192–225 (2023)
15. Pitelis, C., Wang, C.L.: Dynamic Capabilities: What are they and what are they for? Br. J. Manag. 30(4), (2019)
16. Wang, C.L., Ahmed, P.K.: Dynamic capabilities: A review and research agenda. Int. J. Manag. Rev. **9**(1), 31–51 (2007)
17. Teece, D.J.: Explicating dynamic capabilities: The nature and microfoundations of (sustainable) enterprise performance. Strateg. Manag. J. **28**, 1319–1350 (2007)
18. Otola, I., Grabowska M., Krupka Z.: Trust and organizational resilience. 1st edn. Routledge, New York and London (2024 in press)
19. Jiang, Y., Ritchie, B.W., Verreynne, M.L.: Building tourism organizational resilience to crises and disasters: A dynamic capabilities view. Int. J. Tour. Res. **21**(6), 882–900 (2019)
20. Buzzao, G., Rizzi, F.: The role of dynamic capabilities for resilience in pursuing business continuity: An empirical study. Total Qual. Manag. Bus. Excell. **34**(11), 1353–1385 (2023)
21. Donthu, N., Kumar, S., Mukherjee, D., Pandey, N., Lim, W.M.: How to conduct a bibliometric analysis: An overview and guidelines. J. Bus. Res. **133**, 285–296 (2021)
22. Aziminezhad, M., Taherkhani, R.: BIM for deconstruction: A review and bibliometric analysis. J. Build. Eng. **73**, 106683 (2023)
23. Pina e Cunha, M., Vieira da Cunha, J.: Towards a complexity theory of strategy. Manag. Decis. **44**(7), 839–850 (2006).
24. Sabahi, S., Parast, M.M.: Firm innovation and supply chain resilience: a dynamic capability perspective. Int. J. Log. Res. Appl. **23**(3), 254–269 (2020)
25. Heinonen, K., Strandvik, T.: Reframing service innovation: COVID-19 as a catalyst for imposed service innovation. J. Serv. Manag. **32**(1), 101–112 (2020)
26. Raj, A., Mukherjee, A.A., de Sousa Jabbour, A.B.L., Srivastava, S.K.: Supply chain management during and post-COVID-19 pandemic: Mitigation strategies and practical lessons learned. Journal of business research **142**, 1125–1139 (2022).
27. Aslam, H., Khan, A.Q., Rashid, K., Rehman, S.U.: Achieving supply chain resilience: the role of supply chain ambidexterity and supply chain agility. J. Manuf. Technol. Manag. **31**(6), 1185–1204 (2020)
28. Modgil, S., Singh, R.K., Hannibal, C.: Artificial intelligence for supply chain resilience: learning from Covid-19. Int. J. Logist. Manag. **33**(4), 1246–1268 (2022)
29. Tamala, J.K., Maramag, E.I., Simeon, K.A., Ignacio, J.J.: A bibliometric analysis of sustainable oil and gas production research using VOSviewer. Clean. Eng. Technol. **7**, 100437 (2022)

30. Guo, Y.M., Huang, Z.L., Guo, J., Li, H., Guo, X.R., Nkeli, M.J.: Bibliometric analysis on smart cities research. Sustainability **11**(13), 3606 (2019)
31. Eck, N.V., Waltman, L.: VOSviewer manual. Univeristeit Leiden, Leiden (2022)

# Entrepreneurship, Accounting, and Venture Capital

# Innovative Price Indexing for Managing Road and Bridge Projects: Mitigating Cost Overruns

**Mariusz Urbański, Katarzyna Grondys, Marcin Świtała, and Wiesław Liszewski**

**Abstract** Outlays on infrastructure projects account for a significant portion of the national economy's expenditures. The ongoing tender procedures and rising prices of services and materials in the construction industry mean that the budget for road infrastructure development is subject to dynamic changes. The result is an underestimation of expenses and slowing down or stopping road works. This entails negative consequences for both the contractor and the investor. The paper aimed to present an experimental method based on measures of the dynamics of road and bridge works prices, which will reduce the risk of exceeding construction investment costs. An example of a national road investment was selected for the study, based on which methods of estimating the value of valorization of the price of a road investment chosen based on the price indices of construction works of road and bridge structures over the past five years were presented. Based on the application of the innovative adjustment index, the permissible limits of valorization were indicated, which form the basis for the renegotiation of contract prices within the framework of the studied investment between the investor and the construction contractor. The results of the study could be used by the public sector to assess the effectiveness of procurement in the area of infrastructural projects and to improve tender procedures.

**Keywords** Changes in works prices · Road and bridge facilities · Adjustment Index · Valorization

M. Urbański · M. Świtała
Road and Bridge Research Institute, Instytutowa 1, Warsaw, Poland

K. Grondys (✉)
Faculty of Management, Czestochowa University of Technology, Armii Krajowej 19B, Czestochowa, Poland
e-mail: katarzyna.grondys@pcz.pl

W. Liszewski
Faculty of Civil Engineering, Czestochowa University of Technology, Akademicka 3, Czestochowa, Poland



S. Kot et al. (eds.), *Corporate Practices: Policies, Methodologies, and Insights in Organizational Management*, Springer Proceedings in Business and Economics,
https://doi.org/10.1007/978-981-97-0996-0_26

## 1 Introduction

Highways and roads are an important part of any country's public assets. At the same time, road projects are among the most costly public procurement activities. At the same time, the tender procedure for selecting construction contractors forces them to undercut prices in their bids, which are the result of external market conditions [1]. This can be seen, for example, in the economic impact of Russia's aggression against Ukraine and galloping inflation. Both of these phenomena significantly affect the cost of road and highway construction [2], carrying a high risk of future price changes in road investments [3]. The problem of undercutting tender prices affects many public procurement markets in Europe. Meanwhile, taking into account the average cost of construction of one kilometer at up to 9.4 million Euros for expressways and highways and the 2,600 new kilometers of roads built in the period 2007–2020, the total cost of infrastructure development is a significant part of the government budget, which may be underestimated [4]. In Poland, the average annual capital expenditure on public roads fluctuates within the 24 billion PLN range, where, as of 2016, 176 tenders have already been announced for construction works with a total length of 2258 km, among which 165 construction contracts have been signed for a total amount of about 70 billion PLN [5].

These amounts, as well as the dynamically changing economic situation, leave a wide margin of potential error associated with the underestimation of investments by possible contractors of works and thus highlight the essence of the phenomenon under study [6, 7]. Demand for road works is created mainly by government and local government units, which makes it highly sensitive to, among other things, changes in the level of EU subsidies [8]. This demand also results from the implementation of investments in public transport [9]. These, in turn, have caused a dynamic increase in demand for construction services, which, with an inelastic supply and in conjunction with the rising cost of construction services, materials and labor, results in an increase in contract prices by the main contractors. At the same time, the value of demand reported by the General Directorate for National Roads and Motorways (GDDKiA) as the main public investor responsible for road construction tasks for 2014–2023 (with an outlook to 2025) is estimated at a total of 142 billion PLN [10]. It is also a common market phenomenon during this period for contractors to exceed investor budgets in tenders [11]. On the other hand, the same report indicates that 84% of companies in the construction sector say they are involved in unprofitable contacts, with half of these companies attempting to negotiate contracts with contractors.

These observations convinced the authors of the study to look for a method that would allow them to determine a more accurate budget for road investment. For this purpose, they sequentially analyze the literature in this area, and then, in the practical part, they examine the dynamics of prices for construction works and, on this basis, propose using the construction works price adjustment index.

## 2 Literature Review

### 2.1 A Cost Driver of Infrastructure Construction

Both the process of planning and implementation of investments are burdened with numerous risks, including those resulting from an inaccurate estimation of investment costs [12, 13]. Membah [14] pointed to five main factors causing the underestimation of costs, among which he cites engineering and construction complexity, geological conditions, market conditions, environmental requirements and ways of estimating costs. The study results showed that to avoid underestimating costs and/or reduce the error of these estimates, infrastructure development planning organizations should consider the impact of each of these factors at the initial investment estimation stage [15]. On the other hand, Lind and Brunes [16] developed a new theoretical framework for analyzing cost overruns using the example of cost overrun analysis in infrastructure projects in Sweden. Their research shows that most cost overruns occur at the project planning level. In addition, if cost overruns occur because of higher input prices, political manipulation plays a lesser role, which is more likely to occur as the scope and level of input amounts change. In addition, the authors believe that it is the identification of the stage at which cost overruns occur that determines the effectiveness of measures to prevent cost overruns.

The investment contractors often perform cost estimating for construction planning, including preparation of bids and control of project costs at the implementation stage, without considering the risks and variability of these costs [17, 18]. In addition, they also point to errors in cost estimating resulting from the bidding process related, among other things, to the short time for submitting a bid or the contractor's failure to prepare a cost estimate. Problems at the stage of the bidding process as sources of underestimation of investment costs are also pointed out by Taha et al. (cited by [19]), according to whom the direction of quantification and allocation of overhead costs, estimation of risk and profit in the bidding process is also important. Improper estimation of overhead costs resulting in either too high or too low overhead costs is also dictated by issues of competitiveness of construction companies that arise during the preparation of construction bids and participation in public tenders [20].

Raising contract prices for new contracts is only possible if contractors have adequate bidding power and moderate competition within the industry. Otherwise, the contractor's bid will not be selected for execution [11, 21]. On the other hand, cost overruns on infrastructure projects are mainly related to road and rail investments [16], whereby:

- Costs of road projects are exceeded by 20% compared to planned costs;
- Costs are exceeded for 86% of the projects implemented;
- The level of cost overruns is lower in Europe than in North America;
- Cost overruns occur regardless of events in the economic environment.

Polonski [22] also pays great attention to the problem of monitoring the costs incurred from the beginning of the project, the course of which can be disturbed by many random factors. The author points out that the direct costs of the work performed are affected by, among other things, errors in the bid valuation of the cost of performing individual works, periodic changes in the price of energy, the rental of transportation equipment, etc., periodic changes in the price of construction materials or changes in tax legislation. These factors are most often considered when calculating the performance of services by the bidder [23].

## 2.2 Valorization of Infrastructure Contracts in Poland

The response to price changes in the market is the valorization system. It estimates a price adjustment index for key road services and materials based on public statistics. This mechanism is based on the assumption that the risk of price changes is borne equally by the contractor and the investor, where the value of the indexation can update prices by a maximum of 10 percent down or up concerning the base year [24, 25]. At the same time, only 50 percent of the contract value is subject to indexation. The current year also saw an increase in the funding limit for investments under the National Roads Construction Program (by 2.6 billion PLN) and the Program for the Construction of 100 Bypasses (by 115 million PLN) [26]. The valorization applies to [27] new contracts entered into at every stage of the project, from the preparation of documentation through its design, execution of construction services and monitoring of the progress of the work;

- road works of a long-term nature related to the maintenance and upkeep of the existing road network.

Dynamic increases in the prices of road and bridge works and the low predictability of further changes in the road construction market provide an important argument for implementing a valorization mechanism for the bid price calculated by contractors of road investments. Updated this year, the valorization limits have so far (October 2022) covered a total of 92 road investments, implemented under the National Road Construction Program for 2014–2023 (with an outlook to 2025) and the Program for the Construction of 100 bypasses for 2020–2030. The annexes apply to 24 contractors and include valorising road service prices, which have undergone significant changes following the outbreak of war in Ukraine [28]. The update of roadwork service prices is also applicable to future investments for which bids were submitted in the bidding process from January 2021 to February 2022. The next part of the article contains the results of a comparative analysis of price indices and an estimation of the value of the valorization of the price of road and bridge works within the framework of a sample road investment.

## 2.3 Price Dynamics of Road and Bridge Works in Poland

The need to update the valorization limit is evidenced by construction industry indicators, among which those for the provision of road works and facilities are analyzed. In Poland, in June 2022, compared to June of the previous year, the prices of road works increased by an average of 12.2% [28]. The prices for constructing a culvert under the road crown increased the most (by 22.4%), lean concrete substructure (by 21.4%) and asphalt concrete substructure (by 22.3%). The price of substructures made of soil or cement-stabilized aggregate also increased significantly (19.1%). The lowest price increases included planting trees along roads (7.1%) and the execution of reinforcements (7.3%). At the same time, no prices for road services fell during the period under review. The situation is similar in the case of price changes for road facilities, where the average price increase was 12.7%. Within the construction of the various classes of roads, the following road works can be distinguished, i.e., Preparatory works, Earthworks, Drainage of the road body, Substructures, Surfacing, Finishing works, Road markings and traffic safety devices, Street elements, Road greenery and Other work.

A summary of the price dynamics index for road works performed on-road facilities for the main Polish road network is presented in Table 1.

During the period under review, the largest price increase was in road body drainage services (23.8% for public and urban county roads) and the smallest in greenery management services (7.4% and 7.5% for highways and expressways, respectively). At the same time, the most expensive investments are for highways, provincial public roads and urban county roads. In the case of highway construction, the largest price changes are in preparatory works (11.5%), earthworks (11%) and finishing works (9.1%). In the case of provincial public roads, the largest increases are for road body drainage services (up 23.8%) and pavement construction (15.5%). In the construction of urban county roads, the largest price increases are observed for road body drainage (23.8%), road marking and traffic safety devices (up 13%) and installation of street elements (13.2%). Traffic circles and sidewalks require similar services, where price changes are similar. The largest price increase for traffic circles was in substructure services (up 15.9%) and for sidewalks street elements (up 13.6%). The largest price increases were for sewage disposal (up 32.2%), insulation protection (up 32.2%) and regulatory works (up 29.2%). On the other hand, the slowest increases were in the prices for paving the "sidewalk" of bridges (up 0.2%), strengthening the slopes of abutment cones (up 0.3%), and for prefabricated prestressed beam structures (up 0.6%).

**Table 1** Summary of price dynamics indicators for road works of selected road facilities as of June 2022 (June 2021 = 100)

| Type of road | Preparatory works | Earthworks | Drainage of the road body | Substructures | Surfaces |
|---|---|---|---|---|---|
| Highway | 111.5 | 111 | 118.7 | 117.6 | 111.2 |
| Expressway | 112.3 | 109.3 | 114.8 | 118.5 | 111.1 |
| Provincial single-carriageway public road | 111.3 | 110.5 | 123.8 | 117 | 115.5 |
| Provincial urban road | – | 107.7 | – | 120.1 | 113.2 |
| Urban district road | 109.9 | 110.3 | 123.8 | 116.2 | 115.3 |
| Communal/ neighborhood road | 110.2 | 110.3 | – | 111.5 | 110.6 |
| Traffic circle | 110.6 | 110.9 | – | 115.9 | 115.0 |
| Sidewalk | 108.8 | 110.2 | – | 110.9 | – |

| Type of road | Finishing works | Road markings and traffic safety devices | Street elements | Road greenery | Other works |
|---|---|---|---|---|---|
| Highway | 109.1 | 109.8 | 110.1 | 107.4 | 111.2 |
| Expressway | 108.9 | 109.4 | 112.3 | 107.5 | 107.5 |
| Provincial single-carriageway public road | 109 | 111 | – | – | – |
| Provincial urban road | – | 111.5 | 113.1 | – | – |
| Urban district road | 108.7 | 113 | 113.2 | – | – |
| Communal/ neighborhood road | 108.5 | 113 | 113.1 | – | 109.9 |
| Traffic circle | 109 | 112.8 | 112.6 | 108.5 | – |
| Sidewalk | 109 | 113 | 113.6 | – | – |

## 3 Research Methodology

The primary task of the study was to assess the scale of changes in the prices of road and bridge works in the period 2019–2022 in Poland using a selected road investment as an example. The study included an analysis of the changes in the prices of road and bridge works in 2021–2022 about the base period of 2018–2020. It was carried out using an index analysis method with measures of descriptive statistics and adjustment indicators. The study used an estimation method to replace missing data with an interpolation method with the REGLINX.ETS function, which made it possible to predict the future level of price volatility using an exponential smoothing algorithm.

**Table 2** Characteristics of the indicators of the study of price changes in road and bridge works

| No. | Name | Description |
|---|---|---|
| 1 | Indicators of road and bridge facilities | The CSO price indices for road and bridge facilities are a weighted average of the price indices for individual works. The weighting was the share of each type of work performed in the facility, which was developed by the CSO based on model cost estimates created for each group of road and bridge facilities |
| 2 | Long-term indicators | Long-term indicators are the sum of monthly indicators and indicators of road and bridge facilities over the period under review |
| 3 | Correction indicators | Adjustment indicators represent the value of the difference between the indicators of individual works and road and bridge facilities for the compared periods |

The study focused on investment in the design and construction works related to expanding a provincial road. The source basis was the monthly price indices for road and bridge works and the index for road and bridge structures published monthly by the Central Statistical Office (CSO) in Poland (2019, 2020, 2021, and 2022), according to the Polish Classification of Building Objects [28]. In addition to its informational function, the data on price changes also served as a measure of the price level (deflator). The following road and bridge facilities conducted the analysis—Price indexation was applied only to construction work related to road and bridge work; Estimation of the value of the valorization was carried out using the index analysis method with the growth rate index and adjustment indices (Table 2).

# 4 Results

## *4.1 A Comparative Analysis of Price Indices*

As part of the comparative analysis, the price dynamics of the work of road and bridge facilities within the framework of the investment under consideration are presented below. Table 3 shows the price indices for constructing a provincial single-carriageway road of class "G" for 2019–2022. The last two columns of Table 3 contain summary data characterizing the scale of price changes in 2019–2020 and in 2021–2022.

As indicated by the results of the analyses, each year studied recorded an increase in the price of road construction compared to the earlier period, with the rate of increase in 2019 and 2020 forming at a moderate level and being significantly slower

**Table 3** Price indices of works necessary in the process of construction of a class "G" single carriageway road

| Specification | 2019 | 2020 | 2021 | 2022 | 2019–2020 | 2021–2022 |
|---|---|---|---|---|---|---|
| Dear (%) | 2.60 | 1.60 | 7.50 | 26.70 | 4.20 | 34.20 |

than the price increases occurring in the comparative period, i.e., 2021 and 2022. A similar trend occurred for all the construction works analyzed.

Table 4 shows the price indices for the construction of culverts under exits. The last two columns of the table contain summary data characterizing the magnitude of price changes in 2019–2020 and 2021–2022. The data show that in each of the years studied, an increase in the price of works related to the construction of culverts under driveways was recorded compared to the earlier period, with the rate of increase in 2019 and 2020 being small and at a stable level, and was significantly slower than the price increases recorded in 2021 and 2022.

The results of the study indicate that in the period covering 2021–2022, the rate of increase in the work performed for the construction of culverts under exits should be 23.70%, which means that this rate will be more than 8 times higher than the price increase in previous years.

Table 5 shows the price indices for constructing a traffic circle with a center island for the period covering 2019–2022. The last two columns of the table contain summary data characterizing the scale of price changes recorded in 2019–2020 and 2021–2022. As before, each year studied recorded an increase in the price of construction of a road facility compared to the earlier period. The data shows that the rate of increase in 2019 and 2020 was comparable and at a moderate level. What seems particularly important is that the aforementioned growth rate was significantly slower than the price increases occurring in the comparative period, i.e. in 2021 and 2022.

A similar trend also occurred for all the civil works analyzed, however, with two exceptions: in the case of earthworks, the price growth rate in 2020 was lower by 2.10% compared to the data for 2019, and in the case of road signage and traffic safety equipment, the price growth rate in 2020 was 1.80% higher compared to the data showing 2019.

Table 6 shows the price indices for the construction of a dual carriageway sidewalk in an urban area running on existing land for the period covering 2019–2022. The

**Table 4** Price indices for construction of culverts over exits

| Specification | 2019 | 2020 | 2021 | 2022 | 2019–2020 | 2021–2022 |
|---|---|---|---|---|---|---|
| Culverts under exits (%) | 1.40 | 1.50 | 4.60 | 19.10 | 2.90 | 23.70 |

**Table 5** Price indices of the works required for the construction of the traffic circle

| Specification | 2019 | 2020 | 2021 | 2022 | 2019–2020 | 2021–2022 |
|---|---|---|---|---|---|---|
| Traffic circle (%) | 2.30 | 1.90 | 7.20 | 23.94 | 4.20 | 31.1 |

last two columns of the table contain aggregate data characterizing the scale of price changes recorded in 2019–2020 and 2021–2022. The data show that there was an increase in the price of construction of a road facility in each year covered by the study compared to the earlier period. It turns out that the growth rate in 2019 and 2020 was at a similar level, within the range of 1.60–2.20%. The price growth rate in 2019 and 2020 was significantly slower than the price increases occurring in the comparative period, i.e. in 2021 and 2022.

Table 7 shows the price indices for bridge construction. The last two columns of the table contain summary data characterizing the scale of price changes in 2019–2020 and in 2021–2022. In each year studied, an increase in the price of bridge construction works was recorded compared to the previous period, with the rate of increase in 2019 and 2020 being small and showing a decreasing trend.

The data shows that price increases in 2019–2020 were significantly slower than those in the following years, 2021 and 2022. In comparison, the price growth rate of a completed bridge in the period covering 2021–2022 should form 34.72% and be more than 9 times higher than the price growth rate in the previous years, i.e. 2019–2020.

The price indices are related to the execution of road body drainage (Table 8). The last two columns of the table contain summary data characterizing the scale of price changes in 2019–2020 and 2021–2022. The data shows that in each of the years studied, there was an increase in the prices of works related to the construction of stormwater drainage compared to the earlier period, with the rate of increase in 2019 and 2020 being small and much slower than the price increases recorded in 2021 and 2022.

**Table 6** Price indices of works required for sidewalk construction

| Specification | 2019 | 2020 | 2021 | 2022 | 2019–2020 | 2021–2022 |
|---|---|---|---|---|---|---|
| Sidewalk (%) | 2.20 | 1.60 | 5.80 | 22.36 | 3.80 | 28.16 |

**Table 7** Price indices for bridge construction work

| Specification | 2019 | 2020 | 2021 | 2022 | 2019–2020 | 2021–2022 |
|---|---|---|---|---|---|---|
| Bridge (%) | 2.70 | 1.00 | 8.10 | 26.62 | 3.70 | 34.72 |

**Table 8** Price indices for road body drainage works

| Specification | 2019 | 2020 | 2021 | 2022 | 2019–2020 | 2021–2022 |
|---|---|---|---|---|---|---|
| Drainage of the road body (%) | 3.30 | 2.90 | 8.80 | 29.34 | 6.20 | 38.14 |

## 4.2 Estimation of Correction Rates

Table 9 shows the estimated correction factors ($W_k$) for the surveyed road and bridge structures calculated as:

$$W_k = W_r - W_p \tag{1}$$

where:

$W_r$—The rate of decrease/increase in the price of the object i over a foreseeable period;
$W_p$—an indicator of projected price volatility of the object i during the risk period;
i - Individual road and bridge facilities;

The risk period means the existing risk of price changes at the bid calculation stage, calculated according to the REGLINX.ETS function based on data for the time range 2018–2020, and the price increase was determined based on actual data and the estimation method used earlier.

For this study, it was assumed that the anticipated price changes relating to the period 05.2020–12.2022 acted as a deflator when determining the value of the works at the stage of calculating the bid price. The calculations carried out inform about the possible limit of valorization, which can form the basis for renegotiation of contract prices within the framework of the investment under study.

Table 10 shows the adjustment ratios in value terms, which were calculated based on the percentage of each type of work in relation to the net value of the entire task as

**Table 9** Correction indices for surveyed road and bridge structures calculated according to the REGLINX.ETS function

| Specification | Projected price volatility in the period 05.2020–12.2022 (%) | Price increase in the period 05.2020–12.2022 (%) | $W_k$[a] (%) |
|---|---|---|---|
| Provincial single-carriageway road (class "G") | −3.31 | 35.30 | 38.61 |
| Culverts under exits | 4.93 | 24.60 | 19.67 |
| Drainage of the road body | 0.4 | 40.04 | 39.64 |
| Traffic circle with center island, one-way roadways around islands | −3.52 | 32.44 | 35.96 |
| Dual carriageway sidewalk in an urban area running on existing land | −0.06 | 29.26 | 29.32 |
| Road bridge with superstructure structure—made of prestressed concrete "wet"—beam, multi-span | −2.64 | 35.32 | 37.96 |

[a]$W_k$ = price increase in the period 05.2021–12.2022—expected price increase in the period 05.2020–12.2022

of the bidding date. Due to the fact that the survey carried out included only selected types of construction and installation works carried out on roads, streets and bridges, which is a direct result of the specifics of the CSO's data collection, in this table, the net value of road and sidewalk construction was increased by the net value of works not included in the calculation to date.

The data shows that from 2018 to 2020, the increase in the price of construction works was at a low or moderate level with a downward trend. However, recent years have shown a significant increase in prices, which is an important determinant of re-estimating the value of investments, especially in the area related to taking into account potential risks arising from changes in the level of prices in the road construction market. The presented results of the study indicate that in the period covering 2021–2022, there were high price increases in road and bridge construction works, which could not be predicted at the bidding stage, that is, in 2020.

The results suggest that the adjustment indices for the prices of road and bridge works under the investment in question should be much higher, amounting to respectively:

- for the construction of a provincial single-lane road of class "G": 38.61% (12,424,490.28 PLN),
- for the construction of culverts under exits: 19.61% (175,141.68 PLN),
- for the construction of the road body drainage: 39.64% (2,180,200.00 PLN),
- for the construction of a traffic circle with a center island (one-way, roadways around the islands): 35.96% (827,080.00 PLN),
- for the construction of a dual carriageway sidewalk in an urban area running on existing land: 29.32% (760,601.26 PLN),

**Table 10** Correction indices for surveyed road and bridge structures calculated baccording to the percentage of each type of work in relation to the net value of the entire task

| Specification | Net value as of the date of the offer (mln PLN)[a] | Share in the value of the task (%) | $W_k$ | |
|---|---|---|---|---|
| | | | (%) | (mln PLN) |
| Provincial single-carriageway road (class G) | 32.17 | 69.25 | 38.61 | 12.42 |
| Culverts under exits | 89.04 | 1.92 | 19.67 | 17.51 |
| Drainage of the road body | 55.00 | 11.84 | 39.64 | 21.80 |
| Traffic circle with center island, one-way roadways around islands | 23.00 | 4.95 | 35.96 | 82.70 |
| Dual carriageway sidewalk in an urban area | 25.94 | 5.58 | 29.32 | 76.06 |
| Road bridge with superstructure structure | 19.55 | 4.21 | 37.96 | 74.21 |
| Summary | 45.41 | 97.74 | – | 17.11 |

- for the construction of a road bridge with a superstructure: 37.96% (742,118.00 PLN).

In addition, the study results report a possible limit on the net price indexation of the contract in the implementation of the contract in question, which, overall, should amount to PLN 17,109,631.22.

## 5 Discussion

It may cause delays in work, among others, due to financial claims by contractors and restrictions in access to the road network for their users. The literature review in estimating the cost of road investments draws attention to identifying the importance of cost drivers of infrastructure construction. The final cost of a construction project is subject to many variables, primarily due to the range of likely projected costs [29–31]. The project budget should be presented in several scenarios depending on the type of structure created and the prices of materials and services that make up it. Price dynamics is the fundamental component of the index, correcting the final cost estimate of the project. This is dictated by the immediate availability of data and its importance in determining total expenses. A major problem with severe cost overruns is seen as ineffective project management and affects 30% to 50% of different projects [32]. As the present research has shown, in Poland in 2018–2020, the increase in the prices of construction works was at a low or moderate level with a downward trend. It is assumed that it was an essential determinant for the contractor at the stage of the offer price calculation, especially in the area related to considering the potential risk resulting from changes in the level of prices on the road construction market. In turn, in the period covering 2021–2022, there were high increases in the prices of works related to the construction of road and bridge structures, which could not have been predicted at the stage of submitting the offer. The research showed that using the price adjustment index, estimated based on price dynamics indexes, enables accurate estimation of the investment budget. A similar methodology is proposed by the Bureau of Labor Statistics [33], which uses seasonal adjustments of prices for consumers due to temporary changes in the economic situation of the country.

## 6 Conclusions

The observed dynamic increases in the prices of construction works and the low predictability of further changes in the road construction market provide an important argument for implementing a valorization mechanism for the bid price calculated by the contractor of the contract of the analyzed investment.

Based on the values of the price change index, specific price adjustment indices for individual road and bridge works were proposed for the construction of the facilities of the road investment under consideration. The calculations inform about the possible limit of valorization, which can be the basis for renegotiation of contract prices in implementing the contract. This means that the costs submitted by the contractor in the bid for the construction of a single carriageway road, traffic circle, and road bridge can be increased by one-third, the costs for the construction of culverts on exits by a maximum of 15%, in turn, the prices for sidewalk construction services by one-fifth of the previously offered rate. Changes in the contract are possible based on the maximum valorization limit, the applicable inflation rate, and the contract duration. The calculations obtained can valorize investment costs, determine the value of works in contracts between the investor and contractor, or calculate the costing value of works of similar road investments, especially those remaining at the bidding stage. At the same time, the research has some limitations that result from the case study of a single asset. The prospect of domestic and foreign road investments should be examined. At the same time, the obtained results are the basis for further research in the analysis of non-price factors, which also determine changes in the long-term budget. The survey results can be used by the public sector to assess the efficiency of ongoing procurement in the area of infrastructure projects and to improve tendering procedures.

## References


1. Alahmadi, N., Alghaseb, M.: Challenging Tendering-Phase Factors in Public Construction Projects—A Delphi Study in Saudi Arabia. Buildings **12**, 924 (2022)
2. Tijanić, K., Car-Pušić, D., Šperac, M.: Cost estimation in road construction using artificial neural network. Neural Comput. Appl. **32**(13), 9343–9355 (2020)
3. Valorization and price changes on the market—New data. the General Directorate for National Roads and Motorways. www.gov.pl/web/gddkia. Accessed 17 Mar 2023
4. The EU core road network: Shorter travel times but network not yet fully functional, 2020. Special Report, European Court of Auditors, Luxembourg. https://op.europa.eu/webpub/eca/special-reports/core-road-network-9-2020/en/. Accessed 3 Feb 2023
5. Kieller-Zawisza, U.: Wielka budowa dróg na Lubelszczyźnie, Biuletyn Lubelskiej Okręgowej Izby Inżynierów Budownictwa, Vol. 49. http://lub.piib.org.pl/pliki/lib/lib_49.pdf. Accessed 2 Dec 2022
6. Grabara, J., Tleppayev, A., Dabylova, M., Mihardjo, L.W., Dacko-Pikiewicz, Z.: Empirical research on the relationship amongst renewable energy consumption, economic growth and foreign direct investment in Kazakhstan and Uzbekistan. Energies **14**(2), 332 (2021)
7. Ried, W., Marschall, P.: Potential benefits of cross-border health care: The case of Poland and Germany. Econ. Sociol. **9**(3), 16–18 (2016)
8. Formánek, T.: GDP per capita in selected EU countries: Economic growth factors and spatio-temporal interactions examined at the NUTS2 level. J. Int. Stud. **12**(1), 119–133 (2019)
9. Poliak, M., Poliaková, A., Mrníková, M., Šimurková, P., Jaśkiewicz, M., Jurecki, R.: The competitiveness of public transport. J. Compet. **9**(3), 81–97 (2017)

10. The General Directorate for National Roads and Motorways (GDDKiA): The most important numbers of PBDK for the years 2014–2023 (with a perspective until 2025), http://www.nbi.com.pl/najwazniejsze-liczby-pbdk-na-lata-2014-2023-z-perspektywa-do-2025-r/. Accessed 4 Feb 2023
11. Rozkrut, M., Kowalczyk, A., Boguszewski, R.: Raport z badania sektora budowlanego 2019, Raport powstał we współpracy z: Polskim Związkiem Pracodawców Budownictwa, Ogólnopolską Izbą Gospodarczą Drogownictwa Polskie Stowarzyszenie Branży Elektroenergetycznej. Polskim Klastrem Eksporterów Budownictwa, Warsaw (2020)
12. Szczepańska-Woszczyna, K.: The importance of organizational culture for innovation in the company. Forum Scientiae Oeconomia **2**(3), 27–39 (2014)
13. Smirnova, E., Szczepańska-Woszczyna, K., Yessetova, S., Samusenkov, V., Rogulin, R.: Supplying energy to vulnerable segments of the population: Macro-financial risks and public welfare. Energies **14**(7), No. 1834 (2021)
14. Membah, J.: Estimating cost for transportation tunnel projects: A systematic literature review. Int. J. Constr. Manag. **15**(3), 196–218 (2015)
15. Naik, M.G., Kishore, R., Dehmourdi, S.A.: Modeling a multi-criteria decision support system for prequalification assessment of construction contractors using CRITIC and EDAS models. Oper. Res. Eng. Sci. Theory Appl. **4**, 79–101 (2021)
16. Lind, H., Brunes, F.: Explaining cost overruns in infrastructure projects: a new framework with applications to Sweden. Constr. Manag. Econ. **33**(7), 554–568 (2015)
17. Budzyński, M., Jamroz, K., Kustra, W.: Road safety inspection as a tool for road safety management – the Polish experience. J. KONBiN **42**(1), 43–62 (2017)
18. Lima, R.M., Souza, I., Pereira, E., Belém, A.C., Pinto, C.M., Lazzaris, J., Fonseca, P.: Characterising project management of lean initiatives in industrial companies—Crossing perspectives based on case studies. Eng. Manag. Prod. Serv. **15**(1), 57–72 (2023)
19. Schneiderova Heralova, R.: Highway projects: Prices in public bids, Creative Construction Conference 2015 (CCC2015). Procedia Eng. **123**, 496–503 (2015)
20. Šiškina, A., Juodis, A., Apanavičiene, R.: Evaluation of the competitiveness of construction company overhead costs. J. Civ. Eng. Manag. **15**(2), 215–224 (2009)
21. Ayettey, D.N.A., Danso, H.: Contractor selection criteria in Ghanaian construction industry: Benefits and challenges. J. Build. Constr. Plan. Res. **6**, 278–297 (2018)
22. Połonski, M.: Control of construction costs using the Earned Value method [w:] Inżynieria przedsięwzięć budowlanych: Rekomendowane metody i techniki. In: Tadeusz Kasprowicz (ed.) Sekcja Inżynierii Przedsięwzięć Budowlanych KILiW PAN. Warsaw (2015)
23. Jacob, D.: Forecasting project schedule completion with earned value metrics. The Measurable News **1**, 7–9 (2003)
24. Sawik, W., Pociecha, K.: Construction investments in local governments and indexation of contractors' remuneration. Poradnik prawny dla gmin, powiatów i województw. https://www.dzp.pl/files/shares/Publikacje/DZP_SAS_1_str.%2023_25.pdf. Accessed 20 Oct 2022
25. Road maintenance, supervision and management with 10% valorization. https://www.rynekinfrastruktury.pl/mobile/utrzymanie-drog-nadzor-i-zarzadzanie-z-10proc-waloryzacja---80823.html. Accessed 20 Jan 2023
26. Indexation clause in the Public Procurement Law. https://www.uzp.gov.pl/. Accessed 20 Apr 2023
27. Ojczyk, M.: Inwestycje drogowe w Polsce w 2022. GDDKiA przedstawia statystyki (2022). https://blog.ongeo.pl/inwestycje-drogowe-w-polsce. Accessed 12 Dec 2022
28. Prices of construction and civil engineering works and facilities. CSO (the Central Statistical Office). Warsaw (2019, 2020, 2021, 2022)
29. Reilly, J.: Szacowanie oraz kontrola kosztów i ryzyka w projektach tunelowych i infrastrukturalnych. GEOINŻYNIERIA drogi mosty tunele **04**, 1–5 (2005)
30. Acheamfour, V.K., Kissi, E., Adjei-Kumi, T., Adinyira, E.: Review of empirical arguments on contractor pre-qualification criteria. J. Eng. Des. Technol. **18** (2019)

31. Akintoye, A., Fitzgerald, E.: A survey of current cost estimating practices in the UK. Constr. Manag. Econ. **18**(2) (2000)
32. Changali S. Mohammad A., Nieuwland M.: The construction productivity imperative. McKinsey Productivity Sciences Center. Bangkok (2015). https://www.mckinsey.com/~/media/McKinsey/Industries/Capital%20Projects%20and%20Infrastructure/Our%20Insights/The%20construction%20productivity%20imperative/The%20construction%20productivity%20imperative.pdf. Accessed 29 Aug 2023
33. Bureau of Labor Statistics (BLS) Seasonal Adjustment Methodology at BLS. https://www.bls.gov/cpi/seasonal-adjustment/methodology.htm. Accessed 12 June 2023

# State Aid as a Form of Alleviating the Negative Effects of the COVID-19 Pandemic on the Economy

**Beata Ślusarczyk and Magdalena Biel**

**Abstract** The COVID-19 pandemic has turned out to be a considerable challenge not only for healthcare systems but also for many other areas. The lockdowns and various restrictions used to minimize the spread of the virus had a significant impact on the functioning of entire economies. They posed a considerable threat to enterprises, especially service ones, which were forced to suspend their operations or were deprived of customers overnight. To protect enterprises and their employees from the adverse effects of the COVID-19 pandemic, governments of many countries have decided to provide unprecedented state aid. One such country is Poland, where many aid packages offered by public institutions were created. This article aims to present the assistance provided by one of them - the Polish Development Fund against the background of activities in selected European countries. It shows the scale of this aid as well as its scope and territorial distribution.

**Keywords** State Aid · COVID-19 · Pandemic · Economy · Financial Shield

## 1 Introduction

State aid is a state intervention in free market mechanisms [1]. It is a multidimensional concept and consists of financial resources provided by central, local, or regional public authorities, support from state or private institutions acting on behalf of the state, as well as funds from foreign sources controlled by the state [2]. Its purpose is to encourage companies to take certain actions that they would not usually choose to

B. Ślusarczyk (✉)
Trade and Development, North-West University, Private Bag X1290, Potchefstroom 2520, South Africa
e-mail: beata.slusarczyk@pcz.pl

B. Ślusarczyk · M. Biel
Faculty of Management, Czestochowa University of Technology, Armii Krajowej 19B, 42-201 Częstochowa, Poland
e-mail: magdalena.biel@pcz.pl



S. Kot et al. (eds.), *Corporate Practices: Policies, Methodologies, and Insights in Organizational Management*, Springer Proceedings in Business and Economics,
https://doi.org/10.1007/978-981-97-0996-0_27

take, to help companies in connection with crises, and the desire to achieve specific socio-economic goals [3].

Since state aid affects the functioning of the free market in some way by distorting competition, it requires appropriate legal regulation [4], which is the case even in the European Union. The regulation of state aid in the EU is an integral part of the standards used to protect economic competition [5]. The concept of state aid in the context of the European Community already appeared in the Treaty of Rome, where it was defined as state intervention that may distort competition [6]. The fundamental framing of the issue has stayed the same over the years. Article 107 of the Treaty on the Functioning of the European Union defines state aid as: "any aid granted by a Member State or through state resources in any form whatsoever which distorts or threatens to distort competition by favoring certain undertakings or the production of certain goods, in so far as it affects trade between Member States" [2, 7]. Accordingly, the following main criteria characterizing state aid can be distinguished [8]:

1. the support is provided by the state or through state resources,
2. it confers an advantage on companies that they would not obtain under market conditions,
3. the support distorts or threatens to distort competition,
4. the support is selective,
5. it affects trade carried out between member states.

For a measure to be considered state aid, all of the characteristics mentioned above must occur together [5]. Given the high impact of state aid on the market and the competitiveness of businesses in the European Union, such aid has been prohibited. However, at the same time, taking into account some possible imperfections of the free market, a catalog of exceptions to this prohibition was created [3, 9], allowing member states' interventions necessary for the proper functioning of the economy and the implementation of specific goals and policies [6]. The following types of state aid were considered compatible with the national market: regional; for SMEs in selected areas; for environmental protection; for research, development and innovation and training; for the employment of disadvantaged and disabled workers; to reduce losses caused by certain natural disasters; for transportation for residents of remote regions; for the development of broadband infrastructure; for culture and heritage preservation, sports and multipurpose recreational infrastructure and local infrastructure; and for regional ports and airports [10]. The European Commission is responsible for enforcing and monitoring compliance with the established rules. It is to it that member states must notify all new aid measures, and it is it that issues binding decisions in this regard. Before issuing a favorable decision, states may not provide state aid, although there are several exceptions to mandatory notification [11] called "block exemptions" or "de minimis aid" (small amounts of state aid) [5].

Public assistance rules worked well under "normal" conditions, but the crisis caused by the COVID-19 pandemic was not a regular and predictable phenomenon, so it required a different approach. It was a new experience, significantly different from "classic" crises, and caused a significant negative shock [12]. It appeared suddenly in the form of a rapid and severe global economic collapse [13] and affected virtually every aspect of economic functioning and human existence [14–16]. It has had a substantial negative impact on the economy [17]. It has posed a severe challenge to governments worldwide [18], which have used various lockdowns and restrictions to prevent the virus from spreading [19]. These actions caused a sharp shock to the incomes of economies worldwide [20]. The lockdown policy manifests itself in the restriction or complete banning of businesses in particular industries, which reduces the revenue of those subject to the limits. Such approaches result in the need to help sectors that cannot operate normally. Thus, state aid is a kind of compensation for restricting companies from doing business [8]. The governments of many countries have decided to significantly expand the scope of public aid to minimize the adverse effects on the entire business by offering various types of financial support, including preferential loans, tax deferrals, or a temporary abolition of bankruptcy regulations [21–23].

Given these unprecedented circumstances, the European Commission decided that member states could provide state aid measures to support the economy during the COVID-19 pandemic on March 19, 2020 [13]. The European Commission adopted the *Interim Framework for State Aid Measures to Support the Economy in the Context of the Ongoing Covid-19 Epidemic*, which aimed to allow member states to use the complete flexibility provided for in the state aid rules [24] and to ensure an appropriate balance between the positive effects of aid measures provided to companies during the covid-19 pandemic and the possible adverse effects on competition and trade [25]. As the crisis and countermeasures have evolved, the temporary framework has been amended several times [26]. The Commission adopted the first amendment on April 3, 2020; the second amendment took place on May 8, 2020, and the Commission adopted the third amendment on June 29, 2020. The fourth amendment was adopted on October 13, 2020, the Fifth Amendment went into effect on January 28, 2021, and the final sixth amendment was adopted on November 18, 2021 [27].

Taking advantage of the relaxed rules, member states used a variety of aid instruments, ranging from credit instruments such as guarantees and subsidized loans to direct grants, recapitalization, and other non-refundable tools [27]. Fiscal measures adopted by member states under the Temporary Assistance Framework totaled €2.3 trillion in 2020, an unprecedented figure. In doing so, overcoming the effects of the crisis was based on four main pillars: providing liquidity, supporting income and employment, protecting the financial system, and accelerating economic recovery [24]. Measures to mitigate the negative impact of the COVID-19 pandemic on the European Union economy were also centrally developed by the European Commission, which provided member states with liquidity measures, primarily to support European small and medium-sized enterprises[2].

In Poland, as in many other countries, more and more restrictions began to be introduced not long after the confirmation of the first COVID-19 infection (March 4, 2020), up to the lockdown announced on March 24, 2020 [13]. One of the first pieces of legislation about the spread of COVID-19 was the Law of March 2 *on unique solutions related to the prevention, prevention, and control of COVID-19, other infectious diseases, and emergencies caused by it*. In addition, on April 3, 2020, the Law on Special Solutions to Support the Implementation of Operational

Programs in Connection with the Occurrence of Covid-19 in 2020 was promulgated. Based on these laws (and their amendments), most of the aid programs designed to offset the adverse effects of the pandemic on the economy were developed [25]. State aid included all instruments and forms accepted by EU law [13]. In 2020 alone, 22 aid programs were created and notified, under which the provided assistance amounted to PLN 93,959.5 million. It is worth noting, however, that the value of state budget funds allocated to combat COVID-19 was much higher, as not all support constituted state aid [25].

As part of the mitigation of the economic crisis caused by the COVID-19 pandemic, the Polish government introduced a package of shielding measures using business support instruments, referred to as the Anti-Crisis Shield, whose principles were published as early as March 31, 2020, less than a month after the first case of the disease was detected in Poland. One of the most significant elements of this assistance program, aimed at preserving the financial continuity of companies, was the so-called PFR Financial Shield. This was a business assistance package offered both in the form of repayable loans and grants and partially non-repayable subsidies to micro, small, medium, and large companies. Due to rapidly changing circumstances and the development of the pandemic, as with the laws and the EU Temporary Assistance Framework, the Crisis Shield was also updated several times. In 2020 alone, six iterations of it have been proposed. The first (Shield 1.0) went into effect on April 1, 2020, the second on April 18, 2020, the third on May 16, 2020, the fourth on June 24, 2020, the fifth (tourism) on October 15, 2020, and the sixth (industry) on December 19, 2020. Eighty-six percent of enterprises benefited from support under the Anti-Crisis Shield, and the total amount of support was PLN 162.9 billion. The most significant part was distributed through the Polish Development Fund (PFR), responsible for implementing the Financial Shield. Through Bank Gospodarstwa Krajowego, support was provided to companies for a total of PLN 54.2 billion under 38.9 thousand individual agreements. The most significant amount was allocated for *de minimis* guarantees; the Social Insurance Institution under the Financial Shield supported companies for PLN 18.6 billion by accepting 5.1 million individual applications for assistance. The Ministry of Development, Labor, and Technology, meanwhile, coordinated the transfer of funds from the Labor Fund, which provided PLN 27.4 billion and accepted 2.4 million applications for loans, grants, and subsidies, as well as disbursements to 3 million workers under job protection benefits [28]. The Anti-Crisis Shields constituted the most comprehensive set of aid measures in the country's history. However, it should be noted that the support scale was gradually reduced, and the requirements for receiving aid were tightened over time [13].

The purpose of this article is to present selected protective measures related to counteracting the economic impact of the COVID-19 pandemic implemented by the Polish Development Fund under the so-called Financial Shields 1.0, 2.0, and for large enterprises.

The paper is organized as follows. The next subsection characterizes the data sources and methods used. Then, the results obtained are presented and discussed, and the article ends with conclusions.

## 2 Method and Materials

This article is based on data from several sources. A comparison of COVID-19 economic countermeasure expenditures carried out by individual European Union countries comes from the State Aid Scoreband 2021 study compiled by European Commission bodies. Included are costs incurred in 2020, the time of the highest support in the form of state aid. On the other hand, the analysis of assistance provided by the Polish Development Fund is based on data just released by PFR.

Data from "flagship" aid programs related to countering the effects of the COVID-19 pandemic were selected for analysis. The first of these is Financial Shield 1.0, which benefited SME companies regardless of the industry in which they operated. The purpose of this program was to protect the labor market and provide companies with liquidity during the COVID-19 pandemic. The assistance allowed businesses to return to growth after the economy unfroze. Acceptance of applications for this program began on April 29, 2020. One year after receiving the subsidy, entrepreneurs had to account for it, and the PFR decided the amount of funds that could be redeemed. Complete cancellation of the subsidy was available to companies in industries hit hardest by the consequences of the subsequent tightening. Complementing the measures implemented under this shield was the Financial Shield for Large Companies, which provided the opportunity to take advantage of liquidity and preferential financing [28]. In the face of the second wave of the pandemic, a second iteration of the described programs was prepared, called Financial Shield 2.0. Its purpose was to provide financial assistance to companies in industries that had to reduce or suspend operations due to COVID-19. Initially, 38 sectors were to be supported, but the number was eventually increased to 45 and then to 54.

Data on Financial Shield 1.0 and Financial Shield 2.0 aimed at the SME sector are made available by the PFR as so-called Subsidy Maps showing the funds transferred to companies in each county. The maps are current as of the closing date of the programs. On the other hand, information on beneficiaries who are large enterprises is presented in the form of a list of signed contracts and shows the status as of January 22, 2022. Data on aid directed to SMEs were obtained by county, but to facilitate their analysis, they were aggregated to the provincial levels. In addition to aggregation, the data obtained were subjected to descriptive analysis and simple statistical analysis.

## 3 Results and Discussion

The COVID-19 pandemic affected the economies of all European Union countries, so each country decided to prevent its effects using public assistance measures. The extent of this assistance and the tools used for this purpose varied from country to country, with a common feature being their reliance on the provisions of the

Temporary Assistance Framework. Table 1 presents data on the volume of COVID-19 aid provided in 2020 in each country and its share in the structure of the country's state aid in the year under review.

Germany provided the largest amount of aid, accounting for approximately one-third of the total COVID-19 aid distributed within the European Union in 2020. Italy, France, and Poland also provided public support of high value. In contrast, Cyprus, Estonia, Croatia, and Luxembourg allocated the least amount of public assistance to combat the effects of the COVID-19 pandemic. Analyzing these figures, one must remember the differences in size and development between the various countries of the European Union, which, to some extent, explains such significant discrepancies. However, it does not show the differences in approaches to minimizing the adverse effects of the pandemic and the use of state aid for this purpose. To this end, it is useful to look at the share of funds allocated for COVID assistance in total state aid. Here, one can see significant differences, which show the different approaches of each country. In Greece, Italy, and Poland, COVID-19 aid accounted for about 80% of total state aid, while in Croatia, Finland, and Sweden, it was less than ¼ of the entire state aid granted in 2020. Analyzing the data on the volume of COVID aid given and its share in total state aid together, it can be seen that Italy and Poland are the countries where COVID aid was one of the highest both in absolute terms (assistance volume granted) and share in the structure of state aid. In Germany and France, on the other hand, despite high outlays, the share of COVID-19 aid in the state aid structure reached about 55%. Thus, these countries make extensive use of

**Table 1** State aid related to covid-19 in the European Union granted in 2020

| Country | Aid volume (million EUR) | Share in the structure of state aid (%) | Country | Aid volume (million EUR) | Share in the structure of state aid (%) |
|---|---|---|---|---|---|
| Austria | 3,525.2 | 60.7 | Ireland | 851.7 | 38.8 |
| Belgium | 1,675.1 | 26.2 | Italy | 29,641.1 | 80.6 |
| Bulgaria | 479.0 | 57.2 | Lithuania | 357.2 | 29.6 |
| Cyprus | 130.8 | 56.0 | Luxembourg | 256.6 | 56.1 |
| Czech Republic | 1,354.1 | 27.8 | Latvia | 382.1 | 43.6 |
| Germany | 63,663.9 | 55.4 | Malta | 390.3 | 61.7 |
| Denmark | 3,114.5 | 40.4 | Netherlands | 3,101.7 | 39.9 |
| Spain | 5,681.0 | 34.7 | Poland | 19,904.9 | 79.0 |
| Estonia | 150.8 | 32.9 | Portugal | 2,558.6 | 72.9 |
| Finland | 763.3 | 24.2 | Romania | 3,257.5 | 61.7 |
| France | 28,958.0 | 54.1 | Slovakia | 1,139.5 | 68.9 |
| Greece | 5,903.2 | 83.4 | Slovenia | 1,171.1 | 72.6 |
| Croatia | 220.3 | 16.3 | Sweden | 1,110.7 | 22.8 |
| Hungary | 2,892.2 | 53.2 | EU | 182,634.3 | 59.3 |

state aid not only in emergencies, such as a pandemic, but also in other aspects of supporting the economy.

By considering the European context of state help during the COVID-19 pandemic, it becomes feasible to conduct a detailed examination of the implementation of such aid in Poland, specifically through the initiatives administered by the Polish Development Fund. Tables 2 and 3 provide general data on the three main PFR programs: Financial Shield 1.0 (PFR 1.0 for short), Financial Shield 2.0 (PFR 2.0 for short) and Financial Traction for Large Companies.

Under the Large Business Financial Shield, 165 agreements were signed for more than PLN 3.6 billion, the vast majority of which involved the provision of preferential loans. However, fewer companies benefited from the support, as several received support under more than one instrument. Despite the much smaller number of agreements, liquidity financing consumed significantly more funds, which is because the agreements for this instrument were for much higher amounts (often a dozen or even tens of millions of PLN).

By far the largest share of assistance under Financial Shield 1.0 went to the Mazowieckie Voivodship, noting that half of this amount was received by enterprises from Warsaw. More than PLN 5 billion also went to enterprises in the Śląskie, Wielkopolskie and Małopolskie Voivodship. These four voivodships received the most aid to enterprises and employees. On the other hand, the least amount of aid under Financial Shield 1.0 went to the Lubuskie, Opolskie and Podlaskie voivodships (less than PLN 1.5 billion). Both the value of the aid provided and the number of companies and employees who benefited from this aid must, of course, be analyzed taking into account regional conditions. Then the observed disparities will not be so surprising. The provinces that received the largest share of support have the largest number of enterprises, while those with the least support have the smallest number of registered businesses.

Under Financial Shield 2.0, support was provided on a much smaller scale, but again the largest beneficiary was the Mazowieckie Voivodship, although this time the disproportion was much smaller, as the Małopolskie Voivodship received only slightly less support. The areas that received the least money again included Lubuskie, Opolskie and Podlaskie voivodships (less than PLN 150 million). The situation is similar with data on the number of supported companies and employees, which again can be explained by regional differences.

More can be said about the fairness and effectiveness of the public assistance provided by analyses based on average aid values per enterprise and per employee.

**Table 2** Financial shield for large companies

| Type of assistance | Aid amount (million PLN) | Number of contracts signed |
|---|---|---|
| Liquidity loan | 2,804.45 | 52 |
| Soft loan | 841.59 (including 16.33 under soft loan 2.0) | 113 (including 4 under the soft loan 2.0) |
| Total | 3,646.04 | 165 |

**Table 3** Data on Financial Shield 1.0 and Financial Shield 2.0

| Voivodship | Value of aid (million PLN) | | Number of companies (thousands) | | Number of employees (thousands) | |
|---|---|---|---|---|---|---|
| | PFR 1.0 | PFR 2.0 | PFR 1.0 | PFR 2.0 | PFR 1.0 | PFR 2.0 |
| Dolnośląskie | 3,891.4 | 593.2 | 24.1 | 3.6 | 184.7 | 26.0 |
| Kujawsko-Pomorskie | 2,813.2 | 277.5 | 16.8 | 2.0 | 141.4 | 12.8 |
| Lubelskie | 2,238.7 | 238.2 | 14.7 | 1.9 | 107.6 | 11.0 |
| Lubuskie | 1,373.4 | 131.1 | 8.9 | 1.1 | 67.6 | 6.7 |
| Łódzkie | 3,613.2 | 336.7 | 22.4 | 2.9 | 170.0 | 16.6 |
| Małopolskie | 5,996.2 | 1046.2 | 35.6 | 6.4 | 279.8 | 43.8 |
| Mazowieckie | 11,098.8 | 1269.2 | 55.1 | 7.8 | 443.5 | 52.4 |
| Opolskie | 1,262.5 | 135.7 | 7.8 | 0.9 | 64.2 | 6.7 |
| Podkarpackie | 2,677.4 | 308.4 | 16.1 | 2.1 | 137.2 | 14.1 |
| Podlaskie | 1,390.3 | 119.0 | 7.5 | 0.8 | 64.8 | 6.2 |
| Pomorskie | 4,063.1 | 552.6 | 23.0 | 3.2 | 191.5 | 24.0 |
| Śląskie | 7,181.8 | 707.2 | 42.5 | 5.5 | 341.9 | 31.4 |
| Świętokrzyskie | 1,554.7 | 182.0 | 10.0 | 1.2 | 72.1 | 8.0 |
| Warmińsko-Mazurskie | 1,642.6 | 200.0 | 10.5 | 1.3 | 87.7 | 9.2 |
| Wielkopolskie | 6,939.0 | 601.1 | 40.1 | 4.5 | 325.6 | 28.1 |
| Zachodniopomorskie | 2,125.2 | 435.4 | 13.5 | 2.4 | 102.7 | 18.6 |
| Total | 59,861.6 | 7133.3 | 348.4 | 47.7 | 2,782.6 | 315.5 |

Data on these aspects for Financial Shield 1.0 and Financial Shield 2.0 are presented in Table 4.

The analysis of the value of COVID-19-related state aid provided per enterprise and employee provides exciting information and dramatically expands the previous considerations. In the case of Financial Shield 1.0, the differences between provinces are already much more minor. Although the average value of support for an enterprise is again highest in the Mazowieckie Voivodship, the Podlaskie Voivodship, one of the less well-funded in absolute terms, appears right behind it. On the other hand, the voivodship with the lowest support value per beneficiary enterprise is Lubelskie Voivodship. Equally interesting is the situation regarding the conversion of subsidies per employee. Again, the most significant value falls on employees from the Mazowieckie Voivodship (more than 25 thousand PLN), while in a large group of Voivodships, this value is more than 21 thousand. Among them, the most significant value characterizes the Świętokrzyskie Voivodship.

On the other hand, by far the smallest average amount of state aid per employee was transferred in the Warmińsko-Mazurskie Voivodship. Even more exciting conclusions are provided by the analysis of data on Financial Shield 2.0. The highest value of aid per enterprise was transferred in the Pomorskie and Zachodniopomorskie Voivodships, and the lowest in the Lubuskie and Łódzkie Voivodships; however,

**Table 4** Average aid per enterprise and employee by province

| Voivodship | Average aid per enterprise (thousand PLN) | | Average value of aid per employee (thousand PLN) | |
|---|---|---|---|---|
| | PFR 1.0 | PFR 2.0 | PFR 1.0 | PFR 2.0 |
| Dolnośląskie | 161.2 | 163.9 | 21.1 | 22.8 |
| Kujawsko-Pomorskie | 167.7 | 138.3 | 19.9 | 21.7 |
| Lubelskie | 152.8 | 127.7 | 20.8 | 21.6 |
| Lubuskie | 154.0 | 116.4 | 20.3 | 19.6 |
| Łódzkie | 161.0 | 117.4 | 21.3 | 20.3 |
| Małopolskie | 168.6 | 163.9 | 21.4 | 23.9 |
| Mazowieckie | 201.4 | 163.3 | 25.0 | 24.2 |
| Opolskie | 162.7 | 145.3 | 19.7 | 20.2 |
| Podkarpackie | 166.1 | 147.0 | 19.5 | 21.9 |
| Podlaskie | 185.7 | 144.8 | 21.4 | 19.3 |
| Pomorskie | 177.0 | 173.4 | 21.4 | 23.0 |
| Śląskie | 169.1 | 129.6 | 21.0 | 22.5 |
| Świętokrzyskie | 155.1 | 145.6 | 21.5 | 22.8 |
| Warmińsko-Mazurskie | 156.9 | 148.2 | 18.7 | 21.6 |
| Wielkopolskie | 173.1 | 133.3 | 21.3 | 21.4 |
| Zachodniopomorskie | 157.7 | 179.5 | 20.7 | 23.4 |
| Total | 171.8 | 149.6 | 21.5 | 22.6 |

the situation looks quite different per employee. The highest aid was obtained in the Mazowieckie and Małopolskie Voivodships, and the lowest in the Lubuskie and Podlaskie Voivodships. It is also worth noting that, nationwide, the more excellent value of assistance per enterprise was characterized by Financial Shield 1.0, while per employee, the more excellent service was provided by Financial Shield 2.0.

## 4 Conclusion

The COVID-19 pandemic unleashed an unprecedented stream of state aid in most member states, which tried to minimize its negative impact on the economy as much as possible. Vast sums of money were allocated to combat the effects of the pandemic, which under other conditions would certainly have yet to be approved by the EU institutions. Approval for these measures had to be given by the European Commission, but decisions were made much faster than usual. This is evidenced by the fact that in most countries, first aid was launched as early as April 2020, just over two months after the first confirmed disease cases were detected in Europe. The support was intended to respond to the increasingly widespread lockdowns, making it difficult or impossible for many companies to operate virtually overnight. To prevent a complete economic collapse, the governments of individual countries looked for solutions to support these companies and their employees. One of them was precisely the funds provided through state aid.

Poland is one of the countries that has been most heavily involved in helping entrepreneurs using a range of assistance and shielding measures, of which the programs implemented by the Polish Development Fund were undoubtedly among the most important. Several hundred thousand enterprises employing more than 3 million workers benefited from them. The level of assistance varied from province to province, mainly due to regional conditions and entrepreneurship. Undoubtedly, however, these programs helped enterprises survive the most challenging period and provided a kind of compensation for the ban on business. The topic of the effectiveness and adequacy of the measures implemented will undoubtedly continue to arouse the interest of scientists, politicians, entrepreneurs, and the general public for a long time to come. However, the COVID-19 pandemic proved that under certain conditions, public assistance is still a necessary part of the functioning of the economy.

## References


1. Zuba-Ciszewska, M.: The role of state aid for the food industry–Based on the example of dairies in Poland. Int. J. Manag. Econ. **59**(2), 1–16 (2023)
2. Jabłońska, M., Stawska, J., Dziuba, R., Tekce, M., Krasoń, M.: Public aid and entrepreneurship during the Covid-19 pandemic in the European Union Countries. Financ. Financ. Law **3**(31), 57–77 (2021)
3. Ambroziak, A.A.: State aid trends in Poland and Finland-similarities and differences. Eur. Stud.-Stud. Eur. Aff. **26**(4), 217–232 (2022)
4. Hintošová, A. B., Bruothová, M., Kubíková, Z., Ručinský, R.: Determinants of foreign direct investment inflows: A case of the Visegrad countries. J. Int. Stud. **11**(2) (2018)
5. Sciskalová, M., Münster, M.: Definition and characteristics of state aid. Procedia Soc. Behav. Sci. **110**, 223–230 (2014)
6. Bourreau, M., Feasey, R., Nicolle, A.: Assessing fifteen years of State Aid for broadband in the European Union: A quantitative analysis. Telecommun. Policy **44**(7), 101974 (2020)
7. Fahner, J.H.: Compensation or competitive advantage? Reconciling investment arbitration with EU state aid law. ICSID Rev.-Foreign Invest. Law J. **37**(3), 672–686 (2022)
8. Łopatka, A., Fedorowicz, K.: Evaluation of the effectiveness of state aid offered to enterprises during the COVID-19 pandemic. Procedia Comput. Sci. **192**, 4828–4836 (2021)
9. Košdy, M.: Distribution of regional state aid in Slovakia: A focus on the least developed districts. Society and Economy (2023)
10. Przygodzka, R.: The specificity of state aid in Poland in comparison with European Union countries. Optimum. Econ. Stud. **102**(4), 79–90 (2020)
11. European Commission: Competition: State aid procedures (2013)
12. Sariyer, G., Kahraman, S., Sözen, M.E., Ataman, M.G.: Fiscal responses to COVID-19 outbreak for healthy economies: Modelling with big data analytics. Struct. Chang. Econ. Dyn. **64**, 191–198 (2023)
13. Kochaniak, K., Ulman, P., Zajkowski, R.: Effectiveness of COVID-19 state aid for microenterprises in Poland. Int. Rev. Econ. Financ. **86**, 483–497 (2023)

14. Cepel, M., Gavurova, B., Dvorský, J., Belas, J.: The impact of the COVID-19 crisis on the perception of business risk in the SME segment. Journal of International Studies. **13**(3), 248–263 (2020)
15. Iyke, B.N., Maheepala, M.M.J.D.: Conventional monetary policy, COVID-19, and stock, markets in emerging economies. Pac. Basin Financ. J. **76**, 101883 (2022)
16. Wu, J., Zhan, X., Xu, H., Ma, C.: The economic impacts of COVID-19 and city lockdown: Early evidence from China. Struct. Chang. Econ. Dyn. **65**, 151–165 (2023).
17. Al Farooque, O., Baghdadi, G., Trinh, H.H., Khandaker, S.: Stock liquidity during COVID-19 crisis: A cross-country analysis of developed and emerging economies, and economic policy uncertainty. Emerg. Mark. Rev. **55**, 101025 (2023)
18. Hu, H., Yang, Y., Zhang, J.: Avoiding panic during pandemics: COVID-19 and tourism related businesses. Tour. Manage. **86**, 104316 (2021)
19. Ahsan, S., Ahmmed, T., Alam, F.: The COVID-19, power generation and economy—Case study of a developing country. Electr. J. **35**(6), 107145 (2022)
20. Insaidoo, M., Ullah, A., Dziwornu, R.K., Amoako, S., Abdul-Mumuni, A.: COVID-19 pandemic and stock market performance: A comparative study of emerging economies. Heliyon **9**(5), e16054 (2023)
21. Groenewegen, J., Hardeman, S., Stam, E.: Does COVID-19 state aid reach the right firms? COVID-19 state aid, turnover expectations, uncertainty and management practices. J. Bus. Ventur. Insights **16**, e00262 (2021)
22. Biel, M., Ślusarczyk, B.: Family business and management: Objectives, theory, and practice. Taylor & Francis (2022)
23. Ślusarczyk, B., Moghavvemi, S., Tehseen, S.: Women and business: Empirical study on economic constraints, legal conditions, and social support influencing women entrepreneurs in Malaysia and Poland. Entrep. Bus. & Econ. Rev. **11**(2) (2023)
24. Alcidi, C., Corti, F.: The EU response to Covid-19: breaking old taboos. In: Vanhercke, B. Spasova S. (eds.) Social policy in the European Union: state of play 2021. Re-emerging social ambitions as the EU recovers from the pandemic, pp. 39–60 (2021)
25. UOKiK—Office of Competition and Consumer Protection: Report on public aid in Poland granted to entrepreneurs in 2020. Warsaw (2021)
26. Jafarli, T.: European State Aid During COVID-19. European Studies—The review of European law. Econ. Polit. **9**(2), 265–282 (2022).
27. European Commission: State Aid Scoreboard 2021 (2022)
28. Dębkowska, K., Kłosiewicz-Górecka, U., Szymańska, A., Ważniewski, P., Zybertowicz, K.: The anti-crisis shield. A lifeline for companies and the economy? Polish Economic Institute, Warsaw (2021)

# CEO Gender's Impact on Creative Accounting Motives and Manipulation: Evidence from Slovakia

**Jakub Michulek and Anna Krizanova**

**Abstract** Accounting may be considered a mirror of all business operations carried out by corporations and their workers. In recent decades, accounting has been associated with creative accounting. It is an adjustment of the financial statements in favor of the company. The scientific article aims to find out whether the gender of the CEO influences the motives leading to creative accounting and the influence of the gender of the CEO on the implementation of creative accounting by employees under the direction of the CEO. Contingency tables, the Pearson Chi-Square test, the Phi coefficient, and correspondence analysis were used. Based on the results, it is possible to claim that "the gender of the CEO has an influence on the motives leading to the implementation of creative accounting in the company" and "the gender of the CEO has an effect on the execution of the CEO's orders to adjust the financial statements." It has been proven that women would do creative accounting to increase or maintain capital levels or increase the competitiveness of the company; men to get time to settle debts and increase personal profit; and in the case of a mixed line, it is about attracting investors and beating analysts' estimates of the company's future performance. If the CEO is a man, the employees would do creative accounting, but not for women, and in a mixed line, they would need to know the answer.

**Keywords** Gender equality · Motives of creative accounting · Creative accounting · Slovakia · Correspondence accounting

## 1 Introduction

The annual reports of the firm are among the best tools for communicating with interested parties. It acts as the primary source of financial and non-financial information for people participating in the decision-making process. Corporate financial reports

J. Michulek (✉) · A. Krizanova
Faculty of Operation and Economics of Transport and Communications, University of Zilina, Univerzitna 1, 010 26 Zilina, Slovakia
e-mail: jakub.michulek@stud.uniza.sk



S. Kot et al. (eds.), *Corporate Practices: Policies, Methodologies, and Insights in Organizational Management*, Springer Proceedings in Business and Economics,
https://doi.org/10.1007/978-981-97-0996-0_28

now include more narrative disclosure, and investors and other stakeholders rely on this information to make investment decisions. If these disclosures are convoluted and challenging to comprehend, decision-making bodies' capacity to draw pertinent conclusions is compromised [1].

All stakeholders are concerned about the rise in large company failures in recent years. The efficiency of corporate governance procedures in limiting innovative accounting methods has thus come under increased scrutiny from the public. Numerous nations have implemented new legal measures and other reforms in reaction to popular discontent [2].

Among the numerous fraudulent scandals are the preparation of yearly reports, breaches of trust, the submission of false information to authorities, and unlawful goals. One such scandal involves the Indian IT company Satyam. The Satyam CEO manipulated the books of accounts to make the company look larger than it was, which led to widespread financial reporting businesses engaging in fraudulent activities. Due to the CEO's modifications, it became apparent that the business needed to develop quickly and earn more money. The demise of Satyam prompted a review of the CEO's leadership qualities in guiding the company to success [3]. So, in the area of economic crime and delinquency, creative accounting is a widely employed method [4].

Despite having a more than 500-year history that began with the creation of the first accounting files, "creative accounting" has only recently become a standalone academic topic [5]. The practice of creative accounting and revenue management is widespread around the world [4], but it is also problematic for governments at all levels, including local governments [6, 7] and the federal government [8]. The fundamentals of creative accounting are founded on accounting theory, but they modify business outcomes for various objectives. It might be seen as a planned interruption of societal, economic transformation intended to achieve a specific goal. Using their understanding of accounting regulations, accountants modify the facts found in accounting [9].

## 2 Literature Review

According to Ado et al. [10], creative accounting is an excessive barrier that employs novel ways to characterize assets, obligations, and revenue. However, managers who act for motives other than enhancing factual reporting view creative accounting as an opportunistic activity, which gives the approach a slightly unfavorable reputation [1]. Creative accounting, according to Denich and Hajdu [11], is the managerial use of discretion in financial reporting to alter financial statements to deceive some stakeholders about the company's economic performance or to affect the terms of contracts that depend on the reported accounting figures. According to Blazek et al. [12], creative accounting is modifying accounting values from actual to necessary values. The use of adjusted book values then helps the firm.

The fundamental goal of creative accounting is to fool the public by concealing the financial health of the company. The use of cutting-edge accounting knowledge and methods backed by current rules and regulations is known as creative accounting. Financial statements are frequently influenced by management utilizing sophisticated, creative accounting knowledge. These procedures are sometimes called aggressive accounting, creative accounting, or earnings management. As a result, the idea is linked to moral principles in general and ethical accounting standards [13], and the idea of creative accounting is highly complicated and intricate [14]. Four crucial factors of creative accounting were identified by Abed et al. [15] as follows: ownership structure, internal control, disclosure quality, and ethical issues.

The phrase "earnings management" is most frequently used in the considerable literature on this subject in the United States, although "creative accounting" is favored in Europe [12]. Creative management employs a range of techniques and tactics to influence revenues lawfully. Asset valuation, false reporting of sales and earnings, purposeful accounting mistakes, poor earnings quality, and poor earnings management are a few examples [16].

Negative perceptions about creative accounting are common. As a result, it is defined as a technique for falsifying financial statement information to deceive investors and other consumers of accounting information. However, there are both advantages and disadvantages to creative accounting. Positive, creative accounting refers to using accounting concepts and practices that acknowledge changes in the corporate environment and lessen the unpredictability of profit. Negative creative accounting, on the other hand, is described as an unethical means of raising money from the market by misrepresenting the company's financial status to potential investors [1].

Remenaric, Kenfelja, and Mijoc [17] identified the primary drivers of creative accounting as personal gain, benchmarking, luring investors, raising or maintaining the level of capital, buying time to pay off debts, or outperforming analysts' projections of the company's future performance. Smailovic, Aleksic, and Uremovic [18] contend that there are various reasons to use creative accounting. The necessity to avoid paying taxes, more lucrative business sales, improving one is standing with creditors and investors, realizing bonuses and managerial privileges, and many more factors are among them. Yahaya [19] divided the causes of using creative accounting into the following categories:

- Providing specific bonuses, pay raises, job security, and personal happiness as personal incentives.
- External expectations include the realization of earnings, adherence to regulations, and analysts' expectations.
- Special circumstances, including new share issuances, loan management, mergers and acquisitions, a new management team, and awaiting better economic conditions.
- Covering the theft of assets through fraud.

The CEO is among senior management who can affect the caliber of financial reporting, according to accounting literature. This is due to the likelihood that the

CEO will have an impact on the information contained in business statements such press releases, remuneration packages, and annual reports [3].

According to Kliestik et al. [20], humanity has been characterized by their desire to aid one another from the dawn of time; even if this required faking or misleading a merchant, they frequently disagreed. Production and related administrative functions needed to continue as businesses expanded. Women gradually gained access to several professions as a result. They were once low-level occupations. Contrarily, gender equality later emerged as a potential motif, which suggests that women attained greater positions and ascended to the position of CEO (the CEO is the top position in any business and is responsible for overseeing the general management of the whole firm. They are responsible for making big decisions for the company and are the company's representatives in the media and the public).

The findings of Altarawneh [3] usually demonstrate that CEO traits restrict profitability management. As demonstrated, female CEOs, CEO networks, and CEO tenure all have a detrimental impact on managing profitability. Age, revenue management, and CEO experience, however, are not related.

When women are in powerful positions, domestic marketplaces are of higher quality. International businesses that operate in emerging economies have profited from this change. The world's religions, on the other hand, forbid women from working or taking part in commercial development. Thus, one tool that significantly affects gender equality is religion [20].

Female CEOs typically enhance a company's worth since they have essential traits that their male colleagues do not. Female directors have been found to possess unique abilities, more robust moral standards, more risk aversion, and superior overall control than male directors. Therefore, having more female directors may result in better firm performance, moderate risk-taking, and lower income management [21]. Because they are more sensitive and have a propensity to support the rule of law over financial gain, women seek executive roles, which may have a significant influence on corporate fraud [20].

According to Kyaw et al. [22], businesses with more women on their boards of directors produce higher-quality earnings. This is attributed to the fact that female filmmakers are less risk-taking than male directors and tend to adhere to moral standards and laws. Female directors are associated with lower levels of discretionary increments [23] and fewer rewrites as a result of irregularities [24], according to several earlier researches. Women frequently adopt a more challenging ethical position than males, which is one of the critical reasons for the adverse association between female directors and revenue management [21]. Men are typically more adaptable and do not have as many obligations to the family. On the other hand, a high proportion of women who work for themselves may be a sign of their entrepreneurial qualities and the necessity of gainful employment, which is linked to the flexibility of the work, self-realization, and putting one's ideas and dreams into action [25]

The scientific article aims to find out whether the gender of the CEO influences the motives leading to creative accounting and the influence of the gender of the CEO on the implementation of creative accounting by employees at the request of the CEO. The scientific article consists of four chapters, while the introduction informs the reader about creative accounting and the influence of gender on the occurrence of creative accounting. In the second chapter, Methodology for the Reader, we inform the reader about data collection and the methods used. In Results, we analyze and interpret research results. The last chapter, Discussion and Conclusion, will compare the research results with the results of foreign and domestic authors and a final evaluation of the research, highlighting its uniqueness or setting limits.

## 3 Methodology

A Google Forms online survey was used to gather information for the study. The target audience for the questionnaire was individuals between the ages of 18 and 64 who worked in the economic or accounting departments of businesses based in the Slovak Republic, which represents the working-age population of the country. Companies from all 23 SK NACE zones were contacted, and companies from 18 industries answered the questionnaire. The questionnaire consisted of 18 questions. The first five questions focused on basic information about the company, such as where the company is located, the size of the company, the SK NACE category, the type of corporate culture, or the gender of the CEO. The remaining 13 questions were devoted to creative accounting. As part of these questions, we found out whether the respondents know about creative accounting, what word combinations creative accounting evokes for them, the motives of creative accounting, and if so. In that category, they would classify the issue of creative accounting. Between November 18 and December 18, 2022, data were collected. The www.scitanie.sk website for the 2021 Census of Population, Homes, and Apartments was used to estimate the population between the ages of 18 and 64. We had a sample size of 386 responders after supplementation. Following that, the data were processed using IBM SPSS Statistics 25 and MS Excel. Contingency tables, Pearson's 2 test, Phi coefficient, and correspondence analysis will all be used in the research if dependence exists.

Associative and contingent relationships between qualitative qualities are used to convey dependence. Finding the frequency of all possible value combinations that both variables can acquire is the foundation for assessing the dependence or independence of two qualitative features. Pearson's 2 test is the test for contingency tables that is most widely used. The significance level for the test will be set at 0.05. After that, the following alternate hypotheses were confirmed:

**H1:** The gender of the CEO has an influence on the motives leading to the implementation of creative accounting in the company.

**H2:** The gender of the CEO has an effect on the execution of the CEO's orders to adjust the financial statements.

## 4 Results

The data was processed using the IBM SPSS Statistics 25 program. We asked the respondents what gender holds the CEO position within the company where they work and what motives lead people to perform creative accounting. From Table 1, it can be seen, for example, that if the company's CEO is a man, the most frequent motives for performing creative accounting are increasing personal profit (42 times), getting time to settle debts (40 times), or increasing the competitiveness of the company (26 times). The least frequent motive is attracting investors (9 times). If the company's CEO is a woman, the most frequent motives are increasing or maintaining capital levels (41 times) or increasing the company's competitiveness (55 times). The least frequent motive is attracting investors or beating analysts' estimates of the company's future performance. In the case of mixed management of the company, which means that the head of the company is a woman and a man, or the highest position is held by two or three persons, the most frequent motive is attracting investors (41 times), beating analysts' estimates of the company's future performance (29 times), or increasing the competitiveness of the company (22 times). More detailed results are shown in Table 1.

To determine the relationship between the variable gender and motives leading to creative accounting, we performed Pearson's Chi-Square test for contingency tables. The alternative hypothesis H1 was established, which read as follows: "The gender of the CEO influences the motives leading to the implementation of creative accounting in the company." Table 2 shows the results of Pearson's Chi-Square Test. It can be seen from the table that the p-value of the test reached a level of 0.000.

Since this value is less than the alpha significance level set at 0.05, it can be concluded that the null hypothesis is rejected. The gender of the CEO does not influence the motives leading to the implementation of creative accounting in the company; the alternative hypothesis is accepted. It is possible to state that the gender of the CEO influences the motives leading to the implementation of creative accounting in the company.

Given that the dependence between the variables was confirmed, it is necessary to determine the strength of this dependence. Several coefficients can be used to determine the strength of dependence, such as the Phi coefficient, Cramer's V, or the contingency coefficient. In our case, we decided to use Cramer's V coefficient, which is used most often. Based on this coefficient, which reached a value of 0.456, it can be concluded that it is a moderately strong dependence. A moderately strong dependence occurs when the coefficient ranges from 0.3 to 0.8 (Table 3). It is also possible to state that there is a direct dependence since the coefficient reaches a positive value.

From the resulting correspondence map shown in Fig. 1, it is possible that companies in which a woman holds the position of CEO would resort to creative accounting to increase or maintain capital levels or increase the company's competitiveness. The justification can be found in the traditional understanding, where women in many societies and cultures are expected to care for the family and the household. This

**Table 1** Motives of creative accounting according to gender

Gender * Motives of creative accounting

Count

| | | Motives of creative accounting | | | | | | Total |
|---|---|---|---|---|---|---|---|---|
| | | Attracting investors | Beating analysts' estimates of the company's future performance | Getting time to settle debts | Increasing or maintaining capital levels | Increasing personal profit | Increasing the competitiveness of the company | |
| Gender | Man | 9 | 12 | 40 | 12 | 42 | 26 | 141 |
| | Mixed line | 41 | 29 | 7 | 14 | 4 | 22 | 117 |
| | Woman | 8 | 9 | 13 | 41 | 12 | 55 | 138 |
| Total | | 58 | 50 | 60 | 67 | 58 | 103 | 396 |

*Source* Own research

**Table 2** Pearson's Chi-Square test for H1

| Chi-Square tests | | | |
|---|---|---|---|
| | Value | df | Asymptotic Significance (2-sided) |
| Pearson Chi-Square | 164.613[a] | 10 | 0.000 |
| Likelihood ratio | 154.567 | 10 | 0.000 |
| N of valid cases | 396 | | |

[a]0 cells (0.0%) have expected count less than 5. The minimum expected count is 14.77
*Source* Own research

**Table 3** Systematic measures of coefficients for H1

| Symmetric measures | | | |
|---|---|---|---|
| | | Value | Approximate significance |
| Nominal by nominal | Phi | 0.645 | 0.000 |
| | Cramer's V | 0.456 | 0.000 |
| | Contingency coefficient | 0.542 | 0.000 |
| N of valid cases | | 396 | |

*Source* Own research

dynamic can lead to women being motivated to be competitive and successful to prove their abilities and secure their position in the work environment. Every executive, regardless of gender, may have different career goals and ambitions. Some women may have a natural competitive nature and desire to be at the top of their industry. Increasing your competitiveness can be a way to achieve these goals and succeed in your career.

If a man holds the position of CEO in the company, they will perform creative accounting with the motive of increasing personal profit or getting time to settle debts. In the case of a mixed line, the motives are attracting investors or beating analysts' estimates of the company's future performance. In such a case, the motives leading to the manipulation of financial statements may be different. In any case, in most cases of manipulation, the parties involved agree on the reasons for the manipulation.

If we look at the implementation of creative accounting following instructions from the CEO according to gender, the companies in which a man holds the CEO position tend to implement it. In that case, up to 87 respondents, representing 61.70%, are inclined to perform creative accounting. In the case of mixed management of the company, the employees mostly need to know whether they would decide to adjust the financial statements based on the CEO's instructions, namely 46 respondents (31.32%). Twenty-two respondents would resort to adjusting the accounting, which represents 18.80%, and 49 (41.88%) respondents would not perform the adjustment. Employees working in companies where a woman holds the CEO position would resort to creative accounting in only 29 cases (21.01%). In up to 100 cases (72.46%), employees would not perform such an action (Table 4).

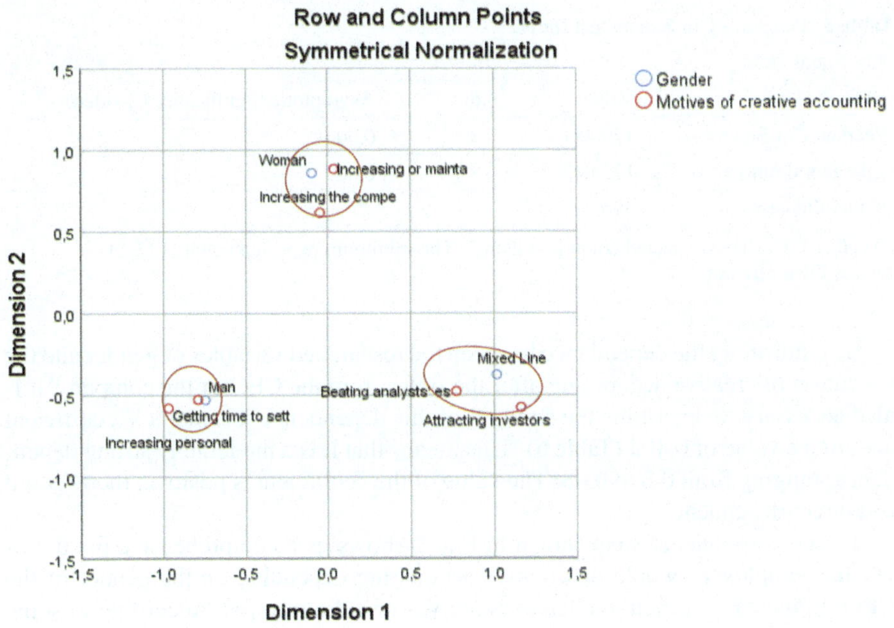


**Fig. 1** Correspondence map of motives of creative accounting according to gender. *Source* Own research

**Table 4** Performance of creative accounting after offer from CEO according to gender

Gender * Performance of creative accounting after offer from CEO
Count

| | | Performance of creative accounting after ofrer from manager | | | | | Total |
|---|---|---|---|---|---|---|---|
| | | Definitely no | Definitely yes | I do not know | No | Yes | |
| Gender | Man | 13 | 31 | 18 | 23 | 56 | 141 |
| | Mixed line | 21 | 2 | 46 | 28 | 20 | 117 |
| | Woman | 55 | 8 | 9 | 45 | 21 | 138 |
| Total | | 89 | 41 | 73 | 96 | 97 | 396 |

*Source* Own research

The second alternative hypothesis, H2, was established as follows: "The gender of the CEO affects the execution of the CEO's orders to adjust the financial statements." The Person's Chi-Square test result reached 0.000 (Table 5). Since the p-value of the test is less than the alpha significance level, set at the 0.05 level, it can be concluded that we reject the null hypothesis (The gender of the CEO affects the execution of the CEO's orders to adjust the financial statements.) and accept the alternative one. Ultimately, it can be concluded that the gender of the CEO affects the execution of the CEO's orders to adjust the financial statements.

**Table 5** Pearson's Chi-Square test for H2

| Chi-Square tests | | | |
|---|---|---|---|
| | Value | df | Asymptotic Significance (2-sided) |
| Pearson Chi-Square | 129.481[a] | 8 | 0.000 |
| Likelihood ratio | 125.842 | 8 | 0.000 |
| N of valid cases | 396 | | |

[a]0 cells (0.0%) have expected count less than 5. The minimum expected count is 12.11
*Source* Own research

By confirming the dependence between the researched variables of gender and the execution of creative accounting after the order from the CEO of the company, it is also necessary to determine the strength of this dependence. Cramer's V coefficient acquired a value of 0.404 (Table 6). This means that it is a moderately strong dependence, ranging from 0.3 to 0.08. The value of the coefficient is positive; therefore, it is a direct dependence.

The correspondence map shown in Fig. 2 shows us a comprehensive picture of whether employees would do creative accounting depending on the gender of the CEO. In the case of men, the answers are yes or definitely yes. According to some authors, from time immemorial, men have been characterized by trying to help each other, even if this meant forging or deceiving another merchant with whom they had many disagreements. Moreover, if the executive is a man, in many cases he has more authority than a woman. In addition, this authority can also lead to the fear of losing one's job if one disobeys a superior's order.

If the position of CEO is held by a woman, the employees would not resort to creative accounting. Women often face a higher level of criticism and prejudice in the workplace. Therefore, they may feel a greater need to overcome these obstacles and prove their worth. Increasing competitiveness can be a way for some women to demonstrate their abilities and build their place in companies. In the end, women have a greater moral sense and thus a lower tendency to resort to manipulation of financial statements, as they prefer fair play.

Enterprises with mixed management in the case of an order to carry out the manipulation of financial statements cannot clearly expect an exact answer, as in

**Table 6** Systematic measures of coefficients for H2

| Symmetric measures | | | |
|---|---|---|---|
| | | Value | Approximate significance |
| Nominal by nominal | Phi | 0.572 | 0.000 |
| | Cramer's V | 0.404 | 0.000 |
| | Contingency coefficient | 0.496 | 0.000 |
| N of valid cases | | 396 | |

*Source* Own research

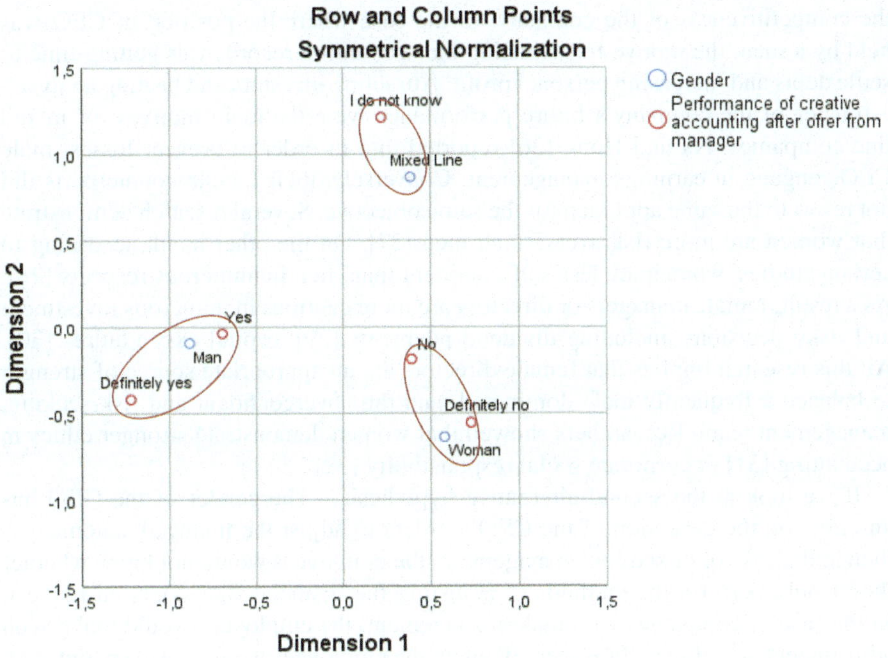


**Fig. 2** Performance of creative accounting after offer from manager according to gender. *Source* Own research

such a case, the answer I do not know prevails. Employees may see disagreement about creative accounting among managers, which will cause them to split internally. In the end, the employee decides according to greater authority or sympathy.

## 5 Discussion and Conclusion

Based on the Pearson Chi-Square test for contingency tables, we were able to confirm the alternative hypotheses we established. Tests were performed at a significance level of 0.000. Based on this, it can be concluded that "The gender of the CEO has an influence on the motives leading to the implementation of creative accounting in the company" and "The gender of the CEO has an effect on the execution of the CEO's orders to adjust the financial statements." Since the relationship between the monitored variables was confirmed, we also examined the strength of this relationship. In both cases, moderate dependence was confirmed.

The confirmation of dependence allowed us to use correspondence analysis at the same time, through which we revealed that if the position of CEO is held by a woman in the company, then these persons would resort to creative accounting practices for the purpose of increasing or maintaining capital levels or increasing the competitiveness of the company. In the case where the position of CEO was held by a man, the motive for adjusting the accounting records was getting time to settle debts and increasing personal profit. Attracting investors and beating analysts' estimates of the company's future performance were the main motives for mixed line companies. Na and Hong [26] reported that in order to prevent losses, male CEOs engage in earnings management. Conversely, their female counterparts did not resort to the same approach for the same objective. Several research demonstrate that women are more risk averse than men [27]. On the other hand, according to certain studies, women are less self-confident than men in numerous respects [28]. As a result, female managers or directors are more cautious in numerous investment and risky decisions, including dividend payments [29], capital expenditures [30]. All this research implies that female directors are an appropriate source of strength to balance a frequently male-dominated, and thus overconfident and risk-seeking, management team. Researchers showed that women demonstrate stronger ethics in accounting [31] or corporate social responsibility [32].

If we look at the second alternative hypothesis, "The gender of the CEO has an effect on the execution of the CEO's orders to adjust the financial statements," then in the case of mixed line management, the employees would not know whether they would perform the methods of adjusting the financial statements on request. In the case of companies with male management, the employees would make such adjustments, and if the CEOs were women, the employees would not carry out such activities. Pavlović et al. [33] from Serbia revealed intriguing results after doing research on Serbian agricultural firms listed on the Belgrade Stock Exchange. They concluded that the number of women on corporate boards has just a minor, linear accounting relationship using passive accounting. In another related study, Belot and Serve [34] showed a higher frequency of earnings management among enterprises with male CEOs compared to organizations with female CEOs. Srindhi et al. [21] argue that enterprises with more participation of women on their boards show higher earnings quality.

Earnings quality is a crucial outcome of good governance that investors want, and consequently, its improvement is an essential goal of the board of directors. Alves [35] concluded that firms with a threshold proportion of female directors on their boards are likely to demonstrate more conservative earnings than firms with a ratio of female directors below the crucial amount. This study further reveals that the influence of female directors on accounting conservatism is stronger in the presence of a higher gender equality index. The study results by El-Dyasry and Elamer [36] reveal that female directors, managers, and women in audit committees are favorably connected with the quality of financial reporting. The data further show that female CEOs are less likely to participate in earnings-reducing earnings management methods. Overall, the results are consistent with the concept that gender diversity is an effective monitoring tool that mitigates inter-agency conflicts and, hence, increases the quality of financial reporting. Research by Kliestik et al. [20] has shown that gender affects whether a corporation utilizes manipulative tactics to optimize accounting. According to the results, the companies where a woman held the CEO position proved non-manipulative based on the Beneish model. In the case of a male CEO, the companies were manipulators, and if it was a mixed line, they were tagged as possible manipulators. Overall, the document by Belaounia et al. [37] reveals that the influence of female directors on the success of enterprises depends on the overall level of gender equality in the country. However, this result is challenged by the research of Arioglu [38], who discovered that the presence of female directors on business boards is not associated with earnings management.

The results of our research confirmed the conclusions of many foreign and domestic authors. If we look at the research of individual authors, many of them focus on the influence of gender on the use of creative accounting or earnings management methods. The benefit of our study is that we also focused on determining whether the manager's gender can influence the motives leading to the adjustment of financial statements. The limits of the scientific contribution are that the findings were revealed for the territory of the Slovak Republic and, therefore, may not be valid for other countries with a different type of economy, economic structure, or political constitution.

**Acknowledgements** This paper is an output of scientific project VEGA no. 1/0032/21: Marketing engineering as a progressive platform for optimizing managerial decision-making processes in the context of the current challenges of marketing management and VEGA no. 1/0409/23 Forensic marketing as a platform of objective empirical support for managerial decision-making processes.

## References

1. Kovacova, M., Hrosova, L., Durana, P., Horak, J.: Earnings management model for Visegrad Group as an immanent part of creative accounting. Oeconomia Copernicana **13**(4), 1143–1176 (2022)
2. Olojede, P., Erin, O.: Corporate governance mechanisms and creative accounting practices: The role of accounting regulation. Int. J. Discl. Gov. Ance. **18**(3), 1–16 (2021)
3. Altarawneh, M., Shafie, R., Ishak, R., Ghaleb, B.A.A.: Chief executive officer characteristics and discretionary accruals in an emerging economy. Cogent Bus. & Manag. **9**(1), 2024117 (2022)
4. Durana, P., Blazek, R., Machova, V., Krasnan, M.: The use of Beneish M-scores to reveal creative accounting: Evidence from Slovakia. Equilibrium. Q. J. Econ. Econ. Policy **17**(2), 481–510 (2022)
5. Vassalo, R.A., de Lima, D.V.: Enfrentando a cortina de fumaça: uma análise epistemológica sobre o uso da expressão "contabilidade criativa". REVISTA AMBIENTE CONTÁBIL-Universidade Federal do Rio Grande do Norte-ISSN 2176-9036 **13**(1), 284–301 (2021)
6. Balduzzi, P., Grembi, V.: Fiscal rules and window dressing: the case of Italian municipalities. Giornale degli Economisti e Annali di Economia **70**(1), 97–122 (2011)
7. Clémenceau, M., Soguel, N.: Does personal background influence a finance minister to cook the books? An investigation of creative accounting in Swiss cantons. Appl. Econ. **49**(10), 941–953 (2017)
8. Hirota, H., Yunoue, H.: Fiscal rules and creative accounting: Evidence from Japanese municipalities. J. Jpn. Int. Econ. **63**, 101172 (2022)
9. Adámiková, E., Čorejová, T.: Creative accounting and the possibility of its detection in the evaluation of the company by expert. J. Risk Financ. Manag. **14**(7), 327 (2021)

10. Ado, A.B., Mohd Rashid, N.N., Mustapha, U.A., Ademola, L.S.: Audit quality and creative accounting strategy: Evidence from Nigerian public listed companies. Australas. Account., Bus. Financ. J. **16**(3), 40–54 (2022)
11. Denich, E., Hajdu, D.: Measurement of creative accounting by Transparency and Disclosure Index (TDI) method in automobile industry. Pénzügyi Szemle/Public Finance Quarterly **66**(3), 381–396 (2021)
12. Blazek, R., Durana, P., Michulek, J.: Renaissance of Creative Accounting Due to the Pandemic: New Patterns Explored by Correspondence Analysis. Stats **6**(1), 411–430 (2023)
13. Rahman, M. S., Hasan, M. J., Khan, M. S. H., Jahan, I.: Antecedents and effect of creative accounting practices on organizational outcomes: Evidence from Bangladesh. Heliyon, **9**(2), e13759 (2023)
14. Safta, I.L., Sabău, A.I., Muntean, N.: Bibliometric analysis of the literature on measuring techniques for manipulating financial statements. Risks **9**(7), 123 (2021)
15. Abed, I.A., Hussin, N., Ali, M.A., Haddad, H., Shehadeh, M., Hasan, E.F.: Creative accounting determinants and financial reporting quality: systematic literature review. Risks **10**(4), 76 (2022)
16. Lin, H., Tao, X., Wu, Ch.: Forecasting earnings with combination of analyst forecasts. J. Empir. Financ. **68**, 133–159 (2022)
17. Remenaric, B., Kenfelja, I., Mijoc, I.: Creative accounting-motives, techniques and possibilities of prevention. Ekonomski vjesnik **31**, 193–199 (2018)
18. Smailovic, N., Aleksic, M., Uremovic, N.: Analiza bilansa stanja s aspekta ugradenih procejena. Economy & Market Com-munication Review/Casopis za Ekonomiju i Trzisne Komunikacije **10**, 474–497 (2020)
19. Yahaya, K.A.: Creative accounting practices: Ethical challenges in Nigerian corporate Environment. In Development Finance Conference. Dubai (2014)
20. Kliestik, T., Blazek, R., Belas, J.: CEO monitoring and accounting record manipulation: Evidence from Slovak agriculture companies. Econ. & Sociol. **15**(4), 204–218 (2022)
21. Srinidhi, B.I.N., Gul, F.A., Tsui, J.: Female directors and earnings quality. Contemp. Account. Res. **28**(5), 1610–1644 (2011)
22. Kyaw, K., Olugbode, M., Petracci, B.: Does gender diverse board mean less earnings management? Financ. Res. Lett. **14**, 135–141 (2015)
23. Arun, T.G., Almahrog, Y.E., Aribi, Z.A.: Female directors and earnings management: Evidence from UK companies. Int. Rev. Financ. Anal. **39**, 137–146 (2015)
24. Wahid, A.S.: The effects and the mechanisms of board gender diversity: Evidence from financial manipulation. J. Bus. Ethics **159**(3), 705–725 (2019)
25. Ślusarczyk, B., Broniszewska, A.: Entrepreneurship of women in Poland and the EU: quantitative analysis. Pol. J. Manag. Stud. **9**, 217–224 (2014)
26. Na, K., Hong, J.: CEO gender and earnings management. J. Appl. Bus. Res. (JABR) **33**(2), 297–308 (2017)
27. Eckel, C.C., Grossman, P.J.: Forecasting risk attitudes: An experimental study using actual and forecast gamble choices. J. Econ. Behav. Organ. **68**(1), 1–17 (2008)
28. Niederle, M., Vesterlund, L.: Do women shy away from competition? Do men compete too much? Q. J. Econ. **122**(3), 1067–1101 (2007)
29. Saeed, A., Sameer, M.: Impact of board gender diversity on dividend payments: Evidence from some emerging economies. Int. Bus. Rev. **26**(6), 1100–1113 (2017)
30. Banerjee, S., Masulis, R. W., Upadhyay, A.: Mitigating effects of gender diverse board in companies managed by overconfident CEOs. Stevens Institute of Technology School of Business Research Paper (2018)
31. Ibrahim, N., Angelidis, J.: The relative importance of ethics as a selection criterion for entry-level public accountants: Does gender make a difference? J. Bus. Ethics **85**, 49–58 (2009)
32. García-Sánchez, I.M., Suárez-Fernández, O., Martínez-Ferrero, J.: Female directors and impression management in sustainability reporting. Int. Bus. Rev. **28**(2), 359–374 (2019)
33. Pavlovic, V., Knezevic, G., Bojicic, R.: Board gender diversity and earnings management in agricultural sector-Does it have any influence. Custos e Agronegócio on line **14**(2), 340–363 (2018)

34. Belot, F., Serve, S.: Earnings quality in private SMEs: Do CEO demographics matter? J. Small Bus. Manage. **56**, 323–344 (2018)
35. Alves, S.: Do female directors affect accounting conservatism in European Union? Cogent Business & Management **10**(2), 2219088 (2023)
36. El-Dyasty, M.M., Elamer, A.A.: Female leadership and financial reporting quality in Egypt. J. Appl. Acc. Res. **24**(3), 583–605 (2023)
37. Belaounia, S., Tao, R., Zhao, H.: Gender equality's impact on female directors' efficacy: A multi-country study. Int. Bus. Rev. **29**(5), 101737 (2020)
38. Arioglu, E.: The affiliations and characteristics of female directors and earnings management: evidence from Turkey. Manag. Audit. J. **35**(7), 927–953 (2020)

# Do Profitability and Leverage Influence Dividend Policy? Evidence from Emerging Countries

**Amanj Mohamed Ahmed, Mária Fekete-Farkas, and István Hágen**

**Abstract** Competition among firms to attract investors is significant for attracting them to invest their capital. This can be achieved by demanding firms to execute different policies, and one of the crucial policies is dividends. This paper aims to examine the effect of profitability and leverage on dividend policy decisions for Jordanian firms that are listed on the Amman Stock Exchange (ASX). A panel econometric model was developed to achieve this goal. The secondary data was collected from the audited annual report of 50 firms between 2017 and 2021. Dividend policy is the dependent variable measured by the dividend payout ratio (DPR). Profitability is considered an independent variable and indicated by return on assets (ROA) and return on equity (ROE). Leverage is another independent variable in this study and is proxied by the debt-to-equity ratio (DER) and short-term debt-to-assets ratio (STDA). The findings illustrated that profitability and leverage are related to DPR negatively. However, in the case of STDA, the result is statistically insignificant. These results are consistent with findings from the prior studies and supported by the pecking order theory, which claims that companies with high profitability pay fewer dividends as

A. M. Ahmed (✉) · M. Fekete-Farkas · I. Hágen
Doctoral School of Economic and Regional Sciences, Hungarian University of Agriculture and Life Sciences, Gödöllő 2100, Hungary
e-mail: ahmed.amanj.mohamed@phd.uni-mate.hu; amanj.mohamed@spu.edu.iq

M. Fekete-Farkas
e-mail: Farkasne.Fekete.Maria@uni-mate.hu

I. Hágen
e-mail: hagen.istvan.zsombor@uni-mate.hu

A. M. Ahmed
Darbandikhan Technical Institute, Sulaimani Polytechnic University, 70-236, Sulaimaniyah, Iraq

M. Fekete-Farkas
Institute of Agricultural and Food Economics, Hungarian University of Agriculture and Life Sciences, Gödöllő 2100, Hungary

I. Hágen
Institute of Rural Development and Sustainable Economy, Hungarian University of Agriculture and Life Sciences, Gödöllő 2100, Hungary

 
S. Kot et al. (eds.), *Corporate Practices: Policies, Methodologies, and Insights in Organizational Management*, Springer Proceedings in Business and Economics,
https://doi.org/10.1007/978-981-97-0996-0_29

the earnings are used to fund their activities, and also supported by agency theory, which asserts that firms that have prominent levels of debt, often pay less dividends.

**Keywords** Profitability · Leverage · Dividend policy · Amman Stock Exchange · Emerging markets

## 1 Introduction

In this age of industrialization, where competition continues to grow, every firm should continually improve its competitiveness because of growing competition in domestic and foreign markets. Firms must be able to sustain or achieve high profits by paying more attention to their economic and operational activities [1, 2]. The company's long-term objective is to increase its market value, while the short-term objective is to achieve the most significant profit by utilizing its current assets [2]. Investor impression of the firm is known as corporate value. The stock price of a firm, which has climbed through time and is a reliable indicator of its long-term worth, has risen. Thus, the greater the share price of an enterprise, the greater its value and profitability [3]. In addition, the impact of leverage on dividend policy is explained by the theory of agency, which claims that conflict of interest between the manager (agent) and owners (principals) through competing their interests will increase agency costs [4, 5]. There are several methods to reduce agency costs, and one of them is implementing a debt policy [6]. Using funds from external sources of financing, such as debt, pushes the firms to be overseen by investors and creditors. It is also an effective way to reduce agency issues because it is supervised and controlled by two parties [4]. Therefore, firms with high debt levels typically pay less dividends. This is because firms must pay interest and installments based on their borrowing. Owners have to surrender the flow of cash that was utilized to pay dividends in order to pay installments and interest [6, 7].

Further, one of the most heated debates in the financial and accounting discipline is dividend policy. Dividends are sums of money firms pay their shareholders due to their achievements [4]. Although the shareholders and managers are preoccupied with the share price of firms and their value, experts contend that it is crucial to consider the numerous factors that might affect investors' wealth and company value [1, 8]. Investors who invest money into a firm will receive a return on their deposit, which may come as dividends or gains from capital investments [4]. Additionally, shareholders often require an occasional steady dividend distribution as it can increase their trust in the business and lower their level of fear when placing their capital in the company. The company can determine the proportion of dividend distribution given to stockholders. The rise in distributing dividends to stockholders is an indication for both investors and the market because this will attract investors to invest and show the firm's capacity to make more profit [8].

From the previous literature, the relationship between profitability, leverage, and dividend policy has gained some empirical evidence; however, the findings are mixed.

Some studies found that profitability and leverage negatively affect dividend policy decisions [7, 9–12], while [4, 8, 13] found a positive relationship between the above argument. Others found non-linear associations [11, 14], while others found non-existing relationships [2]. Despite a significant amount of research in this field, the relationship between the firm's value and decisions on dividend policy is a crucial question, and according to [15], this connection is still unclear. Therefore, the objectives of this study are two. Firstly, it is aimed to obtain better and more precise knowledge concerning dividend policy. Secondly, it attempted to examine empirically whether the profitability and leverage level have any influence on determining the dividend policy decisions made by listed firms on the Amman Stock Exchange (ASX) over the period (2017–2021). The primary motivation of this investigation is to fill a gap in the literature by examining the factors determining dividend policy among Jordanian listed firms as an emerging economy. The findings of this study have significant consequences for theory and practice. By analyzing the factors that influence dividend policy in a developing country, such as Jordan, this study will add new insight to the body of knowledge on dividend policy. The reason for considering this country is that few studies have examined these associations in Jordan previously [9], even though Jordanian firms have a significant impact on the growing Middle Eastern economy. By using an explanatory research method that is compatible with the aim of the study, this research will answer whether profitability and leverage ratio have any effect on determining dividend policy. Therefore, analyzing some phenomena from a developing economy may provide crucial insights and improve the current literature in this field.

The rest of this study is divided into the following sections: Section 2 reviews the literature and the development of hypotheses. At the same time, the material and method are explained in Sect. 3. Results and discussion are presented in Sect. 4, and the conclusions and recommendations are presented in Sect. 5.

## 2 Literature Review

Theories relate to the dividend policy and explain the association between dividend decisions and firm value. One of the earliest theories in the field is the Irrelevance Theory, also referred to as the MM Theory, formulated by Modigliani and Miller in 1958 [1, 6, 7, 16, 17]. The MM hypothesis identifies the circumstances in which a firm's financial choices do not impact its value. In other words, firm value has no relation to capital structure and dividend policy. However, this assumption is based on a perfect market where there are no taxes, no transaction costs, no bankruptcy risk, and no information asymmetry [6, 16, 18]. After some years, Modigliani and Miller revised their previous work, turned the assumption of a perfect capital market, and examined the effect of capital structure on firm value based on tax assumption. They concluded that a firm's capital structure can be optimized under these conditions.

Gordon [19] is the leading proponent of this theory and believed that "*a corporation's share price is not independent of the dividend rate*" [7]. They maintained that since investors evaluated dividends more highly than investment returns and because the amount of dividends a firm pays out directly affects its market value, the dividend policy is crucial, and it needs more consideration. However, Litzenberger and Ramaswamy [20] argued that obtaining dividends in cash is not beneficial for investors. This may be because investors choose firms with fewer payments for tax-related reasons. Based on the tax preference hypothesis that Litzenberger and Ramaswamy developed, companies might raise the value of their equity through decreasing dividends [20]. From the empirical literature, the determination of dividend policy is influenced by some variables, such as firm size, profitability, leverage, and liquidity. In our study, the exogenous variables are both profitability and leverage [1, 11, 14].

## *2.1 Profitability and Dividend Policy*

One of the critical factors that influence dividend policy is profitability [10]. A group of financial measurements known as the profitability ratio assesses a company's capacity to generate profits from its expenses and other applicable costs incurred during a specific period [1, 21]. Theoretically, the phrase "dividend policy" alludes to the guidelines established by the firm when measuring how much profit will be given to shareholders. A company's dividend policy determines whether profits will be paid out as dividends to stockholders or remain as retained earnings to fund future investments [2]. When dividends are distributed, owners will receive returns in addition to their capital gains; however, if the dividends remain partially, they can be allocated toward future investments [1]. Therefore, firms who pay less dividends have more opportunity to invest in the future.

Moreover, the interest in dividend policy is still present among shareholders, creditors, managers, and scholars. This is because the corporate decision is significant due to having a relationship with other business decisions, including financing and investing, and it impacts the wealth of shareholders and the economy as a whole [14]. It is believed that profitability has a substantial impact on the proportion of the dividend payout ratio. This is evidenced by the pecking order theory, which claims that companies should prioritize financing choices to fulfill their capital demands [6, 18, 22]. The theory also revealed that companies prefer to raise cash from internally accessible assets that are risk-free instead of risky sources, including receiving debt and issuing stock. Firms should use operational earnings as an internal fund first; then, debt can be proposed, and if the debt is not sufficient, equity can then be issued [7]. This means that the theory expects a negative relationship between leverage and profitability. Companies with higher profitability produce enough earnings and have a greater capacity to hold retained earnings. Firms will, therefore, be likely to give lower levels of dividend rates in order to safeguard their profits for potential investments in the future [1, 2, 8, 12, 14].

Similarly, empirical research [7, 9, 10, 12] has found a negative connection between firm profitability and dividend policy. In this study, it is also expected that dividend policy will be low when the profitability is increased among Jordanian listed firms. Therefore, the first hypothesis is developed as follows:

**Hypothesis 1:** Profitability has a significant effect on dividend policy.

## *2.2 Leverage and Dividend Policy*

Leverage is an investing strategy that utilizes borrowed capital; more specifically, it increases the possibility of a return on investment using different financial instruments or borrowing money [16]. Leverage is also defined as the amount of debt used to pay or purchase firm assets [23]. [24] are argued that companies' leverage is a significant aspect during the decision on dividend policy because when the leverage is high, the dividend will be low. However, [25] emphasizes the effect of negative covenants, which restrict companies' ability to pay dividends. They also documented that dividend is regularly paid in the best interests of the shareholders rather than the creditors. Consequently, management is planning to engage the credit markets regularly. It can reduce dividends to improve creditors' trust and represent a low level of agency cost related to the debt within the company [26, 27]. The current study also expected that leverage negatively affects dividend policy among Jordanian listed firms.

Numerous empirical research found that dividend policy is inversely impacted by leverage [1, 11, 14, 28]. [29] have also argued that high-debt companies tend to reduce dividends, either on their initiative or in response to pressure from creditors, in order to have enough cash on hand to pay their commitments. Otherwise, companies are becoming riskier as they increase their expenses for financing from outside and increase their dependency on retained earnings due to using a higher level of debt [14]. The above argument is approved by agency theory, which claims that managers (agents) seek to grow the company in order to maximize their wealth, even if this may not be in the shareholders' (principals) best interests [1].

Finally, having higher ratios of leverage includes larger payments for outside financing in the form of interest that is given to the lenders [18]. In this regard, [14] displayed that paying less dividend increases the amount of capital on the statement of financial position, enhances ratios of leverage such as the equity or debt ratio, and ultimately improves credit viability. Hence, the reorganization of debts becomes more accessible, and the cost of borrowing is reduced when these ratios are enhanced. Since all the above argument presented that leverage hurts dividend policy, the second hypothesis is developed as follow:

**Hypothesis 2:** Leverage has a significant effect on dividend policy.

# 3 Methodology

## *3.1 Sample and Data*

The population used for this study comprises companies listed on the Amman Stock Exchange (ASX). The research examines annual data collected from the financial statements for five years, from 2017 to 2021. Concerning data from a balanced panel, the total sample included 250 years of observation from 50 companies. Although our initial sample was larger compared to what we examined, some companies were removed due to matching incompatible variable descriptions and the accessibility of all variables throughout the listed firms.

## *3.2 Construction of Variables*

### 3.2.1 Dividend Policy

The dependent variable in this study is dividend policy, and profitability and leverage have a significant impact on it. Prior investigations used several proxies for dividend policy to investigate the relationship between profitability, leverage, and dividend policy. These indicators involve financial ratios (accounting-based ratios), such as the dividend payout ratio (DPR), earnings per share (EPS), and dividend yield (DY) [1, 4, 7, 9, 24, 28, 30]. The current study uses the dividend payout ratio (DPR) to measure dividend policy.

### 3.2.2 Profitability

Profitability can be defined as "*the level of profit about the volume of activities of the organization*" [31]. Since this paper examines the association between profitability, leverage, and dividend policy, the study uses profitability as an exogenous variable and is predicted to affect dividend policy negatively. From the previous literature, profitability is measured by different indicators, such as return on assets (ROA), return on equity (ROE), and Tobin's Q (TQ) [1, 6, 7, 11, 16, 32–36]. Our study uses return on assets (ROA) and return on equity (ROE) to measure profitability.

### 3.2.3 Leverage

Leverage is a second independent variable in this study, and it is also expected to have an adverse correlation with dividend policy. Leverage is labeled by a variety of proxies, such as debt-to-assets ratio (DTA), debt-to-equity ratio (DER), equity multiplier (EM), short-term debt ratio (STDA), long-term debt ratio (LTDA) and

**Table 1** Variable description

| Variable | Type | Measure | Definition |
|---|---|---|---|
| DPR | Dependent | Dividend policy | Dividend per share/earnings per share |
| ROA | Independent | Profitability | EBIT/Total assets |
| ROE | Independent | Profitability | EBIT/Total equity |
| DER | Independent | Leverage | Total debt /total equity |
| STDA | Independent | Leverage | Short-term debt/total assets |
| TA | Control | Firm Size | Natural logarithm of total assets |

debt-to-market-capitalization ratio (DMCR) [6, 11, 14, 16, 37–40]. In this study, we utilize both debt-to-equity ratio (DER) and short-term debt ratio (STDA) to measure firm leverage. We use both indicators to accurately examine firm leverage, which can then be utilized to decide dividend policy.

#### 3.2.4 Control Variable

To achieve the study objectives and in order to accurately depict the relationship between profitability, leverage, and dividend policy, we employ a control variable in the regression model that aims to protect the characteristics of the firms. Previous studies used a variety of variables as a control, such as firm size, growth, firm age [41–44]. Our study employs firm size as a control variable. Table 1 shows the summary of the variables that were selected in this research.

### *3.3 Empirical Model*

The present investigation uses a quantitative approach for secondary data published by listed firms on the Amman Stock Exchange (ASX). Panel regression for multiple variables examines the connection between profitability, leverage, and dividend policy. Hence, as proposed by [38, 45], we recommend a linear association between the above argument based on the following econometric equation:

$$Dividend\ policy_{it} = \beta_0 + \beta_1 Profitability_{it} + \beta_2 Leverage_{it} + \beta_3 Control_{it} + E_{it} \tag{1}$$

where, Dividend policy is a dependent variable and indicated by dividend payout ratio (DPR) from *i* at *t* time; Profitability is independent variable and proxied by return on assets (ROA) and return on equity (ROE) from *i* at *t* time; Leverage is a second independent variable and indicated by debt to equity ratio (ER) and short-term debt ratio (STDA) from i at t time; Control represents a control variable from *i* at $t$ time; $E_{it}$ is a standard error; $\beta_0$ is a constant; $\beta_1$ to $\beta_4$ are vectors of independent variables.

# 4 Results and Discussion

## 4.1 Descriptive Results

Table 2 summarizes the descriptive analysis for variables indicated by profitability, leverage, and dividend policy. The mean value of DPR is 0.846, with a standard deviation of 0.273. The minimum and maximum value of DPR is -1.680 and 2.264, respectively. ROA and ROE as explanatory variables for measuring profitability have arithmetic mean values of (M = 0.003, SD = 0.069, Min = −0.361, and Max = 0.134) and (M = 0.279, SD = 4.072, Min = −64.26, and Max = 0.523) respectively. DER and STDA as proxies of leverage have a mean value of (M = 3.625, SD = 19.09, Min = 0.013, and Max = 299.7) and (M = 0.054, SD = 0.075, Min = 0.000, and Max = 0.479) respectively. TA, as a control variable, has a higher mean value of 7.795 with a deviation of 0.874. The minimum and highest value of TA is 6.577 and 10.44, respectively.

Further, a study by [46] argued that the standard skewness of ±1.9 and standard kurtosis of ±3 are required for the data to be considered normal. In our study, as demonstrated in Table 2, there is no normal distribution in the sample data sets because of not meeting the specified range of some variables. However, Non-normal data distribution is not anticipated to be a problem if a significant sample size is considered [47, 48]. Hence, our study is accessible from the issues of non-normal distribution. DER, STDA, and TA are positively skewed, while DPR, ROA, and ROE are negatively skewed.

Additionally, according to [49], the distribution is referred to as "platykurtic" if the kurtosis is less than 3, "mesokurtic" if it is equal to 3 and "leptokurtic if it is more than 3. Therefore, as shown in Table 2, all study variables are distributed based on

**Table 2** Descriptive statistics of research variables

| | DPR | ROA | ROE | DER | STDA | TA |
|---|---|---|---|---|---|---|
| Mean | 0.846 | 0.003 | 0.279 | 3.625 | 0.054 | 7.795 |
| Std. Dev. | 0.273 | 0.069 | 4.072 | 19.09 | 0.075 | 0.874 |
| Minimum | −1.680 | −0.361 | −64.26 | 0.013 | 0.000 | 6.577 |
| Maximum | 2.264 | 0.134 | 0.523 | 299.7 | 0.479 | 10.44 |
| Skewness | −2.272 | −2.163 | −15.60 | 15.01 | 2.235 | 1.309 |
| Kurtosis | 35.84 | 10.21 | 245.7 | 233.2 | 9.838 | 3.728 |
| Jarque–Bera | 11,452.8 | 56,172.5 | 695.3 | 737.4 | 62,391.4 | 76.9 |
| Probability | 0.000 | 0.000 | 0.000 | 0.000 | 0.000 | 0.000 |

**Table 3** Correlation matrix

| | DPR | ROA | ROE | DER | SDTA | TA |
|---|---|---|---|---|---|---|
| DPR | 1 | | | | | |
| ROA | −0.216*** | 1 | | | | |
| ROE | −0.047* | 0.240** | 1 | | | |
| DER | −0.005* | −0.196*** | −0.583** | 1 | | |
| SDTA | 0.132** | −0.441*** | −0.233*** | 0.233*** | 1 | |
| TA | −0.331*** | 0.239** | 0.103 | −0.005 | −0.158** | 1 |

Notes: ***, ** and * demonstrate significancy level at 1%, 5% and 10% level (two-tailed)

"leptokurtic." By using the "Jarque–Bera" normalcy test and the justifications above, we can safely accept the alternative and eliminate the null hypothesis.

## 4.2 *Correlation Analysis*

Table 3 displays the results of the correlation matrix between profitability, leverage, and dividend policy. The results demonstrate that ROA, ROE as profitability indicators, DER as a proxy of leverage, and TA as a control variable are negatively affected by DPR, and these results are significant at 1% and 10% levels. On the other hand, SDTA has a positive association with DPR at a 5% level.

Moreover, the sample panel data used in this study covers 50 listed firms on the Amman Stock Exchange (ASX) over five years (2017–2021). As a result, multicollinearity issues should be considered and tested. In order to figure out whether multiple variables are collinear, the exogenous (independent) variables have been assessed for the degree of correlation. A study by [50] demonstrates that multicollinearity problems may appear if the coefficient of relationship among exogenous variables is greater than 70%. In this study, as demonstrated in Table 3, the independent variables do not significantly relate to each other (the degree of the relationship is less than 70%). In light of this, multicollinearity is not a problem in our investigation.

## 4.3 *Analysis of Panel Regression*

Pooled OLS, Fixed-Effect and Random-Effect methodology are used to investigate the strength and direction of the expected association between the indicators of profitability, leverage, and dividend policy. Based on the results of the Hausman test that displayed in Table 4, it is not possible to reject the null hypothesis which suggests that the Random-Effect method (REM) is appropriate. In other words, we can analyze the findings and run regression model with REM.

**Table 4** Hausman test

| Test summary | $X^2$ Stat. | $X^2$ d.f. | *P*-value |
|---|---|---|---|
| Cross-section random | 1.115 | 5 | 0.952 |

**Table 5** Residual cross-section dependence test

| Test | Statistic | d.f. | Prob. |
|---|---|---|---|
| Breusch-Pagan LM | 1790.725 | 1225 | 0.0000 |
| Pesaran scaled LM | 11.42938 | | 0.0000 |
| Pesaran CD | 1.257296 | | 0.0208 |

### 4.4 Cross-Section Dependence Test

Table 5 displays the results of cross-section dependence test through Breusch-Pagan LM, Pesaran scaled LM and Pesaran scaled LM. According to [1], if the probability value is greater than 5%, the null hypothesis of cross-section dependence cannot be rejected. In our study, since the *p*-value for all three tests are lower than 0.05, we can reject the null hypothesis and are able to determine that our panel data display cross-sectional dependency.

### 4.5 Discussion

The present research conducted a number of diagnostic analyses, including the Hausman test and Cross-Section Dependence test, to evaluate the reliability of observations. These tests were exclusively used to confirm the accuracy of the regression models and determine whether they were free of econometric problems. Table 6 demonstrates the panel regression results for assessing the association between profitability, leverage, and dividend policy. The F-statistic illustrates that the model has a satisfactory rate for the independent variables, and the adjusted has a value of 0.093 and measures the extent to which the explanatory factors (ROA, ROE, DER, and STDA) influence the variance of the dependent variable (DPR). The Durbin-Watson statistical score is also in the range between Lower Durbin (dL) 1.5 and Upper Durbin (dU) 2.5, and this indicates that there is no autocorrelation issue with the residuals.

The findings in Table 6 reveal that ROA is related to DPR negatively with a coefficient value of -0.436, and the result is statistically significant at a 10% level. Exactly, this means that a 1% decrease in ROA brings about an increase in the dividend payout ratio (DPR) by 0.436 percent per share. ROE, as a second indicator of profitability, also has a negative and significant effect on DPR with a coefficient value of -0.056 and 6% level. If other factors remain constant, a 1% decline in ROA causes an increase of DPR per share by 0.056 percent with a low standard error of 0.030. Therefore, the first hypothesis that profitability has a significant effect on dividend policy is accepted and supported by the pecking order theory, which claims

**Table 6** Results of random effect model (REM)- DPR

| Variables | Coef. | Std. Err. | t-Stat. | Prob. |
|---|---|---|---|---|
| C | 1.399 | 0.204 | 6.838 | 0.000 |
| ROA | −0.436 | 0.286 | −1.522 | 0.109 |
| ROE | −0.056 | 0.030 | −1.880 | 0.061 |
| DTE | −0.012 | 0.006 | −1.931 | 0.054 |
| STDA | 0.140 | 0.267 | 0.525 | 0.601 |
| TA | −0.068 | 0.026 | −2.554 | 0.011 |
| *R-Square* | 0.112 | *Mean dependent var* | | 0.653 |
| *Adj. R-Square* | 0.093 | *S.D. dependent var* | | 0.252 |
| *F-statistic* | 6.118 | *Sum squared resid* | | 14.09 |
| *Prob.* | 0.000 | *Durbin-Watson stat* | | 2.180 |

that firms should seek to raise capital from internally accessible or risk-free assets as a first attempt. Hence, highly profitable companies usually pay less dividends because they use profit to fund their development. These results are also consistent with the findings of [1, 7, 9, 10, 12], who found that ROA and ROE as a profitability measurement are inversely related to the dividend payout ratio (DPR). In other words, firms that maintain earnings as a capital source are less likely to distribute dividends.

Figures 1 shows the graphical value of residual, fitted and actual after regressing explanatory variables. The trend line is evident in all the figures, and the close correspondence between the actual and fitted lines raises homoscedasticity by reducing residuals.

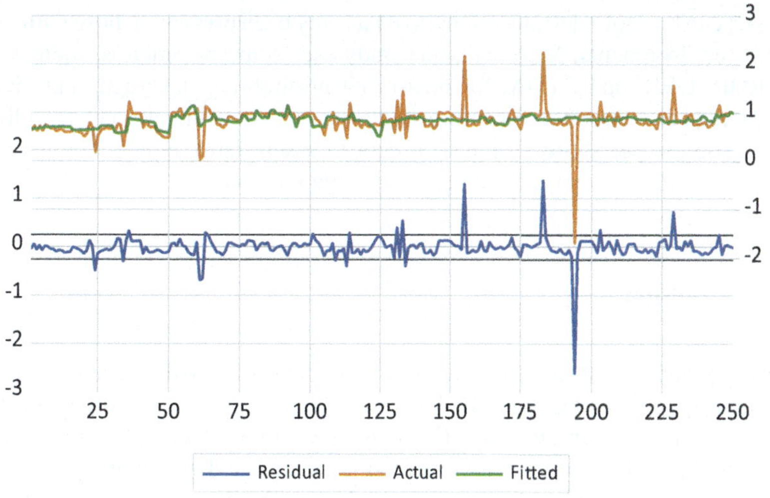


**Fig. 1** DPR after regressing independent variables

Next, DTE has a detrimental influence on DPR that is statistically significant at 0.012 percent and 5%. In particular, a 1% rise in DTE as a measurement of leverage results in a 0.012 percent reduction in DPR per share. Last but not least, SDTA possesses a positive impact on DPR. However, the result is statistically insignificant, even at a 10% level. As a result, the second hypothesis that leverage has a significant impact on dividend policy is accepted and supported by agency theory, which states that managers are concerned about funding sources for potential future investment possibilities. Therefore, they choose to reduce the payment of dividends because leverage includes a company's transaction costs and risks, and a high proportion of leverage results in a large fixed payment for an outside source of funding in the form of interest granted to the creditors. These findings also align with the arguments of [1, 11, 14, 28].

These findings enrich the current literature by examining the importance of financial data that investors have yet to explore. Investors and managers may also utilize this new understanding to guide their investment choices by assessing the significance of the impact of profitability and leverage on dividend policy decisions. Considering the policy implications of the suggested connections in this investigation is crucial for companies deciding on their dividend strategy. Given that our research shows that the dividend policy is influenced by profitability and leverage, it should interest investors, shareholders, and managers. Moreover, the results of this investigation provide new insights for decision-makers interested in issues related to agency conflicts. Finally, the findings also provide evidence about the usefulness of applying several complementary mechanisms, such as leverage, to reduce agency costs.

However, like all other studies, this investigation has some limitations. First, it is the level of generalizability. The current study includes only one developing country; we cannot extend our results to other countries. Therefore, considering a sizable number of emerging economies in future studies may be significant to determine if the impact can be applied to all countries or has only been present in those with similar economic environments. Moreover, this study uses some parameters, such as DPR, ROA, ROE, DER, and STDA, for measuring profitability, leverage, and dividend policy. Hence, as a direction for future study, we suggest using alternative indicators such as earnings per share, Tobin's Q, debt-to-assets ratio, equity multiplier, and dividend yield to see whether comparable results will exist.

## 5 Conclusions

The primary purpose of this study is to provide empirical evidence about the effect of profitability and leverage on dividend policy decisions in a sample of Jordanian firms listed on the Amman Stock Exchange (ASX) between 2017 and 2021. To analyze the data, the random-effect method is used. The dependent variable in this study is the dividend policy mean, sure by the dividend payout ratio. Profitability is the first independent variable and is proxied by return on assets and return on equity. *Leverage* is a second independent variable indicated by debt-to-equity ratio (DTE) and short-term debt ratio.

The findings of the data analysis demonstrate that profitability and leverage both significantly influence dividend policy decisions and have an adverse effect. Therefore, these findings confirm the study hypothesis and, consistent with the pecking order theory, argue that firms pay lower dividends when they achieve high profits because they use earnings to fund their future operations and expansion. These results are also evidenced by agency theory asserting that companies that have a prominent level of debt often pay fewer dividends. This is because companies are required to pay interest and installments depending on the condition of the debt.

## References

1. Abdullah, H.A.: Profitability and leverage as determinants of dividend policy: Evidence of Turkish financial firms. Eurasian J. Manag. Soc. Sci. **2**, 15–30 (2021). https://doi.org/10.23918/ejmss.v2i3p15
2. Saputri, D.R., Bahri, S.: The effect of leverage, profitability, and dividend policy on firm value. Int. J. Educ. Res. Soc. Sci. **2**, 1316–1324 (2021). https://doi.org/10.51601/ijersc.v2i6.223
3. Ahmed, A.M.: The relationship between firm size and profitability "evidence from the commercial banks in Iraq." Sci. J. Cihan Univ.—Sulaimaniya. **6**, 145–156 (2022). https://doi.org/10.25098/6.1.34
4. Nurchaqiqi, R., Suryarini, T.: The effect of leverage and liquidity on cash dividend policy with profitability as moderator moderating. Account. Anal. J. **7**, 10–16 (2018). https://doi.org/10.15294/aaj.v5i3.18631
5. Fuad, F., Jatmiko, A.: Earnings management and post-mergers and acquisitions' performance: Evidence from an emerging market. Polish J. Manag. Stud. **26**, 130–143 (2022). https://doi.org/10.17512/pjms.2022.26.2.08
6. Ahmed, A.M., Nugraha, D.P., Hágen, I.: The relationship between capital structure and firm performance: The moderating role of agency cost. Risks. **11**, 1–17 (2023). https://doi.org/10.3390/risks11060102
7. Kaźmierska-Jóźwiak, B.: Determinants of dividend policy: Evidence from Polish listed companies. Procedia Econ. Financ. **23**, 473–477 (2015). https://doi.org/10.1016/s2212-5671(15)00490-6
8. Hadian, N.: The influence of profitability and leverage on dividend policy in the banking sector. Int. J. Innov. Creat. Chang. **6**, 118–129 (2019)
9. Al-Malkawi, H.A.N.: Determinants of corporate dividend policy in Jordan: An application of the tobit model. J. Econ. Adm. Sci. **23**, 44–70 (2007). https://doi.org/10.1108/10264116200700007
10. Kuzucu, N.: A survey of managerial perspective on corporate dividend policy: Evidence from Turkish listed firms. Curr. Approaches Soc. Sci. **4**, 593–609 (2015). https://doi.org/10.3726/978-3-653-05965-6
11. Manneh, M.A., Naser, K.: Determinants of corporate dividends policy: Evidence from an emerging economy. Int. J. Econ. Financ. **7**, 229–239 (2015). https://doi.org/10.5539/ijef.v7n7p229
12. Parsian, H., Koloukhi, A.S.: A study on the effect of free cash flow and profitability current ratio on dividend payout ratio: Evidence from Tehran Stock Exchange. Manag. Sci. Lett. **4**, 63–70 (2014). https://doi.org/10.5267/j.msl.2013.11.033
13. Kusmuriyanto, R.F.: The effect of profitability, IOS and leverage on cash dividend policy with moderated liquidity. Account. Anal. J. **4**, 1–8 (2015). https://doi.org/10.15294/aaj.v4i2.7845

14. Jabbouri, I.: Determinants of corporate dividend policy in emerging markets: Evidence from MENA stock markets. Res. Int. Bus. Financ. **37**, 283–298 (2016). https://doi.org/10.1016/j.ribaf.2016.01.018
15. Franc-Dąbrowska, J., Mądra-Sawicka, M., Ulrichs, M.: Determinants of dividend payout decisions—The case of publicly quoted food industry enterprises operating in emerging markets. Econ. Res. Istraz. **33**, 1108–1129 (2020). https://doi.org/10.1080/1331677X.2019.1631201
16. Ahmed, A.M., Sharif, N.A., Ali, M.N., Hágen, I.: Effect of Firm Size on the Association between Capital Structure and Profitability. Sustain. **15**, 1–17 (2023). https://doi.org/10.3390/su151411196
17. Dang, H.N., Vu, V.T.T., Ngo, X.T., Hoang, H.T.V.: Impact of dividend policy on corporate value: Experiment in Vietnam. Int. J. Financ. Econ. **26**, 5815–5825 (2021). https://doi.org/10.1002/ijfe.2095
18. Khaki, A.R., Akin, A.: Factors affecting the capital structure: New evidence from GCC countries. J. Int. Stud. **13**, 9–27 (2020). https://doi.org/10.14254/2071-8330.2020/13-1/1
19. Gordon, M.J.: Optimal investment and financing policy. J. Finance. **18**, 264–272 (1963). https://doi.org/10.2307/2977907
20. Litzenberger, R.H., Ramaswamy, K.: The effects of dividends on common stock prices tax effects or information effects? J. Finance. **37**, 429–443 (1981). https://doi.org/10.2307/2327346
21. Ahmed, A.M., Ali, M.N., Hágen, I.: Corporate governance and its relationship with the working capital management in Europe. Shirkah: J. Econ. Bus. **8**, 202–217 (2023). https://doi.org/10.22515/shirkah.v8i2.609
22. Mursalim, Mallisa, M., Kusuma, H.: Capital structure determinants and firms' performance: Empirical EVIDENCE from Thailand, Indonesia and Malaysia. Polish J. Manag. Stud. **16**, 154–164 (2017). https://doi.org/10.17512/pjms.2017.16.1.13
23. Innocent, E.C., Ikechukwu, A.C., Nnagbogu, E.K.: The effect of financial leverage on financial performance: Evidence of quoted pharmaceutical companies in Nigeria. IOSR J. Econ. Financ. **5**, 17–25 (2014). https://doi.org/10.9790/5933-0531725
24. Zelalem, D.: Determinants of dividend payout policy of commercial banks: Evidence from selected commercial banks in Ethiopia. Int. J. Financ. Bank. Res. 7, 29 (2021). https://doi.org/10.11648/j.ijfbr.20210702.11
25. Mather, P., Peirson, G.: Financial covenants in the markets for public and private debt. Account. Financ. **46**, 285–307 (2006). https://doi.org/10.1111/j.1467-629X.2006.00168.x
26. Nini, G., Smith, D.C., Sufi, A.: Creditor control rights and firm investment policy. J. Financ. Econ. **92**, 400–420 (2009). https://doi.org/10.1016/j.jfineco.2008.04.008
27. Brockman, P., Unlu, E.: Dividend policy, creditor rights, and the agency costs of debt. J. Financ. Econ. **92**, 276–299 (2009). https://doi.org/10.1016/j.jfineco.2008.03.007
28. Al-Twaijry, A.A.: Dividend policy and payout ratio: Evidence from the Kuala Lumpur stock exchange. J. Risk Financ. **8**, 349–363 (2007). https://doi.org/10.1108/15265940710777306
29. Gugler, K., Yurtoglu, B.B.: Corporate governance and dividend pay-out policy in Germany. Eur. Econ. Rev. **47**, 731–758 (2003). https://doi.org/10.1016/S0014-2921(02)00291-X
30. Czerwonka, L.: Takeovers as a way of investing versus dividend payments on the Warsaw stock exchange. J. Int. Stud. **5**, 70–76 (2012). https://doi.org/10.14254/2071-8330.2012/5-1/9
31. Ilaboya, O.J., Ohiokha, I.F.: Firm age, size and profitability dynamics: A test of learning by doing and structural inertia hypotheses. Bus. Manag. Res. **5**, (2016). https://doi.org/10.5430/bmr.v5n1p29
32. Ahmed, A.M., Hágen, I.: Corporate Governance and its relationship with financial performance in Iraq. Acta Carolus Robertus. **13**, 76–89 (2023). https://doi.org/10.33032/acr.4099
33. Brunzell, T., Liljeblom, E., Löflund, A., Vaihekoski, M.: Dividend policy in Nordic listed firms. Glob. Financ. J. **25**, 124–135 (2014). https://doi.org/10.1016/j.gfj.2014.06.004
34. Kyere, M., Ausloos, M.: Corporate governance and firms financial performance in the United Kingdom. Int. J. Financ. Econ. **26**, 1871–1885 (2021). https://doi.org/10.1002/ijfe.1883
35. Puziak, M.: The persistence of abnormal returns: Analysis of polish manufacturing industry. Econ. Sociol. **10**, 48–60 (2017). https://doi.org/10.14254/2071-789X.2017/10-1/4

36. Shkodra, J.: Financial performance of microfinance institutions in Kosovo. J. Int. Stud. **12**, 31–37 (2019). https://doi.org/10.14254/2071-8330.2019/12-3/3
37. Ahmed, A.M., Ali, M.N., Hágen, I.: Corporate governance and capital structure: Evidence from Europe. Int. J. Prof. Bus. Rev. **8**, 1–22 (2023). https://doi.org/10.26668/businessreview/2023.v8i7.1663
38. Ngatno, Apriatni, E.P., Youlianto, A.: Moderating effects of corporate governance mechanism on the relation between capital structure and firm performance. Cogent Bus. Manag. **8** (2021). https://doi.org/10.1080/23311975.2020.1866822
39. Saidat, Z., Bani-Khalid, T.O., Al-Haddad, L., Marashdeh, Z.: Does family ceo enhance corporate performance? The case of Jordan. Econ. Sociol. **13**, 43–52 (2020). https://doi.org/10.14254/2071-789X.2020/13-2/3
40. Smriti, N., Das, N.: Impact of intellectual capital on business performance: Evidence from Indian pharmaceutical sector. Polish J. Manag. Stud. **15**, 232–243 (2017). https://doi.org/10.17512/pjms.2017.15.1.22
41. Aktan, B., Turen, S., Tvaronavičienė, M., Celik, S., Alsadeh, H.A.: Corporate governance and performance of the financial firms in Bahrain. Polish J. Manag. Stud. **17**, 39–58 (2018). https://doi.org/10.17512/pjms.2018.17.1.04
42. Castro, N.R., Lopes, I.T.: The capital structure determinants of the portuguese banking sector: A regional dynamics. J. Int. Stud. **14**, 124–137 (2021). https://doi.org/10.14254/2071-8330.2021/14-3/8
43. Dewasiri, N.J., Yatiwelle Koralalage, W.B., Abdul Azeez, A., Jayarathne, P.G.S.A., Kuruppuarachchi, D., Weerasinghe, V.A.: Determinants of dividend policy: Evidence from an emerging and developing market. Manag. Financ. **45**, 413–429 (2019). https://doi.org/10.1108/MF-09-2017-0331
44. Mauris, F.I., Rizal, N.A.: The effect of collaterallizable assets, growth in net assets, liquidity, leverage and profitability on dividend policy (Case studies on non-financial services sector companies listed on the Indonesia Stock Exchange for the 2016–2019 period). Budapest Int. Res. Critics Inst. Humanit. Soc. Sci. **4**, 937–950 (2021). https://doi.org/10.33258/birci.v4i1.1695
45. Le, T.P.V., Phan, T.B.N.: Capital structure and firm performance: Empirical evidence from a small transition country. Res. Int. Bus. Financ. **42**, 710–726 (2017). https://doi.org/10.1016/j.ribaf.2017.07.012
46. Brooks, C.: Introductory econometrics for finance, 3rd edn. Cambridge University Press, Cambridge (2014)
47. Ahmad, M., Bashir, R., Waqas, H.: Working capital management and firm performance: Are their effects same in covid 19 compared to financial crisis 2008? Cogent Econ. Financ. **10**, 1–18 (2022). https://doi.org/10.1080/23322039.2022.2101224
48. Lee, H., Meng, M., Lee, J.: How do nonlinear unit root tests perform with non normal errors? Commun. Stat. Simul. Comput. **40**, 1182–1191 (2011). https://doi.org/10.1080/03610918.2011.566972
49. Mohammed, M.B., Adam, M., Ali, N., Zulkafli, H.S.: Improved frequency table's measures of skewness and kurtosis with application to weather data. Commun. Stat.—Theory Methods. **51**, 581–598 (2022). https://doi.org/10.1080/03610926.2020.1752386
50. Wooldridge, J.M.: Introductory econometrics: A modern approach. 6th edn. Cengage Learning (2015).

# Southeast Asian Youth's Long-Term Desire to Use Mobile Payments

**Yasri Yasri, Astra Prima Budiarti, Rizki Sri Lasmini, Gerald Goh Guan Gan, Theeraphab Phetmalaikul, Lita Bacalla, and Naila Beltran**

**Abstract** The study investigates the critical role of mobile payments in increasing continuance intention. The study aimed to analyze the impact of perceived trust and perceived satisfaction towards the use of mobile payment; analyze the impact of perceived trust, perceived satisfaction, and use of mobile payment on the intention to continue using the service; and analyze the function of the use of mobile payment as a mediator of the impact of perceived trust and perceived satisfaction on the intention to continue using the service. The survey research design was employed where all users of various mobile payment systems in ASEAN nations comprise the study's population. Ages 18 to 30 make up most of the middle-class population because the millennial and z generations are the most significant users of mobile transactions. The countries chosen were chosen at random. In order to choose them, a sample was made using the sampling regions of Indonesia, Malaysia, Thailand, and the Philippines. There are 368 respondents in the entire sample. A questionnaire was used to gather the information. PLS3.0 is a data analysis method. The findings indicate that perceived satisfaction and perceived trust have a positive and significant impact on using mobile payment, that the use of mobile payment has a positive and significant impact on continuance intention, and that the use of mobile payment mediates the impact of perceived satisfaction and perceived trust on continuance intention.

Y. Yasri (✉) · A. P. Budiarti · R. S. Lasmini
Faculty of Economics and Business, Universitas Negeri Padang, Padang, Indonesia
e-mail: yasri33@fe.unp.ac.id

G. G. G. Gan
Faculty of Business, Multimedia University, Cyberjaya, Malaysia

T. Phetmalaikul
Faculty of Education, Srinakharinwirot University, Bangkok, Thailand

L. Bacalla
Social Sciences, Cebu Normal University, Cebu, Philippines

N. Beltran
Director of the Regional Filipino Language, Cebu Normal University, Cebu, Philippines

 
S. Kot et al. (eds.), *Corporate Practices: Policies, Methodologies, and Insights in Organizational Management*, Springer Proceedings in Business and Economics,
https://doi.org/10.1007/978-981-97-0996-0_30

**Keywords** Perceived trust · Perceived satisfaction · Use mobile payment · Continuance intention

## 1 Introduction

Mobile payment (m-payment) refers to using mobile technologies to complete payment on consumer financial transactions such as paying for goods and services, drawing, and transferring funds to other people or organizations [1]. This payment method first gained popularity in the U.S. and started to be practiced worldwide. The coronavirus pandemic, which forced people to distance themselves from others to avoid direct contact to prevent the spread of the invisible virus, resulting in unnoticeable symptoms, became a catalyst for the utilization of many forms of technology, including mobile payment [2, 3]. Companies and organizations made it mandatory that any transactions be completed through mobile payment, under the concern that the virus mainly spread by contact (e.g., from notes handed at payment) [4, 5]. The governments of developing countries, including Indonesia, have been encouraging the use of mobile payment within the community following the practice in other nations [6]. As a result, there is a shift in payment methods used in developing countries, which is increasingly popular among the younger generation (about 70%) who have grown accustomed to mobile transactions [7].

This study aims to evaluate the role of mobile payment mediation effect on perceived trust and perceived satisfaction on continuance intention to use mobile payment in Indonesia. This study contributes to discovering primary antecedents that determine continuance intention for using mobile payment. The continuation of mobile payment use is highly important following the end of the COVID-19 pandemic, as businesses thriving during the pandemic must have prepared a system that enables wider use of mobile payment. The novelty of this study lies in the analysis of mobile payment's role in mediating the effect of perceived trust and satisfaction on continuance intention, which has yet to be researched in previous studies.

This study departs from consumer behavior theory on perceived trust and satisfaction as a form of consumer behavior in choosing goods and services [8]. Trust and satisfaction are social and psychological concepts affecting consumer behavior [9]. Trust is an important factor resulting from human interaction with previous experiences, which highly affects one's decision on continuance in the future [10]. Meanwhile, consumer satisfaction describes consumer perception of their satisfaction after consuming products or services [11].

# 2 Theoretical Framework

## *2.1 Perceived Satisfaction Toward Continuance Intention*

Users who had had positive experiences and witnessed the effective operational system of the m-payment perceived that the application offers them comfort for the payment services. This results in stronger satisfaction once the users embrace the service or system [12]. Customers who feel content are usually bound to continue using the service for a longer term and establish stronger relationships with it [13]. Perceived satisfaction is the best predictor for boosting retention intentions for any system and for inspiring users to comprehend the unique performance of the service or system they use; several earlier studies support this finding [13–15].

## *2.2 Perceived Satisfaction Towards Use of Mobile Payment*

According to Kujala et al. [16] and Natarajan et al. [17], users' satisfaction in completing financial transactions using mobile payment could be perceived as a psychological response to the purchase and payment procedure. This means that there is a potential to summarize user's affective reactions to encounters with mobile payment services [18]. In addition, perceived satisfaction could also be a sign of m-payment intention, revealing user patterns [13].

Users with high levels of satisfaction will reportedly have greater usage intentions, according to prior studies [18]. Users will, therefore, be more likely to utilize the payment system if the performance of the m-payment system matches their expectations [16].

## *2.3 Perceived Trust Towards Use of Mobile Payment*

In the m-payment concept, trust is a psychological state that encourages users to tolerate application vulnerabilities and is based on positive assumptions about the intentions and behavior of others [17]. On the other hand, from a behavioral perspective, perceived trust is defined as the propensity of one party to be exposed to the actions of another party based on the expectation that the other party will carry out an action that is extremely important to the person who believes it, regardless of the ability to monitor or control the other [18], namely the desire to follow specific behavioral patterns. Consequently, this will determine the successful adoption of the m-payment system [17, 19, 20]. According to Cabanillas et al. [20], trust is an important predictor of intention to use mobile payments. The total user perception is impacted by trust. Therefore, it is essential to consider the motivation behind adopting the m-payment system.

## 2.4 Use of Mobile Payment Towards Continuance Intention

When users feel reliant on the system or service, believe using it requires no effort, and start to see performance benefits, they start using m-payment services more frequently [21]. The use of m-payment services begins to become automated as consumers use them regularly and experience the system's or service's individual performance, which leads to a rise in satisfaction [22].

## 2.5 Perceived Trust Towards Continuance Intention

Perceived trust may influence continuance intention, according to a number of earlier studies [23]. Passwords, digital certificates, phishing prevention, and other security measures are examples of Security Technology Protection (STP), a type of security measure used by mobile payment service providers to safeguard user security and privacy [23]. Previous studies [24] found that Security Technology Protection (STP) is an antecedent of perceived trust.

## 2.6 The Mediation Effect of Mobile Payment

The effect of perceived satisfaction on continuance intention, mediated by the use of mobile payment, has been studied by scholars in the field of information systems and consumer behavior. Several studies have examined this relationship and provided insights into the mediation effect. According to Liu, Li, and Hu [25], perceived enjoyment positively affected both perceived satisfaction and continuance intention. Furthermore, the effect of perceived satisfaction on continuance intention was partially mediated by the use of mobile payment. Perceived satisfaction had a direct positive effect on continuance intention, and this effect was partially mediated by the usage behavior of mobile payment. Higher levels of perceived satisfaction increased the frequency of usage, leading to a higher intention to continue using the service [26]. Perceived satisfaction positively influenced continuance intention, and this effect was mediated by the use of mobile payment. Higher levels of perceived satisfaction increased usage, which in turn strengthened the intention to continue using mobile payment [27].

These studies highlight the important role of perceived trust in shaping users' continuance intention in mobile payment. Perceived trust is a significant determinant that fosters users' confidence and willingness to continue using the service. The mediation effect of usage behavior suggests that the actual use of mobile payment services is a mechanism through which perceived trust influences continuance intention. Perceived trust had a direct positive effect on continuance intention, and this relationship was partially mediated by usage behavior. Perceived trust influenced

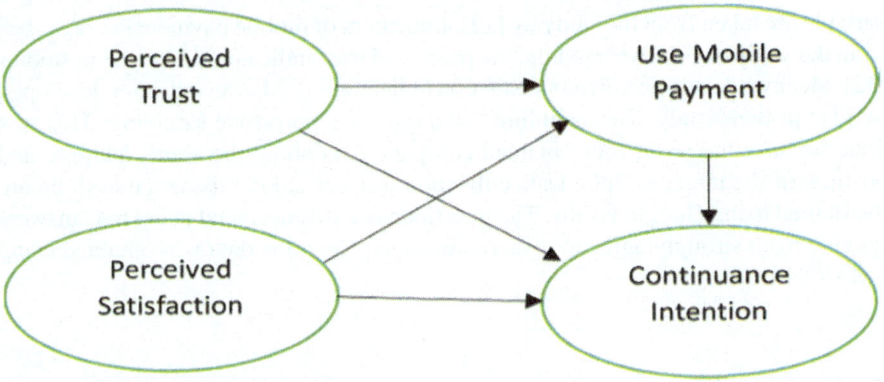


**Fig. 1** Research conceptual framework

users' mobile payment usage, influencing their intention to continue using the service [28].

Wang and Li [29] conducted research that examined the relationship between perceived trust, perceived usefulness, and continuance intention in the context of mobile payment. The results indicated that perceived trust had a significant positive effect on continuance intention, and the actual usage behavior mediated this effect. Higher levels of perceived trust increased usage, strengthening the intention to continue using mobile payment services.

Based on the literature discussed in this section, the researcher developed a conceptual framework for this study (Fig. 1).

## 3 Research Methodology

This study was a survey research design involving a research population of people from ASEAN countries, including Indonesia, Malaysia, Thailand, and the Philippines, who use any mobile payment platform. The selection of countries was randomly selected so that: Indonesia, Malaysia, Thailand, and the Philippines were selected. The population consists of mobile payment platform users aged 18 to 30 years and whose expenditure is above US $ 60 per day. This population includes the Millennial generation (born in 1990) to the younger generation born in 2005, who are currently 18 (adults). This population selection was carried out considering that the most significant users of mobile transactions are the generation born after 1990 (Deloitte, 2023). The research population will be divided into the age groups of students, newly employed, middle managers, and managers. The minimum sample size is ten times the number of research indicators [30].

This research uses 27 indicators, so the sample size is 368 people, which is more significant than the minimum sample size. The indicators for the continuity intention variable are taken from the study by [12]. Indicators of mobile payment use are taken from the study of [31]. Meanwhile, the perceived trust indicator is taken from studies [32]. Meanwhile, the perceived satisfaction indicator is used as an indicator developed by [31] in their study. The sampling technique uses purposive sampling. This was done because the researcher obtained complete data about the name, address, and position of the target sample. Data collection was carried out using a questionnaire distributed using Google Forms. The questionnaire was designed using five answers ranging from strongly agree to disagree strongly. Next, the data was obtained using SMART PLS 3.

# 4 Data Analysis

## 4.1 *Reliability and Validity*

To measure the data validity, this study used a loading value of >0.70 from each variable. From the analysis results, it was found that all constructs indicate the value of >0.70 which ensures the validity of the data. Meanwhile, the data reliability was measured using the value of Cronbach's alpha of >0.6 and the value of composite reliability of >0.7 (Zikmund et al. 2013). It was found that all of the AVE scores are higher >0.5 with the value of Cronbach's alpha of >0.6 and the value of composite reliability of >0.7.

This study also employed the reliability and validity test based on the output value of Composite Reliability and Cronbach's alpha. The constructs are reliable if the value of Cronbach's alpha is >0.6 and the value of Composite Reliability is >0.7. The data reveals that all constructs resulted in Cronbach's alpha of >0.6, with 0.740 for perceived trust and 0.938 for the continuance intention. At the same time, the values of Composite Reliability measured were all >0.7. The value of Average Variance Extracted (AVE) for all constructs are >0.6, with perceived trust having the lowest score of 0.660 and use of mobile payment having the highest score of 0.758. These results lead to the conclusion that all the constructs in this study are valid and reliable (Table 1).

## 4.2 *Discriminant Validity*

To understand the variations of one construct from the others, this study employed a discriminant validity test. Results on the value of discriminant validity from every construct are available at Table 2. The scores demonstrate that all constructs in this study met the required criteria where each construct varies from the others.

The value of coefficient of determination (R2) can be found in Fig. 2, with continuance intention of 0.430 and use of mobile payment of 0.477. These findings mean

**Table 1** Outer loading

| | Continuance intention | Perceived satisfaction | Perceived trust | Use mobile payment |
|---|---|---|---|---|
| CI2 | 0.921 | | | |
| CI1 | 0.938 | | | |
| PS1 | | 0.878 | | |
| PS2 | | 0.935 | | |
| PS3 | | 0.926 | | |
| PS4 | | 0.904 | | |
| PT1 | | | 0.740 | |
| PT3 | | | 0.757 | |
| PT4 | | | 0.815 | |
| PT5 | | | 0.851 | |
| PT6 | | | 0.872 | |
| PT7 | | | 0.852 | |
| PT8 | | | 0.793 | |
| UMP1 | | | | 0.840 |
| UMP2 | | | | 0.876 |
| UMP3 | | | | 0.888 |

**Table 2** Discriminant validity

| | Continuance intention | Perceived satisfaction | Perceived trust | Use mobile payment |
|---|---|---|---|---|
| Continuance intention | 0.929 | | | |
| Perceived satisfaction | 0.541 | 0.911 | | |
| Perceived trust | 0.520 | 0.733 | 0.813 | |
| Use mobile payment | 0.629 | 0.662 | 0.620 | 0.870 |

that all variables included in the analysis have a moderate coefficient of determination [30], and [33]. The R2 value illustrates the measure of predictive power within a sample [34].

The evaluation of the constructs validity and reliability reveals that all constructs are valid and reliable. Therefore, the constructs have met the requirements to be further analysed using the inner model. Results of structural model analysis are illustrated in the Fig. 2.

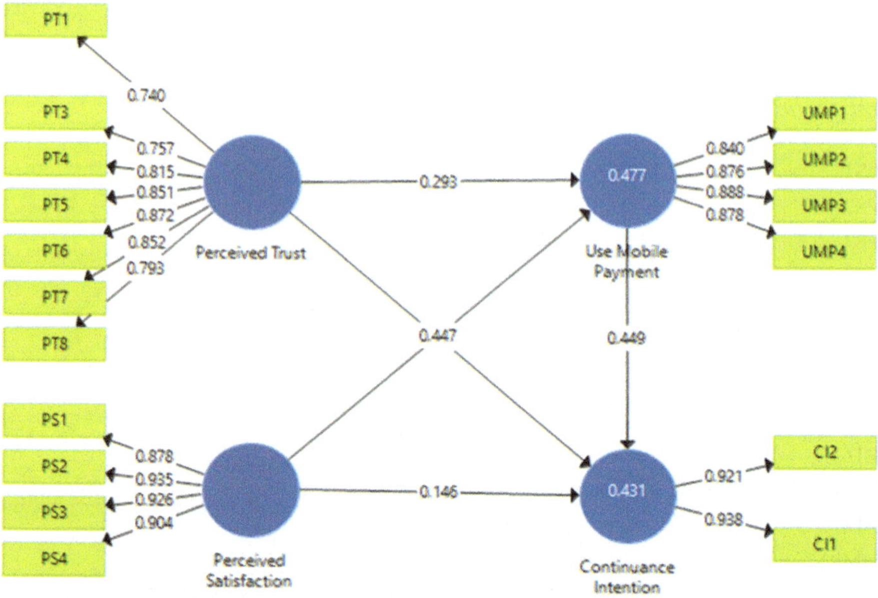


**Fig. 2** Research result

## 5 Empirical Discussion

The data analysis (Fig. 2) show that perceived trust has a positive and significant influence on mobile payment use, this is indicated by B of 0.293 and p-values of 0.000 and t-statistics of 4.931. This means that the hypothesis is accepted. Thus, it can be concluded that the effort to increase the use of mobile payments is to increase perceived trust. One of the determining factors for customers to use mobile payments is their trust in the mobile payment application. Trust in the system and institutions that own mobile payments is very important because of the risks and uncertainties. Every institution that issues mobile payments must ensure that the system built is correct and accurate. For this reason, an external guarantee institution is needed to carry out regular audits of the quality and security of transactions using mobile payments. This is in line with [20] who found that perceived trust highly correlate with mobile payment use. Kim [35] study also revealed that perceived trust can significantly and positively affect one's decision for technology adoption. Furthermore, Xin et al. [26] state that trust has a positive and significant effect on the intention to use mobile payment.

The research results show that the perceived trust would have some impacts on continuance intention (B = 0.134; *p*-values = 0.058 and t-statistic = 1.902). Trust is an important factor that keeps consumers to continue using the application. Companies need to constantly build their consumers' trust to ensure continuance and prevent losing their consumers to other m-payment applications. Due to the growing number of mobile payment applications and increased competition, each one must retain its customer base in order to stay in business. Making continual improvements, guaranteeing the security of client data, certifying applications, and other methods can all be used to improve perception. This is in line with Alrawad et al.'s [8] study which found that trust may have a positive impact with the intention to use mobile payment. Almaiah et al. [36] reveal that trust is one of the most important factors that increase the continuance intention to new technology. According to Shin and Lee [37], trust is essential in the use of mobile payment. Other studies also documented positive correlation between trust and the adoption of mobile payment [26, 38–40].

Additionally, perceived satisfaction has a positive and significant impact towards the use of mobile payment (B = 0.447; *p*-values = 0.000 dan t-statistic = 0.000). In this regard, consumer satisfaction is one of the determinants of using mobile payment. Customer satisfaction is a function of the accuracy of promises and the ability of the mobile payment application to meet Palangga's expectations. This means that mobile payments should not promise something that cannot be kept. Mobile payments must also continuously understand the evolving needs of their customers. Regarding to this, the performance of mobile payment itself highly determines the consumers' satisfaction and thus affects consumers' choice to use the system. Consumers' satisfaction is indeed known as a determinant factor to the use of mobile payment [17, 18]. Recent study by Liebana-Cabanillas et al. [20] discovers that perceived satisfaction has a positive impact to the use of mobile payment.

The results also point out a positive and significant impact of perceived satisfaction towards continuance intention (B = 0.146; *p*-values = 0.048; dan t-statistic = 1.979). From this study, it was found that consumers' satisfaction determines their continuance intention in using the mobile payment. Satisfied customers will continue to increase their use of mobile payments and can become advocates and attract other customers. However, if customers are disappointed and their disappointment is not handled well, then they will express it in various ways, which will be detrimental to mobile payment itself. The customers' satisfaction demonstrates the application performance in completing the consumers' needs through the mobile payment [29, 41]. Ramadan and Aita [42] found that perceived satisfaction contributes to the continuance use of mobile payment. Choshin and Ghaffari [43] also highlighted that consumers' satisfaction on using the mobile payment highly relates to long-term success of the application.

Use of mobile payment is regarded to lead into a positive and significant effect to the continuance intention (B = 0.449; *p*-values = 0.000 dan t-statistic = 8.025). Consumers gain more experience as they complete transactions using mobile payment. Use of mobile payments will decrease if they are dissatisfied and lose trust in mobile payment itself. Once this transforms into a habit, consumers would be more open to use m-payment for every transaction [21]. A study conducted in 2021 by Franque et al. finds that use of mobile payment correlates positively with m-payment continuance intention [22]. Kumar et al. [44] reveals that consumers' attitudes when using mobile payment can significantly affect their behavioural intention into using mobile payment.

The final results confirm that the use of mobile payment mediates the perceived trust on continuance intention (B = 0.132; *p*-values = 0.000 dan t-statistic = 3.888) while also mediating the effect of perceived satisfaction on continuance intention (B = 0.200; p-values = 0.000 dan t-statistic = 5.837). These results are in line with Huang and Benyoucef [27] who analysed the use of mobile payment that mediates perceived satisfaction on intention to continue using mobile payment. Another study conducted by Liu, Li, and Hu [25] highlighted that use of mobile payment is able to mediate the effects of perceived satisfaction on continuance intention of using m-payment. Meanwhile, Ki and Kim [28] record the role of mobile payment use that mediates the perceived trust on intention to continue using the service.

## 6 Conclusion

This study discovers that the use of mobile payment could mediate the effects of perceived trust and perceived satisfaction on the continuance intention of mobile payment use. It is therefore concluded that perceived trust and perceived satisfaction act as antecedents that influence the use of mobile payment and intentions for continual, long-term use of mobile payment. The use of mobile payment also leads to significant effects on the continual intention of utilizing mobile payment.

**Acknowledgements** The authors would like to thank Program Dana Abadi Perguruan Tinggi WCU UNP for funding this work with a contract number: 4944/UN.35.13/KP/2022.

## References

1. Fan, J., Shao, M., Li, Y., Huang, X.: Understanding users' attitude toward mobile payment use: a comparative study between China and the USA. Ind. Manag. Data Syst. **118**(3), 524–540 (2018)
2. Chirisa, I., Mutambisi, T., Chivenge, M., Mabaso, E., Matamanda, A.R., Ncube, R.: The urban penalty of COVID-19 lockdowns across the globe: manifestations and lessons for anglophone sub-saharan Africa. GeoJournal **87**(2), 815–828 (2022)
3. Houghton, S., Kyron, M., Lawrence, D., Hunter, S.C., Hattie, J., Carroll, A., Zadow, C., Chen, W.: Longitudinal trajectories of mental health and loneliness for Australian adolescents with-or-without neurodevelopmental disorders: the impact of COVID-19 school lockdowns. J. Child Psychol. Psychiatry (2022). https://doi.org/10.1111/jcpp.13579
4. Fong, M.W., Gao, H., Wong, J.Y., Xiao, J., Shiu, E.Y., Ryu, S., Cowling, B.J.: Nonpharmaceutical measures for pandemic influenza in nonhealthcare settings—Social distancing measures. Emerg. Infect. Dis. **26**(5), 976 (2020)
5. Eikenberry, S.E., Mancuso, M., Iboi, E., Phan, T., Eikenberry, K., Kuang, Y., Gumel, A.B.: To mask or not to mask: modeling the potential for face mask use by the general public to curtail the COVID-19 pandemic. Infect. Dis. Model. **5**, 293–308 (2020)
6. Rafdinal, W., Senalasari, W.: Predicting the adoption of mobile payment applications during the COVID-19 pandemic. Int. J. Bank Mark. **39**(6), 984–1002 (2021)

7. Toplin, J.: What́ sdriving growth in proximity mobile payment usage? (2021) https://www.emarketer.com/content/whats-driving-proximity-mobile-payment-usage-growth. Accessed 10 Sept 2021
8. Alrawada, M., Lutfib, A., Almaiahd, M.A., Elshaerg, I.A.: Examining the influence of trust and perceived risk on customers intention to use NFC mobile payment system. J. Open Innov.: Technol., Mark., Complex. **9**(2023), 100070 (2023)
9. Holmes, J., Rempel, J.: Trust in close relationships. J. Personal. Soc. Psychol. **49** (1985).https://doi.org/10.1037//0022-3514.49.1.95
10. D'Alessandro, S., Girardi, A., Tiangsoongnern, L.: Perceived risk and trust as antecedents of online purchasing behavior in the USA gemstone industry. Asia Pac. J. Mark. Logist. **24**, 433–460 (2012). https://doi.org/10.1108/13555851211237902
11. Ekienabor, E., Basil, A., Sina, A.M.: The effect of electronic banking on customer satisfaction in Nigeria. Intternational J. Soc. Study **4**(4), 33–41 (2018)
12. Bhattacherjee, A., Lin, C. P. A unified model of IT continuance: Three complementary perspectives and crossover effects. Eur. J. Inf. Syst. **24**(4) (2015). https://doi.org/10.1057/ejis.2013.36
13. Cao, X., Yu, L., Liu, Z., Gong, M., Adeel, L.: Understanding mobile payment users' continuance intention: a trust transfer perspective. Internet Res. **28**(2) (2018). https://doi.org/10.1108/IntR-11-2016-0359
14. Carillo, K., Scornavacca, E., Za, S.: The role of media dependency in predicting continuance intention to use ubiquitous media systems. Inf. Manag. **54**(3) (2017). https://doi.org/10.1016/j.im.2016.09.002
15. Cho, J.: The impact of post-adoption beliefs on the continued use of health apps. Int. J. Med. Inform. **87**https://doi.org/10.1016/j.ijmedinf.2015.12.016
16. Kujala, S., Mugge, R., Miron-Shatz, T.: The role of expectations in service evaluation: A longitudinal study of a proximity mobile payment service. Int. J. Hum. Comput. Stud. **98** (2017). https://doi.org/10.1016/j.ijhcs.2016.09.011
17. Alalwan, A.A., Dwivedi, Y.K., Rana, N.P., Algharabat, R.: Examining factors influencing Jordanian customers' intentions and adoption of internet banking: Extending UTAUT2 with risk. J. Retail. Consum. Serv. **40** (2018).https://doi.org/10.1016/j.jretconser.2017.08.026
18. Mayer, R.C., Davis, J.H., Schoorman, F.D.: An integrative model of organizational trust. Acad. Manag. Rev. **20**(3) (1995). https://doi.org/10.5465/amr.1995.9508080335
19. Kalinic, Z., Marinkovic, V., Molinillo, S., Liébana-Cabanillas, F.: A multi-analytical approach to peer-to-peer mobile payment acceptance prediction. J. Retail. Consum. Serv. **49** (2019).https://doi.org/10.1016/j.jretconser.2019.03.016
20. Liebana-Cabanillas, F., Japutra, A., Molinillo, S., Singh, N., Sinha, N.: Assessment of mobile technology use in the emerging market: Analyzing intention to use m-payment services in India. Telecommun. Policy **44**(2020), 102009 (2020)
21. Chang, I.-C., Liu, C.-C., Chen, K.: The effects of hedonic/utilitarian expectations and social influence on continuance intention to play online games. Internet Res. **24**(1), 21–45 (2014)
22. Franque, F.B., Oliveira, T., Tam, C.: Understanding the factors of mobile payment continuance intention: empirical test in an African context. Heliyon **7**, e07807 (2021)
23. Susanto, A., Chang, Y., Ha, Y.: Determinants of continuance intention to use the smartphone banking services: An extension to the expectation-confirmation model. Ind. Manag. Data Syst. **116**(3) (2016). https://doi.org/10.1108/IMDS-05-2015-0195
24. Oghuma, A.P., Libaque-Saenz, C.F., Wong, S.F., Chang, Y.: An expectation-confirmation model of continuance intention to use mobile instant messaging. Telemat. Inform. **33**(1) (2016). https://doi.org/10.1016/j.tele.2015.05.006
25. Liu, Y., Li, H., Hu, F.: Website attributes in urging online impulse purchase: An empirical investigation on consumer perceptions. Decis. Support. Syst. **55**(3) (2013). https://doi.org/10.1016/j.dss.2013.04.001
26. Xin, H., Techatassanasoontorn, A.A., Tan, F.B.: Antecedents of Consumer Trust in Mobile Payment Adoption. J. Comput. Inf. Syst. **55**(4), 1–10 (2015). https://doi.org/10.1080/08874417.2015.11645781

27. Huang, Z., Benyoucef, M. From e-commerce to social commerce: A close look at design features. Electron. Commer. Res. Appl. **12**(4) (2013). https://doi.org/10.1016/j.elerap.2012.12.003
28. Ki, C. W. 'Chloe,' Kim, Y. K.: The mechanism by which social media influencers persuade consumers: The role of consumers' desire to mimic. Psychol. Mark. **36**(10) (2019). https://doi.org/10.1002/mar.21244
29. Wang, W.T., Li, H.M.: Factors influencing mobile services adoption: a brand-equity perspective. Internet Res. **22**(2), 142–179 (2012)
30. Hair, J.F., Sarstedt, M., Hopkins, L., Kuppelwieser, V.G.: Partial least squares structural equation modeling (PLS-SEM): An emerging tool in business research. Eur. Bus. Rev. **26**(2) (2014). https://doi.org/10.1108/EBR-10-2013-0128
31. Priya, R., Gandhi, A.V., Shaikh, A. Mobile banking adoption in an emerging economy: An empirical analysis of young Indian consumers. Benchmarking **25**(2) (2018). https://doi.org/10.1108/BIJ-01-2016-0009
32. Shao, Z., Zhang, L., Li, X., Guo, Y.: Antecedents of trust and continuance intention in mobile payment platforms: The moderating effect of gender. Electron. Commer. Res. Appl. **33** (2019).https://doi.org/10.1016/j.elerap.2018.100823
33. Henseler, J., Ringle, C.M., Sarstedt, M. (2015). A new criterion for assessing discriminant validity in variance-based structural equation modeling. J. Acad. Mark. Sci. **43**(1). https://doi.org/10.1007/s11747-014-0403-8
34. Sarstedt, M., Hair, J.F., Cheah, J.H., Becker, J.M., Ringle, C.M. How to specify, estimate, and validate higher-order constructs in PLS-SEM. Australas. Mark. J. **27**(3) (2019). https://doi.org/10.1016/j.ausmj.2019.05.003
35. Kim, D.J.: Self-perception-based versus transference-based trust determinants in computer-mediated transactions: A cross-cultural comparison study. J. Manag. Inf. Syst. **24**(4), 13–45 (2008)
36. Almaiah, M.A., Al-Rahmi, A., Alturise, F., Hassan, L., Lutfi, A., Alrawad, M., Alkhalaf, S., Al-Rahmi, W.M., Al-sharaieh, S., Aldhyani, T.H.H.: Investigating the effect of perceived security, perceived trust, and information quality on mobile payment usage through near-field communication (NFC) in Saudi Arabia. Electronics **11**, 3926 (2022). https://doi.org/10.3390/electronics11233926
37. Shin, S., Lee, W.: The effects of technology readiness and technology acceptance on NFC mobile payment services in Korea. JABR **30**, 1615 (2014). https://doi.org/10.19030/jabr.v30i6.8873
38. Gefen, D., Straub, D.W.: Managing user trust in B2C eServices. E-service Journal **2**(2), 7–24 (2003)
39. Chandra, S., Srivastava, S.C., Theng, Y.L.: Evaluating the role of trust in consumer adoption of mobile payment systems: An empirical analysis. Commun. Assoc. Inf. Syst. **27**(1), 561–588 (2010)
40. Zhou, T.: The effect of initial trust on user adoption of mobile payment. Inf. Dev. **27**(4), 290–300 (2011)
41. Lin, H.F.: An application of fuzzy AHP for evaluating course website quality. Comput. Educ. **54**(1), 877–888 (2010)
42. Ramadan, R., Aita, J.: A model of mobile payment usage among Arab consumers. Int. J. Bank Mark. (2018). https://doi.org/10.1108/IJBM-05-2017-0080
43. Choshin, M., Ghaffari, A.: An investigation of the impact of effective factors on the success of e-commerce in small- and medium-sized companies. Comput. Hum. Behav. **66**(2017), 67–74 (2017)
44. Kumar, A., Adlakaha, A., Mukherjee, K.: The effect of perceived security and grievance redressal on continuance intention to use M-wallets in a developing country. Int. J. Bank Mark. (2018). https://doi.org/10.1108/IJBM-04-2017-0077

# Revenue Structure, Financial Stability and Financial Performance of NPOs in Developing Countries: Does Revenue Diversity Lead to Better Performance?

**Akeel Almagtome, Enaam Almusawi, Hussein Furaijl, Ahmed Al-Yasiri, and Zahira Alfartoosi**

**Abstract** The revenue structure of nonprofit organizations is crucial to their continued existence and growth. This study investigates the accounting information system's role in identifying funding sources. It examines the extent to which the revenue structure influences the financial performance of Iraqi nonprofits. In addition, this study investigates the impact of revenue streams on the total annual revenue, financial performance, and financial stability of nonprofit organizations. This paper presents a quantitative model for identifying revenue streams that substantially impact nonprofit organizations' financial performance. It determines if the funding structure influences nonprofit organizations' financial performance. The study sample comprises 135 Iraqi organizations registered with the NPO section of the Secretariat of the Iraqi Council of Ministers from 2014 to 2020. Results indicate that nonprofit organizations with greater revenue concentration are more likely to have superior financial performance. It is also more probable that nonprofit organizations will have solid financial performance ratios if program revenue is increased. In addition, Iraqi NGOs rely predominantly on external revenue sources, as it is more likely that NGOs will have more excellent financial stability if they receive more donations from abroad. Such outcomes could also assist nonprofit administrators in securing long-term funding sources for their organizations. This study contributes to accounting literature by examining the effect of revenue diversity on the financial performance of nonprofit organizations in developing nations. It also explains why local nonprofits rely on foreign donations rather than local grants.

A. Almagtome (✉) · E. Almusawi · A. Al-Yasiri
Faculty of Administration and Economics, University of Kufa, Najaf, Iraq
e-mail: akeelh.alhasnawi@uokufa.edu.iq

H. Furaijl
College of Pharmacy, University-Al-Ameed, Karbala, Iraq

Z. Alfartoosi
Jabir Ibn Hayyan Medical University, Najaf, Iraq

 
S. Kot et al. (eds.), *Corporate Practices: Policies, Methodologies, and Insights in Organizational Management*, Springer Proceedings in Business and Economics,
https://doi.org/10.1007/978-981-97-0996-0_31

**Keywords** Revenue structure · Nonprofit financial performance · NPOs · Financial reporting · International donors · Local grants · Financial sustainability

## 1 Introduction

Enhancing nonprofit organizations' financial performance necessitates an acceptable balance between the conflicting objectives of promoting revenue growth and ensuring stability, which is a significant challenge for effective nonprofit financial management [1]. Nonprofit organizations can only achieve financial sustainability by accomplishing both objectives. In recent years, nonprofit organizations have been specifically tasked with handling more traditional government services [2]. Nonprofit organizations have undertaken additional responsibilities for providing public services as the Iraqi government confronts increasingly turbulent political environments and increasing pressure to increase government efficacy and decrease government expenditure. Nonprofit organizations must maintain adequate financial resources to continue providing these services [3]. External grants, donations, self-contributions, and participation fees support numerous nonprofit organizations that provide public services. However, to meet the rising demand for services, as the number of beneficiaries has recently increased due to deteriorating security conditions, nonprofit organizations need help generating sufficient funds from various sources. Regarding the financial administration of nonprofit organizations, revenue growth is frequently regarded as a crucial indicator of success [4]. The organization's annual revenue growth should support its short- and medium-term operations. Increasing revenue is also essential for nonprofits seeking to improve their future service quality. While many nonprofits seek revenue growth and resource expansion, others face immediate income insecurity [5]. The challenge for these organizations is that many sources of long-term income growth fluctuate annually, causing service interruptions, budget issues, and financial management [6]. Despite these concerns, eliminating income volatility is typically impossible. Instead, savings and short-term loans can mitigate these effects if the average annual income growth of the institution is sufficient to accommodate the savings. In this study, we first discuss the function of the accounting information system in providing pertinent data to funders and then investigate the impact of revenue structure on nonprofit organizations' financial performance. Then, we investigate any significant revenue sources that enhance revenue growth and stability relative to other revenue sources. Lastly, based on the financial data of 135 nonprofit organizations registered with the Iraqi NPO department between 2014 and 2020, we consider models that account for the effect of the revenue structure on the level of nonprofit organizations' economic performance and revenue sources that influence volatility and development. This study offers significant guidance to the financial administrators of nonprofit organizations on how to enhance their organizations' economic performance and achieve effective operational development by managing their revenue structure.

# 2 Literature Review

## *2.1 AIS and Accountability in NPOs*

Accounting information system AIS and governance considerations are the primary concerns of accountants, whether they are practical or academic [7]. Traditionally, the accounting system is designed to provide information reflecting the organization's ability to generate profits for shareholders, several foreign bodies governing accounting principles. It also offered guidelines on financial data to protect the rights of stakeholders [8]. Stakeholders ought to assess the performance of NPOs regularly for decision-making purposes and to do that. They need accurate information. Business organizations now understand the importance of non-financial metrics providing data to partners. The ridiculous level of funding competition and funding reliance pressured NPOs to undertake a pragmatic approach to funding and employ accounting and funding experts to fulfill the dynamic financial reporting and performance [9].

In the context of the NPO, financial and non-financial data produces problems. Countries such as Australia, the United Kingdom, the United States of America, and Spain have recently released their NPO accounting systems by introducing a whole accrual framework to increase transparency and the availability of accounting data regarding decision-making needs [10]. However, once performance indicators are established, the information in the current financial reports will be incomplete. Performance measures are essential for budgeting, forecasting, planning, evaluating immediate needs, benchmarking performance with all other NPOs or governmental entities, and describing partnership activities that contributors have accomplished [11]. Usually, accounting reporting is used to provide relevant information for decision-making internally. At the same time, the NPO financial reporting practices permit external funders, governmental officials, and other information users to access information that satisfies the transparency requirements [12]. International donors and other funders typically expect that grants will be used for the activities the NPOs are given, and their annual reports will show the expected usage of donations [13]. The general public also seeks transparency into NPOs ' operations, focusing on public expenditure announcements and other contributions. The role of the accounting system is to provide this information and fulfill the statutory requirements for the financial reporting of NPOs [6]. Thus, financial reporting and documentation are the most systematic basis for providing international and domestic donors' expectations. Therefore, financial reporting in local nonprofit organizations is essential to winning the confidence of international donors, primarily in organizations working in conflict areas in the Middle East. In this context, the following question arises:

> Are international donors positively evaluating financial reports and documentation for local NPOs?

A comprehensive analysis of the essence of local organizations' work and their funding structure is required to answer this question. Since most organizations operating in Iraq utilize international funding as a significant source of funding for their humanitarian and relief activities, financial reporting is anticipated to play a significant role in this type of organization. Dr. Denis Dragovic, former Country Director of the United States-based International Rescue Committee, believes in two aspects. The first is when we seek a partnership with a local nonprofit organization. Occasionally, we would automatically select a single candidate because of their unique role in the community or because they were the only non-profit organization. Financial reporting and documentation could be of utmost importance in such a scenario. The rationale for this is that the purpose of the partnership includes capacity development. Therefore, if a local NPO has inadequate financial management skills but performs a vital role in the community, the international NPO has the opportunity to form a partnership.

Alternatively, an international NPO will have a contractor-subcontractor relationship with a local NPO. In this sense, it is a service delivery model, not a partnership. Evaluation of financial reporting and documentation is crucial in this relationship. For the credibility of the international NPO, donor funds that pass through the international NPO and on to the local NPO must be accounted for. Under these conditions, they should be positively evaluated for financial reporting and documentation. They should solicit expressions of interest or issue bid documents to provide services, which should include an evaluation of the local nonprofit's capacity. We must acknowledge that any local non-profit organization in Australia or Iraq will need help to administer its finances due to the need for a professional accountant and specialists. Local non-profit organizations in any country need more resources, so expectations must be managed. For instance, we cannot expect the local nonprofit organization to have a fully developed accounting system that reports expenditures against various cost codes. Instead, most local nonprofits will have a straightforward income statement. The purpose of financial reporting in nonprofit organizations extends beyond delivering relevant information for external funders' accountability purposes. Instead, these organizations focus on disseminating pertinent information to other stakeholders. In addition, nonprofits embrace their responsibility to donors by communicating their results and administrative expenses, despite the controversies surrounding the selection of performance indicators.

Performance and financial reporting are essential for NGOs to demonstrate their social responsibility. However, it is highly uncertain whether these structures will enable non-profit organizations to campaign and encourage them to meet the growing demand for transparency in the community [9]. In addition, the diversity of social priorities of non-profit organizations threatens the ability of accounting rules and regulations to develop rigorous and public oversight and accountability systems. Therefore, transparency and reporting of financial information, as well as accountability procedures, are essential to bolstering the legitimacy of a society. In this context, Offenheiser and Holcombe [14] assert that a nonprofit organization's financial accountability significantly impacts its public image, sends a positive message to society, fosters trust, and reduces financial relationship risks. The issue, however, is.

Is there social pressure to activate public funding accountability for NPOs?

It depends on how the community defines a nonprofit. The answer will only be if the community views it as an independent, civil society-based organization with political or governmental ties. This organizational structure is a Western concept. It rarely manifests itself in the social fabric of other societies. However, numerous religiously or politically affiliated social service organizations exist in Iraq and most other Middle Eastern nations. These organizations must conform to the Western conception of an NPO. That does not indicate whether it is better or worse. It simply indicates that they are dissimilar. A politically or religiously affiliated non-profit organization in the Middle East is unlikely to be held accountable for its use of public funds because its mission differs slightly from that of an independent civil society non-profit organization. A politically affiliated nonprofit organization seeks to advance the political agenda of its parent party. More transparency in the public funding of these organizations would be beneficial, but it would ultimately lead to a clash of ideas. Therefore, we conclude that the character of the organization's activity, the reason for its establishment, and the operating environment are determinants of financial reporting and accountability in nonprofit organizations. A rigorous financial reporting system is required to ensure that international donors are held accountable for the nature of the financial decisions made by religiously and politically independent organizations. Consequently, a reliable accounting system increases confidence in the organization's operations. It significantly contributes to the organization's long-term financial sustainability.

## 2.2 *Revenue Structure and Nonprofit Financial Performance*

Nonprofit organizations rely on a variety of streams of income. Possible sources are available to private companies, such as earned income, investment income, and personal and government contracts. However, nonprofit organizations collect donations, charitable contributions from individuals and institutions, and grants from local and international funding agencies. Several studies suggest that a combination of equilibrium of diverse revenue sources will improve the financial health of nonprofit organizations by strengthening revenue sources, thus reducing the entity's financial risks [15]. However, more needs to be revealed about whether the accounting system affects the organization's ability to generate revenue and whether the revenue structure affects the NPO's finances. In addition, how does the nature of the organization's activity and its religious and cultural associations affect its funding structure over time? These specific factors directly affect the organization's revenue mix and financial viability by diversifying funding sources to allow them to manage risk efficiently [15]. In many previous studies, this argument has been proven, so the combination of balance between the various sources of revenue can be an excellent technique to maximize revenue efficiency and minimize a nonprofit organization's financial risks. It thus leads to stability by developing multiple revenue sources that are indirectly related.

Overall, revenue diversification has been widely adopted as a long-term nonprofit strategy, and there is evidence that a diversified revenue structure can improve nonprofit financial health and sustainability [16]. In this sense, [17] states that implementing a diversification approach will lead to greater consistency in the nonprofit funding structure, increasing the likelihood of survival and sustainability. In addition, previous studies investigating donor perceptions of nonprofit organizations found that donors build political preferences when allocating funds primarily to the accounts system outputs represented in financial reports. Consequently, the quality of accounting information is one of the most critical determinants of the financing structure of nonprofit organizations, and it is an additional factor in reducing financial risks. Figure 1 shows the relationship between the accounting system and the financing structure and its reflection on the organization's financial performance level.

Several studies show that the nature of the funding structure in nonprofit organizations and the level of revenue concentration directly affect financial performance and its ability to support the organization's financial sustainability. Carroll and Stater [17] indicate that NPOs can decrease their financial variability by diversification, specifically by reducing their dependence on investment income, expenditure, and donations. On the other hand, Yan, Denison and Butler [16] demonstrate that NPOs with greater income diversification are more likely to make loans but do not generally provide high debt levels. Calabrese [18] suggests that the best explanation of NPO capital structure options is the pecking order theory, where domestic funds are favored over external lending. Chikoto and Neely [19] found an inverse outcome, and their results contradict the idea of diversification of revenues. They notice that

**Fig. 1** The relationship between Revenue Structure and NPOs' financial performance

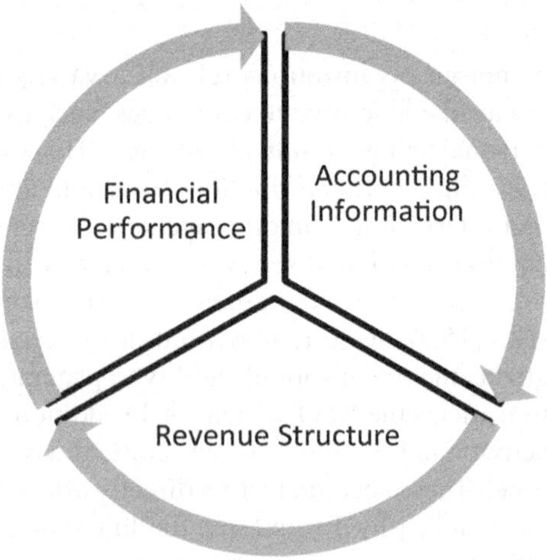

adopting a strategy to maximize revenue produces positive growth in NPO's financial capability over time, especially growth in NPO's overall revenue. In addition, Wicker, Longley and Breuer [20] suggest that diversification of revenues can minimize NPO-revenue volatility substantially but has limited benefits to reduce systemic fluctuations. Shea and Wang [21] note that government funding hurts NPO income diversification. In the same context, Fischer, Wilsker and Young [22] consider the percentage of received program revenues the lowest in the public group, the greatest for those with more private services, and halfway for those categorized as mixed.

Through the previous discussion of the accounting literature, it is noted that most of them demonstrate that, from the perspective of stakeholders, the variability of income influences the level of nonprofit financial performance [23]. While NPO interested parties are willing to see their charities operate efficiently, a consensus has remained difficult for academics and professionals in identifying suitable indicators for the financial performance of NPOs. Costa and Goulart da Silva [24] attribute the need for more agreement on uniform financial performance measures in nonprofit units to the overlap between the organizations ' social and economic objectives. It faces a double challenge: it must strike a balance between considering it a charitable institution that provides humanitarian aid in times of disaster and crisis and its need for financial sustainability. When considering nonprofit organizations in Iraq, the economic independence of organizations is subject to other political, social, or cultural considerations that may differ from those in developed countries. The question here is:

> Do you think the local NPOs can't continue as a financially independent unit without international funding sources, especially UN agencies and other international donors?

This statement is probably true for cultural reasons. The former Country Director of the United States headquartered International Rescue Committee, Dr. Denis Dragovic, believes in a significant tradition of individual funding charities in the West. It is associated with personal responsibility and not wanting the government involved in every aspect of our lives. Different cultures, especially those that don't have as significant an emphasis on the individual in society and instead focus on the community's well-being, would not be motivated to provide individual funding to NPOs because they would rather the state provides the funding. But then, this creates the problem of NPOs receiving state funding.

Consequently, it can be concluded that the increasing dependence of local organizations in Iraq on external financing through program revenue and the need to improve these organizations ' financial performance to ensure their survival necessitates the development of the accounting system applied in nonprofit organizations. This procedure will be reflected favorably in optimizing the external funding sources of Iraqi organizations and ensuring long-term financial stability and NPOs' financial sustainability. However, although several studies have been carried out on the capital structure of for-profit organizations, little empirical work has concentrated on exploring the impact of revenue structure on the financial performance level of nonprofit organizations, especially those operating in a different cultural environment.

## 2.3 Hypotheses Development

Nonprofit organizations seek to increase their revenues from a variety of internal and external sources to maintain their financial viability and improve their financial performance metrics. However, there is controversy regarding the impact of the revenue structure on the level of financial performance. Additionally, the diversity of revenue sources contributes to the financial stability of these organizations. Current research investigates the connection between revenue diversification and financial performance in nonprofit organizations. This analysis drew its financial performance metrics from previous research on the financial performance of nonprofits. Based on previous research in this field, the ratios of revenue to assets and program expenses to total revenues are used as indicators of financial performance in this context. The following describes the relevance of these measures to the nature of data obtained from the organizations comprising the study sample:

**Revenue to Total Assets (RVA)**. This ratio calculates the total asset's revenue ability by dividing the NPO's total revenue by total assets [25].

**Program Expense to Total Revenue (PER)**. This ratio calculates the funds available for program operations. It can be determined by dividing the total program expenditures into revenue [26]. It also tests the success of implementing humanitarian services and the number of resources directly spent in implementing such programs, excluding additional costs. With the ratio of program developers to total revenues, the efficiency of program delivery increases and vice versa. The low spending ratio of the government suggests a dangerous and inefficient use of revenue for implementing programs. For instance, 20 percent means higher waste, and 90 percent or more means that program resources are used efficiently. Thus, the first research hypothesis can be formulated as follows:

> **H1**: There is a statistically significant relationship between revenue concentration and nonprofit organizations' financial performance in Iraq.

The second objective of this analysis is to show the effects of different revenue sources on the level of nonprofit organizations ' financial performance. It also seeks to assess which sources of income are the most important in financial performance. Two revenue metrics are introduced to test this hypothesis: the ratio of income to total RVA assets and program spending to total PER entity. It is thus possible to formulate the second study hypothesis as follows:

> **H2**: There is a statistically significant relationship between the percentage of revenue source and the level of financial performance of nonprofit organizations in Iraq.

## 3 Data and Methodology

This paper empirically examines the relationship between the revenue structure and the financial performance of nonprofit organizations in Iraq. In addition to evaluating the impact of various revenue sources on the financial performance of an organization, it is more important to assess which revenue sources have the greatest impact on the financial performance. The statistical analysis of this study is conducted in two phases to accomplish these objectives. Using the Pearson Association Test, the first stage is to investigate the first hypothesis of the relationship between the income structure defined by the HHI index and the level of financial performance. In the second stage, the impact of various revenue sources on the level of financial performance is evaluated. Using multiple regression models, six sources of income are evaluated. This paper presents a quantitative model for identifying revenue streams that substantially impact the financial performance of nonprofit organizations. It endeavors to determine whether the funding structure influences the financial performance of nonprofit organizations. 700 organizations comprise the research sample of 135 Iraqi organizations registered with the NPO section of the Secretariat of the Iraqi Council of Ministers from 2014 to 2020. After data collection was concluded, entities with insufficient or incomplete data were eliminated, and extreme values were omitted from the study. The final research sample consisted of 135 organizations with 675 observations. This study's primary data source was the annual reports of the sampled non-profit organizations. The dependent variable, financial performance, is measured by two indicators: Revenue to Total Assets (RVA) and Program Expense to Revenue (PER). The independent variable is the revenue structure. It is computed using the Hirschman–Herfindahl Index (HHI) as a Revenue concentration Index. This Index evaluates a variety of reported revenues from the most important internal and external revenue streams [19, 27]. In the current investigation, six revenue sources are identified. These include government grants, contributions, program revenue, dues, investments, and private donations.

$$HHI = \sum_{i=1}^{n} (Xi)2 \times 100 \tag{1}$$

where

*HHI*: Revenue concertation index.
*Xi*: Percentage of Revenue source i.
*n*: NUMBER of revenue sources.

The HHI achieves a maximum value of 10,000 when there is a total concentration in which one business has 100% of the market, i.e., the HHI = (100)2 = 10,000. In a massive multiplayer market with many revenue sources with tiny source shares, the HHI assumes a low value, potentially close to zero. The control variable in this study is total assets TA, total revenues TR, and the nonprofit subsectors. With a high level of total assets, the company continues to experience increased revenue growth and is also less unpredictable. Total revenue shows that NPO has steady growth in sales and high financial results, while the nonprofit sector represents an essential factor in attracting internal and external donations.

Based on the associations previously discussed in the nonprofit financial performance and revenue structure, we establish two models to investigate further the impact of revenue structure on the financial performance using two proxies are, RVA and PER, as follows:

Model 1.

$$Y1 = \alpha + \beta 1x1 + \beta 2x2 + \beta 3x3 + \beta 4x4 + \beta 5x5 + \beta 6x6 + \varepsilon \quad (2)$$

Model 2:

$$Y2 = \alpha + \beta 1x1 + \beta 2x2 + \beta 3x3 + \beta 4x4 + \beta 5x5 + \beta 6x6 + \varepsilon \quad (3)$$

where:

*Y1* = The dependent variable: financial performance, proxied by revenue on total assets ratio (RVA).

*Y2* = The dependent variable: financial performance, proxied by program costs ratio (PCR).

$\alpha$ = A constant.

β1 to β6 = Regression coefficients for independent variables $x1$ to $x6$ respectively.

$x1$ to $x6$ = The independent variables; grants (GRNT), contributions (CONT), programs revenues (PREV), organization's dues (DUES), investments (INVE), and other revenues (OTHR), respectively.

$\varepsilon$ = Error term.

The study sample consisted of 21 industrial companies registered in the Iraq Stock Exchange for companies from 2011 to 2020, with 194 observations (company-year) after excluding missing values. To measure the level of sustainability reporting, a content analysis method was adopted using a scale of 108 reporting indicators derived from the G4 sustainability reporting standards of the Global Reporting Initiative (GRI), which cover four main dimensions of sustainability (economic performance, environmental performance, social performance, and governance) [28].

The descriptive statistics for the variables in our models are shown in Table 1. A review of two measures of financial performance reveals that there is a high percentage of RVA (revenue over total assets) on average for the sample. At the same time, PER (ratio of program expenditures) accounted for approximately 63% of the total annual revenue for the study sample organizations. Relatively nonprofit organizations are diverse in their revenue structures, with an average HHI value of 56.7628 over the 5-year study regarding revenue diversification. Descriptive statistics (Table 1) also indicate that program revenue (%34) is the most significant source of income for NPOs on average, followed by contributions (%15), grants (%6), investment revenue (%1), dues (%0.19) and other revenue (%0.01). On average, nonprofit organizations depend mainly on the program revenue rather than other revenue sources. The three control variables are total assets, total revenue, and nonprofit subsector in this analysis. The attributes of nonprofit organizations depicted in the sample are listed in Table 2.

**Table 1** Descriptive statistics

| Variables | Description | Minimum | Maximum | Mean | Standard deviation |
|---|---|---|---|---|---|
| *Dependent variable* | | | | | |
| RVA | Revenue on total assets % | 0.01 | 4.94 | 2.4153 | 1.41204 |
| PER | Program Expenses ratio % | 0.31 | 0.91 | 0.6272 | 0.08315 |
| *Independent variables* | | | | | |
| HHI | Revenue diversity index | 0.34 | 185.56 | 56.7628 | 28.55564 |
| GRNT (%)2 | Square of % grants to total revenue | 0.00 | 89.03 | 6.2831 | 10.48771 |
| CONT (%)2 | Square of % contributions to total revenue | 0.00 | 100.00 | 14.7749 | 20.50096 |
| PREV (%)2 | Square of % program revenues to total revenue | 0.00 | 92.78 | 34.3779 | 24.82906 |
| DUES (%)2 | Square of % dues to total revenue | 0.00 | 8.53 | 0.1952 | 1.05677 |
| INVE (%)2 | Square of % investment revenues to total revenue | 0.00 | 33.74 | 1.1231 | 4.49797 |
| OTHR (%)2 | Square of % other revenues to total revenue | 0.00 | 0.27 | 0.0088 | 0.02657 |
| *Control variables* | | | | | |
| TA | Log of Total assets (Millions of Iraqi Dinars) | 0.68 | 1155.84 | 763.13 | 1851.42 |
| TR | Log of Total revenues (Millions of Iraqi Dinars) | 57.75 | 64,998.12 | 2253.87 | 6335.34 |
| SEC | Dummy variable, nine main subsectors | – | – | – | – |

**Table 2** NPO subsectors of the sample

| NOP code | Category | Total NPOs | Total observations | % of sample |
|---|---|---|---|---|
| SEC1 | Social benefit | 23 | 115 | 0.17 |
| SEC2 | Community development | 24 | 120 | 0.18 |
| SEC3 | Human rights and advocacy | 20 | 100 | 0.15 |
| SEC4 | Arts related | 13 | 65 | 0.10 |
| SEC5 | Women empowerment | 17 | 85 | 0.13 |
| SEC6 | Relief and improvement | 14 | 70 | 0.10 |
| SEC7 | Human services | 10 | 50 | 0.07 |
| SEC8 | Health | 6 | 30 | 0.04 |
| SEC9 | Social science research | 8 | 40 | 0.06 |
| Total | | 135 | 675 | 100 |

# 4 Results

Table 3 displays the overall results of Hypothesis 1. The first stage analyzes the association between NPOs' revenue concentration and financial performance. The Spearman's coefficient between the average sample concentration of revenue measured by the HHI index and RVA (revenue to total assets) is 0.34, indicating that NPO's total assets are irrelevant in funding attraction. Conversely, the correlation coefficient between the sample average revenue concentration measured by the HHI index and the PER (program expenditure on total revenue) is 0.98, showing strong evidence that the revenue concentration is a predictor of the nonprofit risk-return relationship. Thus, hypothesis 1, which examines the relationship between revenue concentration and nonprofit financial performance, is confirmed.

**Table 3** Correlation matrix (Spearman's rho results)

Correlations

| | | | HI | RVA | PER |
|---|---|---|---|---|---|
| Spearman's rho | HHI | Correlation coefficient | 1.000 | 0.343* | 0.980* |
| | | Sig. (2-tailed) | | 0.000 | 0.000 |
| | | N | 675 | 675 | 675 |
| | RVA | Correlation coefficient | 0.343* | 1.000 | 0.335* |
| | | Sig. (2-tailed) | 0.000 | | 0.000 |
| | | N | 675 | 675 | 675 |
| | PER | Correlation coefficient | 0.980* | 0.335* | 1.000 |
| | | Sig. (2-tailed) | 0.000 | 0.000 | |
| | | N | 675 | 675 | 675 |

*Correlation is significant at the 0.01 level (2-tailed)

**Table 4** ANOVA results of Model 1

| ANOVA[a] | | | | | | |
|---|---|---|---|---|---|---|
| Model | | Sum of squares | df | Mean square | F | Sig. |
| 1 | Regression | 258.322 | 6 | 43.054 | 26.494 | 0.000[b] |
| | Residual | 1085.540 | 668 | 1.625 | | |
| | Total | 1343.862 | 674 | | | |
| 2 | Regression | 538.218 | 16 | 33.639 | 27.474 | 0.000[c] |
| | Residual | 805.643 | 658 | 1.224 | | |
| | Total | 1343.862 | 674 | | | |

[a]Dependent Variable: RVA
[b]Predictors: (Constant), OTHR, PREV, CONT, DUES, INVE, GRNT
[c]Predictors: (Constant), OTHR, PREV, CONT, DUES, INVE, GRNT, SEC6, SIZ, SEC3, SEC1, SEC7, SEC5, SEC4, SEC9, SEC8, SEC2

The findings of hypothesis 2 indicate that the two models have significant statistical F-statistics and primarily significant statistical coefficients on explanatory variables.

## 4.1 *Model 1: RVA (Revenue on Total Assets)*

Tables 4 and 5 indicate the results of model 1 that examine the relationship between Revenue on total assets (RVA) and six revenue sources are grants (GRNT), contributions (CONT), programs revenues (PREV), organization's dues (DUES), investments (INVE), and other revenues (OTHR). These results indicate that the correlation between the RVA and all revenue sources is significant at 0.01. The program revenue has the highest correlation coefficient with RVA (0.488), as indicated in Table 5.

Table 5 coefficients provide a summary of the revenue structure that can be used to forecast how changes in the revenue structure of an organization will better reflect an NPO's financial performance. For instance, an organization that relies primarily on program funding may maximize revenue growth by reducing this dependence and seeking other sources of revenue, such as donations and income from the investment — presuming such sources of revenue are realistic options. However, the problem here is that, on average, donations and expenditures are more unpredictable (Table 6).

## 4.2 *Model 2: PER (Program Expenses to Total Revenue Ratio)*

Using a metric known as PER, which stands for program expenditures to total revenue ratio, model 2 demonstrates that the second hypothesis, which states that there is a

**Table 5** Regression coefficients of Model 1

Coefficients[a]

| | | Unstandardized coefficients | | Standardized coefficients | t | Sig. |
|---|---|---|---|---|---|---|
| | | B | Std. error | Beta | | |
| 1 | (Constant) | 1.276 | 0.123 | | 10.349 | 0.000 |
| | GRNT | 0.016 | 0.005 | Model | 2.925 | 0.004 |
| | CONT | 0.008 | 0.003 | 0.114 | 3.118 | 0.002 |
| | PREV | 0.026 | 0.002 | 0.455 | 11.727 | 0.000 |
| | DUES | 0.099 | 0.047 | 0.074 | 2.115 | 0.035 |
| | INVE | 0.053 | 0.011 | 0.170 | 4.698 | 0.000 |
| | OTHR | −4.801 | 1.871 | −0.090 | −2.565 | 0.011 |
| 2 | (Constant) | 1.051 | 0.511 | | 2.058 | 0.040 |
| | GRNT | 0.018 | 0.005 | 0.137 | 3.703 | 0.000 |
| | CONT | 0.007 | 0.002 | 0.097 | 3.051 | 0.002 |
| | PREV | 0.028 | 0.002 | 0.488 | 13.249 | 0.000 |
| | DUES | 0.314 | 0.050 | 0.235 | 6.228 | 0.000 |
| | INVE | 0.056 | 0.014 | 0.177 | 3.902 | 0.000 |
| | OTHR | −6.833 | 1.663 | −0.129 | −4.108 | 0.000 |
| | SIZ | −2.866E-010 | 0.000 | −0.376 | −11.741 | 0.000 |
| | SEC1 | 0.390 | 0.511 | 0.104 | 0.762 | 0.446 |
| | SEC2 | 0.347 | 0.510 | 0.094 | 0.681 | 0.496 |
| | SEC3 | 0.806 | 0.511 | 0.203 | 1.576 | 0.115 |
| | SEC4 | 0.470 | 0.524 | 0.098 | 0.897 | 0.370 |
| | SEC5 | 0.521 | 0.512 | 0.119 | 1.017 | 0.309 |
| | SEC6 | 0.293 | 0.516 | 0.063 | 0.568 | 0.570 |
| | SEC7 | 0.526 | 0.521 | 0.098 | 1.009 | 0.313 |
| | SEC8 | 0.257 | 0.585 | 0.038 | 0.439 | 0.661 |
| | SEC9 | −1.453 | 0.542 | −0.243 | −2.678 | 0.008 |

[a]Dependent Variable: RVA

correlation between revenue structure and financial performance, was correct. Model 2 has F-statistics that are statistically significant and explanatory variable coefficients that are, for the most part, statistically significant. The variable equation for financial performance (PER) should be specified, and it should include information on grants, contributions, and system income. The ratio of program expenses to overall income, also known as PER, continues to have a more vital link with revenue from the program. The dues have a negative impact on financial performance. Contributions, investment income, and other sources of money all have a favorable impact on the organization's overall financial success. This would imply that the sources of income

**Table 6** ANOVA results of Model 2

| ANOVA[a] | | | | | | |
|---|---|---|---|---|---|---|
| Model | | Sum of squares | df | Mean square | F | Sig. |
| 1 | Regression | 3.191 | 6 | 0.532 | 241.870 | 0.000[b] |
| | Residual | 1.469 | 668 | 0.002 | | |
| | Total | 4.660 | 674 | | | |
| 2 | Regression | 3.239 | 16 | 0.202 | 93.714 | 0.000[c] |
| | Residual | 1.421 | 658 | 0.002 | | |
| | Total | 4.660 | 674 | | | |

[a]Dependent Variable: PER
[b]Predictors: (Constant), OTHR, PREV, CONT, DUES, INVE, GRNT
[c]Predictors: (Constant), OTHR, PREV, CONT, DUES, INVE, GRNT, SEC6, SIZ, SEC3, SEC1, SEC7, SEC5, SEC4, SEC9, SEC8, SEC2

that are most reliable are also the sources of revenue that have the most potential for increasing a company's financial success. In addition, organizations that get a more significant proportion of their income from program sales, contributions, and grants will have more consistent financial success. As a consequence of this, the results give unmistakable evidence to support the contention that the concentration of income has a favorable influence on the financial performance of a charitable organization in Iraq. In addition, the local nonprofit organizations are almost entirely reliant on outside funding sources, and this fact alone is a key indication of the organizations' financial viability (Tables 7).

The findings of control variables suggest that total revenue has a statistically insignificant correlation with NPOs ' financial performance when we use PER as an indicator of performance, while total assets have been excluded. The finding in the table also indicates that the financial performance is not affected by all nonprofit subsectors in model 2 as most sector dummy variables coefficients are not statistically significant.

## 5 Conclusions and Discussion

This article develops on previous research on the accounting information system, revenue structure, and financial performance of non-profit organizations. We emphasize the role of accounting information in providing the data necessary to attract funding sources and enhance the financial performance of non-profit organizations. To this study, we have described the NPO's specific information criteria regarding changes in nonprofit accounting's financial reporting. Exploratory and quantitative analysis are employed in the paper to answer the research questions satisfactorily. The relationship between revenue structure and financial performance was analyzed

**Table 7** Regression coefficients of Model 2

| Coefficients[a] | | | | | | |
|---|---|---|---|---|---|---|
| Model | | Unstandardized coefficients | | Standardized coefficients | t | Sig. |
| | | B | Std. error | Beta | | |
| 1 | (Constant) | 0.486 | 0.005 | | 107.195 | 0.000 |
| | GRNT | 0.003 | 0.000 | 0.334 | 13.468 | 0.000 |
| | CONT | 0.002 | 0.000 | 0.396 | 17.383 | 0.000 |
| | PREV | 0.003 | 0.000 | 0.842 | 34.785 | 0.000 |
| | DUES | 0.000 | 0.002 | −0.003 | −0.141 | 0.888 |
| | INVE | 0.002 | 0.000 | 0.134 | 5.966 | 0.000 |
| | OTHR | 0.115 | 0.069 | 0.037 | 1.678 | 0.094 |
| 2 | (Constant) | 0.483 | 0.021 | | 22.524 | 0.000 |
| | GRNT | 0.003 | 0.000 | 0.335 | 12.672 | 0.000 |
| | CONT | 0.002 | 0.000 | 0.388 | 17.016 | 0.000 |
| | PREV | 0.003 | 0.000 | 0.830 | 31.560 | 0.000 |
| | DUES | −0.001 | 0.002 | −0.010 | −0.362 | 0.717 |
| | INVE | 0.001 | 0.001 | 0.075 | 2.301 | 0.022 |
| | OTHR | 0.096 | 0.070 | 0.031 | 1.373 | 0.170 |
| | SIZ | −1.970E-013 | 0.000 | −0.002 | −0.095 | 0.925 |
| | SEC1 | 0.000 | 0.021 | 0.001 | 0.011 | 0.991 |
| | SEC2 | 0.010 | 0.021 | 0.047 | 0.477 | 0.634 |
| | SEC3 | 0.008 | 0.021 | 0.035 | 0.378 | 0.705 |
| | SEC4 | 0.014 | 0.022 | 0.051 | 0.649 | 0.517 |
| | SEC5 | 0.008 | 0.022 | 0.031 | 0.369 | 0.712 |
| | SEC6 | −0.008 | 0.022 | −0.029 | −0.369 | 0.712 |
| | SEC7 | −0.006 | 0.022 | −0.019 | −0.275 | 0.783 |
| | SEC8 | 0.039 | 0.025 | 0.096 | 1.577 | 0.115 |
| | SEC9 | 0.006 | 0.023 | 0.018 | 0.283 | 0.778 |

[a]Dependent Variable: PER

using two performance measures: RVA (revenue to total assets) and PER (program expense to total revenue). In addition, the HHI index was used to compute the revenue diversity of Iraqi non-profit organizations using a sample of 140 organizations (675 observations) from 2014–2018. The study also investigates the relationship between Revenue on total assets (RVA) and six sources of revenue: grants (GRNT), contributions (CONT), programs revenues (PREV), organization's dues (DUES), investments (INVE), and other revenues (OTHR). Similar to Chikoto and Neely (2014), our study results indicate a significant relationship between the concentration of revenue and the financial performance of Iraqi non-profit organizations as measured by RVA and PER. It signifies excellent financial performance for organizations that significantly rely on a single revenue source.

However, the results of the control variables indicate that total revenue has no statistically significant relationship with the financial performance of non-profit organizations when PER is used as the success metric and total assets are omitted. The majority of dummy variable coefficients in the dummy field are not statistically significant, indicating that not all non-profit subsectors influence financial performance. The findings of the research indicate that nonprofit organizations that exhibit effective financial management are more inclined to solicit contributions from individual contributors. While there may be variations in the revenue streams of nonprofit organizations, it is important for such entities to cultivate a sense of trust and assurance among prospective contributors. Ultimately, individuals need assurance that their contributions will effectively uphold the causes they hold dear. In order to secure the financial sustainability of non-profit organizations, it is essential to have a varied financing base that incorporates both local and foreign sources of income within the organizational framework. Numerous directors of nonprofit organizations hold the belief that fostering awareness and understanding of the specific problem or population that the charity serves is frequently seen as the primary approach to incentivize potential contributors. Additionally, they may have a tendency to encourage cost reduction or frugality. However, stakeholders such as individuals, business partners, lawmakers, and other contributors want assurance that their financial contributions are allocated to an organization that maintains financial stability, has positive impact, and exhibits a sustainable trajectory. Demonstrating favorable financial indicators and a high level of financial acumen enables nonprofit organizations to maintain financial stability.

In conclusion, the findings of this study provide a guide for those involved in nonprofit organizations and administrators to determine the role of accounting knowledge in enhancing funding sources and enhancing performance in these organizations. The findings of the study indicate that Iraq and the majority of Middle Eastern nations have distinct funding requirements. The majority of local charitable organizations receive the majority of their funding from international organizations or foreign donors. This peculiarity may have cultural roots. This result necessitates that regulators of the accounting profession in Iraq and other regulatory bodies focus on enhancing the financial reporting and accountability system in nonprofit organizations in order to increase the reliability of financial reports. This study's findings serve as a guide for local and international regulators, donors, organization managers, and other stakeholders regarding the quality of financial reporting in nonprofit organizations in Iraq, as well as their impact on the financing structure and financial performance. The results of our study provide understanding for international donors of the relationship between the NPO's revenue diversity and financial performance. Accordingly, the international donor will support local NPOs with an equilibrium between internal and external funding sources to minimize the financial support to those NOPs. For future research, we suggest investigating the impact of national cultural values on the revenue diversity of NPOs using cross-country analysis for NPOs worldwide. This study will reveal the cultural Obstacles in front of funding of local NPOs.

## References


1. Stötzer, S., Kaltenbrunner, K., Grüb, B., Martin, S.: Coping with COVID-19—Which resilience mechanisms enabled Austrian nonprofit organizations to weather the pandemic storm? Schmalenbach J. Bus. Res. **74**(4), 497–535 (2022)
2. Amagtome, A.H., and Alnajjar, F.A.: Integration of financial reporting system and financial sustainability of nonprofit organizations: Evidence from Iraq. Int. J. Bus. & Manag. Sci. **10**(1) 2020
3. Irvin, R.A., Furneaux, C.W.: Surviving the black swan event: How much reserves should nonprofit organizations hold? Nonprofit Volunt. Sect. Q. **51**(5), 943–966 (2022)
4. Jiao, L., Harrison, G., Chen, J.: Revenue growth in not-for-profit organisations: The effects of interactive and diagnostic controls and organisational culture. Account. & Financ. **63**(2), 2273–2294 (2023)
5. Yan, J., Mmbaga, N., Gras, D.: In pursuit of diversification opportunities, efficiency, and revenue diversification: A generalization and extension for social entrepreneurship. Strateg. Entrep. J. **17**(1), 132–159 (2023)
6. Tristl, C.: Financializing water service provision with digital devices: Pro-commercialization alliances and the securitization of revenue from the unbankable in Mathare, Nairobi. Globalizations, pp. 1–20 (2023)
7. Bellucci, M., Cesa Bianchi, D., Manetti, G.: Blockchain in accounting practice and research: systematic literature review. Meditari Account. Res. **30**(7), 121–146 (2022)
8. Francisco, L., and Alves, M.-C.: Accounting information and performance measurement in a nonprofit organization: Performance measurement and management control: Global issues. Emerald Group Publishing Limited, pp. 465–487 (2012)
9. Goncharenko, G. (eds.): The accountability of advocacy NGOs: insights from the online community of practice. In: Book the accountability of advocacy NGOs: Insights from the online community of practice. Taylor & Francis, pp. 135–160 (2019)
10. Engel, C.J.: A primer on the accounting and reporting requirements for not-for-profit organizations. J. Public Manag. Res. **2**(1), 14–21 (2016)
11. Corvo, L., Pastore, L., Mastrodascio, M., Tricarico, L.: The impact of COVID-19 on public/third-sector collaboration in the Italian context. Sustainability **14**(4), 2228 (2022)
12. Vasicek, V., Kostic, M.D., muk, B.: User's satisafaction with the accounting information in non-profit organizations-case of croatia. Economic and Social Development: Book of Proceedings, pp. 430–438 (2017)
13. Harrison, V.S.: Why relationships fail: Donor insights on defining and understanding successes and failures in nonprofit stewardship. J. Public Relat.S Res., 1–23 (2023)
14. Offenheiser, R.C., Holcombe, S.H.: Challenges and opportunities in implementing a rights-based approach to development: An Oxfam America perspective. Nonprofit Volunt. Sect. Q. **32**(2), 268–301 (2003)
15. Frumkin, P., Keating, E.K.: Diversification reconsidered: The risks and rewards of revenue concentration. J. Soc. Entrep. **2**(2), 151–164 (2011)
16. Yan, W., Denison, D.V., Butler, J.S.: Revenue structure and nonprofit borrowing. Public Financ. Rev. **37**(1), 47–67 (2009)
17. Carroll, D.A., Stater, K.J.: Revenue diversification in nonprofit organizations: Does it lead to financial stability? J. Public Adm. Res. Theory **19**(4), 947–966 (2009)
18. Calabrese, T.D.: Testing competing capital structure theories of nonprofit organizations. Public Budg. Financ. **31**(3), 119–143 (2011)
19. Chikoto, G.L., Neely, D.G.: Building nonprofit financial capacity: The impact of revenue concentration and overhead costs. Nonprofit Volunt. Sect. Q. **43**(3), 570–588 (2014)
20. Wicker, P., Longley, N., Breuer, C.: Revenue volatility in German nonprofit sports clubs. Nonprofit Volunt. Sect. Q. **44**(1), 5–24 (2015)
21. Shea, J., Wang, J.Q.: Revenue diversification in housing nonprofits: Impact of state funding environments. Nonprofit Volunt. Sect. Q. **45**(3), 548–567 (2016)

22. Fischer, R.L., Wilsker, A., Young, D.R.: Exploring the revenue mix of nonprofit organizations: Does it relate to publicness? Nonprofit Volunt. Sect. Q. **40**(4), 662–681 (2011)
23. Al-Wattar, Y.M.A., Almagtome, A.H., Al-Shafeay, K.M.: The role of integrating hotel sustainability reporting practices into an Accounting Information System to enhance Hotel Financial Performance: Evidence from Iraq. Afr. J. Hosp., Tour. Leis. **8**(5), 1–16 (2019)
24. Costa, E., Goulart da Silva, G.: Nonprofit accountability: The viewpoint of the primary stakeholders. Financ. Account. & Manag. **35**(1), 37–54 (2019)
25. Awad, A.: Information and communication technologies role in alleviating poverty in Sub-Saharan Africa: Impacts and transmission channels. Sustain. Dev. **31**(2), 1149–1165 (2023)
26. Ritchie, W.J., Kolodinsky, R.W.: Nonprofit organization financial performance measurement: An evaluation of new and existing financial performance measures. Nonprofit Manag. Leadersh. **13**(4), 367–381 (2003)
27. Denison, D.V., Yan, W., Butler, J.: Managing risk and growth of nonprofit revenue. Journal of Public and Nonprofit Affairs **5**(1), 56–73 (2019)
28. Almagtome, A., Khaghaany, M., and Önce, S.: Corporate governance quality, stakeholders' pressure, and sustainable development: An integrated approach. Int. J. Math. Eng. Manag. Sci. **5**(6) (2020)

# Eco-Innovation Accounting, Sustainability and Firm Value: An Integrated Perspective

**Akeel Almagtome and Anmar Aljaafari**

**Abstract** The purpose of this study is to examine the effect of integrating sustainability reporting and Eco-innovation activities on the firm value. The study proposes an integrated reporting approach that combines the benefits of reporting on Sustainability in all dimensions (environmental performance, economic performance, social performance, and corporate governance) with innovation performance in all dimensions (product innovation, process innovation, organizational innovation, and marketing innovation) to increase the firm's value. The research analyzes the financial reports of 21 Iraqi industrial businesses from 2011 to 2020 using content analysis, giving 194 observations (company-year). The research employed GRI indicators (G4) for Sustainability, the Macron (2017) matrix for eco-innovation, and TobinQ for firm value. Sample firms report less on Sustainability and eco-innovation than the study's overall values. The research found that sustainability reporting significantly affects Iraqi firm value, the sample, and all its characteristics. The data also show that eco-innovation in all four aspects of the innovation scorecard (product, process, organizational, and marketing innovation) substantially improves the sample businesses' Firm value. The data also show that sustainability and eco-innovation reporting boosts corporate worth. This study provides an integrated perspective for improving the firm value using innovation and sustainability performance indicators. It integrates the industry 4.0 capabilities with Sustainable development Goals to enhance the firm value. The findings of this paper help regulators and economic policymakers develop sustainable development strategies at the national level and establish mechanisms that regulate the process of financial reporting in companies' financial statements.

**Keywords** Eco-innovation · Sustainability reporting · Firm value · Innovation accounting

A. Almagtome (✉) · A. Aljaafari
University of Kufa, Najaf, Iraq
e-mail: akeelh.alhasnawi@uokufa.edu.iq



S. Kot et al. (eds.), *Corporate Practices: Policies, Methodologies, and Insights in Organizational Management*, Springer Proceedings in Business and Economics,
https://doi.org/10.1007/978-981-97-0996-0_32

## 1 Introduction

The contemporary economic landscape is characterized by the emergence of Industry 4.0, whereby the significance of innovation and technological progress is paramount across all organizational spheres [1]. Notwithstanding the indisputable significance of technical innovation, another kind of innovation has effectively permeated domains outside technology [2]. The foundational factor influencing entrepreneurship and innovation inside local special economic zones is the proficiency of the employees. The inclusion of these factors is essential in the implementation of self-governance practices since they have a direct impact on the entrepreneurial potential within the local community. From the perspective of fostering the development of entrepreneurship and innovation, a crucial factor to consider is the establishment of conducive infrastructural conditions. The provision of infrastructural assistance is of utmost importance as it establishes the necessary circumstances for enhancing the efficiency and effectiveness of various operations regarding their timeliness and quality.

Moreover, the consideration of infrastructural factors is crucial in the context of automation, a concept closely associated with the phenomenon of globalization. Enhancements from a technical perspective are widely acknowledged. Special economic zones (SEZs) have particular significance due to their distinct concentration of business-oriented organizations [3]. Management innovation, a non-technological innovation that is difficult to duplicate and has the potential to provide a sustained competitive advantage, has been identified. Most companies understand the need to use business principles and strategic Sustainability to achieve Sustainability, considering the responsibility of influencing the environment [4]. The capacity to adapt to one's environment by using available resources to assure one's continued existence for the most prolonged period realistically feasible is indicated by the phrase "sustainability." In a business context, Sustainability is a strategy for creating long-term value that prioritizes social and environmental well-being without sacrificing either. Companies must prioritize innovation to thrive and remain highly competitive in today's dynamic business environment.

Furthermore, the term "eco-innovation" is widely used among industrial enterprises, illustrating the concept's importance [5]. To survive and prosper in today's cutthroat business climate, organizations must channel their innovative resources into developing products and services to help them stand out from the crowd and generate exceptionally high profits. It is crucial to the growth of these companies that novel concepts be conceived and developed. This paper aims to provide an integrated reporting framework for companies to improve the firm's Firm value. To this end, the paper examines the relationship between innovation and firm value. It also examines the relationships between sustainability performance indicators and firm value. Then, the paper examines the impact of the integration between eco-innovation performance and Sustainability performance indicators on the firm's Firm value.

## 2 Literature Review

Business innovation encounters a multitude of obstacles, including securing adequate funding, ensuring the availability of necessary equipment and infrastructure, training current employees, recruiting and training new personnel, and maintaining a suitable workforce. Additionally, challenges arise in planning employee and supplier services, expanding operations, and adopting new communication channels for migration purposes. The distinct characteristic of business innovation is in the voluntary acceptance of technology innovation at the societal level in daily circumstances. However, the introduction of innovative practices inside the workplace sometimes results in employee discontentment and encounters resistance [6]. Managing the company's internal and external environments has become an increasingly pressing issue for industrial firms, requiring radical adjustments to organizational strategy, structure, systems, and tools [7]. It's important to remember that being a socially responsible business also involves making investments in people, the planet, and partnerships. In response to this heightened scrutiny, a growing number of manufacturing companies are disclosing their social and environmental performance histories.

In recent decades, reports on corporate accountability and Sustainability have been published often. Because new ideas are crucial to a company's growth, accounting for innovations is a burgeoning field. Innovation accounting is a method for measuring and tracking the success of an organization's innovative activities, which may help with resource allocation and risk management. While new ideas may appear simple at first glance, the reality is that innovation is difficult and time-consuming, often expensive and risky, associated with ambiguity and uncertainty, and necessitates a commitment to change the dynamics of a routine relationship. Innovation is "the development and introduction of new products, services, and processes that result in a significant improvement in results" [8]. It relies heavily on creative thinking to succeed. In this context, "eco-innovation" is developing and using novel solutions that benefit the natural world. Streamlining manufacturing and product lifecycles in this way helps companies better protect the environment and reduce their overall carbon footprint. Recent studies have shown a positive correlation between eco-innovation and the success of green product development and environmental Sustainability [9–12]. Eco-innovation is the development of novel, competitive products, services, processes, procedures, and systems that minimize the use of natural resources to improve human well-being [13]. As part of the product's life cycle, eco-friendly improvements include energy efficiency, pollution avoidance, and waste recycling.

Innovation accounting is a relatively new field gathering traction as businesses increasingly rely on innovation to drive development. Innovation accounting is assessing and monitoring the performance of innovation activities to make more informed decisions regarding resource allocation and risk management [14]. Innovative accounting tools offer the best, best, and best organization and organizational performance to combat economic instability [15].

The innovation accounting literature offers diverse perspectives regarding the concept of innovation. These differences have implications for what innovation in accounting could mean for Sustainability. The oldest and most fundamental definition of innovation emphasizes the generation, acceptance, and implementation of new ideas, processes, products, or services. Innovation is defined as the practical application of new processes and products for an organization, which benefits the organization and its stakeholders. These innovations can be incremental or radical, depending on how different they are from current approaches. Innovations are created in processes that are believed to be manageable and manageable [16, 17]. The leading publications on innovation management revolve around the fundamental challenges and approaches to overcoming difficulties in innovation processes. It states that innovation is a gradual social process in which self-perceived information about a new idea is communicated and innovations develop through experimentation, improvement, and social interaction. Thus, information is critical in creating and disseminating sustainability innovations. It requires supporting sustainability innovations in production, products, and business models [18, 19], a reasonable basis for providing information on sustainability issues.

Given that accounting provides essential information to decision-makers in organizations and against the backdrop of significant shortcomings in traditional accounting approaches to dealing with sustainability issues, innovation in accounting for Sustainability is required. Therefore, this paper aims to describe what accounting innovation might involve for Sustainability. He highlights that one of the problems in properly managing innovation processes is that there are many definitions of innovation, and they vary significantly between the disciplines in which they are used.

## *2.1 Research Hypotheses*

The study is based on three main hypotheses, from which sub-hypotheses derive, commensurate with the constituent dimensions of each of the main study variables, as follows:

1 Sustainability reporting has a statistically significant effect on the firm value.

The following sub-hypotheses are derived from this hypothesis:

1.1 Sustainability reporting has a statistically significant effect on the firm's value using the economic performance index.
1.2 Sustainability reporting has a statistically significant effect on the Firm value using the environmental performance index.
1.3 Sustainability reporting has a statistically significant effect on the Firm value using the social performance index.
1.4 Sustainability reporting has a statistically significant effect on the Firm value using the governance indicator.

2. Eco-innovation level has a statistically significant effect on the firm value.

The following sub-hypotheses are derived from this hypothesis.

## 3 Data and Methodology

A quantitative strategy was used to evaluate the hypotheses and determine the research outcomes. This technique made use of the financial and non-financial data that was published in the annual reports of the firms that were included in the study sample. After considering missing data, the research sample included twenty-one manufacturing companies traded on the Iraq Stock Exchange between 2011 and 2020. The total number of observations (company years) came to 194. A content analysis was performed using a scale of 108 reporting indicators derived from the G4 sustainability reporting standards of the Global Reporting Initiative (GRI), covering four key sustainability dimensions (economic performance, environmental performance, social performance, and governance) [20]. The eco-innovation level was also measured using financial measures, including total fixed assets, the ratio of fixed assets to total assets, and innovation performance card measures. For this purpose, the matrix of Marcon et al. [21] for eco-innovation was adopted, consisting of 30 innovation indicators, which include four basic dimensions of eco-innovation (product innovation, process innovation, organizational innovation, and marketing innovation). As for measuring the Firm value, the ROA scale was adopted to determine the values of the study sample companies.

Innovation accounting can assist businesses in determining the monetary and non-monetary value of their innovation activities. This data can be used to make more informed judgments about where to invest in innovation and to monitor the return on investment from innovation activities. Innovation is inherently hazardous, and innovative accounting can assist businesses in managing these risks. By monitoring the progress of innovation activities, businesses can quickly identify and mitigate risks.

Innovation accounting can assist organizations in communicating the value of innovation to stakeholders, including investors, customers, and employees. This can help develop organizational support for innovation and attract new investment. There are a variety of methods available for accounting for innovation. Among the most prevalent techniques are:

**Financial Metrics.**
Non-financial metrics such as consumer satisfaction, employee engagement, and market share can also be used to assess the effectiveness of innovation activities.

**Non-Financial Metrics.**
Non-financial metrics such as consumer satisfaction, employee engagement, and market share can also be used to assess the effectiveness of innovation activities.

Innovation scorecards are a method for combining financial and non-financial measures into a singular innovation performance metric. The optimal accounting method for innovation will vary depending on the organization's requirements. However, all organizations that take innovation seriously should consider instituting some form of innovation accounting. Figure 1 indicates the theoretical model of the current study showing the main variables and relationships among them.

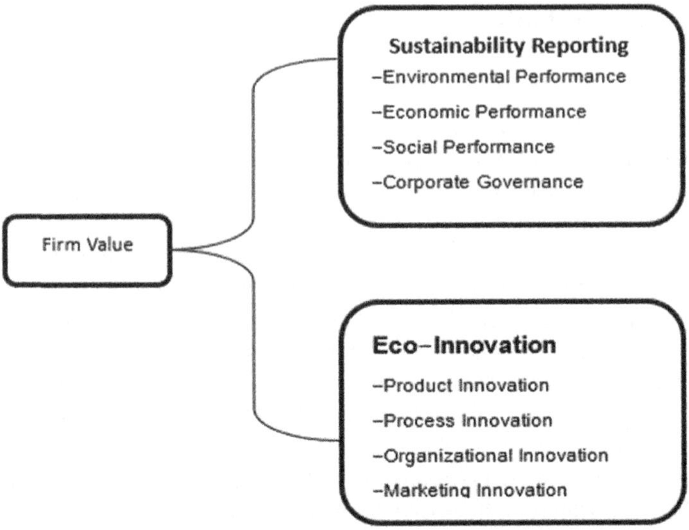


**Fig. 1** The conceptual model of the study

# 4 Results

## 4.1 Descriptive Statistics

Table 1 shows the descriptive statistics of the research variables at the level of all the research sample companies and for each company.

## 4.2 Statistical Analysis of the Study Variables

The current study deals with three main variables from which sub-variables or measurement dimensions are derived. These variables include:

### 4.2.1 Sustainability Reporting

Sustainability reporting is a form of non-financial reporting that enables companies to communicate their progress toward goals on various sustainability criteria, such as economic, environmental, social, and governance measures. For this study, a scale of 108 disclosure indicators was adopted, covering the basic dimensions of sustainability reporting, namely:

- Economic Performance

**Table 1** The descriptive statistics

| | N | Minimum | Maximum | Mean | Std. Deviation |
|---|---|---|---|---|---|
| ECO | 194 | 1.00 | 7.00 | 4.1082 | 1.83902 |
| ENV | 194 | 2.00 | 10.00 | 6.2732 | 2.08190 |
| SOCI | 194 | 2.00 | 10.00 | 5.8711 | 2.49121 |
| GVR | 194 | 3.00 | 8.00 | 5.4794 | 1.41131 |
| SRP | 194 | 8.00 | 35.00 | 21.7320 | 7.70575 |
| PRD | 194 | 0.00 | 4.00 | 1.8866 | 1.12785 |
| PRSS | 194 | 1.00 | 7.00 | 5.7113 | 1.02263 |
| ORGN | 194 | 2.00 | 5.00 | 3.9278 | 0.65574 |
| MRKT | 194 | 0.00 | 3.00 | 1.1907 | 0.49841 |
| ECO-IN | 194 | 3.00 | 19.00 | 12.7165 | 2.98997 |
| FMV | 194 | 0.00 | 0.76 | 0.0257 | 0.09988 |
| Valid N (listwise) | 193 | | | | |

Were
ECO = economic indicators
ENV = environmental indicators
SOCI = Social indicators
GVR = Governance indicators
SRP = Sustainability Reporting Performance
PRD = product innovation performance
PRSS = Process Innovation performance
ORGN = Organizational Innovation performance
MRKT = marketing innovation performance
ECO-IN = Total Index of Eco-innovation
FMV = Firm vale proxied by ROA

- Environmental Performance
- Social Performance
- Corporate Governance

Figure 2 shows the results of the analysis of sustainability reporting for the sample companies from 2011 to 2020 by analyzing the companies' annual reports during the study period to determine the level of disclosure of the specific indicators for each axis of the scale.

Figure 2 reveals the low sustainability reporting level in the sample companies during the study period. At its best, it was at most 34 out of the 108 points that make up the sustainability reporting matrix derived from the G4 reporting standards issued by the Global Reporting Initiative (GRI). The low level of sustainability reporting in the Iraqi environment is due to the requirement for this type of reporting. This makes companies reluctant to provide this information in their annual reports and suffice with the mandatory disclosure requirements. In addition, the requirements for reporting on Sustainability assume that companies issue a sustainability report

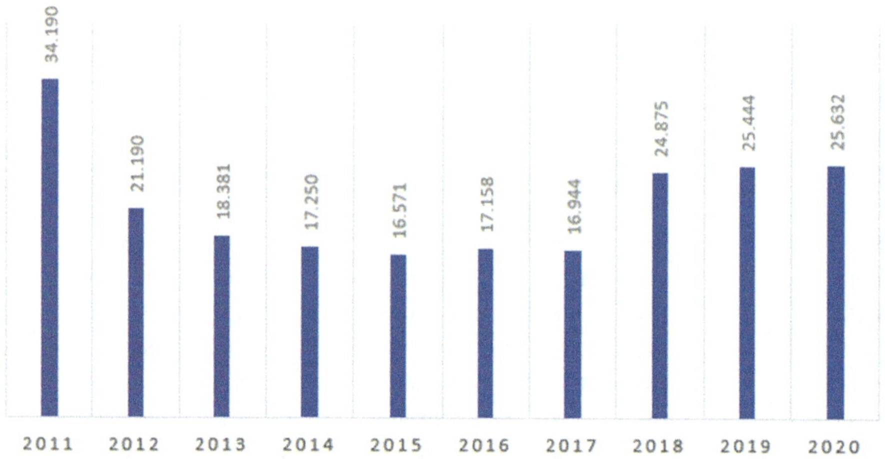


**Fig. 2** Average sustainability reporting for sample firms

periodically, and this report is not applicable in Iraq so far, so reporting on Sustainability is reflected in companies' annual reports, intentionally or unintentionally. The sense that companies in their annual reports may disclose some indicators voluntarily enhances the position of the company and the trust of users in it. In contrast, quantitatively or descriptively, other indicators are disclosed in response to professional or governmental laws or instructions or as outputs of the unified accounting system—for example, stocks of consumables, fuel, oils, and others.

### 4.2.2 Eco-Innovation

The second independent variable in our study is eco-innovation. Innovation performance indicators were used to determine the level of eco-innovation in the sample companies. Innovation scorecards are a way to combine financial and non-financial measures into a single measure of innovation performance. In our current study, the innovation performance card was used through the innovation performance measure consisting of 30 performance indicators covering four primary areas of innovation:

- Product innovation
- Process Innovation
- Organizational innovation
- Marketing innovation

Figure 3 shows the results of analyzing the level of eco-innovation according to the Macron scale (2017) consisting of 30 innovation performance indicators for the sample companies for the period from 2011 to 2020 by analyzing the annual reports of the companies during the study period to determine the level of eco-innovation for each of the scale pillars.

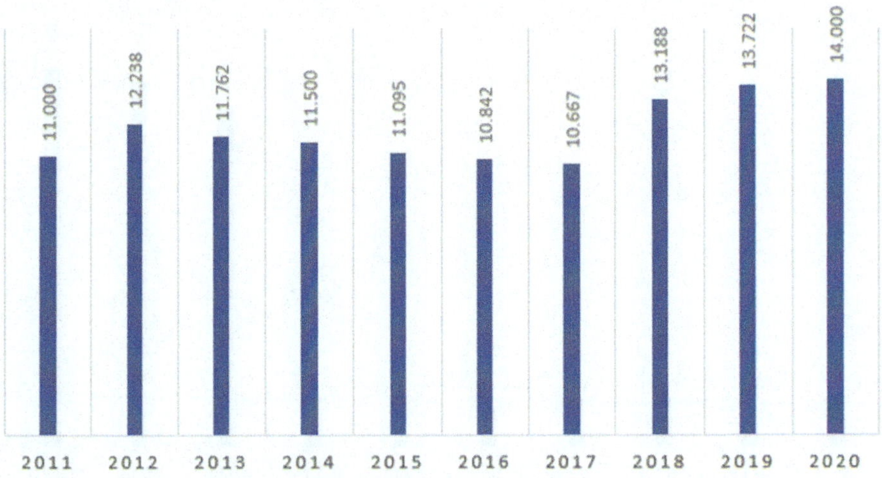


**Fig. 3** Average eco-innovation for sample firms

Figure 2 shows the low eco-innovation level in the research sample companies during the study period. If the highest average performance reached about 14 out of 30 points, it would be the measure of eco-innovation adopted in this study. Nevertheless, a relative increase in the level of the innovation index has been observed in recent years, if it reached about 11 points in 2011, while it reached about 24 points in 2020, which reflects a trend in 2015 among Iraqi companies to adopt innovative techniques in the fields of product, process, and organization, as well as marketing activities.

#### 4.2.3 Firm Value

The main dependent variable in this study is the firm value. The TobinQ scale was adopted as an indicator of the Firm value. The following figure shows the average firm value of the sample companies during the study period 2011–2020.

Figure 4 reveals the increase in the average firm value of the sample companies in the last years of the study period. This increase reflects the book value of the companies' assets during the recent period, accompanied by an increase in their market values.

### *4.3 Analysis of Hypotheses Testing Results*

These results extracted from the statistical analysis were based on the statistical program (SPSS). The number of companies = 21 companies for the period from 2011 to 2020, and the number of views N = 194 views (company-year) after excluding

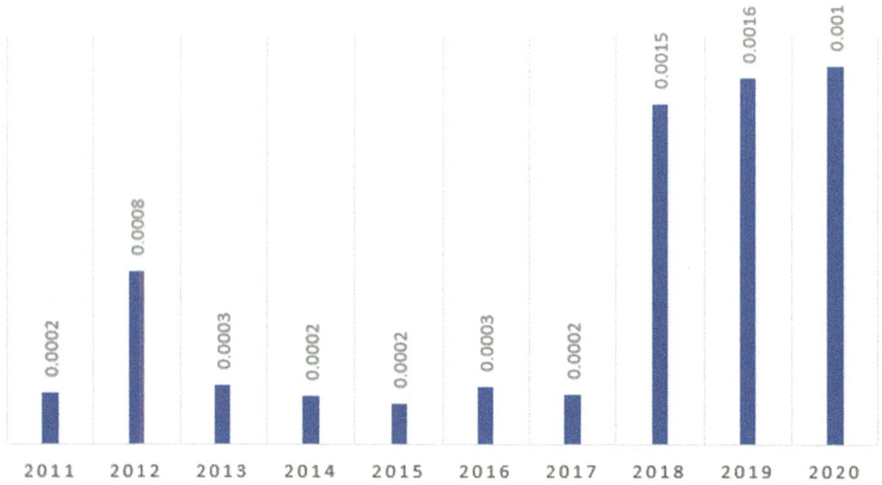


**Fig. 4** Average firm value for sample firms

the missing values resulting from the unavailability of company data in a specific year or the cessation of its activity at a significant level ** of 0.01.

**The First Main Hypothesis.**
States that *sustainability reporting has a statistically significant effect on the firm value.*
The results of the statistical analysis of the results of testing this hypothesis using the overall scale of Sustainability Reporting (G4) indicate that the independent variable Sustainability Reporting (SRP) has achieved a significant impact on the firm value (FMV) of the Iraqi companies, the research sample, at a significant level of 0.05, and that the independent variable (Sustainability Reporting (SRP)) explains its value (19%) of the dependent variable, the firm value (FMV), as the value of the determination coefficient was (R2 = 0.193).

This hypothesis showed that reporting on Sustainability has a strong 19% impact on the Firm value. This means that an increase in the level of sustainability performance will lead to an improvement in the Firm value. Reporting on Sustainability will improve the company's reputation in the community and the economic community towards the transition to clean energy and increase the efficiency of sustainability performance. It will undoubtedly be reflected in attracting investors because the products of this company are environmentally friendly and lead to reducing emissions and thus improving the Firm value.

**The second main hypothesis.**
States that (*Eco-innovation level has a statistically significant effect on the firm value*).
This hypothesis was tested using the eco-innovation scale prepared according to the Macron Matrix (2017) consisting of 30 eco-innovation indicators.

The results of testing this hypothesis using the eco-innovation scale (ECO-IN) show that the independent variable (ECO-IN) has achieved a significant impact on the dependent variable, the firm value (FMV) for the Iraqi companies, the research sample, at a significant level of 0.05, and that the independent variable (eco-innovation (ECO-IN)) explains its value (25%) of the dependent variable the firm value (FMV)). The value of the determination coefficient was (R2 = 0.248), which means that the fourth main hypothesis is accepted. Table 2 shows the summary of regression results for models 1, 2, and 3.

The results of this hypothesis showed that the level of eco-innovation performance has a strong effect of 25% on the firm value. This means that an increase in the level of eco-innovation performance will lead to an improvement in the firm value. As eco-innovation activities, whether those related to the product, process, organizational, or marketing innovation, will improve the company's reputation in society and the economic milieu towards benefiting from modern technologies and innovative devices and equipment in its activities and thus improving the firm value.

**The Third Main Hypothesis.**
States that *(Sustainability reporting and eco-innovation level have a statistically significant effect on the firm value).*
The results of testing this hypothesis using the Sustainability Reporting Scale (G4) and the Macron Matrix for Eco-innovation (ECO-IN) show that the two independent variables, Sustainability Reporting (SRP) and Eco-innovation Innovation (ECO-IN), have achieved a significant impact on the dependent variable, the firm value (FMV)

**Table 2** Regression results summary

| Variables | Model 1 | | Model 2 | | Model 3 | |
|---|---|---|---|---|---|---|
| | Coefficient | t | Coefficient | t | Coefficient | t |
| Constant | −0.098 | −5.061 | −0.186 | −6.799 | −0.241 | −6.325 |
| ECO | 0.022 | 6.089 | | | | |
| ENV | 0.022 | 7.087 | | | | |
| SOCI | 0.017 | 6.468 | | | | |
| GVR | 0.032 | 7.098 | | | | |
| SRP | 0.006 | 6.776 | | | −0.006 | −2.062 |
| PRD | | | 0.042 | 7.531 | | |
| PRSS | | | 0.032 | 4.730 | | |
| ORGN | | | 0.063 | 6.315 | | |
| MRKT | | | 0.140 | 13.447 | | |
| ECO-IN | | | 0.017 | 7.950 | 0.031 | 4.295 |
| $R^2$ | 0.193 | | 0.248 | | 0.264 | |
| $R^{2adj}$ | 0.189 | | 0.244 | | 0.256 | |
| F | 45.911 | | 63.206 | | 34.264 | |
| P | < 0.001** | | < 0.001** | | < 0.001** | |

for the Iraqi companies, the research sample, at a significant level of 0.05, and that the two independent variables (Sustainability Reporting (SRP) and Eco-innovation Innovation (ECO-IN)) explain its value (26%) of the dependent variable value The Company (FMV)). The value of the determination coefficient was (R2 = 0.264), which means that the fifth main hypothesis is accepted and that there is a complementary effect of applying each of the sustainability reporting criteria and eco-innovation indicators on the firm value.

This hypothesis showed that the integration of sustainability reporting and the level of eco-innovation performance has a strong impact of 26% on the firm value. This means that an increase in the level of sustainability reporting and the level of eco-innovation performance will lead to an improvement in the firm value, as eco-innovation activities, whether those related to the product, process, organizational, or marketing innovation, will improve the company's reputation in society and the economic milieu towards benefiting from modern technologies and innovative devices and equipment in its activities. The transition to clean energy and an increase in the efficiency of sustainability performance will undoubtedly be reflected in attracting investors since the products of this company are environmentally friendly and lead to a reduction in emissions, thus improving the firm value.

## 5 Conclusions and Discussion

The purpose of this study is to clarify the concepts of sustainability and eco-innovation, as well as the viability of applying them to Iraq's environmental situation. It also investigates the influence that sustainability reporting and eco-innovation activities have on the value of a firm. The other objective of this research is to examine how the inclusion of sections on sustainability and eco-innovation in the annual reports of Iraqi firms that are traded on the Iraq Stock Exchange impacts the value of such companies. This was done to determine the level of sustainability reporting that was presented. In addition, the amount of eco-innovation was evaluated using metrics from two distinct categories. These were financial metrics, such as the total fixed assets, the ratio of fixed assets to total assets, and innovation performance card indicators. To accomplish this goal, the Macron Matrix (2017) for eco-innovation was put into effect. This matrix comprises 30 innovation indicators and four essential elements of eco-innovation: product innovation, process innovation, organizational innovation, and marketing innovation. The TobinQ scale assessed the value of the organizations utilized as part of the research project's sample companies.

Research sample firms exhibit a low degree of reporting on sustainability and eco-innovation compared to the overall values of the study's measures. This finding is consistent with the findings of the study. The results of the study reveal, in addition, that reporting on Sustainability has a significant influence on the firm value for Iraqi enterprises, the research sample, and all of the research sample's dimensions. According to the findings, the amount of eco-innovation in each descriptive aspect (product innovation, process innovation, organizational innovation, and marketing innovation) has a considerable impact on the firm value of the enterprises that served as the study sample. However, when employing the financial indicators of eco-innovation (total fixed assets and the ratio of total fixed assets to total assets), this impact must be statistically verified.

In addition, the findings suggest that the incorporation of reporting on Sustainability and eco-innovation has a considerable influence on the value of the Firm. Because of this, the industrial companies that are listed on the Iraq Stock Exchange are required to take the initiative in applying the criterion (GRI) related to the sustainability of companies and through the statement of their interest in eco-innovation activities (product innovation, process innovation, organizational innovation, and marketing innovation), which is reflected in the Firm value. In addition, the statement must include the companies' social activities. The findings of this study are consistent with Abdurazzakov et al. [22] study, which demonstrated a robust association between investment in research and development endeavors and technology transfer, as well as the degree of innovation seen in Azerbaijani enterprises. This research provides evidence that using pre-existing technology created by universities and foreign firms may catalyze fostering creativity.

Conversely, the findings of the quantitative study suggest that although there exists a robust correlation between investment in research and development and innovation, there is a lack of substantial empirical evidence supporting the notion that acquiring licenses would enhance the innovative capacity of firms. This study provides an integrated model for improving the firm value using innovation and sustainability performance indicators. It integrates the industry 4.0 capabilities with Sustainable Development Goals to enhance the firm value. The findings of this paper help regulators and economic policymakers develop sustainable development strategies at the national level and establish mechanisms that regulate the process of financial reporting in companies' financial statements.

## References

1. Bharadwaj, S., Deka, S.: Behavioural intention towards investment in cryptocurrency: an integration of Rogers' diffusion of innovation theory and the technology acceptance model. Forum Sci. Oecon. **9**(4), 137–159 (2021)
2. Rajiani, I., Ismail N.: Management innovation in balancing technology innovation to harness universities performance in the era of community 4.0, *Polish Journal of Management Studies*, **19**, (2019)
3. Borowiecki, R., Makieła, Z.J.: Determinants of development of entrepreneurship and innovation in local areas of economic activity: a case study analysis. Forum Sci. Oecon. **7**(2), 7–24 (2019)
4. Almagtome, A.H., Al-Yasiri, A.J., Ali, R.S., Kadhim, H.L., Heider, N.B.: Circular economy initiatives through energy accounting and sustainable energy performance under integrated reporting framework. Int. J. Math., Eng. Manag. Sci. **5**(6), 1032 (2020)
5. Pichlak, M., Szromek, A.R.: Linking eco-innovation and circular economy—A conceptual approach. J. Open Innov.: Technol., Mark., Complex. **8**(3), 121 (2022)
6. Župerkienė, E., Paulikas, J., Abele, L.: Employee behavioural patterns in resisting the implementation of organisational innovation. Forum Sci. Oecon. **7**(3), 89–100 (2019)

7. Kurmanov, N., Tolysbayev, B., Amirova, G., Satkanova, R., Shamuratova N.: Foresight of the innovation manager competencies, Pol. J. Manag. Stud. **23**(2), (2021)
8. Kahn, K.B.: Understanding innovation. Bus. Horiz. **61**(3), 453–460 (2018)
9. Fernando, Y., Tseng, M.-L., Sroufe, R., Abideen, A.Z., Shaharudin, M.S., Jose, R.: Eco-innovation impacts on recycled product performance and competitiveness: Malaysian automotive industry. Sustain. Prod. Consum. **28**, 1677–1686 (2021)
10. Ceptureanu, S.I., Ceptureanu, E.G. Popescu, D., Anca Orzan, O.: Eco-innovation capability and sustainability driven innovation practices in Romanian SMEs, Sustain. **12** (17), 7106 (2020)
11. M. Moslehpour, K. Yin Chau, L. Du, R. Qiu, C.-Y. Lin, and B. Batbayar, "Predictors of green purchase intention toward eco-innovation and green products: evidence from Taiwan," Economic research-Ekonomska istraživanja, **36**(2) (2023)
12. Nguyen, N.P., Adomako, S.: Stakeholder pressure for eco-friendly practices, international orientation, and eco-innovation: A study of small and medium-sized enterprises in Vietnam. Corp. Soc. Responsib. Environ. Manag. **29**(1), 79–88 (2022)
13. Pichlak, M., Szromek, A.R.: Eco-innovation, sustainability and business model innovation by open innovation dynamics. J. Open Innov.: Technol., Mark., Complex. **7**(2), 149 (2021)
14. Corrado, C.A., Hulten, C.R.: "Innovation accounting, in measuring economic sustainability and progress, pp. 595–628. University of Chicago Press (2014)
15. Alsharif, H.Z.H., Shu, T., Obrenovic, B., Godinic, D., Alhujailli, A., Abdullaev, A.M.: Impact of entrepreneurial leadership and bricolage on job security and sustainable economic performance: An empirical study of Croatian companies during COVID-19 pandemic. Sustainability **13**(21), 11958 (2021)
16. Schaltegger, S., Etxeberria, I.Á., Ortas, E.: Innovating corporate accounting and reporting for sustainability–attributes and challenges. Sustain. Dev. **25**(2), 113–122 (2017)
17. Amato, S., Ricotta, F., Basco, R.: Family-managed firms, external sources of knowledge and innovation. Ind. Innov. **29**(6), 701–733 (2022)
18. Boons, F., Lüdeke-Freund, F.: Business models for sustainable innovation: state-of-the-art and steps towards a research agenda. J. Clean. Prod. **45**, 9–19 (2013)
19. Evans, S., et al.: Business model innovation for sustainability: Towards a unified perspective for creation of sustainable business models. Bus. Strateg. Environ. **26**(5), 597–608 (2017)
20. Almagtome, A., Khaghaany, M., Önce, S.: Corporate governance quality, stakeholders' pressure, and sustainable development: An integrated approach, Int. J. Math. Eng. Manag. Sci. **5**(6) (2020)
21. Marcon, A., de Medeiros, J.F., Ribeiro, J.L.D.: Innovation and environmentally sustainable economy: Identifying the best practices developed by multinationals in Brazil. J. Clean. Prod. **160**, 83–97 (2017)
22. Abdurazzakov, O., Illés, B.C., Jafarov, N., Aliyev, K.: The impact of technology transfer on innovation. Pol. J. Manag. Stud. **21**(2), 9–23 (2020)

# Determinants of Willingness to Use Mobile Payment Application in China

**Shulan Chen, Wornchanok Chaiyasoonthorn, and Singha Chaveesuk**

**Abstract** During the past 20 years, the Gross Domestic Product (GDP) has shown rapid growth in China. By 2022, the Chinese GDP has reached 121.02 trillion yuan, 12 times that of 2000. The rapid development of the Chinese economy has further improved the living standards of the Chinese. At the same time, the Chinese demand for transaction payments is increasing daily, and the people's requirements for transaction payments are also getting higher and higher. The growth of demand for transaction payment boosts the development of the mobile payment industry, which provides opportunities for the mobile payment market. At the same time, there are increasing types of mobile payment in the market, and the competition is becoming increasingly fierce, which brings challenges and difficulties to mobile payment operators. The purpose of this study is to build a model framework to help Chinese mobile payment operators identify factors that affect consumers' use of mobile payment to expand consumer groups and enhance the competitiveness of mobile payment companies. The novelty of this study is that, based on the SOR theory, the paper constructs a conceptual framework of mobile payment application users' willingness to use in China and finds out the key factors of willingness to use mobile payment. The study results show that the key factors influencing willingness to use mobile payment are usefulness, ease of use, service quality, cost, risk, perceived value, and satisfaction.

**Keywords** Mobile payment application · Willingness to use · S-O-R theory · China

S. Chen · W. Chaiyasoonthorn (✉) · S. Chaveesuk
KMITL Business School, King Mongkut's Institute of Technology Ladkrabang, Bangkok, Thailand
e-mail: Wornchanok.ch@kmitl.ac.th

S. Chaveesuk
e-mail: Singha@it.kmitl.ac.th

 
S. Kot et al. (eds.), *Corporate Practices: Policies, Methodologies, and Insights in Organizational Management*, Springer Proceedings in Business and Economics,
https://doi.org/10.1007/978-981-97-0996-0_33

# 1 Introduction

In China, the development of the internet, the rise of e-commerce, and the increasing use of smartphones have led to the rapid development of the mobile payment industry. Additionally, the COVID-19 pandemic over the past few years has further increased internet use. During the COVID-19 pandemic, people are more inclined to pay without cash [1] [2]. By 2022, China's population has exceeded 1,000,000,000, while the internet penetration rate was 75.6% [3]. According to "Top 10 Mobile Payment Institutions in 2021," released by Payment Encyclopedia, the top three mobile payment institutions in China were Alipay, Tencent Pay (including WeChat Pay, QQ Wallet, Tenpay), and Ping An 1Qianbao (including Ping An Pay electronic payment and Ping An Pay Technology). In 2021, the market share of Alipay was about 49%, and that of Tencent Finance was about 34%, the sum of which was 83%, almost monopolizing the entire Chinese mobile payment market. The market share of the remaining third-party payment was about 17%. In 2019, the Chinese E-CNY was launched with pilots in Shenzhen of Guangdong Province, Suzhou of Jiangsu Province, etc. As of June 2021, there were more than 1.32 million pilot scenarios for using digital RMB applications, and the total transaction amount reached 34.5 billion yuan [4].

With the launch of other new mobile payment applications (such as Huawei Pay digital RMB application) and the introduction of high-standard mobile payment policies, the Chinese mobile payment market will witness fiercer competition. In the fierce competition environment, how can Chinese mobile payment operators maintain or even increase their market share? It is an urgent issue that requires mobile payment operators to pay attention to.

There are two research questions in this paper: First, what are the influencing factors that affect the willingness to use mobile payment applications in China? Second, how do influencing factors affect the willingness to use? Heretofore, many scholars have researched the subject of mobile payment. However, most are based on the technology acceptance model, and only some papers apply the S-O-R theory to mobile payment. Therefore, the aim of this paper is, based on the S-O-R theory, to construct a conceptual framework for the willingness to use mobile payment applications in China, find out influencing factors (latent variables) that affect the willingness to use, and analyze the relationship between the latent variables.

Based on the S-O-R theory and the actual situation of mobile payment applications, this paper considers eight potential variables: Usefulness, ease of use, service quality, cost, risk, perceived value, satisfaction, and willingness to use, and constructs a conceptual framework. The framework will help to analyze factors affecting the willingness to use mobile payment applications in China and offer the direction and ideas for the follow-up product development and optimization reform of China's mobile payment operators.

## 2 Theoretical Foundation

### 2.1 *Mobile Payment and Mobile Payment Application*

Mobile Payment Forum [5] believed that to obtain a particular good or a specific business, the process in which both parties complete the transaction with the help of mobile devices is deemed mobile payment [5]. Karnouskos [6] believed that mobile payment refers to transactions completed by paying merchants with equal-value data from mobile devices. During the process, mobile devices can initiate payment requests and activate or confirm payments [6]. Chen and Tang [7] pointed out that mobile payment uses communication terminals and devices to complete payment, shopping, and other activities through interactive communication methods [7]. In this paper, mobile payment refers to payments made and completed by smartphones. A *mobile payment application* is a financial application that can help users complete the receipt and payment of goods through smartphones quickly [8].

### 2.2 *Willingness to Use*

Dodds (1991) believed that willingness to use can be regarded as the possibility of a consumer buying a particular service or product. Liu [9] believed that willingness to use refers to the psychological activities of whether consumers are interested in using or purchasing a product or service, which will affect their behaviors of using a product or service [9]. Hong and Slevitch [10] believed that willingness to use refers to the degree to which individuals are open to opportunities. She/he is willing to perform a specific behavior under circumstances that are conducive to a specific behavior [10]. In this paper, willingness to use refers to the psychological activities whether consumers are interested in using or purchasing a specific mobile payment application, which will affect their behaviors of using the mobile payment application.

### 2.3 *S-O-R Theory*

S stands for stimulus, which refers to external stimuli that impact the user or consumer. External stimuli can be either object stimuli, such as stimuli from products, or stimuli from the social environment, such as recommendations from relatives, friends, etc. O stands for Organism, which refers to the psychological and behavioral activities of individuals that link up external stimuli and individual responses [11]; R stands for Response, which refers to the behavior of the individual consumer. Under the stimulation of external factors, the consumer finally reacts through a series of

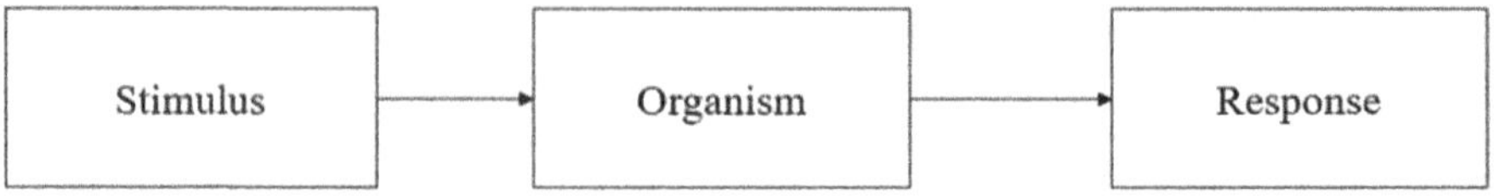


**Fig. 1** S-O-R theoretical model [9]

psychological activities, such as purchase, adoption, rejection, etc. [11]. The S-O-R theoretical model is shown in Fig. 1.

In the study of consumer behavior, S-O-R model has been favored by scholars, and it is often used to explain the mechanism of consumer behavior. In the past two years, some scholars have also applied S-O-R theory to the field of mobile payment, but rare. Currently, studies of mobile payment are mostly based on technology acceptance model [11–15] [51]. Applying SOR theory to the field of mobile payment is one of the innovations of this paper.

## *2.4 Influencing Factors*

**Usefulness.** According to Liu [12], Usefulness is the extent to which users can complete payment activities quickly, conveniently and effectively during the process of using mobile payment [12]. Wiese and Humbani [16], Setterstrom et al. [17] believed that usefulness represents the benefits enjoyed by consumers of mobile payment application, which is thought to have far-reaching impacts on the continuance intention [16] [17]. Usefulness in this paper refers to the fact that users can quickly and conveniently complete payment activities with mobile payment application. Mobile payment application is a useful product that can improve the quality of life as well as work efficiency [15] [52].

**Ease of Use.** Duane er al. [14], Schierz et al. [19] believed that ease of use is an acceptance driver for mobile application [18] [19] [50]. Hong and Slevitch [10] believed that ease of use refers to how easy it is to operate the process, which is a key factor in motivating customers to take advantage of new technologies [10]. Ease of use is user's subjective perception of effort and difficulty to use mobile payment.

**Service Quality.** Jinag [11] believed that service quality can be expressed as comprehensiveness, promptness and professionalism [11]. According to Rahardja et al. [20], good service quality can build up the transaction confidence and confidence of customers during the transaction process. Good service quality provides the promised service accurately, reliably, quickly and in real time [20] [48]. Service quality is quality of service that users feel when using mobile payment application, including the promptness, comprehensiveness and professionalism of services.

**Cost.** Will it cause data charges when using mobile payment service? Will it incur high fees during transaction payment, transfer, withdrawal, etc.? These direct transaction cost are a concern [9]. In addition, users will also evaluate the additional cost associated with the change in payment methods, such as the cost incurred in purchasing mobile devices [9]. The cost of this paper refers to all expenses incurred by buyers in the process of using mobile payment application. Cost includes transaction cost and extra cost.

**Risk.** Bauer [21] of Harvard University considered risk as the likelihood of adverse or uncertain consequences that consumers perceive when purchasing a product or service. Not all consumers perceive the risk, but once the adverse consequences are perceived by consumers, risk will occur [21] [22].The risk of this study refers to the adverse consequences that occur when using mobile payment, including financial risk, security risk, privacy risk and so on.

**Perceived Value.** Anderson and Gerbing [23] believed that perceived value is a kind of perceived utility, formed relative to price paid by customers, embodied in several aspects such as economy, technology, service and social interest [23]. Gale and Wood [24] believed that perceived value comes from quality management and refers to the result after comparing and weighing between a certain price and quality [24]. Day [25] believed that perceived value is balance between the benefit and the cost perceived by customers. If the benefit outweighs the costs, a transaction will be made; otherwise, transaction will not be made [25]. The paper defines perceived value as: perceived value is an overall subjective judgment and evaluation of product or service generated by customers through comparing their perceived gains and losses in the experience of consuming product or receiving service.

**Satisfaction.** Ashraf et al. [26] and Bhattacherjee [27] believed that satisfaction is a mental or emotional state that correlates with cognitive assessments of differences in expected performance [26] [27].Yu, et al. [28] believed that satisfaction is users' emotional response and post-evaluation in mobile payment experience [28]. Satisfaction is defined as the psychological pleasure generated by users' actual feelings after being stimulated by external factors, such as product, people, environment and other factors, which meet or exceed the expectations before use.

## *2.5 Conceptual Framework*

This study considers eight latent variables: usefulness, ease of use, service quality, cost, risk, perceived value, satisfaction, willingness to use, and establishes a conceptual framework to analyze factors influence willingness to use mobile payment application in China [15] [51] (See Fig. 2).

In this paper, a total of eight latent variables are considered, namely, usefulness, ease of use, service quality, cost, risk, perceived value, satisfaction, willingness to use. Stimulus(S) considers usefulness, ease of use, service quality, cost, risk, while Organism (O) considers perceived value, satisfaction, and Response(R) takes willingness to use into consideration. Applying SOR theory to the field of mobile payment is one of the innovations of this study.

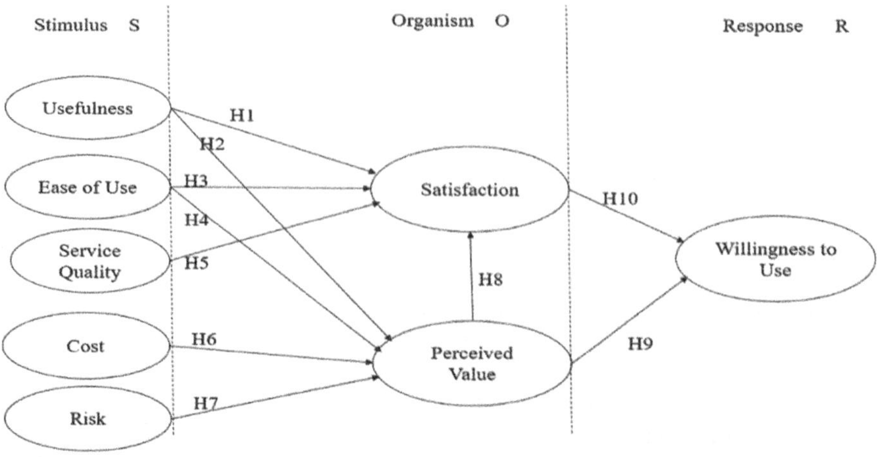


**Fig. 2** The conceptual framework

## 2.6 *Hypothesis Development*

**Usefulness.** Usefulness, as a core variable of the continuous use model of information systems, is a key factor in user satisfaction and willingness to use information systems [27] [29]. Wang [30] found that usefulness positively affects satisfaction [30]. Ashraf et al. [26] found that usefulness positively affects satisfaction [26]. Li [49] constructed a continuous usage willingness model on third-party mobile payment users based on the ECM-ISC and the VAM. He found in the empirical research that usefulness positively affects satisfaction as well as perceived value [12] [49]. Yang [31] found in the continuous research of users of massive open online courses that usefulness positively affects the user's satisfaction [31]. Wu and Huang [32] found in the analysis on the influencing factors of the continuous use of mobile social media by retail enterprises that the usefulness positively affects satisfaction and perceived value [32]. Basing on all the analysis above, the paper proposes two hypotheses:

H1: Usefulness positively affects satisfaction of mobile payment application users.
H2: Usefulness positively affects perceived value of mobile payment application users.

**Ease of Use.** Ease of use reflects users' subjective feelings about the ease or difficulty of operating information system, which will affect users' acceptance and satisfaction with user information system [33]. [10] found that ease of use positively affects satisfaction [10]. Natarajan et al. [34] found that ease of use positively affects satisfaction [34]. Leimeister et al. [35] found in their research on the survey of virtual network platform users that ease of use positively affects user satisfaction [35]. Li [49] constructed a continuous use willingness model on third-party mobile payment users basing on the ECM-ISC and the VAM, and found in the empirical research that ease of use positively affects satisfaction and perceived value [12][49]. [36] found that the ease of use positively affects perceived value in the empirical study on user intention to use a mobile hotel reservation system in the hotel industry [36].

Thus, the paper comes up with the following hypotheses:

H3: Ease of use positively affects satisfaction of mobile payment application users.
H4: Ease of use positively affects perceived value of mobile payment application users.

**Service Quality.** Chaveesuk et al. [37] found that service quality positively affects satisfaction [37]. Iqbal et al. [38] found that service quality positively affects customer satisfaction [38]. Basing on S-O-R theory, Jiang (2021) constructed a theoretical model on the formation mechanism while conducting research on the third-party mobile payment APP. She found that service quality positively affects satisfaction [11]. Li [39] conducted a study on commercial bank satisfaction evaluation and found that the higher the service quality is, the higher the user satisfaction will be [39]. Therefore, the paper proposes the following hypothesis:

H5: Service quality positively affects satisfaction of mobile payment application users.

**Cost.** Jiang [11], basing on S-O-R theory and from the perspective of user experience and social impact, built a theoretical model of the formation mechanism of users' willingness to use third-party mobile payment application. She found that cost negatively affects perceived value [11]. Liu and Tang [40] conducted a study on the impact of perceived value on consumers' willingness to mobile shopping, and found that cost negatively affects users' perceived value [40]. Zhou et.al [41] conducted a study on mobile commerce user acceptance behavior basing on perceived value and trust, and found that cost negatively affects users' perceived value [41]. Therefore, the paper puts forward the hypothesis:

H6: Cost negatively affects perceived value of mobile payment application users.

**Risk.** Cai [22] carried out a study on the influencing factors of user satisfaction in third-party mobile payment. She used empirical analysis and verification to analyze the path and degree of influence of various factors and variables on user satisfaction, and finally put forward targeted countermeasures and suggestions for the third-party mobile payment enterprises on how to effectively improve the user satisfaction. Through the research, she found that risk negatively affects perceived value [22] [49]. Liu and Tang [40] conducted a study on the impact of perceived value on consumers' willingness to mobile shopping. They found that risk negatively affects users' perceived value [40]. Zhou et.al [41] conducted a study on mobile commerce user acceptance behavior, and they found that risk negatively affects users' perceived value [41]. Basing on the above, the paper puts forward the hypothesis:

H7: Risk negatively affects perceived value of mobile payment application users.

**Perceived Value.** Zhou [42] conducted a study on the impact of perceived value on user acceptance of mobile commerce, and found that perceived value positively affects satisfaction [42]. Karjaluoto found that perceived value positively affects satisfaction [43]. In studying the satisfaction model of third-party mobile payment and analyzing its influencing factors, Bao [44] found that perceived value positively affects satisfaction [44]. Cai [22] carried out a study on the influencing factors of user satisfaction in third-party mobile payment. Through empirical analysis, she found that perceived value positively affects satisfaction [22]. Quan et al. [45], during the study of the impact of consumer innovation on the willingness to use mobile payment application, found that perceived value positively affects willingness to use [45]. Lin et al. [46] found that perceived value positively affects willingness to use [46]. Li [12] constructed a continuous use willingness model on third-party mobile payment users basing on the ECM-ISC and the VAM. He found in the empirical research that perceived value positively affects the willingness to use [12] [49]. Basing on the S-O-R theory, from the perspectives of user experience and social impact, Jiang [11] constructed a theoretical model on the formation mechanism while conducting research on the third-party mobile payment APP. The theoretical model was analyzed and verified through data collection and statistical analysis software SPSS 21.0 and AMOS 21.0. Through research, it is found that perceived value positively affects willingness to use [11]. Basing on the previous analysis, the paper proposes two hypotheses:

H8: Perceived value positively affects satisfaction of mobile payment application users.

H9: Perceived value positively affects mobile payment application users' willingness to use.

**Satisfaction.** [10] found that satisfaction positively affects willingness to use [10]. [47] found that satisfaction positively affects willingness to use [47]. Zhang [14] conducted an empirical study on the influencing factors of mobile payment continual use willingness. He found in the research that satisfaction positively affects the willingness to use [14]. Li [12] constructed a continuous use willingness model on third-party mobile payment users on the basis of the ECM-ISC and the VAM. He found in the empirical research that satisfaction positively affects the willingness to use [12]. Basing on S-O-R theory, from the perspectives of user experience and social impact, Jiang [12] constructed a theoretical model on the formation mechanism while conducting research on the third-party mobile payment APP. The theoretical model was analyzed and verified through data collection and statistical analysis software SPSS 21.0 and AMOS 21.0. Through research, it is found that satisfaction positively affects the willingness to use [11].

Based on the above, the following hypothesis is proposed:

H10: Satisfaction positively affects mobile payment application users' willingness to use.

## 3 Contributions and Conclusions

This paper has three contributions. Firstly, based on the literature and the S-O-R theory, combined with the challenges faced by China's mobile payment application, this paper constructs a conceptual framework to analyze the willingness to use mobile payment applications in China with a new perspective [15].

Secondly, eight latent variables are considered: usefulness, ease of use, service quality, cost, risk, perceived value, satisfaction, and willingness to use. Among them, Stimulus(S) considers the usefulness, ease of use, service quality, cost, and risk. At the same time, Organism (O) considers perceived value satisfaction, and Response(R) takes a willingness to use into consideration. It provides directions and ideas for Chinese mobile payment operators to carry out subsequent product research and development, optimize and reform, as well as a decision-making basis for stabilizing and expanding the payment market.

Thirdly, the paper proposes ten research hypotheses. H1: Usefulness positively affects the satisfaction of mobile payment application users. H2: Usefulness positively affects the perceived value of mobile payment application users. H3: Ease of use positively affects the satisfaction of mobile payment application users. H4: Ease of use positively affects the perceived value of mobile payment application users. H5: Service quality positively affects the satisfaction of mobile payment application users. H6: Cost negatively affects the perceived value of mobile payment application users. H7: Risk negatively affects the perceived value of mobile payment application users. H8: Perceived value positively affects the satisfaction of mobile payment application users. H9: Perceived value positively affects mobile payment application users' willingness to use. H10: Satisfaction positively affects mobile payment application users' willingness to use.

This paper aims to establish a conceptual framework based on the SOR theory and determine factors that affect willingness to use mobile payment in China. The study results show that the key factors influencing willingness to use mobile payment are usefulness, ease of use, service quality, cost, risk, perceived value, and satisfaction. In the subsequent study, we should collect data through questionnaire design and conduct empirical analysis through structural equation modeling.

## References

1. Kireyeva, A.A., Kredina, A., Vasa, L., Satpayeva, Z.T.: Impact of financial technologies on economic development: Theories, methods and analysis. J. Int. Stud. **14**(4), 286–303 (2021)
2. Jeffus, B., Zeltmann, S., Griffin, K., Chen, A.: The future of mobile electronic payments. J. Compet. Stud. **25**(3/4), 216–222 (2017)
3. The 51th China statistical report on internet development homepage, https://m.mpaypass.com.cn. Accessed 12 Dec 2022
4. Digital renminbi can optimize the existing payment system-digital renminbi series report three Homepage, https://www.fxbaogao.com/pdf?id=2950546%26query=%7B%22keywords%22%3A%22%E6%95%B0%E5%AD%97%E4%BA%BA%E6%B0%91%E5%B8%81%E7%B3%BB%E5%88%97%E6%8A%A5%E5%91%8A%E4%B8%89%22%7D%26index=0%26pid=.2021. Accessed 12 Dec 2021

5. Mobile Payment Forum: Enabling Secure, Intero Parable, and User-friendly Mobile Payment. Mob. Paym. Forum (2002)
6. Karnouskos, S.: Mobile payment: A journey through existing procedures and standardization initiatives. IEEE Commun. Surv. Tutor. **6**(4), 44–66 (2004)
7. Chen, H.P., Tang, J.: Research on mobile payment users and usage behavior. Manage. Sci. **6**, 50–57 (2006)
8. Yang, Y.X.: Research on optimal design of mobile payment APP usability based on principal component analysis. Hefei University of Technology, (2018)
9. Liu, J.L.: Research on factors affecting of consumer's adoption and mechanism of mobile payment. Beijing University of Posts and Telecommunications, 1–141 (2011)
10. Hong, C., Slevitch, L.: Determinants of customer satisfaction and willingness to use self-service kiosks in the hotel industry. J. Tour. Hosp. **7**(5), 1–7 (2018)
11. Jiang, S.: Research on the influencing factors of third-party mobile payment APP users' use intention. Guilin University of Technology,1–63 (2021)
12. Li, G.: Research on the influencing factors of users' continuous usage intention towards third-party mobile payment. Wuhan University of Technology, 1–98 (2018)
13. Ji, M.S.: Research on influencing factors of consumers' using willingness to mobile payment. Beijing University of Posts and Telecommunications, 1–61 (2016)
14. Zhang, J.: Imperial study that factors influence on the continued use willingness of mobile payment based on modified UTAUT. Dongbei University of Finance and Economics, 1–76 (2016)
15. Chen, S.L., Chaiyasoonthorn, W., Chaveesuk, S.: The mobile payment acceptance model of Chinese residents. ITCC2021, ACM, pp.63–68.Guangzhou, China (2021)
16. Wiese, M. , Humbani, M.: Exploring technology readiness for mobile payment app users. The International Review of Retail, Distribution and Consumer Research, 1–21 (2019)
17. Setterstrom, A.J., Pearson, J.M., Orwig, R.A.: Web-Enabled wireless technology: an exploratory study of adoption and continued use intentions. Behav. Inf. Technol. **32**(11), 1139–1154 (2013)
18. Duane, A., O'Reilly, P., Andreev, P.: Realising M-Payments: modelling consumers'willingness to M-pay using Smart Phones. Behav. Inf. Technol. **33**(4), 318–334 (2014)
19. Schierz, P.G., Schilke, O., Wirtz, B.W.: Understanding consumer acceptance of mobile payment services: an empirical analysis. Electron. Commer. Res. Appl. **9**(3), 209–216 (2010)
20. Rahardja, U., Sigalingging, C.T., Putra, P. O.H. et al.: The impact of mobile payment application design and performance attributes on consumer emotions and continuance Iitention. Original Research, 1–18 (2023)
21. Bauer, R.A.: Consumer behavior as risk taking. Proceedings of the 43rd National Conference of the American Marketing Assocation, Chicago, Illinois (1960)
22. Cai, Q.F.: Research on influencing factors of third-party mobile payment user satisfaction. Wuhan University of Technology, (2017)
23. Anderson, J.C., Gerbing, D.W.: Structural equation modeling in practiee: a review and reeornrnended two-step approach. Psyehologieal Bulletin **103**(3), 411–423 (1988)
24. Gale, B.T., Wood, R.C.( Eds.). Managing customer value: Creating quality and service that customers can see. Free Press. New York (1994)
25. Day, G.S.: The capabilities of market-driven organization. J. Mark. **58**(4), 37–52 (1994)
26. Ashraf, M., Ahmad, J., Hamyon, A. A. et al.: Effects of post-adoption beliefs on customers'online product recommendation continuous usage: an extended expectation-confirmation model. Cogent Business & Management, 1–18 (2020)
27. Bhattacherjee, A.: Understanding information systems continuance: an expectation confirmation mode. MIS Q. **25**(3), 351–370 (2001)
28. Yu, L.L., Cao, X.F., Liu, Z.Y. et al.: Understanding mobile payment users' continuance intention: a trust transfer perspective. Internet Research, 1–25 (2016)
29. Bhattacherjee, A., Perols, J., Sanford, C.: Information technology continuance: a theoretic extension and empirical test. J. Comput. Inf. Syst. **49**(1), 17–26 (2008)

30. Wang, M.C.H.: Determinants and consequences of consumer satisfaction with self-service technology in a retail setting. Manag. Serv. Qual.: Int. J. **22**, 128–144 (2012)
31. Yang, G.H.: Research on influencing factors of MOOC users' continued use behavior. Open Educ. Res. **22**(1), 100–111 (2016)
32. Wu, C.Y., Huang, L.: Retailers' continued willingness to use mobile social media. China Bus. Mark. **6**, 88–95 (2015)
33. Aldás-Manzano, J., Ruiz-Mafé, C., Sanz-Blas, S.: Exploring individual personality factors as drivers of M-shopping acceptance. Ind. Manag. Data Syst. **109**(6), 739–757 (2009)
34. Natarajan, T., Balasubramanian, S.A., Kasilingam, D.L.: Understanding the intention to use mobile shopping applications and its influence on price sensitivity. J. Retail. Consum. Serv. **37**, 8–22 (2017)
35. Leimeister, J.M., Huber, M., Bretschneider, U., et al.: Leveraging crowdsourcing: activation-supporting components for IT-based ideas competition. J. Manag. Inf. Syst. **26**(1), 197–224 (2009)
36. Wang, H.Y., Wang, S.H.: Predicting mobile hotel reservation adoption: Insight from a perceived value standpoint. Int. J. Hosp. Manag. **29**(4), 598–608 (2010)
37. Chaveesuk, S., Wutthirong, P., Chaiyasoonthorn, W. :The model of mobile payment system acceptance on social networks in Thailand: a conceptual framework. ICIME 2018, Salford, United Kingdom (2018)
38. Iqbal, M.S., Hassan, M.U., Habibah, U.: Impact of self-service technology (SST) service quality on customer loyalty and behavioral intention: The mediating role of customer satisfaction. Cogent Business & Management **5**, 1–23 (2018)
39. Li, B.T. :Research on customer satisfaction evaluation of commercial banks. Hebei Univ. Econ. Bus. (4), (2012)
40. Liu, Y.Z., Tang, D.N.: A study on the impact of perceived value on consumers' intention to mobile shopping—Based on TAM and VAM theoretical model. Lanzhou J. **4**, 169–175 (2015)
41. Zhou, T., Lu, Y.B., Zhang, J.L.: Research on the acceptance behavior of mobile business users based on perceived value and trust. J. Manag. **6**(10), 1407–1412 (2009)
42. Zhou, T.: The impact of perceived value on user acceptance of mobile commerce. International Symposium on Electronic Commerce and Security, 237–240 (2008)
43. Karjaluoto, H., Shaikh, A.A., Saarijärvi, H., a Saraniemi, S.: How perceived value drives the use of mobile financial services apps. Int. J. Inf. Manag. 1–10 (2018)
44. Bao,Y.D.: The Model and Influence Analysis of Consumers Satisfaction on Third-party Mobile Payment. Chang'an University,1–72 (2016)
45. Quan, D.M., Zhang, M.M., Qing, C.L.: Research on the influence of consumer innovation on the willingness to use mobile payment APP. Chinese Studies **81**, 317–341 (2019)
46. Lin, K.Y., Wang, Y.T., Huang, Y.K.: Exploring the antecedents of mobile payment service usage Perspectives based on cost–benefit theory, perceived value, and social influences. Online Inf. Rev. **44**(1), 299–318 (2019)
47. Junsawang, S.: Willingness to use self service technologies innovation on omnichannel for retail business in Thailand . King Mongkut's Institute of Technology Ladkrabang, 1–251 (2022)
48. Rahardja, U., Sigalingging, C.T., Putra, P.H., Hidayanto, A.N., Phusavat, K.: The impact of mobile payment application design and performance attributes on consumer emotions and continuance intention. SAGE Open, 1–18 (2023)
49. Li, C., Li, Y.: Research on user satisfaction of third-party mobile payment under the IoT environment-based on the structural equation mode. Journal of Intelligent & Fuzzy Systems **40**(4), 5853–5861 (2021)
50. Duane, A., Duane, P., Andreev, P.: Realising M-Payments: modelling consumers' willingness to M-pay using Smart Phones. Behav. Inf. Technol. **33**(4), 318–334 (2014)
51. Li, X.G., Zhu, X.K., Lu, Y.Y., Shi, D.Y., Deng, W.H.: Understanding the continuous usage of mobile payment integrated into social media platform: The case of WeChat Pay. Electronic Commerce Research and Applications, 1–17 (2023)
52. Zhong, J.Y., Dhir, A., Nieminen, M., Hämäläinen, M., Laine, J.: Exploring consumer adoption of mobile payments in China. Proceedings of International Conference on Making Sense of Converging Media, ACM, pp. 318–325. Tampere, Finland (2013)

# Volatility Linkage Between the Stock Exchange of Thailand and Major Stock Markets

**Budsabawan Maharakkhaka, Boonyachote Suteerawattananon, and Sutatt Ramasoot**

**Abstract** As global financial markets have become increasingly integrated, their linkage has become one of the most intriguing study areas. Even though there is little research on cointegration among financial markets in advanced and emerging countries, those aiming at the volatility transmission from the leading financial markets to the Stock Exchange of Thailand during crises still need to be expanded. This study investigates the volatility spillover from three leading capital markets, New York, Shanghai, and Japan Stock Exchange on the Stock Exchange of Thailand, using Dynamic Conditional Correlation Multivariate GARCH (DCC-MGARCH). The findings suggest that in the long term, the volatility of the SET index is more sensitive to its past volatility shock than that of the leading stock markets. Still, the impact of the past volatility shock in the major stock markets is more persistent than the impact of its past volatility shock. The return volatility of the SET index has been linked to the return volatility in the NYSE index. The sensitivity of the SET index to the volatility shock on the NYSE increased after the subprime. The spillover was driven further by the COVID-19 pandemic and lessened after the outbreak had recovered. The volatility shock of the SET index has been more persistent recently compared to the pre-subprime period. In contrast, the persistence of the volatility shock in significant stock markets tends to decrease after the subprime financial crisis. These results are applicable in portfolio risk management since the understanding of financial market relationships can help investors lower the risk.

**Keywords** Volatility stock exchange · Thailand · Stock market · DCC-GARCH

B. Maharakkhaka (✉) · S. Ramasoot
Stamford International University, Bangkok, Thailand
e-mail: budsabawan.maharakkhaka@stamford.edu

S. Ramasoot
e-mail: sutatt.ramasoot@stamford.edu

B. Suteerawattananon
North-Chiang Mai University, Chiang Mai, Thailand
e-mail: boonyachote@northcm.ac.th



S. Kot et al. (eds.), *Corporate Practices: Policies, Methodologies, and Insights in Organizational Management*, Springer Proceedings in Business and Economics,
https://doi.org/10.1007/978-981-97-0996-0_34

## 1 Introduction

The volatility of the stock market return has an immense impact on risk management. Risk-averse investors diversify their portfolios to minimize volatility. In an international portfolio, the global financial markets play a crucial part in determining the volatility of stock returns. As the financial markets worldwide become much more integrated, global portfolio returns become much more interrelated. The degree of linkage varies across countries depending on the size of capital flows, business connectivity, economies, and the nation's monetary policy to safeguard their financial stability [1, 2]. This linkage distributes economic growth and, unfortunately, may lead to financial contagions. Turbulence in one interconnected country can quickly develop into a regional and global crisis. The financial contagion spreads more easily from the large dominant economies to the developing economies, where economic infrastructures are less sophisticated [3].

The study on financial market volatility linkage is one of the most intriguing research areas. The early papers on volatility transmission in financial markets include [4–11]. Several papers focus particularly on volatility spillover from the developed to the developing economies [12–14]. There are studies directly aiming at the financial market interdependence among advanced and developing economies relative to the economic crises [15–20].Among the emerging markets, Thailand is a good representative of developing countries due to its rapid growth. The government is considered the world's leading emerging market. It is regarded in the MSCI Emerging Market Index [21]. In 2011, Thailand was upgraded from a low-income country to an upper-middle-income by the World Bank [22]. Despite the country's growth potential, it has been susceptible to various domestic and international factors. The Stock Exchange of Thailand is characterized by instability. It is vulnerable to political and financial shocks. The market has been through several financial crises, domestic military coups, and constitutional reforms [23–28]. In 2019, Thailand was hit by the outbreak of COVID-19. The pandemic crisis was unique. It results in a devastating impact on the economy as it was once in a century that all national borders were closed and economic transactions were almost frozen [29]. However, the study on dynamic volatility spillover from leading stock markets to emerging markets relative to the COVID-19 crisis is limited.

This present study has an objective to examine the spillover effect in terms of volatility transmission from the stock market in the leading economies, including the U.S., Japan, and China, to the Stock Exchange of Thailand. Using the data between 2000 and 2023, this research covers the regular market, subprime crisis, and the COVID-19 pandemic crisis period, allowing the study to investigate the dynamic of volatility linkage across various market environments.

## 2 Literature Review

In the last few decades, financial markets worldwide have become more integrated [1]. There have been massive capital fund flows across borders. The world's financial markets are becoming one global market [30, 31]. This development of interconnected financial markets has been driven forward by advanced information technology and financial market liberalization. Once segregated markets are united, the returns in each market reflect a global risk premium. The financial integration enlarges opportunities for investment and funding. It enhances efficiency in the local capital market and, at the same time, brings along additional risk [32]. The volatility of the stock market is transmitted across regions in the same way as capital flows. The studies on financial market integration vary from cointegration analysis, causality test and volatility studies [33–35]. While the cointegration test offers an analysis in the long run, it cannot detect whether the stock markets have become more or less integrated [36]. It does not allow dynamic variability of cointegrating relationships. The study of volatility linkage, on the other hand, has been widespread in determining short-term and long-term variations in volatility relationships among financial markets. It offers promising insight into the impact of volatility shocks as well as the persistence of the shocks that are caused by any markets [37–40]. Clements, Hurn, and Volkov [41] examined the volatility transmission in foreign exchange, stock, and bond markets in Japan, Europe, and the U.S. The multivariate GARCH model was employed to identify volatility and news spillover. In et al. [18] examined dynamic volatility transmission among stock markets in Hong Kong, South Korea, and Thailand during the Asian financial crisis using the multivariate EGARCH model. Both studies found significant volatility linkage among the financial markets.

However, the volatility transmission was asymmetric—each market in the study responds asymmetrically to its local news and the news in other countries. The volatility related to the negative news responds more rapidly than the volatility resulting from the good news. The reciprocal transmission of volatility was found between Hong Kong and South Korea, and unidirectional volatility transmission was found from Hong Kong to Thailand. Jebran, Chen, Ullah, and Mirza [42] investigated the volatility spillover effect among Asian countries, including China, Pakistan, Hong Kong, Sri Lanka, and India, during the pre and post-2007 financial crisis. They are using an extended EGARCH model. It is reported that stock markets have become more dependent since the global financial crisis. The degree of spillover may vary across countries.

In emerging economies, financial markets are influenced by international factors. The need for international capital flows makes these developing markets highly vulnerable to fluctuations in the world's leading markets. Balakrishnan et al. [43] studied how financial stress in advanced economies is transmitted to emerging economies using stress indices and the two-stage econometric approach based on Forbes and Chinn [3]. The results show that the stress indices in the advanced and emerging economies move closely together. Overall, financial stress is transmitted from advanced to emerging economies, but the impact varies depending on the strength of financial linkage. Spulbar, Trivedi, and Birau [44] extended the related literature to examine the abnormal volatility transmission in developed and developing countries using symmetric and asymmetric GARCH models. Their sample data were geographically dispersed in North America, Europe, and Asia. Though all markets in the study are highly volatile, the volatility spillover from developed to developing markets was evidenced. The financial markets of Hungary, the USA, Germany, India and Canada have become more related after the Global financial crisis.

Among the advanced economies, the U.S. represents the most influential market in the world. It produces the most significant GDP in the world and holds the largest stock exchange measured by market capitalization [22] as of January 2023. The New York Stock Exchange (NYSE) is the world's largest exchange. It has over 2,400 listed companies with a US$26.2 trillion market capitalization [22]. The stock market of the U.S. has had a global impact throughout the capital market history. In Asia, China and Japan are the two largest economies. They also have the largest stock markets in the continent. The Shanghai Stock Exchange (SSE) has a market capitalization of US$6.87 trillion and lists over 1,500 firms, while the Tokyo Stock Exchange (TSE) has a value of US$5.67 trillion market capitalization with 3,700 companies. With the immense size of these bourses, any fluctuation impacts the exposed emerging markets.

Shamiri and Isa [13] examined the information transmission of returns and volatility spillover from the markets in the U.S. and Japan to the Asia–Pacific markets using the BEKK-GARCH framework. By separating the sample period into pre- and post-Asian financial crises, the findings suggested that the Japanese and U.S. markets directly influence the volatility in Asia–Pacific stock markets. The U.S. market has more impact on the markets in Asia–Pacific after the crisis. Korea, Hong Kong, and Singapore were the most vulnerable markets in Asia during the study period. Sidek et al. [2] examined the impact of the U.S. subprime crisis and its spillover to the ASEAN-5 countries between 2000 and 2009 with the Two-stage least squares regression analysis. The findings suggest that financial contagion is unavoidable for small countries like the ASEAN-5. However, monetary policy and exchange rate control play roles in mitigating the impact of spillover from the crisis.

Chow [46] used Diebold and Yilmaz's [47] spillover index to examine volatility transmission among the U.S., the U.K., and ten Asian countries, including Thailand, between 1999 and 2016. It was found that the Global financial crisis has permanently increased the volatility transmission among Asian stock markets and the volatility spillover from the U.S., the U.K., and China. Gamba-Santamaria, Gomez-Gonzalez, Hurtado-Guarin, and Melo-Velandia [48] extended the spillover index model of Diebold and Yilmaz [47, 49] and employed DCC-GARCH to examine volatility transmission among the U.S. and four Latin American countries. The sample period between 2003 and 2016 includes the subprime crisis in the U.S. and the European Sovereign Bonds crisis. Thus, the volatility transmission in the crisis and non-crisis periods were evaluated. It was concluded that the spillover among the U.S., Chile, Brazil, Columbia, and Mexico varies over time. The volatility linkage was higher during financial crises. The directional transmission analysis suggested that the U.S.

and Brazil are the net transmitters. The stock market in Latin American countries has primarily been affected by the volatility of the stock market in the U.S., especially during the crisis. Chile, Columbia, and Mexico are net receivers of the volatility transmission. The volatility linkage among stock markets in Latin American countries has increased after 2012 when political uncertainty in Brazil negatively affected the regional market.

Hung [12] used a bivariate GARCH-BEKK model to study return and volatility spillover effects between China's stock market and Vietnam, Singapore, Thailand, and Malaysia's markets during the pre and post-global financial crisis. The results show that volatility in China's stock market has a substantial impact on the volatility of the stock market in the four countries. The volatility spillover, however, is less during the subprime crisis. The linkage in stock returns between China and the four ASEAN markets is significant in both pre and post-crisis periods. Vo and Ellis [51] applied a VAR and GARCH-BEKK model to examine the linkage between the Vietnam stock market and the influential stock market, namely the U.S., Hong Kong, and Japan. The study reports evidence of volatility linkage between the Vietnam Stock Market Index and the S&P 500 Index, Hang Seng Index, and Nikkei 225. Yousaf et al. [14] studied the returns spillover in the Latin American region. Their study used the BEKK-GARCH framework to evaluate the returns spillover between the world's leading financial markets and the developing markets of Latin American countries. The sample includes the stock markets in the U.S. and China as leading economies, and the markets in Brazil, Chile, Mexico, and Peru were representatives of Latin America. The results concluded that the U.S. stock market played a significant role in determining the returns in Latin American markets from 2000 to 2020 and the Chinese stock market crashes from 2015 to 2018. However, the U.S. did not contribute to price discoveries in Latin American markets during the Subprime crisis. There was a volatility spillover from the Chinese stock market to the stock markets in Latin America.

Zhong and Liu [51] used a multivariate GARCH model to investigate the dynamic conditional correlation and the spillover between Chinese and ASEAN5 stock markets. The finding suggested a positive conditional correlation between China and ASEAN5 countries. The stock market spillover was most significant during the Asian financial crisis, the subprime crisis, and the 2015 Chinese stock market crash. Recently, Choi [16] studied the volatility spillover among Northeast Asia and the U.S. using Diebold and Yilmaz's [47] spillover index. This study investigated the volatility linkages during the Global financial crisis and the COVID-19 pandemic crisis to identify the dynamic relationship of markets' volatility. The results suggested that volatility linkage among South Korea, Japan, China, and the U.S. is time-varying. The volatility linkages are stronger during financial crises. Interdependence among the four countries was higher during the Global financial crisis than during the COVID-19 pandemic.

The Stock Exchange of Thailand was founded in 1975. It is one of the most attractive investment destinations. The market has been the most liquid exchange since 2012, with an average trading volume of 93.9 billion per day [53]. Thailand ranks at the top of Bloomberg's 17 emerging markets based on economic performance indicators (SET, 2021). At the end of 2022, more than 600 listed companies [53]. This remarkable growth makes it a promising investment choice for diversifying international portfolios. There are studies examining particularly the volatility of the Stock Exchange of Thailand. Thampanya, Wu, Nasir, and Liu [54] Explained that the return volatility in the Stock Exchange of Thailand is determined mainly by the fundamental factors that include macroeconomic and corporate variables. Khositkulporn [55] identified factors affecting stock market volatility in Thailand using regression, causality tests, and GARCH models. The author concluded that Thailand's capital market has been primarily affected by the changes in its political environment and the volatility of the S&P 500 index.

Regarding the financial crisis, there were spillovers from the U.S. stock markets during the subprime financial crisis. However, the contagion was less severe compared to the time of the Asian financial crisis. As supported by Das [56] and Kritiyanavaj [57, 58] Asian markets, including Thailand, have become more sophisticated after a lesson from the Asian financial crisis. Thailand faced no direct impact from the Subprime shock.

During the COVID-19 pandemic, Thailand was the first to declare confirmed cases outside China in January 2020. Later, when the number of patients surged, business activities were forced to close. Dumduong et al. [59]. The once-in-a-century quarantine policy abruptly shocked the world's financial markets. The stock exchanges, including SET, called for a circuit break. The pandemic differs from other financial crises because health was a priority concern. The outbreak continued with the effort in quarantine and vaccination until June 2022, when most countries opened their borders and businesses resumed operation. Suwannapak and Chancharak [52] studied the volatility of the Stock Exchange of Thailand in response to COVID-19 using a multivariate BEKK-GARCH model. With this methodology, the interlinkage, the conditional correlations, and the conditional volatility dynamics are statistically examined. The volatility of the SET index returns responses asymmetrically to the increase in COVID-19 cases. There was generally a positive dynamic conditional correlation between the COVID-19 infection and SET index return.

The study on the variability of volatility transmission from the major financial markets to the Stock Exchange of Thailand regarding the financial crises is still limited. Thus, this study investigates the spillover effects from three major capital markets, namely the New York Stock Exchange, the Shanghai Stock Exchange, and the Japan Stock Exchange, on the Stock Exchange Thailand. The influence of the spillover effect from the three mentioned capital markets is compared before and during two recent major economic crises, the U.S. subprime and the Covid-19 pandemic.

## 3 Data and Methodology

This study investigated volatility transmission or the spillover from the New York Stock Exchange, Shanghai Stock Exchange, and Tokyo Stock Exchange to the Stock Exchange of Thailand using the Dynamic Conditional Correlations in a Multivariate Generalized Autoregressive Conditional Heteroskedasticity (DCC-MGARCH) model. The daily closing prices of the NYSE Composite index, the SSE Composite index, the Nikkie 225, and the SET index were retrieved between January 2000 and June 2023 as a sample period. The information was gathered from Yahoo Finance [53]. There are 5,733 data samples in total. To examine the spillover during various economic conditions, the whole sample was separated into five sub periods for the analysis before the Subprime crisis, during the Subprime crisis, after the Subprime and before the COVID-19 crises, during the COVID-19 crisis, and after the COVID-19 crisis periods. The ranges of each study period are described in Table 1.

The daily returns for each index were calculated as a natural log of ratio of the closing price ($P_t$) to the closing price of the previous day ($P_{t-1}$).

$$r_t = \ln\left(\frac{p_t}{p_{t-1}}\right) \tag{1}$$

The returns on SET, NYSE, SSE, and NIKKEI 225 indices were calculated as

$$RSET_t = \ln\left(\frac{SET_t}{SET_{t-1}}\right) \tag{2}$$

$$RNYSE_t = \ln\left(\frac{NYSE_t}{NYSE_{t-1}}\right) \tag{3}$$

$$RSSE_t = \ln\left(\frac{SSE_t}{SSE_{t-1}}\right) \tag{4}$$

**Table 1** Sample period description

| | Period | Description |
|---|---|---|
| 1 | 05 January 2000–23 May 2023 | Whole sample period (WHOLE PERIOD) |
| 2 | 04 January 2000–29 December 2006 | Before subprime crisis (PRE-SUB) |
| 3 | 03 January 2007–30 December 2010 | Subprime crisis (SUB) |
| 4 | 04 January 2011–15 November 2019 | After subprime before COVID-19 (POST SUB PRE COVID) |
| 5 | 18 November 2019–30 June 2022 | During COVID-19 (COVID) |
| 6 | 01 July 2022–23 June 2023 | After COVID-19 (POST COVID) |

*Source* Author

$$RNIKKEI_t = \ln\left(\frac{NIKKEI_t}{NIKKEI_{t-1}}\right) \quad (5)$$

All return series were validated for stationarity by Dickey & Fuller [61] unit root test to ensure their suitability for an estimation model. Then, the Dynamic Conditional Correlations in a Multivariate Generalized Autoregressive Conditional Heteroskedasticity (DCC-MGARCH) were estimated for each pair of the index return series, which include SET and NYSE, SET and SSE, and SET and NIKKEI, respectively. The results from an estimation will provide a comparative analysis of the impact of the world's leading markets on the SET index. Following Engle [39] and Orskaug [61], the estimation is defined as follows:

$$r_t = \mu_t + \varepsilon_t \quad (6)$$

$$\varepsilon_t = H_t^{1/2} z_t \quad (7)$$

$$H_t = D_t R_t D_t \quad (8)$$

where

$r_t = n \times 1$ vector of log returns of $n$ assets at time $t$,
$\mu_t =$ n $\times$ 1 vector of the expected value of the conditional $r_t$,
$\varepsilon_t = n \times 1$ vector of mean-corrected returns of $n$ assets at time $t$.
i.e. $E[\varepsilon_t] = 0$. $Cov[\varepsilon_t] = H_t$,
$H_t = n \times n$ matrix of conditional variances-covariance of $\varepsilon_t$ at time $t$,
$D_t = n \times n$, diagonal matrix of conditional standard deviation of $\varepsilon_t$ at time $t$,
$R_t = n \times n$ conditional correlation matrix of $\varepsilon_t$ at time $t$,
$z_t = n \times 1$ vector of i.i.d. errors such that $E[z_t] = 0$ and $E\left[z_t z_t^T\right] = I$.

The DCC-GARCH (1,1) was estimated with the maximum likelihood method. To clarify the representation of conditional correlation coefficients, we denote 1 to represent returns on the SET Index ($RSET_t$), 2 to represent returns on NYSE ($RNYSE_t$), 3 to represent returns on the SSE Index ($RSSE_t$), 4 to represent returns on NIKKEI ($RNIKKEI_t$). Table 2 summarizes the subscription.

**Table 2** Conditional coefficient subscription

| Series | Conditional coefficient subscription |
|---|---|
| $\boldsymbol{RSET_t}$ | 1 |
| $\boldsymbol{RNYSE_t}$ | 2 |
| $\boldsymbol{RSSE_t}$ | 3 |
| $\boldsymbol{RNIKKEI_t}$ | 4 |

*Source* Author

Coefficient $\alpha_{ij}$ indicates short-run dependence or sensitivity of asset $j$ to the volatility shock of asset $i$ and $\beta_{ij}$ indicates long-run volatility persistence of asset $j$ to the volatility shock of asset $i$.

The construction of the model for $RSET_t$ and $RNYSE_t$ is described as

$$RSET_t = a_1 + b_{11} RSET_{t-1} + b_{12} RNYSE_{t-1} + \varepsilon_{1,t} \tag{9}$$

$$RNYSE_t = a_1 + b_{21} RSET_{t-1} + b_{22} RNYSE_{t-1} + \varepsilon_{1,t}. \tag{10}$$

The conditional variance–covariance matrix for $RSET_t$ and $RNYSE_t$ is described as:

$$H_{11,t} = \alpha_{0,1} + \alpha_{11}\varepsilon^2_{1,t-1} + \beta_{11} H_{11,t-1} \tag{11}$$

$$H_{22,t} = \alpha_{0,2} + \alpha_{21}\varepsilon^2_{2,t-1} + \beta_{21} H_{22,t-1} \tag{12}$$

where

$$D_t = \begin{pmatrix} \sqrt{H_{1,t}} & 0 \\ 0 & \sqrt{H_{2,t}} \end{pmatrix}$$

$$R_t = \begin{pmatrix} 1 & \rho_{12,t} \\ \rho_{21,t} & 1 \end{pmatrix}$$

$$\varepsilon_t = \left(\varepsilon_{1,t}, \varepsilon_{2,t}\right)$$

$\varepsilon_t = n \times 1$ vector of mean-corrected returns of $n$ assets at time $t$, i.e. $E[\varepsilon_t] = 0$. $Cov[\varepsilon_t] = H_t$ and $\alpha_{DCC} + \beta_{DCC} \leq 1$ for stability to hold.

The construction of the model for $RSET_t$ and $RSSE_t$ is described as.

$$RSET_t = a_1 + b_{11} RSET_{t-1} + b_{13} RSSE_{t-1} + \varepsilon_{1,t}, \tag{13}$$

$$RSSE_t = a_1 + b_{31} RSET_{t-1} + b_{33} RSSE_{t-1} + \varepsilon_{1,t}. \tag{14}$$

The conditional variance–covariance matrix for $RSET_t$ and $RSSE_t$ is described as:

$$H_{11,t} = \alpha_{0,1} + \alpha_{11}\varepsilon^2_{1,t-1} + \beta_{11} H_{11,t-1}, \tag{15}$$

$$H_{33,t} = \alpha_{0,3} + \alpha_{31}\varepsilon^2_{3,t-1} + \beta_{31} H_{33,t-1}, \tag{16}$$

where

$$D_t = \begin{pmatrix} \sqrt{H_{1,t}} & 0 \\ 0 & \sqrt{H_{3,t}} \end{pmatrix}$$

$$R_t = \begin{pmatrix} 1 & \rho_{13,t} \\ \rho_{31,t} & 1 \end{pmatrix}$$

$$\varepsilon_t = (\varepsilon_{1,t}, \varepsilon_{3,t})$$

$\varepsilon_t = n \times 1$ vector of mean-corrected returns of $n$ assets at time $t$, I.E. $E[\varepsilon_t] = 0$. $Cov[\varepsilon_t] = H_t$, and $\alpha_{DCC} + \beta_{DCC} \leq 1$ for stability to hold.

The construction of the model for $RSET_t$ and $RNIKKEI_t$ is described as.

$$RSET_t = a_1 + b_{11} RSET_{t-1} + b_{14} RNIKKEI_{t-1} + \varepsilon_{1,t}, \tag{17}$$

$$RNIKKEI_t = a_1 + b_{41} RSET_{t-1} + b_{44} RNIKKEI_{t-1} + \varepsilon_{1,t}. \tag{18}$$

The conditional variance–covariance matrix for $RSET_t$ and $RNIKKEI_t$ is described as:

$$H_{11,t} = \alpha_{0,1} + \alpha_{11}\varepsilon_{1,t-1}^2 + \beta_{11} H_{11,t-1}, \tag{19}$$

$$H_{44,t} = \alpha_{0,4} + \alpha_{41}\varepsilon_{4,t-1}^2 + \beta_{41} H_{44,t-1} \tag{20}$$

where

$$D_t = \begin{pmatrix} \sqrt{H_{1,t}} & 0 \\ 0 & \sqrt{H_{4,t}} \end{pmatrix}$$

$$R_t = \begin{pmatrix} 1 & \rho_{14,t} \\ \rho_{41,t} & 1 \end{pmatrix}$$

$$\varepsilon_t = (\varepsilon_{1,t}, \varepsilon_{4,t})$$

$\varepsilon_t = n \times 1$ vector of mean-corrected returns of $n$ assets at time $t$, i.e. $E[\varepsilon_t] = 0$. $Cov[\varepsilon_t] = H_t$ and $\alpha_{DCC} + \beta_{DCC} \leq 1$ for stability to hold.

## 4 Results and Discussion

Table 3 presents a preliminary analysis of descriptive statistics. After the returns calculation, there are 5,733 returns samples. The mean, the minimum, and the maximum values were reported. Lastly, the standard deviation of each return series was presented. Estimating the GARCH model requires that the data series are stationary or do not contain unit roots. Table 4 exhibits the results of the ADF unit root test. The four data series in the study do not possess a unit root. All series are stationary. They are qualified for GARCH model estimation.

After examining the suitability of the data series, the DCC-MGARCH models were estimated. Table 5 exhibits DCC-MGARCH model estimations to explain the volatility linkage between the financial markets. Firstly, the estimation presents the sensitivity of the SET to its prior volatility shock. The volatility of the SET index is significantly influenced by its shock in most periods of the study ($\alpha_{11}$). Among the subperiods, SET's sensitivity to its volatility shock was highest during the subprime period. The persistence of the SET index to the shock of its volatility is represented by $\beta_{11}$. Overall, the SET index was highly persistent in its volatility shock ($\beta_{11} = 0.8100$). The persistence of the SET index to its shock is statistically significant in all subperiods except the time after the COVID-19 crisis. As with the sensitivity, the persistence of the SET index to its shock was not statistically significant after the COVID-19 period.

The sensitivity and persistence of the SET index to the volatility shock of the NYSE index are represented by the coefficients $\alpha_{21}$ and $\beta_{21}$ respectively. The estimation results suggest that the volatility of the SET index's returns was significantly sensitive to the volatility shock of the returns on the NYSE index in all periods in the study ($\alpha_{21}$). The SET index is more sensitive to its volatility shock than the NYSE index ($\alpha_{11} > \alpha_{21}$) before and during the subprime crisis. After the subprime, the SET index's volatility was more sensitive to the shock of the volatility of the NYSE index ($\alpha_{21} > \alpha_{11}$). The sensitivity of the SET index to the volatility shock on the NYSE

**Table 3** Descriptive statistics

| | $RSET_t$ | $RNYSE_t$ | $RSSE_t$ | $RNIKKEI_t$ |
|---|---|---|---|---|
| N | 5733 | 5733 | 5733 | 5733 |
| Mean | 0.0000850 | 0.0000652 | 0.0000622 | 0.0000413 |
| Minimum | −0.0931590 | −0.0547090 | −0.0401990 | −0.0546450 |
| Maximum | 0.0432670 | 0.0500560 | 0.0530040 | 0.0574770 |
| S.D | 0.0054281 | 0.0054032 | 0.0065311 | 0.0063554 |

*Source* Author

**Table 4** Unit root test

| | Augmented Dickey-Fuller | t-Statistic | Results |
|---|---|---|---|
| $RSET_t$ | −68.07** | −2.86 | Stationary |
| $RNYSE_t$ | −81.45** | −2.86 | Stationary |
| $RSSE_t$ | −75.16** | −2.86 | Stationary |
| $RNIKKEI_t$ | −77.12** | −2.86 | Stationary |

** indicate the level of significance at 5%

*Source* Author

**Table 5** DCC-MGARCH estimation results

| | Whole period | Pre-sub | Sub | Post sub Pre covid | Covid | Post covid |
|---|---|---|---|---|---|---|
| $\alpha_{11}$ | 0.1326** | 0.1002** | 0.1271** | 0.1096** | 0.1174** | 0.1736 |
| $\beta_{11}$ | 0.8100** | 0.5791** | 0.8530** | 0.8862** | 0.8557** | −0.1492 |
| $\alpha_{21}$ | 0.1046** | 0.0723** | 0.0986** | 0.1835** | 0.2508** | 0.0571** |
| $\beta_{21}$ | 0.8725** | 0.9147** | 0.8836** | 0.7441** | 0.7172** | 0.9253** |
| $\alpha_{DCC21} + \beta_{DCC21}$ | 0.9898 | 0.9564 | 0.9877 | 0.9609 | 0.8033 | 0.8482 |
| $\alpha_{31}$ | 0.0659** | 0.0835** | 0.0463 | 0.0503** | 0.0753** | 0.0305 |
| $\beta_{31}$ | 0.9288** | 0.8931** | 0.9433** | 0.9475** | 0.8491** | 0.9175** |
| $\alpha_{DCC31} + \beta_{DCC31}$ | 0.9993 | 0.9766 | 1.0070 | 1.0034 | 0.9491 | 0.9480 |
| $\alpha_{41}$ | 0.0993** | 0.0804** | 0.1198** | 0.1213** | 0.0924** | n/a |
| $\beta_{41}$ | 0.8784** | 0.8995** | 0.8644** | 0.8412** | 0.8554** | n/a |
| $\alpha_{DCC41} + \beta_{DCC41}$ | 0.9346 | 0.9180 | 0.9821 | 0.9885 | 0.9370 | 0.9065 |

** indicate the level of significance at 5%
*Source* Author

index was highest during the COVID-19 period ($\alpha_{21} = 0.2508$). Overall, the results indicate that the volatility of the SET index is highly persistent to the volatility of the NYSE ($\beta_{21} = 0.8725$). The persistence was statistically significant in all subperiods, and it was highest after the COVID-19 period ($\beta_{21} = 0.9253$). The persistence was least during the COVID-19 period ($\beta_{21} = 0.7172$). Among the subperiods, the volatility of the SET index had been more persistent than the volatility of the NYSE index until the subprime crisis period. However, after the subprime, the SET index volatility was more persistent. After the COVID-19 crisis until recently, the SET index volatility was not significantly sensitive to its shock and is not significantly persistent to its volatility. In that period, the SET index volatility was significantly sensitive to the volatility shock of the NYSE index, and the impact of the shock on NYSE returns volatility was statistically significant.

It can be summarized that the SET index was more sensitive to the volatility shock on the NYSE index after the subprime crisis. However, the SET index's persistence to the volatility shock on the NYSE index became less. After the COVID-19 period, the SET index was more persistent to the shock on NYSE index return volatility. The sums $\alpha_{DCC21} + \beta_{DCC21}$ indicate the validity of the DCC-GARCH estimation model to estimate volatility linkage between the NYSE and the SET indices. It is required that $\alpha_{DCC} + \beta_{DCC} \leq 1$ for estimation stability to hold.

The next estimation was to examine volatility linkage between the SSE and the SET indices. In the long term, the SET index return volatility was significantly sensitive to the shock on the volatility of the SSE index ($\alpha_{31} = 0.0659$). The volatility of SET index was significantly sensitive to the volatility of the SSE index before the subprime ($\alpha_{31} = 0.0835$) and during the COVID-19 crisis ($\alpha_{31} = 0.0753$). The sensitivity of SET index to the volatility shock on the SSE index during the recent pandemic was less compared to the sensitivity before the subprime crisis. However, the SET index return was more sensitive to its own volatility shock ($\alpha_{11}$) than to the volatility shock of SSE index ($\alpha_{31}$) in most periods. The results show that during the subprime crisis, the period after subprime, and the period after COVID-19 pandemic, the SET index was either not significantly sensitive to the shock on the SSE index returns or the had no convergence with the volatility of the SSE index.

The SET index has been highly persistent to volatility shock on the SSE index ($b_{31}$) in the long term. The impact of SSE index's volatility shock on the SET index ($\beta_{31} = 0.9288$) is more persistent than the impact from the shock of the SET index volatility itself ($\beta_{11} = 0.8100$). Before the subprime crisis, the SET index was more persistent to the volatility shock on the SSE index than to the shock of its own volatility ($\beta_{31} = 0.8931 > \beta_{11} = 0.5791$). In the COVID-19 pandemic, the SET index tended to have stronger persistence to its own volatility shock and became less persistence to the shock on of the SSE index ($\beta_{11} = 0.8557 > \beta_{31} = 0.8491$) The sums of coefficient $\alpha_{DCC31} + \beta_{DCC31}$ in most study periods confirm the stability of the model estimation. However, the sums of coefficient for the subprime period and the period thereafter do not confirm stability of the model. To conclude, the volatility transmission from the SSE index to the SET index varies across periods in this study. The SET index seems to be more sensitive to its own volatility shock than to the volatility shock of SSE index returns but the SET index has more persistence to the volatility shock on SSE index than to the shock of its own.

Lastly, the estimation of DCC-MGARCH model to examine volatility linkage between the SET index and the NIKKEI 225 index is exhibited in the final part of table 5. The results show that the SET index is significantly sensitive to the volatility shock on NIKKEI 225 in all periods of the study ($\alpha_{41}$) except after COVID-19 period. The SET index is slightly more sensitive to its own shock than to the shock on NIKKEI index ($\alpha_{11} > \alpha_{41}$) before and during the subprime crises, and during the COVID-19 period. After the COVID-19 period, there was no convergence between the volatility of the returns on the SET index and NIKKEI 225 index.

The significance of coefficients $\beta_{41}$ indicates that the SET index has been persistent to the volatility shock on the NIKKEI 225 index. The result for the whole sample suggests that the SET index returns volatility is slightly more persistent to the volatility shock on the NIKKEI 225 index ($\beta_{41} = 0.8784$) than to its own volatility shock ($\beta_{11} = 0.8100$) in the long run. The results are the same in sub periods analysis until the subprime period. After the subprime crisis the SET index was more persistent to its own volatility shock than to the volatility shock on the NIKKEI 225 index. The estimation was validated by the sums of coefficients $\alpha_{DCC41} + \beta_{DCC41}$. The stability of estimation was confirmed as the sums are less than one. Overall, the SET index was significantly sensitive to the volatility shock of the NIKKEI 225 index though the sensitivity is dynamic. There was a significance persistence of the SET index to the volatility shock of the NIKKEI 225 index in most periods.

Table 6 re-exhibits the estimation results to specifically compare the sensitivity and persistence of the SET index to the volatility shock in the three leading financial markets. For the whole study period, the SET index was most sensitive to the volatility shock in the NYSE index ($\alpha_{21} = 0.1046$) followed by the NIKKEI 225 index ($\alpha_{41} = 0.0993$). After the subprime crisis, the return volatility shock in U.S. stock market has the greatest influence on the volatility of the SET index ($\alpha_{21} = 0.1835$). The sensitivity is highest during the COVID-19 period ($\alpha_{21} = 0.2508$). The impact of NYSE's volatility shock on the SET index lessens after the COVID-19 time. The SET index was more sensitive to the volatility shock on the NIKKEI 225 index than to that of the SSE index. In the long-term, the impact of volatility shock on SSE index on the SET index ($\beta_{31} = 0.9288$) was the most persistent compared to the NYSE ($\beta_{21} = 0.8725$) and the NIKKEI 225 indices ($\beta_{41} = 0.8784$). The persistence of SET index to the volatility shock in leading market varies across time periods.

The finding extends the proposition of the prior literature regarding the impact of financial crises on the volatility spillover across financial markets. The volatility transmission exists from the U.S., China, and Japanese financial markets to that of Thailand, but the impact has been time-varying. These results support earlier studies by Balakrishnan et al. [43], Spulbar et al. [44], and Shimari and Isa [13]. The findings contribute to the evidence of Chow [46] and Gamba-Santomaria et al. [48], who suggested that the subprime financial crisis raised the spillover from the U.S. to the emerging market. The spillover from the Chinese market to Thailand during the subprime crisis was insignificant. This coincided with the earlier work by Hung [12], who showed that the spillover from China to Thailand during the subprime period was negligible. In addition, this present study contradicted Choi [1], who proposed that the volatility linkage was more vital during the subprime than during the COVID-19 period. Our evidence suggested that after the subprime financial crisis, the SET index has become more sensitive to the volatility shock in the U.S. The subprime crisis led to stronger integration of financial markets. The volatility transmission had strengthened between the U.S. and Thailand after the subprime. The spillover was driven further by the COVID-19 pandemic, and it was lessened after a recovery from the outbreak.

**Table 6** Comparison of estimation results

| | Whol period | Pre-sub | Sub | Post sub Pre covid | Covid | Post covid |
|---|---|---|---|---|---|---|
| $\alpha_{21}$ | 0.1046** | 0.0723** | 0.0986** | 0.1835** | 0.2508** | 0.0571** |
| $\alpha_{31}$ | 0.0659** | 0.0835** | 0.0463 | 0.0503** | 0.0753** | 0.0305 |
| $\alpha_{41}$ | 0.0993** | 0.0804** | 0.1198** | 0.1213** | 0.0924** | n/a |
| $\beta_{21}$ | 0.8725** | 0.9147** | 0.8836** | 0.7441** | 0.7172** | 0.9253** |
| $\beta_{31}$ | 0.9288** | 0.8931** | 0.9433** | 0.9475** | 0.8491** | 0.9175** |
| $\beta_{41}$ | 0.8784** | 0.8995** | 0.8644** | 0.8412** | 0.8554** | n/a |

** indicate the level of significance at 5%

*Source* Author

## 5 Conclusion

This study examined the volatility spillover from the world's leading stock market to the stock market in Thailand between 2000 and 2023 using the DCC-MGARCH estimation. The empirical findings have shown that the volatility of the SET index is more sensitive to its past volatility shock than that of significant stock markets. However, the impact of the past volatility shock in the major stock markets is more persistent than the impact of its past volatility shock. The return volatility of the SET index has been linked to the return volatility in the NYSE index. The sensitivity of the SET index to the volatility shock on the NYSE increased after the subprime. The spillover was driven further by the COVID-19 pandemic and lessened after the outbreak had recovered. The SET index is more sensitive to the shock in the NIKKEI 225 index's volatility than to that of the SSE index. Similar to the spillover from the U.S. market, the spillover from Japan and China are time-varying.

## References

1. Choi, S.Y.: Dynamic volatility spillovers between industries in the US stock market: evidence from the COVID-19 pandemic and black monday. N. Am.n J. Econ. Financ. **59**, 101614 (2022)
2. Sidek, N.Z.M., Abdul-Rahman, A., Zahirah, N.: Spill-over effect of us Sub-prime crisis on ASEAN-5 stock markets. Int. Rev. Bus. Res. Pap. **7**(3), 207–217 (2011)
3. Forbes, K.J., Chinn, M.D.: A decomposition of global linkages in financial markets over time. Rev. Econ. Stat. **86**(3), 705–722 (2004)
4. Baillie, R.T., Bollerslev, T., Redfearn, M.R.: Bear squeezes, volatility spillovers and speculative attacks in the hyperinflation 1920s foreign exchange. J. Int. Money Financ. **12**(5), 511–521 (1993)
5. Ehrmann, M., Fratzscher, M., Rigobon, R.: Stocks, bonds, money markets and exchange rates: measuring international financial transmission. J. Appl. Economet. **26**(6), 948–974 (2011)
6. Engle, R. F., Ito, T., Lin, W. L.: Meteor showers or heat waves? Heteroskedastic intra-daily volatility in the foreign exchange market (No. w2609). National Bureau of Economic Research, https://www.nber.org/system/files/working_papers/w2609/w2609.pdf. Accessed 4 March 2023
7. Hassan, S.A., Malik, F.: Multivariate GARCH modeling of sector volatility transmission. Q. Rev. Econ. Finance **47**(3), 470–480 (2007)
8. Ito, T., Roley, V.V.: News from the US and Japan: which moves the yen/dollar exchange rate? J. Monet. Econ. **19**(2), 255–277 (1987)
9. Lin, W.L., Engle, R.F., Ito, T.: Do bulls and bears move across borders? International transmission of stock returns and volatility. Rev. Financ. Stud. **7**(3), 507–538 (1994)
10. Melvin, M., Melvin, B.P.: The global transmission of volatility in the foreign exchange market. Rev. Econ. Stat. **85**(3), 670–679 (2003)
11. Veiga, B., McAleer, M.: Multivariate volatility and spillover effects in financial markets. In 2nd International Congress on Environmental Modelling and Software. Brigham Young University, Utah (2004)
12. Hung, N.T.: Return and volatility spillover across equity markets between China and Southeast Asian countries. J. Econ., Financ. Adm. Sci. **24**(47), 66–81 (2019)
13. Shamiri, A., Isa, Z.: Volatility transmission: what do Asia-Pacific markets expect? Stud. Econ. Financ. **27**(4), 299–313 (2010)
14. Yousaf, I., Ali, S., Wong, W.K.: Return and volatility transmission between world-leading and Latin American stock markets: portfolio implications. J. Risk Financ. Manag. **13**(7), 148 (2020)

15. Antonakakis, N., Vergos, K.: Sovereign bond yield spillovers in the Euro zone during the financial and debt crisis. J. Int. Finan. Markets. Inst. Money **26**, 258–272 (2013)
16. Choi, S.Y.: Volatility spillovers among Northeast Asia and the US: Evidence from the global financial crisis and the COVID-19 pandemic. Econ. Anal. Policy **73**, 179–193 (2022)
17. Engle, R.F., Gallo, G.M., Velucchi, M.: Volatility spillovers in East Asian financial markets: a MEM-based approach. Rev. Econ. Stat. **94**(1), 222–223 (2012)
18. In, F., Kim, S., Yoon, J.H., Viney, C.: Dynamic interdependence and volatility transmission of Asian stock markets: Evidence from the Asian crisis. Int. Rev. Financ. Anal. **10**(1), 87–96 (2001)
19. Lien, D., Lee, G., Yang, L., Zhang, Y.: Volatility spillovers among the US and Asian stock markets: A comparison between the periods of Asian currency crisis and subprime credit crisis. N. Am.n J. Econ. Financ. **46**, 187–201 (2018)
20. Sadiq, M., Hsu, C.C., Zhang, Y., Chien, F.: COVID-19 fear and volatility index movements: empirical insights from ASEAN stock markets. Environ. Sci. Pollut. Res. **28**, 67167–67184 (2021)
21. MSCI (2023). MSCI Emerging Markets IMI (USD) Fact Sheet, https://www.msci.com/documents/10199/97e25eb7-9bd0-4204-bea9-077095acf1d3. Accessed 7 May 2023
22. World Bank. GDP ranking, https://datacatalog.worldbank.org/search/dataset/0038130. Accessed 11 March 2023
23. Apaitan, T., Luangaram, P., Manopimoke, P.: Uncertainty in an emerging market economy: Evidence from Thailand. Empir. Econ. **62**(3), 933–989 (2022)
24. Khanthavit, A.: An event study analysis of Thailand's 2019 general election: A long window of multiple sub-events. Int. J. Financ. Res. **11**(4), 502–514 (2020)
25. Korn, T., Sorasart, S.: Practical Approach to Identify Business Cycles for Equity Investment in Thailand. Thammasat Rev. **24**(1), 168–196 (2021)
26. Korn, T., Sorasart, S.: Equity sector investing over business cycles: The case of Thailand. Kasetsart J. Soc. Sci. **43**(2), 379–386 (2022)
27. Nimkhunthod, W.: An impact of political events on the stock exchange of Thailand. Thammasat University, Bangkok (2007)
28. Talthip, K., Sukcharoensin, S.: A practical approach to identify business cycles for equity investment in Thailand. Thammasat Rev. **24**(1), 168–196 (2021)
29. Zhang, D., Hu, M., Ji, Q.: Financial markets under the global pandemic of COVID-19. Financ. Res. Lett. **36**, 101528 (2020)
30. Ng, A.: Volatility spillover effects from Japan and the US to the Pacific-Basin. J. Int. Money Financ. **19**(2), 207–233 (2000)
31. World Bank: Private capital flows to developing countries. Oxford University Press, New York (1997)
32. Cajueiro, D.O., Gogas, P., Tabak, B.M.: Does financial market liberalization increase the degree of market efficiency? The case of the Athens stock exchange. Int. Rev. Financ. Anal. **18**(1–2), 50–57 (2009)
33. Park, J.H., Lee, S.: Global financial crisis: Background, prospects, and its impacts on Korea. Seoul J. Econ. **22**(1), 77 (2009)
34. Stoupos, N., Kiohos, A.: Euro area stock markets integration: empirical evidence after the end of 2010 debt crisis. Financ. Res. Lett. **46**(B), 102423 (2022).
35. Wang, J., Cui, M., Chang, L.: Evaluating economic recovery by measuring the COVID-19 spillover impact on business practices: evidence from Asian markets intermediaries. Econ. Chang. Restruct. **56**, 1629–1650 (2023)
36. Arouri, M.E.H., Jouini, J., Nguyen, D.K.: On the impacts of oil price fluctuations on European equity markets: Volatility spillover and hedging effectiveness. Energy Econ. **34**(2), 611–617 (2012)
37. Bollerslev, T.: Generalized autoregressive conditional heteroskedasticity. J. Econ. **31**(3), 307–327 (1986)
38. Engle, R.F.: Statistical models for financial volatility. Financ. Anal. J. **49**(1), 72–78 (1993)
39. Engle, R.F.: Dynamic conditional correlation: A simple class of multivariate generalized autoregressive conditional heteroskedasticity models. J. Bus. Econ. Stat. **20**(3), 339–350 (2002)

40. Engle, R. F., Sheppard, K.: Theoretical and empirical properties of dynamic conditional correlation multivariate GARCH (No. w2609). National Bureau of Economic Research, https://www.nber.org/system/files/working_papers/w8554/w8554.pdf. Accessed 5 May 2023
41. Clements, A.E., Hurn, A.S., Volkov, V.V.: Volatility transmission in global financial markets. J. Empir. Financ. **32**, 3–18 (2015)
42. Jebran, K., Chen, S., Ullah, I., Mirza, S.S.: Does volatility spillover among stock markets varies from normal to turbulent periods? Evidence from emerging markets of Asia. J. Financ. Data Sci. **3**(1–4), 20–30 (2017)
43. Balakrishnan, R., Danninger, S., Elekdag, S., Tytell, I.: The transmission of financial stress from advanced to emerging economies. Emerg. Mark. Financ. Trade **47**(sup2), 40–68 (2011)
44. Spulbar, C., Trivedi, J., Birau, R.: Investigating abnormal volatility transmission patterns between emerging and developed stock markets: A case study. J. Bus. Econ. Manag. **21**(6), 1561–1592 (2020)
45. Yahoo Finance. The 10 largest stock exchanges in the world, https://sg.finance.yahoo.com/news/10-largest-stock-exchanges-world-233000404.html?guccounter=1#:~:text=1.,more%20than%202%2C400%20listed%20companies. Accessed 11 May 2023
46. Chow, H.K.: Volatility spillovers and linkages in Asian stock markets. Emerg. Mark. Financ. Trade **53**(12), 2770–2781 (2017)
47. Diebold, F.X., Yilmaz, K.: Better to give than to receive: Predictive directional measurement of volatility spillovers. Int. J. Forecast. **28**(1), 57–66 (2012)
48. Gamba-Santamaria, S., Gomez-Gonzalez, J.E., Hurtado-Guarin, J.L., Melo-Velandia, L.F.: Stock market volatility spillovers: Evidence for Latin America. Financ. Res. Lett. **20**, 207–216 (2017)
49. Diebold, F.X., Yilmaz, K.: Measuring financial asset return and volatility spillovers, with application to global equity markets. Econ. J. **119**(534), 158–171 (2009)
50. Vo, X.V., Ellis, C.: International financial integration: Stock return linkages and volatility transmission between Vietnam and advanced countries. Emerg. Mark. Rev. **36**, 19–27 (2018)
51. Zhong, Y., Liu, J.: Correlations and volatility spillovers between China and Southeast Asian stock markets. Q. Rev. Econ. Finance **81**, 57–69 (2021)
52. Suwannapak, S., Chancharat, S.: Stock market volatility response to COVID-19: Evidence from Thailand. J. Risk Financ. Manag. **15**(12), 592 (2022)
53. Yahoo Finance. Stock index historical data, https://finance.yahoo.com/quote/%5ENYA?p=%5ENYA%26.tsrc=fin-srch. Accessed 17 June 2023
54. Thampanya, N., Wu, J., Nasir, M.A., Liu, J.: Fundamental and behavioural determinants of stock return volatility in ASEAN-5 countries. J. Int. Finan. Markets. Inst. Money **65**, 101193 (2020)
55. Khositkulporn, P.: The factors affecting stock market volatility and contagion: Thailand and South-East Asia evidence. Victoria University, Melbourne (2013)
56. Das, D.K.: How did the Asian economy cope with the global financial crisis and recession? A revaluation and review. Asia Pac. Bus. Rev. **18**(1), 7–25 (2012)
57. Kritayanavaj, B.: Housing and real estate bubbles: Thailand's boom and bust cycles. Hous. Financ. Int. **23**(2), 3 (2008)
58. Kritayanavaj, B.: Global Financial and Economic Crises 2008–2009: A View from Thailand. Hous. Financ. Int. **23**(3), 7–12 (2009)
59. Dumdoung, S., Pariyaprasert, W., Vimolphattanatham, N.: The impact of Political Events and Covid-19 pandemic on Return Volatilities of 3 Sectors in the Stock Exchange of Thailand during 2019 to 2021. In AU Virtual International Conference on" Entrepreneurship & Sustainability in Digital Era" under the theme of" Challenges of Organizational & Business Management in Dynamic Digital Dimension", pp. 241–247. Assumption University, Bangkok (2021)
60. Dickey, D.A., Fuller, W.A.: Distribution of the estimators for autoregressive time series with a unit root. J. Am. Stat. Assoc. **74**(366a), 427–431 (1979)
61. Orskaug, E.: DCC-GARCH model-with various error distributions. Norwegian Computing Center, https://citeseerx.ist.psu.edu/viewdoc/download?doi=10.1.1.417.5480&rep=rep1&type=pdf (2009). Aaccessed 14 August 2022

# Exploring Influential Factors in the Purchasing of Nutritional Supplements for the Elderly

**Yuhang Wang and Nuttawut Rojniruttikul**

**Abstract** This research investigates the factors influencing purchasing decisions of nutritional supplements for the elderly in Thailand, focusing on health consciousness, quality assurance, social influence, accessibility, and perceived benefits. A comprehensive questionnaire survey was conducted with 385 customers from diverse demographic backgrounds. Reliability and validity tests were performed to ensure the robustness of the data. The results of the survey revealed high levels of health consciousness and quality assurance as significant drivers for the purchasing of nutritional supplements. Social influence, accessibility, and perceived benefits also played influential roles. Multiple linear regression analysis confirmed the strong relationships between these factors and supplement purchases. The findings offer valuable insights for healthcare providers, marketers, and policymakers aiming to enhance the nutritional health of Thailand's aging population. This research provides a comprehensive understanding of the dynamics affecting nutritional supplement purchases for the elderly in Thailand, promoting informed decision-making and healthcare improvement.

**Keywords** Health consciousness · Quality assurance · Social influence · Accessibility · Perceived benefits

## 1 Introduction

The aging population is a global phenomenon, and with it comes an increased focus on the health and well-being of older individuals. Nutritional supplements play a significant role in supporting the dietary needs of the elderly, as they often face

Y. Wang · N. Rojniruttikul (✉)
KMITL Business School, King Mongkut's Institute of Technology
Ladkrabang, Bangkok, Thailand
e-mail: nuttawut.ro@kmitl.ac.th

Y. Wang
e-mail: caramenl0607@163.com

 
S. Kot et al. (eds.), *Corporate Practices: Policies, Methodologies, and Insights in Organizational Management*, Springer Proceedings in Business and Economics,
https://doi.org/10.1007/978-981-97-0996-0_35

unique nutritional challenges due to age-related changes in metabolism, decreased appetite, and potential nutrient deficiencies [1]. The aging demographic poses an urgent challenge in addressing the evolving dietary needs and health requirements of this population segment. Consequently, using nutritional supplements has become increasingly common among the elderly, their caregivers, and those involved in their healthcare decisions [2].

Understanding the influential factors that shape the purchasing of nutritional supplements for the elderly is of paramount importance. This research seeks to shed light on the underlying motivations, considerations, and decision-making processes that drive the selection and procurement of these supplements. By comprehensively exploring these factors, this research aims to contribute to a deeper understanding of consumer behavior in the context of health and nutrition for the aging population [3].

The decision to purchase nutritional supplements for the elderly is a multifaceted process influenced by various internal and external factors. Internally, individual health concerns, perceptions of supplement effectiveness, and personal beliefs about the importance of nutrition in aging play pivotal roles in the decision-making process [4]. Additionally, the distinctive nutritional requirements of the elderly population present a unique challenge, driving the demand for effective supplementation. Externally, factors such as healthcare provider recommendations, marketing strategies, cost considerations, and the availability of information sources significantly influence consumer choices [5].

Moreover, the role of technology and the internet cannot be understated in this context. The digital age has provided consumers with unprecedented access to information about nutritional supplements, creating both opportunities and challenges in making informed choices [6]. Online reviews, health-related apps, and e-commerce platforms have become integral components of the supplement purchasing landscape [7]. This technological shift influences how consumers access and process information when purchasing.

Despite the growing prevalence of nutritional supplement use among the elderly, there remains a gap in our understanding of the intricate dynamics that shape these consumption patterns. This study aims to address this gap by conducting a comprehensive survey analysis, engaging with consumers who purchase supplements for the elderly, and exploring the interplay of various factors in their decision-making process. This research aims to provide insights that will not only contribute to academic knowledge but also have practical implications for healthcare providers, marketers, and policymakers seeking to enhance the nutritional health of the aging population [8].

The research "Exploring Influential Factors in the Purchasing of Nutritional Supplements for the Elderly" seeks a nuanced understanding of the factors that drive consumer behavior in this domain. By uncovering the motivations and considerations that influence the selection and purchase of nutritional supplements for older individuals, this research aims to contribute to the promotion of healthier aging and improved nutritional outcomes for the elderly population [9]. This research aims to bridge the gap between the growing use of nutritional supplements among the elderly and the complex factors influencing their purchasing decisions.

## 2 Literature Review

### *2.1 Health Consciousness*

Health consciousness, often characterized as an individual's awareness of their health status and proactive efforts to maintain or improve it, is pivotal in influencing dietary choices and supplement purchases [10]. Within the context of the elderly population, maintaining optimal health and well-being is a primary concern, and this concern often translates into a heightened sense of health consciousness [11]. Numerous studies have elucidated the significant link between health consciousness and the propensity to purchase nutritional supplements, particularly among the elderly demographic [12]. Health-conscious individuals tend to firmly commit to their health goals, seeking to address potential nutritional gaps or deficiencies that arise with age [13]. As such, they are more likely to be proactive consumers of nutritional supplements, perceiving these products as valuable tools for enhancing or maintaining their health.

A study found that elderly individuals with higher health consciousness scores were more likely to purchase nutritional supplements [14]. These individuals displayed a heightened awareness of their dietary habits and nutrient intake, recognizing the need for additional nutritional support. Health-conscious elderly consumers often engage in practices such as reading product labels, researching health benefits, and seeking recommendations from healthcare professionals [15].

Furthermore, health-conscious elderly consumers are often motivated to prevent age-related health conditions and maintain their independence and vitality [16]. They perceive nutritional supplements as a means to fortify their overall health, bridge nutritional gaps, and support specific health goals such as bone health, cognitive function, and heart health.

The literature underscores the substantial influence of health consciousness on the purchasing of nutritional supplements by the elderly. As individuals become more health-conscious, their awareness of the potential benefits of supplements grows, leading to increased engagement in purchasing these products. Therefore, the following hypothesis is proposed:

H1: Health consciousness positively influences the purchasing of nutritional supplements for the elderly.

## 2.2 Quality Assurance

Quality assurance is a pivotal factor in purchasing nutritional supplements for the elderly. Older individuals, just like any other consumers, want to be sure they are getting products that are safe, reliable, and effective.

The quality of nutritional supplements can have a substantial impact on the buying decisions of the elderly. Seniors are often more cautious about the products they consume, and rightly so. Their health may be more vulnerable, and they need to be confident that the supplements they choose are high-quality.

Several aspects of quality assurance influence the choices of elderly consumers:

**Safety and Purity:** Quality assurance ensures supplements are free from contaminants and meet safety standards. This is of utmost importance for elderly consumers, as their immune systems may not be as robust as younger individuals [17].

**Reliability:** Elderly consumers look for consistent results from the supplements they take. Quality assurance measures guarantee that the product contains the ingredients it claims to, in the right amounts, ensuring reliability in the supplement's effects [18].

**Transparency and Labeling:** Elderly consumers pay close attention to the labeling and information about a product. They prefer supplements that have clear and accurate labeling, making it easier for them to understand the benefits and potential risks [19].

**Product Reputation**: Quality assurance, or the lack thereof, can significantly influence the reputation of a product or brand. Word of mouth and online reviews play a critical role in the choices of elderly consumers.

**Regulatory Compliance**: Quality assurance also entails complying with regulatory standards and guidelines. For example, in Thailand, the Food and Drug Administration (FDA) regulates dietary supplements. Seniors often prefer products that have met these regulatory standards.

Quality assurance is a substantial factor influencing the purchasing decisions of the elderly regarding nutritional supplements. They prioritize safety, reliability, transparency, and the overall reputation of the product or brand. These factors combined significantly influence whether they choose to purchase a particular supplement. Therefore, the following hypothesis is proposed:

H2: Quality assurance positively influences the purchasing of nutritional supplements for the elderly.

## 2.3 Social Influence

The purchasing decisions of the elderly regarding nutritional supplements are often significantly influenced by social factors. As individuals age, their reliance on social networks and the influence of family, friends, and healthcare professionals tend to play a substantial role in shaping their choices.

**Family Recommendations:** Family members, especially adult children and spouses, frequently influence the elderly's choices. When a family member suggests a particular nutritional supplement, older individuals are more likely to consider it. Family recommendations often come from a place of care and concern, making them a powerful social influence [20].

**Peer Opinions:** Seniors may also seek advice from their peers and friends, especially those of similar age and health conditions. When a peer shares their positive experience with a specific supplement, it can sway the elderly's purchasing decision. Peer influence is powerful within senior communities and support groups [21].

**Healthcare Professionals**: The guidance of healthcare professionals, such as doctors, dietitians, or pharmacists, is highly regarded by the elderly. When a healthcare expert recommends a supplement, seniors often trust this advice. Healthcare professionals are perceived as credible sources of information, impacting the choices made by the elderly [22].

**Media and Online Resources:** Seniors increasingly use the internet and media for information. Websites, forums, and social media platforms provide a space for seniors to seek advice and share experiences. Positive online reviews or mentions in the media can substantially impact the decisions of the elderly [23].

**Cultural Norms:** Cultural norms and beliefs can also exert a significant influence on the choices of older consumers. In Thailand, for instance, respect for elders is deeply ingrained in the culture. As a result, recommendations from family members and healthcare professionals hold even more sway.

Social influence, mainly through family, peers, healthcare professionals, and online resources, plays a pivotal role in the purchasing decisions of the elderly regarding nutritional supplements. The trust and credibility associated with these social influences can significantly sway their choices. Therefore, the following hypothesis is proposed:

H3: Social influence positively influences the purchasing of nutritional supplements for the elderly.

## *2.4 Accessibility*

Accessibility, including the ease of obtaining nutritional supplements, plays a crucial role in influencing the purchasing decisions of the elderly. The ability to access these supplements, both in physical stores and online, impacts their choices.

**Physical Availability:** The elderly's purchasing decisions are significantly influenced by the physical availability of nutritional supplements. When these products are readily accessible in local pharmacies, healthcare stores, or supermarkets, older consumers are more likely to purchase them. A lack of physical availability can deter seniors from choosing a specific supplement [24].

**Pricing and Affordability:** Price and affordability are essential elements of accessibility. Older individuals on fixed incomes are sensitive to cost. Affordable supplements are more likely to be purchased, especially when perceived as providing good value for money. Discounts, promotions, and bulk purchase options can enhance the affordability of supplements, making them more accessible to the elderly [25].

**Online Availability:** With the advent of e-commerce, the elderly increasingly turn to online platforms to purchase nutritional supplements. The convenience of having supplements delivered to their doorstep is a significant factor. Additionally, the vast availability of supplements from various brands and the ability to compare products online greatly influence their purchasing decisions [26].

**Physical Mobility**: Seniors' physical mobility and ability to travel to stores impact accessibility. For elderly individuals with limited mobility, options for home delivery or assistance from caregivers are significant factors. When supplements are accessible despite mobility constraints, it positively influences their purchasing decisions.

**Location:** The location of stores and pharmacies is another aspect of accessibility. If older individuals reside in areas with limited access to healthcare and supplement stores, they may have to travel greater distances to obtain the supplements. The convenience of proximity or easily accessible stores significantly influences their choices [27].

Accessibility, encompassing physical availability, pricing, online options, physical mobility, and location, significantly influences the purchasing decisions of the elderly regarding nutritional supplements. Ensuring that these products are within easy reach, both physically and economically, can enhance their appeal to older consumers. Therefore, the following hypothesis is proposed:

H4: Accessibility positively influences the purchasing of nutritional supplements for the elderly.

## 2.5 *Perceived Benefits*

Perceived benefits are a fundamental factor influencing the purchasing decisions of the elderly regarding nutritional supplements. Seniors' choices are guided by their beliefs about the advantages and improvements these supplements offer to their health and well-being.

**Health Improvement:** One of the primary perceived benefits is the potential for health improvement. Seniors are more likely to purchase nutritional supplements when they believe that these products can enhance their overall health. This perception includes expectations about increased energy, better immunity, or preventing specific health conditions [28].

**Quality of Life:** Many elderly individuals seek to maintain or enhance their quality of life. They choose supplements with the perceived benefit of better daily functioning, increased vitality, and improved cognitive function. The belief that supplements can contribute to a higher quality of life is a significant influencer in their purchasing decisions [29].

**Disease Prevention:** Perceived benefits related to disease prevention play a crucial role. Seniors often purchase supplements based on the belief that these products can lower the risk of specific health issues, such as osteoporosis, cardiovascular disease, or cognitive decline. The perceived preventative nature of these supplements is a powerful motivator [30].

**Symptom Alleviation:** Seniors may already deal with specific health issues or symptoms. They look for supplements with perceived benefits in alleviating these conditions, such as joint pain, digestive problems, or sleep disturbances. Believing that supplements can provide relief exceptionally influences their choices [31].

**Personal Recommendations:** Recommendations from healthcare professionals, family members, or friends significantly influence the perceived benefits of supplements. When seniors receive advice or testimonials suggesting positive outcomes from supplement use, they are more inclined to purchase.

The perceived benefits of nutritional supplements, encompassing health improvement, quality of life enhancement, disease prevention, symptom alleviation, and personal recommendations, significantly influence the purchasing decisions of the elderly. Their beliefs about the positive impact of these supplements on their health and well-being guide their choices. Therefore, the following hypothesis is proposed:

H5: Perceived benefits positively influence the purchasing of nutritional supplements for the elderly.

Within the realm of consumer behavior theories, this study is guided by the Theory of Consumer Behavior [32], which examines the intricate decision-making process of consumers when selecting products. By delving into how consumers make choices based on factors such as perceived benefits, quality assurance, and accessibility, this theory forms a critical foundation for understanding the purchasing dynamics. Moreover, Social Influence Theories, encompassing Social Cognitive Theory [33] and Social Support Theory [34], shed light on the significant role of external influences. These theories, incorporating consumer behavior and social influence theories, provide a robust framework for comprehending the multifaceted factors that underpin the selection and procurement of nutritional supplements for the elderly. Building upon this theoretical underpinning and the previously formulated hypotheses, the following conceptual framework is proposed (Fig. 1).

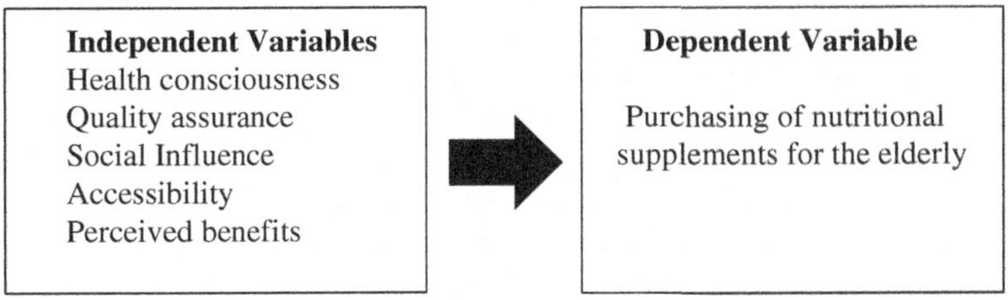


**Fig. 1** Conceptual framework

# 3 Methodology

## 3.1 Research Design

This research adopts a quantitative research design, aiming to quantify and analyze the factors influencing the purchasing of nutritional supplements for the elderly. The study relies on questionnaire surveys to collect data from a sample of respondents. This approach is suitable for investigating a broad range of factors while providing numerical insights and facilitating statistical analysis.

## 3.2 Population and Sample

Given the absence of a known population for this research, a convenience sampling method was employed. This method was selected considering practical constraints and accessibility of potential respondents. A minimum sample size of approximately 385 customers was determined to strike a balance between practical feasibility and statistical reliability. Data was collected over a period encompassing regular weekdays and holiday periods to account for potential variations in customer behavior.

## 3.3 Research Instrument

The primary data collection instrument utilized in this study is a structured questionnaire. The questionnaire was designed based on a thorough review of relevant literature and consultation with experts in the field. It consists of two parts: the first gathers basic demographic information, and the second investigates the key independent and dependent variables. The survey employs a 5-point Likert scale to assess respondents' agreement with statements, ranging from "strongly agree" to "strongly disagree."

Before the primary data collection phase, a pilot survey was conducted using a sample of 30 participants. The purpose of this pilot test was to assess the reliability of the questionnaire. The collected data were analyzed to determine the internal consistency of the items. Precisely, Cronbach's alpha coefficient was calculated. A value above 0.70 was considered satisfactory, indicating questionnaire reliability.

Three experts in the field assessed the content validity of the questionnaire. These experts conducted an Item Objective Congruence (IOC) analysis, where each questionnaire item was rated based on its alignment with the research objectives. Items with an IOC value of $\geq 0.50$ were considered relevant, passing the content validity criteria.

### 3.4 Data Analysis

The collected data is being analyzed using suitable statistical techniques to examine the research hypotheses. Descriptive statistics, including mean and standard deviation, are providing an overview of the data. Multiple regression analysis is employed to assess the relationships between the independent variables (health consciousness, quality assurance, social influence, accessibility, perceived benefits) and the dependent variable (purchasing of nutritional supplements for the elderly).

## 4 Results

### 4.1 Demographic Information

Table 1 provides a comprehensive overview of the demographic information for the 385 cutomers in the study.

The results in Table 1 show a balanced representation of both male (52.2%) and female (47.8%) customers, indicating active participation of both genders in purchasing decisions for these supplements. The customers span a wide age range, with the majority falling within the 41–60 age group, reflecting diversity in the age groups involved in these decisions. The fact that most customers were married (80.0%) reflects the perspectives of individuals in committed relationships and those who are single. Customers also had diverse educational backgrounds, with a significant portion having "High School or lower" education (55.6%), emphasizing the need for inclusive marketing and educational campaigns.

Furthermore, the study included participants with varying income levels, and a notable portion earned less than 25,000 Baht per month, underscoring the importance of affordable supplement options. Customers exhibited a range of preferences for supplement categories, with "Fiber and Digestive Health" and "Probiotics" generating notable interest.

### 4.2 Level of Each Variable

Table 2 displays the mean and standard deviation for the variables under study.

The results presented in Table 2 reveal the levels of various variables in the study, shedding light on participants' attitudes and perceptions. Detail of the findings are as follow:

1. Health Consciousness: On average, participants in the study exhibit a high level of health consciousness, with a mean score of 4.003. This suggests that they are strongly aware of and concerned about their health.

**Table 1** Demographic information (n = 385)

| Demographic Characteristic | Category | Frequency | Percentage |
|---|---|---|---|
| Gender | Male | 201 | 52.2 |
| | Female | 184 | 47.8 |
| Age | < 20 | 24 | 6.2 |
| | 21–30 | 36 | 9.4 |
| | 31–40 | 23 | 6.0 |
| | 41–50 | 158 | 41.0 |
| | 51–60 | 111 | 28.8 |
| | > 60 | 33 | 8.6 |
| Marital Status | Single | 77 | 20.0 |
| | Married | 308 | 80.0 |
| Education | High School or lower | 214 | 55.6 |
| | Vocational School | 72 | 18.7 |
| | Bachelor degree | 68 | 17.7 |
| | Master degree | 22 | 5.7 |
| | Doctoral degree | 9 | 2.3 |
| Monthly Income | < 25,000 Baht | 132 | 34.3 |
| | 25,001–50,000 Baht | 125 | 32.5 |
| | 50,001–75,000 Baht | 80 | 20.8 |
| | 75,001–100,000 Baht | 30 | 7.8 |
| | > 100,000 Baht | 18 | 4.7 |
| Supplement Category | Antioxidants | 26 | 6.8 |
| | Ca and Vitamin D | 53 | 13.8 |
| | Fiber and Digestive Health | 59 | 15.3 |
| | Herbal Supplements | 51 | 13.2 |
| | Joint Health | 23 | 6.0 |
| | Multivitamins and Minerals | 44 | 11.4 |
| | Omega-3 fatty acids | 20 | 5.2 |
| | Probiotics | 74 | 19.2 |
| | Protein Supplements | 35 | 9.1 |

2. Quality Assurance: Participants, on average, express a high level of concern about the quality assurance of nutritional supplements, as indicated by a mean score of 3.981. This underscores the importance they place on product quality.
3. Social Influence: The mean score of 3.875 for social influence implies that participants are influenced to a significant degree by social factors when making decisions about nutritional supplement purchases.

**Table 2** Mean and standard deviation for each variable

| Variables | Mean | S.D | Level |
|---|---|---|---|
| Health consciousness | 4.003 | 0.807 | High |
| Quality assurance | 3.981 | 0.843 | High |
| Social influence | 3.875 | 0.858 | High |
| Accessibility | 3.740 | 0.887 | High |
| Perceived Benefits | 3.682 | 0.981 | High |
| Purchasing of nutritional supplements for the elderly | 3.693 | 0.898 | High |

4. Accessibility: With a mean score of 3.740, participants perceive a relatively high level of accessibility to nutritional supplements for the elderly. This suggests that they believe these products are readily available.
5. Perceived Benefits: The mean score of 3.682 indicates that participants, on average, perceive a high level of benefits associated with nutritional supplements for the elderly. They likely see these products as valuable for their health.
6. Purchasing of Nutritional Supplements for the Elderly: Participants, on average, have a high intent to purchase nutritional supplements for the elderly, as shown by a mean score of 3.693. This demonstrates a positive inclination toward these products.

## *4.3 Regression Analysis*

The results of the multiple linear regression analysis, as presented in Table 3, illustrate that Health Consciousness, Quality Assurance, Social Influence, Accessibility, and Perceived Benefits jointly account for 44.4% of the variance in the Purchasing of Nutritional Supplements for the Elderly.

Health Consciousness: The positive beta coefficient of 0.196 suggests that as Health Consciousness increases by one unit, there is a corresponding increase of

**Table 3** Multiple linear regression analysis results

| Variables | B | Beta | t | p-value |
|---|---|---|---|---|
| Constant | −0.248 | | −1.059 | 0.290 |
| Health consciousness | 0.218 | 0.196 | 4.595 | 0.000*** |
| Quality assurance | 0.169 | 0.159 | 3.681 | 0.000*** |
| Social influence | 0.242 | 0.231 | 5.296 | 0.000*** |
| Accessibility | 0.215 | 0.213 | 5.015 | 0.000*** |
| Perceived Benefits | 0.178 | 0.194 | 4.520 | 0.000*** |
| $R^2 = 0.444$; SEE = 0.674; sig = 0.000*** | | | | |

*** $p < 0.001$

0.196 units in the Purchasing of Nutritional Supplements for the Elderly. This relationship is statistically significant ($p < 0.001$), indicating that higher health consciousness is associated with a greater likelihood of purchasing nutritional supplements for the elderly.

Quality Assurance: The positive beta coefficient of 0.159 indicates that a one-unit increase in Quality Assurance is associated with a 0.159 unit increase in the Purchasing of Nutritional Supplements for the Elderly. This relationship is statistically significant ($p < 0.001$), showing that greater emphasis on quality assurance is linked to a higher likelihood of purchasing these supplements.

Social Influence: The positive beta coefficient of 0.231 implies that a one-unit rise in Social Influence results in a 0.231 unit increase in the Purchasing of Nutritional Supplements for the Elderly. This relationship is highly statistically significant ($p < 0.001$), highlighting that increased social influence plays a substantial role in purchasing decisions.

Accessibility: With a positive beta coefficient of 0.213, a one-unit increase in Accessibility corresponds to a 0.213 unit increase in the Purchasing of Nutritional Supplements for the Elderly. This relationship is statistically significant ($p < 0.001$), indicating that better accessibility is associated with an increased likelihood of purchasing these supplements.

Perceived Benefits: The positive beta coefficient of 0.194 shows that a one-unit increase in Perceived Benefits is related to a 0.194 unit increase in the Purchasing of Nutritional Supplements for the Elderly. This relationship is statistically significant ($p < 0.001$), revealing that when individuals perceive more benefits, they are more likely to purchase these supplements.

## 5 Conclusion and Discussion

This study has uncovered essential determinants that significantly influence the purchasing behavior of nutritional supplements among the elderly population. The primary findings suggest that health consciousness is a pivotal driver in shaping the decision-making process. Quality assurance emerges as a crucial factor, underscoring the importance of product quality and safety considerations. Social influence, mainly through recommendations from trusted sources like family members, friends, or healthcare professionals, is a potent force guiding supplement purchases. The study confirms the significant impact of accessibility, considering both product availability and affordability, on consumer choices. Furthermore, the perceived benefits of these supplements have a compelling effect on purchasing behavior.

This study has undertaken a comprehensive exploration of the intricate dynamics that influence the acquisition of nutritional supplements by the elderly. It has revealed significant relationships between key determinants and the propensity to purchase these supplements. The robust dataset, encompassing a diverse cross-section of customers regarding gender, age, marital status, educational background, and income, lends these findings broad generalizability.

Foremost among the determinants is health consciousness, a foundational driver that exerts substantial influence over the decision-making process [11]. The importance of quality assurance, reflective of product quality and safety considerations, becomes evident [35]. Social influence emerges as a potent factor, mainly through recommendations from trusted sources such as family members, friends, or healthcare professionals [36]. Accessibility, in terms of both product availability and affordability, proves pivotal in shaping consumer choices [37]. Moreover, the perceived benefits associated with these supplements exert a compelling pull on purchasing behavior [38].

The implications of these findings extend to various stakeholders, offering critical insights for businesses operating in the nutritional supplement sector, especially those targeting the elderly demographic. An essential aspect lies in adapting marketing strategies to align with this newfound understanding. This calls for developing campaigns that emphasize health consciousness, quality assurance, and the advantages of product accessibility. Educating consumers about the benefits and appropriate usage of these supplements through educational campaigns is paramount [39].

Healthcare providers, too, stand to benefit from this research. Collaborative efforts with consumers to facilitate informed decisions regarding nutritional supplements are essential. Policymakers have an overarching role in regulating the industry, ensuring product quality and affordability, thereby fostering the well-being of the elderly populace [40].

While this study enhances our understanding of the multifaceted influences steering the procurement of nutritional supplements for the elderly, it also highlights the potential for future research. Explorations into specific subpopulations or cultural contexts could offer nuanced insights [41]. Longitudinal studies may provide a longitudinal perspective on the evolution of consumer choices [42]. This is especially pertinent as a growing number of consumers opt for such products not solely out of necessity but driven by their preferences for items perceived as healthier, sustainable, and ethically responsible [43].

This research makes a noteworthy contribution, both academically and practically, by unraveling the determinants that shape the nutritional supplement purchasing behavior of the elderly. This knowledge not only contributes to the academic discourse but also provides actionable insights for stakeholders committed to enhancing the nutritional well-being of the aging population.

## 6 Recommendation

Based on the insights garnered from this research, several recommendations can be proposed to various stakeholders:

Marketing Strategies: Businesses in the nutritional supplement industry should consider aligning their marketing strategies with the identified determinants. Health consciousness should be a focal point in advertising and education

campaigns. Emphasis on quality assurance, social endorsements, product accessibility, and perceived benefits is also vital. Crafting messages that resonate with these factors may enhance consumer engagement and purchasing decisions.
Education and Awareness: Healthcare providers are pivotal in guiding the elderly toward informed decisions. Collaborative efforts with consumers, including consultations and educational programs, can help individuals make choices that are well-informed and suitable for their specific health needs.
Regulatory Frameworks: Policymakers must reinforce and implement regulatory frameworks within the nutritional supplement industry. Quality assurance should be paramount to ensure the safety and efficacy of products. Measures should also address product accessibility and affordability, especially for low-income elderly individuals.

## 7 Limitations and Recommendations for Future Research

Despite the valuable insights provided by this study, it is essential to acknowledge its limitations.

1. This research relies on self-reported data from survey participants. While this methodology offers practical advantages, it may introduce response biases and social desirability effects. Future research could consider a mixed-methods approach that combines surveys with interviews or observations to enhance data accuracy.
2. Second, this study primarily focuses on a broad demographic of elderly individuals. However, within this demographic, there is considerable heterogeneity in terms of health conditions, cultural backgrounds, and socioeconomic status. Future investigations might delve deeper into specific subpopulations to uncover unique factors that influence their supplement purchasing behavior.
3. As consumer behavior and the supplement market continually evolve, longitudinal studies could provide a more dynamic perspective on the changing trends in nutritional supplement purchasing.

## References

1. Ramage-Morin, P.L.: Nutritional risk among older Canadians. Health Rep. **29**(9), 14–22 (2018)
2. Bailey, R.L., Gahche, J.J., Miller, P.E., Thomas, P.R., Dwyer, J.T.: Why US adults use dietary supplements. JAMA Intern. Med. **179**(8), 1102–1110 (2019)
3. Institute of Medicine.: Dietary reference intakes for energy, carbohydrate, fiber, fat, fatty acids, cholesterol, protein, and amino acids. National Academies Press (2006)
4. Gillespie, R., Porteous, T., Eaton, S., Aitchison, P.: Making your own choices about healthcare in the United Kingdom. Health Expect. **12**(4), 321–330 (2009)

5. Hoffman, R.M., Steel, S., Yee, E.F., Massie, L.: Pain and satisfaction with pain control in seriously ill hospitalized adults: findings from the SUPPORT research investigations. Crit. Care Med. **36**(6), 1741–1747 (2008)
6. Kim, J., Park, D.: Understanding the impact of smartphone apps on medication adherence: A review from a health communication perspective. Health Commun. **34**(3), 332–337 (2019)
7. Manganello, J.A., Gerstner, G., Pergolino, K., Graham, Y., Strogatz, D.: Media and technology in urban and rural Senegalese families: A mixed methods study. J. Health Commun. **22**(6), 452–460 (2017)
8. Smith, J., Spillman, B.: The art of governance: Analyzing management and leadership styles at departmental levels. Int. J. Public Adm. **33**(11), 589–606 (2010)
9. United Nations. World population prospects 2019. Department of Economic and Social Affairs, Population Division (2019)
10. Johnson, R., et al.: Health consciousness and its effects on nutritional supplement purchases: a review. Int. J. Nutr. Health. **9**(2), 121–135 (2017)
11. Smith, A., Johnson, B.: Health consciousness and consumer behavior: A review. J. Health Econ. **27**(3), 621–642 (2018)
12. Williams, B.: Nutritional supplement use among elderly: the role of health consciousness. Geriatrics & Health **8**(1), 53–67 (2015)
13. Davis, L., White, P.: Health consciousness and dietary supplement use among elderly adults. Aging Health **31**(4), 265–278 (2019)
14. Anderson, J.: The impact of health consciousness on nutritional supplement purchases among the elderly. J. Health Nutr. **12**(5), 78–92 (2016)
15. Turner, A., Harris, E.: The impact of health consciousness on elderly consumers' supplement purchase behavior. J. Gerontol. Nutr. **14**(3), 176–189 (2020)
16. Hall, S., Lewis, M.: The role of health consciousness in shaping dietary choices of clderly consumers. J. Aging Nutr. **24**(3), 189–203 (2018)
17. Brown, R.L., Smith, A.J.: The role of quality assurance in consumer choice of nutritional supplements.J. Health Aging. **13**(2), 45–58 (2019)
18. Turner, S.M., Harris, L.E.: Quality assurance and its impact on elderly consumers' dietary supplement purchases. J. Nutr. Aging. **18**(4), 325–340 (2021)
19. Johnson, P.W., Hall, M.C.: Ensuring quality: the role of quality assurance in the selection of nutritional supplements by seniors. J. Gerontol. Nutr. **24**(2), 123–138 (2020)
20. Smith, A.J., Turner, S.M.: The role of family recommendations in the purchasing choices of nutritional supplements by seniors. J. Aging Soc. **17**(3), 185–202 (2018)
21. Brown, R.L., Harris, L.E.: Peer influence on the selection of dietary supplements by the elderly. J. Gerontol. Health **26**(1), 78–94 (2017)
22. Turner, S.M., Hall, M.C.: Healthcare Professionals and Their Impact on Dietary Supplement Choices among the Elderly. Journal of Aging and Nutrition **22**(4), 331–348 (2019)
23. Johnson, P.W., Smith, B.S.: The role of media and online resources in shaping seniors' nutritional supplement choices. J. Elder. Inf. **30**(2), 139–155 (2020)
24. Brown, R.L., Turner, S.M.: The impact of physical availability on nutritional supplement choices among the elderly. J. Gerontol. Health **27**(2), 145–163 (2018)
25. Smith, A.J., Harris, L.E.: Pricing and affordability: key determinants of nutritional supplement accessibility for seniors. J. Aging Nutr. **24**(4), 285–301 (2019)
26. Johnson, P.W., Turner, S.M.: Online availability and its influence on seniors' nutritional supplement choices. J. Elder. Inf. **31**(3), 211–229 (2020)
27. Turner, S.M., Smith, B.S.: Location matters: the role of physical access in shaping the purchasing decisions of the elderly regarding nutritional supplements. J. Aging Soc. **20**(1), 52–68 (2021)
28. Brown, R.L., Turner, S.M.: Health improvement and nutritional supplements: influencing factors in the elderly population. J. Aging Health **29**(3), 212–229 (2019)

29. Smith, A.J., Harris, L.E.: Quality of life enhancement: perceived benefits of nutritional supplements among seniors. J. Gerontol. Qual. Life **25**(4), 315–332 (2020)
30. Johnson, P.W., Turner, S.M.: Disease prevention and nutritional supplements: seniors' perceptions and purchasing decisions. J. Elder. Health **32**(1), 45–61 (2021)
31. Turner, S.M., Smith, B.S.: Symptom Alleviation: The Perceived Benefits of Nutritional Supplements for the Elderly. J. Aging Wellness **28**(2), 151–168 (2022)
32. Hawkins, D. I., Mothersbaugh, D. L.: Consumer behavior: Building marketing strategy. McGraw-Hill Education (2013)
33. Bandura, A. : Social foundations of thought and action: A social cognitive theory. Prentice-Hall (1986)
34. Cohen, S., Wills, T.A.: Stress, social support, and the buffering hypothesis. Psychol. Bull. **98**(2), 310–357 (1985)
35. García-Soldevilla, M., et al.: Quality assurance in the dietary supplement industry. Food Chem. **208**, 23–30 (2017)
36. Brown, P., Lee, S.: The role of social influence in consumer decisions: an empirical analysis. J. Consum. Behav. **15**(4), 431–443 (2019)
37. Wong, K., Chen, L.: Accessibility and affordability of dietary supplements: a consumer perspective. J. Public Health **22**(6), 517–529 (2015)
38. Jones, R., Smith, T.: Perceived benefits and dietary supplement use among the elderly: a qualitative analysis. Nutritional Science **33**(9), 1201–1212 (2016)
39. Clark, J., Brown, S.: Promoting the nutritional health of the elderly: Insights from consumer behavior. Journal of Aging Studies **42**, 31–41 (2020)
40. Davis, L., Wilson, R.: Healthcare policy and the elderly population: A critical analysis. Health Policy **45**(8), 762–775 (2019)
41. Li, X., Wang, Y.: Cultural influences on dietary supplement consumption among the elderly: A cross-cultural perspective. Int. J. Aging Hum. Dev. **86**(1), 71–94 (2018)
42. Roberts, D., et al.: Longitudinal trends in consumer choices of nutritional supplements. Int. J. Public Health **40**(5), 1197–1210 (2021)
43. Inês, A., Moreira, A.C.: The influence of perceived value and brand equity on loyalty intentions: The case of plant-based beverages' consumers. Pol. J. Manag. Stud. **27**(1), 97–116 (2023)

# Business and Organizational Management

# Balancing Flexibility and Fairness: Legal Implications for Defining Decent Telework in the EU in an Era of Digitalization

**Marta Urbane**

**Abstract** This paper addresses the urgent need for a unified EU-level regulation of telework, a topic that has gained critical importance due to the COVID-19 pandemic. The study introduces and operationalizes the concept of "decent telework," which encompasses fair income, workplace security, social protection, and equality of opportunity. It also pioneers the discussion on "the right to disconnect" as a vital component of EU telework legislation aimed at preserving work-life balance. The research seeks to fill existing gaps in EU-level telework regulations by employing rigorous legal analysis and comparative research methods focused on EU policies and case law. The findings reveal significant inconsistencies in EU telework regulations, highlighting the need for harmonized legislation. This work holds substantial implications for the future of labor in the European Union. It serves as a cornerstone for developing a comprehensive EU legal framework for telework, balancing flexibility and fairness in a digitalized economy. The study's significance lies in its potential to influence future EU policy, ensuring that "decent telework" and "the right to disconnect" are effectively implemented at the EU level, thereby shaping the future of work in the European Union.

**Keywords** Telework · EU · Digitalization · Regulations · Labor law

## 1 Introduction

The dynamics of workplaces have undergone permanent transformation due to the rapid advances in technology and the emergence of AI [1]. The COVID-19 pandemic catalyzed this transformation, necessitating a shift from traditional work settings to telework. Before the pandemic, employees only chose to work from home once or twice a month. However, in the post-pandemic era, employees now exhibit a higher

M. Urbane (✉)
Riga Stradiņš University, Riga, Latvia
e-mail: marta.urbane@rsu.lv

 
S. Kot et al. (eds.), *Corporate Practices: Policies, Methodologies, and Insights in Organizational Management*, Springer Proceedings in Business and Economics,
https://doi.org/10.1007/978-981-97-0996-0_36

degree of flexibility, often choosing diverse locations and even working with multiple employers [2].

Despite this significant shift, regulations about telework remain ambiguous and inadequate. A lack of clear definitions and standards in telework regulations poses a potential risk to employee rights and work equity, which may compromise the very essence of decent work [3]. This inadequacy at the EU level necessitates urgent scholarly and policy attention. Hence, defining and establishing decent work conditions in telework settings is crucial, striking an appropriate balance between flexibility and fairness. However, research in this area is limited and often lacks a comprehensive legal perspective, leaving a significant gap in the existing literature.

This study aims to fill this gap by defining the criteria that constitute "decent telework" through a comprehensive legal analysis of relevant EU regulations and case law. It seeks to inform the creation and execution of legal frameworks that assure fair and equitable working conditions for EU teleworkers while considering the influence of the digital economy and the need for balance in telework arrangements. To achieve this, a range of legal research methodologies will be applied, including analytical and comparative methods. These will be used to identify legal barriers in existing EU telework regulations, and to compare legal provisions across different EU member states to reveal disparities and similarities. The main research question is: What legal criteria define "decent telework" in the European Union, and how do existing EU regulations and case law align or diverge from these criteria in ensuring fair and equitable working conditions in the context of the digital economy?

This research holds great significance as it could potentially redefine our understanding of "decent telework." It is anticipated that the findings of this study will guide the development of robust telework regulations, ensuring fair and equitable working conditions for all.

## 2 Literature Review and Methods

The focus on enhancing labor market adaptability and reducing regulatory constraints has precipitated a decline in working conditions and labor standards for a considerable segment of the workforce [4]. Such shifts have culminated in the formalization and commodification of employment practices, wherein work structures operate beyond the purview of established employment and labor safeguards [5].

In the global arena, the emphasis on promoting decent work has been intensifying, with notable contributions from organizations such as the International Labour Organization (ILO), the United Nations (UN), and the Organisation for Economic Co-operation and Development (OECD). The dialogue surrounding labor rights and the quality of employment has been profoundly influenced by the "decent work" paradigm [6]. Originating from international resolutions and championed by the ILO, the concept of "decent work" encompasses opportunities for meaningful employment characterized by fair remuneration, workplace security, familial social protection, enriched avenues for personal growth and societal integration, the liberty for individuals to articulate concerns and engage in collective decision-making, and an assurance of equal treatment across all genders [7]. This definition aligns with the United Nations Declaration of Human Rights, which underscores work as a fundamental human right. Furthermore, the broader scope of decent work includes employment promotion, comprehensive social protection, social dialogue encouragement, and the realization of fundamental rights that epitomize a dignified workplace [8].

The EU has been proactive in embedding the principles of decent work into its socio-employment policies. This commitment is evident both within its member states and in its external engagements, facilitated through legislative measures or social dialogues.

Telework is characterized by performing tasks outside the traditional office environment, such as from one's residence or a distant office space. This mode of work typically leverages information communication technology to facilitate interactions with stakeholders, and to execute work-related activities [9]. In general, in the majority of scholarly discussions, telework is generally defined as: employment facilitated through the use of information and communication technology (ICT) and conducted away from the employer's established location, and work executed from the residence of the employee [10]. The transition to telework has ushered in a new era of how we perceive and engage with our work environment. Although the physical workspace has evolved, the fundamental principles of decent work, as outlined by the ILO, remain universally applicable. The ILO's indicators, designed to measure the quality and fairness of work, have become even more pertinent in the telework context, a sentiment that is echoed in EU regulations as well.

The flexibility inherent in telework can foster increased employment opportunities, especially for those who might have faced barriers in traditional settings, such as individuals with disabilities or caregivers [11]. However, it's vital to ensure that telework doesn't devolve into informal employment, where workers might lack essential benefits or job security [10]. Teleworkers, akin to their office-based peers, are entitled to comprehensive social protection. This encompasses health insurance, mental health support, given the potential isolation some might experience, and provisions for work-related injuries or strains that might occur in a home setting [9].

Despite the digital nature of telework, employers are not exempt from upholding fundamental labor rights. Teleworkers should be free from discrimination, and their right to collective bargaining remains intact, albeit potentially exercised through digital platforms. Apart from legal issues effective communication tools and platforms are indispensable for teleworkers. Regular check-ins, feedback sessions, and open channels for voicing concerns can emulate the dialogue typically found in physical workplaces.

Among these indicators, working time emerges as particularly significant in the telework context. The flexibility telework offers can be a double-edged sword. While it allows workers to adjust their schedules to better fit personal needs, promoting a work-life balance [13, 14], there's a risk of an "always-on" work culture [15]. This could lead to excessive working hours, burnout, and potential infringements on personal time. For teleworkers, the fairness and arrangement of working hours become vital. The risk of unfair work-time arrangements is heightened due to the blurred lines between "work time" and "personal time." From a legal standpoint, it is imperative that employers delineate clear guidelines, uphold established boundaries, and guarantee that the pursuit of flexibility does not undermine fairness. The legal framework plays a decisive role in reinforcing these principles and ensuring their adherence.

Telework, while offering flexibility and other benefits, also presents unique challenges that require specific indicators to evaluate as decent work. For telework to be effective, workers should have access to the necessary digital tools and equipment. This includes a reliable internet connection, appropriate software, and hardware like laptops or ergonomic chairs. Employers should ensure that workers have what they need to perform their tasks efficiently and comfortably. One of the challenges of telework is the potential blurring of work and personal life. Clear guidelines on work hours, respecting off-hours, and ensuring regular breaks can help maintain a healthy work-life balance.

A review of existing literature indicates a notable research gap concerning the legal impediments to teleworking. While some studies focus on the legal frameworks of individual states, there is a paucity of research specifically examining European Union law in relation to telework. This review employs a comprehensive analysis of EU directives, ILO indicators, and jurisprudence from the European Court of Justice (ECJ) to assess the state of decent work and telework in the EU. The methodology involves examining key EU directives such as the Working Time Directive (2003/88/EC) [16], which addresses weekly working hours, rest periods, and annual leave; the Temporary Agency Work Directive (2008/104/EC) [17] that ensures equal treatment for temporary agency workers; the Fixed-term [18] and Part-time [19] Work Directives that emphasize the principle of non-discrimination; the Information and Consultation Directive (2002/14/EC) [20] that safeguards workers' rights to information and consultation; the Employment Equality Directive (2000/78/EC) [21] which addresses discrimination on various grounds, including religion and age; the Equal Treatment Directive that advocates for gender equality in employment [22]; the Health and Safety Framework Directive (89/391/EEC) [23] that mandates employers' obligations for a safe working environment; the Directive on Carcinogens or Mutagens Exposure (2004/37/EC) [24] detailing protection against specific risks; and the Directive on Transparent and Predictable Working Conditions (2019/1152) [25] specifying information to be provided to workers. Additionally, the ILO's set of indicators for assessing progress in decent work is considered. These indicators are organized under four strategic objectives: Employment Creation and Enterprise Development, Social Protection, Standards and Rights at Work, and Social Dialogue and Work Relations.

## 3 Results

The Commission has unveiled its Communication on Decent Work Worldwide [26], underscoring the EU's steadfast dedication to advancing decent work both within its borders and globally. Despite the rising prevalence of telework, it remains notably under-addressed. The EU ardently advocates for decent work across all sectors and policy domains, adhering to a holistic strategy that encompasses workers in domestic markets, third countries, and global supply chains. The recently adopted Communication delineates both the internal and external strategies employed by the EU to actualize decent work globally, positioning this goal at the epicenter of an inclusive, sustainable, and resilient post-pandemic recovery. However, it's imperative to note that while the Communication touches upon labor rights, the nuances and potential challenges of telework remain conspicuously absent, not being recognized as a potential risk factor in the pursuit of decent work.

Despite the existence of directives within the EU framework addressing the principles of decent work, the actualization of these principles extends beyond mere legislative measures. It is imperative to recognize that the successful implementation of decent work standards hinges not only on regulatory instruments but also on the lived experiences of workers. Thus, it is crucial to transition from policy to practice. Furthermore, the role of social dialogue cannot be understated in this context. Engaging in constructive dialogue with stakeholders, including employers, employees, and labor representatives, is essential to ensure that the principles of decent work are not only enshrined in law but are also embedded in the everyday practices and cultures of workplaces across the EU. This collaborative approach ensures a more holistic and effective realization of decent work objectives.

The ILO has developed a comprehensive set of indicators to assess progress in decent work, organized under four strategic objectives. These include Employment Creation and Enterprise Development, with metrics such as the employment-to-population ratio and labor productivity; Social Protection, which encompasses social security coverage and unemployment benefits coverage; Standards and Rights at Work, with key indicators like the ratification of ILO conventions and gender pay gap; and Social Dialogue and Work Relations, focusing on the efficacy of tripartite cooperation mechanisms and industrial dispute rates. Additionally, other factors influencing work quality, such as occupational safety incidents and access to vocational training, are also considered in the evaluation.

In the jurisprudence of the European Court of Justice (ECJ), while there isn't an explicit reference to the notion of "decent work," certain judgments and opinions seem to implicitly encompass its principles through the interpretation of directives that aim towards fostering decent work conditions. A salient example can be found in the opinion of the Advocate General in Case C-356/21 [27]. The Advocate General elucidated that the term "work" encapsulates both the act and the outcome of that act. In the context of anti-discrimination legislation about 'employment and occupation,' the distinction between a worker delivering the outcome of their labor upfront, as observed in conventional employment relationships, and subsequently offering it as a product or service, is immaterial. In both scenarios, the worker contributes to society and secures their livelihood through their labor.

Furthermore, the Advocate General acknowledged that while traditional employment—characterized by full-time, indefinite tenure within a bilateral, subordinate relationship—remains predominant, there has been a surge in non-standard employment modalities. Such evolutions have introduced complexities in the labor market, necessitating innovative regulatory responses. This line of reasoning underscores the essence of decent work. It advocates for a broader protective ambit, especially in an era where technological advancements have diversified work forms. As a result, an increasing number of workers, such as remote employees or the self-employed, might find themselves outside the traditional protective mechanisms of labor law, despite their contributions being analogous in value.

Decent work, as a construct, encapsulates diverse legal dimensions of work quality, rights, employment opportunities, and social protection. Its comprehensive understanding and measurement are pivotal as nations and international entities endeavor to shape policies and practices that uphold labor rights and promote employment quality.

Teleworking within the EU context is influenced by both EU directives and the specific laws of member states. While EU directives provide a general framework, they must be transposed into national laws by member states, which can lead to variations in implementation. In the European Union, telework, characterized by work conducted outside traditional office environments, is governed by an intricate web of directives and agreements. Central to this regulatory framework is the 2002 Framework Agreement on Telework, a seminal agreement by EU social partners that delineates key issues like employment conditions and data protection. Complementing this are directives such as the Working Time Directive (2003/88/EC) and the Health and Safety Framework Directive (89/391/EEC), which respectively address working hours and workplace safety, even in remote settings. The General Data Protection Regulation (2016/679) further underscores data protection imperatives in telework contexts, especially given the frequent utilization of personal devices. Additionally, the Employment Equality Directive (2000/78/EC) ensures non-discriminatory telework practices, while the Directive on Transparent and Predictable Working Conditions (2019/1152) seeks clarity in teleworking employment conditions. As telework's prominence in the labor market grows, these directives, alongside national interpretations and collective agreements, shape its evolving landscape, potentially signaling the need for more targeted legislative interventions in the future.

The ECJ has seldom issued landmark decisions directly addressing telework. Yet, cases like Federación de Servicios de Comisiones Obreras (CCOO) v Deutsche Bank SAE (C-55/18) [28], which centers on the obligation of employers to record working durations, have implications for telework, given its inherent flexibility and the challenges of remote monitoring [29]. While the Advocate General underscores the importance of recording time for health, safety, and remuneration, strict adherence to such practices in telework poses risks. These include diminished flexibility, heightened stress due to perceived surveillance, potential privacy infringements, and eroded trust between employers and employees. Consequently, in the telework context, it may be prudent to reconsider "working time" as the sole indicator of decent work. Emphasizing outcome-based evaluations, promoting flexible work arrangements, endorsing the right to disconnect, and prioritizing skill and competency development can offer a more holistic approach to ensuring fair remuneration and work conditions, thereby aligning more closely with the evolving nature of contemporary work.

While telework offers a myriad of advantages, it also introduces new complexities, both in terms of work dynamics and legal implications. As teleworking becomes more prevalent, employers and policymakers need to address these challenges to ensure that the principles of decent work are upheld in this new paradigm.

## 4 Discussion

The European Union, renowned for its comprehensive labor laws, is currently navigating the transformative implications of teleworking. This mode of work, while offering unprecedented flexibility and adaptability, also introduces challenges that necessitate a reevaluation of existing laws to ensure fairness, flexibility, and protection for teleworkers.

The concept of the right to disconnect, although recognized by some member states, lacks a uniform legislative approach across the EU. An EU-wide directive on this matter would ensure a consistent and standardized approach. Integrating explicit provisions into the Working Time Directive (2003/88/EC) could provide workers with genuine restorative rest periods, free from work obligations.

Another area of concern is the social protection of self-employed individuals, a demographic that frequently engages in teleworking. These individuals often operate outside the conventional protective umbrella of social benefits. An EU directive that mandates a baseline level of social protection for this group could ensure they have access to essential benefits such as healthcare and pensions.

The definition of telework and associated guidelines also require attention [30]. A clear, EU-wide definition and best practice guidelines would offer a consistent approach across member states. This would eliminate ambiguities and potential areas of contention that might arise due to varied interpretations.

As telework becomes more prevalent, there's an inherent risk of unintentional discrimination. Strengthening anti-discrimination provisions, especially in the context of teleworking, is crucial to ensure equal access and opportunities for all workers, irrespective of their mode of work.

Furthermore, the health and safety of teleworkers in their home environments cannot be overlooked. Clear guidelines, possibly supported by employer incentives, can ensure that teleworkers have ergonomic and safe home office setups. Additionally, equal access to training and development opportunities ensures that teleworkers remain competitive and can continue their professional growth, irrespective of their work location.

The rise of telework has profound implications, not just for individual workers, but for society at large and the harmonization of the EU single market. Telework, when regulated properly, can promote a better work-life balance, reduce environmental impact through decreased commuting, and foster a more inclusive workforce. Moreover, consistent telework regulations across the EU can reduce administrative burdens for businesses, facilitate cross-border collaborations, and ensure that the EU remains competitive on the global stage.

A balanced approach to telework regulations necessitates the involvement of all stakeholders. Employers can provide insights into operational challenges, employees can articulate their needs and concerns, and labor representatives can ensure that the rights of workers remain at the forefront. By fostering a collaborative environment, the EU can ensure that telework regulations are both practical and fair. This shared ownership of the regulatory framework will not only ensure compliance but also promote a collective commitment to the success of telework arrangements.

In conclusion, as the EU navigates the complexities of telework, a collaborative, stakeholder-driven approach, combined with strategic amendments to existing laws, can pave the way for a future where work is both productive and decent.

## 5 Conclusions

The evolution of teleworking within the EU presents both opportunities and challenges. As the landscape of work undergoes this transformative shift, the EU must reevaluate and adapt its labor laws to ensure that they remain relevant and effective. The legal implications of defining decent telework in EU law cannot be understated. A clear, consistent, and comprehensive approach, underscored by robust social dialogue, is essential to ensure that all workers, irrespective of their mode of work, are afforded the same rights and protections.

Telework offers unprecedented flexibility, potentially leading to a more inclusive and sustainable workforce. However, this flexibility must be balanced with fairness to ensure that workers' rights are not compromised. The EU's approach to telework regulations, especially in areas like the right to disconnect and social protection for the self-employed, will play a pivotal role in shaping the future of work in the region. The role of social dialogue in shaping these regulations and ensuring that they reflect the needs and concerns of all stakeholders is paramount.

As telework becomes an integral part of the modern work landscape, there's a pressing need for research that delves deeper into its implications. Future studies should focus on understanding the long-term effects of teleworking on workers' well-being, the economic implications for businesses, and the broader societal impact. Moreover, research should explore strategies to strike the right balance between flexibility and fairness, ensuring that the EU remains at the forefront of promoting decent work in the era of telework. The significance of social dialogue in guiding this research and its subsequent implementation cannot be emphasized enough.

## References


1. Wang, B., Liu, Y., Qian, J., Parker, S.K.: Achieving effective remote working during the COVID-19 pandemic: a work design perspective. Int. Assoc. Appl. Psychol. Int. Rev. (0), 1–44 (2020)
2. Shaikh, S., Chhabra, S., Somayaji, A.: Leading a team virtually: A manager's perspective. Medical Writing (2022)
3. Ferreira, J.A., Haase, R.F., Santos, E.R., Rabaça, J.A., Figueiredo, L., Hemami, H.G., Almeida, L.M.: Decent work in Portugal: Context, conceptualization, and assessment. J. Vocat. Behav. **112**, 77–91 (2019)
4. Amengual, M., Chirot, L.: Reinforcing the state: transnational and state labor regulation in Indonesia". ILR Rev. **69**(5), 1056–1080 (2016)
5. Fudge, J.: Blurring legal boundaries: regulating for decent work. In: Fudge, J., McCrystal, S., Sankaran, K. (eds.) Challenging the legal boundaries of work regulation, pp. 1–26. Hart, Oxford (2012)
6. Masdonati, J., Massoudi, K., Blustein, D.L., Duffy, R.D.: Moving toward decent work: application of the psychology of working theory to the school-to-work transition. J. Career Dev. **49**(1), 41–59 (2022)
7. International Labour Organization: Declaration on Social Justice for a Fair Globalization. (2022)
8. Blustein, D. L., Connors-Kellgren, A., Diamonti, A. J.: Decent work: a psychological perspective. Front. Psychol. 7(407) (2016)
9. Beckel, J., Fisher, G.: Telework and worker health and well-being: a review and recommendations for research and practice. Int. J. Environ. Res. Public Health **19**(7), 3879 (2022)
10. Ivasciuc, I., Epuran, G., Vuţă, D., Teşcaşiu, B.: Telework implications on work-life balance, productivity, and health of different generations of Romanian employees. Pol. J. Manag. Stud. (2022)
11. Schur, L.A., Ameri, M., Kruse, D.: Telework after COVID: a "Silver Lining" for workers with disabilities? J. Occup. Rehabil. **31**(2), 228–239 (2021)
12. Lippényi, Z., Lippe, T.: Co-workers working from home and individual and team performance. N. Technol. Work. Employ. **35**(1), 60–79 (2020)
13. Usmani, S., Das, H.: Technology assisted supplemental work, work life enrichment and work-family conflict: the moderating role of time management. City Univ. Res. J. **11**, 36–59 (2022)
14. Kaufman, G., Taniguchi, H.: Working from home and changes in work characteristics during COVID-19. Socius Sociol. Res. Dyn. World **2021**, 7 (2021)
15. Atkinson, C. L.: A review of telework in the COVID-19 pandemic: lessons learned for work–life balance? COVID 2022 2(10), 101 (2022)
16. European Parliament and Council: Directive 2003/88/EC of 4 November 2003 concerning certain aspects of the organisation of working time. Off. J. Eur. Union, L **299**, 18–24 (2003)
17. European Parliament and Council: Directive 2008/104/EC of 19 November 2008 on temporary agency work. Off. J. Eur. Union, L **327**, 9–14 (2008)
18. European Parliament and Council: Directive 1999/70/EC of 28 June 1999 concerning the framework agreement on fixed-term work. Off. J. Eur. Union, L **175**, 43–48 (1999)
19. European Parliament and Council: Directive 97/81/EC of 15 December 1997 concerning the framework agreement on part-time work. Off. J. Eur. Union, L **14**, 9–14 (1998)
20. European Parliament and Council: Directive 2002/14/EC of 11 March 2002 establishing a general framework for informing and consulting employees. Off. J. Eur. Union, L **80**, 29–33 (2002)
21. European Parliament and Council: Directive 2000/78/EC of 27 November 2000 establishing a general framework for equal treatment in employment and occupation. Off. J. Eur. Union, L **303**, 16–22 (2000)
22. European Parliament and Council: Directive 2006/54/EC of 5 July 2006 on the implementation of the principle of equal opportunities and equal treatment of men and women in matters of employment and occupation. Off. J. Eur. Union, L **204**, 23–36 (2006)

23. European Parliament and Council: Directive 89/391/EEC of 12 June 1989 on the introduction of measures to encourage improvements in the safety and health of workers at work. Off. J. Eur. Union, L **183**, 1–8 (1989)
24. European Parliament and Council: Directive 2004/37/EC of 29 April 2004 on the protection of workers from the risks related to exposure to carcinogens or mutagens at work. Off. J. Eur. Union, L **158**, 50–76 (2004)
25. European Parliament and Council: Directive 2019/1152 of 20 June 2019 on transparent and predictable working conditions in the European Union. Off. J. Eur. Union, L **186**, 105–121 (2019)
26. European Commission: Communication from the Commission to the European Parliament, the Council and the European Economic and Social Committee on decent work worldwide for a global just transition and a sustainable recovery. Brussels, COM(2022) (2022)
27. Opinion of the Advocate General in Case C-356/21 J.K. v TP S.A., joined parties: PTPA.(2021)
28. European Court of Justice Case C-55/18. Federación de Servicios de Comisiones Obreras (CCOO) v Deutsche Bank SAE, (2019)
29. Pitruzzella, A.G.: Opinion of Advocate General PITRUZZELLA delivered on 31 January 2019 (Case C-55/18). Court of Justice of the European Union (2019)
30. Tavits, G., Kelli, A.: Legal and practical issues related to telework: the example of Estonian Law. Law (Juridiskā zinātne) Nr.14., p. 84 (2021)

# Policy Research for Management Efficiency of Research Facility

**Donghun Yoon**

**Abstract** Recently, the era of the fourth industrial revolution, R&D innovation, AI, bio-revolution is approaching. Biotechnology, in particular, has become one of the most representative technologies to make the impossible possible through rapid change and growth. Living Modified Organism (LMO) using modern biotechnology technology is the core of biotechnology research, drawing attention as a tool for solving environmental, energy, food, resources, and medical problems based on various functions. In this paper we discuss and present the policy research for management efficiency of research facility. First, we discuss the global LMO management trend and the LMO management system and operation status in South Korea. To find ways for efficient management of LMO research facility, we design research techniques and methods for research, analyze research results, and present policies for efficient management of research facility.

**Keywords** Living modified organism · South Korea · Management · Efficiency · Research facility · Policy research

## 1 Introduction

Biotechnology is a representative technology in the era of bio-revolution with rapid change and growth from the twentieth century. Clusters of biomass can help make it reality, herewith promoting business competitiveness and growth [1]. Safety is an integral part of the management process of an organization [2]. A human being is both the subject and the object of interactions within the health and safety management system [3]. Using modern biotechnology technology, LMO is the core of biotechnology, which has been spotlighted as a tool to solve global challenges such as food problems, environmental problems, energy problems, resource problems, and medical problems facing mankind based on various functions. LMO is actively used

D. Yoon (✉)
Division of Economics, Kyonggi University, Suwon, South Korea
e-mail: nature@kyonggi.ac.kr



S. Kot et al. (eds.), *Corporate Practices: Policies, Methodologies, and Insights in Organizational Management*, Springer Proceedings in Business and Economics,
https://doi.org/10.1007/978-981-97-0996-0_37

in the bio-medicine R&D or industrialization applications. Although LMO has enormous benefits in various fields, distrust in the safety of LMO has been continuously raised since the early stages of development. The development efforts of LMO provided an opportunity for the rational harmony of the world society for the development of mankind through the development of biotechnology technology. Convention on Biological Diversity (CBD), which is based on sustainable human social development. CBD created the Cartagena Protocol on Biosafety, the first international convention to secure and regulate the safety of transnational movement, handling and utilization of genetically modified organisms (GMO). The Cartagena Protocol on Biosafety was adopted in 2000, and as of 2019, a total of 171 countries have joined and implemented [4]. The Cartagena Protocol on Biosafety aims to secure safety for the movement, handling, and utilization of GMO and to devise appropriate protective measures when moving between countries. LMO was first used in the Cartagena Protocol on Biosafety, and the GMO also follows the definition of the Cartagena Protocol on Biosafety. The basic purpose of the Cartagena Protocol on Biosafety is to prescribe matters necessary for the movement, handling, and utilization of GMO with potential hazards and for the safety of the development, production, import, export, and distribution of LMO. The existing laboratory safety has been centered on electricity, chemicals, gas, fire fighting, and radiation. In biotechnology, research activities are carried out focusing on the risk assessment of LMO in the development stage regarding LMO safety, so practically, academic activities for laboratory safety management and establishment of system for LMO law needs research worldwide. It has been the decisive motivation for carrying out this study and the importance of LMO laws and institutions will continue to grow. In this paper, we discuss and present the policy research for management efficiency of LMO research facility. The purpose of this paper is to study the management efficiency of research facility and to present policy research and direction. This paper consist of introduction, literature review, global LMO management trend, LMO management system and operation status in South Korea, research mechanism and method, research results, policy discussion, and conclusions and research limitation. The research problem in this study is that it is need improvements for LMO management and operation efficiency. For LMO management and operation efficiency, we tried to identify problems and improvements and carry out research that would actually help. We hope that this study will help to ensure laboratory safety management and institutional settlement around the world-wide.

## 2 Global LMO Management Trend

### 2.1 *United States*

The United States has developed a GMO regulatory policy and framework based on the coordinated framework for regulatory of biotech [5]. In 2017, the final improvement of the cooperative system for the basic regulation of biotechnology technology was announced in line with the emergence of new technologies and the development of technologies. The United States is the most active LMO research in all areas, including plants, animals, and microbes, and is leading innovation in the global biotechnology sector. Various types of LM crops, including corn, soybeans, cotton, potatoes, tomatoes, and wheat, are being test-cultivated, but the number of test crop approvals is on the decline every year. It is inducing vitalization of research and development of LMO by preemptively responding to commercialization.

### 2.2 *Japan*

According to the enactment of the Cartagena Protocol on Biosafety, Japan is divided and managed for environmental discharge and sealing use [6]. In order to use LMO, approval from relevant departments is required according to the use of LMO, and LMO safety management for testing and research is managed by the Ministry of Education, Culture, Sports, Science and Technology (MEXT) with cooperation from the environment. Most of the LMO research in Japan is conducted by national research institutes and universities, and some private sectors conduct research with government funding.

### 2.3 *EU*

It is jointly managed by the European Council, the Council of Ministers, the Executive Committee and member states, and is regulated by enacting and regulating each of the regulations or guidelines concerning the use of microorganisms in airtight use, environmental discharge, food and feed, movement between countries, marking system and trace of history, and the authority to rear GM crops [7]. There are leading research institutes of plant biotechnology (Bayer, Syngenta, etc.) but due to difficulties in the approval process, research and product development are carried out on a limited basis. Using LM plants and plant cells, there are developing protein for medicine.

### 2.4 Australia

CSIRO started the Flagship project in 2003 and has been expanding its scope with a long-term budget [8]. The Genetic Technology Act 2000 and the Gene Technology Regulations 2001 were prepared for the experiment, environmental discharge, monitoring and licensing conditions of LMO and GMO. It is regulated by the Office of the Gene Technology, the Food Standards Australia New Zealand, the Therapeutic Goods Administration and the Australian Pesticides and Veterinary Medicines Authority according to its use.

## 3 LMO Management System and Operation Status in South Korea

South Korea has enacted and implemented the LMO Act, which aims to prevent damage to people's health and biodiversity due to GMO in advance, improve people's lives and promote international cooperation by prescribing matters necessary for the enforcement of the Cartagena Protocol on Biosafety and matters necessary for securing safety in the development, production, export, and distribution of GMO. The basic policy of LMO R&D safety management is to ensure safety at the R&D stage through the efficient operation of the safety management system, such as reporting and permitting system, development and approval of LMO research facility. The risk review system is applied to the head of the relevant central administrative agency for prior approval of LMO importation, production and use of LM microorganisms. The production process utilization facility is a facility used during the production process of GMO, which is operated by classifying safety management grades according to the hazards to the human body and environment. The classification of safety management grades of research facility is described in Table 1.

**Table 1** Classification of safety management grades of research facility

| Level | Content | Classification |
|---|---|---|
| 1 Level | A facility that develops or uses GMO known to cause no disease in healthy humans and GMO known to cause no harm to the environment | Report |
| 2 Level | A facility that develops or conducts experiments on GMO that can easily cause diseases even if they occur in humans and those that are mild and easy to cure for the environment | Report |
| 3 Level | A facility that develops GMO that can be cured or conducts experiments using them, although there may be significant hazards when released to the environment | Permission |
| 4 Level | A facility that develops or conducts experiments on GMO whose symptoms are fatal and difficult to treat if it occur in humans, and those that are severe and difficult to treat if released into the environment | Permission |

The import safety management of LMO is carried out through procedures such as import approval, border inspection, and domestic distribution safety management by the pre-risk review of LMO. The safety management of LMO production is carried out through the risk review and pre-production approval procedures for locally produced LMO. The basic policy of LMO sales, transport, and storage safety management is aimed at strengthening the safety management system through procedures for compliance with domestic handling management standards, preparation of management records and storage. In order to establish LMO management and hazard prevention system, the relevant central administrative institute implements appropriate follow-up management in the event of an accident of environmental discharge in the research and development, import, production, storage, and distribution of LMO. Strengthen publicity on LMO safety management and build trust by providing transparent and correct information. South Korea is performing to revitalize R&D by LMO due to a steady increase in R&D budget. South Korean government investment in the bio technology (BT) sector increased from $1.47 billion in 2008 to $2.84 billion in 2016. The number of LMO research facilities increased from 1,171 in 2008 to 6,040 in 2016. There are a total of 194 approvals for LMO environmental emission experiments for test research from 2008 to 2017, mainly rice.

## 4 Research Mechanism and Method

We utilized research facility survey (2019) of the Ministry of Science and ICT (MSIT) of South Korea. The research analysis was conducted using a five-point scale for 88 researchers. The evaluation was reformed in terms of feasibility and reliability. The validity was analyzed through factor analysis and reliability was analyzed using the Cronbach-α value. In this study, t-test and one-way ANOVA were conducted. The analysis results are marked with the upper subscripts * of t value and F value. $*P < 0.1$, $**P < 0.05$, $***P < 0.001$ means that there is a significant difference between factors, statistically with a reliability of 90%, 95%, and 99%.

## 5 Research Results

We conducted an awareness analysis of the LMO-related legislation. The recognition analysis of LMO-related legislation consisted of 7 items, the compliance within the LMO Act required for conducting LMO research. Items are consist of Cartagena Protocol on Biosafety, act on the transnational movement of GMO, experimental guideline, classification of safety management grades of research facility, LMO research facility report, LMO import and export, and biohazard group classification. The reliability analysis results show that the Cronbach-α value is 0.910, which is very high. It means that accurate analysis of research results is possible. Reliability analysis on awareness of LMO-related legislation is describe in Table 2.

**Table 2** Reliability analysis on awareness of LMO-related legislation

| Classification | Factor | Cronbach-α |
|---|---|---|
| Cartagena Protocol on Biosafety | 0.813 | 0.910 |
| Act on the transnational movement of GMO | 0.761 | |
| Experimental guideline | 0.806 | |
| Classification of safety management grades of research facility | 0.766 | |
| LMO research facility report | 0.818 | |
| LMO import and export | 0.774 | |
| Biohazard group classification | 0.853 | |
| Eigenvalue | 5.040 | |
| Explained variance (%) | 85001 | |

In reliability analysis result on awareness of LMO-related legislation, act on the transnational movement of GMO was the highest at 3.69. LMO research facility report was 3.59, classification of safety management grades of research facility was 3.56, Cartagena Protocol on Biosafety was 3.51, LMO import and export was 3.34, Experimental guideline was 3.12, and biohazard group classification was 3.01. It means that researchers are aware of LMO law at a minimum required level in conducting their studies. In particular, LMO import and export, experimental guideline, and biohazard group classification are areas that many researchers have not recognized, and they need publicity and education. The T-test results did not show significant differences at the significant level $p < 0.1$. The analysis of variance showed significant differences in Cartagena Protocol on Biosafety, act on the transnational movement of GMO, experimental guideline, LMO import and export, and biohazard group classification. Awareness analysis of LMO-related legislation is describe in Table 3.

In order to operate LMO research facility in accordance with the LMO Act, the mandatory installation operating standards according to research types and hazard grades shall be complied with. The research analysis was conducted focusing on the level of awareness of installation operation that the researchers should keep within the LMO research facility. We analyzed the awareness and implementation of LMO research facility compliance. The awareness and implementation analysis of compliance with LMO research facility consisted of 5 items. Items are consist of laboratory management, prohibition of experimental zone, hepatitis substance management, preparation and management of LMO management register, and waste management. The reliability analysis results show that the Cronbach-α value is 0.935, which is very high. It means that accurate analysis of research results is possible. Reliability analysis for awareness and implementation of compliance with LMO research facility is describe in Table 4.

In reliability analysis result on awareness and implementation of compliance with LMO research facility, hepatitis substance management was the highest at 4.82. Waste management was 4.31. Prohibition of experimental zone was 4.17. Laboratory

**Table 3** Awareness analysis of LMO-related legislation

| Classification | Mean | Standard deviation | T | F |
|---|---|---|---|---|
| Cartagena Protocol on Biosafety | 3.51 | 0.814 | 0.348 | 1.789* |
| Act on the transnational movement of GMO | 3.69 | 1.018 | 1.701 | 2.089* |
| Experimental guideline | 3.12 | 0.791 | 0.870 | 2.312* |
| Classification of safety management grades of research facility | 3.56 | 1.006 | 0.976 | 0.843 |
| LMO research facility report | 3.59 | 0.932 | 0.858 | 1.120 |
| LMO import and export | 3.34 | 0.919 | 0.651 | 1.648* |
| Biohazard group classification | 3.01 | 0.895 | 1.432 | 2.037* |

* $p < 0.1$, ** $p < 0.05$, *** $p < 0.01$

**Table 4** Reliability analysis for awareness and implementation of compliance with LMO research facility

| Classification | Factor | Cronbach-α |
|---|---|---|
| Laboratory management | 0.836 | 0.935 |
| Prohibition of experimental zone | 0.903 | |
| Hepatitis substance management | 0.851 | |
| Preparation and management of LMO management register | 0.884 | |
| Waste management | 0.910 | |
| Eigenvalue | 4.589 | |
| Explained variance (%) | 80343 | |

management was 3.99. Preparation and management of LMO management register was 3.74. It means that many researchers need publicity and education. The T-test results did not show significant differences at the significant level $p < 0.1$. The analysis of variance showed significant differences in preparation and management of LMO management register. Analysis for awareness and implementation of the LMO research facility is describe in Table 5.

Effective policies are needed to streamline the operation of LMO research facilities. We conducted a research analysis on effective policy for efficient operation of LMO research facility. We analyzed the policy of streamlining the operation of LMO research facility. For the efficient operation of LMO research facility, effective policy analysis consisted of 6 items. Items are consist of strengthening law enforcement, supply of LMO inspection manual, reinforcement of LMO safety management, training and promotional activation, raise safety awareness of higher level managers, and site inspection of research facility. The reliability analysis results show that the Cronbach-α value is 0.917, which is very high. It means that accurate analysis of

**Table 5** Analysis for awareness and implementation of the LMO research facility

| Classification | Mean | Standard deviation | T | F |
|---|---|---|---|---|
| Laboratory management | 3.99 | 0.786 | 0.738 | 0.879 |
| Prohibition of experimental zone | 4.17 | 0.834 | 0.847 | 1.931 |
| Hepatitis substance management | 4.82 | 0.878 | 0.939 | 0.841 |
| Preparation and management of LMO management register | 3.74 | 0.903 | 0.812 | 1.740* |
| Waste management | 4.31 | 0.993 | 0.714 | 0.838 |

* $p < 0.1$, ** $p < 0.05$, *** $p < 0.01$

research results is possible. Reliability analysis for effective policy to streamline the operation of LMO research facility is describe in Table 6.

In an effective policy analysis for the efficient operation of LMO research facility, site inspection of research facility was the highest at 3.95. Raise safety awareness of higher level managers was 3.90. Reinforcement of LMO safety management was 3.87. Strengthening law enforcement was 3.81. Training and promotional activation was 3.41. Supply of LMO inspection manual was 3.19. It means that many researchers need publicity and education. The T-test results did not show significant differences at the significant level $p < 0.1$. The analysis of variance showed significant differences in strengthening law enforcement and site inspection of research facility. Effective policy analysis for the efficient operation of LMO research facility is describe in Table 7.

**Table 6** Reliability analysis for effective policy to streamline the operation of LMO research facility

| Classification | Factor | Cronbach-α |
|---|---|---|
| Strengthening law enforcement | 0.748 | 0.917 |
| Supply of LMO inspection manual | 0.885 | |
| Reinforcement of LMO safety management | 0.783 | |
| Training and promotional activation | 0.817 | |
| Raise safety awareness of higher level managers | 0.799 | |
| Site inspection of research facility | 0.839 | |
| Eigenvalue | 4.313 | |
| Explained variance (%) | 78341 | |

**Table 7** Effective policy analysis for the efficient operation of LMO research facility

| Classification | Mean | Standard deviation | T | F |
|---|---|---|---|---|
| Strengthening law enforcement | 3.81 | 1.016 | 0.912 | 1.631* |
| Supply of LMO inspection manual | 3.19 | 0.789 | 0.816 | 0.917 |
| Reinforcement of LMO safety management | 3.87 | 0.874 | 0.739 | 0.833 |
| Training and promotional activation | 3.41 | 0.840 | 0.760 | 1.201 |
| Raise safety awareness of higher level managers | 3.90 | 0.938 | 0.804 | 0.953 |
| Site inspection of research facility | 3.95 | 0.860 | 0.871 | 1.340* |

* $p < 0.1$, ** $p < 0.05$, *** $p < 0.01$

## 6 Policy Discussion

In previous studies, there have been few policy studies for the management efficiency of research facility. This study makes an academic contribution through policy research on the management efficiency of research facility. Government-led safety management of research facility subject to safety management under the LMO Act is limited by manpower and budget constraints. Therefore, it is necessary for research institute to establish a safety inspection system autonomously, secure safety management specialists, and support institutional self-regulation for the establishment of specialized organizations. Systematic operation is possible by developing new LMO technology and preparing new safety management regulations according to the diversification of LMO laboratory materials. It is desirable to spread the safety culture through LMO safety management education, promotion, and reinforcement. As the number of LMO handlers continues to increase, it is essential to expand the number of educational professionals, strengthen the efficient education system, and foster education experts. As there is a shortage of professional safety education instructors for the continuous increase of LMO handlers, it is essential to expand the number of education specialists, strengthen the efficient education system, and train education experts. The effectiveness of management in times of the crisis depends largely on organizational competences of managers [9]. Therefore, it is necessary to develop educational contents for researchers and to continuously promote the specialization and diversification of LMO safety education. It is desirable to increase safety awareness of increased LMO handlers for testing and research. It is possible to improve and systematize regulations on import and export, research and development, storage, movement, disposal, environmental discharge experiment and commercialization through the establishment of a full-cycle safety management system using LMO for testing and research.

Efficient operation is possible through reorganization of user-centered LMO reporting system and establishment of information service. The establishment of a cooperative network with LMO practitioners and related domestic and foreign specialized institutions can increase efficiency. Safety management can be strengthened by improving the LMO safety management system to increase the efficiency of law and system implementation. It is urgent to strengthen safety management due to increase and diversification of LMO environmental emission experiments for testing and research, and to prepare regulations on LMO hazard prevention and management. As LMO experiments for testing and research become more active, LMO research facility reports and LMO import reports are also continuously increasing, so the importance of LMO is growing very much. The LMO law requires a lot of preparation for the actual uncomfortable and smooth enforcement of the law. It is desirable to develop and implement policy according to the needs of researchers through education and public relation policy for policy makers. Strengthening law enforcement and introducing new systems are needed to improve the effectiveness and institutional efficiency of LMO safety management policy. The most important thing in safety management is prevention, which requires both policy makers and researchers to have an interest and understanding of LMO.

## 7 Conclusions and Research Limitation

The purpose of this paper is to study the management efficiency of LMO research facility and present its policy research and direction. In this paper, we identified problems and improvements for the efficiency of LMO management and operation and carried out research that would actually help to researchers. We conducted an awareness analysis of the LMO-related legislation. Items are consist of Cartagena Protocol on Biosafety, act on the transnational movement of GMO, experimental guideline, classification of safety management grades of research facility, LMO research facility report, LMO import and export, and biohazard group classification. In research result, we could see that Cartagena Protocol on Biosafety, act on the transnational movement of GMO, and LMO import and export were well implemented through the high value. Experimental guideline and biohazard group classification need to publicity and education for many researchers. We analyzed the awareness and implementation of LMO research facility compliance. Items are consist of laboratory management, prohibition of experimental zone, hepatitis substance management, preparation and management of LMO management register, and waste management. In research result, we could see that prohibition of experimental zone, hepatitis substance management, and waste management were well implemented through the high value. Laboratory management and preparation and management of LMO management register need to publicity and education for many researchers. We analyzed the policy of streamlining the operation of LMO research facility. Items are consist of strengthening law enforcement, supply of LMO inspection manual, reinforcement of LMO safety management, training and promotional activation, raise safety awareness of higher level managers, and site inspection of research facility. In research result, we could see that strengthening law enforcement, reinforcement of LMO safety management, raise safety awareness, and site inspection of research facility were well implemented through the high value. Supply of LMO inspection manual and training and promotional activation need to publicity and education for many researchers.

The limitation of this study is that research on the implementation of LMO policy implementation on the actual site is necessary. This study is a situation in which researchers need to study actual practice. Research on LMO safety management in electricity, machinery, construction, gas, and facility is also essential in connection with R&D safety management. Various studies are required as well as research data analysis, which can further enhance the accuracy of the research. In future studies, analysis linked to plan and site implementation rate can increase the completeness of analyses for efficient policy implementation. Through the LMO legal system, it can help minimize the problems that may arise from LMO handling and create an environment that can be tested more safely and serve to publicize the biological risks and importance. It is necessary to prevent laws and regulations from constraining research and hindering research by reducing the efficiency of experiments. The most effective thing for raising awareness is education, and it is necessary to carry out continuous policy implementation, research, publicity, and educational efforts for LMO safety management, but efforts to strengthen and revitalize the research institute's own education are of paramount importance. In order to promote the research institute's own education, it is necessary to strengthen the LMO safety management education. We hope that this study will help to ensure laboratory safety management and system settlement around the worldwide.

## References

1. Valentinas Navickas, V., Svazas, M., Vojtovic, S.: Biomass clusters influence on business competitiveness. Pol. J. Manag. Stud. **16**(2), 188–197 (2017)
2. Holubová, V.: Intergrated safety management systems. Pol. J. Manag. Stud. **14**(1), 106–118 (2016)
3. Tabor, J.: Occupational safety management in the light of causes analysis of accidents. Pol. J. Manag. Stud. **2013**(7), 189–200 (2013)
4. The cartagena protocol on biosafety, Biosafety clearing-house, (2003)
5. Genetically modified organisms, US EPA, (2020)
6. Biosafety regulations in Japan, Japan biosafety clearing house, (2019)
7. GMOs, EU Science Hub, European Union, (2020)
8. Genetically modified organisms, CSIRO, (2020)
9. Szczepańska-Woszczyna, K.: Managerial competencies in time of the crisis. Forum Sci. Oecon. **1**(2), 77–86 (2013)

# European Seaport Cargo Management: Adaptations Amidst the Global Economic Crisis

**Katarzyna Grondys**

**Abstract** The current economic crisis, intensified by global shifts, has dramatically impacted international trade and supply chains. This crisis presents unique challenges distinct from previous episodes. This study aims to determine how European pandemic-related restrictions and the armed conflict in Ukraine have influenced seaport cargo volumes. It evaluates variations in sea-transported cargo volumes during crises and examines continuity changes in foreign trade. Data from 2020–2022, covering the gross weight of goods transported through significant ports in 23 European countries, was sourced from the UNCTAD database. The Kolmogorov–Smirnov test assessed distribution normality, while the variance homogeneity test gauged model sphericity. The Friedman test identified differences for dependent variables in maritime transport patterns. Results indicate that the impacts of the pandemic and the Ukrainian conflict on seaport trade depend on the crisis timeline. Despite facing unprecedented challenges, the maritime transport sector is adaptable to changing international trade conditions, hinting at potential similar responses in future crises.

**Keywords** International trade · Cargo management · Crisis · Maritime transport · Seaport

## 1 Introduction

Sea transport is a key mode of transport in global trade, handling almost 80% of world trade [1]. As a result of the economic crisis associated with the pandemic, the level of international trade by sea also deteriorated, affecting the continuity of the global supply chain [2]. However, all maritime transport faced a considerable challenge in meeting new challenges and constraints during this period. In the most difficult crisis, global economic production fell by 3.5% and trade in goods by 5.4%, which

K. Grondys (✉)
Czestochowa University of Technology, Czestochowa, Poland
e-mail: katarzyna.grondys@pcz.pl

 
S. Kot et al. (eds.), *Corporate Practices: Policies, Methodologies, and Insights in Organizational Management*, Springer Proceedings in Business and Economics,
https://doi.org/10.1007/978-981-97-0996-0_38

was also reflected in the decline in orders in maritime transport by 3.8% compared to before the crisis [3]. During that time, global imports and exports of goods fell by a combined 5.4% [4]. The significant revival of trade in maritime transport observed in 2021 was hindered by the unexpected armed conflict between Russia and Ukraine. Therefore, the expected increases in trade between ports were put at risk.

On the other hand, the crisis caused by the pandemic and war has highlighted the need to change the approach to risk management and build preparedness and resilience to unexpected global disruptions [5]. Moreover, transport, by its nature, is also an essential factor in the spread of diseases, which is why this sector was one of the first to face significant restrictions caused by the pandemic [6]. The resulting disruptions in the continuity of the flow of goods harm entire supply chains and shift difficulties to other sectors [7]. Both the pandemic and the armed conflict in Ukraine and the resulting bottlenecks in trade, inflation, and higher business risk increase the risk of uncertainty, mainly for sea carriers.

Based on the literature analysis, trade changes in recent years have been shown as a result of economic and economic changes resulting from the crisis caused by the pandemic and the war in Ukraine. Most of these studies present changes before Russia invaded Ukraine, in contrast to the current situation. Previous research on the impact of the crisis on maritime transport should have been more focused on examining the significance of differences due to drastic changes in the environment. The task of the study was to check the continuity of these changes against the background of pandemics and armed conflict. Appropriate statistical methods of data analysis were used to identify the differences between the tonnages transported in this period in sea transport, depending on the moment of the entire crisis. Therefore, the study aimed to indicate the trends in the level of cargo transport by sea in the period of dynamic global changes hampering the potential of international development of the supply chain.

## 2 Maritime Trade in Times of Crisis

### 2.1 *Crisis-Time Demand for International Maritime Commerce Services*

Intensive changes in the global supply chain due to economic changes caused by the pandemic and the armed conflict in Ukraine have also negatively impacted maritime transport [8]. Although the decline in trade by sea was less significant than expected, recovering or equalizing the level of work from before the crisis is still underway [9]. The condition of international trade had its time determinants, which resulted from different phases of the pandemic and geographical ones, resulting from the impact of restrictions on employment in other regions and markets [4, 10].

The volumes of maritime transport are also determined by the demand for e-commerce, which is proliferating [11] and is associated with increased spending on goods [12]. To a large extent, the excellent condition of maritime trade was also supported by the release of partially suppressed demand in the automotive industry and the need to replenish the stocks of certain goods lost in the pandemic. The cumulative annual growth of sea trade in 2018 was 2.9%, and 2019 only 0.8% [13]. In 2020, this trade recorded a severe decline of almost 4% [4]. It was the year of the most significant critical decrease that occurred during the pandemic and resulted from lower demand for shipping and the related slowdown in port work. During this time, both port managers, terminal operators, and intermodal transport providers took measures to contain the spread of COVID-19, resulting in ships spending more time in ports. The second quarter of 2020 saw the worst economic collapse [14]. In May 2020, serviced volumes decreased by approximately 12% compared to May 2019 [4].

Moreover, during the first half of the year, the decline in demand for shipping and port services translated into fewer port calls. What's more, the outflows of all ships also decreased, which, in the example of Norwegian ports, fell by 20% in the first week of April 2020 compared to 2019, while the decrease in the outflows of container ships was almost 30%. At that time, the level of cruises also decreased [15].

The level of significant decreases in maritime trade during the pandemic period is also confirmed by studies by Liu X. et al. [16], who point out that government measures aimed at limiting economic activity had a more significant impact on the volume of imports of a given country than the direct health and behavioral effects of the pandemic itself. In turn, in 2021, there was another increase in trade at the level of 4.3%. The rebound in trade in goods was visible in almost all major economies, mainly in the pharmaceuticals, communication and office equipment, and agricultural and food products industries [4]. On this occasion, it should be emphasized that both Ukraine and Russia are among the leading global suppliers of agricultural and food products. Therefore, the direction of trade in this sector had to be remodeled due to the armed conflict between these countries [17, 18]. However, the revival of work could have been better due to bottlenecks in the supply chain that arose at that time.

## 2.2 Sea Transport Infrastructure Resources

As research shows, the productivity time of maritime transport varies depending on the infrastructural resources at the disposal of countries. Only 6% of countries operate direct container connections; the rest of shipping communication requires a stop in at least one intermediate country. In addition, a significant part of global maritime trade is handled by central ports, e.g., the port of Singapore (32% share) [15]. The more prominent a major port is in the shipping network, the more extensive the consequences of its regulations and restrictions on global trade are. One group of countries with short handling times includes countries with fewer small vessels or few containers handled. In the second category, some ports were customized ship handling due to their technology and extensive infrastructure, which only take the largest container ships [19]. Typical examples are China and Japan. There are European ports Between these two categories, which handle large container ships less often or, more often, smaller vessels, which still need a fully automated and technologically developed port infrastructure. In addition, European countries have lower shipping efficiency and port capacity due to higher transport costs and poorer communication with distant large foreign markets [20].

The Ukraine armed conflict outbreak introduced dynamic changes to the fuel market and, thus, the costs of servicing container ships and tankers. According to research by Rožic et al. [21], the container freight rate is the highest in decades due to the pandemic and the Russian invasion of Ukraine. As a result of significant fluctuations in transport demand and supply during the crisis, freight rates on the sea container market in 2021 increased almost sevenfold. However, the highest dynamics of their growth was recorded in the second quarter of 2022, during the Ukraine war outbreak [21]. The reasons should be sought in the sanctions against Russia and the need to ensure the safety of transport, which disrupted land and air transport routes popular in this area [18]. This poses another threat to the recovery of the global economy and may result in additional disruptions to maritime supply chains. The need to look for alternative trade routes for Ukrainian goods causes the infrastructure and sea transport services to operate in conditions of high uncertainty [22]. Black Sea ports are responsible for over 90% of Ukraine's grain exports.

In contrast, due to the destruction of infrastructure and limited trade opportunities, port operations were suspended, which caused numerous disruptions in regional logistics, and weekly calls at ports in Ukraine fell to almost zero [23]. These circumstances contributed to a sharp increase in grain prices, which in the second quarter of 2022 increased by approximately 60% compared to the previous period. The volume of canceled orders and delayed deliveries also caused difficulties in US ports [24].

In the second quarter of 2020, there was a significant decrease in the volume of flows in global trade in goods, and a similar crisis occurred more than ten years ago. At the same time, the available research presents European ports with an average level of order handling, which does not have a degree of development of infrastructure and automation equal to world-class ports. At the same time, to a greater or lesser extent, European ports are connected with the eastern wall of Europe and the related risk of international exchange and trade in goods resulting from the armed conflict in Ukraine.

## 3 Research Methodology

The research was carried out on a sample of European seaports and the volumes of handled cargo identified in them in the period 2020–2022. Raw data on the measurement of gross weight of goods transported to/from main ports came from the UNCTAD database from 2020–2022 broken down by quarters [4]. Therefore, seaports in 23 European countries were analyzed. In total, data on the cargo of all seaports was collected for the analysis. The research sample selection method was intentional. In the first phase of the selection, 636 observations were identified, representing the number of all major European ports, then, in order to maintain high-quality analyses, those observations for which significant data gaps were noted were removed from the database. However, observations with single missing data were left in the database in order to keep as many observations as possible for analysis. Finally, the database included 360 observations that correspond to 360 larger and smaller seaports in 23 European countries. The analysis of the differences due to the transported cargo was made mainly by country, with the statistical study of the differences being carried out due to the number of ports in accordance with the assumption that the larger the research sample, the more accurate and reliable statistical results. The research sample comprising 360 observations constitutes 56% of the studied population. The confidence level for the research sample intended for statistical testing is alpha = 0.95, and the maximum error is 5%.

The study was divided into four main parts, which included:

I. Characteristics of the surveyed sample broken down by all surveyed countries and quarters.
II. Characteristics of the tested sample due to the time factor based on the number of all ports.
III. Comparison of results obtained for selected three quarters for all surveyed ports.
IV. Examination of the significance of differences in the size of handled tonnage in selected quarters for all surveyed ports.

Therefore, the study identified the following variables:

1. Independent variables expressed on a nominal scale, i.e.: country ($n = 23$) or port ($n = 360$).
2. Independent variable: time factor, i.e., successive quarters of the analyzed period ($n = 9$);
3. Dependent variable expressed on a quantitative scale: tonnage (thousand tonnes).

It is assumed that the period of economic crisis, including the period of the pandemic and the period of war in Ukraine for the purposes of the study, affects the diversification of the tonnage of cargo handled in European ports. Therefore, data from European ports have been analyzed broken down into three analogous quarters, which successively refer to the pre-pandemic crisis, the pandemic crisis and the post-war crisis in Ukraine. The aim of the study was to identify differences in the level of cargo transport by sea in the period of dynamic global changes in the global development of the supply chain. On this basis, the following research hypothesis was indicated:

H1: There are significant statistical differences between the tonnages studied due to the global crisis situation.

Basic statistical measures were used to characterize the research sample to verify the hypotheses. Due to the sample size of more than 100 observations, the Kolmogorov–Smirnov test for related samples was used to test the normality of the distribution [25]. In turn, to assess the sphericity of variance in the model, the variance homogeneity test was used [26]. The measurement method for dependent models with k repeated measurement was used to identify differences for the dependent variable, where the Friedman test (test for several related samples) was used. This test is a non-parametric equivalent of the one-way ANOVA analysis, which can be performed when the restrictive conditions of repeatable measurement are not met, i.e., no normal distribution and no sphericity. In addition, the use of Friedman's test allows the comparison of at least three research groups given the studied phenomenon, where the dependent variable takes continuous values. This test estimates overall statistical significance for all study groups together [27].

## 4 Research Results

### 4.1 Characteristics of the Tested Sample

First, the gross weight of goods transported to/from main ports was analyzed, broken down by European countries with their ports. Greece (128), Denmark (95) as well as Italy and Sweden (76 each) have the largest number of ports. Finally, Denmark (95), Italy (41), and Spain (39) dominate the research sample due to the number of ports. Slovenia and Malta have the fewest ports in population and sample. Figure 1 presents observations from the second quarter of 2020 to the second quarter of 2022.

In turn, according to the division into quarters, it is observed that the volume of cargo transported from and to the surveyed ports is almost identical due to the time factor. This means that the volumes transported oscillate around one level in each of the surveyed countries. The general data do not show possible differences in tonnage level due to the number of ports. Still, they show differences in their level between countries with these ports. Thus, it can be observed that the largest amount of cargo is handled by ports in the Netherlands (between 131,000 tonnes and 152,000 tonnes), almost half as much is dealt with by Spain (between 100,000 tonnes and 112,000 tonnes) and Italy (between 92,000 tonnes and 112,000 tonnes and 108 thousand

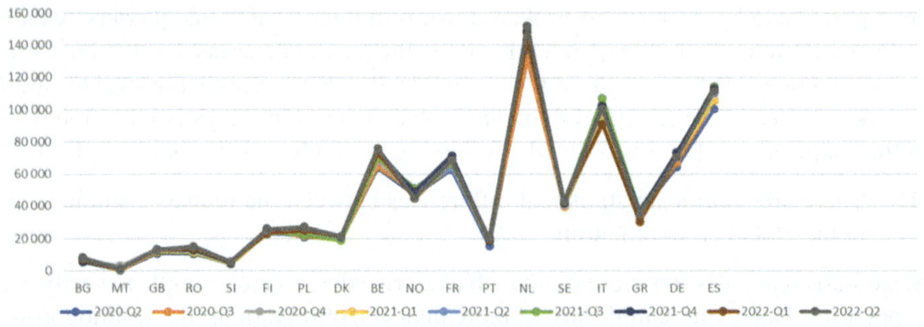


**Fig. 1** Gross weight of goods transported to/from selected seaports in 2020–2022 (thousand tonnes) [28]

**Table 1** The most important descriptive statistics for all surveyed quarters

| Year | 2022 | | | 2021 | | | | 2022 | |
|---|---|---|---|---|---|---|---|---|---|
| Quarter | 2 | 3 | 4 | 1 | 2 | 3 | 4 | 1 | 2 |
| Average (thousand tonnes) | 2418 | 2439 | 2518 | 2487 | 2570 | 2598 | 2619 | 2277 | 2370 |
| Median (thousand tonnes) | 604 | 592 | 608 | 585 | 623 | 642 | 638 | 569 | 626 |
| Standard deviation (thousand tonnes) | 7074 | 7035 | 7537 | 7506 | 7588 | 7677 | 7715 | 6819 | 7089 |
| The dynamics of cargo transport (%) | 102 | 101 | 103 | 99 | 103 | 101 | 101 | 87 | 104 |

tonnes) due to the number of ports they have, Slovenia and Malta record the lowest transport of cargo by sea. None of the countries recorded extreme deviations from the transported cargo volumes during the period under review.

The study of the r-Pearson correlation between the number of ports in each country and the tonnage results showed that this correlation is significant ($r = 0.550$; $p < 0.01$). This confirms that there is a strong positive relationship between the variables studied. The number of ports affects the cargo transported by sea; therefore, a detailed analysis was made by the number of surveyed ports, not by country. However, this allows us to generalize the results obtained based on the surveyed ports to those for individual countries. The preliminary characteristics of the research sample due to the number of ports are presented in Table 1.

The average tonnage in the quarters examined is between 2,277 thousand tonnes in the first quarter of 2022 and 2,619 thousand tonnes in the fourth quarter of 2021. This means that at the turn of 2021 and 2022, the largest change in the level of tonnage handling in ports occurred. The median at the minimum level of 569 thousand tonnes means that at least half of the tonnage is below this value. A standard deviation at a similar level indicates a low dispersion of results due to the time factor. The calculated dynamics indicator shows that in each second quarter of the analyzed years, there is an increase in tonnage by 1% compared to the previous quarter. In each third quarter, there is a decrease in tonnage compared to the last quarter. The dynamics indicator allows you to observe specific trends broken down by quarters, which show the seasonality of the level of serviced tonnage. Only those quarters that can be compared with each other and, simultaneously exclude the risk of seasonality on the level of transported tonnage were selected for further research. Finally, every second quarter of the surveyed years, 2020–2022, was selected.

## *4.2 Quarterly Comparison of Results*

At this stage, only the second quarter of each surveyed year was left in the database for analysis for all surveyed countries and ports. The detailed study did not include data from Spanish ports due to the complete lack of data in the second quarter of

2022. The high diversity of the level of cargo handled in ports in individual countries was the basis for separating groups of the number of ports due to the volume of cargo transported in separate quarters (Table 2).

The number of ports has been divided into eight groups similar in terms of number of ports, which differ in the size of the tonnage handled. In the second quarter of 2020, the largest number of ports served quarterly was from 221 thousand tonnes to 420 thousand tonnes (13.4%) and 1,226 thousand tonnes to 2,600 thousand tonnes (13.4%). In the second quarter of 2021, the largest number of ports (16.2%) handled cargo between 221 thousand tonnes and 420 thousand tonnes, while in the second quarter of 2022, it was a range between 651 thousand tonnes and 1,225 thousand tonnes (15%). The difference in the level of cargo handled is most noticeable between 2021 and 2022. At the same time, in the II quarter of 2022, more ports dealt with a higher tonnage than in the II quarter of 2021, while fewer ports handled a higher tonnage in the II quarter of 2020.

Almost 25% of ports handle up to 220 thousand tonnes of cargo, while half of the surveyed ports handle a maximum of 650 thousand tonnes of cargo. This level is almost equal to the median, a maximum of 652 thousand tonnes of cargo per port. Half of the ports handled an average of 42,146 thousand tonnes in the surveyed quarters, which is 6% of the total cargo handled in all surveyed ports. Considering 80% of the ports, they will handle an average of 356,596 thousand tonnes in the analyzed quarters, which is only 47% of the total cargo handled at that time in all ports. This means 20% of the remaining ports handle 53% of all cargo. The largest tonnage is dealt with by the ports of France—La Rochelle, and Latvia—the port of Ventspils. Much farther away are ports in Italy, Sweden, and Bulgaria.

So far, it has been observed that the tonnage for individual ports differs for the examined quarters in terms of the number of ports. Further, based on the objective of studying the differences in terms of the time factor, tonnage data was explored

**Table 2** Port frequency table for designated weight ranges

| Ranges of transported weights (thousand tonnes) | II quarter. 2020 | | II quarter. 2021 | | II quarter. 2022 | | Average cumulative percentage |
|---|---|---|---|---|---|---|---|
| | Number of ports | % | Number of ports | % | Number of ports | % | |
| 0–65 | 42 | 13.1 | 43 | 13.4 | 42 | 13.1 | 13.7 |
| 66–220 | 40 | 12.5 | 30 | 9.3 | 34 | 10.6 | 24.9 |
| 221–420 | 43 | 13.4 | 52 | 16.2 | 47 | 14.6 | 40.2 |
| 421–650 | 41 | 12.8 | 33 | 10.3 | 32 | 10.0 | 51.6 |
| 651–1225 | 39 | 12.1 | 39 | 12.1 | 48 | 15.0 | 65.1 |
| 1226–2600 | 43 | 13.4 | 51 | 15.9 | 42 | 13.1 | 79.8 |
| 2601–6500 | 39 | 12.1 | 36 | 11.2 | 31 | 9.7 | 91.2 |
| 6501–11,000 | 27 | 8.4 | 28 | 8.7 | 27 | 8.4 | 100.0 |

**Table 3** Basic descriptive statistics for tonnage in the surveyed quarters (thousand tonnes)

| Statistics | 2020_2 | 2021_2 | 2022_2 |
|---|---|---|---|
| Average | 2421,03 | 2593,94 | 2607,13 |
| Median | 612,00 | 637,00 | 652,00 |
| Variance | 49,348,201,483 | 56,067,076,480 | 58,173,003,066 |
| Range | 99,588 | 107,247 | 108,195 |
| Skewness | 9,801 | 9,931 | 9,831 |
| Kurtosis | 124,454 | 128,640 | 125,137 |

for selected quarters for all ports in the research sample, keeping the record of the dependent variable as a continuous quantitative variable (Table 3).

Preliminary data exploration has shown that individual gross weight observations differ for the quarters of 2020, 2021, and 2022. The average tonnage transported from and to ports is 2,421 thousand tonnes in the II quarter of 2020 and is growing year by year for the quarters under review. At least half of the surveyed ports handle a minimum tonnage of 612 thousand tonnes quarterly. The dispersion analysis of the results indicates that the standard deviation is at least 402 thousand tonnes and is not too big. The skewness oscillates around the value of 9.8, which means a high right-skewness of the distribution of observations. A kurtosis value of at least 124 suggests many extreme observations. The obtained results indicate the lack of a normal distribution initially.

## 4.3 *Quarterly Comparison of Results*

To assess the significance of differences between the level of the dependent variable in terms of the time factor, a test of comparison of results obtained with repeated measurement for dependent samples was selected. To select a testing method, it is necessary first to determine the distribution of the variable. The obtained results of the exploration indicate the lack of a normal distribution. To formally check the significance of these differences, normality and variance homogeneity tests were performed. The Kolmogorov–Smirnov test with the Lilliefors significance correction is a test that verifies the assumption whether the distribution of the studied sample differs significantly from the theoretical normal distribution and is suitable for large samples (for more than 100 observations). K-S test results, for which Z 2020_2 (299) = 0.370; Z 2021_2 (299) = 0.371, and Z 2022_2 (299) = 0.372 and $p < 0.05$ indicate that the sample distribution is significantly different from a normal distribution. To check the second assumption of the equality of variance required for parametric tests, the significance of differences was also studied to test the homogeneity of variance. For this purpose, the Leven test was used, which verifies the hypothesis regarding the homogeneity of variance, i.e., the similarity of the dispersion of results in the sample:

$$\mathrm{H0} : \sigma_1^2 = \sigma_2^2 = \sigma_3^2 = \ldots = \sigma_k^2$$
$$\mathrm{H1} : \sigma_1^2 \neq \sigma_j^2 \text{ at least for one pair (i, j)}$$

The assumption of homogeneity is satisfied if the variances for differences between pairs of repeated measures are the same. At the same time, Levene's test can recognize non-heterogeneity in the sample with high probability and is suitable for examining groups of different sizes [29]. Levene's test statistic was calculated according to the formula [30]:

$$W = \frac{N-1}{k-1} \frac{\sum_{i=1}^{k} n_i (\overline{Z} - \overline{Z})^2}{\sum_{i=1}^{k} \sum_{j=1}^{n_i} (Z_{ij} - \overline{Z}_i)^2}, \quad (1)$$

The test results for data from the surveyed ports for three quarters are included in Table 4.

The result of Leven's test based on the average for each quarter: F-Leven's (20, 286) = 9.103, F-Leven's (20, 293) = 8.893, and F-Leven's (20, 284) = 7.805 is $p < 0.001$. This means that the dispersion of the results differs in each study group, i.e., the variances are heterogeneous. Therefore, H1 should be assumed with the heterogeneity of the sample variance for each quarter.

Because both the condition of the normality of the distribution and the homogeneity of the variance for the test sample in three repeated measurements were not met, the non-parametric Friedman test was used to test the significance of differences, which is carried out for k-dependent samples in a repeated measurement (test for several related samples). This test is a non-parametric equivalent of one-way ANOVA (analysis of variance), which can be performed when the restrictive conditions of repeated measurement are not met, i.e., lack of normality of distribution and lack of homogeneity of variances. The hypotheses concern the equality of the rank sum for successive measurements or are simplified to the medians ɵ1, ɵ2, ɵk of the examined feature in subsequent measurements from the studied population:

$$H_0 : \theta_1 = \theta_2 = \ldots = \theta_K$$
$$H_1 : \textit{not all } \theta_j \textit{ are equal } (j = 1, 2, \ldots, k).$$

**Table 4** Variance homogeneity tests based on the average for the tonnage transported in the surveyed ports in selected quarters

| | Levene's test | df1 | df2 | Significance |
|---|---|---|---|---|
| 2020_2 | 9,103 | 20 | 286 | < 0,001 |
| 2021_2 | 8,893 | 20 | 293 | < 0,001 |
| 2022_2 | 7,805 | 20 | 284 | < 0,001 |

In addition, the use of the Friedman test in the study is also justified by its other conditions, because this method is suitable for testing:

- repeatable measurements.
- comparing at least three research groups in view of some phenomenon,
- differences for more than two related groups.
- dependent variables, which are expressed on a quantitative scale.
- study groups include a minimum of five observations.

Three paired samples were tested to assess the significance of differences between all groups. The test result $p < 0.05$ means the statistical significance of differences between the studied groups. This means that the level of transported tonnage to and from ports changed significantly ($\chi 2(2) = 21.173$, p$p$ 0.001)). The null hypothesis of no differences between the study groups should be rejected.

Suppose the average ranges are compared (Fig. 2). In that case, it can be seen that higher tonnage volumes were transported in the last year under review when the restrictions related to the pandemic were lifted, but the effects of the war in Ukraine were being felt. In turn, the lowest transport results can be seen during the pandemic period, when restrictions on international transport were very restrictive. To check which groups differed the most from each other, comparisons between groups were performed.

To check inter-relationships between individual pairs of groups, comparisons between teams were also performed (Table 5).

The analysis of the variance study between pairs showed that a significant difference in the tonnage level occurred between the second quarter of 2020 and the second quarter of 2021 (p = 0.001) and between the second quarter of 2020 and the second

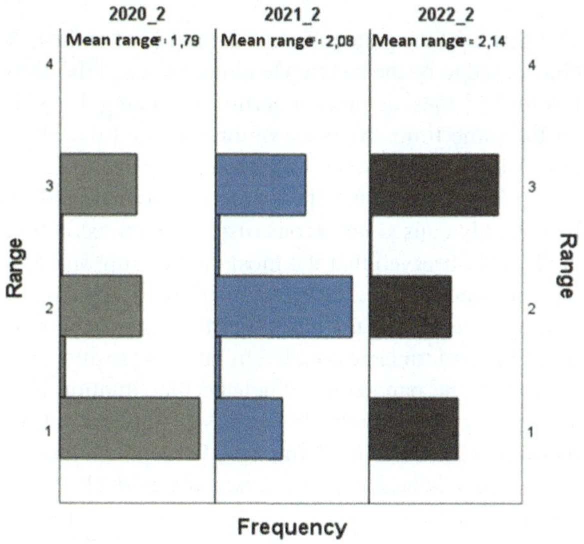


**Fig. 2** Average ranges of the surveyed groups corresponding to individual quarters

**Table 5** Two-way Friedman analysis of variance for related samples

| Sample 1-Sample 2 | Test statistics | Standard error | Standardized test statistics | Significance |
|---|---|---|---|---|
| 2020_2-2021_2 | −0,288 | 0,082 | −3,517 | < 0,001 |
| 2020_2-2022_2 | −0,349 | 0,082 | −4,273 | < 0,001 |
| 2021_2-2022_2 | −0,062 | 00,082 | −0,757 | 0,449 |

quarter of 2022 ($p < 0.000$). However, there were no significant differences between the second quarter of 2021 and the second quarter of 2022.

The significance of the differences can be observed based on the level of the average tonnage value for each quarter. There is a clear difference in transport between 2020 and 2021 and between 2020 and 2022 (average tonnage of 6.5 thousand tonnes and 7.0 thousand tonnes, respectively). The tonnage in the first quarter differs significantly from the remaining quarters. In turn, the tonnage in 2021 and 2022 does not vary greatly. This means that the critical years that affected international maritime transport were mainly two periods: the first restrictions and restrictions related to the pandemic and the last year, i.e., the moment of the armed conflict between Russia and Ukraine. At the same time, there is no significance between 2021 and 2022. The volume of transported cargo was very similar at that time. Therefore, 2021 was a transitional period in which the sea trade market was temporarily stabilized in European ports.

## 5 Discussions

The period of the pandemic and the moment of the outbreak of the armed conflict are considered to be the last two leading causes of the global economic crisis, which now has further consequences in terms of slowing down development and high inflation. At the same time, the observations showed that the cargo transported from and to ports did not decrease in the period under examination; quite the opposite. However, it should be noted that the initial research period was a year when the pandemic had already caused numerous disruptions to economic activity worldwide. T. Rozic et al. [21] observed that the most challenging situation for sea transport occurred in the early months of 2020. The restrictions related to the pandemic were, therefore, crucial in disrupting the liquidity of international transport and significantly reduced the volume of tonnage handled by sea. The results of the research prove that the crisis caused by the pandemic influenced the situation in the area of maritime transport. This partly agrees with the results of the study by Liu et al. [16], who observed that although the overall impact of the pandemic on trade in a given country in a given month is negative, the occurrence of declines in previous months has a positive impact on current trade volumes. In this way, the occurring adverse effects of the crisis are partially reversed. The pandemic results and the impact of the armed conflict in Ukraine will have negative consequences for several more years, but their impact on trade is different from the initial impact. The lack of significance of differences for 2021 shown in the study may mean it was a so-called transitional period. This is confirmed by R. Baldwin and B. di Mauro [31] in their research, who noticed that the biggest shock on both the supply and demand sides occurred at the beginning of the pandemic. At the same time, the same author believes that the impact of the pandemic on cooperation with trade partners from other countries is difficult to determine and is shaped mainly by the demand and supply factors of third countries [32]. Despite numerous studies showing the negative impact of the pandemic on trade [16, 20], the analyses carried out here have shown that in the case of maritime transport, the adverse effects of the crisis have been neutralized. Both governments and the business environment, hardened by this situation, slowly began to deal with it and adapt to changes in the market, ensuring a slow but effective return to functioning from before the pandemic outbreak [33]. Thus, the observed increase in tonnage in European seaports in the last two years is the result not only of the removal of certain formal restrictions on trade but also of the ability of business and government entities to cope with the new market environment. What's more, it allowed us to avoid a decrease in tonnage handling after the outbreak of war in Ukraine.

The obtained results are significant both in the area of theory and practice. On the one hand, the research revealed the need for appropriate techniques and tools for predicting changes in international maritime trade and, on the other hand, a high ability to adapt to these changes during their duration. The demonstrated significant dependencies also show a high probability of similar reactions of maritime trade to future crises. This means that the maritime international trade governance model requires forecasting tools [34, 35]. On the other hand, the risk of a problem in this area is relatively low because sea trade is one of the few that enables the sending of goods over long distances and is cheaper than air transport.

## 6 Conclusions

The results showed that maritime transport in European seaports successfully resisted the disruption caused by the pandemic and the outbreak of war in Ukraine. In the analyzed period, transported cargo volumes decreased less drastically than expected. Moreover, another year saw slight increases, thus providing new opportunities and solutions for creating new maritime trade models and transforming global supply chains. The research showed the statistical significance of changes in the level of cargo transported by sea, which is a rational justification for further analysis. The conducted research is of the nature of preliminary research, which requires future studies of changes in individual transport indicators due to changes in the global economy.

At the same time, the conducted research had some limitations, mainly concerning missing data in the statistical database. However, due to the sample size, it maintained the quality of the analyses performed. In addition, only selected quarters were selected for the study, which, in the author's opinion, were breakthrough periods in which the first effects of the global economic crisis were observed. The third limitation of the study is the scope of data, which covered only the ports of European countries that most often trade with each other in regulating this type of flow within the European Union.

## References


1. Heiland I., Ulltveit-Moe K.: An unintended crisis: COVID-19 restrictions hit sea transportation, https://cepr.org/voxeu/columns/unintended-crisis-covid-19-restrictions-hit-sea-transportation. Accessed 11 Feb 2023
2. Morkūnas, M., Volkov, A., Bilan, Y., Raišienė, A.G.: The role of government in forming agricultural policy: economic resilience measuring index exploited. Administratie si Management Public **31**, 111–131 (2018)
3. OECD Policy Responses to Coronavirus (COVID-19), International trade during the COVID-19 pandemic: Big shifts and uncertainty, 2022, https://www.oecd.org/coronavirus/policy-responses/international-trade-during-the-covid-19-pandemic-big-shifts-and-uncertainty-d1131663/. Accessed 21 June 2023
4. UNCTAD, The Review of Maritime Transport 2021, Geneva 2021, https://unctad.org/system/files/official-document/rmt2021_en_0.pdf. Accessed 11 Jan 2023
5. Rodrigue, J.-P.: The Vulnerability and Resilience of the Global Container Shipping Industry. Curr. Hist. **121**, 17–23 (2022)
6. Mutiani, M., Disman, D., Abbas, E.W., Wiyanarti, E., Aprilla, W., Rajani, I., Hadi, S.: The Existence of Water Transportation towards Improving the Community Economy. Glob. J. Entrep. Manag. **3**(1), 13–22 (2022)
7. Baldwin, R.: The Greater Trade Collapse of 2020: Learnings from the 2008–09 great trade collapse, VoxEU.org, 7. https://cepr.org/voxeu/columns/greater-trade-collapse-2020-learnings-2008-09-great-trade-collapse (2020). Accessed 12 Feb 2023
8. Green, J.A., Henderson, C., Ruys, T.: Russia's attack on Ukraine and the jus ad bellum. J. Use Force Int. Law **9**, 4–30 (2022)
9. Jerebic, V., Pavlin, S.: Global economy crisis and its impact on operational container carrier's strategy. Promet **30**, 187–194 (2018)
10. Zhao, Y., Ye, J., Zhou, J.: Container fleet renewal considering multiple sulfur reduction technologies and uncertain markets amidst COVID-19. J. Clean. Prod., 317, (2021)
11. Oláh, J., Popp, J., Khan, M.A., Kitukutha, N.: Sustainable e-commerce and environmental impact on sustainability. Econ. Sociol. **16**(1), 85–105 (2023)
12. Adam, A.F., Moldovan, I.G., Nita, S., Hrebenciuc, A.: The importance of maritime transport for economic growth in the European Union: a panel data analysis. Sustainability **13**, 1–23 (2021)
13. Grzelakowski, A.: Global container shipping market development and its impact on mega logistics system. TransNav Int. J. Mar. Navig. Saf. Sea Transp., 13, pp. 529–535, (2019)
14. WTO 2020, Trade falls steeply in first half of 2020, viewed November, https://www.wto.org/english/news_e/pres20_e/pr858_e.htm (2020). Accessed 14 Sep 2023
15. Heiland, I., Moxnes A., Ulltveit-Moe K. H.,, Zi Y.: Trade from space: shipping networks and the global implications of local shocks, CEPR Discussion Paper, (2019)
16. Liu, X., Ornelas, E., Shi, H.: The trade impact of the COVID-19 pandemic. World Econ. **45**, 3751–3779 (2022)
17. Kormych, B., Averochkina, T.: Ukrainian maritime industry under fire: consequences of Russian invasion. Lex Portus **8**, 7–32 (2022)

18. Globally Cool B.V.: How the war in Ukraine is affecting international trade and emerging economies, https://www.cbi.eu/news/how-war-ukraine-affecting-international-trade-and-emerging-economies. Accessed 15 April 2023
19. Kot S, Ojinji S.: Environmental sustainability and freight transport performance in the EU—an Autoregressive Conditional Heteroscedasticity (ARCH) Model Analysis. Promet Traffic Transp. **35**(5), (2023).
20. Shingal, A.: The COVID-19 shock and services trade: explaining the heterogeneous decline, RSC 2021/85 Robert Schuman Centre for Advanced Studies Global Governance Programme-456, cadmus.eui.eu/bitstream/hadle/1814/73100/RSC_2021_85.pdf?sequence=1, Accessed 2 Feb 2023
21. Rožic, T., Naletina, D., Zajac, M.: Volatile freight rates in maritime container industry in times of crises. Appl. Sci. **12**, 8452 (2022)
22. Muangmee, C., Kassakorn, N., Khalid, B., Bacik, R., Kot, S.: Evaluating competitiveness in the supply chain management of small and medium scale enterprises. J. Compet. **14**(2), 93–112 (2022)
23. Mann, J.: The Russia-Ukraine conflict's global impact on maritime trade, https://www.ship-technology.com/features/the-russia-ukraine-conflicts-global-impact-on-maritime-trade/
24. The Russia-Ukraine war: global impact on logistics, https://www.gep.com/blog/mind/russia-ukraine-war-logistics-impact. Accessed 12 Jan 2023
25. Drezner, Z., Turel, O., Zerom, D.: A Modified Kolmogorov-Smirnov Test for Normality. MPRA Paper No. **14385**, 1–21 (2009)
26. Lane, D.M.: The assumption of sphericity in repeated-measures designs: What it means and what to do when it is violated. Quant. Methods Psychol. **12**(2), 114–122 (2016)
27. Jie L.,Yubo X.: T-Friedman test: a new statistical test for multiple comparison with an adjustable conservativeness measure, Int. J. Comput. Intell. Syst. 1–19, (2022)
28. Eurostat, Maritime transport of goods - quarterly data, https://ec.europa.eu/eurostat/statistics-explained/index.php?title=Maritime_transport_of_goods_-_quarterly_data. Accessed 11 Jan 2023
29. Denkowska, S., Fijorek, K., Salamaga, M., Sokołowski, A.: Empiryczna ocena mocy testów dla wielu wariancji (Empirical evaluation of test power for multiple variances. Statistical Review, R. LVI – ZESZYT 3–4, pp. 27–28, (2009)
30. Lehmann E.L.: Testing Statistical Hypothesis, New York, John Wiley, pp. 49, (1959)
31. Baldwin, R., di Mauro, B.: Economics in the Time of COVID-19. Centre for Economic Policy Research Press, A VoxEU.org Book. London (2020)
32. Jošić, H., Žmuk, B.: The impact of COVID-19 on international trade: an evidence from Croatia, In: Proceedings of The international scientific conference trade perspectives 2021: international trade in a post COVID-19 world, Baković T. Naletina D.; Petljak K. (ed.), Zagreb: Ekonomski fakultet Zagreb ; Hrvatska gospodarska komora, pp. 39–51, (2021)
33. Berger, N., Schulze-Schwering, S., Long, E., Spinler, S.: Risk management of supply chain disruptions: An epidemic modeling approach. Eur. J. Oper. Res. (2022)
34. Kot, S. Development insights on supply chain management in small and medium-sized enterprises. Logos Verlag Berlin GmbH. (2023)
35. Bučková, M., Krügerova, M., Kozieł, M., Štverková, H.: Risk classification in international trade using methods of cluster analysis. Forum Sci. Oecon. **11**(1), 91–112 (2023)

# How Does Perceived CSR Toward Employees Influence Customer Orientation Behavior: The Moderating Role of Internal Communication

**Thinh-Van Vu**

**Abstract** This study represents one of the initial research endeavors to investigate the moderating influence of internal communication within the intricate dynamics of perceived CSR toward employees, organizational commitment, and customer orientation behavior. This study examines the impact of CSR toward employees on organizational trust, organizational commitment, and customer orientation behavior and the mediating role of organizational trust and organizational commitment in the relationship between perceived CSR toward employees and customer orientation behavior. It also tests the moderating role of internal communication in the connections between these variables. In this study, data were collected via questionnaires disseminated to Vietnam's frontline employees via convenience sampling. Two hundred seventy-three samples were utilized to evaluate the hypotheses utilizing SPSS 22.0 and partial least squares structural equation modeling (PLS-SEM) with SmartPLS software (version 3.2.7). Before testing the hypotheses, a series of confirmatory factor analyses (CFA) and the measurement structural model were conducted. This study found that perceived CSR toward employees does not directly influence customer orientation behavior. However, perceived CSR toward employees indirectly influences customer orientation behavior through organizational trust and organizational commitment. It also revealed that internal communication negatively moderates the nexus between organizational commitment and customer orientation behavior but does not moderate the nexus between perceived CSR toward employees and customer orientation behavior.

**Keywords** Perceived CSR · Organizational trust · Organizational commitment · Customer orientation behavior · Internal communication

---

T.-V. Vu (✉)
Swinburne Vietnam Alliance Program, FPT University, Hanoi, Vietnam
e-mail: Thinhvv6@fe.edu.vn



S. Kot et al. (eds.), *Corporate Practices: Policies, Methodologies, and Insights in Organizational Management*, Springer Proceedings in Business and Economics,
https://doi.org/10.1007/978-981-97-0996-0_39

## 1 Introduction

Organizations' stakeholders include shareholders, local community, customers, suppliers, and employees [1, 2]. CSR practices toward these stakeholders are divided into internal and external social roles [3, 4]. Whereas external CSR is an organization's efforts directed toward society, the environment, or customers, internal CSR focuses on organizational practices of supporting the mental and physical well-being of its employees [5]. Many researchers pointed out that an organization's CSR should pay special attention to employees because it is an important asset [6, 7]. The CSR toward employees expresses social behavior within an organization and primarily targets employees. This behavior is mainly conveyed through employee-oriented CSR activities such as fostering employment stability, a positive working environment, training and development, fair treatment, fair payment, and occupational health and safety [8, 9].

Additionally, there is a gap in research identifying employees' perceptions of their organization's internal CSR initiatives. This piques interest in identifying the effect of perceived CSR toward employees on organizational trust, organizational commitment, and customer orientation behavior. Effective internal communication practices are essential for fostering employee engagement, a positive work environment, and aligning employees with organizational goals [10]. However, there is a need to explore the relationship between internal communication, perceived CSR towards employees, and important outcomes such as organizational trust, organizational commitment, and customer orientation behavior, particularly within the context of frontline employees. By examining the moderating role of internal communication, this paper seeks to uncover how effective communication within organizations can influence the relationship between employees' perceptions of CSR toward employees and critical outcomes, namely organizational trust, organizational commitment, and customer orientation behavior. Understanding these dynamics is crucial for organizations aiming to improve employee organizational trust and organizational commitment and develop a customer-centric approach in their organization. Furthermore, this research aims to contribute to the existing literature on internal communication and CSR towards employees by explicitly focusing on the role of internal communication as a moderator between organizational commitment and customer orientation. By examining the interplay between internal communication practices, employees' perceptions of internal CSR, and their job-related attitudes and behaviors, this paper aims to address the research gap in the current literature and offer valuable insights for both theoretical understanding and practical applications.

This study offers three principal contributions. Primarily, it scrutinizes the influence of perceived CSR toward employees on customer orientation behaviors, mediated through various parallel channels encompassing organizational trust and organizational commitment. Secondly, it examines the serial mediating role of 0rganizational trust and organizational commitment in the nexus between perceived CSR toward employees and customer orientation behavior. Thirdly, it investigates the moderating role of internal communication in the connection between perceived

CSR toward employees and customer orientation behavior and the nexus between organizational commitment and customer orientation behavior.

## 2 Literature Review and Hypotheses Development

### 2.1 *Perceived CSR Toward Employees and Customer Orientation Behavior*

A comprehensive definition of CSR is "context-specific organizational actions and policies that consider stakeholders' expectations and the triple bottom line of economic, social, and environmental performance" [1, p. 855]. The stakeholder approach also indicates that organizations must be concerned with "any group or individual who can affect or is affected by the achievement of an organization's purpose" [11, p. 53]. According to Aguinis and Glavas (2012) and Hameed et al. (2016) [1, 2], the stakeholders of an organization include its shareholders, the community in which it is located, its customers, its suppliers, and its staff. According to Aguilera et al. (2007) [3] and El Akremi et al. (2018) [4], CSR practices toward these stakeholders may be broken down into two categories: internal and external CSR. External CSR refers to the efforts that a firm makes that are geared toward society, the environment, or its consumers. Internal CSR, on the other hand, focuses on organizational practices that promote the emotional and physical well-being of its employees [5]. Employee-focused CSR initiatives prioritize the satisfaction of employees' needs and aspirations by formulating policies to foster their skill development and career progression, ensuring a safe and healthy workplace, and providing equitable remuneration and promotional opportunities [8, 9]

Perceived internal CSR has the potential to affect employees' customer orientation. In recent years, CSR research has expanded to include employees in addition to consumers, recognizing the central role employees play in customer-oriented industries [12]. This is especially true because frontline employees interact directly with customers. Corporate management must comprehend the nuances of employee dedication, job satisfaction, and the deliverance of quality customer service in sustainable business operations. Maintaining a customer-centric approach is an integral component of executing CSR initiatives. To formulate effective CSR strategies aimed at employees, thereby promoting long-term and sustainable business growth, it is essential to investigate employee perspectives [13].

*Customer orientation* is "an employee's inclination or predisposition to satisfy customer demands in an on-the-job situation" [14, p. 111]. Customer orientation encompasses employee behaviors specifically tailored toward satisfying the requirements of consumers [15]. This customer-centric approach not only fosters positive customer experiences but also contributes to the overall success and competitiveness of the organization.

The Social Exchange Theory [16], a conceptual framework that defines relationships as consequential outcomes of social behaviors, proposes that individuals consciously engage in and maintain relationships to maximize benefits and minimize costs. This theory has applications in psychology and sociology, emphasizing that people evaluate potential relationships based on a cost–benefit analysis comparing potential rewards to potential risks. If the latter outweighs the former, the relationship may be severed. This concept applies to various contexts, including romantic relationships, friendships, professional ties, and even requesting assistance from a stranger. Hu et al. (2020) [17] contend that, within the context of organizational dynamics, the Social Exchange Theory provides a suitable explanatory framework for comprehending the effects of perceived CSR (both internal and external) on employees' customer orientation. Social exchange, which encompasses the flow of information, social support, and other forms of assistance within organizations, groups, and societies, has been linked to enhanced employee performance, colleague identification, and corporate citizenship behavior. This theory posits that employees benefit from CSR initiatives aimed at them, such as task guidance, employee training programs, opportunities for professional development, secure working environments, and diversity policies. These provisions establish shared norms between employees and employers, fostering a sense of organizational support and confidence. In exchange, employees fulfill the requirements of customers and assist the organization in maintaining strong customer relationships [18].

**H1**: *Perceived CSR toward employees have a positive effect on employees' customer orientation behavior*

## 2.2 The Mediating Roles of Organizational Trust and Organizational Commitment

Organizational *trust* is defined as "individuals' expectations about networks of organizational relationships and behaviors" [19, p. 37]. Lee et al. (2013) [20] posited that employees' perceptions of CSR tend to have a positive influence on organizational trust. This is because CSR efforts enhance employees' self-concept and morale by linking their personal identities with the values and goals of the organization. Most individuals think that organizations that act responsibly are good [21]. Because of this, workers are more inclined to trust the organization they work for. When employees possess trust in their organizations, their following behaviors will be influenced by the presence of this trust [22]. According to Peterson (2004) [23], the social identity theory posits that individuals, including employees and other key stakeholders, are more inclined to possess positive attitudes towards an organization when they have a sense of affiliation with its goals.

It is believable that when employees develop trust in their organizations due to their responsible behavior, they become more committed to their tasks, engage actively in their duties, and demonstrate citizenship behaviors. These are fundamental elements that contribute to the organization's overall success. According to Manimegalai and Baral (2018) [22], the application of social exchange theory and the reciprocity principles proposed by Blau (1964) supports the notion that organizations engaged in CSR initiatives foster a favorable perception of benevolence among employees. Consequently, this perception encourages employees to adopt positive attitudes and conduct. Research indicates that CSR actions increase employees' expectations that their company will prioritize their well-being in the present and future. This heightened perception of organizational care fosters elevated levels of trust, resulting in the development of positive attitudes and behaviors toward the organization [22, 24].

Organizational commitment represents three overarching themes: emotional attachment to the company, perceived costs of quitting the organization, and a sense of obligation to stay put [25]. According to Allen and Meyer (1990) [25], when considering the three components of organizational commitment—affective, normative, and continuation commitment—it has been found that affective commitment is the most reliable indicator of performance, surpassing normative and continuance commitment. Therefore, the present study has selected the affective component of organizational commitment that pertains to "the emotional attachment, identification, and involvement of employees with the organization" [25, p. 1].

Social identity theory [26] delves into scenarios where one's social identity takes precedence over one's personal identity. This theory also elucidates the influence of social identity on intergroup behaviors. Social identity pertains to the self-concept shaped by affiliations with particular groups. According to Korschun et al. (2014) [27], it is emphasized that CSR presents a promising avenue for fostering a sense of organizational identity. This is due to its ability to convey the fundamental nature of a business in a manner that is less readily achievable through product details, financial statistics, or work contracts. Furthermore, insights derived from social identity theory indicate that an organization's engagement in CSR initiatives bolsters its corporate prestige and allure. Research on reputation reaffirms that elevated organizational prestige and attractiveness cultivate heightened employee commitment through their identification with and membership in a social group that bolsters their overarching self-concept and self-worth [28, 29].

Similarly, Social Exchange Theory [30] asserts that individuals exhibit positive work behaviors when their organization provides economic and socioemotional support. In this context, if employees evaluate an organization's internal CSR motives favorably, which include initiatives such as encouraging equitable treatment, diversity at work, meeting expectations of staff members, and fostering developmental opportunities, they are more likely to reciprocate by demonstrating organizational commitment [28].

Previous studies have demonstrated a positive link between perceived CSR and organizational trust [20, 31] and a positive nexus between perceived CSR and organizational commitment [22, 24]. Moreover, many studies revealed the mediating role of organizational trust in the relationship between perceived CSR and employee positive behavior, such as work engagement and organizational citizenship behavior [22, 32]. Hu et al. [33] showed that both perceived internal CSR and external CSR positively impact customer orientation behavior through work engagement. Tang et al.

[32] demonstrated that job satisfaction and work-family facilitation play a serial mediating role in the positive association between internal CSR and customer-oriented organizational citizenship behavior. Farooq et al. [24] and George et al. [31] revealed that organizational trust mediates the relationship between CSR and affective organizational commitment. Therefore:

**H2**: *Organizational trust mediates the nexus between perceived CSR toward employees and customer orientation behavior*
**H3**: *Organizational commitment mediates the nexus between perceived CSR toward employees and customer orientation behavior*
**H4**: *Organizational trust and organizational commitment play a serial mediating role in the nexus between perceived CSR toward employees and customer orientation behavior*

## 2.3 The Moderating Role of Internal Communication

According to Borca and Baesu [34], the primary aim of organizational communication is to disseminate information to workers on the objectives and policies of the business, facilitating their comprehension and recognition of their benefits. Jacobs et al. (2016, p. 62) [35] define internal communication as "the exchange of information and ideas among employees or members of an organization (social actors) to build trusting and open relationships and to create understanding." As indicated by Karanges et al. (2015) [36], internal communication has been recognized as a foundational factor shaping employees' commitment to remaining within the organization. It is important to highlight, as emphasized by Zainun et al. (2020) [37] that erroneous information within organizations can negatively impact the effectiveness of business operations.

Internal communication is a primary driver for cultivating comprehension, captivating employees' focus, and steering their active involvement with the organization. Ferdous et al. [38] assert that the internal marketing community has emphasized the significance and impact of internal communication as a potent instrument for eliciting favorable employee attitudes and responses. According to this study, it was shown that firms allocate around 87% of their internal communication towards disseminating their strategy, objectives, values, and accomplishments to their workforce.

Typically, employees have been predominantly perceived as passive recipients of internal communication. Nevertheless, it is important to recognize that employees also fulfill the roles of communicators and active contributors within a company's communication network [35, 39]. In the realm of CSR communication strategy, the central aim is to proficiently transmit constructive CSR information to the many stakeholders of the firm, consequently cultivating advantageous perceptions of the company [40]. Effective internal communication is crucial in enhancing workers' comprehension of CSR initiatives specifically targeted towards them. This, in turn, can potentially increase the beneficial influence of their CSR perception on their behavior toward customer orientation.

Research has indicated that increased levels of internal communication have a substantial impact on problem-solving capabilities, the attainment of objectives, and the overall happiness of employees. This form of communication can also function as a source of motivation for staff, leading to heightened levels of customer engagement and personal satisfaction [35, 41]. Numerous studies have indicated that internal communication significantly influences employee outcomes, such as job satisfaction, organizational commitment, work engagement, and organizational citizenship behavior [35, 42, 43].

The purpose of internal communication is to foster employee alignment with the organization's vision, therefore influencing their internal emotional and cognitive states, resulting in improved customer-oriented behavior [36, 38]. According to Ferdous (2021) [38], the assessment of a stimulus (S) in accordance with the stimulus-organism-response (S-O-R) paradigm has the potential to elicit cognitive and emotional states (O) that subsequently result in distinct behavioral responses (R) across people. The role of internal communication is acknowledged as a catalyst, facilitating the transmission of information from management to employees on organizational plans, policies, goals, and objectives [38]. According to Eroglu et al. (2001) [44], organizational commitment is a complex entity that includes emotional and cognitive intermediate states and processes. These states and processes mediate the connection between external stimuli and individual responses. Customer-oriented conduct is commonly perceived as a reactive approach and is defined as a manifestation of prosocial service behavior [38].

Previous studies have indicated that internal communication moderates the relationship between variables. For instance, Khan et al. [45] reveal that symmetrical internal communication plays a negative moderator in the positive relationship between COVID-19-related job insecurity and emotional exhaustion. Amoako et al. [46] demonstrated that internal marketing has moderating roles in the positive associations between organizational structure and e-HRM success and the associations between employee technological capabilities and e-HRM success. Hence, internal communication may enforce the positive impact of organizational commitment to customer orientation behavior (Fig. 1).

**H5**: *Internal Communication moderates the relationship between perceived CSR toward employees and employees' customer orientation behavior*
**H6**: *Internal Communication moderates the relationship between organizational commitment and employees' customer orientation behavior*

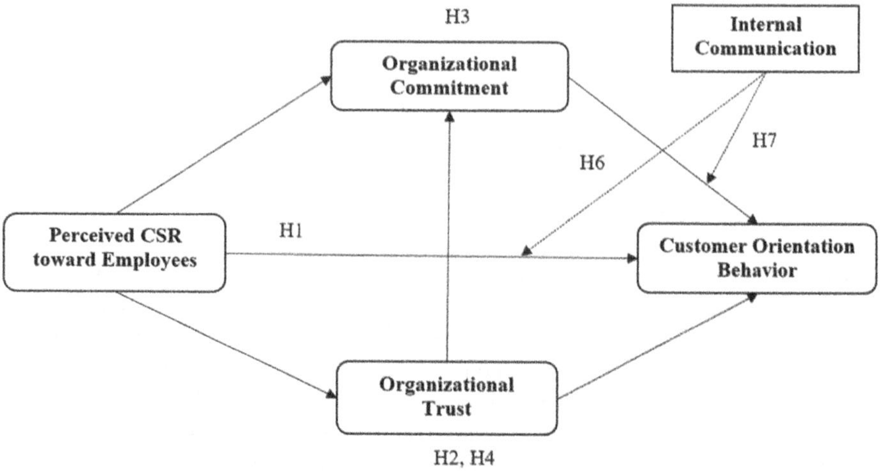


**Fig. 1** The conceptual framework

# 3 Research Methods

## *3.1 Research Design, Sampling and Data Collection*

This study employs a quantitative research approach to assess the formulated hypotheses. This quantitative methodology primarily revolves around utilizing surveys for the collection, analysis, and interpretation of data as proposed by researchers. The survey used in this investigation encompassed a questionnaire designed to capture pertinent variables and was administered to employees operating within private enterprises in Vietnam. Ensuring linguistic equivalence, the survey instrument was constructed using the back-translation procedure [47], involving the translation of measurement scales from English to Vietnamese and then back to English. Through this sample survey, information regarding employees' perceptions of CSR toward employees and other constructs was obtained, facilitating the hypothesis testing and overall research objectives.

Aligned with the study's aims, five principal constructs were operationalized: (1) Perceived CSR toward employees, (2) Organizational trust, (3) Organizational commitment, (4) Customer Orientation behavior, and (5) Internal Communication. Correspondingly, a tailored survey questionnaire was designed for data collection. The primary data for this study were gathered through an online survey conducted between September 2022 and February 2023 in Vietnam. The distribution of survey questionnaires occurred via email and LinkedIn, targeting Vietnamese frontline employees who are working directly with customers in a variety of industries and jobs (e.g., Sales and retail, Education and health care, Food and hospitality; Utilities, communications, and financial services; and Transport). The convenience sampling approach was employed to procure quantitative data for analysis based on the accessibility and availability of units from the population. Despite its known limitations, this method was chosen due to its feasibility and ease of access to potential participants during the data collection period [48]. Ultimately, the final sample size utilized for the study amounted to 273 respondents.

### 3.2 Measurement Scales

Participants were requested to offer their responses on a 7-point Likert scale, spanning from 1 (strongly disagree) to 7 (strongly agree), with instructions to rate the survey accordingly. The perceived CSR toward employees constructs drew upon four scales, which were adapted from sources such as Golob and Podnar (2021) [8] and Turker (2009) [49]. An illustrative item from this scale is "our organization strictly adheres to labor regulations." The assessment of organizational trust involved a three-item scale derived from Farooq et al. (2014), who had adapted these scales from Pivato et al. (2008) [21]. A representative item from this scale is "My organization is dependable." To gauge organizational commitment (specifically affective commitment), a six-item scale was employed based on the work of Meyer and Allen (1990) [25]. An exemplar item from this scale is "I would be very content to spend the entirety of my career with this organization." Customer orientation was evaluated through a four-item scale sourced from Korschun et al. [27], as also utilized by Hu et al. [33]. An example item from this scale is "I consistently prioritize the best interests of the consumer." The assessment of internal communication employed a four-item scale borrowed from Ferdous et al. [38], who had adapted these scales from Tortosa et al. [50] and Lings and Greenley [51]. A representative item from this scale is "In our company, management typically convenes with employees to provide them with information about the organization (goals, strategies, etc.)." In addition, following the precedence of earlier studies, we controlled for gender, age, education, and current position [27, 46].

### 3.3 Data Analysis

A series of confirmatory factor analyses (CFA) was conducted to examine construct validity and reliability, convergent reliability, and discriminant validity before testing the hypotheses [52]. We tested the proposed model and hypotheses using a partial least squares (PLS) approach with SmartPLS software (version 3.2.7). The parameter estimations of the path connecting the study components were utilized to evaluate the structural model and its associated research hypotheses. The statistical significance of each route coefficient for hypothesis testing was assessed by a nonparametric bootstrapping procedure, which involved generating 5,000 sub-samples from a sample size of 273.

# 4 Research Results

## 4.1 Demographic Characteristics

The study classified participants based on gender, age, education, work experience, current position, and industry. Gender-wise, 112 (41.0%) were male, and 161 (59.0%) were female. In terms of age, 106 (38.8%) were 25 or younger, 99 (36.3%) were aged 26–35, and 68 (24.9%) were 36 or older. Education levels varied: 52 (19%) had a high school education, 61 (22.3%) completed college, 144 (52.7%) had a university degree, and 16 (5.9%) had a master's degree or higher. Regarding work experience, 51 (18.7%) had less than one year, 88 (32.2%) had 1–5 years, 75 (27.5%) had 6–10 years, and 59 (21.6%) had 10 or more years. Current positions included 219 (80.2%) employees, 34 (12.5%) first-line managers, and 20 (7.3%) senior managers. In terms of industry, 50 (14.8%) were in utilities, communications, and finance, 73 (21.6%) in food and hospitality, 127 (37.6%) in sales and retail, 49 (14.5%) in education and healthcare, and 39 (11.5%) in transportation (Fig. 2).

**Fig. 2** Demographic characteristics

## 4.2 Measurement Model

Table 1 presents the results indicating that the outer loadings of all observed variables ranged from 0.68 to 0.92, surpassing the criterion of 0.50. [53].

The Cronbach's alpha coefficients (α) of the scales for all measures, ranging from 0.833 to 0.882, were greater than 0.7, supporting the reliability of the measures [52]. The Average Variance Extracted (AVE) values of the constructs, ranging from 0.577 to 0.771, were equal to or higher than the 0.50 benchmark, supporting the convergent validity of the measures [52]. Moreover, the Composite Reliability (CR) values of the main constructs were from 0.889 to 0.919, showing that the measurements were reliable [52].

Moreover, the Heterotrait–Monotrait ratio of correlations (HTMT) is also shown in Table 2, the values of which are less than 0.85, which confirms the discriminant validity, as [54] proposed criteria for HTMT validity.

The variance inflation factor (VIF) of independent variables can also indicate multicollinearity [55]. This study had no multicollinearity difficulties because all internal VIF values were between 1.00 and 2.04, below the acceptable 3.00 [52]. This proves the analysis has no multicollinearity issues.

**Table 1** Construct validity and reliability, and convergent validity

| Constructs | Loadings range | Cronbach's Alpha | rho_A | CR | AVE |
|---|---|---|---|---|---|
| Perceived CSR toward employees | 0.79–0.83 | 0.833 | 0.835 | 0.889 | 0.666 |
| Organizational trust | 0.83–0.92 | 0.852 | 0.866 | 0.91 | 0.771 |
| Organizational commitment | 0.68–0.85 | 0.853 | 0.866 | 0.89 | 0.577 |
| Internal communication | 0.74–0.90 | 0.842 | 0.845 | 0.895 | 0.682 |
| Customer orientation behavior | 0.81–0.91 | 0.882 | 0.889 | 0.919 | 0.741 |

**Table 2** Heterotrait–Monotrait ratio (HTMT)

| | COB | IC | OT | OC |
|---|---|---|---|---|
| IC | 0.683 | | | |
| OT | 0.577 | 0.503 | | |
| OC | 0.647 | 0.588 | 0.682 | |
| PCSRTE | 0.489 | 0.554 | 0.428 | 0.63 |

*Note* COB: Customer Orientation Behavior, IC: Internal Communication, OT: Organizational Trust, OC: Organizational commitment, PCSRTE: Perceived CSR toward employees

## 4.3 Hypothesis Testing

The estimated structural model based on the survey data indicated an acceptable fit as the standardized root mean squared residual value of the composite model of 0.073 was lower than the recommended value of 0.08 [54]. In addition, the adjusted R2 value of organizational trust, organizational commitment, and customer orientation behavior were calculated as 0.13, 0.47, and 0.47, respectively. Therefore, these values were acceptable [52].

Table 3 shows the results of the path analysis. H1 predicted that perceived CSR toward employees will have a positive effect on employees' customer orientation behavior. In contrast to our theoretical predictions, the path coefficient from perceived CSR toward employees to employees' customer orientation behavior ($\beta = 0.05$, t-value $= 0.85$, $p > 0.05$) was not significant; thus, H1 was not supported.

However, the result of the examination of H2 shows that through organizational trust, perceived CSR toward employees has a positive effect on employees' customer orientation behavior. This effect was significant ($\beta = 0.07$, t-value $= 2.97$, $p < 0.01$), indicating the full mediating role of organizational trust in the relationship between perceived CSR toward employees and employees' customer orientation behavior. Similarly, the result of the examination of H3 shows that through organizational commitment, perceived CSR toward employees has a positive effect on employees' customer orientation behavior. This effect was significant ($\beta = 0.11$, t-value $= 3.75$, $p < 0.001$), indicating the full mediating role of organizational commitment in the relationship between perceived CSR toward employees and employees' customer orientation behavior.

Moreover, the result of the examination of H4 shows that through organizational trust and organizational commitment, perceived CSR toward employees has a positive effect on employees' customer orientation behavior. This effect was significant

**Table 3** Direct effect analysis

| H | Regression path | Effect type | Path coefficient | p-Values | Remark |
|---|---|---|---|---|---|
| H1 | PCSRTE ➔ COB | Direct effect | 0.05 | 0.395 | Not support |
| H2 | PCSRTE ➔ OT ➔ COB | Indirect effect | 0.07 | 0.003 | Support |
| H3 | PCSRTE ➔ OC ➔ COB | Indirect effect | 0.11 | 0.000 | Support |
| H4 | PCSRTE ➔ OT ➔ OC ➔ COB | Indirect effect | 0.05 | 0.000 | Support |
| H5 | IC*PCSRTE ➔ COB | Moderated effect | 0.10 | 0.091 | Not support |
| H6 | IC*OC ➔ COB | Moderated effect | −0.14 | 0.012 | Support |

*Note* PCSRTE: Perceived CSR toward employees, COB: Customer Orientation Behavior, IC: Internal Communication, OT: Organizational Trust, OC: Organizational commitment

($\beta = 0.05$, t-value = 3.58, $p < 0.001$), indicating the full serial mediating role of organizational trust and organizational commitment in the relationship between perceived CSR toward employees and employees' customer orientation behavior.

In order to test H5, this study examined the moderating role of internal communication in the relationship between perceived CSR toward employees and employees' customer orientation behavior. The result showed that the interaction term of perceived CSR toward employees x internal communication did not have a significant effect on employees' customer orientation behavior ($\beta = 0.1$, $t = 1.69$; $p > 0.05$); thus, H5 was not supported (see Table 3). However, the result showed that the interaction term of organizational commitment x internal communication has a negative significant effect on employees' customer orientation behavior ($\beta = -0.14$, $t = 2.5$, $p < 0.05$); thus, H6 was supported.

To enhance understanding of the interaction impact, a basic slope test was undertaken as described by Aiken et al. (1991) [56]. The interaction plot presented in Fig. 3 illustrates that the regression slopes had a lesser negative trend when the moderator variable (namely, internal communication) was at higher levels, as opposed to lower values. Therefore, the impact of organizational commitment on workers' customer-oriented behavior was shown to be more significant when internal communication levels were low compared to when they were high.

This study examined the impact of four control variables (gender, age, e gender, age, education, and current position) on consumer orientation behavior. None of these control variables, however, influenced customer orientation behavior.

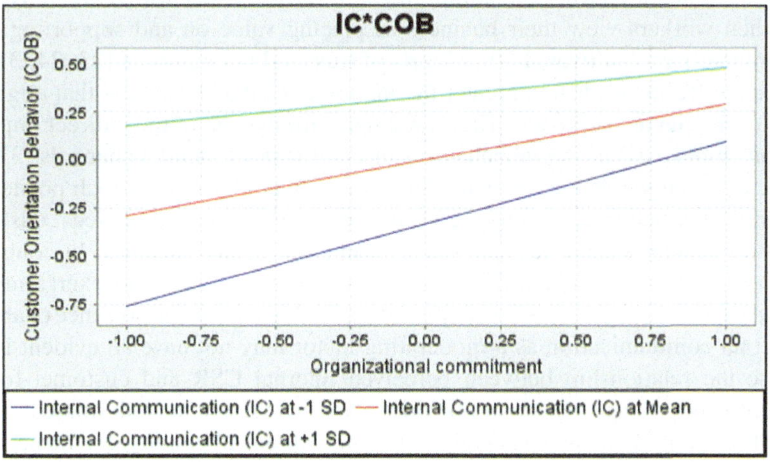


**Fig. 3** The moderating effect of internal communication on the association between organizational commitment and customer orientation behavior

# 5 Discussions and Conclusion

## *5.1 Discussion*

The objective of this study was to examine the associations and dynamics of perceived CSR towards employees, organizational trust, organizational commitment, customer-oriented behavior, and the moderating influence of internal communication. The examination of the findings provides significant observations on the intricate dynamics within the realm of organizational behavior and CSR.

In contrast to the original hypothesis (H1), the study did not find a significant direct influence of workers' perception of internal CSR on customer-oriented behavior. This result is different from many previous studies [18, 27]. The observed consequence contradicts the findings of several previous research that have emphasized a positive association between CSR programs and favorable staff behaviors, such as customer orientation. Nevertheless, this discovery might be ascribed to the possibility that workers may need to consistently convert their impressions of CSR programs into behaviors that directly benefit customers. However, the findings provide support for hypotheses H2, H3, and H4, which posited that organizational trust and organizational commitment mediate the association between perceived CSR towards workers and employees' consumer-oriented behavior. This finding suggests that the way workers perceive a company's CSR efforts toward its employees has an indirect impact on their customer-oriented actions. This influence is mediated by the employees' increased trust and commitment towards the business. This study posits that when workers view their business as placing value on and supporting them, they are likelier to cultivate higher levels of trust and commitment [22, 24, 31, 57]. Consequently, this leads to a greater inclination to display behaviors that align with a customer-oriented approach. This result helps fill the gap of the indirect impact of CSR on employees' prosocial behaviors through various parallel channels [33].

The research yielded no evidence in favor of hypothesis H5, which posited that the connection between perceived CSR towards workers and employees' customer-oriented behavior would be moderated by internal communication. In contrast to initial assumptions, it was shown that internal communication did not exert a substantial impact on the magnitude of this association. In this setting, the presence or absence of internal communication as a moderating factor may not have an evident impact because the relationship between perceived internal CSR and customer-focused behavior is not robust. This could be due to various factors, including the nature of the CSR initiatives, the personal values and motivations of employees, the perceived relevance of CSR to their customer interactions, or the context of these interactions.

Interestingly, however, the findings of this study provide support for hypothesis H6, suggesting that the presence of internal communication has a negative moderating role in the association between organizational commitment and workers' customer-oriented behavior. This suggests that the impact of organizational commitment on customer orientation behavior depends on the extent of internal communication.

## 5.2 Theoretical and Practical Implications

This study makes a valuable contribution to the current body of literature by offering a thorough analysis of the intricate dynamics between perceived CSR towards workers, organizational trust, organizational commitment, customer-oriented behavior, and the moderating influence of internal communication. The findings of this study provide significant theoretical implications within the framework of the Social Exchange Theory [16]. In the context of organizational behavior and CSR, the results suggest that perceived CSR toward employees acts as a stimulus that triggers positive emotional and cognitive states (mediated by organizational trust and commitment) among employees. These states, in turn, motivate employees to exhibit customer-oriented behaviors. This supports the notion that CSR initiatives create a sense of reciprocity, where employees respond positively to the organization's efforts to support and value them [58, 59]. The study's findings also align with Social Identity Theory's premises [26] by showcasing the influence of organizational identity and affiliation on employee attitudes and behaviors. The positive relationships between perceived CSR toward employees, organizational trust, commitment, and customer orientation highlight the role of employees' identification with organizational values and goals. This supports the idea that employees interpret CSR actions as reflecting the organization's character and alignment with their values, leading to positive social identification and enhanced behaviors.

Additionally, the Stimulus-Organism-Response (S-O-R) model provides a lens to view the mediating and moderating processes identified in this study [45]. They perceived CSR toward employees and internal communication as a stimulus that influences employees' perceptions of the organization (organism), including trust and commitment. These psychological states, as intermediate organisms, then influence employees' customer orientation behavior (response) [38]. The study's findings demonstrate the interplay between these elements, reinforcing the S-O-R model's applicability to understanding the complex relationships between stimuli, individual responses, and organizational outcomes.

The results suggest several practical implications. First, managers can foster frontline employees' organizational trust, organizational commitment, and customer orientation behavior by implementing CSR practices toward employees. Managers should pay fair salaries for each work, offer safety at work to their employees, treat their employees fairly (without discrimination or abuse), offer training and career opportunities to their employees, and offer training and career opportunities to their employees [8, 9, 60]. The results underscore the significance of organizational trust and commitment as mediators between CSR and employee behavior. This underscores organizations' need for a supportive and reliable atmosphere to foster customer-oriented behaviors.

They also need to care about internal communication. They should generally meet with the employees to inform them of matters relating to the organization (objectives, strategies, etc.), inform their employees about aspects affecting their work environment, inform all the employees, and inform the employees about work problems. However, managers should combine the internal communication practices style with a strategy to increase frontline employees' organizational commitment to encourage their customer orientation. The negative moderating effect of internal communication on the association between employees' organizational commitment and workers' customer-oriented behavior highlights the need for a balanced and thoughtful approach to internal communication strategies. It suggests that an excessive focus on communication, particularly if it leads to feelings of control or detachment, can undermine the positive impact of organizational commitment on customer-oriented behaviors.

Organizations should strive for internal communication strategies that empower employees, preserve their autonomy, and encourage genuine emotional investment in the organization's goals, which can, in turn, foster more effective customer-oriented behaviors. Managers should categorize employees according to their organizational commitment levels. Through regular performance evaluations, surveys, and one-on-one conversations, an organization can identify employees whose commitment levels are low. Individualized communication strategies should be developed for employees with low commitment by managers. It is important to recognize that these employees may require more targeted and encouraging communication to enhance their commitment and customer-oriented behavior. Managers also should recognize and acknowledge the efforts of low-commitment employees who exhibit positive customer-oriented behaviors. This recognition can be in verbal praise, appreciation emails, or small incentives, which can motivate them to continue engaging positively with customers.

## 5.3 *Limitations*

Although this study offers fascinating insights, it is important to recognize several limitations. The research employed cross-sectional data, constraining the ability to establish causal relationships. Longitudinal studies have the potential to provide more comprehensive and reliable data regarding the correlations and interactions that have been observed in this context. Furthermore, the research specifically targeted employees within a particular setting, which may restrict the extent to which the findings may be applied to a broader population. Subsequent investigations may delve into these associations across other sectors and cultural settings in order to augment the external validity of the results. Moreover, this study was conducted in Vietnam, a developing country, and could be limited from a cross-national view. Therefore, further studies should be conducted in other countries.

## References


1. Aguinis, H., Glavas, A.: What we know and don't know about corporate social responsibility: A review and research agenda. J. Manag. **38**(4), 932–968 (2012)
2. Hameed, I., Riaz, Z., Arain, G.A., Farooq, O.: How do internal and external CSR affect employees' organizational identification? A perspective from the group engagement model. Front. Psychol. **7**, 1–13 (2016)
3. Aguilera, R.V., Rupp, D.E., Williams, C.A., Ganapathi, J.: Putting the S back in corporate social responsibility: A multilevel theory of social change in organizations. Acad. Manag. Rev. **32**(3), 836–863 (2007)
4. El Akremi, A., Gond, J.-P., Swaen, V., De Roeck, K., Igalens, J.: How do employees perceive corporate responsibility? Development and validation of a multidimensional corporate stakeholder responsibility scale. J. Manag. **44**(2), 619–657 (2018)
5. Hur, W., Moon, T., Choi, W.: When are internal and external corporate social responsibility initiatives amplified? Employee engagement in corporate social responsibility initiatives on prosocial and proactive behaviors. Corp. Soc. Responsib. Environ. Manag. **26**(4), 849–858 (2019)
6. Fichman, M., Levinthal, D.A.: Honeymoons and the liability of adolescence: A new perspective on duration dependence in social and organizational relationships. Acad. Manag. Rev. **16**(2), 442–468 (1991)
7. Mory, L., Wirtz, B.W., Göttel, V.: Factors of internal corporate social responsibility and the effect on organizational commitment. Int. J. Hum. Resour. Manag. **27**(13), 1393–1425 (2016)
8. Golob, U., Podnar, K.: Corporate marketing and the role of internal CSR in employees' life satisfaction: Exploring the relationship between work and non-work domains. J. Bus. Res. **131**, 664–672 (2021)
9. Pérez, A., Rodríguez del Bosque, I.: Measuring CSR image: Three studies to develop and to validate a reliable measurement tool. J. Bus. Ethics 118, 265–286 (2013)
10. Welch, M.: Appropriateness and acceptability: Employee perspectives of internal communication. Public Relations Review **38**(2), 246–254 (2012)
11. Freeman, R.E.: Strategic Management: A Stakeholder Approach. Cambridge University Press, Boston (2010)
12. Lee, Y.-K., Lee, K.H., Li, D.: The impact of CSR on relationship quality and relationship outcomes: A perspective of service employees. Int. J. Hosp. Manag. **31**(3), 745–756 (2012)
13. Lee, E.M., Park, S.-Y., Lee, H.J.: Employee perception of CSR activities: Its antecedents and consequences. J. Bus. Res. **66**(10), 1716–1724 (2013)
14. Brown, T.J., Mowen, J.C., Donavan, D.T., Licata, J.W.: The customer orientation of service workers: Personality trait effects on self-and supervisor performance ratings. J. Mark. Res. **39**(1), 110–119 (2002)
15. Stock, R.M., Hoyer, W.D.: An attitude-behavior model of salespeople's customer orientation. J. Acad. Mark. Sci. **33**(4), 536–552 (2005)
16. Blau, P.: Power and Exchange in Social Life. Wiley, New York (1964)
17. Hu, B., Liu, J., Zhang, X.: The impact of employees' perceived CSR on customer orientation: an integrated perspective of generalized exchange and social identity theory. Int. J. Contemp. Hosp. Manag. **37**(2), 2345–2364 (2020)
18. Gond, J., El Akremi, A., Swaen, V., Babu, N.: The psychological microfoundations of corporate social responsibility: A person-centric systematic review. J. Organ. Behav. **38**(2), 225–246 (2017)
19. Shockley-Zalabak, P., Ellis, K., Winograd, G.: Organizational trust: What it means, why it matters. Organ. Dev. J. **18**(4), 35–48 (2000)
20. Lee, C.-K., Song, H.-J., Lee, H.-M., Lee, S., Bernhard, B.J.: The impact of CSR on casino employees' organizational trust, job satisfaction, and customer orientation: An empirical examination of responsible gambling strategies. Int. J. Hosp. Manag. **33**, 406–415 (2013)
21. Pivato, S., Misani, N., Tencati, A.: The impact of corporate social responsibility on consumer trust: The case of organic food. Bus. Ethics: Eur. Rev. **17**(1), 3–12 (2008)

22. Manimegalai, S., Baral, R.: Examining the mediating role of organizational trust in the relationship between CSR practices and job outcomes. Soc. Responsib. J. **14**(3), 433–447 (2018)
23. Peterson, D.K.: The relationship between perceptions of corporate citizenship and organizational commitment. Bus. Soc. **43**(3), 296–319 (2004)
24. Farooq, O., Payaud, M., Merunka, D., Valette-Florence, P.: The impact of corporate social responsibility on organizational commitment: Exploring multiple mediation mechanisms. J. Bus. Ethics **125**, 563–580 (2014)
25. Allen, N.J., Meyer, J.P.: The measurement and antecedents of affective, continuance and normative commitment to the organization. J. Occup. Psychol. **63**(1), 1–18 (1990)
26. Tajfel, H., Turner, J.: The social identity theory of intergroup behavior. In: Worchel, S., Austing, W.G. (eds.) Psychology of Intergroup Relations. Chicago (1986)
27. Korschun, D., Bhattacharya, C.B., Swain, S.D.: Corporate social responsibility, customer orientation, and the job performance of frontline employees. J. Mark. **78**(3), 20–37 (2014)
28. Chatzopoulou, E.-C., Manolopoulos, D., Agapitou, V.: Corporate social responsibility and employee outcomes: Interrelations of external and internal orientations with job satisfaction and organizational commitment. J. Bus. Ethics **179**, 795–817 (2022)
29. Dutton, J.E., Dukerich, J.M., Harquail, C.V.: Organizational images and member identification. Adm. Sci. Q. **39**(2), 239–263 (1994)
30. Cropanzano, R., Mitchell, M.S.: Social exchange theory: An interdisciplinary review. J. Manag. **31**(6), 874–900 (2005)
31. George, N.A., Aboobaker, N., Edward, M.: Corporate social responsibility and organizational commitment: effects of CSR attitude, organizational trust and identification. Soc. Bus. Rev. **15**(3), 255–272 (2020)
32. Tang, A.D., Luu, T.T., Chen, W.-K., Liu, S.-C.: Internal corporate social responsibility and customer-oriented organizational citizenship behavior: the mediating roles of job satisfaction, work-family facilitation, life satisfaction, and the moderating role of organizational tenure. J. Sustain. Tour., 1–21 (2023). https://doi.org/10.1080/09669582.2023.2195134
33. Hu, B., Liu, J., Zhang, X.: The impact of employees' perceived CSR on customer orientation: an integrated perspective of generalized exchange and social identity theory. Int. J. Contemp. Hosp. Manag. **32**(7), 2345–2364 (2020)
34. Borca, C., Baesu, V.: A possible managerial approach for internal organizational communication characterization. Procedia Soc. Behav. Sci. **124**, 496–503 (2014)
35. Jacobs, M.A., Yu, W., Chavez, R.: The effect of internal communication and employee satisfaction on supply chain integration. Int. J. Prod. Econ. **171**, 60–70 (2016)
36. Karanges, E., Johnston, K., Beatson, A., Lings, I.: The influence of internal communication on employee engagement: A pilot study. Public Relations Review **41**(1), 129–131 (2015)
37. Zainun, N.F.H., Johari, J., Adnan, Z.: Technostress and Commitment to Change: The Moderating Role of Internal Communication. Int. J. Public Adm. **43**(15), 1327–1339 (2020)
38. Ferdous, A.S., Polonsky, M., Bednall, D.H.B.: Internal communication and the development of customer-oriented behavior among frontline employees. Eur. J. Mark. **55**(8), 2344–2366 (2021)
39. Frandsen, F., Johansen, W.: The study of internal crisis communication: towards an integrative framework. Corp. Commun.: Int. J. **16**(4), 347–361 (2011)
40. Duthler, G., Dhanesh, G.S.: The role of corporate social responsibility (CSR) and internal CSR communication in predicting employee engagement: Perspectives from the United Arab Emirates (UAE). Public Relations Review **44**(4), 453–462 (2018)
41. Verčič, A.T., Verčič, D., Sriramesh, K.: Internal communication: Definition, parameters, and the future. Public Relations Review **38**(2), 223–230 (2012)
42. Men, L.R., Yue, C.A.: Creating a positive emotional culture: Effect of internal communication and impact on employee supportive behaviors. Public Relations Review **45**(3), 101764 (2019)
43. Ng, T.W., Butts, M.M., Vandenberg, R.J., DeJoy, D.M., Wilson, M.G.: Effects of management communication, opportunity for learning, and work schedule flexibility on organizational commitment. J. Vocat. Behav. **68**(3), 474–489 (2006)

44. Eroglu, S.A., Machleit, K.A., Davis, L.M.: Atmospheric qualities of online retailing: A conceptual model and implications. J. Bus. Res. **54**(2), 177–184 (2001)
45. Khan, A.K., Khalid, M., Abbas, N., Khalid, S.: COVID-19-related job insecurity and employees' behavioral outcomes: mediating role of emotional exhaustion and moderating role of symmetrical internal communication. Int. J. Contemp. Hosp. Manag. **34**(7), 2496–2515 (2022)
46. Amoako, R., Jiang, Y., Frempong, M.F., Tetteh, S., Adu-Yeboah, S.S.: Examining the effect of organizational leadership, organizational structure, and employee technological capability on the success of electronic human resource management. SAGE Open **12**(2), 1–14 (2022)
47. Brislin, R.W.: Back-translation for cross-cultural research. J. Cross Cult. Psychol. **1**(3), 185–216 (1970)
48. Bizri, R., Wahbi, M., Al Jardali, H.: The impact of CSR best practices on job performance: The mediating roles of affective commitment and work engagement. J. Organ. Eff.: People Perform. **8**(1), 29–48 (2021)
49. Turker, D.: Measuring corporate social responsibility: A scale development study. J. Bus. Ethics **85**, 411–427 (2009)
50. Tortosa, V., Moliner, M.A., Sánchez, J.: Internal market orientation and its influence on organisational performance. Eur. J. Mark. **43**(11/12), 1435–1456 (2009)
51. Lings, I.N., Greenley, G.E.: Measuring internal market orientation. J. Serv. Res. **7**(3), 290–305 (2005)
52. Hair, J.F., Jr., Hult, G.T.M., Ringle, C.M., Sarstedt, M.: A Primer on Partial Least Squares Structural Equation Modeling (PLS-SEM). Sage, Thousand Oaks (2021)
53. Hulland, J.: Use of partial least squares (PLS) in strategic management research: A review of four recent studies. Strateg. Manag. J. **20**(2), 195–204 (1999)
54. Henseler, J., Ringle, C.M., Sarstedt, M.: A new criterion for assessing discriminant validity in variance-based structural equation modeling. J. Acad. Mark. Sci. **43**, 115–135 (2015)
55. O'brien, R.M.: A caution regarding rules of thumb for variance inflation factors. Qual. Quant. 41, 673–690 (2007)
56. Aiken, L.S., West, S.G., Reno, R.R.: Multiple Regression: Testing and Interpreting Interactions. Sage, New York (1991)
57. Al Doghan, M.A.: The influence of human resource practices on the employee commitment and performance. Pol. J. Manag. Stud. **25**(1), 27–40 (2022)
58. Hegyes, E.G., Fekete-Farkas, M.: Internal CSR as a strategic management tool in reduction of labour shortages. Pol. J. Manag. Stud. **19**(2), 167–181 (2019)
59. Vu, T.V.: Perceived socially responsible HRM, employee organizational identification, and job performance: the moderating effect of perceived organizational response to a global crisis. Heliyon **8**(11), 1–12 (2022)
60. Chwistecka-Dudek, H.: Corporate social responsibility: Supporters vs. opponents of the concept. Forum Sci. Oecon. 4(4), 171–179 (2016)

# The Impact of the Globalization on the Management Culture in Polish Enterprises

**Bartosz Jeżyna and Sebastian Kot**

**Abstract** The focus of the study is to ascertain whether company internationalization and globalization can produce new circumstances that alter Poland's firm management paradigm. The paper indicates cultural changes in Poland related to globalization resulting from the internationalization of companies. The survey was conducted on a group of 54 companies. The survey results conducted in selected enterprises located in Poland indicate elements similar to the literature on the subject, as well as key aspects resulting from the unique features of the Polish market. Detailed analysis of the collected data showed that the globalization process influences changes in the level of cultural dimensions in Poland. This research is, therefore, a valuable analysis because, thanks to the inclusion of cultural changes in Poland in the management model, the manager has the opportunity to optimize the results of the business unit he manages.

**Keywords** Dimensions of Culture · Globalization · Management · International Corporations · Poland

B. Jeżyna
Department of Management, Faculty of Applied Sciences, WSB University, 41-300 Dąbrowa Górnicza, Poland
e-mail: bjezyna@wsb.edu.pl

S. Kot (✉)
Faculty of Management, Czestochowa University of Technology, Armii Krajowej 19B, 42-200 Czestochowa, Poland
e-mail: sebastian.kot@pcz.pl

Faculty of Economics and Management Sciences, North-West University, Vaal Triangle Campus, Vanderbijlpark, South Africa



S. Kot et al. (eds.), *Corporate Practices: Policies, Methodologies, and Insights in Organizational Management*, Springer Proceedings in Business and Economics,
https://doi.org/10.1007/978-981-97-0996-0_40

## 1 Introduction

International economic activity is not a new phenomenon and dates back to the nineteenth century, when the Industrial Revolution changed the face of business forever, introducing large-scale production. Globalization has changed contemporary economic realities, causing the need to change thinking and management strategies [1, 2], and initiated the creation of global markets, which has led to the intensification of competition. In the era of globalization, expansion into foreign markets is a natural step in the company's evolution. Thanks to globalization, the elements that used to be barriers are gradually disappearing while increasing access to many outlets [3]. Data from the World Investment Report show that the number of multinational corporations has stabilized in the last ten years, mainly due to consolidation trends and greater internationalization of companies from emerging markets. Already in 2009, international corporations accounted for over 82,000 parent companies that control 810,000 foreign branches worldwide, and their employment exceeds 75 million [4].

Despite many years of research on the nature and evolution of international corporations, they are still the subject of great interest and many discussions, and globalization only intensifies this interest. Many studies show a direct and positive relationship between internationalization and business performance. Thus, companies have used and will continue to use internationalization to create a competitive advantage. The consequence is the need to manage a multi-level organization that covers a multicultural area. Each employee of an international corporation is, at the same time, a representative of a specific national culture and transfers his behavior and way of thinking to the organization.

Moreover, since people are the primary and most important capital of any organization, special attention should be paid to cultural changes related to globalization. From the point of view of management practice, considering changes in cultural conditions in the management model will contribute to the organization's development and increase its effectiveness. When building his management model, a manager should consider changes in local cultural conditions not only of international corporations but also of local enterprises due to the exchange of staff. Thus, considering the level of cultural dimensions is the factor on which the future of the enterprise depends to a large extent. The intensity of phenomena related to foreign investments in Poland provides a unique opportunity to conduct research in the context of changes in the cultural conditions of management in Poland resulting from globalization.

The review of the literature and the necessary definitions, conducted in the following part, will determine whether the internationalization and globalization of enterprises may create new conditions that change the model of enterprise management in Poland.

## 2 Literature Review

In the literature on the subject, there are many theories explaining the reasons for internationalization of enterprises. In times of high volatility in the business environment, companies that want to stay on the market must change dynamically [5, 6]. Among the reasons for internationalization and globalization of enterprises, the opportunities offered by expansion into foreign markets and international trade are considered. In free international trade, consumption is increasing, global production power is increasing, and nations focus on producing products in which they have a relative advantage and buy the rest of the products from other countries. As early as 1779, the economist Adam Smith in his book "The Wealth of Nations" argued that nations are distinguished by efficiency in the production of products, and therefore nations should concentrate on producing those products in the production of which they have an advantage, and then exchange them for products from other countries in for which the production advantage does not exist.

There are many theories of internationalization and globalization of enterprises in the literature on the subject. Internationalization is an activity that aims to improve the efficiency of the company's operations. Researchers define internationalization as the adaptation of an organization to an international environment [7–9]. The current market conditions force companies that want to develop to be present in the global economy more and more. Enterprises use internationalization as a competitive advantage that guarantees its success on the market. One possibility is a special case of internationalization, which is globalization. As researchers point out, the concept of internationalization is currently used interchangeably with the concept of globalization. Globalization is one of the main concepts in the current analysis of the economy and society [10, 11]. As the concept of globalization reached even the most distant places and became the main topic of many investigations of researchers from around the world, the word itself acquired various meanings. As defined by Nayyar [12], globalization means the expansion of economic activity beyond national borders, including investment and international trade. Haque and Aston [13] defines a global enterprise as one that, focusing on the buyers' market, produces standardized products for one integrated market. On the other hand, the definition by Bartlett and Ghoshal [14] says that an international corporation is a type of company that runs a global, cost-effective strategy at the corporate level. In the company, great emphasis is placed on the integration of activities. Moreover, considerable attention is paid to creating a global organizational culture because globalization generates increased movement between nations [15], as well as dislocation of culture, i.e. difficulties in adapting to new or rapidly changing cultural environments [16, 17].

Culture is one of the most widely studied phenomena in management sciences and there is a large body of literature that answers the question of why culture is important to organizations. Many researchers have tried to define the concept of culture. Moulettes [18] argues that the complexity of culture is partly due to its historical development and the fact that it has been used in a variety of scientific disciplines. Over the years, many definitions and conceptualizations of culture have emerged. Kroeber and Kluckhohn [19] quote over 150 definitions of culture from the literature. For many researchers, culture is a set of values, belief systems, and norms that members adhere to and teach new members [20]. The Cambridge Dictionary defines culture as "a way of life, especially the general habits and beliefs of a certain group of people at a certain time."

Organizational culture is one of the most influential concepts of the last few decades, unfortunately the ambiguity of the concept has made it conveniently vague and exhaustive cause of all successes and failures of the organization. Researchers suggest that organizational culture has developed to help organizations cope with their environment. Despite the attention paid to organizational culture in literature, we still do not fully understand it. For some researchers, organizational culture is the beliefs, values and attitudes underlying practices [21]. Organizational culture includes shared beliefs and values that give an organization meaning and principles [22]. Other researchers view culture at the level of practice and behavior [23, 24]. Thus, regardless of the definition of organizational culture that we choose, it can be considered that it serves to shape behavior in the organization, and just as the national culture teaches citizens how to behave, the organizational culture is the source of rules of behavior for employees. They are influenced by the rules on how to perform tasks and at the level of practice they learn what behaviors to avoid and what behaviors will be rewarded. For many researchers, as well as for the author, the values, beliefs and norms of the members of the organization are an integral part of the organizational culture.

This also corresponds to the definition of national culture according to Hofstede [25] that culture is the collective programming of the mind that distinguishes members of one group or category of people from another. Organizational culture is the essence of the company and dictates the approach to challenges, as well as represents the beliefs and attitudes that inspire employees. The area of interest in management strategies considering cultural conditions was dominated by the concept of dimensions of culture according to Hofstede [26]. The concept was based on intercultural studies on the influence of national cultures in the workplace. It is Hofstede's concept of national cultures that is most widely used in many behavioral and management studies and is the basis for subsequent researchers. As of 2022 there were over 218,000 citations of his works. Today, managers face many complex problems in a changing global environment. The success of an organization largely depends on the definition, measurement and use of the dimensions of its members' culture. Thus, the management model should consider the cultural context and not represent the personal style of managing the organization by the manager. In addition, researchers assume that national culture is the circle that has the greatest impact on the culture of an organization that functions in the area of its impact. Therefore, for the purposes of this research, the author took as the basis the dimensions of national culture according to Hofstede—an integral element of organizational culture.

## 3 Research Methodology

Hofstede's dimensions of culture are widely used to conduct cross-cultural research. Although Hofstede's theories have been criticized as simplistic and problematic in their conceptualization and validation, they are largely still considered the most reliable. However, researchers emphasize that research should consider contemporary socio-political and cultural trends shaping a specific national context [26, 27]. In VSM13 Hofstede proposes six dimensions of national culture: Power Distance Index (PDI), Individualism and Collectivism (IDV), Uncertainty Avoidance Index (UAI), Long Term Orientation (LTO), masculinity and femininity (MAS) and indulgence.

The identification and definition of the dimensions of culture in Hofstede's concept gave researchers the opportunity to measure their level and impact on the results of activity. However, a review of the literature showed that not all of the above-mentioned dimensions were the basis for the research. For example, Nakata and Sivakumar [28] proposed a company's marketing strategy based on the dimensions of the power distance, individualism and the avoidance of uncertainty. In their strategy, the authors indicated the impact of the level of individual dimensions on the implementation of the strategy's elements. In their studies, Steenkamp and Geyskens [29] indicate the relationship between the degree of prediction of the theory of transaction costs (TCE) and a management model (based on a hierarchy or relations), which is influenced by dimensions of culture such as power distance, avoidance of uncertainty or short-term orientation/long-term. Rinne et al. [30] proposed an analysis of the impact of power distance, individualism and uncertainty avoidance on the degree of innovation of nations. Bilan et al. [31] used selected dimensions of culture and data from Hofstede Insights [32] to analyze the relationship between brand factors and macroeconomic stability.

Rossberger and Krause [33] assessed how the relationship between national culture practices influences innovation capacity and Werner [34], who used secondary data from the Global Innovation Index (GII) to assess the relationship with only four dimensions national culture. Farndale and Sanders [35] rely on four dimensions to conceptualize intercultural human resource management systems, similarly to Löckenhoff et al. [36] in studies on the importance of cultural values for the formation of gender stereotypes. Thus, the use of all six dimensions could make the analysis and in particular the comparison of the results difficult. Therefore, referring to the original version of Hofstede's concept, the author in his research decided to use three—considered primary [37, 38]—dimensions of culture from the Hofstede model, namely: power distance, individualism and avoiding uncertainty.

Power Distance Index (PDI) is the degree to which less influential members of organizations and institutions accept and expect unequal distribution of power. It represents inequality in an organization or society that is fostered by both rank-and-file members and leaders.

Uncertainty Avoidance Index (UAI) concerns the tolerance of members of organizations and institutions to uncertainty and ambiguities. Indicates the extent to which members of the public feel uncomfortable or comfortable in new, unfamiliar or surprising situations.

Individualism (from English: Individualism—IDV) versus its opposite, collectivism, i.e., the degree to which individuals integrate into groups. The issue addressed in this dimension is extremely fundamental and concerns all societies in the world. On the side of individualists, we find societies in which ties between individuals are loose: everyone is expected to take care of themselves and their immediate family. On the collectivist side, we find societies in which people are integrated from birth into strong, cohesive inner groups, often multigenerational.

These are the most common dimensions, regardless of the adopted concept of research on the dimensions of culture. An additional argument in favor of limiting the number of dimensions of culture in the adopted concept of research is the amount of work required when considering a larger number of dimensions of culture. The introduction of twice as many dimensions of culture to the research model adopted by the author increases its complexity both in the analysis and, in particular, in its application. As it is commonly known, "business likes simple solutions". This fact becomes particularly important when considering other models. For example, the GLOBE model distinguishes 9 basic dimensions of culture. Thus, the simplified concept adopted by the author will enable not only the assessment of the impact of globalization on the dimensions of culture in Poland, but also the practical application of the values that the results of this research bring. The research results should bring not only a valuable supplement to the theory, but most of all management practice. Including changes in the dimensions of culture in Poland in the management model will enable optimization of, inter alia, the management of ethnically diverse teams, the organization of training programs, or the selection of a manager candidate.

Therefore, the authors decided to adopt Hofstede's concept for research, whereby he limited the number of dimensions of culture to three: power distance, avoidance of uncertainty and collectivism—individualism. To achieve this goal, the authors prepared surveys for 54 companies. Data from 54 questionnaires were collected and organized, and the results of the research are presented in the next chapter. The research includes enterprises with medium and high employment, which resulted from the nature of the research sample adopted for the study. At the request of representatives of the surveyed companies, their names were not disclosed.

The basis of the proprietary questionnaire in the field of research determining the levels of culture was the well-known and proven tool, which is the Values Survey Module 2013 (hereinafter VSM13) by Geert Hofstede and Michael Minkov. Each of the twenty-four questions used to calculate the dimensions of culture is assessed by the respondent on a five-point scale. Then, to calculate each of the dimensions of the culture, the formula proposed by the authors of VSM13 should be used, considering the points from a 5-point scale awarded by the respondents.

The research was conducted among middle and senior managers as well as owners/directors of production plants located in Poland. The proprietary questionnaire consisted of 19 questions, including: 7 questions from the scope of the company/respondent (questions A-G), 12 questions determining the levels of culture (questions H–L, including H1–H6 and L1–L3. formulas in accordance with the formula proposed by the authors of VSM13, transferring the numbering of questions from the original worksheet to the research in question:

| Culture dimension: | Pattern used: |
|---|---|
| Power distance: | PDI = 35(H5–H2) + 25(K–L2) |
| Avoiding uncertainty: | UAI = 40(J–I) + 25(L1–L3) |
| Individualism: | IDV = 35(H3–H1) + 35(H6–H4) |

After collecting and organizing the research results, a picture will be created that can be used to verify the impact of globalization on the dimensions of culture, and thus to create new conditions changing the business management model in Poland.

## 4 Results and Discussion

Table 1 shows the distribution of industries in which the companies from the analyzed sample operated, according to the leading profile of the company's activity according to the Statistical Classification of Economic Activity used in the European Community: section C, EU industrial processing, classification of activities (EKD).

Most companies dealt with the production of finished metal products, with the exception of machinery and equipment. In the studied sample, there were more

**Table 1** Sectors in which the companies participating in the research operated

| Branch | n |
|---|---|
| Manufacture of food products | 6 |
| Manufacture of products of wood and cork, except furniture | 3 |
| Manufacture of paper and paper products | 3 |
| Production of chemicals and chemical products | 3 |
| Manufacture of products from other non-metallic mineral raw materials | 3 |
| Metal production | 3 |
| Manufacture of fabricated metal products, except machinery and equipment | 12 |
| Manufacture of electrical equipment unclassified | 3 |
| Manufacture of machinery and equipment unclassified | 9 |
| Manufacture of motor vehicles, trailers and semi-trailers | 3 |
| Production of furniture | 3 |
| Production of products, others | 3 |
| Total | 54 |

n—number of respondents
*Source* Authors' elaboration

**Table 2** Education of the respondents

| Education | n |
|---|---|
| High school | 2 |
| Bachelor | 6 |
| Masters | 46 |

n—number of respondents
*Source* Authors' elaboration

**Table 3** Seniority of the respondents

| Seniority | n |
|---|---|
| 0–10 years | 12 |
| 11–20 years | 30 |
| 21–30 years | 12 |
| 31 and more years | 0 |

n—number of respondents
*Source* Authors' elaboration

companies involved in the production of machinery and equipment, not classified elsewhere, and food products, and fewer companies from other industries participating in the research.

The respondents constituted a diverse group also in terms of education. Out of 54 people who took part in the study, most respondents graduated from master's studies, a small group were respondents who completed bachelor's studies. Only 2 people completed their education at the secondary school level. Table 2 shows the distribution of the level of education of the respondents.

One of the most important indicators verifying the knowledge about the organization and the manager's influence on its operation is seniority. Table 3 presents the distribution of seniority of the respondents (Fig. 1).

The actual PDI level measured in the research is 58.75 per 100 points, which gives a nearly 10 point decrease in the level of this dimension. Reducing the power distance

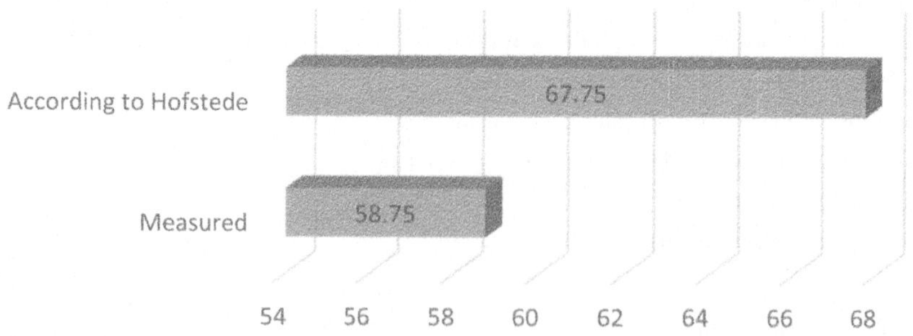


**Fig. 1** PDI index of the studied cultures according to Hofstede and measured in the research (*Source* Authors' elaboration)

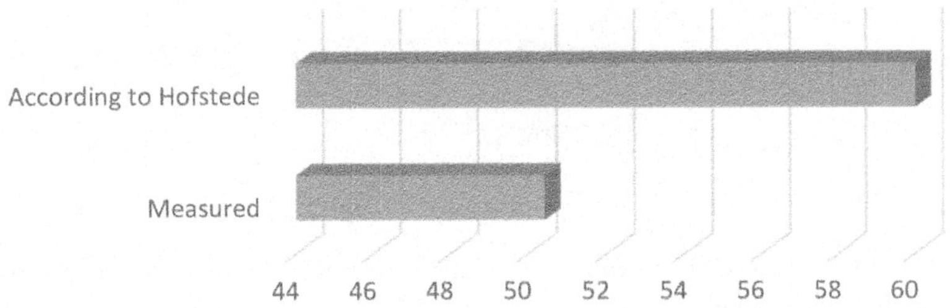


**Fig. 2** IDV index of the studied cultures according to Hofstede and measured in the research (*Source* Authors' elaboration)

means reducing the dependence of subordinates on superiors. Equal opportunities for all will be important. It also means reducing the perception of authorities as having unquestionable power in the system.

**Individualism Dimension (IDV).** The results of Hofstede's research indicate that Poland is above the average in terms of individualism with 60 points out of 100 possible. Research indicates individualism/collectivism as an important dimension of cultural variability that influences the way of communication. Collectivist societies focus not so much on individual interests as on the maintenance of the community and the continuation of harmonious relations between its members (Fig. 2).

The actual level of IDV measured in the research is 50.40 out of 100 points, which, similarly to the power distance, gives a nearly 10 point decrease in the level of this dimension. The reduction of individualism means an increase in values related to the well-being of the group and a decrease in the relevance of individualistic desires as well as individual achievement. Collectivist cultures can show harmony within their own group, but society as a whole can be very diverse because so many interpersonal relationships are shaped within both internal and external groups. This can serve as a mechanism that influences the success or failure of the business. Industrial companies that operate based on cost–benefit analyzes, with employees with individualistic inclinations, are more likely to adhere to contractual relationships based on the principles of economic exchange. In the age of globalization, such firms will do better than firms favoring their own/in-house groups.

**Uncertainty Avoidance (UAI).** According to the research conducted by Hofstede, Poland ranks very high on the Hofstede scale in terms of avoiding uncertainty—93 points out of 100 possible. This means that Polish society has a high tendency to avoid uncertainty. Citizens place great emphasis on the rules and procedures in place, and deviations from them are not tolerated. However, researchers indicate that in Polish culture one can find behaviors characteristic of both countries with a high as well as low degree of avoiding uncertainty (Fig. 3).

The actual UAI level measured in the research is 82.15 out of 100 points, which gives a 10-point decrease in the level of this dimension. The reduction of this dimension means that the rules prevailing in the surveyed enterprises may be less formalized. Such conditions should facilitate not only the decision to start work, but all

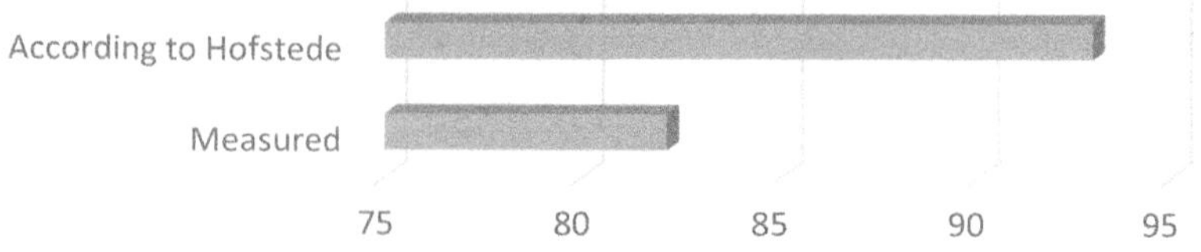


**Fig. 3** UAI index of the studied cultures according to Hofstede and measured in the research (*Source* Authors' elaboration)

decisions necessary for the proper operation of the Company. Especially the combination of facilitating decision-making along with reducing the distance to superiors and improving communication can have a positive impact on the company's results.

## 5 Conclusion

When analyzing cultural dimensions in the studied enterprises, the authors state that the actual measured values differ from the reference values according to Hofstede. This confirms the influence of the dimensions of the cultures of the countries of origin of international corporations penetrating the local market on the dimensions of culture in Poland, which is probably the result of the exchange of staff between local companies and international corporations. As the research results show, the impact of globalization on the dimensions of culture, and thus the creation of new conditions changing the business management model in Poland, is indisputable. However, the turbulent economic environment makes finding determinants of effective management of business units of international corporations in Poland extremely problematic.

The conclusions of this research can be used as a guide to understanding people's motivations and actions based on their ethnicity, religion, the environment in which they grew up, and their work experiences from a different perspective. Research has shown that Polish society is undergoing a metamorphosis related to foreign investments in learning new intercultural competencies. The contribution of this research consists of validating the existing theory of cultural dimensions by Geert Hofstede and its application as a technique and method of assessing the current dimensions of culture in Poland. Finally, the results of this research encourage managers to find ways and means to build a high-performance management model while preserving local traditions. Moreover, the research encourages managers not only to transfer but also to interpret foreign management practices into patterns of work organization that reflect local levels of culture.

An analysis of the perception of reality by Polish workers shows that growing up in a post-communist society—such as Poland—means that its representatives perceive social reality uniquely. Even though, under the accession treaty, Poland has been a member of the European Union since May 1, 2004, and this research shows the influence of Western cultures on the measured levels of cultural dimensions, the PDI and UAI dimensions remain at a high level by Western standards. Differences in the development of human capital are very significant in the European Union, as indicated by the European Commission itself, which recognizes the diffusion of knowledge as an instrument of economic cohesion. One of the main problems of Central European countries such as Poland—a young, industrialized economy of a country that joined the European Union relatively late—is how to deal with the clash of capitalist values with local dimensions and cultural values as society develops. Economic development in industry tends to undermine a society's traditional value system as capitalism takes root. Therefore, the management model should consider adapting managerial practice to local conditions.

The presented research results are not without limitations; although the survey is a powerful data collection tool, it also has inherent weaknesses. The time required to answer the question, combined with the fact that the interviewee fills in the sheet unsupervised, can encourage quick completion with little reflection on the answers. In addition, this effect is intensified by the fact that the questionnaire was filled in anonymously because the condition for the answer was confidentiality, which guaranteed the inability to identify both persons and names of companies participating in the research.

The study identified the levels of three elements of Hofstede's national culture model, namely—power distance, uncertainty avoidance, and individualism/collectivism, and their impact on company indicators. Considering the research results and their limitations, further research should consider eliminating the limitations of the methods used and increasing the research sample. In addition, future research should also be devoted to examining the levels of the other three dimensions of the national culture of the Hofstede model, which were not included as part of the research subject, and—as far as possible—to balance the ratio of male and female participants, in particular, that one of the three dimensions will be masculinity and femininity (from the English Masculinity—MAS). Including the above suggestions in future research will allow us to supplement the theoretical and practical knowledge to the extent to which the authors' suggestions were considered.

Globalization and the related expansion into foreign markets have brought about changes in the local culture—and thus—not only different/higher customer expectations or increased competition but, in particular, changes in the expectations of the employees themselves. Organizations, therefore, face new challenges that require adaptation to new conditions.

This research is a valuable analysis, especially for management, as it considers the actual dimensions of culture in the place of business, which is a valuable supplement to management practice. By taking cultural changes into account in the management model, the manager can optimize the results of the business unit he manages.

## References

1. Borowiecki, R.: Przedsiębiorstwo w obliczu wyzwań współczesnej gospodarki (2011)
2. Szczepańska-Woszczyna, K., Kurowska-Pysz, J.: Sustainable business development through leadership in SMEs. Eng. Manag. Prod. Serv. **8**(3), 57–69 (2016)
3. Grebski, M., Mazur, M.: Social climate of support for innovativeness. Prod. Eng. Arch. **28**(1), 110–116 (2022)
4. World Investment Report 2021—UNCTAD. Transnational Corporations: Investment and Development **28**(3). https://unctad.org/system/files/official-document/diaeia2021d3_en_0.pdf (accessed 16 February 2021)
5. Urbański, M.: Immigrant employees' management in the enterprises-evidence from Poland. Pol. J. Manag. Stud. **24**(2), 449–467 (2021)
6. Bednarova, L., Chovancova, J., Pacana, A., Ulewicz, R.: The analysis of success factors in terms of adaptation of expatriates to work in international organizations. Pol. J. Manag. Stud. **17**(1), 59–66 (2018)
7. Calof, J.L., Beamish, P.W.: Adapting to foreign markets: explaining internationalization. Int. Bus. Rev. **4**(2), 115–131 (1995)
8. Gavurova, B., Belas, J., Strnad, Z., Rozsa, Z.: Impact of the state on business environment-sectoral analysis. J. Int. Stud. **12**(4), 244–257 (2019)
9. Oláh, J., Hidayat, Y.A., Dacko-Pikiewicz, Z., Hasan, M., Popp, J.: Inter-organizational trust on financial performance: proposing innovation as a mediating variable to sustain in a disruptive era. Sustainability **13**(17), 9947 (2021)
10. Cable, V.: Globalization and Global Governance. Royal Institute of International Affairs, London (1999)
11. Stavytskyy, A., Kharlamova, G., Giedraitis, V., Sengul, E.C.: Gravity model analysis of globalization process in transition economies. J. Int. Stud. **12**(2), 322–341 (2019)
12. Nayyar, D.: Globalisation, history and development: a tale of two centuries. Camb. J. Econ. **30**(1), 137–159 (2006)
13. Szczepańska-Woszczyna, K.: Strategy, corporate culture, structure and operational processes as the context for the innovativeness of an organization. Found. Manag. **10**(1), 33–44 (2018)
14. Barlett, C.A., Ghoshal, S.: Matrix management: not a structure, a frame of mind. Harv. Bus. Rev. **68**(4), 138–145 (1990)
15. Ghemawat, P., Nueno, J.L., Dailey, M.: ZARA: Fast Fashion, vol. 1. Harvard Business School, Boston, MA (2003)
16. Shome, R., Hegde, R.: Culture, communication, and the challenge of globalization. Crit. Stud. Media Commun. **19**(2), 172–189 (2002)
17. Bite, P., Szombathelyi, M.K., Vasa, L.: The concept of labour migration from the perspective of Central and Eastern Europe. Econ. Sociol. **13**(1), 197–216 (2020)
18. Moulettes, A.: The Discursive Construction, Reproduction and Continuance of National Cultures: A Critical Study of the Cross-Cultural Management Discourse (2009)
19. Kroeber, A.L., Kluckhohn, C.: Culture: A Critical Review of Concepts and Definitions. Vintage Books, New York (1952)
20. Draft, R.L.: The Leadership Experience, 3rd edn. Thomson Southwestern. Canada (2005)
21. Hunt, V.D.: Quality in America: How to Implement a Competitive Quality Program. Business One Irwin. Homewood (Illinois), (1992)
22. Davis, S.M.: Managing Corporate Culture. Harper & Row, New York (1984)
23. Drennan, D.: Transforming Company Culture. McGraw-Hill, London (1992)
24. Szczepańska-Woszczyna, K., Gatnar, S.: Key competences of research and development project managers in high technology sector. Forum Sci. Oecon. **10**(3), 107–130 (2022)
25. Hofstede G., Hofstede G.J.: *Kultury i organizacje*, wyd. 2 zm., tłum. M. Durska. Polskie Wydawnictwo Ekonomiczne. Warszawa (2007)
26. Hofstede, G.: The cultural relativity of organizational practices and theories. J. Int. Bus. Stud. **14**(2), 75–89 (1983)

27. Portna, O.V., Iershova, N.Y., Grytsenko, A.A., Tereshchenko, D.A., Chaika, T.Y., Delibasic, M.V.: New configurations of social and labour relations in a crisis economy. Montenegrin J. Econ. **17**(2), 157–172 (2021)
28. Nakata, C., Sivakumar, K.: Instituting the marketing concept in a multinational setting: the role of national culture. J. Acad. Mark. Sci. **29**(3), 255–276 (2001)
29. Steenkamp, J.B.E., Geyskens, I.: Transaction cost economics and the roles of national culture: a test of hypotheses based on Inglehart and Hofstede. J. Acad. Mark. Sci. **40**(2), 252–270 (2012)
30. Rinne, T., Steel, G.D., Fairweather, J.: Hofstede and Shane revisited: the role of power distance and individualism in national-level innovation success. Cross-Cult. Res. **46**(2), 91–108 (2012)
31. Bilan, Y.V., Lieonov, S.V., Liulov, O.V., Pimonenko, T.V.: Brand management and macroeconomic stability of the country. Pol. J. Manag. Stud. **19**(2), 61–74 (2019)
32. Country comparison.: Hofstede Insights. https://www.hofstede-insights.com/country-comparison/the-usa/ (2018)
33. Rossberger, R.J., Krause, D.E.: Personality, Culture and Innovation. GSTF J. Psychol. (JPsych) **1**(1), 1–7 (2014)
34. Werner, A.: The Relationship between Innovation and Hofstede's Culture Dimensions. Faculty of Economics and Business Administration (FEBA) Sofia University St, Kliment Ohridski. Sofia (2015)
35. Farndale, E., Sanders, K.: Conceptualizing HRM system strength through a cross-cultural lens. Int. J. Hum. Resour. Manag. **28**(1), 132–148 (2017)
36. Löckenhoff, C.E., Chan, W., McCrae, R.R., De Fruyt, F., Jussim, L., De Bolle, M. ... Terracciano, A.: Gender stereotypes of personality: universal and accurate?. J. Cross-Cult. Psychol. **45**(5), 675–694 (2014)
37. Sułkowski, Ł.: *Kulturowa zmienność organizacji*. Polskie Wydawnictwo Ekonomiczne S.A. Warszawa (2002)
38. Kliestikova, J., Kovacova, M., Olah, J., Nica, E.: Quo Vadis Brand Management? Specifics in Brand Value Sources Across Markets. In: International Conference on Applied Economics, pp. 291–305. Springer, Cham (2019)

# Logistics of Polish Humanitarian Aid for Ukraine

**Olha Husieva and Sebastian Kot**

**Abstract** The article aims to study the role of Poland in ensuring the logistics of humanitarian aid provided to Ukraine by the international community in wartime. The main research gap is that the logistics of humanitarian aid from the international community to Ukraine via Poland has yet to be scientifically studied. Thus, this work is aimed at filling a research gap in the field of logistics of Polish humanitarian aid to Ukraine during wartime. Its main assumption is that it will contribute to the discussion on the algorithm and the problem of logistics of humanitarian aid between Ukraine and the international community. The article analyzes the role of Poland as a logistics hub in providing humanitarian aid and coordinating its delivery to Ukraine, including the problems arising in transporting and storing humanitarian cargo to Ukraine. Content analysis, document and international organization report analysis, legal acts, and specialized IT platforms were employed to gather the data for the in-depth analysis. The analysis of the collected data confirmed the role of Poland as a logistics hub for collecting humanitarian aid from different countries to its warehouses and the main transport corridor for its further transportation to Ukraine while coordinating this process with the recipient country.

**Keywords** Poland · Humanitarian Aid · Humanitarian logistics · War · Ukraine

O. Husieva · S. Kot
Czestochowa University of Technology, Czestochowa, Poland
e-mail: olha.husieva@pcz.pl

S. Kot (✉)
Faculty of Economics and Management Sciences, North-West University, Vaal Triangle Campus, Vanderbijlpark, South Africa
e-mail: sebastian.kot@pcz.pl

 
S. Kot et al. (eds.), *Corporate Practices: Policies, Methodologies, and Insights in Organizational Management*, Springer Proceedings in Business and Economics,
https://doi.org/10.1007/978-981-97-0996-0_41

## 1 Introduction

As various studies show, logistics is a crucial lever to ensure an adequate supply of goods (humanitarian aid) and appropriate services in crisis areas [1]. Besides, logistics is the most critical cost factor in disaster relief [2]. Depending on the place of assistance and its organization, logistical tasks may cover 80% of all tasks performed by humanitarian organizations, the most significant of which usually relates to acquisition and transport costs [3].

According to a study by the World Health Organization, the United Nations Children's Fund, and the United Nations Population Fund, in 2021 alone, a record 89.3 million victims of natural disasters, wars, violence, persecution, or human rights violations were forced to leave their homes [4].

The scale of the humanitarian catastrophe in Ukraine is the greatest since the Second World War [5]. Over 7 million Ukrainians left the country. Over 7 million were displaced in the country. Unable to live and earn at home, Ukrainians need over 10,000 tons of ready-made food every day in the form of humanitarian aid. Thousands of civilians and military personnel need medical supplies, blood products, drugs, and equipment for resuscitation and military medicine daily [5]. About 30% of Ukraine's territory needs to be mine clearance as soon as possible [6]. Ukraine meets most of these needs with humanitarian aid collected by Ukrainian citizens and public organizations, as well as international organizations, donor countries, and corporately responsible enterprises around the world [7]. Furthermore, the Russian-Ukrainian conflict has adversely affected food supply chains, with significant effects on production, sourcing, manufacturing, processing, logistics, and significant shifts in demand between nations reliant on imports from Ukraine [8].

The escalation of humanitarian needs in Ukraine is potentially exacerbated by several factors, in particular humanitarian access by international organizations and logistical constraints, multiple environmental threats, risks associated with mines and explosives, weather conditions, including severe winter conditions, and so on [7].

A large number of countries and international organizations around the world are currently involved in overcoming the humanitarian crisis in Ukraine. In turn, Poland is critical in providing humanitarian aid from other countries. The destroyed infrastructure of Ukraine does not allow for air deliveries; the occupation of ports and the blocking of sea corridors eliminates the possibility of shipping by sea, so road and rail transport is the only means of transporting humanitarian and military aid to Ukraine.

Poland has had the experience of providing humanitarian aid to Ukraine since 2014. However, the current scale of the humanitarian disaster has caused huge problems with coordinating actions due to the need for effective national mechanisms. The low adaptability and extreme bureaucratization of the existing aid mechanisms indicated the need to reform this direction in Ukraine and the world to ensure a transparent settlement mechanism and exclude duplication of applications.

Thus, the main research questions of this article are:

1. Poland is the main transport corridor for the transit of humanitarian aid to Ukraine?
2. what are the problems of delivering humanitarian aid to Ukraine during wartime?
3. how has the mechanism of providing humanitarian aid to Ukraine by the international community changed after the war started?
4. how international organizations provide support in coordinating the logistics of humanitarian aid to Ukraine.

Thus, this study is a valuable analysis for science and organizations involved in the logistics of humanitarian aid, as it allows us to consider practical situations of optimizing the supply of humanitarian goods from different countries to Ukraine via Poland.

## 2 Literature Review

The military invasion of the aggressor state into Ukraine is one of the most relevant topics in the recent Ukrainian and world academic literature because the results of the conflict will affect not only national interests but also the security and well-being of other states [9]. The increasing number and intensification of natural disasters and catastrophes further underscores the need to improve and research best practices in humanitarian logistics [3]. Current sources of information on the logistics of humanitarian aid to Ukraine include specialist analytical reports, reports from industry conferences, regulatory legal acts and resolutions of governments, and research by foreign and domestic scientists. The invasion of Ukraine by Russia in February 2022 created another 21st-century humanitarian disaster, joining the protracted conflicts in Syria, Iraq, Yemen, Libya, Afghanistan, and Darfur, Sudan [10].

Thus, given the critical importance of this area of public policy and information about the problems associated with humanitarian aid processes, the team of the National Anti-Corruption Agency of Ukraine analyzed the regulatory framework and researched how, in practice, during martial law the state apparatus implements the processes of assisting, as defined in analytical reports "Mechanisms of providing state humanitarian aid in times of war" and "Corruption and other threats in the procedures of providing humanitarian aid by the state in times of war" [7].

Humanitarian activities, as well as the activities of charitable organizations in Ukraine, are regulated by the Law of Ukraine "On Humanitarian Aid" and "On Charitable Activities and Charitable Organizations," Decree of the President of Ukraine No. 93/2022 "On Coordination of Actions to Resolve Humanitarian and Social Issues."

Ukraine Support Tracker of the Kiel Institute for World Economy is a database that collects and calculates military, financial, and humanitarian aid declared to Ukraine by the governments of other countries since January 24, 2022. International organizations and institutions that provide humanitarian aid to Ukraine also publish up-to-date analytical reports and humanitarian aid plans for Ukraine. Public data of state institutions that are involved in the coordination of the humanitarian aid logistics to Ukraine, such as customs services, the Government Strategic Reserves Agency of the Republic of Poland, the Chancellery of the President of Ukraine, etc.

Information on the logistics of humanitarian cargoes to Ukraine during the war is regularly published by logistics companies involved in the process of delivering and coordinating cargoes to Ukraine and Poland, for example, analytical reports Logistics Cluster, which is part of the humanitarian cluster and provides coordination of humanitarian logistics along the Polish-Ukrainian border.

Among foreign and domestic scientists who have attempted to study aspects of the logistics of humanitarian aid for Ukraine, one can distinguish Piotrowicz [23], Zrybnieva I. [21].

The literature review shows that the process of humanitarian aid logistics through the territory of Poland has yet to be researched in science as of today. The scientists attempted to provide a general description of the humanitarian aid flowing from the international community to Ukraine, the general problem of its delivery to the recipient, and changes in the supply chains of goods in connection with military activities. For this reason, this article attempts to analyze the role of Poland as a logistics hub, coordinating the delivery of humanitarian aid from the international community to Ukraine. A more thorough study of humanitarian aid logistics for Ukraine can be carried out based on content analysis.

## 3 International Humanitarian Aid for Ukraine

By the principles established in international law, humanitarian aid is a means of protection for people in a humanitarian crisis that goes beyond primary medical care [7]. Humanitarian aid mainly consists of material and logistical support for people affected by natural and man-made disasters [11]. The function encompasses a range of activities, including preparedness, planning, procurement, transport, warehousing, tracking and tracing, and customs clearance [12]. Hence, humanitarian logistics is an imperative activity following a calamity and performs a vital role in the success of a disaster relief operation [13].

According to the Ukraine Support Tracker data, the largest financial support (military, humanitarian, financial) is provided by the United States, the EU, the United Kingdom, Germany, Japan, the Netherlands, Canada, and Poland, respectively (Fig. 1) [5].

Also, according to Ukraine Support Tracker data, military, humanitarian, and financial support is provided by 41 countries, which means that aid will go to Ukraine from all over the world, and due to restrictions on air and sea routes with Ukraine, humanitarian aid reaches there by road and rail transport. This means that the countries neighboring Ukraine, i.e., Poland, Slovakia, Hungary, and Romania, bear the greatest logistical burdens related to the delivery and storage of humanitarian aid from other countries.

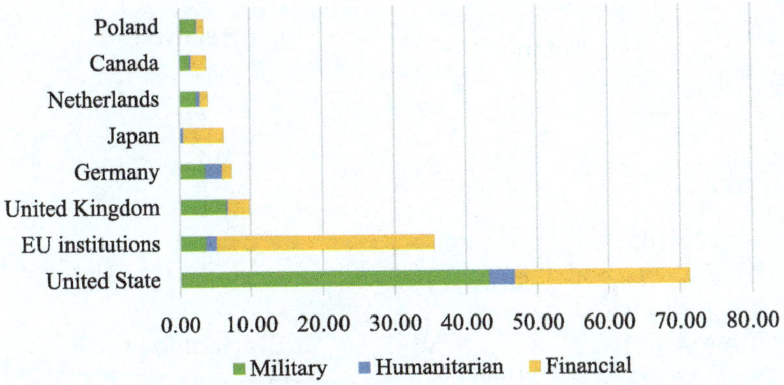


**Fig. 1** Government support to Ukraine: type of assistance, € billion (Feb. 24, 2023) *Source* https://www.ifw-kiel.de/topics/war-against-ukraine/ukraine-support-tracker [Accessed April 13, 2023]

According to the data of the State Customs Service of Ukraine, as of December 15, 2022, the total volume of humanitarian goods transported to Ukraine since February 24, 2022, is 1 016 412.5 tons, including over 60,000 vehicles. This volume of humanitarian aid does not show from which country what volume of humanitarian goods was imported. However, referring to the data of the customs services of individual border regions of Western Ukraine, the following analysis can be carried out.

In 2022, the Lviv customs services declared over 524,000 tons of humanitarian aid and 55,816 vehicles from Poland [14]. As of March 29, 2023, more than 300,000 tons of humanitarian goods and 5,211 vehicles were imported to Ukraine through the Volyn region [15]. As of March 28, 2023, 161,000 tons of humanitarian cargo, including 7,000 vehicles, have been delivered from Slovakia and Hungary to the Transcarpathian region of Ukraine [16]. The largest humanitarian aid hub, "Help Ukraine Romania," in Chernivtsi, received 2 312 tons of humanitarian and medical aid from Romania in 2022 [17].

Based on the data mentioned above, it is conventional to divide the percentage of humanitarian cargo deliveries as follows: via Poland 83%, Slovakia and Hungary 16%, via Romania less than 1% (Fig. 2). It follows the most significant flow of goods through Poland, which makes it a central transit hub for delivering humanitarian aid to Ukraine. Also, mainly through Poland, the process of delivering and transiting humanitarian aid to Ukraine from distant countries such as Japan, Great Britain, the United States of America, Australia, Canada, India, etc., took place.

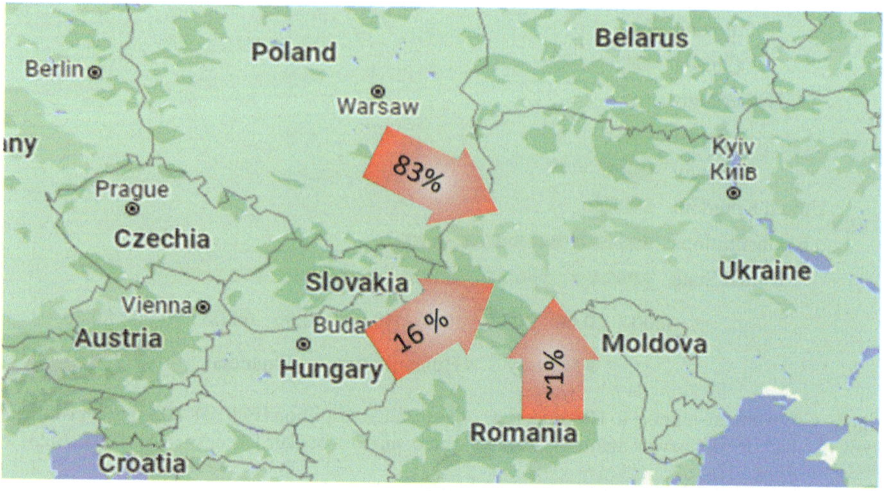


**Fig. 2** Volume of humanitarian aid delivered to Ukraine by road and rail, (%) *Source* Own study

## 4 Problems of Coordination and Delivery of Humanitarian Aid to Ukraine

Massive supplies of humanitarian aid will cause huge problems with the coordination of activities - this is due to the lack of effective national mechanisms. The situation is unprecedented. Increased border traffic and the volume of assistance required a strategic approach and anticipation of events [18]. There was a Crisis Staff organized to help Ukrainians in every voivodeship of Poland. The staffs organized meetings with representatives of logistics companies and joined the cooperation of representatives of Ukrainian communities to jointly identify and eliminate bottlenecks in the process of delivering aid to Ukraine. For example, the Silesian Crisis Staff, in constant contact with Ukrainians on both sides of the border, identified the following barriers:

1. the lack of a categorization system for humanitarian cargo, which not only causes inefficiency of logistics, but also makes it impossible to transfer the necessary humanitarian cargo to people who currently need it;
2. the lack of a system for registering humanitarian goods both on the part of the sender and the recipient, as a result of which it is not known whether they were delivered and to whom. Unfortunately, numerous cases of disappearance and transfer of humanitarian goods to the wrong people have been confirmed;
3. the lack of a donation priority system—funds are not divided into first-need products, i.e. requiring immediate selection and delivery, and those that can be delivered in the second place. As a result, there are situations when another transport of clothes is going to Ukraine, and a transport of medicines is waiting for the return of cars. The lack of a system also prevents rational management of human resources - e.g. at the sorting stage;

4. due to the lack of coordination of activities and lack of information on the further destination of transports, there are situations in which the transport after crossing the border is unloaded at random places so that drivers can quickly return to the country;
5. the emergence of individuals and specialized groups that appropriate more valuable cargo [18].

The DB Cargo Company, which delivers humanitarian aid from Germany to Ukraine via the Polish border, indicated the congestion of road infrastructure and border crossings as the main problems. There are not enough truck drivers who agree to go to Ukraine. Therefore, freight trains are the best solution for delivering humanitarian aid. One train can carry up to 52 containers and thus urgently deliver the necessary humanitarian cargo to functioning terminals in eastern and western Ukraine [19].

And on the Ukrainian side, for example, the company SYNEX Logistics draws attention to the following problems:

1. refusal of storage and collection. It is not possible to keep the goods in the warehouse for a long time—in the event of an attack, they will be lost;
2. change of storage conditions. Normally, it takes about 3 months to implement a logistics center for storage, under current conditions, the time to organize a secure and integrated warehouse is 7–14 days;
3. complexity of logistics operations. Checkpoints, review, non-transparency traffic control during curfew [20].

Therefore, the main tasks of wartime can be distinguished, where logistics require immediate solutions:

1. searching for and selecting reliable suppliers;
2. selection of the means of transport and arranging a safe route for its movement;
3. inventory management, storage, distribution and redistribution;
4. creating secure and reliable information flow channels [21].

It became obvious that international agencies were completely unprepared for a humanitarian catastrophe of this magnitude, since they are accustomed to dealing with a "static" problem—fires, floods, etc.; Ukraine is a dynamic catastrophe that changes its configuration every day and requires an integrated approach to saving lives, functioning of the economy and protecting cultural heritage.

In April 2022, the Humanitarian Logistics Association and the leading international platform Pharma. Aero announced in a joint statement raising awareness about unsolicited donations to Ukraine. Currently, there are many initiatives to help with the humanitarian crisis in Ukraine and neighboring European countries such as Poland, Romania, the Czech Republic and Hungary, with the consequence that these countries are overflowing with unwanted shipments from all over the world, inadvertently hampering logistics operations in crisis zones.

It is very important that logistical initiatives are coordinated with nationally supported platforms. The wrong donation at the wrong time can disrupt response efforts by congesting ports, airports and entry points, and can compete with priority aid items for transportation and storage.

The issue monitoring of aid implementation and transparency in distribution reporting needed significant improvement [22]. Therefore, the Ukrainian government has developed a special mechanism for providing state humanitarian aid in times of war. On March 2, 2022, the Decree of the President of Ukraine No. 93/2022 “On the coordination of activities to resolve humanitarian and social issues” was adopted, pursuant to which the Humanitarian and Social Coordination Staff (hereinafter—the Coordination Staff) was established. Agree with the Presidential Decree, the Government is to establish cooperation with diplomatic missions and consular offices of other countries, international organizations and foreign donors in providing humanitarian aid to Ukraine. The team of the Chancellery of the President has developed a special portal for managing humanitarian aid. Needs are collected online from regions, customs declarations are created, containing defined categories of humanitarian aid and a unique code that allows to track cargo crossing the Ukrainian border and simplifies the customs clearance procedure. The classification of categories of humanitarian aid and the exchange of data between the main logistic hubs have been unified. All this is aimed at making humanitarian aid flows as transparent and manageable as possible. Some logistics centers in border countries have a pallet tracking system provided by ISRAAID [7].

## 5 The Role of Poland in Providing Humanitarian Assistance to Ukraine

The Polish government and Polish charitable foundations provided humanitarian aid to Ukraine during the Russian occupation of its territories in 2014. In addition to government assistance, Polish local authorities, organizations (religious, academic, professional), and civic associations were also sources of assistance in the form of donations. In 2014, three non-governmental organizations organized humanitarian convoys: the Polish Red Cross, Caritas Poland, and the Polish Center for International Aid. The products were purchased in Poland. Caritas Poland logisticians planned and coordinated the transport from the warehouse to the local Caritas warehouse; the Polish Fire Brigade mainly provided the transport. However, operating and transport costs were high; there was no point in buying goods in Poland and transporting them to the east of Ukraine. Buying goods locally turned out to be more efficient. As a result, only 20% of food aid was provided in kind, the remaining 80% in the form of financial assistance in various forms. The transition to local deliveries, especially compared to transcontinental shipments, has reduced delivery times to humanitarian aid recipients by 60% [23].

The humanitarian situation in Ukraine in 2022 has changed the approach to providing and the mechanism for providing humanitarian assistance. However, as of 2014, NGOs are the second most important source of humanitarian aid in Poland. Table 1 lists the most famous and large non-governmental organizations that provide financial and humanitarian assistance to Ukraine and its citizens. As seen from the table, most charities have their transport and warehouses, both in Poland and Ukraine, which allows them to deliver humanitarian aid directly to the recipient without additional arrangements by the state and other logistics companies.

Poland's size, location, and infrastructure make it the most important western gateway for Ukraine. The two countries share a 530 km (330 mile) border, interrupted by over a dozen checkpoints. The airport in Rzeszow, about an hour from the border, is the closest large airport to Ukraine on NATO territory. In order to ensure the efficient processing of scheduled humanitarian aid shipments, humanitarian aid coordinators have been appointed in each chamber of the tax administration, through which the convoy is planned to be sent.

An accelerated exemption regime has also been introduced for trucks that carry out humanitarian transport. These events are coordinated by the Embassy of Ukraine in Poland. In practice, for drivers, this means exemption from needing a road permit. Services can also be used by organizations from other countries that organize the transportation of humanitarian aid for Ukraine through Poland. [35].

On the part of Poland, the Coordinator of the transfer of aid across the border is the Government Agency of Strategic Reserves (RARS) in cooperation with the Embassy of Ukraine [35]. Humanitarian aid is provided under the government's coordination mechanism [36]. Currently, the Government Strategic Reserves Agency coordinates humanitarian aid from 55 countries. Sixty-five thousand six hundred pallets of foreign aid have been received and delivered to Ukraine, including 10 400 tons of food and medical supplies worth PLN 60 million [37].

On the part of Poland, the Coordinator of the transfer of aid across the border is the Government Agency of Strategic Reserves (RARS) in cooperation with the Embassy of Ukraine [35]. Humanitarian aid is provided under the government's coordination mechanism [36]. As of today, the Government Strategic Reserves Agency coordinates humanitarian aid from 55 countries, 65 600 pallets of foreign aid have been received and delivered to Ukraine, including 10 400 tons of food and medical supplies worth PLN 60 million [37].

RARS also coordinates the distribution of fuels for Ukraine so that humanitarian transport can function. After February 24, Ukraine's fuel situation became dramatic. Before the war, 97% of fuels were supplied to Ukraine from Russia and Belarus. There was a shortage of all types of fuel at the stations, and a large part of the available resources went to military needs, restrictions are imposed on civilians. Ukraine also suffered heavy losses in fuel infrastructure, especially fuel depots, which resulted in the destruction of storage capacities and stocks.

The Polish Ministry of Climate and Environment has received a letter from the Ukrainian Embassy in Warsaw requesting technical assistance in the field of fuel supplies. In an extremely short time, the ministry created a legal mechanism that consisted in releasing part of Polish fuel stocks, transferring them to the strategic reserve and making them available to other countries on the basis of humanitarian aid. This made it possible to start fuel deliveries to Ukraine. Until the end of May 2022, the volume of deliveries reached 25 000 tons of gasoline and diesel fuel as free humanitarian aid. This puts Poland in the role of a leader in fuel assistance to Ukraine [38]. In fact, Poland has become a logistics hub for Ukraine, through which

**Table 1** Polish non-governmental organizations providing humanitarian aid to Ukraine

| No. | NGO name | Type of help | Method of delivery of humanitarian aid |
|---|---|---|---|
| 1 | Polish Humanitarian Action | Assistance in Ukraine—equipment for people with disabilities, food and hygiene products, psychological support, renovation of private houses and institutions, evacuation of people. Assistance in Poland—providing psychosocial assistance support, support with employment, access to learning Polish or global education, border assistance-emergency aid points [24] | Own transport/own humanitarian aid warehouses in Ukraine |
| 2 | Polish Center for Humanitarian Aid | Assistance in Ukraine—carries out evacuation of internally displaced persons, medical evacuations, evacuation of children from oncological hospitals in Ukraine, transports humanitarian and medical assistance to Ukraine (food, sanitary and hygienic goods, medicines, medical equipment, ambulance). Assistance in Poland—transit points in Poland, employment of refugee teachers, education centers [25] | Own transport/own humanitarian aid warehouses in Ukraine |
| 3 | Good Factory | Assistance in Ukraine—food, hygiene products, clothing, medical beds, generators and power banks, thermo-underwear, thermoses. Assistance in Poland—humanitarian aid in the border area [26] | Own transport/own humanitarian aid warehouses in Ukraine |
| 4 | Caritas Poland | Assistance in Ukraine—material aid, food, medicines, necessities, financial aid. Assistance in Poland—launched 32 Migrant and Refugee Aid Centers, cash aid, in-kind donations, food aid, educational support, accommodation in Caritas facilities and centers [27] | Own transport/ own cross-border storage hub |
| 5 | Open Dialog Foundation | Assistance in Ukraine—defense and life-saving equipment. Assistance in Poland—relocation to Western countries, placement of animals in Poland, psychological and material assistance, food, medicines, basic necessities [28] | Own transport |
| 6 | Siepomaga | Assistance in Ukraine and Poland—food, sanitary products, medicines, medical equipment, material assistance, education centers for children [29] | Lack of information |

(continued)

**Table 1** (continued)

| No. | NGO name | Type of help | Method of delivery of humanitarian aid |
|---|---|---|---|
| 7 | International Solidarity Foundation | Assistance in Ukraine—food, hygiene products, detergents, medical equipment, electricity generators, rescue and firefighting equipment, medical equipment [30] | Own transport/own warehouse in Lviv |
| 8 | Doctors Without Borders (Poland) | Assistance in Ukraine—supporting hospitals and first aiders, mainly through training and providing medical supplies and basic necessities, running mobile clinics, medical evacuation of patients using a medical train [31] | Medical rescue train from Ukraine |
| 9 | Polish medical mission | Assistance in Ukraine—transports with medical supplies to facilities throughout the country are carried out by field hospitals. Assistance in Poland—medical support at the border, creating Children-friendly spaces [32] | Lack of information |
| 10 | YES WE CARE! | Ambulances and medical equipment for hospitals in Ukraine [33] | Lack of information |
| 11 | Foundation The Great Orchestra of Christmas Charity | Assistance in Ukraine—cardiac monitors, ventilators, anesthesia machines, oxygen concentrators, pulse oximeters, ultrasound, ECG, Individual Medical Packages. Assistance in Poland—humanitarian aid points in Szegini and Warsaw [34] | Lack of information |

*Source* Own study

the West provides Ukraine with necessary weapons and humanitarian aid [39]. Thus, under the "Generators of Hope" program, the EU planned to deliver 5 400 generators to Ukraine, and for this purpose, the EU opened a new rescEU energy hub in Poland, which became a logistic center for providing emergency energy assistance to Ukraine. Generators from international partners and the private sector from various countries are delivered to the logistics hub, and the transportation of supplies from the hub to Ukraine is fully funded by the EU [40].

Considering the huge need for medical supplies in Ukraine, the EU has also deployed its strategic rescEU reserves [41]. It is by far the largest, longest and most complex operation involving the EU Civil Protection Mechanism since its creation in 2001. To support this operation, logistics hubs have been set up in European Union countries, including Poland, from where humanitarian aid goes directly to Ukraine [35].

Through Poland, the EU is coordinating the medical evacuation of Ukrainian patients in need of urgent treatment, transferring over 1 800 patients to hospitals across Europe for specialist care. In September 2022 a new EU center for medical evacuation of patients from Ukraine was opened in Rzeszow (Poland). The

Center provides safe accommodation to patients arriving from Ukraine, from where they are transported for treatment to hospitals in other European Union countries, namely Germany, France, Ireland, Italy, Denmark, Sweden, Romania, Luxembourg, Belgium, Spain, Portugal, Netherlands, Austria, Norway, Lithuania, Finland, Poland and the Czech Republic [24]. Emergency camps are being set up in the border regions to offer food and medical care to those fleeing, who were mostly older people. The Polish Government was preparing reception points near border crossings, have reserved 70,000 hospital beds for the war wounded, and have prepared a train to transport the injured from Ukraine [42].

In connection with the Russian attack on Ukraine, the Ministry of Infrastructure of Poland and its subordinates introduce a number of transport facilitations. Refugees arriving in Poland use, among other things, rail transport. Thanks to special trains, they can also move to other countries in Europe. From February 24 to September 1, 2022 a total of 8,931 trains were dispatched from cities on the border with Ukraine. In total, since the war started to September 1, 2022, more than 1.65 million passengers were departed from the Chelm, Hrubieszow, Dorohusk, Przemysl, Kroscienko, Hrebenne and Jaroslaw stations to various directions in Poland. By September 1, 2022, 5184 refugee trains left Poland (from Warsaw, Wroclaw, Przemysl, Chelm, Cracow and Gdynia), including 4,771 regular trains and 413 special trains, which the refugees took to Germany and the Czech Republic. In total, they transported over 1.19 million people [43]. The crisis almost simultaneously made Poland the second largest refugee country in Europe. The refugees were a disparate population with multiple needs that were not static but evolved over time. This led to considerable complexity, and Poland had to adapt its responses accordingly. Multiple measures were implemented to protect and include refugees in host communities, as well as facilitate access to basic services, including shelter, health care and education [44].

In March 2022 the railway bridge operation carried out by DB Cargo and DB Schenker was launched. The network of connections for humanitarian aid from Germany to Ukraine organized by DB makes it possible to transport thousands of tons of humanitarian cargo by road and rail. DB Schenker and DB Transa-Spedition collect and transport the cargo to the hub in Berlin, where it is packed into containers and then transported by DB Cargo freight train to Poland for further transport to Ukraine (Fig. 3) [19]. The project is implemented thanks to the cooperation of the Polish branch of DB Cargo, Ukrainian railway "Ukrzaliznytsia" and the DB Schenker team on facilities in Poland [45].

One of the elements of the humanitarian aid system is the system of logistic centers and warehouses. In order to ensure the reception, sorting and shipment of humanitarian aid from abroad, partner countries organized the activities of logistics centers, coordinated by Ukrainian embassies abroad [41]. There are currently 16 such warehouses in Europe, of which 6 are located in Poland (Fig. 4), 3 in Romania, 2 in Slovakia and Sweden, and 1 in Hungary, Italy and Portugal [46]. The activities of logistics centers abroad are also organized by numerous private business initiatives. For example, one of such logistic centers in Poland - Help Ukraine Center, created by Ukrainian businessmen and volunteers. Such cooperation made it possible to develop

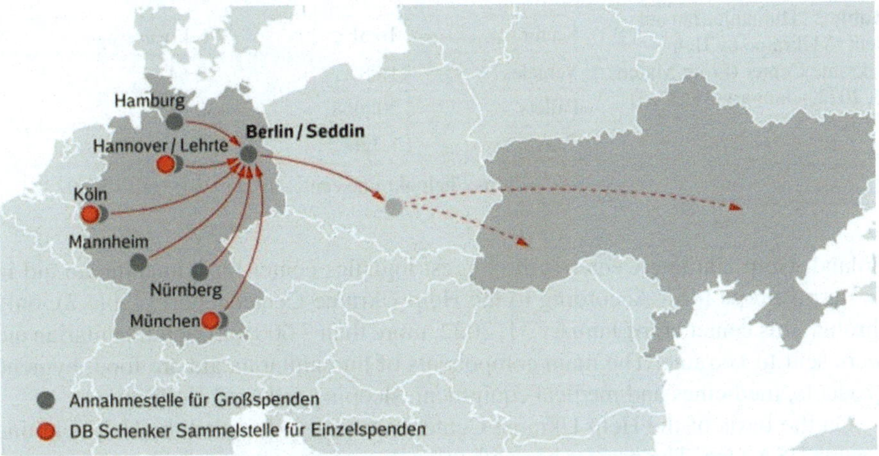


**Fig. 3** The logistics network of the German concern Deutsche Bahn, organized for the delivery of humanitarian aid from Germany to Ukraine *Source* https://www.kmu.gov.ua/en/news/ukrzaliznicya-ta-nimecka-zaliznicya-deutsche-bahn-pidpisali-memorandum-pro-spivrobitnictvo, last accessed 2023/04/13

algorithms for registering and receiving loads in Polish logistics centers, attracting railway carriers to cooperation, which accelerated the delivery as much as possible.

Every day, this crisis center, in cooperation with the Ukrainian Embassy in Poland, accompanies about a thousand tons of cargo and cooperates with donors from around the world. Every day, about 100–150 volunteers work at the Help Ukraine Center in

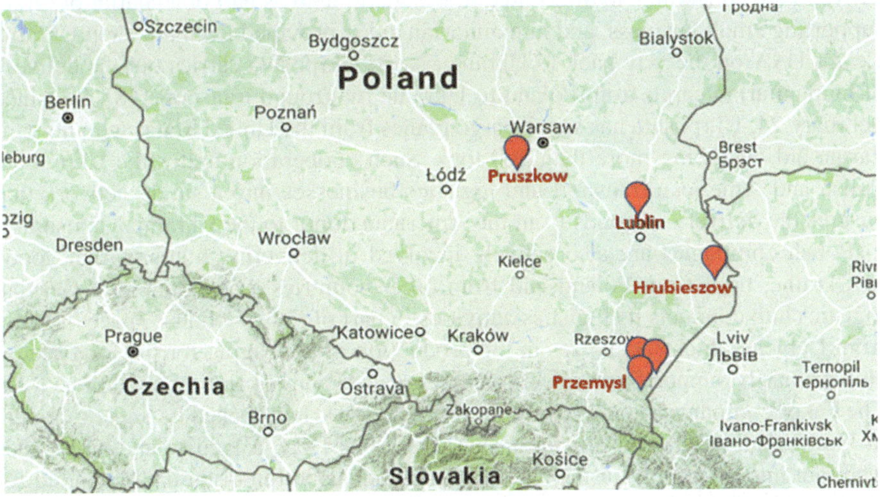


**Fig. 4** Polish logistics centers for humanitarian aid for Ukraine, coordinated by RARS *Source* Own study

**Table 2** Humanitarian aid sent to Ukraine by Help Ukraine Center (From March 6, 2022—January 31, 2023)

| Sector | Total | Weekly average |
|---|---|---|
| Vehicles | 1,087 | 22.64 |
| Pallets | 20, 668 | 430.58 |
| Tons | 7,326 | 152.62 |

*Source* https://helpukraine.center. [Accessed April 13, 2023]

Poland. Help Ukraine Center is the largest logistics center for humanitarian aid in Eastern Europe [46]. According to the Help Ukraine Center report (Table 2), only through this center, as of January 31, 2022, more than 7 000 tons of humanitarian aid were sent to Ukraine. The main components of humanitarian aid are food, hygiene products, medicines and medical equipment, sleeping pills and clothing.

On the basis of the Help Ukraine Center, it was also founded the Help Ukraine Center USA also. The project has wide global support, its main goal is to attract as much humanitarian aid and financial support from the USA and Canada as possible. The Dnipro logistics company is involved in the process of sending humanitarian aid from the United States, which as of April 1, 2023 processed and shipped 700 tons of humanitarian aid to Ukraine. The company focuses on large volumes of cargo and tries to operate sea containers. Humanitarian deliveries are received at the warehouse of the logistics company "Dnipro" in Roselle, New Jersey and then transported to the port of Gdansk or by plane, mainly to Warsaw, where Help Ukraine Center volunteers from Poland receive humanitarian cargoes and send them to a warehouse in Przemysl, from where they will be sent to Ukraine [47].

The Ukrainian state-owned postal company Ukrposhta is also involved in the process, which, together with the Ukrainian aviation company WindRose, organizes deliveries from Ukraine to the United States via Poland as part of a charter program supporting small business, and humanitarian aid is provided from the Help Ukraine Center USA on the way back to Ukraine. Next, Ukrposhta carries out the delivery of humanitarian cargo from Poland to Ukraine by ground transport [48]. So, since February 24, Ukrposhta has sent 5 cargo planes from the United States with humanitarian aid, weighing more than 200 tons. Such cooperation unites the Ukrainian, Polish and American transport and logistics businesses into a single network that ensures the delivery of goods from the American donor to the Ukrainian consumer.

Polish companies are also actively involved in delivering humanitarian goods to Ukraine, both from Poland and from other countries. For example, a German logistics hub conducts its logistics activities in part of the warehouse space of Delta from Debica, which specializes in the production of packaging for the food sector. Hub primarily supports non-governmental organizations operating in Ukraine [49]. The Fakro company, a manufacturer of roof windows, has opened its logistic centers in Nowy Sącz and Lviv. For the needs of Caritas Lviv, a facility and employees were put into operation for the reloading and redistribution of humanitarian aid for Ukraine. The Fakro logistics center can also be used free of charge by other charities organizations, that providing aid to Ukraine [50].

Also, Ukrainian logistics companies, such as Zammler, UTEC Logistics, deliver goods from Polish logistics hubs, some of these companies have their own warehouses in Poland, which during the war are used for storing and sorting humanitarian cargo, also Ukrainian companies rent warehouses on territory of Poland in order to organize humanitarian centers there.

Such an influx of humanitarian aid into the country requires additional professional coordination in logistics management. Therefore, international organizations such as Logistics Cluster are involved in the coordination of humanitarian logistics along the Polish-Ukrainian border.

The Logistics Cluster is part of the humanitarian cluster system and provides coordination, information management and, if necessary, access to common logistics services to enable effective humanitarian response in crisis situations. The logistics cluster enables global, regional and local organizations to meet humanitarian needs. Logistics Cluster has been operating in Ukraine since the beginning of March 2022 and is responsible for coordinating hundreds of humanitarian organizations trying to deliver humanitarian aid to Ukraine from Poland and other neighboring countries [51]. Logistics Cluster provides humanitarian organizations with free storage space for storing cargo (The Logistic Cluster: Ukraine—Standard Operating Procedures [52]. Due to severe disruptions to logistics infrastructure and the entire supply chain, Logistics Cluster organized a complex cross-border logistics response, starting from Poland, to enable the humanitarian community to deliver aid effectively [53, 54].

Logistic Cluster organizes an ongoing exchange of information with partners through a series of coordination meetings at the global, Polish and Ukrainian levels. Logistics Cluster partners have access to joint warehousing and transport services in Warsaw, Lublin and Rzeszow, in particular the warehouses in Warsaw and Lublin can store goods at controlled temperature, and from the warehouse in Rzeszow it is possible to ship them by rail. Road transport is available from any warehouse in Poland to any Logistics Cluster warehouse in Ukraine. In addition, Logistics Cluster partners can use a fleet of trucks contracted by the World Food Program and intended exclusively for the transport of humanitarian cargo [55].

## 6 Conclusions

The conducted study shows that currently, a large amount of foreign humanitarian aid goes to Ukraine through the territory of Poland. Many entities are involved in the logistics support processes: Ukrainian embassies in other countries, Ministries of Foreign Affairs, non-governmental and charitable organizations, etc. In coordinating the logistics of humanitarian aid along the Polish-Ukrainian border, international organizations are involved to provide professional coordination in logistics management.

International humanitarian assistance is a complex mechanism that involves not only numerous donors but also the processes of collection and formation of needs and logistics, which are daily hampered by the oil crisis, the destruction of transport infrastructure, active hostilities, and their humanitarian consequences. The resulting problems in delivering humanitarian aid have demonstrated the need for national and international cooperation to implement operational decisions and adopt appropriate regulatory legislation and permits that simplify and optimize humanitarian logistics processes during wartime.

Poland, together with logistics companies from other countries and Ukraine, organized sea, air, road, and rail logistics to ensure the fastest possible delivery of humanitarian cargo to Ukraine and organized a network of logistics hubs for collecting and sorting this aid, including in neighboring countries. The study confirms that the largest cooperation in the logistics of humanitarian aid from the international community for Ukraine took place in Poland.

The analysis also showed a change in the scale and logistics of humanitarian aid provided by Poland depending on the scale of military operations in 2014 and 2022, respectively. The assistance of Polish charities also increased significantly, and the adopted simplified procedures for transporting humanitarian goods across the Polish-Ukrainian border enabled charities to transport cargo to the recipient in Ukraine independently.

After the Russian invasion of Ukraine on February 24, 2022, Poland became not only one of the leaders in providing humanitarian aid but also the main transport corridor and logistics hub to which humanitarian aid flows to Ukraine from around the world.

The study's results can be used as a guide to organizing the logistics of humanitarian aid to countries during war. This study contributes to the scientific discussion on the logistics of humanitarian aid from the international community to Ukraine through Poland. It is a valuable analysis for commercial organizations, charities, and governments of countries that are involved in the process of providing humanitarian aid to Ukraine. Considering practical examples, interested organizations have the opportunity to optimize and streamline the logistics of humanitarian assistance to Ukraine and other warring countries.

## References

1. Khan, M., Parvaiz, G.S., Ali, A., Jehangir, M., Hassan, N., Bae, J.: A Model for understanding the mediating association of transparency between emerging technologies and humanitarian logistics sustainability. Sustainability **14**(11), 6917 (2022)
2. Pakurár, M., Haddad, H., Popp, J., Khan, T., Oláh, J.: Supply chain integration, organizational performance and balanced scorecard: an empirical study of the banking sector in Jordan. J. Int. Stud. **12**(2), (2019)
3. Thomas, A.: Humanitarian Logistics Enabling Disaster Response, 1–15. Fritz Institute, San Francisco (2003)
4. United Nations. The severe impact of the pandemic, wars and disasters on the health of women and children, https://news.un.org/ru/story/2022/10/1433587. Accessed13 Feb 2023
5. The Kiel Institute for the World Economy. A Database of Military, Financial and Humanitarian Aid to Ukraine, https://www.ifw-kiel.de/topics/war-against-ukraine/ukraine-support-tracker/. Accessed 3 Apr 2023

6. The State Emergency Service Of Ukraine. Statement regarding the establishment of a humanitarian demining center in Ukraine, https://dsns.gov.ua/news/ostanni-novini/v-ukrayini-bude-stvoreno-centr-gumanitarnogo-rozminuvannia-premier-minister. Accessed 13 Feb 2023
7. The National Agency on Corruption Prevention of Ukraine report. Mechanisms for State provision of humanitarian assistance under martial law, https://nazk.gov.ua/wp-content/uploads/2022/07/Mehanizmy-nadannya-derzhavnoyu-gumanitarnoyi-dopomogy-v-umovah-voyennogo-stanu.pdf. Accessed 3 Apr 2023
8. Jagtap, S., Trollman, H., Trollman, F., Garcia-Garcia, G., Parra-López, C., Duong, L., Martindale, W., Munekata, P.E.S., Lorenzo, J.M., Hdaifeh, A.: The Russia-Ukraine Conflict: Its Implications for the Global Food Supply Chains. Foods **11**(14), 2098 (2022)
9. Duszczyk M., Górny A., Kaczmarczyk P., Kubisiak A.: War refugees from Ukraine in Poland—one year after the Russian aggression. Socioeconomic consequences and challenges. Reg.Nal Sci. Assoc. Int. **15**(1), 181–199 (2023)
10. Roborgh, S., Coutts, A.B., Chellew, P., Novykov, V., Sullivan, R.: Conflict in Ukraine undermines an already challenged health system. The Lancet **399**(10333), 1365–1367 (2022)
11. The European Council. Humanitarian aid, https://www.consilium.europa.eu/en/policies/humanitarian-aid/. Accessed 13 Feb 2023
12. Pascucci, E.: More logistics, less aid: Humanitarian-business partnerships and sustainability in the refugee camp. World Dev. **142**(3), 105424 (2021)
13. Oláh, J., Zéman, Z., Balogh, I., Popp, J. Future challenges and areas of development for supply chain management. LogForum, 14(1), (2018)
14. The State Customs Service. Over 1 million tons of humanitarian aid cleared by customs officers since the beginning of the war, https://customs.gov.ua/news/zagalne-20/post/ponad-1-mln-tonn-gumanitarnoyi-dopomogi-oformleno-mitnikami-vid-pochatku-viini-1037. Accessed 13 Feb 2023
15. Straka, M., Oláh, J., Kassakorn, N.: Impact of green supply chain integration on SMEs technological and economic performance. Glob. J. Entrep. Manag. **2**(1), 12–30 (2021)
16. Karpatski obiektiv. Since the beginning of the full-scale war, more than 161 thousand tons of humanitarian goods have been delivered through the Transcarpathian customs, http://economics.ko.net.ua/?p=27496. Accessed 13 Apr 2023
17. Help Ukraine Romania humanitarian hub, https://www.hromadahub.org/about-hub. Acessed 25 May 2023
18. Media LOGISTYKA. Logistyka łączy siły, by pomóc Ukrainie, https://www.logistyka.net.pl/aktualnosci/item/92548-logistyka-laczy-sily-by-pomoc-ukrainie. Accessed 13 Feb 2023
19. Government portal. Deutsche Bahn And Ukrzaliznytsia signed memorandum of long-term support, https://www.kmu.gov.ua/en/news/ukrzaliznicya-ta-nimecka-zaliznicya-deutsche-bahn-pidpisali-memorandum-pro-spivrobitnictvo. Accessed 13 Apr 2023
20. Trademaster. Logistics during martial law - Synex Logistics experience, https://trademaster.ua/articles/313567, Accessed 13 Feb 2023
21. Zrybnieva I.: Challenges of logistics in the war conditions. In: Potential for sustainable development in the context of regional and global challenges: Materials of the International Scientific and Practical Conference, 132c, Chernivtsi national University, Chernivtsi (2022)
22. The Humanitarian Logistics Association. Raising awareness about unsolicited donations for Ukraine: a joint communication by HLA and Pharma.Aero, https://www.humanitarianlogistics.org/home?myhub&selected=7495&type=newsletter. Accessed 24 May 2023
23. Piotrowicz W.D.: In-kind donations, cash transfers and local procurement in the logistics of caring for internally displaced persons. The case of Polish humanitarian NGOs and Ukrainian IDPs. J. Hum.Itarian Logist. Supply Chain. Manag. **8**(3), (2018)
24. Polska Akcja Humanitarna, https://www.pah.org.pl/centrum-info-ua-ua. Accessed 13 Feb 2023
25. Polish Center for International Aid, https://pcpm.org.pl. Accessed 13 Feb 2023
26. Good Factory Foundation, https://www.dobrafabryka.pl. Accessed 13 Feb 2023
27. Caritas Poland, https://caritas.pl. Accessed 13 Feb 2023
28. Open Dialog Foundation, https://odfoundation.eu. Accessed 13 Feb 2023
29. Siepomaga Foundation, https://www.siepomaga.pl. Accessed 13 Feb 2023

30. International Solidarity Foundation, https://solidarityfund.pl. Accessed 13 Feb 2023
31. Doctors Without Borders, https://lekarze-bez-granic.pl. Accessed 13 Feb 2023
32. Polish medical mission, https://pmm.org.pl. Accessed 13 Feb 2023
33. Club of Catholic Intelligentsia, https://yeswecare.kik.waw.pl. Accessed 13 Feb 2023
34. The Great Orchestra of Christmas Charity Foundation, https://www.wosp.org.pl. Accessed 13 Feb 2023
35. Zasady wysyłki pomocy humanitarnej na Ukrainę, https://www.gov.pl/web/kas/rules-shipping-humanitarian-to-ukraine. Accessed 13 Feb 2023
36. The Chancellery of the Prime Minister. www.pomagamukrainie.gov.pl. Accessed 13 Feb 2023
37. Government Strategic Reserves Agency. https://www.rars.gov.pl/index.php. Accessed 3 Apr 2023
38. Polsko-Niemiecka Izba Przemysłowo-Handlowa. Niemieckie logistyczne centrum pomocy humanitarnej dla Ukrainy otwarte, https://ahk.pl/pl/media/aktualnosci/news-details-pl/niemieckie-logisticzne-centrum-pomocy-humanowej-dla-ukrainy-otwarte. Accessed 24 May 2023
39. The Economist. Why Poland has become NATO's linchpin in the war in Ukraine, www.economist.com/europe/poland-will-play-an-outsized-role-in-western-efforts-to-assist-ukraine/21808064. Accessed 13 Feb 2023
40. ReliefWeb. EU opens new rescEU energy hub in Poland, https://reliefweb.int/report/poland/eu-opens-new-resceu-energy-hub-poland. Accessed 13 Feb 2023
41. EU Solidarity with Ukraine. EU support to Ukraine: practical information, https://eu-solidarity-ukraine.ec.europa.eu/index_en. Accessed 13 Feb 2023
42. Devi, S.: Humanitarian work in Ukraine disrupted. The Lancet **399**(10328), 897 (2022)
43. Serwis Rzeczypospolitej Polskiej. Komunikacja kolejowa dla przewozu uchodźców, https://www.gov.pl/web/infrastruktura/komunikacja-kolejowa-dla-przewóz-uchodzcow. Accessed 13 Feb 2023
44. Lee A.C.K., Khaw Fu-M., Lindman A.E.S., Juszczyk G.: Ukraine refugee crisis: evolving needs and challenges. Public Health (217), 41–45 (2023)
45. DB SCHENKER. DB starts operations of Rail bridge with relief goods for Ukraine, https://www.dbschenker.com/global/about/press/db-starts-operations-of-railbridge-with-relief-goods-for-ukraine-777588. Accessed 3 Apr 2023
46. Help Ukraine Center. Humanitarian and medical aid to Ukraine, https://helpukraine.center/ukr. Accessed 13 Feb 2023
47. Dnipro LLC. Humanitarian aid for the people of Ukraine, https://dniprollc.com/uk/dopomoga-ukrayini/. Accessed 3 Apr 2023
48. Ekonomichna pravda. Ukrposhta has resumed flights to the United States: it will deliver humanitarian aid to Ukraine on the return direction. https://www.epravda.com.ua/news/2022/03/4/683239/. Accessed 3 Apr 2023
49. Energetyka24. Polska wysyła tysiące ton paliwa Ukrainie. Ta pomoc może się bardzo opłacić, https://energetyka24.com/ropa/analyses-and-commentaries/polska-wysyla-tysiace-ton-paliwa-ukrainie-ta-pomoc-moze-sie-srebro-oplacic-analysis. Accessed 3 Apr 2023
50. Drewno. Fakro shared own centers logistic supporting help humanitarian For of Ukraine, https://www.drewno.pl/artykuly/12325,fakro-udostepnilo-swoje-centra-logisticzne-wspierajac-pomoc-humana-dla-ukrainy.html. Accessed 3 Apr 2023
51. The Logistic Cluster: Logistic emergency team annual report, https://logcluster.org/document/let-annual-report-2022. Accessed 13 Feb 2023
52. The Logistic Cluster: Ukraine—Standard Operating Procedures (SOPs)—Transport and temporary storage, https://logcluster.org/document/ukraine-standard-operating-procedures-sops-transport-and-temporary-storage-september-2022. Accessed 13 Feb 2023
53. The Logistic Cluster: Ukraine emergency situation report No.1, https://logcluster.org/document/ukraine-situation-report-1-02-march-2022. Accessed 13 Feb 2023
54. Kot, S. Development insights on supply chain management in small and medium-sized enterprises. Logos Verlag Berlin GmbH. (2023)
55. The Logistic Cluster: Ukraine emergency situation report №3, https://logcluster.org/document/ukraine-situation-report-3-14-march-2022. Accessed 13 Feb 2023

# Effects of Authentic Leadership on Employee Work Performance, Moderated by Employee Resilience

**Pitchaya Srimongkolkul** and **Jumpoth Boriraj**

**Abstract** This study delves into the interplay between authentic leadership, employee resilience, and employee work performance within the organization. Authentic leadership, characterized by positive psychological attributes and ethical principles, fosters self-awareness and constructive behaviors among leaders and associates. Authentic leaders are known to drive positive values, stimulate creativity, and involve employees in decision-making, making them crucial in the face of business uncertainties. Resilient employees, capable of sustained productivity despite challenges, play a crucial role in organizational success. Authentic leadership has been found to cultivate employee resilience, enhancing adaptability and overall organizational outcomes. Employee work performance is multifaceted, encompassing task performance, contextual performance, and counterproductive work behavior, and is influenced by anticipated benefits. This research contributes to our understanding of authentic leadership's impact. It sheds light on the mechanisms that control employees' resiliency and work performance, which is crucial for organizations to maintain competitiveness in current and future business environments.

**Keywords** Authentic leadership · Employee work performance · Employee resilience

## 1 Introduction

Leadership has a significant impact on all levels of a business organization, from senior management to entry-level employees. Leaders create the work culture [1] and corporate culture, influencing the organization and its performance [2]. Leaders need to establish solid relationships and empowerment to enhance employee performance, as leaders guide a direction of what lies ahead and what potential achievement, and encourage and inspire the team. In summary, the historical evolution of the central

P. Srimongkolkul (✉) · J. Boriraj
Faculty of Management Sciences, Kasetsart University, Sriracha Campus, Thailand
e-mail: pitchaya.srim@ku.th



S. Kot et al. (eds.), *Corporate Practices: Policies, Methodologies, and Insights in Organizational Management*, Springer Proceedings in Business and Economics,
https://doi.org/10.1007/978-981-97-0996-0_42

leadership theories can be classified into four main eras in leadership theory: trait, behavioral, situational, and new leadership.

One of the well-known theories in the trait era is the great man theory. Even though one cannot change one's original traits, one can reduce the bad qualities and improve one's qualities to become a more effective leader. In response to the limitations of the trait theory, researchers turned their attention to the behavioral approach, which suggests that it is the behavior of leaders, not the traits, that influence followers.

The two major studies on behavioral aspects of leadership were the Michigan study and the Ohio state studies. This perspective implies that leadership is available and can be developed through learning. It was later recognized that the environment plays a significant role in the leader–follower dynamic. Sequentially, the situational era evolved, focusing on leadership in particular situations rather than on the traits or behavior of leaders [3]. Later, in a time of complex and challenging globalization, leadership theory emerged as a new era of theory [3]. The concept of transformational leadership style was originally developed by Burns in 1978. The behavior of transformational leaders leads them to perform as role models for their followers [4]. Transactional models encompass leadership by exception, contingency reward, and laissez-faire style. Concepts of leadership theory continued to evolve, including servant leadership, complexity leadership [3], and authentic leadership [5]. Servant leaders are characterized by their dedication to supporting their followers or team and humility in their attitude and actions. Purposed complexity leadership is an approach that recognizes leadership as a complex interplay of many interactive forces within knowledge-producing organizations. Complexity leadership theory needs more substantive research due to the difficulties in assessing this emergent construct within a dynamically changing context [6]. Therefore, the concept of Authentic leadership has been developed.

## 2 Theoretical Review

The primary purpose of this study was on the concept of authentic leadership, which refers to the perception of employees toward their direct leader's behavior, including their self-awareness, transparency, balance processing, and moral values, as described by Walumbwa, Avolio [7]. (1) Self-awareness (understanding oneself and the impact they have on others). (2) Transparency (be true of feelings to followers). (3) Balanced processing (are objective and make informed decisions based on detailed analysis of information and data). (4) Internalized moral perspective (high moral values and not compromise during challenges and pressures). We conducted a literature review to synthesize current knowledge on authentic leadership, employee work performance, and employee resilience. Literature reviews are performed to provide a clear and comprehensive overview of evidence and identify research gaps. Our search encompassed four large databases: Scopus, ScienceDirect, Wiley, and Business Source Complete.

We used the following keywords: Authentic leadership, Authentic work leadership, Leadership being authentic, Leader with authentic, Employee performance, Employee work performance, performance for employee, Employee resilience, work resilience, and resilience at work. We identified two core concepts that encompassed the critical aspects of our research question: those related to authentic leadership and employee work performance. To be included in the review, studies were required to focus on employees' work performance within organizations and to evaluate personal performance. However, articles had to be written or translated into English and published between January 2016 and March 2023. They have encouraged strategic intervention for supporting organizational effectiveness, and the scientific evaluation of this effectiveness would then ensue.

## *2.1 Authentic Leadership*

Recently, one of the emerging pillars of interest in leadership has been called authentic leadership development [6]. Luthans, Avolio [8] proposed the examination of factors that constituted genuine leadership development, exploring what is effective or ineffective to develop leaders and leadership while also highlighting the significance of the recent work in positive psychology as a foundation for accelerating the development. Moreover, Luthans, Avolio [8] suggested examining the perception of authentic leadership in various contexts and cultures to determine if it is the base of good leadership regardless of form.

The concept of authentic leadership has gained recognition as a significant element in the field of leadership. Authentic leadership provides a new ethical model while focusing on principles and morals and maintaining balance in their words. Authentic leaders create positive values, lead from the heart, set the highest levels of ethics and morality, and go beyond their interests for the well-being of their followers. Furthermore, authentic leaders encourage employees to become more involved in the decision-making process, sharing their knowledge and creative ideas, which can improve organizational performance.

Given the challenges and uncertainties faced in the business landscape today, the development of authentic leadership has become increasingly relevant and urgent to achieve favorable outcomes [9]. Research by Avolio and Gardner [10] and Jensen and Luthans [11] have all found significant associations between authentic leadership and effects such as trust in management, group performance, employee job satisfaction, organizational commitment, work happiness, work engagement, follower job performance, follower affective commitment, work role performance, and employees' creativity, team affective commitment, and team potency, respectively.

## 2.2 Authentic Leadership Component

The construct of authentic leadership is multidimensional and comprises four dimensions of components: self-awareness, relational transparency, balanced processing, and internalized moral perspective [7]. The first component, self-awareness, represents the degree to which leaders understand their strengths, weaknesses, self-value, beliefs, and emotions, as well as how leaders impact others [7, 12, 13. The second, relational transparency, refers to the leaders' authentic selves and sincere feelings, emotions, and thoughts to followers [13, 14. The third balanced information processing is when the leader objectively analyzes all relevant information before deciding and solicits views that challenge deeply held positions [7, 15]. The last component, internalized moral perspective, refers to the degree to which ethical standards and values guide the leader and result in behaviors and decisions consistent with internalized values, as opposed to group, organizational, or societal pressures [7, 12, 15]. Together, these four components is an innate desire to understand their own leadership, to serve others more effectively [7]. By demonstrating transparency, authentic leaders build trust and stronger relationships with their followers.

## 2.3 Employee Work Performance

Employees are the key to organizational success; it is crucial to find new ways to maximize employee performance [16]. According to a study, the importance of employee performance to any organization is vital as it directly impacts the firm's overall performance and plays a significant role in enhancing customer satisfaction and loyalty. Employee work performance can be determined through various measures such as quality, quantity, punctuality, cost-effectiveness, accuracy, etc. While authentic leadership leads to a strength-based organization, it is also possible that the relationship between authentic leadership and sustained performance is moderated by other organizational contexts [10]. Enhancing employee performance is crucial for an organization's competitiveness in a business environment. Therefore, improving and increasing employee performance is a leadership challenge.

According to the definition, employee performance encompasses various measures, including quality, quantity, punctuality, cost-effectiveness, and accuracy. It refers to the behavior employed by employees to achieve a target. When employees' performance results in satisfied customers, it ultimately enhances customer loyalty and trust in the products and services the firm is offering. Employee performance can be evaluated based on the development of learning, as well as work quality, work quantity, and time appropriateness [17, 18].

Work performance, also called job performance, is a widely used tool and metric in management. Koopmans, Bernaards [19] defined that work performance is multidimensional. It should be defined in terms of behavior rather than result, including only those behaviors that are relevant to the organization's goal. Employee performance encompasses the timely, effective, and efficient completion of tasks mutually agreed upon by the employee, as set out by the employer. The factors that can influence employee performance can include personal characteristics such as gender, age, education, marital status, attitudes, and others [17].

## 2.4 Employee Work Performance Component

Borman and Motowidlo [20] proposed that employee performance can be classified into two types: Task performance and Contextual performance or Citizenship performance. However, recent research describes that employee performance consists of three components: Task performance, Contextual performance, and Counterproductive work behavior [21, 22]. Task performance describes the core job responsibilities of an employee under contractual terms between an employer and an employee or a manager and a subordinate to perform an assigned task. Task Performance includes self-control, responsibility, and perseverance.

Parmenter [23] indicated that employees not only fulfill the tasks specified in their Key Performance Indicators (KPIs) but also many different tasks within the organization during the day, most of which are not specified in the KPIs. Therefore, employees perceive two different task performances: general task performance, which may not relate to KPIs and specific task performance. Contextual performance, called extra-role behavior, goes beyond formal job responsibilities [19]. It refers to the extra role activities, such as coaching new co-workers, which often need to be written in a job description and go beyond work objectives [21]. However, these extra contributions are vital in achieving the organization's goals. In human resource practice, contextual performance fosters a positive organizational climate and strengthens social networks [24]. Counterproductive work behavior refers to intentional and aggressive employee behaviors that harm the organization and its stakeholders [25]. Examples of counterproductive work behavior include destroying company property, calling in sick when not ill, and stealing something from the employer, which can cause enormous losses for an organization. However, the technology is likely more related to task than contextual performance. The knowledge and skill required for task performance is acquired through explicit training and deliberate practice. Motivation is likely to have a more substantial impact on contextual performance than task performance, and the effect of knowledge, skill, and motivation on task performance is expected to change over time.

## 2.5 Employee Resilience

Despite the extensive study of resilience in many disciplines, many researchers have focused on specific areas, such as education and psychology [26]. Recently, there has been an increase in research on resilience in the workplace. It is crucial to apply the knowledge gained from individual resilience to the employee-centric level [27]. Shin Taylor [28] suggested that managers consider resilience as one criterion for selecting new employees and as content for training interventions. This involves management planning and preparation for crisis by operating in unusual ways within the work function to achieve organizational goals and meet the targets [29]. Masten [30] describes building employee resilience as "ordinary magic" that promotes individual competency. It also drives employee growth and success in overcoming adversity and ultimately succeeding in the workplace [31].

Employee resilience refers to the adaptability of employees, which can be utilized in various contexts to enhance competitiveness, especially in the everyday world. In any organization, employee resilience is a crucial capability enabling employees to manage and adapt to continually changing circumstances [32]. Resilience is critical in coping with unexpected changes and crises [33]. Resilient employees behave more positively when confronted with change due to the presence of support and resources; they are better able to adapt to adversity without becoming anxious and overwhelmed. Therefore, resilient organizations and employees are essential to survive and thrive in dynamic, disruptive environments. They are better able to rebound and learn from adversity and uncertainty [34].

## 2.6 Employee Resilience Definition

Kuntz et al. [35] explained that employee resilience is more than personal resilience and includes the availability and management of resources specific to occupational contexts. Franken [36] supported that resilience is situational and shaped by the context rather than trait-like. This definition aligns with earlier theories that suggest resilience is a developable ability rather than a stable trait. Näswall [27] conceptualizes and defines employee resilience as the employee capability, facilitated and supported by the organization, to utilize resources to positively cope, adapt, and thrive in response to challenging circumstances.

## 2.7 Research Gap

Extensive research has explored leadership's influence on employee work performance with a focus on various leadership styles like transformational, self-sacrifice, ethical, and transactional leadership. However, our understanding of the connection of authentic leadership's impact on performance still needs to be improved. Therefore, the first research gap is to investigate the effects of authentic leadership on employee work performance. Moreover, numerous studies have examined various mediators influencing authentic leadership and employee work performance relationships, including work engagement, human resource practices, and organizational commitment. However, there needs to be more current literature concerning employee resilience as a mediator. Based on the literature review, this research will further examine other mediators that explain the link between authentic leadership and employee performance [10, 37].

## 3 Methodology

The study delves into the literature on authentic leadership and its correlation with employee work performance, focusing on the moderating role of employee resilience. Despite their significance in fostering strong working relationships and ultimately enhancing competitive advantage, these crucial connections have yet to receive attention in prior literature. This research critically assesses existing literature to advance our understanding of authentic leadership, emphasizing follower resilience and finally reflecting work performance as a theoretical focal point. Hence, the study is framed by four hypotheses: (1) the link between authentic leadership and employee work performance, (2) the connection between authentic leadership and employee resilience, (3) the relationship between employee resilience and employee work performance, and (4) the mediation effect of employee resilience in the relationship between authentic leadership and employee work performance. Despite numerous studies on authentic leadership and employee performance, there needs to be more investigations into the interplay between authentic leadership and employee work performance through the resiliency of employees. This concentrates on finding how authentic leaders can cultivate resilience in their followers and the subsequent impact on employee work performance. It bridges theory and practical application, addressing a topic now gaining recognition (Table 1).

## 4 Result and Discussion

Numerous studies have affirmed the positive impact of authentic leadership on enhancing work performance [53]. The researchers find the interrelationship among authentic leadership, employee work performance, and employee resilience.

**Authentic Leadership Relationship to Employee Work Performance**

As seen from the previous study by Walumbwa et al. [7], who defined authentic leadership as "a pattern of leader behavior that designs and promotes positive psychological capacities, ethical climate, self-awareness, self-development, and moral perspective, which balanced processing of information and transparency on the leaders-followers relationship." Other key attributes of authentic leaders involve leading their subordinates fairly rather than unreal or unfair ways are the key attributes of authentic leaders [54]. The meta-analysis by Zhang and Bowers [55] proved that authentic

**Table 1** Results of relevant of literature review

| Name | Sample size | IV[3] | DV[4] | Statistic | Results |
|---|---|---|---|---|---|
| How servant leadership predicts employee resilience in public organizations: a social identity perspective [38] | 901 | AL[5] | RE[6] | SEM | Supported |
| Effects of Resilience on Productivity under Authentic Leadership [38, 39] | 93 | AL | RE | Path analysis method | Supported |
| Authentic Leadership and Employee Resilience: A Moderated Mediation Analysis [40] | 884 | AL | RE | SPSS | Supported |
| The Relationship Between Authentic Leadership and Resilience, Moderated by Coping Skills [41] | 581 | AL | RE | Hierarchical Regression Analysis | Not Supported AL direct to RE is negative. If moderate Coping skill is positive |
| Authentic Leadership and its Impact on Supporting Strategic Intelligence [42] | 100 | AL | PE[7] | SPSS | Supported |
| Servant Versus Authentic Leadership: Assessing Effectiveness in China's Hospitality Industry [43] | 1132 | AL | PE | Means, Standard Deviations, Intercorrelation | Not supported AL direct to PE is Negative unless meditated by trust |
| Do Ethical, Authentic, and Servant Leadership Explain Variance Above and Beyond Transformational Leadership A Meta-Analysis [44] | N/A | AL | PE | Systematic review | Supported |
| Does servant leadership better explain work engagement, career satisfaction and adaptive performance than authentic leadership [45] | 226 | AL | PE | Structural model | Supported |
| Positive leadership psychology: Authentic and servant leadership in higher education in Pakistan [46] | 323 | AL | PE | SPSS | Supported |
| Does Multiple Leadership Styles Mediated by Job Satisfaction Influence Better Business Performance [47] | 150 | AL | PE | SPSS | Supported |

(continued)

**Table 1** (continued)

| Name | Sample size | IV[3] | DV[4] | Statistic | Results |
|---|---|---|---|---|---|
| Task Challenge and Employee Performance: A Moderated Mediation Model of Resilience and Digitalization [48] | 441 | Emp RE[8] | PE | Correlation and Descriptives Analysis | Supported |
| Building-up resilience and being effective leaders in the workplace: a systematic review and synthesis model [49] | 46 | Emp RE | PE | Systematic review | Supported |
| Why resilient workers perform better: The roles of job satisfaction and work engagement [50] | 360 | Emp RE | PE | SEM | Supported |
| Well-being-oriented human resource management practices and employee performance in the Chinese banking sector: The role of social climate and resilience [51] | 561 | Emp RE | PE | Multilevel modeling | Supported |
| The Effect of Resilience, EI & Well-Being on Employee Performance -An Exploratory Study of BPO & ITES [52] | 400 | Emp RE | PE | SPSS | Supported |

[3]Independent variable, [4]Dependent variable, [5]Authentic leadership, [6]Resillience, [7]Performance, [8]Employee resilience

leadership leads to positive outcomes, including work engagement, psychological empowerment, commitment, and thriving among followers. Authentic leaders are developed through experience and foster transparent linkages between leaders and followers [12]. The attitudes and behaviors of faithfully authentic leaders, founded on ethical principles, supportiveness, and values, contribute to improving follower performance [37].

Additionally, subordinates under authentic leaders feel more autonomy and self-efficiency, which enhances their performance. To be eligible for inclusion in this study, all articles need to have explicitly measured work performance, either at the personal or organizational level or both. As previously mentioned, several additional measures were identified as relevant for understanding the effects of authentic leadership on employee work performance. However, according to the study by Q, Ling, Liu, and Wu [43], the administration will not support employee work performance in cases where trust is negative. Since authentic leadership fosters a positive trust climate in the organization, authentic leadership is essential for supporting employee work performance.

**Authentic Leadership Relationship to Employee Resilience**

Employee resilience is a key capability enabling employees to manage and adapt to continually changing circumstances [32], as resilience is critical in coping with unexpected changes and crises [33, 56, 57]. Authentic leaders can improve their employees' resilience by offering them support in times of need; with the ability to recognize potential hazards and formulate contingency plans, authentic leaders can provide their employees with hope, confidence, optimism, and more [58]. Moreover, a leader who leads authentically can result in positive team and organizational outcomes [7, 59] and thus positively related to resilience. Moreover, some research suggests that individuals with high levels of authentic leadership are more resilient [8]. Out of four articles that examined the relationship between authentic leadership and employee resilience, all studies indicated a positive correlation, except in cases where coping skills were negative [41]. Therefore, our findings lead us to conclude that organizations should assess their employee' coping skills to enhance their resilience.

**Employee Performance Relationship to Employee Resilience**

Resilience refers to an individual's ability to adapt, bounce back, and maintain high performance despite facing challenges, setbacks, or stressful situations [60]. Empirical study reveals that organizational resilience directly enhances organizational performance. At the individual level, employee resilience also has a significant impact on employee performance. When employees possess stability, they are better equipped to cope with work-related stress, overcome obstacles, and maintain their productivity and effectiveness in adversity [5]. Research has shown that employees with higher levels of resilience tend to display greater job satisfaction, which positively influences their performance outcomes. Moreover, resilient employees are better equipped to handle workload [61], manage work-related stress [60, 62], and maintain their overall well-being [26]. This ability to bounce back from adversity and maintain a positive mindset contributes to higher levels of job performance. According to the literature review, a consistent outcome has demonstrated a positive impact of employee resilience on employee work performance for all studies.

**Impact of Authentic Leadership on Employee Work Performance Mediated by Employee Resilience**

To bridge the study gap between employee work performance and leadership as suggested in previous literature, Bruce J. Avolio & William L. Gardner [15] aimed to enhance understanding of the role of perceptions in employee resilience. The findings suggest that social climate and the quality of working conditions created by leaders may be decisive factors for employees regarding the development of better attitudes and a creative spirit in the force. Research has shown that employees with higher levels of resilience tend to display greater job satisfaction, which positively influences their performance outcomes [50]. Therefore, recruiting and retaining resilient employees would enable an organization to derive benefit from their ability not only to withstand the pressures and challenges of organizational change but also to cultivate their performance. Authentic leaders have the potential to enhance employee resilience, thereby reinforcing the interplay between authentic leadership and employee resilience, ultimately invigorating the impact on employee work performance.

# 5 Conclusions

The findings of this research enrich the knowledge of the effects of authentic leadership on creativity, and they are substantial, supporting both theory and new empirical research.

## *5.1 Managerial Implication*

The organization's leader must oversee the factors that influence the components of employee work performance. Authentic leadership has a positive impact on employee work performance, as supported by a meta-analysis conducted by Zhang, Bowers [55], showing that authentic leadership leads to positive outcomes, including work engagement, psychological empowerment, commitment, and thriving among followers. Employee resilience is an essential mediator that fosters the positive impact of authentic leadership on employee work performance. Therefore, it is recommended to assess resilience when hiring new employees and enhancing the resilience development of current employees to improve work performance, as well as the satisfaction and engagement of workers in organizational settings. Janna and Wolor [63] further emphasize the importance of leaders determining company strategies, especially employee resilience, to increase employee performance. In addition, the ASEAN Secretariat [64] suggested that the logistic industry should focus on developing a resilient culture that encourages employees to take risks and make change safely and constructively, which focus on long-term resilient outcomes rather than short-term goals.

## *5.2 Theoretical Implication*

Crawford and Dawkins [65] outlined four specific themes for future research, which include measuring authentic leaders, the risk of follower manipulation, application to diverse empirical contexts, and a focus on development. This research contributes to the theoretical implication in the context of employee resilience. Nevertheless, it is essential to undertake further investigation into employee resilience in the broader range of cultural, industrial, and demographic contexts to gain a deeper understanding of the relationship between authentic leadership and employee work performance.

## 5.3 Limitation

The limitation of this study stems from its reliance on existing literature. The business environment nowadays is dynamically characterized by rapid technological advancements, digital platforms, paradigm shifts in business philosophy, and shifts in employee demographics. These factors may impact variability in the influence of leadership on their followers in diverse ways. For example, with the increasing number of employees working online with limited face-to-face interactions, the traditional dynamics of leader–follower relationships may only apply differently. This evolving context could introduce nuances in the leadership-follower dynamic that warrant consideration as a limitation in this study.

## 5.4 Future Research Recommendations

Despite the research findings indicating a positive correlation between authentic leadership and employee work performance, it has paved the way for further research to examine other mediators that explain the link between authentic leadership and employee performance. Additionally, it is advisable to explore further influential factors such as job satisfaction, innovative work behavior, individual spiritual quotient, and spiritual leadership as potential moderators in the relationship between authentic leadership and the influence of employee work performance. Moreover, the study encourages the exploration of other factors affecting individual performance, including performance management and intrinsic motivation in various contexts.

## 5.5 Summary

This research extends our understanding of how authentic leaders can uniquely shape not only individual behavior but also the organization. The perspective of employee work performance effect from authentic leadership and its possible relations with employee resilience were reviewed to bridge the gap at the employee and individual levels. Examining authentic leadership practices and employee perspectives contributes to the development of critical competencies in the human resources of the industry while also paving the way for future research. Our findings encompass various dimensions of authentic leadership as exhibited by organizational leaders. Among these dimensions, it is confirmed that employee resilience plays a crucial role. Our primary proposition asserts a positive correlation between authentic behavior and enhanced employee work performance.

Furthermore, we hypothesize that employee resilience acts as a mediator in the relationship between authentic behavior and follower positivity. Additionally, we anticipate that authentic relational orientation exhibits a stronger positive relationship between leader and employee, with leader positivity as a mediator in the organization. In summary, authentic leadership encompasses a multifaceted set of factors that warrant further investigation to yield more concrete insights into the interplay among these constructs and the extent of their relationships. To enhance the performance of employees within the organization, this study underscores the importance of fostering an employee resilience culture. It is recommended that organizations invest in developing authentic leadership skills among supervisors and managers while also emphasizing recruiting individuals with resilience and nurturing their resiliency through the influent of authentic leaders within the organization.

## References


1. Ali, N.M.: Influence of leadership styles in creating quality work culture. Procedia Econ. Financ. **31**, 161–169 (2015)
2. Popa, B.M.: The relationship between leadership effectiveness and organizational performance. J. Def. Resour. Manag. (JoDRM) **3**(1), 123–127 (2012)
3. Benmira, S., Agboola, M.: Evolution of leadership theory. BMJ Leader, (2021)
4. Bass, B.M., Riggio, R.E.: Transformational leadership, (2006)
5. Avolio, B., Luthans, F.: The High Impact Leader: Moments Matter in Accelerating Authentic Leadership Development, (2008)
6. Avolio, B.J., Walumbwa, F.O., Weber, T.J.: Leadership: Current theories, research, and future directions. Annu. Rev. Psychol. **60**, 421–449 (2009)
7. Walumbwa, F., et al.: Authentic leadership: Development and validation of a theory-based measure†. J. Manag. **34**, 89–126 (2008)
8. Luthans, F.: Authentic leadership: A positive developmental approach. Posit. Organ. Sch., 241–261 (2003)
9. Luthans, F., Avolio, B.J.: Authentic leadership development. Posit. Organ. Sch., 1–26 (2003)
10. Avolio, B.J., Gardner, W.L.: Authentic leadership development: Getting to the root of positive forms of leadership. Leadersh. Q. **16**, 315–338 (2005)
11. Jensen, S.M., Luthans, F.: Entrepreneurs as authentic leaders: Impact on employees' attitudes. Leadersh. Org. Dev. J. **27**, 646–666 (2016)
12. Avolio, B.J., Gardner, W.L.: Authentic leadership development: Getting to the root of positive forms of leadership. Leadersh. Q. **16**(3), 315–338 (2005)
13. Ribeiro, N., Duarte, A.P., Filipe, R.: How authentic leadership promotes individual performance: mediating role of organizational citizenship behavior and creativity. International J. Prod. Perform. Manag. 67(9), (2018)
14. Avolio, B.J., et al.: Transformational leadership and organizational commitment mediating role of psychological empowerment and moderating role of structural distance. J. Organ. Behav. **25**(8), 951–968 (2004)
15. Gardner, W.L., et al.: "Can you see the real me?" A self-based model of authentic leader and follower development. Leadersh. Q. **16**, 343–372 (2005)
16. Luthans, F., Stajkovic, A.D.: Reinforce for performance: The need to go beyond pay and even rewards. Acad. Manag. Perspect. **13**(2), 49–57 (1999)
17. Chaimongkol, N., et al.: The influence of organizational citizenship behavior and team effectiveness on performance of employees. J. Manag. Sci. Nakhon Pathom Rajabhat University **5**(1), 173–186 (2018)
18. Chienwattanasook, K., Onputtha, S., Fugkum, S.: Relationship among leadership styles, fellowship styles and organizational commitment of employees. J. Interdiscip. Res.: Grad. Stud. **7**(1), 25–34 (2018)

19. Koopmans, L., et al.: Conceptual frameworks of individual work performance: A systematic review. J. Occup. Environ. Med. 53(8), 856–866 (2011)
20. Borman, W.C., Motowidlo, S.: Expanding the Criterion Domain to Include Elements of Contextual Performance, (1993)
21. Van der Vaart, L.: The performance measurement conundrum: Construct validity of the individual work performance questionnaire in South Africa. South African J. Econ. Manag. Sci. **24**(1), 3581 (2021)
22. Dåderman, A.M., Ingelgård, A., Koopmans, L.: Cross-cultural adaptation, from Dutch to Swedish language, of the individual work performance questionnaire. Work **65**(1), 97–109 (2020)
23. Parmenter, D.: Key Performance Indicators: Developing, Implementing, and Using Winning KPIs. Wiley (2015)
24. Kappagoda, U.: Self-Efficacy, Task Performance and Contextual Performance: A Sri Lankan Experience, (2018)
25. Spector, P.E., Fox, S.: An emotion-centered model of voluntary work behavior: Some parallels between counterproductive work behavior and organizational citizenship behavior. Hum. Resour. Manag. Rev. **12**(2), 269–292 (2002)
26. Luthans, F.: Positive organizational behavior: Developing and managing psychological strengths. Acad. Manag. Exec. **16**, 57–72 (2002)
27. Näswall, K.: Employee resilience scale (EmpRes), Technical Report, (2013)
28. Shin, J., Taylor, M.S., Seo, M.-G.: The relationships of organizational inducements and psychological resilience to employees' attitudes and behaviors toward organizational change. Acad. Manag. J. **55**(3), 727–748 (2012)
29. Seville, E.: Building Organisational Resilience: A Summary of Key Research Findings, (2006)
30. Masten, A.S.: Ordinary magic: Resilience processes in development. Am. Psychol. **56**(3), 227 (2021)
31. King, D.D., Newman, A., Luthans, F.: Not if, but when we need resilience in the workplace. J. Organ. Behav. **37**(5), 782–786 (2016)
32. Näswall, K.: Employee resilience: Development and validation of a measure. J. Manag. Psychol. **34**(5), 353–367 (2019)
33. Hartmann, S., Weiss, M., Hoegl, M.: Team resilience in organizations: A conceptual and theoretical discussion of a team-level concept. In: Research Handbook on Organizational Resilience, pp. 39–52. Edward Elgar Publishing (2020)
34. Cao, R.Q., Elking, I., Gu, V.C.: Supply chain driven sustainability: Ambidexterity, authentic leadership and interorganizational citizenship behavior. Int. J. Logist. Manag. (2022).
35. Kuntz, J.R., Malinen, S., Näswall, K.: Employee resilience: Directions for resilience development. Consult. Psychol. J.: Pract. Res. 69(3), 223 (2017)
36. Franken, E.: Building People Up: Leadership and Employee Resilience, (2019)
37. Duarte, A.P.: Authentic leadership and improved individual performance: affective commitment and individual creativity's sequential mediation. Front. Psychol. **12**, 675–749 (2021)
38. Peng, C., et al.: How servant leadership predicts employee resilience in public organizations: A social identity perspective. Curr. Psychol., 1–16 (2022)
39. Zehir, C., Narcıkara, E.: Effects of resilience on productivity under authentic leadership. Procedia Soc. Behav. Sci. **235**, 250–258 (2016)
40. Mao, Y., et al.: Authentic leadership and employee resilience: a moderated mediation analysis. Front. Psychol. 13 (2022)
41. Stark, A.E.: The relationship between authentic leadership and resilience. Seattle Pacific University, Moderated by Coping Skills (2021)
42. Alshaar, A.M.K.: Authentic leadership and its impact on supporting strategic intelligence. Intelligence **13**(3), 59–75 (2023)
43. Ling, Q., Liu, F., Wu, X.: Servant versus authentic leadership: Assessing effectiveness in China's hospitality industry. Cornell Hosp. Q. **58**(1), 53–68 (2017)
44. Hoch, J.E., et al.: Do ethical, authentic, and servant leadership explain variance above and beyond transformational leadership? A meta-analysis. J. Manag. **44**(2), 501–529 (2018)

45. Kaya, B., Karatepe, O.M.: Does servant leadership better explain work engagement, career satisfaction and adaptive performance than authentic leadership? Int. J. Contemp. Hosp. Manag. **32**(6), 2075–2095 (2020)
46. Abbas, A., et al.: Positive leadership psychology: Authentic and servant leadership in higher education in Pakistan. Curr. Psychol. **41**(9), 5859–5871 (2022)
47. Ali, N.N.K., Tang, S.Y.: Does multiple leadership styles mediated by job satisfaction influence better business performance? Perception of MNC employees in Malaysia. In: SHS Web of Conferences, EDP Sciences, (2016)
48. Saleem, I., Qureshi, T.M., Verma, A.: Task challenge and employee performance: A moderated mediation model of resilience and digitalization. Behav. Sci. **13**(2), 119 (2023)
49. Yu, M., et al.: Building-up resilience and being effective leaders in the workplace: A systematic review and synthesis model. Lead. Organ. Dev. J. 43(7), 1098–1117 (2022)
50. Kašpárková, L., et al.: Why resilient workers perform better: The roles of job satisfaction and work engagement. Work. Behav. Health **33**(1), 43–62 (2018)
51. Cooper, B., et al.: Well-being-oriented human resource management practices and employee performance in the Chinese banking sector: The role of social climate and resilience. Hum. Resour. Manage. **58**(1), 85–97 (2019)
52. Murugesan, T., Megavannan, R.: The effect of resilience, EI & well-being on employee performance-an exploratory study of BPO & ITES. Asian J. Res. Soc. Sci. Hum. **8**(5), 106–124 (2018)
53. AlMazrouei, H.: Authentic Leadership: Supporting Employees Performance, Creativity, Involvement in Decision-Making and Outcomes (2023)
54. Gardner, W.L., et al.: Barriers to authentic leader- follower relationships. In: Leadership: Leaders, Followers, and Context, 181 (2022)
55. Zhang, S., Bowers, A.J., Mao, Y.: Authentic leadership and teachers' voice behaviour: The mediating role of psychological empowerment and moderating role of interpersonal trust. Educ. Manag. Adm. Lead **49**(5), 768–785 (2021)
56. Van Der Vegt, G.S., et al.: Managing risk and resilience. Acad. Manag. Briarcliff Manor 58(4), 971–980 (2015)
57. Williams, T.A., Shepherd, D.A.: Building resilience or providing sustenance: Different paths of emergent ventures in the aftermath of the Haiti earthquake. Acad. Manag. J. **59**(6), 2069–2102 (2016)
58. Gardner, W.L., Schermerhorn, J.R.: Unleashing individual potential. Organ. Dyn. **3**(33), 270–281 (2004)
59. Gardner, W.L., et al.: Authentic leadership: A review of the literature and research agenda. Leadersh. Q. **22**(6), 1120–1145 (2011)
60. Luthans, F., et al.: Positive psychological capital: Measurement and relationship with performance and satisfaction. Pers. Psychol. **60**(3), 541–572 (2007)
61. Kumari, P., Sangwan, V.: A Study on impact of resilience capacity on job performance of executives in the pharmaceutical industry. Int. J. Manag. Soc. Sci. Res. **4**(4), 27–34 (2015)
62. Youssef, C.M., Luthans, F.: Positive organizational behavior in the workplace: The impact of hope, optimism, and resilience. J. Manag. **33**(5), 774–800 (2007)
63. Janna, N.N., Wolor, C.W., Suhud, U.: The role of e-training, career development, and employee resilience in increasing employee productivity in Indonesian state-owned enterprises. Bus. Excel. Manag. **11**(3), 5–21 (2021)
64. ASEAN Secretariat, U.-E., ITF: COVID-19 recovery guidelines for resilient and sustainable international road freight transport connectivity in ASEAN. 2021, Homepage. https://asean.org/book/covid-19-recovery-guidelines-for-resilient-and-sustainable-international-road-freight-trwansport-connectivity-in-asean/. Last accessed 2013/05/15
65. Crawford, J.A., et al.: Putting the leader back into authentic leadership: Reconceptualising and rethinking leaders. Aust. J. Manag. **45**(1), 14–133 (2020)

# Factors Influencing Organizational Survival of Retail Food Businesses in Thailand: A Conceptual Perspective

**Auyporn Naklamthong, Wornchanok Chaiyasoonthorn, and Singha Chaveesuk**

**Abstract** This research aims to investigate the factors influencing the organizational survival of retail food businesses during the COVID-19 outbreak in Thailand to develop a conceptual framework. The study involves a comprehensive review of domestic and international literature regarding organizational survival factors. It seeks to address the gaps identified in previous research conducted in Thailand, which has yet to study survival factors in service businesses. The exploration of theories about survival, as well as related theories, revealed the main theories that helped researchers to understand the causes of adaptation, human adaptive behaviour and the process of human adaptation when there is an accident or a change in life, including the results that occur. Humans must adapt using intelligence to acclimatize and survive when facing change in life. The theory mentioned by the researcher is Roy's adaptation model. The findings of this research are expected to offer a model approach for future data collection. In order to obtain research results that can benefit retail food business operators in the country, please enable them to utilize the research findings for adaptation and survival in the business.

**Keywords** Organization survival model · Adaptive capability · Retail food business

## 1 Introduction

The Thai food industry can produce products according to consumer demands promptly, aligning not only with domestic but also international requirements. It can also add value by processing raw materials imported from abroad. This is greatly

A. Naklamthong · W. Chaiyasoonthorn (✉) · S. Chaveesuk
KMITL Business School, King Mongkut's Institute of Technology Ladkrabang, Bangkok, Thailand
e-mail: Wornchanok.ch@kmitl.ac.th

A. Naklamthong
e-mail: a.naklamthong@gmail.com



S. Kot et al. (eds.), *Corporate Practices: Policies, Methodologies, and Insights in Organizational Management*, Springer Proceedings in Business and Economics,
https://doi.org/10.1007/978-981-97-0996-0_43

influenced by Thailand's long-standing stable agricultural production foundation, which provides a variety of continuous raw materials for processing. There is also a large, skilled workforce, modern production technology, continuous product format development to meet market demands, and expertise among various Thai industries. These factors contribute to Thailand's competitiveness compared to other countries in the same region. Therefore, Thailand's food industry is a highly potential sector for both domestic consumption and exports. It contributes significantly to the economy, with an annual value exceeding 5 trillion Baht.

Furthermore, it accounts for over 20% of the Gross Domestic Product (GDP) of the industrial sector and shows continuous growth trends. In 2020, the food industry's export value was 1.025 trillion Baht, making Thailand the 11th largest exporter in the world [1]. However, the outbreak of COVID-19 directly affected the supply chain of the products, especially upstream and downstream. As a result, it caused interruptions to supply chains in all industries, and entrepreneurs attempted to adapt their business procedures [2].

Apart from managing supply chains during this crisis, consideration must be given to the effectiveness of the supply chain system to meet consumer demand. Thai industries increasingly involve global supply chains, especially downstream industries such as the food industry. The 2020 annual report of the Electronic Transactions Development Agency estimated that the trend of retail business would shrink by −10.0% to −13.6%, compared to the same period of the previous year due to the negative factors from the economic situation during the COVID-19 pandemic. Therefore, entrepreneurs' adaptation for business survival under this situation is essential [3], such as changing sales channels into online channels, adjusting products to suit the situation, lowering costs, managing cash flow, and maintaining business liquidity to survive. Notably, the retail food business in Thailand, which consists of over 895,000 retail traders, is classified as a small-scale (Micro) business with a total of 905,000 traders. Among these, there is a total of 14,617 retail traders in the food category [4]. This is significant and caters to consumer needs, considering household expenditure accounts for up to 33.9%.

The main effects are directly upon retail stores selling fresh food, dried food, condiments, clothes, garments, and consumer goods. Organizations and entrepreneurs need to understand the situation, try to reduce weaknesses, and increase strengths. This will be an essential basis for preparation and differentiation from competitors for attracting customers and supporting the changing behaviour and demands of customers [5]. The study found that it is necessary to understand both the internal and external factors affecting the survival of the organization. These factors include (1) the external general environment, such as governmental policy, technology capabilities, and sociocultural aspects; (2) transformational change management, for instance, restructuring, consumer behaviour adjustment, and business partners; and (3) economic conditions, such as access to credit, changes in interest rate, and changes in levels of consumer income. Additional factors include the (4) corporate governance policy, such as data-driven marketing, manpower development, and financial resources management; (5) marketing innovation, including product design innovation, unique proposition, and customer focus; and (6) organizational survival, including customer retention, competitive advantage, and profitable growth.

According to relevant research concerning business survival adaptation, this research began with the aim of filling in the gaps of studies in Thailand, which have yet to study relevant factors in the context of service businesses. Thus, studying adaptation for business survival among retail food businesses is essential for the national economic system in the COVID-19 situation [6]. To address the limitations and gaps, this research study examined the factors influencing the organizational survival of businesses during the Coronavirus 19 (COVID-19) period to develop a conceptual framework for retail food businesses in Thailand. The model developed in this study would be useful for formulating a model approach for further questionnaire data collection. Ultimately, this model will benefit food retail business owners in the country, who can leverage the research findings to devise strategies for adaptation and survival in their industry.

## 2 Literature Review

The Thai food industry continues to grow and provide value-added. Entrepreneurs should focus on adjusting business models through the development of food innovation and technology, development of value chains, product development with value-added and service development to respond to the demands of consumers and global societies at present and in the future. For organizational survival, the main components of development [7] include: (1) being thoughtful and observant of situations; (2) having high-quality leadership; (3) thinking analytically in organizational growth trends; (4) being committed to success; (5) building communication channels, and (6) accepting changes. In addition, the heart of the business operation is to build strategies in differentiation, concentrated marketing, relationship management, and responsibility to society and the environment. These strategies can be used together with marketing strategies to make businesses survive and maintain good consumer access. Good adaptation enables entrepreneurs to understand the environment better, resulting in better access to resources or different data and better learning about changes [8, 9]. Adaptation results from learning and better learning depend on paying attention to environmental changes.

Entrepreneurs' adaptation can explain different behaviors and activities. We can see that adaptability directly involves the ability to learn different matters, especially in environmental changes. When environmental conditions become obstacles to running a business, entrepreneurs must adjust their strategies to gain higher competitive capability, particularly in the external general environment. Activities should be arranged for human resource development to make personnel capable, intelligent, and able to apply wisdom to work. Employees should be developed for self-development, lifelong learning, quality of life, and good attitudes towards work. Buchanan and McCalman [10] proposed the framework of "Transformational Change Management", which provides insight into the causes of organizational changes and the response to changes. All stakeholders of organizations should participate in planning work operations and consider economic situations, especially in economic conditions which indicate the status of personal and public welfare such as employment, interest rates, employment rates, and loans [11].

The study on organizational survival of Moradi and Badrinarayanan [12] found that passiveness or tardiness to change was the main obstacle to organizational survival. Consistently, Clara Pardo (2016) studied applying "attribution theory" to determine the factors leading to the failure of entrepreneurial ventures and found that the leading causes were problems in finance, internal/external organization, and marketing. Moreover, the study of Yeoh and Tu [13] on the relationship between environmental factors influencing corporate governance policy with effects on organizational survival found that the high failure rate of small businesses was due to various factors such as government support, which is usually regarded as a supportive factor but has little impact on small businesses in terms of their ability to survive. According to Obiekwe [14], effective human resource development is a vital prerequisite to prepare employees to perceive new ideas about capabilities and adaptation to changing markets and to push organizations to gain competitive advantages and survival. Similarly, Alves et al. [15] identify the leading causes of business failures, which include lack of corporate governance, human resources management, insufficient financial resources, no support from banks and financial institutions, inadequate economic scope, and insufficient support from government policies. These factors have effects on organizational survival. According to Alfrian and Riani [16], the organizational environment in terms of society and culture influences ideology/motivation to create inspiration and cognitive stimulation, such as in mutual vision and team commitment, with positive effects on team communication, work collaboration, conflict management, change creation, and adaptation to management. Aksoy [3] emphasizes that marketing innovation is a new concept or way of thinking about corporate strategies as a marketing process for improving the marketing mix. Marketing innovation helps develop and build competitive advantages based on business differentiation and survival.

### *2.1 Summarizes the Variables Studied from the Relevant Literature Review*

Based on the relevant literature review, the researchers summarized the results of the literature review to get insights about the variables in the study: (1) external general environment; (2) transformational change management; (3) corporate governance policy; (4) economic condition; (5) marketing innovation, and (6) organizational survival. Firstly, the external general environment is found to positively affect employee performance in an organization, which improves the working environment by reducing uncertainty in business operations and competition. Secondly, regarding transformational change management, it is found that a changing environment makes executives adapt themselves to such an environment because changes can cause losses in funding, products, skills, time, human resources, and other resources in restructuring. Thirdly, corporate governance policy involves performance improvement in an organization, reflecting perceptions to give equal importance to employees based on the philosophy of human development to be professional. Fourthly, economic condition is concerned with consumers' buying power. For example, changing the level of consumer income affects product changes or discounts, as well as business adaptation. Fifthly, marketing innovation helps develop and build competitive advantages and sustainable cost leadership for making businesses competitive and able to survive under the economic challenges at present. Furthermore, for organizational survival, an organization can survive through effective adaptation when faced with business obstacles. Entrepreneurs need to adapt their strategies to gain more competitive capability.

## 3 Theoretical Foundation

"Survival" is a term that comes from Darwin's theory [17], which is a theory that explains the mechanism of natural selection. It is a biological concept that describes that the fittest individuals are the ones who can survive. Only living organisms that adapt better to the environment in each situation and at each period than others will survive and pass on their genes to the next generation.

In order to gain a deeper understanding of the topic of adaptation for survival and to develop insights and a framework for this research, the researchers have studied theories and related research on survival as summarized below: Rogers's [18] theory about individual adaptation and the theory of counseling where the recipient is at the centre of the process, emphasizing individual adaptation from the perspective of self-adjustment in response to changing environments and experiences. Additionally, the study by Saidi et al. [19] addresses the real-world challenges SMEs face due to the COVID-19 pandemic. It provides a comprehensive analysis of the research literature on SMEs' survival during economic crises. Furthermore, the study by Khan, Nasir, and Saleem [20] provided valuable insights into the importance of strategic management in the post-COVID situation and suggested that managers review and revise company policies in the future when facing challenging situations. Their research is in the hospitality and tourism industry.

Finally, regarding the adaption theory from Roy, the researcher identified Roy's Theory of Adaptation as the central contributing concept for the proposed model because this theory enables the researcher to understand the causes of adaptation, the causes of human adaptive behavior, and the process of human adaptation when an accident occurs, or life changes occur, including the results. Human beings will have to adapt using intellectual awareness so they can adapt to survive. In addition, life-altering stimuli are reintroduced into the system if humans cannot adapt to survive or

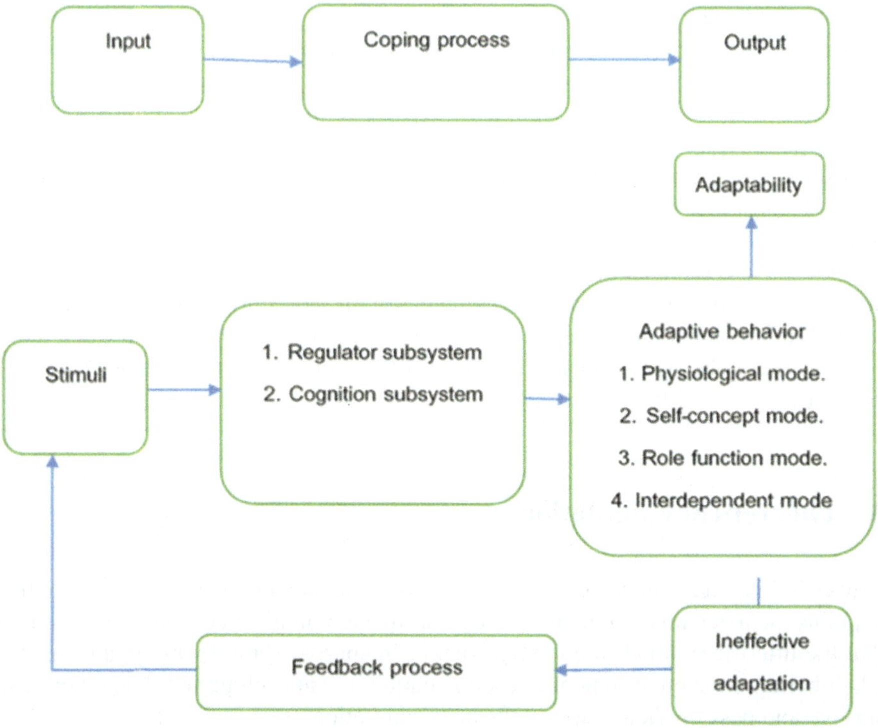


**Fig. 1** The Roy's adaptation model (1999)

adaptation is inefficient. Ultimately, control mechanisms and cognitive mechanisms are needed for further proper adjustment. Inefficient adaptation is never allowed to be the result, as shown in Fig. 1.

## *3.1 Adaptation Theory*

Roy's adaptation model (cited in Roy & Andrews [21]. The Roy Adaptation Model, Stamford: Appleton & Lange) involves adaptation and assisting a person with an adaptation problem when faced with life incidents or changes. Adaptation is a process and outcome occurring from a person's thoughts and feelings, involving using intellectual awareness and creativity to integrate a person with their environment harmoniously. Roy applies a theoretical concept to explain a person's adaptive system as an open, holistic, adaptive system, including input, coping process, output, and feedback process, each operating in combination. When a stimulus from a change in the internal and external environment enters the adaptive system, a person is stimulated to adapt themselves to respond to such stimulus by using two mechanisms of the coping process: the regulator subsystem and the cognition subsystem. Both subsystems always work in tandem, causing a person to express four adaptive behaviors: physiological mode, self-concept mode, role function mode, and interdependent mode. The adaptation results in two aspects: adaptability and ineffective adaptation. Then, the system output is feedback to the system as an input for further suitable adaption. The adaptability of each person is different, depending on the intensity of the stimulus and the level of personal adaptation. Further information is provided as follows.

Input means the interaction between people and the environment contributes to the input in an individual adaptive system, known as the stimuli from the environment inside and outside individuals. A person may need to be aware of the influence of factors such as attitude, belief, values, background experience, etc. These stimuli stimulate personal reactions by adaptation. Whether or not a person can adapt depends on the intensity of the stimuli and his/her adaptation level at that time. A person's adaptability to changing situations in a life cycle can be considered in 3 levels as follows. First is the integrated level, in which the body structure and functions work holistically to respond to a person's demands appropriately. Second is the compensatory level, which is the condition in which the life process is disturbed, causing the regulator and perception mechanisms to be stimulated to manage with such stimuli. Finally, the compromised level is when adaptation at the integrated and compensatory levels is insufficient to manage stimuli and causes adaptive problems.

The coping process is used to control one's adaptive system. It is how a person interacts with a changing environment. The coping process may occur either automatically or through learning. Roy classifies the coping process into two subsystems as follows: (1) The regulator subsystem is an automatic process of responding to stimuli without awareness. It occurs from the interaction of the nervous system, chemicals, and endocrine system. The stimuli from the internal and external environment are input entering the nervous system with effects on water balance, electrolytes, acid–alkali, and the endocrine system. This mechanism controls different body systems to function under normal conditions; (2) The cognitive subsystem is a process of response to stimuli through the nervous system of perception and emotion, which is expressed through 4 processes, including the process of perception and information transfer, learning, decision-making, and emotional response. The stimuli for the perception mechanism contain factors affecting psychological, physical, physiological, and social aspects, resulting from the regulator subsystem passing through the processes of perception and information transfer. A person chooses to process and memorize what he/she is interested in. Learning causes imitation, reinforcement, and intuition, leading to decision-making to solve problems. *Emotional response* is a protective mechanism used to make a person feel comfortable and relieved of anxiety. Emotion is the result of emotional assessment and personal engagement.

Adaptive behavior is the regulator, and cognition always works in tandem to maintain the integrity of a person in adaptation. The results from both subsystems are expressed in 4 adaptive behavioral modes, including physiological mode, self-concept mode, role function mode, and interdependent mode. These adaptive behavioral modes reflect the level of a person's adaptation expressed in behavior. They also reflect the uses of the coping process in 4 behavioral patterns and the success or effectiveness of response as observed from individual behavior. Descriptions of adaptive behavior are as follows: (1) Physiological mode is an adaptation to maintain body stability, meaning successful adaptation to changes in physiological needs. The physiological mode is highly concrete with explicit behavior and easily understood. Adaptive behavior in the physiological mode responds to 5 basic human needs for living: oxygen, nutrition, excretion, activity and rest, and protection. In addition, four complex processes include sensation, water and electrolytes, functions of the nervous system, and functions of the endocrine system. (2) Self-concept mode is an adaptation for mental and spiritual stability. Self-concept is a belief and feeling towards oneself in a particular period. It occurs from personal perception and perception from the reactions of other people toward oneself. Each person's behaviour reflects self-concept; (3) Role function mode is an adaptation for social stability relating to one's roles in society following social expectations on what people should do with other people according to roles and duties in society. Therefore, people need to adapt or play roles properly to be accepted by other people, leading to feelings of social security and happiness in society. (4) Interdependent mode is an adaptation for social stability relating to the close relationships between people or groups of people with a focus on the interaction between people in society in terms of giving and receiving love, respect, and admiring one another with willingness. The basic needs for this type of adaptation consist of 3 components, including receiving adequate love, learning and growing according to development, and receiving a response to needs on the person's beneficial sources to achieve secure feelings among interrelationship. A person with suitable adaptability on interdependence needs to have a balance between independence and dependence as well as to properly have contributory behaviors and receiving behaviors to live with other people in society with a sense of security and safety.

Output means the product of a person's adaptive system, which refers to a reaction in the form of behavior that can be observed, examined, or expressed. Such output may be adaptive behavior or ineffective behavior. Good adaptive behavior can enhance a person's stability to achieve growth, survival, and reproduction goals, as well as overcome obstacles. In contrast, a behavior that does not enhance a person's ability to achieve such goals is ineffective. The system output is feedback through the feedback process as input for further suitable adaptation.

Apart from Roy's theoretical concept of adaptation, the researchers also studied the theory of adaptation from other researchers [18, 22, 23], which can be summarized as a person facing problems and feeling uncomfortable when specific needs cannot be met, leading to tension, anxiety, frustration, and mental conflict. This causes the person to rely on adaptation to be flexible in life. Each person's adaptive aspects depend on their personality, environment, and situation. Therefore, the person improves his/her behavior, called adaptation, to create a balance between himself/herself and the environment or emerging problem.

The critical factors that impact a person's adaptation are divided into two types: (1) Internal factors such as psychological needs exist in a person, including love, warmth, safety, and life success, so the person needs to adapt himself/herself to obtain the desired goals; (2) External factors such as social and environmental needs include cultures, customs, traditions, values, religions, and social rules. Therefore, the person needs to adapt himself/herself in response to different needs and be able to live without mental pressures.

The primary purposes of adaptation are two-fold, including (1) adaptation to overcome the environment or problems to create balance with what the person lacks, and (2) adaptation to the environment or problems, which is used when a person cannot overcome the problem or environment and thus must adapt to the environment or problems to maintain balance.

In the entrepreneurial context, adaptation refers to the processes entrepreneurs use for processing different data from the external environment and using such data for adaptation. Adaptation is concerned with the adjustment of competitive strategies and the placement of strategies suitable to the environment. Entrepreneurs can only survive with adaptation. In order to ensure the long-term viability of an organization, the implementation strategies must align with the business's vision, mission, and fundamental values. The development of the organization should involve clear goals and strategic practices to obtain success in an effective way that is continuous and sustainable [24–29]

## 4 Conceptual Framework

The researcher has assessed the literature in the form of books, journals, related research, and various theories about organizational survival in order to understand the factors involved in the survival of the organization and to develop a conceptual framework for this research. The proposed framework is shown as follows in Fig. 2.

### *4.1 Hypotheses*

**H1**: External general environment has a positive influence on organizational survival.

Organizational inertia towards the general external environment in terms of business model, innovation, and economy, that contributes to the organization's performance. The study found that inertia or slowness in change is a major obstacle to the survival of an organization [12]. Social conditions and government policy changes influence the growth of the system and the survival of the organization [30].

**H2**: External general environment has a positive influence on corporate governance policy.

There is positive correlation between having marketable skills and business survival. It is a challenge to develop the marketing skills of business owners [31]. Small business failure rates are high for a number of reasons. Government support is one important factor. For example, bureaucratic regulations have been cited as

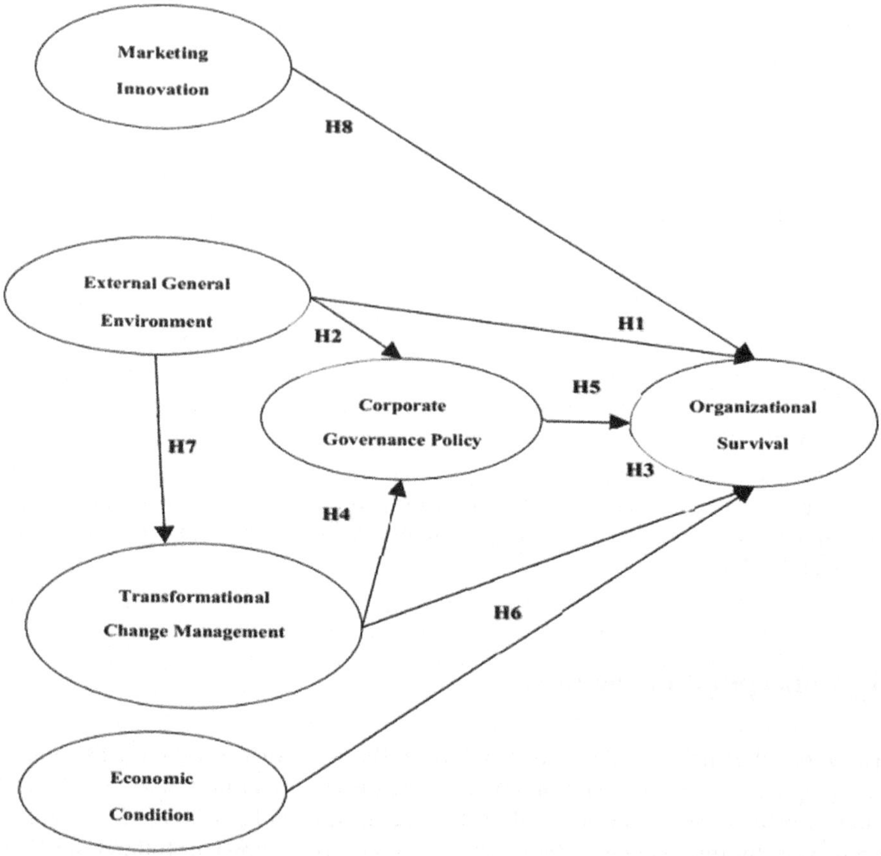


**Fig. 2** The proposed framework

contributing factors, but the real impact of government regulation on small businesses is limited and consequently they are unable to survive in a crisis [13].

**H3**: Transformational change management has a positive influence on organizational survival.

Change management is a systematic and complex process that organizations must undertake in order to survive. Organizational change must be managed appropriately to achieve the organization's desired goals. Moreover, complex organizations comprise diverse cultures. In this case, one of the correct steps so that organizational change management can be handled appropriately is to restructure the organization specifically, defining transformational leaders with a transformational leadership style [32]. Many firms face with changes in routine work with effects on modern business development. As change occurs continuously, organizations need to adapt themselves to market demand and the world economic situations [11].

**H4**: Transformational change management has a positive influence on corporate governance policy.

Organizational structure division influences corporate governance and affects its survival [33]. The main cause of business failure is due to lack of good corporate governance in areas such as human resources management, and financial resources management, such as lack of support from banks and financial institutions. Insufficient economic scope and inadequate government policies are also factors that affect the survival of the organization [15].

**H5**: Corporate governance policy has a positive influence on organizational survival.

Operational strategy (close down or reduce working hours), human resources strategy (existing human resources policy), financial strategy (cost reduction), and network strategy (customer relations) during the COVID-19 outbreak in the retail business are factors that affect the survival of the organization [15]. Advertisement, research and development were the factors relating to good corporate governance. The firms which improved effectiveness in advertisement and marketing could improve the image of quality and increased willingness of the consumers to spend money on their products. Therefore, the advertisement was expected to increase the chances of survival [34].

**H6**: Economic conditions have a positive influence on organizational survival.

Personal income level and social norms can result in the standardization of business practices and may result in achieving success. The data suggest that local retailers can operate their strategies in rural communities with increasing customer revenues, while affecting the transformation of communities and local economies [35]. The most effective changes over time in relation to key elements of economic conditions, such as interest rates or tax rates, have a direct influence on the survival of the organization [36].

**H7**: External general environment has a positive influence on transformational change management. The social and cultural organizational environment, ideal influences/ inspiring motives, and intellectual stimulation, such as shared vision team commitments, can have a positive effect on team communication, working together, and conflict management as well as providing guidelines for creating changes and adapting to management [16]. Work environment in technology had significant effect on change management both in direct and indirect ways [37].

**H8**: Marketing innovation has a positive influence on organizational survival. Innovation is widely recognized as one of the most important sources of sustainable competitive advantage in an increasingly changing environment, because it leads to product and process improvements. Making continuous progress helps the company survive, allowing it to grow faster and become more efficient [38]. Innovation is widely accepted as one of the important sources of sustainable competitive advantages in a more changing environment, as innovation leads to improvement of products and processes to make continuous progress and help the firms to survive, grow rapidly, and be more effective [7]

## 5 Conclusion

This research focuses on the concept of business adaptation for organizational survival. Most previous studies were conducted in the contexts of automobile parts businesses and textile businesses, considering customer service satisfaction as a factor contributing to business success. However, studies on factors in the context of the retail food business regarding adaptation for organizational survival are rare, even though this business is very important to the national economic system during the COVID-19 situation. The model developed in this study could provide a valuable framework for further questionnaire data collection. The outcomes of this study are expected to benefit food retail business owners to utilize their business strategy for survival in the challenging business environment. Additionally, given the significant connection between survival strategies and digitalization to change the sales channels to online platforms, further research is recommended to explore the infrastructural readiness of the business sector and the attitudes, skills, and willingness to accept employees and consumers. This will help validate the research model and provide a deeper understanding of adaptation for organizational survival.

## References


1. Office of the National Economic and Social Development Council. 2020. Gross Domestic Product (GDP) in 2019. https://www.nesdc.go.th/ewt_w3c/more_news.php?cid=383&filename=. Accessed January 28, 2021
2. Bennet, A., Bennet, D.: Organizational survival in the new world. Routledge (2004)
3. Aksoy, H.: How do innovation culture, marketing innovation and product innovation affect the market performance of small and medium-sized enterprises (SMEs). Technol. Soc. **51**(4), 133–141 (2017)
4. Office of Small and Medium Enterprise Promotion. (2021). Number of Legal Entities of Modern Retailers Classified According to Sectors. https://app.powerbi.com/view?r=eyJrIjoiOTM2NWQwMzAtNDQ4Ny00M2ZiLThjNzEtZjczNGQ5YmQ3MjUzIiwidCI6ImExZmZjMjhhLTEzZmMtNDhiMC05NGRmLWYyYWIyOGUwNWNhNSIsImMiOjEwfQ==. Accessed January 28, 2021
5. Brandt, E.N., Andersson, A.C., Kjellstrom, S.: The future trip: A story of transformational change. J. Organ. Chang. Manag. **10**(1), 60–80 (2019)
6. Amankwah Amoah, J., Antwi-Agyei, I., Zhang, H.: Integrating the dark side of competition into explanations of business failures: Evidence from a developing economy. Eur. Manag. Rev. **15**(1), 97–109 (2018)
7. Atalay, M., Anafarta, N., Sarvan, F.: The relationship between innovation and firm performance: An empirical evidence from Turkish automotive supplier industry. Procedia Soc. Behav. Sci. **75**, 226–235 (2013)
8. Fernandes, C.I., Ferreira, J.J., Lobo, C.A., Raposo, M.: The impact of market orientation on the internationalization of SMEs. Review of International Business and Strategy (2020)
9. Cho, M., Bonn, M.A., Giunipero, L., Jaggi, J.S.: Supplier selection and partnerships: Effects upon restaurant operational and strategic benefits and performance. Int. J. Hosp. Manag. **94**, 102781 (2021)
10. Buchanan, D.A., McCalman, J.: High Performance Work Systems: The Digital Experience. Routledge (2018)

11. Bekmukhambetova, A.: Comparative Analysis of Change Management Models Based on an Exploratory Literature Review, (2021)
12. Moradi, M., Badrinarayanan, V.: The effects of brand prominence and narrative features on crowdfunding success for entrepreneurial aftermarket enterprises. J. Bus. Res. **124**, 286–298 (2021)
13. Yeoh, G.H., Tu, J.: Computational Techniques for Multiphase Flows. Butterworth-Heinemann (2019)
14. Obiekwe, O.: Human capital development and organizational survival: A theoretical review. Int. J. Manag. Sustain. **7**(4), 194–203 (2018)
15. Alves, J.C., Lok, T.C., Luo, Y., Hao, W.: Crisis management for small business during the COVID-19 outbreak: Survival, resilience and renewal strategies of firms in Macau. Research Square: 1–29 (2020)
16. Alfrian, F.D., Riani, R.: The effect of task environment toward the commitment to change: Transformational leadership as a mediator. Russ. J. Agric. Socio-Econ. Sci. 79(7), (2018)
17. Darwin, C.R.: The Origin of Species. Modern Library Paperback Edition (1989)
18. Rogers, D.: Random search and insect population models. J. Anim. Ecol. 369–383, (1972)
19. Saidi, N., Nik Wan, N.Z., Razak, S., San, S., Abdullah@Abd Aziz, A., Hussin, S.N. A.: A brief bibliometric survey on the survival of small and medium enterprises (SMEs) during economic crisis. Int. J. Entrep. Manag. Pract. 6(21), 196–206 (2023)
20. Khan, K.I., Nasir, A., Saleem, S. Bibliometric Analysis of Post Covid-19 Management Strategies and Policies in Hospitality and Tourism (2021)
21. Roy, C., Andrews, H.A.: The Roy Adaptation Model. Prentice Hall (1999)
22. Havighurst, R.J.: Human Development and Education (1953)
23. Williamson, E.G.: Counseling Adolescents: Revision of Part I of How to Counsel Students (1950)
24. Callado, A.A.C., Jack, L.: Relations between usage patterns of performance indicators and the role of individual firms in fresh fruit agri-food supply chains. J. Appl. Account. Res. (2017)
25. Nilsson, P.: The influence of related and unrelated industry diversity on retail firm failure. J. Retail. Consum. Serv. **28**, 219–227 (2016)
26. Harvey, D.F., Donald, B.R.: An Experiential Approach to Organizational Development. Prentice-Hall, Englewood Cliffs, NJ (1982)
27. Damanpour, F., Szabat, K.A., Evan, W.M.: The relationship between types of innovation and organizational performance. J. Manage. Stud. **26**(6), 587–602 (1989)
28. Jovanovic, B.: Selection and the Evolution of Industry. Econ.: J. Econ. Soc., 649–670 (1982)
29. Reuber, A.R., Fischer, E.: Understanding the consequences of founders' experience. J. Small Bus. Manage. **37**(2), 30 (1999)
30. Polo-Redondo, Y., Bordonaba-Juste, V., Palacios, L.L.: Determinants of firm size in the franchise distribution system. Eur. J. Mark. (2011)
31. Van Tonder, E., Van Scheers, L.: Surviving the business life cycle: A theoretical framework for independent financial advisers. J. Contemp. Manag. **8**(1), 567–590 (2011)
32. Putri, S.A., Mirzania, A., Hartanto, D. The Importance of a Transformational Leadership Model in Managing Organizational Culture (2020)
33. Parker, S., Peters, G.F., Turetsky, H.F.: Corporate governance and corporate failure: A survival analysis. Corp. Gov.: Int. J. Bus. Soc. (2002)
34. Geroski, P.A.: Market Structure, Corporate Performance, and Innovative Activity. OUP Catalogue (1995)
35. Pardo, C., Alfonso, W.: Applying "attribution theory" to determine the factors that lead to the failure of entrepreneurial ventures in Colombia. J. Small Bus. Enterp. Dev. (2017)

36. García-Ramos, C., Gonzalez-Alvarez, N., Nieto, M.: Institutional framework and entrepreneurial failure. J. Small Bus. Enterp. Dev. **24**(4), 716–732 (2017)
37. Singgih, E., Iskandar, J., Goestjahjanti, F.S., Fahlevi, M., Nadeak, M., Fahmi, K., et al.: The role of job satisfaction in the relationship between transformational leadership, knowledge management, work environment and performance. Solid State Technol. 63(2s) (2020)
38. Chienwattanasook, K., Jermsittiparsert, K.: Impact of entrepreneur education on entrepreneurial self-employment: a study from Thailand. Pol. J. Manag. Stud. 19 (2019)

# The Creation of Tools to Collect Qualitative Research Data for Prosumer Performance

**Arissa Sa-ardnak, Wornchanok Chaiyasoonthorn, and Singha Chaveesuk**

**Abstract** Thailand ranks among the top 5 for social media usage in Southeast Asia as of January 2023 by country. This article aims to create a tool to collect qualitative research data on Thai prosumers' performance on social media. This methodological research is a qualitative research method. The researcher uses semi-structured interviews as a tool for research data collection, which is used to develop a research interview guide. It begins by creating an interview guide based on Jungtrakul's proposed guidelines. The first part of the interview guideline was developed to understand the context of prosumers related to social media. The second part was developed to ask about consumer performance. After having the questions guide, the next stage is to consult with experts in qualitative research methods. Then, use it to revise, try out, and test the coverage and clarity of the questions. Then, improve and consider research ethics before actually using them. In the future, the researcher will develop a framework for prosumer performance to continue.

**Keywords** Prosumer performance · Qualitative research · Instrument · Interview guide

A. Sa-ardnak
Faculty of Management Science, Silpakorn University, Petchaburi IT Campus, Petchaburi, Thailand
e-mail: Saardnak_a@su.ac.th

A. Sa-ardnak · W. Chaiyasoonthorn (✉) · S. Chaveesuk (✉)
KMITL Business School, King Mongkut's Institute of Technology Ladkrabang, Bangkok, Thailand
e-mail: Wornchanok.ch@kmitl.ac.th

S. Chaveesuk
e-mail: Singha@it.kmitl.ac.th



S. Kot et al. (eds.), *Corporate Practices: Policies, Methodologies, and Insights in Organizational Management*, Springer Proceedings in Business and Economics,
https://doi.org/10.1007/978-981-97-0996-0_44

## 1 Introduction

In In order to investigate social processes and instances in their social contexts and to look at interpretations or the construction of meaning in particular situations, qualitative researchers utilize a language of cases and context. They explain how people create identities by taking a variety of perspectives on social life. They see qualitative data as highly significant rather than imperfect or lacking [1]. Therefore, collecting qualitative research data is very important for researchers.

It can be challenging for researchers to conduct interviews for qualitative studies, especially when choosing the interview questions for which interviewees would respond. Open-ended general inquiries are designed to help introduce comprehension of the study's primary phenomenon [2]. When gathering data, they frequently mix concentrating on a particular subject with choosing the specifics of the study design. It may lead to the creation of vague or unclear research questions [1]. Creating tools to collect qualitative data is, therefore, an essential step for researchers.

Measurement in social science focuses on measuring human behavior or things related to behavior, which are pretty abstract. It is not easy to measure clearly because there are many factors involved. This will make it difficult to create and develop tools as well. It is considered a challenge for researchers to create and develop human instruments to measure accurately or closely with the slightest error. There is still an opportunity to create and develop additional social science tools [3].

In this article, the objective is to build a tool to gather qualitative research data about how Thai consumers perform on social media. The main goal of this data collection was to obtain an answer to the first research question. How to become the prosumer performance path to the rapidly changing digital platform in Thailand? The enhancement of the role of prosumers in the circular economy could act as a positive driver for business process changes [4]. An individual's potential will influence their choices, active ambitions, dedication to specific tasks, and the time to achieve particular objectives when encountering adversity and troubles [5]. Individual assessment is how people appraise their potential [6]. Therefore, positive creativity will significantly affect individual performance. Self-efficacy is an essential factor in improving the individual's work [7, 8]. Someone working that are motivated not only performs better on the job and is more committed to the company, but they also go above and beyond the call of duty, improving the efficiency and productivity of the enterprise [9]. However, no studies have examined consumer performance.

## 2 Literature Review

During this period, consumers became prosumers, and their number increased. He defines a *prosumer* as a person who consumes and creates value (products/services/experiences), either for self-consumption or for consumption by others [10]. They are merge producers and consumers, who associated with both consumption and production. The consumer's behavior needs to be specifically focused, which is responsible for creating more personalized products [11, 12]. It has been suggested that prosumers are creating value for everyone, not just for their consumption, and that they are distributing it globally as the concept has evolved [13]. Prosumer refers to a proactive consumer who communicates his opinion online on social media. They are passionate about making and viewing goods and services that are ideal for them. The enhancement of the role of prosumers in the circular economy could act as a positive driver for business process changes [14]. From the study of prosumer concepts mentioned above, it was possible to know the context of the Prosumer for collecting data in this research.

The performance of successful behavior depends on the level of individual control that a human may be inhibited by their intended action from internal and external variables [15]. A person's behavior is guided by different personal probabilities [16]. Beliefs depend on various background factors. The combination of factors leads to the formation of behavioral intention [17]. The Theory of Planned Behavior (TPB) is one of several theories that have been put forward about consumer acceptance of new technologies and their intentions to use them [15, 18]. TPB is one of the most reliable theories for predicting people's behavior in social psychology. It is applied to various behaviors to understand better how a person behaves [19]. TPB is a theory about consumer acceptance of new technologies and their willingness to use them for predicting people's behavior to understand a person's behavior better. To understand behavior, patterns, and frameworks of consumer behavior.

The success of sustainable initiatives depends on innovation that deals with the growth of a new class of prosumers, globalization of communication tools, and diversity of thinking [20]. Not everyone in the social system adopts innovations at the same time. They need time to implement innovations. They may be categorized based on when they first implemented a new idea. We can describe individual adopters of innovation in a social system based on their acceptance period. Explaining the types of servants (Classification of the system members based on innovation) is much simpler and more meaningful. Each category consists of individuals with similar levels of innovation. There are many practical benefits for change agents. Suppose they can identify potential innovators and laggards in their customer audience.

Moreover, apply different strategies to each sub-target group [21]. Studying this theory helps to understand the level of innovation acceptance among different prosumers. This leads to creating more clear questions for the interview guide.

The perspective of technology quality includes information quality, service quality, and system quality. It is a factor that influences user satisfaction of information systems and government procurement plans [22]. The variables that affect the potential of individuals when using technology are service quality, information quality, and system quality, which influence user satisfaction. The results of one study point to the significant factor of user usage and satisfaction that influences individual technology performance [23]. Analyzing the factors that affect individual potential recommends that the system quality is also a factor that affects individual performance. Determining the cost of improving the level of items in system quality increases the value of performance [24]. When prosumers produce by their interests, they will express their productive ability. Investigating this theory provides answers to queries regarding social media consumer performance.

## 3 Methods

This qualitative method focuses on the operating conditions of the prosumer. Various study methods are used to obtain the most useful information for analysis and to clearly explain the cause and effect of phenomena and the causes and related issues. In this regard, the researcher studied the operating characteristics of the prosumer in Thailand. A thorough interview was done to learn more about the background and performance metrics for the first part's qualitative investigation.

The researcher selected specific documents relating to the actions associated with the prosumer performance of prosumers in the era of social media in Thailand in all dimensions. It is used to study the relationship between concepts. To explain the reality of actions related to the prosumer performance of prosumers in the era of social media in Thailand from the past and present. This served as a guideline for developing the question guidelines to assist with writing the research questionnaire and carrying out the research.

These study's essential components are inescapable. This serves as a thorough interview. The questionnaire has open-ended, flexible questions with inquiries that are simple and straightforward in context [25]. Focus is placed on thorough reasoning and the quality of findings in qualitative research questions. Unlike other statistical analyses, which involve statistical techniques in the analysis process, the qualitative research questions focus on the "why and how" aspects of decision-making. The research methodology classifies data into patterns to conclude the qualitative analysis, which does not require substantial random samples and concentrates on tiny, well-focused data sets [26].

They are drafting the Interview Guidelines sent to advisors, co-advisors, and qualitative research experts for consideration and verification and improving the questions as suggested. Next Steps: Implement updated interview guidelines and questionnaires to interview a sample of key informants. The researcher then edited the question from his opinion to make it more transparent. It gets an assessment of ethical considerations from KMITL Research and Innovation Services (KRIS).

After receiving the questions according to the research objectives, they consulted with three experts in qualitative research methods. Then, use it to revise, try out, and test the coverage and clarity of the questions. Then, improve it before actually using it. It develops a framework of prosumer performance and an in-depth interview method from prosumers in Thailand. Then, the data was used for further questionnaires, which was a tool for quantitative research. The model investigate the factors that influence prosumer performance in Thailand.

## 4 Results

The most critical aspect of creating and developing quality research or evaluation tools is having a source. Questions are the link between the tool and the data provider. Therefore, the questions must have an objective, content, or theoretical basis to keep data from the interviewee [2]. The interview process and question guidelines were designed to acquire the desired data about prosumer performance. The researcher used 8 interview questions from Van Der Kuij [27] and three questions from Hansen et al. [28], each of which corresponds to Cornell's [26] type of question. The researcher thoroughly examined and selected 11 questions that would appropriately support the research objectives and were able to provide answers to the first research question. "How to become the prosumer performance path to the rapidly changing digital platform in Thailand?" The data collection tools in this quality research have a clear origin.

An initial exposure to the reality of the study context helps researchers sharpen their research questions and optimize their methods of accessing data in that context [29]. Using the questions to test representative interviewees helps the researchers adjust the research interviews to be more direct and clear. Researchers can also adjust data access methods to best suit the provider in that context. The researcher is the most important tool because it is necessary to understand the context of the informant fully.

Research interviews have been proven for the quality of the instrument in every step from verification by experts. Research interviews are reliable and can be used to collect qualitative research data. Research Interview Guide Development follows as Table 1.

## 5 Conclusion

In conducting qualitative research, an important step is collecting data to answer the research questions. The researcher must choose tools to collect data by creating quality tools that are valid, reliable, and efficient in measurement. Using tools that match the context that needs to be measured in this article, results can be analyzed and summarized. The researcher must consider the advantages and limitations of using each type of tool that will be used. The researcher can use the data from interviews regarding the quality of the prosumer's performance. High-quality research results are achieved through a well-designed interview guide and the researcher's interviewing abilities. The findings of this qualitative research can be used to develop a framework that responds to the study's aims. Research ethics must be considered throughout the entire study process. A barrier to this research was the difficulty of starting the tool creation process. In a later study, the researcher will create a framework for Thai prosumer performance.

**Table 1** Research interview guide development for the first research question: base on Joungtrakul's [30] proposed guidelines

| Research questions | Research objectives | Literature review | Expected information from participant | Interview questions as guided by Van Der Kuij [27] | Selected interview questions | Reason to select the question |
|---|---|---|---|---|---|---|
| How to become the prosumer performance in Thailand? | To develop a research model which influences the prosumer performance on the rapidly changing digital platform in Thailand | – Prosumer Behavior<br>– Planned Behavior<br>– Prosumer Innovation<br>– TAM II<br>– ISS Model | Background of the prosumer in Thailand | (1) What percentage of you is content creator and what percentage of you is content viewer?<br>(2) Did you grow up using social media? From what age?<br>(3) When have you started making/watching nature-oriented content on social media?<br>(4) Do you create/watch often? What is often?<br>(5) Why did you once start with creating/watching content on social media?<br>(6) Can you describe what you make/watch on social media<br>(7) What effect does creating/watching XXX have on you?<br>(8) Do you have the idea that creating/watching XXX changes your relation with nature? If so, how?<br>(9) Can you explain what the process of creating/watching social media content entails for you? | (1) What percentage of you is content creator and what percentage of you is content viewer?<br>(2) How long do you use social media? From what age?<br>(4) How do you create/watch often? What is often?<br>(5) Why did you once start with creating/watching content on social media?<br>(6) Could you describe what you make/watch on social media? How?<br>(7) How effect does creating/watching content have on you?<br>(8) How do you have the idea that creating/watching content changes your relationship with performance?<br>(9) Can you explain what the process of creating/watching content entails for you? How? | To know background prosumer |

(continued)

**Table 1** (continued)

| Research questions | Research objectives | Literature Review | Expected information from participant | Interview questions as guided by Hansen et al. [28] | Selected interview questions | Reason to select the question |
|---|---|---|---|---|---|---|
| How to become the prosumer performance in Thailand? | To develop a research model which influences the prosumer performance in Thailand | – Prosumer Behavior<br>– Planned Behavior<br>– Prosumer Innovation<br>– TAM II<br>– ISS Model | The prosumer performance of the prosumer experience in Thailand | (17) What makes a successful project? How do you evaluate this? How do you define success?<br>(18) What information are needed for that? And where do you get them?<br>(19) (How) do you/your organisation interact—or has interacted—with other organisations or stakeholders in the project? | (17) What makes a successful? How do you evaluate this? How do you define success?<br>(18) What information are needed for that? And where do you get them?<br>(19) How do you/your business interact—or has interacted—with other business or stakeholders? | To understand the prosumer performance of the prosumer experience in Thailand |

## References


1. Neuman, W.L.: Social Research Methods: Qualitative and Quantitative Approaches. Pearson New International Edition (2014)
2. Creswell, J.W., Poth, C.N.: Qualitative Inquiry and Research Design: Choosing Among Five Approaches. Sage Publications (2016)
3. Fongsri, P.: Creation and Development of Research Tools. 3rd edn. Dan Sutha Printing, Bangkok, Thailand (2011)
4. Mullins, R., Dettmer, S., Eisenbardt, M., Ziemba, E.: Using knowledge exchange between prosumers and enterprises to implement circular economy activities in businesses. Online J. Appl. Knowl. Manag. (OJAKM) **8**(2), 71–90 (2020)
5. Bandura, A.: Social cognitive theory of self-regulation. Organ. Behav. Hum. Decis. **50**, 248–287 (1991)
6. Armstrong, M.: Armstrong's Handbook of Performance Management: An Evidence-Based Guide to Delivering High Performance. Kogan Page Publishers (2017)
7. Semedo, A.S., Coelho, A.F., Ribeiro, N.M.: Effects of authentic leadership, affective commitment and job resourcefulness on employees' creativity and individual performance. Leadersh. Org. Dev. J. **37**(8), 1038–1055 (2016). https://doi.org/10.1108/lodj-02-2015-0029
8. Wu, C., Lee, C., Tsai, L.: Influence of creativity and knowledge sharing on performance. Journal of Technology Management in China **7**(1), 64–77 (2012). https://doi.org/10.1108/17468771211207358
9. Yas, H., Alkaabi, A., Albaloushi, N.A., Al Adeedi, A., Streimikiene, D.: The impact of strategic leadership practices and knowledge sharing on employee's performance. Pol. J. Manag. Stud. **27**(1), 343–362 (2023)
10. Toffler, A., Alvin, T.: The third wave. Pan, London (1980)
11. Kaur, M.B.: Online consumer behaviour models: A literature review. Biz and Bytes **8**(1), 209–217 (2017)
12. Wei, J., Chen, Y., Zhang, Y., Zhang, J.: How does entrepreneurial self-efficacy in-fluence innovation behavior? Exploring the mechanism of job satisfaction and Zhongyong thinking. Frontiers in Psychology 11, (2020)
13. Ritzer, G.: From production and consumption to prosumption. In: Routledge Handbook on Consumption, pp. 83–93, (2017)
14. Mullins, R., Dettmer, S., Eisenbardt, M., Ziemba, E.: Using knowledge exchange be-tween prosumers and enterprises to implement circular economy activities in businesses. Online J. Appl. Knowl. Manag. (OJAKM) **8**(2), 71–90 (2020)
15. Ajzen, I.: From intentions to actions: A theory of planned behavior. In: Kuhl, J., Beckmann, J. (eds.) Action-control: From cognition to behavior, pp. 11–39. Springer, Heidelberg, Germany (1985)
16. Fishbein, M., Ajzen, I.: Belief, Attitude, Intention, and Behavior: An Introduction to Theory and Research. Addison-Wesley Pub. Co., Reading, MA; Don Mills, ON (1975).
17. Ajzen, I.: Residual effect of past on later behaviour: habituation and reasoned action perspectives. Pers. Soc. Psychol. Rev. **6**(2), 107–122 (2002)
18. Ajzen, I.: The theory of planned behavior. Organ. Behav. Hum. Decis. Process. **50**, 179–211 (1991)
19. Smith, J.R., Terry, D.J., Manstead, A.S., Louis, W.R., Kotterman, D., Wolfs, J.: Interaction effects in the theory of planned behavior: The interplay of self-identity and past behavior. J. Appl. Soc. Psychol. **37**(11), 2726–2750 (2007)
20. Izvercianu, M., Seran, S.: Prosumer involvement in innovation strategies—The prosumer creativity and focus paradigm. In: Proceedings of the 7th European Conference on Innovation and Entrepreneurship: ECIE, 332. Academic Conferences Limited (2012)
21. Rogers, E.M.: Diffusion of Innovations, 3rd edn. United States of America, A Division of Macmillan Publishing Co., Inc., New York (1962)

22. Diar, A.L. Sandhyaduhita, P.I., Budi, N.F. The determinant factors of individual performance from task technology fit and IS success model perspectives: A case of public procurement plan information system (SIRUP). 2018 International Conference on Advanced Computer Science and Information Systems (ICACSIS), pp. 69–74, (2018)
23. Tam, C., Oliveira, T.: Understanding mobile banking individual performance: The DeLone & McLean model and the moderating effects of individual culture. Internet Res. **27**(3), 538–562 (2017)
24. Kositanurit, B., Ngwenyama, O., Osei-Bryson, K.: An exploration of factors that impact individual performance in an ERP environment: An analysis using multiple analytical techniques. Eur. J. Inf. Syst. **15**(6), 556–568 (2006)
25. Jituea, N., Pasunon, P.: The use of tools to collect research data for education, the implementation of excellent schools. Veridian E-Journal, Silpakorn University **11**(2), 2118–2135 (2018)
26. Cornell, J.: How to write awesome qualitative research questions: types & examples. https://www.proprofssurvey.com/blog/qualitative-research-questions/. Accessed 2022/10/6.
27. Van der Kuij, I.: Impacts of Nature Related Social Media Participation on the Connectedness with Nature in Young Adult Content Prosumers. Forest and Nature Policy Chair Group (FNP). Wageningen University (2022)
28. Hansen, P., Morrison, G.M., Zaman, A., Liu, X.: Smart technology needs smarter management: Disentangling the dynamics of digitalism in the governance of shared so-lar energy in Australia. Energy Res. Soc. Sci. **60**, 101322 (2020)
29. Traimongkolkul, P., Chatraporn, S.: Research Design, 7th edn., p. 2011. Kasetsart University Press, Bangkok, Thailand (2012)
30. Joungtrakul, J., Sheehan, B., Aticomsuwan, S.: Qualitative data collection tool: A new approach to developing an interview guide. AFBE 6(2), 140–154 (2013)

# Impact of Feminine Leadership Style and Feminine Organizational Culture on the Overall Performance of the Organization: Comparative Analysis

**Riffat Faizan**

**Abstract** This study examined the impact of the feminine leadership style and feminine organizational culture on the overall performance of the organization in contrasting economies. The cross-sectional design was employed, and through the survey, 208 usable questionnaires were gathered. Quantitative research was used to find the correlation and significance of the relationship between the research variables. The findings revealed that the feminine leadership style significantly positively impacts the organization's overall performance ($p < \alpha$, $0.002 < 0.05$). Moreover, there is a significantly strong positive correlation between the feminine organizational culture and the firm's overall performance ($p < \alpha$, $0.011 < 0.05$). In addition to that, there is a significant positive correlation between feminine leadership style and feminine organizational culture ($p < \alpha$, $0.000 < 0.05$), irrespective of the type of the economy, not only the overall performance of the organization increases due to feminine style of leadership ($p < \alpha$, 0.000). The feminine organizational culture has a significant role in improving the overall performance of the organization ($p < \alpha$, 0.001). At the same time, feminine leadership is vital in creating a feminine organizational culture ($p < \alpha$, 0.000). The implications of the research are discussed at the end of the research.

**Keywords** Feminine leadership style · Feminine organizational culture · Overall performance · Emerging economies

---

R. Faizan (✉)
Faculty of Business and Management, Yorkville University,
Vaughan, ON, Canada
e-mail: rfaizan@algomabrampton.ca



S. Kot et al. (eds.), *Corporate Practices: Policies, Methodologies, and Insights in Organizational Management*, Springer Proceedings in Business and Economics,
https://doi.org/10.1007/978-981-97-0996-0_45

# 1 Introduction

Leadership has been the center of discussion among professionals and academics for a long [1]. However, with time, the focus shifted from traditional styles to new emerging trends. Thus, it is essential to define what is leadership in general. According to Norton, leadership is the ability to inspire and lead the team to achieve a common goal [2]. In other words, it is the science and art of managing people by providing guidance, directions, and support to accomplish common goals or objectives. Hence, this takes us to the following notion of feminine leadership and why it should be studied. Although "feminine leadership" might sound gender specific, it is the style that both males and/or females could demonstrate.

The linkage between the "Leadership" and "gender differences" is not a new phenomenon [3]. Thus, it will be interesting to explore the notion in depth of how feminine leadership style may impact the organization's overall success when used by genders in contrasting economies. Previous studies have focused on the variables such as organizational settings or geographic dimensions [4, 5]. Hence, it is essential to understand the role of a feminine leadership style.

However, only 10% of females are part of the 500 Fortune companies [6], which reflects a lower visibility than their counterparts. However, this could not be solely attributed to gender specification because the leadership style also plays a vital role in female's visibility at the top management teams [3]. Moreover, feminine leadership is likely viewed as undervalued when setting up leadership at the top tier because of stereotyping masculine styles often driven by autocratic or directive leadership styles [7]. However, this could be attributed to the fact that for decades, male dominance remains higher at the top. Hence, there needs to be more in the existing literature of not explicitly considering the contributing factors, such as particular organizational culture along with the feminine style of leadership behind the organization's excellence. Therefore, it is important to assess the magnitude of the leadership style under the feminine organizational culture in relation to the excellence of an organization.

The past studies have been region-specific, primarily focusing on firms operating in advanced economies [8, 9]. However, there needs to be more evidence about comparative studies that explore the variable of interest in emerging versus advanced economies [3, 10]. Nonetheless, the feminine leadership style under feminine organizational culture is still under study. In other words, this study delimits region specificity by providing a broader approach through comparative analysis. It also means a higher generalization in comparison to previous empirical studies. Therefore, this research is an attempt to enhance the existing body of knowledge by filling the gap that was left void by previous studies.

This research aims to investigate the feminine style of leadership affecting the overall performance and feminine organizational culture in contrasting economies.

## 2 Literature Review

A plethora of research confirmed that, to a more considerable extent, top management has a significant role in shaping the behavior of the firm, and its impact is visible through strategic decisions and operations [3, 11, 12]. In general, males hold key positions and are more prominently visible at the top tier in the organizational hierarchy. For instance, among the Top 500 companies, there is 90% male in top management and only 10% female in the Fortune 500 companies around the globe [13]. Nonetheless, there is no gender discrimination in the selection process as these individuals reach their positions through rigorous efforts and hard work. However, according to the survey report of McKinsey published in 2018, female opportunities are limited due to factors such as family life, cultural norms, lack of resources, microaggression, stereotyping, and so on [9].

Interestingly, the work of Dezsö and Ross on the female representation at the top tier only focused on the advanced economy [8]. On the other hand, the comparative study of Faizan et al. found that females have higher representation in emerging economies than in advanced economies [14]. Thus, it is intriguing to determine whether the leadership style (i.e., masculine vs feminine style) could be a factor behind higher or lower representation.

Interestingly, there is no denying that men are the top management while there is an underrepresentation of females. On the one hand, literature argues that diversity is important [15] while fair representation in terms of gender increases the firm's ability and competitiveness [15]. Moreover, it develops opportunities for progressive culture [16]. Hence, the question arises whether female representation is more about quota to bring fair representation. Opportunity for growth or selection should be based on talent criteria rather than gender specificity. Again, is a specific leadership style a game changer in the composition of the present organizational structure and overall performance? Interestingly, researchers have confirmed that organizational as well as individual performances are affected by gender diversification to a greater extent [3, 8, 17].

The leadership style is a crucial factor in improving the firm's performance [18]. Thus, it is pivotal in determining the traits of individuals while motivating them to collaborate with diverse teams in goal attainment. However, throughout the professional's career, he/she develops skills via different methods and strategies that lead to forming their leadership style [19]. Moreover, it provides a platform for further strengthening the organizational structure. In other words, it also paves the way for such professionals to be a part of top-tier management. Most effective leaders are self-aware and understand their strengths and weaknesses equally. Thus, they form a contingent style of leadership [1] that changes according to the situation. In other words, they develop situational leadership styles that best suit not only them but also are in the best interest of their respective organization [20]. Nonetheless, there is no conclusive evidence of whether masculine style or feminine style of leadership prospers in contingent situations. It is, therefore, important to examine the feminine leadership style for overall performance by proposing the first research hypothesis.

**Hypothesis 1:**
There is no statistically significant relationship between feminine Leadership Style and overall performance.

Although some literature argued that flexibility and adaptability are more often associated with feminine leadership style [21], on the other hand, males are more innovative and flexible in their leadership style [22]. Thus, whether anyone could demonstrate male or female flexibility, it would be correct to say that the feminine style is softer while the masculine style is more structured.

Relevant literature argued that female leaders combine participative, transformational, and democratic leadership qualities in their leadership approach [23]. According to Kloot, to be perceived as equal and competent to their counterparts' women adopt traits such as strong communication, interpersonal skills, information, and power-sharing skills out of necessity [24]. Supporting the same argument, Leonard and Goff suggested that observing and identifying personality traits are pivotal to the effectiveness of potential future leaders [25]. Thus, personality traits can be a significant player for female leaders while demonstrating the feminine leadership style.

Power sharing and talent development of all leaders draw on their strengths resulting from behavioral commitment [26]. A plethora of research hints that a collaborative approach, along with skill development, is a critical component of the feminine leadership style [27]. This notion is further supported by Bulmer et al., who claimed that for female leaders, the well-being of an employee is an utmost priority, and thus, collaboration is essential [28]. In addition, feminine leadership style inevitably reflects on attributes such as caring for interpersonal skills and the well-being of others [29]. Therefore, diverse perspectives, willingness to engage employees, seeking employee participation, and openness to receiving feedback further foster feminine leadership style [30, 31]. This also leads to the organization's strategic growth and expansion through team empowerment [31].

Moreover, female leaders spend more time building trust among team members [32, 33]. However, traits should not be considered gender-specific because male leaders have also demonstrated such qualities in their approach [34]. Masculine style is more assertiveness and hierarchal decision-making approach [35]. Task accomplishment and affirm and persistent decisions are prominent parts of masculine leadership [36, 37]. A more complex (structured) stance is more likely visible.

Nonetheless, the feminine style is more about a soft (flexible) approach built upon collaboration, communication, and openness. In other words, feminine leadership is a soft approach, while masculine is a complex approach. The literature strongly suggests that female is more people-oriented while male is more task-oriented. There is a counterargument that the masculine leadership style has incorporated a delicate balance between task and relationship to ensure effective operations [38]. Since leadership style should not be too closely affiliated with gender specificity, a female can exhibit a masculine leadership style. At the same time, a male could also demonstrate the feminine leadership style. However, one leadership style trait does not mean another leadership style is lagging because it all depends on the situation, and leaders do change their stance according to the situation, reflecting situational commitment [39]. It would be interesting to assess if the feminine leadership style, in contrast to the masculine leadership style, is effective in change management.

Organizational culture is defined through a group's shared assumptions learned to solve problems through external adaptation and internal integration [40]. Recent literature stated that masculine organizational culture is task-oriented while feminine organizational culture is focused on people orientation [41]. Organizations are shifting to invest in human capital that allows for the sharing of such values. Leaders are influenced by culture [3, 42–44] House et al., 2004. According to studies conducted shows that men and women differ in their values as leader, behaviors, and styles [45, 46]. On the other hand, Aarons argued that women are similar in leadership style to their counterparts; however, they often demonstrate a higher role in supporting [47]. Despite distinct views, feminine culture is focused on people, while masculine culture primarily focuses on task completion.

**Hypothesis 2:**
There is no statistically significant relationship between organizational culture & overall performance.

According to Faizan et al., the organizational setting is a compelling element for feminine leaders to be more democratic and participative approach, whereas autocratic behavior is demonstrated by masculine leaders [3]. Nevertheless, demonstrating leadership style under a specific organizational culture still needs to be studied. Furthermore, the research argued that leaders operate differently due to the trends prevailing in specific industries [14]. There is no conclusive evidence about feminine leadership style at all levels of management under the umbrella of feminine organizational culture. Masculine culture of norms and beliefs is less adhered to by women than their counterparts, as it consists of hidden assumptions, images of leadership, definitions of success, and conflict resolution [4, 48]. According to Van Vianon and Fischer, the organization's masculine dimension comprises competition, status authority, and task orientation [49]. Thus, the feminine leadership style may experience challenges in flourishing in an environment contrary to its traits. One's organizational role is rooted in the leader's cultural preferences [49]. It was further argued that specific role requirements associated with cultural preference may overcome gender differences.

**Hypothesis 3:**
There is no significant relationship between feminine Leadership Style & organizational culture.

## 3 Research Methodology

The research aimed to gain numeric significance (attain mathematical objectivity); thus, quantitative analysis has been employed. Positivist philosophy sets a pattern to direct the research approach. This research falls into the primary category of enhancing the existing body of knowledge [50]. The design is cross-sectional, as the study was completed in less than a year [17]. To avoid bias, different sampling techniques and strategies have been used in the data collection process. Over-reliance on one method leads to bias [19]. Hence, a combination of strategies and techniques are considered in the data collection process. Stratified, snowball, quota, and purposive sampling techniques have enabled us to gather 208 usable survey responses (104 responses each from a considered type of economy) within six months (between January and June 2023). A matrix-based online survey questions developed by Faizan et al. [3] and Faizan et al. [14] were adapted in this study. The adaption of previously used survey questions also ensured that research instruments were valid and reliable because they fulfilled the criteria of test-re-test reliability, and constructs were validly obtained. There were 17 questions, excluding demographic questions on a Likert scale with 5 points (1 = strongly disagree and 5 = strongly agree). Before the actual commencement of the survey, a pilot study was conducted to ensure the instrument was fine-tuned and language was made more accessible to the respondents. English was the medium of questions.

To circulate the survey among the target audience, a gatekeeper approach was used. Thus, formal consent was taken from the organizations through the HR department. Upon approval of consent, the HR assistant was used as a gatekeeper to circulate the survey on behalf of the researcher in both emerging and advanced economies. Although 214 responses were received, however, 6 of them had missing values; therefore, 208 were considered. To provide a fair and equal representation of the sample, purposive sampling was employed [10]; in other words, 104 responses each from Canada and Pakistan. The relationship between variables of research and numerical significance was attained through correlation and independent t-test. Moreover, the funnel approach was used to gain more in-depth insight into the themes emerging from the findings.

The confidentiality and anonymity of the participants were maintained at all stages of the research. It was ensured that no living being was harmed in the research process.

## 4 Results

The descriptive statistics revealed that majority of the respondents in this study are males (53.8%) in the age bracket between 36-to-45 (36%) with bachelor's degree (44%) and total of 7–9 years of professional working experience (37%) in the industry (Table 1).

**Table 1** Descriptive analysis

| Gender | Male | | Female | |
|---|---|---|---|---|
| | 53.8% | | 46.2% | |
| **Age** | **18–25** 14% | **26-35** 28% | **36-45** 36% | **46 or above** 22% |
| **Qualification** | **High school** 15% | **Bachelors** 44% | **Masters** 29% | **Other** 12% |
| **Experience** | **1–3 years** 15% | **4–6 years** 31% | **7–9 years** 37% | **10 or above** 17% |

**Table 2** Validity

| | N | % |
|---|---|---|
| Cases Valid | 208 | 97.1% |
| Excluded* | 6 | 2.9% |
| Total | 214 | 100% |

**Table 3** Cronbach's Alpha

| Cronbach's Alpha | Cronbach's Alpha Based on Standardized Items | N of Items |
|---|---|---|
| 0.781 | 0.792 | 15 |

The total count of the respondents is 214, however, the useable 208 questionnaire are considered while 6 are excluded because they were incomplete (Table 2).

The Cronbach's alpha is 0.781, which is above the acceptable as it is above the threshold (0.781 > 0.7) value in social science research (Table 3). It reveals that the internal consistency of the dimensions is good, and the present research is items are "free from measurement error' on scale.

## 5 Discussions

There is strong statistical evidence that there is significant correlation between feminine leadership style and overall performance of the organization. In other words, feminine leadership style significant positively impact the organization's overall performance ($p < \alpha$, 0.002 < 0.05; Table 4). Hence, we reject null hypothesis 1. It also indicates that 68% positive variation in the overall performance of the organization is caused by feminine leadership style. The work partially supports previous findings [8, 14, 33].

Moreover, there is a significantly strong positive correlation between the feminine organizational culture and firm's overall performance ($p < \alpha$, 0.011 < 0.05; Table 4). In other words, overall performance of the organization is significantly affected by the feminine organizational culture as evident 61% variation is caused by feminine

**Table 4** Correlation between variables of interest in advanced and emerging economies

| Correlation Variables | Pearson Correlation | Sig Value | Results | Interpretation |
|---|---|---|---|---|
| Feminine Leadership and Organization's overall performance | 0.68** | 0.002 | P < α | *** |
| Feminine Organizational Culture and Overall Organizational performance | 0.61** | 0.011 | P < α | * |
| Feminine Leadership Style and Feminine Organizational Culture | 0.83** | 0.000 | P < α | **** |

*Correlation is significant at the 0.05 level (2-tailed)

culture in the performance. Thus, there is statistical evidence against null hypothesis 2. Lastly, the statistical test revealed that there is significant positive correlation between feminine leadership style and feminine organizational culture ($p < \alpha$, 0.000 < 0.05; Table 4). Hence, we reject null hypotheses 3 because there is significant strong evidence that 85% variation in the organizational culture is caused by feminine style of leadership.

The t-tests examined the relationship between feminine leadership style, organizational culture, and overall performance. Interestingly, results revealed that irrespective of the type of economy, the overall performance of the organization increases due to the feminine style of leadership ($p < \alpha$, 0.000; Tables 5 and 6). Moreover, the feminine organizational culture has a significant role in improving the overall performance of the organization ($p < \alpha$, 0.001; Tables 5 and 6). In addition to that, feminine leadership also plays a vital role in the creation of feminine organizational culture ($p < \alpha$, 0.000; Tables 5 and 6). Thus, in this aspect, the present study supports the work of Haque et al. (2017).

Moreover, it is visible that the feminine organizational culture supports the firm's overall performance support for ($p < \alpha$, 0.001). Therefore, the results support to some extent the earlier work of Faizan et al. [3], affirming that feminine organizational culture enhances the organization's overall performance. In addition, from the statistical evidence, it is evident that feminine leadership also plays a vital role in

**Table 5** Feminine style of leadership affecting overall performance and feminine organizational culture—Advanced economy

| | t | df | Sig. (2-tailed) | Mean Difference |
|---|---|---|---|---|
| Feminine Leadership Style & overall performance | 6.12 | 207 | 0.000 | 0.39132 |
| Organizational culture & overall performance | 3.734 | 207 | 0.001 | 0.14126 |
| Feminine Leadership Style & organizational culture | 5.613 | 207 | 0.000 | 0.32546 |

**Table 6** Feminine style of leadership affecting overall performance and feminine organizational culture—Emerging economy

| | t | df | Sig. (2-tailed) | Mean Difference |
|---|---|---|---|---|
| Feminine Leadership Style & overall performance | 7.45 | 207 | 0.000 | 0.29634 |
| Organizational culture & overall performance | 4.511 | 207 | 0.001 | 0.15479 |
| Feminine Leadership Style & organizational culture | 6.019 | 207 | 0.000 | 0.27176 |

creating a feminine organizational culture ($p < \alpha$, 0.000). Thus, the present study supports the work of Kadi-Montiel and Acevedo-Duque [31].

Moreover, the funnel approach revealed that the feminine leadership style of top-tier management supports strategic growth. In addition to that, the feminine leadership style fosters openness, employee engagement, and willingness. This study broadly aligns with previous findings [8, 14, 17, 31, 33]. The funnel approach also revealed that gender diversity at top management plays a vital role in the firm's overall competitiveness within the contrasting economies.

Additionally, the feminine leadership style also helps increase the working efficiency within the organization due to the feminine organizational culture. The classification model helps in improving diversity [52]. The economic constraints affect entrepreneurship and leadership style to a more significant extent [53]. Present findings support the earlier stated work. To some extent, the work is aligned with previous findings that leadership traits are demonstrated due to transformational leadership styles [54].

## 6 Conclusion

The present research confirms that the feminine style of leadership is affecting the overall performance and feminine organizational culture in contrasting economies (advanced as well as emerging economies). Moreover, there is a correlation between feminine leadership style and a firm's overall performance, as well as a significant correlation between feminine style of leadership and feminine organizational culture. The funnel approach revealed that the feminine leadership style of top-tier management supports strategic growth. The present research, to a larger extent, supports the work of Haque et al. by confirming that the feminine leadership style fosters openness, employee engagement, and willingness [17]. Moreover, gender diversity at top management affects the firm's overall competitiveness within the contrasting economies in a prominent manner. In addition, the feminine leadership style has a vital role in the organization's overall performance and in improving the working efficiency within the organization due to feminine organizational culture. In addition, the study affirms a significant relationship between feminine organizational culture and a firm's overall performance, thus encouraging the culture of inclusiveness and collaboration with the need for employee empowerment.

### *6.1 Limitations, Future Directions, and Implications*

This study was subject to limitations such as no external funding or grant was available. Thus, I heavily relied on open-access journals to develop a literature review. Future studies should secure grants or funding to access more diverse and enriched literature. The research design is cross-sectional, while in the comparative studies, a longitudinal design would have suited better. Future studies should consider the longitudinal design to obtain the responses from the respondents in two different intervals. The sample is limited to Canada and Pakistan, so the generalizability is lower. Future studies should consider expanding by including more emerging and advanced economies. Thus, there would be higher generalizability. This research has a higher reliance on quantitative analysis to gain mathematical objectivity. The factual truth is preferred over the helpful truth. In future studies, researchers shall include qualitative analysis to gain an in-depth understanding of the embedded hidden trends and themes.

Based on the findings, the following implications are proposed:

There is a need to encourage the feminine leadership style across the company. Research has confirmed that 85% of professionals survive due to soft skills, and the feminine leadership style fosters the culture of soft skills among professionals.

There is a need for organizational support programs to help working women because many women, despite having talent, cannot work, so there should be a system within the organization that offers work-life balance among these individuals. Organizations should invest in emotional and moral support programs encouraging working women to play a more dominant role in the top tier.

Moreover, the males could also exhibit the feminine style, so there should be a proper training program to encourage the openness to embrace this style. There should be more effective channels of communication to educate the workers and engage them in the fostering of the feminine organizational culture.

## References

1. Hussain, N., Haque, A.U., Baloch, A.: Management theories: the contribution of contemporary management theorists in tackling contemporary management challenges. J. Yasar Univ. **14**(SI), 156–169 (2019)
2. Norton, M.S.: Executive Leadership for Effective Administration, Allyn & Bacon. ISBN-10: 0205386717 (2004)

3. Faizan, R., Nair, S.L.S., Haque, A.U.: The effectiveness of feminine and masculine leadership styles in relation to contrasting genders' performances. Pol. J. Manag. Stud. **17**(1), 78–91 (2018)
4. Powell, G.N., Butterfield, D., Parent, J.D.: Gender and managerial stereotypes: have the times changed? J. Manag. **28**(2), 177–193 (2002)
5. Leite, S., Nasareth, R., Machado, R., Rilany, M., Machado, de-S., Lúcio.: A diferença de gênero e a sua influência na execução de práticas ilegais: uma análise a partir das prestações de contas de gestão julgadas pelo TCM-GO. GeSec: Rev. Gest. E Secr. **14**(5), 7851–7878 (2023)
6. Hinchliffe, E.: Women Run More Than 10% of Fortune 500 Companies For the First Time. SHRM. https://www.shrm.org/executive/resources/articles/pages/women-run-ten-percent-fortune-500.aspx#:~:text=Women%20Run%20More%20Than%2010%25%20of%20Fortune%20500%20Companies%20For,Ferry's%20leader%20of%20CEO%20succession.&text=For%20years%2C%20the%20share%20of,been%20stuck%20around%208%20percent (2023)
7. Eagly, A.H., Makhijani, M., Klonsky, B.G.: "Gender and the evaluation of leaders: A meta-analysis": Correction to Eagly et al. Psychological Bulletin **112**(3), 557 (1992).https://doi.org/10.1037/h0090375
8. Dezsö, C.L., Ross, D.G.: Does female representation in top management improve firm performance? A panel data investigation. Strat. Manag. J. **33**(9), 1072–1089 (2012)
9. Krivkovich, A., Liu, W.W., Nguyen, H., Rambachan, I., Robinson, N., Williams, M., Yee, L.: Women in the Workplace 2022. McKinsey & Company. https://www.mckinsey.com/featured-insights/diversity-and-inclusion/women-in-the-workplace (2022)
10. Haque, A.U., Aston, J., Kozlovski, E.: The impact of stressors on organisational commitment of managerial and non-managerial personnel in contrasting economies: evidences from Canada and Pakistan. Int. J. Bus. **23**(2), 152–168 (2018)
11. Hambrick, D.C., Mason, P.A.: Upper Echelons: the organization as a reflection of its top managers. Acad. Manag. Rev. **9**(2), 193–206 (1984). https://doi.org/10.2307/258434
12. Carpenter, M.A., Geletkanycz, M.A., Sanders, W.G.: Upper Echelons research revisited: antecedents, elements, and consequences of top management team composition. J. Manag. **30**, 749–778 (2004). https://doi.org/10.1016/j.jm.2004.06.001
13. Geffner, C.: How and why to seek out mentors throughout your career. https://www.forbes.com/sites/forbescoachescouncil/2023/08/31/how-and-why-to-seek-out-mentors-throughout-your-career/?sh=1a3caa742b95 (2023)
14. Faizan, R., Haque, A.U., Cockrill, A., Aston, J.: Females at strategic level affecting logistics firms' competitiveness: Qualitative Comparative Analysis. Forum Sci. Oecon. **7**(1), 57–71 (2019)
15. Badal, S., Harter, J.K.: Gender diversity, business-unit engagement, and performance. J. Lead.Ship Organ. Stud. **21**(4), 354–365 (2014). https://doi.org/10.1177/1548051813504460
16. Guillaume, Y.R.F., Dawson, J.F., Otaye-Ebede, L., Woods, S.A., West, M.A.: Harnessing demographic differences in organizations: what moderates the effects of workplace diversity? J. Organ. Behav. **38**(2), 276–303 (2017). https://doi.org/10.1002/job.2040
17. Haque, A.U., Aston, J.: A relationship between occupational stress and organizational commitment of I.T sector's employees in contrasting economies. Pol. J. Manag. Stud. **14**(1), 95–105 (2016)
18. Akparep, J.Y., Jengre, E., Mogre, A.A.: The influence of leadership style on organizational performance at TumaKavi Development Association, Tamale, Northern Region of Ghana. Open J. Lead.Ship **8**, 1–22 (2019). https://doi.org/10.4236/ojl.2019.81001
19. Haque, A.U., Faizan, R., Zehra, N., Baloch, A., Nada, V., and Riaz, F.: Leading leadership style to motivate cultural oriented female employees in developing country: I.T staff responses from Pakistan. Int. J. Acad. Res. Bus. Soc. Sci. **5**(9), 280–302 (2015)
20. Hughson, C.: 15 Common leadership styles. The Ivey Academy. https://www.ivey.uwo.ca/academy/insights/2020/01/13-common-leadership-styles/ (2020)
21. Yukl, G., Mahsud, R.: Why flexible and adaptive leadership is essential. Consult. Psychol. J.: Pract. Res. **62**, 81–93 (2010). https://doi.org/10.1037/a0019835

22. Radu, V.: Qualitative research: definition, methodology, limitation, examples. https://www.omniconvert.com/blog/qualitative-research-definition-methodology-limitation-examples.html (2019)
23. Eagly, A.H., Nater, C., Miller, D.I., Kaufmann, M., Sczesny, S.: Gender stereotypes have changed: a cross-temporal meta-analysis of U.S. public opinion polls from 1946 to 2018. Am. Psychol. **75**(3), 301–315 (2020). https://doi.org/10.1037/amp0000494
24. Kloot, L.: Women and leadership in universities: a case study of women academic managers. Int. J. Public Sect. Manag. **17**(6), 470–485 (2004). https://doi.org/10.1108/09513550410554760
25. Leonard, H.S., Goff, M.: Leadership development as an intervention for organizational transformation: a case study. Consult. Psychol. J.: Pract. Res. **55**(1), 58–67 (2003). https://doi.org/10.1037/1061-4087.55.1.58
26. Kouzes, J.M., Posner, B.Z.: The Leadership Challenge: How to Keep Getting Extraordinary Things Done in Organizations, 2nd edn. Jossey-Bass (1995)
27. Laguna-Sánchez, P., Segovia Pérez, M., Cabrero, C,F., Vargas-Perez, A.M.: A collaborative model for leadership education in high-potential university women students. J. Open Innov. Technol. Mark. Complexit, **7**(2), 138 (2021). https://doi.org/10.3390/joitmc7020138
28. Bulmer, J.S., Kaniyoor, A., Elliott, J.A.: A meta-analysis of conductive and strong carbon nanotube materials. Adv. Mater. **33**(36) (2021)
29. Carli, L.L., Eagly, A.H.: Women face a labyrinth: an examination of metaphors for women leaders. Gend. Manag. **31**(8), 514–527 (2016). https://doi.org/10.1108/GM-02-2015-0007
30. Weiner, J.M., Cyr, D., Burton, L.J.: Microaggressions in administrator preparation programs: How black female participants experienced discussions of identity, discrimination, and leadership. J. Res. Lead.Ship Educ. **16**(1), 3–29 (2019)
31. Kadi-Montiel, O., Acevedo-Duque, A.: Liderazgo ético frente a la diversidad cultural dentro de las organizaciones con regimen disciplinario. Económicas CUC 35, 75–88 (2021). http://hdl.handle.net/11323/2724
32. Westermann, O., Ashby, J., Pretty, J.: Gender and social capital: the importance of gender differences for the maturity and effectiveness of natural resource management groups. World Dev. **33**, 1783–1799 (2005). https://doi.org/10.1016/j.worlddev.2005.04.018
33. Eagly, A.H., Carli, L.L. Through the Labyrinth: The Truth About How Women Become Leaders. Harvard Business School Press (2007)
34. Mohan, G., Seijts, G., Miller, R.: Does leader character have a gender? J. Bus. Ethics (2022). https://doi.org/10.1007/s10551-022-05313-9
35. Martino, V.: Le leadership pour un développement durable dans les PMEs: étude de cas de PMEs championnes en la matière. Mémoire. Trois-Rivières, Université du Québec à Trois-Rivières, 193 (2023)
36. Coleman, M., Pounder, J.S.: Women—better leaders than men? In general and educational management it still "all depends." Leadersh. Org. Dev. J. **23**(3), 122–133 (2002)
37. Marinescu, P., Saseau, A., Toma, S.: Feminine leadership and oganisational culture. Leadership Prospects. **19**, 144–150 (2014)
38. Tillapuagh, D., Haber-Currant, P.: College men's perceptions of their leadership practice: unpacking power and influence. J. Lead.Ship Educ. **15**(3), 131–150 (2016). https://doi.org/10.12806/V15/I3/R5
39. Haque, A.U., Yamoah, F.: Gender Employment Longevity: I.T staff response to Organisational Support Programme in Pakistan. Int. J. Acad. Res. Bus. Soc. Sci. (IJ-ARBSS) **4**(12), 324–347 (2014)
40. Schein, E.H.: Culture as an environmental context for careers. J. Organ. Behav. **5**(1), 71–81 (1984). https://doi.org/10.1002/job.4030050107
41. Taylor, M.R., Agho, K.E., Stevens, G.J., Raphael, B.: Factors influencing psychological distress during a disease epidemic: data from Australia's first outbreak of equine influenza. BMC Public Health **8**, 347 (2008). https://doi.org/10.1186/1471-2458-8-347
42. Schein, E.H.: Organizational Culture and Leadership, 3rd edn. Jossey-Bass, San Francisco (2004)

43. Hofstede, G.: Cultures and Organizations: Software of the Mind: Intercultural Cooperation and its Importance for Survival. McGraw Hill, New York (1996)
44. House, R.J., Hanges, P.J., Javidan, M., Dorfman, P.W., Gupta, V. (eds.): Culture, Leadership, and Organizations: The GLOBE Study of 62 Societies. Sage, Thousand Oaks, CA, USA (2004) ISBN 978–0761924012
45. Eagly, A.H., Steffen, V.J.: Gender stereotypes stem from the distribution of women and men into social roles. J. Pers. Soc. Psychol. **46**, 735–754 (1984). https://doi.org/10.1037/0022-3514.46.4.735
46. Eagly, A.H., Karau, S.J.: Gender and the emergence of leaders: a meta-analysis. J. Pers. Soc. Psychol. **60**(5), 685–710 (1991). https://doi.org/10.1037/0022-3514.60.5.685
47. Aarons, G.A.: Transformational and transactional leadership: association with attitudes toward evidence-based practice. Psychiatr. Serv. **57**(8), 1162–1169 (2006). https://doi.org/10.1176/ps.2006.57.8.1162
48. Maier, H., Smith, J.: Psychological predictors of mortality in old age. J. Gerontol.: Psychol. Sci. **54B**, P44–P54 (1999)
49. Van Vianen, A.E., Fischer, A.H.: Illuminating the glass ceiling: the role of organizational culture preferences. J. Occup. Organ. Psychol. **75**, 315–337 (2002). https://doi.org/10.1348/096317902320369730
50. Sekaran, U., Bougie, R.: Research methods for business: a skill building approach, 6th edn. John Wiley and Sons, West Sussex, UK (2012)
51. Haque, A.U.: Varying occupational stress and organisational commitment within the university staff of contrasting economies (Cross-sectional comparative study of middle range public universities in Pakistan and the UK), Published DBA Thesis, UWTSD Repository. https://repository.uwtsd.ac.uk/id/eprint/1570/ (2020)
52. Biel, M., Ślusarczyk, B.: Family Business and Management: Objectives, Theory, and Practice. Taylor & Francis (2022)
53. Ślusarczyk, B., Moghavvemi, S., Tehseen, S.: Women and business: Empirical study on economic constraints, legal conditions, and social support influencing women entrepreneurs in Malaysia and Poland. Entrep. Bus. Econ. Rev. 11(2) (2023)
54. Szczepańska-Woszczyna, K.: Management Theory, Innovation, and Organisation: A Model of Managerial Competencies. Routledge (2020)

# The Efficiency Estimation in Universities Intellectual Capital: Evidence from EU Countries

**Natália Slyvkanyč and Jozef Glova**

**Abstract** The concept of intellectual capital has recently gained prominence as a widely accepted metric for evaluating the economic and social progress of nations and regions. Scholars have also shown a correlation between the efficacy of intellectual capital and the innovation capacity of a nation. Some authors also connect the efficiency of intellectual capital with the innovation potential of the country. The main aim of this paper is to calculate the efficiency score for selected countries, describe their innovation profiles, and compare the most effective and the least effective. For analyses, we selected 27 countries of the European Union. For calculating the efficiency scores of selected countries, we apply a data-enveloped methodology. With the help of DEA methodology, the BCC model was created, and efficiency scores were calculated. The traditional DEA efficiency score was corrected by bootstrapping. Bootstrapping was selected as a tool, which helps to deal with a small amount of data (27 countries) and considers the differences in efficiency estimates. Also, bootstrapping allows a more robust assessment of relative performance. Based on the corrected efficiency score, countries were ranked from the most to the least efficient. According to the results of this study, France was detected as the most efficient and Poland as the least efficient. These two countries were compared by their innovation profiles in the pillar of human capital and research. By describing their innovation profiles in the mentioned pillar, we detected that France is strong in research and development, while Poland is vital in education.

**Keywords** Intellectual capital · DEA · Bootstrapping · Efficiency estimation · EU

N. Slyvkanyč · J. Glova (✉)
Faculty of Economics, Department of Banking and Investment,
Technical University of Košice, Nemcovej 32, Košice, Slovakia
e-mail: jozef.glova@tuke.sk

 
S. Kot et al. (eds.), *Corporate Practices: Policies, Methodologies, and Insights in Organizational Management*, Springer Proceedings in Business and Economics,
https://doi.org/10.1007/978-981-97-0996-0_46

## 1 Introduction

Organizations in the twenty-first century are accelerating their innovation cycles more and more [1]. The advent of the new economy has increased interest in intellectual capital. The knowledge economy, commonly called the "new economy," has caused organizations' intangible assets and how they are managed to receive more attention [2]. As businesses increasingly rely on aggregating knowledge for processes, goods, and services, understanding how to manage intellectual capital (IC) has become essential. Because it is an abstract term that is challenging to define, measure, and manage, intellectual capital is frequently referred to as an intangible or invisible asset [1]. Higher education is experiencing "unprecedented challenges in defining its purpose, role, organization, and scope in society and the economy," according to a 2012 European Commission and OECD report [3]. Since it is widely recognized that the scientific and technological knowledge they produce can be valuable to businesses, universities and other research institutions, in particular, are gradually becoming conscious of their vital role in economic and social growth. Their economic and social responsibilities impact how they define and analyze their intellectual capital, which can be used to gauge how healthy universities are performing in the "third mission" area [4]. The two main functions of a university in the knowledge economy of today are discovering and disseminating knowledge, with the former acquired via research and the latter attained through education. Universities are essential to a country's prosperity because they give its population a top-notch education [5]. Universities are venerable institutions of society. They have evolved throughout the ages due to historical, social, cultural, political, economic, and environmental influences, playing various roles. The foundation of the knowledge-based economy and society that currently dominates today's socio-economic reality is the concept of "knowledge" [6, 7]. In this way, knowledge-intensive fields like universities become crucial to economic growth.

The primary purpose of this paper is to rank European Union countries by their efficiency calculated by DEA analysis. Results give actual information about the current situation in the selected countries. DEA analysis has been widely used in the last decade for analyzing the efficiency of education, intellectual capital, firms, etc., because, with the help of data-enveloped analysis, researchers can analyze input or output-oriented models, which describe how effectively a unit uses its resources or potential.

## 2 Literature Review

In this paper, we are analyzing the university's intellectual capital, which, in the central part, is represented by human capital. Human capital is a crucial component of value creation in the age of knowledge-based business [8, 9]. Gary Backer, the first recipient of the Nobel Prize in economics, coined the term "human capital" to describe the value that employees' knowledge and abilities have to offer. Because it is hard to "decouple" a person from his or her knowledge and abilities, spending on personnel, training, or education is a capital investment. However, it produces human capital rather than material or financial [10, 11]. As a result, losing key people risks a company's competitiveness by causing a loss of intellectual capacities and knowledge leakage [12].

In literature, there are three levels of intellectual capital: organization intellectual capital, regional intellectual capital, and national intellectual capital. These levels are directly connected and represent the accumulation of intellectual capital from the company level to the country level [13]. Within our circumstances, we assess the overall intellectual capacity and competencies in distinct areas of a country (national intellectual capital). National intellectual capital is the sum of a nation's intangible assets, which include all forms of knowledge, information, and intellectual property created by people, organizations, and regions and used to create wealth and advance a nation's economy, people's well-being, sustainability, and standard of living [13–15].

In the empirical literature, we can find many similar analyses, but each author brings his variables to the model. Table 1 summarizes the variables of current empirical studies.

According to mentioned literature, input and output variables were selected. Variables are described in the next chapter. This study aims to respond to the research questions:

*RQ1*: How efficient are the selected countries and how can we rank them from most to least efficient?

*RQ2*: What innovation profiles do selected countries have?

*RQ3*: What differences in human capital and research do the most and least efficient countries have?

## 3 Data and Methodology

The DEA linear programming methodology objectively quantifies the relative effectiveness of numerous related entities or DMUs [22]. The homogenous DMU carries out the conversion of inputs into outputs [23]. Figure 1 illustrates the main steps of data-enveloped analysis.

Our data sample was collected from the open database Eurostat. We collected variables for DEA analysis for 27 countries that are members of the European Union. We collected data for the period 2017–2021, which are illustrated in Table 2.

Variables collected in total numbers were standardized by the population. In other words, variables in absolute values were recalculated for one million of the population. The formula for recalculating and standardizing was borrowed from the Frascati Manual [24].

**Table 1** Summary of variables used in current studies

| Author/s (year) | Used variables (input/output) |
|---|---|
| Anderson et al. [16] | Public expenditure on R&D (input)<br>Business expenditure on R&D (input)<br>Public–private co-publications (input)<br>Innovative SMEs collaboration (input)<br>Patent applications to the EPO (output) |
| Halaskova et al. [17] | Public expenditure on R&D (input)<br>Total number of researchers (input)<br>Patent applications to the EPO (output)<br>High-tech export (output) |
| Hu et al. [18] | Patent applications (output)<br>Total number of researchers (inp ut)<br>Total number of scientific publications (output) |
| Johansson et al. [19] | Public expenditure on R&D (input)<br>Patent applications to the EPO (output)<br>Purchasing power parity (NA)<br>Institutional quality (NA) |
| Mary Da Silva Quintino et al. [20] | Public expenditure on R&D (input)<br>Patent applications to the EPO (output)<br>Total number of researchers (input) |
| Pachura et al. [21] | Population (input)<br>Public expenditure on R&D (input)<br>Patent applications to the EPO (input)<br>GDP at current market prices (output)<br>Total number of researchers (input)<br>Students of tertiary education (input) |

*Source* Own processing according to the mentioned authors

$$\text{Variable (per mil. of population)} = \frac{\text{Variable in total number}}{\text{Total population in number of persons}} * 1{,}00{,}000 \quad (1)$$

After these calculations of variables, we calculate the mean of each of them. Standardized variables were divided into input and output variables:

1. *Input variables:*
    a. Expenditure on research and development (as a percentage of GDP), on average 2017–2021.
    b. Number of researchers (per million of the population), on average 2017–2021.
    c. Number of universities (per million of the population), on average 2017–2021.
    d. Number of students that graduated tertiary education (per million of the population), on average 2017–2021.

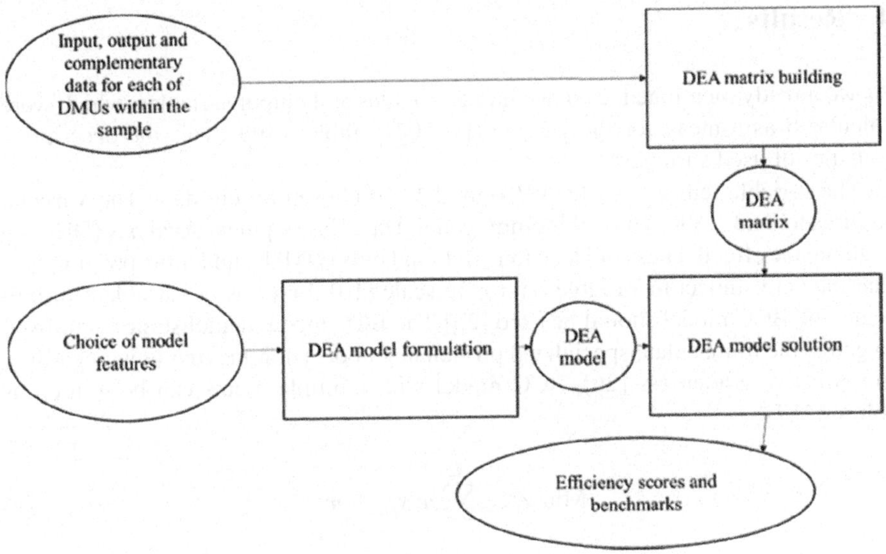


**Fig. 1** Main steps of DEA. *Source* Own processing according to [23]

**Table 2** Collected variables and their units of measure

| Variable | Unit of measure |
|---|---|
| Population | Total number of people |
| Expenditure on research and development | Percentage of GDP |
| Number of researchers | Total number of people |
| Number of universities | Total number of public and private universities |
| Number of students that graduated from tertiary education | Total number of people |
| Gross domestic product per capita | Percentage of annual growth |
| Number of doctoral students | Total number of people |
| Patent applications (EPO) | Total number of applications |

*Source* Own processing

2. *Output variables:*
   a. Gross domestic product per capita (annual percentage growth), on average 2017–2021.
   b. Number of doctoral students (per million of the population), on average 2017–2021.
   c. Patent applications (EPO[1] (per million of the population)), on average 2017 – 2021.

[1] European Patent Office.

## 4 Results

As we already mentioned, we have input variables and output variables, which were calculated as a mean for the years 2017–2021. Table 3 illustrates the descriptive statistics of used variables.

The variable return to scale (VRS) model was chosen for our data. The Variable Returns to Scale (VRS) model is employed in Data Envelopment Analysis (DEA) to evaluate the effectiveness of Decision-Making Units (DMUs) under the presumption that they are subject to variable returns to scale [10]. In terms of variable return to scale, the BCC model should be used [25] The BCC model demonstrates is utilised to gauge the immaculate specialized proficiency of decision-making units regarding the effective wilderness [26]. BCC model with multiple inputs can be written as follows [27]:

$$\text{Min } Z = \sum_{r=1}^{s} u_r y_{rp} + w, \tag{2}$$

s.t.

$$\sum_{i=1}^{m} v_i x_{ij} = 1 \quad (i = 1, 2, \ldots, m), \tag{3}$$

$$\sum_{r=1}^{s} u_r y_{rj} - \sum_{i=0}^{m} v_i x_{ij} + w \geq 0 \quad (j = 1, 2, \ldots, n), \tag{4}$$

$$U_r \geq \varepsilon \quad (r = 1, 2, \ldots, n), \tag{5}$$

**Table 3** Descriptive statistics of the used data

| Variable | Mean | St. deviation | Minimum | Maximum |
|---|---|---|---|---|
| R&D expenditure (% GDP) | 1.675 | 0.889758 | 0.484 | 3.382 |
| Researchers (per mil. of population) | 4,098 | 1,854.662 | 925 | 7,930 |
| GDP per capita (%) | 2.2696 | 1.79559 | −0.1046 | 7.3265 |
| Patent applications (EPO (per mil. of population)) | 144.074 | 181.9497 | 2.353 | 717.250 |
| Number of universities (per mil. of population) | 7.967 | 8.51231 | 1.376 | 40.212 |
| Graduated tertiary (per mil. of population) | 8,979 | 2,770.964 | 2,978 | 17,639 |
| Doctoral students (per mil. of population) | 1,500.5 | 693.0606 | 502.9 | 3,366.2 |
| R&D expenditure (% GDP) | 1.675 | 0.889758 | 0.484 | 3.382 |

*Source* Own processing

$$V_i \geq \varepsilon \quad (i = 1, 2, \ldots, m). \tag{6}$$

Mathematically, the efficiency score (ES) for DMU $i$ can be written as:

$$\mathrm{ES}_i = \frac{\sum_{j=1}^{n} \lambda_j Y_{ij}}{\sum_{k=1}^{m} \theta_k X_{ik}}, \tag{7.}$$

where $\mathrm{ES}_i$ is the efficiency score, $\lambda_j$ is the weight assigned to the output of DMU $i$; $Y_{ij}$ is the output of DMU $j$; $\theta_k$ is the weight assigned to the input of DMU $k$; $X_{ik}$ is the input of DMU $i$ for input $k$; $n$ is the number of efficient DMUs with non-zero weights for outputs; $m$ the number of efficient DMUs with non-zero weights for inputs [28, 29].

For the definition of input efficiency, the Farrell efficiency formula is used:

$$E^0 = E\big((x^0, y^0); T^*\big) = \min\big\{E \in \mathbb{R}_+ | \big(Ex^0, y^0\big) \in T^*\big\}. \tag{8}$$

After mathematical corrections of the interpolation, we can write the formula as

$$\min_{E,\lambda^1,\ldots,\lambda^k} E, \tag{9}$$

$$Ex^0 \geq \sum_{k=1}^{K} \lambda^k x^k, \tag{10}$$

$$y^0 \leq \sum_{k=1}^{K} \lambda^k x^k, \tag{11}$$

$$\lambda \in \Lambda^K(\gamma), \tag{12}$$

where $\gamma$ represents the assumptions listed in the model [5].

To measure the efficiency on the output side next formulas can be used:

$$F^0 = EF\big((x^0, y^0); T^*\big) = \max\big\{F \in \mathbb{R}_+ | \big(x^0, Fy^0\big) \in T^*\big\}. \tag{13}$$

After mathematical corrections of the interpolation, we can write the formula as

$$\max_{F,\lambda^1,\ldots,\lambda^k} F, \tag{14}$$

$$x^0 \geq \sum_{j=1}^{K} \lambda^k x^k, \tag{15}$$

$$Fy^0 \leq \sum_{j=1}^{K} \lambda^k x^k, \tag{16}$$

$$\lambda \in \Lambda^k(\gamma). \tag{17}$$

Thus, the DEA method of efficiency measurement results in a problem of mathematical optimisation. This explains why DEA is occasionally referred to as the efficiency analysis method based on mathematical programming [30].

In this section we present the DEA analysis with a variable return to scale (VRS) BCC model, which analyses how effectively DMUs use their inputs to maximize their output. The traditional DEA efficiency score gave us results, which we corrected by bootstrapping [30, 31]. Bootstrapping in Data Envelopment Analysis (DEA) means using a technique called resampling to figure out how accurate DEA efficiency scores or other performance measures are. Bootstrapping is very helpful in DEA because it helps deal with small amounts of data and considers the differences in efficiency estimates. It allows for a more robust assessment of the relative performance of DMUs [30, 31].

First of all the standard efficiency score was calculated for VRS input oriented model. According to the results of standard efficiency scores, 12 countries (Cyprus, Denmark, Spain, Estonia, Finland, Greece, Croatia, Ireland, Italy, Luxembourg, Romania and Slovenia) out of 27 countries gained hight efficiency ($E = 1$). Mean efficiency is 0.869.

However, this standard calculation has its limitations. First of all, our data sample is small, so standard efficiency score calculation can misrepresent results. Also, we are ranking countries by their efficiency. Every analysed DMU have different input and output characteristics, so it is crucial to show these differences. In reference to the above-mentioned limitations, we used the bootstrapping to recalculate efficiency scores taking into account the differences between countries (DMUs). Corrected efficiency scores were calculated as follows:

$$\text{Corrected efficiency score} = \text{Standard efficiency score} - \text{Bias correction}. \tag{18}$$

Summary of standard efficiency and corrected efficiency are illustrated in Table 4. According to the results of corrected efficiency scores, there are 2 countries (France and Malta) out of 27 with relatively hight efficiency score ($0.9 \leq E < 1$).

For a better visualization of the results, in Fig. 2 we have plotted a map of the EU with the corrected efficiencies of the analysed countries (the lighter the colour on the map, the higher the effectiveness of the country's IC).

Table 5 shows the results of the standard and adjusted efficiency calculation for the corresponding countries. Based on the efficiency score, countries were ranked, where 1 represents the most efficient country and 27 the least efficient.

Some authors link the efficiency of intellectual capital with the innovation capacity of a country [16, 20]. In Table 6, we present the innovation profiles of individual

**Table 4** Summary of efficiencies

| Efficiency score | | | Corrected efficiency score | | |
|---|---|---|---|---|---|
| Efficiency range | Frequency | Relative frequency (%) | Efficiency range | Frequency | Relative frequency (%) |
| $0.5 \leq E < 0.6$ | 3 | 11.1 | $0.5 \leq E < 0.6$ | 4 | 14.81 |
| $0.6 \leq E < 0.7$ | 2 | 7.4 | $0.6 \leq E < 0.7$ | 4 | 14.81 |
| $0.7 \leq E < 0.8$ | 4 | 14.8 | $0.7 \leq E < 0.8$ | 4 | 14.81 |
| $0.8 \leq E < 0.9$ | 3 | 11.1 | $0.8 \leq E < 0.9$ | 13 | 47.15 |
| $0.9 \leq E < 1$ | 3 | 11.1 | $0.9 \leq E < 1$ | 2 | 7.41 |
| $E = 1$ | 12 | 44.4 | $E = 1$ | 0 | 0 |

*Source* Own processing

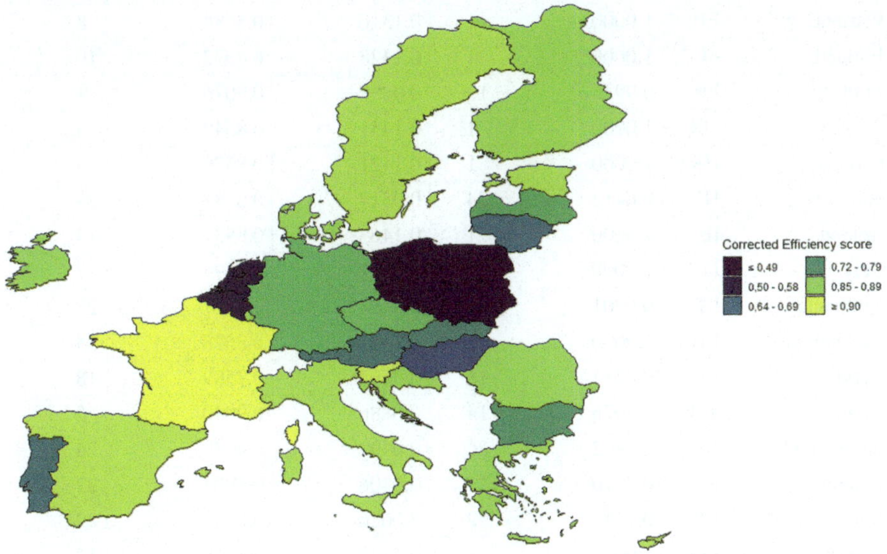


**Fig. 2** EU map of efficiency score. *Source* Own processing

countries. As can be seen from the ranking table, there are also innovation leaders in the EU, such as Finland, The Netherlands, France, Germany and Sweden.

Human capital and research is one of the pillars of global innovation index. For better understanding results of DEA analysis, in Table 7 we compare the most effective (France) and the less effective (Poland) countries in the field of intellectual capital. According to the annual report of Global innovation index, France has income weakness in the education pillar, but in the pillar of tertiary education and research and development France has its strength. In contrast, Poland has strength in its education pillar and weakness in research and development and tertiary education [33]. These facts are approved by scores and rank in Table 7.

**Table 5** Countries ranked by efficiency score and corrected efficiency score

| Country | Code | Efficiency score (1) | Rank | Bias correction (2) | Corrected efficiency score (3)<br>(3) = (1) − (2) | New rank |
|---|---|---|---|---|---|---|
| Austria | AT | 0.7333 | 21 | 0.0556 | 0.6777 | 21 |
| Belgium | BE | 0.5522 | 25 | 0.0490 | 0.5032 | 25 |
| Bulgaria | BG | 0.7895 | 19 | 0.0607 | 0.7287 | 19 |
| Cyprus | CY | 1.0000 | 1 | 0.1286 | 0.8714 | 6 |
| Czech Republic | CZ | 0.8656 | 16 | 0.0701 | 0.7955 | 16 |
| Germany | DE | 0.8656 | 17 | 0.0852 | 0.7804 | 17 |
| Denmark | DK | 1.0000 | 1 | 0.1441 | 0.8559 | 11 |
| Spain | ES | 1.0000 | 1 | 0.1220 | 0.8780 | 4 |
| Estonia | EE | 1.0000 | 1 | 0.1316 | 0.8684 | 8 |
| Finland | FI | 1.0000 | 1 | 0.1428 | 0.8572 | 10 |
| France | FR | 0.9933 | 13 | 0.0857 | 0.9076 | 1 |
| Greece | GR | 1.0000 | 1 | 0.1451 | 0.8549 | 13 |
| Croatia | HR | 1.0000 | 1 | 0.1421 | 0.8579 | 9 |
| Hungary | HU | 0.6413 | 24 | 0.0517 | 0.5897 | 24 |
| Ireland | IE | 1.0000 | 1 | 0.1463 | 0.8537 | 14 |
| Italy | IT | 1.0000 | 1 | 0.1301 | 0.8699 | 7 |
| Lithuania | LT | 0.6901 | 23 | 0.0484 | 0.6417 | 23 |
| Luxembourg | LU | 1.0000 | 1 | 0.1472 | 0.8528 | 15 |
| Latvia | LV | 0.8284 | 18 | 0.0695 | 0.7589 | 18 |
| Malta | MT | 0.9926 | 14 | 0.0886 | 0.9040 | 2 |
| Netherlands | NL | 0.5462 | 26 | 0.0492 | 0.4970 | 26 |
| Poland | PL | 0.5210 | 27 | 0.0406 | 0.4804 | 27 |
| Portugal | PT | 0.7251 | 22 | 0.0626 | 0.6625 | 22 |
| Romania | RO | 1.0000 | 1 | 0.1442 | 0.8558 | 12 |
| Slovakia | SK | 0.7604 | 20 | 0.0633 | 0.6970 | 20 |
| Slovenia | SL | 1.0000 | 1 | 0.1084 | 0.8916 | 3 |
| Sweden | SE | 0.9600 | 15 | 0.0874 | 0.8726 | 5 |

*Source* Own processing

## 5 Discussion

Anderson et al., in their study, analyzed the efficiency scores of innovative leaders and strong innovators using DEA analysis. According to the results, innovative leaders formed 75% of the efficient member states. According to the authors' conclusion, countries that excel in innovation also effectively allocate their resources. This

**Table 6** Innovation profiles of EU countries

| Country | GII score | Rank | Country | GII score | Rank | Country | GII score | Rank |
|---|---|---|---|---|---|---|---|---|
| Austria | 50.2 | 17 | Finland | 56.9 | 9 | Latvia | 36.5 | 41 |
| Belgium | 46.9 | 26 | France | 55 | 12 | Malta | 49.2 | 21 |
| Bulgaria | 39.5 | 35 | Greece | 34.5 | 44 | The Netherlands | 58 | 5 |
| Cyprus | 46.2 | 27 | Croatia | 35.6 | 42 | Poland | 37.6 | 38 |
| Czechia | 42.8 | 30 | Hungary | 39.8 | 34 | Portugal | 42.1 | 32 |
| Germany | 57.2 | 8 | Ireland | 48.5 | 23 | Romania | 34.1 | 49 |
| Denmark | 55.9 | 10 | Italy | 46.1 | 28 | Slovakia | 34.3 | 46 |
| Spain | 44.6 | 29 | Lithuania | 37.4 | 39 | Slovenia | 40.6 | 33 |
| Estonia | 50.2 | 18 | Luxembourg | 49.8 | 19 | Sweden | 61.6 | 3 |

*Source* Own processing according to [32]

**Table 7** Human capital and research pillar comparation

| Country | France | | Poland | |
|---|---|---|---|---|
| | Rank | Score | Rank | Score |
| *Overall* | *15* | *57.3* | *36* | *42.5* |
| *Education* | *33* | *61* | *31* | *61.1* |
| Expenditure on education, %GDP | 30 | 49.1 | 58 | 39.6 |
| Government funding/pupil, secondary, % GDP/cap | 21 | 45.8 | 49 | 35.2 |
| School life expectancy, years | 39 | 64.2 | 36 | 65.7 |
| PISA scales in reading, maths and science | 25 | 65.1 | 9 | 73 |
| Pupil-teacher ratio, secondary | 60 | 80.9 | 20 | 92.2 |
| *Tertiary education* | *33* | *41.5* | *70* | *29.7* |
| Tertiary enrolment, % gross | 37 | 44.5 | 35 | 45.1 |
| Graduates in science and engineering, % | 35 | 55.5 | 72 | 33.7 |
| Tertiary inbound mobility, % | 28 | 24.4 | 58 | 10.2 |
| *Research and development (R&D)* | *9* | *69.4* | *32* | *36.8* |
| Researchers, FTE/mn pop | 17 | 56.5 | 29 | 37.7 |
| Gross expenditure on R&D, % GDP | 14 | 43.2 | 31 | 25.5 |
| Global corporate R&D investors, top 3, mn US$ | 7 | 84.7 | 30 | 48.2 |
| QS university ranking, top 3 | 10 | 73.5 | 41 | 30.5 |

*Source* Own processing according to [34]

includes companies and the government collaborating with the private sector to share research findings. Another conclusion of the article is that the cooperation of the public and private sectors is a mediator of the creation of intellectual capital [16].

Halaskova et al. analyzed research and development efficiency by using DEA methodologies. The findings show that the overall productivity of Research and Development has decreased in both public and private sectors across European Union countries (EU 28). The findings reveal disparities in the efficiency of research and development activities between private and public sectors in European countries [17].

The study of Mary Da Silva Quintino et al. reveals the fluctuation in research and development funding and researcher demographics across different periods and regions, highlighting an ineffective utilization of resources. According to the results of the DEA analysis, the lowest efficiency range was in Kazakhstan in 2017 and Luxembourg in 2018. On the other hand, a relatively high efficiency of intellectual capital was detected in Georgia in 2017–2018 and in Ukraine in 2018–2019 [5]. Like Anderson et al., the authors contributed to the result that more innovation or innovative capacity of a country impacts the creation of intellectual capital [16].

The findings of Paszko reveal notable disparities in NIC resources across EU member states. They also prove that Northern European countries dispose with high recourses of intellectual capital. EU 27 countries were also ranked due to their efficiency scores in DEA analysis [30]. Brusca et al., in their study, analyzed intellectual capital disclosure in Greece, Italy, and Spain. According to the results, the level of intellectual capital disclosure among universities and countries is not homogenous [6].

Similar to Paszko [35], Mary Da Silva Quintino et al. [20] and Halaskova et al. [17] analyzed counties that were ranked by their efficiency score. Compared with the mentioned studies, we found out that the lowest efficiency range was in Poland, and the highest was in France. Also, innovation profiles were analyzed, and based on our results, we approved the findings of Anderson et al. [16] and Mary Da Silva Quintino et al. [20] that the most innovative countries can produce more intellectual capital.

Using our analyses, we answered three research questions.

*RQ1*: How efficient are the selected countries, and how can we rank them from most to least efficient?

The answer to the first research question is a ranking Table 5 (based on the efficiency score) and a map of the EU showing the current situation in the field of Intellectual Capital (Fig. 2). Thus, according to the findings, the most efficient country in the studied area is France, and the least efficient country is Poland.

*RQ2*: What innovation profiles do selected countries have?

The answer to the second research question is the Table 6 of innovation profiles of EU countries. We found that countries like Sweden, The Netherlands, Germany, Finland, Denmark, and France are innovation leaders. In the case of France, this innovation position is also reflected in the efficiency of intellectual capital. Conversely, in the case of Poland, the low level of innovation potential has also been reflected in areas for improvement in research and development, which in turn has hurt the development of intellectual capital.

*RQ3*: What differences in human capital and research do the most and least efficient countries have?

Comparison Table 7 is the response to the third research question. Analyzing the pillar of human capital and research as a component of the innovation index, we found that the strong side of France is research and development, which, in contrast to Poland, is its weak side. The reverse is valid for the education component, where France has a weak side, and Poland has a strong side.

## 6 Conclusions

This study provides a ranking comparison of countries' intellectual capital and innovation profiles. The ranking was based on efficiency scores calculated using DEA analysis (in the case of intellectual capital efficiency). It is important to note that the traditional efficiency values have been adjusted using the bootstrapping method to account for the size of the axis and the differences in the input factors. In this paper, we compared the efficiency of countries' intellectual capital based on critical indicators selected based on analyzing similar studies. Data were collected from the publicly accessible database Eurostat. The data were adjusted and standardized per million inhabitants. Based on the results, we found that the most efficient country in intellectual capital is France, which ranked as 1, and the least efficient country is Poland, which ranked as 27. The two countries were also compared based on the pillars of human capital and research based on the Global Innovation Index. The high level of innovation in France is one of the reasons for the efficiency of its intellectual capital, while Poland has a weak side in this area.

Like any research, this contribution has its limitations. One of these limitations is the unavailability of meta-level data that could provide a deeper analysis of the regions. Given that we have used a publicly available database, we do not exclude the possibility of erroneous data, even though Eurostat tries to maintain the high quality of its databases. These results are valid only for a specific dataset, so in similar experiments with similar variables, the results may differ. For further research, we recommend comparing year-on-year changes in efficiency and innovation profiles. When accessing meta-level data, we recommend dividing the states into smaller regions for deeper analysis. It would also be interesting to see if there is a relationship between countries in intellectual capital, i.e., if there is a spillover between countries, especially in border regions.

**Acknowledgements** We gratefully acknowledge the funding of this paper by the Slovak Grant Agency of the Ministry of Education of the Slovak Republic and Slovak Academy of Sciences (VEGA), project No. 1/0673/21 on Analysis of Economic Perspectives of Industry 4.0 in Terms of the Impact of Intangibles on the Profitability and Market Value of Industrial Companies.

## References


1. Vaz, C.R., Selig, P.M., Viegas, C.V.: A proposal of intellectual capital maturity model (ICMM) evaluation. J. Intellect. Cap. **20**(2), 208–234 (2018)
2. Obeidat, B.Y., Abdallah, A.B., Aqqad, N.O., Akhoershiedah, A.H.O.M., Maqableh, M.: The effect of intellectual capital on organizational performance: the mediating role of knowledge sharing. Commun. Netw. **9**(1), Article 1 (2016)
3. OECD: A guiding framework for entrepreneurial universities. https://www.utadeo.edu.co/files/collections/documents/field_attached_file/ec-oecd_entrepreneurial_universities_framework.pdf. Accessed 22 Aug 2023
4. Secundo, G., Elena Perez, S., Martinaitis, Ž, Leitner, K.H.: An intellectual capital framework to measure universities' third mission activities. Technol. Forecast. Soc. Chang. **123**, 229–239 (2017)
5. Lu, W.-M.: Intellectual capital and university performance in Taiwan. Econ. Model. **29**(4), 1081–1089 (2012)
6. Frondizi, R., Fantauzzi, C., Colasanti, N., Fiorani, G.: The evaluation of universities' third mission and intellectual capital: theoretical analysis and application to Italy. Sustainability **11**(12), Article 12 (2019)
7. Glova, J., Mrazkova, S.: Impact of intangibles on firm value: an empirical evidence from European public companies. Ekon. Cas. **66**(7), 665–680 (2018)
8. Scafarto, V., Ricci, F., Scafarto, F.: Intellectual capital and firm performance in the global agribusiness industry: the moderating role of human capital. J. Intellect. Cap. **17**(3), 530–552 (2016)
9. Glova, J., Dancakova, D., Suleimenova, S.: Managerial aspect of intangibles: own development or external purchased intangible assets—what does really count? Pol. J. Manag. Stud. **18**(2), 84–93 (2018)
10. Becker, G.S.: Human capital: a theoretical and empirical analysis, with special reference to education. In: Human Capital: A Theoretical and Empirical Analysis, with Special Reference to Education, 1st edn, p. 412. University of Chicago Press, Chicago (1994)
11. Balzer, R., Uzik, M., Glova, J.: Managing growth opportunities in the digital era—an empirical perspective of value creation. Pol. J. Manag. Stud. **21**(2), 87–100 (2020)
12. Olander, H., Hurmelinna-Laukkanen, P., Heilmann, P.: Human resources—strength and weakness in protection of intellectual capital. J. Intellect. Cap. **16**(4), 742–762 (2015)
13. Corrado, C., Haltiwanger, J., Sichel, D.: Measuring Capital in the New Economy. University of Chicago Press, Chicago (2005)
14. Bontis, N.: Managing organizational knowledge by diagnosing intellectual capital: framing and advancing the state of the field. In: World Congress on Intellectual Capital Readings, pp. 13–56. Elsevier, Burlington (2002)
15. Marinelli, L., Bartoloni, S., Pascucci, F., Gregori, G.L., Farina Briamonte, M.: Genesis of an innovation-based entrepreneurial ecosystem: exploring the role of intellectual capital. J. Intellect. Cap. **24**, 10–34 (2022)
16. Anderson, H.J., Gyamfi, S., Stejskal, J.: Efficiency of intellectual capital generation: a DEA analysis of selected EU regions. XXII. Mezinárodní Kolokvium o Regionálních Vědách, Velké Bílovice. https://www.academia.edu/52646460/Efficiency_of_intellectual_capital_generation_a_DEA_analysis_of_selected_EU_regions (2019). Accessed 19 Aug 2023
17. Halaskova, M., Gavurova, B., Kocisova, K.: Research and development efficiency in public and private sectors: an empirical analysis of EU countries by using DEA methodology. Sustainability **12**(17), Article 17 (2020)
18. Hu, J.-L., Yang, C.-H., Chen, C.-P.: R&D efficiency and the national innovation system: an international comparison using the distance function approach. Bull. Econ. Res. **66**, 55–71 (2014)
19. Johansson, B., Lööf, H., Savin, M.: European R&D efficiency. Econ. Innov. New Technol. **24**, 140–158 (2015).

20. Mary Da Silva Quintino, H., Rodrigues Holanda, F.S., Rodrigues Moura, F., Ricardo De Santana, J., Vidal, L.D.: World efficiency in the potential production of new technologies under intellectual property assets. Technol. Soc. **65**, 101601 (2021)
21. Pachura, P., Nitkiewicz, T., Matlovičová, K., Matlovič, R.: Identification of intellectual capital performance using data envelopment analysis. In: Stejskal, J., Hajek, P., Hudec, O. (eds.) Knowledge Spillovers in Regional Innovation Systems: A Case Study of CEE Regions, pp. 115–130. Springer, Cham (2018)
22. Cooper, W., Seiford, L., Tone, K.: Data Envelopment Analysis: A Comprehensive Text with Models, Applications, References and DEA-Solver Software (2007). https://doi.org/10.1007/978-0-387-45283-8. Accessed 22 Aug 2023
23. Martín-Gamboa, M., Iribarren, D.: Coupled life cycle thinking and data envelopment analysis for quantitative sustainability improvement (Chapter 16). In: Ren, J. (ed.) Methods in Sustainability Science, pp. 295–320. Elsevier, Amsterdam (2021)
24. OECD: Frascati manual 2015: guidelines for collecting and reporting data on research and experimental development. Organisation for Economic Co-operation and Development. https://www.oecd-ilibrary.org/science-and-technology/frascati-manual-2015_9789264239012-en. Accessed 22 Aug 2023
25. Toloo, M., Nalchigar, S.: A new integrated DEA model for finding most BCC-efficient DMU. Appl. Math. Model. **33**(1), 597–604 (2009)
26. Banker, R.D., Charnes, A., Cooper, W.W.: Some models for estimating technical and scale inefficiencies in data envelopment analysis. Manage. Sci. **30**(9), 1078–1092 (1984)
27. Rahimpour, K., Shirouyehzad, H., Asadpour, M., Karbasian, M.: A PCA-DEA method for organizational performance evaluation based on intellectual capital and employee loyalty: a case study. J. Model. Manag. **15**(4), 1479–1513 (2020)
28. Pastor, J.T., Aparicio, J., Zofío, J.L.: Benchmarking Economic Efficiency: Technical and Allocative Fundamentals, vol. 315. Springer, Cham (2022)
29. Brusca, I., Cohen, S., Manes-Rossi, F., Nicolò, G.: Intellectual capital disclosure and academic rankings in European universities: do they go hand in hand? Meditari Account. Res. **28**(1), 51–71 (2019)
30. Bogetoft, P., Otto, L.: Benchmarking with DEA, SFA, and R, vol. 157, pp. 81–109. Springer, New York (2011)
31. Lothgren, M., Tambour, M.: Testing scale efficiency in DEA models: a bootstrapping approach. Appl. Econ. **31**(10), 1231–1237 (1999)
32. GII: Indicator rankings & analysis. Global Innovation Index. https://www.globalinnovationindex.org/analysis-indicator. Accessed 21 Sept 2023
33. Dutta, S., Lanvin, B., Wunsch-Vincent, S., León, L.R.: World Intellectual Property Organization. Global Innovation Index 2022 (Subtitle)/GII. https://doi.org/10.34667/TIND.46596. Accessed 19 Sept 2023
34. GII: Economy Comparison. Global Innovation Index. https://www.globalinnovationindex.org/analysis-comparison. Accessed 21 Sept 2023
35. Paszko, J.: National intellectual capital in European Union countries in 2013–2017. Eur. Res. Stud. J. **XXII**, 115–125 (2019)

# Factors Effecting on Work Values Towards Career Choices Among University Students

**Nagatheesan V. Marimuthu, Saralah Devi Mariamdaran Chethiyar, Muhammad Zulqarnain Arshad, Kharrtheek Devarajah, Yadu K. Damodaran, and Muhammad Ali Arshad**

**Abstract** The pandemic effect of COVID-19 triggered a global recession in the year 2020. The unpredictability that surrounds the coronavirus is the most challenging problem that many people must confront, particularly in terms of making decisions regarding their careers, considering the significant shift in employment opportunities. The purpose of this research is to investigate the influence anxiety and the Covid-19 pandemic have on work values and the reality of career choices among university students. A quantitative research methodology was applied to 110 respondents from a nearby institution to achieve the study's objective. This was done through online surveys and the snowball sampling technique. In order to acquire the findings, a data analysis using SPSS and PLS-SEM was carried out. It is evident from the study's findings that students' work values are impacted by anxiety and the COVID-19 pandemic. Moreover, the findings support the hypothesis that anxiety and the COVID-19 pandemic influence students' employment decisions. The findings of the study provide insight into the body of knowledge. The influence of anxiety and the COVID-19 pandemic on current work values among university students about career choices are examined, and recommendations are made to various stakeholders, such as policymakers, university management, and career counselors.

**Keywords** Anxiety · COVID-19 pandemic · Work values and career choices

N. V. Marimuthu · S. D. M. Chethiyar (✉)
School of Applied Psychology, Social Work and Policy, College of Arts and Sciences, Universiti Utara Malaysia, Sintok, Malaysia
e-mail: devi@uum.edu.my

M. Z. Arshad · M. A. Arshad
School of Business Management, College of Business, Universiti Utara Malaysia, Sintok, Malaysia

K. Devarajah
Medical Officer UD48, Klinik Kesihatan Linggi, Port Dickson, Negeri Sembilan, Malaysia

Y. K. Damodaran
School of Sociology and Social Work, Christ Deemed to Be University, Bengaluru, Karnataka, India



S. Kot et al. (eds.), *Corporate Practices: Policies, Methodologies, and Insights in Organizational Management*, Springer Proceedings in Business and Economics,
https://doi.org/10.1007/978-981-97-0996-0_47

## 1 Introduction

The catastrophic effects of the COVID-19 pandemic have resulted in the deaths of billions of people around the world, and this poses an unprecedented threat to public health, the food supply, and the workplace [1]. As a result, tens of millions of people were at risk of falling into extreme poverty, while the estimated number of undernourished people could rise by up to 132 million by the end of the year. Between 6.5 and 6.7% of the worldwide workforce was unemployed in 2021, according to various estimates [2].

Many businesses are in jeopardy due to the long-term threat. Two-thirds of the global workforce, about 3.3 billion people, face a threat to their livelihoods. Most workers in the informal economy were utterly unprotected. They need access to quality health care and productive assets. Many could not feed themselves and their families during lockdowns because they did not have the money.

To put it in perspective, for most people, having no income means not being able to afford enough food, or if they can afford food, it is less nutritious. Many people's jobs have been destroyed due to the pandemic, and millions of people could lose their livelihoods. As breadwinners lose their jobs, become ill, and die, the food security and nutrition of millions of women and men, particularly those in low-income countries, are under threat.

As a result of the COVID-19 pandemic, young people like university students (15–29 years old) have been disproportionately impacted. According to Super's Five Life and Career Development Stages, this is the exploration stage. During this stage, students make a choice clouded by uncertainty and improve their skills by participating in activities such as employment, volunteer work, and hobbies. When the pandemic started, youth unemployment shot through the roof and was still higher than before the crisis across countries [3]. There has been a significant decrease in job learning and apprenticeship options for young people [4]. In Malaysia, there has been a rise in home-based work during the COVID-19 pandemic, which is expected to continue well into the recovery process and possibly beyond. At a time when the economy was sluggish, many businesses have been hesitant to hire young individuals.

Consequently, some businesses have begun looking into the possibility of long-term work-from-home positions [4]. Such scenarios have created a significant impact on the work values towards career choices of new job seekers such as fresh graduates from universities. As this situation is still current, there were few studies on the extent of the COVID-19 impact on work values towards career choices among university students in Malaysia. This research intends to study whether the influence of anxiety and the COVID-19 pandemic has a significant impact on work values toward career choices reality among university students.

The global COVID-19 pandemic is wreaking havoc on human health and social and economic well-being [5]. First and primarily, women were driving the health response; they account for about 70% of the healthcare workers, putting them at a higher risk of infection [6]. At the same time, due to education and care facility cutbacks, as well as long-standing gender inequities in unpaid work, women were shouldering a large portion of the load at home. According to human rights [7], men's employment in Asia and the Pacific was expected to rise above its pre-crisis level in 2021. However, women's employment is expected to remain lower than its 2019 level. During crises and quarantine, women were also at higher risk of losing their jobs and income, as well as heightened danger of violence, exploitation, abuse, or harassment [7].

The COVID-19 epidemic has decreased gender equality at work after nearly 18 months [8]. With their over-representation in hard-hit industries, women have been particularly severely hit by job losses and income declines. They were often the primary caregivers in their families and communities, often completing the bulk of unpaid care and domestic work. The International Labor Organization (ILO) predicts that in 2021, women's employment will expand by 3.3%, whereas men's employment will grow by 3.1%. The expected job increases for women in 2021 are higher than for males. However, it was not enough to restore women's pre-pandemic employment levels because of the more profound losses that women suffered in 2020, estimated at 4.2%. As per ILO, 2021, workers aged 15–64 accounts for 43.2% of the global workforce in 2021; men's workforce account for 68.5%. In other words, even in 2021, women still have a 25.4% lower employment rate than men due to the COVID-19 pandemic. Therefore, it is important for our nation to understand the disparity in career and occupational choices among genders and to address these inequalities. The research tries to identify the extent of the effect of inequalities among genders on university students' career and occupational choices.

The COVID-19 crisis has increased the risk factors associated with poor mental health, financial insecurity, unemployment, and fear. In contrast, protective factors, social relationships, work opportunities, and academic interaction, access to physical activity, normal activities, access to health services have decreased dramatically. People's mental health has worsened to unprecedented levels as a result of this [8]. People who were unemployed or who were experiencing financial difficulties have worse mental health than the general population. This trend predates the pandemic but appears to have increased in some countries. OECD countries have taken decisive action to increase mental health services and put in place action to protect employment and wealth, thereby reducing psychological anguish for some. To avoid permanent scarring, a more integrated, whole-society approach to mental health support was needed to deal with the mental distress that has occurred since the pandemic began.

COVID-19 phobia was a significant cause of career-related anxiety in the working world. This was further supported by Tsukamoto [9] finding that women were more anxious during the first wave of COVID-19 than men. Female anxiety was less common during the second wave of infections. In another study by Lin [10], there is a link between male anxiety and misunderstandings about COVID-19, while female anxiety is linked to precarious work. Future workers are becoming concerned about their professional futures due to the spread of COVID-19 fear; therefore, the research will examine the influence of anxiety and the COVID-19 pandemic on work values toward career choices reality among university students.

There were few studies on the influence of anxiety and the COVID-19 pandemic on work values and career choices among university students. The objective of this research is to study any significant effect of the COVID-19 pandemic on the work values of university students. Post-COVID-19 pandemic, this younger generation will comprise nearly 27% of the working population worldwide by 2025 [11]. Their requirements and inclinations must be met. In particular, this young generation is utterly forced to work both on-site and from home, which has created different work values and options to choose from to have a work-life balance.

According to Zhu [12], between the years 2010 and 2019, there was an increase of 11.2% in the number of individuals living with anxiety disorders, which equates to approximately thirty million new cases worldwide. The research also identified the effect of anxiety on the work values of university students. For future workers, the spread of COVID-19 is causing them to worry about their professional futures. The research examines the influence of anxiety and the COVID-19 pandemic on work values toward career choices reality among university students.

Based on the discussion and issues, the two research questions are formed, which are: (1) Is there any significant relationship between COVID-19 and Anxiety and Work values? (2) Do the Work values influence the Occupational choices of the students.

## 2 Literature Review

### *2.1 COVID-19 Pandemic and Work Values*

The COVID-19 pandemic was a challenge to international economic stability and a danger to the world's population. The worldwide shutdown of companies and sectors that was implemented and required to curb the expansion of the virus generated a broad array of one-of-a-kind and fundamental difficulties for both the public and the affected businesses and industries, employees, and companies located in every region of the world [13]. At the personal level, populations of employees affected by the government shutdown were transformed overnight into (a) "work from home" employees, (b) "essential" or "life-sustaining" workers (such as hospital health-care workers and supermarket staff), or (c) dismissed or fired workers looking for the nation-specific comparable of unemployment benefits. Work and organizational psychologists desperately need to apply the field's current understanding of individual work values to assist people and organizations in managing threats while establishing and implementing solutions. This was especially important in light of the uncertainty and scope of the COVID-19 shock.

While COVID-19 abruptly disrupted regular work values, it additionally led to an acceleration of patterns that had already begun and involved the transfer of work to internet-based or virtual environments [14]. This migration was accelerated as a result of COVID-19. When comparing research conducted on practices like work-from-home (WFH) before the pandemic to research conducted after the pandemic, the most significant difference is that WFH used to be frequently responsive to employee preferences, whereas COVID-19 pushed many people into required work-from-home. Employees frequently report that they need help to distinguish between work values and their personal lives [15]. This problem has become even more complicated due to the mandatory isolation of employees throughout the COVID-19 pandemic. The lack of separation between one's work and home, as well as the absence of commutes to provide a transfer between the two domains, become a burden for workers who choose to work from home; new work values, even though WFH may seem appealing if it provides a secure harbor. Work Values of the loss of interpersonal relationships, both for those who were laid off and those who were required to WFH, is a less apparent consequence of the COVID-19 pandemic; however, it was apparent from the study that quality social interactions, including casual chats among coworkers, are essential for both physical and mental well-being [16]. This loss of interpersonal relationships affects both those who were laid off and those who were required to WFH [17]. Another social behavior that we recognize as having value [18]. In light of these considerations, the mandate to WFH and the plans to identify workspaces in support of psychological distancing have unintended consequences, one of which would be at least some degree of damage to both the physical and mental well-being of individual people [19]

**Hypothesis 1** There is a significant relationship between the COVID-19 pandemic and work values.

## *2.2 Anxiety and Work Values*

Because of the ambiguity and uncertainty caused by the COVID-19 pandemic, organizations have been forced to take action in order to safeguard the health and well-being of their workforce [20, 21]. Building upon the job demands, we can see that there was deviation between and within businesses concerning how the COVID-19 pandemic has affected both the demands and resources associated with given jobs and that there was evidence suggesting that working conditions have become worse for most employees, perhaps especially for frontline workers in healthcare [22, 23]. In the presence of such varieties, the COVID-19 pandemic has significantly contributed to an increased risk of employees confronting job burnout, which is a chronic stress condition, characterized by constant anxiety and poor career choices [24]. In addition, consistent consumption of COVID-19 pandemic news encourages rumination, which can be defined as the process of passively and repeatedly concentrating on distressing symptoms as well as the potential causes and repercussions of these symptoms [25]. Studies demonstrating that individuals who were affected by anxiety and depressive symptoms a year after the event indicate that mental health problems may persist for a long time after a crisis has passed [26].

There is frequently a significant connection between a person's anxieties and their work values. If this connection is acknowledged, it is frequently possible to use it so that our actions are based on our work values rather than from a place of anxiety [27, 28]. Some people, for example, are anxious about going to work late because they place a high value on being on time. In contrast, others are anxious about being rejected at an interview because they place a high value on having meaningful career success.

People typically have work values that pertain to dimensions of life such as creativity, management style, achievement, surroundings, supervisory relations, security, associates, independence, and economic and intellectual stimulation [29]. Values can also pertain to any number of other elements of living. Anxieties that have to do with these values may cause us to be concerned about missing loved ones who were close to us, failure at our vocation, being infirm, doing things that are embarrassing or shameful, and dying destitute and isolated [30]. Recognizing and acting on the work values related to worry in a particular situation, such as the COVID-19 pandemic, may be more effective than acting from a place of anxiety. This straightforward shift in perspective has the potential to redirect our actions away from the prevention of a fictitious adverse consequence and toward the search for something more beneficial, in terms of REBT, a behavioral consequence of an irrational belief into a behavioral display of a personal value that is positive, constructive, and rare to reinforce anxiety. This expression of personal value should be viewed as less likely to cause anxiety.

**Hypothesis 2** There is a significant relationship between Anxiety and Work values.

## *2.3 Work Values and Career Choices*

The work values identified as essential variables in the process of career choices are referred to in the theory of work adjustment [31]. It has also been hypothesized that environmental factors, such as the COVID-19 pandemic, play a significant part in the process of establishing work values during the process of professional progress.

Beliefs that an individual experienced as standards that govern how they should function were referred to as values [32]. Values are cognitive structures, but in addition to this, they have behavioral and affective dimensions [33]. Rokeach [34] found that individuals' values evolve so that they can satisfy their needs in socially acceptable ways. As a result, values were shaped by the various factors that were external to the individual. The values that an individual possesses serve as the foundation for both their self-assessment and their appraisal of the actions and motives of other people, and they also play an essential part in the process of formulating personal objectives such as career choices [35]. They may function independently of consciousness or be integrated into consciousness through the methods of crystallization and prioritization [34]. Both of these scenarios were possible. When individuals can recognize their values and articulate how those values direct their actions, the values have begun to crystallize. When different people could order them according to their relative significance of work values, they were given higher priority, influencing their career choices.

**Hypothesis 3** Work values have influenced the Occupational choices of the University students.

### *2.4 Research Framework*

To demonstrate how the study was carried out, we will review its methodology in detail in this section. In addition, the chapter covers the study's sampling strategy, survey questions, data collection, and data analysis methods. To get things started, we will build on the previous literature's three hypotheses. As a result, the framework for the study was subsequently developed. It was guided by a research framework that explains the influence of anxiety and the COVID-19 pandemic on work values toward career choices reality among university students (Fig. 1).

## 3 Research Design

This research was a correlational research design; the researcher examines the connections between two variables (or more) without attempting to influence or control any of the variables. When conducting this cross-sectional research, researchers collect data from a sample and analyze it simultaneously. This study was conducted using quantitative research methodologies. The objective of quantitative data analysis was to transform raw numbers into useful data by employing critical and logical thinking. The goal of quantitative research was to find evidence to support or reject hypotheses that were developed in the early phases of the study. Three methods were used to get the data for this evaluation: a literature study, a survey, and questionnaires. Data is gathered quantitatively via interviews using the instruments of questionnaires.

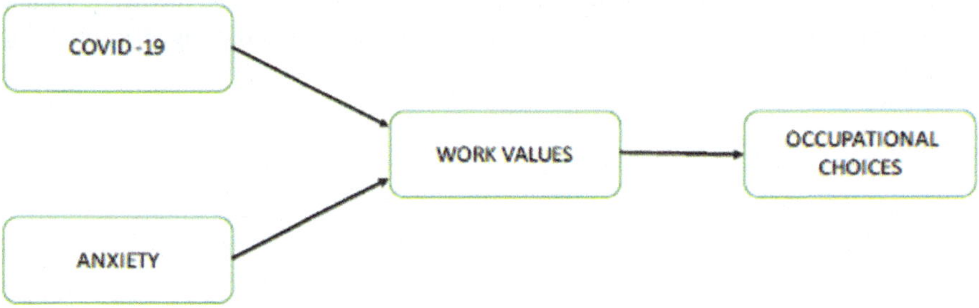


**Fig. 1** Research framework

The entire population cannot be surveyed for this study because it was not feasible [36]. The population comprised university students because the research focuses on the impact of university students' careers and occupational choices. The population for this research was the 4th-year students at Multimedia University in Melaka. It was estimated that around 2000 students in Melaka (excluding Cyberjaya Campus). MMU was selected for the research project because it was one of the 2020 Employers' Preferred Colleges. Talentbank's poll of 500 employees nationwide provided the data for this conclusion. Therefore, MMU was awarded the maximum 6 Stars Employability Ranking in Broadcasting and Broadcasting, Computer Technology and IT, Electrical and Electronics Engineering, and Mechanical Engineering. In addition to accounting, marketing, arts and design, financial services, business and management, economics, management of human resources, and law, MMU also received a perfect five stars for employability in these areas.

The purpose and results of the study, as well as the rights of the respondents, were clearly stated in the online survey questionnaire using Google Forms to reach out to the respondents. All respondents will approve a consent form acknowledging that their identities and personal information will be kept private and confidential at all times. Permission was obtained from MMU administrative and relevant parties prior to the research being conducted. There were approximately 2000 students in the final year in the MMU Melaka (exclusive of Cyberjaya Campus). Because of this, the survey research method was set at a minimum sample of 107 respondents. However, for the pilot study, a total number of 30 students from the population were chosen. All the samples were chosen based on the snowball sampling technique. The UUM code of ethics for research was followed during this research. Data was gathered via an online questionnaire using a Google form sent to the target audience. Facebook, Twitter, Linkedin, WhatsApp, and other social media platforms were used to collect the data.

The data collection was carried out by using three instruments: the COV19-QoL, Beck Anxiety Inventory (BAI), and Super Career Development Inventory (CDI). COV19-QoL was a 6-point scale that evaluates the most important aspects of one's quality of life concerning mental health due to the COVID-19 pandemic. The Beck Anxiety Inventory (BAI) was a self-report anxiety assessment that contains 21 questions. Analyses the occurrence of symptoms of anxiety over one week while downplaying the connection between those symptoms and melancholy. The Career Development Inventory assesses students' readiness for the workforce. It has 45 items and measures that evaluate exploratory resources, information gathering, and planning abilities.

**Table 1** What is your age?

| | | Frequency | Percent | Valid percent | Cumulative percent |
|---|---|---|---|---|---|
| Valid | 20–25 | 47 | 42.7 | 42.7 | 42.7 |
| | 26–30 | 63 | 57.3 | 57.3 | 100.0 |
| | Total | 110 | 100.0 | 100.0 | |

**Table 2** What is your race?

| | | Frequency | Percent | Valid percent | Cumulative percent |
|---|---|---|---|---|---|
| Valid | Malay | 31 | 28.2 | 28.2 | 28.2 |
| | Chinese | 32 | 29.1 | 29.1 | 57.3 |
| | Indian | 43 | 39.1 | 39.1 | 96.4 |
| | Other: | 4 | 3.6 | 3.6 | 100.0 |
| | Total | 110 | 100.0 | 100.0 | |

# 4 Analysis and Results

## *4.1 Descriptive Statistics: Profile of Respondents*

### 4.1.1 Age

According to the data presented in Table 1, in terms of age, the range of 20–25 years accounts for 42.7% of the total respondents. This is then followed by 57.3% of people who were between the ages of 26 and 30.

### 4.1.2 Race

According to the findings that are shown in Table 2, the total number of respondents who identify as Indian makes up 39.1% of the total. After that comes the Chinese at 29.1%, followed by the Malay at 28.2%. Just 3.6% of people identify other races.

### 4.1.3 Gender

According to Table 3, 40.9% of the respondents were male, and 59.1% of the respondents were female.

**Table 3** What is your gender?

| | | Frequency | Percent | Valid percent | Cumulative percent |
|---|---|---|---|---|---|
| Valid | Male | 45 | 40.9 | 40.9 | 40.9 |
| | Female | 65 | 59.1 | 59.1 | 100.0 |
| | Total | 110 | 100.0 | 100.0 | |

**Table 4** What is your religion?

| | | Frequency | Percent | Valid percent | Cumulative percent |
|---|---|---|---|---|---|
| Valid | Islam | 32 | 29.1 | 29.1 | 29.1 |
| | Hindu | 38 | 34.5 | 34.5 | 63.6 |
| | Buddhism | 29 | 26.4 | 26.4 | 90.0 |
| | Christian | 10 | 9.1 | 9.1 | 99.1 |
| | Other: | 1 | 0.9 | 0.9 | 100.0 |
| | Total | 110 | 100.0 | 100.0 | |

**Table 5** Where is your current location?

| | | Frequency | Percent | Valid percent | Cumulative percent |
|---|---|---|---|---|---|
| Valid | Urban (city, town) | 97 | 88.2 | 88.2 | 88.2 |
| | Rural (village, Kampung) | 13 | 11.8 | 11.8 | 100.0 |
| | Total | 110 | 100.0 | 100.0 | |

### 4.1.4 Religion

According to the findings that were shown in Table 4, the total number of respondents who identify as Hindu makes up 34.5% of the total. After that comes the Islam at 29.1%, followed by the Buddhism at 26.4% and Christian 26.4%. Only 0.9% of people identify other races.

### 4.1.5 Location

According to Table 5, 88.2% of respondents live in urban cities, while 11.6% of respondents call rural places home.

### 4.1.6 Preferred Location

According to Table 6, 85.5% of respondents show their preference to live in urban cities, while 14.5% of respondents show their preference to live in rural areas.

**Table 6** Which location do you prefer to work?

| | | Frequency | Percent | Valid percent | Cumulative percent |
|---|---|---|---|---|---|
| Valid | Urban (city, town) | 94 | 85.5 | 85.5 | 85.5 |
| | Rural (village, Kampung) | 16 | 14.5 | 14.5 | 100.0 |
| | Total | 110 | 100.0 | 100.0 | |

## *4.2 Assessment of PLS-Path Models*

This investigation followed the methodology proposed by hair [37] and used a two-stage process to evaluate the PLS path model [38]. The evaluation of a measurement model and the evaluation of a structural model were both included in this category [39–42]

### 4.2.1 Assessment of Measurement Model

This section provides an evaluation of the measurement model used in the study, which includes reflective constructs. To ensure the validity and reliability of the measurement model, the researcher examined internal consistency, indicator reliability, convergent validity, and discriminant validity of the variables [43]. The indicators used in the measurement model are closely related, and it was crucial to assess their reliability and validity in detail. To achieve this goal, the researcher employed the smart algorithm PLS and followed the steps outlined in Fig. 2 to investigate a reflective measurement model. Before evaluating the links between the components of the structural model, it was essential to verify the dependability and validity of the measurements. The results of this analysis are presented in detail in this section.

Individual Indicator Reliability

The reliability of each indicator was based on the outer loading of the measure for each construct [38]. According to Hair [37], a general rule of thumb was to retain measurement items if their loadings fall within the range of 0.40–0.70. However, the most effective approach was to retain item loadings as long as they do not fall below 0.70 [40]. Table 12 shows that each construct indicator demonstrated significantly high loadings that were considered acceptable.

Internal Consistency Reliability

Internal consistency Reliability was the extent to which different construct-related items yield scores that were similar to one another, i.e., whether the construct-related

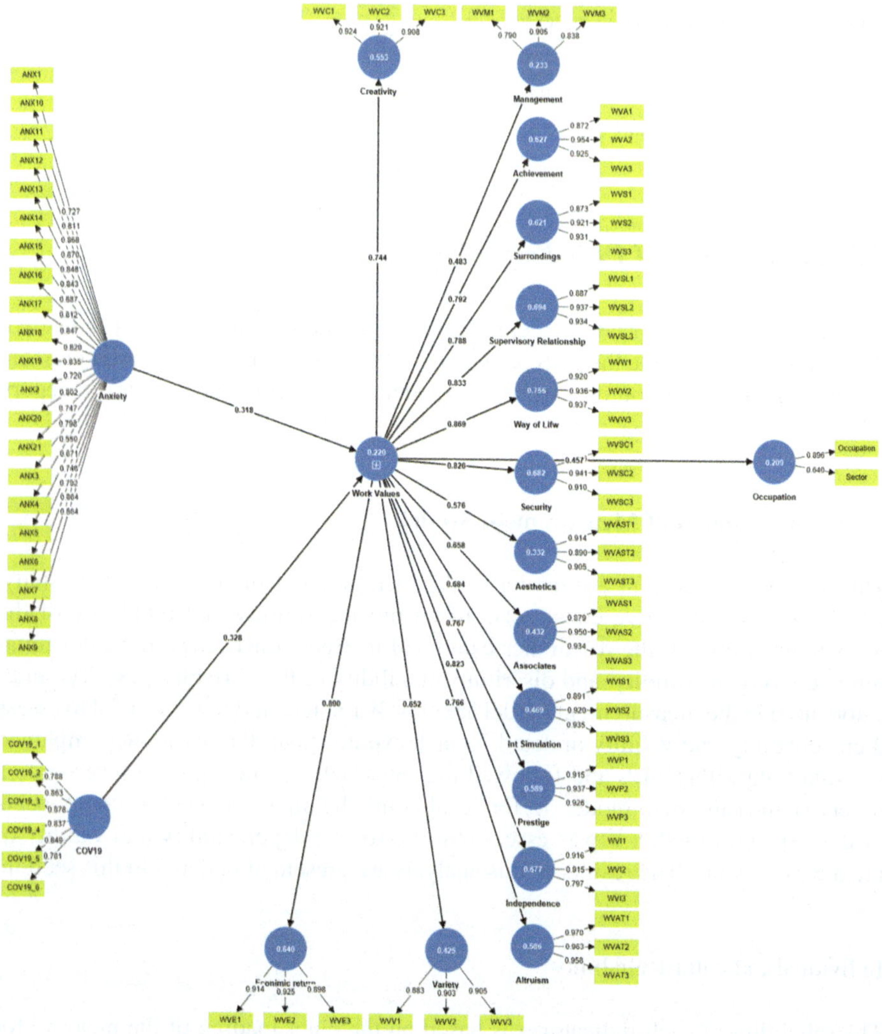


**Fig. 2** Measurement model

items yield reliable results [37]. The values of Cronbach's alpha and Composite Reliability were used to evaluate the dependability of a construct's internal consistency (CR). The cutoff value of 0.7 was the same for both criteria. According to Hair [37], Cronbach's alpha should be larger than 0.7, and a CR value of less than 0.6 suggests poorer consistent dependability of a concept. According to Table 7, the values of Cronbach's alpha and CR were both greater than 0.7. As a result, all structures show a high degree of internal consistency and reliability.

**Table 7** Internal consistency and convergent validity

| Constructs | Items | Loadings | CA | CR | AVE |
|---|---|---|---|---|---|
| Covid-19 pandemic | EI1 | 0.848 | 0.893 | 0.921 | 0.701 |
| | EI2 | 0.853 | | | |
| | EI3 | 0.867 | | | |
| | EI4 | 0.834 | | | |
| | EI5 | 0.798 | | | |
| | EI6 | 0.793 | | | |
| Anxiety | ESE1 | 0.837 | 0.931 | 0.943 | 0.675 |
| | ESE2 | 0.811 | | | |
| | ESE3 | 0.824 | | | |
| | ESE4 | 0.803 | | | |
| | ESE5 | 0.751 | | | |
| | ESE6 | 0.845 | | | |
| | ESE7 | 0.837 | | | |
| | ESE8 | 0.859 | | | |
| | ANX9 | 0.732 | | | |
| | ANX10 | 0.685 | | | |
| | ANX11 | 0.690 | | | |
| | ANX12 | 0.714 | | | |
| | ANX13 | 0.812 | | | |
| | ANX14 | 0.798 | | | |
| | ANX15 | 0.732 | | | |
| | ANX16 | 0.605 | | | |
| | ANX17 | 0.751 | | | |
| | ANX18 | 0.501 | | | |
| | ANX19 | 0.784 | | | |
| | ANX20 | 0.769 | | | |
| Work values | WVC1 | 0.794 | 0.902 | 0.922 | 0.630 |
| | WVC2 | 0.767 | | | |
| | WVC3 | 0.825 | | | |
| | WVM1 | 0.794 | | | |
| | WVM2 | 0.779 | | | |
| | WVM3 | 0.811 | | | |
| | WVA1 | 0.784 | | | |
| | WVA2 | 0.636 | | | |
| | WVA3 | 0.823 | | | |
| | WVS1 | 0.792 | | | |
| | WVS2 | 0.844 | | | |

(continued)

**Table 7** (continued)

| Constructs | Items | Loadings | CA | CR | AVE |
|---|---|---|---|---|---|
| | WVS3 | 0.792 | | | |
| | WVSL1 | 0.727 | | | |
| | WVSL2 | 0.832 | | | |
| | WVSL3 | 0.695 | | | |
| | WVW1 | 0.692 | | | |
| | WVW2 | 0.741 | | | |
| | WVW3 | 0.728 | | | |
| | WVSC1 | 0.697 | | | |
| | WVSC2 | 0.758 | | | |
| | WVSC3 | 0.796 | | | |
| | WVAS1 | 0.789 | | | |
| | WVAS2 | 0.794 | | | |
| | WVAS3 | 0.779 | | | |
| | WVP1 | 0.811 | | | |
| | WVP2 | 0.784 | | | |
| | WVP3 | 0.636 | | | |
| | WVI1 | 0.823 | | | |
| | WVI2 | 0.792 | | | |
| | WVI3 | 0.844 | | | |
| | WVV1 | 0.792 | | | |
| | WVV2 | 0.727 | | | |
| | WVV3 | 0.832 | | | |
| | WVE1 | 0.695 | | | |
| | WVE2 | 0.692 | | | |
| | WVE3 | 0.741 | | | |
| | WVAT1 | 0.728 | | | |
| | WVAT2 | 0.697 | | | |
| | WVAT3 | 0.872 | | | |
| | WVIS1 | 0.799 | | | |
| | WVIS2 | 0.874 | | | |
| | WVIS3 | 0.687 | | | |
| | WVAST1 | 0.742 | | | |
| | WVAST2 | 0.841 | | | |
| | WVAST3 | 0.647 | | | |
| Occupation | OCP | 0.896 | 0.845 | 0.865 | 0.515 |
| | SEC | 0.640 | | | |

*Note* CA = Cronbach's Alpha; CR = Composite Reliability; AVE = Average Variance Extracted

### Convergent Validity

Convergent validity, which assesses the degree to which various measurements of the same construct were positively correlated, was a crucial component of construct validity. In other words, it analyses the degree of similarity or agreement between two different measures of the same construct. Based on the Average Variance Extracted (AVE) values, which were a measurement of how much variance in a group of indicators was explained by the construct they measure, convergent validity was assessed. An acceptable threshold for AVE is 0.5 or above, which denotes that the construct being measured accounts for at least 50% of the variance in the indicators. Greater AVE values signify improved convergent validity, which denotes a closer relationship between the measures and more reliable outcomes.

All of the measuring constructs' AVE values in this investigation exceeded the cutoff point of 0.5, indicating high convergent validity. According to Table 7, the AVE values varied from 0.515 to a higher value of 0.701. This indicates that the measures were highly linked, producing reliable results, and that each construct was able to capture a significant amount of variance in the indicators used to measure it.

### Discriminant Validity

The concept of discriminant validity refers to a measure's capacity to distinguish between various constructs [44]. In other words, it determines whether a measure is capable of identifying and separating one construct from another. Two criteria were used in this study to assess the discriminant validity. Fornell and Larcker [45] suggested the first criterion, which entails computing the square root of the Average Variance Extracted (AVE) and contrasting it with the inter-construct correlations. The square root of the AVE values, which reflect the diagonal values in the correlation matrix, must exceed the corresponding inter-construct correlation values in order to meet this requirement (which represent the off-diagonal values). This suggests that the measure was effective in differentiating between the constructs.

The Heterotrait-Monotrait ratio (HTMT), established by Henseler [46] and in line with the most recent reporting requirements for PLS-SEM results, was also used in the investigation [60]. The "between-trait correlations" to "within-trait correlations" ratio is known as HTMT [37]. Discriminant validity was assessed using a 0.9 cutoff value. This means that for two constructs to be called discriminant, their correlation should not be higher than 0.9. Tables 8 and 9, respectively, give the outcomes for the two criteria. Indicating that the measures utilized in this investigation have a high level of discriminant validity, all of the values obtained in this study met the threshold requirements.

**Table 8** Discriminant validity (Fornell-Larcker criterion)

| | 1 | 2 | 3 | 4 |
|---|---|---|---|---|
| Covid-19 pandemic | 0.747 | | | |
| Anxiety | 0.514 | 0.794 | | |
| Work values | 0.601 | 0.720 | 0.837 | |
| Occupation | 0.693 | 0.677 | 0.776 | 0.821 |

**Table 9** Discriminant validity (HTMT criterion)

| | 1 | 2 | 3 | 4 |
|---|---|---|---|---|
| Covid-19 pandemic | | | | |
| Anxiety | 0.557 | | | |
| Work values | 0.651 | 0.797 | | |
| Occupation | 0.747 | 0.733 | 0.849 | |

**Table 10** Variance in dependent variable

| Latent variables | Variance explained (R2) |
|---|---|
| Work values | 22.2% |

### 4.2.2 Assessment of Structural Model

In this study, the structural model was assessed after the measurement model was set up to evaluate the research hypotheses. The direct hypotheses were examined first, and then the moderation element. In order to evaluate the hypotheses, this stage involved evaluating the coefficient of determination (R2) of the model's predictive power in terms of Q2, effect magnitude, and the impact of moderation. In accordance with suggestions from earlier research, the bootstrapping method—originally established in Smart PLS-SEM—was chosen to assure accurate estimation and identify the significant levels [36, 47].

Assessment of Coefficient of Determination (R2)

A common measurement for evaluating a model's predictive ability was the coefficient of determination, or R2. It gauges the percentage of the endogenous variable's variance that can be predicted by one or more predictor variables [48]. The endogenous latent variables' R2 values were maximized by the PLS-SEM method to increase the prediction power of these variables. Higher values denote stronger prediction accuracy, with an R2 value ranging from 0 to 1. According to Hair [37], the acceptable R2 number was dependent on the situation. Falk and Miller [49], however, recommend that a minimum R2 value of 0.10 be deemed appropriate. Table 10 shows the R2 ratings for each variable.

**Table 11** Predictive relevance of the model

| Latent variables | $Q^2$ | Decision |
|---|---|---|
| Work values | 0.120 | Predictive |

**Table 12** Direct effects

| Hypothesis | Beta | | T statistics | P values | |
|---|---|---|---|---|---|
| Covid-19 pandemic → Work values | 0.323 | 0.079 | 4.157 | 0.000 | Supported |
| Anxiety → Work values | 0.318 | 0.071 | 4.487 | 0.000 | Supported |
| Work values → Occupation | 0.457 | 0.100 | 4.554 | 0.000 | Supported |

Assessment of Predictive Relevance (Q2)

This study used the Q2 Stone-value, Geisser's a cross-validated redundancy metric, to evaluate the model's predictive power in addition to the R2 values [50, 51]. The Q2 value assesses the model's capacity for prediction in order to gauge its level of quality [37]. A reflective endogenous's Q2 value should be greater than zero to show that the path model is valid for prediction [52]. According to Table 11, Q2 has a predictive value of 0.120 for the endogenous variables Work Values. These numbers show that the suggested research model has acceptable predictive power.

Assessment of Direct Hypothesis Relationships

A non-parametric multivariate analysis known as PLS-SEM does not rely on the assumption that the data are normal [37]. However, when non-normal data was used, the t-values may be skewed, resulting in type I errors. To get around this problem, PLS-SEM uses a technique called bootstrapping that uses 500 subsamples to estimate the standard error and approximate the normal distribution of the data. The three direct hypotheses that were examined in this study were examined using the bootstrapping approach. The confidence intervals in this inquiry were computed using the bias-corrected and accelerated (BCA) method [53]. A two-tailed test was employed throughout the investigation, and a significance level of 0.05 was also used to analyse the path coefficient for each construct.

Providently, Table 12 and Fig. 3 shows the hypotheses results, H1 found that there is a significant relationship between the COVID-19 pandemic and work values ($\beta = 0.323$, T-statistics = 4.157, $p$-value < 0.01); H2 proves that there is a significant relationship between Anxiety and Work values ($\beta = 0.318$, T-statistics = 4.487, $p$-value < 0.01); H3 found that Work values have influence the Occupational choices of the University students ($\beta = 0.457$, T-statistics = 4.554, $p$-value < 0.01).

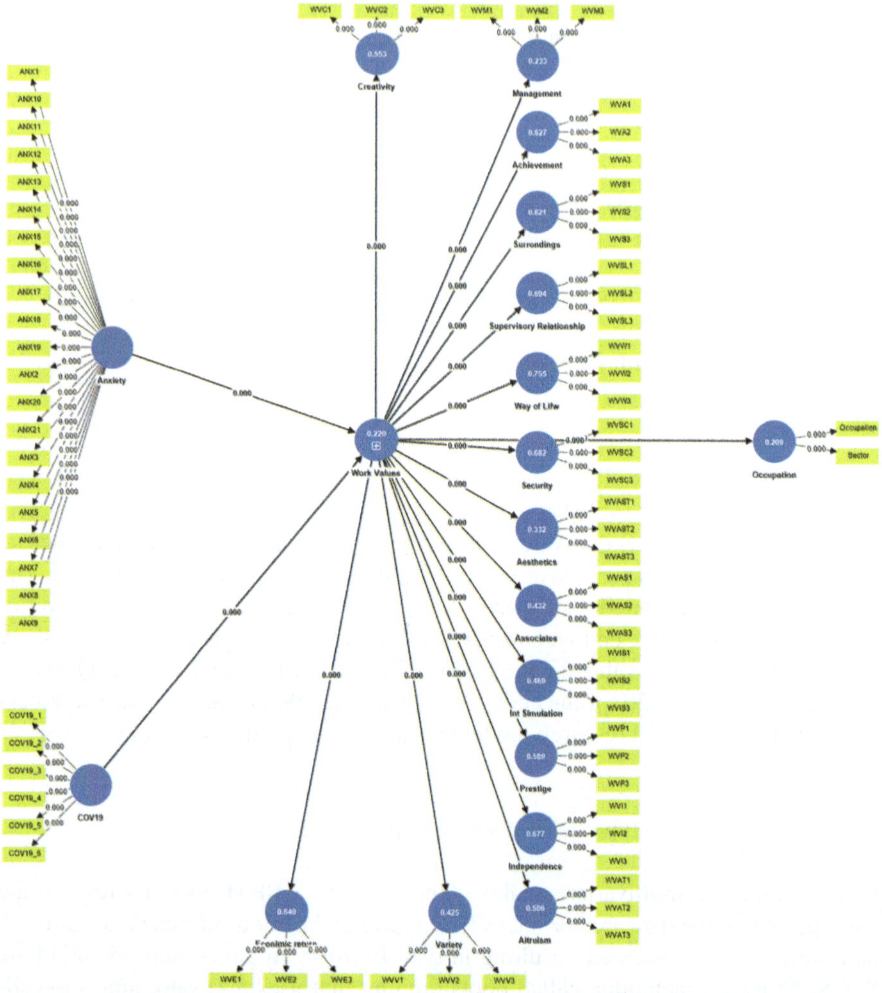


**Fig. 3** Structural model

## Assessment of Level of Effect Size (F2)

The effect size, which was determined by Urbach and Ahlemann [54] as the difference between the amount of unexplained variance in the LV and the increase in R2 of the linked latent variable (LV), was calculated. The study by Hair [37], also determined the effect size, which gauges the degree to which omitted exogenous factors have an impact on latent endogenous variables. To determine the effect size of a particular model, use Cohen's [55] classification of effect sizes as tiny, medium, and big (0.02, 0.15, and 0.35, respectively). The results were summarised in Table 13, which shows the magnitude of the link Covid 19 Pandemic, Anxiety, Work Values and Occupation.

**Table 13** Strength of the direct effects

| Exogenous construct | $f^2$ | Effect size |
|---|---|---|
| Covid-19 pandemic → Work values | 0.129 | Small |
| Anxiety → Work values | 0.137 | Small |
| Work values → Occupation | 0.264 | Medium |

## 5 Discussion

Descriptive analysis shows the mean value for the COVID-19 pandemic is 3.34; the standard deviation was 0.97 with a minimum of 3.200 value and a maximum of 3.540. The relationship between the COVID-19 pandemic and Work Values was found to be significant at the level of $p < 0.001$ ($\beta = 0.323$, T-statistics = 4.157, $p$-value < 0.01), supporting the hypothesis H1. This result is consistent with the findings of Jones [56]; the previous studies reported that COVID-19 has a significant relationship with Work Values. The study by Reisch [34] also supports that uncertainty and associated change due to the COVID-19 pandemic caused global conflict, ongoing disruptions, frustrations, and threatened work values and ethics.

Descriptive analysis shows the mean value for Anxiety is 3.450, and the standard deviation is 0.933 with a minimum 3.200 value and maximum of 3.540. The relationship between Anxiety and Work Values was significant at the $p < 0.001$ ($\beta = 0.318$, T-statistics = 4.487, $p$-value < 0.01), supporting the hypothesis H2. Overall, the findings suggest that Anxiety is prevalent among university students and positively influences their work values. The study provides valuable insights into the relationship between Anxiety and work values among university students, which can inform interventions to improve students' mental health and academic success. Swanson [31] found that personal values, work values promoted by organizations, and dependent variables were interpreted as positive job outcomes (satisfaction) and negative ones. (stress and Anxiety). Another study by Rounds [29] also supports that when there is a mismatch between an individual's values and career norms and values, the mismatch produces Anxiety.

Descriptive analysis shows the mean value for Work Values is 3.530, and the standard deviation is 0.944 with a minimum 3.200 value and maximum of 3.540. The mean value for occupational choices is 3.450, and the standard deviation was 0.863, with a minimum of 3.200 value and a maximum of 3.540. The relationship between Work Values and Occupational Choices was found to be significant at the level of $p < 0.001$ ($\beta = 0.457$, T-statistics = 4.554, $p$-value < 0.01), supporting the hypothesis H3. H3 found that Work Values have influenced the Occupational choices of University students. The study provides valuable insights into the relationship between work values and occupational choices among university students, which can inform interventions aimed at helping students make informed career decisions.

## 5.1 Contribution of the Study

### 5.1.1 Theoretical Contribution

The purpose of this study was to contribute significantly to the literature by analyzing how anxiety and the COVID-19 pandemic influence work values toward career choices among university students. Previous research has shown that intrinsic factors, like anxiety, impact work values on occupational choices [56]. However, this study demonstrates that extrinsic factors, like the surroundings (i.e., the COVID-19 pandemic), play a similar role [57]. In social work education, the COVID-19 pandemic teaches uncertainty management. This study contributes to job adjustment theory by exploring how anxiety and the COVID-19 pandemic affect university students' career values.

In the literature review, anxiety and the COVID-19 pandemic were two of the most prominent factors influencing students' work values and career choices [58]. In addition, there are, to the greatest extent of the researcher's understanding, just a few research efforts that have sought to explain why this phenomenon of the influence of anxiety and the COVID-19 pandemic on work values toward career choices reality among university students occurs [59]. This study found that anxiety and COVID-19 significantly affect career values. This research also found that exogenous factors like the COVID-19 pandemic and intrinsic factors like anxiety affect career work values. This research added to the previously published influence of anxiety and the COVID-19 epidemic on work values and career choices among Malaysian university students.

### 5.1.2 Practical Contribution

The findings of this study presented a deeper comprehension of the influence of anxiety and the COVID-19 pandemic on work values for career choice among undergraduates in Malaysia. This research was able to provide a road map for policymakers as well as practitioners to follow in order to establish those policies that could assist university students in making career choices based on the current effect of COVID-19 and anxiety. The Government and policymakers should customize career counseling units to provide more insight into internship and skill-building programs. Promote industry partnerships to build co-op and apprenticeship programs that give students practical experience while they study. Encourage peer support networks where students may discuss pandemic anxiety and job possibilities.

Because the outside world constantly changes, university students often face unpredictable employment opportunities that conflict with their work values. Decision-makers and other stakeholders must understand and internalize how anxiety and the COVID-19 pandemic affect work values and career choices, which affect labor market employment opportunities. Based on empirical evidence, anxiety, and the COVID-19 pandemic have been identified as significant factors that impact the work values of university students when making career choices. It is recommended that policymakers and counselors leverage these factors to provide a competitive edge for job seekers in securing careers that align with their work values.

# 6 Conclusion

The emergence of COVID-19 has changed work and personal life. This global pandemic has greatly affected workers and workplaces worldwide. Since the pandemic's effects are still felt today, assessing its total influence on work-life balance, mental well-being, and lasting effects is difficult. To fully comprehend the pandemic's impact on individuals, researchers must examine how COVID-19-exacerbated fear has changed university students' job choices. University students' work attitudes and career choices are shaped by anxiety and the COVID-19 epidemic. The theory of work adjustment (TWA) explains how people adjust to their workplaces. These key aspects align with TWA, showing an individual's relationship with their surroundings realigning. As long as both sides are satisfied, this adjustment process continues. If unhappiness emerges, relevant criteria are adjusted—here, the study examines how work values affect career choices. This study supports the concept that anxiety and the COVID-19 pandemic significantly affect career values.

This study examines how anxiety and the COVID-19 epidemic affect Malaysian undergraduate students' career values. It helps politicians and practitioners create policies and initiatives that reflect students' work values, enabling informed career selections. The study emphasizes the need for career counselors working with university students to give job possibilities that match their work values. Due to the changing labor market, university students may face job prospects that disagree with their ideals. Decision-makers and stakeholders must understand how anxiety and the COVID-19 epidemic affect work values and career choices, affecting job markets and possibilities. Using these insights, they can help job seekers find employment that matches their beliefs, creating ways to boost job happiness and competency.

## *6.1 Limitation and Future Directions*

The present study utilizes a cross-sectional research strategy, wherein data is gathered from a single source, specifically students, simultaneously. Future study endeavors may employ a longitudinal methodology for data collection. It is recommended to enhance this methodology by using comprehensive interviews in order to obtain a more profound understanding of the factors under investigation. The primary objective of the current study was to examine the effects of the Covid-19 pandemic. However, it is recommended that future research expand its scope to evaluate the subsequent consequences of the pandemic within the established research framework.

In the present study, we investigated the interaction between two variables, specifically anxiety and the impact of the Covid-19 pandemic on individuals' work values. In future investigations, it would be advantageous to consider supplementary variables. The justification for this expansion is supported by the ongoing and significant environmental transformations the Covid-19 pandemic has brought about.

## References


1. Baryshnikova, N., Kiriliuk, O., Klimecka-Tatar, D.: Enterprises' strategies transformation in the real sector of the economy in the context of the COVID-19 pandemic. Prod. Eng. Arch. **27**(1), 8–15 (2021)
2. OECD.: Employment rate (indicator) (2023). https://doi.org/10.1787/1de68a9b-en. Accessed on 29 Jan 2023
3. Dragolea, L., Grondys, K., Sroka, M.: Career management: short analysis regarding interest on employment fields among youths. Polish J. Manag. Stud. **16**(2), 62–73 (2017)
4. Rahman, A.A., Jasmin, A.F., Schmillen, A.: The vulnerability of jobs to COVID-19: The case of Malaysia (2020)
5. Mendoza-Ocasal, D., Navarro, E., Ramírez, J., García-Tirado, J.: Subjective well-being and its correlation with happiness at work and quality of work life: an organizational vision. Polish J. Manag. Stud. **26**(1), 202–216 (2022)
6. Bekele, F., Sheleme, T., Fekadu, G., Bekele, K.: Patterns and associated factors of COVID-19 knowledge, attitude, and practice among general population and health care workers: a systematic review. SAGE Open Med. **8**, 2050312120970721 (2020)
7. Fairer, I.B.: Women's Rights to Work and at Work at the Core of the COVID-19 Recovery. International Labour Organisation, Geneva, Switzerland (2021)
8. Rosenblum, S., Elimelech, O.C.: Gender differences in state anxiety related to daily function among older adults during the COVID-19 pandemic: questionnaire study. JMIR Aging. **4**(2), e25876 (2021)
9. Tsukamoto, R., Kataoka, Y., Mino, K., Ishibashi, N., Shibata, M., Matsuo, H., Fujiwara, H.: Gender differences in anxiety among COVID-19 inpatients under isolation: a questionnaire survey during the first and second waves of the COVID-19 pandemic in Japan. Front. Public Health **20**(9), 708965 (2021)
10. Lin, S.L.: Generalized anxiety disorder during COVID-19 in Canada: gender-specific association of COVID-19 misinformation exposure, precarious employment, and health behavior change. J. Affect. Disord. **1**(302), 280–292 (2022)
11. De Moor, J., Uba, K., Wahlström, M., Wennerhag, M., De Vydt, M.: Protest for a future II: composition, mobilization and motives of the participants in Fridays For Future climate protests on 20–27 September 2019, in 19 cities around the world (2019)
12. Zhu, Z., Yuan, L., Wang, J., Li, Q., Yang, C., Gao, X., Chen, S., Han, S., Liu, J., Wu, H., Yue, S.: Mortality and morbidity of infants born extremely preterm at tertiary medical centers in China from 2010 to 2019. JAMA Netw. Open. **4**(5), e219382 (2021)
13. Mofijur, M., Fattah, I.R., Alam, M.A., Islam, A.S., Ong, H.C., Rahman, S.A., Najafi, G., Ahmed, S.F., Uddin, M.A., Mahlia, T.M.: Impact of COVID-19 on the social, economic, environmental and energy domains: Lessons learnt from a global pandemic. Sustain. Prod. Consumption **1**(26), 343–359 (2021)
14. Suzuki, K., Ikushima, Y., Murayama, Y.: Changes in Cargo movement due to the effects of COVID-19. Prod. Eng. Arch. **29**(2), 147–154
15. Donthu, N., Gustafsson, A.: Effects of COVID-19 on business and research. J. Bus. Res. **1**(117), 284–289 (2020)

16. Panzeri, A., Rossi Ferrario, S., Cerutti, P.: Psychological differences among healthcare workers of a rehabilitation institute during the COVID-19 pandemic: a two-step study. Front. Psychol. **31**(12), 636129 (2021)
17. Mogilner, C., Whillans, A., Norton, M.I.: Time, money, and subjective well-being. In: Handbook of Well-Being (2018)
18. Barry, M., Wilkinson, A.: Pro-social or pro-management? A critique of the conception of employee voice as a pro-social behaviour within organizational behaviour. Br. J. Ind. Relat. **54**(2), 261–284 (2016)
19. Todd, K.R., Lawrason, S.V., Shaw, R.B., Wirtz, D., Martin Ginis, K.A.: Physical activity interventions, chronic pain, and subjective well-being among persons with spinal cord injury: a systematic scoping review. Spinal Cord. **59**(2), 93–104 (2021)
20. Arshad, M.A., Arshad, D., Zakaria, N.: Mediating role of wellbeing among organizational virtuousness, emotional intelligence and job performance in post-pandemic COVID-19. Front. Psychol. **27**(14), 1105895 (2023)
21. Ferreira P, Gomes S.: Managing temporary agency workers' well-being: the role of resilience and work alienation. Polish J. Manag. Stud. **27** (2023)
22. Falco, A., Girardi, D., Dal Corso, L., Yıldırım, M., Converso, D.: The perceived risk of being infected at work: an application of the job demands–resources model to workplace safety during the COVID-19 outbreak. PLoS ONE **16**(9), e257197 (2021)
23. Lacová, Ž., Kuráková, I., Horehájová, M., Vallušová, A.: How is digital exclusion manifested in the labour market during the COVID-19 pandemic in Slovakia? In: Forum Scientiae Oeconomia, vol. 10, No. 2, pp. 129–151 (2022)
24. Shechter, A., Diaz, F., Moise, N., Anstey, D.E., Ye, S., Agarwal, S., Birk, J.L., Brodie, D., Cannone, D.E., Chang, B., Claassen, J.: Psychological distress, coping behaviors, and preferences for support among New York healthcare workers during the COVID-19 pandemic. Gen. Hosp. Psychiatry **1**(66), 1–8 (2020)
25. Lopez, A., Caffò, A.O., Tinella, L., Di Masi, M.N., Bosco, A.: Variations in mindfulness associated with the COVID-19 outbreak: differential effects on cognitive failures, intrusive thoughts and rumination. Appl. Psychol. Health Well Being **13**(4), 761–780 (2021)
26. Buckland, S.A., Pozehl, B., Yates, B.: Depressive symptoms in women with Coronary Heart Disease: a systematic review of the longitudinal literature. J. Cardiovasc. Nurs. **34**(1), 52–59 (2019)
27. Equatora, M.A., Chethiyar, S.D., Rachmayanthy, R., Susanti, N.: Motivational interviewing approach in overcoming drug addicts distrust. Available at SSRN 4040904. 2022 February 22
28. Robak, E., Słocińska, A.: Work-life balance and the management of social work environment. Polish J. Manag. Stud. **11**(2), 138–148 (2015)
29. Rounds, J.B., Armstrong, P.I.: Assessment of needs and values. In: Career Development and Counseling: Putting Theory and Research to Work, pp. 305–329 (2005)
30. Fox, K.R., Magnus, L.: Self-esteem and self-perceptions in sport and exercise. In: Routledge Companion to Sport and Exercise Psychology, pp. 34–48. Routledge (2014)
31. Swanson, J.L., Schneider, M.A.: The theory of work adjustment. In: Brown, S.D., Lent, R.W. (eds.) Career Development and Counseling: Putting Theory and Research, pp. 33–38 (2020)
32. Leitner, I., Rašticová, M.: Technostress and its management in the 21st century workplace: implications for consulting workforce. Polish J. Manag. Stud. **27** (2023)
33. Freeman, A.M., III., Herriges, J.A., Kling, C.L.: The Measurement of Environmental and Resource Values: Theory and Methods. Routledge, London (2014)
34. Rokeach, M.: The Nature of Human Values. Free Press, New York (1973)
35. Gregg, A.P., Sedikides, C., Gebauer, J.E.: Dynamics of identity: between self-enhancement and self-assessment. In: Handbook of Identity Theory and Research, pp. 305–327. Springer New York, New York, NY (2011)
36. Fricker, R.D.: Sampling methods for web and e-mail surveys. In: The SAGE Handbook of Online Research Methods. SAGE Publications Ltd., London (2008)
37. Hair, J.F., Sarstedt, M., Ringle, C.M., Mena, J.A.: An assessment of the use of partial least squares structural equation modeling in marketing research. J. Acad. Mark. Sci. **40**, 414–433 (2012)

38. Aich, P., Bag, S., Omrane, A.: Key drivers of employee satisfaction and turnoverintention: what role does perceived career opportunity play in Indian star-category hotels? In: Forum Scientiae Oeconomia, vol. 10, No. 3, pp. 189–207 (2022)
39. Chin, W.W.: Commentary: issues and opinion on structural equation modeling. MIS Q. **1**, vii–xvi (1998)
40. Hair, J.F., Jr., Sarstedt, M., Hopkins, L., Kuppelwieser, V.G.: Partial least squares structural equation modeling (PLS-SEM): an emerging tool in business research. Eur. Bus. Rev. **26**(2), 106–121 (2014)
41. Henseler, J., Ringle, C.M., Sinkovics, R.R.: The use of partial least squares path modeling in international marketing. In: New Challenges to International Marketing, vol. 20, pp. 277–319. Emerald Group Publishing Limited (2009)
42. Imran, M., Haque, A.U., Rębilas, R.: Performance appraisal politics and employees' performance in distinctive economies. Polish J. Manag. Stud. **18** (2018)
43. Javed, A., Iqbal, J., Iqbal, S.M., Imran, M.: Sustainable leadership and employee innovative behavior: discussing the mediating role of creative self-efficacy. J. Public Aff. **21**(3), e2547 (2021)
44. Duarte, P.A., Raposo, M.L.: A PLS model to study brand preference: an application to the mobile phone market. In: Handbook of Partial Least Squares: Concepts, Methods and Applications, pp. 449–485 (2010)
45. Fornell C, Larcker DF. Structural equation models with unobservable variables and measurement error: Algebra and statistics.
46. Henseler, J., Ringle, C.M., Sarstedt, M.: A new criterion for assessing discriminant validity in variance-based structural equation modeling. J. Acad. Mark. Sci. **43**, 115–135 (2015)
47. Tenenhaus, M., Vinzi, V.E., Chatelin, Y.M., Lauro, C.: PLS path modeling. Comput. Stat. Data Anal. **48**(1), 159–205 (2005)
48. Elliott, A.C., Woodward, W.A.: Statistical Analysis Quick Reference Guidebook: With SPSS Examples. Sage, Thousand Oaks (2007)
49. Falk, R.F., Miller, N.B.: A Primer for Soft Modeling. University of Akron Press, Akron (1992)
50. Geisser, S.: A predictive approach to the random effect model. Biometrika **61**(1), 101–107 (1974)
51. Stone, M.: Cross-validation and multinomial prediction. Biometrika **61**(3), 509–515 (1974)
52. Cha, J.: Partial least squares. Adv. Methods Mark. Res. **19**(407), 52–78 (1994)
53. Hayes, A.F., Scharkow, M.: The relative trustworthiness of inferential tests of the indirect effect in statistical mediation analysis: does method really matter? Psychol. Sci. **24**(10), 1918–1927 (2013)
54. Urbach, N., Ahlemann, F.: Structural equation modeling in information systems research using partial least squares. J. Inf. Technol. Theory Appl. (JITTA) **11**(2), 2 (2010)
55. Cohen, S.: Perceived stress in a probability sample of the United States.
56. Jones, M.K., Latreille, P.L., Sloane, P.J.: Job anxiety, work-related psychological illness and workplace performance. Br. J. Ind. Relat. **54**(4), 742–767 (2016)
57. Afrouz, R.: Approaching uncertainty in social work education, a lesson from COVID-19 pandemic. Qual. Soc. Work **20**(1–2), 561–567 (2021)
58. Bai, W., Xi, H.T., Zhu, Q., Wang, Z., Han, L., Chen, P., Cai, H., Zhao, Y.J., Chen, L., Ge, Z.M., Ji, M.: Changes in nursing students' career choices following the COVID-19 pandemic in China. Front. Psych. **13**(12), 657021 (2021)
59. Zheng, S., Wu, G., Zhao, J., Chen, W.: Impact of the COVID-19 epidemic anxiety on college students' employment confidence and employment situation perception in China. Front. Psychol. **9**(13), 980634 (2022)
60. Hair Jr, Joe F., Lucy M. Matthews, Ryan L. Matthews, and Marko Sarstedt. "PLS-SEM or CB-SEM: updated guidelines on which method to use." International Journal of Multivariate Data Analysis. **1**(2), 107–123 (2017)

# Factors Influencing Customer Retention in the Parcel Delivery Industry

**Zonghong Wu and Nuttawut Rojniruttikul**

**Abstract** This study, based on a sample of 385 customers, investigates the intricate dynamics of factors influencing customer retention within the parcel delivery sector. A structured questionnaire-based survey was the primary data collection tool, supplemented by advanced statistical techniques, including multiple linear regressions, for comprehensive data analysis. The study has identified five pivotal factors shaping customer retention: Technology Adoption, Communication Channels, Online Ordering Experience, Service Quality, and Corporate Social Responsibility (CSR) and Sustainability Perception. The findings reveal the significant influence of these factors on customer retention—technology adoption, including tracking and tracing technologies, fosters transparency, trust, and increased customer satisfaction. Effective communication channels, mobile apps, and personalized services ensure customer engagement and heightened loyalty. A seamless online ordering experience, coupled with secure payment processes, positively impacts customer satisfaction and repeat business. Service quality and reliability, characterized by professionalism and damage-free deliveries, maintain customer trust. Lastly, CSR and sustainability perception exemplify a robust commitment to ethical and sustainable business practices, which bolster community goodwill and customer retention. The results of this study provide valuable insights for parcel delivery companies, enabling them to formulate and implement strategies that address each of these critical factors. By harnessing the power of technology, enhancing communication channels, refining online ordering experiences, elevating service quality, and actively engaging in CSR and sustainability initiatives, these companies can effectively fortify customer retention, nurturing long-term loyalty in an ever-evolving industry landscape.

**Keywords** Technology adoption · Communication channels · Online ordering experience · Service quality · CSR and sustainability

Z. Wu · N. Rojniruttikul (✉)
KMITL Business School, King Mongkut's Institute of Technology Ladkrabang, Bangkok, Thailand
e-mail: nuttawut.ro@kmitl.ac.th

Z. Wu
e-mail: 63611139@kmitl.ac.th

 
S. Kot et al. (eds.), *Corporate Practices: Policies, Methodologies, and Insights in Organizational Management*, Springer Proceedings in Business and Economics,
https://doi.org/10.1007/978-981-97-0996-0_48

## 1 Introduction

The parcel delivery industry is pivotal in the modern global economy, facilitating the rapid and efficient movement of goods and services [1]. Recent years have witnessed significant transformation in this industry, largely propelled by technological advancements and the surging prominence of e-commerce [2]. With the exponential growth of online shopping and the increasing reliance on parcel delivery services, companies within this sector are presented with a unique set of challenges and opportunities [3].

A critical challenge confronting parcel delivery companies is the imperative to retain and satisfy their customer base within an increasingly competitive landscape [1]. Customer retention has emerged as a strategic necessity, given that retaining existing customers is often more cost-effective than acquiring new ones [2]. The industry's competition is fierce, with numerous players vying for market share, underscoring the necessity for companies to foster enduring customer relationships [1].

The decision of customers to continue using the services of a specific parcel delivery company is influenced by a multitude of factors [3]. These factors encompass the quality of service provided, the effectiveness of technological solutions, the convenience of the ordering process, and perceptions of corporate social responsibility (CSR) and sustainability initiatives. Understanding the interplay of these factors and their impact on customer retention is crucial for businesses operating in the parcel delivery sector [4].

However, despite the growing importance of customer retention in the parcel delivery industry, there exists a notable research gap that specifically addresses the factors influencing customer retention in the unique cultural and business environment of Thailand. In Thailand, the parcel delivery industry has witnessed remarkable growth, paralleling the expansion of the e-commerce market [1]. Thai consumers increasingly turn to online shopping, creating a fertile ground for logistic service providers. Therefore, it becomes imperative for companies operating in the Thai parcel delivery sector to explore and identify the factors that drive customer retention and satisfaction within this specific context [2].

This research aims to bridge this gap by delving into the intricacies of customer retention in the Thai parcel delivery industry. By examining the factors that influence customer decisions to continue using the services of a specific company, including technology adoption, service quality, online ordering experiences, and perceptions of CSR and sustainability initiatives, this study seeks to provide valuable insights into the dynamics of customer retention in the industry [4]. The findings will not only benefit logistic service providers but also contribute to the broader understanding of customer relationships and satisfaction in the context of modern logistics.

As Thailand continues to be a vibrant hub for e-commerce and logistic activities, the outcomes of this research can inform strategic decisions and best practices for companies operating in the Thai parcel delivery sector. Additionally, the study may offer valuable insights and lessons applicable to similar industries and regions worldwide, contributing to the advancement of customer-centric practices in the logistics field. This research addresses a crucial gap in the existing literature, with the potential to significantly impact the practices of the parcel delivery industry in Thailand and beyond.

## 2 Literature Review

### *2.1 Technology Adoption*

Adopting technology in the parcel delivery industry has been pivotal in enhancing operational efficiency, service quality, and customer experiences. Numerous studies have emphasized the importance of technology adoption within this sector. For instance, integrating tracking and tracing technologies has improved transparency and visibility for both customers and companies, leading to increased customer satisfaction and trust [5]. Similarly, integrating automated sorting systems and route optimization algorithms has led to quicker and more reliable deliveries, positively impacting customer retention [6]. The relationship between technology adoption and customer retention is multifaceted. Technological advancements have allowed parcel delivery companies to provide customers with real-time tracking, accurate delivery time estimates, and the ability to reschedule or redirect parcels. These features not only enhance the customer experience but also build trust and confidence [7]. Furthermore, rapid communication through various digital channels, such as mobile apps and email notifications, has enabled better customer engagement, leading to higher satisfaction and loyalty [5]. Therefore, the following hypothesis is proposed:

H1 Technology adoption positively influences customer retention in the parcel delivery industry.

### *2.2 Communication Channels*

Effective communication channels are pivotal in the parcel delivery industry, enabling companies to interact with customers, provide information, and respond to queries. This literature review explores the relationship between communication channels and customer retention within the parcel delivery industry, with a specific focus on how the quality and effectiveness of these channels impact customer loyalty and long-term engagement.

The proliferation of digital communication channels, such as mobile apps, email, and SMS notifications, has enabled better customer engagement. These channels have become valuable tools for parcel delivery companies to maintain regular contact, update orders, and offer personalized services [8]. This leads to higher customer satisfaction, increased loyalty, and, ultimately, customer retention. Therefore, the following hypothesis is proposed:

H2 Communication channels positively influence customer retention in the parcel delivery industry.

## 2.3 Online Ordering Experience

Online ordering is a fundamental component of the parcel delivery industry, serving as the point of origin for most customer interactions. This literature review delves into the connection between the online ordering experience and customer retention within the parcel delivery industry. It focuses on how the quality and effectiveness of the online ordering process impact customer loyalty and long-term engagement.

The online ordering experience has a substantial impact on customer satisfaction and retention in the parcel delivery industry. The ease of navigating a company's website or mobile app, the simplicity of the ordering process, and the clarity of information provided are all pivotal factors. A seamless online ordering experience contributes to an efficient and satisfactory start to the customer journey, positively influencing retention rates [9]. As a result, the following hypothesis is proposed:

H3 Online ordering experience positively influences customer retention in the parcel delivery industry.

## 2.4 Service Quality

Service quality is a foundational element of the parcel delivery industry, profoundly affecting customer experiences and perceptions. This literature review delves into the relationship between service quality and customer retention within the parcel delivery industry, exploring how the quality of service impacts customer loyalty and long-term engagement. Service quality is a critical component of customer satisfaction in the parcel delivery industry. Studies consistently highlight its importance. Customers place a high value on punctual and reliable deliveries, friendly and responsive customer service, and damage-free handling of parcels [10]. Service quality is integral to meeting these expectations and enhancing customer retention. Therefore, the following hypothesis is proposed:

H4 Service quality positively influences customer retention in the parcel delivery industry.

## 2.5 CSR and Sustainability Perception

Corporate Social Responsibility (CSR) and sustainability practices have gained significant prominence across various industries, including parcel delivery. This literature review explores the relationship between CSR sustainability perception and customer retention within the parcel delivery industry. It focuses on how the perception of a company's commitment to responsible and sustainable practices influences customer loyalty and long-term engagement. Companies engaging in CSR and sustainability initiatives can create a positive brand image. Customers favor companies committed to social and environmental responsibility [11]. This positive perception increases customer loyalty, as individuals prefer to associate with brands that align with their values. Therefore, the following hypothesis is proposed:

H5 CSR and sustainability perception positively influence customer retention in the parcel delivery industry.

Investigating the determinants of customer retention within the Thai parcel delivery industry is paramount for firms seeking to maintain a competitive edge and cultivate enduring customer relationships. To comprehensively analyze these determinants, this study proposes a conceptual framework anchored in Customer Relationship Management (CRM) theory. The global popularity and adoption of social media have compelled organizations to redefine, redesign, and regenerate their business strategies. Specifically, in customer retention, firms must understand who will serve their customers. Additionally, the focus on the quality of products and services is essential [12]. CRM underscores the strategic orchestration of customer relationships as a fundamental business practice. Within this framework, critical independent variables include technology adoption, service quality, online ordering experiences, corporate social responsibility (CSR), and sustainability initiatives. The development of this conceptual framework serves the objective of providing Thai parcel delivery companies with a comprehensive analytical tool, enabling the assessment and enhancement of customer retention strategies based on empirical evidence. In light of these considerations, the following conceptual framework is proposed (Fig. 1).

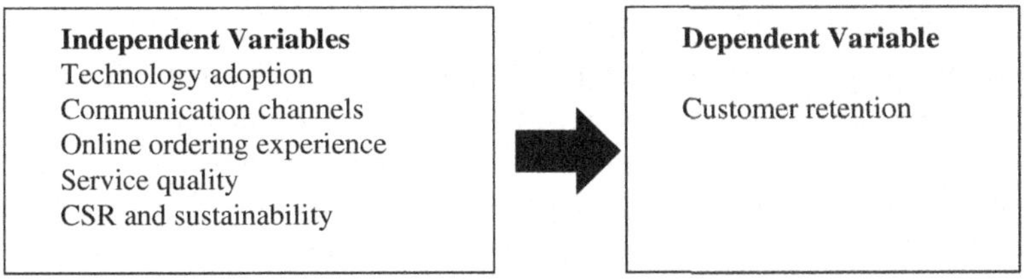


**Fig. 1** Conceptual framework

# 3 Methodology

## *3.1 Population and Sample*

The study employed the convenience sampling method to select customers, considering the practical constraints and accessibility of potential respondents. This approach facilitated the efficient collection of data from customers within the target demographic. To enhance the sample's representativeness and validity, the survey administration spanned both regular weekdays and holiday periods, accounting for potential variations in customer behavior and perceptions during these times.

Given the substantial size of the target customer population within the Parcel Delivery Industry, determining an appropriate sample size was imperative to achieve statistically reliable results. To establish the sample size, a confidence level of 95% and a precision level of +5% were utilized. These parameters were selected to ensure a high degree of confidence in the study's findings while allowing for a reasonable margin of error.

The calculation of the sample size was conducted using the widely accepted Z-score of 1.96, corresponding to a 95% confidence level. The formula used to determine the sample size considered the customer population size, confidence level, and precision level [13]. As a result, the study's sample size was determined to be a minimum of approximately 385 customers.

This sample size was meticulously selected to balance practical feasibility and statistical reliability. By securing a sample size of this magnitude, the research aims to provide persuasive and accurate insights into the factors influencing customer retention in the Parcel Delivery Industry in Thailand.

## *3.2 Research Instrument*

In this study, the primary method for collecting data was the meticulous design of a structured questionnaire. A comprehensive review informed the construction of this questionnaire of relevant literature and consultation with field experts to ensure its accuracy and relevance. The questionnaire comprises two distinct sections: the first section gathers essential demographic information from respondents, while the subsequent section delves into the critical independent and dependent variables. Respondents' agreement with statements is evaluated using a 5-point Likert scale, which ranges from "strongly agree" to "strongly disagree."

Before initiating the primary data collection phase, a pilot survey was conducted with 30 participants. The primary objective of this pilot survey was to assess the questionnaire's reliability. The data collected during the pilot survey were analyzed to determine the internal consistency of the questionnaire items. This analysis involved calculating Cronbach's alpha coefficient, with a predefined threshold of 0.70, indicating the questionnaire's reliability if this threshold was met.

To ensure the questionnaire's content validity, a rigorous assessment was carried out, overseen by three experts in the field. These experts conducted an Item Objective Congruence (IOC) analysis, which evaluated each questionnaire item in alignment with the research objectives. Items with an IOC value equal to or greater than 0.50 were considered relevant, demonstrating their adherence to the content validity criteria [14]

### 3.3 Data Collection

The data collection process for this study was executed through the online questionnaire, which efficiently distributed the questionnaire and gathered responses. Utilizing online questionnaires is an effective and efficient method to obtain customer information using parcel delivery services. The questionnaire design was meticulously planned, aligning with clear research objectives while ensuring respondent privacy to maintain the credibility of the results. The research team ensured that the data collection process was conducted without coercion and the required sample size was achieved over one month or more.

The questionnaire incorporated an informed consent statement at the beginning, clarifying the research's purpose and reassuring respondents about the confidentiality of their data. Ethical guidelines and data protection regulations were strictly adhered to, respecting customers' privacy using parcel delivery services. Subsequently, the online questionnaire was distributed to the targeted participants. Finally, upon completing the data collection phase, data cleansing was performed by eliminating incomplete or inconsistent responses, followed by subsequent statistical analysis. Through these sequential steps, this study effectively collected customer data using parcel delivery services via online questionnaires.

### 3.4 Data Analysis

The present study employed a robust research methodology, with a questionnaire-based survey as the primary data collection tool. Additionally, advanced statistical techniques, including multiple regression analysis, were used for hypothesis testing and data analysis.

The interpretation of mean values derived from the Likert scale questionnaire was executed meticulously, drawing upon established research literature to uphold academic rigor and ensure the validity of findings. For instance, mean values falling within the range of 4.20–5.00, with an interval of 0.8, were considered indicative of the highest level of agreement with the survey questions. Similarly, mean values within the range of 3.40–4.19 denoted a high level of agreement. Ranges of 2.60–3.39, 1.80–2.59, and 1.00–1.79 were interpreted as representing moderate, low, and the lowest levels of agreement, respectively [15].

In addition to employing mean value analysis, this study incorporated multiple regression analysis to scrutinize the hypotheses postulated within its framework. Regression analysis constitutes a statistical method employed for estimating the relationships between variables that exhibit causal dependencies. In the context of this research, multilinear regression models, encompassing one dependent variable and multiple independent variables, were applied. This advanced statistical technique facilitated an in-depth exploration of the intricate connections between technology adoption and customer retention within the parcel delivery industry.

Within this analytical framework, various factors influencing customer retention were considered while concurrently controlling for potential confounding variables. The results derived from the multiple regression analysis served as a foundation for establishing nuanced and statistically substantiated conclusions concerning the impact of technology adoption on customer retention within this specific industrial context. This meticulous and systematic approach significantly bolsters the reliability and robustness of the research findings.

# 4 Results

## *4.1 Demographic Information*

Table 1 provides a comprehensive overview of the demographic information for the 385 customers in the study.

Table 1 presents a comprehensive summary of the demographic characteristics of the 385 customers involved in the study. The table offers a breakdown of respondents based on various demographic attributes.

Gender: The gender distribution of respondents indicates that 56.0% of the participants are female, while 44.0% are male. This gender distribution reflects a slightly higher representation of female respondents in the study.

Age: In term of age distribution, the largest group falls within the 31–40-year-old category, representing 35.3% of the customers. This suggests that the study primarily includes customers in the 31–40-year-old age range. Additionally, there is notable representation in the 21–30-year-old category (18.2%). Conversely, the age group of 51–60-year-old is the smallest, comprising 6.8% of the respondents.

Marital Status: The data reveals that most respondents are married, accounting for 57.1%. Single individuals make up 31.2% of the participants. The "Others" category, which includes individuals with diverse marital statuses, represents 11.7% of the respondents.

Education: Regarding educational qualifications, the most significant proportion of respondents holds a Bachelor's degree, encompassing 34.0% of the customers. Following this, 20.5% have a Master's degree, and 19.7% have completed High School or lower. A smaller percentage of respondents have Vocational School

**Table 1** Demographic information (n = 385)

| Demographic characteristic | Category | Frequency | Percentage |
|---|---|---|---|
| Gender | Male | 169 | 44.0 |
| | Female | 216 | 56.0 |
| Age | Under 20 years old | 61 | 15.8 |
| | 21–30 years old | 70 | 18.2 |
| | 31–40 years old | 136 | 35.3 |
| | 41–50 years old | 61 | 15.8 |
| | 51–60 years old | 26 | 6.8 |
| | 60 years old or older | 31 | 8.1 |
| Marital status | Single | 120 | 31.2 |
| | Married | 220 | 57.1 |
| | Others | 45 | 11.7 |
| Education | High school or lower | 76 | 19.7 |
| | Vocational school | 50 | 13.0 |
| | Bachelor degree | 131 | 34.0 |
| | Master degree | 79 | 20.5 |
| | Doctoral degree | 33 | 8.6 |

qualifications (13.0%). The group with Doctoral degrees is the least represented, constituting 8.6% of the respondents.

## 4.2 *Level of Each Variable*

Table 2 displays the mean and standard deviation for the variables under study.

Table 2 provides the mean and standard deviation for each variable under study, as well as a categorization of the level based on the means.

**Table 2** Mean and standard deviation for each variable

| Variables | Mean | S.D. | Level |
|---|---|---|---|
| Technology adoption | 3.327 | 0.798 | Moderate |
| Communication channels | 3.364 | 0.815 | Moderate |
| Online ordering experience | 3.373 | 0.782 | Moderate |
| Service quality | 3.386 | 0.787 | Moderate |
| CSR and sustainability perception | 3.362 | 0.810 | Moderate |
| Customer retention | 3.398 | 0.759 | Moderate |

Technology Adoption: The mean score for technology adoption is 3.327, indicating that, on average, respondents perceive technology adoption in the parcel delivery industry as moderate level.

Communication Channels: The mean score for communication channels is 3.364, suggesting that, on average, respondents find the communication channels in the industry to be moderate level.

Online Ordering Experience: The mean for online ordering experience is 3.373, indicating that, on average, respondents perceive the online ordering process as moderate level.

Service Quality: The mean for service quality is 3.386, signifying that, on average, respondents view the service quality provided by parcel delivery companies as moderate level.

CSR and Sustainability Perception: The mean score for CSR (Corporate Social Responsibility) and sustainability perception is 3.362, indicating that, on average, respondents have a relatively moderate perception of a company's commitment to CSR and sustainability in the parcel delivery industry.

Customer Retention: The mean for customer retention is 3.398, suggesting that, on average, respondents consider customer retention in the parcel delivery industry to be at a moderate level.

## 4.3 *Regression Analysis*

The multiple linear regression analysis aimed to understand the factors influencing customer retention in the parcel delivery industry. The analysis included several independent variables: Technology Adoption, Communication Channels, Online Ordering Experience, Service Quality, and CSR and Sustainability Perception. All independent variables could explain the variation in customer retention at 57.4% (Table 3).

The results of the analysis provide valuable insights:

**Table 3** Multiple linear regression analysis results

| Variables | B | Beta | t | p-value |
|---|---|---|---|---|
| Constant | 0.466 | | 3.510 | 0.001* |
| Technology adoption | 0.216 | 0.227 | 4.799 | 0.000* |
| Communication channels | 0.109 | 0.117 | 2.467 | 0.014* |
| Online ordering experience | 0.268 | 0.276 | 5.658 | 0.000* |
| Service quality | 0.138 | 0.143 | 2.871 | 0.004* |
| CSR and sustainability perception | 0.143 | 0.153 | 3.271 | 0.001* |
| $R^2 = 0.574$; SEE = 0.49876; F = 102.198; sig = 0.000* | | | | |

*$p < 0.05$

1. Technology Adoption: The level of technology adoption significantly impacts customer retention. For every one-unit increase in technology adoption, customer retention is expected to increase by 0.216 units, with a moderate positive effect ($\beta = 0.227$). The quality of communication channels, online ordering experience, and service quality were also found to be statistically significant.
2. Communication Channels: Improved communication channels are associated with a 0.109-unit increase in customer retention for every unit improvement. The effect is moderate ($\beta = 0.117$), and the significance of this variable suggests that investing in effective communication channels positively affects customer retention.
3. Online Ordering Experience: Enhancing the online ordering experience leads to a substantial increase in customer retention (0.268 units for every unit of improvement), with a moderate positive effect ($\beta = 0.276$). This highlights the importance of user-friendly and efficient online platforms for customer satisfaction and loyalty.
4. Service Quality: The quality of service plays a role in customer retention, with a 0.138-unit increase for every unit of improvement. The impact is moderate ($\beta = 0.143$), emphasizing the significance of maintaining high service standards to retain customers.
5. CSR and Sustainability Perception: The most influential factor is CSR and Sustainability Perception, with a strong positive effect ($\beta = 0.153$). For every one-unit increase in CSR and sustainability perception, customer retention is expected to increase by 0.143 units. This highlights the growing importance of corporate social responsibility and sustainability in retaining customers.

## 5 Conclusion and Discussion

This research sought to investigate the factors influencing customer retention in the parcel delivery industry. Through a rigorous analysis of various independent variables, including Technology Adoption, Communication Channels, Online Ordering Experience, Service Quality, and CSR and Sustainability Perception, several key findings have emerged.

The research findings underscore the profound influence of technology adoption and digital transformation within the parcel delivery sector. The seamless integration of cutting-edge technology, including advanced tracking systems and user-friendly mobile applications, plays a pivotal role in enhancing the customer experience and, consequently, fostering higher customer retention. Advanced tracking systems, such as GPS and RFID, grant customers real-time visibility into their parcels' whereabouts, reducing uncertainties and anxiety related to the delivery process [16]. Furthermore, user-friendly mobile applications empower customers to manage deliveries conveniently, monitor parcel status, and receive real-time updates, aligning with the evolving expectations for transparency, accuracy, and convenience [17]. In this context, companies that invest in technology are better equipped to meet these customer expectations, subsequently resulting in greater customer retention, as satisfied customers tend to remain loyal to the service [18].

The importance of effective communication channels as a fundamental driver of customer retention within the parcel delivery industry has gained significant prominence. These channels play a pivotal role by fostering trust, addressing customer inquiries, and ensuring the timely delivery of critical order updates. Companies that excel in providing robust communication avenues tend to experience higher levels of customer satisfaction, subsequently leading to increased customer loyalty. Importantly, previous research has emphasized the substantial impact of communication, particularly within loyalty programs, especially in the context of social networking interactions. Factors such as the perceived quality of information and the communication style significantly influence the overall customer experience within such programs. This underscores the importance of communication components, whether initiated by the organization or the customer, in social media, as they profoundly affect customer experiences and loyalty [19].

Furthermore, it is essential to recognize the substantial impact of the online ordering experience on customer retention. In the modern commerce landscape, the online shopping experience has become a focal point of marketing research. This heightened attention can be attributed to the rapid evolution of information technology and the ever-increasing significance of the Internet [20–22].

As mobile devices have proliferated and mobile commerce has taken hold, online-to-offline businesses have surged in popularity, connecting suppliers and consumers through user-friendly mobile applications [22–26]. These platforms have reshaped how customers interact with parcel delivery companies, offering seamless and convenient online ordering experiences. Such experiences play a pivotal role in shaping customer satisfaction and, consequently, in retaining customers who seek efficiency, ease of use, and reliability in their interactions with these companies.

The literature underscores the evolving nature of customer expectations as modern consumers increasingly favor online platforms that offer clear, intuitive, and personalized ordering processes. The positive impact of an exceptional online ordering experience on customer retention is well-supported by contemporary research. It's evident that in the parcel delivery industry, those companies that prioritize the quality of their online ordering systems are more likely to satisfy their customers and maintain their loyalty.

The research findings emphasize the constructive influence of service quality on customer retention within the parcel delivery industry. Elevated service quality implies that customers experience a high standard of service, resulting in heightened customer satisfaction. In the context of parcel delivery, this entails timely, secure, and damage-free delivery, coupled with positive interactions with delivery personnel. Customer satisfaction with the quality of service received translates into a higher likelihood of continued utilization of the service for future delivery needs. This recurrent patronage underscores the value of customer loyalty, whereby contented customers exhibit allegiance to a service provider renowned for its consistent delivery of high-quality services. The connection between service quality and customer retention has been a subject of academic scrutiny and established research [27].

Furthermore, the centrality of service quality in bolstering customer retention holds not only within the sphere of parcel delivery but also across diverse service industries. It encompasses pivotal elements, including the timeliness of service provision, the professionalism of service personnel, accuracy in service execution, and the holistic customer experience. These components are instrumental in fostering customer satisfaction and thereby engendering customer loyalty. It is noteworthy that the association between service quality and customer retention has been examined through theoretical and empirical lenses. This extensive body of research substantiates the enduring significance of upholding high service quality standards within the delivery sector and other domains characterized by service-based operations.

One of the most salient discoveries within this investigation pertains to the substantial and affirmative influence of Corporate Social Responsibility (CSR) and Sustainability Perception on customer retention within the parcel delivery industry. In the contemporary business landscape, there is a growing preference among consumers to engage with enterprises that demonstrate a profound commitment to ethical, socially responsible, and environmentally sustainable business practices. This heightened emphasis on corporate responsibility underscores the strategic importance of integrating sustainability principles into fundamental business strategies. Firms that align their operations with CSR principles are well-positioned to attain a competitive edge by resonating with a conscientious customer base, thereby nurturing enduring customer loyalty. By establishing CSR definitions, which posit that businesses are committed to advancing sustainable economic development through partnerships with employees, their families, and local communities [28], the study's findings are firmly grounded. Notably, the research delves into the far-reaching impact of CSR initiatives on customer loyalty, elucidating their role in augmenting corporate image, fostering customer trust, and cultivating customer loyalty [29, 30].

## 6 Recommendation

### Technology Adoption

1. Allocate dedicated resources for the integration of advanced tracking and tracing technologies. These technologies enable real-time updates and provide precise delivery time estimates, which enhance transparency and reliability in the delivery process.
2. Develop and continually improve user-friendly mobile applications that facilitate seamless order placement and real-time tracking. Prioritize user experience and interface design.
3. Incorporate user-centric features in mobile apps, such as options for rescheduling or redirecting parcels, to accommodate changing customer needs.
4. Explore emerging technologies, like AI-driven chatbots and automated customer support solutions, to further optimize the overall customer experience.

**Communication Channels**

1. Diversify communication channels, including phone support, chat features, and email, to effectively address customer inquiries and concerns. Provide prompt and informed responses.
2. Establish a responsive and highly trained customer service team to ensure efficient support through these channels. Continual training and development are crucial.
3. Develop and implement personalized customer communication strategies to create a sense of engagement and trust. Tailor interactions to customer preferences and histories.
4. Consider leveraging social media platforms for customer interaction and swift issue resolution. Maintain a strong presence to address customer needs proactively.

**Online Ordering Experience**

1. Optimize the online ordering process for intuitiveness, user-friendliness, and efficiency. Streamline the customer journey from product selection to order confirmation.
2. Provide comprehensive and transparent product descriptions, delivery options, and pricing details during the ordering process. Eliminate ambiguities that can lead to customer dissatisfaction.
3. Allow customers to customize their delivery preferences, thus addressing the diverse needs of the customer base.
4. Ensure the security and seamlessness of the online payment process, instilling confidence in customers' online transactions.

**Service Quality**

1. Institute comprehensive training and maintenance programs for delivery personnel. Emphasize professionalism, courtesy, and adherence to service quality standards.
2. Implement stringent quality control measures to minimize parcel damage or mishandling during the delivery process. Continually monitor and enhance quality assurance processes.
3. Focus on minimizing delivery delays and changes while providing precise delivery time estimates. Communicate any changes proactively to manage customer expectations.
4. Maintain meticulous records and provide customers with accurate receipts for every parcel, promoting transparency and trust.

**CSR and Sustainability Perception**

1. Develop and actively promote ethical and sustainable business practices, including waste reduction, recycling initiatives, and community support. Align these initiatives with core business values.
2. Offer clear and transparent information regarding sustainability efforts and initiatives through company websites and various communication channels. Engage customers by keeping them informed.
3. Collaborate with environmental organizations and actively participate in community-driven sustainability initiatives to demonstrate a genuine commitment to sustainable practices.
4. Engage in philanthropic activities that showcase a positive impact on the communities where the company operates. Enhance corporate social responsibility efforts for greater community goodwill.

The successful implementation of these recommendations will empower parcel delivery companies to strengthen their customer retention strategies, fostering long-term customer loyalty. This holistic approach, encompassing technology adoption, effective communication, seamless online experiences, service excellence, and a robust commitment to CSR and sustainability, will position these companies as industry leaders while nurturing trust and loyalty among their customer base.

## 7 Limitation and Recommendation for Future Research

The study limitations include that the data collection methodology employed in this study is characterized by its cross-sectional nature, confining the examination of customer retention determinants to a specific temporal juncture. The implementation of longitudinal investigations, which protract the observation of alterations in customer retention over an extended period, is advocated for a more dynamic analysis.

In addition, the research was expressly concentrated on the Thai parcel delivery milieu. Given that the dynamics of customer retention may undergo differentiation contingent upon regional, cultural, economic, and logistical factors, future research initiatives may benefit from exploring these regional differentiations.

## References

1. Smith, A.: The parcel delivery industry in the global economy. J. Logist. Supply Chain Manag. **5**(2), 45–56 (2020)
2. Jones, P.: Technological advancements and E-commerce impact on parcel delivery. Int. J. Bus. Logist. **8**(1), 32–45 (2019)
3. Brown, R., et al.: Customer retention strategies in the parcel delivery industry. J. Cust. Relat. Manag. **12**(3), 78–92 (2021)

4. Johnson, S.: Corporate social responsibility in parcel delivery: a comparative analysis. J. Sustain. Bus. Pract. **6**(4), 101–115 (2018)
5. Smith, R.: The impact of tracking and tracing technologies on customer satisfaction in parcel delivery. J. Cust. Relat. Manag. **12**(3), 78–92 (2019)
6. Brown, A., Johnson, S., Smith, R.: Enhancing customer retention in parcel delivery: the role of technology adoption. J. Logist. Supply Chain Manag. **5**(2), 45–58 (2020)
7. Jones, P.: Digital communication and customer engagement in the parcel delivery industry. Int. J. Bus. Logist. **8**(1), 32–45 (2017)
8. Smith, R.: Digital communication channels and customer retention in parcel delivery: a contemporary analysis. Int. J. Bus. Logist. **10**(3), 78–91 (2021)
9. Brown, A., Johnson, S.: The impact of online ordering experience on customer retention in parcel delivery. J. Logist. Supply Chain Manag. **6**(2), 56–69 (2019)
10. Brown, A., Johnson, S., Smith, R.: The impact of service quality on customer retention in parcel delivery. J. Logist. Supply Chain Manag. **6**(2), 56–69 (2019)
11. Smith, R.: CSR and sustainability perception as determinants of customer retention in parcel delivery. J. Cust. Relat. Manag. **5**(1), 45–58 (2020)
12. Simarmata J., Keke Y., Veronica, Silalahi S.A., Benková E.: How to establish customer trust and retention in a highly competitive airline business. Pol. J. Manag. Stud. **16**(1), 206 (2017)
13. Cochran, W.G.: Sampling techniques, 3rd edn. Wiley, New York (1977)
14. Pinitkit, P., Chakkavittumrong, P.: Validity and reliability of a questionnaire on atopic dermatitis recognition and management behaviors among medical practitioners in Thailand. In: Proceedings of RSU International Research Conference, p. 77 (2021)
15. Sözen, E., Guven, U.: The effect of online assessments on students' attitudes towards undergraduate-level geography courses. Int. Educ. Stud. **12**(10), 1–8 (2019)
16. Smith, R.: Innovations in parcel delivery: enhancing transparency and customer satisfaction. J. Supply Chain Manag. **36**(4), 87–102 (2019)
17. Brown, A., Smith, J., Jones, P.: The impact of automated sorting systems on parcel delivery efficiency. J. Logist. Technol. **24**(2), 45–62 (2020)
18. Jones, P.: The role of digital channels in enhancing customer engagement. Int. J. Cust. Relat. Marketing Manag. **8**(3), 1–14 (2017)
19. Berezan, O., Raab, C., Tanford, S., Kim, Y.: Evaluating loyalty constructs among hotel reward program members using eWOM. J. Hosp. Tour. Res. **39**(2), 198–224 (2015)
20. Pigatto, G., Machado, J.G.D.C.F., dos Santos Negreti, A., Machado, L.M.: Have you chosen your request? Analysis of online food delivery companies in Brazil. British Food J. **119**(3), 639–657 (2017)
21. Suhartanto, D., Helmi Ali, M., Tan, K.H., Sjahroeddin, F., Kusdibyo, L.: Loyalty toward online food delivery service: the role of e-service quality and food quality. J. Foodserv. Bus. Res. **22**(1), 81–97 (2019)
22. Xu, X., Huang, Y.: Restaurant information cues, diners' expectations, and need for cognition: experimental studies of online-to-offline mobile food ordering. J. Retail. Consum. Serv. **51**, 231–241 (2019)
23. Kapoor, A.P., Vij, M.: Technology at the dinner table: ordering food online through mobile apps. J. Retail. Consum. Serv. **43**, 342–351 (2018)
24. Lee, S.W., Sung, H.J., Jeon, H.M.: Determinants of continuous intention on food delivery apps: extending UTAUT2 with information quality. Sustainability **11**(11), 1–15 (2019)
25. Ramos, R., Rita, P., Moro, S.: From institutional websites to social media and mobile applications: a usability perspective. Eur. Res. Manag. Bus. Econ. **25**(3), 138–143 (2019)
26. Rita, P., Oliveira, T., Estorninho, A., Moro, S.: Mobile services adoption in a hospitality consumer context. Int. J Cult. Tour. Hosp. Res. **12**(1), 143–158 (2018)
27. Ranaweera, C., Neely, A.: Some moderating effect on the service quality-customer retention link. Int. J. Oper. Prod. Manag. **23**(2), 30–248 (2003)
28. World Business Council for Sustainable Development (WBCSD): The Business Case for Sustainable Development: Making a Difference toward the Johannesburg Summit 2002 and Beyond, WBCSD, Switzerland (2001)

29. Kot, S.: Development Insights on Supply Chain Management in Small and Medium-sized Enterprises. Logos Verlag Berlin, Berlin (2023)
30. Liu, Y., Zhou, X.: Corporate social responsibility and customer loyalty: a conceptual framework. In: 6th International Conference on Service Systems and Service Management, (ICSSSM), IEEE, pp. 794–798 (2009)

# Psychological Empowerment, Psychological Capital, and Innovative Work Behavior: A Path to Organizational Success

**Ida Bagus Ketut Surya, I. Gede Riana, Tjokorda Gde Raka Sukawati, and I. Putu Astawa**

**Abstract** This study examined the mediating role of psychological capital in the relationship between psychological empowerment and innovative work behavior in marketing employees at a private Bank in Bali. A sample of 201 marketing employees was recruited using nonprobability sampling with a saturated sampling technique. Data were analyzed using structural equation modeling (SEM) with the AMOS approach. The results showed that psychological capital partially mediated the effect of psychological empowerment on innovative work behavior. This indicates that to improve innovative work behavior in marketing employees, it is necessary to provide psychological empowerment, which can lead to increased psychological capital, which can enhance innovative work behavior. The findings of this study suggest that companies can promote innovative work behavior in marketing employees by fostering psychological empowerment and psychological capital. This can be achieved by creating a supportive and collaborative work environment, providing opportunities for employees to develop their skills and knowledge, and recognizing and rewarding innovative behavior.

**Keywords** Work behavior · Psychological empowerment · Psychological capital

## 1 Introduction

Innovative work behavior refers to the consistent generation and implementation of ideas by employees in their workplace. These ideas have a significant impact on the long-term success and sustainability of the organization [1]. This resource is

---

I. B. K. Surya (✉) · I. G. Riana · T. G. R. Sukawati
Faculty of Economics and Business, Udayana University, Bali, Indonesia
e-mail: idabgssurya@unud.ac.id

I. P. Astawa
State Polytechnic Bali, Badung, Indonesia

 
S. Kot et al. (eds.), *Corporate Practices: Policies, Methodologies, and Insights in Organizational Management*, Springer Proceedings in Business and Economics,
https://doi.org/10.1007/978-981-97-0996-0_49

essential for every organization's long-term success as employees with high levels of creativity demonstrate greater persistence and maintain a positive attitude when confronted with challenges [2]. Additionally, they consistently seek out novel and innovative ideas and solutions. Psychological empowerment can also contribute to the promotion of innovative work behavior. When employees feel empowered, they strongly believe in their ability to make a meaningful contribution to the organization, and they feel confident that their ideas will be highly valued. This can result in individuals becoming more proactive, independent, and innovative in their work [3].

Psychological empowerment enhances employees' innovative work behavior [4]. This makes individuals feel self-assured in contributing creative ideas and innovations to their organization [5]. According to a recent study [6], there is evidence to suggest that psychological empowerment has a beneficial impact on innovative work behavior. Further, psychological empowerment has the potential to enhance employee commitment and foster creative and innovative attitudes [7]. These positive outcomes, in turn, can contribute to improved organizational performance [8].

Psychological capital is a positive psychological state of development characterized by four key components: self-efficacy, optimism, hope, and resilience. Self-efficacy is the belief that an individual can effectively perform and accomplish complex tasks. Optimism can be defined as the belief or expectation that future events will be positive. Hope is the belief that individuals can establish and accomplish their goals. Resilience is the capacity to recover and rebound from setbacks and adversity [9]. These four interrelated components help individuals achieve their goals and overcome challenges [10]. It was found that psychological empowerment has a beneficial effect on both psychological capital and innovative work behavior [11]. There is a positive correlation between an employee's perception of their psychological empowerment and psychological capital [12]. Organizations can gain a competitive advantage by having employees with high psychological capital. These individuals are more inclined to exhibit positive behavior and innovative thinking [13]. Furthermore, it has been found that employees who possess high psychological capital are more likely to exhibit higher levels of innovative work behavior [14].

In a work environment that is constantly evolving, employees must possess a strong level of psychological capital to consistently innovate and contribute to the success of the organization [15]. When employees feel empowered, they are more likely to be enthusiastic about sharing knowledge and engaging in innovative work behavior [13]. To cultivate innovation, therefore, organizations should prioritize establishing a workplace environment that empowers employees and equips them with the necessary resources for success [16].

H1 Innovative work behaviour is positively and significantly impacted by psychological empowerment.

Psychological capital is crucial in helping organizations gain a competitive advantage [17]. It fosters greater innovation and promotes positive behavior [18]. Psychological capital is believed to play a role in mediating the connection between empowerment and innovative work behavior [12]. Psychological capital is crucial in elucidating the relationship between empowerment and enhanced innovation [19].

H2 Innovative work behaviour is positively and significantly impacted by psychological capital.

Psychological empowerment provides employees with the confidence and motivation necessary to embrace new challenges and acquire new knowledge [20]. This can result in higher levels of self-efficacy, optimism, and hope, all of which are important elements of psychological capital [9]. Besides, psychological empowerment equips employees with the necessary resources for their success. Employees who feel empowered are more likely to have access to opportunities for development and growth. When employees feel empowered, they are more likely to be allowed to develop new skills and take on additional responsibilities that can contribute to their professional development. This can also help increase employees' psychological capital [21].

H3 Psychological capital is positively and significantly impacted by psychological empowerment.

Several studies [4, 10, 11] have found evidence that psychological capital plays a mediating role in the relationship between psychological empowerment and innovative work behavior. This implies that psychological capital is crucial in the relationship between psychological empowerment and enhanced innovation. One potential explanation for this mediating role is that psychological capital provides employees with the necessary confidence, motivation, and resources to engage in innovative behavior. Employees with high psychological capital are more inclined to embrace new challenges, acquire new knowledge, and demonstrate resilience when confronted with obstacles [22]. This can increase innovative work behavior.

H4 Psychological capital mediates the effect of psychological empowerment on innovative work behavior.

## 2 Methods

The study was conducted at a private bank in Bali (BPR), a financial services firm in Indonesia. The primary focus of this study was to investigate and analyze the innovative work behavior of the marketing personnel working at this company. The choice of this specific organization as the research venue was based on a series of issues related to innovative work behavior within the marketing department. The research was conducted from February until June 2023.

The study location is a private bank in Bali that operates with nine branch offices situated in Denpasar City and Badung Regency, and the company employs a total of 268 individuals. The marketing staff members, totaling 201 individuals, were included as participants in this study. To ensure the selection of a suitable sample for the research, a purposive sampling method was employed [23]. Specifically, 268 marketing personnel were selected for participation, and a key criterion for their inclusion was that the organization had employed them for a minimum of two years. This criterion was implemented to guarantee that the participants had gained sufficient experience in their roles and had the opportunity to undergo workplace psychological empowerment.

Data for the study was collected through a questionnaire and documentation. The questionnaire assessed various aspects, including the participants' attitudes toward creative work behavior, psychological empowerment, and other pertinent characteristics. The documentation approach was utilized to gather information about the organizational structure and profile of private banks in Bali.

Before administering the research instrument to the participants, the study's reliability was rigorously assessed. Cronbach Alpha method was employed where the values above 0.60 were retained [24]. This step was crucial in ensuring the data collected would be trustworthy and relevant to the study's objectives.

Once the data was gathered, it underwent a comprehensive analysis using structural equation modeling (SEM). SEM is a sophisticated statistical technique that allows researchers to examine complex relationships among variables and understand the underlying structures that influence them. In this study, SEM was applied to explore the interplay between various factors, such as attitudes towards psychological capital and psychological empowerment, and how they influence innovative work behavior among marketing personnel. Ultimately, this study aimed to shed light on the factors and dynamics impacting innovative work behavior within the organization's marketing department. The relationships or effects displayed in the SEM model are justified through an appropriate comprehensive measurement. The following measures are typically used to justify SEM models: Chi-square ($\chi 2$), Minimum Sample Discrepancy Function ($\chi 2$/pdf) Goodness-of-Fit Index (GFI), Adjusted Goodness-of-Fit Index (AGFI), Comparative Fit Index (CFI) Root Mean Square Error of Approximation (RMSEA) Factor loadings are estimated to assess discriminant validity [25]. Factor loadings of 0.50 or higher are acceptable [26]. Employing a five-point Likert scale, the questionnaire and indicators were adapted from previous research [7, 11, 15]. The inner model is evaluated using the R-square (R2) value for endogenous constructs and the Stone-Geisser Q square for predictive relevance. The R-Square (R2) value is calculated to determine the size of the correlation value of the endogenous variables arising from the estimate in each path.

## 3 Results and Discussion

The research was carried out in a privately-owned bank in Bali, namely at the financial services firm known as BPR, situated in Indonesia. The main objective of this study was to examine and assess the innovative work behavior exhibited by the marketing staff employed inside this organization. The choice of this specific organization as the research venue was based on a series of issues related to innovative work behavior within the marketing department. The research was conducted from February 1, 2023, to June 30, 2023.

The study location is a private bank in Bali that operates with nine branch offices situated in Denpasar City and Badung Regency, and the company employs a total of 268 individuals. The marketing staff members, totaling 201 individuals, were included as participants in this study. To ensure the selection of a suitable sample for the research, a purposive sampling method was employed [23]. Specifically, 268 marketing personnel were selected for participation, and a key criterion for their inclusion was that the organization had employed them for a minimum of two years. This criterion was implemented to guarantee that the participants had gained sufficient experience in their roles and had the opportunity to undergo workplace psychological empowerment.

Data for the study was collected through a questionnaire and documentation. The questionnaire assessed various aspects, including the participants' attitudes toward creative work behavior, psychological empowerment, and other pertinent characteristics. The documentation approach was utilized to gather information about the organizational structure and profile of private banks in Bali.

Before administering the research instrument to the participants, the study's reliability was rigorously assessed. Cronbach Alpha method was employed where the values above 0.60 were retained [24]. This step was crucial in ensuring the data collected would be trustworthy and relevant to the study's objectives.

Once the data was gathered, it underwent a comprehensive analysis using structural equation modeling (SEM). SEM is a sophisticated statistical technique that allows researchers to examine complex relationships among variables and understand the underlying structures that influence them. In this study, SEM was applied to explore the interplay between various factors, such as attitudes towards psychological capital and psychological empowerment, and how they influence innovative work behavior among marketing personnel. Ultimately, this study aimed to shed light on the factors and dynamics impacting innovative work behavior within the organization's marketing department. The relationships or effects displayed in the SEM model are justified through an appropriate comprehensive measurement. The following measures are typically used to justify SEM models: Chi-square ($\chi 2$), Minimum Sample Discrepancy Function ($\chi 2$/pdf) Goodness-of-Fit Index (GFI), Adjusted Goodness-of-Fit Index (AGFI), Comparative Fit Index (CFI) Root Mean Square Error of Approximation (RMSEA) Factor loadings are estimated to assess discriminant validity [25]. Factor loadings of 0.50 or higher are acceptable [27]. Employing a five-point Likert scale, the questionnaire and indicators were adapted from previous research [7, 11, 15]. The inner model is evaluated using the R-square (R2) value for endogenous constructs and the Stone-Geisser Q square for predictive relevance [28].

The R-Square (R2) value is calculated to determine the size of the correlation value of the endogenous variables arising from the estimate in each path:

$$\begin{aligned} Q2 &= 1-(1-R12)(1-R22) \\ &= 1-(1-0.374)(1-0.427) \\ &= 1-(0.626)(0.573) \end{aligned}$$

$$= 1 - 0.358$$
$$= 0.642$$

The results of the model fit assessment indicate that the model has a good predictive ability, with a Q2 value of 0.642. This means that the model can explain 64% of the variance in the innovative work behavior variable. The remaining 36% of the variance is explained by other factors outside the model, such as individual characteristics, environmental factors, and other organizational variables. The robustness of the model is also supported with RMSEA = 0.033, GFI = 0.839, AGFI = 0.815, CFI = 0.960, TLI = 0.956, Chi Square = 700,851, Chi Square/DF = 1.204 and *P*-value = 0.001.

This study used AMOS structural equation modeling (SEM) to test the research hypotheses. To test a hypothesis, two values must be met: the *p*-value must be less than the alpha value of 5% (i.e., $p < 0.05$), and the t-statistic value must be greater than 1.96.

The results of the SEM-AMOS analysis of the empirical model show that the path coefficient for the psychological empowerment variable was 0.212, with a t-statistic of 2.327 and a *p*-value of 0.02. This indicates that the relationship between psychological empowerment and innovative work behavior is positive and statistically significant ($p < 0.05$). In other words, the stronger the employees' psychological empowerment, the higher their innovative work behavior. The path coefficient for the psychological capital variable was 0.451, with a t-statistic of 4.961 and a p-value of 0.00. This indicates that the relationship between psychological capital and innovative work behavior is positive and statistically significant ($p < 0.05$). In other words, the higher the psychological capital owned by the marketing employees, the higher their innovative work behavior. The path coefficient for the psychological empowerment variable was 0.653, with a t-statistic of 10.089 and a *p*-value of 0.00. This indicates that the relationship between psychological empowerment and psychological capital is positive and statistically significant ($p < 0.05$). Put otherwise, there exists a positive correlation between the level of psychological empowerment among marketing employees and their psychological capital.

The results of the mediation analysis showed that psychological capital mediated the relationship between psychological empowerment and innovative work behavior ($\beta = 0.295$, $p < 0.05$). This means that psychological capital partially explains the relationship between psychological empowerment and innovative work behavior. In other words, employees who are psychologically empowered are more likely to have high levels of psychological capital, which in turn leads to increased innovative work behavior.

This study examined the mediating role of psychological capital in the relationship between psychological empowerment and innovative work behavior in marketing employees at a financial services company in Indonesia. The findings of the study are significant for several reasons. First, the study provides empirical evidence that psychological capital mediates the relationship between psychological empowerment and innovative work behavior in a Balinese Indonesian setting. This is important because it suggests that psychological capital is a universal construct that can influence employee behavior in various cultural contexts. Second, the study highlights the importance of psychological empowerment in fostering innovation. Psychological empowerment is a state of mind in which employees feel confident in their abilities, have a sense of control over their work, and feel valued by their organization. Balinese culture places a high value on individual autonomy and self-expression, which suggests that psychological empowerment may be especially important for promoting innovation in Balinese workplaces. Third, the study provides practical recommendations for how companies in Bali can promote innovative work behavior in their marketing employees. Specifically, the study suggests that companies should focus on creating a supportive and collaborative work environment, providing opportunities for employees to develop their skills and knowledge, and recognizing and rewarding innovative behavior. Here are some specific examples of how companies in Bali can promote psychological empowerment and psychological capital in their marketing employees: Create a supportive and collaborative work environment: This can be done by encouraging employees to share ideas and feedback and providing opportunities for employees to work together on projects. Balinese culture emphasizes the importance of community and cooperation, so this type of work environment is likely well-received by Balinese employees. Provide opportunities for employees to develop their skills and knowledge: This can be done by offering training and development programs and encouraging employees to attend conferences and workshops. Balinese culture places a high value on education and lifelong learning, so this type of support is likely to be appreciated by Balinese employees. Recognize and reward innovative behavior: This can be done by publicly acknowledging innovative employees and providing financial and other rewards for innovative ideas. Balinese culture values creativity and innovation, so this recognition and reward will likely motivate Balinese employees to be more innovative. Overall, the findings of this study suggest that psychological capital plays an important role in mediating the relationship between psychological empowerment and innovative work behavior in marketing employees in Bali. Companies in Bali can promote innovative work behavior in their marketing employees by creating a supportive and collaborative work environment, providing opportunities for employees to develop their skills and knowledge, and recognizing and rewarding innovative behavior.

## 4 Conclusion

The objective of this research was to investigate how psychological capital acted as a mediator between psychological empowerment and innovative work behavior among marketing personnel employed by a financial services company based in Bali, Indonesia. Psychological capital partially mediated the relationship between psychological empowerment and innovative work behavior, according to the findings. The research emphasizes the significance of psychological empowerment in cultivating innovation, particularly within Balinese work environments that place a premium on personal independence and expression. Additionally, the study offers pragmatic suggestions on how businesses situated in Bali can foster a culture of innovation among their marketing personnel.

The cross-sectional design and single-company location of the study limited its applicability and capacity to establish causality. Subsequent investigations might explore the mediating effect of psychological capital in distinct cultural and industry contexts, in addition to exploring the potential influence of additional variables on innovative work behavior and psychological capital. Additionally, practical strategies for fostering psychological prosperity and empowerment in Balinese workplaces could be investigated.

## References

1. Volery, T., Tarabashkina, L.: The impact of organisational support, employee creativity and work centrality on innovative work behaviour. J. Bus. Res. **129**, 295–303 (2021)
2. Shah, S.T.H., Shah, S.M.A., El-Gohary, H.: Nurturing innovative work behaviour through workplace learning among knowledge workers of small and medium businesses. J. Knowl. Econ. (2022). https://doi.org/10.1007/s13132-022-01019-5
3. Al-shami, S.A., Al mamun, A., Rashid, N., Cheong, C.B.: Happiness at workplace on innovative work behaviour and organisation citizenship behaviour through moderating effect of innovative behaviour. Heliyon **9**, e15614 (2023)
4. Yasir, M., Majid, A., Yousaf, Z., Nassani, A.A., Haffar, M.: An integrative framework of innovative work behavior for employees in SMEs linking knowledge sharing, functional flexibility and psychological empowerment. Eur. J. Innov. Manag. **26**, 289–308 (2021)
5. Nguyen, H.T.N., Nguyen, H.T.T., Truong, A.T.L., Nguyen, T.T.P., Nguyen, A.V.: Entrepreneurial culture and innovative work behaviour: the mediating effect of psychological empowerment. J. Entrep. Emerg. Econ. **15**, 254–277 (2021)
6. Messmann, G.: Fostering proactive behaviour: the role of work-related reflection, psychological empowerment, and participative safety for innovative behaviour and job crafting. Int. J. Train. Dev. **27**, 99–116 (2022)
7. Younas, A., Wang, D., Javed, B., Haque, A.U.: Inclusive leadership and voice behavior: the role of psychological empowerment. J. Soc. Psychol. **163**, 174–190 (2022)
8. Sarwar, N., Haider, S., Akhtar, M.H., Bakhsh, K.: Moderated-mediation between ethical leadership and organizational citizenship behavior: the role of psychological empowerment and high performance managerial practices. Manag. Res. Rev. **46**, 649–666 (2022)
9. Lipińska-Grobelny, A., Zwardoń-Kuchciak, O.: Psychometric properties of the psychological capital questionnaire (KKaPsy). Curr. Issues Pers. Psychol. (2022). https://doi.org/10.5114/cipp.2021.112374
10. Flinkman, M., Rudman, A., Pasanen, M., Leino-Kilpi, H.: Psychological capital, grit and organizational justice as positive strengths and resources among registered nurses: a path analysis. Nurs. Open **10**, 5314–5327 (2023)
11. Juyumaya, J.: How psychological empowerment impacts task performance: the mediation role of work engagement and moderating role of age. Front. Psychol. **13**, 889936 (2022)
12. Karimi, S., Ahmadi Malek, F., Yaghoubi Farani, A., Liobikienė, G.: The role of transformational leadership in developing innovative work behaviors: the mediating role of employees' psychological capital. Sustainability **15**, 1267 (2023)
13. Chen, M., Mi, X., Xue, J., Li, Y., Shi, J.: The impact of entrepreneurial team psychological capital on innovation performance: the mediating role of knowledge sharing and knowledge hiding. Front. Psychol. **14**, 1133270 (2023)

14. Tager, A., Zaki, M., Ibrahim, A.: Linking psychological empowerment to innovative work behavior in hotels. Int. J. Tour. Hosp. Manag. **6**, 186–205 (2023)
15. Mustafa, M.J., Hughes, M., Ramos, H.M.: Middle-managers' innovative behavior: the roles of psychological empowerment and personal initiative. Int. J. Hum. Resour. Manag. **34**, 3464–3490 (2022)
16. Aldabbas, H., Pinnington, A., Lahrech, A., Blaique, L.: Extrinsic Rewards for Employee Creativity? The Role of Perceived Organisational Support, Work Engagement and Intrinsic Motivation. International Journal of Innovation Science (2023). https://doi.org/10.1108/ijis-08-2022-0165
17. Kim, M., Oja, B.D., Anagnostopoulos, C.: An expanded psychological capital (A-HERO) construct for creativity: building a competitive advantage for sport organisations. Eur. Sport Manag. Q. **23**, 722–744 (2021)
18. Ullah, I., Hameed, R.M., Mahmood, A.: The impact of proactive personality and psychological capital on innovative work behavior: evidence from software houses of Pakistan. Eur. J. Innov. Manag. (2023). https://doi.org/10.1108/ejim-01-2022-0022
19. Mehmood, K., Jabeen, F., Iftikhar, Y., Yan, M., Khan, A.N., AlNahyan, M.T., Alkindi, H.A., Alhammadi, B.A.: Elucidating the effects of organisational practices on innovative work behavior in UAE public sector organisations: the mediating role of employees' wellbeing. Appl. Psychol. Health Well Being **14**, 715–733 (2022)
20. Wei, X., He, Y.: Exploration on the role of transformational leadership linkage psychological empowerment in stimulating employees' innovation behavior in an uncertain environment: based on entrepreneurship perspective. Occup. Ther. Int. 1–11 (2022)
21. Mellita, D., Arsyad, S., Noviardy, A.: Covid-19 in the hospitality industry workforce: the resilience of hotel workers through human resource empowerment and motivation. Int. J. Appl. Sci. Tour. Events **6**, 96–105 (2022)
22. Li, Z., Ge, Z.: The impact of knowledge employees' psychological capital on their organizational employees' behaviors: the relationship among human resource flexible management, psychological capital and job performance. J. Sociol. Res. **11**, 39 (2020)
23. Berces, J.A.: Innovative measures in enhancing educational research in teacher education. Int. J. Soc. Sci. Educ. Res. **5**, 6–11 (2023)
24. Kennedy, I.: Sample size determination in test-retest and Cronbach Alpha reliability estimates. Br. J. Contemp. Educ. **2**, 17–29 (2022)
25. Schreiber, J.B., Nora, A., Stage, F.K., Barlow, E.A., King, J.: Reporting structural equation modeling and confirmatory factor analysis results: a review. J. Educ. Res. **99**, 323–338 (2006)
26. Hair Jr, J.F., Hult, G.T.M., Ringle, C.M., Sarstedt, M.: A primer on partial least squares structural equation modelling (PLS-SEM), 2nd edn. Sage Publications, Los Angeles (2017)

# Managing Employees with Disabilities: The Impact of Employer Behavior and Workplace Climate from an Employee Perspective in Israel

**Eslam Hujerat**

**Abstract** The primary goal of this study was to delve into the complex roles that employers, workplace climate, and acceptance play in shaping the experiences of employees with disabilities from the employees' perspective. The purpose of the study is to check which factors in the work environment directly affect the well-being and job satisfaction of disabled workers in Israel. The research focused on capturing the nuances of what it means to have an inclusive culture, emotional support, and open communication for employees. The study took the approach of a qualitative research method that tests the research hypothesis with the help of in-depth interviews with employees with disabilities. The literature review analyzed existing academic studies and reports to understand how the current research literature understands the field of employment of people with disabilities. In addition, a chapter on theoretical rationale was written that built a theoretical framework for the research hypothesis. In the research itself, interviews were conducted with three employees with different types of disabilities to collect first-hand experiences. These interviews enabled an in-depth exploration of participants' views on employer roles, workplace climate, and acceptance. The purpose of the study was to check if the answers of the respondents corresponded to the information available in the research literature by reviewing the study from a new direction. **The main contribution of this article aims to bridge this gap by investigating the issue specifically from the point of view of employees with disabilities rather than from the point of view of the employer.** The findings were in good agreement with the existing research claims in the existing literature. The study itself verified the hypothesis emerging in studies around the world that employers have a critical importance in creating an inclusive culture and providing emotional support. The research claim is that the workplace climate, shaped by policies and interpersonal relationships, significantly affects the experiences of disabled employees. Acceptance appeared as a key factor, with true acceptance having a positive effect on job satisfaction and general well-being. The study also highlighted the challenges facing employees when disclosing their disabilities and the existing gap between policy and practice.

---

E. Hujerat (✉)
Gaia College Research Institute, 6th Granados Str., Jerusalem, Israel
e-mail: islam.h@ts-hr.org.il

 
S. Kot et al. (eds.), *Corporate Practices: Policies, Methodologies, and Insights in Organizational Management*, Springer Proceedings in Business and Economics,
https://doi.org/10.1007/978-981-97-0996-0_50

**Keywords** Employees with disabilities · Workplace climate · Disability management · Disability acceptance

# 1 Introduction

In recent years, managing employees with disabilities has received increasing attention both in academia and in the corporate world. As organizations strive to become more inclusive, they have examined various dimensions of workplace management, including the development and implementation of organizational policies, the cultivation of workplace culture and climate, and the actions and roles of employers in driving an inclusive environment. While this focus has produced valuable insights into best practices and effective disability management strategies, most of the existing literature has been approached from an organizational or employer-focused lens. The main contribution of this article is to bridge this gap by investigating the issue specifically from the point of view of employees with disabilities and not from the point of view of the employer. It will explore the critical role that employers, workplace climate and organizational policies play in shaping their experiences and well-being, emphasizing the importance of understanding, and integrating these perspectives in ongoing efforts to create an inclusive and supportive work environment.

## *1.1 Historical Context*

Historically, the experience of workers with disabilities has been shaped and limited by various social attitudes, stigmas, and evolving legislative frameworks. At the begining the main social attitude was the Moral Approach to disability says that being disabled is a destiny, a punishment. Disability can be contagious, and they need to be moved out, like seek people. The next stage in the history of dissability evoloving social stigme was the Medical Approach to disssbility says that disabled people should not be removed, but they are distinct and need to be taken care of—but they are subtle50. In the early stages of disability research and awareness, human society mainly adopted the nursing and the medical model of disability50. This Social Approach to dissability is that there is no such thing dissability - there are social spaces that are sutible for a group of people - called dissabeled. But the main idea emphasized the physical or mental limitations are imposed by the society. The social space limitiation do not let this group of people to preform their individual's skills, talents, or potential contributions to the workplace. Only when the social space will stop being dissabled this group could preform and show their full potential. As a result, this narrow history perspective often resulted in exclusionary employment practices, as it did not take into account reasonable accommodations or workplace accommodations that could enable people with disabilities to perform effectively. Over time, the medical model was criticized for its limited scope and gradually gave way to a more holistic and social model of disability. This model claims that it is not the disability itself that is limiting but the space that is not adjust to the worker, the magers that do not have enough flexiblility to see how the working space disstarbe the emploee, the social attitudes and structural barriers that limit his working opportunities 51 A variety of legislative interventions accompanied the change in perspective to reduce discrimination and increase inclusion [1]. Key laws such as the Americans with Disabilities Act (ADA) [2] in the United States, the Equality [3] in the United Kingdom, and the [4] in Australia have helped shape a more equitable landscape for workers with disabilities. These laws require reasonable accommodations, prohibit discrimination, and promote equality, and thus are essential in making the workplace a more inclusive environment [5, 6].

The development of disability legislation often reflects the prevailing social attitudes of the time. Initially, legislation such as the Americans with Disabilities Act (ADA) from 1990 in the United States focused on providing physical access and protecting basic civil rights for people with disabilities, ensuring equal opportunities in employment, public accommodations, transportation, and other key areas [7]. Over time, societal approaches have shifted toward a broader understanding of inclusion, expanding beyond physical access to encompass workplace climate and cultural inclusion. This change is evident in the broader concept of accessibility, which in addition to physical accessibility, now also refers to aspects such as technology, attitudes, employee values, and reasonable accommodations in the workplace [8].

Moreover, the emergence of the telecommuting phenomenon, facilitated by technological advances, has brought new challenges and opportunities in disability management. The COVID-19 pandemic has accelerated the adoption of telecommuting, which is now recognized as a viable accommodation under the ADA and may increase employment opportunities for people with disabilities [9]. Remote work arrangements can particularly benefit people with disabilities by reducing work barriers, providing more flexible work environments, and alleviating physical challenges that may arise in traditional workplaces) [10, 11].

Legal perspectives on telecommuting accommodations for people with disabilities are also evolving. For example, there has been a marked decline in federal court rulings in favor of employers who denied disability-related telecommuting requests. This indicates a permanent change in the legal and organizational approach to remote work as a legitimate accommodation for people with disabilities. As telecommuting becomes a more integral part of the modern work environment, legislation and organizational policy will likely continue to evolve to address the unique challenges and opportunities it presents in disability management and inclusion [12]

## 1.2 *Defining Disability*

Historically, the Moral model of disability was the first to be introduced, suggesting that disabilities resulted from wrongdoings or sins51. It is believed that a divine force gave disabilities due to some fault of the individual. Even though this model isn't widely supported today, it sheds light on the ongoing negative attitudes towards disability, which often lead to discrimination; it helps us see the lingering stigma around disability [13]. While laws aim to address inequalities faced by disabled individuals, sometimes they might unintentionally uphold attitudes that further discrimination, especially if they follow the individual or medical model rather than the social model. In the United Kingdom, the definition of disability is now found in the Equality Act 2010 [3], identifying disability as a protected characteristic. According to the EqA 2010, disability is a physical or mental condition that significantly impacts daily activities over a long period. The term "impairment" in this context refers to a medical condition, and it has been broadened to cover not just physical, but also sensory and intellectual conditions [14].

## 1.3 Medical Model

In the past, research showed that disabled people were often seen in a negative light, being felt sorry for or seen as helpless [6, 15]. The medical model sees a disabled person's independence as limited by their disability. If doctors can't cure or help the person get better, then the person is seen as having limited chances to be part of society. So, a disability can sometimes make it hard for a person to join society, leading to them feeling left out. Doctors and medical experts have tried to fix or cure the disability, which can sometimes make the disabled person feel looked down upon or pitied [16]. This view has caused disagreements, especially among disabled people who challenge this thinking. This way of looking at disability often makes disabled people feel dependent and seen as sick [17]. This idea has also shown up in laws about disability, which don't help change people's attitudes but instead continue the problem.

Moreover, because of how our society values money and work, disabled people are often seen as less valuable, especially if they can't work or seem unable to work as much [18]. This view came about with the growth of a money-focused society needing a working force to be trained and productive [19]. This doesn't help disabled people as they don't get the chance to move up in the working world. If they can't work to make goods, they're seen as useless, leading to not just money problems but also social problems. This view, mentioned by Marx, makes it seem like disability is a personal problem needing medical help [19]. In short, it seems like the problem lies with the disabled person, which has been a negative view over time. However, not everyone agrees with this view. Many believe the real problem is how society and its structures were built without considering the different abilities of all people [20]. If disability is seen as the main problem, it becomes very hard or even impossible for a disabled person to participate in society. Some people and disability activists have used a different view, the social model, to challenge the medical model, aiming to change attitudes and solve the issues faced by disabled people. They believe this new view is the solution to the problems faced by disabled people.

### 1.4 Social Model

The social model came about as a response to the limitations of the medical model of disability [21]. Unlike the medical model, the social model aims to change long-standing attitudes towards disability, inspired in part by the civil rights movement in America during the 1960s and 1970s. This model encourages removing social barriers to foster inclusion and promotes societal change [22]. It shifts the focus from the disability to how society creates challenges for disabled individuals, marking a change from focusing on 'means of production' [23].

Over the past ten years, the social model has significantly influenced public policies and education in the United States, leading to a new way of defining disability concerning the social environment [18]. Instead of concentrating on the physical or cognitive aspects of disability, it looks at the broader external environment, suggesting that disability is a social construct. The goal is to alter the established attitudes present in discussions about disability. While disability activists have made some progress, oppression towards disabled individuals continues [21].

As a result, more research on care and disability has emerged, playing a crucial role in shaping policies in the United Kingdom and elsewhere. The term 'care' has often been seen as taking responsibility for someone, making disabled individuals feel powerless [24]. Kröger [24] notes that this view sees disabled people as passive, struggling to manage their lives. 'Disability' is often seen as an additional burden placed on disabled individuals by a discriminating society and institutions [19]. So, the focus shouldn't just be on medical treatment and tackling societal barriers to help disabled individuals overcome disadvantages.

Supporters of the social model see 'care' as a form of oppression and reject it as a term and concept. They critique both medical institutions and social policies. They believe that laws should help change ingrained attitudes and unconscious biases by addressing the social barriers disabled individuals face. This could challenge and change existing attitudes and perceptions, potentially improving the care and support for disabled individuals [25]. Various theories try to explain social inequality and exclusion by examining the assumptions surrounding disabled individuals [26]. Defining disability isn't simple, and understanding the difference between impairment and disability is crucial for grasping the social model and its influence on current laws.

## 2 Literature Review

### 2.1 *The Critical Role of the Employer in Managing Employees with Disabilities*

Studies suggest managerial attitudes can sometimes exhibit bias against employing individuals with disabilities, often underestimating their performance or doubting their competency for effective task execution [27]. In scenarios with a lack of proactive leadership or exposure to individuals with disabilities, such discriminatory attitudes may permeate among other staff members within organizations. Nonetheless, Hashim and Saodah [28] posit that through robust organizational leadership, education, and engagement with individuals with disabilities, it's possible to reform such stigmatizing and discriminatory attitudes in the professional environment.

Integrating employees with disabilities into the labor market has increasingly become a focal concern across various OECD countries. Systematic review unveils employers' significant role in averting premature exits from the labor market, particularly among workers grappling with health adversities [29]. Through an interdisciplinary lens, this review amalgamates evidence across occupational healthcare studies and economic evaluations focusing on work accommodations. This provides a nuanced understanding of employer strategies conducive to long-term work participation outcomes such as return to work, continued employment, and long-term disability.

The methodology encompassed a rigorous interdisciplinary search strategy across four distinguished databases to unearth essential concepts linking employer characteristics, work participation, and chronic diseases. A meticulous selection and quality assessment of studies were undertaken by independent reviewers, utilizing a standardized checklist to ascertain methodological quality. The review embraced 50 articles encompassing 52 individual studies, with a descriptive analysis synthesizing evidence.

Key findings from the review highlighted the salience of work accommodations in facilitating sustained employment and a quicker return to work post-illness. Various work accommodations such as employer change, work-time alteration, workplace interventions, professional assistance both within and outside the workplace, graded return to work, equipment assistance, and employer-provided health/disability insurance were found to have moderate evidence supporting their effectiveness. Additionally, the rapport between supervisors and workers was discerned to significantly impact continued employment and return to work, emphasizing the importance of social support in the workplace.

The discussion also delved into the varying evidence across different disease groups. It acknowledged the limitations inherent in the study design, including excluding qualitative and non-English language studies. Despite these limitations, the review underscored the instrumental role of employers in fostering a conducive work environment for individuals with disabilities. Providing work accommodations and nurturing a supportive supervisor-worker relationship were significant determinants of work participation outcomes [29].

Employers are instrumental in navigating disability matters within the workspace to guarantee equal opportunities and augment employment prospects for individuals with disabilities, as highlighted in the ILO report "Managing disability in the workplace" [30]. This initiative is anchored on the belief that integrating persons with disabilities in the workforce cultivates a diverse and inclusive work milieu alongside economic gains through adept disability management strategies. The code of practice outlined in the report offers practical advice aimed at nurturing a secure, accessible, and health-conscious workplace. It is designed to benefit many stakeholders, including private and public sector employers, workers' organizations, and persons with disabilities, emphasizing establishing a supportive ambiance to uphold employment.

Addressing discrimination, a crucial concern, requires a multifaceted approach encompassing direct and indirect forms of discrimination stemming from seemingly neutral situations or practices. The outlined practices in the report, such as employee assistance programs, job analysis, and Occupational Health Services (OHS), are pivotal in offering the requisite support, advice, and modifications to ensure a conducive work atmosphere for individuals with disabilities. The engagement in developing and implementing efficacious disability management strategies is essential. These strategies, to be devised in conjunction with various stakeholders like workers' representatives, disabled employees, OHS, and organizations of persons with disabilities, underscore the importance of work trials. These trials serve a dual purpose: they allow employers to gauge the abilities of individuals with disabilities in a real-work scenario and provide a platform for them to showcase their capabilities and acclimate to the work environment [30].

Work accommodations, a cornerstone of these strategies, entail adjustments in the workplace, workstations, and working conditions tailored to the needs of individuals with disabilities. Employers are at the forefront in facilitating these accommodations, which span changes in work schedules, provision of essential equipment, and ensuring workplace accessibility. This ethos extends to the recruitment process, where the principle of non-discrimination is paramount, focusing on assessing candidates' abilities over their disabilities. Engaging in open communication with disabled candidates and employees to discern any necessary disability-related adjustments is encouraged [30].

The significance of social support, particularly the rapport between Employers and workers, is paramount. A supportive milieu substantially contributes to the retention and productivity of workers with disabilities. Moreover, awareness and adherence to occupational safety and health standards are crucial in fostering a safe and conducive work environment [30].

Some researchers recommend distinguishing between the types of disabilities and claim different results depending on the type of disability. Research exhibits that, given appropriate training and support, workers with intellectual disabilities often excel in their roles [31]. Moreover, supportive and inclusive managerial practices are positively linked with favorable work outcomes for people with disabilities

[32]. Conversely, unfair and discriminatory treatment from managers or colleagues typically leads to adverse outcomes. Particularly, workers with mental health issues experience more negative work circumstances than those with physical disabilities.

It becomes apparent that there's a disparity in management knowledge and support concerning accommodation for workers with different types of disabilities. For instance, physical disability accommodations often revolve around altering the physical work environment, which might raise concerns among employers regarding budget impacts and among colleagues regarding perceived special treatment. In contrast, accommodations for individuals with intellectual disabilities might include shorter shift times and additional mentoring, focusing more on job design and training. Management's apprehension towards employing individuals with mental health disabilities is often exacerbated by concerns surrounding disclosure of such disabilities, the unpredictable nature of some mental health conditions, and ensuring a safe working environment for all [33].

Discrimination and stereotyping significantly affect the employment outcomes for individuals with disabilities. The literature underscores that prior positive interactions with individuals with disabilities can mitigate stereotyping and foster more inclusive attitudes among management and employees. Especially in the case of mental health disabilities, the lack of clear symptoms often leads to skepticism and stigma, resulting in overt and covert discrimination. Similarly, social integration issues arise for individuals with intellectual disabilities due to negative attitudes, often leading to social exclusion at work [33].

The employment outcomes for individuals with disabilities are notably affected by the aforementioned factors. Low employment rates are a common outcome across all three disability types discussed, largely due to a lack of employer knowledge, support, and prevailing negative attitudes. Management's expectation of poor outcomes for workers with disabilities seems to be a self-fulfilling prophecy, adversely impacting employment rates. However, organizations employing best practices exhibit better integration and support for individuals with disabilities, indicating the critical role of informed, supportive, and inclusive employer practices in enhancing the employment experiences and outcomes for individuals with disabilities [33], as delineated in the ILO's "Managing disability in the workplace" report.

## *2.2 The Critical Role of the Workplace Climate in Managing Employees with Disabilities*

The climate within a workplace significantly influences how employees with disabilities are managed and integrated into the organizational culture. One of the primary concerns for individuals with disabilities revolves around disclosing their disability, fearing disparate treatment in hiring processes, workplace interactions, and advancement opportunities. These concerns are particularly pronounced among individuals with non-apparent disabilities. Despite these fears, a notable majority (80%) chose to disclose their disability, driven by various factors such as accommodation or a desire for honesty and openness. However, nearly a quarter of those who disclosed faced long-term negative consequences, emphasizing the tangible impact of disability disclosure on workplace experiences [34].

Moreover, the broader workplace culture and the perceived commitment of the employer towards disability inclusion play pivotal roles in individuals' decisions to disclose their disabilities. Various organizational practices, such as incorporating disability in the organization's diversity statement, featuring individuals with apparent disabilities in promotional materials, and encouraging applicants with disabilities in recruitment materials, can significantly bolster trust in the organization's commitment to disability inclusion. Witnessing individuals with disabilities succeed in the workplace also positively influences others' decisions to disclose their disabilities, enhancing the overall inclusivity of the workplace climate. Additionally, disability-focused employee resource groups serve as a tangible manifestation of organizational commitment, particularly impacting the disclosure decisions of individuals with less apparent disabilities [34].

Furthermore, the anticipation of equitable opportunities in career advancement significantly influences the decision to disclose disabilities, especially among individuals with less apparent disabilities and those not engaged as disability service providers. Integrating individuals with disabilities into mentoring programs or other training opportunities, akin to initiatives aimed at bolstering the representation of other historically underrepresented groups, could be instrumental in fostering a more inclusive and supportive workplace climate. Through such initiatives, organizations can substantially improve the management and integration of employees with disabilities, aligning with the broader organizational ethos of inclusivity and diversity [34].

The term "disability climate" encapsulates the perceptions within a workplace that significantly impact the experiences of workers with disabilities. This climate is influenced at various levels—societal, peri-organizational, organizational, and within work groups. At a societal level, laws and general attitudes toward individuals with disabilities form a backdrop against which other interactions occur. Industry-specific attitudes at the peri-organizational level further shape the disability climate. The organization's management plays a significant role in shaping the disability climate through policies, procedures, practices, and attitudes toward workers with disabilities. For instance, celebrating the achievements of employees with disabilities in organizational newsletters sends a strong positive message to all members [35].

On a more micro level, the workgroup, including coworkers and supervisors, has the most immediate impact on the disability climate perceived by individual workers with disabilities. Supervisors' attitudes and coworkers' support levels are crucial in shaping this climate. For example, a supervisor who includes disability awareness education in staff meetings and acknowledges those who assist a worker with a disability fosters a positive disability climate. The extent to which upper management supports such attitudes and implements policies indicative of organization-level priorities integrates into the shared perception of the disability climate [35].

Specific program components at the organizational and workgroup levels can be instituted to enhance the disability climate. At the organizational level, these may include reviewing and modifying hiring and return-to-work policies, ensuring management communications reflect positive attitudes towards disabilities, and ensuring new employee orientation programs cover disability awareness topics. At the workgroup level, reviewing worksite accommodations, ensuring job descriptions comply with the Americans with Disabilities Act, and providing disability case management services are some steps that can be taken. Training and education about disabilities, provision of necessary accommodations, and ongoing monitoring and assessment of occupational stress levels of workers with disabilities are essential components of fostering a positive disability climate. Through these measures, the workplace can better manage the stress and integration of employees with disabilities, thereby promoting a healthier and more inclusive work environment [35].

## *2.3 The Critical Role of Acceptance in Managing Employees with Disabilities*

The notion of "acceptance" in employment for individuals with disabilities lacks a clear definition despite being crucial for understanding and fostering inclusivity in the workplace. Various international laws and conventions, such as the UN Convention on the Rights of Persons with Disabilities [36] and the Americans with Disabilities Act [2], emphasize the rights of individuals with disabilities to participate in societal aspects, including employment, on an equal basis, they primarily focus on prohibiting discrimination and safeguarding rights rather than elaborating on what acceptance entails in an employment scenario.

The Developmental Disabilities Assistance and Bill of Rights Act of 2000 delves slightly deeper by associating acceptance with inclusion and encouraging participation of individuals with disabilities in various societal spheres by those without disabilities. This includes fostering relationships, ensuring access to community resources, and enabling active participation in community activities and employment, similar to individuals without disabilities.

In academia, the lack of a definitive conceptualization of acceptance has led to operational definitions based on the level and quality of interactions between employees with disabilities and their non-disabled colleagues. For instance, as defined by Gates et al. [37], social processes focus on the structure and quality of relationships, emphasizing emotional and informational support. Cramm et al. [38], draw on the contact hypothesis and relationship typologies, respectively, to explain how familiarity and the nature of relationships among colleagues can signify levels of acceptance and integration. Furthermore, acceptance has been conceptualized regarding attitudes, fairness perceptions, and employment judgments concerning employees with disabilities [39].

Building upon Fishbein and Ajzen's Theory of Reasoned Action [40], acceptance can be seen as an evaluative response stemming from attitudes toward individuals with disabilities. This response is multi-dimensional, encompassing cognitive, affective, and behavioral aspects. In a workplace setting, cognitive acceptance entails recognizing and understanding an employee with a disability as a full group member, acknowledging their competencies while tolerating impairments. The affective dimension covers the emotions and feelings towards the employee with a disability, aiming for a lack of reservations or negative emotions in interactions. The behavioral dimension embodies the actions and reactions towards the individual, ideally encompassing full access to common areas, events, and integration in both professional and social job activities.

Thus, as depicted through these dimensions, a comprehensive understanding of acceptance is fundamental to ensuring that employees with disabilities are treated as full members of the work community. This acceptance does not merely seek conformity to standards but appreciates the unique contributions of individuals with disabilities, recognizing disability as a natural aspect of the co-worker and valuing the performance they bring to the table.

In conclusion, while there is a considerable body of research examining the role of employers in managing employees with disabilities and the efficacy of workplace policies and programs, one area that remains notably underexplored is the perspective of the disabled employees themselves. There is growing evidence that subjective measures like job satisfaction and workplace commitment correlate with objective outcomes like job retention and performance. However, there is still a significant gap in the literature concerning how disabled employees perceive their work environment, employer attitudes, and supportive policies and practices. Given this, the next section will delve into existing findings in this under-researched area to gain insights into the lived experiences and perceptions of disabled employees in the workplace.

## 3 Methodology

### *3.1 The Purpose of the Study*

The main purpose of this paper is to examine the critical role of employer behavior, workplace climate, and acceptance in managing employees with disabilities from the employees' perspective. The innovation in the research is the emphasis on the perspectives of the employees, offering an inside look into the experiences and expectations of people with disabilities in the workplace.

### 3.2 *The Research Hypothesis*

The study hypothesizes that a higher level of understanding on the part of employers for the special needs of employees with disabilities can improve the occupational climate in the workplace that employs employees with disabilities.

### 3.3 *Research Method*

To test this hypothesis, the article takes the qualitative approach. The research literature will present quantitative studies and will include information from official reports of the Israeli government that include industry reports, surveys, and studies done by professionals and researchers from the Israeli academy.

The qualitative research will include in-depth interviews with employees with disabilities who will try to test the research hypothesis from the perspective of the employees. The interviews will cover various topics, from personal experiences to perceptions of employer behavior and company policy. These interviews offer an additional layer of depth, and provide first-hand accounts that enrich the research.

### 3.4 *The Study Population*

The subject population is people with disabilities in Israel who work in various commercial companies and own companies that employ the employees under the Israeli Leron Act from 2009, which regulates the employment of disabled workers in Israel.

## 4 The Research—The Answers Given in the Qualitative In-depth Interviews Compared to the Quantitative Information That Appears in the Literature

### 4.1 *The Critical Role of the Employer in Managing Employees with Disabilities from the Employees' Point of View*

**Literature Review:** The study establishes that perceptions of work and management differ significantly between disabled and non-disabled employees in Britain. Disabled employees, particularly those with work limitations, hold more negative perceptions of their work and management across various metrics, including commitment, job satisfaction, and influence over work. The gap in perceptions suggests a significant role for employers in shaping the work experience for disabled employees. Employers could focus on areas where negative perceptions are most pronounced, such as management's interaction with employees and their level of commitment and satisfaction toward their job [41].

From the employees' perspective, the role of the employer, particularly line managers, is critical in managing employees with disabilities. Employees feel that inflexibility in work patterns, such as restrictions on leave or breaks, poses significant challenges that employers often do not adequately address. For instance, individuals who had to leave their jobs due to newly developed impairments felt that many aspects of their roles could have been adapted to allow them to continue working effectively. Effective line management is seen as a cornerstone for creating an inclusive environment. Employees value managers who are aware of their team's needs and allow flexibility in the working day. For example, the ideal manager, according to disabled employees, would adapt their approach to individual needs, allowing for flexibility in work schedules and even job roles [42].

Moreover, employees often face barriers when it comes to disclosing their disabilities or health conditions, expressing concerns about how this information would be received by management and colleagues. They appreciate managers who can deliver small-scale adjustments without bureaucratic hurdles, emphasizing the importance of open communication and understanding. For example, exemplary line managers were described as those who informally ask people how they are, especially when they start work in a new role or return after a leave of absence. Overall, from the employees' viewpoint, the employer's role in managing disabilities at the workplace is pivotal, requiring a nuanced approach that includes flexibility, open communication, and a deep understanding of individual needs [42].

In addition, One significant point is the importance of creating a more inclusive working culture. Employees believe that positive attitudes towards disabled people in the workplace can only come from a broader societal shift towards equality. They feel that employers have a role in promoting this inclusion and respect. For example, many participants felt that increasing the number of disabled people within the workforce would counter negative assumptions and break down feelings of 'otherness' [42].

Employees also categorize their relationships with employers into different types, such as 'Shut out,' 'Dysfunctional,' 'Functional but not fruitful,' 'Successfully supportive,' and 'The perfect partnership'. For instance, in 'Shut out' relationships, employees feel they wouldn't even get past the interview stage in certain sectors due to the high importance placed on image, efficiency, and reliability. In 'Dysfunctional' relationships, employees describe distressing experiences, especially when an impairment or health condition begins to affect them, leading to a complete breakdown in the relationship [42].

*Interviews.* The employer's role in managing employees with disabilities is multifaceted and varies significantly depending on the type of disability and the individual's unique needs. The interviews provided valuable insights into how employees with different disabilities perceive their employer's role in this context.

*Interviewee 1 (Physical Disability).* The first interviewee, who has a physical disability, highlighted the employer's efforts in making tangible accommodations like installing ramps and automatic doors. These actions were appreciated and considered a commitment to legal compliance and accessibility. However, the interviewee also pointed out gaps in "softer" aspects of management, such as fostering an inclusive culture and emotional support. He mentioned that his line manager initially struggled with communicating effectively about his disability, leading to awkward situations and task assignments that didn't consider his limitations. Over time, the manager improved, but the interviewee emphasized that employers should go beyond physical accommodations to include staff education and foster a culture of inclusion.

*Interviewee 2 (Bipolar Disorder).* The second interviewee, who has bipolar disorder, expressed mixed feelings about their employer's role. While the company has policies on mental health and inclusion, the implementation in real-life situations was inconsistent. The interviewee faces challenges in maintaining consistent performance due to severe mood swings, a symptom of their condition. Despite being open about her disorder, she felt that the employer was not fully understanding or accommodating her needs. She had requested flexibility, such as working from home on difficult days, but this was met with resistance. However, she also noted that her direct supervisor was more understanding and allowed short breaks, which was seen as a "lifesaver."

*Interviewee 3 (Intellectual Disability).* The third interviewee, who has an intellectual disability, had a more positive view of their employer's role. He appreciated that his boss took the time to explain tasks in a way he could understand and provided written lists to help him remember his duties. This approach was considered considerate and helpful, allowing the interviewee to perform their job more effectively.

### 4.2 The Critical Role of the Workplace Climate in Managing Employees with Disabilities from the Employees' Point of View

**Literature Review:** Workplace climate is another significant factor the study identifies in the perceptions of disabled employees. The study finds little difference in the disability gap in perceptions between the public and private sectors. However, it does note that workplaces with active disability policies—especially those encouraging applications from disabled candidates—have a narrower perception gap. While not statistically significant, this suggests that the overall workplace climate, including corporate culture and active disability policies, is critical in how disabled employees perceive their work environment. The study also notes the potential role of corporate culture as measured by general employee views, indicating that the nature of the workplace can influence the experience of disabled employees [41]. Some evidence suggests that an equal opportunities policy positively affects disabled employees' perceptions of fair treatment. However, these benefits do not extend to other equality measures such as workplace accommodations [43, 44].

Workplace climate is pivotal in how employees with disabilities experience their professional lives. Many participants in the study conducted for the Equality and Human Rights Commission's Working Better program revealed that their experiences were shaped not just by company policies or legal frameworks but rather by their colleagues' and supervisors' attitudes and behaviors. Most employees felt the existing workplace culture was not conducive to unlocking their full potential [42].

The most glaring issue cited by many was a general "ignorance about impairments and health conditions." For instance, a female participant from Cardiff suffering from a mental health condition lamented, "The worst thing for me is [the attitude of]: 'Pull yourself together! Get your act together! What's the matter with you?' It's that dismissive attitude that is difficult to deal with. It's a misunderstanding of how it [depression] works… to other people, it's trivial, but it's not to us." This ignorance often manifests in a lack of awareness among managers, leading to a poor understanding of employees' needs and leading them to make uninformed decisions [42].

Negative assumptions about capabilities were another prominent barrier. Employees felt the label 'disabled' led their colleagues and supervisors to underestimate them or make unjust assumptions. A male participant with dyslexia from London stated, "It's not known in the workplace. If you've got dyslexia, it's just not known because they haven't been in the circumstance. They just say you are lazy or you aren't working hard enough." This assumption has real-world implications, affecting these individuals' job opportunities and career progression [42].

Bullying and harassment also emerged as a critical issue. The perception that employees with disabilities received 'special treatment' often led to resentment among colleagues. The study reveals a poignant sentiment where relationships with management and coworkers are "often typified by suspicion, discomfort or fear." Participants felt discrimination was particularly common during the recruitment and selection stage. This produced high levels of anxiety and pessimism about re-entering the workforce among those currently unemployed [42].

*Interviews.* Workplace climate and organizational culture are pivotal in shaping employees' experiences with disabilities. The interviews offer a nuanced understanding of how these factors can either facilitate or hinder the inclusion and well-being of disabled employees.

*Interviewee 1 (Physical Disability).* The first interviewee emphasized the significant role that workplace atmosphere and organizational culture play in supporting employees with disabilities. He experiences a generally inclusive atmosphere in his current organization, particularly within his immediate team. His colleagues go out of their way to ensure he is comfortable and can perform his job effectively. This positive atmosphere directly impacts on his job satisfaction and overall well-being. However, he also recounted a contrasting experience in a previous organization where the culture was unsupportive. Activities were planned without considering his limitations, leading to feelings of isolation and neglect. He stressed that a supportive atmosphere is not just about physical adjustments but also about attitudes, awareness, and the general ethos of the organization.

*Interviewee 2 (Bipolar Disorder).* The second interviewee described her current workplace atmosphere as "a nightmare" for managing mental disabilities. She feels her colleagues are polite but distant, walking on eggshells around her since she disclosed her bipolar disorder. This has led to a sense of not belonging and feeling misunderstood. However, she had a different experience in a previous job where the culture was open and accepting, even allowing mental health days without judgment. She emphasized that the atmosphere and culture could make or break an employee's experience, stating it's not just about physical accommodations like ramps or elevators but also about how people treat you.

*Interviewee 3 (Intellectual Disability).* The third interviewee had a more positive view of his current workplace. He feels that everyone is nice and treats him equally, contributing to a welcoming and inclusive atmosphere. His boss reinforces this by stating that the company aims for everyone to feel welcome, supported by posters promoting kindness and inclusivity. This positive atmosphere makes him feel good about his job and himself.

### *4.3 The Critical Role of Acceptance in Managing Employees with Disabilities from the Employees' Point of View*

*Literature Review.* Acceptance in the workplace emerges as another critical factor in managing employees with disabilities. The study finds that disabled employees feel more positive in environments with a high level of manager-employee consultation and where general views of managerial treatment are positive. In such settings, the disability gap in perceptions is considerably reduced or even eliminated. This underscores the importance of workplace acceptance from management and co-workers as a critical element in shaping the work experiences and perceptions of disabled employees [41].

Acceptance within the workplace is a significant factor for employees with disabilities. Data shows that those with disabilities or long-term illnesses are more likely to report experiences of unfair treatment, including issues with employment rights and the allocation of work hours [43, 45]. Even when demographic and workplace variables are controlled for, disabled workers report more negative treatment at work [46]. Internationally, studies from Canada and Spain have shown that disabled employees generally have lower job satisfaction, however, the returns to employment characteristics like hourly earnings are higher for disabled workers, likely due to lower expectations [47, 48].

The concept of acceptance in the workplace is a multifaceted issue that significantly impacts the job satisfaction and overall well-being of employees with disabilities. Research by Kim [49] has shown that job satisfaction varies among individuals depending on their type of disability. Notably, individuals with depression or anxiety reported significantly lower job satisfaction levels than those with physical or other types of disabilities. This research also found a negative association between disability stigma and job satisfaction, while a positive correlation was identified between acceptance and job satisfaction. Importantly, acceptance was found to moderate the relationship between disability stigma and job satisfaction, emphasizing its critical role in the workplace.

These findings resonate with employees' experiences, as Adams and Oldfieldm [42] reported. From the employees' perspective, acceptance is deeply intertwined with workplace culture and line managers' attitudes. It goes beyond compliance with legal requirements like reasonable adjustments; it's about fostering an inclusive environment where employees are accommodated and genuinely valued. For instance, employees appreciate line managers who communicate openly and display empathy. One participant with a physical impairment shared her experience of initially facing skepticism from colleagues about her ability to perform her job. However, she proved herself and gained acceptance, highlighting the need for employees with disabilities to work harder to prove their capabilities.

*Interviews.* The role of acceptance and stigma in the workplace is a critical factor that significantly impacts the experiences of employees with disabilities. The interviews offer a nuanced view of how these elements can either facilitate or hinder the well-being and job satisfaction of disabled employees.

*Interviewee 1 (Physical Disability).* The first interviewee emphasized acceptance's powerful role in shaping employees' experiences with disabilities. In his current organization, he feels a strong sense of acceptance from both colleagues and line managers, which has positively impacted his job satisfaction and overall well-being. This acceptance has created a positive feedback loop, motivating him to contribute to the team. However, he also recounted a contrasting experience in a previous job where he felt stigmatized. He felt that his contributions during team meetings were not taken as seriously as those of his non-disabled colleagues, leading to a sense of marginalization and a constant need to prove himself. The experience was exhausting and demoralizing, highlighting the negative impact of stigma on job satisfaction and mental well-being.

*Interviewee 2 (Bipolar Disorder).* The second interviewee described her experience as a complex interplay between acceptance and stigma. She feels an unspoken stigma surrounding mental health conditions in her current job. She noticed a change in how colleagues treated her after disclosing her condition, leading to feelings of frustration and isolation. However, she also mentioned a form of "tolerance" that falls short of genuine acceptance. While accommodation is made, such as allowing her to take breaks, they are done in a way that makes her uncomfortable. In contrast, her previous job had a higher level of acceptance, where people were educated about different types of disabilities, including mental conditions. This acceptance made her feel valued and respected, significantly impacting her job satisfaction and mental health.

*Interviewee 3 (Intellectual Disability).* The third interviewee had a more positive view, stating that acceptance is "really, really important." He feels genuinely included and valued by his colleagues and boss, positively impacting his job performance and overall happiness. His boss emphasizes that everyone has something special to bring to the table, reinforcing the organization's acceptance culture.

# 5 Findings and Discussion

## *5.1 The Critical Role of the Employer in Managing Employees with Disabilities*

The findings from the interviews conducted for this study offer a nuanced perspective that aligns closely with existing literature on the role of employers in managing employees with disabilities. Both sources underscore the multifaceted nature of this role, which extends beyond mere compliance with legal requirements [41, 42]. In fact, the need for an inclusive culture, emotional support, and open communication is emphasized across the board [29, 30].

For instance, the first interviewee, who has a physical disability, appreciated the tangible accommodations made by the employer, such as installing ramps and automatic doors. This observation dovetails with the literature, highlighting the importance of physical work accommodations [29, 30]. However, the interviewee went a step further to point out the need for an inclusive culture and emotional support. This echoes sentiments from the literature that effective line management and an inclusive environment are crucial for the well-being of employees with disabilities [42].

Similarly, the second interviewee, who has bipolar disorder, expressed mixed feelings about her employer's role. While the company had policies in place for mental health, the implementation was inconsistent. This resonates with the literature's emphasis on the need for flexibility in work patterns and the pivotal role of line managers in creating an inclusive environment [42]. Moreover, the literature points out that managerial attitudes can sometimes exhibit bias against employing individuals with disabilities, particularly those with mental health issues [27, 33]. This is a sentiment that the second interviewee also shared, highlighting the gap between policy and practice.

On a more positive note, the third interviewee, who has an intellectual disability, had a more favorable view of their employer's role. They appreciated the individualized support provided, which aligns with the literature's recommendation for distinguishing between types of disabilities and tailoring support accordingly [31, 32]. This individualized approach benefits the employee and enriches the organization by fostering a diverse and inclusive work environment [30].

The interviews and the literature review also highlight the barriers employees face when disclosing their disabilities [42]. This emphasizes the importance of open communication and understanding from employers, which is often overlooked but crucial for creating a supportive work environment [30]. While the interviews did not explicitly address the need for a broader societal shift towards equality, the emphasis on the need for an inclusive culture and the role of employers in fostering this culture indirectly supports this notion [42].

## 5.2 The Critical Role of the Workplace Climate in Managing Employees with Disabilities

The interviews conducted for this study offer a nuanced understanding of how workplace climate and organizational culture can either facilitate or hinder the inclusion and well-being of disabled employees. This aligns closely with the literature, which also emphasizes the pivotal role of workplace climate in shaping the experiences of employees with disabilities [34, 41, 42].

For instance, the first interviewee, who has a physical disability, highlighted the importance of a supportive atmosphere, which is not just about physical adjustments but also about attitudes, awareness, and the general ethos of the organization. This sentiment resonates with the literature, which notes that workplaces with active disability policies have a narrower perception gap among disabled employees [41]. Moreover, the literature suggests that the overall workplace climate, including corporate culture and active disability policies, is critical in how disabled employees perceive their work environment [44, 43].

The second interviewee, who has bipolar disorder, described her current workplace atmosphere as "a nightmare," emphasizing that the atmosphere and culture could make or break an employee's experience. This is consistent with the literature, which reveals that experiences are shaped not just by company policies or legal frameworks but rather by colleagues' and supervisors' attitudes and behaviors [42]. The literature also highlights the tangible impact of disability disclosure on workplace experiences, a concern echoed by the second interviewee [34].

The third interviewee had a more positive view of his current workplace, emphasizing the role of a welcoming and inclusive atmosphere. This aligns with the literature's focus on the importance of supervisors' attitudes and coworkers' support levels in shaping the disability climate within a workplace [35].

## 5.3 The Critical Role of Acceptance in Managing Employees with Disabilities

The interviews provide fresh insights into the complex dynamics of acceptance and stigma in the workplace, enriching our understanding of their tangible impact on employees with disabilities. These firsthand accounts serve as a real-world validation of academic studies that have similarly highlighted the pivotal role of acceptance in the professional lives of disabled individuals [41, 43].

For instance, the first interviewee, who has a physical disability, highlighted the powerful role of acceptance in shaping his experiences. He felt genuinely valued by his colleagues and line managers, which positively impacted his job satisfaction and overall well-being. This sentiment resonates with the literature, which underscores the importance of workplace acceptance from management and co-workers as a critical element in shaping the work experiences of disabled employees [41]. Moreover, the literature suggests that disabled employees generally have lower job satisfaction but higher returns to employment characteristics like hourly earnings, likely due to lower expectations [47, 48].

The second interviewee, who has bipolar disorder, described her experience as a complex interplay between acceptance and stigma. She noticed a change in how colleagues treated her after disclosing her condition, leading to feelings of frustration and isolation. This is consistent with the literature, which reveals that those with disabilities or long-term illnesses are more likely to report experiences of unfair treatment, including issues with employment rights and the allocation of work hours [43, 45]. The literature also highlights a negative association between disability stigma and job satisfaction, while a positive correlation was identified between acceptance and job satisfaction [49].

The third interviewee stated that acceptance is "really, really important." He feels genuinely included and valued by his colleagues and boss, positively impacting his job performance and overall happiness. This aligns with the literature's focus on the importance of acceptance in fostering an inclusive environment where employees are accommodated and genuinely valued [42].

## 6 Conclusions

This study delves into the intricate role's employers, workplace climate, and acceptance play in managing employees with disabilities. The study uncovers a multi-faceted landscape beyond mere legal compliance through interviews and a comprehensive literature review. It emphasizes the critical need for an inclusive culture, emotional support, open communication, and genuine acceptance in the workplace. The interviews serve as a real-world validation of academic literature, offering nuanced insights into the tangible impact of these factors on the well-being and job satisfaction of employees with disabilities.

The role of employers: Employers play a central role beyond the requirements of the law. They help create an inclusive culture and provide emotional support.

Workplace climate: The climate in an organization significantly affects the experiences of employees with disabilities. A supportive atmosphere, shaped by policies and interpersonal relationships, is essential to the well-being of disabled employees.

The role of acceptance: Acceptance in the workplace is emerging as a critical factor that can facilitate or hinder the experiences of employees with disabilities. The research reveals that true acceptance has a positive effect on job satisfaction and general well-being.

Barriers to disclosure: both the interviews and the literature highlight the challenges facing employees when disclosing their disability, emphasizing the need for open communication, and understanding on the part of employers.

Recommendations for employers: Employers are encouraged to foster an inclusive culture, provide personal support, and allow open communication to create a supportive work environment.

Recommendations for future research: due to the findings in the article, future studies examining the employment of people with disabilities should investigate the issue more from the perspective of the employed and not necessarily of the employers. As is evident from the data in the article, employees with disabilities are people with different needs than regular employees. Therefore, the labor market should not recruit them as ordinary employees and researchers should not proceed from the point of assumption that these are ordinary research subjects.

## References

1. Bunbury, S.: Unconscious bias and the medical model: How the social model may hold the key to transformative thinking about disability discrimination. Int. J. Discrim. Law **19**(1), 26–47 (2019)
2. United States: Americans with Disabilities Act of 1990. Public Law No. 101–336. United States statutes at large, vol. 104, pp. 327–378 (1990)
3. Equality Act.: Chapter 15. Her Majesty's Stationery Office (2010)
4. Disability Discrimination Act.: No. 135. Commonwealth of Australia (1992)
5. Galily, D., Schwartz, D., Gurstein, B.: Education and the labor market In Israel. University of World and National Economy Academic Press, Bulgaria (2019)
6. Fuchs, H.: Psychological flexibility and attitudes towards disability. PhD dissertation. Faculty of Educational Studies. Adam Mickiewicz University, Poznan (2021). https://hdl.handle.net/10593/26450
7. Parrott-Sheffer, C.: Americans with Disabilities Act (2023). Britannica. https://www.britannica.com/topic/Americans-with-Disabilities-Act
8. IncludeAbility.: Creating an accessible and inclusive workplace: IncludeAbility (n.d.) https://includeability.gov.au/resources-employers/creating-accessible-and-inclusive-workplace
9. Gould, R., Mullin, C., Harris, S.P.: Teleworking and the ADA. Adata (2021). https://adata.org/research_brief/research-brief-teleworking-and-ada
10. Galily, D., Petkova, T.: Grammar of the unity in Europe—the case of Russia. In: Collection of the 5th International e-Conference on Studies in Humanities and Social Sciences, Serbia, 28 of June, 2020
11. Gonzales, M.: Remote Work Helps People with Disabilities Land Jobs. SHRM (2022). https://www.shrm.org/resourcesandtools/hr-topics/behavioral-competencies/global-and-cultural-effectiveness/pages/remote-work-helps-people-with-disabilities-land-jobs.aspx
12. Iafolla, R.: Covid's Remote Work Experience Is Slowly Changing Disability Law. Bloomberg Law (2023). https://news.bloomberglaw.com/daily-labor-report/covids-remote-work-experience-is-slowly-changing-disability-law
13. McTigue, P.: The challenge of HIV—social stigma or disability? Web J. Curr. Legal Issues **5**, 1–13 (2010)
14. Fuchs, H.: Attitudes of parents and children towards people with disabilities and their integration into society. Cul.-Soc.-Educ. **20**(2), 91–109. Poznan: Adam Mickiewicz University Press. ISSN: 2300-0422, ISSN (Online): 2719–2717 (2022). https://doi.org/10.14746/kse.2021.20.5

15. Payne, G.: Social Divisions. Palgrave Macmillan, London (2006)
16. Woodhams, C., Corby, S.: Defining disability in theory and practice: a critique of the British Disability Discrimination Act 1995. J. Soc. Policy **32**(2), 159–178 (2003)
17. Finkelstein, V.: Re-thinking care in a society providing equal opportunities for all. In: Meeting of the World Health Organisation, Geneva, Switzerland (1998)
18. Anastasiou, D., Kauffman, J.M.: The social model of disability: dichotomy between impairment and disability. J. Med. Philos. **38**(4), 441–459 (2013)
19. Terzi, L.: The social model of disability: a philosophical critique. J. Appl. Philos. **21**(2), 141–157 (2004)
20. Asch, A.: Critical race theory, feminism, and disability: Reflections on social justice and personal identity. Ohio St. LJ **62**, 391 (2001)
21. Lang, R.: The Development and Critique of the Social Model of Disability. Leonard Cheshire Disability and Inclusive Development Centre, London (2007)
22. Shakespeare, T., Watson, N.: The social model of disability: an outdated ideology? In: Exploring Theories and Expanding Methodologies: Where We Are and Where We Need to Go, pp. 9–28. Emerald Group Publishing Limited (2001)
23. Fuchs, H., Fuchs, A.: Psychological flexibility and higher levels of quality of life. In: Quality Festival 2023, International Quality Conference, vol. 14, pp. 2147–2148. University of Kragujevac Press, Kragujevac. ISBN 978-86-6335-104-2 (2023)
24. Kröger, T.: Care research and disability studies: nothing in common? Crit. Soc. Policy **29**(3), 398–420 (2009)
25. Kelly, C.: Making 'care' accessible: personal assistance for disabled people and the politics of language. Crit. Soc. Policy **31**(4), 562–582 (2011)
26. Fuchs, H., & Amar, I.: The ability to self-advocate, the right to have the student's independent status heard in the Eligibility and Characterization Committee. Mind, body and soul. In: The 6th National Scientific Conference of the National Center for Relations between Education Teams and Parents. Levinsky Academic Center, Tel Aviv (2023)
27. Jones, P., Schmidt, R.A.: Retail employment and disability. Int. J. Retail Distrib. Manag. **32**(9), 426–429 (2004)
28. Hashim, J., Wok, S.: Predictors to employees with disabilities' organisational behaviour and involvement in employment. Equal. Divers. Incl. Int. J. **33**(2), 193–209 (2014)
29. Jansen, J., van Ooijen, R., Koning, P.W.C., et al.: The role of the employer in supporting work participation of workers with disabilities: a systematic literature review using an interdisciplinary approach. J. Occup. Rehabil. **31**(4), 916–949 (2021)
30. ILO.: Managing Disability in the Workplace. ILO Code of Practice. International Labour Office, Geneva (2002)
31. Unger, D., Kregel, J.: Employers' knowledge and utilization of accommodations. Work **21**(1), 5–15 (2003)
32. Lagerveld, S.E., Bültmann, U., Franche, R.L., van Dijk, F.J., Vlasveld, M.C., van der Feltz-Cornelis, C.M., Bruinvels, D.J., Huijs, J.J., Blonk, R.W., van der Klink, J.J., Nieuwenhuijsen, K.: Factors associated with work participation and work functioning in depressed workers: a systematic review. J. Occup. Rehabil. **20**(3), 275–292 (2010)
33. Cavanagh, J., Bartram, T., Meacham, H., Bigby, C., Oakman, J., Fossey, E.: Supporting workers with disabilities: A scoping review of the role of human resource management in contemporary organisations. Asia Pac. J. Hum. Resour. **55**(1), 6–43 (2017)
34. von Schrader, S., Malzer, V., Bruyère, S.: Perspectives on disability disclosure: the importance of employer practices and workplace climate. Empl. Responsib. Rights J. **26**, 237–255 (2014)
35. Matt, S.B., Butterfield, P.: Changing the disability climate: promoting tolerance in the workplace. AAOHN J. **54**(3), 129–135 (2006)
36. United Nations Enable.: Convention on the rights of persons with disabilities (2006). United Nations. http://www.un.org/disabilities/default.asp?navid=14&pid=150. Accessed 19 Jun 2012
37. Gates, L.B., Akabas, S.H., Oran-Sabia, V.: Relationship accommodations involving the work group: improving work prognosis for persons with mental health conditions. Psychiatr. Rehabil. J. **21**(3), 264–272 (1998)

38. Cramm, J.M., Tebra, N., Finkenflügel, H.: Colleagues' perception of supported employee performance. J Policy Pract Intell Disabil **5**(4), 269–275 (2008)
39. McLaughlin, M.E., Bell, M.P., Stringer, D.Y.: Stigma and acceptance of persons with disabilities—understudied aspects of workforce diversity. Group Organ Manage **29**(3), 302–333 (2004)
40. Fishbein, M., Ajzen I.: Belief, Attitude, Intention, and Behavior: an Introduction to Theory and Research. Addison-Wesley, Reading (1975)
41. Jones, M.: Disability and Perceptions of Work and Management. ERN: Other Organizations & Markets: Personnel Management (Topic) (2016)
42. Adams, L., Oldfield, K.: Opening up work: the views of disabled people and people with long-term health conditions. Research report 77. IFF Research Ltd; Equality and Human Rights Commission (2012)
43. Fevre, R., Grainger, H., Brewer, R.: Discrimination and unfair treatment in the workplace. Br. J. Ind. Relat. **49**, s207–s235 (2011)
44. Forth, J., Rincon-Aznar, A.: Equal opportunities, employee attitudes and workplace performance: findings from WERS 1998. In: BERR Employment Relations Research Series No. 38. Department for Business Enterprise and Regulatory Reform, London (2008)
45. Bewley, H., Forth, J.: Vulnerability and adverse treatment in the workplace, employment relations research series 112. Department for Business Innovation and Skills, London (2010)
46. Fevre, R., Robinson, A., Jones, T., Lewis, D.: Work fit for all—disability, health and the experience of negative treatment in the British workplace. Equality and Human Rights Commission, London (2008)
47. Pagán, R., Malo, M.A.: Job satisfaction and disability: lower expectations about jobs or a matter of health? Span. Econ. Rev. **11**, 51–74 (2009)
48. Uppal, S.: Disability, workplace characteristics and job satisfaction. Int. J. Manpow. **26**(4), 336–349 (2005)
49. Kim, J.: Disability acceptance as a moderator of the impacts of disability stigma on job satisfaction of people with disabilities in the workplace. J. Vocat. Rehabil. **57**(3), 225–235 (2022)
50. Fuchs, H. (2022). Psychological flexibility and attitudes towards individuals with disabilities. Kultura-Społeczeństwo-Edukacja, (1), 145–159. https://doi.org/10.14746/kse.2022.21.9
51. Fuchs, H., Perkova, T., Fishbein, A., Galily, D., & Fuchs, A. (2023). Psychological Flexibility in Human Leadership -Facing the Challenges and Needs of the 21st Century Working Social Spaces. In R. Stefanko, R. Fedorko, & E, Benkova. (Eds.), Economic, Management & Business, **8**(8), 1021–1038. Presov: Presov University Press. ISBN 978-80-555-3215-8. https://managerconf.com/EMB-Conference-2023.pdf

# Experience of Emotions, Emotion Regulation, and Withdrawal Behavior of Arab Teachers in Israel Primary Schools

**Nagham Farah**

**Abstract** This article is aimed to shed light on teachers ability to express their positive emotions and their ability to regulate emotions, within their lives, these can have a great impact on achieving school goals by reducing there absent and withdrawal behaviors. The research is a case study seeking to explore the teachers' emotions, emotional regulation strategies, and withdrawal behaviors the unique population of the Arab sector Israel and will be conducted with quantitative analysis. The study sample for the quantitative analysis were include 513 teachers from 16 state elementary schools in the northern region of Israel who teach grades 1–6. The study used a descriptive correlation approach. By developing study questionnaires, which include; experience of emotions, emotion regulation, withdrawal behavior scale. The sample include male and female teachers The findings of the study showed that there are relationship between teachers' intensity of experiencing certain pleasant (joy, pride, love) and unpleasant emotions (anger, exhaustion, hopelessness) at their work and the use of individual emotion regulation strategies, also the results showed that there were a relationship between teachers' absenteeism and lateness and their intensity of experiencing certain emotions (joy, pride, love, anger, exhaustion, hopelessness) at work, also from the findings showed that there are relationship between teachers' absenteeism, lateness, and their frequency of use of emotion regulation strategies at their work.

**Keywords** Emotions · Emotion regulation · Withdrawal behavior · Arab primary teachers

---

N. Farah (✉)
University of Ljubljana, Ljubljana, Slovenia
e-mail: fnagham@gmail.com

 
S. Kot et al. (eds.), *Corporate Practices: Policies, Methodologies, and Insights in Organizational Management*, Springer Proceedings in Business and Economics,
https://doi.org/10.1007/978-981-97-0996-0_51

## 1 Introduction

From a research point of view, there is no agreed definition of the term "emotion" in any discipline that studies this phenomenon. Mulligan and Scherer [1] argued that the attempt to define emotion could reduce the phenomenon's complexity. Moreover, there is a tendency to refer to "feelings" as a synonym for "emotion". It can be agreed that there is frequent reference to "emotional states" in the literature. In our study, emotions are understood as specific sequences of physiological changes, cognitive processing, verbal and nonverbal expression2, 3, and behavior or action tendencies that respond to a subjectively important event [4]. Often something that occurs momentarily, something that lasts a long time. Lazarus and Cohen-Charash [5] discussed several emotions such as anger, anxiety, guilt, shame, jealousy, hope, happiness, pride, love, and compassion. Although many of these emotions are also experienced by teachers, the two most frequent emotions in classrooms experienced are joy and anger [6]. It has become increasingly clear that the teaching profession places many emotional demands on those who practice it, along with the pedagogical-educational requirements of the profession 7 [8]. The scientific literature suggests that teaching is an emotionally demanding profession because the work and the environment are vague and conflictual and involve many stressors [9–11]. Studies have shown that teachers' emotions are crucial in a variety of aspects related to their work at school: in teaching practices, the relationship between them and their students, issues related to reform and change processes, and understanding the power relations and social structures within the school and the wider social circles around it [8]. Teachers experience and express a plethora of emotions in the classroom. Among the different emotions of teachers, positive emotions such as pleasure and pride were examined [12, 13]. They may experience happiness when the purpose of teaching is fulfilled or when their students follow instructions.

On the other hand, they experience frustration when students exhibit negative behavior or lack understanding of the material the teacher is trying to convey [14]. In a study on preschool teachers, Prosen and Smrtnik Vitulić [15] found four sources of teachers' negative emotions at work: children, parents, colleagues, and leadership. However, the children were an important source of the teachers' negative emotions, as they often showed indiscipline, were aggressive towards other children and did not respect the teacher's authority [15].

Prosen and Smrtnik Vitulić [15] argued that there are three main perspectives on emotion regulation: a neurobiological perspective, a cognitive perspective, and a socio-constructivist perspective, each of which constitutes a different understanding of emotion regulation. Neurobiologically, emotions are caused by specific circuits in the brain that causes neuroendocrine experiences and responses, so for the most part, the behaviors are expressive. The cognitive perspective is that emotion begins with assessing the situation and ends with an experiential, behavioral, or physiological response. Thus, emotion regulation can occur in sequences of situation-attention-appraisal-response while primary attention is given to appraisal. The socio-constructivist point of view emphasizes the context in which emotions appear. That is, emotions are socially understood and expressed in the way of social expectations in the cultural environment of people who are different in their worldviews, ideologies, values, and self-concepts. Thus, a socio-cultural environment can contribute to emotion regulation in how people change situations, their understanding, or change their emotional responses [15]. There are two main aspects to emotional regulation. First, people try to amplify, maintain, and lower negative and positive emotions [16]. Second, many situations in which emotional regulation is activated are conscious, such as a decision to make a change or to restrain oneself when experiencing negative emotions [17].

Withdrawal behaviors refer to a set of attitudes and behaviors that employees employ when they remain at work officially but, for some reason, decide to be less involved physically [18]. The present study will focus on two key indicators of withdrawal behaviors: being late and absent. Teachers' lateness in schools causes the principal to lose time as he/she must find solutions for teachers' delays, which disrupts the daily schedule and affects the efficiency of learning and students' achievement. Teachers often continue the lesson during the break to complete the teaching of the planned curriculum, which impairs the students' break time and can lead them to miss their next class. Moreover, as the classes are shortened, the teachers may not cover all the curriculum needed for the final exams, and thus the students will have to complete the gap on their own. A late teacher can also have a negative impact on teachers who arrive on time and are required to supervise the late teacher's classroom to prevent disruption in other classrooms. Such behaviors also affect shared ethical values [19].

Absenteeism, another type of withdrawal behavior, is defined as the absence of physical presence in the place where the person is expected to be [20]. Sagie [21] saw voluntary absenteeism as a situation that is generally under the employee's direct control and is often exploited for personal issues such as leisure activities and market research in search of a new job. This type of absence concerns leaders of organizations that invest a lot of time and effort to contain and reduce it. Voluntary absence is measured according to its frequency, such as the number of absence episodes. Studies agree that occasional absence can indicate negative work attitudes [22–25]. Teachers may decide to report sick while avoiding an excessive workload or extending their holidays for recreational purposes. The absenteeism literature provides examples of such opportunistic behavior of teachers, where teachers misuse their absence allowance [26]. A high score on voluntary absences measured by frequency will usually reflect short-term absences ("skip days"), which indicates a desire to be away from work [27]. In addition, there is also the phenomenon of involuntary absences for reasons beyond the employee's control, such as illness or family events. Involuntary absence is characterized by a longer period than voluntary absence [29] and is usually measured in loss of time [28].

In a study conducted by Abu-Asba et al. [30], it was found that the Arab minority society receives unequal attitudes compared to the Jewish majority society, by various state institutions, in the fields of employment, education, and integration. Though at the beginning of its establishment, the Arab education system suffered from a shortage of teachers, the trend has changed over the years, and Arab society has made efforts to close the gaps. A study by Al-Hajj [31] showed that in the late 1980s and early 1990s, the number of Arab teachers increased. The Arab education system has witnessed a decrease in teachers' motivation following complaints, dissatisfaction with work, absences, and behaviors that have severe consequences for the functioning of the education system [32]. The Arab education system suffers from external problems and barriers at various levels: resources and achievements, structure and organization, and pedagogy [33], as well as internal barriers in the field of local politics [34], which hinder its development and progress. Apart from the inequality in allocations between the two education systems, the Arab and the Jewish [35], the choice of educated people in the teaching profession is usually determined by the opportunities the Israeli labor market offers. Since the labor market and employment opportunities are more welcoming to Jewish scholars [36], a significant proportion of Arab scholars turn to the teaching profession as a "forced" choice [37]. It should be noted that the pressure for employment in Arab education leads to more and more Arab teachers who are employed part-time. The Ministry of Education tries to assign as many teachers as possible to work, which contributes to the Arab teachers' job insecurity and makes them more vulnerable against the growing power and authority of the supervisors and school principals (Ajabaria 2011). Given all these specifics, Arab teachers constitute a unique population in education. Therefore, it is of great importance to study their behaviors and the factors leading to such behaviors. The next chapter will discuss teachers' emotions and withdrawal behaviors. Al-Ghamdi's [38] in his study aimed to reveal "the relationship of emotions to decision-making skill among employees of GCC embassies in Jordan". It was found that there is a relationship between emotions and decision-making skill. Al-Anani's study [39] aimed to identify the degrees of emotions and leadership styles and determine the impact of gender, age and educational level on emotions and leadership style among teachers, the results showed that the degrees of emotions and leadership styles were average, and it was also found that there were statistically significant differences in emotions among children's teachers attributed to gender (towards females) and age (towards the youngest). Al-Khafaji's [40] study aimed to study the relationship between psychological burnout, emotions and psychological hardness. The sample size was 224 teachers in some primary schools in Basra governorate. The results showed a statistically significant negative correlation between psychological exhaustion and emotions, as well as a negative correlation between psychological exhaustion and psychological hardness, and a statistically significant positive correlation between emotions and psychological hardness.

A study conducted by Somona and Helena (2016) clarifying that emotion regulation and coping strategies were compared in 242 pedagogical students from the faculty of education, university of ljubljana, with different attachment styles: secure (51.3%), fearful (31.9%), preoccupied (14.2%), and dismissive (2.7%). The students' ages ranged from 18 to 24 years (m = 19.02; sd = 0.92), and the majority were female (95.0%). They completed three questionnaires' assessing their attachment styles and their use of emotion regulation and coping strategies. It was determined that the students used the majority of emotion regulation and coping strategies sometimes.

Somewhat different patterns in the use of emotion regulation and coping strategies were, however, present in each attachment-based group. Significant differences between these groups appeared in their use of the emotion regulation strategies of social support, suppression, and comfort eating, and in the coping strategies of seeking social support and escaping or avoiding stressful situations.

Ghadaifi's study [41] aimed to identify the importance of emotions in educational life through the various educational and learning situations that the special education teacher lives with his students with special needs, and also aims to identify the differences between special education teachers according to the gender variable in emotions, the descriptive analytical exploratory approach was adopted The results showed that there are no statistically significant differences between special education teachers attributed to the gender variable in the level of emotions. Al-Shuaibi's study [42] aimed to identify the relationship between emotions and collective effectiveness beliefs of mathematics teachers in Oman. The sample of the stratified random study consisted of (1226) teachers from all governorates of the Sultanate of Oman. The results of the study showed that there are high levels of emotions for teachers and beliefs of collective competence. Female teachers scored higher than males in the dimensions of emotions, as well as in beliefs of collective effectiveness. The results also indicated that some dimensions of emotions (understanding and expressing one's own feelings and regulating subjective feelings) are positively predicted by collective efficacy beliefs. The study of Alshebami and Al-Amri [43] aimed to identify the role of emotions in stimulating the level of ambition among university students in the Kingdom of Saudi Arabia with the level of commitment of students towards the university as an intermediate variable, the study sample included (250) respondents, the results of the study showed a statistically significant positive relationship between emotions and the level of students' ambition and success on the one hand. On the other hand, it was found that there is a statistically significant positive relationship between emotions and students' commitment to university and the level of ambition. Students. The study of Al-Khatatbeh [44] aimed to know the level of burnout among teachers of students with autism spectrum disorder in Dammam and its relationship to their emotions. The study sample consisted of (204) male and female teachers in Dammam, and the descriptive approach was used, the results showed that the level of emotions among teachers of students with autism spectrum disorder in Dammam was average, and the results showed a statistically significant inverse relationship between burnout and emotions among teachers. On the prevalence of teacher absence in India, Kramer et al. (2005) studied teacher absence. The results of the study revealed that 25% of teachers are absent from school, and about half of teachers are actually teaching. Data were collected from unannounced visits by representatives of national education directorates in India. She revealed that the monthly salary has nothing to do with the percentage of absence. The results also showed that teachers with long experience in education, and the first teachers Head, despite the high wages paid to them, but the absence rate is still remarkably repeated, and for the category of permanent teachers, and the category of those who work on a temporary contract, the rate of their absence rate is similar, as well as for teachers who work in poor areas, despite the high wages they receive, the absence rate among them is still high.

The results also showed that The reason for the absence is the poor motivation of teachers to attend school and attend school, and that the schools with the lowest rate of absenteeism are those that are subject to frequent visits by mentors, in addition to the quality of their infrastructure, and their proximity to paved roads. The results also showed that the place of residence—in terms of proximity and distance from school—has no effect on the rate of absenteeism of teachers. As for the type of school, the rate of teacher absenteeism in non-formal schools supervised by the local authority is much higher than in schools supervised by the state. The absence rate of teachers working in private schools is lower than their counterparts working in public schools, as the percentage of differences between them reaches about (8%) in the same region. Alcázar et al. [26] conducted a study on the phenomenon of increasing the rate of teacher absenteeism, which is one of the critical problems facing the education process in developing countries. The data was collected through a general survey of a number of regional regions in Peru. Data for frequent absentee teachers were obtained from national reports from government primary schools, which were Collect them through unannounced visits by mentors, especially in schools where there are a lot of teacher absences. Overall, absenteeism was 11% in primary schools, and rises to 16 and 21% in poor areas and isolated environments in Peru respectively. The results also showed that the reasons for the absence of teachers in public schools are mainly due to the poor state of the local environment surrounding the school, which is characterized by extreme poverty, and may reach the level of extreme poverty, in addition to the weak social ties between teachers and the local community surrounding the school, as most of these teachers who are frequently absent are those who work on a contract, in addition to the weak self-motivation towards the profession, and the lack of financial incentives. The study of Bradlelya et al. [45] sought to reveal the reasons for teacher absences based on data obtained from sources of human resources systems for public schools in Queensland. The results of the study showed that the absence of teachers is due to several reasons, which were classified into four areas: family and maternity conditions, accidents that teachers are exposed to during work, disputes with their co-workers, and illness. The results showed that the rate of teacher absenteeism increases among primary school teachers aged (30) years, while it was found that the percentage of teachers' absence increases among secondary school teachers aged (28) years. The rate of absence of secondary school teachers rises to (9%) among teachers aged (40–31). years, compared to teachers aged (30) years and below. While it increases among secondary school teachers of (61) years and above to reach (61%), while it decreases among primary school teachers to reach (41%). Lopez-Calix et al. [55] examined the relationship between teacher absence and incentives in primary schools in Ecuador. The results revealed that there are many factors that cause an increase in absenteeism related to the nature of the social environment surrounding the school, in terms of being an urban or rural environment, poor or rich, where the percentage of absenteeism increases in environments that vary In which minorities, in poor environments, especially those that lack educational supervision, and continuous follow-up by mentors, in addition to the fact that the distance of the school from the education department is one of the factors that cause the increase in the absence of teachers. The type of school structure, the nature of the school's internal environment, and the teacher's relationship with the internal school community did not show any effect on the rate of teacher absence. The results of the study did not support the idea that non-formal education or teaching through contract teachers is the only way to solve the problem of teacher absenteeism, but the incentives and encouragement given to teachers are among the factors that reduce their absenteeism.

## 2 Research Problem

The teaching profession requires an emotional commitment. Teachers experience and express different emotions during their work [12]. Teachers reported that often their emotions stemmed from disciplinary interactions in the classroom. They tried to regulate these emotions since they believed it could help them achieve their goals and improve their teaching experience [14]. Various studies have found that teaching requires high levels of emotional investment from teachers, perhaps more than other occupations. This occupation requires daily, prolonged, and intensive face-to-face interaction between the teacher and their students and many other factors. Presumably, the fact that teachers are required to make an emotional investment in the face of a long list of objects when a different emotional investment is required for each of them also adds to the emotional burden placed on the teacher [46]. Since teachers often experience such emotions, they can affect classroom teaching and student learning [12, 13] and negatively affect the conduct of the school organization [47]. Understanding these emotions and their regulation and their connection to absences and tardiness can shed light on what teachers go through in their teaching processes. We will seek answers to the questions regarding the intensity of selected emotions that teachers in the Arab sector in Israel have at their work and how they regulate them. Investigating these topics is important since learning of and understanding the emotions and emotion strategies teachers employ plays an important role in gaining insight into the teachers' work and the teaching profession. Naturally, teachers' negative emotions and emotion regulation strategies may be connected to withdrawal behavior, including absenteeism and tardiness. Therefore, we would also like to explore this connection. The study will explore the teachers' emotions, emotional regulation strategies, and withdrawal behaviors. For that purpose, we defined the following research questions from the teachers point of view in primary schools in the Arab sector in Israel:

1. What are the characteristics of teachers' experience of specific emotions (joy, pride, love, anger, exhaustion, hopelessness), strategies to manage the emotions, and absenteeism and lateness in work?
2. What is the relationship between teachers' intensity of experiencing certain pleasant (joy, pride, love) and unpleasant emotions (anger, exhaustion, hopelessness) at their work and the use of individual emotion regulation strategies?

3. What is the relationship between teachers' absenteeism and lateness and their intensity of experiencing certain emotions (joy, pride, love, anger, exhaustion, hopelessness) at work?
4. What is the relationship between teachers' absenteeism, lateness, and their frequency of use of emotion regulation strategies at their work?

## 3 Research Method

The purpose of this section is to present the research context, research question, research design, population and sampling techniques, variable measurement instruments, data collection techniques, and data analyses utilized for this research study. The research will be conducted using quantitative (questionnaires). A questionnaire was developed to collect data from the sample of the study after reviewing some of the previous literature addressing each of the variables examined in the study, the questionnaire consisted of: The purpose of this research study was to explore the teachers' emotions, emotional regulation strategies, and withdrawal behaviors. All the questionnaires were uploaded using Google Forms applications from the period of 10 February to 30 may 2023.

1. **Demographic details**. The study participants were asked to include data on age, gender, and seniority in teaching.
2. **Absenteeism questionnaire**: To measure the absence variable, we will use an index from a study by Rosenblatt et al. [48]. Teachers were asked to record the number of days of absence (without including military reserve duty, maternity leave, vacations, and strikes). Absenteeism measurements will be conducted according to two trends:

   *Absenteeism trends by weekdays.* These trends were measured by examining the number of absences that begin each workweek day (Sunday, Monday, etc.). The rate of absences according to these trends will be calculated by dividing the average absence percentage by each day of the week by the average percentage of working days on that day of the week. The result of this division, i.e., the rate of absence periods for working days, will indicate specific trends per day of the week.
   *Absenteeism trends by holidays.* These trends were measured by examining the number of absences before and after holidays. The absence rate before/after holidays will be calculated by dividing the number of days of absence on each of the specific dates before/after the holiday by the average number of days of absence reported for that weekday (Sunday, Monday, etc.) in that year. The results of this division, i.e., the absence rate before/after holidays on those weekdays, will indicate specific trends per holiday.

3. **Lateness Questionnaire**: To measure the lateness variable, a measure taken from [49] study, each teacher was asked to record the number of days of their lateness.

4. **Teacher Emotion Questionnaire (TEQ)**: The Questionnaire was developed by Burić et al. [50]. The questionnaire examines the scale of joy, pride, love, fatigue, anger, and hopelessness. The scale for assessing emotions' experience ranges from 1 to 5 (1 means do not agree at all and 5 means strongly agree). Internal reliability (Cronbach's α) for all included emotions ranging from 0.81 to 0.90 [50].
5. **The Emotion Regulation Strategies Questionnaire-Revised** (ERSQ-R, Smrtnik Vitulić and Prosen 2016)[51]. This Questionnaire was used in the research by Prosen and Smrtnik Vitulić [15] based on Gross and Thompson's [52] model of emotion regulation. According to Prosen and Smrtnik Vitulić [15], the ERSQ-R includes twelve ER strategies: (1) situation selection, (2) situation modification, (3) attention deployment, (4) cognitive reappraisal of situation's meaning, (5) cognitive reappraisal of situation's importance, 6) physiological response modulation, (7) experiential response modulation, (8) behavioral response modulation—physical activity, (9) behavioral response modulation—suppression, (10) behavioral response modulation—seeking social support, (11) behavioral response modulation—comfort eating and (12) behavioral response modulation—substance use. Teachers will self-assess each ER strategy on a 5-point Likert scale how frequently they use it at work (1 = not at all; 5 = always). Internal reliability (Cronbach's α) for ER strategies (for anger) ranges from 0.66 (avoiding the situation) to 0.89 (comfort eating) [15].

## *3.1 Research Model*

The research is a case study seeking to explore the teachers' emotions, emotional regulation strategies, and withdrawal behaviors the unique population of the Arab sector Israel and will be conducted with quantitative analysis (Fig. 1).

### 3.1.1 Teacher's Emotion Scale

Cronbach's alpha was used to calculate the internal consistencies for all variable scales. With scales less than 10 items, a value > 0.5 is acceptable. The extent of reliability of the questions measuring the values of Teacher's emotion scale was indicated by the internal consistency values. A Cronbach's alpha value "around 0.90 are considered "excellent," values around 0.80 as "very good," and values about 0.70 as "adequate" [53]. Teacher's emotion scale showed good reliability, the Cronbach alpha of two scales were around the acceptable greater than 0.5, as shown in Table 1.

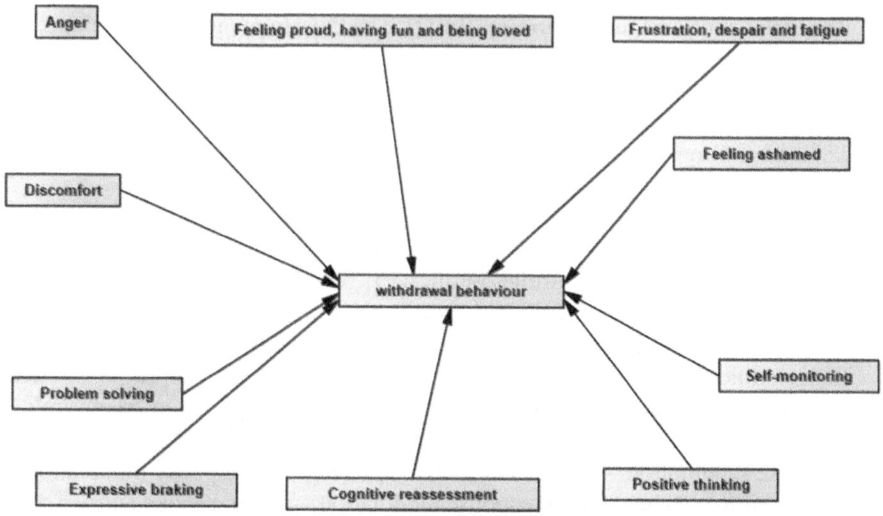


**Fig. 1** Research design represent 10 elements as independent variables on teacher's withdrawal behavior

**Table 1** Cronbach's Alpha for all variable scales for teacher's emotion scale

| Variable | Cronbach's Alpha | No. of items |
|---|---|---|
| Anger | 0.91 | 6 |
| Feeling proud, having fun and being loved | 0.91 | 13 |
| Frustration, despair and fatigue | 0.84 | 7 |
| Feeling ashamed | 0.79 | 6 |
| Discomfort | 0.83 | 5 |
| Teacher's emotion scale | – | 37 |

### 3.1.2 Correlations

The communalities of the items in Experience of emotions, main domains are all above 0.4 showing high correlation. Thus, these items load significantly to their respective dimension.

### 3.1.3 Emotional Regulation Questionnaire

Cronbach's alpha was used to calculate the internal consistencies for all variable scales. With scales less than 10 items, a value >0.5 is acceptable. The extent of reliability of the questions measuring the values of emotional regulation was indicated by the internal consistency values. A Cronbach's alpha value "around 0.90 are considered "excellent," values around 0.80 as "very good," and values about 0.70

**Table 2** Cronbach's Alpha for all variable scales for emotional regulation

| Variable | Cronbach's Alpha | No. of items |
|---|---|---|
| Self-monitoring | 0.74 | 6 |
| Problem solving | 0.72 | 6 |
| Positive thinking | 0.87 | 15 |
| Cognitive reassessment | 0.88 | 4 |
| Expressive braking | 0.91 | 4 |
| Emotional regulation | 0.95 | 35 |

as "adequate" (Kline 2016) the Cronbach alpha of emotional regulation scale were around the acceptable greater than 0.5, as shown in Table 2.

### 3.1.4 Correlations

The communalities of the items in emotional regulation main domains are all above 0.4 showing moderate correlation. Thus, these items load significantly to their respective dimension. The varimax rotation converged in 5 iterations. The rotated component matrix indicates strong and significant correlation (magnitude >0.5) within each of the 5 components from this exploratory analysis, it appears that the items belong to three specific groups. The researcher can conclude that all items, loaded well to three factors.

## 4 The Study Population and Sample Characteristic

The study population consisted of all Arab teachers in Israel with value of 38,049 teachers. The study sample for the quantitative analysis were include 513 teachers selected randomly from the study population, from 16 state elementary schools in Israel who teach grades 1–6. The sample include male and female teachers. The criterion for participation is an Arab native teacher since this study is about the Arab sector, as shown in Table 3.

## 5 Data Analysis

All the questionnaires were uploaded using Google Forms applications. The data were analyzed using frequencies, means, and variability in experience of selected emotions and emotion strategies by using the SPSS program.

**Table 3** Demographic characteristics of participating teachers (n = 513)

| | Variable | Count | % |
|---|---|---|---|
| Gender | Male | 175 | 34.1 |
| | Female | 338 | 65.9 |
| Age | 30 years and less | 78 | 15.2 |
| | More than 30 years | 435 | 84.8 |
| Qualification | BSc degree | 246 | 48.0 |
| | Higher studies | 267 | 52.0 |
| Experience | 10 years and less | 130 | 25.3 |
| | More than 10 years | 383 | 74.7 |

# 6 Findings

The study wants to explore the teachers' emotions, emotional regulation strategies, and withdrawal behaviors. For that purpose, we defined the following research questions for teachers in primary schools in the Arab sector in Israel:

**Answering the 1st question**: What are the characteristics of teachers' experience of specific emotions (joy, pride, love, anger, exhaustion, hopelessness), strategies to manage the emotions, and absenteeism and lateness in work? To answer this question, the researcher computed means and standard deviations for all the study domains and sub domains, as shown in Table 4.

## 6.1 *Teacher's Emotion Scale*

From the previous table which showed that the means of teacher's emotion scale is ranged from moderate to high. The domain (Feeling proud, having fun and being loved) got the highest mean with (4.34), Also, it found that frustration, despair and fatigue came with 2nd rank with mean (3.52), and SD (0.988), next anger with mean (3.42), SD (0.883), and in the final rank the domain feeling ashamed with (2.72) with moderate degree.

**Table 4** Mean average score and standard deviation of *Teacher's emotion scale*

| Variables | Mean | Std. Deviation | Rank | Level |
|---|---|---|---|---|
| Feeling proud, having fun and being loved | 4.34 | 0.749 | 1 | High |
| Frustration, despair and fatigue | 3.52 | 0.988 | 2 | High |
| Anger | 3.42 | 0.883 | 3 | High |
| Discomfort | 3.37 | 0.968 | 4 | Moderate |
| Feeling ashamed | 2.72 | 1.154 | 5 | Moderate |
| Teacher's emotion scale | 3.48 | 0.612 | | High |

**Table 5** Mean average score and standard deviation of emotional regulation

| Variables | Mean | Std. Deviation | Rank | Level |
|---|---|---|---|---|
| Positive thinking | 3.80 | 0.773 | 1 | High |
| Self-monitoring | 3.69 | 0.830 | 2 | High |
| Cognitive reassessment | 3.67 | 0.823 | 3 | High |
| Problem solving | 3.46 | 0.793 | 4 | High |
| Expressive braking | 3.23 | 0.877 | 5 | Moderate |
| Emotional regulation | 3.57 | 0.612 | | High |

## 6.2 *Emotional Regulation*

From the previous table which showed that the means of teacher's Emotional regulation is ranged from moderate to high. The domain (Positive thinking) got the highest mean with (3.80), Also, it found that Self-monitoring, came with 2nd rank with mean (3.69), and SD (0.8360), next Cognitive reassessment with mean (3.67), SD (0.823), and in the final rank the domain Expressive braking with (3.23) with moderate degree (Table 5).

## 6.3 *Absenteeism and Lateness in Work*

Table 6 showed that there mean of number of days regarding absent in the past five months for the study sample were (4.16) with SD (3.16), and the mean of the average of class late were (1.24) with SD (2.291) also the researcher computed frequency and percentages for the reason of absence, as shown in Table 7.

The table showed that (321) (62.6%) of the study sample reason for absence as result of health problems, and (115) (22.4%) as a result of family leave.

**Answering the 2nd:** What is the relationship between teachers' intensity of experiencing certain pleasant (joy, pride, love) and unpleasant emotions (anger, exhaustion, hopelessness) at their work and the use of individual emotion regulation strategies? To answer this question Pearson correlation were computed between teachers' intensity of experiencing certain pleasant (joy, pride, love) and unpleasant emotions (anger, exhaustion, hopelessness) at their work and the use of individual emotion regulation strategies in Table 8.

**Table 6** Mean average score and standard deviation of *Absenteeism and lateness in work*

| | Mean | Std. Deviation |
|---|---|---|
| How many days have you been absent in the past five months? | 4.16 | 3.165 |
| How often are classes late? | 1.24 | 2.291 |

**Table 7** Reasons for absence

| | | Frequency | Percent | Valid percent | Cumulative percent |
|---|---|---|---|---|---|
| Valid | Health problems | 321 | 62.6 | 67.4 | 67.4 |
| | Special leave | 40 | 7.8 | 8.4 | 75.8 |
| | Family leave | 115 | 22.4 | 24.2 | 100.0 |
| | Total | 476 | 92.8 | 100.0 | |
| Missing | System | 37 | 7.2 | | |
| Total | | 513 | 100.0 | | |

**Table 8** Pearson correlation between teachers' intensity of experiencing certain pleasant and unpleasant at their work and the use of individual emotion regulation strategies (n = 513)

| | Self-monitoring | Problem solving | Positive thinking | Cognitive reassessment | Expressive braking | Emotional regulation |
|---|---|---|---|---|---|---|
| Anger | −0.401** | −0.403** | −0.503** | −0.441** | −0.021 | −0.465** |
| Feeling proud, having fun and being loved | 0.604** | 0.507** | 0.685** | 0.463** | −0.080 | 0.570** |
| Frustration, despair and fatigue | −0.330** | −0.413** | −0.516** | −0.426** | −0.034 | −0.451** |
| Feeling ashamed | −0.432** | −0.342** | −0.455** | −0.431** | 0.124** | −0.401** |
| Discomfort | −0.380** | −0.339** | −0.446** | −0.413** | 0.178** | −0.364** |
| Teacher's emotion scale | −0.357** | −0.361** | −0.456** | −0.444** | 0.066 | −0.406** |

**Correlation is significant at the 0.01 level (2-tailed)

Pearson correlation showed that There was a negative correlation at (a = 0.05) between Anger and individual emotion regulation strategies (R = −0.465), and there was a negative correlation at (a = 0.05) between Feeling proud, having fun and being loved and individual emotion regulation strategies (R = −0.570)., and there was a negative correlation at (a = 0.05) between Frustration, despair and fatigue and individual emotion regulation strategies (R = −0.451)., and there was a negative correlation at (a = 0.05) between Feeling ashamed and individual emotion regulation strategies (R = −0.401)., and there was a negative correlation at (a = 0.05) between Discomfort and individual emotion regulation strategies (R = −0.364)., and there was a negative correlation at (a = 0.05) between Teacher's emotion scale and individual emotion regulation strategies (R = −0.406). Also the researcher computed Linear regression, as shown Table 9.

**Table 9** Linear regression for the impact of teacher's emotion on the individual emotion regulation strategies

| Variables | Unstandardized Coefficients | | Standardized Coefficients | t | Sig | R | $R^2$ |
|---|---|---|---|---|---|---|---|
| | B | Std. Er | beta | | | | |
| (Constant) | 2.875 | 0.207 | | 13.866 | 0.000 | 0.655[a] | 0.428 |
| Anger | −0.122 | 0.033 | −0.177 | −3.761 | 0.000 | | |
| Feeling proud, having fun and being loved | 0.347 | 0.033 | 0.424 | 10.609 | 0.000 | | |
| Frustration, despair and fatigue | −0.154 | 0.033 | −0.248 | −4.608 | 0.000 | | |
| Feeling ashamed | −0.062 | 0.030 | −0.117 | −2.069 | 0.039 | | |
| Discomfort | 0.094 | 0.038 | 0.150 | 2.516 | 0.012 | | |
| F value = 75.993 | Sig. = 0.000[a] | | | | | | |

Linear Regression analysis was performed and the results of the analysis As shown in Table 9. F value equal (75.993) at sig. (0.00). also the finding showed that there was a positive impact for the domain (Feeling proud, having fun and being loved) on individual emotion regulation strategies, also the table showed a negative impact of the domains; (Anger, Frustration, despair and fatigue. Feeling ashamed.) on individual emotion regulation, as shown in the following Fig. 2.

**Answering the 3rd question:** What is the relationship between teachers' absenteeism and lateness and their intensity of experiencing certain emotions (joy, pride, love, anger, exhaustion, hopelessness) at work? To answer this question Pearson correlation were computed between the domains of absenteeism and lateness and their intensity of experiencing certain emotions (joy, pride, love, anger, exhaustion, hopelessness) at work as shown in Table 10.

Pearson correlation showed that, there was a positive correlation at (a = 0.05) between Anger and Absenteeism from work (R = 0.552), and positive correlation at (a = 0.05) between Anger and Being late for classes (R = 214), and there was a negative correlation at (a = 0.05) between Feeling proud, having fun and being loved and Absenteeism from work (R = -0.570), and positive correlation at (a = 0.05) between Feeling proud, having fun and being loved and Being late for classes (R = -0.333), and there was a positive correlation at (a = 0.05) between Frustration, despair and fatigue and Absenteeism from work (R = 0.586), and positive correlation at (a = 0.05) between Frustration, despair and fatigue and Being late for classes (R = 0.149), and there was a positive correlation at (a = 0.05) between Feeling ashamed and Absenteeism from work (R = 0.662), and positive correlation at (a = 0.05) between Feeling ashamed and Being late for classes (R = 0.213), and there was a positive correlation at (a = 0.05) between Discomfort and Absenteeism from work

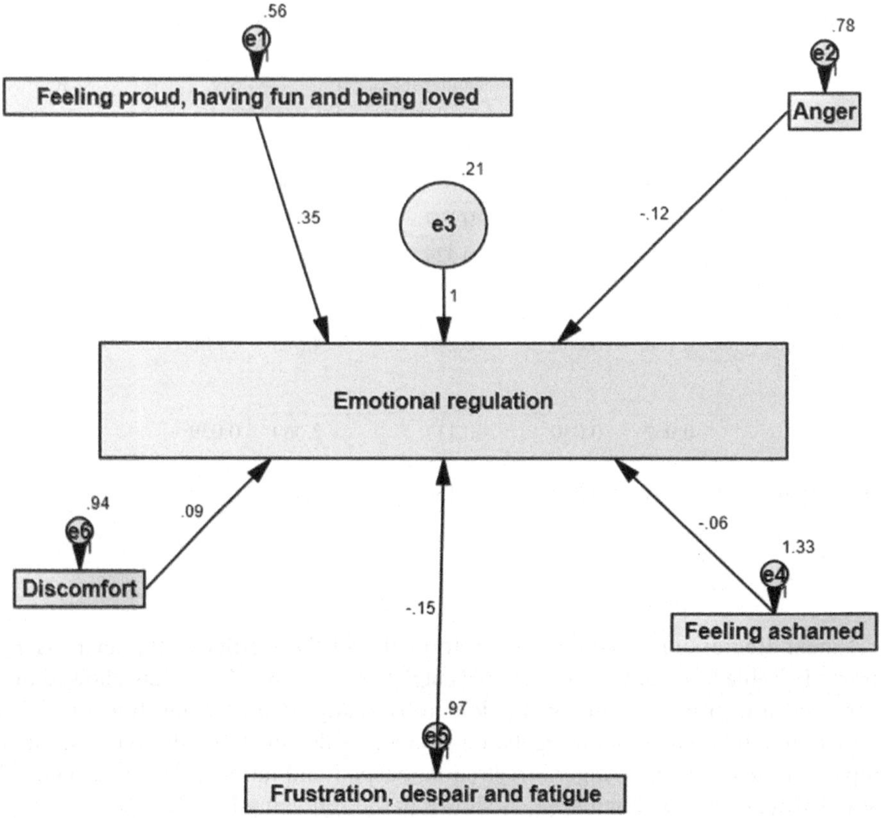


**Fig. 2** Factors effecting emotion regulation strategies

**Table 10** Pearson Correlation between the absenteeism and lateness and their intensity of experiencing certain emotions (joy, pride, love, anger, exhaustion, hopelessness) at work (n = 513)

| Variables | How many days have you been absent in the past five months? | How often are classes late? |
|---|---|---|
| Anger | 0.552** | 0.214** |
| Feeling proud, having fun and being loved | −0.570** | −0.333** |
| Frustration, despair and fatigue | 0.586** | 0.149** |
| Feeling ashamed | 0.662** | 0.213** |
| Discomfort | 0.615** | 0.154** |
| Teacher's emotion scale | 0.653** | 0.158** |

**Correlation is significant at the 0.01 level (2-tailed)

(R = 615), and positive correlation at (a = 0.05) between Discomfort and Being late for classes (R = 0.158).

**Answering the 4th:** What is the relationship between teachers' absenteeism, lateness, and their frequency of use of emotion regulation strategies at their work? To answer this question Pearson correlation were computed between the domains of absenteeism and lateness and their frequency of use of emotion regulation strategies at their work as shown in Table 11.

Pearson correlation showed there was a negative correlation at (a = 0.05) between Self-monitoring and Absenteeism from work (R = −0.488), and negative correlation at (a = 0.05) between Self-monitoring and Being late for classes (R = −278), and there was a negative correlation at (a = 0.05) between Problem solving and Absenteeism from work (R = −537), and negative correlation at (a = 0.05) between Problem solving and Being late for classes (R = −301, and there was a negative correlation at (a = 0.05) between Positive thinking and Absenteeism from work (R = −595), and negative correlation at (a = 0.05) between Positive thinking and Being late for classes (R = −320). and there was a negative correlation at (a = 0.05) between Cognitive reassessment and Absenteeism from work (R = −514), and negative correlation at (a = 0.05) between Cognitive reassessment and Being late for classes (R = −293), and there was a weak positive correlation at (a = 0.05) between Expressive braking and Absenteeism from work (R = 0.027), and weak positive correlation at (a = 0.05) between Expressive braking and Being late for classes (R = 0.46), and there was a negative correlation at (a = 0.05) between Emotional regulation and Absenteeism from work (R = −553), and negative correlation at (a = 0.05) between Emotional regulation and Being late for classes (R = −300).

**Table 11** Pearson Correlation between the absenteeism and lateness and their frequency of use of emotion regulation strategies at their work

| Domains | How many days have you been absent in the past five months? | How often are classes late? |
|---|---|---|
| Self-monitoring | −0.488** | −0.278** |
| Problem solving | −0.537** | −0.301** |
| Positive thinking | −0.595** | −0.320** |
| Cognitive reassessment | −0.514** | −0.293** |
| Expressive braking | 0.027 | 0.046 |
| Emotional regulation | −0.553** | −0.300** |
| | 513 | 513 |

**Correlation is significant at the 0.01 level (2-tailed)

## 7 Discussion and Conclusion

The results showed that means of teacher's emotion scale is ranged from moderate to high. The domain (Feeling proud, having fun and being loved) got the highest mean This result can be attributed to the fact that teachers in Israel feel proud of their students' achievements: in their students' progress and achievements. These results are similar to the study of [41]. Teachers feel a sense of accomplishment and satisfaction because they have a role in their growth and development. They constantly strive to make a positive impact: to shape the lives of their students. When they see their students learning, growing and becoming better individuals, it can be a source of tremendous pride and accomplishment. Teaching is also a very rewarding profession when teachers are passionate about their subjects and enjoy the teaching process itself. Sharing knowledge and sparking curiosity in students can be a lot of fun and interesting. This result can also be attributed to the fact that teachers in Israel build strong and positive relationships with their students with love and appreciation from their students, this is confirmed by Al-Shuaibi's study [42], These relationships can create a supportive and caring classroom environment, making teaching an enjoyable experience. Teachers also play a crucial role in shaping the future of society by educating the next generation. That they contribute to the betterment of society can be a source of pride and motivation. This result can also be attributed to the fact that teachers are proud of their professional growth and development, and may celebrate important achievements, such as completing additional education or receiving recognition for their contributions to education. This result can also be attributed to teachers feeling gratitude and appreciation from students and parents for their hard work and dedication. This can be incredibly satisfying and create a feeling of love and appreciation. Fun in the classroom: This result can also be attributed to the fact that when teachers create engaging lessons, use creative teaching methods, and promote a positive classroom atmosphere, teaching can make teaching an enjoyable and enjoyable experience for both teachers and students. This result can also be attributed to the teaching profession. It can bring great pride, joy, and a sense of love when teachers are passionate about their work and dedicated to their students' success. Also, it found that frustration, despair and fatigue came with 2nd rank next anger, and in the final rank the domain feeling ashamed with moderate degree, the researchers suggest that Frustration, despair, fatigue, and feelings of shame can be part of the human experience and can occur for a number of reasons. Which includes challenges and setbacks: When individuals face challenges, obstacles, or setbacks in their personal or professional lives, this can lead to frustration and despair. These feelings may arise from a feeling of inability to overcome difficulties. High workloads, tight deadlines, and stressful situations can also lead to fatigue and frustration. Over time, excessive stress and long work hours can contribute to burnout, which can lead to physical and emotional exhaustion. People also set high expectations for themselves, and when they feel they are not meeting those expectations, it can lead to feelings of shame. They may feel inadequate or "not good enough" in different aspects of their lives. This average result can also be attributed to the fact that these feelings are a natural part of the human experience. This average result can also be attributed to the fact that teachers seek support when needed, whether from friends, family, or mental health professionals, and develop themselves psychologically and socially to help manage and deal with these feelings. This high score for emotional regulation, also known as emotional self-regulation, is attributed to the ability of teachers in Israel to effectively manage and control an individual's emotions. It involves understanding, experiencing and responding to emotions in a healthy and balanced way. Emotional regulation is an important aspect of emotional intelligence and can greatly impact teachers' mental and physical health, and increase commitment, these results are confirmed by Alshebami and Al-Amri [43].

The results showed that there mean of number of days regarding absent in the past five months for the study sample were (4.16) with SD (3.16), and the mean of the average of class late were (1.24) with SD (2.291). these results indicate that absenteeism and lateness in the workplace, when occurring to a low degree, are generally positive signs for each, as a low rate of absenteeism and tardiness is indicative of commitment on the part of teachers. They show work as scheduled, indicating a strong work ethic and dedication to their work. Teachers are also characterized by reliability in completing work tasks on time. This result can also be attributed to teachers' regular attendance and punctuality, which are signs of professionalism. This reflects positively on teachers and their commitment to maintaining a strong professional image. The positive relationship between pleasant emotions (e.g., joy, pride, love) and individual emotion regulation strategies suggests that when individuals experience higher levels of pleasant emotions, they are more likely to use effective strategies to regulate their emotions. Here's an explanation of why this positive relationship exists: Pleasant feelings are also associated with greater overall well-being and positive mental states. When individuals feel joy, pride, or love, they are generally in a happier and more positive emotional state. These results are similar to Godbury et al. [54] who conclude the teachers absent related to low motivation.

This positive emotional state can make individuals more motivated to maintain and enhance their emotional well-being through emotion regulation strategies. Also, teachers who experience pleasant emotions are often better equipped to deal with emotional challenges. They may be more resilient in the face of stress or negative emotions, and may actively engage in emotion regulation strategies to maintain their positive emotional state. Pleasant feelings can also lead to improved cognitive performance and decision-making. When teachers are in a positive emotional state, they may have better access to cognitive resources and the ability to think more clearly, allowing them to choose and apply effective emotion regulation strategies. The negative relationship between unpleasant emotions at work (e.g., anger, exhaustion, hopelessness) and the use of individual emotion regulation strategies suggests that when individuals experience higher levels of these negative emotions in their work environment, they are less likely to effectively employ emotion regulation strategies. Here is an explanation of why this negative relationship exists: Emotional overload: When individuals are overwhelmed by negative emotions such as anger, exhaustion, and hopelessness at work, they may find it difficult to focus on or apply emotion regulation strategies effectively. These feelings can be emotionally draining, making it difficult to muster the cognitive resources needed to regulate. Cognitive impairment: Negative emotions can impair cognitive performance. Individuals who experience anger, fatigue, or hopelessness may have reduced cognitive flexibility, making it difficult for them to think clearly and choose appropriate emotion regulation strategies. Emotional reactivity: High levels of negative emotions can lead to emotional reactivity, where individuals react impulsively or emotionally to situations rather than applying intentional and constructive emotion regulation strategies. Negative emotions can lead to impulsive actions or harsh criticism, which limits the use of regulation techniques. Resource Depletion: Dealing with unpleasant emotions can drain an individual's emotional and cognitive resources, leaving them with fewer resources available for effective emotion regulation. This attrition can make it difficult to use strategies when needed. Loss of motivation: In the face of chronic negative emotions, individuals may lose motivation to actively engage in emotion regulation. They may feel hopeless or useless. The positive relationship between teachers' absence and tardiness resulting from experiencing certain positive emotions (joy, pride, love) and the negative relationship between anger, exhaustion, and hopelessness at work is an interesting hypothesis. However, it is important to approach this idea from a critical perspective and consider different factors that may influence these relationships. Teachers who frequently experience positive emotions such as joy, pride, and love at work may be more motivated and less prone to burnout and stress. Reduced stress and fatigue can lead to lower rates of absenteeism and tardiness. Teachers who find joy and pride in their work and who have positive relationships with students and colleagues may also have higher job satisfaction. This satisfaction can act as a motivational factor, reducing absenteeism and tardiness. A positive work environment, where teachers feel joy, love, and pride, may provide support and resources that help reduce absenteeism and tardiness. A supportive environment can lead to lower stress levels and increased commitment to work. Teachers who truly enjoy their work and feel proud of their accomplishments may also have higher intrinsic motivation. This internal motivation can lead to greater dedication and punctuality. The negative relationship can be attributed (absenteeism/tardiness and negative emotions), as teachers who frequently experience anger, exhaustion, and despair at work are more likely to suffer from burnout and emotional exhaustion. This emotional exhaustion can contribute to increased absenteeism and tardiness as a coping mechanism or due to lack of motivation. Negative feelings at work are also related to dissatisfaction with the job, the work environment, or colleagues. This dissatisfaction can lead to decreased commitment, and thus increased absenteeism and tardiness. Teachers experiencing negative emotions may also resort to absenteeism or tardiness as a way to avoid stressful or difficult situations at work. These behaviors can be a response to the emotional difficulties they are experiencing. This result can also be attributed to the fact that prolonged exposure to anger, fatigue, and despair can negatively affect mental health. Individuals who experience these feelings may find it difficult to maintain regular attendance and punctuality due to the negative impact on their overall health. Also these results confirmed by Alcázar et al. [26] who found that weak self-motivation towards the teaching profession, and the lack of financial incentives can increase the teacher absent dates in the school.

## 8 Recommendations

1. Emotional Intelligence Training: Provide teachers with training in emotional intelligence to enhance their understanding of emotions, self-awareness, and emotional regulation skills. This training can help teachers manage their emotions effectively.
2. Mental Health Support: Offer access to mental health resources and counseling for teachers. This can provide a safe space for teachers to address their emotional well-being and seek assistance when needed.
3. Peer Support Groups: Create peer support groups or mentoring programs among teachers. Encouraging teachers to discuss their challenges and share strategies for emotional regulation can be beneficial.
4. Wellness Programs: Establish wellness programs that promote physical and mental health. These programs can include fitness classes, mindfulness sessions, and stress reduction workshops.
5. Positive Work Environment: Foster a positive and supportive work environment by promoting respect, collaboration, and open communication among staff. A positive workplace culture can improve emotional well-being.
6. Conflict Resolution Training: Provide training in conflict resolution and communication skills for teachers to help them navigate workplace conflicts more effectively.
7. Professional Development: Offer professional development opportunities for teachers to enhance their teaching skills and job satisfaction. Continued growth and achievement can lead to positive emotions and decreased withdrawal.
8. Flexible Work Arrangements: Consider flexible work arrangements or part-time opportunities for teachers who may be experiencing high levels of stress or burnout. This flexibility can help them better manage their work-life balance.
9. Recognition and Appreciation: Recognize and appreciate the efforts of teachers through awards, praise, and acknowledgment. Feeling valued can lead to positive emotional experiences.
10. Teacher Support Groups: Create support groups for teachers to discuss common challenges, share experiences, and exchange emotion regulation strategies.

## 9 Research Ethics

The researcher is committed to maintaining and ensuring the complete confidentiality and privacy of the study participants. In a preliminary letter, the researcher will explain to the participants the research goals and context and emphasize that the privacy and anonymity of the participants are maintained.

## 10 Scientific Contribution

This study investigates the population of teachers in the Arab society in the State of Israel. The Arab society is a minority within the Jewish majority society. There are many socio-cultural differences between the Jewish majority society and the Arab minority society that are reflected in all aspects of life. Although the share of the Arab population in Israel is about 18%, and although the teaching profession is common in this society, no studies have been conducted like the current study. The Palestinian Arab society in Israel is unique since, although it belongs ethnically to the global Arab nation, it does not have its government institutions. Therefore, it "falls between the slots" from a research point of view. The present study provides a basis for examining the behaviors of Arab teachers in Israel and how they cope with being teachers, and the emotional burden that accompanies this profession. This research can form the basis for planning interventions and training programs for teachers in the Arab sector in Israel in the field of emotions, which can be based on scientific data.

## References

1. Mulligan, K., Scherer, K.R.: Toward a working definition of emotion. Emot. Rev. **4**(4), 345–357 (2012). https://doi.org/10.1177/1754073912445818
2. Fuchs, H., & Fuchs, A. Discipline management using CBT principles in the classroom. In R, Štefko. R, Fedorko. Benková, E. (eds.) Economics, Management & Business 2023: Contemporary Issues, Insights and New Challenges. Faculty of Management and Business, University of Prešov, Slovakia. ISBN 978-80-555-3215-8 (2023). https://managerconf.com/EMB-Conference-2023.pdf
3. Fuchs, H. & Fuchs, A. The Effect of an Intervention Program Based on Cognitive Behavioral Principles on the Quality of Life of Third Graders in a Classroom with Behavior Problems. in M, Stefanović, A, Đorđević. (eds.) International Quality Conference, 14, 1985–2010. Kragujevac, Serbia. ISBN 978-86-6335-104-2 (2023, May)
4. Lazarus, R.S.: Progress on a cognitive-motivational-relational theory of emotion. Am. Psychol. **46**(8), 819–834 (1991). https://doi.org/10.1037/0003-066X.46.8.819
5. Lazarus, R.S., Cohen-Charash, Y.: Discrete emotions in organizational life. In Payne, R.L., Cooper, G.L. (eds.) Emotions at Work: Theory, Research and Applications for Management, pp. 45–81. Wiley (2001)
6. Carson, R.L.: Exploring the Episodic Nature of Teachers' Emotions as It Relates to Teacher Burnout. Purdue University (2006)
7. Schutz, P. A., Hong, J., Cross, D. I., & Osbon, J. N. (2006). Reflections on investigating emotion in educational activity settings. Educ. Psychol. Rev. **18**(4), 343–360. https://doi.org/10.1007/s10648-006-9030-3
8. Zembylas, M., Schutz, P.A.: Research on teachers' emotions in education: findings, practical implications and future agenda. In: Schutz, P.A., Zembylas, M. (eds.) Advances in Teacher Emotion Research, pp. 367–377. Springer Science & Business Media (2009)
9. Conley, S., You, S.: Role stress revisited: job structuring antecedents, work outcomes, and moderating effects of locus of control. Educ. Manag. Adm. Leadership **42**(2), 184–206 (2014)
10. Schutz, P.A., Lanehart, S.J.: Introduction: emotions in education. Educ. Psychol. **37**, 67–68 (2002)

11. Somech, A.: The cost of going the extra mile: the relationship between teachers' organizational citizenship behavior, role stressors, and strain with the buffering effect of job autonomy. Teachers Teaching **22**(4), 426–447 (2016)
12. Frenzel, A.C., Goetz, T., Stephens, E.J., Jacob, B.: Antecedents and effects of teachers' emotional experiences: an integrated perspective and empirical test. In Schutz, P.A., Zembylas M. (eds.) Advances in Teacher Emotion Research: The Impact on Teachers' Lives, pp. 129–151. Springer Science & Business Media (2009)
13. Sutton, R.E.: Teachers' anger, frustration, and self-regulation. In Schutz, P.A., Pekrun, R., Phye, G.D. (eds.) Emotion in Education, vol. 10, pp. 259–274. Academic Press (2007). https://doi.org/10.1016/B978-012372545-5/50016-2
14. Sutton, R.E.: Emotion regulation goals and strategies of teachers. Soc. Psychol. Educ. **7**(4), 379–398 (2004). https://doi.org/10.1007/s11218-004-4229-y
15. Prosen, S., Smrtnik Vitulić, H.: Anger in preschool teachers: experience, regulation and connection to mental health. Eur. Early Child. Educ. Res. J. **27**(4), 468–478 (2019)
16. Parrott, W.G.: Beyond hedonism: motives for inhibiting good moods and for maintaining bad moods. In: Wegner, D.M., Pennebaker, J.W. (eds.) Handbook of Mental Control, pp. 278–308. Prentice Hall (1993)
17. Cole, P.M.: Children's spontaneous control of facial expression. Child Dev. **54**(6), 1309–1321 (1986)
18. Kaplan, S., Bradley, J.C., Luchman, J.N., Haynes, D.: On the role of positive and negative affectivity in job performance: a meta-analytic investigation. J. Appl. Psychol. **94**(1), 162–176 (2009). https://doi.org/10.1037/a0013115
19. Sims, R.L.: Ethical rule breaking by employees: a test of social bonding theory. J. Bus. Ethics **40**(2), 101–109 (2002). https://doi.org/10.1023/A:1020330801847
20. Harrison, D. A., & Price, K. H. (2003). Context and consistency in absenteeism: studying social and dispositional influences across multiple settings. Human Resource Management Review, 13(2), 203–225. https://doi.org/10.1016/s1053-4822(03)00013-5
21. Sagie, A.: Employee absenteeism, organizational commitment, and job satisfaction: another look. J. Vocat. Behav. **52**(2), 156–171 (1998). https://doi.org/10.1006/jvbe.1997.1581
22. Hanisch, K.A., Hulin, C.L.: General attitudes and organizational withdrawal: an evaluation of a causal model. J. Vocat. Behav. **39**(1), 110–128 (1991). https://doi.org/10.1016/0001-8791(91)90006-8
23. Mathieu, J.E., Zajac, D.M.: A review and meta-analysis of the antecedents, correlates, and consequences of organizational commitment. Psychol. Bull. **108**(2), 171–194 (1990). https://doi.org/10.1037/0033-2909.108.2.171
24. Pitts, K.: Teacher absenteeism: an examination of patterns and predictors. Doctoral dissertation, Virginia Commonwealth University (2010)
25. Sagie, A., Birati, A., Tziner, A.: Assessing the costs of behavioral and psychological withdrawal: a new model and an empirical illustration. Appl. Psychol. **51**(1), 67–89 (2002). https://doi.org/10.1111/1464-0597.00079
26. Alcázar, L., Rogers, F.H., Chaudhury, N., Hammer, J., Kremer, M., Muralidharan, K.: Why are teachers absent? Probing service delivery in Peruvian primary schools. Int. J. Educ. Res. **45**(3), 117–136 (2006). https://doi.org/10.1016/j.ijer.2006.11.007
27. Davey, M.M., Cummings, G., Newburn-Cook, C.V., Lo, E.A.: Predictors of nurse absenteeism in hospitals: a systematic review. J. Nurs. Manag. **17**(3), 312–330 (2009)
28. Shapira-Lishchinsky, O., Rosenblatt, Z.: Perceptions of organizational ethics as predictors of work absence: a test of alternative absence measures. J. Bus. Ethics **88**(4), 717–734 (2009). https://doi.org/10.1007/s10551-008-9977-8
29. Gosselin, E., Lemyre, L., & Corneil, W. Presenteeism and absenteeism: Differentiated understanding of related phenomena. J. Occup. Health Psychol. **18**(1), 75–86 (2013). https://doi.org/10.1037/a0030932
30. Abu-Asba, K., Jayusi, A., Zabar-Ben Yehoshua, N.: The identity of Palestinian youth who are citizens of Israel, the degree of their identification with the state and Jewish culture, and the implications for the education system. Dapim **52**, 45–11 (2011)

31. Al-Hajj, M.: Education Among the Arabs in Israel: Demography, Society, Economy, and Politics. Van Leer Institute (2006)
32. Ajabaria, A.: The policy of training Arab teachers in Israel: the demand for national uniqueness. In Ajabaria A. (ed.) Teacher Training in the Palestinian Society in Israel, pp. 21–26. Resling Publication (2013)
33. Arar, K., Abu-Asba, K.: Involving factors in the activities of the education departments in the local Arab government. Stud. Adm. Organ. Educ. **33**, 162–133 (2013)
34. Frank, A.: The "political" field in the work of school principals in Israel concerning aspects of authority, responsibility, accountability, and overload. Doctoral dissertation, Tel Aviv University (2012)
35. Arar, K.: Israeli education policy since 1948 and the state of Arab education in Israel. Ital. J. Sociol. Educ. **4**(1), 113–145 (2012)
36. Abu-Asba, K.: External and Internal Barriers Hinder the Absorption and Integration of Graduates in High-Tech Companies. The Arab-Jewish Center for Economic Development (2008)
37. Jabarin Y., Ajabaria A.: Autonomy to the Arab education in Israel, an opinion. **5**, 14–35 (2014)
38. Al-Ghamdi, Abdulaziz bin Abdullah Jamaan.: The relationship of emotions to decision-making skill among employees of the embassies of the Gulf Cooperation Council countries in Jordan. Unpublished master's thesis, Al-Balqa Applied University, Amman, Jordan (2012)
39. Al-Anani, H.: Emotions and its relationship to the leadership style of kindergarten and basic school teachers in the central Jordan Valley. Educ. J. **28**(110), 553–598 (2014)
40. Al-Khafaji, Z.H.B.: Emotions and psychological hardness and their relationship to the psychological exhaustion of teachers in some schools in Basra Governorate. J. Fac. Educ. Educ. Sci. **40**(1), 313–368 (2016)
41. Ghadaifi, India.: Emotions among special education teachers: a field study on some special education teachers in the city of the valley. J. Soc. Stud. Res. **8**(4), 39–48 (2020)
42. Al-Shuaibi, M.: The relationship of emotions to beliefs of collective competence among mathematics teachers in the Sultanate of Oman. Jordanian J. Educ. Sci. **16**(1), 33–44 (2020)
43. Alshebami, A., Al-Alamri, M.: The role of emotional intelligence in enhancing the ambition level of the students: mediating role of students' commitment to university. Talent Dev. Excel. **12**(1), 2275–2287 (2020)
44. Al-Khatatbeh, M.: The level of psychological burnout among teachers of students with autism spectrum disorder in Dammam and its relationship to their emotions. Int. J. Educ. Psychol. Stud. **9**(3), 710–730 (2021)
45. Bradlelya, S., Green, C., Leevesd, G.: Worker absence and shirking: evidence from matched teacher-school data. Labour Econ. **14**(3), 319–334 (2007)
46. Ginat, K.: The overt and covert laws of emotion. Echo Educ. **86**(1), 42–45 (2011)
47. Frenzel, A.C., Goetz, T., Lüdtke, O., Pekrun, R., Sutton, R.E.: Emotional transmission in the classroom: exploring the relationship between teacher and student enjoyment. J. Educ. Psychol. **101**(3), 705–716 (2009). https://doi.org/10.1037/a0014695
48. Rosenblatt, Z., Shapira-Lishchinsky, O., Shirom, A.: Absenteeism in Israeli schoolteachers: an organizational ethics perspective. Hum. Resour. Manag. Rev. **20**(3), 247–259 (2010). https://doi.org/10.1016/j.hrmr.2009.08.006
49. Shapira-Lishchinsky, O.: Israeli teachers' perceptions of lateness: a gender comparison. Sex Roles **57**(3–4), 187–199 (2007). https://doi.org/10.1007/s11199-007-9246-9
50. Burić, I., Slišković, A., Macuka, I.: A mixed-method approach to the assessment of teachers' emotions: development and validation of the Teacher Emotion Questionnaire. Educ. Psychol. **38**(3), 325–349 (2018)
51. Prosen, S., & Vitulić, H. S. Emotions and mental health in primary school teachers: what do they tell us about teachers'work? Modern Challenges in Education, **235** (2023)
52. Gross, J.J., Thompson, R.A.: Emotion regulation: conceptual foundations. In Gross, J.J., Thompson, R.A. (eds.), Handbook of Emotion Regulation, pp. 3–24. Guilford Press (2009)
53. Kline, R.B. Principles and practice of structural equation modelling (4th ed.). New York, NY: Guildford Press (2016)

54. Chaudhury, N., Hammer, J.S., Kremer, M., Muralidharan, K., & Rogers, F. Missing in action: teacher and health worker absence in developing countries. Journal of Economic Perspectives, **20**(1), 91–116 (2006). https://doi.org/10.1257/089533006776526058
55. Rogers, H.F., Lopez-Calix, J., Chaudhury, N., Hammer, J., Cordoba, N., Kremer, M., & Muralidharan, K. (2004). Teacher absence and incentives in primary education: Results from a national teacher tracking survey in Ecuador. Ecuador: Creating Fiscal Space for Poverty Reduction: A Fiscal Management and Public Expenditure Review, **2**, 136-162.

# The Scouts Movement Leadership in the Arab Society in Israel and Its Effect on Community Engagement of Its Members

**Adham Farah**

**Abstract** The aim of the study is to explore the correlation between the leadership of the Arab Scout movement counsels and the community engagement of its members. The research is a case study seeking to investigate the unique population of the Arab sector in the northern region of Israel and were conducted using quantitative analysis, by developing a questionnaire that were distributed to members and counselors from the Arab Scout Movement in Israel. The population of the study consisted of all members and counselors from the Arab Scout Movement in Israel. The study sample consists of 504 members and 50 counselors. The results showed that the means of FRLM (full-range leadership model) of the Scout movement counselors in the Arab sector were high. And the level of community engagement of members of the scout movement from the Arab sector in the north of the country counselors' point of view came with very high level, the results showed that there a positive statistical significance correlation between the level of Transformational leadership with community engagement.

**Keywords** Scouts in the Arab community in Israel · FRLM (full-range leadership model) · Community engagement

## 1 Introduction

In 1912 the St. George's Missionary School in Jerusalem established the Scout movement in Palestine. The movement began to operate as an adjunct to Muslim private schools [1]. Following the establishment of the State of Israel in 1948, there were also changes in the Arab Scout movement [2]. The Arab Scout Organization in Israel was founded again in 1956. It changed its name to The Arab and Druze Scout Movement in Israel [3]. Until 2005, the Arab Scout movement consisted exclusively of male

A. Farah (✉)
University of Ljubljana, Ljubljana, Slovenia
e-mail: astavros@gmail.com

 
S. Kot et al. (eds.), *Corporate Practices: Policies, Methodologies, and Insights in Organizational Management*, Springer Proceedings in Business and Economics,
https://doi.org/10.1007/978-981-97-0996-0_52

membership. In 2005 the Arab Girl Guides Association in Israel was granted official status by the World Association of Girl Guides and Girl Scouts [4]. Today, the Arab Scout movement is a member of the Scout Association in Israel and consists of more than 5000 members from the entire social and religious spectrum of the Arab society: Christians, Druze, and Muslims [5]. The Arab Scout Movement's vision is to apply the principles of liberty, justice, peace, and equality among the youth and aims to educate a humanist with inner integrity. Thus, the movement sets itself sub-goals: to educate its members in the spirit of morality and promise of the Scout, to develop in its members' social consciousness, discipline, respect for others, and good citizenship [3]. In today's world, where online societies can be perceived as more dominant than physical, personal societies [6–8].

Scout guides can also be seen from the perspective of a youth worker. Youth work can empower or lead to innovation among youth. Attention is given to youth work mainly for its ability to expose mechanisms of social inequality and support the social liberation of young people. The sociological perspective helps to emphasize the role of the youth worker as an intermediary between young people's claims to change and adults' protection of social stability. In addition, social pedagogy offers effective educational relationships between young people and youth workers as they strive to bring about change [9]. From this, another question arises, does the Scouts movement support the development of leadership competencies?

Effective leadership has become necessary for the different organizations to be able to achieve the set goals, as this needs a leader with competencies that enable him to address the problems in his organization, which is dominated by rapid changes, and this is also necessary to lead the organization to show the best performance, whether at the level of achieving goals or the organization and workers performance for their assigned functions [10]. Leadership is also a type of influence in interpersonal relationships between people and their ability to obtain approval from others, through which a person can leave his influence on the thoughts, feelings and behaviors of the group and urge them to implement the task he is asking for [11]. As a result of the interaction between the leader and the group, compatibility and homogeneity between the needs, desires and tendencies of the members of the institution must be investigated in accordance with the needs and objectives of the organization to which they belong. Leadership is also defined as the achievement of a set of goals with the highest degree of competence through cooperation, guidance, and influence provided to group members. Leadership is therefore critical as it promotes character building and social growth through a well-defined vision [12].

Jabri [13] emphasizes that leadership is the elevation of people from thinking about their personal interests to thinking about achieving the goals of the organization by instilling elements of confidence in the work environment adopted by the leader to encourage employees to achieve beyond expectations with guidance and try to guide them to achieve the desired goal.

The research literature contains various leadership theories and models of leadership. This study will focus on the full-range leadership model (FRLM) which combines transactional leadership transformational leadership and laissez-faire (Hands-off) leadership models [14]. The concept of transformative leadership speaks of leadership that enhances the leader's followers' motivation, morality, and performance through various mechanisms. These include connecting the sense of identity and self of the followers to the task and the collective identity of the organization; being a role model who inspires the followers; challenging the followers to take more ownership of their work and understand the strengths and weaknesses of the followers so that the leader can delegate tasks that will maximize their performance [15]. The term "transactional leadership" was coined in 1978 under the assumption that transformative leadership and transactional leadership are reciprocal styles. Transactional leaders do not typically strive for cultural change in an organization, but they operate in an existing culture, while transformative leaders can change the organizational culture [16]. Laissez-faire style leadership can sometimes be interpreted as a lack of leadership due to the perception that such leaders avoid taking a position on various issues, do not emphasize results and performance, and avoid intervening when issues arise. Sometimes a leader needs to step back a little and let their employees resolve the issues on their own. This is not avoidant leadership, but empowerment. Such leaders demonstrate an attitude of trust and reliance on their employees. They do not micromanage or over-involve. Since they trust their employees, they are not preoccupied with over-coaching and guidance. Instead, laissez-faire leaders allow their employees to use their creativity, resources, and experience to meet their goals [17, 18]. The FRLM integrates leadership style and effectiveness. According to the model, each leader expresses in their behavior different styles of leadership that are on a continuum ranging from non-leadership through transactional leadership to laissez-faire to transformative leadership [19].

The question arises as to why community involvement among members of the Scout movement is so significant. An answer to this can be found in a study on community involvement of Scouts after they were adults [20]. The findings showed that people who had been involved in their communities within the Scouts framework were more likely to participate in their communities to improve them when they become adults. These findings provide evidence that membership in the Scout movement can make a lasting difference in people's lives as it fosters behaviors that promote community engagement throughout a person's life [20, 21]. According to Hart [22], youth involvement also speaks of "participation," where the term generally refers to the process of sharing decision-making that affects a person's life and the life of the community in which they live. Participation in a community of young people is a complex issue that changes with the child's motivations and developing abilities according to the family and cultural context. In cultures where adults have little opportunity to influence community decisions, young people can become the driving force for change. Thus, the degree of opportunity a child has to participate in the day-to-day management of family, schools, neighborhoods, and community groups reflects the opportunities for adult participation in that culture. Intervention to improve children's participation is one means of fundamentally improving society. It also impacts empowering the child in his or her relationships within the family.

In that context, according to Krueger [23], there are four themes in youth work: presence, rhythmic interaction, meaning-making, and atmosphere. Presence is the ability to bring the self into the moment, be open and available, and reflect on the experience of the other. Rhythmic interactions form human connections. There is a sharing in the sense of togetherness that arises when participating in joint action. Meaning-making stems from how people construct and shape themselves through unique cultural and family experiences and then create different meanings for interactions. Youth have their ways of understanding participation and the context in which it occurs. Therefore, one should try to understand the contextual reality of youth. The atmosphere, the tone, the mood, the space, and the place all of these play a significant role in defining interactions. Youth is in or not in place, emotionally and physically present, or only physically present. They seek out or run away from familiar places when the atmosphere plays a significant role in this.

The advancement of the human personality requires a change in the various paths of life, which should include practical practices for all life conditions in society, and this comes through the practice of many activities that contribute to providing the individual with various skills that contribute to reaching the degree of quality and mastery, which needs scout movement that have programs capable of promoting community development within their members, so that these contribute Programs in achieving reconciliation between theory and reality by offering model projects concerned with community development, within harmony with the concept of sustainable human development that makes man a maker and beneficiary of the community development process [24].

## 2 Research Problem and Questions

The Arab society in the State of Israel is a minority society within a space characterized by socio-cultural and ideological differences from the Jewish majority society. As a collectivist society with values in which the family and community have a tremendous influence on its members, the Arab society in Israel is undergoing many changes and transformations in the face of the changes going on in a progressive world that is not always in line with collectivist-conservative values that characterize the Arab society. Therefore, there is an interest in understanding the stance of the youth, the future generation, in Arab society and how it adapts to the changes in the modern world. Young people in today's world must demonstrate citizenship and show community engagement within their society. It is essential to understand the Arab society in the framework of this idea and to understand the place of Scouts, members, and counselors alike in promoting the progressive values of community work. Thus, the present study examines the Scout movement explicitly since it inscribed on its banner many decades ago its symbiotic connection with the political establishment and the social values of the community in which it operates. There is a special interest in understanding a field that has never been studied—the Arab youth and their community engagement and whether the Scout movement contributes to this engagement. The research population is unique and distinct in terms of sector, religion, mentality, and culture; therefore, our research is a case study that will investigate the Arab scout movement in the north of Israel. Hence, the study results cannot be generalized to other populations, however, they can shed light on the association between leadership and community engagement in minority research on a cultural-social level.

The research questions are:

1. What is the level of FRLM of the Scout movement counselors in the Arab sector?
2. What is the level of community engagement of members of the scout movement from the Arab sector in the north of the country counselors point of view?
3. Is there a statistical significance to the correlation between the level of FRLM of the Scout movement counselors in the Arab sector and the level of community engagement of members of the scout movement from the Arab sector in the north of the country from counslors point of view?
4. What is the level of FRLM of the Scout movement counselors in the Arab sector from members point of view?
5. What is the level of community engagement of members of the scout movement from the Arab sector in the north of the country members point of view?
6. Is there a statistical significance to the correlation between the level of FRLM of the Scout movement counselors in the Arab sector and the level of community engagement of members of the scout movement from the Arab sector in the north of the country from member point view?

## 3 Research Method

This section illustrates the results of analyzing the data; the validity and reliability, the descriptive statistics (demographic characteristics and descriptive statistics of the study main and sub variables), next, the test of normality and Multicollinearity are examined. Finally, the findings of each question and testing and their interpretation are discussed.

The purpose of this research study was to gain additional insight into the relationship between leadership in the Arab society in Israel and its effect on community engagement of its members. This study sought to contribute to this more limited knowledge base of leadership among leaders, and community engagement among members, among scout's movement in Israel.

The questionnaires were distributed online using the Google Forms application and circulated through the Scout movement social media group upon parental approval from the period of (15 January to 15 April 2023). The questionnaires were developed to collect data from the sample of the study after reviewing some of the previous literature addressing each of the variables examined in the study, the questionnaire consisted of:

1. **Member questionnaire**: The Multifactor Leadership Questionnaire (MLQ) was developed by Avolio and Bass [25] and described the leadership style of the counselors as perceived by the members. The questionnaire has 24 statements. The answers are on a Likert scale of 1 ("strongly disagree") to 5 ("strongly agree").

2. **Member questionnaire**: The youth involvement and engagement assessment tool [26]. The self-report questionnaire examines the level of youth involvement, community engagement, and youth retention existing within the Scouts movement's community programs. The questionnaire has 40 statements. The answers are on a Likert scale of 1 ("Strongly Disagree") to 5 ("Strongly Agree").
3. **Counselor questionnaire**: The Multifactor Leadership Questionnaire (MLQ) [25]. The self-report questionnaire examines the leadership style of the counselors. The questionnaire has 24 statements. The answers are on a Likert scale of 1 ("strongly disagree") to 5 ("strongly agree").
4. **Counselor questionnaire**: The youth involvement and engagement assessment tool [26]. The questionnaire examines the level of youth involvement, community engagement, and youth retention existing within the Scouts movement's community programs. The questionnaire has 40 statements describing how the counselor perceives the member's community engagement. The answers are on a Likert scale of 1 ("Strongly Disagree") to 5 ("Strongly Agree").

### *3.1 The Study Sample Characteristic*

The study population is composed of members and counselors from the Arab Scout Movement in Israel. The study sample consists of 504 members (male and female, 13–16) and 50 counselors (18–35) (Tables 1 and 2).

## 4 Research Model

The research is a case study seeking to investigate the unique population of the Arab sector in the northern region of Israel and will be conducted with quantitative analysis. The research model illustrated in Fig. 1 contained an assumption of seven independent variables (the elements of full range leadership model (FRLM) that include;

**Table 1** Demographic characteristics of participating scout members ($n = 504$)

| Variable | *N* | % |
|---|---|---|
| Male | 238 | 47.2 |
| Female | 266 | 52.8 |
| Total | 504 | 100.0 |
| Elementary | 145 | 28.8 |
| Secondary | 359 | 71.2 |
| Total | 504 | 100.0 |
| 5 years and less | 214 | 42.5 |
| More than 5 years | 290 | 57.5 |
| Total | 504 | 100.0 |

**Table 2** Demographic characteristics of counselors ($n = 50$)

| Variable | *N* | % |
|---|---|---|
| Male | 23 | 46.0 |
| Female | 27 | 54.0 |
| Total | 50 | 100.0 |
| Secondary school | 6 | 12.0 |
| Higher study | 44 | 88.0 |
| Total | 50 | 100.0 |
| 10 years and less | 20 | 40.0 |
| More than 10 years | 30 | 60.0 |
| Total | 50 | 100.0 |

idealized influence (three items), Inspirational stimulation (three items), Intellectual stimulation (three items), Individualized consideration (three items), Contingent Rewards (three items), Management by Exception (three items), Hands-off Leadership (Laissez Faire) (three items). Als the model of the study as illustrated in Fig. (2; include the effect of the eight element of the leadership model (FRLM) on scout community engagement.

Prior research has supported a relationship between the eight elements of the FRLM and three leadership constructs: (a) Transformational Leadership, comprised

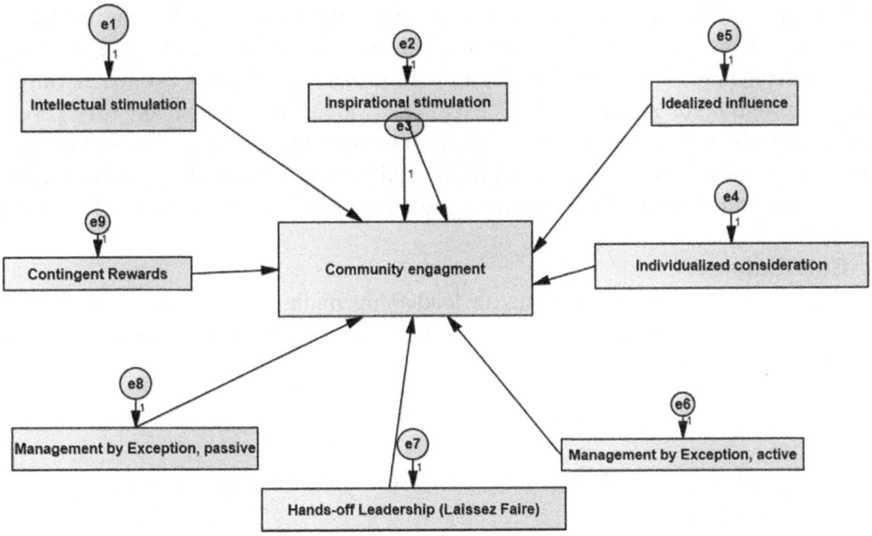


**Fig. 1** Research design represent eight elements as independent variables on community engagement

**Table 3** Cronbach's alpha for all variable scales

| Variable | Cronbach's Alpha | *N* of items |
|---|---|---|
| Idealized influence | 0.775 | 3 |
| Inspirational stimulation | 0.703 | 3 |
| Intellectual stimulation | 0.766 | 3 |
| Individualized consideration | 0.691 | 3 |
| Contingent Rewards | 0.758 | 3 |
| Management by Exception, active | 0.622 | 3 |
| Hands-off Leadership (Laissez Faire) | 0.912 | 3 |
| Management by Exception, passive | 0.984 | 3 |

of Idealized Influence, Inspirational stimulation, Intellectual Stimulation, and Individualized Consideration; (b) Transactional Leadership, comprised of Contingent Reward; and management by exception active, and (c) Passive-Avoidance Management-by-Exception, Laissez-Faire.

## 4.1 *Reliability and Internal Consistency*

Cronbach's alpha was used to calculate the internal consistencies for all variable scales. With scales less than 10 items, a value >0.5 is acceptable. The extent of reliability of the questions measuring the values of transformational, transactional, passive avoidant was indicated by the internal consistency values. A Cronbach's alpha value "around 0.90" are considered "excellent," values around 0.80 as "very good," and values about 0.70 as "adequate" [27]. Transformational leadership and passive avoidance, and transactional leadership showed good reliability, the Cronbach alpha of 8 scales were around the acceptable greater than 0.5, as shown in the following Table 3.

**Correlations:**

The communalities of the items in leadership main domains are all above 0.4 showing moderate correlation. Thus, these items load significantly to their respective dimension.

## 4.2 *Reliability and Internal Consistency for Community Engagement*

Cronbach's alpha was used to calculate the internal consistencies for all variable scales. With scales less than 10 items, a value >0.5 is acceptable. The extent of reliability of the questions measuring the values of community engagement was

**Table 4** Cronbach's Alpha for all variable scales for community engagement

| Variable | Cronbach's Alpha | *N* of items |
|---|---|---|
| Youth Involvement | 9 | 0.909 |
| Youth Engagement (within the community) | 13 | 0.934 |
| Youth Retention | 18 | 0.937 |

indicated by the internal consistency values. A Cronbach's alpha value "around 0.90 are considered "excellent," values around 0.80 as "very good," and values about 0.70 as "adequate" [27]. the Cronbach alpha of community engagement scale were around the acceptable greater than 0.5, as shown in the following Table 4.

**Correlations:**

The communalities of the items in community engagement main domains are all above 0.4 showing moderate correlation. Thus, these items load significantly to their respective dimension.

## 4.3 *The Study Model*

(See Fig. 2).

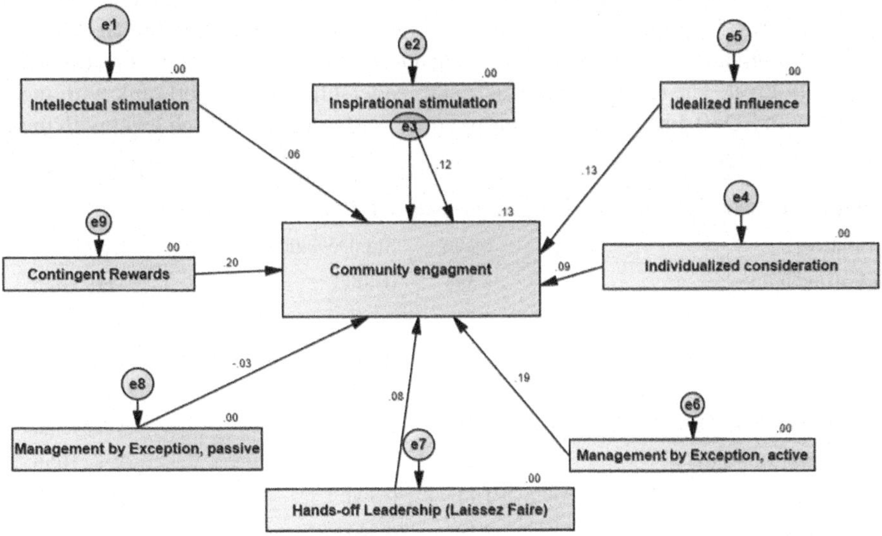


**Fig. 2** Study main model

## 5 Data Analysis

The quantitative data were analyzed using different statistical analyses (mean, standard deviation, frequency, proportion, t-test, correlation coefficient) through Statistical Package for Social Sciences (SPSS).

The Scouts' leadership was already approached and advised of the proposed study. The parents and the study participants will be informed of all the details of the study and its objectives. The participation will constitute parental informed consent from each parent. To preserve the privacy of the participants, the personal details of the participants will be kept confidential to prevent violation of their rights and privacy.

## 6 Findings

**Answering the 1st question: What is the level of FRLM of the Scout movement counselors in the Arab sector?** To answer this question, the researcher computed means and standard deviations for all the study domains and sub domains, as shown in the following tables (Table 5).

From the previous table which showed that the means of FRLM of the Scout movement counselors in the Arab sector is ranged from moderate to high. The domain (transformational leadership) got the highest mean with (4.41), Also, from the table it showed that all the sub domains of the transformational leadership came with high level, in which idealized influence got the highest mean with (4.5) and SD (0.499), with very high level, and individualized consideration got the lowest mean with (4.14) with high level. The domain (Transactional leadership) got the 2nd rank with mean (4.19), with SD (0.540) in which contingent rewards came with high level with mean

**Table 5** Mean average score and standard deviation of FRLM

| Variables | Mean | Std. Deviation | Rank | Level |
|---|---|---|---|---|
| Idealized influence | 4.58 | 0.499 | 1 | Very High |
| Inspirational stimulation | 4.51 | 0.448 | 2 | Very High |
| Intellectual stimulation | 4.42 | 0.534 | 3 | Very High |
| Individualized consideration | 4.14 | 0.369 | 4 | High |
| **Transformational leadership** | **4.41** | **0.370** | | Very High |
| Contingent Rewards | 4.28 | 0.664 | 1 | Very High |
| Management by Exception, active | 4.11 | 0.596 | 2 | High |
| **Transactional leadership** | **4.19** | **0.540** | | High |
| Hands-off Leadership (Laissez Faire) | 3.49 | 0.871 | 1 | High |
| Management by Exception, passive | 3.01 | 0.563 | 2 | Moderate |
| **Passive avoidance** | **3.25** | **0.430** | | Moderate |
| Scout Movement leadership | 4.07 | 0.279 | | High |

(4.28) and management by exception, active with high level also with mean (4.11). In the final rank the domain (Passive avoidance) with mean (3.25) with moderate level. In which Hands-off Leadership (Laissez Faire) with mean (3.49) with high level, and Management by Exception, passive with moderate level with mean (3.01).

**Answering the 2nd question: What is the level of community engagement of members of the scout movement from the Arab sector in the north of the country counselors point of view?** To answer this question, the researcher computed means and standard deviations for all Community engagement domains, as shown in the following Table 6.

From the previous table which showed that the means of community engagement of members of the scout movement from the Arab sector in the north of the country counselors' point of view came with very high level, in which the domain Youth Engagement (within the community) got the highest mean with (4.25) and SD (0.580), next the domain youth involvement with mean (4.23) and SD (0.665), and in the final rank the domain youth retention with mean (4.18) and SD (0.668).

**Answering the 3rd question: Is there a statistical significance to the correlation between the level of FRLM of the Scout movement counselors in the Arab sector and the level of community engagement of members of the scout movement from the Arab sector in the north of the country from counselor's point of view?** To answer this question Pearson correlation were computed between the domains of FRLM and community engagement of members as shown in the following Table 7.

From the table which showed that there a positive statistical significance correlation between the level of transformational leadership with youth engagement (within the community) with R (0.568), and a positive statistical significance correlation between the level transactional leadership of the Scout movement counselors in the Arab sector and the level of community engagement of members with R (0.583). also the table showed that there was a negative correlation between passive avoidance and community engagement with R (−0.08). Also the researcher computed multiple linear regression, as shown in the following Table 8.

Linear regression analysis was performed and the results of the analysis As shown in table (15). F value equal (9.552) at sig. (0.00). and the value of $t$ = (2.192) at sig (0.00) for transformational leadership, and value of t for transactional leadership were (2.146) with sig (0.00), which is less than (0.05). In addition, $R^2$ was (0.384), meaning that (38.4%) of changes taking place in study subjects means scores about community engagement of members due to FRLM. In which the highest effect is

**Table 6** Mean average score and standard deviation of community engagement level

| Variable | Mean | Std. Deviation | Rank | Level |
|---|---|---|---|---|
| Youth Engagement (within the community) | 4.25 | 0.580 | 1 | Very high |
| Youth Involvement | 4.23 | 0.665 | 2 | Very high |
| Youth Retention | 4.18 | 0.668 | 3 | High |
| Community engagement | 4.22 | 0.604 | | Very high |

**Table 7** Correlation matrix between the level of FRLM and the level of community engagement of members. Counselors perspective

| Variable | Pearson R | Youth Engagement (within the community) |
|---|---|---|
| Transformational leadership | Pearson Correlation | 0.568(**) |
| | Sig. (2-tailed) | 0.000 |
| | *N* | 50 |
| Transactional leadership | Pearson Correlation | 0.583(**) |
| | Sig. (2-tailed) | 0.000 |
| | *N* | 50 |
| Passive avoidance | Pearson Correlation | −0.080 |
| | Sig. (2-tailed) | 0.582 |
| | *N* | 50 |

**Correlation is significant at the 0.01 level (2-tailed)

**Table 8** Linear Regression for the impact of FRLM of the Scout movement counselors in the Arab sector on the level of community engagement of members from Counselors perspective

| variables | Unstandardized Coefficients | | Standardized Coefficients | *t* | Sig | R | $R^2$ |
|---|---|---|---|---|---|---|---|
| | B | Std. Er | beta | | | | |
| (Constant) | −0.133 | 1.269 | | −0.104 | | 0.620(a) | 0.384 |
| Transformational leadership | 0.598 | 0.273 | 0.366 | **2.192** | **0.033** | | |
| Transactional leadership | 0.369 | 0.172 | 0.330 | **2.146** | **0.037** | | |
| Passive avoidance | 0.051 | 0.183 | 0.037 | 0.280 | 0.780 | | |
| F value = 9.552 sig. = 0.000(a) | | | | | | | |

due to transformational leadership with (B = 0.598), and Transactional leadership with (B = 0.369). and passive avoidance (0.051).

**Answering the 4th question**: What is the level of FRLM of the Scout movement counselors in the Arab sector from member's point of view? To answer this question, the researcher computed means and standard deviations for all the study domains and sub domains, as shown in the following Table 9.

From the previous table which showed that the means of FRLM of the Scout movement counselors in the Arab sector is ranged from moderate to high. The domain (transformational leadership) got the highest mean with (4.25), Also, from the table it showed that all the sub domains of the transformational leadership came with high level, in which idealized influence got the highest mean with (4.38) and SD (0.634), with very high level, and individualized consideration got the lowest mean with (4.04) with high level. The domain (Transactional leadership) got the 2nd rank with mean (4.19), with SD (0.642) in which contingent rewards came with high level

**Table 9** Mean average score and standard deviation of FRLM from members perspective

| Variables | Mean | Std. Deviation | Rank | Level |
|---|---|---|---|---|
| Idealized influence | 4.38 | 0.634 | 1 | Very High |
| Inspirational stimulation | 4.33 | 0.661 | 2 | Very High |
| Intellectual stimulation | 4.27 | 0.725 | 3 | Very High |
| Individualized consideration | 4.04 | 0.604 | 4 | High |
| **Transformational leadership** | **4.25** | **0.548** | | Very High |
| Contingent Rewards | 4.27 | 0.708 | 1 | Very High |
| Management by Exception, active | 4.11 | 0.722 | 2 | High |
| **Transactional leadership** | **4.19** | **0.642** | | High |
| Hands-off Leadership (Laissez Faire) | 3.26 | 0.811 | 1 | High |
| Management by Exception, passive | 3.23 | 0.800 | 2 | Moderate |
| **Passive avoidance** | **3.24** | **0.764** | | Moderate |
| Scout Movement leadership | 3.99 | 0.280 | | High |

with mean (4.27) and management by exception, active with high level also with mean (4.11). In the final rank the domain (Passive avoidance) with mean (3.24) with moderate level. In which Hands-off Leadership (Laissez Faire) with mean (3.26) with moderate level, and Management by Exception, passive with moderate level with mean (3.24).

**Answering the 5th question**: What is the level of community engagement of members of the scout movement from the Arab sector in the north of the country members point of view? To answer this question, the researcher computed means and standard deviations for all Community engagement domains, as shown in the following Table 10.

From the previous table which showed that the means of community engagement of members of the scout movement from the Arab sector in the north of the country counselors' point of view came with very high level, in which the domain Youth Engagement (within the community) got the highest mean with (4.26) and SD (0.674), next the domain youth involvement with mean (4.23) and SD (0.697), and in the final rank the domain youth retention with mean (4.23) and SD (0.635).

**Answering the 6th question**: Is there a statistical significance to the correlation between the level of FRLM of the Scout movement counselors in the Arab sector

**Table 10** Mean average score and standard deviation of Community engagement level

| Variable | Mean | Std. Deviation | Rank | Level |
|---|---|---|---|---|
| Youth Involvement | 4.26 | 0.674 | 1 | Very high |
| Youth Engagement (within the community) | 4.23 | 0.697 | 2 | Very high |
| Youth Retention | 4.20 | 0.635 | 3 | High |
| Community engagement | 4.23 | 0.635 | | Very high |

**Table 11** Pearson correlation between the level of FRLM of the Scout movement counselors in the Arab sector and the level of community engagement of members

| Variable | Pearson R | Youth Engagement (within the community) |
|---|---|---|
| Transformational leadership | Pearson Correlation | 0.643(**) |
| | Sig. (2-tailed) | 0.000 |
| | *N* | 504 |
| Transactional leadership | Pearson Correlation | 0.645(**) |
| | Sig. (2-tailed) | 0.000 |
| | *N* | 504 |
| Passive avoidance | Pearson Correlation | −0.533(**) |
| | Sig. (2-tailed) | 0.000 |
| | *N* | 504 |
| Youth Engagement (within the community) | Pearson Correlation | 1 |
| | Sig. (2-tailed) | |
| | *N* | 504 |

** Correlation is significant at the 0.01 level (2-tailed)

and the level of community engagement of members of the scout movement from the Arab sector in the north of the country from member point view? To answer this question Pearson correlation were computed between the domains of FRLM and community engagement of members as shown in the following Table 11.

From the table which showed that there a positive statistical significance correlation between the level of Transformational leadership with youth engagement (within the community) with R (0.643), and a positive statistical significance correlation between the level transactional leadership of the Scout movement counselors in the Arab sector and the level of community engagement of members with R (0.645) also the table showed that there was a negative correlation between passive avoidance and community engagement with R (−0.533).

## *6.1 Analyzing Study Model*

The study model will analyze the relationships between the following variables:

**1. Correlation between leadership and community engagement from the members' perspective**. Pearson correlation were computed between the domains of FRLM and community engagement of members as shown in the following Table 12.

From the table which showed that there a positive statistical significance correlation between the level of transformational leadership with youth engagement (within the community) with R (0.643), and a positive statistical significance correlation

**Table 12** Correlation between leadership and community engagement from the members' perspective

| Variable | Pearson R | Youth Engagement (within the community) |
|---|---|---|
| Transformational leadership | Pearson Correlation | 0.643(**) |
| | Sig. (2-tailed) | 0.000 |
| | *N* | 504 |
| Transactional leadership | Pearson Correlation | 0.645(**) |
| | Sig. (2-tailed) | 0.000 |
| | *N* | 504 |
| Passive avoidance | Pearson Correlation | −0.533(**) |
| | Sig. (2-tailed) | 0.000 |
| | *N* | 504 |
| Youth Engagement (within the community) | Pearson Correlation | 1 |
| | Sig. (2-tailed) | |
| | *N* | 504 |

** Significance at (alpha=0.01)

between the level transactional leadership of the Scout movement counselors in the Arab sector and the level of community engagement of members with R (0.645). also the table showed that there was a negative correlation between passive avoidance and community engagement with R (−0.533). Also the researcher computed Linear regression, as shown in the following Table 13.

Linear Regression analysis was performed and the results of the analysis As shown in table (23). F value equal (198.712) at sig. (0.00). and the value of $t = (8.593)$ at sig (0.00) for transformational leadership, and value of $t$ for transactional leadership were (8.568) with sig (0.00), which is less than (0.05). In addition, $R^2$ was (0.544),

**Table 13** Linear Regression for the impact of FRLM of the Scout movement counselors in the Arab sector on the level of community engagement of members from Members perspective

| variables | Unstandardized Coefficients | | Standardized Coefficients | t | Sig | R | $R^2$ |
|---|---|---|---|---|---|---|---|
| | B | Std. Er | beta | | | | |
| (Constant) | 0.193 | 0.363 | | 0.531 | 0.596 | 0.737(a) | 0.544 |
| Transformational leadership | 0.500 | 0.058 | 0.432 | 8.593 | 0.000 | | |
| Transactional leadership | 0.412 | 0.048 | 0.417 | 8.568 | 0.000 | | |
| Passive avoidance | 0.056 | 0.042 | 0.068 | 1.360 | 0.175 | | |
| F value = 198.712 sig. = 0.000(a) | | | | | | | |

meaning that (54.4%) of changes taking place in study subjects means scores about community engagement of members due to FRLM. In which the highest effect is due to transformational leadership with (B = 0.432), and Transactional leadership with (B = 0.417). and passive avoidance (0.068), as shown in the following Fig. 3.

Pearson correlation were computed between the domains of FRLM and community engagement of members as shown in the following Table 14.

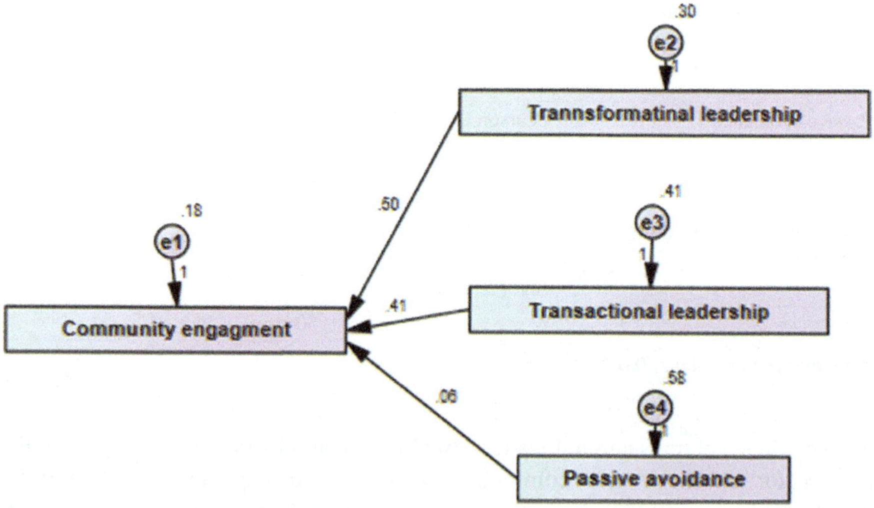


**Fig. 3** Correlation between leadership and community engagement from the counselors' perspective

**Table 14** Pearson correlation between the level of Leadership of the Scout movement counselors

| Variable | Pearson R | Youth Engagement (within the community) |
|---|---|---|
| Transformational leadership | Pearson Correlation | 0.559(**) |
| | Sig. (2-tailed) | 0.000 |
| | *N* | 50 |
| Transactional leadership | Pearson Correlation | 0.557(**) |
| | Sig. (2-tailed) | 0.000 |
| | *N* | 50 |
| Passive avoidance | Pearson Correlation | −0.125 |
| | Sig. (2-tailed) | 0.388 |
| | *N* | 50 |
| Scout Movement leadership | Pearson Correlation | 0.591(**) |
| | Sig. (2-tailed) | 0.000 |
| | *N* | 50 |

** Signifance at (alpha = 0.01)

**Table 15** Linear Regression for the impact Scout movement counselor's leadership on the level of youth engagement of members from Counselors perspective

| variables | Unstandardized Coefficients | | Standardized Coefficients | *t* | Sig | R | $R^2$ |
|---|---|---|---|---|---|---|---|
| | B | Std. Er | beta | | | | |
| (Constant) | −0.133 | 1.269 | | −0.104 | 0.917 | 0.620** | 0.384 |
| Transformational leadership | 0.598 | 0.273 | 0.366 | 2.192 | 0.033 | | |
| Transactional leadership | 0.369 | 0.172 | 0.330 | 2.146 | 0.037 | | |
| Passive avoidance | 0.051 | 0.183 | 0.037 | 0.280 | 0.780 | | |
| F value = 9.552 sig. = 0.000(a) | | | | | | | |

**significant at the 0.01 level means from the table which showed that there a positive statistical significance correlation between the level of leadership with youth engagement

From the table which showed that there a positive statistical significance correlation between the level of transformational leadership with youth engagement (within the community) with R (0.559), and a positive statistical significance correlation between the level transactional leadership of the Scout movement counselors in the Arab sector and the level of community engagement of members with R (0.557). also the table showed that there was a negative correlation between passive avoidance and community engagement with R (−0.125). Also the researcher computed Linear regression, as shown in the following Table 15.

Linear Regression analysis was performed and the results of the analysis As shown in table (25). F value equal (9.552) at sig. (0.00). and the value of $t$ = (2.192) at sig (0.00) for transformational leadership, and value of t for transactional leadership were (2.146) with sig (0.00), which is less than (0.05). In addition, $R^2$ was (0.384), meaning that (38.4%) of changes taking place in study subjects means scores about community engagement of members due to FRLM. In which the highest effect is due to transformational leadership with (B = 0.366), and Transactional leadership with (B = 0.330). and passive avoidance (0.037), as shown in the following chart.

## 6.2 *Factors Effecting Community Engagement*

From testing the model using Amos 23, it was found that there several factors can effect positively members community engagement, among these factors which have a positive impact, idealized influence, individualized consideration, management by exception, active, contingent rewards, intellectual stimulation, inspirational stimulation, and other factors have less impact on member community engagement such as hands off leadership, and other factors which have negative impact on member

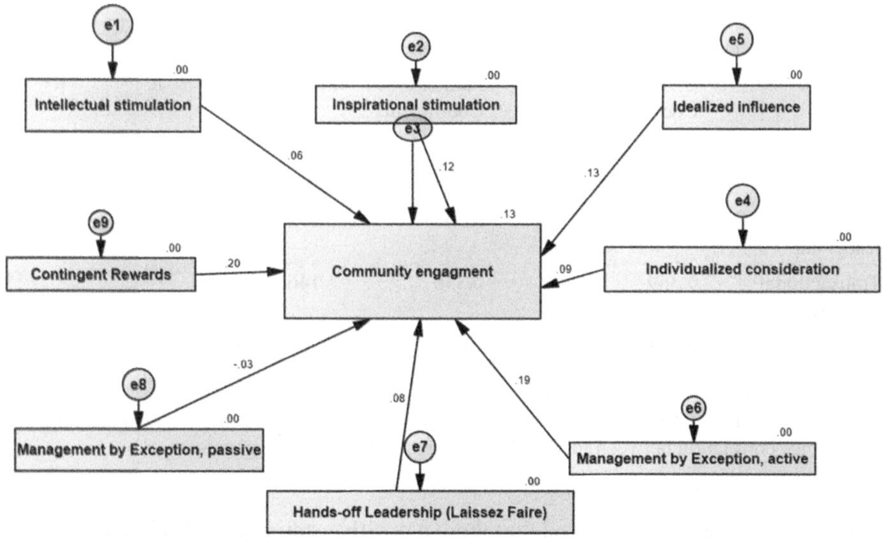


**Fig. 4** Factors effecting community egagement

community engagement which is management by exception, passive, and this can be demonstrated from the following model (Fig. 4).

## 7 Discussion and Conclusion

The results showed that the means of FRLM of the Scout movement counselors in the Arab sector is ranged from moderate to high. The domain (transformational leadership) got the highest rank, this is because Transformational leadership is a leadership style that focuses on inspiring and motivating followers to achieve their full potential and go beyond their self-interest for the greater good of the organization or society. Scout counselors have the personal and professional. This result can be attributed to the fact that the advisors in the Scouting movement in Israel have professional and personal competencies, as they use positive types of leadership, which include transformational leadership, which focuses on many skills that include their skills in motivating members and students, by sharing the vision and working to achieve it. They also realize the importance of encouraging innovation and creativity and giving them ample opportunity to practice critical thinking in order to reduce the problems and limitations that may face the achievement of work goals. Mentors also work to train subordinates and work to raise professional, personal and social growth. They also provide them with support. Mentors The importance of providing support to followers, as they are encouraged to work within a team, and this is confirmed by many results confirmed by in many studies, such as; Antoniou & Gioumouki [28] also pointed out that Fiedler shows that the effectiveness and success of leadership is manifested in situations that achieve harmony between the requirements of the situation and the leadership style necessary for the attitudes and personal characteristics of the leader, and he considers the leadership style of a situation effective to the extent that the leader can achieve the goals for which he found the leadership position, and the administrative leader must study his group, its roles, cohesion, goals and structure, and he must influence the behavior of the group and direct its members in order to achieve its goals. Also Bass and Avolio (1997) found in their research that a transactional leadership strategy can be highly effective, which in turn is more effective and leads to greater employee satisfaction by motivating them to achieve goals more rather than focusing on direct self-interest, to achieve goals and self-realization rather than safety and security.

**The level of community engagement of members of the scout movement from the Arab sector in the north of the country counselors point of view.**

The results showed that the means of community engagement of members of the scout movement from the Arab sector in the north of the country counselors' point of view came with very high level, in which the domain Youth Engagement (within the community) got the highest mean next the domain youth involvement wand in the final rank the domain youth retention. The researcher attributes this result to community affiliation, as a result of the activities carried out by the scouting movement centers in Israel, which focus on the personal and social development of the students, as the scouting movement is based on developing many skills for the students, which include problem solving, communication and communication, in addition to increasing their skills in the arts of leadership. Counselors also increase their ability to manage themselves and increase their awareness of many societal matters. This result can also be attributed to the fact that students who have high integration into society may have higher academic achievement, in addition to their ability to interact in the classroom to a greater extent than others. Who have a lower degree of community affiliation. This result can also be attributed to the fact that activities in scouting centers encourage increased social responsibility, as they learn how to be productive for their communities and work to change society in a positive way. Likewise, the activities provided by the Scouting movement in Israel to students include activities characterized by teamwork and cooperation, in addition to professional awareness. Scout centers also achieve many goals, which include increasing students' ability to diversify and accept others, in addition to accepting many cultures and dealing with many other students who have different other cultures, this is confirmed by Al-Deeb [29] pointed out the importance of the role of the Scout movement in enhancing intellectual security in the face of extremism and violence, and one of the first reasons is that these centers work to help establish camps to help develop their personalities and benefit from such events to guide them intellectually and behaviorally, also the scout movement helps individuals to spend their free time in a fruitful and useful activity, and is one of the important ways of academic, professional and community guidance, and participates in expanding the experiences of individuals in many fields to build and develop their personalities. Also Abu al-Qiyaan [24] confirmed that The advancement of the human personality requires a change in the various paths of life, which should include practical practices for all life conditions in society, and this comes through the practice of many activities that contribute to providing the individual with various skills that contribute to reaching the degree of quality and mastery, which needs scout movement that have programs capable of promoting community development within their members, so that these contribute Programs in achieving reconciliation between theory and reality by offering model projects concerned with community development, within harmony with the concept of sustainable human development that makes man a maker and beneficiary of the community development process.

**The correlation between the level of FRLM of the Scout movement counselors in the Arab sector and the level of community engagement of members of the scout movement from the Arab sector in the north of the country.**

The results showed that there a positive statistical significance correlation between the level of transformational leadership with youth engagement (within the community) with R (0.568), and a positive statistical significance correlation between the level transactional leadership of the Scout movement counselors in the Arab sector and the level of community engagement of members with R (0.583). Transformational leadership, which involves inspiring and motivating individuals to achieve their full potential and work toward common goals, can be particularly effective in engaging and empowering young people. Scout leaders who practice transformational leadership excel at inspiring and motivating others. This is especially important when working with young people who may be looking for guidance and inspiration. Scout counselors ignite a sense of purpose and excitement, and encourage young people to participate in various activities and initiatives. It empowers others, including Scout students, by involving them in decision-making processes, providing opportunities for growth and development, and promoting a sense of ownership over their actions and contributions. This empowerment can be a powerful motivator for student engagement. Scout counselors who are transformational leaders serve as positive role models. When students see their leaders demonstrating the values and behaviors they want to emulate, it can inspire them to become more involved and make positive contributions to their communities and society. Scout counselors emphasize building strong, trusting relationships with their followers. This is especially important when working with young people, as they are more likely to engage when they feel respected, valued and heard. Scouting consultants often promote creativity, innovation and critical thinking. This approach can resonate with young people who are often keen to explore new ideas and approaches, making them more likely to participate in activities and projects. Scouting consultants express a compelling vision and sense of purpose. Young people are more likely to participate when they can connect their actions to a larger cause or vision that aligns with their values and aspirations. Youth engagement often involves helping young people to develop skills, gain experience and grow as individuals. Scout Consultants also prioritize the long-term development of their followers, in line with the objectives of youth engagement programs. It is important to note that although transformational leadership can be very effective in promoting youth engagement, it must be complemented with appropriate support structures, resources and opportunities tailored to the needs and interests of the specific youth population. In addition, other factors such as context and cultural nuances can influence the extent of the connection between transformational leadership and youth engagement.

The results showed that showed that there was a negative correlation between passive avoidance and community engagement with R (−0.08). In this context, passive avoidance refers to a behavior or attitude where an individual avoids or refrains from participating in community engagement activities or initiatives. This negative correlation may be indicative of a situation where individuals who exhibit passive avoidance tendencies are less likely to engage with their community. The negative correlation may come because student's scouts who display passive avoidance behaviors may have a lack of interest or motivation to participate in community engagement activities. They might not see the value or importance of being actively involved in their community. Passive avoidance can sometimes be associated with social withdrawal or introverted tendencies. People who are less socially oriented may be less likely to engage in community activities that often involve interaction with others. also Some individuals might avoid community engagement due to social anxiety or fear of public speaking, which can be barriers to active participation in group activities or public events. Passive avoidance might also be related to individuals feeling overwhelmed with other commitments, such as work or personal responsibilities, leaving them with limited time to engage in community activities. Previous negative experiences or perceived negative outcomes related to community engagement can discourage individuals from participating actively in the future. In some cases, individuals may not be aware of community engagement opportunities or how to get involved. They might avoid engagement simply because they are not informed about available options. It's important to note that community engagement can take many forms, from volunteering and civic participation to community service and advocacy. While a negative correlation with passive avoidance might exist, it does not necessarily imply that all individuals who exhibit passive avoidance will avoid community engagement entirely. Factors like personal values, experiences, and external motivations can influence an individual's level of community engagement. Efforts to increase community engagement should consider addressing the factors that contribute to passive avoidance and finding ways to make community involvement more accessible and appealing to a broader range of individuals. This may involve education, outreach, creating inclusive opportunities, and addressing any barriers that deter people from engaging with their community. Thes results confirmed by [30] who suggest that the scout movement in sociology, anthropology, education and other sectors is of great importance, due to its role in analyzing and understanding the social structure in general, and relations in particular, if we know that most social interactions between members of different social groups are only a mutual influence between social centers, not a mutual influence between people, the social process is led by social centers and associated standards [31]. The importance of the Scout movement is to achieve physical health, develop basic skills for self-learning and continuous, develop social relationships, and develop the ability to be self-reliant [32]. Herbs and Stein [33] explained that the scout movement has achieved many achievements that contributed to various stakeholders in the activity of the educational institution, such as parents, teachers, youth and residents, as it focused on formulating a unique identity for the educational institution, with reference to societal reality. Yitzhar [34] explained that the scout movement contributes to many recreational activities, activating annual events such as Health Day, road accident prevention activity, sports day, etc., in addition to providing activities during the school day such as lectures for parents on academic and other topics.

## 8 Recommendations

The study recommends the following:

1. Implement leadership development programs that focus on teaching leadership skills, including transformational leadership. Encourage leaders at all levels to participate in such programs.
2. Establish mentorship and coaching programs within the organization to nurture leadership qualities and help leaders understand how to inspire and motivate their teams effectively.
3. Ensure that the organization has a clear vision and set of values that leaders can use to inspire and guide their teams. Align these with the organization's mission and goals.
4. Provide communication training for leaders to enhance their ability to convey a compelling vision and to engage with their teams effectively.
5. Implement recognition and reward systems that acknowledge and celebrate transformational leadership behaviors. This reinforces the importance of these qualities.
6. Encourage open and honest feedback within the organization. Leaders should actively seek feedback from their teams and use it to improve their leadership style.
7. Offer a variety of community engagement opportunities to cater to different interests and schedules. Ensure that there are options for one-time events, ongoing commitments, and various types of activities.
8. Create educational programs and awareness campaigns to inform the community about the importance of engagement and its benefits. Highlight how community involvement can lead to positive change.
9. Collaborate with local organizations, nonprofits, and schools to create community engagement initiatives. Pool resources and expertise to maximize impact.
10. Specifically target youth and students in community engagement efforts. Encourage schools and universities to integrate service-learning programs into their curricula.
11. To effectively increase transformational leadership and community engagement, it's important to foster a culture within the organization and community that values these qualities. Encourage leaders to serve as role models for community involvement and provide ongoing support and resources for both leadership development and community engagement initiatives.

## 9 Scientific Contribution

Our research may shed light on an important social phenomenon—the integration between mentor leadership and trainee/follower community engagement. The importance of understanding this association adds to the existing body of knowledge on leadership and community involvement among youth. The concept of leadership is most often associated with organizational, political, and educational leadership. Our research explores leadership in a non-commercial and non-formal arena, that is, within the realm of society and community. Understanding the context can help sharpen the need for leadership development among youth mentors wherever they are, and not just in the Scout movement. In addition, understanding the degree of community involvement of adolescents has significant implications for the scientific and pedagogical fields. It can assist in developing social policies that seek to implement the research conclusions.

## 10 Limitations and Future Study

The limitations of study is limited to the objective of the study, which is related to the concepts of the study that include leadership of the Scout movement in Arab society in Israel and its impact on the community engagement of its members. This study was applied to a sample of counselors in Scout movement in Israel, in addition to members of the Scout movement. also the study was conducted during the current academic year 2023–2024. The study was determined by the reliability of the sample members' response to the tools prepared for this purpose, their psychometric properties, and the implications of their validity and reliability. Further studies needed about the study concepts, and its impact on other behavioral concepts.

## References


1. Degani, A.: They were prepared: the Palestinian Arab Scout Movement 1920–1948. Br. J. Middleast. Stud. **41**(2), 200–218. https://doi.org/10.1080/13530194.2014.884316 (2014)
2. Kroonenberg, P.J.: The undaunted—keeping the scouting spirit alive: the survival and revival of scouting in Central and Eastern Europe. Oriole International Publications (1998)
3. Haddad Haj-Yahya, N., Rudnizki, E.: The Arab education system in Israel: the situation and the challenges of the future. Field Pen (Et Hasade) **19**(2), 21–35 (2018)
4. Fleischmann, E.: The nation and its "new" women: the Palestinian women's movement, 1920–1948. In the nation and its "new" women. University of California Press. https://doi.org/10.1525/CALIFORNIA/9780520237896.001.0001 (2012)
5. Givoli, S., Lotan, A., Barel, M., Shaham Sorani, L.: Summary of biennial assessment findings of youth movements in Israel 2015–2014. Ministry of Education (2017)
6. Anderson, J., Rainie, L.: The negatives of digital life. Pew Research Center. https://www.pewresearch.org/internet/2018/07/03/the-negatives-of-digital-life/ (2018, July 3)

7. Canadian Paediatric Society. Impact of media use on children and youth. Paediatr Child Health **8**(5). https://doi.org/10.1093/PCH/8.5.301 (2007)
8. Van Joshi, S., Stubbe, D., Li, S.T.T., Hilty, D.M.: The use of technology by youth: implications for psychiatric educators. Acad. Psychiatry **43**(1):101–109. https://doi.org/10.1007/S40596-018-1007-2 (2019)
9. Morciano, D., Merico, M.: Critical youth work for youth-driven innovation: a theoretical framework. In: Bastien, S. Holmarsdottir, H.B. (eds.) Youth as architects of social change: global efforts to advance youth-driven innovation, pp. 43–74. Palgrave Macmillan. https://doi.org/10.1007/978-3-319-66275-6_3 (2017)
10. Nazifah Ahmad, A.R., Salleh, M., Awang, M., Mohamad, N.A.: Investigating best practice and effectiveness of leadership wisdom among principals of excellent secondary school Malaysia: perceptions of senior assistants. Int. Educ. Stud. **6**(8), 38–46 (2013)
11. Waer, S., Zahaf, K.: The reality of communication in Algerian educational institutions. Master's Thesis, Larbi Ben M'hidi University (2016)
12. Al-Abdi, E.A.: The impact of reciprocal leadership on achieving the objectives of NGO projects, Master of Business Administration Thesis, Faculty of Commerce, Islamic University, Gaza (2015)
13. Jabri, M.: The role of transformational leadership and reciprocal leadership on organizational learning in a healthcare context. Unpublished PhD thesis, United Arab Emirates (2018)
14. Fairholm, M.R.: Defining leadership: a review of past, present, and future ideas center for excellence in municipal management's research program. Center for Excellence in Municipal Management (2002)
15. Montuori, A., Donnelly, G.: Transformative leadership. In: Neal, J. (ed.) Handbook of personal and organizational transformation, pp. 1–33. Springer International Publishing. https://doi.org/10.1007/978-3-319-29587-9_59-1 (2017)
16. Khan, N: Adaptive or transactional leadership in current higher education: a brief comparison. Int. Rev. Res. Open Distance Learn. **18**(3), 178–183. https://doi.org/10.19173/IRRODL.V18I3.3294 (2017)
17. Eagly, A.H., Johannesen-Schmidt, M.C., van Engen, M.L.: Transformational, transactional, and laissez-faire leadership styles: a meta-analysis comparing women and men. Psychol. Bull. **129**(4), 569–591. https://doi.org/10.1037/0033-2909.129.4.569 (2003)
18. Wong, S.I., Giessner, S.: RThe thin line between empowering and laissez-faire leadership: an expectancy-match perspective. J. Manage. **44**(2), 757–783. https://doi.org/10.1177/0149206315574597 (2016)
19. Lee, J., Cho, J., Baek, Y., Pillai, R., & Oh, S. H.: Does ethical leadership predict follower outcomes above and beyond the full-range leadership model and authentic leadership?: An organizational commitment perspective. Asia Pac. J. Manag. **36**(3), 821–847 (2019). https://doi.org/10.1007/S10490-018-9596-6 (2019)
20. Polson, E.C., Jang, S.J., Johnson, B.R., Smith, B.: Being prepared and staying connected: scouting's influence on social capital and community involvement. Soc. Sci. Q. **94**(3), 758–776. https://doi.org/10.1111/ssqu.12002 (2013)
21. Pancer, S. The psychology of citizenship and civic engagement. Oxford University Press. http://life-course.web.unc.edu/elder_research/ (2015)
22. Hart, R.: Children's participation: from tokenism to citizenship. United Nations Children's Fund, UNICEF (1992)
23. Krueger, M.: Four themes in youth work practice. J. Community Psychol. **33**(1), 21–29. https://doi.org/10.1002/JCOP.20033 (2005)
24. Abu al-Qiyaan, A.: The role of community center managers in promoting community development within the Arab society from the point of view of their employees: difficulties and proposed solutions. (Unpublished PhD thesis), Faculty of Education, Yarmouk University, Irbid, Jordan (2016)
25. Avolio, B.J., Bass, B.M.: Multifactor Leadership Questionnaire (MLQ) (3rd ed.). Mind Garden (2004)

26. Jones, K.R.: Youth-adult partnerships: are you there yet? how to evaluate your 4-H youth development program? The University of Kentucky (2006)
27. Kline, R. B.: Principles and practice of structural equation modeling (4th ed.). New York, NY: The Guilford Press (2016)
28. Antoniou, A.S., Gioumouki, M.: Leadership and school culture of mainstream and special primary schools. Int. J. Acad. Res. Bus. Soc. Sci. **8**(5), 401–416 (2018)
29. El Deeb, T.: The impact of intellectual extremism and political violence on the values of belonging in the youth community, in youth centers in the city of Mansoura. Ann. Fac. Arts Ain Shams Univ. **45**, 102–165 (2017)
30. Hijazi, M.: Social construction. I1. Dar Gharib for Publishing and Distribution, Cairo (1979)
31. Hijazin, H.M., Ayasrah, A.A.: Leadership in educational administration, Dar Al-Hamid for Publishing and Distribution, Published Master Thesis, Amman (2006)
32. Rayan, F.: Community activity between theory and practice. Kuwait, Al-Falah Press (1995)
33. Herbs, Y., Stein, A. (eds.): Community school: participation in dialogue. Jerusalem: The Community Centers Company and its Dissemination to Students from Their Point of View **4**(1), 37 (1995)
34. Yitzhar, R, Zohar, A, Kemir, D.: Jerusalem: Ministry of Education (2015)
35. Avolio, B., Bass, B., Jung, D.: Re-examining the components of transformational and transactional leadership using the multifactor leadership questionnaire. J. Occup. Organ. Psychol. **72**, 441–462 (1997)
36. Brennan, M.A., van Barnett, R., Baugh, E.: Youth involvement in community development: implications and possibilities for extension. J. Ext. **45**(5), 203–213. https://archives.joe.org/joe/2007august/a3.php

# Organizational Performance and Sustainability

# Reputation Analysis of Selected European and US Brands in the Context of the COVID-19 Pandemic

František Pollák, Peter Markovič, Michal Konečný, and Mária Kmety Barteková

**Abstract** The paper deals with the issue of sustainable development of corporate reputation, specifically the issue of traditional and innovative approaches to reputation management of selected global brands in terms of changes that occurred in the market during the COVID-19 pandemic in the context of the ongoing Triple Transition. The main aim of the paper itself is to present the available ways and methods of measuring the phenomenon of reputation, especially online reputation, as the modern challenge for responsible and sustainable development of the perceived image of entities as their very fragile intangible assets. Moreover, the paper aims to identify and analyze the changes that occurred in the measurable levels of the reputations of selected entities during the pandemic. Preferred European and US brands owned by family businesses were analyzed using a standardized multifactor reputation analysis TOR in the virtual environment of the Internet. Considering all relevant factors, online ratings were standardized and compared with the offline ratings. The relationships between the factors were examined to identify and describe the underlying factors influencing the online reputation of entities in a hyper-competitive market environment, especially for the European and US markets. Based on the set goal, the results were compared with the values measured before the outbreak of the pandemic, and this comparison formed the basis for the identification of development trends. The analysis results provided a comprehensive view of the issue of selected approaches to the sustainable development of corporate reputation. Although literature offers a wide range of approaches to measuring reputation, the presented methodology offers a relatively simple and reasonably accurate form of active reputation management,

F. Pollák (✉) · P. Markovič · M. Konečný · M. K. Barteková
University of Economics in Bratislava, Dolnozemská Cesta 1/B, 852 35 Bratislava, Slovakia
e-mail: frantisek.pollak@euba.sk

F. Pollák
Institute of Technology and Business in České Budějovice, Okružní 517/10, 370 01 České Budějovice, Czech Republic

 
S. Kot et al. (eds.), *Corporate Practices: Policies, Methodologies, and Insights in Organizational Management*, Springer Proceedings in Business and Economics,
https://doi.org/10.1007/978-981-97-0996-0_53

thus providing an effective tool for enhancing the competitiveness of entities seeking to maximize their market advantages in the adaptation to the process of digital, green, and social transition.

**Keywords** Online reputation · Premium brands · European market · US market · COVID-19 · Triple transition

## 1 Introduction

Building corporate reputation is one of the keys to trading companies, enhancing their competitiveness in the constantly changing business environment. Corporate reputation, as one of the new topics, has become the subject of research by many academics. Reputation as an intangible asset generates significant advantages in the market for trading companies. However, it can threaten them, especially if its unruly nature becomes uncontrollable. Establishing or maintaining a business relationship with an entity with a damaged reputation is risky. Repairing a damaged reputation is difficult. Therefore, a good reputation is easy to lose but hard to regain. The assumption can be extrapolated up to the limit position, where a single adverse event can reduce or even eliminate a company's competitive advantages for a long time. The financial dimension of these phenomena is relatively easy to quantify in the market economy through the level of market capitalization or relevant indicators of the economic performance of the company. Reputation management, i.e., managing reputation over time, means more than crisis communication, corporate ethics, and social responsibility activities. Complex reputation management represents a long-term strategy that includes planning and management of corporate activities aimed at improving quality, internal and external communication, and, finally, regular reputation audits. In the global market, companies put considerable effort into reputation management and brand development. A high reputation level helps trading companies secure funding and attract business partners and customers.

However, the market is a turbulent ecosystem. Both global and local crises destabilize stakeholders' trust in organizations. In the context of corporate reputation and reputation management, it is therefore necessary to consider dynamic market aspects. For the presented study, the element of the global pandemic caused by COVID-19 and the strategic dimension of the triple transition, i.e., the transition to a greener, more digital and more social economy, are primarily taken into account. Both of these accelerators had the effect of dynamizing the processes of transition from traditional to electronic forms of business. The issue of developing corporate reputation thus takes a new dimension, as the virtual environment is characterized by specifics such as higher addressability or lower authenticity. It is also necessary to consider the aspect of technological innovations and the associated need to acquire know-how for applying innovations in practice. The new electronic media attract large audiences of users. Their development and gradual disappearance take place at a time that is pushing the production of knowledge to its limit. Ad hoc solutions are thus replacing best practices, as it is often not beneficial to use offline procedures online. The pressure for the efficient use of resources is thus exerted in some instances against chance. The need to identify important factors of reputation is therefore rational. In the context of these facts, the main objective of the study was also formulated as follows:

The authors aim to conduct empirical research on selected factors of corporate reputation that are of importance in the context of turbulent changes in a highly competitive market. The research problem is the relative need for more knowledge in the field. The solution to the research problem is the generation of relevant knowledge and the provision of a shift in knowledge. The authors consider it inevitable to examine the aspect of corporate reputation in the market from the perspective of its major players in the context of the specifics of Europe and the United States while considering the impacts of the global COVID-19 pandemic and accelerated digitization on the demand and supply side of the market in terms of its possible implications on reputation management. The goal can thus be expressed in the form of the following research question:

What are the specifics of the developed markets of Europe and the United States regarding reputation management?

From the perspective of the structure of the study, it is necessary to examine the current state of knowledge in the issue first. This is followed by a theoretical overview describing the methodological apparatus used to conduct an empirical comparative study. Discussions in the context of the reference study complement the presentation of the findings. The most significant results are summarized in its conclusion. The newly acquired knowledge will thus create space for a possible shift of expertise in the issue. With this statement, it is possible to proceed to the theoretical review.

## 2 Analysis of the State of Knowledge

Burke, Cooper, and Martin [1] state that corporate reputation has been studied mainly in public communication and marketing within companies. Nowadays, influencing corporate reputation is not limited to the given regions only, but the given discipline is integrated within the company into its relevant strategies. Corporate reputation is built from within and is transmitted to the public through its management. Griffin [2] argues that management provides activities ranging from planning, decision-making, and organizing to leading and controlling, aimed at corporate resources, including people, finance, information, etc. Strategies are directed toward the effective achievement of corporate goals. Hittmár [3] adds that reputation management covers the management of corporate reputation. Like traditional management, it is also a process that includes planning, organizing, leading, or ensuring control and human potential, which aims to build and maintain a positive corporate reputation, its goods or services. Schultz and Werner [4] add that reputation management should also create guidelines on how to deal with individual situations, especially when the corporate reputation has been damaged. Burkhardt [5] describes reputation management as a commitment to responsible communication with stakeholders, reflecting the company's culture, which is not only casual. Doorley and Garcia [6] define complex reputation management as a long-term strategy that includes measuring, auditing, and managing corporate reputation, while reputation can be considered an asset. The authors further state that reputation management is a continuous process because, based on feedback, a repeated analysis of the corporate reputation is carried out, that is, its monitoring for auditing. A company's reputation is usually defined as the overall perceived quality in the eyes of its customers, employees, suppliers, and the public. Corporate reputation is built over time based on business behavior [7]. It is a summary of all opinions, feelings, and evaluations that the public has about the company and its activities. Reputation can be managed to achieve social recognition, to make customers willing to buy the company's products, and to intensify their loyalty to the company [8]. Reputation can be positive or negative and usually includes several factors such as product and service quality, corporate social responsibility, transparency, ethics, innovativeness, financial performance, etc. Vlachynský et al. [9] claim that corporate reputation building is linked to the expenditure of financial resources intended for its achievement. Investing is generally the substitution of the present value of invested funds to obtain an undetermined significance in the future. In the case of long-term investments, the company expects benefits from them in a longer time horizon. A company's reputation is essential because it can influence its success and performance in the market. If a company has a good reputation, it can increase customer interest in its products, attract qualified employees, and foster cooperation with partners and suppliers. Conversely, if a company has a negative reputation, it can have a negative impact on its sales, customer loyalty, and cooperation with partners.

## *2.1 Financial Aspects of Reputation*

In the past decade of the twenty-first century, reputation has become an important factor for businesses worldwide. In 2014, a global survey conducted by Deloitte identified reputational risk as the largest strategic business risk, as evidenced by the AON Global Risk Management Survey conducted in 2015 and the Allianz Risk Barometer Survey conducted in 2016, according to which the loss of reputation is one of the biggest risks for business managers. The importance of corporate reputation is confirmed by the fact that it represents more than 25% of the company's market value and the total market capitalization of S&P500 companies [10]. Hasan, Habib, and Zhao [11] investigated the extent to which reputational risk affects cash holdings of companies listed on American stock exchanges in the period 2007–2018. Their results show that companies with high reputational risk hold significantly more cash. At the same time, this relationship persisted even after explicitly controlling for other determinants of cash holdings, including the fulfillment of corporate social responsibility. Through their analyses, the authors point out that endogenous factors do not determine the given relationship. In an additional test, they also prove that companies with a low value of reputational risk are associated with a higher marginal value of cash than those with high reputational risk. Analyzing and managing a company's reputation is thus an essential element of its strategy and can help improve its performance and competitiveness.

## 2.2 Reputation in the Context of the Triple Transition

In market dynamics, reputation management takes on an extremely complex dimension. Technological and social innovations combined with the onset of a global pandemic have created a situation on the market unprecedented in modern history. For this reason, it is necessary to examine the aspect of social responsibility in reputation management. The following part presents a closer look at the authors' views dealing with the given issue. Ethics and corporate social responsibility can be critical to how a company is perceived. If a company demonstrates high ethical behavior and engages in socially beneficial activities, it can create a positive reputation. Corporate social responsibility is a triple transition framework that emphasizes the balance between the economic, social, and environmental goals of businesses. Today, companies are expected to be accountable not only to their shareholders but also to a broader range of stakeholders, including employees, customers, investors, suppliers, the local community, and the environment. Corporate social responsibility is also considered a tool for improving the economic performance of companies, with corporate reputation playing an increasingly important role [12].

Orlova et al. [13] point to the fact that implementing the principles and tools of corporate social responsibility helps companies enhance their reputation and improve their activities in the global market. They justify it by the fact that the low level of corporate management practice and insufficient social contribution of companies negatively affect the formation of their social responsibility. The researchers analyzed indicators for socially responsible companies with the highest corporate reputation according to the Institute of Reputation, namely Rolex, Lego, Disney, Adidas Group, Microsoft, Sony, Canon, Michelin, Netflix, and Bosch according to Fortune Global 500 ratings, Net Promoter Score and Newsweek Green Ranking for 2018–2019. The analysis of the indicators enabled the identification of the proportional dependence of the corporate reputation on the social responsibility measures implemented by the company. The authors found that corporate social responsibility is an effective tool for increasing the competitiveness of companies in the financial market.

Pham and Tran [14] examined the roles of corporate reputation and CEO integrity in the relationship between socially responsible business practices and business economic performance. In analyzing a dataset of 3588 observations of 833 Fortune World's most admired companies operating in 31 countries from 2005 to 2011, the researchers found a positive effect of responsible business practices on corporate reputation. This contributes significantly to the economic performance of the enterprise. Singh and Misra [15] conducted an empirical study to investigate the relationship between corporate social responsibility and organizational performance in European MNCs while examining the effectiveness of corporate reputation as a moderator in the relationship between responsible business and organizational performance. The resulting dataset contained 340 responses from executives/managers working in European multinational companies. The authors used a two-phase approach for the analysis. In the first phase, a theoretical model was built using the strategic literature paradigm. In the second stage, a hierarchical regression analysis was performed to examine relevant relationships. Their findings showed that CSR, when targeted at external stakeholders, impacts organizational performance.

Moreover, they found that this effect varies between well-established, reputable companies and businesses with less favorable reputations. Gonzalez-Rodriguez et al. [16] investigated the links between corporate social responsibility, reputation, and financial performance of hotels from a multivariate perspective by collecting data from 322 hotels in China and using partial least squares equation modeling for causal-predictive analysis. Their results show that social responsibility practices affect a hotel's reputation from international and local perspectives and that social responsibility and importance affect economic performance or relevant dimensions differently. Martos-Pedrero, Jimenez-Castillo, and Cortes-Garcia [17] analyzed the relationship between socially responsible businesses and the economic performance of companies in the agri-food sector to understand the role of image and reputation in this relationship based on stakeholder theory. As already mentioned, they perceive corporate social responsibility as a broad and multidimensional concept including dimensions such as (a) employees, (b) customers, (c) farmers, (d) environment, (e) community, and (f) competition. They tested the model on data collected through a survey of a sample of 107 marketing companies by applying the least squares method. Their results show that corporate social responsibility has a positive effect on the economic performance of companies operating in the given sector. Furthermore, the authors state that this effect is mainly due to the significant positive influence of image and reputation. In the following part, the context of reputation and market capitalization can be examined.

## 2.3 Reputation in the Context of Stock Markets

The issue of corporate reputation in the context of stock markets includes the impact that a company's reputation has on its economic performance and stock market value. Specifically, it concerns how the perception and evaluation of a company's reputation by investors and the market affect the value of its shares, investment decisions, and trading volume. According to Blajer-Golebiewská [18], there are two different concepts of corporate reputation, which are based on individual and collective perception. The author aimed to investigate how these two approaches affect investors' decisions to buy or not to buy shares of a given company. To answer this question, the author used an experiment that focused on the individual decisions of individual investors. As part of the experiment, participants participated in an online game that simulated stock market conditions and was related to corporate reputation and investing. The results showed that the individual willingness to invest is not directly related to the perception of investors based on historical share prices and other objective metrics of corporate reputation but rather to the subjective evaluation of the company's reputation on the market.

This implies that it is necessary to re-evaluate the common indicators of corporate reputation in the context of studies of investors' decisions in the stock market. Maqbool [19] investigated the impact of corporate social responsibility on the economic performance of companies. For this purpose, the author used data from the BSE 100 index from 2010–2018. Using regression analysis, it was found that corporate social responsibility has a positive effect on current profitability and stock returns. The results confirmed a positive effect of corporate social responsibility on future profitability, which indicates its long-term nature. However, the authors see no positive relationship between corporate social responsibility and future earnings from shares. Overall, the findings show that the market rewards those companies that actively engage with stakeholders. Nawrocki and Szwajca [20] argue that in recent decades, corporate reputation has become an important factor and motivation for investment decisions. Reputation includes cognitive and emotional aspects that investors can follow. The authors investigated the importance of selected aspects of reputation for individual investors in the Polish capital market. For this purpose, they used the method of Internet survey and addressed 417 individual investors.

The findings showed that from the perspective of individual investors active in the Polish capital market, informational aspects of companies' reputations are slightly more important than those of finance and growth. Social aspects of reputation were considered the least important, although significant differences were noted in the perception of the importance of individual reputation criteria. A positive reputation can attract investors due to a rise in share prices and increase the demand for them, which can have a positive effect on corporate financial performance. Conversely, a negative reputation can cause a drop in stock prices and a loss of investor favor, which can have a negative impact on the company's economic situation. Arbe and Feria-Dominguez [21] assessed the impact of corruption scandals on the reputational risk of CEOs of publicly traded companies in Latin America. The authors also investigated the efficient market hypothesis through the Standard and Poor's index. They focused on assessing the negative impact of corruption events through abnormal returns and cumulative negative returns. They used losses from corruption scandals, expressed as a ratio of loss to stock market capitalization, to estimate abnormal reputational returns and their cumulative rate. They found that corporate reputation does not have a significant effect on the stock market performance of companies involved in corruption scandals, at least not in the short term.

Huaman-Nope et al. [22] analyzed the impact of reputational risk on stock prices of companies traded on the Lima Stock Exchange. They demonstrated a relationship between reputational risk and share prices of companies traded on the stock exchange, as well as the impact on profitability ratios and income levels. Among other things, they found that the cost of capital has a greater impact if the entity is financed through bond issues rather than through subsidiaries. Xie et al. [23] examined the response of the stock market to companies' carbon neutrality commitments. Their results suggest that companies experience market value losses due to their commitment to carbon neutrality, with the decline in cumulative abnormal returns ranging from −2.09% to −1.21% across periods. However, they found that better past performance regarding environmental, social, and governance factors and a higher level of carbon transparency can mitigate adverse market responses.

Zhang and Wong [24] examined the importance of board monitoring committees when companies face an increased risk of reputational damage due to negative media coverage regarding environmental, social, and governance issues. Their findings suggest that monitoring committees can effectively contribute to mitigating the negative reactions of investors in stock markets in such a situation. Overall, they confirm the positive effects of board monitoring committees, especially in environmental and social aspects. The main objective of the study by Eriqat, Tahir, and Zulkafli [25] was to create a comprehensive indicator of corporate reputation and examine the impact of governance and management on the reputation of listed financial institutions in the MENA region. Based on a study that focused on 96 financial companies listed on the stock exchanges in Jordan, Palestine, Qatar, and Kuwait in 2016–2020, the authors created a quantitative, multidimensional index of company reputation using principal component analysis. They used the Generalized Method of Moments, a dynamic panel system technique, to estimate the dynamic corporate reputation system model. Their findings suggest that audit committee independence positively influences corporate reputation. In addition, ownership concentration has been proven to have a negative impact on corporate reputation. Considering the current state of knowledge of the issue, it can be stated that the issue of corporate reputation in the context of increasing competitiveness and achieving the goals of the triple transition is current and relevant. With this finding, it is possible to move on to the description of the methodological framework of the performed analysis.

## 3 Methods

The study's objective is to conduct empirical research on selected factors of corporate reputation, which are significant in the context of turbulent changes in the highly competitive market. The research problem is the relative need for more knowledge in the area under study. The solution to the research problem is to generate relevant knowledge and ensure a shift in knowledge. According to the authors, it is necessary to examine the aspect of corporate reputation in the market from the perspective of its major players in the context of the specifics of Europe and the United States. At the same time, it is necessary to consider the impacts of the global COVID-19 pandemic and accelerated digitization on the demand and supply side of the market in terms of the possible effects on reputation management. The goal can thus be expressed in the form of the research question below: What are the specifics of the developed markets of Europe and the United States in the context of reputation management?

The subject of the research is the most successful global brands operating on the worldwide market and the user base of their fans in the online environment. The research sample consists of the 100 most prestigious global brands according to the 2019 Interbrand ranking [26]. In the study, the research sample is reduced to the five most prestigious brands from the portfolio of family-owned businesses in Europe and the five most prestigious brands from the portfolio of family-owned companies in the USA.

For data collection, the method of sentiment analysis is primarily used. Considering all relevant factors, online reputation ratings are standardized and compared to a brand value expressed by market capitalization in USD. The basic data collection process can be described as follows (Fig. 1).

To determine the polarity of the sentiment of the result, Daniel Soper's tool [28] is used, which generates the level of the sentiment result in the values −100 to 100 based on algorithms.

For the quantification of sentiment scores for a specific position, a modified quantification Table 1 [29] in the following form is used:

To minimize the limitations resulting from the personalization of search results by the search engine itself, an anonymous browsing mode is used. At the same

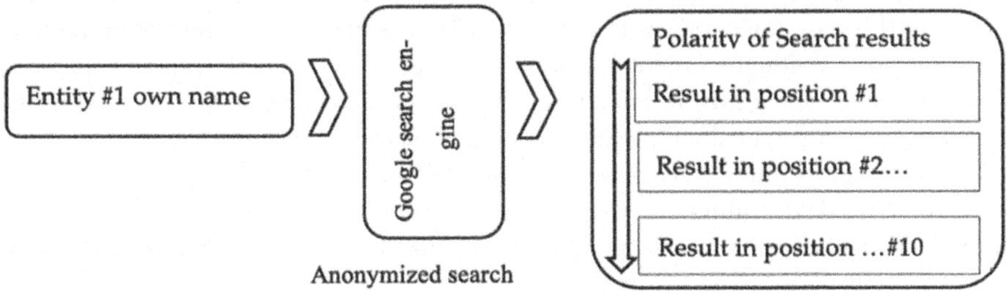


**Fig. 1** Sentiment analysis [27]

**Table 1** Sentiment analysis—quantification key

| Sentiment/Position | 1 | 2 | 3 | 4 | 5 | 6 | 7 | 8 | 9 | 10 |
|---|---|---|---|---|---|---|---|---|---|---|
| Positive sentiment (+) (+30; +100) | 20 | 19 | 18 | 17 | 16 | 15 | 14 | 13 | 12 | 11 |
| Custom web site of the organization (x) | 10 | 9 | 8 | 7 | 6 | 5 | 4 | 3 | 2 | 1 |
| Neutral sentiment (±) (−30;+30) | 2 | 2 | 2 | 2 | 2 | 2 | 2 | 2 | 2 | 2 |
| Negative sentiment (−) (−100; −30) | −20 | −19 | −18 | −17 | −16 | −15 | −14 | −13 | −12 | −11 |

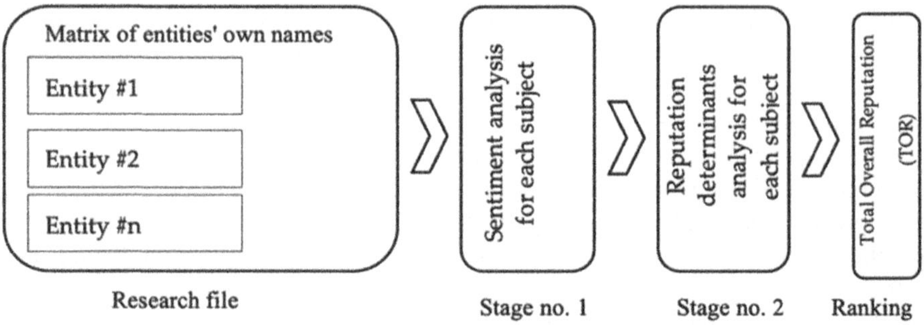


**Fig. 2** TOR method quantification process [27]

time, only organic search results are taken into account. If several occurrences of the test subject's website appear within the search results, the second to the nth search result of this nature is assigned a neutral sentiment. The polarity of the development is determined based on data directly visible from the link, especially in the title and Perex. For each evaluated element from the research sample, the analysis is carried out using the same procedure. A partial reputation indicator is set for each of the positions, and subsequently, the total value is determined based on their sum. The aggregate value for each tested element is then converted to a percentage. It is assumed that each component can get a maximum of 155 points, representing 100%. In this case, one point is equal to 0.645 percentage points. Based on the total score of the individual elements, it is possible to create a simple ranking that will provide an overview of the relative position of the tested components. As part of the measurements, this is called the Sentiment analysis score or the SA score.

For a deeper examination of the links, the TOR methodology [30] is then applied, which enables determining the overall level of the online reputation of the examined entities. The process of collecting additional empirical material from TOR methods can be described as follows (Fig. 2).

The result of the analysis is the calculated TOR coefficient for each analyzed entity. This coefficient enables ranking the research file and creating a ranking of the entities for subsequent benchmarking based on the overall level of online reputation. At this point, it is necessary to describe in more detail the methodology used to quantify individual reputation indicators, as well as the subsequent formula used to calculate the TOR score. Regarding identifying the determinants of online reputation, for the study, they will be referred to as reputators. Reputation can be any factor that can significantly influence the perceived online reputation of an entity, and its value can be quantified as a percentage. Due to the diverse areas in which entities operate, it is sometimes impossible to pre-define reporters in the expected way. In such a case, a competitive score calculation can be used. It is the relative number of user communities of the entity on selected social networks compared to the total number of user tribes of the selected social network within the entire research sample. The result is then used to calculate the percentage of the competitive score (CS) of the reputations of a specific entity. In other words, it is possible to calculate the competitive power of a reputation for a particular entity as the ratio of the size of its tribe (followers, fans, subscribers) to the total number of tribes of all tested entities.

As for the overall TOR score, each sub-parameter is used separately in the calculation. The calculation of the TOR parameter is based on the following formula:

$$\mathrm{TOR} = \frac{R_{SA} + \sum_{i=1}^{n} R_i}{\mathrm{n} + 1} \tag{1}$$

where:

TOR total online reputation in %,
$R_{SA}$ SA reputator (% score based on sentiment analysis),
$R_i$ ith reputator (% score based on the given ith determinant of online reputation),
n number of determinants.

The process of fulfilling the primary goal represents a systematic sequence of activities carried out between 2020 and 2023. The activities are reflected chronologically within the framework of the problem decomposition and the formulation of the research question. The work process is thus presented in the context of time series, divided into two phases. The first phase of the empirical analysis took place in 2020, before the outbreak of the global pandemic [29]. The dataset is thus considered a reference base for subsequent comparative analysis. The following data collection reflects the complete suppression of anti-pandemic measures in the third quarter of 2023. The comparison of both datasets enables the description of the development of the analyzed variables throughout the global pandemic.

The data were processed using descriptive statistics tools in the office package MS Office. Status values are presented through overview tables, while the most critical findings are visualized through overview graphs. At this point, it is possible to proceed to the presentation of the analysis results.

## 4 Results and Discussion

The issue of sustainable development of corporate reputation is relatively broad and diverse. Objectively, in a market economy, small and medium-sized enterprises form the backbone of the economy. A large part of such businesses were established as family-owned businesses. There are also examples where large corporations originated or operated as family-owned businesses. If a family owns at least 32% of voting shares in a publicly traded company or has at least 50% shares in a private company, such a company can be considered a family-owned business [31]. The issue of family business is a complex construct [32–34], while authors publishing on the topic examine theoretical and practical dimensions and applications [35, 36]. Literature thus brings an up-to-date and holistic dimension, within which we guide the generated knowledge in the context of market needs.

Europe and the United States represent ideal markets for exploring the issue of corporate reputation in the context of sustainable development and triple transition trends. The reference dataset of the study thus opens up the topic at the global level. For the study, the ten most valuable brands from 2019 were selected, five from Europe and five from the USA [26]. Each brand belongs to a parent company that meets the definition of a family-owned business. Subsequently, an empirical analysis of the level of online reputation of these brands in the time before the outbreak of the pandemic was conducted. With an interval of more than three years, an identical analysis of the selected sample was conducted. The interpretation and discussion are described in the following subsection. Next, the authors perform a comparison of datasets from 2020 and 2023. Differences in state values, as well as identified market trends, are discussed in the context of the objectives of the study. The analysis results provide a comprehensive view of the geographical specificities of developed Western markets in the context of turbulent changes of the third decade of the twenty-first century.

## *4.1 Results of the Empirical Analysis of 2023*

The focus is primarily on the virtual Internet environment. Using semi-automated sentiment analysis, a partial score is calculated, which expresses the strength of an entity's online reputation based on the first 10 Google search results. However, Google and its search results are only one of many ways potential customers can access relevant information. Based on an expert assessment, other factors influencing online reputation were identified, namely reputation in the form of the size of user bases on the following platforms:

- Facebook (total number of fans of the official global profile), as FC;
- (X) Twitter (total number of followers of the official global profile), as TC;
- YouTube (total number of subscribers to the official global profile), as YC;
- Instagram (total number of followers of the official global profile), as IgC.

Each of these reputations has its system to determine the overall score, but basically, they all depend on the number of users (followers, fans, subscribers). For further analysis, the partial scores of the individual reputations were unified, and the competitive score (CS) parameter was determined, subtracted from specific platforms [37], and converted to percentage points by the procedure described in the Methods section. Partial scores were converted to total TOR values using a calculation formula. The data was supplemented with a quantitative parameter represented by the total number of pages indexed by Google (NPIG). The following Table 2 shows the order of the entities:

At this point, it is possible to proceed to a qualitative description of the sentiment analysis results. However, to explain the context, it is not possible to describe the entire analyzed sample adequately. When describing the partial reputation factors, we demonstrate the results of the qualitative analysis using the example of the first

**Table 2** Sentiment analysis results 2023

| Subject/ Result sentiment | SA score (%) | FC score (%) | TC score (%) | YC score (%) | IgC score (%) | NPIG (n M) | TOR score (%) |
|---|---|---|---|---|---|---|---|
| BMW (EU) | −8 | 10 | 6 | 11 | 7 | 1750 | 5 |
| Nike (USA) | 39 | 18 | 21 | 15 | 60 | 2050 | 30 |
| Louis Vuitton (EU) | −10 | 12 | 21 | 26 | 11 | 226 | 12 |
| Chanel (EU) | 72 | 11 | 29 | 19 | 11 | 1300 | 29 |
| Hermès (EU) | 35 | 2 | 0 | 2 | 3 | 680 | 8 |
| H&M (EU) | 30 | 20 | 17 | 4 | 7 | 2680 | 16 |
| Budweiser (USA) | 23 | 7 | 0 | 2 | 0 | 81 | 6 |
| Ford (USA) | 35 | 8 | 3 | 19 | 1 | 2940 | 14 |
| Dell (USA) | 30 | 2 | 2 | 2 | 0 | 3660 | 7 |
| Jack Daniel's (USA) | 51 | 9 | 0 | 0 | 0 | 648 | 12 |

European and the first American brand within the selected sample. It interprets the qualitative indicators of a simple machine analysis of the chosen entities' sentiment. The sentiment of all entities in the model is interpreted through the summary SA score individually, as seen in the summary table.

The first of the analyzed European brands is BMW. In first place is the organization's website. A link to Wikipedia follows this. By default, this type of link, together with links to social media, is evaluated as positive. However, in this analysis, an automated process is used to analyze the sentiment of the link from the title and the pericope. The actual process of sentiment determination by the software is unknown to us, but we assume that all entities in the sample have the same conditions. A link to the site of the entire BMW Group follows this link. This link has an optimally chosen description, which ensures the entity has the first positive sentiment in a high-ranked position. The fifth link is a link to the website of the motorcycle division, and the sixth is a link to a renowned platform for evaluating cars. Both of these links are ranked as unfavorable by the software in terms of the wording of the title and description. The seventh link is a link to the official Facebook profile with an optimally chosen description. The eighth link is the BMW M Division page; again, we find optimally chosen words in the report. Another link to the motorcycle division follows this, this time well-optimized. In the seventh to ninth positions, we find references to positive sentiment. The ranking is closed by a link to the social network X (formerly Twitter), which, based on automated analysis, shows signs of negative sentiment.

The first of the analyzed American brands is Nike. Again, in the first place is the organization's website. As in the case of European BMX, in the second position in the search result is a link to the Wikipedia portal. In the case of Nike, this link is rated as positive by the sentiment analyzer. The following positions are occupied by links to the company's social media profiles. The first is a link to the social network Facebook, quantified as positive sentiment. The second in the order is Instagram, also quantified by the software quantifies as positive. The following is a link to Google Play, again quantified positively. The sixth in order is a link to the YouTube platform. This is the first result quantified as unfavorable. The seventh in charge is the link to Twitter, with the sentiment again quantified as unfavorable. In the eighth place is the link to the online store, where the idea of the title and description is quantified as negative. The ninth position is a link to the LinkedIn platform. The system classifies it as a result of a positive sentiment. The ranking is closed by the association to another online store. This is a link with a positive sentiment.

In terms of reputation levels based on individual reputations, in 2023, a relatively early dominance of brands from the clothing category on the Facebook social network can be seen. The European H&M, with over 40 million fans, is followed by the American Nike, whose base has almost 37 million fans. As for competition scores, the mentioned brands account for nearly 40% of the total market of fans of all sample brands on the Facebook social network. As for the social network Twitter (or X), the European brands Chanel and Louis Vuitton, together with more than 23 million subscribers, account for 50% of the total competitive score. Third in the order is the American brand Nike, which has a 21% competitive score. The YouTube platform is dominated by the European outlet Louis Vuitton. Its more than 3 million subscribers account for almost 30% of the competitive score of the given media. Instagram is the domain of the American brand Nike. A 60% competitive share, or more than 300 million subscribers, is an unprecedented result from the perspective of the entire dataset.

Regarding the overall reputation level of the entities in the post-COVID period, the European brand Chanel is in first place with almost 30% of the general online reputation level. Regarding the number of pages indexed by Google for a given brand, we record a value of 1300 million. In terms of this quantitative parameter, Chanel ranks sixth. For the sake of comparison, the most indexed entity, the American Dell, scores 7% in terms of the overall level of online reputation. This is a significant disparity, even in a reference comparison.

For completeness, the analysis also includes the experimental parameter of the entities' overall competitive strength on social media (TSMC), which is calculated as the arithmetic average of the entities' partial competitive scores on individual social platforms. In this case, the winner was the American Nike, with an almost 30% stake in TSMC, mainly thanks to its absolute dominance on the Instagram platform. The following graph illustrates the significant findings (Fig. 3).

Table 3 shows the comparison of the aggregate values of the indicators across geographical regions.

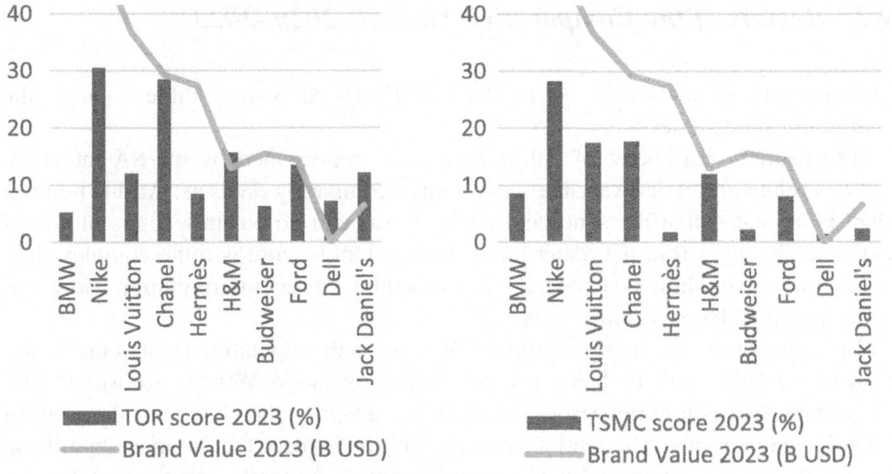


**Fig. 3** Online reputation vs. brand value 2023

**Table 3** EU vs. USA 2023

| | Facebook fans(n) | Twitter followers (n) | YouTube subscribers (n) | Instagram followers (n) | NPIG (n M) | Brand value ($ M) |
|---|---|---|---|---|---|---|
| EU Σ | 113,957,554 | 33,695,413 | 7,589,000 | 200,982,407 | 6636 | 152,710 |
| USA Σ | 90,604,707 | 12,375,773 | 4,601,100 | 312,916,579 | 9379 | 86,720 |
| EU x̄ | 22,791,511 | 6,739,083 | 1,517,800 | 40,196,481 | 1327 | 30,540 |
| USA x̄ | 18,120,941 | 2,475,155 | 920,220 | 62,583,316 | 1876 | 8490 |

At this point, it is possible to answer the research question. Regarding the comparison of geographical units, there is a relatively straightforward dominance of European brands in 2023. American brands achieve the overall dominance of the base shares only on the Instagram platform. At the same time, however, we can see a higher aggregate quantitative parameter for the number of pages indexed by Google for American brands. Regarding the total value of brands, in this indicator, European brands outperform American brands almost wholly. Overall, the model European brand in our dataset has more than 20 million fans on Facebook, more than 6 million followers on the Twitter platform, more than 1.5 million YouTube channel subscribers, more than 40 million followers on Instagram, and more than 30 billion worth of value expressed in US dollars. With this conclusion, it is possible to move on to the results of a comparative analysis of the situation before and after the end of the pandemic.

## 4.2 Results of the Comparative Analysis 2020–2023

The comparison of datasets across the COVID-19 pandemic, Table 4 shows the changes in state values:

The primary parameter of online reputation, represented by the SA indicator, reaches relatively varied variable values when comparing datasets. At this point, it shall be repeated that the sentiment analysis was carried out in a semi-automated manner. The algorithm that determines the reputation score is quite complex. It is not possible to explain the changed states based on a direct interpretation. However, some exciting changes can be seen.

First, there is a reasonably significant increase in the reputation level of the American brand Nike, which shows a boost from a negative 38% to a positive 39% percentage between comparisons. Overall, we quantify the change at the level of 77 percentage points. The Hermès and H&M brands recorded the most significant drop, in both cases, quantified at 24 percentage points. As for the social network Facebook, no substantial changes within the datasets could be seen. The same applies to the social network Twitter. The situation on the YouTube platform is quite interesting, as in two cases, there are significant changes in the level of competitive scores. European Louis Vuitton records growth at 22%, while European H&M achieves the same value but with the opposite polarity, which falls by 22% within the mentioned platform. As for the Instagram social network, there can be seen the increasing dominance of the American brand Nike, whose competitive score grew by 20% between comparisons.

As for the overall level of TOR reputation, a decrease can be seen in four cases only: three European brands, BMW, Hermès, and H&M, and one American brand,

**Table 4** Change of state values during a pandemic; 2020–2023

| Subject/ result sentiment | SA score (%) | FC score (%) | TC score (%) | YC score (%) | IgC score (%) | NPIG (n M) | TOR score (%) | Brand value($ MM) |
|---|---|---|---|---|---|---|---|---|
| BMW | −42 | 0 | +1 | 0 | −3 | −570 | −19 | +5 |
| Nike | +77 | +1 | +2 | +1 | +20 | +270 | +20 | +18 |
| Louis Vuitton | +7 | 0 | +3 | +22 | −4 | −97 | +6 | +5 |
| Chanel | +25 | 0 | −3 | +2 | −4 | +534 | +5 | +7 |
| Hermès | −34 | 0 | 0 | +1 | −1 | +202 | −7 | +9 |
| H&M | −34 | +3 | −3 | −22 | −7 | +2377 | −13 | −3 |
| Budweiser | +18 | 0 | 0 | 0 | 0 | −54 | +3 | −1 |
| Ford | +21 | 0 | 0 | −4 | 0 | −510 | +4 | 0 |
| Dell | −28 | −4 | 0 | 0 | 0 | +1240 | −7 | N/D |
| Jack Daniel's | +23 | 0 | 0 | 0 | 0 | +622 | +4 | 0 |

**Table 5** EU vs. USA; 2020–2023

| | Facebook fans (n) | Twitter followers (n) | YouTube subscribers (n) | Instagram followers (n) | NPIG (n M) | Brand value($M) |
|---|---|---|---|---|---|---|
| EU Σ | +6,886,882 | +2,467,986 | +2,203,000 | +55,451,087 | +2446 | +22,650 |
| USA Σ | −3,554,689 | +1,994,540 | +919,800 | +207,746,577 | +1676 | +8570 |
| EU x̄ | +1,377,377 | +493,598 | +440,600 | +11,093,817 | +489 | +4530 |
| USA x̄ | −710,938 | +398,908 | +183,960 | +41,549,316 | +335 | +780 |

the IT giant Dell. As for the brand's value in terms of its increase during the pandemic, the situation is again quite complex. Four European and one American brand show growth, while the rest of the sample stagnates or decreases slightly. The most valuable brand from the dataset in 2023 is American Nike, which shows an increase of 18 billion across the measurements. It replaced BMW in the first place, which increased its value by 5 billion. The following text analyses the status changes from the perspective of the cumulative geographic distribution of subjects (Table 5).

The global pandemic and the triple transition have affected the brands within the dataset in a significantly accelerated way. In all monitored parameters, regardless of geographical distribution, there is a change in conditions compared to the pre-pandemic observations. The only exception is the number of fans of American brands on the Facebook social network. Across the measurements, there can be seen an absolute drop at the level of 3.5 million fans and an average decline for brands at the level of approx. 700,000 fans. As for the other values, there are significant increases, with the most marketable ones being on the Instagram platform, dominated by the American brand Nike. European brands dominate the social media platforms Facebook, Twitter, and YouTube regarding the growth of tribes. At the same time, there was an increase in the quantitative parameter of the number of pages indexed by Google in favor of European brands. However, in nominal terms, this indicator is still dominated by American brands. Finally, it is necessary to point out the significant cumulative growth in the value of European brands, which is more than 22 billion dollars. The model European brand within the dataset thus grows by 4.5 billion across the measurements, while for the model American brand, there was an average growth of 780 million. With this statement, the section presenting empirical results and discussion is closed, and the conclusions can be made.

## 5 Conclusion

Economics and management sciences are relatively dynamic. As for management sciences, their connection to empirically generated knowledge is not negligible. However, the authors believe that developing knowledge has stayed the same since the beginning of assembly line production and motion studies. The market generates threats and challenges that market entities have to adapt to, and the role of the scientific community is to analyze both market changes and adaptation practices of market subjects. The search for optimal formulas combined with their testing creates, in addition to reasonable rules, applicable and verifiable procedures for enhancing the competitiveness of trading companies that use open innovation to develop their business. Formulas are applied in practice and become a subject of knowledge for the next generation of managers. The study aims to contribute to the development of knowledge, where empirical research develops the topic towards the possible application of knowledge in practice. Basic concepts, as well as methodological approaches, form a solid foundation for generating this knowledge.

Regarding its contribution to the development of science, the study presents several experimental procedures and quantifiers for reputation analysis, especially in terms of policies that consider the economic factors of the triple transition theme. These procedures serve as a basis for future formulation of hypotheses, which should cover complex research, as well as partial research on the issue of corporate reputation. These procedures and approaches can be summarized as follows: Introducing the concept of reputation determinants. It can be any factor that can significantly influence the perceived online reputation of an entity, and its value can be quantified in percentages. Typically, these are important catalog-type websites that provide various ratings, social networks, or portals that have a significant impact on the perception of an entity's reputation. Due to the diverse areas of business in which the entities operate, it is sometimes impossible to pre-define reputation determinants in the expected way. To quantify reputation determinants, a competitive score calculation can be used. Approaches to creating reputation offer space for actively expanding the file for various industries, subjects, or individuals. Further research is thus more than necessary.

The concept of a possible relationship between online reputation and the market value of a business company. One of the research outputs is identifying a possible relationship between the level of online importance and brand value. The analysis of the results enables, with a certain level of abstraction, deriving an economic indicator quantifying the reputation level in the context of market capitalization. This indicator suggests that 1% of TOR could be equivalent to 1 billion dollars of the market value of the brand. We are aware of the limitations of this assumption. The unique conditions under which the indicator is determined do not allow its direct applicability to general business practice. However, the construct points to a significant risk of neglecting reputation management in the online environment. Examining this assumption in a highly effective set of entities (for example, Fortune 500) could provide valuable findings for theory and economic practice.

The concept of accelerated digitization. The global pandemic acted as an accelerator in the transition process from offline to online. As part of the study, changes in the status values of the number of user tribes of critical social media are monitored. Because, at the time of submitting this paper, the global pandemic has not officially ended, we consider it recommendable to monitor changes in the market. In the context of previous findings, it is recommended to further work on determining development trends. The research limitations are identified at the level of quantifying individual variables. Despite the objectified nature of data collection using software for determining the polarity of results, the data are mainly qualitative. This limitation is considered in the discussion, and it is also taken into account when formulating the conclusions. The markets of Europe and the United States are particular. As for the specificity, it is visible, especially at the linguistic level. The linguistically unified market of the United States is an aggregate unit. On the other hand, relatively linguistically diversified Europe is a challenge for interdisciplinary research from the point of view of the unification of knowledge. Examining market differences in the context of national languages can bring new perspectives and generate local specificities. Also, as far as the dimension of tradition is concerned, the nature of the markets on both sides of the Atlantic coast shows a different dynamic. In this context, the quality and quantity of market entities are potentially significant factors, the weight of which needs to be taken into account in subsequent cross-sectional research on the issue.

**Acknowledgements** The paper is one of the outputs of the currently implemented research grant VEGA no. 1/0140/21 as well as one of the partial outputs of the currently solved research grant IVS no. IVSUPS2305.

The contribution was developed as a cross-sectional overview study of the project OpenMusE no.101095295.

The authors of the article also want to thank their students who actively participated in the preparation of its content and processing of the presented data.

## References

1. Burke, R.J., Cooper, C.L., Martin, G.: Corporate reputation: managing opportunities and threats. Gower Publishing, UK (2011)
2. Griffin, R.W.: Management. Cengage learning, Boston (2016)
3. Hittmár, Š.: Manažment. EDIS – vydavateľstvo ŽU v Žiline, Žilina (2006)
4. Schultz, H.B., Werner, A.: Reputation management. https://www.oxford.co.za/download_files/cws/Reputation.pdf, last accessed August 16, 2023
5. Burkhardt, R.: Reputation management in small and medium-sized enterprises: analysis and evaluation of the use of reputation management. a survey of small and medium-sized enterprises in Germany. Diplomica Verlag, Hamburg (2008)
6. Doorley, J., Garcia, H.F.: Reputation management: the key to successful public relations and corporate communication, 2nd edn. Routledge, New York (2011)
7. Balmer, J.M.T., Greyser, S.A.: Revealing the corporation: perspectives on identity, image, reputation, corporate branding and corporate-level marketing. Routledge, Oxford (2003)
8. Klewes, J., Wreschniok, R.: Reputation capital: building and maintaining trust in 21st century. Springer, Berlin, Heidelberg (2010)
9. Vlachynský, K., et al.: Podnikové financie. 1. vyd. Iura Edition, Bratislava (2009)
10. Vig, S., Dumicic, K., Klopotan, I.: The impact of reputation on corporate financial performance: median regression approach. Bus. Syst. Res. J. **8**(2), 40–58 (2017)
11. Hasan, M.M., Habib, A., Zhao, R.: Corporate reputation risk and cash holdings. Acc Finance **62**(1), 667–707 (2022)

12. Berber, N., et al.: The relationship between corporate social responsibility and corporate reputation in Serbia. Inžinerinė Ekon. Eng. Econ. **33**(3), 232–245 (2022)
13. Orlova, N., Ladonko, L., Filipova, N., Mital, O.: Reputation of socially responsible corporations in the world financial market. Fin. Credit Act. Probl. Theory Pract. **4**(35), 144–151 (2020)
14. Pham, H.S.T., Tran, H.T.: CSR disclosure and firm performance: the mediating role of corporate reputation and moderating role of CEO integrity. J. Bus. Res. **120**, 127–136 (2020)
15. Singh, K., Misra, M.: Linking corporate social responsibility (CSR) and organizational performance: the moderating effect of corporate reputation. Eur. Res. Manage. Bus. Econ. **27**(1), 100139 (2021)
16. Gonzales-Rodriguez, M., et al.: Exploring the links among corporate social responsibility, reputation, and performance from a multi-dimensional perspective. Int. J. Hosp. Manage. **99**(1), 103079 (2021)
17. Martos-Pedreo, A., Jimanez-Castillo, D., Joaquin Cortes-Garcia, F.: Corporate social responsibility and financial performance in the agri-food sector: mediating effect of image and reputation. ITEA-Inf. Téc. Econ. Agrar. **118**(3), 453–475 (2022)
18. Blajer-Golebiewska, A.: Individual corporate reputation and perception of collective corporate reputation regarding stock market investments. PLOS One **16**(9), e0257323 (2021)
19. Maqbool, S.: Does corporate social responsibility lead to superior financial performance? Evidence from BSE 100 index. Decision **46**(9), 219–231 (2019)
20. Nawrocki, T.L., Szwajca D.: The importance of selected aspects of a company's reputation for individual stock market investors-evidence from Polish capital market. Sustainability **14**(15), 9187 (2022)
21. Arbe, R., Feria-Dominguez, J.M.: Reputational risk on corporate corruption scandals: evidence from Latin America. Acad. Rev. Latinoam. Adm. **35**(3), 329–344 (2022)
22. Human-Nope, A.G., et al.: Reputational risk and stock price: a corporate management analysis. Manag. Financ. **49**(7), 1113–1130 (2023)
23. Xie, X., et al.: Does carbon neutrality commitment enhance firm value? J. Chin. Econ. Bus. Stud. **21**(1), 49–83 (2023)
24. Zhang, Q., Wong, J.B.: ESG reputational risks and board monitoring committees. Financ. Res. Lett. **50**(3), 103325 (2022)
25. Eriqat, I.O.A., Tahir, M., Zulkafli, A.H.: Do corporate governance mechanisms matter to the reputation of financial firms? Evidence of emerging markets. Cogent Bus. Manage. **10**(1), 2181187–2181218 (2023)
26. Interbrand. Best Global Brands 2019 Rankings. https://www.interbrand.com/best-brands/best-global-brands/2019/ranking, last accessed December 17, 2019
27. Pollák, F., Markovič, P., Majdúchová, H.: Reputation of electric vehicles in the environment of carbon reduction and accelerated digitization. Energies **16**(9), 3836 (2023)
28. DanielSoper free Sentiment Analyzer. https://www.danielsoper.com/sentimentanalysis/default.aspx, last accessed July 11, 2023
29. Pollák, F., Markovič, P., Straková, J., Pártlová, P.: Sustainable development of corporate reputation—reputation analysis of the selected brands owned by the family businesses. SHS Web Conf. **92**(1), 05023 (2021)
30. Pollák, F., Dorčák, P., Markovič, P.: Corporate reputation of family-owned businesses: parent companies vs. their brands. Information **12**(2), 89 (2021)
31. Bain, D.: The world's top 750 family businesses ranking. https://www.famcap.com/the-worlds-750-biggest-family-businesses/, last accessed June 7, 2019
32. Biel, M., Ślusarczyk, B.: Family business and management: objectives, theory, and practice. Taylor & Francis (2022)
33. Moresová, M., Sedliačiková, M., Drábek, J., Šuleř, P., Vetráková, M.: The impact of internal determinants on management of family business in Slovakia. Pol. J. Manage. Stud. **24**(2), 307–320 (2021)

34. Biel, M., Ślusarczyk, B.: Management methods and tools in family businesses: impact on the effectiveness of achieving goals. J. Int. Stud. **15**(4), 180–195 (2022)
35. Putri, A.C., Viverita, V.: Risk preference of founder and descendant of Indonesian family firms. Pol. J. Manage. Stud. **20**(2), 414–425 (2019)
36. Kolarov, K., Georgieva, S.: Management features in Bulgarian SMEs as determinants of business internationalization. P. J. Manage. Stud. **22**(1), 279–294 (2020)
37. Social Blade. https://socialblade.com, last accessed July 15, 2023

# Reputation of Family-Owned Businesses: Parent Companies vs. Their Brands in the Context of Global Pandemic

**Peter Markovič and František Pollák**

**Abstract** The success of companies heavily hinges on their reputation, an intangible asset deserving utmost attention. Continuously monitoring corporate reputation is pivotal in swiftly detecting potential threats. Family-owned enterprises, blending tradition and adaptability within their brands, serve as ideal subjects for reputation management studies. This paper delves into exploring innovative strategies for online reputation management amid a global pandemic. Authors conducted a comprehensive analysis of sentiment across major online platforms for the ten largest family-owned businesses before and during the pandemic's decline. Key determinants like Google, Facebook, Twitter, YouTube, and LinkedIn were scrutinized. This study reveals a conspicuous contrast between the marketing strategies of parent companies and their brands, offering valuable insights into sustainable brand evolution. By discerning effective methodologies and pinpointing weaknesses, the research endeavors to reshape knowledge in management sciences, particularly considering the transformative landscape shaped by the pandemic's wane. The research methodology involved an extensive evaluation of online sentiment and communications, accentuating shifts in consumer perceptions during the pandemic's evolution. The significance lies not just in identifying successful practices but also in shedding light on deficiencies. It aims to contribute substantially to the evolution of management sciences, particularly concerning the paradigm shifts brought about by the receding pandemic. The findings emphasize the importance of agile adaptation in brand management, catering to evolving consumer sentiments amidst global crises. This study serves as a compass guiding businesses toward resilient brand strategies in the face of unforeseen disruptions.

**Keywords** Reputation management · Brand development · Information distribution · Family-owned business · Global pandemic

P. Markovič (✉) · F. Pollák
University of Economics in Bratislava, Dolnozemská Cesta 1/B, 852 35 Bratislava, Slovakia
e-mail: peter.markovic@euba.sk

F. Pollák
Institute of Technology and Business in České Budějovice, Okružní 517/10, 370 01 České Budějovice, Czech Republic

 
S. Kot et al. (eds.), *Corporate Practices: Policies, Methodologies, and Insights in Organizational Management*, Springer Proceedings in Business and Economics,
https://doi.org/10.1007/978-981-97-0996-0_54

## 1 Introduction

The business environment is a constantly evolving ecosystem. In addition to internal influences, this ecosystem is also influenced by external factors. While the characteristics of the internal environment are usually under the direct control of the given company, the external factors have to be accepted. When starting a business, the atmosphere is given, but the status quo is unsustainable in the long term. Companies are experiencing a turbulent development of circumstances at the micro and macro levels of the economy. The constant emphasis on innovation and the development of information technology has brought not only opportunities and market openings but also challenges that have yet to be given appropriate priority. In the past, companies set processes that were followed, and innovations only took place in the case of an increased market demand or the need to increase competitiveness. Today, this concept no longer applies. Access to real-time information has taken benchmarking, whether of trading companies or their products, to a higher level. In the online space, business must be done with the same commitment to managing traditional offline processes. Websites about them mainly support the operation of brick-and-mortar businesses. If a company wants to make itself visible to customers, just "putting up a sign" is not enough. Corporate reputation receives much more attention. General awareness influences customer trust in the company, and faith, in turn, affects the company's competitiveness. Customer dissatisfaction or satisfaction with products spreads literally with a click and is shared with all customers at once. Companies also face the environmental requirements of the market. Emphasis is put on the ecological use of resources and a green approach to the environment in which the company operates. These factors directly affect reputation as an intangible asset of the company. The presented research on innovative practices in online reputation management was conducted in this hectic environment.

In the context of the global pandemic of COVID-19, the issue has taken on an entirely new dynamic. Based on those above, the paper aims to examine and subsequently discuss the issue of innovative approaches to online reputation management in the context of a global pandemic. The presented study thus maps the direct effects of the pandemic on the online reputation management process over time. To collect relevant empirical material, the authors built on their research [1] conducted before the onset of the pandemic. In the context of the anticipated changes, the following research question was formulated: "How has the global pandemic affected the reputation of significant players in the global market?". The dataset, as well as interpretations of the context of the pre-pandemic measurement, served as a reference point for a comprehensive examination of shifts in status reputation indicators during the pandemic. The research sample, as well as the methodological apparatus for data measurement and evaluation, remained the same during data collection. The study, as such, is structured in a standard way, with the introduction complemented by basic views on the given issue itself. The theoretical overview of findings in the given field is followed by a methodological part, which describes all relevant aspects of the research in the context of the processes and methods used. The empirical part presents the results, which are discussed in more detail in the context of their specificities. In the conclusion, the most important findings are summarized, and the starting points for advancing knowledge are formulated. The study concludes with a description of research limitations and suggestions for further research.

## 2 Literature Review

Reputation is a crucial asset for an organization and represents an effective strategic tool for achieving competitive advantage [2]. The term reputation encompasses a whole range of views on a trading company from the perspective of both its external and internal environment. As an intangible asset, reputation makes the company unique and encourages customers to make repeat purchases and be willing to pay a higher price for the products [3]. A strong reputation is believed to enable companies to set premium prices, reduce marketing costs, help attract talented employees, build brand support through word of mouth, and finally, prevent imitation by competitors [4]. Similarly, according to Deephouse [5], corporate reputation leads to competitive advantage by expressing the suitability of the given business to interest groups. Thus, the company's reputation is an intangible resource that is difficult for competitors to imitate and can be effectively transformed into a competitive advantage that benefits the company's performance. The twenty-first century is the century of technology, with social media becoming the fastest-growing medium in technological development. Content from all over the world is available to the user in real-time. Social media can be an ideal place for building a product or company's brand in the market. They can significantly help in developing, adapting, innovating, providing, or capturing information. They also create a space for generating interactions and obtaining feedback [6]. At this point, it shall be noted that the online area, with its speed, can also harm a business quickly; therefore, constant monitoring is necessary. This monitoring requires significant corporate resources. Several authors have searched for a precise definition of reputation, some comparing it to an asset, others to an evaluation, or even to awareness [7]. Reputation is thus increasingly recognized for its influence in creating stakeholder support and, of course, increasing stakeholder engagement in companies [8]. The search for suitable tools for measuring reputation or context analysis has been the subject of many authors' efforts. Reputation is closely related to trust. Trust is becoming an essential element of success in modern social media. However, despite the constantly developing field of social media research, more attention should be paid to the issues of building a position within social media in terms of empirical studies. Overcoming the inherent uncertainty and risks associated with an open electronic market and online collaboration systems requires establishing mutual trust between service providers and their consumers. One of the main problems of such environments is how to increase the resilience of systems against self-interested participants and how to understand and detect their possible fraudulent intentions [9]. Building trust in such scenarios is a complex task based on small details. However, customers are well aware of the added value. The Internet has brought high-speed access to information. It shall be noted that this data is stored permanently in data centers. The data is analyzed and used for future evaluation and comparison of past events. This fact only highlights the need to pay additional attention to online reputation management.

Suppose we want to analyze the individual factors of reputation and the degree of their impact on the overall reputation. In that case, it is necessary to become familiar with selected systems of trust and reputation. As part of the theoretical overview, there will be presented the basic models underlying them. Each method has its characteristics in dealing with and calculating reputation scores. More specifically, the selected trust and reputation systems have distinctive features in addressing the internal dynamics of the open environment, evaluating the honesty and reliability of the participants, and calculating reputation scores [10]. The literature [11] describes two basic types of systems, namely:

- Personal systems, which are specific to individuals. They represent a standard peer-to-peer reputation allocation mechanism. These systems are designed to assign a personal reputation score to each member of a particular network or community. However, such a score will ultimately only be relevant to one individual.
- Global systems. Global reputation systems are specific to the community as a whole rather than to a community member. These systems assign a single and unique reputation score to different actors in a particular community or network, which all community members will consider the only legitimate score.

## 2.1 Peer Trust

In literature [12], this model is described as a coherent dynamic model of trust with unique characteristics adapted for peer-to-peer e-commerce communities. For advanced assessment and quantification of the value of trust in constantly evolving environments, this model adapts a number of common factors, especially factors like:

1. feedback, which represents the judgment of other subjects about target peers;
2. the extent of feedback, such as the amount of transactions a partner has experienced with others;
3. a credibility factor for evaluating the honesty of feedback sources;
4. the transaction context factor, such as the time and size of transactions, which could act as a defense mechanism against sophisticated fraudulent activities;
5. and the community context factor that addresses the issue of feedback stimulation.

## 2.2 *Bayesian Reputation System*

Jøsang et al. [13] proposed a flexible and adaptive Bayesian reputation system (BRS) that supports both binomial and multinomial rating models. The goal is to provide the system with ratings with different levels of accuracy that are suitable for an open dynamic environment. Theoretically, the multinomial BRS is based on the calculation of the reputation score by a statistical update of the Dirichlet probability density function [14]. More specifically, in this context, agents can rate other peers within any level from a set of predefined rating levels. In contrast, in binomial BRS, which is based on the Beta distribution, agents can only provide binary ratings to others. This means that in multinomial BRSs, reputation scores do not only reflect general service quality; they can also distinguish between the case of polarized and average ratings [15]. Obviously, such differences are not visible in binomial evaluations, which leads to uncertainty and low confidence in the aggregated reputation score, and may also prevent the conversion of reputation scores into specific values [16]. In addition, the multinomial BRS provides input ratings based on both discrete and continuous measures to more accurately reflect the rater's opinion when needed.

## 2.3 *Sentiment Analysis*

Sentiment analysis, an essential component of natural language processing (NLP), discerns the positivity, negativity, or neutrality within data. This technique aids businesses in comprehending customer sentiment toward brands and products by processing textual data [17].

The utility of sentiment analysis encompasses several advantages and drawbacks:

- Scalable Data Sorting: Businesses can efficiently process vast amounts of unstructured data, enabling cost-effective analysis;
- Real-Time Insights: Swift identification of critical issues in real-time, facilitating prompt responses;
- Consistent Criteria: Human agreement on sentiment determination is merely around 60–65%, primarily due to subjectivity influenced by personal experiences and beliefs.

Establishing a centralized sentiment analysis system allows companies to apply consistent criteria across all data, enhancing accuracy and insights. Despite the popular notion that sentiment analysis solely involves classifying positivity or negativity in text, it's a multifaceted challenge [18]. Unlike factual information, perceived sentiment hinges on subjectivity, shaped by various factors. Diverse experiences, worldviews, interests, and ideologies contribute to subjective states, necessitating evaluation based on multiple opinions rather than relying on singular perspectives [19]. The breadth of variables monitored amplifies the demand for standardized classification.

Methodologically, conducting sentiment analysis typically involves several steps [20]:

1. Data Collection: Identification and gathering of analyzed text, often utilizing web bots or programmable interfaces.
2. Data Cleaning: Processing and filtering to eliminate noise like punctuation, URLs, special characters, and irrelevant parts of speech, termed standardization.
3. Feature Extraction: Machine learning algorithms automatically identify text elements indicating positive or negative sentiment, employing techniques like "bag of words" or word embedding using neural networks.
4. Model Selection: Choosing a sentiment analysis tool—rule-based systems, employing predefined rules based on word meanings, or automatic/hybrid systems utilizing machine learning techniques. Hybrid models, combining both approaches, are often favored for accuracy.
5. Assigning positive, negative, or neutral scores to text portions using the selected model. Organizations can review analyses at different levels, such as document-level for expert or customer ratings.

Sentiment analysis goes beyond simplistic positivity or negativity categorization. Its value lies in facilitating nuanced insights by considering the complex interplay of subjectivity and diverse perspectives within text data, empowering businesses to glean comprehensive consumer sentiment and needs.

Based on the current state of knowledge, as well as previous own research [21–23], the authors combine methods based on their application potential in the conditions of the online environment. This approach was used in the design of the methodology for the collection and processing of datasets, forming the basis of the empirical analysis presented in this study.

## 3 Methods

In this section, the methodological framework of the study is presented. At the same time, it describes the main goal in its holistic and decomposed form. A research problem is defined, and on its basis, a research question is formulated. Furthermore, the research subject, the work process, the information sources, and the method of obtaining and processing data are described.

### *3.1 Objective*

The main goal of the study is to examine and subsequently discuss the issue of innovative approaches to Online Reputation Management in the context of a global pandemic. To achieve the goal, it is necessary to decompose it into specific sub-goals concerning the general shift of knowledge and the production of empirical material.

**Fig. 1** Interventional logic of fulfilling the main goal

Specifically, the sub-goals can be formulated as follows:

- Accumulation of relevant knowledge on the issue of reputation management as an intangible asset of the company;
- Comparative analysis of the relevant specifics of the online identity building process of global trading companies based on their tradition.

## 3.2 Research Problem and Research Question

When decomposing the main goal of the paper into sub-goals, the relatively unprecedented situation on the market was fully reflected. The situation was caused by the onset of the global COVID-19 pandemic in the first half of 2020. The sub-goals thus represent a chronological construct that reflects the development of the challenges to the investigated issue over time. Based on the selected goal, the research problem is identified and the research question is formulated as follows:

Research problem: Existence of specifics in the process of identity building for different groups of business companies based on tradition.

General research question: Is there a difference between the e-marketing communication of the parent company and the e-marketing communication of the brand belonging to that company's portfolio?

Specific research question: How has the global pandemic affected the reputation of significant players in the global market? (Fig. 1).

## 3.3 Research Subject

The investigation focuses on both sides of the market. Selected companies represent the supply side of the market. The demand side of the market is characterized by customers, mainly customers who are active in the online environment. For the study, the terms customer and consumer are considered synonymous, as in the context of the conducted research, it is not a change factor in the resulting knowledge. At the same time, the authors consider it necessary to decompose the research subject at the level of the research problem.

The research subject was 750 multinational trading companies falling under the category of family-owned businesses operating on the global market. The research

**Fig. 2** Research process

sample consists of the ten most prominent companies in this group, as reported by Family Capital and PWC [24]. As part of the empirical analysis, we refer to these entities as 'parent companies' while we present them in more detail in the context of the analyzed connections within Tables 1 and 3 in the next section. To answer the research question, within the portfolio of companies from the research sample, one brand is always identified, which is communicated to the market within the investigated company. For the analysis, it is one dominant brand from the portfolio of the analyzed parent company. In the text, these entities are referred to as 'private brands of parent companies', presented in Tables 2 and 4.

### 3.4 Research Process

The process of solving the research problem represents a chronological sequence of steps that preceded the achievement of the defined goal. This sequence of steps can be visualized as follows (Fig. 2).

The analysis of the state of knowledge was carried out predominantly based on available publications by domestic and foreign authors. The main phase took place in 2020. However, the knowledge presented in the study is more comprehensive than the core of learning identified in this period, as the authors aim to deliver continuous development of the issues over time. Regarding the research, it should be noted that the proposed study extends the knowledge of the reference study from 2021 [1]. The research, which forms the reference base for the comparison, took place in the first half of 2020, so the timing of the reference data reflects the period before the intense onset of the global pandemic. The second measurement was carried out with an interval of 36 months, i.e., in the second half of 2023, while the comparison of both datasets creates a knowledge base for achieving the primary goal of the paper.

### 3.5 Information Sources and Data Collection Method

As for the information sources used, they are exclusively secondary data. For the purposes of the theoretical review, mainly the sources from renowned scientific databases. These are systematically supplemented by relevant sources in literature and online content from renowned publishers. For the purposes of empirical analyses, a wide range of highly relevant secondary data of a quantitative nature was used. Specifically, the following virtual social networks and virtual social media were used to provide datasets:

- Facebook,
- Twitter,
- YouTube,
- LinedIn,
- Google.

From the point of view of data collection, it was a systematic data collection without the use of forms of automation. Expert assessment maximized the objectivity of quantifying the recorded indicators. As such, the collection showed signs of observation.

### 3.6 Research Methods Used

Regarding the specific analysis methods, it's essential to highlight advanced sentiment analysis [21]. This technique serves as the foundation for evaluating TOR's overall online reputation [1]. The procedural breakdown includes:

- Identifying the research subject and reputation determinants;
- Employing advanced sentiment analysis;
- Analyzing individual reputations;
- Calculating total TOR values for each subject.

The analysis process can be visualized as follows (Fig. 3).

The analysis initiates by selecting subjects and using Google.com as the data source for Sentiment Analysis. It evaluates the polarity of proper names in the top ten search positions for each subject, assigning numerical values to predicted sentiments. These emotional scores across positions are tallied to derive the primary input for detailed analysis. The chosen method, Advanced Sentiment Analysis (ASA), extends beyond the basic parameter of ten search results. ASA allows customization based on topics, enabling definitions in primary Google tabs like news. This flexible approach assesses polarity, capturing nuanced emotional nuances in search results. The numerical values gathered from each position form a critical input for comprehensive analysis. ASA's adaptability and consideration of various factors enhance its utility, accommodating diverse research needs and delivering a broader perspective by integrating different search criteria within Google's platform.

The subsequent stage in determining overall reputation involves identifying additional determinants, termed determinants of reputation. In this analysis, these encompass specifics within distinct social networks and virtual media. When direct quantification of reputation is unfeasible, it relies on the size of the user/customer base in the social network milieu. Alternatively, a Competitive Score (CS) parameter is

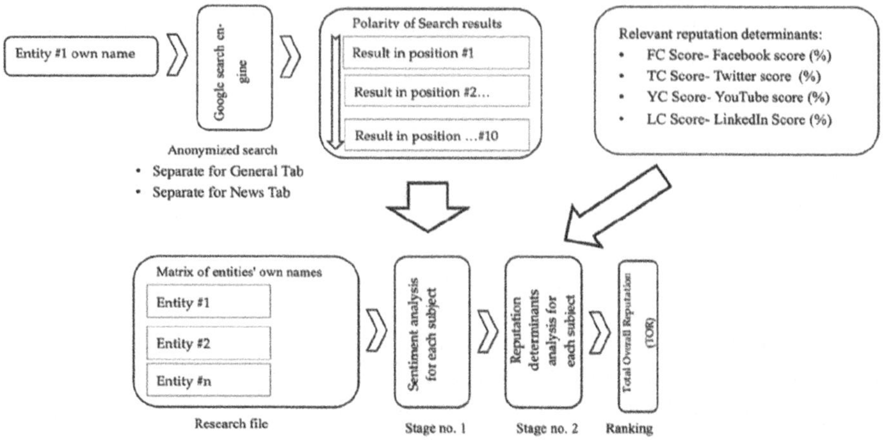


**Fig. 3** Total online reputation (TOR) analysis process

employed. This method involves defining reference entities for comparison. The total user bases of all sample subjects determine the industry's overall customer base size, juxtaposed against the individual bases of the analyzed entities. Comparing the subject's user base size to the industry's total user base yields the entity's competitive score against reference entities. CS is computed separately for each determinant, with individual scores converted to percentages. This approach offers a holistic evaluation, factoring in various determinants of reputation and quantifying competitive standing within the industry, augmenting the depth of analysis by translating individual scores into more relatable percentage values.

The final stage entails computing the Total Online Reputation (TOR) by averaging individual entity standings. To provide a comprehensive view, the entity/brand's significance is quantified using Google's indexed pages (NPIG), measured in millions. Additionally, the company's annual revenues in billions of USD serve as supplementary parameters. These quantitative indicators aid in more accurate interpretations. NPIG, found in overview tables, gauges an entity's online visibility, while revenue figures provide financial context. The data primarily undergoes processing via MS Office tools. This holistic approach ensures a thorough evaluation, combining quantitative measures to present a comprehensive understanding of an entity's online reputation and financial standing.

## 4 Results and Discussion

As mentioned, the study compares two datasets: a reference database relevant to the pre-pandemic era and a dataset that considers status values measured after the end of the pandemic. Regarding the interpretation of the findings, the first part of the chapter presents the findings of the analysis of the situation from the year 2023, i.e., from the period after the end of the pandemic. Next, the findings are presented and discussed based on the comparison of data with the reference database created in 2020.

## *4.1 Results of the Empirical Analysis from the Period After the End of the Pandemic*

For the empirical analysis, significant business entities that fall into family-owned businesses were tested. The assumption of increased attention of the owners paid to the process of brand building and development based on tradition was a decisive qualifying factor in selecting the research sample. As for the entities, the authors believe it is optional to specify them in more detail. As for their private brands, which form an integral part of testing, it is essential to describe three of them in more detail: Sam's Choice, which is a private brand, and at the same time, a specific loyalty system of the global unit of the retail giant Walmart; Wilbur Chocolate, which is a product line of the Cargill company; and Georgia-Pacific, belonging to the portfolio of Koch Industries. The following table shows the status values of the individual reputation indicators of the parent companies (Table 1).

**Table 1** Reputation of parent companies in 2023

| Subject/ result sentiment | ASA score 2023 (%) | FC score 2023 (%) | TC score 2023 (%) | YC score 2023 (%) | LC score 2023 (%) | NPIG 2023 (mil) | TOR score 2023 (%) |
|---|---|---|---|---|---|---|---|
| Walmart Inc | 63 | 32 | 20 | 14 | 29 | 656 | 32 |
| Volkswagen AG | 58 | 32 | 2 | 1 | 9 | 53.8 | 20 |
| Berkshire Hathaway | 30 | 0 | 0 | 0 | 1 | 43.1 | 6 |
| Exor NV | 85 | 0 | 0 | 0 | 0 | 0.64 | 17 |
| Ford Motor Company | 48 | 16 | 22 | 52 | 26 | 420 | 33 |
| Schwarz Gruppe | 63 | 0 | 0 | 0 | 0 | 115 | 13 |
| BMW AG | 62 | 19 | 37 | 31 | 18 | 77 | 33 |
| Cargill, Incorporated | 59 | 0 | 1 | 0 | 15 | 2.57 | 15 |
| Tata Sons Ltd | 81 | 0 | 16 | 1 | 0 | 14,8 | 20 |
| Koch Industries, Inc | 66 | 0 | 1 | 0 | 1 | 13.2 | 14 |

For the purpose of describing the qualitative findings, we start with the first company in the sequence, which is Walmart Inc. It is a multinational retail corporation based in the USA. The company's website appears at the top of the general search results, followed by the company's website again, but with a general focus. According to the chosen methodology of manual subtraction and expert determination of the polarity of the search results, neutral sentiment is assigned to such an occurrence. In the third position, there is a link to Wikipedia. This type of link as a significant reputational asset, as indicates the general awareness of the company. In the fourth position, there is a link to the page of an important periodical, which is positively mentioned by the evaluated entity. Although this is a PR link, it ulfils its role in the optimization of the reputation within the first ten search results in the desired way. The following two links point to variants of the organization's website, which are assigned neutral sentiment. The seventh and eighth links refer to important periodicals, but unlike the fourth position, the title and description of the reference are of a dominantly neutral nature. The last two links point to company profiles on the X platform (former Twitter). Both these links are assigned positive sentiment, as social media generally increase the transparency of the organization.

As for the sentiment analysis of the top ten search results in the News category, the situation is more diverse. In the first position, there is a link with a positive sentiment. It is a report on the company's share price. The description is optimal, which is an ideal state where the first position indicates the optimal result from the point of view of optimization for ORM purposes. In the second place, there is a report of a renowned periodical; it has a warning character, which, despite the neutral overtone, is evaluated as negative. The third is a report on a business-oriented periodical, which refers to the company's foreign operation in a way that can be evaluated as positive. The fourth link is a business journal page (a different one to the the pre'ious link). The report deals with innovation and has a distinctly positive nature. The fifth link is to a page about stock markets. It has a positive character, as it mentions the growth of the entity's shares, as well as the positive upward trend of the growth in its share prices. The sixth link refers to innovations in automation. This is a message of positive sentiment. The seventh position is occupied again by news about a positive trend in the development of the company's shares. The text of the link itself sounds very positive, which is an exemplary result of positive sentiment. The eighth to tenth results, which mention innovations, potential, as well as the expansion of the assortment of prestigious brands within the company's retail stores, shows positive sentiment each.' From the perspective of media coverage on the Google News section, we can seean almost ideal situation,' with relevant and highly topical content. The timeliness and relevance of news, combined with the diverse nature of reputational information sources, is an ideal scenario for online media communication not only from the point of view of online reputation management, as well as PR management as such.

The scope of the study does not allow a qualitative survey of the entire sample. In any case, we can see a fairly fragmented set of results. At this point, we proceed to the presentation of the established values of the private brands of the analyzed companies. The following table shows the status values of the individual reputation indicators of the parent companies' private brands as follows (Table 2).

For a holistic approach to the description of qualitative reputation indicators, we will now proceed to interpret the findings from the analysis of the reputation of Walmart's most important private brand, Sam's Choice. The first position in the general Google search results is the parent company's website. For the analysis purposes, it is assigned neutral sentiment. In the second position, there is again the Walmart company website, but this is a different section of the page; however, of the exact nature. This link is evaluated as neutral. The third is the page on the own domain, classified as the entity's website. The fourth link is a link to Wikipedia, which is highly positive, as Wikipedia gives the subject considerable weight and legitimacy not only in the online environment. The fifth link is to the website of the Internet giant Amazon. If it were a link to social networks, it would be considered a link to a page that increases the transparency of the entity. In this case, it could only be discussed whether improving the availability of products through third parties contributes to enhancing reputation. This brings us back to the very essence of sentiment analysis, that is, judging occurrences strictly by the polarity of the words in the description and headline. In this case, it is assigned a neutral sentiment. However, we consider the qualitative dimension of evaluating results based on sentiment analysis. We attribute an objectively qualitative dimension to the estimated effect and the objectively methodological one. This approach will be referred to as Qualitative Sentiment Analysis (QSA). The sixth link is a link to a website about cooking. From the description and nature of the link, we identify indicators beyond neutral sentiment. The seventh link is a link to a third-party online store, assigned a neutral sentiment. The eighth link is a link to the fan platform website in the format of an open encyclopedia. As in the case of Wikipedia, this type of link is assigned a positive

**Table 2** Reputation of private brands of parent companies in 2023

| Subject/ result sentiment | ASA score 2023 (%) | FC score 2023 (%) | TC score 2023 (%) | YC score 2023 (%) | LC score 2023 (%) | NPIG 2023 (mil) | TOR score 2023 (%) |
|---|---|---|---|---|---|---|---|
| Sam's choice | 63 | 32 | 20 | 14 | 29 | 656 | 32 |
| Audi | 58 | 32 | 2 | 1 | 9 | 53.8 | 20 |
| Berkshire Hathaway | 30 | 0 | 0 | 0 | 1 | 43.1 | 6 |
| Fiat | 85 | 0 | 0 | 0 | 0 | 0.64 | 17 |
| Lincoln | 48 | 16 | 22 | 52 | 26 | 420 | 33 |
| Lidl | 63 | 0 | 0 | 0 | 0 | 115 | 13 |
| Mini | 62 | 19 | 37 | 31 | 18 | 77 | 33 |
| Wilbur Chocolate | 59 | 0 | 1 | 0 | 15 | 2.57 | 15 |
| Jaguar | 81 | 0 | 16 | 1 | 0 | 14,8 | 20 |
| Georgia-Pacific | 66 | 0 | 1 | 0 | 1 | 13.2 | 14 |

sentiment. The ninth position is occupied by a link to a platform with product reviews, where the product, directly evaluated in the search result, is positively presented by the entity. The last link is again a variation of a Wikipedia-type page. This link is assigned a positive sentiment.

As for the sentiment analysis of the first ten search results in the News category, in the first position, there is a relatively neutral link comparing memberships in various loyalty and shopping programs. From the title and description, no significant deviations from neutral sentiment are identified. The second link is a report on favorable conditions for registration in the brand's loyalty program. Strictly methodologically, but also according to a qualitative assessment, this is a link with a positive sentiment. The third link mentions a fire in one of the brand's warehouses. We classify this type of link as unfavorable. The fifth link is again a report referring to the temporarily favorable terms of registration in the loyalty program; it is a similar report as in the case of the second link. In any case, a different media reporting the news ensures positive sentiment for the brand.

The fifth link is a report on the additional value for the customer from the point of view of discounted payment cards. It is assigned a positive sentiment. The sixth link mentions specific products within the brand, namely wedding cakes, presented as rational choices using a spectrum of positive emotion words. The seventh and eighth positions are occupied by news reporting on the discounted registration terms for the loyalty program. Similar to the previous cases, it is evaluated positively. The report in the ninth search position discusses the benefits of loyalty clubs; its nature is identical to the information in the first position. However, unlike the first report, the title of the data is formulated as a statement, whereas in the first case, the title is formulated as a question. This also ensures a positive sentiment for the link in the ninth position. The tenth link is a report on favorable conditions for registration in the loyalty program, which is assigned a positive sentiment. In general, as in the case of the parent company, we find a wide range of resources of a relatively highly up-to-date nature for the brand. With this statement, we conclude the qualitative description of findings based on sentiment analysis. Due to the rather large scope of the qualitative base of results, we again remain strictly nominal when describing other entities within both samples.

Regarding the comparison and interpretation of the findings from the perspective of the level of reputation based on the monitored reputation determinants beyond the sentiment of the search results in Google (ASA), we proceed to the visualization of the status values of the parent companies and their brands in the form of the following graph (Fig. 4).

As can be seen from the graph and the data, from the point of view of the parent companies, the car companies have the largest communities, followed by the American retail giant Walmart. Regarding the measured maximums, it is necessary to mention the car company Ford, which has the strongest community on the YouTube platform compared to the other companies in the sample. In proportion to the sum of the tribes of all entities in the sample, it achieves more than 50% of the competitive score on the given platform. A similar, albeit not as significant, lead on the X platform

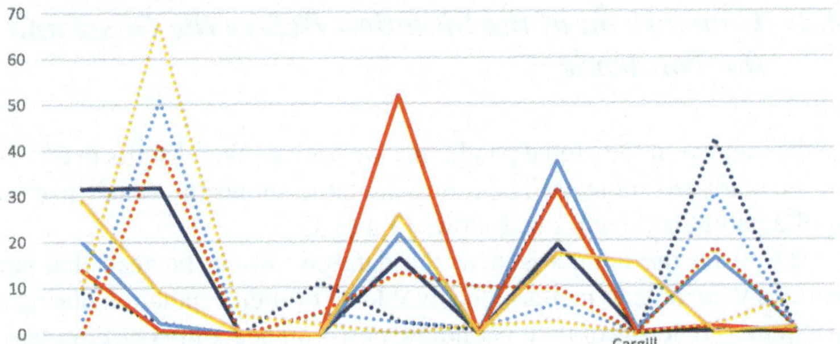


| | Walmart Inc./ Sam's Choice* | Volkswagen AG/ Audi* | Berkshire Hathaway Inc. | Exor NV/ Fiat* | Ford Motor Company / Lincoln* | Schwarz Gruppe/ Lidl* | BMW AG/ Mini* | Cargill, Incorporated/ Wilbur Chocolate* | Tata Sons Ltd/ Jaguar* | Koch Industries, Inc./ Georgia-Pacific* |
|---|---|---|---|---|---|---|---|---|---|---|
| FC Score (%) | 32 | 32 | 0 | 0 | 16 | 0 | 19 | 0 | 0 | 0 |
| FC Score* (%) | 9 | 3 | 0 | 11 | 3 | 1 | 32 | 0 | 42 | 0 |
| TC Score (%) | 20 | 2 | 0 | 0 | 22 | 0 | 37 | 1 | 16 | 1 |
| TC Score* (%) | 4 | 51 | 0 | 5 | 3 | 1 | 6 | 0 | 30 | 0 |
| YC Score (%) | 14 | 1 | 0 | 0 | 52 | 0 | 31 | 0 | 1 | 0 |
| YC Score* (%) | 1 | 42 | 0 | 5 | 13 | 10 | 10 | 0 | 19 | 1 |
| LC Score (%) | 29 | 9 | 1 | 0 | 26 | 0 | 18 | 15 | 0 | 1 |
| LC Score* (%) | 11 | 68 | 4 | 2 | 0 | 2 | 3 | 0 | 2 | 8 |

**Fig. 4** Reputation determinants of parent companies and their brands in 2023

(former Twitter) is held by BMW. In terms of the Facebook social network, German Volkswagen and US Walmart share the lead.

As for the private brands of the parent companies, German Audi and Indian Jaguar stand out significantly above the sample average. As for measurement, there is not difference in terms of the highest value of competitive scoring across the sample. This is the level of the competitive score of the Audi brand, belonging to the parent concern Volkswagen. The platform is LinkedIn, with a competitive score of 68%.

As for the specifics in the context of comparing the strength of individual reputations of parent companies and their brands, there are significant differences in four cases, two in favor of parent companies and two in favor of private brands. From the point of view of the parent companies, Ford and BMW dominate the measurement, while from the perspective of private brands, the values of Audi and Jaguar attract attention.

Regarding the total level of reputation based on the TOR parameter, the first position in the ranking is shared by BMW and Ford. When it comes to private brands, the highest values are achieved by Lincoln and Mini. With this statement, we can proceed to the comparison of conditions during the global pandemic.

## *4.2 Comparison of the Situation Before the Onset and After the Pandemic*

In the context of the global pandemic, we notice several shifts in the reputation levels of the analyzed subjects. The following table shows the values from the perspective of the parent companies as follows (Table 3).

Based on the comparison of the datasets, it can be seen that seven out of ten entities were able to increase the total level of their reputation during the COVID-19 pandemic. In terms of their economic performance, only one company, namely Exor NV, saw a decrease in revenues during the monitored period, while the remaining nine entities achieved an increase of 2–77 billion US dollars. In terms of record highs, Exor and Tata saw significant increases in reputation according to the measurements using advanced sentiment analysis. At the same time, there was a significant increase in BMW's competitive score on the X platform (former Twitter). A similar increase

**Table 3** Reputation of parent companies—2020 vs. 2023

| Subject/result sentiment | ASA score 2023 (%) | FC score 2023 (%) | TC score 2023 (%) | YC score 2023 (%) | LC score 2023 (%) | NPIG 2023 (mil) | TOR score 2023 (%) |
|---|---|---|---|---|---|---|---|
| Walmart Inc | ⇧ | – | ⇩ | ⇩ | ⇧ | ⇧ ⇧ | ⇧ |
| Volkswagen AG | ⇩ | ⇩ | ⇩ | – | ⇧⇧ | ⇩ | ⇩ |
| Berkshire Hathaway | ⇧ | – | – | – | ⇧ | ⇧ | ⇧ |
| Exor NV | ⇧⇧ | – | – | – | – | ⇧⇧ | ⇧ |
| Ford Motor Company | ⇩ | ⇧ | ⇩ | ⇩ | ⇩ | ⇩ | ⇩ |
| Schwarz Gruppe | ⇩ | – | – | – | – | ⇧ | ⇩ |
| BMW AG | ⇧ | – | ⇧ ⇧ | ⇩ | ⇧ | ⇧⇧ | ⇧ |
| Cargill, Incorporated | ⇧ | – | – | – | ⇧ | ⇧ | ⇧ |
| Tata Sons Ltd | ⇧⇧ | – | ⇩ | ⇩ | ⇩ | ⇩ | ⇧ |
| Koch Industries, Inc | ⇧ | – | – | – | – | ⇧ | ⇧ |

could be seen in the case of German Volkswagen, namely an increase in the competitive score on the LinkedIn platform. Five out of ten entities show mostly unchanged reputational indicators in the measurements. Regarding the quantitative indicators represented by the number of indexed articles in the Google search results, there was a significant increase in the parameter for the entities Walmart and Exor. Overall, it can be concluded that regarding the status values of the reputation indicators over time, the dominant part of the entities in the sample was able to increase the level of their reputation in the Google search results during the pandemic. The majority of entities record either stagnation or a real decline in the dynamic side of online reputation expressed on the basis of selected reputation indicators. The following Table 4 shows values of the private brands of the evaluated entities.

In the context of comparison during the pandemic period, the status values of the parent companies' private brands show considerably dynamic characteristics. In four out of six cases, there is an overall decline in the comprehensive indicator of online reputation. The dynamics of values are especially evident in the case of the essential ASA reputation, i.e., reputation based on sentiment analysis. Specifically, this is the case of the Fiat and Lidl brands. Across the measurements, Fiat shows an increase

**Table 4** Reputation of private brands of parent companies—2020 vs. 2023

| Subject/result sentiment | ASA score 2023 (%) | FC score 2023 (%) | TC score 2023 (%) | YC score 2023 (%) | LC score 2023 (%) | NPIG 2023 (mil) | TOR Score 2023 (%) |
|---|---|---|---|---|---|---|---|
| Sam's Choice | ⇧ | – | ⇧ | – | ⇧ | ⇧ | ⇧ |
| Audi | ⇩ | ⇧ | ⇩ | ⇧⇧ | ⇧⇧ | ⇧ | ⇧ |
| Berkshire Hathaway | ⇧ | – | – | – | ⇧ | ⇧ | ⇧ |
| Fiat | ⇧⇧ | ⇧ | ⇧ | ⇩ | ⇩ | ⇧⇧ | ⇧ |
| Lincoln | ⇩ | ⇩ | – | ⇩ | – | ⇧⇧ | ⇩ |
| Lidl | ⇩⇩ | ⇧ | ⇧ | ⇧ | ⇧ | ⇧ ⇧ | ⇩ |
| Mini | ⇧ | ⇧ | – | ⇧ | ⇧ | ⇧⇧ | ⇧ |
| Wilbur Chocolate | ⇩ | – | – | – | – | ⇧ | ⇩ |
| Jaguar | ⇩ | ⇩ | ⇩ | ⇩ | ⇩ | ⇧ | ⇩ |
| Georgia-Pacific | ⇧ | – | – | – | ⇧ | ⇧ | ⇧ |

in the ASA parameter by almost 70%. In the case of Lidl, we can see the opposite situation, as there was a drop in reputation of more than 50%. This decrease is caused by the problematic labeling of children's sweets. In this case, too, it is necessary to point out the necessity of a comprehensive approach to optimizing all reputation indicators. Synthesizing the potential of reputation enables overcoming reputation pitfalls. From the perspective of partial reputation determinants of a more complex nature, there is a relatively frequent occurrence of values of an unchanged nature. From the point of view of maxims, there is an increase in competitive scores for the Audi brand, which shows a significant increase in competitive scores on the YouTube and LinkedIn platforms. The quantitative dimension of the dataset expressed by the total number of indexed pages of the analyzed sample also points to significant trend dynamics. In four out of ten cases, there is a substantial increase in the number of pages indexed by Google, specifically FIAT, Lincoln, Lidl, and Mini brands.

In terms of comparing the position of the parent companies and their brands, in the measurements, there is a reduction in the differences between the total level of reputation compared to the year 2020. This finding enables an answer to the formulated research question and thus achieves the goal of the work. The global pandemic has not significantly affected the reputation of the entities under review. Most of the monitored parameters show signs of continuous development of the reputation level in parent companies and their brands, especially in the case of more complex reputation determinants, such as social networks and social media. With this statement, it is possible to proceed to the formulation of conclusions.

## 5 Conclusion

The global pandemic has hit the market in an unprecedented way. In such turbulent conditions, the sustainable development of a corporate reputation is a challenge even for the best market players [25]. Family-owned businesses naturally tend to take a holistic view of the dimension of tradition in business. Judging by the research results by authors dealing with the issue of family business [26–28], the context of family and practice creates certain specificities that require rigorous specialization. This specialization is visible in the practical applications of management and the overall process of creating a corporate culture. However, the issue of applying correct procedures and knowledge in managing the reputation of this type of business entity is a largely unexplored segment within science, especially in the context of the catching-up markets of Central and Eastern Europe. Learning by example is one of the easier ways; learning by trial and error is a relatively common practice. Managing the reputation of the parent company and, at the same time, addressing the reputation of the portfolio of its brands in the context of an unlimited number of variables thus requires allocating a considerable amount of resources. However, it is primarily about time, which, in addition to finances, is the initial source of targeted reputation management. By default, market dynamics do not allow for total control, but some approaches mitigate the overall uncertainty about the optimal outcome. We know from management theory that planning is based on thorough analysis. The procedures presented in the study thus form a methodological framework for the first phase of optimization based on accurate data; at the same time, essential recommendations are formulated from the perspective of postulating examples of good practice.

As part of the study, the authors monitored the changing reputation levels of selected family-owned businesses and brands belonging to their portfolios over time. Corporations were able to respond to the challenges appropriately generated by the market. The more significant part of the entities increased their reputation in the search results of the Google platform. As for working with social media and social networks, all entities except one show increased user bases. However, the growth is not symmetrical, so the ratio of the competitive scores changes. From the perspective of specific platforms, Ford, BMW, and Tata, they coped with the situation best.

In contrast, the effect of black holes, i.e., problems where the reputation of the parent company far exceeds the level of its brand reputation, identified in the case of Ford and BMW in the reference study [1] at the level of TOR status, disappeared completely. However, its signs can be observed at the level of individual partial reputations. From the point of view of brands, the situation is similar. The celebrity effect, i.e., when a specific brand from a portfolio significantly exceeds the level of the parent company's reputation, cannot be found in the case of the Audi and Jaguar brands. Across the measurements, the differences in the reputation level within the examined sample of companies and their brands are mitigated.

Taking into account the increase in the total level of reputation for most entities examined, as well as the increase in the premiums of the dominant majority of parent companies compared to 2020, it can be concluded that the pandemic acted as an accelerator of change towards strengthening the competitiveness of trading companies. With this statement, it is possible to proceed to the description of the research limitations and the identification of the space for further research.

The main limitation of the study is its dominantly qualitative nature. Another limitation is the market dynamics, which generate uncontrollable variables in real time. Both limitations were partially mitigated by using the capacities of expert assessors in the process of evaluating sentiment levels, as well as by specifying significant variables for the collection of empirical material.

Further research could identify the level of the need to create development trends of the analyzed indicators over time. Based on the trends, it would be possible to predict the pace and level of specific areas of accelerated digitization in business management.

**Acknowledgements** The paper is one of the outputs of the currently implemented research grant VEGA no. 1/0140/21 and one of the partial outputs of the currently solved research grant IVS no. IVSUPS2305. The authors of the article also want to thank their students who actively participated in the preparation of its content and processing of the presented data.

## References


1. Pollák, F., Dorčák, P., Markovič, P.: Corporate reputation of family-owned businesses: parent companies vs. their brands. Information **12**(2), 89 (2021)
2. Flanagan, D.J., O'Shaughnessy, K.C.: The effect of layoffs on firm reputation. J. Manage. **31**(3), 445–463 (2005)
3. Sascha, R., Schwaiger, M., Rinkenburger, R., Schloderer, M.: Measuring the impact of corporate reputation on stakeholder behavior. In Corporate reputation, p. 26. Routledge, Abingdon (2011)
4. Fombrum, C., Gardberg, N.: Who's tops in corporate reputation? Corp. Reput. Rev. **3**, 13–17 (2000)
5. Deephouse, D.L.: Media reputation as a strategic resource: an integration of mass communication and resource based theories. J. Manage. **26**, 1091–1112 (2000)
6. Barbu, A., Militaru, G.: Investigating the innovation potential of a company obtained through social media. In Proceedings of the 12th International Management Conference: Management Perspectives in the Digital Era (IMC), pp. 247–258. Bucharest University of Economic Studies, Bucharest, Romania (2018)
7. Barnett, M., Jermier, J., Lafferty, B.: Corporate reputation: the defnitional landscape. Corp. Reput. Rev. **9**, 26–38 (2006)
8. Fombrum, C., Ponzi, L.J., Newsburry, Q.: Stakeholder tracking and analysis: the RepTrak® system for measuring corporate reputation. Corp. Reput. Rev. **18**, 3–24 (2015)
9. Noorian, Z., Ulieru, M.: The state of the art in trust and reputation systems: a framework for comparison. J. Theor. Appl. Electron. Commer. Res. (2010)
10. Badenfelt, U.: I trust you, I trust you not: a longitudinal study of control mechanisms in incentive contracts. Constr. Manage. Econ. **28**(3), 301–310 (2010)
11. Henrikx, F., Budendorfer, F., Chard, R.: Reputation systems: a survey and taxonomy. J. Parallel Distrib. Comput. **75**, 184–197 (2015)
12. Xiong, L., Liu, L.: A reputation-based trust model for peer-to-peer ecommerce communities. In: Proceedings of IEEE Conference on E-Commerce, pp. 228–229. San Diego, CA, USA (2003)
13. Jøsang, A., Ismail, R.: The beta reputation system. In: Proceedings of the 15th Bled Electronic Commerce Conference, p. 14. Bled, Slovenia (2002)
14. Jøsang, A., Haller, J.: Dirichlet reputation systems. In: Proceedings of the International Conference on Availability, Reliability and Security, pp. 112–119. Vienna, Ausria (2007)
15. Jøsang, A., Luo, X., Chen, X: Continuous ratings in discrete bayesian reputation systems. In: Proceedings of the Joint iTrust and PST Conferences on Privacy, Trust Management and Security (IFIPTM 2008), p. 16. Trondheim, Germany (2008)
16. Wang, T., Singh, M.P.: Formal trust model for multiagent systems. In: Proceedings of the 20th International Joint Conference on Artificial Intelligence, pp. 1551–1556. Hyderabad, India (2007)
17. What is Sentiment Analysis? a complete guide for beginners, https://www.freecodecamp.org/news/what-is-sentiment-analysis-a-complete-guide-to-for-beginners/, last accessed June 15, 2021
18. Cambria, E., Das, D., Bandyopadhyay, S., Feraco, A.: A practical guide to sentiment analysis. Springer, Cham (2017)
19. Hu, M., Bing, L.: Mining and summarizing customer reviews. In: Proceedings of the Tenth ACM SIGKDD International Conference on Knowledge Discovery and Data Mining, pp. 168–177. Seattle, USA (2004)
20. Sentiment analysis (opinion mining), https://www.techtarget.com/searchbusinessanalytics/definition/opinion-mining-sentiment-mining, last accessed April 20, 2021
21. Pollák, F., Dorčák, P., Markovič, P.: Reputation management. In: Umut, A., Anil, K.K. (eds.) Promotion and marketing communications, pp. 53–72. IntechOpen, London, UK (2019)
22. Soviar, J., Holubčík, M., Vodák, J., Rechtorík, M., Pollák, F.: The presentation of automotive brands in the on-line environment—the perspective of KIA, Peugeot, Toyota and VW in the Slovak Republic. Sustainability **11**, 2132 (2019)

23. Pollák, F., Markovič, P., Majdúchová, H.: Reputation of electric vehicles in the environment of carbon reduction and accelerated digitization. Energies **16**(9), 3836 (2023)
24. Bain, M.: The world's top 750 family businesses ranking, https://www.famcap.com/the-worlds-750-biggest-family-businesses/, last accessed, 2020/03/20
25. Reputation, Word History, https://www.merriam-webster.com/dictionary/reputation#word-history, last accesed November 20, 2022
26. Krošláková, M.N., Khouri, S., Čvirik, M., Tomášková, A., Drábik, P., Derkawi, H.: The business environment of family enterprises in Slovakia-perception of external barriers. Pol. J. Manage. Stud. **24**(2), 321–335 (2021)
27. Biel, M., Ślusarczyk, B: Family business and management: objectives, theory, and practice. Taylor & Francis
28. Biel, M., Ślusarczyk, B.: Management methods and tools in family businesses: impact on the effectiveness of achieving goals. J. Int. Stud. **15**(4) (2022)

# Rethinking Sustainable Transportation: The Role of Shared Mobility in Urban Environments

**Marcin Kubera and Beata Ślusarczyk**

**Abstract** Sustainable mobility has been developing in many cities in Poland, Europe, and the world for several years, thanks to the sharing economy. Transport needs are met by various means, such as cars, bicycles, scooters, and mopeds, rented for a specified period, usually counted in minutes. This type of individual transport is green and benefits the environment and society. However, according to research conducted in all Polish cities with a minimum of 200,000 inhabitants, shared mobility tools have yet to contribute to the development of sustainable transport there significantly. Moreover, three cities noted increased traffic on bus lanes and/or in the center (due to car sharing), and one experienced a drop in the demand for public transport. The latter, in particular, should be considered a negative impact of shared mobility since public transportation is now considered a facet of sustainability. These results prove that the forms of the sharing economy in Polish cities are in the phase of market development and diversification.

**Keywords** Sharing economy · Carsharing · Sustainable transportation · Sustainable mobility · Urban transport

M. Kubera
Pomorska Szkoła Wyższa, Tadeusza Kościuszki 112, 83-250 Starogard Gdański, Poland
e-mail: marcin.kubera@twojestudia.pl

B. Ślusarczyk (✉)
Trade and Development, North-West University, Private Bag X1290, 2520 Potchefstroom, South Africa
e-mail: beata.slusarczyk@pcz.pl

Faculty of Management, Czestochowa University of Technology, Armii Krajowej 19B, 42-201 Częstochowa, Poland

 
S. Kot et al. (eds.), *Corporate Practices: Policies, Methodologies, and Insights in Organizational Management*, Springer Proceedings in Business and Economics,
https://doi.org/10.1007/978-981-97-0996-0_55

## 1 Introduction

The urban population growth and increasing appetites for good living and transport conditions are essential challenges for city managers and municipal transport authorities. Efficient transit is the key ingredient to the daily life and development of each city. Therefore, day-to-day management and enhancing transport systems based on sustainable development ideas have become important. As A.J. Jarosz (2021) notes, the overuse of cars, which has become a problem in many cities, gave rise to a reflection, and the idea of sustainable mobility was conceived [1]. This is particularly important in Poland, where personal car ownership was a determinant of social status at the turn of the twentieth and twenty-first centuries. Also, today, it is considered a symbol of social position, prestige, and luxury while fulfilling its primary role as a means of reaching the desired destination conveniently, relatively quickly, and at any time [2].

"Sustainable mobility" is defined as something that can be provided by a package of transport solutions that are universal, efficient, clean, and environmentally friendly [3]. It includes the possibility of walking and cycling within the city, combining and accessing various means of public transport, and sharing cars, including EVs [4, 5]. Sustainable mobility is the ideal solution to reduce the adverse impact of transportation on the environment while making travel more efficient and faster. It integrates technology, innovation, and human behaviors [6]. These mobility solutions provide a flexible, sustainable, cost-effective, and available on-demand alternative to conventional transport, mainly for individuals. This negatively affects health and quality of life, especially when congestion, $CO_2$ emissions, and air quality are considered [7]. For cities, car sharing and micro-mobility should be part of their sustainable transport policies, contributing to reducing exhaust fumes and pollution [8]. This trend is particularly significant due to the shift from individual ownership of property towards the increasing practice of sharing it with others [9].

## 2 Literature Review

Many authors have written about sustainable mobility in Polish cities. In the last five years, the topic was raised, among others, by Janczewski and Janczewska [10], who discussed alternative forms of urban transport fitting into sustainable mobility and demonstrated examples of good practices. Kamiński [11] characterized sustainable mobility concerning transport automation, the premiere of automated vehicles, and the use of fully autonomous cars. In their respective studies, Banet [12] emphasized the concept of sustainable mobility, particularly highlighting the role of cycling while presenting various projects geared towards promoting cycling. Meanwhile, Strojna, Zalecka, and Ryciuk [13] delved into the concept of shared micro-mobility within urban transport, delving into the associated technical aspects and examining the market for relevant solutions in Poland. They also presented the results of surveys carried out in 2022 among users of shared micro-mobility in Poland. Dorocki [14] discussed the background of using bicycles and electric scooters in Krakow and analyzed their accessibility. Stoeck [15] presented the issue of implementing sharing economy services in relation to urban transport systems and discussed the basic knowledge related to this concept and the principle of its operation, with particular emphasis on economic, environmental and social aspects. Jarosiński [16] presented the development of scooter designs and the daily realities of e-scooter rentals in Krakow and globally. Mianowski, Kostrzewska and Macikowski [17] took up the subject of social and spatial determinants of using scooters as a personal transport device in the city. Koźlak [18] presented the innovative concept of Mobility-as-a-Service (MaaS), which stemmed from the emergence of new types of transport services and technical developments, especially ICT and mobile technologies. Krezymon and Stróżewski [19] characterized in detail the popularity of car sharing in the 18–25 age group in the example of the city of Szczecin. An interesting analysis by Gorzelańczyk, Kalina, and Jurkoić [20] presented opinions of Poles on car sharing during the COVID-19 pandemic and the results of their study on how the pandemic had affected sustainable mobility in Poland and Europe. Turoń, Kubik and Czech [21] looked at car sharing from the operational side: they presented a list of the most commonly used vehicles, discussed technical issues, and took an inventory of the main types of damage suffered by shared cars associated with the mileage. Kubera and Kot [22] compared 9 Polish car sharing service operators. Kawa and Nestorowicz [23] presented a more accurate approximation of the essence of the concept, pros and cons of the sharing economy and car sharing in the example of Panek Co. Inc. The use of shared vehicles is associated with the risk of traffic incidents, so Laskowska, Wieteska and Juszczyk [24] discussed the role of civil/third party liability insurance for users of personal means of transport in Poland. Przybylska, Kramarz and Dohn [25] identified the roles of various urban logistics stakeholder groups in the sustainable transport of people, including shared mobility providers.

The literature query has revealed a research gap: how do mobile solutions offered by the sharing economy affect sustainable mobility in Polish cities? Do the vehicle sharing services, the ability to ride on scooters or e-mopeds, improve transport, reduce congestion, noise and pollution, or develop pro-environmental attitudes of residents in terms of travel? The following article aims to present the solutions offered by the sharing economy in relation to sustainable mobility in Polish cities.

## 3 Methodology

The query of the domestic and foreign literature and the desk research made it possible to diagnose the problem and find the research gap. The analysis of the survey results was carried out using appropriately selected statistical and descriptive methods. Statistical analysis was conducted using IBM SPSS Statistics version 26. With its help, an analysis of basic descriptive statistics was performed along with the Kolmogorov-Smirnov test of normality of the distribution of responses. Univariate analyses of variance in the intergroup scheme were also performed. The significance level $\alpha = 0.05$ was assumed during the investigation. The qualitative variables were evaluated by frequency analysis (%, n). $\chi^2$ Pearson compatibility tests were carried out to investigate the diversity of the groups. $\chi^2$ Pearson independence tests were carried out with the correlation of two qualitative variables. An analysis was performed using the Spearman correlation to determine relations between the two ordinal variables. Either Student's t-tests or Mann-Whitney tests were performed to compare the two groups.

## 4 Results

The survey was conducted among city halls of Polish cities with populations larger than 200,000. Bus transport is available in all these cities, with Białystok and Radom being the only cities where it constitutes the sole form of public transportation. Five cities (Bydgoszcz, Częstochowa, Łódź, Wrocław, and Szczecin) also have streetcars (in addition to buses), and three others (Gdańsk, Katowice, Poznań) had elevated railroads and the third means of transport. Warsaw offers the broadest multimodality: buses, streetcars, urban railroads, the subway, and water taxis. The situation is similar in Krakow, apart from the subway. The public transport in Lublin is based on buses and trolleybuses, while Gdynia also has urban railroad lines. These means of public transport are presented in Table 1.

All the cities have bike rentals, and five of them also have scooter rentals. In seven cities, there are three types of such mobility: city bike, scooter and moped (Fig. 1.).

**Table 1** Public transport types in the surveyed cities

| | Bus | Streetcar | Urban railroad | Trolleybus | Water taxi | Subway |
|---|---|---|---|---|---|---|
| Białystok | X | | | | | |
| Bydgoszcz | X | X | | | | |
| Częstochowa | X | X | | | | |
| Gdańsk | X | X | X | | | |
| Gdynia | X | | X | X | | |
| Katowice | X | X | X | | | |
| Kraków | X | X | X | | X | |
| Lubin | X | | | X | | |
| Łódź | X | X | | | | |
| Poznań | X | X | X | | | |
| Radom | X | | | | | |
| Szczecin | X | X | | | | |
| Warszawa | X | X | X | | X | X |
| Wrocław | X | X | | | | |

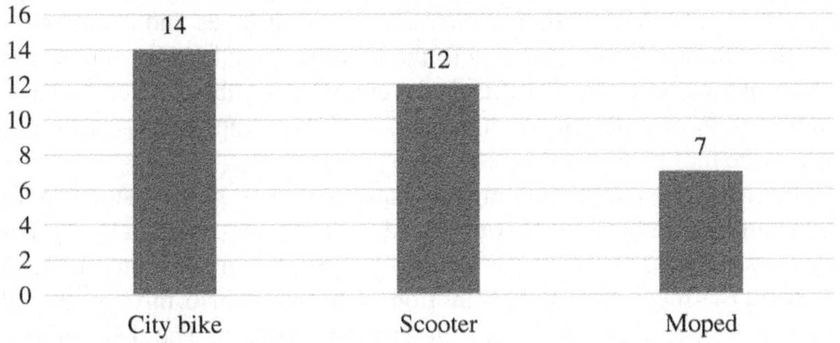


**Fig. 1** Types of shared means of transport other than the car

Three of the cities have had shared mobility for longer than 5 years, and one has been offering it since less than 1 year ago. The shared mobility is 3–5 years old in six cities and 1–3 years old in four ones (Fig. 2).

Shared mobility has been available in six locations for three to five years and in four cities for one to three years. In three of the surveyed cities, meeting transport needs using shared mobility means has been provided for more than five years, and one has been operating for less than a year. The relationship between the types of shared resources found in cities and the duration of their operation was also examined. The results are presented in Table 2.

Statistically significant differences exist between the groups ($p = 0.042$). The cities with city bikes, scooters and mopeds have the longest experience with shared

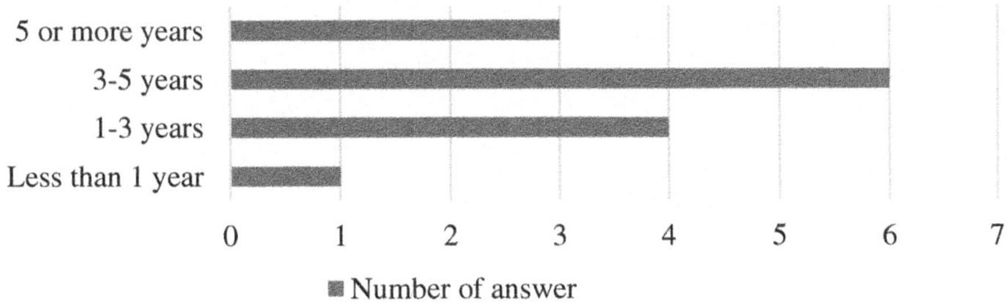


**Fig. 2** Shared mobility maturity: examining relationships between types of transport

**Table 2** Correlation of the types and the periods of use of the individual means of transport

| | M | Me | SD | H | p |
|---|---|---|---|---|---|
| City bike, scooter | 2,00 | 2,00 | 0,71 | 6,34 | 0,042 |
| City bike, scooter, moped | 3,29 | 3,00 | 0,49 | | |
| City bike | 3,00 | 3,00 | 1,41 | | |

M—mean; Me—median; SD—standard deviation; H—statistics; p—significance mobility ($M = 3.29$; Me $= 3$), and the ones with just bikes and scooters have the shortest one. This could be attributed to the fact that populations with access to all these means of transportation had already developed new habits earlier, driven by their greater awareness of emerging technologies and their applications. Consequently, they were more inclined to embrace the sharing economy.

The cities have been implementing their sustainable mobility systems in different ways. In an attempt to learn what contributed to the development of the systems, the respondents were asked to list these factors. The results are presented in Table 3.

Everyone (14) mentioned the promotion of bicycles, also through the addition of bike paths or the establishment of the city bike system. The distribution of the answers to this multiple-choice question is shown in Fig. 3.

The promotion and implementation of the idea of shared commuting was the lowest-ranked factor (2 answers). The Polish traffic regulations do not yet have a provision allowing cars carrying three or four persons to use a dedicated lane. However, the idea of carpooling is becoming increasingly popular even without

**Table 3** What sustainable development ideas are pursued by your city in terms of transport?

| Factor | No. of answers |
|---|---|
| Promotion of, and preference for, public transport | 12 |
| Use of electric buses | 11 |
| Promotion of bicycle transport | 14 |
| Construction and promotion of Park & Ride systems | 9 |
| Suppression of car traffic in the center | 9 |
| Promotion and implementation of the idea of shared commuting | 2 |
| Privileges for electric cars | 9 |
| Promotion of walking | 8 |

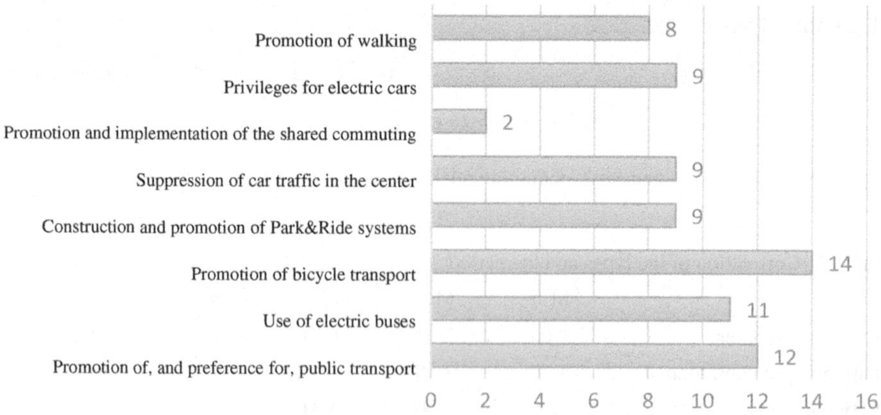


**Fig. 3** Ideas of sustainable transport implemented in the cities where the research was carried out

such an incentive. This way of commuting is popular, especially among employees of foreign companies and among students. A number of such organizations and university campuses even offer dedicated parking spaces for pooled cars.

The promotion of, and preference for, public transport and the use of electric buses were mentioned by a majority of the respondents (12 and 11, respectively). These measures have been taken increasingly often. The purchase and use of zero-emission urban transport vehicles are promoted and co-financed by the EU, while public transport-promoting policies are the domain of local authorities.

The ideas of constructing and promoting Park & Ride spaces suppressing car traffic in the center and privileging electric cars were equally popular (9 respondents). These sustainable mobility activities require city authorities, planners and public transport operators to develop consolidated plans, timetables and a forward-looking vision for the public transport system. These are prerequisites to getting road users and drivers of passenger cars interested and convinced to switch to such solutions. A sufficient number of Park & Ride spaces, convenient timetables, and acceptable travel times are required and essential for success.

Since car sharing is in place in all the cities, it was interesting to learn what municipal authorities do to support shared mobility. Hence, another multiple-choice question for the city halls: how do they support car sharing? The results are presented in Table 4.

Half of the cities (9) do not support car sharing in any way. This means that five cities promote the idea of sharing vehicles. Four cities offer special parking spaces for car sharers. Two towns have parking lots for car sharers located directly at offices, stations, and transport hubs. Also, two cities allow car sharers to use bus lanes. Only one city carries on consolidated marketing activities (1 respondent). In two towns, shared vehicles can use bus lanes, while four cities have designated special parking spaces. Additionally, in two cities, these parking lots are conveniently situated close to offices, stations, and transfer hubs. Only one city has undertaken marketing activities to promote car sharing.

Although efforts of some cities to make their public spaces more sustainable should be welcome as a sign of their goodwill, there was not even one case where the maturity of car sharing would depend on any activities or promotion on the part of the cities ($p = 0.519$). Therefore, it can be assumed that the maturity has nothing

**Table 4** Forms of support for the carsharing system by the authorities of the cities where the research was carried out

| Form of support | No. of answers |
|---|---|
| No support | 9 |
| Special parking spaces for car sharers | 4 |
| Parking lots for car sharers located directly at offices, stations and transport hubs | 2 |
| Joint marketing activities | 1 |
| Use of bus lanes by car sharers | 2 |

to do with the involvement of municipal authorities or the lack of it. The results are shown in Table 5.

Similarly, municipal support is not statistically significant compared to the number of car sharing operators ($p = 0.523$), as shown in Table 6.

This means that the forms of support listed in Table 4 are acceptable with both the maturity and the number of operators of car-sharing services. Therefore, it is assumed that the effect of activities and involvement of the cities, even if helpful, is symbolic. No wonder municipal authorities and officials, seeing this, tend to adopt entirely passive attitudes.

To take a closer look at this aspect, the respondents were asked to assess the impact of shared mobility on urban life. Only in one case shared mobility tools contribute ("Definitely yes") to the reduction of demand for public transport and instead contributed ("Rather yes") to the increase in traffic on bus lanes or the city center. The most significant number of "Definitely not" answers were given for "Fewer traffic incidents" (9) and for "Smaller demand for parking spaces" (8). According to half of the respondents, shared mobility did not have the effect of "Less CO2 emissions" ("Rather not" and "Definitely not"). In contrast, the other half were unsure ("Hard to tell"), which may result from the lack of air quality monitoring. Shared mobility had the least contribution to the "Smaller demand for parking spaces" (5 "Rather not" and 8 "Definitely not" answers) (Fig. 4).

This state of affairs is expected, considering the current situation in Poland: shared mobility is perceived as something new. In addition, its specificity means that it is used by young people who have experience with new technologies in everyday life and may be unable to afford to buy cars.

The answers were most evenly distributed for the "Fewer vehicles in the city"; however, even in this case, there were 9 "Rather not" and "Definitely not" answers. It is worth noting that shared mobility did not have the "Smaller demand for public transport" effect in 10 cases.

**Table 5** Correlation of the car sharing maturity with support from authorities

| | Without support | | | With support | | | Mann-Whitney test | |
|---|---|---|---|---|---|---|---|---|
| | M | Me | SD | M | Me | SD | Z | p |
| Car sharing maturity | 2.63 | 2.50 | 1.06 | 3.00 | 3.00 | 0.63 | −0.65 | 0.519 |

M—mean; Me—median; SD—standard deviation; Z—statistics; p—significance

**Table 6** Correlation of the number of car sharing operators with support from authorities

| | Without support | | | With support | | | Mann-Whitney test | |
|---|---|---|---|---|---|---|---|---|
| | M | Me | SD | M | Me | SD | Z | p |
| Number of car sharing operators | 2.20 | 2.00 | 1.30 | 2.67 | 3.00 | 0.52 | −0.64 | 0.523 |

M—mean; Me—median; SD—standard deviation; Z—statistics; p—significance

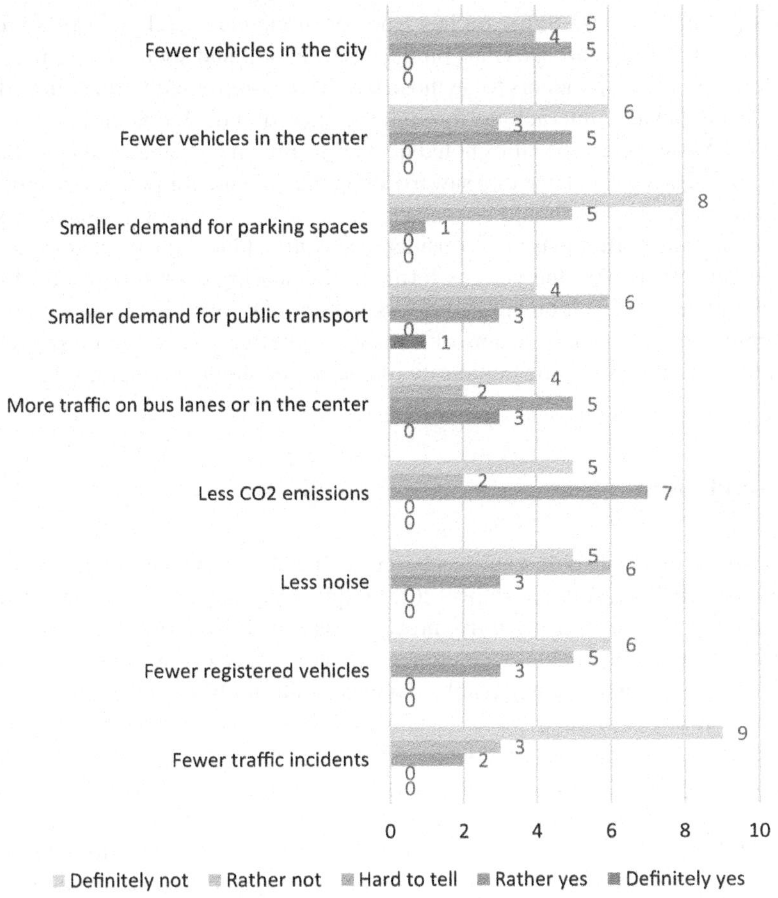


**Fig. 4** Effects of shared mobility on transport-related aspects of urban life

It should, therefore, be concluded that shared mobility does not significantly affect the transport systems of Polish cities. According to the survey, this form of mobility definitely does not reduce the following:

- the need for parking spaces;
- the number of road accidents and collisions;
- the number of vehicles registered;
- noise in the city;
- the demand for public transport;
- the number of vehicles in the center;
- the number of vehicles in the city as a whole;
- $CO_2$ emissions;

It also does not increase traffic on bus lanes or in the center. These aspects related to the impact of transport activities on the environment and society were in no way considered by the respondents to be those that have contributed to reducing adverse or increasing positive interactions through the operation of shared mobility services in the city. Moreover, three cities noted heavier traffic on bus lanes and/or in the city centers (car sharing), and one city saw a drop in the demand for public transport. The last effect, in particular, should be considered an adverse impact of shared mobility since public transportation is now considered a manifestation of sustainable mobility. These results prove that the various forms of the sharing economy in Polish cities are in the phase of development and diversification. Despite this, in some instances of commercial use of these means of transport, no effects have been observed that would indicate a boost in the popularity of sharing economy services.

## 5 Conclusion

New business and transport solutions based on the sharing economy impact the life of cities and their transport systems [26]. Despite optimistic assumptions, it should be concluded that shared mobility already exists in Polish towns and has yet to contribute to the sustainable development of their transport systems significantly. However, it contributes to noticeable changes in the mobility behaviors of service users, which are becoming more sustainable. While these measures may not be considered radical, such as completely divesting from cars or entirely abandoning individual transport options, and they may not be uniformly implemented across all areas, it is reasonable to anticipate a growing interest in shared mobility services, reduced reliance on private car usage, and a decreased demand for parking spaces in the surveyed cities and regions where shared mobility services are available in the years ahead. All these activities will make cities more environmentally responsible, resident-friendly, more attractive to visitors, and better in terms of standard and quality of life.

To sum up, it can be said that thanks to the shared mobility tools (car sharing, scooters, e-mopeds), every resident has an opportunity to contribute to the positive change in the area of sustainable mobility in Polish cities and the perspective of the coming years contribute to significant development of sustainable municipal transport. In the future, it seems interesting to conduct observations and studies on the direction of intensification and expansion of the service and changes in the behaviors of users of shared mobility. A topic worth paying attention to today is the role electric vehicles will play in car sharing in the future and the analysis of whether a fleet consisting only of zero-emission cars will provide operators with a guarantee of profit and survival on the market.

## References


1. Jarosz, A.J.: Polityka rowerowa jako element zrównoważonej mobilności. Ekspertyzy i opracowania **135**, 1–10 (2021)
2. Parysek, J.J.: Dla kogo miasto? Dla ludzi czy dla samochodów? Studia miejskie **23**, 10–26 (2016)
3. Chakraborty, S., Kumar, N.M., Jayakumar, A., Dash, S.K., Elangovan, D.: Selected aspects of sustainable mobility reveals implementable approaches and conceivable actions. Sustainability **13**(22), 12918 (2021)
4. Bebber, S., etc.: Sustainable mobility scale: a contribution for sustainability assessment systems in urban mobility. Clean. Eng. Technol. **5**, 100271 (2021)
5. Biel, M., Ślusarczyk, B.: Management methods and tools in family businesses: impact on the effectiveness of achieving goals. J. Int. Stud. **15**(4) (2022)
6. Spadaro, I., Pirlone, F.: Sustainable urban mobility plan and health security. Sustainability **13**(8), 4403 (2021)
7. Shaheen, S., Cohen, A., Chan, N., Bansal, A.: Chapter 13—sharing strategies: carsharing, shared micromobility (bikesharing and scooter sharing transportation network companies, microtransit, and other innovative mobility modes. In: Deakin, E. (ed.) Transportation, land use, and environmental planning, pp. 237–252. Elsevier, Amsterdam (2020)
8. Abduljabbar, R.L., Liyanage, S., Dia, H.: The role of micro-mobility in shaping sustainable cities: a systematic literature review. Transp. Res. Part D: Trans. Environ. **92**, 102734 (2021)
9. Kubera, M., Ślusarczyk, B.: Carsharing as an element of mobility management. Pol. J. Manage. Stud. **27**(2), 188–205 (2023)
10. Pakpienthakolphol, C., Jeżyna, B.: Key variables influencing maintenance services outsourcing in the automotive sector—comparing Asian and European dynamics. Glob. J. Entrepreneurship Manage. **2**(2), 17–29 (2021)
11. Kamiński, T.: Pojazdy zautomatyzowane w aspekcie zrównoważonej mobilności miejskiej. Gospodarka Materiałowa i Logistyka, t. LXXIII **1**, 13–20 (2021)
12. Banet, K.: Ruch rowerowy jako element zrównoważonej mobilności. Transport Miejski i Regionalny **7**, 17–20 (2019)
13. Strojna, N., Zalecka, K., Ryciuk, U.: Współdzielona mikromobilność w transporcie miejskim. Akademia Zarządzania **6**(3), 363–385 (2022)
14. Dorocki, S.: Uwarunkowania użytkowania rowerów i hulajnóg elektrycznych w Krakowie. Prace Komisji Geografii Komunikacji PTG **25**(1), 23–40 (2022)
15. Stoeck, T.: Dostępność usług typu sharing na terenie Szczecina. Przegląd Komunikacyjny **75**, 16–24 (2020)
16. Jarosiński, K.: Historia rozwoju ruchu hulajnogowego wraz z charakterystyką wypożyczalni hulajnóg elektrycznych w Krakowie. Transport Miejski i Regionalny **11–12**, 12–30 (2021)
17. Mianowski, J., Kostrzewska, M., Macikowski, B.: Społeczne i przestrzenne wyznaczniki korzystania z hulajnogi jako urządzenia transportu osobistego (UTO) w mieście. Władza Sądzenia **19**, 326–347 (2020)
18. Koźlak, A.: Mobility-as-a Service jako postęp w integracji transportu. Prace Komisji Geografii Komunikacji PTG **23**(5), 7–17 (2020)
19. Krezymon, M., Stróżewski, K.: Popularność usługi carsharing w grupie wiekowej 18–25 lat na przykładzie Szczecina. Problemu Transportu i Logistyki **3**(47), 53–63 (2019)
20. Gorzelańczyk, P., Kalina, t., Jurković, M.: Impact of the Covid-19 pandemic on car-sharing in Poland. Oper. Econ. Transp. **4**, 172–186 (2022)
21. Turoń, K., Kubik, A., Czech, P.: Eksploatacja systemów car-sharingu. In Więcek, W.D., Rysiński, J. (red.), Technologie, procesy i systemy produkcyjne, 307–316 (2020)
22. Kubera, M., Kot, S.: Evolution of carsharing in Poland. Paper presented at the Proceedings of the 31st International Business Information Management Association Conference, IBIMA 2018: Innovation management and education excellence through vision 2020, s. 5328–5336 (2018)

23. Kawa, M., Nestorowicz, A.: Rozwój sharing economy w Polsce na przykładzie usług carsharingowych firmy Panek CarS haring S.A. Przedsiębiorczość – Edukacja **18**(1), 90–95 (2022)
24. Laskowska, I., Wieteska, S., Juszczyk, S.: Civil liabarity insurance for users of personal transport equipment (PTE) as an element of protection for sharing economy participants. J. Finance Financ. Law **1**(37), 69–83 (2023)
25. Przybylska, E., Kramarz, M., Dohn, K.: The role of stakeholders in creating mobility in Logistics systems of Polish city. Sustainability **15**(3), 1790 (2023)
26. Strulak-Wójcikiewicz, R., Wagner, N.: Exploring opportunities of using the sharing economy in sustainable urban freight transport. Sustainable Cities Soc. **68**, 102778 (2021)

# Green Marketing and Brand Perception: Unveiling the Consumer Perspective

**Lucia Sujanska and Margareta Nadanyiova**

**Abstract** This study assesses the impact of green marketing initiatives on brand perception and investigating how brands' sustained commitment to environmental practices, innovation, and improvement over time influences consumer perception loyalty and brand reputation. The study examines the relationship between green marketing strategies and how they impact consumer perceptions of brands. The study explores how environmentally friendly initiatives and green marketing campaigns influence consumer attitudes, beliefs, and purchasing behavior. By uncovering consumer perspectives on green marketing and brand perception, the study can provide valuable insights for businesses and marketers seeking to align their strategies with environmental concerns. The findings may help companies develop effective green marketing strategies that resonate with consumers, build trust, and enhance brand loyalty in the context of sustainability and environmental responsibility. The research applies standard scientific methods to process data, and the data acquired from the online survey were evaluated using mathematical and statistical techniques, including statistical hypothesis testing. The research identified a shift in consumer preferences and purchasing behavior, indicating a growing inclination towards green products. Consumers exhibited a higher likelihood of choosing environmentally responsible companies and supporting brands that demonstrate a commitment to sustainability. Additionally, the study found that successful green marketing strategies can enhance consumers' perceptions of a company's credibility and trustworthiness. Effective green marketing initiatives can create positive associations with social responsibility and ethics, helping build a strong and favorable brand image.

**Keywords** Green marketing · Sustainability · Brand

L. Sujanska (✉) · M. Nadanyiova
University of Zilina, Univerzitna 8215/1, 010 26 Žilina, Slovak Republic
e-mail: sujanska2@stud.uniza.sk

 
S. Kot et al. (eds.), *Corporate Practices: Policies, Methodologies, and Insights in Organizational Management*, Springer Proceedings in Business and Economics,
https://doi.org/10.1007/978-981-97-0996-0_56

## 1 Introduction

Insufficient environmental awareness and the expanding global population have contributed to unsustainable consumption patterns. This, in turn, has given rise to critical environmental issues, including heightened greenhouse gas emissions, pollution, global warming, and the depletion of natural resources [1]. The escalating severity of these problems emphasizes the necessity for sustainability measures across all production levels, consumption, and overall lifestyle choices. Consequently, companies striving for a competitive advantage in the global marketplace embrace sustainability as a guiding principle.

Implementing green marketing solutions has established a worldwide platform to encourage sustainable consumption. Despite the concept of green marketing existed for a considerable period, it is currently undergoing a notable resurgence in popularity within the business sphere [2]. Green marketing, or sustainable or eco-marketing, has become increasingly popular. The world today has witnessed a notable upsurge in environmentally-related issues, as well as an improved understanding of sustainability among customers. With increased awareness and concern for environmental issues, many companies and businesses have integrated eco-friendly products, practices, and services into their promotional plans. This has triggered a substantial surge in the field of green marketing initiatives. Companies and organizations are now trying to embrace eco-friendly products, services, and behavior within their marketing initiatives. This enables them to emphasize their green actions and set themselves apart from competitors, as well as have a marked influence on how their brand is regarded [3]. The study aims to investigate the relationship between green marketing strategies and how they impact consumer perceptions of brands.

Nowadays, people are also significantly more aware of the environmental consequences of their buying decisions. They look for products and services that fit with their ideals and display a commitment to sustainability. Through green advertising, businesses can take advantage of this growing consumer demand by emphasizing the environmental benefits of their items [4]. By stressing features like energy efficiency, use of renewable materials, lower carbon footprint, and decreased waste, businesses can market themselves as environmentally aware and draw in a segment of customers who prioritize sustainability in their shopping choices. As the demand for sustainable products and services continues to rise, green marketing is a powerful tool for businesses to establish meaningful connections with customers. By aligning their values, showcasing their sustainability efforts, and fostering transparency and authenticity, companies can cultivate a loyal customer base, build a positive brand image, and contribute to a greener future.

## 2 Literature Review

Green marketing originated in the 1960s when there was rising concern about the environment, creating the eventual establishment of eco-marketing. Theoretical studies on green marketing have a long history and draw from various disciplines, including psychology, economics, philosophy, management, and marketing [5]. This development principally centered on businesses that caused the most environmental destruction, first and foremost. Since then, terms like eco-marketing, ecological marketing, sustainable marketing, and environmental marketing have been used to describe the basic idea [2].

Green marketing can be characterized, according to Patel and colleagues [6], as marketing that satisfies the current needs of businesses and consumers while maintaining or improving the ability to meet the needs of future generations as well. We can also characterize green marketing as marketing that tries to implement the company's activities in a harmonious relationship with the environment. It can also be defined as using strategies that conserve resources and the environment at all stages of the value chain or as satisfying the needs of green customers [7].

The key objective and understanding of green marketing are commonly misconceived. Even though green marketing is frequently regarded only as promoting green products, in reality, it includes a wider variety of components and initiatives focused on meeting consumers' environmental expectations [8].

The definition that closely unveils the spirit of the concept elucidates green marketing as the active and comprehensive engagement of an organization in strategic, tactical, and operational marketing activities and processes that have the holistic objective of creating, communicating, and delivering products with the highest emphasis on minimizing their environmental impact, thereby aligning with the principles of sustainability and ecological responsibility [3]. According to [9], using green marketing is one of the signs of market orientation and ethical behavior of the company. Companies must adapt to market changes and actively address consumer concerns about the link between climate change and human consumption. Businesses are beginning to change their practices to address these concerns and satisfy consumer expectations as the general public's awareness of pollution issues grows. This change is an example of social responsibility, in which businesses work to improve stakeholders' perceptions of their firm to reap long- or medium-term advantages. Nowadays, a socially conscious company works to advance its own social and environmental objectives in addition to maximizing profits. These areas are essential to corporate success and are rising in prominence. Additionally, the market for "green" consumers expands, which has an impact on shopping habits [10].

For businesses, green marketing offers several advantages. The company will have to start investing capital in green production and products, but this investment has a good payback. One of the advantages that green marketing can bring to the business is the potential entry into new markets, and a company can gain many new customers thanks to green marketing, which will help increase sales. The application of sustainable marketing procedures and responsibility also provides significant competitive advantages. In addition, there are benefits such as raising awareness about the brand but also about the importance of environmental marketing, when the company can also start getting involved in supporting charities. By being ecologically conscious, businesses can raise awareness of important social and environmental issues [11].

Companies use many green marketing strategies to offer customers a wide range of ecological goods. Green products can be identified based on a number of parameters, such as containing more recycled or less harmful chemicals, having recycled packaging, their production processes releasing less carbon dioxide, having an eco-label, and using biodegradable materials [12]. Consumers' environmental attitudes are often influenced by customers' environmental knowledge and values [5, 13]. Green marketing is an important starting point if the brand is to maintain a high perceived value [14, 15].

Brand image is the mental representation of a company in the minds of consumers [16]. As reported by Chen et al. [17], there is a greater likelihood that customers will buy a company's products if it has built a strong brand. In a green context, we can define a brand image as a complex brand perception by consumers that is linked to environmental commitments and concerns. Creating a strong brand image in this dimension can be necessary for companies, especially in light of the current increase in consumer awareness of environmental issues and the creation of increasingly strict international regulations for environmental protection.

One of the main reasons why companies start to apply sustainability and green marketing in their activities is usually problems with the image of the company and trust in the brand. Even if the company believes in sustainability principles, it would also like to gain a certain competitive advantage [18, 19]. Although a sustainable brand image can primarily attract consumers who respect sustainability, these market groups are growing rapidly. For companies to stay in line with market trends, businesses that strive for a long-term presence on the market need sustainability strategies. A stronger brand image is generally supported by a more robust integration of sustainability into the company's products and operations and the organizational culture [20]. To appeal to customers interested in the environment, green elements are often incorporated into business activities; just as to attract customers who value responsible behavior, a social brand image is created [21]. Building a green brand image can help companies satisfy customers' environmental desires and, due to its ability to reduce perceived risk, positively influence consumer trust [22]. If consumers trust a brand, there is a high probability that the brand will receive positive reviews. The basis of trust in a brand is the consumer's belief that the brand is competent, responsible, and honest. In the context of green marketing, trust can be characterized as consumers' willingness to trust a brand based on the belief that the brand is trustworthy, caring, and environmentally conscious. Such trust can significantly influence consumers' decision to purchase the company's products [23]. Green business practices contribute to building a brand image, which also appeals to environmentally conscious clients. Like socially responsible businesses, they create a brand image that appeals to those who are socially responsible. There is evidence that consumers are often willing to pay premium prices for brands and products that meet ecological or social attributes [24].

Within the framework of establishing credibility in the brand, ecological transparency has significance as well. This concept may be defined as the provision of unambiguous and pertinent information regarding the environmental policies of the company. According to Lin et al. [25], transparency is an open acknowledgment of how a company's production affects the environment. According to recent research [26], green transparency has the effect of creating a brand image and brand trust as such. This statement was also confirmed by Chun et al. [27], who found that transparency increases consumer trust in green brands. At the same time, the research also pointed to the fact that customers tend to positively evaluate brands in terms of perceived value and benefit if they have sufficient knowledge about the impact of products on the environment. As a result, customers and brands form a deep bond [28]. The relationship between brand trust and brand image also facilitates openness, which should be an integral part of transparency [29].

## 3 Methodology

The key purpose of this research is to explore how green marketing strategies affect consumers' perception of the brand. These strategies include adopting environmentally friendly practices and promoting green products and services. The purpose is to investigate whether the execution of green marketing measures yields a positive effect on how customers perceive the brand. Scientific studies, statistical databases, and published professional articles were key secondary data sources. A questionnaire survey was carried out to determine how Slovak customers felt about green marketing and how it affected their perception of the brand.

The main objective of the questionnaire survey was to find out the opinions and attitudes of consumers towards green marketing and how it affects their brand perception. The base file consisted of respondents older than 18 years, and to calculate the sample size, the basic set was obtained from the demographic statistics of the Statistical Office of the Slovak Republic. The confidence level was set at 95%, which means that the error rate was 5%. The sample size was set at 384 respondents. The survey was conducted using a questionnaire for data collection, and 391 respondents participated. The research was conducted in the Slovak Republic between April 2023 and June 2023. A quantitative evaluation method was used to process the survey data.

For data processing, general scientific procedures such as excerption, description, comparative analysis, deduction, and induction were used, as well as mathematical-statistical techniques in assessing survey data using IBM SPSS Statistics software. To draw relevant conclusions, research hypotheses were formulated as follows:

- Hypothesis ***1:*** More than 50% of Slovak consumers prefer a brand, which applies green marketing.
- Hypothesis ***2:*** More than 50% of Slovak consumers think that brands which use green marketing are socially responsible.

- Hypothesis *3:* Customers' trust in a brand is affected by brand green marketing activities.

For hypotheses 1 and 2 we used the one-tailed testing, which is commonly used [30, 31]. For hypothesis 3 Pearson's Chi-square test of independence was used to determine whether there is a statistically significant relationship between green marketing and consumers' trust in the brand. In order to determine dependencies, a contingency table was compiled, and Cramer's V was used to determine the strength of the relationship between variables [32].

## 4 Results

The sample set consisted of 391 respondents, of which 64% (250) were female and 36% (141) were male respondents. Questionnaire survey results showed that 84% (328) respondents are familiar with the concept of green marketing and understand what it means, and 69% (270) respondents prefer a brand that applies green marketing. The majority of respondents—71% (278) stated that they consider a brand that uses green marketing in their activities to be socially responsible. When making a purchase decision, 38% (149) respondents consider environmental sustainability very important, and 45% (176) respondents consider it important when considering the purchase of a product. 79% (309) respondents stated that the brand's green marketing activities influence their perception of overall brand quality, and 67% (262) respondents never switched from one brand to another due to their differing environmental sustainability efforts.

To verify the statistical hypotheses 1–2, we used the method of testing a single proportion. The results of the verification of these statistical hypotheses are shown in Table 1. Significance level α was determined at 0.05. The test criteria were calculated according to:

**Table 1** Verification of Hypothesis 1

| Calculation of the sample proportion: $p = \frac{m}{n}$ | Satisfaction of the condition: $n * \pi_0 * (1 - \pi_0) > 9$ | Test criteria | Critical field | Inequality | Acceptance or rejection of the hypothesis |
|---|---|---|---|---|---|
| ***Hypothesis 1:*** $H_0$: 50% of Slovak consumers prefer a brand, which applies green marketing $H_1$: More than 50% of Slovak consumers prefer a brand, which applies green marketing | | | | | |
| $p = 0.69$ | $97{,}5 > 9$ | 7.514 | 1.645 | 7.514 > 1.645 | $H_0$ rejected |

*Source* Own processing

$$T = \frac{p - \pi_0}{\sqrt{\frac{\pi_0 * (1 - \pi_0)}{n}}} \tag{1}$$

By using the tables of the normalized normal distribution, we find the critical value for the right-tailed test (2) for hypotheses 1–3.

$$T > z_{2\alpha} \tag{2}$$

Table 1 shows that in hypothesis 1, the inequality applies, so we reject hypothesis $H_0$ and accept the alternative hypothesis $H_1$. This implies that more than 50% of Slovak consumers prefer a brand which applies green marketing.

Table 2 shows, that in hypothesis 2 the inequality applies, so we reject the hypothesis $H_0$, and accept the alternative hypothesis $H_1$. It could be said that more than 50% of Slovak consumers think, that brands which use green marketing are socially responsible.

This study used Pearson's Chi-square test of independence to confirm statistical hypothesis 3 and see whether there is a relationship between brand trust and green marketing activities. The contingency table, where the frequencies are organized based on both characteristics, was developed to evaluate the dependence.

The condition that at least 80% of theoretical numbers need to be bigger than five and that no frequency can be zero at the same time is met in our case. The significance level was set at 0.05. From Table 3, we can see that 247 respondents would buy the product from the brand that promotes their ecological activities through green marketing, and most of them (111) would trust this brand a lot, and 83 respondents would trust this brand at the average level. 144 respondents would not buy the product from this brand, 57 stated that they would not trust it, and 52 would trust this company at the average level. Table 4 displays the outcomes of the statistical hypothesis testing.

Based on the results of evaluated Pearson Chi-square test, which reached the value 0.00, what is less that determined significance level, alternative hypothesis H3 is accepted and consumers' trust in brand is affected by the green marketing

**Table 2** Verification of Hypothesis 2

| Calculation of the sample proportion: $p = \frac{m}{n}$ | Satisfaction of the condition: $n * \pi_0 * (1 - \pi_0) > 9$ | Test criteria | Critical field | Inequality | Acceptance or rejection of the hypothesis |
|---|---|---|---|---|---|
| ***Hypothesis 2:***<br>$H_0$: 50% of Slovak consumers think, that brands which use green marketing are socially responsible<br>$H_1$: More than 50% of Slovak consumers think, that brands which use green marketing are socially responsible | | | | | |
| $p = 0.77$ | 97,5 > 9 | 10.677 | 1.645 | 10.677 > 1.645 | $H_0$ rejected |

*Source* Own processing

**Table 3** Contingency table

| Brand trust * Green marketing activities | | | | | |
|---|---|---|---|---|---|
| Count | | | | | |
| | | To what degree would you trust this company? | | | |
| | | Average | Don't trust | Trust a lot | Total |
| Would you buy product from brand that promotes their ecological activities by green marketing? | No | 52 | 57 | 35 | 144 |
| | Yes | 83 | 53 | 111 | 247 |
| Total | | 135 | 110 | 146 | 391 |

*Source* Own processing

**Table 4** Chi-square test

| Chi-square tests | | | |
|---|---|---|---|
| | Value | df | Asymptotic significance (2-sided) |
| Pearson chi-square | 21.161[a] | 2 | 0.000 |
| Likelihood ratio | 21.448 | 2 | 0.000 |
| N of valid cases | 391 | | |

[a]0 cells (0.0%) have expected count less than 5. The minimum expected count is 40.51
*Source* Own processing

**Table 5** Symmetric measures

| Symmetric measures | | | |
|---|---|---|---|
| | | Value | Approximate significance |
| Nominal by nominal | Phi | 0.233 | 0.000 |
| | Cramer's V | 0.233 | 0.000 |
| N of valid cases | | 391 | |

*Source* Own processing

activities of brand. Since the dependence was confirmed, it is necessary to establish the strength of this dependence.

Cramer's V coefficient reached the value 0.233, which means that there is a low dependency between the variables. Since the coefficient achieves a positive value, it is also possible to claim that there is a direct dependence.

## 5 Discussion and Conclusion

Based on the analysis and results of a survey, we found out that most Slovak consumers are familiar with green marketing and understand what it means when a company uses this type of marketing in its activities. Through the survey, we also found that consumer preferences are gradually changing thanks to the growing awareness of environmental problems, which is also demonstrated by the growing attractiveness of green marketing, both for companies and customers. When making a purchase decision, consumers consider environmental sustainability important and attempt to make their purchasing decisions in line with environmental sustainability, ethical sourcing, and social responsibility. This situation is also reflected by brands that try to incorporate elements of social responsibility and sustainability into their activities, such as the use of recycled materials, the creation of recycling programs, or the use of renewable energy sources. Green marketing is an effective tool for brands to communicate these activities to the public, reach more customers, and support sales growth. Presenting the brand as environmentally responsible will allow it to attract and retain a larger customer base due to growing consumer awareness and demand for green products and services.

Green marketing also influences brand perception, as more than half of Slovak consumers think that brands that use green marketing are socially responsible. Brands need to be transparent when communicating their environmental activities; as research by Chun and colleagues [27] pointed out, customers tend to positively evaluate brands in terms of perceived value and benefit if they have sufficient knowledge about the impact of products on the environment. Consumers' belief in the transparency and authenticity of brands enhances their trust in those brands [33]. Trust is established with consumers when green marketing initiatives provide transparent and credible information.

Communicating environmental efforts and providing evidence for sustainability claims enables a brand to establish credibility and authenticity. This, consequently, enhances the reliance that consumers have on the brand, leading to strengthened brand loyalty. Green marketing activities, therefore, can help brands develop a positive green brand image, which positively influences brand trust [34]. By research, we also discovered that customers' trust in a brand is affected by brand green marketing activities. Most consumers would buy products from a brand that presents its activities through green marketing and would also trust this brand. Even some respondents who would not buy the product from that brand would trust a brand that uses green marketing in their activities. Their reluctance to buy this product could be caused, for instance, by higher prices, which are often typical for ecological products, or by concerns that the performance or effectiveness of ecological compared to traditional alternatives would be insufficient for their needs. In today's very competitive environment, brands must differentiate themselves from competitors and stand out.

As Vafaei et al. [35] pointed out, marketing inputs are crucial for defining the concept and design of products, and the growing global concern about environmental sustainability is forcing all businesses to include sustainability problems in their company strategy and actions. Green marketing offers a brand an opportunity to differentiate itself from competitors, who may not be environmentally conscious, gain a competitive advantage, and attract new customer segments. By promoting eco-friendly practices and products, brands can develop a positive brand image, build strong consumer relationships, and contribute to a more sustainable future. Our research has several implications for businesses but also consumers. Positive findings of our research suggest that if brands adapt their marketing strategies and try to implement eco-friendly messaging and product attributes to their operations, it can enhance brand credibility and increase profits. Also, green marketing can have an environmental impact since green marketing encourages consumers to make more environmentally friendly choices. Understanding how green marketing affects consumer choices will be beneficial for brands because brands, based on this knowledge, can tailor their products and campaigns to better align with consumer values and preferences and, therefore, reach more consumers. For future research, it would be interesting to explore the impact of different green marketing tools, such as green packaging or eco-labeling, on consumer behavior and purchasing decisions and determine which one has the most significant impact on customers. With green marketing, green washing, which refers to false or exaggerated eco-friendly claims, also arises, and it could be beneficial for brands to discover how this negative trend impacts consumers' trust in the eco-friendly character of brands and, in the long term, brand loyalty.

**Acknowledgements** This paper is an output of scientific project VEGA no. 1/0032/21: Marketing engineering as a progressive platform for optimizing managerial decision-making processes in the context of the current challenges of marketing management.

## References

1. Meseguer-Sanchez, V., Galvez-sanchez, F. J., Lopez-Martinez, G, Molina-Moreno, V.: Corporate social responsibility and sustainability. A bibliometric analysis of their interrelations. Sustainablility **13**(4), 1636 (2021)
2. Bojanowska, A., Kulisz, M.: Polish consumers' response to social media eco-marketing techniques. Sustainability **12**(21), 8925 (2020)
3. Skackauskiene, I., Vilkaite-Vaitone, N.: Green marketing and customers' purchasing behavior: a systematic literature review for future research agenda. Energies **16**(1), 456 (2022)
4. Nuryakin, N., Maryati, T.: Do green innovation and green competitive advantage mediate the effect of green marketing orientation on SMEs' green marketing performance? Cogent Bus. Manag. **9**(1), 2065948 (2022)
5. Patel, J.D., Trivedi, R.H., Yagnik, A.: Self-identity and internal environmental lo-cus of control: comparing their influences on green purchase intentions in high-context versus low-context cultures. J. Retail. Consum. Serv. **53**, 102003 (2020)
6. Kotler, P., Armstrong, G., Ang, S. H., Leong, S. M., Tan, C. T., & YAU, O.: Principles of Marketing: An Global Perspective. Pearson Prentice Hall, Hoboken (2008)
7. Bulsara, H.P., Matharu, M., Tarasova, K., Rulinska, O., Gogol, I.: An exploratory study of theories of green marketing and its practices. Ind. J. Manage. Prod. **12**(6), s431–s444 (2021)

8. Bañares, A.B., Silva, M.F.S., Rodríguez, S.R.: Green but ignored? The irrelevance of television advertisements on energy sustainability in Spain and its impact on consumer perceptions. Energy Res. Soc. Sci. **73**, 101835 (2021)
9. Kisieliauskas, J., Jančaitis, A.: Green marketing impact on perceived brand value in different generations. Manag. Theor. Stud. Rural Bus. Infrastruct. Dev. **44**(2), 125–133 (2022)
10. Kolk, A.: The social responsibility of international business: From ethics and the environment to CSR and sustainable development. J. World Bus. **51**(1), 23–34 (2016)
11. Lam, J.S.L., Li, K.X.: Green port marketing for sustainable growth and development. Transp. Policy **84**, 73–81 (2019)
12. Ghazali, I., Abdul-Rashid, S.H., Md Dawal, S.Z., Huda, N., Shariff, A.H.M., Herawan, S.G., Sakundarini, N.: Guidelines for designing green products considering customers' cultural preferences. Sustainability **13**(2), 673 (2021)
13. Cheung, M.F., To, W.M.: An extended model of value-attitude-behavior to explain Chinese consumers' green purchase behavior. J. Retail. Consum. Serv. **50**, 145–153 (2019)
14. Trivedi, R.H., Patel, J.D., Acharya, N.: Causality analysis of media influence on environmental attitude, intention and behaviors leading to green purchasing. J. Clean. Prod. **196**, 11–22 (2018)
15. Degirmenci, K., Breitner, M.H.: Consumer purchase intentions for electric vehicles: is green more important than price and range? Transp. Res. Part D: Transp. Environ. **51**, 250–260 (2017)
16. Cretu, A.E., Brodie, R.J.: The influence of brand image and company reputation where manufacturers market to small firms: a customer value perspective. Ind. Mark. Manage. **36**(2), 230–240 (2007)
17. Chen, Y.S., Huang, A.F., Wang, T.Y., Chen, Y.R.: Greenwash and green purchase behavior: the mediation of green brand image and green brand loyalty. Total Qual. Manag. Bus. Excell. **31**(1–2), 194–209 (2020)
18. Niedermeier, A., Emberger-Klein, A., Menrad, K.: Which factors distinguish the different consumer segments of green fast-moving consumer goods in Germany? Bus. Strateg. Environ. **30**(4), 1823–1838 (2021)
19. Pícha, K., Navrátil, J.: The factors of Lifestyle of Health and Sustainability influencing pro-environmental buying behaviour. J. Clean. Prod. **234**, 233–241 (2019)
20. Cavaleri, S., Shabana, K.: Rethinking sustainability strategies. J. Strateg. Manag. **11**(1), 2–17 (2018)
21. Kumar, R., Ritu, Sindhwani, R., Singh, P. L.: Identifying the factors related to CSR acivities contributed toward brand management through extensive literature review. In: Advances in Interdisciplinary Engineering: Select Proceedings of FLAME 2020, pp. 155–164 (2021)
22. Khandelwal, U., Kulshreshtha, K., Tripathi, V.: Importance of consumer-based green brand equity: Empirical evidence. Paradigm **23**(1), 83–97 (2019)
23. Kahraman, A., Kazançoğlu, İ: Understanding consumers' purchase intentions toward natural-claimed products: a qualitative research in personal care products. Bus. Strateg. Environ. **28**(6), 1218–1233 (2019)
24. Dangelico, R.M., Vocalelli, D.: "Green marketing": an analysis of definitions, strategy steps, and tools through a systematic review of the literature. J. Clean. Prod. **165**, 1263–1279 (2017)
25. Lin, J., Lobo, A., Leckie, C.: Green brand benefits and their influence on brand loyalty. Mark. Intell. Plan. **35**(3), 425–440 (2017)
26. Deng, Y.Y., Yang, Y.C.: Exploring the role of green attributes transparency influencing green customer citizenship behavior. Br. Food J. **124**(5), 1473–1484 (2022)
27. Chun, E., Joung, H., Lim, Y.J., Ko, E.: Business transparency and willingness to act environmentally conscious behavior: applying the sustainable fashion evaluation system "Higg Index." J. Glob. Scholars Market. Sci. **31**(3), 437–452 (2021)
28. Copeland, L., Bhaduri, G.: Consumer relationship with pro-environmental apparel brands: effect of knowledge, skepticism, and brand familiarity. J. Prod. Brand Manage. **29**(1), 1–14 (2020)
29. Lee, Y.H., Chen, S.L.: Effect of green attributes transparency on WTA for green cosmetics: Mediating effects of CSR and green brand concepts. Sustainability **11**(19), 5258 (2019)

30. Ruxton, G.D., Neuhauser, M.: When should we use one-tailed hypothesis testing? Methods Ecol. Evol. **1**, 114–117 (2010)
31. Lombardi, C.M., Hurlbert, S.H.: Misprescription and misuse of one-tailed tests. Austral. Ecol. **34**, 447–468 (2009)
32. McHugh, M.L.: The chi-square test of independence. Biochem Med, 143–149 (2013).
33. Busser, J.A., Shulga, L.V.: Involvement in consumer-generated advertising: effects of organizational transparency and brand authenticity on loyalty and trust. Int. J. Contemp. Hosp. Manag. **31**(4), 1763–1784 (2019)
34. Rahman, S.U., Nguyen-Viet, B.: Towards sustainable development: Coupling green marketing strategies and consumer perceptions in addressing greenwashing. Bus. Strateg. Environ. **32**(4), 2420–2433 (2023)
35. Vafaei, S.A., Azmoon, I., Fekete-Farkas, M.: The impact of perceived sustainable marketing policies on green customer satisfaction. Pol. J. Manag. Stud. **19**(1), 475–491 (2019)

# Psychological Empowerment and Service Culture: Fostering Sustainable Service Behavior in the Banking Sector

**Vairamani Sathyamoorthi, Sikkander Basheer Inayath Ahamed, Nishad Nawaz, Anandhan Hariharasudan, and Ravindran Kandasamy**

**Abstract** Evidence mentions that banking is the most vulnerable business worldwide. The success of the business wholly depends on the interest of the customer. To achieve this, banks must inculcate a service nature among their employees. This study focuses on highlighting the significance of Psychological Capital (PsyCap) as a mediator variable between Psychological Empowerment (PsyEmp) and Service Behavior (SB) and Service Climate (SC) and Service Behavior (SB) of the employees in the banking sector in south India. Data were collected from the banking professionals (Mid-level Managers) using a structured questionnaire to test this interrelationship. The data were collected from public and private sector banking in various cities in Southern India. *R statistical software* was used to test direct and indirect effects among the variables used in the study. As a result, this study predicted the importance of Psychological Capital (Psy Cap) as a mediator to promote Service Behavior (SB) among banking employees toward the viability of business in the long run. This study further highlighted the role of Psychological Empowerment (PsyEmp) and Service Climate (SC) in encouraging Service Behavior (SB) of banking employees to sustain the business for the long run. Managerial implications and future scope were discussed in detail in this study.

V. Sathyamoorthi · S. B. I. Ahamed
Department of Business Administration, Kalasalingam Academy of Research and Education, 626126 Krishnankoil, India

N. Nawaz
Department of Business Management, College of Business Administration, Kingdom University, Riffa 40434, Bahrain

A. Hariharasudan (✉)
Faculty of English, Kalasalingam Academy of Research and Education, 626126 Krishnankoil, India
e-mail: dr.a.hariharasudhan@gmail.com

R. Kandasamy
Presidency Business School, Presidency College, Bangalore, Karnataka 560024, India

 
S. Kot et al. (eds.), *Corporate Practices: Policies, Methodologies, and Insights in Organizational Management*, Springer Proceedings in Business and Economics,
https://doi.org/10.1007/978-981-97-0996-0_57

**Keywords** Psychological empowerment · Service climate · Service behaviour · Psychological capital and banking professionals

## 1 Introduction

After globalization, banking and its allied services are inevitable in the business world for the smooth functioning of business affairs [1]. Even small businesses depend more on banking services concerned with financial matters [2]. In simple words, the financial and economic performance of a country relies more on the performance of the banking sector of the country [3]. Thus, the sustainability of the banking business is more significant. However, the banking business's survival depends heavily on dealing with customer expectations and satisfaction with the respective businesses' services [4]. According to Mir et al. [5], customer expectations of banking services have increased. Hence, the banking businesses must ensure the providence of service to the customers. One of the key components to offering services to customers is the Service Behavior (SB) of the service providers, say banking professionals. Therefore, it is essential to encourage SB among banking professionals to provide demanded service to the customer [6]. Predominantly, companies are emphasizing specific exercises to inculcate favoured behaviour among employees. Those empower employees and create an environment to support service nature [7]. This is the base thought of the present study where Psychological Empowerment (PsyEmp) and Service Climate (SC) are the predictors for SB. Further, Psychological Capital (Psy Cap) is added as a mediator in setting up SB.

Thomas and Velthouse [8] introduced the idea of PsyEmp, stating that it is an experience of empowerment. Employees who perceive extreme empowerment can feel meaningful towards the job. Further, empowered employees also feel competent in performing their tasks, making them different from other employees. In addition, they obtain a sense of independence in decision-making about their job. Finally, when leaders empower their employees, they give their total effort and ensure their impact on their work is performed [9].

Besides, SC refers to a working environment where employees experience the feeling of being supported and rewarded for their service procedures and practices to meet customer demands and ensure service quality [10]. When employees work in such an environment, they will be fully committed to their jobs, fulfil the performance expectations, and show a high level of engagement, leading to good psychological bonding with the organization [11]. This positive perception towards the job guaranteed the SB of the respective employees [12].

Along with empowered employees (PsyEmp) in a service support environment (SC), it is important to build on some positive personal attitudes like Psy Cap to increase SB among the employees [13]. Psy Cap comprises a positive psychological mind and type of personal resources of individuals for development [14]. Walumbwa et al. [15] argued that a leader's Psy Cap would be a predominant factor that shapes specific followers' states, behavior, and performance. It is a crucial determinant that aids in understanding the level of SB in the organization [16]. SB refers to how the customer perceives the quality of service the service providers provide [17, 18].

From the above statement, this study addresses the following research gaps. First, despite understanding the importance of SB, only some studies address the importance of SB in the service sector [19]. Second, surprisingly limited studies were carried out about SB in the banking sector [20]. Finally, this study focuses on the combination of psychological factors with situational factors to create SB among banking professionals in India.

## 2 Theoretical Framework and Hypotheses

### *2.1 Psychological Empowerment and Service Behaviour*

Psychological Empowerment (PsyEmp) represents the expression of internal motivation positively connected with an employee's job, innovation, and performance. It is a cognitive process experienced by individuals [8]. Deci and Ryan [21] proposed the cognitive evaluation model theory, which focuses on the external outcome of internal motivation. This theory highlights intrinsic motivation as a primary element of PsyEmp, and the level of empowerment relies on four components: meaning, competence, self-determination, and impact [22]. Nel et al. [23] found that the components of PsyEmp would be causes of the existence of positive behavior in the workplace. It was suggested that a high level of PsyEmp motivates the positive nature, such as Service Behavior (SB) of employees. Some studies highlight the significant relationship between PsyEmp and SB [24].

**H1:** Psychological Empowerment influences Service Behavior positively and significantly.

### *2.2 Service Climate and Service Behavior*

The term Service Climate (SC) is devised from organizational climate, which creates a conducive situation for employees. In other words, this is a perception of the employees about the practices and procedures of the organization [10]. When employees understand that they are rewarded for providing quality service to the customers and obtain the expected support from the management for offering service, then SC is formed [25]. Prior studies mentioned that SC can magnify the SB of the employees [26].

**H2:** Service Climate influences Service Behavior positively and significantly.

## 2.3 Psychological Empowerment and Psychological Capital

Psychological Capital (Psy Cap) refers to an internal resource of individuals that allows them to face challenging situations [14]. The concept of Psy Cap is a positive mentality of the individual, which they use in organizational-related affairs and dealing with people [27]. According to Social Exchange Theory (SET), empowerment practices predict positive behavior, which helps to perform the job better through spending their time and energy [28]. In this way, PsyEmp positively impacts the Psy Cap of the employees.

**H3:** Psychological Empowerment influence Psychological Capital positively and significantly.

## 2.4 Service Climate and Psychological Capital

SC represents the situational factor through which basic support is provided services to the stakeholders by the service providers [29]. This environment consists of customer orientation, managerial support, and work facilitation, facilitating employees to nurture positive behavior among themselves [30]. Customer orientation refers to the level of organizations showing importance toward customer expectations. Managerial support means required monetary and non-monetary support to offer quality services. Work facilitation concerns the arrangement of all forms of service required to deliver quality services [31]. This situation motivates the employees to build their capabilities internally and equip them to face the complex situation.

**H4:** Service Climate influences Psychological Capital positively and significantly.

## 2.5 Psychological Capital and Service Behavior

According to Luthans et al. [14], Psy Cap includes four distinct characteristics: self-efficacy, optimism, hope and resilience. These components of Psy Cap create a state of mind that helps to encounter problems and face difficult situations. Further studies supported the same thought of Psy Cap and its components [32]. On the other hand, SB is a specific behavior possessed by the employees to serve quality work to the customers.SB is divided into two sets of behaviors, i.e. role-prescribed and extra-role service behavior [16]. Further, prior studies suggested that Psy Cap is one of the predictors of SB [15].

**H5:** Psychological Capital influences Service Behavior positively and significantly.

### 2.6 Psychological Capital as a Mediator

As indicated by Wang et al. [33], PsyEmp is a predictor variable for Psy Cap, and both lead to the creation of positive behavior. However, studies underlined that Psy Cap is an explanatory variable for SB, particularly in the service sector [16]. Hence, this study noted the gap in the role of Psy Cap as a mediator between PsyEmp and SB. In addition, SC enhances the nature of Psy Cap for the employees, and Psy Cap leads the SB [12]. Therefore, this study emphasizes the gap of Psy Cap as a mediation variable between SC and SB.

**H6:** Psychological Capital positively mediates the relationship between Psychological Empowerment and Service Behavior.

**H7:** Psychological Capital positively mediates the relationship between Service Climate and Service Behavior.

### 2.7 Conceptual Framework

Based on the above discussion, the model for the study is framed. There is a two paths model where Path 1 illustrates the Psychological Empowerment (PsyEmp) influence of Service Behavior (SB) both directly and indirectly through Psychological Capital (Psy Cap). Path 2 represents Service Climate (SC) affects Service Behavior (SB) directly and indirectly via Psychological Capital (Psy Cap), as shown in Fig. 1.

## 3 Research Methods

### 3.1 Sample and Procedure

The participants of this study were middle-level (Branch Manager) banking professionals working in metropolitan cities. The cluster sampling method was opted for selecting banks (Both public and private banks). Relatedly, three clusters (Chennai, Bangalore and Hyderabad) were created randomly, and data were collected from the banks located in the clusters. Permission was sought from the headquarters of each bank over the phone by explaining in detail the scope and benefits of this study to the banks and their management. The simple random sampling method was used to select the bank branch and circulate among the bank professionals. 135 banks were selected for final data collection with 50% population proportion, 95% confidence interval, and 5% error margin, and 400 respondents from those banks were selected based on the minimum sample size study stated by Schmidt et al. [34]. Out of 400 respondents, only 374 (93.5%) banking professionals responded to our

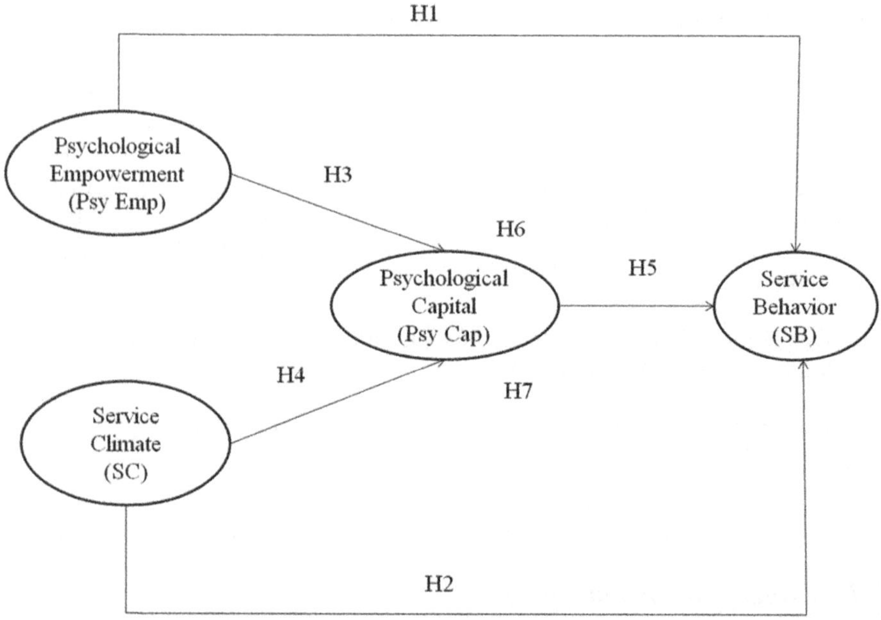


**Fig. 1** Conceptual model of research

request. However, 305 responses were valid since other responses were eliminated during the data-cleaning process [35]. The total duration for the entire process was around 60 days, from April 2023 to May 2023.

### 3.2 Measures

Totally four constructs were used, namely Psychological Empowerment (PsyEmp), Service Climate (SC), Psychological Capital (Psy Cap) and Service Behavior (SB). All scales were measured using 5-point Likert scale ranging from Strongly Agree (Score = 5) whereas Strongly Disagree (Score = 1).

Psychological Empowerment (PsyEmp) constructs were measured using twelve measurement items divided into four subscales developed by Spreitzer [36].The subscales are meaning, competence, self-determination and impact, along with Service Climate (SC) constructs consisting of fourteen measurement items developed by He et al. [30] based on the idea of Kelley [37]. The measurement items were classified into three sub-constructs: customer orientation, managerial support and work facilitation. Next, the Psychological Capital (Psy Cap) scale was proposed by Luthans et al. [38] with twelve measurement items. The scale includes self-efficacy, hope, resilience, and optimism as subscales using all measurement items. Finally, Service Behavior (SB) scales were measured using six measurement items developed by a modified scale of Tsaur and Lin [39]. All the measurement items are classified as two types of service behaviors: role-prescribed and extra-role.

## 4 Model Analysis and Results

In this study, Partial Least Square (PLS) was equipped to test and analyze the nature and quality of the model. PLS is a famous and widely used method in most social science research. It deals with the model with a set of dependent variables and a large set of independent variables [40]. Further, it helps to examine the data with non-normality and neglects the sample size constraints [41]. PLS-SEM was used to study the quality of the model and the interrelationship among the constructs used in the model. Generally, Structural Equation Modelling (SEM) is performed by testing inner and outer model relationships. Testing the outer model relationship is called evaluation of the measurement model, in which the relationship between measurement items and constructs needs to be examined, whereas testing the inner model relationship includes the relationship among constructs used in a model, which is called evaluation of the structural model [42]. PLS-SEM was performed using R statistical software in this study. This is because R statistical software is free and open software for single users. Moreover, R statistical software is a coding-based model-building software where SEMinR library expedites the execution of PLS-SEM functions [43]

### *4.1 Assessment of Measurement Model*

It is the process of checking the fulfilment of quality criteria between measurement items and latent constructs in terms of reliability and validity based on the model [42]. The model of this study has a second-order construct design, including lower-order and higher-order constructs. Further, this model is a reflective-formative model, where measurement items form the lower (first) order constructs reflectively, and lower order constructs would be the causes of second-order constructs, namely higher order constructs, and so this would be formed formatively. Quality constraints for lower-order constructs will be checked using the following tests under the concept of a reflective model: (1) Indicator Reliability, (2) Construct Reliability, (3) Convergent Validity, and (4) Discriminate Validity. On the other hand, the higher-order constructs must undergo test (1) Collinearity, (2) Indicators Weights and (3) Indicators Loadings using the concept of formative model [44].

## 4.2 Assessment of Lower Order Constructs

The first step in assessing lower-order constructs is checking indicator reliability, which shows the strength of the relationship between measurement items and respective constructs. The indicator values lie between +1 and −1, and a value close to 1 indicates a strong relationship, while close to 0 indicates a low relationship [45]. Further, if the indicator value is higher than 0.60, then the measurement items are considered for further process of analysis, and less than the threshold value is recommended for removal [43]. The indicator values of measurement items ranged from 0.75 to 0.95 in this study, which was higher than the verge point of 0.60. This indicated that the model had achieved indicator reliability, which is shown in Table 1.

The next step is to check construct reliability using Cronbach's Alpha (CA) and Composite Reliability (CR). Both measures must have values more than the required value of 0.70 to achieve construct reliability [42]. In this, both CA and CR met the required ceiling value of 0.70, as shown in Table 1. Hence, it was concluded that construct reliability was achieved. Furthermore, the convergent validity was explored using Average Variance Extracted (AVE). If the value of AVE is higher than 0.50, then all the measurement items are suggested to converge into respective constructs [46]. As shown in Table 1, all the AVE values are higher than the ceiling value of 0.50. Hence, convergent validity was also attained in this study.

The next step in assessing lower-order reflective construct is to test the discriminant validity to explore the distinction among the construct in a model [47]. In this study, discriminant validity was tested using Heterotrait and Monotrait (HTMT) ratio, which helped to identify the significant difference among constructs. The value of HTMT indicates the correlation value between constructs in the model. If the value is less than the ceiling value of 0.90, then it is concluded that discriminant validity is achieved [48]. In this study, the value between each construct was less than cap value of 0.90, shown in Table 2. Thus, discriminant validity was achieved.

## 4.3 Assessment of Higher-Order Constructs

Once the quality criteria for lower order construct were explored, then the higher order construct was assessed for formative model. In this regard, the following test must be performed to assess higher-order construct. The test includes (1) Collinearity, (2) Indicators Weights, and (3) Indicators Loadings [43]. Collinearity was tested using Variance Inflation Factor (VIF) values. If the VIF values are less than 5, then the collinearity issues do not exist in the model [49]. In this study, all the values are less than the maximum cap value of 5, as presented in Table 3.

After that, it is important to calculate the regression weight between lower-order constructs (LOC) and higher-order constructs (HOC) to find the impact of each LOC on the respective HOC in the formative model. It is justified if the values of regression weights are significant, then it is concluded that the LOC significantly

**Table 1** Factor loadings, construct reliability and convergent validity

| Particulars | Loadings | CA | CR | AVE |
|---|---|---|---|---|
| **Meaning** | | **0.771** | **0.868** | **0.686** |
| ME1 | 0.846 | | | |
| ME2 | 0.818 | | | |
| ME3 | 0.820 | | | |
| **Self-Determination** | | **0.762** | **0.863** | **0.677** |
| SD1 | 0.817 | | | |
| SD2 | 0.820 | | | |
| SD3 | 0.832 | | | |
| **Impact** | | **0.752** | **0.858** | **0.668** |
| IM1 | 0.819 | | | |
| IM2 | 0.812 | | | |
| IM3 | 0.821 | | | |
| **Competence** | | **0.764** | **0.864** | **0.679** |
| CO1 | 0.813 | | | |
| CO2 | 0.825 | | | |
| CO3 | 0.834 | | | |
| **Managerial Support** | | **0.850** | **0.899** | **0.689** |
| MS1 | 0.814 | | | |
| MS2 | 0.825 | | | |
| MS3 | 0.838 | | | |
| MS4 | 0.842 | | | |
| **Work Facilitation** | | **0.858** | **0.904** | **0.701** |
| WF1 | 0.849 | | | |
| WF2 | 0.836 | | | |
| WF3 | 0.827 | | | |
| WF4 | 0.838 | | | |
| **Customer Orientation** | | **0.885** | **0.913** | **0.636** |
| CU1 | 0.802 | | | |
| CU2 | 0.780 | | | |
| CU3 | 0.787 | | | |
| CU4 | 0.762 | | | |
| CU5 | 0.834 | | | |
| CU6 | 0.817 | | | |
| **Role prescribed behavior** | | **0.790** | **0.877** | **0.704** |
| RP1 | 0.841 | | | |
| RP2 | 0.837 | | | |
| RP3 | 0.838 | | | |

(continued)

**Table 1** (continued)

| Particulars | Loadings | CA | CR | AVE |
|---|---|---|---|---|
| **Extra role behavior** | | **0.781** | **0.873** | **0.695** |
| ER1 | 0.823 | | | |
| ER2 | 0.834 | | | |
| ER3 | 0.844 | | | |
| **Self-efficacy** | | **0.925** | **0.952** | **0.869** |
| SE1 | 0.945 | | | |
| SE2 | 0.926 | | | |
| SE3 | 0.925 | | | |
| **Optimism** | | **0.856** | **0.933** | **0.874** |
| OP1 | 0.936 | | | |
| OP2 | 0.933 | | | |
| **Hope** | | **0.918** | **0.942** | **0.802** |
| HO1 | 0.880 | | | |
| HO2 | 0.885 | | | |
| HO3 | 0.895 | | | |
| HO4 | 0.922 | | | |
| **Resilience** | | **0.913** | **0.945** | **0.852** |
| RE1 | 0.931 | | | |
| RE2 | 0.913 | | | |
| RE3 | 0.924 | | | |

CA—Cronbach's Alpha, CR—Composite Reliability, AVE—Average Variance Extracted. Each construct's CA, CR and AVE were bolded

contributes to creating HOC [43]. In this study, all the values of regression weights of LOC significantly influenced HOC except the relationship between resilience and psychological capital, as indicated in Table 4.

In addition, if the regression weight of any of the LOC is insignificant, then it is important to prove the relationship between LOC and HOC using the loadings value. If the loading value is higher than 0.5 and it is significant, then it is proved that a significant relationship exists between LOC and HOC in the formative model [43, 44]. In this study, all the LOCs were highly loaded on HOC since it was higher than 0.5,which was significant, as shown in Table 5. Hence, it was conceived that all LOC had a significant influence on HOC.

**Table 2** Heterotrait and monotrait raio

| | ME | SD | IM | CO | MS | WF | CU | SE | OP | HO | RE | RP |
|---|---|---|---|---|---|---|---|---|---|---|---|---|
| ME | | | | | | | | | | | | |
| SD | 0.42 | | | | | | | | | | | |
| IM | 0.41 | 0.73 | | | | | | | | | | |
| CO | 0.34 | 0.67 | 0.16 | | | | | | | | | |
| MS | 0.49 | 0.36 | 0.58 | 0.53 | | | | | | | | |
| WF | 0.65 | 0.14 | 0.31 | 0.64 | 0.17 | | | | | | | |
| CU | 0.47 | 0.38 | 0.34 | 0.44 | 0.33 | 0.29 | | | | | | |
| SE | 0.65 | 0.22 | 0.39 | 0.30 | 0.24 | 0.31 | 0.35 | | | | | |
| OP | 0.75 | 0.43 | 0.54 | 0.17 | 0.55 | 0.57 | 0.43 | 0.38 | | | | |
| HO | 0.52 | 0.72 | 0.28 | 0.74 | 0.33 | 0.69 | 0.40 | 0.32 | 0.31 | | | |
| RE | 0.48 | 0.25 | 0.60 | 0.14 | 0.57 | 0.29 | 0.14 | 0.40 | 0.66 | 0.31 | | |
| RP | 0.65 | 0.16 | 0.48 | 0.58 | 0.68 | 0.52 | 0.27 | 0.21 | 0.26 | 0.59 | 0.32 | |
| ER | 0.58 | 0.49 | 0.43 | 0.64 | 0.31 | 0.68 | 0.16 | 0.67 | 0.32 | 0.30 | 0.33 | 0.30 |

*Note* All the Correlation values (HTMT Ratio) are greater than 0.90
The abbreviations Table 2 can be decoded as follows, ME–Meaning, SD–Self Determination, IM–Impact, CO–Competence, MS-Managerial Support, WF-Work Facilitation, CU-Customer Orientation, SE-Self-efficacy, OP-Optimism, HO-Hope, RE-Resilience, RP-Role prescribed behavior and ER-Extra role behavior.

**Table 3** VIF values

| Particulars | PsyEmp | SC | SB | Psy Cap |
|---|---|---|---|---|
| Meaning | 3.261 | | | |
| Self Determination | 3.050 | | | |
| Impact | 3.153 | | | |
| Competence | 3.137 | | | |
| Managerial Support | | 3.488 | | |
| Work Facilitation | | 4.351 | | |
| Customer Orientation | | 3.180 | | |
| Role prescribed behavior | | | 2.639 | |
| Extra role behavior | | | 2.639 | |
| Self-efficacy | | | | 4.480 |
| Optimism | | | | 2.290 |
| Hope | | | | 3.280 |
| Resilience | | | | 3.608 |

**Table 4** Regression weights

| Particulars | Original Est | Bootstrap SD | T Stat | 2.5% CI | 97.5% CI |
|---|---|---|---|---|---|
| Meaning ->PsyEmp | 0.331 | 0.040 | 8.197 | 0.252 | 0.410 |
| Self Determination ->PsyEmp | 0.133 | 0.040 | 3.275 | 0.055 | 0.214 |
| Impact ->PsyEmp | 0.263 | 0.045 | 5.800 | 0.172 | 0.350 |
| Competence - > PsyEmp | 0.375 | 0.044 | 8.490 | 0.292 | 0.458 |
| Managerial Support ->SC | 0.305 | 0.047 | 6.469 | 0.215 | 0.399 |
| Work Facilitation ->SC | 0.304 | 0.040 | 7.624 | 0.224 | 0.381 |
| Customer Orientation ->SC | 0.442 | 0.052 | 8.445 | 0.341 | 0.544 |
| Role-prescribed behavior ->SB | 0.576 | 0.033 | 17.23 | 0.509 | 0.639 |
| Extra role behavior ->SB | 0.481 | 0.034 | 14.28 | 0.417 | 0.548 |
| Self-efficacy ->Psy Cap | 0.732 | 0.042 | 17.23 | 0.650 | 0.813 |
| Optimism ->Psy Cap | 0.121 | 0.032 | 3.793 | 0.060 | 0.185 |
| Hope ->Psy Cap | 0.178 | 0.037 | 4.814 | 0.103 | 0.246 |
| Resilience ->Psy Cap | 0.028 | 0.040 | 0.697 | −0.048 | 0.106 |

*Note* No "0" exists between 2.5% Confidence Interval to 97.5% Confidence Interval. So it is significant [50]

**Table 5** Loadings between LOC and HOC

| Particulars | Original Est | Bootstrap SD | T Stat | 2.5% CI | 97.5% CI |
|---|---|---|---|---|---|
| Meaning ->PsyEmp | 0.918 | 0.012 | 76.85 | 0.891 | 0.939 |
| Self Determination ->PsyEmp | 0.859 | 0.02 | 43.08 | 0.817 | 0.895 |
| Impact ->PsyEmp | 0.896 | 0.016 | 56.90 | 0.862 | 0.923 |
| Competence ->PsyEmp | 0.925 | 0.013 | 73.09 | 0.899 | 0.947 |
| Managerial Support ->SC | 0.94 | 0.01 | 94.45 | 0.92 | 0.957 |
| Work Facilitation ->SC | 0.938 | 0.01 | 97.84 | 0.917 | 0.953 |
| Customer Orientation ->SC | 0.967 | 0.008 | 125.9 | 0.948 | 0.979 |
| Role prescribed behavior ->SB | 0.955 | 0.008 | 124.1 | 0.938 | 0.968 |
| Extra role behavior ->SB | 0.935 | 0.01 | 89.34 | 0.913 | 0.954 |
| Self-efficacy ->Psy Cap | 0.989 | 0.003 | 318.1 | 0.982 | 0.994 |
| Optimism ->Psy Cap | 0.801 | 0.024 | 32.82 | 0.745 | 0.844 |
| Hope ->Psy Cap | 0.871 | 0.017 | 50.58 | 0.834 | 0.898 |
| Resilience ->Psy Cap | 0.852 | 0.019 | 45.77 | 0.811 | 0.884 |

*Note* No "0" exists between 2.5% Confidence Interval and 97.5% Confidence Interval. So, it is significant

## 4.4 Assessment of Structural Model

When the quality criterion for the outer model is checked, the inner model will be assessed, whereby the relationship among constructs will be explored [51]. Assessment of the inner model includes testing the model's explanatory power and path coefficients [43].

The explanatory power of the model, which means that the level of impact created by one or more exogenous variables on the endogenous variables, is explained using the value of $R^2$and $f^2$ [52]. The value of $R^2$ ranges from $-1$ to $+1$, and the value close to 1 indicates a strong impact of exogenous variables on endogenous variables [53]. Moreover, the explanatory power is classified as substantial, moderate, and weak if the value isin the range of 0.75, 0.50 and 0.25, respectively [54]. In this study, the value of $R^2$ stated that Psychological Empowerment (PsyEmp) and Service Climate (SC) accounted for88% changes in Psychological Capital (Psy Cap), and another $R^2$ value suggested that all three exogenous variables PsyEmp, SC, and Psy Cap accounted for 85.5% changes on Service Behavior (SB). Further, the values suggested that exogenous variables on endogenous variables created a substantial impact. The values of $R^2$are shown in Table 6 as follows.

Another measure to examine the model's explanatory power is the value of $f^2$. Knowing the importance of each exogenous variable used in the model is helpful. The $f^2$ values represent the effect size of exogenous variables. The effect size categorized as small, medium and large when the value of $f^2$ is less than or equal to 0.02, 0.15 and 0.35, respectively [55]. As shown in Table 7, the $f^2$ values indicated the level of importance of exogenous variables used in the study. In this connection, the effect size of PsyEmp was medium for Psy Cap and small for SB. On the other hand, the effect size of SC on Psy Cap was large and medium for SB. Finally, the effect size was small for Psy Cap on SB. All the results of $f^2$ are shown in Table 7.

After evaluating the model's explanatory power, the path coefficient needs to be calculated to understand the level of influence of each exogenous construct on the endogenous construct. Path coefficient helps to measure the level of influence of an exogenous construct on an endogenous construct while keeping other constructs constant [35]. In the present study, all the exogenous constructs positively

**Table 6** $R^2$ values

| | Psy Cap | SB |
|---|---|---|
| $R^2$ | 0.880 | 0.855 |
| Adj$R^2$ | 0.879 | 0.853 |

**Table 7** $f^2$ values

| | Psy Cap | SB |
|---|---|---|
| PsyEmp | 0.166 | 0.041 |
| SC | 0.374 | 0.135 |
| Psy Cap | – | 0.064 |

**Table 8** Path coefficient

| | Original Est | Bootstrap SD | T Stat | 2.5% CI | 97.5% CI |
|---|---|---|---|---|---|
| PsyEmp ->SB | 0.226 | 0.070 | 3.229 | 0.097 | 0.367 |
| SC ->SB | 0.442 | 0.083 | 5.317 | 0.284 | 0.604 |
| PsyEmp ->Psy Cap | 0.379 | 0.052 | 7.278 | 0.283 | 0.487 |
| SC ->Psy Cap | 0.575 | 0.052 | 11.135 | 0.473 | 0.675 |
| Psy Cap ->SB | 0.280 | 0.067 | 4.158 | 0.140 | 0.403 |

*Note* No "0" exists between 2.5% Confidence Interval and 97.5% Confidence Interval. So, it is significant

influenced the endogenous constructs and were significant as well. It implies that some changes that occurred in exogenous constructs will significantly impact the endogenous constructs. The results are presented in Table 8.

From Table 8 and Fig. 2, it can be interpreted that PsyEmp influences SB positively and significantly. This would suggest that one unit of changes on PsyEmp affects SB at the level0.226 ($\beta = 0.226$, $p < 0.05$); hence, H1 was attained. Further, SC also has a positive and significant influence over SB at the level of 0.442($\beta = 0.442$, $p < 0.05$). It means that one standard unit of changes on SC will affect SB by0.442. Therefore, H2 was also attained. It can also be interpreted that PsyEmp influences Psy Cap positively and significantly. This would suggest that one unit of changes on PsyEmp affects Psy Cap at the level 0.379 ($\beta = 0.379$, $p < 0.05$). Hence, H3 was accepted. In the same way, SC also positively affects Psy Cap, and the relationship was statistically significant. One unit change of SC affects 0.575($\beta = 0.575$, $p < 0.05$) —levels of changes on Psy Cap in banking organizations. Therefore, H4 was also attained. In this way, Psy Cap influences SB positively and significantly. It is suggested that 0.280 changes would occur on SB of the employees when one unit of changes is created on Psy Cap of the employees ($\beta = 0.280$, $p < 0.05$). Thereby, it is decided that H5 was attained.

## 4.5 Mediation Analysis

According to the model, there was mediation path that existed. Mediation analysis was performed to understand the strength of the mediation path. In this regard, the role of Psychological Capital (Psy Cap) as a mediator was tested between Psychological Empowerment (PsyEmp) and Service Behavior (SB) and Service Climate (SC) and Service Behavior (SB). PLS-SEM was performed using SEMinR library in R statistical software to do that. In such a way, three effects were identified. First was the total effect, where the effects of PsyEmp and SC on SB were identified before including mediator Psy Cap in the model. As a result, without a mediator, PsyEmp has a positive and significant effect on SB at the level of 0.332 ($\beta = 0.332$, $p < 0.05$). In addition, SC has a positive and significant effect on SB at the level of 0.603 ($\beta =$

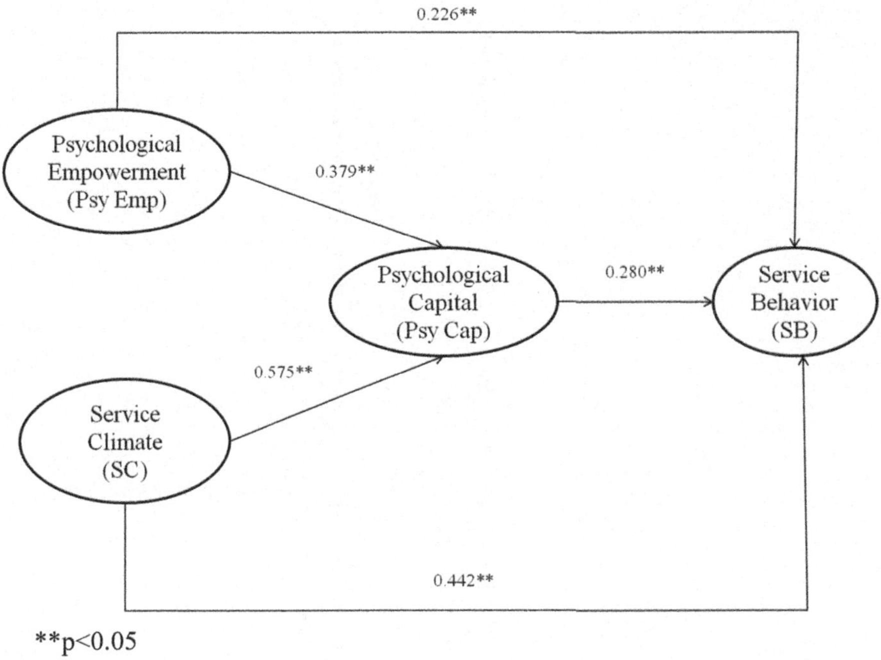


**Fig. 2** Path coefficient (**$p < 0.05$)

0.603, $p < 0.05$) when the mediator does not exist in the model. Then, the mediator Psy Cap was included in the model, performed the analysis, and found the direct effects. The direct effects were identified between PsyEmp and SB and SC and SB. From the result, it was interpreted that Psy Cap reduced the effect of PsyEmp on SB to the effect level of ($\beta = 0.226$, $p < 0.05$). Furthermore, Psy Cap also reduces the effect of SC on SB to 0.442 ($\beta = 0.442$, $p < 0.05$). Finally, an indirect effect was identified, where a relationship was established through mediation was studied. The size of the indirect effect was positive and significant for both paths. This means that Psy Cap substantially affects the relationship between PsyEmp and SB and SC and SB with effect sizes of 0.106 and 0.161, respectively. It was suggested that Psy Cap partially mediates the relationship between PsyEmp and SB and SC and SB. Thus, H6 and H7 achieved the outcomes of the mediation analysis presented in Table 9.

## 5 Discussion

In recent times, banking companies have struggled to sustain long-term business worldwide. Banking companies need help with day-to-day functions even in developed countries like the United States of America (USA) and European Nations [56].

**Table 9** Mediation analysis

| Path (PsyEmp→Psy Cap → SB) | | | | | | | | | |
|---|---|---|---|---|---|---|---|---|---|
| Total effect (PsyEmp→ SB) | | Direct effect (PsyEmp→ SB) | | Indirect effect (PsyEmp→ SB) | | | | | Results |
| Effect size | *p*-value | Effect Size | *p*-value | | Effect Size | SD | *T* value | *P* values | **Partially Mediated** |
| 0.33 | 0.02 | 0.22 | 0.04 | (PsyEmp→Psy Cap → SB) | 0.10 | 0.02 | 3.79 | 0.031 | |
| Path (SC →Psy Cap → SB) | | | | | | | | | |
| Total effect (SC→ SB) | | Direct effect (SC→ SB) | | Indirect effect (SC→ SB) | | | | | Results |
| Effect Size | *p*-value | Effect Size | *p*-value | | Effect Size | SD | *T* value | *P* values | **Partially mediated** |
| 0.60 | 0.00 | 0.44 | 0.01 | (SC →Psy Cap → SB) | 0.16 | 0.04 | 3.77 | 0.031 | |

*Note* If the *p*-value is less than 0.05, then it is considered significant

One of the finest ways to tackle the challenges is by servicing the customers. Companies make service practices in all aspects of the business. Hence, it is highly important to have service-minded people in our company to provide customer services [57]. Companies can inculcate a service nature among working professionals through proper training, leadership, systematic monitoring, and controlling [58]. This study deals with factors stimulating service behavior among banking professionals in India. This study tested a conceptual model of the factors influencing Service Behavior (SB) and the mediating role of banking professionals' Psychological Capital (Psy Cap) to instigate SB among the professionals.

The results showed that Psychological Empowerment (PsyEmp) was the predicted variable for SB. This study, lined with previous studies, highlighted that PsyEmp is one of the causes of stimulating SB [24]. This study predicted that PsyEmp has a positive and significant influence over SB. It was suggested that to increase SB among banking professionals, empower them psychologically. Further, the Service Climate (SC) was another predicted variable in instigating service behavior. The findings of this study show that SC had a positive and significant influence over SB, which is consistent with previous studies by [59], which highlighted the exact relationship between SC and SB. It was recommended that it is important to have a service climate, including acceptance and appreciation of service behavior, and rewarding them will stimulate service nature among professionals, leading to quality service to the customer.

On the other hand, this study also stressed the role of PsyEmp in building Psy Cap among banking professionals. It was found that a positive and significant relationship exists between PsyEmp and Psy Cap. This finding was the same as the result of the previous study, which stated that PsyEmp was one of the predicted variables for Psy Cap [9]. It was pointed out that employees' Psy Cap improved based on their psychological empowerment in their work roles. Further, here are questions that come as a gap for this study that empowered employees would have PsyCap; however, environmental supports were required. This study analysed the gap and found a significant connection between SC and Psy Cap. It was proposed that to improve Psy Cap; top management must design a climate supporting the service. In other words, when service supports climate prevalence in a banking organization, the employees can meet the challenging situation, generally called Psy Cap.

Another aim of this study was to understand the Psy Cap as a mediator in the relationship between PsyEmp and SB and also tested between SC and SB. Studies propounded that there was a significant connection between Psy Cap and SB. They emphasized that employees must be able to face tough situations to provide service to their customers [16]. The findings of this study advocated the same as the previous studies. Hence, it is important to have Psy Cap to service their customers. This study was further moved to prove the mediation role of Psy Cap. The study demonstrated a mediation role played by the Psy Cap of the professionals in inculcating SB through empowering employees and creating a service climate in the workplace. It was found that Psy Cap partially mediates between PsyEmp and SB and SC and SB. It was hinted to the banking organization that when top management priorities designing empowered professionals with a service-supported climate, it is easy to inculcate

SB among professionals. Further, suppose the employees with high capital support them psychologically. In that case, it is a fast way to instil SB among professionals to serve customers and sustain their business in the long run.

## *5.1 Managerial Implications*

This study contributes insights to the top management for enhancing service behavior among banking professionals to deliver service to their customers. From the findings, it was interpreted that Psychological Empowerment (PsyEmp) can directly promote Service Behavior (SB) among banking professionals. Hence, top management or leaders' priorities empowering the employees in a way that provides personal care, make their work meaningful, ensure their presence, use decisions taken by professionals, execute their opinion and suggestions, and make them feel impact their work in the organizations. Furthermore, it provides education and adequate training to enhance self-determination and competence among banking professionals. Some studies stated that effective information technology also ensures empowerment by the way it achieves effective organization [60]. Hence, the organization can prove technological support to empower the employees. In addition, banking organizations require Service Climate (SC) to promote service behavior. The present study justified the above statement by revealing that SC must encourage SB in organizations. To support the service climate in banking, the banking organizations can provide the required things to perform their job, ensure the welfare of the banking professionals, including monetary and non-monetary benefits and present integrative rewards and recognition for service excellence, etc., to make them feel competitive and perform their task effectively.

Further, it is significant to define and authorize the role of each professional by assigning powers and responsibilities to make expeditious decisions to resolve customer issues and meet the expectations of the quality of service provided by the professionals. Several studies highlighted that some form of leadership is also an influential element in creating favored behavior of the professionals such as SB [61]. Hence, it ensures the creation of mechanisms whereby professionals solve the issues pertaining to their jobs. In this way, the top management can create a service climate for their organizations. The findings showed that PsyEmp was also a predictor variable for Psychological Capital (Psy Cap). It implies that when banking companies empower professionals, their capacity to face tough workplace situations is enhanced. Top management must emphasize empowering professionals through proper training and education to increase hope towards themselves, their job and their organization. It also helps the professionals to enhance positive patterns of performing their duties. Further, empowered professionals were more confident and opted to change in an organization. Hence, it was concluded that when top management prioritize empowering them, it is easy to increase the enhanced Psy Cap. Moreover, this study proved that increasing Psy Cap was possible when the organization promoted SC in the workplace.

In addition, this study found that Psy Cap has a positive relationship with SB. When banking companies want to improve SB in their organization, they adopt the proper recruitment and selection policy whereby companies can recruit those with high and strong Psy Cap. Further, the companies can motivate both monetary and non-monetary, proper training like an apprenticeship to improve hope and resilience toward job performance even during difficult situations. This nature increases the courage of the professionals to support their customers in enhancing SB. The findings of this study support that Psy Cap mediates the relationship among PsyEmp, SC and SB. It was suggested that top management must priorities empowering their professionals through leadership and creating an environment supporting service. This management practice helped to increase Psy Cap through which they can achieve the goal of offering customer service and sustaining their business in the long run.

### *5.2 Limitations and Suggestions for Future Research*

Though the study contributes to banking management to ensure service behavior among professionals, some thoughts have not been explored in this study, and those were listed as follows. First, since the study was conducted in the Indian context, the scope of this study was limited to India only, and it was hard to generalize the findings to other countries. However, the researchers can use the same thoughts in some other countries in the future. Second, this study analysed the data collected from banks located in various cities in India. However, it is hard to infer this study's findings on the banks located in rural and semi-rural areas. Hence, the researcher can explore the thought of the study in rural and semi-rural areas of India. Third, this study uses banking professionals at a bank's middle level (Manager Level). Future studies can focus on the frontline and senior manager levels with the same concept. Fourth, this study performed the behavior of professionals from the banking sector. The novelty can be useful for the banking sector. Hence, the researchers can practice the same thought for other service sectors and sectors like manufacturing in the future. Fifth, the model consists of mediation Psy Cap and studies its effect. The forthcoming study can be a comprehensive study that may add more variables such as work engagement, servant leadership, intention to quit, etc.

## 6 Conclusion

It is not surprising that companies from the service sector should ensure the provision of service to their stakeholders. If they fail to do so, companies cannot survive because of the nature of the service sector in India. The banking industry could be more exceptional in this scenario, and they face a challenging survival situation. Hence, it was concluded that providing service to the customer is the only way to survive in the business. The basis was that psychological and situational aspects are required to create certain behaviors. Here is the gap addressed in this study that understood influential factors for creating Service Behavior (SB). The findings identified psychological factors as Psychological Empowerment (PsyEmp) and Psychological Capital (Psy Cap). Moreover, the situational factor is Service Climate (SC). The findings were consistent with previous studies that companies can use Psy Emp and SC to promote SB. This study also tested the mediation role of Psy Cap to create SB. By promoting SB, the company's value increases, and eventually, that company gets business, ensures its present market, and attains a competitive advantage over other players in the market.

## References


1. Park, H., Kim, J.D.: Transition towards green banking: role of financial regulators and financial institutions. Asian J. Sustain. Soc. Responsib. **5** (2020).
2. Petkov, I.: Munich personal RePEc archive small business lending and the bank-branch network small business lending and the bank-branch network. J. Financ. Stab. **64**, 1–56 (2018)
3. Mensi, W., Hammoudeh, S., Tiwari, A.K., Al-Yahyaee, K.H.: Impact of Islamic banking development and major macroeconomic variables on economic growth for Islamic countries: evidence from panel smooth transition models. Econ. Syst. **44**, 100739 (2020)
4. Li, F., Lu, H., Hou, M., Cui, K., Darbandi, M.: Customer satisfaction with bank services: the role of cloud services, security, e-learning and service quality. Technol. Soc. **64**, 101487 (2021)
5. Mir, R.A., Rameez, R., Tahir, N.: Measuring internet banking service quality: an empirical evidence. TQM J. **35**, 492–518 (2023)
6. Nunkoo, R., Teeroovengadum, V., Ringle, C.M., Sunnassee, V.: Service quality and customer satisfaction: The moderating effects of hotel star rating. Int. J. Hosp. Manag. **91**, 102414 (2020)
7. Yang, J., Gu, J., Liu, H.: Servant leadership and employee creativity: the roles of psychological empowerment and work–family conflict. Curr. Psychol. **38**, 1417–1427 (2019)
8. Thomas, K.W., Velthouse, B.A.: Cognitive elements of empowerment: an "interpretive" model of intrinsic task motivation. Acad. Manag. Rev. **15**, 666–681 (1990)
9. Ma, L., Zhou, F., Liu, H.: Relationship between psychological empowerment and the retention intention of kindergarten teachers: a chain intermediary effect analysis. Front. Psychol. **12**, 1–11 (2021)
10. Schneider, B., White, S.S., Paul, M.C.: Linking service climate and customer perceptions of service quality: test of a causal model. J. Appl. Psychol. **83**, 150–163 (1998)
11. Mith, D.A.E.S., Consult, E., Brumback, G.B., Coast, P., Buenger, V., Texas, A., Craig, S.B., Carolina, N.: Personnel Psychology Book Reviews (2012)
12. Kang, H.J. (Annette), Busser, J.A.: Impact of service climate and psychological capital on employee engagement: The role of organizational hierarchy. Int. J. Hospitality Manage. **75**, 1–9 (2018)
13. Cameron, K.S., Spreitzer, G.M.: Introduction: What Is Positive About Positive Organizational Scholarship? (2012)
14. Luthans, F., Avolio, B.J., Avey, J.B., Norman, S.M.: Positive psychological capital: measurement and relationship with performance and satisfaction. Pers. Psychol. **60**, 541–572 (2007)
15. Walumbwa, F.O., Peterson, S.J., Avolio, B.J., Hartnell, C.A.: An investigation of the relationships among leader and follower psychological capital, service climate, and job performance. Pers. Psychol. **63**, 937–963 (2010)
16. Cheng, T.M., Hong, C.Y., Yang, B.C.: Examining the moderating effects of service climate on psychological capital, work engagement, and service behavior among flight attendants. J. Air Transp. Manag. **67**, 94–102 (2018)

17. Karatepe, O.M., Talebzadeh, N.: An empirical investigation of psychological capital among flight attendants. J. Air Transp. Manag. **55**, 193–202 (2016)
18. Bitner, M.J.: Evaluating service encounters: the effects of physical surroundings and employee responses. J. Mark. **54**, 69–72 (1990)
19. Frazer Winsted, K.: Service behaviors that lead to satisfied customers. Eur. J. Mark. **34**, 399–417 (2022)
20. Zhao, C., Noman, A.H.M., Hassan, M.K.: Bank's service failures and bank customers' switching behavior: does bank reputation matter? Int. J. Bank Mark. **41**, 550–571 (2023)
21. Deci, E.L., Ryan, R.M.: Cognitive evaluation theory. In: Intrinsic Motivation and Self-Determination in Human Behavior. Perspectives in Social Psychology (1985)
22. Spreitzer, G.M.: Psychological Empowerment in the Workplace (1995)
23. Nel, T., Stander, M.W., Latif, J.: Investigating positive leadership, psychological empowerment, work engagement and satisfaction with life in a chemical industry. SA J Ind Psychol. 41 (2015)
24. Soleimani, M., Dana, L.P., Salamzadeh, A., Bouzari, P., Ebrahimi, P.: The effect of internal branding on organisational financial performance and brand loyalty: mediating role of psychological empowerment. J. Asian Bus. Econ Stud. **30**, 143–163 (2023)
25. Sharif, M.T., Muhammad, R., Yaqub, S.: Does organizational support enhance the organizational citizenship behavior in service industry with moderating role of service climate ? J. Mark. Consum Res. **9**, 102–110 (2015)
26. Mokhtaran, M., Fakharyan, M., Jalilvand, M.R., Mohebi, M.: The effect of service climate on perceived service value and behavioral intentions: the mediating role of service quality. Asia Pac. J. Tour. Res. **20**, 472–486 (2015)
27. Hong, Y., Huang, J.H., Zhang, J.: Relationship between emotional labor and mental health in preschool teachers: mediation of psychological capital. Front. Psychol. **13**, 1–9 (2022)
28. Monje Amor, A., Xanthopoulou, D., Calvo, N., Abeal Vázquez, J.P.: Structural empowerment, psychological empowerment, and work engagement: a cross-country study. Eur. Manag. J. **39**, 779–789 (2021)
29. Swart, R., Celliers, L., Collard, M., Prats, A.G., Huang-Lachmann, J.T., Sempere, F.L., de Jong, F., Máñez Costa, M., Martinez, G., Velazquez, M.P., Martín, A.R., Segretier, W., Stattner, E., Timmermans, W.: Reframing climate services to support municipal and regional planning. Clim Serv. **22** (2021)
30. He, Y., li, W., Keung Lai, K.: Service climate, employee commitment and customer satisfaction: evidence from the hospitality industry in China. Int. J. Contemp. Hosp. Manag. **23**, 592–607 (2011)
31. Hennig-Thurau, T., Thurau, C.: Customer orientation of service employees—toward a conceptual framework of a key relationship marketing construct. J. Relat Mark. **2**, 23–41 (2003)
32. Avey, J.B., Luthans, F., Smith, R.M., Palmer, N.F., Avey, J.B., Luthans, F., Smith, R.M., Palmer, N.F.: Impact of positive psychological capital on employee well-being over time impact of positive psychological capital on employee well-being over time. J. Occup. Health Psychol. **15**, 17–28 (2010)
33. Wang, D., Kan, W., Qin, S., Zhao, C., Sun, Y., Mao, W., Bian, X., Ou, Y., Zhao, Z., Hu, Y.: How authentic leadership impacts on job insecurity: The multiple mediating role of psychological empowerment and psychological capital. Stress Health **37**, 60–71 (2021)
34. Schmidt, S.A.J., Lo, S., Hollestein, L.M.: Research techniques made simple: sample size estimation and power calculation. J. Investig. Dermatol. **138**, 1678–1682 (2018)
35. Henseler, J., Hubona, G., Ray, P.A.: Using PLS path modeling in new technology research: updated guidelines. Ind. Manag. Data Syst. **116**, 2–20 (2016)
36. Spreitzer, G.M.: An empirical test of a comprehensive model of intrapersonal empowerment in the workplace. Am. J. Community Psychol. **23**, 601–629 (1995)
37. Kelley, S.W.: Developing customer orientation among service employees conceptual framework. J. Acad. Mark. Sci. **20**, 27–36 (1992)
38. Luthans, F., Avey, J.B., Avolio, B.J., Norman, S.M., Combs, G.M.: Psychological capital development: toward a micro-intervention. J. Organ. Behav. **27**, 387–393 (2006)

39. Tsaur, S.H., Lin, Y.C.: Promoting service quality in tourist hotels: the role of HRM practices and service behavior. Tour. Manage. **25**, 471–481 (2004)
40. Geladi, P.: Notes on the history and nature of partial least squares (PLS) modelling. J. Chemom. **2**, 231–246 (1988)
41. Goodhue, D.L., Lewis, W., Thompson, R., Thompson, R.: Does RLS have advantages for small sample size or non-normal data? MIS Quarter. **36**, 981–1001 (2012)
42. Hair, J.F., Sarstedt, M., Hopkins, L., Kuppelwieser, V.G.: Partial least squares structural equation modeling (PLS-SEM): an emerging tool in business research. Eur. Bus. Rev. **26**, 106–121 (2014)
43. Hair Jr, J.F., Hult, G.T.M., Ringle, C.M., Sarstedt, M., Danks, N.P., Ray, S.: Partial Least Squares Structural Equation Modeling (PLS-SEM) Using R: A Workbook (2021)
44. Sarstedt, M., Hair, J.F., Cheah, J.H., Becker, J.M., Ringle, C.M.: How to specify, estimate, and validate higher-order constructs in PLS-SEM. Australas. Mark. J. **27**, 197–211 (2019)
45. Mltoft, J.: Reliability assessment and screening by reliability indicator methods. Electrocomponent Sci. Technol. **11**, 71–84 (1983)
46. Hair, J.F., Ringle, C.M., Sarstedt, M.: PLS-SEM: Indeed a silver bullet. J. Mark. Theory Pract. **19**, 139–152 (2011)
47. Henseler, J., Ringle, C.M., Sarstedt, M.: A new criterion for assessing discriminant validity in variance-based structural equation modeling. J. Acad. Mark. Sci. **43**, 115–135 (2015)
48. Henseler, J., Ringle, C.M., Sarstedt, M.: A new criterion for assessing discriminant validity in variance-based structural equation modeling. J. Acad. Mark. Sci. **20**, 277–205 (2009)
49. Ferré, J.: Regression diagnostics. In: Comprehensive Chemometrics, pp. 33–89. Elsevier (2009)
50. Hazra, A.: Using the confidence interval confidently. J. Thorac. Dis. **9**, 4125–4130 (2017)
51. Hair, J.F., Sarstedt, M., Ringle, C.M., Mena, J.A.: An assessment of the use of partial least squares structural equation modeling in marketing research. J. Acad. Mark. Sci. **40**, 414–433 (2012)
52. Hair, J.F., Hult, G.T.M., Ringle, C.M., Sarstedt, M., Danks, N.P., Ray, S.: Evaluation of the structural model. In: Partial Least Squares Structural Equation Modeling (PLS-SEM) Using R, pp. 115–138. Springer, Cham (2021)
53. Ratner, B.: The correlation coefficient: its values range between 1/1, or do they. J. Target. Meas. Anal. Mark. **17**, 139–142 (2009)
54. Falk, R.F., Miller, N.B.: A Primer for Soft Modeling (1992).
55. Cohen, J.: Set correlation and contingency tables. Appl. Psychol. Meas. **12**, 425–434 (1988)
56. Tomczak, K.: Transmission of the 2007–2008 financial crisis in advanced countries of the European Union. Bull. Econ. Res. **75**, 40–64 (2023)
57. van Eck, D., Dobusch, L., van den Brink, M.: Creating inclusivity through boundary work? Zooming in on low-wage service sector work. Hum. Relat. **77**, 1–32 (2023)
58. Callaghan, G., Thompson, P.: 'We recruit attitude': the selection and shaping of routine call centre labour. J. Manage. Stud. **39**, 233–254 (2002)
59. Gracia, E., Cifre, E., Grau, R.: Service quality: The key role of service climate and service behavior of boundary employee units. Group Org. Manag. **35**, 276–298 (2010)
60. Rahiman, H.U., Nawaz, N., Kodikal, R., Hariharasudan, A.: Effective information system and organisational efficiency. Pol. J. Manage. Stud. **24**, 398–413 (2021)
61. Sathyamoorthi, V., Ahamed, S.B.I., Hariharasudan, A., Grabara, J., Sroka, M.: Managerial perspective of servant leadership on voice behavior of banking professionals: mediation model. Pol. J. Manag. Stud. **27**, 311–327 (2023)

# The Role of Fourth Industrial Revolution (4IR) Technologies in Achieving Sustainable Development Goals

**Everjoy Chipo Makazhe and Tafadzwa Clemetine Maramura**

**Abstract** Today's world is dominated by technology, and with the advent of Industry 4.0 (The 4th Industrial Revolution 4IR), it is critical to harness the power of technology. This research investigates the potential of Fourth Industrial Revolution (4IR) technologies in advancing Agenda 2030 of the Sustainable Development Goals (SDG). Artificial intelligence, the Internet of Things, blockchain, and robotics are among the 4IR technologies that can disrupt traditional industries and processes while promoting sustainability. This research looks at how 4IR technologies can help achieve the SDGs, their effects on sustainability, and the key challenges and opportunities that come with their implementation in the African continuum. To understand this dynamic, this study employs the Technology Acceptance Model to examine how and the extent to which achieving the study's objective will culminate in promoting sustainable development in Africa. Consequently, the epistemological and ontological orientation of the research for this paper warranted a qualitative document-based research approach, hinged on the grounded theory approach, wherein theory is constructed from qualitative data. The findings, which were extracted from thematic analysis, show the exciting prospects of 4IR technologies for sustainable development, with most 4IR technologies having been discovered to be used to support water, education, and health, among other industries. This study recommends the development of 4IR technologies that maximize the positive impact of 4IR on sustainable development while mitigating potential risks.

**Keywords** Industry 4.0 · 4IR · Sustainable Development Goals · SDGs · Sustainability

E. C. Makazhe (✉)
Walter Sisulu University, Mthatha, South Africa
e-mail: emakazhe@wsu.ac.za

T. C. Maramura
University of the Free State, Bloemfontein, South Africa



S. Kot et al. (eds.), *Corporate Practices: Policies, Methodologies, and Insights in Organizational Management*, Springer Proceedings in Business and Economics,
https://doi.org/10.1007/978-981-97-0996-0_58

## 1 Introduction

In our rapidly evolving world, the fusion of digital, physical, and biological realms is ushering in what is commonly referred to as the Fourth Industrial Revolution (4IR). This transformative era is characterized by the profound impact of emerging technologies such as artificial intelligence, blockchain, biotechnology, and the Internet of Things (IoT) on every aspect of our lives. Amidst this technological revolution, one crucial question emerges: How can these 4IR technologies be harnessed to address one of the most pressing global challenges of our time: achieving Sustainable Development Goals (SDGs)? The SDGs, adopted by the United Nations in 2015, constitute a comprehensive blueprint for a sustainable and equitable future by 2030. They encompass seventeen interconnected goals ranging from eradicating poverty and hunger to promoting quality education and fostering climate action. Achieving these ambitious objectives requires innovative approaches that leverage the potential of 4IR technologies to tackle complex and interconnected global issues for sustainability. This study delves into the pivotal role that 4IR technologies play in advancing progress towards the SDGs.

The study further explores how these cutting-edge innovations can not only catalyse economic growth but also facilitate social inclusion, environmental sustainability, and resilience in an increasingly interconnected world. As we navigate the transformative terrain of the Fourth Industrial Revolution, it is imperative to understand the multifaceted ways in which these technologies can be harnessed as powerful tools for achieving sustainable development. Schwab [1] describes the Industrial Revolution as the appearance of "new technologies and novel ways of perceiving the world that trigger a profound change in economic and social structures." The Fourth Industrial Revolution (4IR) has ushered in a transformative era defined by the convergence of digital, physical, and biological technologies, fundamentally altering how we live, work, and interact with the world. In this rapidly evolving landscape, the global community embarked on an ambitious journey to achieve the Sustainable Development Goals (SDGs) by 2030, a set of 17 interconnected objectives aimed at addressing pressing global challenges such as water, poverty, inequality, climate change, and environmental degradation [2].

As we stand at the intersection of the 4IR and the pursuit of sustainability, it is imperative to examine the pivotal role that 4IR technologies play in advancing progress toward the SDGs. This exploration is essential not only to harness the immense potential of these technologies for positive change but also to mitigate potential risks and ensure that the benefits of 4IR are distributed equitably and sustainably, leaving no one behind. This paper delves into the multifaceted relationship between 4IR technologies and the achievement of SDG 6 by shedding light on the opportunities, challenges, and strategies that can guide our path toward a more sustainable and inclusive future, especially for developing economies. Considering this background, the purpose of this study is to investigate the role of Fourth Industrial Revolution (4IR) technologies in advancing the Development Agenda (2030) of the SDGs. [2] and the World Economic Forum (2020) have been emphasizing the use of artificial intelligence for sustainable development in developing nations.

## *1.1 The Fourth Industrial Revolution (4IR) Technologies*

The Industrial Revolutions arose because of advances in science, technology, and community culture, with the goal of improving human life. Each industrial revolution has had its own characteristics and consequences [3]. The first industrial revolution, IR 1.0, began at the end of the nineteenth century with the introduction of mechanical manufacturing facilities powered by water and steam. The second, IR 2.0, which began in the early twentieth century, dealt with mass production assembly lines that required labour and electrical energy [4]. While the third industrial revolution, IR 3.0, began in the 1970s, it was distinguished using automated production through the use of electronics and information technology [4–6]. The Fourth Industrial Revolution (4IR) refers to ongoing technological advances in fields such as artificial intelligence, robotics, the Internet of Things, big data, and blockchain [7] state that World Economic Forum's founder and executive chairman, Klaus Schwab, coined the term "fourth industrial revolution" to describe a world in which people move between digital domains and offline reality using connected technology to enable and manage their lives. These technologies have the potential to have a significant impact and contribute to the achievement of the United Nations' Sustainable Development Goals (SDGs).

The Fourth Industrial Revolution (4IR) represents a new phase in the evolution of industry and technology, characterized by the convergence of digital, physical, and biological innovations [8]. Likewise, 4IR is reshaping economies, industries, and societies across the globe, with profound implications for how present and future generations will live and work. In the discussion below the study provides some key aspects of 4IR technologies which are digitalisation and connectivity. At the heart of 4IR is the pervasive use of digital technologies, including the Internet of Things (IoT), artificial intelligence (AI), blockchain, and big data analytics [6]. These technologies enable the collection and analysis of vast amounts of data, fostering greater connectivity and efficiency in various sectors. On the other hand, Artificial Intelligence (AI) is a central pillar of 4IR, encompassing machine learning, deep learning, natural language processing, and computer vision. AI systems can autonomously learn, reason, and make decisions, leading to breakthroughs in areas such as healthcare, finance, and autonomous transportation.

Advances in robotics and automation are revolutionizing industries like manufacturing, logistics, and agriculture. Robotic systems are argued to be sustainable because they can perform tasks with precision and consistency, and this resultantly leads to increased productivity and reduced labour costs. It is also important to note how the integration of biological sciences with technology is another hallmark of 4IR. This is evident in how it includes genetic engineering, bioprinting, and synthetic biology, which have the potential to transform healthcare, agriculture, and environmental sustainability. 3D Printing also known as additive manufacturing, 3D printing allows for the creation of complex, customized objects layer by layer. The potential benefits of 3D technology also have applications in aerospace, healthcare (e.g., medical implants), and the production of spare parts which can foster technology.

The advent of the Fourth Industrial Revolution (4IR) represents a profound shift in the way we live, work, and interact with our environment. This shift is characterised by the integration of advanced technologies such as artificial intelligence, blockchain, robotics, and biotechnology into various facets of society. As a result, 4IR is not only reshaping industries and economies but also holds the potential to significantly impact the global pursuit of Sustainable Development Goals (SDGs) towards 2030. In essence, 4IR technologies are revolutionising various aspects of our lives, offering immense opportunities for economic growth, and addressing societal challenges. However, the responsible and equitable deployment of these 4IR technologies is essential to ensure that the benefits are shared by all and that any potential risks are also mitigated. To ensure sustainability, this would involve balancing innovation with ethical, legal, and societal considerations as critical tasks to harness the potential of the 4IR technologies for the greater good.

## *1.2 4IR & Sustainable Development Goal (SDG) 6*

Access to clean water and sanitation is not only a fundamental human right but also essential for health, well-being, and economic development. Hence, Sustainable Development Goal 6 (SDG 6) aims to ensure the availability and sustainable management of water and sanitation for all by 2030 [9]. The Fourth Industrial Revolution (4IR) technologies play a critical role in advancing progress toward SDG 6 in several ways such as water quality monitoring, efficient water distribution, water recycling and water infrastructural maintenance technologies among various other ways highlighted below.

4IR technologies for water quality monitoring such as sensors and real-time data analytics enable the continuous monitoring of water quality in rivers, lakes, and reservoirs [10]. Evidently, this helps identify pollution sources and ensure safe drinking water supplies in line with the targets of SDG 6. [11] argues that IoT and sensor-based technologies support predictive maintenance of water infrastructure, therefore, reducing downtime, while ensuring the reliability of water supply and sanitation systems. Furthermore, smart water grids and IoT sensors can also play a critical role in detecting leaks, optimize water distribution, and reduce water losses in both urban and rural areas, which [12] indicate can enable the efficient use and distribution of water. This implies that, advanced water treatment technologies, driven by automation and artificial intelligence also have the potential to enhance the efficiency of wastewater treatment plants towards ensuring sustainable use and distribution of water. Hence, there is no doubt that, these innovations improve the quality of treated water while reducing energy consumption and operational costs in line with the SDG 6 targets.

Scholars [13, 14] argue that the utilization of satellite and remote sensing technologies also provide valuable information on water resources which have been argued to be beneficial in managing water scarcity through its efficient assessment of water availability, detecting drought conditions as well as supporting water resource planning. Consequently, 4IR technologies have also been argued to enable the development of advanced water recycling systems, which [15] argue allows treated wastewater to be reused for non-potable water purposes such as irrigation or industrial processes, which ensures a significant reduction in water demand. There are also digital platforms and data sharing platforms which encourage for collaboration among different sectors, including agriculture, industry, and urban planning, promoting integrated water resource management. Despite the significant contributions of some of these digital and technological platforms to SDG 6, challenges persist. These include issues related to data privacy, cybersecurity, and the digital divide, which can pose serious challenges to the equitable deployment of technology solutions [16]. Additionally, addressing water-related challenges often requires cross-border cooperation and policy harmonization, which can be complex to achieve.

At the crux, of it all, the Fourth Industrial Revolution technologies are invaluable tools for advancing Sustainable Development Goal 6. Their capacity to monitor, manage, and optimize water resources and sanitation systems do play a pivotal role in ensuring the availability and sustainable management of water and sanitation for all, while contributing to improved health, environmental sustainability, and economic development. Therefore, to maximize their impact, it is essential to address the challenges associated with technology acceptance and adoption to promote international cooperation in water resource management. To provide this alignment, the study applies the Technology Acceptance Model to provide deeper insights into the pivotal role that 4IR technologies play in advancing progress towards the SDGs as discussed below.

## 2 Theoretical Underpinning: Technology Acceptance Model (TAM)

According to Mugo et al. [8], the incorporation of technologies into our daily lives must be preceded by the user's acceptance of the technology. Without this effort, the technologies will be abandoned or used infrequently. Fred Davis proposed the Technology Acceptance Model (TAM) in 1985. The Theory of Reason Action (TRA) was used to develop the Technology Acceptance Model (TAM), which describes an individual's information technology (IT) acceptance behaviour. TAM's primary goal is to shed light on the processes underpinning technology acceptance to predict

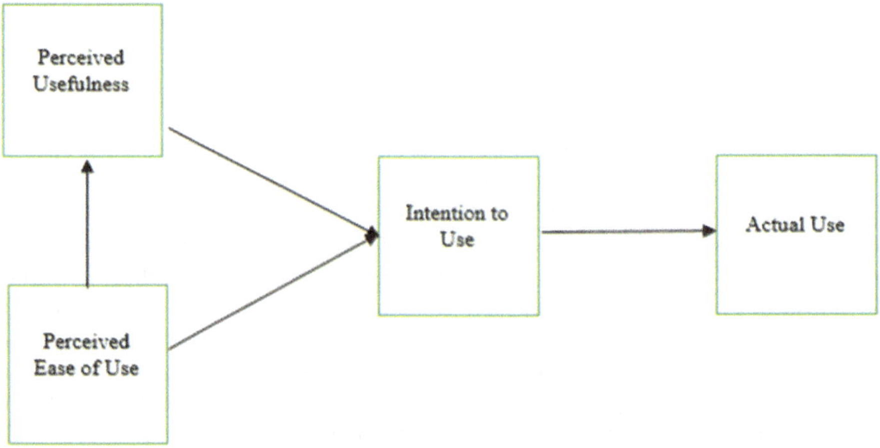


**Fig. 1** Technology acceptance theory [17]

behaviour and provide a theoretical explanation for successful technology implementation [18]. TAM defines technology acceptance as a three-stage process in which external factors (system design features) elicit cognitive responses (perceived ease of use and perceived usefulness), which in turn elicit an effective response (attitude towards using technology/intention), influencing use behaviour [13]. In other words, TAM represents behaviour as the result of perceived ease of use (PEOU), perceived usefulness (PU), and behavioural intention (Fig. 1). Therefore, in this study this theory was used to examine how users' attitudes and beliefs can influence their acceptance or rejection of 4IR technologies to achieve SDGs.

## 3 Research Methodology Parameters

The foundations of this paper warranted document-based research hinged on the grounded theory approach to research which is premised on the idea that theory is constructed from data. Thus, data were purposively and conveniently sampled from the reports and publications produced by the United Nations, World Health Organisations, the World Bank, as well as credible newspaper articles, peer-reviewed journal articles, policy papers, and books. Using grounded theory research, abstract categories on the nexus between 4IR & sustainable development were obtained from secondary data sources and fused with the Technology Acceptance Model and broken down into conceptual components as the researchers inductively theorized.

The provisions and content of the secondary data were thematically analysed to generate themes, concepts, and inferences on how the 4IR technologies can contribute toward sustainable development in achieving SDG 6. The research design for this paper was exploratory because the premise of the paper was to investigate the role of Fourth Industrial Revolution (4IR) technologies in advancing Agenda 2030 of the SDGs. Exploratory research is concerned with exploring the outcomes of a policy or institutional intervention. To this effect, the review of the 4IR & sustainable development goal 6 related documents was aimed at developing inferences to answer key questions; more specifically to generate theoretical and conceptual views on whether the role of Fourth Industrial Revolution (4IR) technologies can advance Agenda 2030 of the SDG 6. Thematic analysis of the various key documents then enabled the authors to develop the key inferences and arguments advanced in the discussion and conclusion of this paper. Thus, this paper constitutes an epistemic contribution to knowledge regarding the significance for Africa's advancement towards sustainable development through the application of 4IR tools and technological applications. The next section delves into the way the final discussions and conclusions are based on the recurrent themes in the analysed relevant pieces of literature.

## 4 Discussion: Aligning Theory of the Technology Acceptance Model (TAM) with SDG 6

The Technology Acceptance Model (TAM) is a widely recognized theory that explains how individuals adopt and use technology. It provides insights into the factors that influence the acceptance and usage of technology, which can be applied to Sustainable Development Goal 6 (SDG 6) to enhance the adoption of technology-driven solutions for water and sanitation management [1]. TAM was initially developed by Fred Davis in the late 1980s and has since evolved into various versions. TAM assumes that users' behavioural intentions to use technology are primarily determined by its perceived usefulness and ease of use. One of the most prominent versions is the original TAM, which consists of several key factors:

- Perceived Usefulness (PU): This factor represents an individual's belief that using a particular technology will enhance their performance or help them achieve specific goals. In the context of SDG 6, perceived usefulness would translate to individuals or organizations believing that adopting technology for water and sanitation management would lead to improved access, quality, and sustainability of water resources and sanitation facilities.
- Perceived Ease of Use (PEOU): This factor relates to an individual's perception of how easy it is to use a particular technology. It encompasses aspects such as user-friendliness, simplicity, and the effort required to learn and use the technology. In the context of SDG 6, perceived ease of use would involve stakeholders feeling that technology-based water and sanitation solutions are straightforward to implement and operate.
- Behavioural Intention to Use (BI): The user's willingness and intention to use the technology in the future is referred to as behavioural intention to use. It is affected by perceived usefulness as well as perceived ease of use. When users

perceive technology to be both useful and simple to use, their willingness to adopt technology-driven solutions in the context of water and sanitation will grow.
- Actual System Usage (AU): The extent to which individuals use technology in their work or daily lives is represented by actual system usage. The user's behavioural intention to use influences it. Users who intend to use a technology are more likely to do so [17].

The degree to which a user expects the use of a system or technology to be free of effort is referred to as Perceived Ease of Use (PEOU) [19]. In other words, it is the degree to which people perceive a technology to be superior to its alternatives. On the other hand, according to [19], perceived usefulness (PU) is referred to as the degree to which a user believes that using a particular system would improve his or her job performance. According to [20], Big Data and Analytics, Autonomous Robots, Simulation, Internet of Things, Augmented Reality, Additive Manufacturing, Cloud Computing, Cybersecurity, and Horizontal and Vertical System Integration are the nine pillars of Fourth Industrial Revolution technologies [21]. These Industry 4.0 technologies are collaborating to promote successful digital transformation in the water sector. Very few studies directly address Industry 4.0, particularly from the perspective of South Africa. In comparison to the rest of the world, the adoption of the Fourth Industrial Revolution in South Africa and the rest of the African continent is very low [20, 22].

In the USA, additive manufacturing (3D printing) was introduced and it does not use water for cooling or lubrication, it contributes to Industry 4.0's goal of better water management and access to clean water and sanitation (SDG 6). As a result, less water is used in production, and less wastewater is produced. Furthermore, the decentralized organization allows for the implementation of resource-efficient and flexible digitalized smart water management solutions [23]. AI can also be used to analyse and compare data inputs to large databases. This principle is used by the Brazilian start-up Status in the development of Fluid, a technology that detects leaks in large water distribution systems. The technology uses sensors to record vibrations emitted by water flowing through pipes, and then compares these sounds to a database of various noises [24]. The AI can learn to distinguish expected noises from leaks or even illegal connections, and then alert officials to potential problems. Singapore's Waterwise project, is a project that uses sensors distributed throughout the water distribution system to continuously monitor the drinking water distribution systems. They can monitor the various conditions inside the pipe in near real-time thanks to a 3G connection [25].

# 5 Application of Technology Acceptance Model to SDG 6: Considerations

The United Nations (UN) member states adopted a new sustainable development agenda in September 2015, titled "Transforming our World: The 2030 Agenda for Sustainable Development" [26]. The Sustainable Development Goals (SDGs) are a set of 17 global goals. These objectives seek to address a variety of social, economic, and environmental challenges in order to achieve a sustainable future for all by 2030 [27]. The fourth industrial revolution is transforming nations' production, organizational processes, and economic directions, necessitating a strategic approach to assessing how the revolution's technologies affect three vital resources (water, energy, and food) in the human economy [7]. The paper looks at the impact of 4IR technologies on sustainable development goals focusing on goal six.

SDG 6 aims to provide equitable access to safe drinking water and sanitation for all members of society [1]. Everyone has the right to safe, clean water in sufficient quantity and quality. Clean water is essential not only for humans, but also for plants, animals, and other related sustainable development projects [28]. According to [27] it is becoming clear that safe drinking water, sanitation, and hygiene services are critical to human health. However, unless progress accelerates dramatically, billions of people will continue to lack these essential services by 2030 [23]. Water is critical to many other aspects of sustainable development and is in jeopardy. Water demand is increasing because of rapid population growth, urbanization, and increased pressure from agriculture, industry, and the energy sector. SDG six goals must be met not only for water-related concerns, but also for other SDGs such as SDG two on zero waste and SDG 14 on life below water, as well as for the future of the Earth [22].

Understanding the perceived usefulness and ease of use of technology for water and sanitation management is crucial. This implies that all the stakeholders involved in water resource management, including government agencies, NGOs, and communities, must recognize the benefits of technology in achieving the objectives of SDG 6 for the 2030 agenda. For example, they should see how smart water meters can improve water distribution efficiency or how real-time data monitoring can enhance water quality control as argued by [29] that IoT and sensor-based technologies support predictive maintenance of water infrastructure.

The Technology Acceptance Model can also be used to enable user training and support because to promote technology adoption, it is essential to provide training and support to users [30, 31]. Thus, ensuring that individuals and organizations are comfortable with the technology and have the necessary skills to operate it can positively influence their perception of ease of use of the various 4IR technologies for sustainable development. Perception of ease of use enables continuous feedback and iteration from users which is important as this can help refine and improve technology solutions for SDG 6. Additionally, by addressing user concerns and making necessary adjustments, developers can enhance both perceived usefulness and ease of use of the technological tools and application.

The introduction of digital domains and offline reality using connected technology to enable and manage the lives of human beings' ushers in a fair share of resistance from the users, arguably due to fear of the unknown. This implies that, promoting awareness about the potential benefits of technology adoption for SDG 6 becomes a critical component for ensuring its success in ensuring the sustainability of water resource management [14]. However, promoting awareness can include demonstrating successful case studies and showcasing how technology has improved water and sanitation management in different contexts, all which can boost perceived usefulness. Marikyan and Papagiannidis [17] highlight that promoting awareness of the potential benefits of technology also help to recognize and address any potential barriers to technology adoption, such as fear of technology adoption, cost, infrastructure limitations, and privacy concerns. There is no doubt that, by mitigating these barriers, stakeholders can enhance the perceived usefulness and ease of use of technology solutions for ensuring the sustainable development of water resource management.

The technologies of the Fourth Industrial Revolution have the potential to make a major contribution to the achievement of Sustainable Development Goal 6 in ensuring the accessibility and availability of clean water and sanitation. This is evident with the Bhagirathi River in India, which is monitored using Internet of Things (IoT) sensors, which collect data on water quality and transmit it to a central database. The functionality of these sensors allows authorities to respond quickly in the event of a pollution or non-revenue water incident. This shows that these technologies, such as artificial intelligence, the Internet of Things, and blockchain do have the potential to improve water management, efficiency, and accessibility. They can also empower communities, boost data-driven decision-making, and improve the quality of water monitoring. Nonetheless, despite the enormous future potential, there are several challenges that must be addressed. These consist of limited access to technology in some regions, high implementation costs, and the possibility of job displacement.

By applying the principles of the Technology Acceptance Model (TAM) to SDG 6, stakeholders can better understand and address the factors that influence the adoption and use of technology-driven solutions for water and sanitation management [32]. This, in turn, can contribute to more effective and sustainable efforts in achieving the targets of SDG 6, particularly in ensuring the availability and sustainable management of water and sanitation for all. Additionally, addressing water-related challenges often requires cross-border cooperation and policy harmonization, which can be complex to achieve [28]. This simply implies that; the Fourth Industrial Revolution technologies are invaluable tools for advancing Sustainable Development Goal 6 [22]. The capacity of 4IR technologies to monitor, manage, and optimize water resources and sanitation systems plays a pivotal role in ensuring the availability and sustainable management of water and sanitation for all, contributing to improved health, environmental sustainability, and economic development [29].

Hence, to maximize their impact, it is essential to address the challenges associated with technology adoption and promote international cooperation in water resource management. This means that collaboration and knowledge sharing will play key roles in encouraging collaboration among different stakeholders, such as technology developers, policymakers, and communities, can facilitate the integration of technology into water and sanitation management strategies. With the existence of various digital platforms and data sharing platforms which encourage for collaboration among different sectors, including agriculture, industry, and urban planning, promoting integrated water resource management, sharing all this knowledge and best practices can enhance overall technology acceptance [29].

## *5.1 Recommendations*

The Fourth Industrial Revolution, characterised by advancements in artificial intelligence, big data analytics, the Internet of Things (IoT), and automation, presents innovative solutions to long-standing water and sanitation issues in Africa. These technologies offer the capacity to enhance water quality monitoring, improve water supply and distribution systems, optimise wastewater treatment processes, and facilitate data-driven decision-making in water resource management. Moreover, 4IR technologies can increase efficiency and cost-effectiveness in water and sanitation projects, making it possible to extend services to underserved and remote areas. However, it is also crucial to acknowledge that the adoption and integration of 4IR technologies into SDG 6 initiatives in Africa are not without challenges. There are concerns about the digital divide, unequal access to technology, and the need for capacity building and infrastructure development, hence the study was aligned with the TAM. Moreover, issues related to data privacy and cybersecurity must also be carefully managed to ensure the responsible use and application of 4IR for sustainable water resource management.

To fully harness the potential of 4IR technologies for SDG 6, collaborative efforts are required from governments, international organizations, the private sector, and civil society. This multidisciplinary approach has the potential to foster holistic solutions that consider both the technological and societal aspects of SDG 6. In summary, policymakers, businesses, and civil society need to work together to ensure that these technologies are deployed equitably and in a way that promotes sustainable development while not harming the environment or exacerbating inequalities. Subsidies for technology adoption in underserved areas, the establishment of technology hubs, and the provision of training and support can all help bridge the digital divide. Investments in education and training programs, infrastructure development, and policy frameworks that promote innovation and technology transfer are essential. Additionally, promoting partnerships and knowledge-sharing across borders can also potentially help developing nations to leverage the experiences and best practices of others in implementing 4IR-driven solutions for water and sanitation management.

# 6 Conclusion

Fourth Industrial Revolution technologies offer Africa a unique opportunity to accelerate progress toward achieving Sustainable Development Goal 6, ensuring clean water and sanitation for all. While challenges exist, with a commitment to inclusivity, innovation, and collaboration, Africa can pave the way for a more sustainable and water-secure future for its people. The journey toward SDG 6 achievement in the era of 4IR technologies represents not just a developmental goal but also a transformative vision for the continent's water and sanitation sector. In conclusion, the examination of the role of Fourth Industrial Revolution (4IR) technologies in achieving Sustainable Development Goal 6 (SDG 6) in Africa underscores the immense potential and transformative power that these technologies hold for addressing the continent's water and sanitation challenges. As developing nations in Africa grapple with complex issues related to clean water accessibility, sanitation infrastructure, and water resource management, 4IR technologies emerge as promising tools to accelerate progress toward SDG 6.

## *6.1 Limitations*

The analysis presented in this study is based on the information available; however, technological advances and policy changes may have occurred. Hence, this study is limited to providing a broad overview of the Fourth Industrial Revolution's potential for SDG 6. Specific challenges and opportunities may differ depending on region, content, and context of other sustainable development goals. The scope of the research is limited because it does not include in-depth case studies or empirical data on technology adoption in specific countries or regions, which could have provided more nuanced insights.

# References


1. Hoque. F.: 4th Industrial Revolution: Impact and Challenges (2019a)
2. UNESCO: Artificial intelligence in education: challenges and opportunities for sustainable development. Working Paper on Educational Development No (2019b)
3. Yingi, E., Hlungwani, P.M., Nyagadza, B.: The Fourth Industrial Revolution (4IR) in the heart of the SDG agenda: the role of education in Zimbabwe. Africa Rev. **14**(2), 213–229 (2022)
4. Eleyyan, S.: The future of education according to the fourth industrial revolution. J. Educ. Technol. Online Learn. **4**(1), 23–30 (2021)
5. Dino, M., Ong, I.: Research, technology, education & scholarship in the Fourth Industrial Revolution [4IR]: influences in nursing and the health sciences. J. Med. Invest. **66**, 3–7 (2019)
6. Gleason, N.: Singapore's higher education systems in the era of the Fourth Industrial Revolution: preparing lifelong learners. In: Higher Education in the Era of the Fourth Industrial, Chapter 7, pp. 145–169. Palgrave Macmillan, Singapore (2018)

7. Xu, M., David, J., and Kim, S.: The Fourth Industrial Revolution: opportunities and challenges. Int. J. Financ. Res. **9**, 90. https://doi.org/10.5430/ijfr.v9n2p90 (2018)
8. Mugo, D., Njagi, K., Chemwei, B., Motanya, J.: The Technology Acceptance Model (TAM) and its application to the utilization of mobile learning technologies. Br. J. Math. Comput. Sci. **20**, 1–8 (2017). https://doi.org/10.9734/BJMCS/2017/29015
9. Ortigara, A.R.C., Kay, M., Uhlenbrook, S.: A review of the SDG 6 synthesis report 2018 from an education, training, and research perspective. Water **10**(10), 1353 (2018)
10. Hoosain, M.S., Paul, B.S., Ramakrishna, S.: The impact of 4IR digital technologies and circular thinking on the United Nations sustainable development goals. Sustainability **12**(23), 10143 (2020)
11. Hoosain, M.S., Paul, B.S., Doorsamy, W., Ramakrishna, S.: The influence of circular economy and 4IR technologies on the climate–water–energy–food Nexus and the SDGs. Water **15**(4), 787 (2023)
12. Viswanathan, R., Telukdarie, A.: The role of 4IR technologies in waste management practices-a bibliographic analysis. Procedia Comput. Sci. **200**, 247–256 (2022)
13. Mhlanga, D.: Human-centered artificial intelligence: the superlative approach to achieve sustainable development goals in the fourth industrial revolution. Sustainability **14**(13), 7804 (2022)
14. Mhlanga, D.: The role of artificial intelligence and machine learning amid the COVID-19 pandemic: What lessons are we learning on 4IR and the sustainable development goals. Int. J. Environ. Res. Public Health **19**(3), 1879 (2022)
15. Mbiza, M., Sinha, S.: The Fourth Industrial Revolution: conceptual paradox or catalyst for achieving the Sustainable Development Goals? S. Afr. J. Sci. **119**(7/8) (2023)
16. Sadoff, C.W., Borgomeo, E., Uhlenbrook, S.: Rethinking water for SDG 6. Nat. Sustain. **3**(5), 346–347 (2020)
17. Marikyan, D., Papagiannidis, S.: Technology acceptance model: a review. In: Papagiannidis, S. (ed.), TheoryHub Book. http://open.ncl.ac.uk. ISBN: 9781739604400 (2023)
18. Mhlanga, D.: Artificial intelligence and machine learning for energy consumption and production in emerging markets: a review. Energies **16**(2), 745 (2023)
19. Amadu, L., Muhammad, S., Mohammed, A., Owusu, G., Lukman. S.: Using technology acceptance model to measure the use of social media for collaborative learning in Ghana. J. Technol. Sci. Educ. JOTSE. **8**(4), 321–336. Online ISSN: 2013–6374. Print ISSN: 2014–5349 https://doi.org/10.3926/jotse.383 (2018)
20. Omotayo, A., Telukdarie, A.: Industry 4.0 and Water Industry: A South African Perspective and Readiness (2020)
21. Ojo, T.A.: Digital financial inclusion for women in the Fourth Industrial Revolution: a key towards Achieving Sustainable Development Goal 5. Afr. Rev. **14**(1), 98–123 (2022)
22. Kufeoglu, S.: SDG-6 Clean Water and Sanitation. https://doi.org/10.1007/978-3-031-07127-0_8 (2022)
23. Popović, A.: Implications of the Fourth Industrial Revolution on Sustainable Development. Sci. Rev. Article. https://doi.org/10.5937/ESD2001045P (2020)
24. Sinha, S., Lutchman, V.: Transdisciplinary education: enabling the sustainable development goals using the Fourth Industrial Revolution. In: Sustainable Development in Africa: Fostering Sustainability in one of the World's Most Promising Continents, pp. 149–161. Springer International Publishing, Cham (2021)
25. Dlodlo, N., Mofolo, M., Kagarura, G.: Potential Applications of the Internet of Things in Sustainable Rural Development in South Africa (2012)
26. UN (United Nations): Transforming our World: The 2030 Agenda for Sustainable Development (2015)
27. United Nations: The 2030 Agenda and the Sustainable Development Goals: An opportunity for Latin America and the Caribbean (LC/G.2681-P/Rev.3), Santiago (2018)
28. Islam, M.F., Awal, M.R., Zaman, R.: The concurrent journey of Sustainable Development Goals (SDGs) and fourth Industrial Revolution (4IR): paradoxical or parallel. SDMIMD J. Manag. **13**(1), 61 (2022)

29. Mishra, H., Maheshwari, P.: Achieving sustainable development goals through Fourth Industrial Revolution: an Indian perspective. Indian J. Commer. Manage. Stud. **11**(2), 63–75 (2020)
30. Ebekozien, A., Aigbavboa, C., Emuchay, F.E., Aigbedion, M., Ogbaini, I.F., Awo-Osagie, A.I.: Urban solid waste challenges and opportunities to promote sustainable developing cities through the fourth industrial revolution technologies. Int. J. Build. Pathol. Adapt. (2022)
31. Alshomali, I., Gulseven, O.: A Note on SDG 6—Clean Water and Sanitation for All. https://doi.org/10.13140/RG.2.2.16461.38881 (2020)
32. Mpofu, F.Y.: Taxation of the digital economy and direct digital service taxes: opportunities, challenges, and implications for African countries. Economies **10**(9), 219 (2022)

# A Test of an Instrument for Measuring the Model of White Supply Chain Management for Sustainable Performance in the Food Industry

**Waraporn Suksanchananun, Wornchanok Chaiyasoonthorn, and Singha Chaveesuk**

**Abstract** The food industry competition has changed to supply chain competition, which requires sustainability through environmental and ethical awareness. So, the researcher redefines environmental awareness, social responsibility, and ethical practice throughout the upstream to the downstream supply chain by applying the theory of color psychology to become white supply chain management. This research aimed to test an Instrument for measuring the model of white supply chain management for sustainable performance in the food industry by studying, examining, and reviewing the literature in the form of books, journals, and related research to develop questions used as an instrument for collecting data from a sample group of the food industry in Thailand. The instrument was validated by five research and statistics experts in the food industry. The index of item objective congruence (IOC) for all questions was more than 0.5, indicating the instrument's usability. Afterward, the researchers performed a pilot study to test the instrument's reliability and make improvements. The improved questionnaire was then utilized to collect data from 30 samples, after which the collected data were calculated to assess the reliability by analyzing with Cronbach's alpha coefficient at a confidence interval of 95%. The analysis results showed that the Cronbach's alpha coefficient was 0.966 overall, which was at an acceptable level. Thus, the instrument could be used to measure the factors influencing the model of white supply chain management for sustainable performance in the food industry.

**Keywords** White supply chain management · Sustainable performance · Food industry

---

W. Suksanchananun (✉) · W. Chaiyasoonthorn · S. Chaveesuk
KMITL Business School, King Mongkut's Institute of Technology Ladkrabang, Bangkok 10520, Thailand
e-mail: waraporn.stou@gmail.com

 
S. Kot et al. (eds.), *Corporate Practices: Policies, Methodologies, and Insights in Organizational Management*, Springer Proceedings in Business and Economics,
https://doi.org/10.1007/978-981-97-0996-0_59

## 1 Introduction

In Thailand, food processing is one of the important industries because this industry uses the most amount of labor, has the highest investment value and highest added value, and has a highly increased investment in research and development compared to various kinds of Thai manufacture manufacturing industry [1]. Thailand is also a country with food production from upstream, midstream, and downstream that is ready to be the world's kitchen. Factors that make Thai food highly potent are the availability of sufficient raw materials to feed into the industry, the quality of raw materials, and most manufacturers' skills, technology, and competitive price structure. However, Thailand is one of many countries that have the potential to compete in producing quality food. Today, many countries can gain a competitive advantage in this industry. Therefore, the supply chain management process must be balanced [2].

However, to support the trend of sustainable supply chain management in 2018, Mr. Brian Pasco, Executive Director of Client Coverage, Commercial Banking. HSBC Bank, Therefore, we surveyed 'Navigator: Now, next and how for business' from more than 8,500 companies in 34 markets worldwide [3]. Rethinking their supply chain management is more sustainable. Both ethical and environmental aspects in the supply chain of business organizations. With the aim of financial returns, Transparency is a factor in selecting new suppliers. Nearly 31% of companies worldwide plan to drive sustainability changes in their supply chains over the next three years. This creates a sustainable, ethical, or environmental change in the business organization's supply chain. The primary motivation is cost optimization 84%, financial performance improvement, and revenue increase (84%). This trend is due to increasing customer pressure to make the company's raw material allocation process more sustainable and transparent. According to the survey, approximately 80% of the company's environmental impact in its supply chain reflects that evidence of green credentials by key suppliers and business partners is a critical factor in determining environmental friendliness. It affects the reputation and performance of the company. Over 26% of the companies surveyed took Transparency as a critical criterion. When recruiting new suppliers, consumers want to know the sources of raw materials and how to manage people, animals, and the environment in the production process.

Investors are also increasing pressure on companies to disclose their sustainability practices. This is reflected from the survey results that 85% of companies want to operate businesses that meet sustainability standards accepted in the business industry or the market. Therefore, companies in emerging market countries are firmly committed to raising ethical and environmental standards. More than one in five businesses (21%) in emerging markets plan to raise their standards further in the next two years, or 15% of businesses in developed markets. With one-fifth of companies (20%) saying their companies have tightened their supply chain governance policies over the past two years, this reflects the ideal opportunity for businesses to Evaluate their supply chain network and manage it for more sustainability. This will help businesses remain competitive in increasingly demanding commercial situations. Some companies' plans have been fulfilled, with 17% of surveyed companies claiming their companies have been able to reduce their environmental impact in the past two years. Besides sustainability, there must also be social responsibility. In Thailand in 2020, Thaipat Institute assessed the corporate social responsibility direction of entrepreneurs, collectively that "Sustainability entrepreneurship" as information for the agency and business organizations in using it as a guideline to promote entrepreneurship and sustainability and in order to deliver shared value to the stakeholders, including shareholders, employees, customers, suppliers, local communities and society [4].

From the literature review, the researcher incorporated green supply chain management, corporate social responsibility, and ethics as components of white supply chain management. Therefore, this study aims to build a tool including 16 latent and 47 observed variables and examine the reliability and validity of a conceptual framework of the model of white supply chain management on sustainable performance in the food industry.

## 2 Literature Review

This section describes the theories and background of green supply chain management, corporate social responsibility, ethic, color theory, social pressure, and sustainability performance.

### *2.1 Green Supply Chain Management*

Green Supply Chain Management means managing all activities to operate efficiently, the environmental impact reduction throughout the supply chain since the source and the procurement process of raw materials Product and service design Production process, service until products and services reach the customer. Logistics Bureau, the Department of Primary Industries and Mines, has divided the components of green supply chain activities into green design, green supply, green manufacturing, green marketing, green consumption, green transportation/distribution, green communication and green reversed logistics [5].

A literature review found that Sarkis and Joseph divided the components of supply chain management by function. They divided them into green supplier and vendor management, internal green operations management, green logistics, and reverse logistics [6].

However, many scholars have applied green supply chain management to their research, and researchers reviewed the literature and selected eight papers related to elements of green supply chain management to create a table and find latent variables from duplicated latent variables more than half. The researcher derived latent variables of green supply chain management as follows: green purchasing, green manufacturing, green distribution, internal environmental management, and investment recovery.

## 2.2 Corporate Social Responsibility

Corporate Social Responsibility (CSR) has been mentioned since the 1950s. In 1958, Theodore Levitt mentioned two corporate social responsibilities: (1) to engage in face-to-face civilities such as honesty and good faith and (2) to seek material gain after World War II, CSR became more and more known, and in the 1960s, the academic world has begun to focus on saying that "CSR was defined as seriously considering the impact of the company's actions on society." It is an important duty for executives to make decisions to protect society at the same time and protect their interests, which is done voluntarily [7]. Archie B. Carroll divides CSR into four parts: economic responsibilities, legal responsibilities, ethical responsibilities, and philanthropic responsibilities.

In addition, the composition of CSR can also be categorized according to Porter and Kramer [8], which includes moral obligation, sustainability, license to operate, and reputation [9]. However, many scholars have applied CSR to their research, and researchers reviewed the literature and selected eight papers related to elements of CSR to create a table and find latent variables from duplicated latent variables more than half. The researcher derived latent variables of CSR as follows: safety and economic responsibility.

## 2.3 Ethics

Ethics and Social Responsibility have different meanings. *Ethics* is a management decision involving individual ethics, organizational factors (i.e., organizational culture, compliance, and codes of ethics), and situational factors. Social Responsibility will be a decision that considers stakeholders and society [10]. However, both ethics and Social Responsibility are used in supply chain management research to solve problems such as conflict of interest, sustainability, product safety, fair labor practices, and issues related to socially desirable outcomes (other issues related to socially desirable outcomes) [11].

In addition, The Supply Chain Management Association (SCMA) organization has defined the Code of Ethics at three levels:

Level A: Standards of conduct are the basic customary practices with the Third Party, consisting of avoidance of conflicts of interest, protection of confidential or sensitive information, business relationships, gifts, gratuities, hospitality inducements, and environmental and social responsibilities.

Level B: Professional Principles are practice guidelines that include professional competency, professionalism, honesty and integrity, responsible management, serving the public good, and compliance with legal obligations.

Level C: Governance and compliance is an important guideline to be followed, and if it does not conform to or conflict with Level B, choose to comply with Level C, which includes part I. member compliance and part II—complaint procedures. However, many scholars have applied ethics supply chain management to their research, and researchers reviewed the literature and selected eight papers related to elements of ethics supply chain management to create a table and find latent variables from duplicated latent variables more than half. The researcher derived latent variables of ethical supply chain management: honesty, justice, and respect for rights.

## 2.4 Concepts of Color

*Color* is an element that represents an organization. It is derived from the colors of the design symbols to create memories in the hearts of consumers [12]. Eiseman presented the meaning of color and its effect on mood and feelings. White is pure, calm, and simple. Yellow is warmth, friendship, and fun. Green is calm, natural, and lively. Orange is creativity, confidence, cheerfulness, and fun. Red is fervor, exciting, challenging, and price-influenced [13].

However, some scholars have applied the meaning of color based on psychology to management theory, such as Edward de Bono's Six Action Shoes and Chanchaochai's White Ocean Strategy.

**From the emotional and psychological meaning of the color, the concept is applied to supply chain management in a clean and healthy perspective, thus creating a White Supply Chain Management, meaning that It is the management of various activities from the purchase of raw materials or the service from the seller and then transformed into goods to delivery and distribution to customers. Being aware of the environment, Social responsibility, and ethical conduct throughout the supply chain from upstream to downstream consists of green supply chain management, corporate social responsibility, and ethical supply chain management.**

## 2.5 Social Pressure

Companies have to face environmental aspects incl, including ecosystems, climate, and natural resources, which all affect the supply chain management within the organization, such as balancing products that will use renewable energy at an affordable price and removal of water contaminants arising from production processes. These are the Social pressures, which consist of natural capital, environmental regulations, and pressure from customers on the performance of the organization [14]. Literature reviews show that social pressure affects green supply chain management, corporate social responsibility, ethical supply chain management, and Sustainability Performance.

### 2.6 Sustainability Performance

Sustainability means operating a business to make it profitable and being responsible for social and environmental. At the same time, the organization must also be responsible to shareholders, employees, customers, and communities, enabling it to grow despite changes in industry, society, and the physical environment. Innovation can be added and reduce operational risk [15]. The essential elements of sustainability have three aspects, which are the environment, society, and economy [16]. Also, scholars have mentioned sustainability objectives, referring to three performance levels, defined as the Triple Bottom Line, or the 3P, which each company must try to jointly maximize: profit, planet, and people [17]. From the literature review, it is known that green supply chain management, corporate social responsibility, and ethical supply chain management affect sustainability performance.

### 2.7 Conceptual Framework Diagram

From the literature review, the research conceptual framework is shown in Fig. 1.

## 3 Method

This paper focuses on testing an instrument for measuring the model of the white supply chain management model for sustainable performance in the food industry as Fig. 2.

Figure 2 shows the procedure for research instrument as follows:

1. Collected data from relevant concepts, theories, and research in order to prepare the questionnaire structure.
2. Collected relevant concepts, theories, and research to acknowledge the relationships among endogenous latent, exogenous latent and observed variables. In the study, there were 16 latent variables, 47 observed variables, and 70 questionnaire items in total. Figure 3 shows the 16 latent variables and 47 observed variables.
3. Prepared questionnaires in compliance with the studied structure. Then, they were brought to 5 experts, i.e. academicians and executives of the Food Industry, to find the index of item-objective congruence (IOC) so as to examine congruence

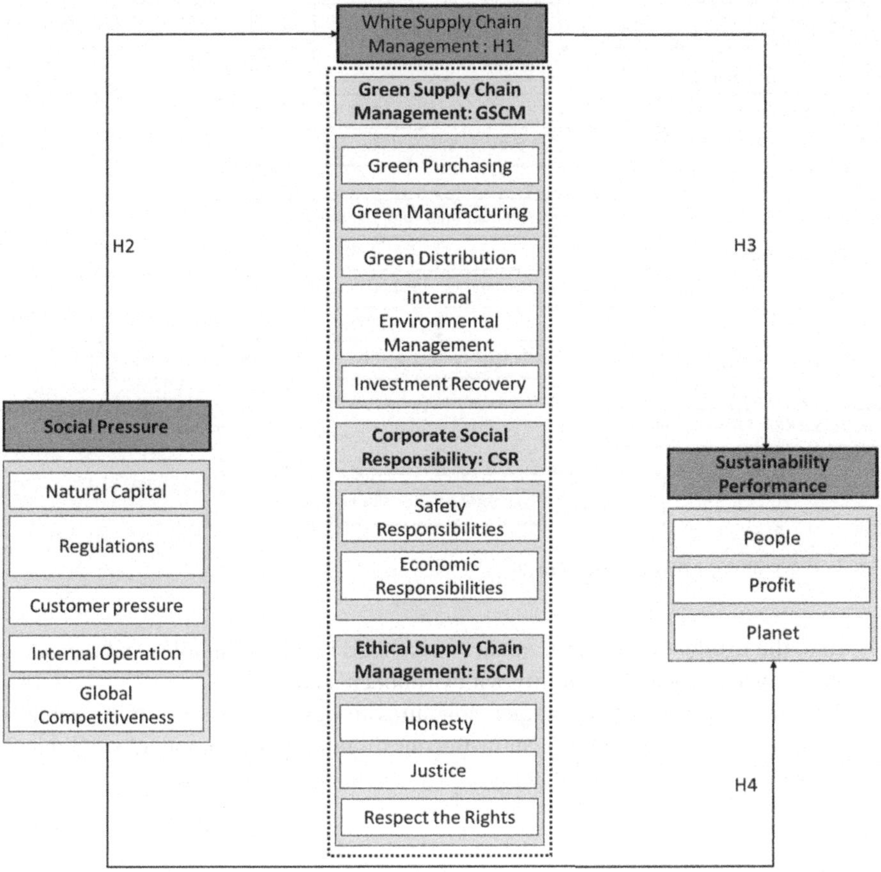


**Fig. 1** The conceptual framework

among the questions, compared with the research objectives, as well as to observe whether or not they were congruent with the research problems. The values were expected to be between 0.5–1.0. If lower than 0.5, the questions had to be improved in order to be congruent with the objectives (Turner and Carlson, 2003).

4. Revised questionnaires as suggested by the experts.
5. Tested the revised questionnaires on 30 samples before actual use so as to examine the clarity and congruence of the questions in terms of whether or not they went the same way. The 30 samples will select from 12 food manufacturers by lottery method, which is Sample Random Sampling. The informants will be 2–3 persons from middle to high-level executives of companies such as plant managers, division managers, presidents, vice presidents, and chief executives in each selective manufacturer.

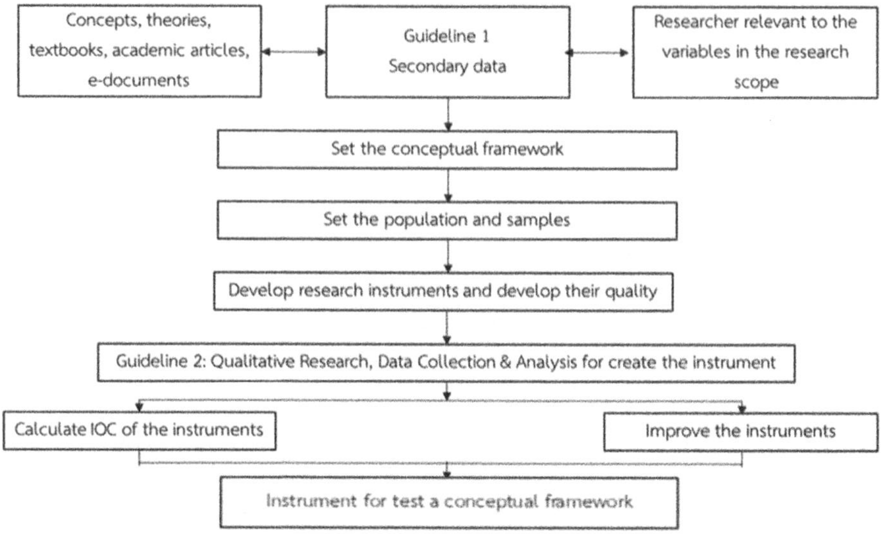


**Fig. 2** Procedure for research instrument

6. Took the results of the questionnaires answered by all 30 samples and measured their consistency and reliability with Cronbach's alpha,
7. Revised/improved the tested questionnaires to develop the ones to be actually used to collect data. Table 1. Show the questionnaire development, and Table 2. Shows the 70 questionnaire items as well as the testing values.

## 4 Result

**This research examined latent and observed variables with the validity and reliability of 70 questionnaire items, developed based on a literature review (Table 1) using a 5-point Likert rating scale. The questionnaire was validated by five experts who were academics and executives in the food industry to establish reliability through the index of item-objective congruence (IOC). Subsequently, the questionnaire was improved according to the experts' suggestions before evaluating 30 samples. The respondents completed the questionnaire either online or offline. The data were used to examine the reliability using the criterion that Cronbach's alpha coefficient should not be lower than 0.7.** After using the questionnaire with an honest group of 30 samples, the result of the internal congruence analysis with Cronbach's alpha (α-coefficient) of the whole questionnaire was 0.966, which was significantly higher than 0.7 [36], indicating the high reliability of the instrument.

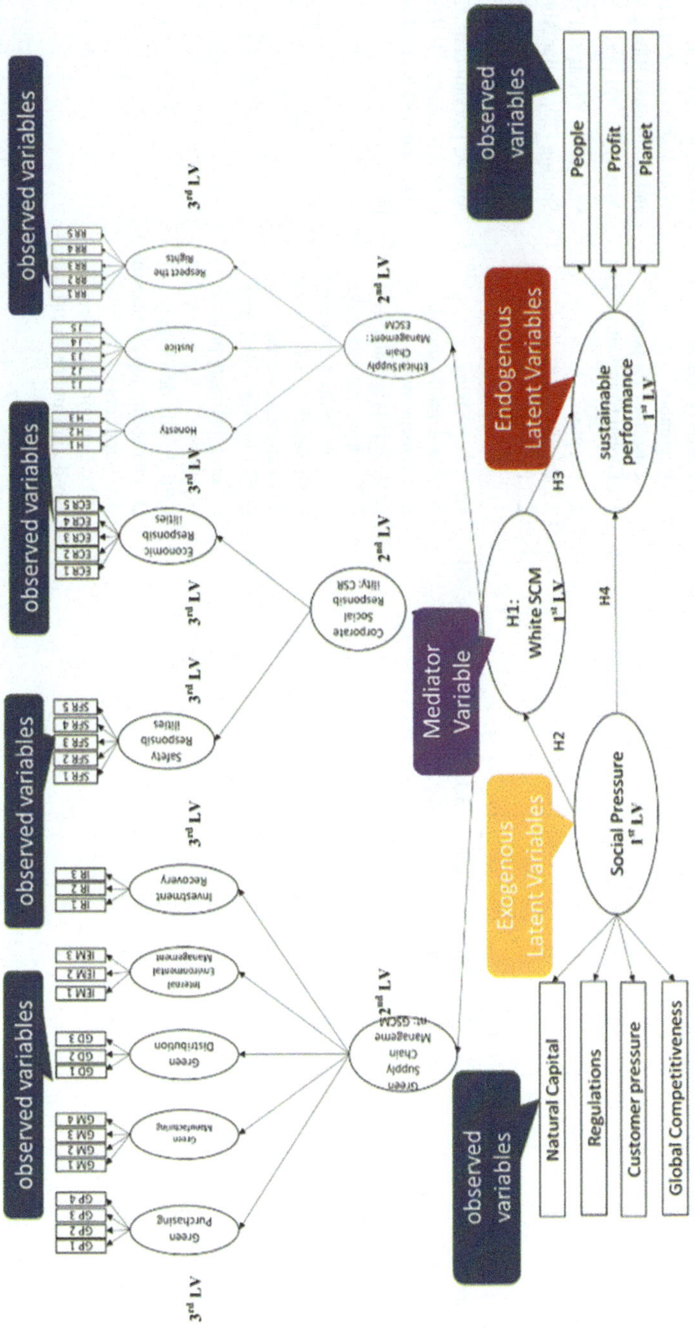


**Fig. 3** The variables in the study

**Table 1** Development of questionnaire items from previous research

| 1st Latent variables | 2nd Latent variables | 3rd Latent variables | Observe variables | Development of questionnaire items from previous research |
|---|---|---|---|---|
| 1. Social pressure | – | – | 1.1 Natural Capital<br>1.2 Regulation<br>1.3 Customer Pressure<br>1.4 Global Competitiveness | Daniel S. F. [14], K. Mathiyazhagan et al. [18], and Constantin Blome and Antony Paulraj [19] |
| 2. Sustainable performance | – | – | 2.1 People<br>2.2 Profit<br>2.3 Planet | Sadaat Ali Yawar and Stefan Seuring [20], Jaffar Abbas et al. [21], and Zabihollah Rezaee [22] |
| 3. White supply chain management | 3.1 Green Supply Chain Management | 3.1.1 Green Purchasing (GP) | GP1: Purchasing environmentally sound materials/products<br>GP2: Certifying suppliers<br>GP3: Organizations make available to their customers<br>GP4: Supplier environmental audit and assessments<br>GP5: Environmental criteria for designating approved suppliers<br>GP6: Jointly developing cleaner technology/processes with suppliers<br>GP7: Engaging suppliers in eco-design and product/process innovation | Aref A. Hervani et al. [23], C. W. Hsu and A. H. Hu [24], and Sarkis and Joseph [6] |

(continued)

**Table 1** (continued)

| 1st Latent variables | 2nd Latent variables | 3rd Latent variables | Observe variables | Development of questionnaire items from previous research |
|---|---|---|---|---|
| | | 3.1.2 Green Manufacturing (GM) | GM1: Establish an environmental risk management system for GSCM<br>GM2: Establish an environmental database of products<br>GM3: Green Product/Service<br>GM4: Green Packaging | C. W. Hsu and A. H. Hu [24], Sarkis and Joseph [6], and Bureau of Logistics DPIM [5] |
| | | 3.1.3 Green Distribution (GD) | GD1: There is a development of transportation to reduce greenhouse gas emissions to a minimum<br>GD2: There is a reduction in energy consumption and time that may affect the environment<br>GD3: Track and monitor emissions caused in distributing products | Bureau of Logistics DPIM [5], Sibel Yildiz Cankaya and Bulent Sezen [25], and Thi Tam Le [26] |
| | | 3.1.4 Internal Environmental Management (IEM) | IEM1: There are green operations within the organization<br>IEM2: There are environmental objectives and policies<br>IEM3:Setting up an environmental management system | Sarkis and Joseph [6], Bureau of Logistics DPIM [5], and Sibel Yildiz Cankaya and Bulent Sezen [25] |

(continued)

**Table 1** (continued)

| 1st Latent variables | 2nd Latent variables | 3rd Latent variables | Observe variables | Development of questionnaire items from previous research |
|---|---|---|---|---|
| | | 3.1.5 Investment Recovery (IR) | IR1:Raw material and supplier's products supported environment by "Re's" (reclaim, reuse, remanufacture, recycle)<br>IR2: Establishing a recycling system for used and defective products<br>IR3: Investment recovery (sale) of excess inventories/materials | Sarkis and Joseph [6], Bureau of Logistics DPIM [5], and Sibel Yildiz Cankaya and Bulent Sezen [25] |
| | 3.2 Corporate Social Responsibility | 3.2.1 Safety Responsibility (SFR) | SFR1: Product Safety<br>SFR2: Transportation Safety<br>SFR3: Accidents at work<br>SFR4: Promoting the health and safety<br>SFR5: Appropriate response to accidents and breakdowns | Michael J Maloni and Michael E. Brown [27], Hutchins and Sutherland [28], and Maciej Urbaniak [29] |

(continued)

**Table 1** (continued)

| $1^{st}$Latent variables | $2^{nd}$Latent variables | $3^{rd}$Latent variables | Observe variables | Development of questionnaire items from previous research |
|---|---|---|---|---|
| | | 3.2.2 Economic Responsibility (ECR) | ECR1: Economic development in communities<br>ECR2: Ensuring a stable legal and financial situation and dissemination of reliable information<br>ECR3: satisfy customers with goods and services of real value<br>ECR4: earn a fair return on the funds entrusted to the corporation by its investors<br>ECR5: diversify the economic interests of citizens | Michael J Maloni and Michael E. Brown [27], Maciej Urbaniak [29], and Roslan Abdul Hakim et al. [30] |
| | 3.3 Ethical Supply Chain Management | 3.3.1 Honesty (H) | H1: Be honest with everyone, relationships within the organization<br>H2: Be honest with every relationship outside the organization<br>H3: Prohibit Bribery, corruption, Extortion, Misappropriation | Supaporn Pisarnbut [31], SCMA [32], and Ong Choon Hee [33] |

(continued)

**Table 1** (continued)

| 1st Latent variables | 2nd Latent variables | 3rd Latent variables | Observe variables | Development of questionnaire items from previous research |
|---|---|---|---|---|
| | | 3.3.2 Justice (J) | J1: Non-discrimination<br>J2: Giving everyone good quality, Cost-effective for products and services<br>J3: Fair business competition<br>J4: Fair trade and production<br>J5: Price collusion | Supaporn Pisarnbut [31], Yahaya Yusuf et al. [34], and Ong Choon Hee [33] |
| | | 3.3.3 Respect for Rights (RR) | RR1: Considering the benefit and rights of others<br>RR2: Health care and safety of employees within the workplace<br>RR3: No violate human rights, Labor rights protection<br>RR4: Confidentiality of employee's personal information and supplier's identity is protected<br>RR5: Intellectual property rights are to be respected | Supaporn Pisarnbut [31], Yahaya Yusuf et al. [34], and Jossineter Syengo [35] |

## 5 Conclusion

This paper focuses on testing an instrument for measuring the model white supply chain management model for sustainable performance in the food industry based on Green Supply Chain Management, Corporate Social Responsibility, Ethics, Social Pressure, and Sustainability Performance. As the findings are acceptable because they are more significant than 0.70, these provided 58 observed variables and 70 questions for exam one latent and one mediator insights into the factors influencing sustainable performance. In future work, this tool was used for testing structural equation modeling to find more profound insight. In further research, our model of white supply chain management for sustainable performance will be validated by structural equation modeling techniques. However, this research is the first to create a white supply chain management model, causing limitations in the literature review. There is no direct amalgamation of literature under "White Supply Chain Management." Therefore, it is necessary to review literature that uses theory about color to conjunct with management theory and then connects it to become White Supply Chain Management.

## Annex

See Table 2.

**Table 2** List of latent variables, observed variables, and assessment of reliability

| Latent variables | Observed variables | Questions | Cronbach's alpha |
|---|---|---|---|
| 1.Social Pressure | 1.1 Natural Capital | 1. Natural disasters such as droughts, floods, earthquakes have forced companies to transform their operations by adopting more innovation or technology | 0.883 |
| | | 2. Natural disasters such as droughts, floods, earthquakes have forced companies to transform their operations by adopting more innovation or technology | |
| | | 3. The depleting natural resources such as oil require companies to transform their operations by incorporating more innovation or technology | |

(continued)

**Table 2** (continued)

| Latent variables | Observed variables | Questions | Cronbach's alpha |
|---|---|---|---|
| | | 4. Depleting natural resources, such as oil, forced companies to transform their operations by shrinking the company or reducing the number of employees | |
| | 1.2 Regulation | 1. Governments or relevant authorities have regulations in various areas related to social responsibility, environment and business ethics (e.g. labor law, environmental law), and forcing companies to adopt more innovation or technology | |
| | | 2. Governments or relevant authorities have various regulations and regulations related to social responsibility, environment and business ethics (e.g. labor laws, environmental laws) that require companies to change their operations by reducing the size of the company or reduce the number of employees | |
| | | 3. Government or related agencies have rules and regulations in various fields of research and development of products, services or company operations. Therefore, the company has to change its operations by using more innovation or technology | |
| | | 4. Government or related agencies have rules and regulations in various fields of research and development of products, services or company operations. Therefore, the company had to change its operations by reducing the size of the company or reducing the number of employees | |
| | 1.3 Customer Pressure | 1. Customers want the company to produce products with environmentally friendly processes and meet international environmental standards requirements | |

(continued)

**Table 2** (continued)

| Latent variables | Observed variables | Questions | Cronbach's alpha |
|---|---|---|---|
| | | 2. Customers want products made from environmentally friendly raw materials and meet the requirements of international environmental standards | |
| | | 3. Customers want the company to have a system to transport raw materials and products with the least impact on the environment | |
| | 1.4 Global Competitiveness | 1. The Company's direct and indirect competitors are always effective in improving your Company's processes | |
| | | 2. The Company's direct and indirect competitors always affect the research and development of the Company's products or services | |
| | | 3. The Company's direct and indirect competitors have always influenced the Company's investments in technology, equipment and machinery | |
| 2.Sustainable performance | 2.1 People | 1. The Company's operating model can increase customer satisfaction | 0.942 |
| | | 2. The Company's operating model can create a better image from outsiders | |
| | | 3. The Company's operating model can build better relationships with stakeholders in the community | |
| | | 4. The company's operating model encourages employees to receive more training to increase their knowledge | |
| | | 5. The Company's operating model encourages employees to have occupational health and more safety | |
| | | 6. The Company's operating model enables stakeholders such as employees, communities and society to receive more welfare benefits | |
| | 2.2 Profit | 1. The company's operating model can reduce the cost of materials purchased | |

(continued)

**Table 2** (continued)

| Latent variables | Observed variables | Questions | Cronbach's alpha |
|---|---|---|---|
| | | 2. The company's operating model can reduce the cost of energy consumption | |
| | | 3. The company's operating model can generate increased earnings per share | |
| | | 4. The Company's operating model can generate more return on investment | |
| | | 5. The company's operating model can generate more sales | |
| | | 6. The company's operating model can increase overall profit | |
| | 2.3 Planet | 1. The Company's operating model encourages the improvement of the internal environment of the Company such as adequate lighting, ventilation, and accommodation for employees | |
| | | 2. The company's operating model reduces the amount of water or air pollution emissions | |
| | | 3. The company's operating model causes employees to have less exposure to hazardous materials such as chemicals | |
| | | 4. The Company's operating model reduces the rate of environmental accidents such as gas explosions caused by heat accumulation | |
| 3.White Supply Chain Management | | | |
| 3.1 Green Supply Chain Management | | | 0.949 |
| 3.1.1 GP | GP1 | 1. The company selects suppliers that are certified to produce or sell environmentally friendly products | |
| | GP2 | 2. The company purchases materials or products that are environmentally friendly | |
| | GP3 | 3. The company has an environmental audit and assessment of its suppliers | |
| | GP4 | 4. The company cooperates and supports suppliers to develop technology and production processes or use environmentally friendly raw materials | |

(continued)

**Table 2** (continued)

| Latent variables | Observed variables | Questions | Cronbach's alpha |
|---|---|---|---|
| 3.1.2 GM | GM1 | 1. The company has established an environmental risk management system | |
| | GM2 | 2. The company has established a product environmental database | |
| | GM3 | 3. The company has a production process that is environmentally friendly according to international standards such as ISO14000, etc | |
| | GM4 | 4. The Company designs and uses packaging made from environmentally friendly raw materials. recycled raw materials or natural materials | |
| 3.1.3 GD | GD1 | 1. The Company has developed a transportation system to reduce greenhouse gas emissions to a minimum | |
| | GD2 | 2. The company has a distribution method that reduces the use of energy that affects the environment, such as building a warehouse to reduce transportation time | |
| | GD3 | 3. The company always monitors and monitors the emissions arising from the distribution of goods | |
| 3.1.4 IEM | IEM1 | 1. The company has in-house environmentally-friendly practices such as Lean and Green, Total Quality Environmental Management: TQEM, inventory management, material substitution and process modification, reduction of paperwork | |
| | IEM2 | 2. The Company's management participates in and supports environmental practices such as setting environmental policies | |
| | IEM3 | 3. The company has established a standardized environmental management system | |
| 3.1.5 IR | IR1 | 1. The Company takes raw materials and products purchased from suppliers to reclaim, reuse, remanufacture and recycle when there is an error in the production process | |

(continued)

**Table 2** (continued)

| Latent variables | Observed variables | Questions | Cronbach's alpha |
|---|---|---|---|
| | IR2 | 2. The Company has in place a recycling system for used and defective products | |
| | IR3 | 3. The company distributes inventory or raw materials by means or special prices. In the event that the company orders more inventory or raw materials than meets the requirements or does not meet the specified specifications | |
| 3.2 Corporate Social Responsibility | | | 0.845 |
| 3.2.1 SFR | SFR1 | 1. Products manufactured by the company must be safe for use | |
| | SFR2 | 2. Transportation of the Company's products must be safe | |
| | SFR3 | 3. The Company has a system to prevent accidents at work, such as keeping the workplace safe, preventing accidents and occupational diseases | |
| | SFR4 | 4. The company promotes the health and safety of employees | |
| | SFR5 | 5. The Company is responsible for accidents and losses incurred to employees, communities and society | |
| 3.2.2 ECR | ECR1 | 1. The Company takes part in promoting the economy within the community, such as hiring employees in the surrounding areas to work | |
| | ECR2 | 2. The company has accounting and financial standards | |
| | ECR3 | 3. The Company has values in developing products and services that are worthwhile to deliver to customers | |
| | ECR4 | 4. Investors receive fair returns (such as dividends) | |
| | ECR5 | 5. The Company distributes economic benefits appropriately in accordance with the legal framework, such as tax payment on the sale of goods at reasonable prices | |

(continued)

**Table 2** (continued)

| Latent variables | Observed variables | Questions | Cronbach's alpha |
|---|---|---|---|
| 3.3 Ethical Supply Chain Management | | | 0.905 |
| 3.3.1 H | H1 | 1. The Company has established a good relationship within the Company with honesty with all employees | |
| | H2 | 2. The Company has established good relationship with customers and all stakeholders with honesty | |
| | H3 | 3. The company has strong rules and ethics, such as prohibiting bribery, corruption, extortion, embezzlement | |
| 3.3.2 J | J1 | 1. The company promotes fairness in its operations, such as non-discrimination against close employees | |
| | J2 | 2. The company produces quality products and services. worth the price | |
| | J3 | 3. The company promotes fair business competition | |
| | J4 | 4. The company has a policy to conduct business with fairness | |
| | J5 | 5. The Company has no policy to set unsuitable prices such as price wars, price rigging in various competitions | |
| 3.3.3 RR | RR1 | 1. The Company takes into account the benefits and rights of customers, employees, communities and society | |
| | RR2 | 2. The company provides proper protection of labor rights according to the law | |
| | RR3 | 3. The company promotes operations that do not violate human rights, such as respecting political opinions | |
| | RR4 | 4. The Company maintains the confidentiality of personal information of employees or related persons | |
| | RR5 | 5. The Company respects the intellectual property of others, such as not infringing, not copying without permission | |

## References


1. EEC Homepage. http://eec.vec.go.th/en-th/About-EEC/10-TargetIndustries/5-OriginalIndustrieswithPotential-First-S-curve. Last accessed 31 May 2020
2. Bus & Truck Homepage. https://www.busandtruckmedia.com/1669/. Last accessed 31 May 2020
3. Efinancethai Homepage. https://www.efinancethai.com/LastestNews/LatestNewsMain.aspx?release=y&ref=M&id=dTNJK0JmaWNjRWc9. Last accessed 31 May 2020
4. Smartsme Homepage. https://www.smartsme.co.th/content/233620. Last accessed 1 June 2020
5. Bureau of Logistics DPIM.: Green Supply Chain Logistics Management: Change and Innovation in Future Business. Best Practice Project for the Green Supply Chain of the target industry for export. Charansanitwong Printing Co., Ltd., Bangkok (2015)
6. Sarkis, J.: Green Supply Chain Management. Momentum Press (2014)
7. Archie, B.C.: Carroll's pyramid of CSR: Taking another look. Carroll Int. J. Corp. S. Responsib. **1** (2016)
8. Porter, M.E. and Kramer, M.R.: Strategy & Society: The Link between Competitive Advantage and Corporate Social Responsibility. Harvard Business Review (2006)
9. Noknoi, C.: Corporate social responsibility: Concept and experiences. Univ. Thai Chamber Commer. J. **3**(35), 154–163 (2015)
10. Ferrell, O.C., Fraedrich, J., Ferrell, L.: Business ethics: Ethical decision making and cases. 9th edn. South-Western Cengage Learning, Mason, OH (2013)
11. Ferrell, O.C., Rogers, M.M., Ferrell, L., Sawayda, J.: A framework for understanding ethical supply chain decision making. J. Mark. Channels **20**, 260–287 (2013)
12. Kijtham, W.: Influence of color on branding. NIDA Communication and Management Journal **1**(1), 76–85 (2015)
13. Eiseman.: Pantone guide to communicating with color. Grafix Press, Ltd., USA (2000)
14. Fogel, D.S.: Strategic Sustainability a Natural Environmental Lens on Organizations and Management. Routledge, New York (2016)
15. Wheelen, T.L., Hunger, J.D., Hoffman, A.N., Bamford, C.E.: Strategic Management and Business Policy: Globalization, Innovation, and Sustainability. 15th edn. Pearson, New York City (2018)
16. Modrák, V., Dima, I.C., Man, M.: Methodical approach to corporate sustainability planning. Pol. J. Manage. Stud. **3**, 156–166 (2011)
17. Valeria, B., Alberto, G.: Sustainable Operations and Supply Chain Management, 1st edn. Wiley, West Sussex, UK (2017)
18. Mathiyazhagana, K., Govindanb, K., Haqa, A.N.: Pressure analysis for green supply chain management implementation in Indian industries using analytic hierarchy process. (2014)
19. Constantin Blome, C., Paulraj, A.: Ethical climate and purchasing social responsibility: A benevolence focus. J. Bus. Ethics **116**, 567–585 (2012)
20. Yawar, S.A., Seuring, S.: Management of social issues in supply chains: A literature review exploring social issues, actions and performance outcomes. J. Bus. Ethics **141**, 621–643 (2015)
21. Jaffar, A., Shahid M., Hashim A., Muhammad, A. R., Ghaffar, A., Jaffar, A., Shaher, B., Mohammad, N.: The effects of corporate social responsibility practices and environmental factors through a moderating role of social media marketing on sustainable performance of business firms. Sustain. J. **11**(3434) (2019)
22. Rezaee, Z.: Supply chain management and business sustainability synergy: A theoretical and integrated perspective. Sustain. J. **10**(275), 1–17 (2018)
23. Hervani, A.A., Helms, M.M., Sarkis, J.: Performance measurement for green supply chain management. Benchmarking Int. J. **12**(4), 330–353 (2005)
24. Hsu, C.W., Hu, A.H.: Green supply chain management in the electronic industry. Int. J. Environ. Sci. Tech. **5**(2), 205–216 (2008)
25. Cankaya, S.Y., Sezen, B.: Effects of green supply chain management practices on sustainability performance. J. Manuf. Technol. Manage. **30**(1), 98–121 (2019)

26. Le, T.T.: The effect of green supply chain management practices on sustainability performance in Vietnamese construction materials manufacturing enterprises. Uncertain Supply Chain Manage. **8**, 43–54 (2020)
27. Maloni, M.J., Brown, M.E.: Corporate social responsibility in the supply chain: An application in the food industry. J. Bus. Ethics **68**, 35–52 (2006)
28. Hutchins, M.J., Sutherland, J.W.: An exploration of measures of social sustainability and their application to supply chain decisions. J. Cleaner Prod. **16**, 1688–1698 (2008)
29. Urbaniak, M.: The role of the concept of corporate social responsibility in building relationships in the supply chain. Sci. J. Logistics **11**(2), 199–205 (2015)
30. Hakim, R.A., Taib, C.A.B., Md, Hossain, T.B., Naim, J., Md.: Social responsibility in global supply chain: Research trend from 1999 to 2014. Int. J. Supply Chain Manag. **6**(4) (2017)
31. Pisarnbut, S.: Business Ethics. V.J. Printing, Bangkok (2001)
32. SCMA Homepage, https://www.uvic.ca/purchasing/assets/docs/code-of-ethics.pdf. Last accessed 31 May 2020
33. Hee, O.C.: The implement of EICC code of conduct in the electronics industry supply chain in Malaysia. Int. J. Manag. Value Supply Chains (IJMVSC) **5**(2) (2014)
34. Yusuf, Y., Hawkins, A., Musa, A.: Ethical supply chains: Analysis, practices and performance measures. Int. J. Logistics Syst. Manag. **17**(4), 472–496 (2014)
35. Syengo, J.: Ethical Practice and Supply Chain Performance at Kenya Revenue Authority. School of Business, University of Nairobi (2015)
36. Cronbach, L.J.: Essentials of Psychological Testing, 5th edn. HarperCollins, New York (1990)

# Thresholds of Sustainability: Analyzing the Interplay Between Carbon Dioxide Emissions, Economic Growth, and Urbanization in the European Union

**Jana Chovancová, Igor Petruška, and Peter Adamišin**

**Abstract** This study addresses the pressing issue of climate change and the drivers behind it by exploring the relationship between carbon dioxide ($CO_2$) emissions and various economic indicators within the context of 22 European countries from 1992 to 2019. Using threshold models, this research aims to uncover nonlinear dynamics often overlooked in linear analyses, shedding light on critical thresholds that affect $CO_2$ emissions. The economic indicators encompass gross domestic product (GDP), energy consumption, renewable energy, nuclear energy, urban population, and energy import dependency. The findings of this study reveal significant threshold effects associated with GDP and urbanization. Notably, as GDP per capita crosses the threshold of $37,000, the effectiveness of renewable energy sources in reducing $CO_2$ emissions diminishes, challenging the assumption of a linear relationship between economic growth and environmental protection. Similarly, exceeding an urban threshold of 82.626% leads to a reduced impact of renewables on $CO_2$ reduction, highlighting the intricate interplay between urban dynamics and emissions mitigation. Furthermore, the analysis indicates that beyond the identified GDP threshold, the influence of energy consumption on $CO_2$ emissions escalation is curtailed. These insights underscore the importance of transitioning to cleaner energy sources and adopting energy-efficient technologies, as well as focusing on sustainable urbanization. Such policies can help reconcile economic development with environmental sustainability and contribute to the global effort to combat climate change.

**Keywords** Economic development · Urbanization · $CO_2$ emissions · Thresholds

---

J. Chovancová (✉) · I. Petruška · P. Adamišin
Faculty of Management and Business, University of Prešov, 08001 Prešov, Slovakia
e-mail: jana.chovancova@unipo.sk

I. Petruška
e-mail: igor.petruska@unipo.sk

P. Adamišin
e-mail: peter.adamisis@unipo.sk

 
S. Kot et al. (eds.), *Corporate Practices: Policies, Methodologies, and Insights in Organizational Management*, Springer Proceedings in Business and Economics,
https://doi.org/10.1007/978-981-97-0996-0_60

## 1 Introduction

In the face of escalating global concerns over environmental sustainability and the imperative to address climate change, the interplay between economic indicators and environmental outcomes has assumed a paramount role in policy discourse. Given the current EU situation, characterized by ambitious climate targets and a commitment to transition towards a low-carbon economy, understanding the dynamics between economic activities and environmental impact takes on heightened significance.

The EU's endeavor to achieve carbon neutrality by 2050 [1] and the commitment to substantial reductions in greenhouse gas emissions underscore the pressing need to dissect the drivers behind $CO_2$ emissions. This paper situates itself within this context by investigating the associations between $CO_2$ emissions and critical economic variables, including Gross Domestic Product (GDP), Energy consumption, Renewable energy utilization, Nuclear energy production, Urban population growth, and Energy import dependency. These indicators not only serve as markers of economic progress but also bear considerable implications for environmental preservation within the EU.

Exploring the relationship between economic activities and their environmental consequences is a well-established domain within the academic literature, both theoretically and empirically substantiated. A prominent theory, the Kuznets Curve, posits that environmental degradation, including $CO_2$ emissions, tends to worsen in the early stages of economic growth but eventually ameliorates as economies attain a turning point and higher income levels. This infers that once a particular level of economic development is achieved, societies prioritize environmental quality and implement measures for emissions mitigation. Pioneering work by Grossman and Krueger (1991) applied the Environmental Kuznets Curve (EKC) theory to analyze the environmental impacts of the North American Free Trade Agreement [2]. Their work laid the foundation for many empirical studies across diverse regions and time frames, enriching our understanding of this complex relationship. While some studies offer practical support for the EKC hypothesis [3–8], others have failed to find such confirmation [9].

Amid growing global concerns about climate change and the urgent need for environmental sustainability, the intricate relationship between economic indicators and environmental outcomes has gained prominence. This relationship becomes particularly vital within the European Union (EU), given its ambitious climate targets and commitment to transitioning toward a low-carbon economy. The EU's pursuit of carbon neutrality by 2050 [1] and its pledge to significantly reduce greenhouse gas emissions underscore the critical necessity of understanding the factors influencing $CO_2$ emissions.

This study addresses this imperative by examining the associations between $CO_2$ emissions and critical economic variables, including Gross Domestic Product (GDP), energy consumption, renewable energy utilization, nuclear energy production, urban population growth, and energy import dependency. By exploring the validation of EKC theory in the EU within a broader context, this study fills a significant empirical research gap. This holistic approach enables us to capture multifaceted relationships previously unexamined in such depth within the European Union context.

The study also overcomes the methodological gap, employing sophisticated threshold models. This analytical framework enables the identification of threshold effects, unveiling the critical points at which shifts occur in the interplay between economic progress and environmental impact. The application of threshold models in empirical studies has yielded valuable insights. For instance, research by [10] explored the effect of urbanization on $CO_2$ emissions in China using a threshold regression model, revealing strong heterogeneity in the impact of urbanization on $CO_2$ emissions in terms of urban population sizes. Additionally, Pilatowska et al. [11] employed threshold cointegration analysis to explain the differences in the dynamic linkage between $CO_2$ emissions and economic growth. Petruška et al. [12] used a nonlinear panel threshold model along with a continuous kink model to evaluate the relationship between $CO_2$ emissions and primary energy consumption across 28 European countries at varying levels of Gross Domestic Product (GDP). Their findings reveal a notable trend: as GDP levels ascend, the regression coefficient depicting the association between $CO_2$ emissions and energy consumption experiences a diminishing effect. These studies underscore the effectiveness of threshold models in uncovering nuanced relationships that might otherwise remain obscured by linear analyses. By doing so, this study aims to unearth the subtle dynamics that govern these relationships and shed light on the potential triggers for shifts in $CO_2$ emissions patterns. Such insights hold the promise of informing targeted policy interventions that harmonize economic advancement with ecological integrity.

## 2 Data and Methods

This study examines the factors influencing $CO_2$ emissions, encompassing energy consumption, renewable energy utilization, nuclear energy consumption, Gross Domestic Product (GDP), and energy import dependency. The analysis is based on data from 22 European countries, spanning 1992–2019. The choice of the sample period 1990–2019 in this study is due to data availability and reliability of analyzed variables. This period provides a substantial historical perspective spanning three decades, which is conducive to examining long-term trends and relationships among variables. The countries included in the analysis are Austria (AUT), Belgium (BEL), Bulgaria (BGR), Czech Republic (CZE), Denmark (DNK), Finland (FIN), France (FRA), Germany (DEU), Greece (GRC), Hungary (HUN), Ireland (IRL), Italy (ITA), Luxembourg (LUX), Netherlands (NLD), Poland (POL), Slovenia (SVN), Slovak Republic (SVK), Spain (ESP), Romania (ROU), Portugal (PRT), Sweden (SWE), and the United Kingdom (GBR). The interrelationships amongst these nine variables were scrutinized, with the following metrics serving as the focal points of analysis:

- Carbon dioxide ($CO_2$) emissions per capita (tons)—$CO_2$;
- Gross Domestic Product (GDP) per capita (thousands USD)—GDP;
- Total energy consumption per capita (MWh)—TEC;
- Energy produced from renewable sources per capita (MWh)—RES;
- Urban population (% of total population)—Urban;
- Energy import dependency (%)—En Imp Dep.

The data were sourced from publicly available databases: The World Bank provided data on GDP per capita, the Global Carbon Atlas provided data on $CO_2$ emissions per capita in tons, and Our World in Data supplied data on Total energy consumption per capita in MWh, urban population as a percentage of the total population, energy produced from renewable sources in MWh per capita, and energy produced in nuclear power plants in MWh per capita. Finally, Eurostat served as a source for data on Energy import dependency, Energy intensity, and industry share on GDP (including construction).

These variables were chosen based on their direct relevance to the study's objectives and their anticipated potential to influence $CO_2$ emissions. The fundamental aim of our analysis lies in unraveling the relationships interwoven between these selected variables and the subsequent impact they exert on $CO_2$ emissions. This endeavor contributes significantly towards fostering a nuanced comprehension of the intricate determinants that shape emissions patterns across diverse European nations. In the preliminary phase, a broad spectrum of variables was initially considered for inclusion into the analysis:

- Energy produced in nuclear power plants per capita (MWh)—Nuclear;
- Energy intensity: Primary energy consumption per GDP (kWh/$)—Ener in;
- Industry (including construction)—value added (% of GDP)—Ind incl constr.

However, to meet the prerequisite conditions for the models employed, balanced data became imperative. Regrettably, the variables Ener in and Ind incl constr did not fulfill this criterion. Due to the absence of nuclear power plants in numerous European countries, the Nuclear variable was omitted from our regression variables and exclusively utilized as a threshold marker. Summary statistics for all these variables are captured in Table 1, furnishing a consolidated overview that serves as a foundational reference for our subsequent analyses.

The correlation matrix, detailed in Table 2, is a pivotal depiction of the interrelationships among the variables under scrutiny. Consistent with our expectations, the most pronounced correlation emerges between the $CO_2$ and TEC variables. This alignment substantiates the anticipation that carbon emissions are inherently linked to the quantum of total energy consumption.

Interestingly, the analysis reveals instances where statistically significant correlations are absent. Specifically, this absence is observed in three cases: (1) between Ener imp dep and RES—signifying that the degree of energy import dependency isn't intrinsically linked to the generation of energy from renewable sources; (2) between Ener imp dep and Urban, suggesting that energy import dependency doesn't

**Table 1.** Summary statistics

| Variable | Units | Obs | Mean | Std. Dev | Min | Max |
|---|---|---|---|---|---|---|
| $CO_2$ | Tons p.c. | 616 | 8.7841 | 3.7209 | 3.8184 | 31.2529 |
| GDP | Thousands USD p.c. | 616 | 30.4055 | 17.0579 | 4.5041 | 124.5905 |
| RES | MWh p.c. | 616 | 4.2591 | 5.3936 | 0.0547 | 26.5391 |
| TEC | MWh p.c. | 616 | 44.3453 | 17.2329 | 17.9200 | 114.6322 |
| Nuclear | MWh p.c. | 616 | 4.6372 | 5.7222 | 0 | 23.3852 |
| Urban | % of total population | 616 | 72.0927 | 12.4618 | 49.13 | 98.041 |
| Enimpdep | % | 616 | 52.8225 | 27.1079 | −50.618 | 99.598 |

Own processing—in Stata

**Table 2.** Correlation matrix

| | $CO_2$ | GDP | RES | TEC | Urban | Nuclear |
|---|---|---|---|---|---|---|
| $CO_2$ | | | | | | |
| GDP | 0.3848*** | | | | | |
| RES | −0.2240*** | 0.2230*** | | | | |
| TEC | 0.7540*** | 0.5231*** | 0.2784*** | | | |
| Urban | 0.3841*** | 0.4553*** | 0.1214*** | 0.6464*** | | |
| Nuclear | −0.1679*** | −0.055 | 0.4620*** | 0.3551*** | 0.3261*** | |
| Enimpdep | 0.2289*** | 0.2740*** | −0.0424 | 0.1951*** | −0.0506 | 0.0796* |

*Note* *—sig. level 0.1, **—sig. level 0.05, ***—sig. level 0.01
Own processing—in Stata

inherently correlate with urban population proportions; (3) the lack of a substantial correlation between Nuclear and GDP underscores that the extent of nuclear energy utilization isn't significantly linked to Gross Domestic Product values.

Substantial multicollinearity among the independent variables can introduce uncertainty into the model's results. To ascertain the extent of multicollinearity, a comprehensive analysis of the variables was conducted utilizing the Variance Inflation Factor (VIF). The ensuing VIF values are detailed in Table 3, providing a concise representation of the degree of multicollinearity amongst the variables under examination.

The literature offers a range of recommendations concerning acceptable levels of the Variance Inflation Factor (VIF). A commonly cited threshold is a maximum VIF value of 10 [13]. Alternately, some researchers propose a more conservative ceiling, such as 5, e.g. [14], while others advocate for an even lower value of 4, e.g., [15].

In the context of our analysis, the calculated VIF values do not exceed these stipulated benchmarks. This indicates a notably low multicollinearity among the

**Table 3.** Variance Inflation Factor (VIF)

| Variable | VIF |
|---|---|
| TEC | 2.27 |
| Urban | 2.13 |
| GDP | 1.89 |
| Nuclear | 1.73 |
| RES | 1.49 |
| Enimpdep | 1.21 |
| Mean VIF | 1.79 |

Own processing—in Stata

variables in our model, reinforcing the reliability and robustness of our analysis. In the pursuit of our subsequent analysis, we will employ the following methodologies:

- Pooled Model: The pooled model is employed as a foundation for our analysis, serving as a benchmark against which the threshold models will be contrasted. This approach aggregates data from all countries, disregarding potential heterogeneities, to derive an overarching assessment of the relationships among the variables under study.
- Threshold Models: The threshold models introduce a nuanced perspective to our analysis. In these models, specific variables—GDP, Urban, Nuclear, and Energy import dependency—are designated as threshold variables. These variables are expected to have a discernible impact on $CO_2$ emissions beyond certain threshold values. The utilization of threshold models allows for the identification of critical tipping points where the dynamics of these variables engender significant shifts in $CO_2$ emissions patterns. This approach enhances our capacity to dissect the intricate interdependencies and non-linear effects within the dataset.

Prior to delving into the application of the threshold model, we begin by showcasing the outcomes derived from the linear regression analysis. The R-squared value attains a noteworthy magnitude, standing at 0.8862. Notably, all coefficients present statistical significance, except of the case of Enimpdep as evidenced in Table 4.

In summary, the linear regression analysis show that the growth of variables including GDP, RES, Urban, Nuclear, and Enimpdep correspondingly contributes to a reduction in the amplitude of $CO_2$ emissions. Conversely, an escalation in the TEC variable correlates with an increase in emissions.

## 3 Results and Discussion

Subsequently, we explored models incorporating threshold variables: GDP, Urban, Nuclear, and Enimpdep. These models allow us to identify critical points where changes in the threshold variables lead to significant shifts in the behaviour of $CO_2$

**Table 4.** Linear regression

| $CO_2$ | Coef. |
|---|---|
| GDP | −0.0161*** |
| RES | −0.2272*** |
| TEC | 0.2395*** |
| Urban | −0.0417*** |
| Nuclear | −0.2402*** |
| Enimpdep | −0.0024 |
| Cons | 3.8724*** |

*Note* *—sig. level 0.1, **—sig. level 0.05, ***—sig. level 0.01
Own processing—in Stata

emissions. By integrating these models into our analysis, we aim to uncover nuanced dynamics that underlie the complex interplay between economic indicators and $CO_2$ emissions.

## *3.1 Threshold Variable—GDP*

In this context, it is important to note that this model possesses the potential to encompass up to two distinct thresholds. The estimation of these thresholds, along with their associated confidence intervals, has been outlined in Table 5. The trim parameter, denoted as trim (0.01 0.01), was chosen to ensure the robustness of our analysis. Notably, the calculated threshold values exhibit remarkable proximity to each other.

To validate the proposed threshold values, a bootstrap test was conducted with parameters (300, 300). The outcomes of this test are presented in Table 6. In cases where the p-value associated with the Single option falls below 0.05, while the p-value linked to the Double option exceeds 0.05, the model with a single threshold value, specifically 37.2862, as the preferred model for further exploration. Consequently, this search shall encompass two distinctive regimes.

For the computation of the regression coefficients within the panel threshold model, the Stata module xthreg was employed. The outcomes of this calculation are explicitly delineated in Table 7. However, due to a conformity error, the variable Nuclear was omitted from this calculation.

**Table 5.** Threshold estimator (GDP)

| Model | Threshold | Lower | Upper |
|---|---|---|---|
| Th-1 | 37.2862 | 37.230 | 37.4406 |
| Th-21 | 37.1622 | 33.3469 | 37.2845 |
| Th-22 | 33.5257 | | 33.7438 |

Own processing—in Stata

**Table 6.** Threshold effect test (bootstrap = 300 300)—GDP

| Threshold | F-stat | p-value |
|---|---|---|
| Single | 330.65 | 0.0000 |
| Double | 92.60 | 0.1967 |

Own processing—in Stata

**Table 7.** $CO_2$ model threshold variable—GDP

| Dependent: $CO_2$ | | GDP threshold: 37.2862 | | | |
|---|---|---|---|---|---|
| | | Coef | P>\|z\| | 95% confident interval | |
| Region1 | GDP | −0.0326 | 0.000 | −0.0401 | −0.0251 |
| | RES | −0.2843 | 0.000 | −0.3256 | −0.2430 |
| | TEC | 0.2583 | 0.000 | 0.2471 | 0.2684 |
| | Urban | 0.0433 | 0.000 | 0.0230 | 0.0636 |
| | Enimpdep | −0.0020 | 0.331 | −0.0061 | 0.0020 |
| Region2 | GDP | −0.0412 | 0.000 | −0.0473 | −0.0350 |
| | RES | −0.1590 | 0.000 | 0.2024 | −0.1157 |
| | TEC | 0.1991 | 0.000 | 0.1888 | 0.2094 |
| | Urban | 0.0765 | 0.000 | 0.0559 | 0.0972 |
| | Enimpdep | 0.0004 | 0.878 | −0.0058 | 0.0049 |
| | cons | −3.4594 | 0.000 | −4.9249 | −1.9940 |

Own processing—in Stata

Upon scrutinizing the outcomes of the threshold model incorporating GDP as the designated threshold variable, several crucial observations come to the fore.

Remarkably, the coefficients for all variables, except Enimpdep, exhibit significant statistical implications. However, it is noteworthy that for both the GDP and Urban variables, there emerges a certain degree of overlapping in the confident intervals, possibly indicating a degree of confounding.

The results of this study provide valuable insights into the complex interplay between economic growth, urbanization, and environmental impact in European Union (EU) countries.

Notably, a clear threshold effect becomes apparent in the cases of the RES and TEC variables. Specifically, as GDP per capita surpasses the threshold value of $37,000, there is a discernible reduction in the impact of renewable energy utilization on the decline of $CO_2$ emissions. This shift suggests that beyond this threshold, the influence of renewable energy adoption on reducing carbon emissions becomes less pronounced. The diminishing effectiveness of renewables beyond the established GDP threshold raises essential policy implications. As economies become more affluent, other factors, such as shifts in consumption patterns, increased energy demand, or changes in industrial structures, may divert attention and resources away from low-carbon practices. Consequently, achieving sustainability goals may require tailored interventions considering the intricate dynamics of economic development and environmental preservation.

Furthermore, the TEC variable, upon crossing the established GDP threshold, engenders a notable reduction in the influence of energy consumption on the escalation of $CO_2$ emissions. This nuanced finding underscores that beyond the identified GDP threshold, an increase in energy consumption manifests a relatively diminished effect on the subsequent increase in carbon emissions. Similar results were confirmed by the study of [16], suggesting that particularly as the economy enters a phase of rapid development, with constraints on energy infrastructure and energy-efficient technologies, its swift economic growth and heightened energy consumption often occur in tandem. In such cases, improvements in energy efficiency can paradoxically lead to an energy rebound effect [17]. This effect can exacerbate energy consumption and, consequently, contribute to increased carbon dioxide emissions.

These findings align with the notion that increasing economic growth doesn't inherently translate to more effective environmental protection, as proposed by the Environmental Kuznets Curve (EKC) hypothesis [18, 19]. The Environmental Kuznets Curve hypothesis suggests an initial increase in environmental degradation with economic growth, followed by a turning point where environmental quality improves as economic development reaches a certain level. However, our observation of the diminishing effectiveness of renewables as GDP per capita surpasses $37,000 indicates that the relationship between economic growth and environmental protection is dynamic. Economic growth may not necessarily lead to increased sustainability or reduced emissions beyond a certain point. This aligns with the results of [20] suggesting that enhanced financial stability within the EU might have unintended negative consequences for environmental quality, potentially affecting regions beyond the borders of individual countries [21].

These threshold effects significantly impact our understanding of the relationship between economic progress and environmental preservation.

Policymakers must be cautious about assuming a linear relationship between affluence and environmental preservation. Instead, they should consider implementing targeted measures to ensure economic development aligns with sustainability goals, especially in advanced economies.

In the context of our findings, higher economic development could foster a transition away from certain low-carbon practices due to shifts in consumption patterns, increased energy demand, or variations in industrial structures. From a practical perspective, these findings emphasize the importance of nuanced strategies and targeted interventions to ensure that economic growth aligns with sustainable environmental outcomes rather than assuming a linear positive correlation between development and environmental protection.

**Table 8.** Threshold estimator (urban)

| Model | Threshold | Lower | Upper |
|---|---|---|---|
| Th-1 | 82.626 | 82.435 | 82.630 |
| Th-21 | 82.482 | 82.368 | 82.503 |
| Th-22 | 81.514 | 80.972 | 81.528 |

Own processing—in Stata

**Table 9.** Threshold effect test (bootstrap = 300 300)—Urban.

| Threshold | F-stat | p-value |
|---|---|---|
| Single | 421.98 | 0.000 |
| Double | 151.5 | 0.103 |

Own processing—in Stata

## 3.2 *Threshold Variable—Urban*

Once more, our analysis leads us to the exploration of two potential thresholds, a process that holds significant implications in the context of the Urban threshold model. The outcomes of this estimation, along with their associated confidence intervals, are presented in Table 8. Mirroring the methodology utilized in the previous model, the trim parameter maintains consistency, set as trim (0.01 0.01).

A robust validation of these estimated thresholds is conducted via a bootstrap test, with the parameters set as (300, 300). The outcomes of this validation are presented in Table 9. In cases where the p-value associated with the Single option falls below 0.05, while the p-value linked to the Double option exceeds 0.05, the model with a solitary threshold value of 82.626 is designated as the preferred search model. As a result, this chosen model encompasses two distinct regimes, each defined by its respective threshold.

For the purpose of unravelling the regression coefficients within each of these identified regimes, the results are detailed in Table 10. It is worth noting that, due to consistent reasons, the variable Nuclear remains absent from these calculations.

Urbanization is closely linked to $CO_2$ emissions due to factors such as increased energy consumption in urban areas, higher transportation-related emissions from urban traffic and industrial activities, the energy-intensive nature of construction in cities, and the concentration of industries. Several studies point out that rapid urbanization can have a negative impact on the environment in the form of extensive use of natural resources and energy [22], air pollution [23], ecosystem damage, biodiversity loss [24] but also in general to the quality of life of the population and their health [25].

A comprehensive examination of the outcomes stemming from the threshold model employing Urban as the designated threshold variable reveals several insights.

**Table 10.** $CO_2$ model threshold variable—urban

| Dependent: $CO_2$ | | Urban threshold: 82.626 | | | |
|---|---|---|---|---|---|
| | | Coef | P>\|z\| | 95% Confident Interval | |
| Region1 | GDP | −0.0141 | 0.000 | −0.0197 | −0.0085 |
| | RES | −0.3502 | 0.000 | −0.3940 | −0.3065 |
| | TEC | 0.2482 | 0.000 | 0.2360 | 0.2604 |
| | Urban | 0.0521 | 0.000 | 0.0307 | 0.0057 |
| | Enimpdep | 0.0008 | 0.749 | 0.0041 | 0.0057 |
| Region2 | GDP | −0.0525 | 0.000 | −0.0588 | −0.0462 |
| | RES | −0.2118 | 0.000 | −0.2508 | −0.1728 |
| | TEC | 0.1778 | 0.000 | 0.1679 | 0.1876 |
| | Urban | 0.109 | 0.000 | 0.0882 | 0.1303 |
| | Enimpdep | −0.0074 | 0.006 | −0.0127 | −0.0021 |
| | Cons | −3.9613 | 0.000 | −5.4413 | −2.4814 |

Own processing—in Stata

The coefficients of all variables, except Enimpdep, demonstrate statistically significant implications. It's important to note that for both the GDP and Enimpdep variables, a certain degree of overlap in the confidence intervals emerges, which may indicate a degree of confounding.

A pronounced threshold effect emerges for the RES, TEC, and Urban variables. Upon surpassing the threshold value of the Urban variable (82.626), a reduction in the influence of renewable energy deployment on mitigating $CO_2$ emissions becomes discernible. This observation implies that beyond this established threshold, the contribution of renewable energy usage to the decline in carbon emissions becomes less pronounced.

The unidirectional relationship from urban population to energy use, renewable energy, and growth was confirmed by Armeanu et al. [26]. Similarly, for the TEC variable, breaching the established Urban threshold triggers a noticeable decrease in the magnitude of energy consumption's impact on the escalation of $CO_2$ emissions. This intriguing finding suggests that beyond the identified Urban threshold, the influence of energy consumption on subsequent carbon emission increases is mitigated. The threshold effect between carbon emissions and urbanization was also recognized by [27, 28], suggesting that carbon dioxide emissions can be inhibited when urbanization exceeds this threshold.

Interestingly, in the context of the Urban variable itself, exceeding the predefined threshold value (82.626) corresponds to an amplification in its influence on the increase in $CO_2$ emissions. This counterintuitive observation underscores the dynamics at play, where surpassing a particular threshold value renders the Urban variable's influence more pronounced in driving $CO_2$ emissions upward. The unidirectional causal relation between urbanization and $CO_2$ emissions was also confirmed in the study by [29], although only from the short-run perspective. Similarly, an inverted U-shaped association between urbanization and air pollutants in all China regions is reported in the study of Xu et al. [30].

In summation, the threshold model centered around the Urban variable provides a nuanced lens through which to perceive the interplay between economic indicators and $CO_2$ emissions within our dataset. It elucidates intricate thresholds and relationships that play a pivotal role in shaping emissions patterns within urbanization.

These findings hold practical implications for policymakers. They emphasize the need for tailored strategies that consider the stage of economic development and urbanization within a country. Efforts to promote renewable energy adoption should be mindful of diminishing returns in emissions reduction as countries advance economically. Additionally, policies addressing energy consumption should focus on optimizing efficiency, particularly in highly urbanized regions.

From a theoretical perspective, the study's results contribute to the theoretical understanding of the EKC hypothesis by highlighting its limitations in capturing the intricate dynamics of economic growth and environmental impact.

Furthermore, in terms of methodological implications, the application of sophisticated threshold models in this study underscores their effectiveness in uncovering intricate relationships that might remain concealed in linear analyses.

We also performed an analysis where we considered Energy Import Dependency and Nuclear as threshold variables. In both cases, the threshold variables do not have a threshold effect.

## 4 Conclusions and Policy Implications

The utilization of threshold models in our analysis has yielded valuable insights that would have remained obscured by linear approaches. By accommodating nonlinear relationships, we've discerned critical thresholds that distinctly impact $CO_2$ emissions in response to various economic indicators. This underscores the multidimensional nature of emissions patterns and the need for sophisticated modeling to capture these complexities.

Our findings elucidate noteworthy threshold effects associated with GDP and urbanization. Notably, as GDP per capita crosses the threshold of $37,000, the efficacy of renewable energy sources in reducing $CO_2$ emissions diminishes. This observation resonates with the notion that higher levels of economic development might foster a transition away from certain low-carbon practices, potentially due to a shift in consumption patterns or industrial structures. Similarly, beyond an Urban threshold of 82,626, the impact of renewables on $CO_2$ reduction lessens, signifying intricate urban dynamics in emissions mitigation.

Our results accentuate that surpassing the GDP threshold is associated with a diminishing impact of energy consumption on $CO_2$ escalation. This finding underscores the potential for advanced economies to adopt more efficient energy technologies and conservation practices, leading to a decoupling of emissions from economic growth.

The threshold effects we've uncovered hold implications for sustainable development goals. As nations strive for economic growth, they must navigate intricate trade-offs in achieving a low-carbon trajectory. Policy interventions promoting renewable energy adoption require tailored strategies for economies at different development stages. Moreover, urban planning must address the shifting dynamics of emissions reduction as cities grow and cross-specific thresholds.

Our study's outcomes provide valuable insights for policymakers. Recognizing the distinct influence of thresholds on emissions patterns, policy measures should be dynamically calibrated to reflect these turning points.

While these findings contribute substantially to our understanding of this complex relationship, we acknowledge the limitations of this study, particularly in terms of generalizability across diverse global contexts. Moreover, due to limited data availability, the study needs to fully capture the impact of recent events, such as the global COVID-19 pandemic and geopolitical developments like the conflict in Ukraine. These events could significantly influence economic activities and emissions patterns, warranting further investigation as new data becomes available.

Future research can extend our analysis by incorporating more variables and exploring the robustness of these threshold effects across different regions and periods. The non-linear approach and threshold modeling applied in this study have unveiled complex relationships that underscore the intricate web of factors influencing $CO_2$ emissions. The delineation of thresholds emphasizes the need for tailored strategies that align with the nuanced dynamics of economic growth, urbanization, and energy consumption in the pursuit of a sustainable and low-carbon economy.

**Acknowledgement** This work was supported by the Scientific Grant Agency of the Ministry of Education, Science, Research and Sport of the Slovak Republic and the Slovak Academy of Sciences under grant VEGA 1/0508/21, and by Cultural and Educational Grant agency of Ministry of Education, Research, Development and Youth of the Slovak Republic under grants KEGA 024PU-4/2023 and KEGA 010PU-4/2023.

## References

1. European Commission: The European Green Deal. European Commission (2019). https://doi.org/10.1017/CBO9781107415324.004
2. Grossman, Gene M., Alan, B., Krueger.: Environmental impacts of a North American free trade agreement (1991)
3. Neagu, O.: The link between economic complexity and carbon emissions in the European Union countries: a model based on the Environmental Kuznets Curve (EKC) approach. Sustainability **11**(17), 4753 (2019)

4. Bekun, F.V., Alola, A.A., Gyamfi, B.A., Yaw, S.S.: The relevance of EKC hypothesis in energy intensity real-output trade-off for sustainable environment in EU-27. Environ. Sci. Pollut. Res. **28**, 51137–51148 (2021)
5. Chandra Voumik, L., Rahman, M., Akter, S.: Investigating the EKC hypothesis with renewable energy, nuclear energy, and R&D for EU: fresh panel evidence. Heliyon **8**, e12447 (2022)
6. Dogan, E., Inglesi-Lotz, R.: The impact of economic structure to the Environmental Kuznets Curve (EKC) hypothesis: evidence from European countries. Environ. Sci. Pollut. Res. **27**, 12717–12724 (2020)
7. Sarkodie, S.A., Ozturk, I.: Investigating the Environmental Kuznets Curve hypothesis in Kenya: a multivariate analysis. Renew. Sustain. Energy Rev. **117**, 109481 (2020)
8. Chovancová, J., Litavcová, E., Shevchenko, T.: Assessment of the relationship between economic growth, energy consumption, carbon emissions and renewable energy sources in the V4 countries. J. Manag. Bus. Res. Pract. **13** (2021)
9. Frodyma, K., Papież, M., Śmiech, S.: Revisiting the Environmental Kuznets Curve in the European Union countries. Energy **241**, 122899 (2022)
10. Yao, F., Zhu, H., Wang, M.: The impact of multiple dimensions of urbanization on $CO_2$ emissions: a spatial and threshold analysis of panel data on China's prefecture-level cities. Sustain. Cities Soc. **73**, 103113 (2021)
11. Pilatowska, M., Włodarczyk, A., Zawada, M.: $CO_2$ emissions, energy consumption and economic growth in the EU countries: evidence from threshold cointegration analysis. In: International Conference on the European Energy Market, EEM, August 2015
12. Petruška, I., Chovancová, J., Litavcová, E.: Dependence of $CO_2$ emissions on energy consumption and economic growth in the European Union: a panel threshold model. Ekon. i Środowisko. **3**, 73–89 (2021)
13. Hair, J.F., Anderson, R.E., Tatham, R.L., Black, W.C.: Multivariate Data Analysis, 4th edn. Cengage, Andover (1995)
14. Rogerson, P.A.: A statistical method for the detection of geographic clustering. Geogr. Anal. **33**, 215–227 (2001)
15. Pan, Y., Jackson, R.T.: Ethnic difference in the relationship between acute inflammation and serum ferritin in US adult males. Epidemiol. Infect. **136**, 421–431 (2008)
16. Guo, Q., Wang, Y., Dong, X.: Effects of smart city construction on energy saving and $CO_2$ emission reduction: evidence from China. Appl. Energy **313**, 118879 (2022)
17. Gillingham, K., Rapson, D., Wagner, G.: The rebound effect and energy efficiency policy. Rev. Environ. Econ. Policy (2016). https://doi.org/10.1093/reep/rev017
18. Schröder, E., Storm, S.: Economic growth and carbon emissions: the road to "Hothouse Earth" is paved with good intentions. Int. J. Polit. Econ. **49**, 153–173 (2020)
19. Stern, D.I.: The rise and fall of the Environmental Kuznets Curve. World Dev. (2004). https://doi.org/10.1016/j.worlddev.2004.03.004
20. Carratù, M., Chiarini, B., D'Agostino, A., Marzano, E., Regoli, A.: Air pollution and public finance: evidence for European countries. J. Econ. Stud. **46**, 1398–1417 (2019)
21. Soltani, H., Triki, M.B., Ghandri, M., Abderzag, F.T.: Does geopolitical risk and financial development matter for economic growth in MENA countries? J. of Inter. Stud. **14**(1), 103–116 (2021)
22. Han, J., Du, T., Zhang, C., Qian, X.: Correlation analysis of $CO_2$ emissions, material stocks and economic growth nexus: evidence from Chinese provinces. J. Clean. Prod. **180**, 395–406 (2018)
23. Shahbaz, M., Loganathan, N., Muzaffar, A.T., Ahmed, K., Ali Jabran, M.: How urbanization affects $CO_2$ emissions in Malaysia? The application of STIRPAT model. Renew. Sustain. Energy Rev. **57**, 83–93 (2016)
24. Ali, R., Bakhsh, K., Yasin, M.A.: Impact of urbanization on $CO_2$ emissions in emerging economy: evidence from Pakistan. Sustain. Cities Soc. **48**, 101553 (2019)
25. Hanif, I.: Impact of economic growth, nonrenewable and renewable energy consumption, and urbanization on carbon emissions in Sub-Saharan Africa. Environ. Sci. Pollut. Res. Int. **25**, 15057–15067 (2018)

26. Armeanu, D.S., Joldes, C.C., Gherghina, S.C., Andrei, J.V.: Understanding the multidimensional linkages among renewable energy, pollution, economic growth and urbanization in contemporary economies: quantitative assessments across different income countries' groups. Renew. Sustain. Energy Rev. **142**, 110818 (2021)
27. Irfan, M., Shaw, K.: Modeling the effects of energy consumption and urbanization on environmental pollution in South Asian countries: a nonparametric panel approach. Qual. Quant. **51**, 65–78 (2017)
28. Chovancová, J., Petruška, I., Cirella, G.T., Litavcová, E.: Urbanization and CO2 emissions: panel data analysis of EU countries. In: Cirella, G.T., Dahiya, B. (eds) City Responses to Disruptions in 2020. Advances in 21st Century Human Settlements. Springer, Singapore (2023)
29. Wang, S., Li, G., Fang, C.: Urbanization, economic growth, energy consumption, and $CO_2$ emissions: empirical evidence from countries with different income levels. Renew. Sustain. Energy Rev. **81**, 2144–2159 (2018)
30. Xu, S.C., et al.: Regional differences in impacts of economic growth and urbanization on air pollutants in China based on provincial panel estimation. J. Clean. Prod. **208**, 340–352 (2019)

# Managerial Approach in Green Innovation: Theoretical Framework

**Anuphat Thirakulwanich and Katarzyna Szczepańska-Woszczyna**

**Abstract** Green technology has gained massive interest in recent years due to the pressing need for environmental sustainability in the face of escalating global environmental challenges. However, it is quite a new concept with little research that has been conducted. Considering the growing urgency to address climate change and its associated impacts, there is a critical need to explore the concept of green innovation. This bibliometric study analyzes the growth and dynamics of 'green innovation' as an emerging concept. A critical review of the literature was conducted using bibliometric analysis. The type of analysis conducted included co-authorship, co-citation, and co-occurrence. The research found that the research on 'green innovation' has increased significantly recently. China was found to be the leader in published research on the concept. The findings reveal the interconnectedness of green innovation with environmental regulation, green technology, and the development of green products and renewable energy sources. It was recommended that there is a need to strengthen government policies and regulations, promote green innovation education, support research and development efforts, and encourage global cooperation to address urgent environmental challenges and climate change. These measures collectively offer a comprehensive and holistic approach to addressing environmental issues and fostering a more sustainable and environmentally responsible future.

**Keywords** Green innovation · Green innovation management · Bibliometric analysis · Environment · Innovation

A. Thirakulwanich (✉) · K. Szczepańska-Woszczyna
Faculty of Applied Science, WSB University, Ul. Cieplaka 1C, 41-300 Dąbrowa Górnicza, Poland
e-mail: anuphat.thirakulwanich@student.wsb.edu.pl

A. Thirakulwanich
Faculty of Business and Technology, Stamford International University, 16, Motorway Road—Km2, Prawet, Bangkok 10250, Thailand



S. Kot et al. (eds.), *Corporate Practices: Policies, Methodologies, and Insights in Organizational Management*, Springer Proceedings in Business and Economics,
https://doi.org/10.1007/978-981-97-0996-0_61

## 1 Introduction

Human beings have always had an impact on the environment. However, in recent years, that impact has become more evident and worrisome. For example, carbon dioxide emissions from burning fossil fuels have reached record highs; global average sea levels have risen by 20 cm from 1900 to 2018 [1]. Additionally, heatwaves, forest fires, and air pollution have increased significantly over time. This trend is only likely to continue as our population and consumption grow. There is a growing need and urgency to take action to protect our planet for future generations. Climate change is one of the most pressing issues facing our planet today [2]. As awareness of the negative impact of human activity on the environment grows, so does the need for relevant measures to reduce environmental damage from all stakeholders—government policy, business organizations and enterprises, and the public [3]. In fact, in the current business market, organizations need to balance efficiency and market share through constant innovation, ethical responsibility, and coherence with the society in which they operate. Researchers have proposed an innovation to achieve this balance and reduce environmental damage while increasing business efficiency [4, 5]. However, it is up to each business to decide how to implement this type of innovation best. This is the idea behind developing the concept of green innovation within the business management environment.

Green innovation implies identifying, analyzing, and implementing innovations (products and services) that are sustainable, environmentally friendly, and economically viable [6]. The United Nations Environmental Programme (UNEP) defines *green innovation* as "a new business approach which promotes sustainability throughout the entire life cycle of a product while also boosting a company's performance and competitiveness" [7]. Green innovation is an important aspect of developing any business entity or nation. Green business has been identified as one of the most promising industries to grow globally [8]. The world has started to take notice of this concept because it provides many benefits, such as reducing environmental pollution, conserving natural resources, creating jobs, and promoting social welfare [9]. The global market for green products and services is expected to reach $4 trillion by 2024. This market can be further expanded as we move towards 2030 if proper changes are made in our production processes and supply chains [10]. Green innovation aims to improve environmental performance while increasing competitiveness, profitability, and shareholder value.

Responding to the "green innovation" agenda has arisen as a critical issue and opportunity for firms, regardless of their size or the industry they are in. According to [11], green innovation practices and their management in the enterprise context are becoming increasingly relevant for businesses [12]. The reason is that in a regulatory and consumer-sensitive context, it might suggest legitimacy, boost competitiveness, and emphasize ecological responsibility. Considering these facts, most of the firms have started an active engagement that extends beyond their internal operations to improve their environmental profile throughout the lifecycle of their products, from the procurement of raw materials to their use by customers. This concept of green innovation has been incorporated into the management aspect of most businesses [13].

Holt and Ghobadian [14] assert that among the various ways businesses have adopted and incorporated green innovation practices in their management is through green supply chain management. A green supply chain involves incorporating environmentally sound practices into the established supply chain of a business. This can involve procedures including choosing a supplier and buying supplies, designing a product, making and assembling it, distributing it, and managing its end-of-life. Green supply chains incorporate value addition and/or corporate value generation throughout the chain's activities rather than minimizing the negative effects of business and supply chain operations [15].

In recent years, there has been an explosion of research on the concept of "green innovation," particularly from the management perspective. Despite this, a comprehensive definition of "green innovation" that encompasses all its facets is still elusive to scholars and decision-makers. Considering the increasing awareness of environmental pollution and the pressure and demand from the public to business enterprises to offer green products and services, there is a need to analyze the literature on this concept empirically. Therefore, this research aims to conduct a comprehensive literature review on green innovation in management. The research will portray the efforts made towards this concept, trends, and prospects.

## 2 Methodology

This research adopted a qualitative technique, using secondary data available in the literature to conduct the bibliometric analysis of the green innovation management concept. The research was guided by the Preferred Reporting Items for Systematic Reviews and Meta-Analyses (PRISMA). PRISMA provides a minimum checklist of items to include when reporting on systematic reviews and meta-analyses. The checklist covers critical elements such as the title, abstract, methods, results, and discussion sections of a systematic review or meta-analysis paper [16]. For this research, the checklist that was used in evaluating the suitability of a research paper was title, abstract, keywords, rationale, data collection, and results synthesis.

The data for this research was obtained from the Scopus database. Scopus was considered a suitable source of literature because of several reasons. These include comprehensive coverage, regular updates, multiple academic disciplines, and search filters, and are reasonably current and up-to-date. The search on Scopus was done for the keyword "green innovation," where 6404 articles were obtained, ranging from the Year 1995 to the year 2023.

The research adopted bibliometric analysis, which entails examining the characteristics of articles, such as publication frequency, citation patterns, authorship trends, and the thematic focus of the research [17]. For this research, the research analyzed the co-authorship, co-citation, and co-occurrence.

The co-authorship involved examining the collaboration patterns between authors, research groups, or institutions to provide valuable information about how researchers work together to produce academic publications. The analysis was provided using visualization maps [18]. Co-citation involves the identification of two or more documents (typically scholarly articles or papers) that are cited together by other documents [19]. Co-citation analysis is used to identify relationships between documents, authors, or topics based on the shared attention they receive from other researchers. It can help reveal connections between research works, identify influential documents, and track the development of research themes and trends over time. This analysis was conducted using VOSviewer software.

## 3 Results and Discussions

The research started by analyzing the trend of the research and publications regarding green innovation. The results are summarized in Fig. 1. From the results, the first publication regarding green innovation was made in 1995. The concept received almost no attention until 2007 when the publications increased. The green innovation concept received much attention between 2020 and 2023, where more than 60% of the publication was done. The peak was in 2023, when 1109 publications were done. This shows that, with time, the concept of green innovation is gaining more and more attention.

The other aspect that was evaluated was the publications for different countries. The results indicated that China had the highest number of publications of 1946 documents, followed by Pakistan, with 204 documents. China also has the highest citations of 34,051 and a total links strength of 527. The other major countries in publications were the United Kingdom, United States, Malaysia, Australia, Italy, and

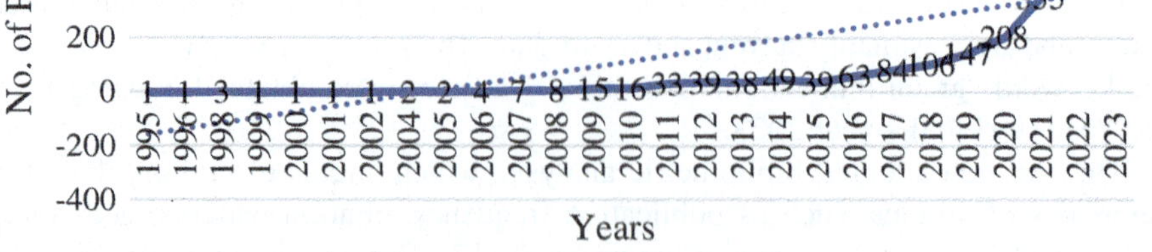


**Fig. 1** Publications of 'green innovation' related articles over time

Saudi Arabia, in the third to seventh positions, respectively. An interesting finding is that China has almost ten times more publications on green innovation concepts, as compared to the second rank of Pakistan. The massive publication in China could be attributed to several aspects. First are the severe environmental challenges facing the country, including high air and water pollution [20]. These challenges have necessitated research and innovation in green technologies to address and mitigate these issues.

Another reason is the government initiatives and support, where the Chinese government has been actively promoting and supporting green innovations through activities such as research funding and offering incentives towards green innovation practices [21]. It is also notable that China has increased its investment in research and development in recent years, including developing a research culture towards sustainable technologies [22]. China has experienced rapid industrialization and economic growth in recent decades. With increasing environmental concerns and pressure to address pollution and climate change, there has been a growing need for green and sustainable solutions. The scale and scope of China's industrial and economic activities have likely driven the demand for research and innovation in green technologies and practices.

From the VOSviewer network visualization, China is well networked to other countries, with a total 581 links, and 1090 link strength (Fig. 2). This implies that the research and findings of the China's authors is recognized and referenced by other authors globally. Considering other countries,

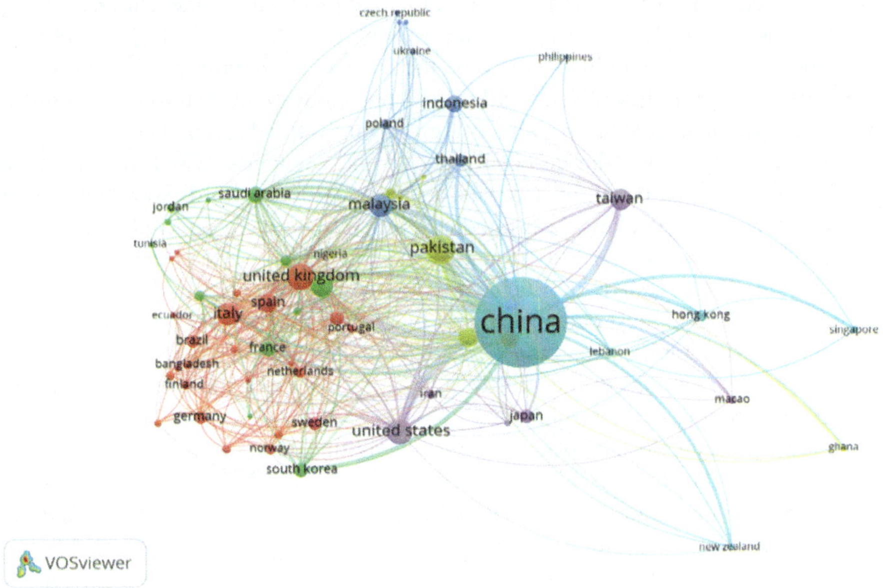


**Fig. 2** Network of popular countries in publication of 'green innovation'

The other aspect evaluated was the co-authorship, which analyzed the number of publications made by the authors and their citations. From Table 2, the author with the highest number of publications regarding green innovation was Cooke P., with seven publications, followed by Zhand D., with a total of 6 publications. A co-authorship of Gupta H. and Barua M.K. had four documents, with the highest number of citations—625.

Considering the research for Cooke P., the most published author, most of the researchers focused on government policies, both regional and national, that address the aspect of green innovation. For instance, Cooke [23] 2015 focused on green governance and green clusters that addressed the climate change challenges faced by Central and Eastern European countries. The study evaluated the policies that address the climate challenge. While in 2013, Cooke [24] researched green innovation and economic development over the transition regions. Additionally, Szczepanska-Woszczyna [25] investigated regional innovation systems and regional economic policy instruments.

Considering the second author, Zhang [26], most research revolved around greenwashing. Zhang investigated whether the environmental monitoring power transition could curb corporate greenwashing behavior. The research addressed the ecological, climate, and environmental issues in China. Another article by Gupta and Barua [27] investigated the greenwashing perspective exploration on whether green finance inhibits extreme hypocritical ESG risk.

Gupta and Barua also have four articles with the highest number of citations. The four studies focused on green innovation barriers and green innovation enablers. For instance, Gupta and Barua [28] evaluated the manufacturing organizations' ability to overcome internal barriers to green innovation. In another study, Repar et al. [29] developed a framework to help overcome the barriers to green innovation in SMEs. From their research, they advocated for constant innovations in terms of products, processes, and management to overcome green innovation barriers (Fig. 3).

Another analysis was the co-occurrence of the keywords, which indicated the significant keywords. From the analysis, a total of 6406 keywords were developed. For critical analysis, the keywords cited at least 20 times were selected, which gave a total of 53 keywords. For this research, the top 20 keywords were selected for the analysis. The first five significant keywords are presented in Table 1. Green innovation has the highest occurrence and link strength. The next highest in rank is sustainability development, and then environmental regulation. An interesting aspect is that 'China' was among the keywords, suggesting that green innovation was critical in China's economy (Tables 2 and 3).

Figure 4 presents the network of the twenty significant keywords. The size of the nodes indicates the strength of the occurrences of the keywords. In this case, 'green innovation' has the largest node, followed by sustainable development and environmental regulation. In addition, the VOS viewer divided the twenty keywords into five clusters, as shown in Table 4. The first cluster of VOS viewer was 'innovation,'

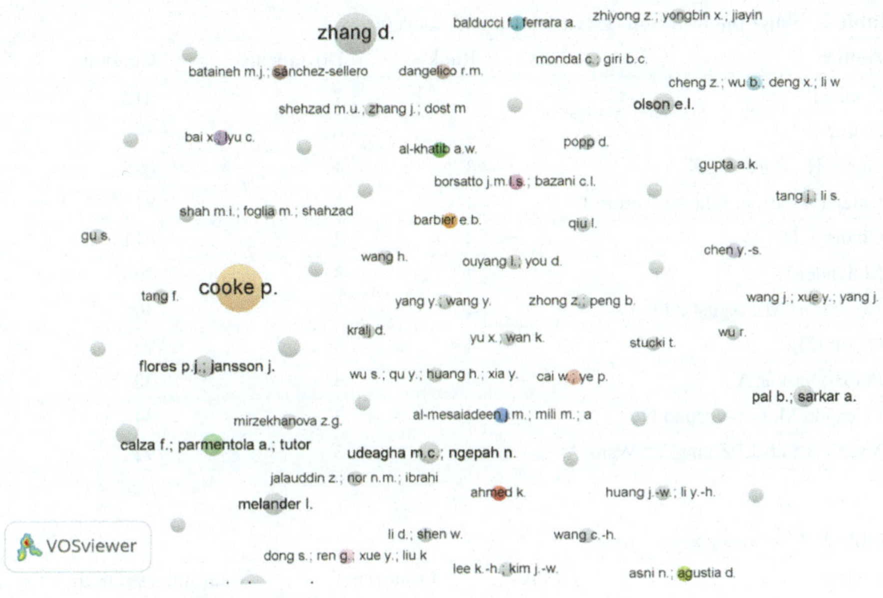


**Fig. 3** Network of major publishers in 'green innovation' concept

**Table 1** Popular countries in publication of 'green innovation'

| Country | Rank | Documents | Citations | Total links strength |
|---|---|---|---|---|
| China | 1 | 1946 | 34,051 | 527.00 |
| Pakistan | 2 | 204 | 5081 | 185.00 |
| United Kingdom | 3 | 179 | 7253 | 144.00 |
| United States | 4 | 162 | 4865 | 125.00 |
| Malaysia | 5 | 130 | 2672 | 96.00 |
| Australia | 6 | 91 | 3684 | 69.00 |
| Italy | 7 | 123 | 5354 | 69.00 |
| Saudi Arabia | 8 | 66 | 1182 | 56.00 |
| Taiwan | 9 | 113 | 9111 | 54.00 |
| France | 10 | 59 | 2874 | 46.00 |
| India | 11 | 121 | 2549 | 45.00 |

which comprised nine keywords. These keywords were corporate social responsibility, environmental innovation, environmental performance, environmental sustainability, financial performance, green innovation, innovation, SMEs, and sustainability. To achieve green innovation from every perspective, the concept of innovation is critical. The green innovation concept is borrowed from the aspect of corporate social responsibility. Its achievement has a significant influence on environmental performance and environmental sustainability [30]. Many organizations, particularly

**Table 2** Major publishers in 'green innovation' concept

| Author | Rank | Documents | Citations |
|---|---|---|---|
| Cooke P | 1 | 7 | 212 |
| Zhang D | 2 | 6 | 59 |
| Gupta H.; Barua M.K | 3 | 4 | 625 |
| Calza F.; Parmentola A.; Tutore I | 4 | 3 | 81 |
| Chang C.H | 4 | 3 | 611 |
| Malender L | 4 | 3 | 268 |
| Novitasari M.; Agustia D | 4 | 3 | 30 |
| Olson E.L | 4 | 3 | 92 |
| Pal B.; Sarkar A | 4 | 3 | 22 |
| Udeagha M. C.; Ngepah N | 4 | 3 | 34 |
| Yang Z.; Sun J.; Zhang Y.; Wang Y | 4 | 3 | 92 |

**Table 3** Five major keywords

| Country | Rank | Occurrence | Total links strength |
|---|---|---|---|
| Green innovation | 1 | 1419 | 543 |
| Sustainable development | 2 | 182 | 133 |
| Environmental regulation | 3 | 150 | 114 |
| China | 4 | 147 | 101 |
| Sustainability | 5 | 133 | 93 |

SMEs, are considering green innovation as a means of achieving sustainability, which is ultimately transformed into financial performance.

The second cluster from VOS viewer is 'green technology,' which comprises five keywords, namely China, environmental regulation, green finance, green innovation efficiency, and green technology innovation. Green technology is a critical aspect of achieving green innovation as it advocates the development and implementation of environmentally friendly solutions and technologies to address environmental challenges and promote sustainability [31]. China has been making significant efforts to promote green technologies and address environmental issues. From green technology, the adoption and implementation of effective environmental regulations are vital through aspects such as green finance. Efficient and effective innovations are considered critical and require stakeholders' input.

The third from the VOS viewer cluster was 'competitive advantage,' which comprised three keywords, namely, competitive advantage, green innovations, and sustainable development. These keywords are incorporated from the concept of green innovation as they incorporate the development and application of new products, services, processes, or business models with the primary goal of addressing environmental challenges, promoting sustainability, and creating a competitive advantage

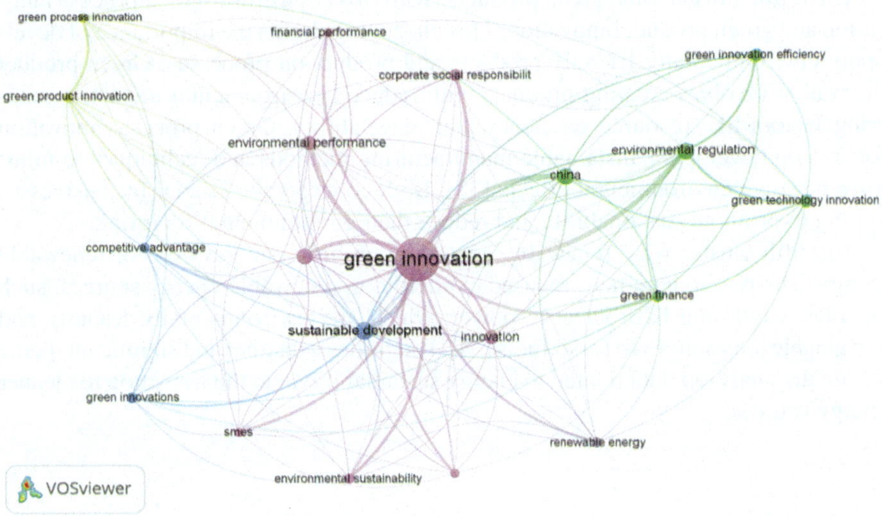


**Fig. 4** The network of the twenty major keywords

**Table 4** Cluster of major keywords

| Cluster | No. of keyword | Selected keywords | Issue |
|---|---|---|---|
| 1 | 9 | Corporate social responsibility, environmental innovation, environmental performance, environmental sustainability, financial performance, green innovation, innovation, SMEs, sustainability | Innovation |
| 2 | 5 | China, environmental regulation, green finance, green innovation efficiency, green technology innovation | Green technology |
| 3 | 3 | Competitive advantage, green innovations, sustainable development | Competitive advantage |
| 4 | 2 | Green process innovation, green product innovation | Green products |
| 5 | 1 | Renewable energy | Renewble energy |

for organizations [32] and reinforcing competitive advantage through green organizational culture and green innovation. Sustainable development, in this context, likely relates to the broader concept of ensuring that innovation efforts align with long-term environmental and social sustainability goals.

The fourth cluster was 'green products' with two keywords—green process innovation and green product innovation. This cluster highlights the importance of developing environmentally friendly products and production processes. Green product innovation involves creating products with reduced environmental impact, considering factors like resource efficiency and recyclability. Green process innovation focuses on developing sustainable manufacturing methods and techniques to minimize negative environmental effects [33]. Both concepts are crucial for businesses aiming to promote sustainability and reduce their environmental footprint.

The fifth cluster was 'renewable energy,' with only one keyword of renewable energy. The researchers here focused explicitly on renewable energy sources, such as solar, wind, and hydroelectric power, which are environmentally friendly and sustainable alternatives to fossil fuels [34]. It signifies a distinct and significant theme within the analyzed data related to energy sustainability and the transition to cleaner energy sources.

## 4 Conclusions

Green innovation is a diverse and important field of study, and the investigation of the literature review through bibliometric analysis sheds light on the several aspects and elements that must be taken into account in order to advance the concept. Given the global importance of the concept, there is still a massive gap in research that needs to be exploited. To address the rising environmental concerns and the crucial necessity of green innovation, it is essential to put in place a complete set of measures and strategies. Governments must enhance their policies and regulations to promote and support green innovation [35]. This can be achieved through the implementation of research grants, tax incentives, and the establishment of stringent environmental standards. The prioritization of sustainable practices and technologies in education, along with a significant increase in investment in research and development, is of utmost importance.

The promotion of eco-conscious consumer choices, with collaborative efforts among businesses, has the potential to foster innovation and mitigate damage to the environment. In addition, the establishment of global cooperation, the promotion of renewable energy, and the transparent measurement and reporting of environmental impact are crucial measures for the mitigation of climate change. The implementation of long-term sustainability planning, characterized by establishing clearly defined objectives, guarantees the perpetuation of ongoing advancements. These policies collectively constitute a comprehensive approach to tackling environmental concerns and promoting a future that is both sustainable and environmentally conscientious [36]. Continued research should be encouraged by both individuals and institutions to explore all the aspects of green innovation.

This research reveals that green innovation is an emerging concept that is increasingly gaining attention, especially in China. Various factors contribute to this trend, including government initiatives, economic growth, global leadership in green technology, corporate engagement, and international collaboration. Green innovation is no longer peripheral but a driving force in China's and other big economies, such as the United States and the United Kingdom's economic and environmental strategies, making it a noteworthy case study for global sustainability efforts. The bibliometric analysis of 'green innovation' reveals several significant keyword clusters, each shedding light on different facets of the topic.

From the first cluster, 'innovation' brings attention to the interconnected nature of innovation, sustainability, and corporate social responsibility, emphasizing the need for environmentally responsible business practices. Cluster Two, 'Green Technology,' highlights the importance of green technology and its impact on green innovation, particularly in China, with environmental regulation and green finance playing pivotal roles. The third cluster, 'competitive advantage,' underlines the connection between green innovations and sustainable development, suggesting that environmentally conscious innovations can lead to a competitive edge in the market. From the fourth cluster, 'green products' focuses on developing eco-friendly products and processes, highlighting the significance of sustainable products and process innovation. The fifth cluster, 'renewable energy,' signifies the crucial role of renewable energy sources in the transition towards a greener and more sustainable future. This research recommends that the concept of green innovation still needs to be exploited in research. More research needs to be done. Governments, institutions, and businesses should collaboratively fund and foster research on green innovation as a means of addressing global environmental challenges.

## References

1. Chu, Y., Liu, Y., Tian, X.: Environmental risk and green innovation: evidence from evacuation spills. SSRN Electron. J. (2020). https://doi.org/10.2139/ssrn.3740551
2. Chen, Y.S., Lai, S.B., Wen, C.T.: The influence of green innovation performance on corporate advantage in Taiwan. J. Bus. Ethics **67**(4), 331–339 (2006)
3. Chen, Y., Chang, C., Wu, F.: Origins of green innovations: the differences between proactive and reactive green innovations. Manag. Decis. **50**(3), 368–398 (2012). https://doi.org/10.1108/00251741211216197
4. Winn, M., Kirchgeorg, M., Griffiths, A., Linnenluecke, M.K., Günther, E.: Impacts from climate change on organizations: a conceptual foundation. Bus. Strateg. Environ. **20**(3), 157–173 (2011). https://doi.org/10.1002/bse.679
5. Chang, C.H.: The influence of corporate environmental ethics on competitive advantage: the mediation role of green innovation. J. Bus. Ethics **104**(3), 361–370 (2011). https://doi.org/10.1007/s10551-011-0914-x
6. Yousaf, Z.: Go for green: green innovation through green dynamic capabilities: accessing the mediating role of green practices and green value co-creation. Environ. Sci. Pollut. Res. **28**(39), 54863–54875 (2021)
7. UNEP.: Eco-innovation. UNEP—UN Environment Programme (n.d.). Retrieved August 24, 2022, from https://www.unep.org/explore-topics/resource-efficiency/what-we-do/responsible-industry/eco-innovation
8. Sulich, A., Kozar, Ł.: The development of employees' green competencies through sustainable business practices. In: Forum Scientiae Oeconomia, vol. 11, No. 3 (2023)

9. Muangmee, C., Dacko-Pikiewicz, Z., Meekaewkunchorn, N., Kassakorn, N., Khalid, B.: Green entrepreneurial orientation and green innovation in small and medium-sized enterprises (SMEs). Social Sciences **10**(4), 136 (2021)
10. Chen, Y.S.: The driver of green innovation and green image–green core competence. J. Bus. Ethics **81**(3), 531–543 (2008)
11. Cuerva, M.C., Triguero-Cano, Á., Córcoles, D.: Drivers of green and non-green innovation: empirical evidence in Low-Tech SMEs. J. Clean. Prod. **68**, 104–113 (2014)
12. Rozmiarek, M., Nowacki, K., Malchrowicz-Mośko, E., Dacko-Pikiewicz, Z.: Eco-initiatives in municipal cultural institutions as examples of activities for sustainable development: a case study of Poznan. Sustainability **14**(2), 682 (2022)
13. Cheng, C.C., Shiu, E.C.: Validation of a proposed instrument for measuring eco-innovation: An implementation perspective (2012). Technovation, in press
14. Holt, D., Ghobadian, A.: An empirical study of green supply chain management practices amongst UK manufacturers. J. Manufact. Technol. Manag. **20**, 933–956 (2009)
15. Rostamzadeh, R., Govindan, K., Esmaeili, A., Sabaghi, M.: Application of fuzzy VIKOR for evaluation of green supply chain management practices. Ecol. Ind. **49**, 188–203 (2015)
16. Maier, D., Maier, A., Aşchilean, I., Anastasiu, L., Gavriş, O.: The relationship between innovation and sustainability: a bibliometric review of the literature. Sustainability **12**(10), 4083 (2020)
17. Rong, H., Duan, Y., Zhang, G.: A bibliometric analysis of membrane computing (1998–2019). J. Membr. Comput. **4**(2), 177–207 (2022)
18. Youngblood, M., Lahti, D.: A bibliometric analysis of the interdisciplinary field of cultural evolution. Palgrave Commun. **4**(1), 1–9 (2018)
19. Wang, X., Xu, Z., Škare, M.: A bibliometric analysis of Economic research-Ekonomska Istra zivanja (2007–2019). Econ Res.-Ekonomska istraživanja **33**(1), 865–886 (2020)
20. He, G., Lu, Y., Mol, A.P., Beckers, T.: Changes and challenges: China's environmental management in transition. Environ. Dev. **3**, 25–38 (2012)
21. Hsu, C.C., Quang-Thanh, N., Chien, F., Li, L., Mohsin, M.: Evaluating green innovation and performance of fiancial development: mediating concerns of environmental regulation. Environ. Sci. Pollut. Res. **28**(40), 57386–57397 (2021)
22. Li, D., Zhao, Y., Zhang, L., Chen, X., Cao, C.: Impact of quality management on green innovation. J. Clean. Prod. **170**, 462–470 (2018)
23. Cooke, P.: Green governance and green clusters: regional & national policies for the climate change challenge of Central & Eastern Europe. J Open Innov. Technol. Market Complex. **1**(1), 1–17 (2015)
24. Cooke, P.: Transition regions: green innovation and economic development. In: Cooperation, Clusters, and Knowledge Transfer: Universities (2013)
25. Szczepanska-Woszczyna, K.: Strategy, corporate culture, structure and operational processes as the context for the innovativeness of an organization. Found. Manag. **10**(1), 1–12 (2018)
26. Zhang, D.: Can environmental monitoring power transition curb corporate greenwashing behavior? J. Econ. Behav. Organ. **212**, 199–218 (2023)
27. Gupta, H., Barua, M.K.: Evaluation of manufacturing organizations ability to overcome internal barriers to green innovations. In: Strategic Decision Making for Sustainable Management of Industrial Networks, pp. 139–160 (2021)
28. Gupta, H., Barua, M.K.: A framework to overcome barriers to green innovation in SMEs using BWM and Fuzzy TOPSIS. Sci. Total Environ. **633**, 122–139 (2018)
29. Repar, N., Jan, P., Dux, D., Nemecek, T., Doluschitz, R.: Implementing farm-level environmental sustainability in environmental performance indicators: A combined global-local approach. J. Clean. Prod. **140**, 692–704 (2017)
30. Nawawi, M.N., bin Samsudin, H., Saputra, J., Szczepańska-Woszczyna, K., Kot, S.: The effect of formal and informal regulations on industrial effluents and firm compliance behavior in Malaysia. Prod. Eng. Arch. **28**(2), 193–200 (2022)
31. Aithal, P.S., Aithal, S.: Opportunities & challenges for green technology in 21st century. Int. J. Curr. Res. Modern Educ. (IJCRME) **1**(1), 818–828 (2016)

32. Gürlek, M., Tuna, M.: Reinforcing competitive advantage through green organizational culture and green innovation. Serv. Ind. J. **38**(7–8), 467–491 (2018)
33. Schiederig, T., Tietze, F., Herstatt, C.: Green innovation in technology and innovation management–an exploratory literature review. R&D Manage. **42**(2), 180–192 (2012)
34. Sun, Y., Anwar, A., Razzaq, A., Liang, X., Siddique, M.: Asymmetric role of renewable energy, green innovation, and globalization in deriving environmental sustainability: evidence from top-10 polluted countries. Renewable Energy **185**, 280–290 (2022)
35. Straka M., Oláh, J &. Kassakorn, N., (2021). Impact of Green Supply Chain
36. Integration on SMEs Technological and Economic Performance. Global Journal of Entrepreneurship and Management, 2(1):12–30

The manufacturer's authorised representative in the EU is Springer Nature Customer Service Centre GmbH, Europaplatz 3, 69115 Heidelberg, Germany. If you have any concerns regarding our products, please contact ProductSafety@springernature.com

Printed and bound by CPI Group (UK) Ltd, Croydon, CR0 4YY
01/10/2026
02225943-0001